THE BIBLE READER

THE
Bible Reader

AN INTERFAITH INTERPRETATION

*With notes from Catholic, Protestant
and Jewish Traditions
and references to Art, Literature, History
and the Social Problems of Modern Man*

Prepared by

WALTER M. ABBOTT, S. J.
RABBI ARTHUR GILBERT
ROLFE LANIER HUNT
J. CARTER SWAIM

THE BRUCE PUBLISHING CO • NEW YORK

GEOFFREY CHAPMAN LTD • LONDON

Geoffrey Chapman Ltd
18 High Street, Wimbledon, London S W 19

Geoffrey Chapman (Ireland) Ltd
5–7 Main Street, Blackrock, County Dublin

Geoffrey Chapman Pty Ltd
44 La Trobe Street, Melbourne, Vic 3000, Australia

The Bruce Publishing Company
850 Third Avenue, New York, New York 10022

Collier-Macmillan Canada Ltd
Toronto, Ontario

Library of Congress Catalog Card Number: 76-93545

PRINTED IN THE UNITED STATES OF AMERICA

Contents

THE NEW TESTAMENT

Contents

ACKNOWLEDGEMENTS

The editors wish to express their appreciation to the publishers and copyright holders of various modern translations of the Scriptures for permission to use selections from their works:

The *Revised Standard Version,* copyright 1946 and 1952, by the Division of Christian Education, National Council of Churches, USA, used with permission, and by agreement with Thomas Nelson & Sons, Camden, New Jersey.

The text of the *Confraternity Edition of the Holy Bible* is reproduced by License of Confraternity of Christian Doctrine, Washington, D.C., the owner of the copyright of said Holy Bible. All rights reserved.

Jewish Publication Society, Philadelphia, Pennsylvania, for selections from *The Holy Scriptures,* copyright 1917, 1945; and also for two selections from *The Torah,* copyright 1962.

Preface

The editors of this book came together eight years ago in a conviction that the preparation of citizens for life today requires an acquaintance with the Bible.

We asked ourselves, what portions of the Bible best contribute to an understanding of our history, our literature, our culture? What persons and ideas in the Bible must the educated man know to understand the allusions he would meet in the classics—and the daily paper—or to understand the development of our social ideals and institutions? What passages of the Bible would acquaint the Christian with Jewish practices at Rosh Hashanah, or Passover, in the synagogue and at home? What portions of Scripture would help the Jew know what Christians affirm at Christmas or Easter? No person can be required to believe or disbelieve, but the facts all must know; if we know more about each other we can hope to live together in harmony.

Together the editors read the Bible and selected those passages we think most important or current in our culture, those passages most associated with our respective religious observances and beliefs. The Christian reader will discover how many of the religious rites of his church have sources in Jewish practice and Scriptures; the Jewish reader will discover that Christians cherish many Jewish ideals and by fidelity to them have helped make them part of the heritage of Western civilization. Attention will be called to passages that have produced varied denominational emphases. We often hear more of our differences, but we should know also what we have in common.

While we were working, two things happened to confirm and widen our efforts: 1. The role of the public school in dealing with religion was clarified by the Supreme Court of the United States in 1963 in its decision in the case of *Abington v. Schempp*. Although it ruled against practices of required worship, the Court added:

> . . . It is insisted that unless these religious exercises are permitted a "religion of secularism" is established in the schools. We agree of course that the State may not establish a "religion of secularism" in the sense of affirmatively opposing or showing hostility to religion, thus "preferring those who believe in no religion over those who do believe." (*Zorach v. Clauson*, 343 U.S., at 314.) We do not agree, however, that this decision in any sense has that effect. In addition, it might well be said that one's education is not complete without a study of comparative religion or the history of religion and its relationship to the advancement of civilization. It certainly may be said that the Bible is worthy of study for its literary and historic qualities. Nothing we have said

here indicates that such study of the Bible or of religion, when presented objectively as part of a secular program of education, may not be effected consistent with the First Amendment.

By the Court's definition, it seems clear that public schools may present to their students a knowledge of the Bible—and of other religious literature—useful to understand our history and institutions, our literature and culture. Through a study of the Bible the school may acquaint the student with ideas and practices of religious groups in his society. In the biblical text the student may find insights on national policies upon which as a citizen he may be called upon to make a decision.

2. While we have been at work, pronouncements from the Vatican Council reflected and furthered a climate encouraging those of us of different faiths to intensify our studies in cooperation with each other.

Persons of all faiths today have the task of absorbing into their world view the astonishing advances of knowledge and technology, to which references are made in our notes. Our notes recognize, too, that we are living in a time when scholars in Ugaritic, Hebrew, Aramaic, Greek and Latin, from which our Bible came, are reaching an increasing agreement as to the exact wording and meaning of the early texts.

Because of the richness of our own experience in reading the Bible together, we know there can be treasures in "living-room dialogue." It has been our experience that Jew, Catholic, and Protestant can consider scriptural questions objectively. Blest with better understanding of the reasons why another believes differently, each of us has enriched his own faith. Readers will find here notes answering some questions we asked of each other.

We have made a beginning in showing the relation of some Bible passages to art, music, literature, politics, philosophy, suggesting in each case a range of viewpoints. We acknowledge that the notes are incomplete. We hope, therefore, that any dissatisfaction with our efforts may inspire you to expand your own; that our selections will send you to the complete Bible in your preferred translation and to your chosen religious leaders for further information and insights.

Walter M. Abbott, S.J.
Rabbi Arthur Gilbert
Rolfe Lanier Hunt
J. Carter Swaim

What is the Bible?

Arnold Schönberg (1874–1951) was an Austrian composer whose twelve-tone music is eagerly followed by today's avant-garde. He has been called "the most important single force" in music in the last half of the twentieth century. One of Schönberg's most discussed works is "Moses and Aron," an atonal opera that deals with two biblical characters whose political roles in the ancient Middle East still instruct man in the twentieth century. Moses believes he has a word from God but finds it difficult to communicate. Aron, on the other hand, is a politician who has neither the depth of experience nor the vision of Moses but he knows how to "sell" the message to the people. The rest of the story can be read in Exodus.

The Bible is a book that binds the world together, by dissolving time. We often gain insight into our behavior as human beings when we look at ourselves as portrayed in the experiences of biblical characters. Our world still witnesses the work of prophetic-type personalities whose vision is far-reaching and of pragmatic men who help make dreams real.

The Bible not only compresses time within the covers of what is now a single volume (in ancient times it circulated on papyrus rolls, so that owning it would be like owning a set of the *Encyclopedia Britannica*); but, in similar compass, it spans the geography of the world. A Chinese boatman identified his own experiences with the story of Noah and the Ark. "I've been through the flood," he said, "and I know it's true." Inside Russia—a land which for half a century has futilely tried to wipe out religion—the greatest discontent of recent years was occasioned by a novel which described an inventor who got himself entangled in the red tape of the Red state and was banished to Siberia because his ambitions ran athwart those of a party official. The author, Vladimir Dudintsev, found his title in an Old Testament phrase echoed in the New Testament: *Not by Bread Alone*.

The Bible is a book of religion and is not authoritative in any other realm. It is not a textbook in mathematics. 1 Kings 7 : 23 describes one of the vessels in the sanctuary as "round, ten cubits from brim to brim . . . and a line of thirty cubits measured its circumference." A schoolboy can figure out that anything which is ten cubits in diameter must be 31.416 cubits in circumference. But this inaccuracy has nothing whatever to do with our eternal salvation. Psalm 19 : 6 assumes that the sun rises at one end of the heavens and makes its circuit to the other end. This is not good astronomy. Isaiah 11 : 12 talks about "the four corners of the earth." We should not want this kind of geography taught in our schools.

Genesis 7 : 11 describes a deluge that resulted when "the windows of the heavens were opened." The U.S. weather bureau has more prosaic ways of analyzing the meteorological factors that lead to a flood. Mark 4 : 31 says that a mustard seed "is the smallest of all seeds on earth." Botanists would not agree to that—but this does not invalidate Jesus' word about the power of a little faith, even though it be as small as a mustard grain. The Bible does not have any geology. The Bible is not a book of metaphysics. Metaphysics, by definition, is what comes after physics—and the Bible has no physics.

Traditionally called the Word of God, the Bible itself claims to contain the words of men who were guided by a power not themselves. A Psalmist says:

> I was dumb and silent,
> I held my peace to no avail;
> my distress grew worse,
> my heart became hot within me.
> As I mused, the fire burned;
> then I spake with my tongue. (Psalm 39 : 2f.)

"The word of the Lord came to Jonah"—and he went to Nineveh. "The word of the Lord" came to Jeremiah—and he stood in the gate, exhorting all: "Amend your ways." The word of the Lord came to the army of Rehoboam, and they changed their plans and went home (1 Kings 12 : 24). The word of the Lord had power beyond the bounds of Judaism. The Chronicler says that, in order "that the word of the Lord by Jeremiah might be accomplished, the Lord stirred up the spirit of Cyrus king of Persia" (2 Chronicles 36 : 22). Paul asked the Thessalonians to join him in prayer "that the word of the Lord may speed on and triumph" (2 Thessalonians 3 : 1).

The Apostles sometimes spoke without a word from the Lord. On one difficult matter, Paul said to the Corinthians: "I have no command of the Lord" (1 Corinthians 7 : 25). "I say, not the Lord. ..." (1 Corinthians 7 : 12). "What I am saying I say not with the Lord's authority but as a fool" (2 Corinthians 11 : 17). Attempting to account for the fact that men did sometimes say more than they had either the wit or the courage to say, the author of 2 Peter 1 : 20 says: "men moved by the Holy Spirit spoke from God."

Some years ago graduating classes often adopted as their motto: "Deeds, Not Words." The men and women of the Bible would never have understood this. For them words are deeds, and nothing is so creative as the spoken utterance. The story of creation is told in these terms. In the midst of darkness and chaos, "God said: 'Let there be light'—and there was light" (Genesis 1 : 3).

> By the word of the Lord the heavens were made,
> and all their host by the breath of his mouth.
> For he spake, and it came to be;
> he commanded, and it stood forth. (Psalm 33 : 6, 9)

We think of a word as something that is to be heard. The men of the Bible were so sure of its reality that they could speak of seeing a word. Habukkuk takes his stand on the watch-tower "to see what God will say" (Habukkuk 2 : 1). The seer in Revelation heard behind him "a loud voice like a trumpet"; then he "turned to see the voice that was speaking" (Revelation 1 : 12). Philo said: "It happens that the voice of men is to be heard, but the voice of God is to be seen, in deeds which the eye appreciates before the ear."

The word comes to us in highly imaginative form, conveyed in figures of speech of every kind, leading us on from the familiar to the unfamiliar. If children are fond of riddles, the Bible uses them, too. Samson employed one to taunt the Philistines (Judges 14 : 12–19). Ezekiel was commanded to "propound a riddle to the house of Israel" (Ezekiel 17 : 2), and Daniel expects that "a king of bold countenance, one who understands riddles, shall arise" (Daniel 8 : 23). If the word "mystery" sometimes occurs in the New Testament (as in 1 Corinthians 15 : 51; Ephesians 1 : 9; 1 Timothy 3 : 9), it is not because its God speaks in conundrums but rather because mystery has been given a new meaning. What once was hidden has now been laid bare. Mystery refers to open secret. Jesus prayed, "I thank thee Father, Lord of heaven and earth, that thou hast hidden these things from the wise and understanding and revealed them to babes" (Matthew 11 : 25).

Fun and play are not often associated with the Bible, but some of the best fun in the world comes from the play on words—and the Bible is full of that. Unhappily, much of this is lost upon the English reader because the pun can rarely be translated. When the word of the Lord came to Jeremiah, saying, "What do you see?" the reply was: "a rod of almond." Then God said: "You have seen well, for I am watching over my word to perform it." This passage (Jeremiah 1 : 11f.) translated into English doesn't make much sense, since in Hebrew the point is made by a play on words, and we should have to translate something like this: "What do you see?" "A wake-tree." "Good! for I am wakeful over my word, to carry it out." When Amos says to his people, "Do not enter into Gilgal . . . for Gilgal shall surely go into exile" (Amos 5 : 5), the point is better made in James Moffatt's translation: "Go not to Gilgal . . . for Gilgal shall have a galling exile." The Tower of Babel is continual reminder of the way in which human pride has made a babble of man's speech.

The daughters of Job, Jemimah, Keziah and Kerenhappuch (Job 42 : 14) become more meaningful when we translate them rather than simply transliterate them: Ringdove, Cassia, and Applescent. Biblical children were often named to commemorate some circumstance of their birth. Isaac means "he laughs"—and this name was bestowed because Abraham thought it a laughing matter that anyone as old as his wife should become a mother. Isaac's twin sons are Esau, or Red (at birth he "came forth red"), and Jacob, or "He takes by the heel" (at birth "his hand had taken hold of Esau's heel"—Genesis 25 : 26). The prophets sometimes gave to their children names which made them living and continuing proclamation of words the prophets wished the people to hear and heed. Isaiah announced that beleaguered Israel's plight was not hopeless: "A remnant shall return" (Isaiah 10 : 21). Therefore he called his son Shearjashub—that is, "A remnant shall return" (Isaiah 7 : 3).

Place names often commemorated the site of some deeply moving personal experience or some profoundly significant national event. The place where Jacob dreamed was named Bethel, or House of God (Genesis 28 : 19). Wandering in the wilderness and unable to drink the brackish water that was available, Moses and his cohorts named the place Marah, or Bitterness (Exodus 15 : 23). A narrow defile where Achan and his family perished was called Achor, or Trouble. The prophet Hosea looked for the time when God would change the Valley of Trouble into the Door of Hope (Hosea 2 : 15).

Because the voice of God is to be seen, the Bible is filled with symbolic actions. Nations today sign a covenant, but the Hebrews "cut a covenant"—that is to say, slew an animal, split it in half, and caused the parties to walk between the halves—token of what would happen to them if they should violate the agreement. To impress upon Jeroboam what was about to happen to the kingdom, Ahijah tore his new garments into twelve pieces, eloquent of division among the tribes (1 Kings 11 : 31). Jeremiah fashioned thongs and yoke-bars and put them on his neck to portray the kind of submission he feared would befall his people with respect to the invading monarch (Jeremiah 27 : 2, 12).

Twentieth-century man will often seek a victim upon whom he can cast blame for all his troubles. The men of the Bible laid their sins upon a goat and sent it into the wilderness. Baptism too is practiced for "the sending away of sins" (cf. Mark 1 : 4). Elemental things like broken bread and poured-out wine become the Bible's symbolic way of expressing death and love.

Seeking to express the inexpressible word, the Bible uses not only symbolic acts but almost every conceivable literary device. It contains fables, census rolls, laws, historical narratives, military chronicles, government annals, poetry of many kinds (nature, romance, dramatic, didactic, work songs, battle songs, hymns for worship), wise sayings, letters, mystic visions.

Unlike other books of religion, the Bible is based on the majesty of what happened. It deals not in ethereal imaginings but in what took place on this very real earth. It is in that sense a book of history—and richer than any other book of history. Its early chapters tell of how God made choice of Abraham and his descendents to be the bearers of his revelation; and of how the promise grew dim when the chosen people became a race of slaves. But God raised up Moses, a deliverer who led the escape from

Pharaoh's bondage. Through a generation of hardship in wilderness wanderings, the disorganized escapees were molded into a nation. Desiring to be like all the nations, Israel had a succession of kings. Solomon tried to outdo at his court the splendour of Oriental monarchs, and the excesses and extravagances of his reign so weakened the nation's vitality that it soon became easy prey to division and foreign invasion.

Carried away captive into exile, the people learned to sing the Lord's song in Babylon's strange land. In these vicissitudes the people hoped for a Messiah who would "slay their foes and lift them high." Released from exile, a remnant returned to the homeland to make a fresh start, trying to rebuild the glory that had been Jerusalem. Many greeted this new venture with enthusiasm, but some "old men who had seen the first house wept with a loud voice when they saw the foundation of this house being laid" (Ezra 3 : 12).

During this period great historic movements were at work beyond the bounds of Judaism. Alexander was spreading Greek culture everywhere and giving the world a common language. The Romans were the next to dream of empire and they linked far-flung provinces together in a network of roads that made travel remarkably easy. Then it was "when the time had fully come, God sent forth his Son" (Galatians 4 : 4). Christians affirm that Hebrew hopes found fulfillment in a child born in Bethlehem. Across Roman roads his apostles sped to carry good news, and their use of the Greek tongue enabled them to be understood everywhere.

Thus it came about that the New Testament was written, not in the Hebrew language, but in Greek. And here is a parable of how the lives of the people of God were bound up with the lives of other nations. The Bible is a book of history, but not of one nation only. In it we study the history of the Hebrews, but their destiny was intertwined with that of all the Middle Eastern empires: Egypt, Babylonia, Assyria, Greece, Rome. In it we read of Hittites and Ninevites, of Medes and Persians, of Edomites and Moabites.

There is a sense in which the Bible is our only book of history. It is the Judeo-Christian religion which has given us the idea of history. The ancient Greeks did not have it. For them everything went round in circles, each age ending just where it had begun.

The Bible assumes that history has a beginning and an end. "In the beginning was the Word," that is to say, God's creative idea, God's expressed purpose of good. Man's role in history is to fulfill God's purpose. At end-time all of man's strivings will be redeemed and God's purpose completed. In the Jewish tradition the establishment of a social order in which men live in peace and security as brothers one with another is considered an essential aspect of this eschatological dream.

Both Jews and Christians recognize that man by himself alone is incapable of achieving this ultimate purpose or of living at all times according to God's creative ideals. Man sins and he must be able to attain forgiveness. He needs the salvation that can come only from God. By faith in God man is able to draw upon resources of power and inspiration that enable him to overcome adversity and to live his life in approximation of God's ideals. Christians believe that the Cross of Jesus Christ now stands at the center of eternity. God's word in the person of Jesus of Nazareth has now come among men enabling the faithful to overcome evil and to be reborn in faith. By New Testament teaching the exalted Christ "must reign until he has put all his enemies under his feet." "Then comes the end when he delivers the Kingdom to God" (1 Corinthians 15 : 24, 25).

The biblical philosophy of history is that time does not represent an endless turning back upon itself. The Bible is a basically optimistic book. Its golden age is not in the past. Its heroes do not sit down and mourn the good old days. They look forward with hope.

Since the Bible makes use of a linear rather than a circular view of history, it is not surprising that its events can be historically dated. The Exodus took place in the time of the Pharaohs. The exile occurred when Nebuchadrezzar was king. The return took place under Cyrus. Jesus was born "in the days of Herod the king" (Matthew 2 : 1). The church continues to confess that Jesus "suffered under Pontius Pilate." From that circumstance arose a new system of dating, based upon the assumption that Christ is the focal point of history. For Christians, everything now is either "B.C." (Before Christ) or "A.D." (in the year of our Lord). Jews, in dissent from this historical centrality given Jesus in the Christian view of history, date events in their religious texts "B.C.E." (Before the Common Era) and "C.E." (the Common Era). Each Rosh Hashanah, the Jewish New Year, Jews also mark another year in their calendar, now more than 5,729 years old.

This is what we mean by saying that the Bible is our only book of history. All other history books are simply commentary upon it. Even the monumental historical summaries undertaken by the men of our time are simply footnotes to the biblical summary:

> But the Lord sits enthroned for ever,
> he has established his throne for judgment;
> and he judges the world with righteousness,
> he judges the people with equity" (Psalm 9 : 7, 8).

While the sacred books of most religions tell of the mysterious doings of a thousand gods and goddesses, the Bible tells of a Creator God who is also the God of Abraham, Isaac and Jacob, Father of Jesus and the prophets, and of all men. No sacred book has in it so many people as the Bible. It is a universal portrait gallery, with pictures of all sorts of men and women: kings and queens and their counselors; judges and reformers; great religious leaders; and common folk in lavish profusion: smallholders and fishermen, tax collectors and carpenters. The heroes of the Bible are not wooden figures of but simple virtue. They are live human beings. They are subject to lust and ambition. They must fight against fear and jealousy. They need to overcome doubt. They commit sin and suffer remorse. In their lives it is possible to find mirrored both the inadequacy and the glory that is man's by virtue of his humanity.

The Bible is a book of history, and its authors and editors tell us something of the historical method employed by them in bringing it to its present form. Not infrequently they name earlier sources to which they had access. The "Book of Jashar" (or the Righteous), cited in Joshua 10 : 13 and 2 Samuel 1 : 18, seems to have been a book of songs celebrating the glory of Israel. Numbers 21 : 14 refers to the "Book of the Wars of the Lord," perhaps another anthology in praise of heroes. 1 Kings 11 : 41 cites "the book of the acts of Solomon," based perhaps upon official archives. There are references to "the Book of the Chronicles of the Kings of Israel" (2 Kings 1 : 18) and "the Book of the Chronicles of the Kings of Judah (2 Kings 8 : 23). 1 Chronicles 29 : 29 lists prophetic sources: "the Chronicles of Samuel the seer, ... the Chronicles of Nathan the prophet, ... the Chronicles of Gad the seer."

Luke 11 : 49 contains a quotation from a book called the "Wisdom of God." The activities of Jannes and Jambres, mentioned in 2 Timothy 3 : 8, were thought by some of the Church Fathers to have been described in a book by that title. Luke tells us in the preface of his Gospel (1 : 1–4) how he went about his work. In order to get at the truth of what happened during the ministry of Jesus, he interviewed eye-witnesses, consulting as many sources as he could, and then prepared "an orderly account." This is an accurate description of the procedure followed by the scientific historian of today.

In general, however, Luke's procedure was not followed by the compilers of the biblical material. If they found two or more stories in circulation, they preferred not to investigate their origins or iron out their discrepancies, but to keep them both. By succeeding generations, too, history was rewritten in the light of changed conditions. Some of the history written after the Hebrew nation broke in two reflects the point of view of Israel, the northern kingdom, some of it that of Judah, the southern. Much of it was revised in the light of the reform carried out under Josiah, reading back into an earlier time practices that represented purer worship. Still later, much of the material was reworked once more by those concerned with the developing importance of the priesthood. The variety of interests evident in these several strands provides us with fascinating data for the reconstruction of the history.

It is but an accident of language that the two parts of the Bible are not called the "old covenant" and the "new covenant." Among us the word *testament* most often occurs in the legal phrase, "the last will and testament." The distinctively Christian addition to the Hebrew Scriptures is not the dying counsel of Jesus. It represents rather what Christians consider the fulfillment of a promise found in Jeremiah 31 : 31, 33: "I will make a new covenant with the house of Israel and the house of Judah.... I will put my law within them, and I will write it upon their hearts."

While Christians believe that God's new covenant with mankind through Jesus as Christ is revealed in the New Testament, they recognize that the New Testament cannot be understood without the Old. The Jewish sources and background for ideas communicated by Jesus are sometimes made known to us only through the material in Hebrew Scripture. Furthermore, as we shall see in this *Bible Reader*, Christian liturgy and ceremonies constantly draw upon Old Testament references and make use of Old Testament prayers—particularly the Psalms.

On their part, Jews believe that the Hebrew Bible remains a vital dynamic source of spiritual instruction for mankind. They do not accept for themselves the Christian claim regarding the New Testament as sacred Scripture. Jews point out that in the post-biblical period—through the writings of the Rabbis in Midrash and Talmud, during the period of Hasidism and to this day—the biblical word has been given an application that provides it with a relevance, a vitality and a contemperaneity unique for world literature. To them, in no way can the Hebrew Bible be considered *Old*.

There are three major divisions of the Old Testament. The earliest section to have been formally recognized as Scripture was the Law. The Hebrew title, *Humash*, "Five Books of Moses," also referred to as Torah, indicates books dealing with the work of Moses rather than books *by* Moses. According to most Bible scholars, these five books of the Law contain the work of many people at many different times.

The Five Books of Moses narrate Hebrew convictions regarding God's creation of the universe and man and recount His covenant with all men through Adam and Noah. In order that God's purpose for mankind may be fulfilled He selects a chosen priest-people. By the quality of their lives, as individuals and in society, the Hebrew people will demonstrate God's power and graciousness. Thus God makes a covenant with Abraham and then, at Sinai, with Moses. He selects as His people the Hebrew slaves whom He has emancipated from Egyptian bondage, even as they accept Abraham as their father, Moses as the law-giver and Yahweh as their God.

The second category of the Hebrew Bible is "the Prophets"—a much more inclusive listing than might be supposed. The distinction we sometimes make between major and minor prophets is not the distinction familiar to the Hebrews. They spoke about the "former prophets" and the "latter prophets." The former prophets include the books which we ordinarily think of as historical, while the twelve "minor"—or shorter—prophets are included by the Hebrews in the latter prophets as but a single book.

The former prophets include Joshua, Judges, Samuel 1 and 2 and Kings 1 and 2. Since books describing the conquest of Canaan, the rule of the judges, and the kings of Israel are referred to as the former prophets, this helps us to understand the true nature of prophecy. Our English *prophet* transliterates a Greek word meaning "one who speaks for another." The prophets were men who spoke for God. The prophets interpreted the past, gave directions for the present, and revealed what might be expected to happen in the future. But whether dealing with the past, the present, or the future, a prophet was distinguished by the forthright way in which he proclaimed the mind of God for a particular historical circumstance.

Prophetic literature is unique by virtue of its power, eloquence and claim on conscience. Distinctively, it recognizes that all of history is the work of God. It insists that the moral climate established by man in his personal life and through his society has a direct consequence on the events of history. The former prophets demonstrate this conviction as they recount the experience of the Hebrews in conquest of their land. When the Hebrews give way to idolatry and immorality they suffer setback and defeat. As they deepen their vision of God's purpose, establish justice in society and live by God's law, they prosper, experience peace and wellbeing.

The pronouncements of the latter prophets appear in Isaiah, Jeremiah, Ezekiel and the Book of the Twelve. Each prophet inveighs against the backsliding and immorality of the people. Each prophet repeats again and again a clear message of Scripture: God judges the deeds of men. But each age brought with it new problems for which new answers had to be given. Each prophet is distinguished by his own insight into the nature of God's rule over men. The prophets instruct the Hebrews: God is Lord over all men, not just of the Hebrews. He can be worshipped in all lands, not just in Palestine. He prefers justice in human behavior, not a false and hypocritical piety. It is not enough to be secure in one's own integrity; man must seek after the peace of his society. Man must establish justice, protect the poor, defend the down-trodden, pursue peace. Moreover, Israel may not think of herself as immune from God's retribution merely because she is chosen of God. To be God's priest-people involves a responsibility of service. Israel must be a light unto nations, she must reflect higher standards of morality. God's justice is universal. He will cause evil nations to fall even as He will punish the Hebrews for their transgressions. But God will never utterly reject His chosen people. A remnant will survive; in their survival God establishes a witness to His graciousness for all of mankind.

The final category of Hebrew Scripture is referred to in Ecclesiasticus as "the other books of our fathers" and "the rest of the books." Later literary works which the Rabbis deemed to have been inspired by the holy spirit and worthy of public reading for spiritual edification were grouped together as "Writings." Jesus referred to them as "the Psalms." The Psalter was the best-known and best-loved work in this collection, and hence can be singled out as representative of the whole. "Writings" also includes works as varied as the Song of Songs, a collection of love songs; Lamentations, an elegiac outpouring of grief over Jerusalem's downfall; Proverbs and Ecclesiastes—poetic renderings of the moral wisdom of that day; Job, a poetic drama concerned with the fact that evil men frequently appear to be rewarded and the good to suffer misfortune.

Works of history are found, too, among the Writings. 1 and 2 Chronicles retell in somewhat glorified fashion events related in earlier narratives. Compare, for example, 2 Samuel 24 : 24 with 1 Chronicles 21 : 25. Ezra and Nehemiah tell of the return from exile and the rebuilding that followed. The historical romance also was used by the Hebrews for the glory of God. Esther describes how a beautiful Jewish maiden and her faithful uncle gained commanding position at the court of the Persian King Ahasuerus (or Xerxes), thereby rescuing the Jewish people from persecution; the story is read in synagogues as a part of the Purim celebration. The idyllic Book of Ruth was written to protest the narrow exclusiveness which led Ezra, upon the return from exile, to order all Jews to put away foreign wives. Finally, the Book of Daniel was included in the writings. Often referred to as one of the minor prophets, it was written too late to be included even among the latter prophets.

Jesus seems to have been especially fond of the Psalms, and their phraseology sounded forth at critical periods of his life. The voice at his baptism, "This is my beloved Son," used the words of Psalm 2 : 7. The Tempter spoke in terms of Psalm 91 : 11: "He will give his angels charge of you." The cry from the cross, "My God, my God, why hast thou forsaken me?" (Matthew 27 : 46) is really the opening words of Psalm 22. This expression of loneliness and desolation is seen in different light when we remember that the whole Psalm was no doubt in his mind. We think of the Beatitudes as distinctive of the ministry of Jesus, yet scattered through the Psalms there are some twenty beatitudes. Probably it was Jesus' own familiarity with the latter which led him to cast part of his teaching in that mold.

We have Jesus' own word for it that he came to fulfill the law, the prophets and the writings. Jesus consciously and deliberately sought to fulfill the grand ideas of the Old Testament. Driving the money-changers from the temple, he cited Isaiah 56 : 7: "For my house shall be called a house of prayer for all peoples." This occurs in a passage descriptive of how foreigners are to be brought to God's holy mountain and be made joyful in his Temple. Thus even as Jesus protested against the commercialism that had invaded the Temple he urged that the Temple be a house of God fit for all men.

Entering the city where he was to die, Jesus proclaimed his

kingship by his choice of animal for the triumphal ride. Kings bent on conquest rode on battle-chargers. *The* King chooses a lowly beast of burden. This is prophecy fulfilled in the grand manner. It is a moving experience to read Isaiah 53 and consider how it was fulfilled in the life and the work of one who "came not to be served but to serve, and to give his life as a ransom for many" (Mark 10 : 45).

Jews, of course, offer other interpretations for these passages. They recognize that their own sufferings and misfortune bring a living reality to the words of Scripture; they hope that by their stripes all men will be healed of prejudice and hatred. Having recognized how bestial, how evil man can become, Jews hope that all men will now turn in penitence to God and recognize an obligation to love one another as the children of the One Father. But there is no false optimism on this account in the Jewish faith. Jews do not believe that the redemption has yet been initiated. They remain ever mindful that until God's messianic Kingdom is established man must learn how to cope with evil and live with fear and uncertainty. In God's Law the Jew finds consolation. It is a way of life.

Christians believe that through the ministry, the sorrows, and the triumph over death by Jesus of Nazareth, the new covenant was gloriously confirmed; the New Testament proclaims the mighty deeds of him "who abolished death and brought life and immortality to light through the gospel" (2 Timothy 1 : 10). After the defection of Judas, the disciples made choice of another to fill out the apostolic company. The one who would be picked, they said, "must become with us a witness to his resurrection" (Acts 1 : 22). The New Testament is given to proclaim the good news that although Jesus was "crucified and killed by the hands of lawless men. . . . God raised him up, having loosed the pangs of death, because it was not possible for him to be held by it" (Acts 2 : 23, 24).

If the books of our English New Testament were arranged in order of origin, the letters of Paul would come first. Paul was a missionary whose life was completely bound up with the life of his converts: "For now we live," he wrote to the people of a city now called Salonika, "if you stand fast in the Lord" (1 Thessalonians 3 : 8). Absent from his friends, he felt as if he had been orphaned (1 Thessalonians 2 : 17 in Greek). It was to keep in touch with his converts and the friends in the churches he had founded that he began to write. The letters he sent are not, for the most part, theological treatises, but answers to specific situations. Each of his letters flies straight to the heart of a local, contemporary crisis.

To Thessalonians, troubled that the expected end of the age had not transpired, Paul wrote that, for those who died in the meantime, they should "not grieve as others do who have no hope"; rather, all were "to do their work in quietness and to earn their own living." When the Galatian churches were in danger of introducing racial distinctions, Paul wrote that in Christ "there is neither Jew nor

Greek . . . neither slave nor free . . . neither male nor female." The
Corinthian letters reveal the heart of Paul as pastor, dealing with the
problems of living the Christian life in a pagan community. The
letter to Romans, dealing with sin and grace, is the nearest thing we
have to a systematic exposition of the Apostle's belief.

Four letters are called "prison epistles." The letter to Ephesians
contemplates the wonders which God in Christ has wrought in and
through the church. Heresies began early, and the letter to
Colossians demonstrates the absurdity of the secret cult, the futility
of ascetic practices, the all-sufficiency of Christ. The letter to
Philemon deals slavery its death blow by insisting that a slave-owner
take back his runaway slave, "no longer as a slave but as a beloved
brother." The letter to Philippians, abounding in evidence of the
affection that existed between a missionary and his converts, has
been called Paul's love letter.

All the letters of Paul were in circulation before a single gospel
attained its present form. The Gospel of Mark, the earliest, seems to
have been based upon the witness which Peter bore; so much of it is
given over to the last week of Jesus' life that it has been called a
"narrative of our Lord's Passion, with an introduction." Matthew
supplements Mark with a great body of teaching material, grouped as
five discourses (Chs. 5 : 3 to 7 : 27; 10; 13; 18; 24 and 25); this gospel
appears first in our English New Testament because its frequent
references to the Old Testament make it a fitting transition to the
New.

Luke, too, took over Mark's outline; to it he adds so many songs of
the nativity that he has been called "the man who gave us
Christmas." In the framework of a travel narrative, depicting Jesus'
journey to Jerusalem, he adds parables demonstrating God's love for
all sorts of people, making this the universal Gospel. The Acts of the
Apostles, the earliest work in church history, is Luke's second
volume. Epitomized in 1 : 8, it tells of the worship and fellowship and
rearranged common life which resulted from the Spirit's outpouring.
John 20 : 31 tells why the fourth Gospel was written: "That you may
believe that Jesus is the Christ, the Son of God, and that believing
you have life in his name."

Further writings appeared in response to further needs. Three
other letters are attributed to Paul: 1 and 2 Timothy and Titus.
Concerned with problems of church government and administration,
they are known as the "pastoral epistles." Though the formal
organization seems to reflect a later time, they appear to be
expansions by his associates of instructions sent by the Apostle to
younger colleagues.

Letters bearing the name of Paul are addressed either to
designated congregations or to individuals. The New Testament
contains other messages addressed to believers everywhere and these
are called "general (or catholic, which means the same thing)

letters." The epistolary form is often only nominal, and many of these appear to be either intended for oral instruction of new Christians or for sermon notes for the deeply moving messages by which their authors bore their witness.

1 Peter tells those persecuted for the faith that the "fiery ordeal" is not to be thought strange: "Christ also suffered for you, leaving you an example, that you should follow his steps." The letter of James discloses the new problems that arose when the church, which began among fishermen, started to make its way among the well-to-do. The letter to Hebrews is sure that anything which can be done by Moses or angels or priests, Jesus can do better. 2 Peter and Jude vividly depict the danger from false prophets and the plight of the wavering. Three letters bear the name of John. 1 John treats of forgiveness that overcomes sin and love that casts out fear. 2 John discloses that false teachers had been going from house to house spreading evil ideas. 3 John reveals how overbearing individuals were trying to arrogate power to themselves.

Though not the last book to have been written, our Bible fittingly comes to its close with an apocalypse. Apocalypse was a literary form as characteristic of the Hebrews as drama was of the Greeks. Time is foreshortened, and in conventional imagery drawn from the realm of nature, God's ultimate triumph over his foes is dramatically portrayed. *Apocalypse* is a Greek word meaning "revelation." It is important to note that Scripture concludes with revelation rather than obfuscation. Revelation is intended to *reveal*, rather than to baffle or confuse. Addressed to Christians undergoing persecution and martyrdom, Revelation encourages the believer to be steadfast by picturing a cosmic conflict in which the outcome is no longer in doubt. The issue has been settled. It is the Lamb and not the lion that triumphs.

Although several times insisting that it is dealing with things immediately at hand, Revelation has always been regarded by the church as picturing in symbolic form the final victory of right over wrong.

Frank Lloyd Wright, describing the architect's ideal of the city that is to be, says it will be "iridescent by day, luminous by night . . . woven of rich glass. . . . Such a city would clean itself in the rain, would know no fire alarm nor any gloom." This sounds like something out of Revelation. "Iridescent by day," he writes, "luminous by night." The seer says: "Night shall be no more; they need no light of lamp or sun." "Woven of rich glass," says Mr. Wright. "Clear as crystal," says the author of Revelation. Such a city, says Mr. Wright, would know no gloom. "Neither shall there be mourning nor crying nor pain any more," says Revelation. Is Frank Lloyd Wright among the apocalyptists? Let us say rather that even for dwellers in the twentieth century the Bible still spells out man's dreams better than man can do himself.

The Bible is a book not only for all times, all places, all peoples, but also for all worlds. It belongs not only to the age that has been and the age that now is, but also to the world that is to be. Man's venture into space may lend new meaning to the eternal purpose, expressed in the Bible, that "the manifold wisdom of God might now be made known to the principalities and powers in the heavenly places" (Ephesians 3 : 10).

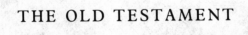
THE OLD TESTAMENT

The Book of Genesis

Genesis is a Greek word meaning "origin," and the Book of Genesis, first in the Bible, recounts the origins of life and society. In Hebrew it is entitled *Bereshith* ("in the beginning"), which is the first Hebrew word.

Genesis narrates the creation of the universe as an act of love by the one God, and asserts the equality and interrelatedness of all human beings by virtue of their descent from Adam, the first man. God then selects out of humankind one to be his chosen—Abraham, father of the people, Israel. Proved worthy in faith and deed Abraham and his seed are the first to witness to the one true God. The remaining chapters of Genesis record the journeys and experiences of the three patriarchs of Israel: Abraham, Isaac, and Jacob.

While Genesis is an ancient account of the beginnings of life as revealed to the Hebrew sages, it does not provide us with the kind of scientific knowledge available through modern physics, biology, chemistry, geology, astronomy, and palaeontology. Concerned with the *why* of man's being, Genesis records the belief of the early Hebrews that the world was not an accident and did not come into being by chance, but was created in love. It is asserted that man is God's most precious creation.

Genesis describes man's sinfulness and God's long patience and graciousness. In the life of one family, the family of Abraham, and in the experience of one people, the people of Israel, Genesis provides insight into the striving of all men, within their humanity, to respond to what they regard as the revealed will of God. Genesis is the first of the "Five Books of Moses." The Five Books taken together are known in Hebrew as *Torah*. (Jews also use the word "Torah" to refer to God's full revelation to man, and as a way of life in keeping with God's Commandments.) Sometimes the Greek word *Pentateuch*, meaning five books, is used as a name for these books.

All churches find in the account of the lives of the Hebrew patriarchs important and enduring lessons. Christians believe that, as participants in the covenant of God, they are heir to the promises made to Israel through the patriarchs. Thus references to Abraham, Isaac, and Jacob and their wives Sarah, Rebekah, Rachel, and Leah are to be found in Christian worship.

For example, both the Protestant Episcopal Book of Common Prayer and the "Divine Office," the official daily prayer of the Catholic church, present selections from Genesis and Exodus about Adam, Noah, Abraham, Joseph, and Moses. In the Catholic liturgy also the names of the patriarchs and the women are mentioned in important ceremonies, such as the Wedding Mass. The Nuptial

Blessing conferred in the Mass on the Day of Marriage contains this prayer for the bride: "May she be the beloved of her husband, as was Rachel; wise, as was Rebecca; long-lived and loyal, as was Sarah." At the end of the Wedding Mass the priest turns to the bridal couple and recites these final good wishes on the part of the Church: "May the God of Abraham, the God of Isaac, and the God of Jacob be with you, and may He fulfill in you His blessing, so that you may see your children's children to the third and fourth generation and afterward possess everlasting and boundless life."

God Creates the World: The First Day

Jews and Christians throughout the centuries have been stirred by this simple and direct description of the world's creation. Out of the void and chaos, God, by His will and word, brought life into being. Here man, the highest of God's creations, will find everything he needs to sustain life, if he uses God's abundance wisely and justly.

Many masterpieces in the arts of our culture find inspiration here, such as Haydn's oratorio "The Creation," based on the first two chapters of Genesis; Michelangelo's painting on the ceiling of the Sistine Chapel in the Vatican (the best-known part of which is probably the finger of God about to touch the finger of Adam, reproduced on a United States postage stamp commemorating the Geodetic Year). Great bronze doors of cathedrals and baptistries (e.g., Ghiberti's 15th-century doors of the baptistry in Florence, Italy) present scenes from the biblical story of creation. Other churches (like San Zeno in Verona, Italy, 12th century) present the creation story in sculptures above the doors.

Genesis 1:1–5

King James Version

In the beginning God created the heaven and the earth.
2 And the earth was without form, and void; and darkness was upon the face of the deep. And the spirit of God moved upon the face of the waters.
3 And God said, Let there be light: and there was light.
4 And God saw the light, that it was good: and God divided the light from the darkness.
5 And God called the light Day, and the darkness he called Night. And the evening and the morning were the first day.

Torah (JPS 1962 translation)

1 When God began to create the heaven and the earth— 2 the earth being unformed and void, with darkness over the surface of the deep and a wind from God sweeping over the water—3 God said, "Let there be light"; and there was light. 4 God saw how good the light was, and God separated the light from the darkness. 5 God called the light Day, and the darkness He called Night. And there was evening and there was morning, a first day.

1:1-5 Bible scholars, noting the similarity between the biblical account of creation and the stories of creation popular among peoples in the time of the Patriarchs, suggest that the differences in these accounts reflect the revelation possessed by the Hebrews. The world was brought into being as an act of love by a God who is above all the forces of nature and is in control of all phenomena. In the Babylonian accounts the world is created out of the struggle of the forces of nature, and man is created as an afterthought, as a slave to the gods. (See Appendix, "The Stories in Genesis and Near Eastern Myths.")

1:1 The Hebrew word *bereshith* can be justifiably translated "when God began to create," suggesting that there is a beginning about which Scripture does not inform us. Also, creation is a *process* initiated by God. Thus translating the word, Hebrew scholars see little conflict between the spiritual truth of the world's creation by God and scientific knowledge concerning the evolutionary processes from which man emerged. **1:2** To distinguish the Jewish concept of holy spirit as a creative and inspirational manifestation of God from the Christian concept of Holy Spirit as a third person of the Trinity, Jewish translators (as in the Jewish Publication Society's *Holy Scripture* of 1917) spell "spirit" uncapitalized. The 1962 Jewish Publication Society translation of the Torah translates the Hebrew word *ruach* as "wind," reminiscent of the early Babylonian mythologies. By his wind God controlled the waters. See Genesis 8:1. **1:5** Note that the day is measured from evening to evening; Jewish holy days commence at sundown the evening before the day of the holiday and conclude at the next sunset. The Jewish calendar marks the passage of time by the moon.

God Creates Man and Woman in His Image: The Sixth Day

Man alone among living creatures on earth has been granted the ability to reason, to probe the secrets of the universe, to make moral judgment, and to communicate values from one generation to another. Jews and Christians believe that by virtue of his divine image man is holy; his divine gifts, however, carry with them commensurate responsibilities to use his own life in service to God and man.

Genesis 1 : 26–31

26 Then God said, "Let us make man in our image, after our likeness; and let them have dominion over the fish of the sea, and over the birds of the air, and over the cattle, and over all the earth, and over every creeping thing that creeps upon the earth." ²⁷ So God created man in his own image, in the image of God he created him; male and female he created them. ²⁸ And God blessed them, and God said to them, "Be fruitful and multiply, and fill the earth and subdue

it; and have dominion over the fish of the sea and over the birds of the air and over every living thing that moves upon the earth." [29] And God said, "Behold, I have given you every plant yielding seed which is upon the face of all the earth, and every tree with seed in its fruit; you shall have them for food. [30] And to every beast of the earth, and to every bird of the air, and to everything that creeps on the earth, everything that has the breath of life, I have given every green plant for food." And it was so. [31] And God saw everything that he had made, and behold, it was very good. And there was evening and there was morning, a sixth day.

1:26 Some Church Fathers saw in the plural reference to God an intimation of the Trinity. The Midrash records a disputation between Christians and Jews on the meaning of this verse. A rabbi was asked how he explained the plural reference to God: "Let *us* make man in *our* image." The rabbi replied that this was clarified by the verse immediately following: "So God created man in *His* image." When the questioners left, the disciples of the rabbi insisted on a further explanation. The rabbi explained that while God alone made Adam of the earth and Eve from one of Adam's ribs, the use of the plural was intended to instruct us that, thereafter, any further procreation would require husband, wife, and the divine presence together (*Genesis Rabbah*). Thus the rabbi invoked a trinity, but not the Trinity of Christian doctrine. **1:27** Compare the Declaration of Independence ("all men are created equal . . . endowed by their Creator with unalienable rights"). The democratic system embodies the view that persons are equal before the law. **1:28** *Be fruitful and multiply.* Jews see the duty of building a home and rearing a family as derived from this passage; it is the first of 613 commandments of the Torah held sacred by Orthodox Jews. Among Christians, discussions of birth control and of procreation as an aim of marriage refer to this verse and to Genesis 2 : 18. **1:31** John Calvin (1509–1564), a leader in the Protestant Reformation, has a chapter on creation in his work, *Institutes of Religion*. He is full of admiration for the order and beauty of the universe: "God has wonderfully adorned heaven and earth with the utmost possible abundance, variety, and beauty, like a large and splendid mansion, most exquisitely and copiously furnished, and exhibited in man the masterpiece of his works by distinguishing him with such splendid beauty and such numerous and great privileges."

God Blesses the Seventh Day
Genesis 2 : 1–3

2 Thus the heavens and the earth were finished, and all the host of them. [2] And on the seventh day God finished his work which he had done, and he rested on the seventh day from all his work which he

had done. ³ So God blessed the seventh day and hallowed it, because on it God rested from all his work which he had done in creation.

    2:1 Saturday, as the seventh day, is observed as a day of prayer, meditation and family reunion by Jews and by some Christians. For Christian observance of Sunday, the first day of the week, see note at Revelation 1 : 10. **2:2** *Rested.* To speak as if God had become fatigued and needed rest, as human beings do, is called "anthropomorphism" (manlike). Jewish and Christian teachers explain that Scripture speaks in the ordinary language of men only in order to be intelligible; man is not to think that God is corporeal, i.e. that He has a body like mortals. **2:3** *Finished.* The author assumes that God's creative work within the universe is never finished. The Hebrew Prayer Book recites: "In His goodness He reneweth creation every day continually."

    In Christian churches, the baptistry and the baptismal font are often in octagonal shape to express the idea that initiation into a supernatural order of grace completes the work of creation. Thus the visible world was made in seven days; an invisible kingdom or order of grace follows.

God Plants a Garden in Eden
Genesis 2:4–17

4 These are the generations of the heavens and the earth when they were created.

    In the day that the LORD God made the earth and the heavens, ⁵ when no plant of the field was yet in the earth and no herb of the field had yet sprung up—for the LORD God had not caused it to rain upon the earth, and there was no man to till the ground; ⁶ but a mist went up from the earth and watered the whole face of the ground—⁷ then the LORD God formed man of dust from the ground, and breathed into his nostrils the breath of life; and man became a living being. ⁸ And the LORD God planted a garden in Eden, in the east; and there he put the man whom he had formed. ⁹ And out of the ground the LORD God made to grow every tree that is pleasant to the sight and good for food, the tree of life also in the midst of the garden, and the tree of the knowledge of good and evil.

    10 A river flowed out of Eden to water the garden, and there it divided and became four rivers. ¹¹ The name of the first is Pishon; it is the one which flows around the whole land of Hav′ilah, where there is gold; ¹² and the gold of that land is good; bdellium and onyx stone are there. ¹³ The name of the second river is Gihon; it is the one which flows around the whole land of Cush. ¹⁴ And the name of the third river is Tigris, which flows east of Assyria. And the fourth river is the Euphra′tes.

15 The LORD God took the man and put him in the garden of Eden to till it and keep it. [16] And the LORD God commanded the man, saying, "You may freely eat of every tree of the garden; [17] but of the tree of the knowledge of good and evil you shall not eat, for in the day that you eat of it you shall die."

2:4 To this point in Genesis, the Hebrew word used for God is *Elohim*; now joined to that word for the first time is the Hebrew *YHWH* (for which, in reading, Hebrews substitute *Adonai*) and translated "Lord." The Rabbis suggested that where Elohim is used it refers to God in His attribute of justice, and wherever YHWH is used God (or "the Lord") assumes an attribute of mercy. The rabbis taught: God realized that man could not endure if his deeds were to be judged alone by God's standard of justice; mercy and forgiveness were also required. Both words for God are combined in this account telling of God's creation of man and man's rule over the Garden of Eden. Some scholars suggest that Genesis describes in two different ways the process by which man was created. Genesis 2:7, 22 relate that man was created from the dust of the earth and woman from man's rib. The scholars claim that this is the account of creation maintained by the historians of the "J" school. Several hundred years later a group of priest historians ("P") rewrote the creation stories. In their account, God created man in His own image . . . male and female he created them (1:27). In the "P" account there is none of the "folklore" concerning dust and rib. (See Appendix: "The Documentary Theory," for a full discussion of the literary sources of the Old Testament as we have it today.)

2:7 *Dust from the earth.* Jewish midrash narrates that God took dust from all corners of the earth and of every color—red, black, and white—in order to teach that all men of whatever place or race are brothers and none may count himself superior (*Pirke R. Eliezer* 11). Another Jewish legend teaches that Adam was created from the dust of the place where the Jerusalem Temple was to be erected. Atonement for human sin was achieved through the sacrifices at that Temple. So God provided that sin would never become a permanent part of human nature (*Genesis Rabbah* 14). In many Christian churches the dust of ashes of the previous year's burned palm leaves are applied to the foreheads of the faithful on Ash Wednesday, first day of "Lent," a forty-day season of penance or self-discipline preceding Easter as a sign of man's mortality. Discussions about capital punishment and "mercy killings" include arguments based on this verse: "If God gives life, is not the right to take life also reserved to God?"

2:8 Various meanings are given to the word "Eden." Ancient versions identify it with a Persian word that originally meant an enclosure or a park. The Hebrew word itself means "delight." In early Jewish religious thought the phrase "Garden of Eden" was descriptive of any place possessing beauty and fertility; eventually it signified the heavenly paradise where the souls of the righteous repose in happiness. Eden may also have referred to the name of a geographical area, Edinu, signifying a plain or steppe, designating the extensive plain watered by the rivers Tigris and Euphrates.

2:15 The Rabbis read into this sentence a divinely ordained lot of man to work. Man was not to taste of the fruit of the tree until he had completed his toil. By labor man fulfills a significant part of his human inheritance from God and contributes to the creation by which the world is made whole and life is given purpose and meaning. Christian theologians generally agree with this teaching, but they add that after "the fall" (cf. Genesis 3:1–24) work became more difficult. Work itself, they hold, is not the consequence of the fall. (See Genesis 1:28; Psalm 104:22; Psalm 127:1–2; Job 8:4.)

2:16 From the eleventh to the fifteenth centuries it was a popular custom to present Bible stories in dramatic form ("Mystery Plays"). One of the most popular of these was the paradise play, about the creation of Adam and Eve and their expulsion from Paradise. A fir tree hung with apples was set up on the stage to represent the Garden of Eden and the tree from which Eve took fruit for Adam to eat. (The Bible does not speak of fir tree or apples; the details developed in popular imagination.) After the mystery plays were forbidden, it became customary to put up a "Paradise tree" in private homes in Germany on Christmas Eve, the popular feast day of Adam and Eve. The modern Christmas tree developed from this fir tree hung with red apples.

2:17 *You shall die.* Some translations read "thou must become mortal." Here we find a source for the idea that death entered human existence with man's sin. Though the evil has been done, the merciful God does not immediately inflict the penalty of death, permitting Adam and Eve to live out the years of their lives. Jewish tradition records that Adam spent forty weeks in prayer seeking forgiveness for his sin. Thus he is seen as a prototype of the penitent sinner. Shortly before Lent, most of the Oriental Churches observe a period of fasting and prayer. It is called the "Fast of Adam" in the Greek Rite, to commemorate this first law of abstinence which God gave to Adam and Eve in Paradise, and to prepare for the coming fast of Lent.

God Creates Woman
Genesis 2 : 18–25

18 Then the LORD God said, "It is not good that the man should be alone; I will make him a helper fit for him." ¹⁹ So out of the ground the LORD God formed every beast of the field and every bird of the air, and brought them to the man to see what he would call them; and whatever the man called every living creature, that was its name. ²⁰ The man gave names to all cattle, and to the birds of the

air, and to every beast of the field; but for the man there was not found a helper fit for him. ²¹ So the LORD God caused a deep sleep to fall upon the man, and while he slept took one of his ribs and closed up its place with flesh; ²² and the rib which the LORD God had taken from the man he made into a woman and brought her to the man. ²³ Then the man said,

> "This at last is bone of my bones
> and flesh of my flesh;
> she shall be called Woman,
> because she was taken out of Man."

²⁴ Therefore a man leaves his father and his mother and cleaves to his wife, and they become one flesh. ²⁵ And the man and his wife were both naked, and were not ashamed.

2:19 In this account of creation, God formed the birds of the air from the ground, but in Genesis 1 : 20 the birds are brought forth from the waters. **2:22** Adam and Eve are honored as saints in the Greek, Syrian, Coptic, and other Eastern churches. This devotion spread from the East to the West, where it became very popular about the tenth century. The Latin Church did not forbid the devotion, but it never officially introduced the feast day (in the Eastern churches the feast day is Christmas Eve). Statues of Adam and Eve may still be seen in many old European churches together with the saints of history. **2:23** *Bone of my bones, and flesh of my flesh*. These words have been interpreted to signify that companionship is an essential aspect of marriage.

Adam and Eve Disobey God

This story is an explanation of the presence of sin in the world. Man, tempted to become "as God, knowing good and evil," disobeys God's commandment. This passage has been understood in a variety of ways by various religious groups. Jews see this story as describing man's first act of disobedience. But they do not hold that man is permanently tainted with guilt as a result; the deadly effect of sin can be removed by true repentance. Jews believe that the soul is created pure and that man, by freedom of will, chooses either to accept God's love or to rebel against Him. Eden did not represent an order of existence on a higher level, from which man fell, for, they point out, "Paradise" is known as the gift at the end of the process of redemption (see Isaiah, chapters 2 and 11). But it is true that death entered the world with Adam's sin. Man was banished from Eden "lest he take also of the tree of life and eat, and live forever" (Genesis 3 : 22). By virtue of sin, according to the Jewish view, man is separated from God. But man can attain life beyond death when his name is linked with the cause of righteousness and obedience to God's law. The story of Adam and Eve recalls, therefore, man's first defiance of divine law. Thereafter in this yet unredeemed world, men will struggle with good and evil, striving toward a time when they will be ultimately reconciled with God and at peace with their fellow men.

In Catholic teaching, Adam and Eve before their fall through sin had a supernatural life, far above the claims of man's nature, a life as adopted children of God destined to enjoy the vision of God in heaven. This life, the "state of original justice," included immunity from irregular desire, ignorance, suffering, death. By their disobedience, "original sin," Adam and Eve forfeited for themselves and their descendants their special life, destiny and gifts. The sin (attributed to Adam as the head of the race) is transmitted to Adam's posterity but is removed by the merits of Jesus the Redeemer, e.g., in the baptism of children. By his incarnation, suffering, death and resurrection, Jesus restored mankind to a supernatural relationship with God, but this does not restore the special gifts such as immunity from death.

The idea of original sin was denied by some Christians, e.g., the Pelagians, fifth-century followers of or adherents to the views of Pelagius, a British monk in the early fifth century, in the sense that they taught that the sin of Adam was not transmitted through inheritance but sin is learned by bad example; they taught that death and suffering were not punishment for sin but the working out of a pure state of nature; that baptism was not for remission of sins but for acceptance into the community of the Church.

The sixteenth-century reformers (e.g., Luther, Calvin) believed in the reality of original sin, but they held that the Scripture meant Adam's natural state of innocence was corrupted and he could do nothing of himself but sin. All Protestants hold with St. Paul that sinful man is "justified" (is reconciled to God, becomes righteous) by the death of Jesus (Romans 5) but their understanding of justice (righteousness) differs as their understanding of the state of original justice differs.

Some of these discussions are reflected in the system of checks and balances in the government established by the Constitution of the United States.

Many Protestants, today, point out that the doctrine of original sin is intended to express the interrelatedness of our humanity. Something has gone wrong with the human nature to which we all are heirs. The biologist speaks of mixed impulses and imperfections which we inherit. The Bible, however, does not base its doctrines upon natural science. Paul's description of his own experience has its parallel in the autobiography of every man: "I do not understand my own actions. For I do not do what I want, but I do the very thing I hate" (Romans 7 : 15).

Many Christians have held that all men are condemned because of the sins of the ancestor. Such a belief is sometimes based upon Romans 5 : 12 in a translation which refers to Adam as one "in whom all men sinned." Other Christians argue that the Greek text says, "because all men sinned"—a statement of the universality of transgression. The solidarity of our race is expressed in Exodus 20 : 5, where God is described as "visiting the iniquity of the fathers upon the children to the third and fourth generation of those who hate me." The corollary of this, however, is that God shows "steadfast love to thousands of those who love me and keep my commandment" (Exodus 20 : 6).

The fact that we cannot escape our membership in the sinful human race is to be held in harmony with Ezekiel's teaching regarding individual responsibility: "The soul that sins shall die. The son shall not suffer for the iniquity of the father, nor the father suffer for the iniquity of the son" (Ezekiel 18 : 20).

Mormons, in the second of their Articles of Faith, say: "We believe that men will be punished for their own sins and not for Adam's transgressions."

From the doctrine of original sin some persons derive a doctrine of "total depravity," meaning that sin is not a mere accumulation of evil dispositions and tendencies, but is an injury to man's will or moral power, making all that he does subject to corruption. Twentieth-century theologians tend to emphasize how even man's best endeavors are often hindered by pride and self-interest. This doctrine in its extreme form has been interpreted to mean that man is utterly incapable of good. The very nature of the temptations which beset man, however, are offered as evidence that the divine image in man has not been wholly lost; few people set out to do evil for evil's sake, but many mistake what is really good. "Whenever I am about to commit any folly," says Bucklaw in Walter Scott's *Bride of Lammermoor*, "he [the devil] persuades me that it is the most necessary, gallant, gentleman-like thing on earth, and I am up to saddle-girths in the bog before I see that the ground is soft."

Genesis 3 : 1–24

3 Now the serpent was more subtle than any other wild creature that the LORD God had made. He said to the woman, "Did God say, 'You shall not eat of any tree of the garden'?" [2] And the woman said to the serpent, "We may eat of the fruit of the trees of the garden; [3] but God said, 'You shall not eat of the fruit of the tree which is in the midst of the garden, neither shall you touch it, lest you die.' " [4] But the serpent said to the woman, "You will not die. [5] For God knows that when you eat of it your eyes will be opened, and you will be like God, knowing good and evil." [6] So when the woman saw that the tree was good for food, and that it was a delight to the eyes, and that the tree was to be desired to make one wise, she took of its fruit and ate; and she also gave some to her husband, and he ate. [7] Then the eyes of both were opened, and they knew that they were naked;

and they sewed fig leaves together and made themselves aprons. 8 And they heard the sound of the LORD God walking in the garden in the cool of the day, and the man and his wife hid themselves from the presence of the LORD God among the trees of the garden. ⁹ But the LORD God called to the man, and said to him, "Where are you?" ¹⁰ And he said, "I heard the sound of thee in the garden, and I was afraid, because I was naked; and I hid myself." ¹¹ He said, "Who told you that you were naked? Have you eaten of the tree of which I commanded you not to eat?" ¹² The man said, "The woman whom thou gavest to be with me, she gave me fruit of the tree, and I ate." ¹³ Then the LORD God said to the woman, "What is this that you have done?" The woman said, "The serpent beguiled me, and I ate." ¹⁴ The LORD God said to the serpent,

"Because you have done this,
    cursed are you above all cattle,
    and above all wild animals;
upon your belly you shall go,
    and dust you shall eat
    all the days of your life.
¹⁵ I will put enmity between you and the woman,
    and between your seed and her seed;
he shall bruise your head,
    and you shall bruise his heel."
¹⁶ To the woman he said,
"I will greatly multiply your pain in childbearing;
    in pain you shall bring forth children,
yet your desire shall be for your husband,
    and he shall rule over you."
¹⁷ And to Adam he said,
"Because you have listened to the voice of your wife,
    and have eaten of the tree
of which I commanded you,
    'You shall not eat of it,'
cursed is the ground because of you;
    in toil you shall eat of it all the days of your life;
¹⁸ thorns and thistles it shall bring forth to you;
    and you shall eat the plants of the field.
¹⁹ In the sweat of your face
    you shall eat bread
till you return to the ground,
    for out of it you were taken;
you are dust,
    and to dust you shall return."

20 The man called his wife's name Eve, because she was the mother of all living. ²¹ And the LORD God made for Adam and for his wife garments of skins, and clothed them.

22 Then the LORD God said, "Behold, the man has become like one of us, knowing good and evil; and now, lest he put forth his hand and take also of the tree of life, and eat, and live for ever"— ²³ therefore the LORD God sent him forth from the garden of Eden, to till the ground from which he was taken. ²⁴ He drove out the man; and at the east of the garden of Eden he placed the cherubim, and a flaming sword which turned every way, to guard the way to the tree of life.

3:1 The *serpent* may hark back to the gigantic serpent in Babylonian mythology who is a cosmic force for evil. But here the serpent is but a creature of God, not a co-equal force of evil. (See Appendix.) In Christian writings the serpent is identified with Satan or the Devil. In the Rabbinic period contemporary with early Christianity (A.D. 200–400), one can find Midrashic legends suggesting that Satan was among the angels cast from heaven. Jewish theologians today are reluctant to recognize such a cosmic force for evil and emphasize instead that evil is a product of human behavior. 3:6 The American constitutional division of powers among legislative, executive and judicial branches of government, with various checks and balances, flows from the view that all men are corruptible and that no man should be tempted with too much power. 3:7 The Geneva Bible, issued in 1560 by English Protestant exiles, derives its popular name, "The Breeches Bible," from its wording here: "They sewed fig leaves together and made themselves breeches." 3:9 The belief that God may speak to man, and man to God, supports the "right of free speech"; by free speech the people are assured of a chance to hear through any man the word which may come from God. 3:15 The Greek version of the Bible translates this passage: "*He* shall bruise your head." A Latin version: "*She* will bruise your head." Thus, some Christians interpret this passage as offering a first vision of the salvation promised the Church in Jesus. The Messiah will conquer the Devil. Catholics understand the feminine gender to refer to Mary, who appears together with her son. The Jewish translation understands this passage to refer in general to the progeny of man—not to a specific redeemer—and it translates the verse: "*They* shall strike at your head." The new Catholic *Jerusalem Bible* renders this passage: "*It* will crush your head." 3:16 When, on the basis of this text, objection was raised to the use of anesthetics in childbirth, the doctor who first began experimentation along this line replied to critics, "But, after all, God before taking woman from man's side caused a deep sleep to fall upon the man" (Genesis 2 : 21). 3:17–19 Because of this passage the need to work has sometimes been explained as a punishment for sin. The prevailing view in Judaism, however, held that work was a commission entrusted to man by God (Genesis 1 : 28); but man is completely dependent on God, for without His help all labor would be in vain (Psalm 127 : 1–2). In the Talmud the Rabbis instruct the faithful: "Labor lends dignity to man" (*Nedarim* 49b). **3:19** The last part of this verse is spoken by the priest each time he puts ashes on the head of a person on the first day of Lent (Ash Wednesday). He says: "Remember, man, that thou art dust, and unto dust thou shalt return." These lines are often heard as part of the funeral ritual of Jews and Christians. **3:21** Despite Adam and Eve's sin, God did not withdraw His concern for them. This account of their punishment is at once followed by an act of lovingkindness. Man is urged to imitate God's ways of love. **3:24** The *cherubim* (plural of "cherub") are not described here, and so artists have used their imaginations. In ancient times they were pictured as winged creatures, half human and half lion. In some traditions they were angelic beings in the form of handsome young men. In Christian art they were depicted this way, often with blue wings and with three pairs of wings. Theologians later figured out nine "choirs" of angels, with the seraphim (with red wings in art) nearest to God and the cherubim next. The seraphim were considered to be absorbed in love, the cherubim in knowledge or contemplation. These ideas explain many references to cherubim in later literature, as in the poems of Dante and Milton. Sometimes, especially in later Christian art, the cherubim were depicted as plump, winged children or babies, and often as only babies' heads with wings.

Cain Commits Murder
Genesis 4 : 1–16

4 Now Adam knew Eve his wife, and she conceived and bore Cain, saying, "I have gotten a man with the help of the LORD." ² And again, she bore his brother Abel. Now Abel was a keeper of sheep, and Cain a tiller of the ground. ³ In the course of time Cain brought to the LORD an offering of the fruit of the ground, ⁴ and Abel brought of the firstlings of his flock and of their fat portions. And the LORD had regard for Abel and his offering, ⁵ but for Cain and his offering he had no regard. So Cain was very angry, and his countenance fell. ⁶ The LORD said to Cain, "Why are you angry, and why has your countenance fallen? ⁷ If you do well, will you not be accepted? And if you do not do well, sin is couching at the door; its desire is for you, but you must master it."

8 Cain said to Abel his brother, "Let us go out to the field." And when they were in the field, Cain rose up against his brother

Abel, and killed him. ⁹Then the LORD said to Cain, "Where is Abel your brother?" He said, "I do not know; am I my brother's keeper?" ¹⁰And the LORD said, "What have you done? The voice of your brother's blood is crying to me from the ground. ¹¹And now you are cursed from the ground, which has opened its mouth to receive your brother's blood from your hand. ¹²When you till the ground, it shall no longer yield to you its strength; you shall be a fugitive and a wanderer on the earth." ¹³Cain said to the LORD, "My punishment is greater than I can bear. ¹⁴Behold, thou hast driven me this day away from the ground; and from thy face I shall be hidden; and I shall be a fugitive and a wanderer on the earth, and whoever finds me will slay me." ¹⁵Then the LORD said to him, "Not so! If any one slays Cain, vengeance shall be taken on him sevenfold." And the LORD put a mark on Cain, lest any who came upon him should kill him. ¹⁶Then Cain went away from the presence of the LORD, and dwelt in the land of Nod, east of Eden.

4:3 Here is the first description of worship in the Scriptures. **4:4** Jewish Midrash, in an effort to explain why Abel's offerings were accepted by God and Cain's were rejected, points to the fact that Abel brought "fat portions"—he took care to offer God his choicest possessions. **4:9** By the question, "Am I my brother's keeper?" a murderer seeks to renounce obligations of brotherhood. The question is not directly answered, but the message of Scripture as a whole clearly asserts the responsibility of men for each other. Cain's question is still heard in debates about social welfare legislation, foreign affairs, etc. **4:13** Cain's plea points to the power of repentance: penitent, he receives God's compassion. **4:14** Blood feuds, a step toward justice, antedated and were made obsolete by the development of courts and police forces. The citizen has some responsibility for law enforcement in any civic system. **4:15** The mark of Cain is understood in Jewish tradition to be an expression of God's forgiving mercy, in that it was by this brand that God protected Cain from a future blood avenger. The Bible does not suggest or imply that skin color was the mark, nor does the text support the idea of "racial inferiority" by virtue of descent from Cain. Nor is there any evidence that the descendants of Cain include Negroes, an interpretation which gained currency in the United States in the heat of Civil War conflicts. Scholars have pointed out that the Kenites, a people known to the Israelites at the time they entered Canaan, were a tattooed people. According to the biblical genealogies the Kenites were descended from the family of Cain. It may be through this account that the Hebrews provided an explanation for the practice of their neighbors in tattooing themselves.

God Sends a Flood

Traditions of a flood are found among many primitive peoples, e.g., Babylonians and American Indians. (See Appendix.) A most popular biblical story, particularly among children, Noah and his ark have also inspired great spirituals, and impressive musical creations such as *The Flood* by Stravinsky and *Noyes Fludde* by Benjamin Britten. *Green Pastures*, the modern American play by Marc Connolly, presents the story in a folk style and language relished by many. Depictions of an ark are found in the catacombs of Rome (second century A.D.), and in a mosaic of a fifth-century synagogue in Gerasa. Raphael used the image of the ark in his paintings in the Vatican, and Gustave Doré's romantic print is world famous.

Genesis 6:9–22; 7:1–5, 11–24; 8:1–12, 15–18, 20–22; 9:17

9 These are the generations of Noah. Noah was a righteous man, blameless in his generation; Noah walked with God. ¹⁰And Noah had three sons, Shem, Ham, and Japheth.

11 Now the earth was corrupt in God's sight, and the earth was filled with violence. ¹²And God saw the earth, and behold, it was corrupt; for all flesh had corrupted their way upon the earth. ¹³And God said to Noah, "I have determined to make an end of all flesh; for the earth is filled with violence through them; behold, I will destroy them with the earth. ¹⁴Make yourself an ark of gopher wood; make rooms in the ark, and cover it inside and out with pitch. ¹⁵This is how you are to make it: the length of the ark three hundred cubits, its breadth fifty cubits, and its height thirty cubits. ¹⁶Make a roof for the ark, and finish it to a cubit above; and set the door of the ark in its side; make it with lower, second, and third decks. ¹⁷For behold, I will bring a flood of waters upon the earth, to destroy all flesh in which is the breath of life from under heaven; everything that is on the earth shall die. ¹⁸But I will establish my covenant with you; and you shall come into the ark, you, your sons, your wife, and your sons' wives with you. ¹⁹And of every living thing of all flesh, you shall bring two of every sort into the ark, to keep them alive with you; they shall be male and female. ²⁰Of the birds according to their kinds, and of the animals according to their kinds, of every creeping thing of the ground according to its kind, two of every sort shall come in to you, to keep them alive. ²¹Also take with you every sort of food that is eaten, and store it up; and it shall serve as food for you and for them." ²²Noah did this; he did all that God commanded him.

7 Then the LORD said to Noah, "Go into the ark, you and all your household, for I have seen that you are righteous before me in this generation. ²Take with you seven pairs of all clean animals, the male

and his mate; and a pair of the animals that are not clean, the male and his mate; ³ and seven pairs of the birds of the air also, male and female, to keep their kind alive upon the face of all the earth. ⁴ For in seven days I will send rain upon the earth forty days and forty nights; and every living thing that I have made I will blot out from the face of the ground." ⁵ And Noah did all that the LORD had commanded him.

11 In the six hundredth year of Noah's life, in the second month, on the seventeenth day of the month, on that day all the fountains of the great deep burst forth, and the windows of the heavens were opened. ¹² And rain fell upon the earth forty days and forty nights. ¹³ On the very same day Noah and his sons, Shem and Ham and Japheth, and Noah's wife and the three wives of his sons with them entered the ark, ¹⁴ they and every beast according to its kind, and all the cattle according to their kinds, and every creeping thing that creeps on the earth according to its kind, and every bird according to its kind, every bird of every sort. ¹⁵ They went into the ark with Noah, two and two of all flesh in which there was the breath of life. ¹⁶ And they that entered, male and female of all flesh, went in as God had commanded him; and the LORD shut him in.

17 The flood continued forty days upon the earth; and the waters increased, and bore up the ark, and it rose high above the earth. ¹⁸ The waters prevailed and increased greatly upon the earth; and the ark floated on the face of the waters. ¹⁹ And the waters prevailed so mightily upon the earth that all the high mountains under the whole heaven were covered; ²⁰ the waters prevailed above the mountains, covering them fifteen cubits deep. ²¹ And all flesh died that moved upon the earth, birds, cattle, beasts, all swarming creatures that swarm upon the earth, and every man; ²² everything on the dry land in whose nostrils was the breath of life died. ²³ He blotted out every living thing that was upon the face of the ground, man and animals and creeping things and birds of the air; they were blotted out from the earth. Only Noah was left, and those that were with him in the ark. ²⁴ And the waters prevailed upon the earth a hundred and fifty days.

8 But God remembered Noah and all the beasts and all the cattle that were with him in the ark. And God made a wind blow over the earth, and the waters subsided; ² the fountains of the deep and the windows of the heavens were closed, the rain from the heavens was restrained, ³ and the waters receded from the earth continually. At the end of a hundred and fifty days the waters had abated; ⁴ and in the seventh month, on the seventeenth day of the month, the ark came to rest upon the mountains of Ar′arat. ⁵ And the waters

continued to abate until the tenth month; in the tenth month, on the first day of the month, the tops of the mountains were seen.

6 At the end of forty days Noah opened the window of the ark which he had made, ⁷and sent forth a raven; and it went to and fro until the waters were dried up from the earth. ⁸Then he sent forth a dove from him, to see if the waters had subsided from the face of the ground; ⁹but the dove found no place to set her foot, and she returned to him to the ark, for the waters were still on the face of the whole earth. So he put forth his hand and took her and brought her into the ark with him. ¹⁰He waited another seven days, and again he sent forth the dove out of the ark; ¹¹and the dove came back to him in the evening, and lo, in her mouth a freshly plucked olive leaf; so Noah knew that the waters had subsided from the earth. ¹²Then he waited another seven days, and sent forth the dove; and she did not return to him any more.

15 Then God said to Noah, ¹⁶"Go forth from the ark, you and your wife, and your sons and your sons' wives with you. ¹⁷Bring forth with you every living thing that is with you of all flesh—birds and animals and every creeping thing that creeps on the earth—that they may breed abundantly on the earth, and be fruitful and multiply upon the earth." ¹⁸So Noah went forth, and his sons and his wife and his sons' wives with him.

20 Then Noah built an altar to the LORD, and took of every clean animal and of every clean bird, and offered burnt offerings on the altar. ²¹And when the LORD smelled the pleasing odor, the LORD said in his heart, "I will never again curse the ground because of man, for the imagination of man's heart is evil from his youth; neither will I ever again destroy every living creature as I have done. ²²While the earth remains, seedtime and harvest, cold and heat, summer and winter, day and night, shall not cease."

9 ¹⁷God said to Noah, "This is the sign of the covenant which I have established between me and all flesh that is upon the earth."

6:15 A cubit is the distance between the elbow and the tip of the fingers, about eighteen inches. The ark would have been about half the length of such great ships as the *Queen Mary* and the *Queen Elizabeth*. **6:22** According to Jewish tradition Noah planted cedar trees and felled them for the building of the ark over a period of 120 years. He continually preached repentance, but the people would not listen to him. In fact, they persecuted him (*Sanhedrin* 108a and *Pirke R. Eliezer* 22). **7:2** By "clean animals" the author may have meant those that were considered ritualistically pure by Jewish law. See Leviticus 11. **7:7** The Christian gospel sees in this account a foreshadowing of events in the end-time, when only those who have taken refuge in the faith will escape the divine judgment. See Luke 17:26 ff. and Matthew 24:37. In 1 Peter 3:20–21 the waters of baptism that save are compared to the salvation brought the eight persons in the ark through water. **8:4** Bible scholars who hold to the documentary theory (see essay in Appendix) find in this flood story a blending of at least two variant versions. In this passage it says that the waters abated at the end of 150 days, whereas 8:6 informs us that Noah opened the porthole at the end of 40 days. In one version, 6:19, Noah is instructed to take two of every living thing into the ark. In another version (7:2), Noah is instructed to take seven pairs of all clean animals and two of animals that are not clean. Many efforts have been made to identify the mountain on which the ark came to rest and to find the remnants of the ark. Some claim the mountain to be Mount Judi, from which the plain of Mesopotamia can be seen. Others suggest it is farther north in Armenia, where Mount Ararat is the commanding peak, 16,945 feet above sea level. In 1829 Mount Ararat was climbed by C. F. Parrot and then again in 1876 by Lord Bryce. Neither found the ark. **9:4** Blood is the symbol of life. According to traditional Jewish teaching, therefore, man may not eat meat until the blood (life) has departed from it entirely, since life is reserved to God. Jewish law forbids the cutting of a limb from a live animal, and it requires a proper ritualistic (kosher) preparation of meat by completely draining the blood from it. **9:4–15** From these verses, by various accepted forms of legal deduction, the rabbis described seven fundamental universal laws (the *Noachide* laws): establishment of courts of justice; prohibition of blasphemy, idolatry, adultery, bloodshed, robbery; eating flesh cut from a living animal (*Sanhedrin* 56a). They considered one who observed these laws to be "pious of the gentiles" and assured of a portion in the world-to-come (*Sanhedrin* 105a).

Noah Curses His Son
Genesis 9 : 18–29

18 The sons of Noah who went forth from the ark were Shem, Ham, and Japheth. Ham was the father of Canaan. ¹⁹ These three were the sons of Noah; and from these the whole earth was peopled.

20 Noah was the first tiller of the soil. He planted a vineyard; ²¹ and he drank of the wine, and became drunk, and lay uncovered in his tent. ²² And Ham, the father of Canaan, saw the nakedness of his father, and told his two brothers outside. ²³ Then Shem and Japheth took a garment, laid it upon both their shoulders, and walked backward and covered the nakedness of their father; their faces were turned away, and they did not see their father's nakedness. ²⁴ When Noah awoke from his wine and knew what his youngest son had done to him, ²⁵ he said,

"Cursed be Canaan;
   a slave of slaves shall he be to his brothers."
²⁶ He also said,
"Blessed by the LORD my God be Shem;
   and let Canaan be his slave.
²⁷ God enlarge Japheth,
   and let him dwell in the tents of Shem;
   and let Canaan be his slave."
28 After the flood Noah lived three hundred and fifty years. ²⁹ All
the days of Noah were nine hundred and fifty years; and he died.

9:21 Good and bad are reported of Noah; the Bible offers no
"whitewash" of its heroes. **9:25** In disputes prior to the Civil War in
the United States, this passage was interpreted in the South to mean
that Negroes, allegedly the descendants of Ham, were condemned to
eternal slavery. The biblical record shows, however, that the sons
and grandsons of Ham became kings and mighty nations; nor were
the Canaanites a colored people. The curse uttered, not by God, but
by Noah under the influence of alcohol, cannot be extended to justify
servitude of Negroes or any people. **9:26** Some biblical scholars
believe that these blessings of Noah may have been written in the
time of King David when both the Hebrews (Shem) and the
Philistines (Japheth) occupied a land formerly in the possession of
the Canaanites, who were now a subject people.

God Divides Mankind into Separate Nations

This tale tries to account for the existence of a divided humanity. In
human pride, according to one view, man seeks to storm the heavens.
In punishment God divides man from his brother into separate
tongues and nationalities. When man tries to replace God as the
ultimate authority, he will find himself in contention with other men.

In another interpretation this tale serves as protest against the
materialistic culture of Babylon, where possessions and buildings
were held in higher regard than human values. The tragic dispersion
of the people is a consequence of this materialistic philosophy of life.

A third view suggests that the building of the tower was a means
used by a primitive and superstitious people to gain security. In
Babylonian mythology the tower may have been considered the
"Gate of God." And so the people placed themselves near a place
where the gods could descend and ascend. The biblical author,
therefore, satirically cites the inadequacy of a pagan tower before the
God of creation.

A fourth less common view notes that God's providence required
that all the ends of the earth be populated, and so he scattered the
peoples all over the earth. This separation of man therefore serves
not as a sign of man's punishment but, rather, reflects upon man's
responsibility to use all of the earth's resources for good.

Genesis 11 : 1–9

11 Now the whole earth had one language and few words. ²And as men migrated from the east, they found a plain in the land of Shinar and settled there. ³And they said to one another, "Come, let us make bricks, and burn them thoroughly." And they had brick for stone, and bitumen for mortar. ⁴Then they said, "Come, let us build ourselves a city, and a tower with its top in the heavens, and let us make a name for ourselves, lest we be scattered abroad upon the face of the whole earth." ⁵And the LORD came down to see the city and the tower, which the sons of men had built. ⁶And the LORD said, "Behold, they are one people, and they have all one language; and this is only the beginning of what they will do; and nothing that they propose to do will now be impossible for them. ⁷Come, let us go down, and there confuse their language, that they may not understand one another's speech." ⁸So the LORD scattered them abroad from there over the face of all the earth, and they left off building the city. ⁹Therefore its name was called Babel, because there the LORD confused the language of all the earth; and from there the LORD scattered them abroad over the face of all the earth.

11:4 In the fifth century B.C. the famous Greek historian Herodotus visited Mesopotamia and described the city of Babylon. Archaeologists today have verified his findings; some believe that his reports and this Bible account describe a temple tower of the Babylonian god Marduk. Archaeologists say the tower rose about 300 feet toward the sky. **11:7** This passage is sometimes used to oppose development of a universal tongue, such as Esperanto. Misunderstandings caused by language difficulties are apparent in sessions of the United Nations. **11:9** "Babel" in Assyrian means "Gate of God." The tower reached to the heavens and so served as the gate of the gods. In popular biblical etymology, however, a word meaning is frequently associated with the sound of the word. Here a Hebrew word meaning "confound" or "confuse" is linked in sound with the word "babel." A play on words can provide an occasion to draw a lesson. In Christian theology the unity of man will be restored in Jesus, at the end of time when the faithful from all nations will be gathered in heaven. See Revelation 7 : 9–10.

God Calls Abram

Through His covenant with Noah, God revealed His concern for all mankind. He placed all men under the authority of His natural law. With the story of Abram—later, chapter 17, to be called "Abraham"—it is now clear that God's universal purpose in the creation will be demonstrated and fulfilled through the life of one family.

Jewish tradition considered Abraham's faith to have been so overflowing with blessing that he rendered "the whole human family one" (*Genesis Rabbah* 39). Jews were instructed to regard "as a disciple of Abram, whosoever has a benign eye, a simple heart and a humble spirit" (*Berachot* 6b).

Jews, Christians, and Muslim regard Abraham as father of their faith.

Abraham has always been one of the key figures in the Christian liturgy. The Offertory of every Catholic Requiem Mass (Mass for the Dead) includes the prayer that the dead may come "into the holy light which Thou didst promise to Abraham and to his seed," and again, at the end of the same prayer: "Grant them, O Lord, to pass from death unto life, which Thou didst promise to Abraham and to his seed." That final phrase in Latin (*quam olim Abrahae promisisti et semini eius*) continues to thrill music lovers everywhere at concert performances of the Requiem Mass (Mozart, Berlioz, Verdi, Fauré, Durufle). The significance of Abraham and the Covenant is communicated powerfully also in Benjamin Britten's *War Requiem*, composed for the new Coventry (England) Cathedral built beside what remained of the old cathedral after its bombing in World War II. These masterpieces continue to give resonance to the saying of Paul, "So you see that it is the men of faith who are the sons of Abraham" (Galatians 3 : 7).

In the Canon of every Catholic Mass, after the Consecration, there is a reference to "the sacrifice of our Patriarch Abraham." Commenting on the phrase, Pope Pius XI said (in September, 1938, to the directors of the Belgian Catholic Radio Agency): "Notice that Abraham is called our Patriarch, our ancestor. Anti-Semitism is incompatible with the thought and sublime reality expressed in this text. It is a movement in which we Christians can have no part whatsoever. ... Anti-Semitism is unacceptable. Spiritually we are Semites."

Genesis 12 : 1–3, 5a, 7

12 Now the LORD said to Abram, "Go from your country and your kindred and your father's house to the land that I will show you. ²And I will make of you a great nation, and I will bless you, and make your name great, so that you will be a blessing. ³I will bless those who bless you, and him who curses you I will curse; and by you all the families of the earth shall bless themselves."

5 And Abram took Sar'ai his wife, and Lot his brother's son, and all their possessions which they had gathered, and the persons that they had gotten in Haran; and they set forth to go to the land of Canaan.

7 Then the LORD appeared to Abram, and said, "To your descendants I will give this land." So he built there an altar to the LORD, who had appeared to him.

12:1 Jewish Midrash recalls that Abram's father, Terah, was an idol-maker (see also Joshua 24 : 2). When still a child, Abram became disillusioned with these lifeless gods. **12:3** The Apostles suggested that Jesus was the fulfillment of this promise to Abraham and his descendants (cf. Acts 3 : 25; Galatians 3 : 8). Paul in Romans 4 : 16–19 numbers Christians as among the "children of Abraham." **12:7** Three promises are made to Abraham: (1) he will become a great nation; (2) all the nations of the earth will be blessed in his seed; (3) his descendants will acquire the land of Canaan. The rest of the narrative recalls how God by miraculous providence rescues Abram and his descendants from one mishap or another until these promises will be fulfilled.

Abram and Sarai Journey to Egypt

Genesis includes two accounts of Abram and Sarai (later called "Sarah") in a circumstance where Abram felt it wise to hide the fact that Sarai was his wife. Some biblical scholars believe that these are two accounts of one episode written by different authors at different periods in history. They point to these passages to demonstrate "the documentary theory" (see Appendix). Here they are, for comparison.

Genesis 12 : 10–20

10 Now there was a famine in the land. So Abram went down to Egypt to sojourn there, for the famine was severe in the land. [11] When he was about to enter Egypt, he said to Sar'ai his wife, "I know that you are a woman beautiful to behold; [12] and when the Egyptians see you, they will say, 'This is his wife'; then they will kill me, but they will let you live. [13] Say you are my sister, that it may go well with me because of you, and that my life may be spared on your account." [14] When Abram entered Egypt the Egyptians saw that the woman was very beautiful. [15] And when the princes of Pharaoh saw her, they praised her to Pharaoh. And the woman was taken into Pharaoh's house. [16] And for her sake he dealt well with Abram; and he had sheep, oxen, he-asses, menservants, maidservants, she-asses, and camels.

17 But the LORD afflicted Pharaoh and his house with great plagues because of Sar'ai, Abram's wife. [18] So Pharaoh called Abram, and said, "What is this you have done to me? Why did you not tell me that she was your wife? [19] Why did you say, 'She is my sister,' so that I took her for my wife? Now then, here is your wife, take her, and be gone." [20] And Pharaoh gave men orders concerning him; and they set him on the way, with his wife and all that he had.

Genesis 20 : 1–7

20 From there Abraham journeyed toward the territory of the Negeb, and dwelt between Kadesh and Shur; and he sojourned in

Gerar. ²And Abraham said of Sarah his wife, "She is my sister." And Abim'elech king of Gerar sent and took Sarah. ³But God came to Abim'elech in a dream by night, and said to him, "Behold, you are a dead man, because of the woman whom you have taken; for she is a man's wife." ⁴Now Abim'elech had not approached her; so he said, "Lord, wilt thou slay an innocent people? ⁵Did he not himself say to me, 'She is my sister'? And she herself said, 'He is my brother.' In the integrity of my heart and the innocence of my hands I have done this." ⁶Then God said to him in the dream, "Yes, I know that you have done this in the integrity of your heart, and it was I who kept you from sinning against me; therefore I did not let you touch her. ⁷Now then restore the man's wife; for he is a prophet, and he will pray for you, and you shall live. But if you do not restore her, know that you shall surely die, you, and all that are yours."

12:10 Egypt was kept fertile by the waters of the Nile River, and so Egyptians suffered famine far less often than the Canaanites, who had to depend on a seasonal rainfall. **12:10** ff. Many students believe that this account was written by the author of the "J" history, because the name for the divinity used here is *YHWH*, translated "Lord", a characteristic of "J." Note that Abram gains by this deception; Sarai is taken into the house of Pharaoh, but God miraculously spares Sarai from defilement. **20:1–7** Where 12 : 10 ff. bears the marks of a "J" account, so here many students believe that this account was written by the author of the "E" history because the Hebrew word for the divinity used in this account is *Elohim*, translated "God." In this passage an effort has been made to idealize the patriarch and to provide a more humanitarian explanation for God's intervention. It is clear that Sarai is not compromised, Abraham is referred to as a prophet; his action is based not alone on fear but because this is a place where "there is no fear of God"; and he has an explanation indicating that, in truth, he had justification to call Sarai his "sister." The Nuzi tablets reveal that it was not uncommon to designate one's wife as "wife-sister." Such status provided the woman with superior privileges and rights over an ordinary wife. Abram, therefore, may have meant no deceit at all in referring to Sarai as his sister; but Jewish biblical authors, centuries later, may have forgotten that ancient custom. **20:2** Abimelech is described as the king of Gerar. In 26 : 1, however, he is described as the king of the Philistines. This would be an anachronism, since the Philistines appeared in Palestine about one thousand years after Abraham. Such a "slip" is used as evidence by those who suggest that the Pentateuch in its present form comes from historians who lived during the period of the monarchy.

Abram and Lot Resolve Their Conflicts Peacefully
Genesis 13 : 1– 2, 5– 13

13 So Abram went up from Egypt, he and his wife, and all that he had, and Lot with him, into the Negeb. 2 Now Abram was very rich in cattle, in silver, and in gold. ⁵ And Lot, who went with Abram, also had flocks and herds and tents, ⁶ so that the land could not support both of them dwelling together; for their possessions were so great that they could not dwell together, ⁷ and there was strife between the herdsmen of Abram's cattle and the herdsmen of Lot's cattle. At that time the Canaanites and the Per'izzites dwelt in the land.

8 Then Abram said to Lot, "Let there be no strife between you and me, and between your herdsmen and my herdsmen; for we are kinsmen. ⁹ Is not the whole land before you? Separate yourself from me. If you take the left hand, then I will go to the right; or if you take the right hand, then I will go to the left." ¹⁰ And Lot lifted up his eyes, and saw that the Jordan valley was well watered everywhere like the garden of the LORD, like the land of Egypt, in the direction of Zo'ar; this was before the LORD destroyed Sodom and Gomor'rah. ¹¹ So Lot chose for himself all the Jordan valley, and Lot journeyed east; thus they separated from each other. ¹² Abram dwelt in the land of Canaan, while Lot dwelt among the cities of the valley and moved his tent as far as Sodom. ¹³ Now the men of Sodom were wicked, great sinners against the LORD.

13:1 Nelson Glueck, president of Reform Judaism's Hebrew Union College in Cincinnati and a distinguished archaeologist, has demonstrated by his excavations in the Negev that the age of Abraham could not be later than the nineteenth century B.C. During that period the Negev, now a desert wasteland, was dotted with hundreds of settlements and caravan roads joining Egypt, Arabia and Canaan. Thus, Abraham could make his journey to the Negev in comparative safety. Dr. Glueck has shown how the Negev residents, by building carefully placed lateral walls, channeled the scant rainwater into terraced fields and into cisterns where it could be collected and saved for a dry season. New Israeli settlements are being built today near or upon the ruins of these ancient villages; and by the same method of water engineering the Israelis seek to reclaim the soil. **13:7** ff. This incident is a part of the history of diplomacy and arbitration—successful ways of handling a dispute.

God Promises Palestine to Abram and His Seed
Genesis 13 : 14– 18

14 The LORD said to Abram, after Lot had separated from him, "Lift up your eyes, and look from the place where you are, northward and

southward and eastward and westward; ¹⁵for all the land which you see I will give to you and to your descendants for ever. ¹⁶I will make your descendants as the dust of the earth; so that if one can count the dust of the earth, your descendants also can be counted. ¹⁷Arise, walk through the length and the breadth of the land, for I will give it to you." ¹⁸So Abram moved his tent, and came and dwelt by the oaks of Mamre, which are at Hebron; and there he built an altar to the LORD.

13:15 Biblical authors were later to explain (Deuteronomy 9 : 4–6) that the Israelites were to occupy Canaan not because of their virtue but, rather, because of the wickedness of the Canaanites. Possession of the land involved moral responsibility. Jewish claim to a national home in Palestine, now established as the State of Israel, reaches back to this promise to Abraham.

Abram Wins a Victory

This passage opens with a description of the military conquest of Palestine by the kings of Shinar, Ellasar, Elam, and Goiim. Lot, son of Abram's brother, who lived in Sodom, was taken captive.

Genesis 14 : 14–24

14 When Abram heard that his kinsman had been taken captive, he led forth his trained men, born in his house, three hundred and eighteen of them, and went in pursuit as far as Dan. ¹⁵And he divided his forces against them by night, he and his servants, and routed them and pursued them to Hobah, north of Damascus. ¹⁶Then he brought back all the goods, and also brought back his kinsman Lot with his goods, and the women and the people.

17 After his return from the defeat of Ched-or-lao'mer and the kings who were with him, the king of Sodom went out to meet him at the Valley of Shaveh (that is, the King's Valley). ¹⁸And Melchiz'edek king of Salem brought out bread and wine; he was priest of God Most High. ¹⁹And he blessed him and said,

"Blessed be Abram by God Most High,
    maker of heaven and earth;
²⁰and blessed be God Most High,
    who has delivered your enemies into your hand!"

And Abram gave him a tenth of everything. ²¹And the king of Sodom said to Abram, "Give me the persons, but take the goods for yourself." ²²But Abram said to the king of Sodom, "I have sworn to the LORD God Most High, maker of heaven and earth, ²³that I would not take a thread or a sandal-thong or anything that is yours, lest you should say, 'I have made Abram rich.' ²⁴I will take nothing but what the young men have eaten, and the share of the men who went with me; let Aner, Eshcol, and Mamre take their share."

14:14 ff. This account appears to be based on ancient records describing the efforts of Mesopotamian chieftains to clear the trade routes to the Red Sea. Abram became involved only in order to rescue his kinsman. At no other place in Scripture is there a reference to his military prowess. The account establishes the Patriarch's connection with Jerusalem, later to become capital city of the united kingdom. Hebrew interpretations see in Melchizedek's blessing of Abram fulfillment of God's promise that Abraham would be a great name. **14:18** The name Melchizedek means "king of righteousness." Salem (meaning "peace") has been variously identified, but most probably refers to Jerusalem. This king-priest, about whom nothing else is known, came to be regarded as the prototype of a priestly ruler belonging to a superior order (cf. Psalm 110 : 4). The author of the Letter to the Hebrews argues from Genesis 14 : 17–20 that Melchizedek was superior to Abraham and the Jewish priests, and that Psalm 110 : 4 is fulfilled in Jesus Christ (Hebrews 7 : 1 ff.). The Communion tradition of bread and wine is attributed to this scene in Genesis, and the event is recalled every day in the Mass (e.g., in the Roman rite, after the Consecration, when the priest prays that God will accept the offering as He accepted "that which Thy high priest Melchizedek offered to Thee, a holy sacrifice, a spotless victim"). In some countries, just before the offertory prayer in the Mass, the people follow an ancient custom of offering bread, wine, candles or money—materials for the sacrifice or for the support of the clergy. Stipends for Masses have the same origin.

God Establishes a Covenant with Abraham
Genesis 17 : 1–21

17 When Abram was ninety-nine years old the LORD appeared to Abram, and said to him, "I am God Almighty; walk before me, and be blameless. ²And I will make my covenant between me and you, and will multiply you exceedingly." ³Then Abram fell on his face; and God said to him, ⁴"Behold, my covenant is with you, and you shall be the father of a multitude of nations. ⁵No longer shall your name be Abram, but your name shall be Abraham; for I have made you the father of a multitude of nations. ⁶I will make you exceedingly fruitful; and I will make nations of you, and kings shall come forth from you. ⁷And I will establish my covenant between me and you and your descendants after you throughout their generations for an everlasting covenant, to be God to you and to your descendants after you. ⁸And I will give to you, and to your descendants after you, the land of your sojournings, all the land of Canaan, for an everlasting possession; and I will be their God."

9 And God said to Abraham, "As for you, you shall keep my covenant, you and your descendants after you throughout their generations. [10] This is my covenant, which you shall keep, between me and you and your descendants after you: Every male among you shall be circumcised. [11] You shall be circumcised in the flesh of your foreskins, and it shall be a sign of the covenant between me and you. [12] He that is eight days old among you shall be circumcised; every male throughout your generations, whether born in your house, or bought with your money from any foreigner who is not of your offspring, [13] both he that is born in your house and he that is bought with your money, shall be circumcised. So shall my covenant be in your flesh an everlasting covenant. [14] Any uncircumcised male who is not circumcised in the flesh of his foreskin shall be cut off from his people; he has broken my covenant."

15 And God said to Abraham, "As for Sar′ai your wife, you shall not call her name Sar′ai, but Sarah shall be her name. [16] I will bless her, and moreover I will give you a son by her; I will bless her, and she shall be a mother of nations; kings of peoples shall come from her." [17] Then Abraham fell on his face and laughed, and said to himself, "Shall a child be born to a man who is a hundred years old? Shall Sarah, who is ninety years old, bear a child?" [18] And Abraham said to God, "O that Ish′mael might live in thy sight!" [19] God said, "No, but Sarah your wife shall bear you a son, and you shall call his name Isaac. I will establish my covenant with him as an everlasting covenant for his descendants after him. [20] As for Ish′mael, I have heard you; behold, I will bless him and make him fruitful and multiply him exceedingly; he shall be the father of twelve princes, and I will make him a great nation. [21] But I will establish my covenant with Isaac, whom Sarah shall bear to you at this season next year."

17:5 In this scriptural passage, God directs Abram toward his new destiny by calling him "Abraham." In the Near Eastern world, a man's name was considered part of his psychic being. To give a person a name is to give him existence. To remove a name is to destroy the essence of a person. Note Deuteronomy 25 : 6, with its stress on the importance of maintaining the identity of a family's name. In Hebrew a most terrifying curse is *Y'mach Sh'mo* ("May his name be blotted out!"). **17:10** *Circumcised.* Circumcision is considered the external sign of God's covenant with Abraham. Among Jews the obligation of religious circumcision is fulfilled only by the performance of the ritual at a religious ceremony on the eighth day after the child's birth. Whatever its original historic source or function, it now signifies for the Jew a consecration to God. Tyrants sought to forbid this rite, but Jews chose death rather than its abandonment (cf. 1 Maccabees 1 : 48, 60; 2 : 46). In the Christian community, baptism replaced circumcision as the badge of membership. **17:19** *Isaac* means *he laughs.* **17:20** In Arabic literature, Ishmael's son Kedar is said to be an ancestor of Mohammed.

God Announces the Birth of Isaac
Genesis 18 : 1–14, 16

18 And the LORD appeared to him by the oaks of Mamre, as he sat at the door of his tent in the heat of the day. [2] He lifted up his eyes and looked, and behold, three men stood in front of him. When he saw them, he ran from the tent door to meet them, and bowed himself to the earth, [3] and said, "My lord, if I have found favor in your sight, do not pass by your servant. [4] Let a little water be brought, and wash your feet, and rest yourselves under the tree, [5] while I fetch a morsel of bread, that you may refresh yourselves, and after that you may pass on—since you have come to your servant." So they said, "Do as you have said." [6] And Abraham hastened into the tent to Sarah, and said, "Make ready quickly three measures of fine meal, knead it, and make cakes." [7] And Abraham ran to the herd, and took a calf, tender and good, and gave it to the servant, who hastened to prepare it. [8] Then he took curds, and milk, and the calf which he had prepared, and set it before them; and he stood by them under the tree while they ate.

9 They said to him, "Where is Sarah your wife?" And he said, "She is in the tent." [10] The LORD said, "I will surely return to you in the spring, and Sarah your wife shall have a son." And Sarah was listening at the tent door behind him. [11] Now Abraham and Sarah were old, advanced in age; it had ceased to be with Sarah after the manner of women. [12] So Sarah laughed to herself, saying, "After I have grown old, and my husband is old, shall I have pleasure?" [13] The LORD said to Abraham, "Why did Sarah laugh, and say, 'Shall I indeed bear a child, now that I am old?' [14] Is anything too hard for the LORD? At the appointed time I will return to you, in the spring, and Sarah shall have a son."

16 Then the men set out from there, and they looked toward Sodom; and Abraham went with them to set them on their way.

18:1 The Rabbis relate this sentence to the preceding selection, i.e., Abraham is recuperating from the operation of circumcision and now God's messengers appear to him. From this they deduced the religious duty and obligation of visiting the sick (cf. Matthew 25 : 36). **18:2** These men are revealed at 19 : 1 to be angels. The Church Fathers understood the presence of the "three" as a foreshadowing of the doctrine of the Trinity. **18:7** The servant is understood by Rabbinical scholars to be the lad Ishmael; Abraham is instructing him in the courtesy of hospitality to strangers. In the Eastern manner, Abraham belittles his offerings, "a morsel of bread," but prepared a feast and waits upon the pleasure of the three strangers. In this case the angels partake of food. In later scriptural writings (e.g., Tobit 12 : 9) angels refuse food. The Rabbis deduced the lesson that it is necessary to conform to the social habits of the people in whose midst one lives. The angels, although they would not ordinarily partake of food, do so out of concern for Abraham and in gratitude for his hospitality. **18:16** As the final gracious act of hospitality Abraham shows the strangers the road and accompanies them until they are safely on their way.

Abraham Pleads with God for Sodom and Gomorrah

In this dialogue with God Abraham demonstrates his concern for justice, even for a people with whom he has no personal ties. The dialogue reveals God's readiness to pardon if only He can do so consistently with justice. Had there been as few as ten righteous men, the cities would have been spared. The work of the righteous provide a redeeming significance beyond their number.

Genesis 18 : 17–21, 23–32

17 The LORD said, "Shall I hide from Abraham what I am about to do, ¹⁸ seeing that Abraham shall become a great and mighty nation, and all the nations of the earth shall bless themselves by him? ¹⁹ No, for I have chosen him, that he may charge his children and his household after him to keep the way of the LORD by doing righteousness and justice; so that the LORD may bring to Abraham what he has promised him." ²⁰ Then the LORD said, "Because the outcry against Sodom and Gomor'rah is great and their sin is very grave, ²¹ I will go down to see whether they have done altogether according to the outcry which has come to me; and if not, I will know."

23 Then Abraham drew near, and said, "Wilt thou indeed destroy the righteous with the wicked? ²⁴ Suppose there are fifty righteous within the city; wilt thou then destroy the place and not spare it for the fifty righteous who are in it? ²⁵ Far be it from thee to do such a thing, to slay the righteous with the wicked, so that the righteous fare as the wicked! Far be that from thee! Shall not the Judge of all the earth do right?" ²⁶ And the LORD said, "If I find at Sodom fifty righteous in the city, I will spare the whole place for their sake." ²⁷ Abraham answered, "Behold, I have taken upon myself to speak to the Lord, I who am but dust and ashes. ²⁸ Suppose five of the fifty righteous are lacking? Wilt thou destroy the whole city for lack of five?" And he said, "I will not destroy it if I find forty-five there." ²⁹ Again he spoke to him, and said, "Suppose forty are found there."

He answered, "For the sake of forty I will not do it." [30] Then he said, "Oh let not the Lord be angry, and I will speak. Suppose thirty are found there." He answered, "I will not do it, if I find thirty there." [31] He said, "Behold, I have taken upon myself to speak to the Lord. Suppose twenty are found there." He answered, "For the sake of twenty I will not destroy it." [32] Then he said, "Oh let not the Lord be angry, and I will speak again but this once. Suppose ten are found there." He answered, "For the sake of ten I will not destroy it."

18:23 The Bible recalls that Abram had spoken with God three times, Genesis 15 : 2, 8; 17 : 17, but each time the matter concerned his own particular destiny. Now that he has been named Abraham, father of a multitude of nations, he is revealed in a profounder character, as a defender of all righteous men. **18:25** Man's ability to trust in God's justice is a central theme of the Hebrew narrative. In Babylonian wisdom literature there are poems that reflect how idolaters in that period despaired at the arbitrariness of their gods. One poem, entitled "Poem of the Righteous Sufferer," bewailed:

What is good in one's sight is evil for a god.
What is bad in one's own mind is good for a god.
Who can understand the counsel of the gods in the midst of heaven?
The plan of a god in deep waters, who can comprehend it?
Where has befuddled mankind ever learned what a god's conduct is?

In contrast, this biblical text points out that even though ten righteous men were not to be found, God would maintain faith with a righteous man. He rescued Lot and his family.

The Angels Visit Sodom
Genesis 19 : 1–13, 24–26, 29

19 The two angels came to Sodom in the evening; and Lot was sitting in the gate of Sodom. When Lot saw them, he rose to meet them, and bowed himself with his face to the earth, [2] and said, "My lords, turn aside, I pray you, to your servant's house and spend the night, and wash your feet; then you may rise up early and go on your way." They said, "No; we will spend the night in the street." [3] But he urged them strongly; so they turned aside to him and entered his house; and he made them a feast, and baked unleavened bread, and they ate. [4] But before they lay down, the men of the city, the men of Sodom, both young and old, all the people to the last man, surrounded the house; [5] and they called to Lot, "Where are the men who came to you tonight? Bring them out to us, that we may know them." [6] Lot went out of the door to the men, shut the door after

him, [7] and said, "I beg you, my brothers, do not act so wickedly.
[8] Behold, I have two daughters who have not known man; let me
bring them out to you, and do to them as you please; only do nothing
to these men, for they have come under the shelter of my roof." [9] But
they said, "Stand back!" And they said, "This fellow came to
sojourn, and he would play the judge! Now we will deal worse with
you than with them." Then they pressed hard against the man Lot,
and drew near to break the door. [10] But the men put forth their
hands and brought Lot into the house to them, and shut the door.
[11] And they struck with blindness the men who were at the door of
the house, both small and great, so that they wearied themselves
groping for the door.

12 Then the men said to Lot, "Have you any one else here?
Sons-in-law, sons, daughters, or any one you have in the city, bring
them out of the place; [13] for we are about to destroy this place,
because the outcry against its people has become great before the
LORD, and the LORD has sent us to destroy it."

24 Then the LORD rained on Sodom and Gomor′rah brimstone
and fire from the LORD out of heaven; [25] and he overthrew those
cities, and all the valley, and all the inhabitants of the cities, and
what grew on the ground. [26] But Lot's wife behind him looked back,
and she became a pillar of salt.

29 So it was that, when God destroyed the cities of the valley, God
remembered Abraham, and sent Lot out of the midst of the
overthrow, when he overthrew the cities in which Lot dwelt.

19:5 *Know them* is a biblical phrase referring to sexual experience. The term "sodomy," sexual relations between men, derives
from the name of the city. Sodomy was considered an abomination to
the Israelites (Leviticus 18 : 22) and punishable by death (Leviticus
20 : 13). Lot fulfills his duty to protect his guests. Only the importance of that duty in his time and place can explain his attitude
toward his daughters, today unthinkable. **19:24** Archaeologists date
the destruction of these cities by earthquake roughly at the time of
Abraham, i.e., between the twenty-first and nineteenth centuries
B.C. The cities were apparently covered over by a collapse of the
earth's crust, affecting the course of the River Jordan and creating
the Dead Sea as it is known today. At its deepest the waters of
the Dead Sea are 1,300 feet deep, but at its southern end, where
these cities are thought to be buried, the Dead Sea is only three to
fourteen feet deep. **19:29** Some Rabbinic scholars suggest that Lot
was spared not because of his own righteousness, but by the merit
of Abraham's faith. Thus a significant biblical concept is underscored: the righteousness of one chosen individual may protect the
lives of others. **19:22** *Zoar* means *little* (see verse 20).

God Fulfills His Promise to Sarah
Genesis 21 : 1–4

21 The LORD visited Sarah as he had said, and the LORD did to Sarah as he had promised. ²And Sarah conceived, and bore Abraham a son in his old age at the time of which God had spoken to him. ³Abraham called the name of his son who was born to him, whom Sarah bore him, Isaac. ⁴And Abraham circumcised his son Isaac when he was eight days old, as God had commanded him.

Abraham Casts Out Hagar and Ishmael
Genesis 21 : 9–21

9 But Sarah saw the son of Hagar the Egyptian, whom she had borne to Abraham, playing with her son Isaac. ¹⁰So she said to Abraham, "Cast out this slave woman with her son; for the son of this slave woman shall not be heir with my son Isaac." ¹¹And the thing was very displeasing to Abraham on account of his son. ¹²But God said to Abraham, "Be not displeased because of the lad and because of your slave woman; whatever Sarah says to you, do as she tells you, for through Isaac shall your descendants be named. ¹³And I will make a nation of the son of the slave woman also, because he is your offspring." ¹⁴So Abraham rose early in the morning, and took bread and a skin of water, and gave it to Hagar, putting it on her shoulder, along with the child, and sent her away. And she departed, and wandered in the wilderness of Beer-sheba.

15 When the water in the skin was gone, she cast the child under one of the bushes. ¹⁶Then she went, and sat down over against him a good way off, about the distance of a bowshot; for she said, "Let me not look upon the death of the child." And as she sat over against him, the child lifted up his voice and wept. ¹⁷And God heard the voice of the lad; and the angel of God called to Hagar from heaven, and said to her, "What troubles you, Hagar? Fear not; for God has heard the voice of the lad where he is. ¹⁸Arise, lift up the lad, and hold him fast with your hand; for I will make him a great nation." ¹⁹Then God opened her eyes, and she saw a well of water; and she went, and filled the skin with water, and gave the lad a drink. ²⁰And God was with the lad, and he grew up; he lived in the wilderness, and became an expert with the bow. ²¹He lived in the wilderness of Paran; and his mother took a wife for him from the land of Egypt.

21:9 When Sarah thought she would have no children, she suggested, in accordance with the customs of that time, that Abraham have a child by Hagar, her maidservant. However, when Sarah herself gave birth to Isaac, she did not wish the right of her son as heir to Abraham to be shared, so she urged Abraham to cast

Hagar and her son out of the household. **21:10** Edmonia Lewis, the first Negro American woman sculptor of reputation, executed in 1875 a marble statue of Hagar, included in the collection of the recently founded Frederick Douglass Institute of Negro Arts and History in Washington, D.C. **21:11** Hurrian tablets from the fifteenth century B.C., uncovered in Nuzi near Haran from whence Abraham came, included legislation permitting a woman to give her maid-servant to her husband if she herself could not bear children. The Hurrian law, however, protected the right of the maidservant. In asking Abraham to cast Hagar out of the house, Sarah may have been breaking the law; hence Abraham's reluctance. Scholars report, however, the existence of an even older Babylonian law that allows the children of a slave-wife to exchange their inheritance rights for freedom. Thus Abraham properly gave Hagar and Ishmael their freedom, while securing the birthright for his son Isaac. Note at 25 : 9 that Ishmael joins Isaac in the burial ceremonies for his father, Abraham. **21:19** God demonstrates his pity on the anguish of the slave mother. She is able to see what had been before her eyes, as it were, but which she had overlooked because of her troubled spirit. A holy fountain at the alleged site of this well is revered by the Muslim faith. Nearby where Abraham left Hagar and Ishmael the famous Kaaba—a Moslem temple—was built. Pilgrimages to these holy places are a significant feature in the Islamic faith.

God Tests Abraham

In Jewish tradition this classic story is referred to as "The Binding of Isaac". Abraham is put to the supreme test. Admittedly, he is devoted to God. But will he also sacrifice that which is most precious to him at God's demand? If Isaac is sacrificed, how then will God fulfill the promises of His covenant? At the last moment God spares Isaac, and Abraham is proved faithful. It is upon the merit of his faithful act that Jews still depend. They invoke this scriptural passage on the New Year (Rosh Hashanah) as they rededicate themselves to God in faith. This passage undoubtedly served to affirm the ancient Hebrews' insistence that child sacrifice as practiced by the nations among whom they lived was evil (cf. Deuteronomy 12 : 31). A willingness to sacrifice life itself in order to remain faithful to God (martyrdom) was inspired among the Jews by invoking this particular passage, although it was spiritual surrender alone that God required. The Church Fathers saw in the sacrifice of Isaac a prefiguring of the Passion of Jesus.

Genesis 22 : 1–19

22 After these things God tested Abraham, and said to him, "Abraham!" And he said, "Here am I." ²He said, "Take your son, your only son Isaac, whom you love, and go to the land of Mori'ah, and offer him there as a burnt offering upon one of the mountains of which I shall tell you." ³So Abraham rose early in the morning, saddled his ass, and took two of his young men with him, and his son Isaac; and he cut the wood for the burnt offering, and arose and went to the place of which God had told him. [4]On the third day Abraham lifted up his eyes and saw the place afar off. [5]Then Abraham said to his young men, "Stay here with the ass; I and the lad will go yonder and worship, and come again to you." [6]And Abraham took the wood of the burnt offering, and laid it on Isaac his son; and he took in his hand the fire and the knife. So they went both of them together. [7]And Isaac said to his father Abraham, "My father!" And he said, "Here am I, my son." He said, "Behold, the fire and the wood; but where is the lamb for a burnt offering?" [8]Abraham said, "God will provide himself the lamb for a burnt offering, my son." So they went both of them together.

9 When they came to the place of which God had told him, Abraham built an altar there, and laid the wood in order, and bound Isaac his son, and laid him on the altar, upon the wood. [10]Then Abraham put forth his hand, and took the knife to slay his son. [11]But the angel of the LORD called to him from heaven, and said, "Abraham, Abraham!" And he said, "Here am I." [12]He said, "Do not lay your hand on the lad or do anything to him; for now I know that you fear God, seeing you have not withheld your son, your only son, from me." [13]And Abraham lifted up his eyes and looked, and behold, behind him was a ram, caught in a thicket by his horns; and Abraham went and took the ram, and offered it up as a burnt offering instead of his son. [14]So Abraham called the name of that place The LORD will provide; as it is said to this day, "On the mount of the LORD it shall be provided."

15 And the angel of the LORD called to Abraham a second time from heaven, [16]and said, "By myself I have sworn, says the LORD, because you have done this, and have not withheld your son, your only son, [17]I will indeed bless you, and I will multiply your descendants as the stars of heaven and as the sand which is on the seashore. And your descendants shall possess the gate of their enemies, [18]and by your descendants shall all the nations of the earth bless themselves, because you have obeyed my voice." [19]So Abraham returned to his young men, and they arose and went together to Beer-sheba; and Abraham dwelt at Beer-sheba.

22:7 Rabbinical tradition suggests that Isaac realized he was to be the offering, and so he shared with his father in this demonstration of faith. A ram's horn, called the *Shofar,* is sounded on the holiest of Jewish festivals, the New Year (Rosh Hashanah) and at the conclusion of the Day of Atonement (Yom Kippur), in recollection of this demonstration of the faith of the Patriarch of Israel.

Abraham Buries Sarah

Genesis 23 : 1–16, 19

23 Sarah lived a hundred and twenty-seven years; these were the years of the life of Sarah. ²And Sarah died at Kir'iath-ar'ba (that is, Hebron) in the land of Canaan; and Abraham went in to mourn for Sarah and to weep for her. ³And Abraham rose up from before his dead, and said to the Hittites, ⁴"I am a stranger and a sojourner among you; give me property among you for a burying place, that I may bury my dead out of my sight." ⁵The Hittites answered Abraham, ⁶"Hear us, my lord; you are a mighty prince among us. Bury your dead in the choicest of our sepulchres; none of us will withhold from you his sepulchre, or hinder you from burying your dead." ⁷Abraham rose and bowed to the Hittites, the people of the land. ⁸And he said to them, "If you are willing that I should bury my dead out of my sight, hear me, and entreat for me Ephron the son of Zohar, ⁹that he may give me the cave of Mach-pe'lah, which he owns; it is at the end of his field. For the full price let him give it to me in your presence as a possession for a burying place." ¹⁰Now Ephron was sitting among the Hittites; and Ephron the Hittite answered Abraham in the hearing of the Hittites, of all who went in at the gate of his city, ¹¹"No, my lord, hear me; I give you the field, and I give you the cave that is in it; in the presence of the sons of my people I give it to you; bury your dead." ¹²Then Abraham bowed down before the people of the land. ¹³And he said to Ephron in the hearing of the people of the land, "But if you will, hear me; I will give the price of the field; accept it from me, that I may bury my dead there." ¹⁴Ephron answered Abraham, ¹⁵"My lord, listen to me; a piece of land worth four hundred shekels of silver, what is that between you and me? Bury your dead." ¹⁶Abraham agreed with Ephron; and Abraham weighed out for Ephron the silver which he had named in the hearing of the Hittites, four hundred shekels of silver, according to the weights current among the merchants.

19 After this, Abraham buried Sarah his wife in the cave of the field of Mach-pe'lah east of Mamre (that is, Hebron) in the land of Canaan.

23:8 ff. The Hittites of the land exposed bodies of the dead to be consumed by animals and vultures. Contrast the practice of embalming in Egypt, cremation in India, the placing of bodies in vaults above ground where the water is near the surface (as in New Orleans) and burial under the sod. Costs of a funeral are a matter of social concern in many lands. **23:9** This cave became the patriarchal family's burying place. In addition to Sarah, others placed there were Abraham, Isaac, Rebekah, Leah and Jacob. The cave is now concealed by an Arab mosque, formerly a church built by the Crusaders.

A Jewish pilgrim of the twelfth century describes a "St. Abraham" church, previously a synagogue, where for a sum of money one could visit the tombs of the patriarchs. **23:11–16** Four hundred shekels of silver are equivalent in the weight then current to 4,650 grams. Today a gram of silver is worth about 3¢. Some scholars say the transaction demonstrates Abraham's intent to make this land the home of his people; it establishes a right of residence in a land in which Abraham's heirs possess legally-acquired property. Thus God's promise in 12 : 7, 13 : 15 and 15 : 7 is beginning to be fulfilled.

Rebekah Is Chosen as Wife to Isaac
Genesis 24:1–7, 9–41, 45–52, 55–61, 63–67

24 Now Abraham was old, well advanced in years; and the LORD had blessed Abraham in all things. ²And Abraham said to his servant, the oldest of his house, who had charge of all that he had, "Put your hand under my thigh, ³and I will make you swear by the LORD, the God of heaven and of the earth, that you will not take a wife for my son from the daughters of the Canaanites, among whom I dwell, ⁴but will go to my country and to my kindred, and take a wife for my son Isaac." ⁵The servant said to him, "Perhaps the woman may not be willing to follow me to this land; must I then take your son back to the land from which you came?" ⁶Abraham said to him, "See to it that you do not take my son back there. ⁷The LORD, the God of heaven, who took me from my father's house and from the land of my birth, and who spoke to me and swore to me, 'To your descendants I will give this land,' he will send his angel before you, and you shall take a wife for my son from there." ⁹So the servant put his hand under the thigh of Abraham his master, and swore to him concerning this matter.

10 Then the servant took ten of his master's camels and departed, taking all sorts of choice gifts from his master; and he arose, and went to Mesopota'mia, to the city of Nahor. ¹¹And he made the camels kneel down outside the city by the well of water at the time of evening, the time when women go out to draw water. ¹²And he said, "O LORD, God of my master Abraham, grant me success today, I pray thee, and show steadfast love to my master Abraham. ¹³Behold, I am standing by the spring of water, and the daughters of the men of the city are coming out to draw water. ¹⁴Let the maiden to whom I shall say, 'Pray let down your jar that I may drink,' and who shall say, 'Drink, and I will water your camels' —let her be the one whom thou hast appointed for thy servant Isaac. By this I shall know that thou hast shown steadfast love to my master."

15 Before he had done speaking, behold, Rebekah, who was born to Bethu'el the son of Milcah, the wife of Nahor, Abraham's brother, came out with her water jar upon her shoulder. ¹⁶The maiden was very fair to look upon, a virgin, whom no man had known. She went

down to the spring, and filled her jar, and came up. ¹⁷ Then the servant ran to meet her, and said, "Pray give me a little water to drink from your jar." ¹⁸ She said, "Drink, my lord"; and she quickly let down her jar upon her hand, and gave him a drink. ¹⁹ When she had finished giving him a drink, she said, "I will draw for your camels also, until they have done drinking." ²⁰ So she quickly emptied her jar into the trough and ran again to the well to draw, and she drew for all his camels. ²¹ The man gazed at her in silence to learn whether the LORD had prospered his journey or not.

22 When the camels had done drinking, the man took a gold ring weighing a half shekel, and two bracelets for her arms weighing ten gold shekels, ²³ and said, "Tell me whose daughter you are. Is there room in your father's house for us to lodge in?" ²⁴ She said to him, "I am the daughter of Bethu'el the son of Milcah, whom she bore to Nahor." ²⁵ She added, "We have both straw and provender enough, and room to lodge in." ²⁶ The man bowed his head and worshiped the LORD, ²⁷ and said, "Blessed be the LORD, the God of my master Abraham, who has not forsaken his steadfast love and his faithfulness toward my master. As for me, the LORD has led me in the way to the house of my master's kinsmen."

28 Then the maiden ran and told her mother's household about these things. ²⁹ Rebekah had a brother whose name was Laban; and Laban ran out to the man, to the spring. ³⁰ When he saw the ring, and the bracelets on his sister's arms, and when he heard the words of Rebekah his sister, "Thus the man spoke to me," he went to the man; and behold, he was standing by the camels at the spring. ³¹ He said, "Come in, O blessed of the LORD; why do you stand outside? For I have prepared the house and a place for the camels." ³² So the man came into the house; and Laban ungirded the camels, and gave him straw and provender for the camels, and water to wash his feet and the feet of the men who were with him. ³³ Then food was set before him to eat; but he said, "I will not eat until I have told my errand." He said, "Speak on."

34 So he said, "I am Abraham's servant. ³⁵ The LORD has greatly blessed my master, and he has become great; he has given him flocks and herds, silver and gold, menservants and maidservants, camels and asses. ³⁶ And Sarah my master's wife bore a son to my master when she was old; and to him he has given all that he has. ³⁷ My master made me swear, saying, 'You shall not take a wife for my son from the daughters of the Canaanites, in whose land I dwell; ³⁸ but you shall go to my father's house and to my kindred, and take a wife for my son.' ³⁹ I said to my master, 'Perhaps the woman will not follow me.' ⁴⁰ But he said to me, 'The LORD, before whom I walk, will send his angel with you and prosper your way; and you shall

take a wife for my son from my kindred and from my father's house; [41] then you will be free from my oath, when you come to my kindred; and if they will not give her to you, you will be free from my oath.'

45 "Before I had done speaking in my heart, behold, Rebekah came out with her water jar on her shoulder; and she went down to the spring, and drew. I said to her, 'Pray let me drink.' [46] She quickly let down her jar from her shoulder, and said, 'Drink, and I will give your camels drink also.' So I drank, and she gave the camels drink also. [47] Then I asked her, 'Whose daughter are you?' She said, 'The daughter of Bethu'el, Nahor's son, whom Milcah bore to him.' So I put the ring on her nose, and the bracelets on her arms. [48] Then I bowed my head and worshiped the LORD, and blessed the LORD, the God of my master Abraham, who had led me by the right way to take the daughter of my master's kinsman for his son. [49] Now then, if you will deal loyally and truly with my master, tell me; and if not, tell me; that I may turn to the right hand or to the left."

50 Then Laban and Bethu'el answered, "The thing comes from the LORD; we cannot speak to you bad or good. [51] Behold, Rebekah is before you, take her and go, and let her be the wife of your master's son, as the LORD has spoken."

52 When Abraham's servant heard their words, he bowed himself to the earth before the LORD.

55 Her brother and her mother said, "Let the maiden remain with us a while, at least ten days; after that she may go." [56] But he said to them, "Do not delay me, since the LORD has prospered my way; let me go that I may go to my master." [57] They said, "We will call the maiden, and ask her." [58] And they called Rebekah, and said to her, "Will you go with this man?" She said, "I will go." [59] So they sent away Rebekah their sister and her nurse, and Abraham's servant and his men. [60] And they blessed Rebekah, and said to her, "Our sister, be the mother of thousands of ten thousands; and may your descendants possess the gate of those who hate them!" [61] Then Rebekah and her maids arose, and rode upon the camels and followed the man; thus the servant took Rebekah, and went his way.

63 And Isaac went out to meditate in the field in the evening; and he lifted up his eyes and looked, and behold, there were camels coming. [64] And Rebekah lifted up her eyes, and when she saw Isaac, she alighted from the camel, [65] and said to the servant, "Who is the man yonder, walking in the field to meet us?" The servant said, "It is my master." So she took her veil and covered herself. [66] And the servant told Isaac all the things that he had done. [67] Then Isaac brought her into the tent, and took Rebekah, and she became his wife; and he loved her. So Isaac was comforted after his mother's death.

24:3 Here is the first of several biblical references to the danger of intermarriage, which was to be avoided to preserve the purity of the Jewish faith from idolatry. **24:7** These are the last words of Abraham recorded in the Bible. Note that at the beginning of his journeys Abraham is full of doubt and questioning (cf. 15 : 2, 8), but now he moves toward death certain of God's fidelity and secure in His providence. **24:12** This is the first prayer of such a personal noncultic nature recorded in the Bible. **24:14** How does one choose a mate or set standards for a bride? Here Eliezer would ask only for a drink for himself; a kindly person, of good character and energy, would be revealed by taking the initiative to draw water for the camels. **24:57** Rabbinic teachings derived from this text the legal precedent that a woman cannot be given away in marriage without her consent. **24:67** The order of the words here: "He took Rebekah, she became his wife, he loved her," evoke comment from Jewish scholars in that it emphasized the importance of the love that *follows*, sustains, and maintains marriage. Parents arrange marriages in many countries; sometimes a dowry goes with the bride, sometimes a price is paid to the family of the bride. In some countries, young people arrange their own marriages, and romantic love is presupposed *before* marriage.

Abraham is Buried with His Wife Sarah
Genesis 25 : 7–11

7 These are the days of the years of Abraham's life, a hundred and seventy-five years. [8] Abraham breathed his last and died in a good old age, an old man and full of years, and was gathered to his people. [9] Isaac and Ish'mael his sons buried him in the cave of Mach-pe'lah, in the field of Ephron the son of Zohar the Hittite, east of Mamre, [10] the field which Abraham purchased from the Hittites. There Abraham was buried, with Sarah his wife. [11] After the death of Abraham God blessed Isaac his son. And Isaac dwelt at Beer-la'hai-roi.

To die at a good old age was regarded in the biblical tradition as a blessing; to die young was a misfortune (Isaiah 38 : 10). There are references in Scripture to a Sheol—an underground gathering place of the dead; the thought provoked terror from which the Lord was petitioned to redeem man (Hosea 13 : 14; Psalm 16 : 10). Not until the close of the biblical period did the Hebrews develop a clear conception of life blessed with immortality and other-worldly reward.

Rebekah Gives Birth to Jacob and Esau
Genesis 25 : 19–34

19 These are the descendants of Isaac, Abraham's son: Abraham was the father of Isaac, [20] and Isaac was forty years old when he took to

wife Rebekah, the daughter of Bethu'el the Aramean of Paddan-aram, the sister of Laban the Aramean. ²¹ And Isaac prayed to the LORD for his wife, because she was barren; and the LORD granted his prayer, and Rebekah his wife conceived. ²² The children struggled together within her; and she said, "If it is thus, why do I live?" So she went to inquire of the LORD. ²³ And the LORD said to her,

> "Two nations are in your womb,
> and two peoples, born of you, shall be divided;
> the one shall be stronger than the other,
> the elder shall serve the younger."

²⁴ When her days to be delivered were fulfilled, behold, there were twins in her womb. ²⁵ The first came forth red, all his body like a hairy mantle; so they called his name Esau. ²⁶ Afterward his brother came forth, and his hand had taken hold of Esau's heel; so his name was called Jacob. Isaac was sixty years old when she bore them.

27 When the boys grew up, Esau was a skilful hunter, a man of the field, while Jacob was a quiet man, dwelling in tents. ²⁸ Isaac loved Esau, because he ate of his game; but Rebekah loved Jacob.

29 Once when Jacob was boiling pottage, Esau came in from the field, and he was famished. ³⁰ And Esau said to Jacob, "Let me eat some of that red pottage, for I am famished!" (Therefore his name was called Edom.) ³¹ Jacob said, "First sell me your birthright." ³² Esau said, "I am about to die; of what use is a birthright to me?" ³³ Jacob said, "Swear to me first." So he swore to him, and sold his birthright to Jacob. ³⁴ Then Jacob gave Esau bread and pottage of lentils, and he ate and drank, and rose and went his way. Thus Esau despised his birthright.

25:21 Like Sarah before her (16 : 1) and Rachel after her (30 : 31), Rebekah was childless. This dramatic tale emphasized that the survival of the Hebrews depended upon the graciousness of God. **25:26** *Jacob* means *he takes by the heel.* **25:30** *Edom* means *red.* **25:31** The birthright entitled the firstborn son to a position of honor and a double share in the family possessions. Rabbinical scholars, concerned that Jacob was taking advantage of his brother, explain that the birthright also provided a position or status which enabled its holder to serve as the family priest and maintain the father's spiritual heritage. Hurrian Tablets, uncovered at Nuzi, describe as common the practice of brothers, negotiating their inheritance. Jacob's behavior therefore may not have been as outrageous as generally understood. In the scriptural reference to the fact that the years of his life were "few and evil" (47 : 9) there is an implicit condemnation of his conduct as unethical.

Isaac Blesses His Sons

Esau the hunter was a man of impulse and instinct. Jacob, more disciplined and restrained, cherished his father's birthright more. Who would inherit the right to be called a patriarch of the people dedicated to God? Jacob was the younger, and his right to that heritage could not be achieved in the natural course of events. Jacob put Esau to the test, and Esau bartered his birthright for a bowl of soup. Then God put Jacob to the test. Only after he has endured trials and tribulations does he become worthy of being a patriarch; he is then given the name "Israel."

Genesis 27 : 1–45

27 When Isaac was old and his eyes were dim so that he could not see, he called Esau his older son, and said to him, "My son"; and he answered, "Here I am." ²He said, "Behold, I am old; I do not know the day of my death. ³Now then, take your weapons, your quiver and your bow, and go out to the field, and hunt game for me, ⁴and prepare for me savory food, such as I love, and bring it to me that I may eat; that I may bless you before I die."

5 Now Rebekah was listening when Isaac spoke to his son Esau. So when Esau went to the field to hunt for game and bring it, ⁶Rebekah said to her son Jacob, "I heard your father speak to your brother Esau, ⁷'Bring me game, and prepare for me savory food, that I may eat it, and bless you before the LORD before I die.' ⁸Now therefore, my son, obey my word as I command you. ⁹Go to the flock, and fetch me two good kids, that I may prepare from them savory food for your father, such as he loves; ¹⁰and you shall bring it to your father to eat, so that he may bless you before he dies." ¹¹But Jacob said to Rebekah his mother, "Behold, my brother Esau is a hairy man, and I am a smooth man. ¹²Perhaps my father will feel me, and I shall seem to be mocking him, and bring a curse upon myself and not a blessing." ¹³His mother said to him, "Upon me be your curse, my son; only obey my word, and go, fetch them to me." ¹⁴So he went and took them and brought them to his mother; and his mother prepared savory food, such as his father loved. ¹⁵Then Rebekah took the best garments of Esau her older son, which were with her in the house, and put them on Jacob her younger son; ¹⁶and the skins of the kids she put upon his hands and upon the smooth part of his neck; ¹⁷and she gave the savory food and the bread, which she had prepared, into the hand of her son Jacob.

18 So he went in to his father, and said, "My father"; and he said, "Here I am; who are you, my son?" ¹⁹Jacob said to his father, "I am Esau your first-born. I have done as you told me; now sit up and eat of my game, that you may bless me." ²⁰But Isaac said to his son,

"How is it that you have found it so quickly, my son?" He answered, "Because the LORD your God granted me success." ²¹ Then Isaac said to Jacob, "Come near, that I may feel you, my son, to know whether you are really my son Esau or not." ²² So Jacob went near to Isaac his father, who felt him and said, "The voice is Jacob's voice, but the hands are the hands of Esau." ²³ And he did not recognize him, because his hands were hairy like his brother Esau's hands; so he blessed him. ²⁴ He said, "Are you really my son Esau?" He answered, "I am." ²⁵ Then he said, "Bring it to me, that I may eat of my son's game and bless you." So he brought it to him, and he ate; and he brought him wine, and he drank. ²⁶ Then his father Isaac said to him, "Come near and kiss me, my son." ²⁷ So he came near and kissed him; and he smelled the smell of his garments, and blessed him, and said,

"See the smell of my son
   is as the smell of a field which the LORD has blessed!
²⁸ May God give you of the dew of heaven,
   and of the fatness of the earth,
   and plenty of grain and wine.
²⁹ Let peoples serve you,
   and nations bow down to you.
Be lord over your brothers,
   and may your mother's sons bow down to you.
Cursed be every one who curses you,
   and blessed be every one who blesses you!"

30 As soon as Isaac had finished blessing Jacob, when Jacob had scarcely gone out from the presence of Isaac his father, Esau his brother came in from his hunting. ³¹ He also prepared savory food, and brought it to his father. And he said to his father, "Let my father arise, and eat of his son's game, that you may bless me." ³² His father Isaac said to him, "Who are you?" He answered, "I am your son, your first-born, Esau." ³³ Then Isaac trembled violently, and said, "Who was it then that hunted game and brought it to me, and I ate it all before you came, and I have blessed him?—yes, and he shall be blessed." ³⁴ When Esau heard the words of his father, he cried out with an exceedingly great and bitter cry, and said to his father, "Bless me, even me also, O my father!" ³⁵ But he said, "Your brother came with guile, and he has taken away your blessing." ³⁶ Esau said, "Is he not rightly named Jacob? For he has supplanted me these two times. He took away my birthright; and behold, now he has taken away my blessing." Then he said, "Have you not reserved a blessing for me?" ³⁷ Isaac answered Esau, "Behold, I have made him your lord, and all his brothers I have given to him for servants, and with

grain and wine I have sustained him. What then can I do for you, my son?" ³⁸ Esau said to his father, "Have you but one blessing, my father? Bless me, even me also, O my father." And Esau lifted up his voice and wept.

39 Then Isaac his father answered him:

> "Behold, away from the fatness of the earth shall your dwelling be,
>
> and away from the dew of heaven on high.
>
> ⁴⁰ By your sword you shall live,
>
> and you shall serve your brother;
>
> but when you break loose
>
> you shall break his yoke from your neck."

41 Now Esau hated Jacob because of the blessing with which his father had blessed him, and Esau said to himself, "The days of mourning for my father are approaching; then I will kill my brother Jacob." ⁴² But the words of Esau her older son were told to Rebekah; so she sent and called Jacob her younger son, and said to him, "Behold, your brother Esau comforts himself by planning to kill you. ⁴³ Now therefore, my son, obey my voice; arise, flee to Laban my brother in Haran, ⁴⁴ and stay with him a while, until your brother's fury turns away; ⁴⁵ until your brother's anger turns away, and he forgets what you have done to him; then I will send, and fetch you from there. Why should I be bereft of you both in one day?"

27:40 Esau is presumed to be an ancestor of the Edomites, a warlike people who thwarted the easy entrance of the Hebrews into Canaan (cf. Numbers 20 : 14–21; Deuteronomy 2 : 4–6). They were defeated in battle 400 years later by King Saul and then again by King David. But in the days of Nebuchadrezzar the Edomites joined in the plunder of Jerusalem (Psalm 137 : 7) and were excoriated by the prophets (Isaiah 34:5–8; Jeremiah 49:7–22). **27:43–45** Proponents of the documentary theory (see Appendix) point out that in these verses Jacob flees his home out of fear of Esau (so says the "J" document); whereas in 28:2 Jacob leaves home to seek a wife from among his kinsfolk (the "P" document, written several hundred years later). In this latter version Jacob's journey is for a "nobler" reason.

Jacob's Dream

Jacob's dream speaks to each man according to his spiritual condition. Rabbinic commentators suggest that it provided the weary and lonely Jacob, in flight for his life, with the assurance that God was not far distant, nor heedless of what man does here on earth. Every spot on earth may be a gate to heaven. The Catholic Church chose this section for the first reading in the special Mass for pilgrims and travelers.

Genesis 28 : 10–22

10 Jacob left Beersheba, and went toward Haran. ¹¹ And he came to a certain place, and stayed there that night, because the sun had set. Taking one of the stones of the place, he put it under his head and lay down in that place to sleep. ¹² And he dreamed that there was a ladder set up on the earth, and the top of it reached to heaven; and behold, the angels of God were ascending and descending on it! ¹³ And behold, the LORD stood above it and said, "I am the LORD, the God of Abraham your father and the God of Isaac; the land on which you lie I will give to you and to your descendants; ¹⁴ and your descendants shall be like the dust of the earth, and you shall spread abroad to the west and to the east and to the north and to the south; and by you and your descendants shall all the families of the earth bless themselves. ¹⁵ Behold, I am with you and will keep you wherever you go, and bring you back to this land; for I will not leave you until I have done that of which I have spoken to you." ¹⁶ Then Jacob awoke from his sleep and said, "Surely the LORD is in this place; and I did not know it." ¹⁷ And he was afraid, and said, "How awesome is this place! This is none other than the house of God, and this is the gate of heaven."

18 So Jacob rose early in the morning, and he took the stone which he had put under his head and set it up for a pillar and poured oil on the top of it. ¹⁹ He called the name of that place Bethel; but the name of the city was Luz at the first. ²⁰ Then Jacob made a vow, saying, "If God will be with me, and will keep me in this way that I go, and will give me bread to eat and clothing to wear, ²¹ so that I come again to my father's house in peace, then the LORD shall be my God, ²² and this stone, which I have set up for a pillar, shall be God's house; and of all that thou givest me I will give the tenth to thee."

28:12 This dream has been the inspiration of many artists. It is the subject of the hymn, "Nearer My God to Thee," and the spiritual, "We Are Climbing Jacob's Ladder," and it is cited in explanations of the mystical experience of prayer. **28:17** Catholics recite this verse at the beginning of the Mass for dedication of a church. **28:19** *Bethel* means *the house of God*. **28:22** This is the earliest reference to the custom of tithing.

Jacob Falls in Love with Rachel
Genesis 29 : 1–6, 10–14

29 Then Jacob went on his journey, and came to the land of the people of the east. ² As he looked, he saw a well in the field, and lo, three flocks of sheep lying beside it; for out of that well the flocks were watered. The stone on the well's mouth was large, ³ and when all the flocks were gathered there, the shepherds would roll the stone from the mouth of the well, and water the sheep, and put the stone back in its place upon the mouth of the well.

4 Jacob said to them, "My brothers, where do you come from?" They said, "We are from Haran." ⁵He said to them, "Do you know Laban the son of Nahor?" They said, "We know him." ⁶He said to them, "Is it well with him?" They said, "It is well; and see, Rachel his daughter is coming with the sheep!"

10 Now when Jacob saw Rachel the daughter of Laban his mother's brother, and the sheep of Laban his mother's brother, Jacob went up and rolled the stone from the well's mouth, and watered the flock of Laban his mother's brother. ¹¹Then Jacob kissed Rachel, and wept aloud. ¹²And Jacob told Rachel that he was her father's kinsman, and that he was Rebekah's son; and she ran and told her father.

13 When Laban heard the tidings of Jacob his sister's son, he ran to meet him, and embraced him and kissed him, and brought him to his house. Jacob told Laban all these things, ¹⁴and Laban said to him, "Surely you are my bone and my flesh!" And he stayed with him a month.

Jacob Marries Leah and Rachel
Genesis 29:15–32

15 Then Laban said to Jacob, "Because you are my kinsman, should you therefore serve me for nothing? Tell me, what shall your wages be?" ¹⁶Now Laban had two daughters; the name of the older was Leah, and the name of the younger was Rachel. ¹⁷Leah's eyes were weak, but Rachel was beautiful and lovely. ¹⁸Jacob loved Rachel; and he said, "I will serve you seven years for your younger daughter Rachel." ¹⁹Laban said, "It is better that I give her to you than that I should give her to any other man; stay with me." ²⁰So Jacob served seven years for Rachel, and they seemed to him but a few days because of the love he had for her.

21 Then Jacob said to Laban, "Give me my wife that I may go in to her, for my time is completed." ²²So Laban gathered together all the men of the place, and made a feast. ²³But in the evening he took his daughter Leah and brought her to Jacob; and he went in to her. ²⁴(Laban gave his maid Zilpah to his daughter Leah to be her maid.) ²⁵And in the morning, behold, it was Leah; and Jacob said to Laban, "What is this you have done to me? Did I not serve with you for Rachel? Why then have you deceived me?" ²⁶Laban said, "It is not so done in our country, to give the younger before the first-born. ²⁷Complete the week of this one, and we will give you the other also

in return for serving me another seven years." ²⁸ Jacob did so, and completed her week; then Laban gave him his daughter Rachel to wife. ²⁹ (Laban gave his maid Bilhah to his daughter Rachel to be her maid.) ³⁰ So Jacob went in to Rachel also, and he loved Rachel more than Leah, and served Laban for another seven years.

31 When the LORD saw that Leah was hated, he opened her womb; but Rachel was barren. ³² And Leah conceived and bore a son, and she called his name Reuben; for she said, "Because the LORD has looked upon my affliction; surely now my husband will love me."

29:20 The depth of Jacob's love is here encompassed in a few words: "They seemed to him but a few days." **29:27** Marriage with two sisters was later forbidden by Jewish law (Leviticus 18 : 18). To Bible scholars the fact that the Hebrew people recorded this event suggests that the patriarchal accounts are indeed based on actual ancient historic events. **29:32** *Reuben* means *See, a son.*

Jacob Gathers a Flock

The arrangement described here favors Laban, and he is at first satisfied. Here is an early account of what has become a science of selective breeding. Although Laban changes the wages ten times within this period, Jacob's skill in the art of eugenics and the graciousness of God assure him success.

Genesis 30 : 22–34, 40–43

22 Then God remembered Rachel, and God hearkened to her and opened her womb. ²³ She conceived and bore a son, and said, "God has taken away my reproach"; ²⁴ and she called his name Joseph, saying, "May the LORD add to me another son!"

25 When Rachel had borne Joseph, Jacob said to Laban, "Send me away, that I may go to my own home and country. ²⁶ Give me my wives and my children for whom I have served you, and let me go; for you know the service which I have given you." ²⁷ But Laban said to him, "If you will allow me to say so, I have learned by divination that the LORD has blessed me because of you; ²⁸ name your wages, and I will give it." ²⁹ Jacob said to him, "You yourself know how I have served you, and how your cattle have fared with me. ³⁰ For you had little before I came, and it has increased abundantly; and the LORD has blessed you wherever I turned. But now when shall I provide for my own household also?" ³¹ He said, "What shall I give you?" Jacob said, "You shall not give me anything; if you will do this for me, I will again feed your flock and keep it: ³² let me pass through all your flock today, removing from it every speckled and spotted sheep and every black lamb, and the spotted and speckled

among the goats; and such shall be my wages. ³³So my honesty will
answer for me later, when you come to look into my wages with you.
Every one that is not speckled and spotted among the goats and
black among the lambs, if found with me, shall be counted stolen."
³⁴Laban said, "Good! Let it be as you have said."

40 And Jacob separated the lambs, and set the faces of the flocks
toward the striped and all the black in the flock of Laban; and he put
his own droves apart, and did not put them with Laban's flock.
⁴¹Whenever the stronger of the flock were breeding Jacob laid the
rods in the runnels before the eyes of the flock, that they might breed
among the rods, ⁴²but for the feebler of the flock he did not lay them
there; so the feebler were Laban's, and the stronger Jacob's. ⁴³Thus
the man grew exceedingly rich, and had large flocks, maidservants
and menservants, and camels and asses.

Jacob Flees Laban
Genesis 31 : 1–9, 14–16, 19–37, 43–55

31 Now Jacob heard that the sons of Laban were saying, "Jacob has
taken all that was our father's; and from what was our father's he
has gained all this wealth." ²And Jacob saw that Laban did not
regard him with favor as before. ³Then the LORD said to Jacob,
"Return to the land of your fathers and to your kindred, and I will
be with you." ⁴So Jacob sent and called Rachel and Leah into the
field where his flock was, ⁵and said to them, "I see that your father
does not regard me with favor as he did before. But the God of my
father has been with me. ⁶You know that I have served your father
with all my strength; ⁷yet your father has cheated me and changed
my wages ten times, but God did not permit him to harm me. ⁸If he
said, 'The spotted shall be your wages,' then all the flock bore
spotted; and if he said, 'The striped shall be your wages,' then all
the flock bore striped. ⁹Thus God has taken away the cattle of your
father, and given them to me."

14 Then Rachel and Leah answered him, "Is there any portion or
inheritance left to us in our father's house? ¹⁵Are we not regarded by
him as foreigners? For he has sold us, and he has been using up the
money given for us. ¹⁶All the property which God has taken away
from our father belongs to us and to our children; now then,
whatever God has said to you, do."

19 Laban had gone to shear his sheep, and Rachel stole her
father's household gods. ²⁰And Jacob outwitted Laban the Aramean,
in that he did not tell him that he intended to flee. ²¹He fled with all
that he had, and arose and crossed the Eu-phra'tes, and set his face
toward the hill country of Gilead.

22 When it was told Laban on the third day that Jacob had fled, [23] he took his kinsmen with him and pursued him for seven days and followed close after him into the hill country of Gilead. [24] But God came to Laban the Aramean in a dream by night, and said to him, "Take heed that you say not a word to Jacob, either good or bad."

25 And Laban overtook Jacob. Now Jacob had pitched his tent in the hill country, and Laban with his kinsmen encamped in the hill country of Gilead. [26] And Laban said to Jacob, "What have you done, that you have cheated me, and carried away my daughters like captives of the sword? [27] Why did you flee secretly, and cheat me, and did not tell me, so that I might have sent you away with mirth and songs, with tambourine and lyre? [28] And why did you not permit me to kiss my sons and my daughters farewell? Now you have done foolishly. [29] It is in my power to do you harm; but the God of your father spoke to me last night, saying, 'Take heed that you speak to Jacob neither good nor bad.' [30] And now you have gone away because you longed greatly for your father's house, but why did you steal my gods?" [31] Jacob answered Laban, "Because I was afraid, for I thought that you would take your daughters from me by force. [32] Any one with whom you find your gods shall not live. In the presence of our kinsmen point out what I have that is yours, and take it." Now Jacob did not know that Rachel had stolen them.

33 So Laban went into Jacob's tent, and into Leah's tent, and into the tent of the two maidservants, but he did not find them. And he went out of Leah's tent, and entered Rachel's. [34] Now Rachel had taken the household gods and put them in the camel's saddle, and sat upon them. Laban felt all about the tent, but did not find them. [35] And she said to her father, "Let not my lord be angry that I cannot rise before you, for the way of women is upon me." So he searched, but did not find the household gods.

36 Then Jacob became angry, and upbraided Laban; Jacob said to Laban, "What is my offense? What is my sin, that you have hotly pursued me? [37] Although you have felt through all my goods, what have you found of all your household goods? Set it here before my kinsmen and your kinsmen, that they may decide between us two."

43 Then Laban answered and said to Jacob, "The daughters are my daughters, the children are my children, the flocks are my flocks, and all that you see is mine. But what can I do this day to these my daughters, or to their children whom they have borne? [44] Come now, let us make a covenant, you and I; and let it be a witness between you and me." [45] So Jacob took a stone, and set it up as a pillar. [46] And Jacob said to his kinsmen, "Gather stones," and they took stones, and made a heap; and they ate there by the heap. [47] Laban

called it Je'garsahadu'tha: but Jacob called it Galeed. [48] Laban said, "This heap is a witness between you and me today." Therefore he named it Galeed, [49] and the pillar Mizpah, for he said, "The LORD watch between you and me, when we are absent one from the other. [50] If you ill-treat my daughters, or if you take wives besides my daughters, although no man is with us, remember, God is witness between you and me."

51 Then Laban said to Jacob, "See this heap and the pillar, which I have set between you and me. [52] This heap is a witness, and the pillar is a witness, that I will not pass over this heap to you, and you will not pass over this heap and this pillar to me, for harm. [53] The God of Abraham and the God of Nahor, the God of their father, judge between us." So Jacob swore by the Fear of his father Isaac, [54] and Jacob offered a sacrifice on the mountain and called his kinsmen to eat bread; and they ate bread and tarried all night on the mountain.

55 Early in the morning Laban arose, and kissed his grand-children and his daughters and blessed them; then he departed and returned home.

31:30 The possession of household gods or teraphim assured the daughters the right to inherit from the property of their father. **31:40** "The Lord watch between me and thee" (KJV). Known as the Mizpah Benediction, these words have often been used to close Christian Endeavor and other Christian youth meetings. In its context, this phrase confirms the agreement between Jacob and Laban, invoking God's discipline upon the one who would break the agreement. **31:47** Laban uses an Aramaic name, Jacob a Hebrew name; both mean *the heap of witness*. **31:49** *mizpah* means *watchpost*.

Jacob Wrestles with the Angel

Jacob has matured in the twenty years since he left his home as a fearful lad; he is ready now to confront Esau, his brother, and make reconciliation. He wishes to establish his home in the Promised Land and to fulfill his obligations to the God of his fathers. Alone and in the dark he wrestles with the angel of God, and he endures. Jacob, "supplanter" of his brother by deceit, now becomes Israel, "champion of God." The encounter with the angel serves as an allegorical reference to the inner struggles and wrestlings of all men as they confront crises in life.

Genesis 32 : 22–32

22 The same night he arose and took his two wives, his two maids, and his eleven children, and crossed the ford of the Jabbok. [23] He took them and sent them across the stream, and likewise everything that he had. [24] And Jacob was left alone; and a man wrestled with

him until the breaking of the day. [25] When the man saw that he did not prevail against Jacob, he touched the hollow of his thigh; and Jacob's thigh was put out of joint as he wrestled with him. [26] Then he said, "Let me go, for the day is breaking." But Jacob said, "I will not let you go, unless you bless me." [27] And he said to him, "What is your name?" And he said, "Jacob." [28] Then he said, "Your name shall no more be called Jacob, but Israel, for you have striven with God and with men, and have prevailed." [29] Then Jacob asked him, "Tell me, I pray, your name." But he said, "Why is it that you ask my name?" And there he blessed him. [30] So Jacob called the name of the place Peni'el, saying, "For I have seen God face to face, and yet my life is preserved." [31] The sun rose upon him as he passed Penu'el, limping because of his thigh. [32] Therefore to this day the Israelites do not eat the sinew of the hip which is upon the hollow of the thigh, because he touched the hollow of Jacob's thigh on the sinew of the hip.

32:24 Using a method of biblical interpretation known as typology (i.e., where events in the Hebrew Scriptures are understood to foreshadow experiences of Jesus or of his Church) Martin Luther suggested that the "pre-existent Christ" was the man with whom Jacob wrestled. *Peniel* means *the face of God*. **32:32** Jacob bears the mark of his struggle, yet he leaves the struggle a redeemed and transformed person.

Jacob and Esau Reconciled
Genesis 33 : 1–5, 8–11, 18–20

33 And Jacob lifted up his eyes and looked, and behold, Esau was coming, and four hundred men with him. So he divided the children among Leah and Rachel and the two maids. [2] And put the maids with their children in front, then Leah with her children, and Rachel and Joseph last of all. [3] He himself went on before them, bowing himself to the ground seven times, until he came near to his brother.

4 But Esau ran to meet him, and embraced him, and fell on his neck and kissed him, and they wept. [5] And when Esau raised his eyes and saw the women and children, he said, "Who are these with you?" Jacob said, "The children whom God has graciously given your servant."

8 Esau said, "What do you mean by all this company which I met?" Jacob answered, "To find favor in the sight of my lord." [9] But Esau said, "I have enough, my brother; keep what you have for yourself." [10] Jacob said, "No, I pray you, if I have found favor in your sight, then accept my present from my hand; for truly to see

your face is like seeing the face of God, with such favor have you received me. ¹¹ Accept, I pray you, my gift that is brought to you, because God has dealt graciously with me, and because I have enough." Thus he urged him, and he took it.

18 And Jacob came safely to the city of Shechem, which is in the land of Canaan, on his way from Paddan-aram; and he camped before the city. ¹⁹ And from the sons of Hamor, Shechem's father, he bought for a hundred pieces of money the piece of land on which he had pitched his tent. ²⁰ There he erected an altar and called it El-El'ohe-Israel.

33:20 The name of the altar means *God, the* God, *of Israel*.

The Story of Joseph

The story of Joseph dramatizes how the divine providence realized its purpose through a complex interaction of human motives, historical chance and natural phenomenon. It is frequently cited as a model short story and has itself inspired a significant series of novels, such as the creative works of Thomas Mann. For historical details on the date of Joseph's rise to power in Egypt see Appendix.

Handel composed two oratorios built around the events in these concluding chapters of Genesis, one entitled *Joseph* and the second *Israel in Egypt*.

Genesis 37 : 2–11

2 This is the history of the family of Jacob.

Joseph, being seventeen years old, was shepherding the flock with his brothers; he was a lad with the sons of Bilhah and Zilpah, his father's wives; and Joseph brought an ill report of them to their father. ³ Now Israel loved Joseph more than any other of his children, because he was the son of his old age; and he made him a long robe with sleeves. ⁴ But when his brothers saw that their father loved him more than all his brothers, they hated him, and could not speak peaceably to him.

5 Now Joseph had a dream, and when he told it to his brothers they only hated him the more. ⁶ He said to them, "Hear this dream which I have dreamed; ⁷ behold, we were binding sheaves in the field, and lo, my sheaf arose and stood upright; and behold, your sheaves gathered round it, and bowed down to my sheaf." ⁸ His brothers said to him, "Are you indeed to reign over us? Or are you indeed to have dominion over us?" So they hated him yet more for his dreams and for his words. ⁹ Then he dreamed another dream, and told it to his brothers, and said, "Behold, I have dreamed another dream; and behold, the sun, the moon, and eleven stars were bowing down to me." ¹⁰ But when he told it to his father and to his brothers, his

father rebuked him, and said to him, "What is this dream that you have dreamed? Shall I and your mother and your brothers indeed come to bow ourselves to the ground before you?" ¹¹ And his brothers were jealous of him, but his father kept the saying in mind.

37:3 *A long robe with sleeves.* The King James Version translates those words as "a coat of many colors," a translation derived from the Greek rendering of the Hebrew text. The 1962 Jewish Publication Society translation, *The Torah*, renders the words as "an ornamented tunic." The coat stimulated jealousy because it symbolized Jacob's intent to make Joseph chief of the tribe upon his death. A coat of ornamentation or color was an insignia of rulership among Semitic chieftains of the time.

Joseph Is Sold into Slavery
Genesis 37 : 12–36

12 Now his brothers went to pasture their father's flock near Shechem. ¹³ And Israel said to Joseph, "Are not your brothers pasturing the flock at Shechem? Come, I will send you to them." And he said to him, "Here I am." ¹⁴ So he said to him, "Go now, see if it is well with your brothers, and with the flock; and bring me word again." So he sent him from the valley of Hebron, and he came to Shechem. ¹⁵ And a man found him wandering in the fields; and the man asked him, "What are you seeking?" ¹⁶ " I am seeking my brothers," he said, "tell me, I pray you, where they are pasturing the flock." ¹⁷ And the man said, "They have gone away, for I heard them say, 'Let us go to Dothan.' " So Joseph went after his brothers, and found them at Dothan. ¹⁸ They saw him afar off, and before he came near to them they conspired against him to kill him. ¹⁹ They said to one another, "Here comes this dreamer. ²⁰ Come now, let us kill him and throw him into one of the pits; then we shall say that a wild beast has devoured him, and we shall see what will become of his dreams." ²¹ But when Reuben heard it, he delivered him out of their hands, saying, "Let us not take his life." ²² And Reuben said to them, "Shed no blood; cast him into this pit here in the wilderness, but lay no hand upon him"—that he might rescue him out of their hand, to restore him to his father. ²³ So when Joseph came to his brothers, they stripped him of his robe, the long robe with sleeves that he wore; ²⁴ and they took him and cast him into a pit. The pit was empty, there was no water in it.

25 Then they sat down to eat; and looking up they saw a caravan of Ish'maelites coming from Gilead, with their camels bearing gum, balm, and myrrh, on their way to carry it down to Egypt. ²⁶ Then Judah said to his brothers, "What profit is it if we slay our brother

and conceal his blood? ²⁷Come, let us sell him to the Ish'maelites, and let not our hand be upon him, for he is our brother, our own flesh." And his brothers heeded him. ²⁸Then Mid'ianite traders passed by; and they drew Joseph up and lifted him out of the pit, and sold him to the Ish'maelites for twenty shekels of silver; and they took Joseph to Egypt.

29 When Reuben returned to the pit and saw that Joseph was not in the pit, he rent his clothes ³⁰and returned to his brothers, and said, "The lad is gone; and I, where shall I go?" ³¹Then they took Joseph's robe, and killed a goat, and dipped the robe in the blood; ³²and they rent the long robe with sleeves and brought it to their father, and said, "This we have found; see now whether it is your son's robe or not." ³³And he recognized it, and said, "It is my son's robe; a wild beast has devoured him; Joseph is without doubt torn to pieces." ³⁴Then Jacob rent his garments, and put sackcloth upon his loins, and mourned for his son many days. ³⁵All his sons and all his daughters rose up to comfort him; but he refused to be comforted, and said, "No, I shall go down to Sheol to my son, mourning." Thus his father wept for him. ³⁶Meanwhile the Mid'ianites had sold him in Egypt to Pot'i-phar, an officer of Pharaoh, the captain of the guard.

37:22 In this verse Reuben is the brother who tries to save Joseph. In 37 : 26 it is Judah who intervenes. (In 42 : 37 Reuben is the noble one, whereas in 43 : 3 it is Judah.) Some scholars suggest that here again is evidence of two strands of history, both maintained in the final editing process. The theory suggests that the verses favoring Reuben were written by a historian who came from the Northern Kingdom—Reuben was a tribe in Israel—while the portion favoring Judah was written by a historian who came from the Southern Kingdom, which derived its name Judah from the largest tribe in that part of Palestine.

Onan Sins

According to the custom of the times, a childless widow was to be taken as a wife into the home of the closest kinsman of the deceased; any child born of that "levirite marriage" would inherit the name and property of the deceased husband. Thus the family name and heritage were preserved (see Deuteronomy 25 : 5 and Ruth 4 : 5). Onan's refusal of this duty to his brother's wife was considered a sin. The term "Onanism" today describes a sexual act where the semen containing the seed of life is purposely wasted.

Genesis 38 : 1–10

38 It happened at that time that Judah went down from his brothers, and turned in to a certain Adullamite, whose name was Hirah.

²There Judah saw the daughter of a certain Canaanite whose name was Shua; he married her and went in to her, ³and she conceived and bore a son, and he called his name Er. ⁴Again she conceived and bore a son, and she called his name Onan. ⁵Yet again she bore a son, and she called his name Shelah. She was in Chezib when she bore him. ⁶And Judah took a wife for Er his first-born, and her name was Tamar. ⁷But Er, Judah's first-born, was wicked in the sight of the LORD; and the LORD slew him. ⁸Then Judah said to Onan, "Go in to your brother's wife, and perform the duty of a brother-in-law to her, and raise up offspring for your brother." ⁹But Onan knew that the offspring would not be his; so when he went in to his brother's wife he spilled the semen on the ground, lest he should give offspring to his brother. ¹⁰And what he did was displeasing in the sight of the LORD, and he slew him also.

38:10 This passage and its meaning have been central in debates on the morality of birth control.

Joseph Is Tempted by Potiphar's Wife
Genesis 39 : 1–20

39 Now Joseph was taken down to Egypt, and Pot'iphar, an officer of Pharaoh, the captain of the guard, an Egyptian, bought him from the Ish'maelites who had brought him down there. ²The LORD was with Joseph, and he became a successful man; and he was in the house of his master the Egyptian, ³and his master saw that the LORD was with him, and that the LORD caused all that he did to prosper in his hands. ⁴So Joseph found favor in his sight and attended him, and he made him overseer of his house and put him in charge of all that he had. ⁵From the time that he made him overseer in his house and over all that he had the LORD blessed the Egyptian's house for Joseph's sake; the blessing of the LORD was upon all that he had, in house and field. ⁶So he left all that he had in Joseph's charge; and having him he had no concern for anything but the food which he ate.

Now Joseph was handsome and good-looking. ⁷And after a time his master's wife cast her eyes upon Joseph, and said, "Lie with me." ⁸But he refused and said to his master's wife, "Lo, having me my master has no concern about anything in the house, and he has put everything that he has in my hand; ⁹he is not greater in this house than I am; nor has he kept back anything from me except yourself, because you are his wife; how then can I do this great wickedness, and sin against God?" ¹⁰And although she spoke to Joseph day after day, he would not listen to her, to lie with her or to be with her. ¹¹But one day, when he went into the house to do his work and none of the men of the house was there in the house, [12] she caught him by his garment, saying, "Lie with me." But he left his garment in her hand, and fled and got out of the house. [13] And when she saw that he had left his garment in her hand, and had fled out of the house, [14] she called to the men of her household and said to them, "See, he has brought among us a Hebrew to insult us; he came in to me to lie with me, and I cried out with a loud voice; [15] and when he heard that I lifted up my voice and cried, he left his garment with me, and fled and got out of the house." [16] Then she laid up his garment by her until his master came home, [17] and she told him the same story, saying, "The Hebrew servant, whom you have brought among us, came in to me to insult me; [18] but as soon as I lifted up my voice and cried, he left his garment with me, and fled out of the house."

19 When his master heard the words which his wife spoke to him, "This is the way your servant treated me," his anger was kindled. [20] And Joseph's master took him and put him into the prison, the place where the king's prisoners were confined, and he was there in prison.

39:8 In Hebrew Bibles musical notations accompany the text. When the biblical portion is read in the synagogue it is generally chanted to a specified melody. The musical notation over the word "refused" is a long, drawn-out note, suggesting that it was not easy for Joseph to turn away from this temptation. Rembrandt several times painted the scene described in verses 11–20. His first version (dated 1655) now hangs in the Mellon Collection, National Gallery of Art, Washington, D.C. Rembrandt, a Christian, lived near the Jewish part of his city and had many Jewish friends. **39:9** Not only does Joseph refrain from disloyalty to his master, but he recognized, the Rabbis stress, that this act of adultery would be a sin against God. Even if Potiphar should never know of the indiscretion, God would. Standards for sexual conduct have varied in different times and cultures. Instead of consenting and then blaming the woman for enticing him, Joseph obeys what he regards as a law of God. He gives an example of the principle that a man is no less responsible for sexual conduct than a woman. **39:12** Joseph fled from sin. The Rabbis teach that sometimes the only way to resist temptation is to turn from it and flee. The thought becomes explicit in James 4 : 7.

Joseph Interprets the Dreams of the Prisoners
Genesis 40 : 1–23

40 Some time after this, the butler of the king of Egypt and his baker offended their lord the king of Egypt. [2] And Pharaoh was angry with his two officers, the chief butler and the chief baker, [3] and he put them in custody in the house of the captain of the guard, in the prison where Joseph was confined. ⁴The captain of the guard charged Joseph with them, and he waited on them; and they continued for some time in custody. ⁵And one night they both dreamed—the butler and the baker of the king of Egypt, who were confined in the prison—each his own dream, and each dream with its own meaning. ⁶When Joseph came to them in the morning and saw them, they were troubled. ⁷So he asked Pharaoh's officers who were with him in custody in his master's house, "Why are your faces downcast today?" ⁸They said to him, "We have had dreams, and there is no one to interpret them." And Joseph said to them, "Do not interpretations belong to God? Tell them to me, I pray you."

- 9 So the chief butler told his dream to Joseph, and said to him, "In my dream there was a vine before me, ¹⁰and on the vine there were three branches; as soon as it budded, its blossoms shot forth, and the clusters ripened into grapes. ¹¹Pharaoh's cup was in my hand; and I took the grapes and pressed them into Pharaoh's cup, and placed the cup in Pharaoh's hand." ¹²Then Joseph said to him, "This is its interpretation: the three branches are three days; ¹³within three days Pharaoh will lift up your head and restore you to your office; and you shall place Pharaoh's cup in his hand as formerly, when you were his butler. ¹⁴But remember me, when it is well with you, and do me the kindness, I pray you, to make mention of me to Pharaoh, and so get me out of this house. ¹⁵For I was indeed stolen out of the land of the Hebrews; and here also I have done nothing that they should put me into the dungeon."

16 When the chief baker saw that the interpretation was favorable, he said to Joseph, "I also had a dream: there were three cake baskets on my head, ¹⁷and in the uppermost basket there were all sorts of baked food for Pharaoh, but the birds were eating it out of the basket on my head." ¹⁸And Joseph answered, "This is its interpretation: the three baskets are three days; ¹⁹within three days Pharaoh will lift up your head—from you!—and hang you on a tree; and the birds will eat the flesh from you."

20 On the third day, which was Pharaoh's birthday, he made a feast for all his servants, and lifted up the head of the chief butler and the head of the chief baker among his servants. ²¹He restored the chief butler to his butlership, and he placed the cup in Pharaoh's hand; ²²but he hanged the chief baker, as Joseph had interpreted to them. ²³Yet the chief butler did not remember Joseph, but forgot him.

40:8 Dream interpretation was a specialized skill in both Egyptian and Mesopotamian cultures. A papyrus, written about 1300 B.C., sets forth the interpretations to be given to every conceivable symbol that might appear in a dream. The biblical text emphasizes, however, that true wisdom is a gift from God, not a magical trick. Thus the faith of a Hebrew confounds the wisest pagan magicians. (Cf. Exodus, chapters 7–8 and Daniel chapter 2.)

Joseph Interprets the Dreams of Pharaoh
Genesis 41 : 1–16, 25–43, 46–49, 53–57

41 After two whole years, Pharaoh dreamed that he was standing by the Nile, ² and behold, there came up out of the Nile seven cows sleek and fat, and they fed in the reed grass. ³ And behold, seven other cows, gaunt and thin, came up out of the Nile after them, and stood by the other cows on the bank of the Nile. ⁴ And the gaunt and thin cows ate up the seven sleek and fat cows. And Pharaoh awoke. ⁵ And he fell asleep and dreamed a second time; and behold, seven ears of grain, plump and good, were growing on one stalk. ⁶ And behold, after them sprouted seven ears, thin and blighted by the east wind. ⁷ And the thin ears swallowed up the seven plump and full ears. And Pharaoh awoke, and behold, it was a dream. ⁸ So in the morning his spirit was troubled; and he sent and called for all the magicians of Egypt and all its wise men; and Pharaoh told them his dream, but there was none who could interpret it to Pharaoh.

9 Then the chief butler said to Pharaoh, "I remember my faults today. ¹⁰ When Pharaoh was angry with his servants, and put me and the chief baker in custody in the house of the captain of the guard, ¹¹ we dreamed on the same night, he and I, each having a dream with its own meaning. ¹² A young Hebrew was there with us, a servant of the captain of the guard; and when we told him, he interpreted our dreams to us, giving an interpretation to each man according to his dream. ¹³ And as he interpreted to us, so it came to pass; I was restored to my office, and the baker was hanged."

14 Then Pharaoh sent and called Joseph, and they brought him hastily out of the dungeon; and when he had shaved himself and changed his clothes, he came in before Pharaoh. ¹⁵ And Pharaoh said to Joseph, "I have had a dream, and there is no one who can interpret it; and I have heard it said of you that when you hear a dream you can interpret it." ¹⁶ Joseph answered Pharaoh, "It is not in me; God will give Pharaoh a favorable answer."

25 Then Joseph said to Pharaoh, "The dream of Pharaoh is one; God has revealed to Pharaoh what he is about to do. ²⁶ The seven good cows are seven years, and the seven good ears are seven years; the dream is one. ²⁷ The seven lean and gaunt cows that came up after them are seven years, and the seven empty ears blighted by the east wind are also seven years of famine. ²⁸ It is as I told Pharaoh,

God has shown to Pharaoh what he is about to do. ²⁹There will come seven years of great plenty throughout all the land of Egypt, ³⁰but after them there will arise seven years of famine, and all the plenty will be forgotten in the land of Egypt; the famine will consume the land, ³¹and the plenty will be unknown in the land by reason of that famine which will follow, for it will be very grievous. ³²And the doubling of Pharaoh's dream means that the thing is fixed by God, and God will shortly bring it to pass. ³³Now therefore let Pharaoh select a man discreet and wise, and set him over the land of Egypt. ³⁴Let Pharaoh proceed to appoint overseers over the land, and take the fifth part of the produce of the land of Egypt during the seven plenteous years. ³⁵And let them gather all the food of these good years that are coming, and lay up grain under the authority of Pharaoh for food in the cities, and let them keep it. ³⁶That food shall be a reserve for the land against the seven years of famine which are to befall the land of Egypt, so that the land may not perish through the famine."

37 This proposal seemed good to Pharaoh and to all his servants. ³⁸And Pharaoh said to his servants, "Can we find such a man as this, in whom is the Spirit of God?" ³⁹So Pharaoh said to Joseph, "Since God has shown you all this, there is none so discreet and wise as you are; ⁴⁰you shall be over my house, and all my people shall order themselves as you command; only as regards the throne will I be greater than you." ⁴¹And Pharaoh said to Joseph, "Behold, I have set you over all the land of Egypt." ⁴²Then Pharaoh took his signet ring from his hand and put it on Joseph's hand, and arrayed him in garments of fine linen, and put a gold chain about his neck; ⁴³and he made him to ride in his second chariot; and they cried before him, "Bow the knee!" Thus he set him over all the land of Egypt.

46 Joseph was thirty years old when he entered the service of Pharaoh king of Egypt. And Joseph went out from the presence of Pharaoh, and went through all the land of Egypt. ⁴⁷During the seven plenteous years the earth brought forth abundantly, ⁴⁸and he gathered up all the food of the seven years when there was plenty in the land of Egypt, and stored up food in the cities; he stored up in every city the food from the fields around it. ⁴⁹And Joseph stored up grain in great abundance, like the sand of the sea, until he ceased to measure it, for it could not be measured.

53 The seven years of plenty that prevailed in the land of Egypt came to an end; ⁵⁴and the seven years of famine began to come, as Joseph had said. There was famine in all lands; but in all the land of Egypt there was bread. ⁵⁵When all the land of Egypt was famished,

the people cried to Pharaoh for bread; and Pharaoh said to all the Egyptians, "Go to Joseph; what he says to you, do." [56] So when the famine had spread over all the land, Joseph opened all the store-houses, and sold to the Egyptians, for the famine was severe in the land of Egypt. [57] Moreover, all the earth came to Egypt to Joseph to buy grain, because the famine was severe over all the earth.

41:8 Many literary masterpieces make use of dreams, e.g., Shakespeare's *Julius Caesar*. Sigmund Freud emphasized the significance of dreams and the usefulness of their interpretation. Research now goes on into the physical processes related to dreams and their importance for mental well-being. **41:14** Joseph shaved prior to his appearance before Pharaoh; the Semites usually wore full beards and shaved only prisoners and slaves. **41:35** ff. Crop surpluses, famines, and food rationing still occasion or accompany national emergencies. Note results reported in Genesis 47 : 13—26: Joseph as a loyal servant to Pharaoh brought to his king all the land handed over by the starving people. This concentration of power tended toward the lessening of individual freedom. Whether such results are necessary consequences of national planning is debatable.

Joseph's Brothers Visit Egypt

The famine spread throughout the world as Joseph had foreseen. Jacob sent his sons from Palestine for food. They did not recognize Joseph. Thus he was able to test them until he was assured that they were devoted to their father's well-being, friendly to and protective of their youngest brother, Benjamin, and in fact repentant of their former misdeed. Then Joseph reveals himself.

Genesis 42 : 1–11, 14, 17–29, 35–38;
43 : 1–3, 6–9, 11–16, 24–34; 44 : 1–14, 18–21, 27–34

42 When Jacob learned that there was grain in Egypt, he said to his sons, "Why do you look at one another?" [2] And he said, "Behold, I have heard that there is grain in Egypt; go down and buy grain for us there, that we may live, and not die." [3] So ten of Joseph's brothers went down to buy grain in Egypt. [4] But Jacob did not send Benjamin, Joseph's brother, with his brothers, for he feared that harm might befall him. [5] Thus the sons of Israel came to buy among the others who came, for the famine was in the land of Canaan.

6 Now Joseph was governor over the land; he it was who sold to all the people of the land. And Joseph's brothers came, and bowed themselves before him with their faces to the ground. [7] Joseph saw his brothers, and knew them, but he treated them like strangers and spoke roughly to them. "Where do you come from?" he said. They said, "From the land of Canaan, to buy food." [8] Thus Joseph knew his brothers, but they did not know him. [9] And Joseph remembered

the dreams which he had dreamed of them; and he said to them, "You are spies, you have come to see the weakness of the land." [10] They said to him, "No, my lord, but to buy food have your servants come. [11] We are all sons of one man, we are honest men, your servants are not spies."

14 But Joseph said to them, "It is as I said to you, you are spies." 17 And he put them all together in prison for three days.

18 On the third day Joseph said to them, "Do this and you will live, for I fear God: [19] if you are honest men, let one of your brothers remain confined in your prison, and let the rest go and carry grain for the famine of your households, [20] and bring your youngest brother to me; so your words will be verified, and you shall not die." And they did so. [21] Then they said to one another, "In truth we are guilty concerning our brother, in that we saw the distress of his soul, when he besought us and we would not listen; therefore is this distress come upon us." [22] And Reuben answered them, "Did I not tell you not to sin against the lad? But you would not listen. So now there comes a reckoning for his blood." [23] They did not know that Joseph understood them, for there was an interpreter between them. [24] Then he turned away from them and wept; and he returned to them and spoke to them. And he took Simeon from them and bound him before their eyes. [25] And Joseph gave orders to fill their bags with grain, and to replace every man's money in his sack, and to give them provisions for the journey. This was done for them.

26 Then they loaded their asses with their grain, and departed. [27] And as one of them opened his sack to give his ass provender at the lodging place, he saw his money in the mouth of his sack; [28] and he said to his brothers, "My money has been put back; here it is in the mouth of my sack!" At this their hearts failed them, and they turned trembling to one another, saying, "What is this that God has done to us?"

29 When they came to Jacob their father in the land of Canaan, they told him all that had befallen them.

35 As they emptied their sacks, behold, every man's bundle of money was in his sack; and when they and their father saw their bundles of money, they were dismayed. [36] And Jacob their father said to them, "You have bereaved me of my children: Joseph is no more, and Simeon is no more, and now you would take Benjamin; all this has come upon me." [37] Then Reuben said to his father, "Slay my two sons if I do not bring him back to you; put him in my hands, and I will bring him back to you." [38] But he said, "My son shall not go down with you, for his brother is dead, and he only is left. If harm

should befall him on the journey that you are to make, you would bring down my gray hairs with sorrow to Sheol."

43 Now the famine was severe in the land. ²And when they had eaten the grain which they had brought from Egypt, their father said to them, "Go again, buy us a little food." ³But Judah said to him, "The man solemnly warned us saying, 'You shall not see my face, unless your brother is with you.' "

6 Israel said, "Why did you treat me so ill as to tell the man that you had another brother?" ⁷They replied, "The man questioned us carefully about ourselves and our kindred, saying, 'Is your father still alive? Have you another brother?' What we told him was in answer to these questions; could we in any way know that he would say, 'Bring your brother down'?" ⁸And Judah said to Israel his father, "Send the lad with me, and we will arise and go, that we may live and not die, both we and you and also our little ones. ⁹I will be surety for him; of my hand you shall require him. If I do not bring him back to you and set him before you, then let me bear the blame for ever."

11 Then their father Israel said to them, "If it must be so, then do this: take some of the choice fruits of the land in your bags, and carry down to the man a present, a little balm and a little honey, gum, myrrh, pistachio nuts, and almonds. ¹²Take double the money with you; carry back with you the money that was returned in the mouth of your sacks; perhaps it was an oversight. ¹³Take also your brother, and arise, go again to the man; ¹⁴may God Almighty grant you mercy before the man, that he may send back your other brother and Benjamin. If I am bereaved of my children, I am bereaved." ¹⁵So the men took the present, and they took double the money with them, and Benjamin; and they arose and went down to Egypt, and stood before Joseph.

16 When Joseph saw Benjamin with them, he said to the steward of his house, "Bring the men into the house, and slaughter an animal and make ready, for the men are to dine with me at noon."

24 And when the man had brought the men into Joseph's house, and given them water, and they had washed their feet, and when he had given them asses provender, ²⁵they made ready the present for Joseph's coming at noon, for they heard that they should eat bread there.

26 When Joseph came home, they brought into the house to him the present which they had with them, and bowed down to him to the ground. ²⁷And he inquired about their welfare, and said, "Is your father well, the old man of whom you spoke? Is he still alive?" ²⁸They said, "Your servant our father is well, he is still alive." And

they bowed their heads and made obeisance. [29] And he lifted up his eyes, and saw his brother Benjamin, his mother's son, and said, "Is this your youngest brother, of whom you spoke to me? God be gracious to you, my son!" [30] Then Joseph made haste, for his heart yearned for his brother, and he sought a place to weep. And he entered his chamber and wept there. [31] Then he washed his face and came out; and controlling himself he said, "Let food be served." [32] They served him by himself, and them by themselves, and the Egyptians who ate with him by themselves, because the Egyptians might not eat bread with the Hebrews, for that is an abomination to the Egyptians. [33] And they sat before him, the first-born according to his birthright and the youngest according to his youth; and the men looked at one another in amazement. [34] Portions were taken to them from Joseph's table, but Benjamin's portion was five times as much as any of theirs. So they drank and were merry with him.

44 Then he commanded the steward of his house, "Fill the men's sacks with food, as much as they can carry, and put each man's money in the mouth of his sack, [2] and put my cup, the silver cup, in the mouth of the sack of the youngest, with his money for the grain." And he did as Joseph told him. [3] As soon as the morning was light, the men were sent away with their asses. [4] When they had gone but a short distance from the city, Joseph said to his steward, "Up, follow after the men; and when you overtake them, say to them, 'Why have you returned evil for good? Why have you stolen my silver cup? [5] Is it not from this that my lord drinks, and by this that he divines? You have done wrong in so doing.' "

6 When he overtook them, he spoke to them these words. [7] They said to him, "Why does my lord speak such words as these? Far be it from your servants that they should do such a thing! [8] Behold, the money which we found in the mouth of our sacks, we brought back to you from the land of Canaan; how then should we steal silver or gold from your lord's house? [9] With whomever of your servants it be found, let him die, and we also will be my lord's slaves." [10] He said, "Let it be as you say: he with whom it is found shall be my slave, and the rest of you shall be blameless." [11] Then every man quickly lowered his sack to the ground, and every man opened his sack. [12] And he searched, beginning with the eldest and ending with the youngest; and the cup was found in Benjamin's sack. [13] Then they rent their clothes, and every man loaded his ass, and they returned to the city.

14 When Judah and his brothers came to Joseph's house, he was still there; and they fell before him to the ground.

18 Then Judah went up to him and said, "O my lord, let your

servant, I pray you, speak a word in my lord's ears, and let not your anger burn against your servant; for you are like Pharaoh himself. [19] My lord asked his servants, saying, 'Have you a father, or a brother?' [20] And we said to my lord, 'We have a father, an old man, and a young brother, the child of his old age; and his brother is dead, and he alone is left of his mother's children; and his father loves him.' [21] Then you said to your servants, 'Bring him down to me, that I may set my eyes upon him.'

27 "Then your servant my father said to us, 'You know that my wife bore me two sons; [28] one left me, and I said, Surely he has been torn to pieces; and I have never seen him since. [29] If you take this one also from me, and harm befalls him, you will bring down my gray hairs in sorrow to Sheol.' [30] Now therefore, when I come to your servant my father, and the lad is not with us, then, as his life is bound up in the lad's life, [31] when he sees that the lad is not with us, he will die; and your servants will bring down the gray hairs of your servant our father with sorrow to Sheol. [32] For your servant became surety for the lad to my father, saying, 'If I do not bring him back to you, then I shall bear the blame in the sight of my father all my life.' [33] Now therefore, let your servant, I pray you, remain instead of the lad as a slave to my lord; and let the lad go back with his brothers. [34] For how can I go back to my father if the lad is not with me? I fear to see the evil that would come upon my father."

> **42:27–28** In this passage the brothers discover the money at the top of their sacks, at the first stopping-place; but at verses 35–36 they discover the money upon their return home, at the bottom of their sacks—an indication perhaps of two versions of the Joseph story edited into one account by a third author at a later date.

Joseph Reveals Himself to His Brothers
Genesis 45 : 1–10, 14–18

45 Then Joseph could not control himself before all those who stood by him; and he cried, "Make every one go out from me." So no one stayed with him when Joseph made himself known to his brothers. [2] And he wept aloud, so that the Egyptians heard it, and the household of Pharaoh heard it. [3] And Joseph said to his brothers, "I am Joseph; is my father still alive?" But his brothers could not answer him, for they were dismayed at his presence.

4 So Joseph said to his brothers, "Come near to me, I pray you." And they came near. And he said, "I am your brother, Joseph, whom you sold into Egypt. [5] And now do not be distressed, or angry with yourselves, because you sold me here; for God sent me before you to preserve life. [6] For the famine has been in the land these two years;

and there are yet five years in which there will be neither plowing nor harvest. ⁷And God sent me before you to preserve for you a remnant on earth, and to keep alive for you many survivors. ⁸So it was not you who sent me here, but God; and he has made me a father to Pharaoh, and lord of all his house and ruler over all the land of Egypt. ⁹Make haste and go up to my father and say to him, 'Thus says your son Joseph, God has made me lord of all Egypt; come down to me, do not tarry; ¹⁰you shall dwell in the land of Goshen, and you shall be near me, you and your children and your children's children, and your flocks, your herds, and all that you have.' "

14 Then he fell upon his brother Benjamin's neck and wept; and Benjamin wept upon his neck. ¹⁵And he kissed all his brothers and wept upon them; and after that his brothers talked with him.

16 When the report was heard in Pharaoh's house, "Joseph's brothers have come," it pleased Pharaoh and his servants well. ¹⁷And Pharaoh said to Joseph, "Say to your brothers, 'Do this: load your beasts and go back to the land of Canaan; ¹⁸and take your father and your households, and come to me, and I will give you the best of the land of Egypt, and you shall eat the fat of the land.' "

45:4 Pope John XXIII in October, 1960, received a group of 130 Jewish leaders with the words: "I am Joseph, your brother," making use of his baptismal name, a welcome demonstrating the brotherhood of Christians and Jews.

Under Joseph's Rule the Pharaoh Obtains All the Land
Genesis 47 : 13–26

13 Now there was no food in all the land; for the famine was very severe, so that the land of Egypt and the land of Canaan languished by reason of the famine. ¹⁴And Joseph gathered up all the money that was found in the land of Egypt and in the land of Canaan, for the grain which they bought; and Joseph brought the money into Pharaoh's house. ¹⁵And when the money was all spent in the land of Egypt and in the land of Canaan, all the Egyptians came to Joseph, and said, "Give us food; why should we die before your eyes? For our money is gone." ¹⁶And Joseph answered, "Give your cattle, and I will give you food in exchange for your cattle, if your money is gone." ¹⁷So they brought their cattle to Joseph; and Joseph gave them food in exchange for the horses, the flocks, the herds, and the asses: and he supplied them with food in exchange for all their cattle that year. ¹⁸And when that year was ended, they came to him the following year, and said to him, "We will not hide from my lord that our money is all spent; and the herds of cattle are my lord's; there is

nothing left in the sight of my lord but our bodies and our lands. ¹⁹ Why should we die before your eyes, both we and our land? Buy us and our land for food, and we with our land will be slaves to Pharaoh; and give us seed, that we may live, and not die, and that the land may not be desolate."

20 So Joseph bought all the land of Egypt for Pharaoh; for all the Egyptians sold their fields, because the famine was severe upon them. The land became Pharaoh's; ²¹ and as for the people, he made slaves of them from one end of Egypt to the other. ²² Only the land of the priests he did not buy; for the priests had a fixed allowance from Pharaoh, and lived on the allowance which Pharaoh gave them; therefore they did not sell their land. ²³ Then Joseph said to the people, "Behold, I have this day bought you and your land for Pharaoh. Now here is seed for you, and you shall sow the land. ²⁴ And at the harvests you shall give a fifth to Pharaoh, and four fifths shall be your own, as seed for the field and as food for yourselves and your households, and as food for your little ones." ²⁵ And they said, "You have saved our lives; may it please my lord, we will be slaves to Pharaoh." ²⁶ So Joseph made it a statute concerning the land of Egypt, and it stands to this day, that Pharaoh should have the fifth; the land of the priests alone did not become Pharaoh's.

Jacob Blesses Ephraim and Manasseh
Genesis 47 : 29 – 31; 48 : 8 – 20

29 And when the time drew near that Israel must die, he called his son Joseph and said to him, "If now I have found favor in your sight, put your hand under my thigh, and promise to deal loyally and truly with me. Do not bury me in Egypt, ³⁰ but let me lie with my fathers; carry me out of Egypt and bury me in their burying place." He answered, "I will do as you have said." ³¹ And he said, "Swear to me"; and he swore to him. Then Israel bowed himself upon the head of his bed.

48 ⁸ When Israel saw Joseph's sons, he said, "Who are these?" ⁹ Joseph said to his father, "They are my sons, whom God has given me here." And he said, "Bring them to me, I pray you, that I may bless them." ¹⁰ Now the eyes of Israel were dim with age, so that he could not see. So Joseph brought them near him; and he kissed them and embraced them. ¹¹ And Israel said to Joseph, "I had not thought to see your face; and lo, God has let me see your children also." ¹² Then Joseph removed them from his knees, and he bowed himself with his face to the earth. ¹³ And Joseph took them both, E'phraim in his right hand toward Israel's left hand, and Manas'seh in his left hand toward Israel's right hand, and brought them near him. ¹⁴ And Israel stretched out his right hand and laid it upon the head of

E'phraim, who was the younger, and his left hand upon the head of Manas'seh, crossing his hands, for Manas'seh was the first-born. [15] And he blessed Joseph, and said,

"The God before whom my fathers Abraham and Isaac walked,
 the God who has led me all my life long to this day,
[16] the angel who has redeemed me from all evil, bless the lads;
 and in them let my name be perpetuated, and the name of my
  fathers Abraham and Isaac;
 and let them grow into a multitude in the midst of the earth."

17 When Joseph saw that his father laid his right hand upon the head of E'phraim, it displeased him; and he took his father's hand, to remove it from E'phraim's head to Manas'seh's head. [18] And Joseph said to his father, "Not so, my father; for this one is the first-born; put your right hand upon his head." [19] But his father refused, and said, "I know, my son, I know; he also shall become a people, and he also shall be great; nevertheless his younger brother shall be greater than he, and his descendants shall become a multitude of nations." [20] So he blessed them that day, saying,

"By you Israel will pronounce blessings, saying,
 'God make you as E'phraim and as Manas'seh;' "
and thus he put E'phraim before Manas'seh.

48:14 This is the first instance in Scriptures of the laying on of hands in blessing. Catholic, Orthodox, and many Protestant churches have kept this symbolic act in certain solemn blessings, as in ordination (cf. Timothy 5 : 22). Jacob intends that the younger son should inherit before the other, and so he crosses his hands, the favored son to be touched by the right hand. By this passage the biblical author accounts for the fact that the tribes of Manasseh and Ephraim acquired status equivalent to those of Jacob's sons; he accounts also for Ephraim's later ascendancy over Manasseh. **48:20** To this day, Jewish fathers will bless their sons on the Sabbath evening and at Bar Mitzvah with the prayer, "God make thee as Ephraim and Manasseh." In interpreting this biblical text, the Rabbis ascribe to the credit of Ephraim and Manasseh the fact that they had abandoned their high station at the court of Egypt in order to identify themselves with their new alien kinsmen, the rustic shepherd immigrants, the sons of Jacob. The Jewish parent prays, therefore, that his sons in like manner will remain true to the heritage of Abraham, Isaac and Jacob.

Jacob Blesses His Sons

Jacob's blessings are represented as a prophetic anticipation of the destinies of all his sons. We cite two examples of these blessings, rendered in poetic form marked by a parallelism of thought characteristic of Hebraic poetry.

Genesis 49 : 1–2, 8–10, 22–26, 28

49 Then Jacob called his sons, and said, "Gather yourselves together, that I may tell you what shall befall you in days to come.

² Assemble and hear, O sons of Jacob,
    and hearken to Israel your father.

⁸ Judah, your brothers shall praise you;
    your hand shall be on the neck of your enemies;
    your father's sons shall bow down before you.
⁹ Judah is a lion's whelp;
    from the prey, my son, you have gone up.
He stooped down, he couched as a lion,
    and as a lioness; who dares rouse him up?
¹⁰ The scepter shall not depart from Judah,
    nor the ruler's staff from between his feet,
until he comes to whom it belongs;
    and to him shall be the obedience of the peoples.

²² Joseph is a fruitful bough,
    a fruitful bough by a spring;
    his branches run over the wall.
²³ The archers fiercely attacked him,
    shot at him, and harassed him sorely;
²⁴ yet his bow remained unmoved,
    his arms were made agile
by the hands of the Mighty One of Jacob
    (by the name of the Shepherd, the Rock of Israel).
²⁵ by the God of your father who will help you,
    by God Almighty who will bless you
with blessings of heaven above,
    blessings of the deep that couches beneath,
    blessings of the breasts and of the womb.
²⁶ The blessings of your father
    are mighty beyond the blessings of the eternal mountains,
    the bounties of the everlasting hills;
may they be on the head of Joseph.
    and on the brow of him who was separate from his brothers."

28 All these are the twelve tribes of Israel; and this is what their father said to them as he blessed them, blessing each with the blessing suitable to him.

49:8 Although Judah was not the eldest son, nor did he possess the birthright, his constancy in defense of his brothers earned him the right of rule. The lion was emblem of the tribe of Judah, signifying the power and speed with which Judah came to the aid of his people. In contemporary synagogues, the emblem of the lion is frequently affixed to the sides of the Tablets of the Law. The word "Jew" describes the descendants of Judah. **49:10** Some commentators find in this verse a Messianic promise. The Jewish Publication Society translation of 1962 renders this verse "so that tribute shall come to him," referring to the tribes of Judah. **49:22** Jacob reserves his most precious blessing for Joseph, who endured the hostility of his brothers, yet remained secure in the care of God. **49:28** Symbols of the Twelve Tribes are strikingly illustrated in stained glass windows that Marc Chagall designed for the Hebrew University Medical Center near Jerusalem.

Joseph Dies in Egypt
Genesis 50 : 15–26

15 When Joseph's brothers saw that their father was dead, they said, "It may be that Joseph will hate us and pay us back for all the evil which we did to him." [16] So they sent a message to Joseph, saying, "Your father gave this command before he died, [17] 'Say to Joseph, Forgive, I pray you, the transgression of your brothers and their sin, because they did evil to you.' And now, we pray you, forgive the transgression of the servants of the God of your father." Joseph wept when they spoke to him. [18] His brothers also came and fell down before him, and said, "Behold, we are your servants." [19] But Joseph said to them, "Fear not, for am I in the place of God? [20] As for you, you meant evil against me; but God meant it for good, to bring it about that many people should be kept alive, as they are today. [21] So do not fear; I will provide for you and your little ones." Thus he reassured them and comforted them.

22 So Joseph dwelt in Egypt, he and his father's house; and Joseph lived a hundred and ten years. [23] And Joseph saw E'phraim's children of the third generation; the children also of Machir the son of Manas'seh were born upon Joseph's knees. [24] And Joseph said to his brothers, "I am about to die; but God will visit you, and bring you up out of this land to the land which he swore to Abraham, to Isaac, and to Jacob." [25] Then Joseph took an oath of the sons of Israel, saying, "God will visit you, and you shall carry up my bones from here." [26] So Joseph died, being a hundred and ten years old; and they embalmed him, and he was put in a coffin in Egypt.

50:26 One hundred and ten years, in Egyptian literary tradition, is the length for a happy and prosperous life.

The Book of Exodus

"Exodus," meaning "a going out" or "departure," is the Greek title of this book. In the Hebrew the title is "Shemoth" meaning "names," from the opening phrase: "And these are the names. . . ."

Genesis describes the lives of the fathers of the Hebrew people; Exodus records their enslavement in Egypt, their deliverance from bondage, the revelation of the Lord at Sinai, and their journey through the wilderness toward the promised Land. By the Exodus and the Covenant at Sinai, Israel became a people, holy to the Lord.

The Book of Exodus also describes their organization of public worship, the revelation of the Ten Commandments and additional moral and social regulations. Having tasted the bitterness of slavery, the Hebrews anticipate a civil order where freedom will be achieved and justice maintained. Religion is linked with morality: God promises freedom to man; He favors righteousness and He humbles oppression. But also He delights in prayer and ritual and demands that man observe both the ceremonial and the moral law.

The Hebrews acknowledge, as few nations have ever done, that their beginnings were humble. They were a slave people. This fact heightens the glory of God's choice. God revealed His Law to a slave people so that all nations may know that it is not through human might or power that man attains salvation; it is rather in faithfulness to God and in acceptance of His Law.

The dramatic account of Israel's bondage and emancipation has inspired a great number of musical compositions. These include Rossini's opera *Moses in Egypt*, Meyerbeer's opera *The Prophet*, Schoenberg's opera *Moses and Aaron*. The Negro spirituals "Go Down Moses" and "Let My People Go" also draw upon the biblical assertion of man's right to freedom.

The Problem of Dating Joseph, the Exodus, and the Conquest

Biblical scholars differ on the dates to be given to such important historic events as the Hebrew migration into Egypt, the career of Joseph, the Pharaoh "who knew not Joseph," the Exodus under Moses, and the conquest of Canaan under Joshua. Archaeological data can support divergent views. Probably a measure of truth is to be found in all the various conflicting explanations, and the Books of Exodus and Joshua compress into one narrative events that transpired over an extended period.

One view is that the Hebrews were part of the Hyksos invasion of Egypt in 1750 B.C. The Hyksos had their capital in the area of Goshen where Jacob and his family settled. Joseph's use of a chariot may testify to his Hyksos affiliation, since the Hyksos were the first to make use of horse and chariot in war.

Another view is built on the fact that Jacob's migration to Goshen was peaceful; Scripture does not describe it as part of a military conquest, such as the Hyksos invasion. Hence it is suggested that the Hebrews entered Egypt during the reign of the monotheist King Ikhnaton, two centuries after the Hyksos. One holding this view notes that the Hebrew words describing the people's obeisance to Joseph: *"Abrech-Venaton"* (Genesis 41:43), translated "Bow the knee!" may really be a Hebrew transliteration for the Greek words meaning "a friend of Ikhnaton." A Theban painting has been discovered that shows a young prince named Meri-re being invested by Ikhnaton with a golden chain, for "he had filled the store houses with spelt and barley."

If the view that the Hebrews were part of the Hyksos invasion of Egypt is accepted, then the King "who knew not Joseph" might be Amasis I, who drove the Hyksos out of Egypt in 1570 B.C. (He would have enslaved those Hebrews who remained in Egypt.) Some scholars believe that many Hebrews left Egypt at that time and participated in an early conquest of parts of Canaan.

If the second view is accepted, that Joseph was a friend of Ikhnaton, and that he was a leader of the Hebrews who had participated in a peaceful migration to Egypt two centuries after the Hyksos, then the Pharaoh "who knew not Joseph" could be Harememheb (1342–1303) the founder of the nineteenth dynasty who wiped out Ikhnaton's religion and may have enslaved the Hebrew followers of the monotheistic Egyptian King. Rameses II of that dynasty (1290–1244) would be the king who ordered the building of storehouses and a capitol city bearing his name. Egyptian records suggest that he used Habiru (Apiru) slaves in that labor. They also indicate that Semitic and non-Semitic slaves were brought into Egypt from the fourteenth to the twelfth century as booty from raids into Canaan. If this view is accepted then the Exodus took place about 1200 B.C.

If there is some truth to both of these theories—and there are still others—then it would appear that the Book of Joshua, describing the conquest of the land of Canaan by the Hebrew tribes, is a fused account, placing in one narration events that extend over a period of time from 1500 B.C. until the invasion under the leadership of Joshua somewhere in the latter half of the thirteenth century B.C.

The suggestion has been offered that the Hebrews entered Canaan in at least three stages: (1) The "Abraham" tribes who entered between 2000–1700 B.C. from the North (i.e., from Mesapotamia) dwelt for a time in the southern Palestinian regions of Hebron and Beersheba and then migrated to Egypt; (2) as part of the Habiru invasion in the fourteenth century B.C. the Hebrews destroyed Jericho and settled in Central Palestine around Shiloh and Shechem; some scholars believe that Joshua was leader of this invasion; (3) an invasion under Moses in the thirteenth century B.C. from the south

(Sinai desert) and from Transjordan. Such scholars, using methods of literary criticism, suggest that the account of the wanderings of the tribes in Numbers 33 preserves a memory of the fourteenth century invasion, when according to archaeological excavations, Moab and Edom were not yet threatening nations; whereas the account in Numbers 21 records the obstacles placed in the way of the Hebrews by Moab and Edom and suggest a thirteenth century date.

Archaeology supports a multiple-invasion theory. Excavations at Jericho indicate that the city was destroyed no earlier than 1400 B.C., but not in the thirteenth century, whereas Debir, Lachish and Eglon are covered under ashes almost three feet thick, destroyed by a conflagration determined to have happened about 1200 B.C.

Once this point in history is passed, biblical history becomes more definite in the dating. Most scholars agree that it was during the period described in Judges and the Books of Samuel that the Hebrews were finally welded into one nation. By the time of David they had all accepted Abraham as their patriarch; and YHWH, revealed to Moses, was the God with whom they made their covenant. So the Habiru nomads finally acquired a land and a God.

Pharaoh Oppresses Israel
Exodus 1 : 1–14, 22; 2 : 1–10

1 These are the names of the sons of Israel who came to Egypt with Jacob, each with his household: ²Reuben, Simeon, Levi, and Judah, ³Is'sachar, Zeb'ulun, and Benjamin, ⁴Dan and Naph'tali, Gad and Asher. ⁵All the offspring of Jacob were seventy persons; Joseph was already in Egypt. ⁶Then Joseph died, and all his brothers, and all that generation. ⁷But the descendants of Israel were fruitful and increased greatly; they multiplied and grew exceedingly strong; so that the land was filled with them.

8 Now there arose a new king over Egypt, who did not know Joseph. ⁹And he said to his people, "Behold, the people of Israel are too many and too mighty for us. ¹⁰Come, let us deal shrewdly with them, lest they multiply, and, if war befall us, they join our enemies and fight against us and escape from the land." ¹¹Therefore they set taskmasters over them to afflict them with heavy burdens; and they built for Pharaoh store cities, Pithom and Ra-am'ses. ¹²But the more they were oppressed, the more they multiplied and the more they spread abroad. And the Egyptians were in dread of the people of Israel. ¹³So they made the people of Israel serve with rigor, ¹⁴and made their lives bitter with hard service, in mortar and brick, and in all kinds of work in the field; in all their work they made them serve with rigor.

22 Then Pharaoh commanded all his people, "Every son that is

born to the Hebrews you shall cast into the Nile, but you shall let every daughter live."

2 Now a man from the house of Levi went and took to wife a daughter of Levi. [2] The woman conceived and bore a son; and when she saw that he was a goodly child, she hid him three months. [3] And when she could hide him no longer she took for him a basket made of bulrushes, and daubed it with bitumen and pitch; and she put the child in it and placed it among the reeds at the river's brink. [4] And his sister stood at a distance, to know what would be done to him. [5] Now the daughter of Pharaoh came down to bathe at the river, and her maidens walked beside the river; she saw the basket among the reeds and sent her maid to fetch it. [6] When she opened it she saw the child; and lo, the babe was crying. She took pity on him and said, "This is one of the Hebrews' children." [7] Then his sister said to Pharaoh's daughter, "Shall I go and call you a nurse from the Hebrew women to nurse the child for you?" [8] And Pharaoh's daughter said to her, "Go." So the girl went and called the child's mother. [9] And Pharoh's daughter said to her, "Take this child away, and nurse him for me, and I will give you your wages." So the woman took the child and nursed him. [10] And the child grew, and she brought him to Pharaoh's daughter, and he became her son; and she named him Moses, for she said, "Because I drew him out of the water."

1:9–10 A minority group is here seen as a threat to the national defense. It is not unusual in a time of crisis for minority groups to suffer injustice. Compare treatment given wartime minority groups in the United States, e.g., Germans in World War I, Japanese in World War II. The extent to which a common language, literature, and race are necessary to national unity is still argued. Minority groups who fled from persecution helped to build the United States; they took inspiration from the biblical account of the liberation of the Hebrews. **2:1–10** This account of Moses' deliverance from the Nile is similar to a Babylonian tale of the birth of King Sargon, the first king of the Akkadian Empire in Mesopotamia, the land from which the early Hebrew patriarchs descended.

Moses Kills an Egyptian Task Master

Moses was reared as an Egyptian in the household of Pharaoh. He did not disavow his people, but identified with them in their pain and suffering.

Exodus 2:11–15

11 One day, when Moses had grown up, he went out to his people and looked on their burdens; and he saw an Egyptian beating a

Hebrew, one of his people. ¹²He looked this way and that, and seeing no one he killed the Egyptian and hid him in the sand. ¹³When he went out the next day, behold, two Hebrews were struggling together; and he said to the man that did the wrong, "Why do you strike your fellow?" ¹⁴He answered, "Who made you a prince and a judge over us? Do you mean to kill me as you killed the Egyptian?" Then Moses was afraid, and thought, "Surely the thing is known."

2:11 Compare Hebrews 11:24 ff.

God Appears to Moses in a Burning Bush

Midian is deep in the southeastern part of the Sinai Peninsula, beyond the jurisdiction of Egypt. There Moses was taken into the house of Jethro, a priest or chieftain of the Midianites. He married Zipporah, daughter of Jethro. He served Jethro faithfully for many years. In the meantime, the Pharaoh Rameses II had passed away, but the new Pharaoh, probably Merenptah, was no less oppressive to the Hebrew people. The Israelites cried out in anguish at their enslavement, now apparently made a permanent condition.

The miracle of the burning bush is understood by some commentators to represent the unceasing, unquenchable call to responsibility felt by Moses in his heart. It is only after this experience and the realization that God would accompany him that Moses feels capable of returning to Egypt to champion the cause of his people.

Exodus 3:1–15, 19–20; 4:1–23, 27–31

3 Now Moses was keeping the flock of his father-in-law, Jethro, the priest of Mid'ian; and he led his flock to the west side of the wilderness, and came to Horeb, the mountain of God. ²And the angel of the LORD appeared to him in a flame of fire out of the midst of a bush; and he looked, and lo, the bush was burning, yet it was not consumed. ³And Moses said, "I will turn aside and see this great sight, why the bush is not burnt." ⁴When the LORD saw that he turned aside to see, God called to him out of the bush, "Moses, Moses!" And he said, "Here am I." ⁵Then he said, "Do not come near; put off your shoes from your feet, for the place on which you are standing is holy ground." ⁶And he said, "I am the God of your father, the God of Abraham, the God of Isaac, and the God of Jacob." And Moses hid his face, for he was afraid to look at God.

7 Then the LORD said, "I have seen the affliction of my people who are in Egypt, and have heard their cry because of their taskmasters; I know their sufferings, ⁸and I have come down to deliver them out of the hand of the Egyptians, and to bring them up

out of that land to a good and broad land, a land flowing with milk and honey, to the place of the Canaanites, the Hittites, the Amorites, the Per'izzites, the Hivites, and the Jeb'usites. ⁹And now, behold, the cry of the people of Israel has come to me, and I have seen the oppression with which the Egyptians oppress them. ¹⁰Come, I will send you to Pharaoh that you may bring forth my people, the sons of Israel, out of Egypt." ¹¹But Moses said to God, "Who am I that I should go to Pharaoh, and bring the sons of Israel out of Egypt?" ¹²He said, "But I will be with you; and this shall be the sign for you, that I have sent you: when you have brought forth the people out of Egypt, you shall serve God upon this mountain."

13 Then Moses said to God, "If I come to the people of Israel and say to them, 'The God of your fathers has sent me to you,' and they ask me, 'What is his name?' what shall I say to them?" ¹⁴God said to Moses, "I AM WHO I AM." And he said, "Say this to the people of Israel, 'I AM has sent me to you.'" ¹⁵God also said to Moses, "Say this to the people of Israel, 'The LORD, the God of your fathers, the God of Abraham, the God of Isaac, and the God of Jacob, has sent me to you': this is my name for ever, and thus I am to be remembered throughout all generations.

19 "I know that the king of Egypt will not let you go unless compelled by a mighty hand. ²⁰So I will stretch out my hand and smite Egypt with all the wonders which I will do in it; after that he will let you go."

4 Then Moses answered, "But behold, they will not believe me or listen to my voice, for they will say, 'The LORD did not appear to you.'" ²The LORD said to him, "What is that in your hand?" He said, "A rod." ³And he said, "Cast it on the ground." So he cast it on the ground, and it became a serpent; and Moses fled from it. ⁴But the LORD said to Moses, "Put out your hand, and take it by the tail"—so he put out his hand and caught it, and it became a rod in his hand— ⁵"that they may believe that the LORD, the God of their fathers, the God of Abraham, the God of Isaac, and the God of Jacob, has appeared to you." ⁶Again, the LORD said to him, "Put your hand into your bosom." And he put his hand into his bosom; and when he took it out, behold, his hand was leprous, as white as snow. ⁷Then God said, "Put your hand back into your bosom." So he put his hand back into his bosom; and when he took it out, behold, it was restored like the rest of his flesh. ⁸"If they will not believe you," God said, "or heed the first sign, they may believe the latter sign. ⁹If they will not believe even these two signs or heed your voice, you shall take some water from the Nile and pour it upon the

dry ground; and the water which you shall take from the Nile will become blood upon the dry ground."

10 But Moses said to the LORD, "Oh, my Lord, I am not eloquent, either heretofore or since thou hast spoken to thy servant; but I am slow of speech and of tongue." ¹¹ Then the LORD said to him, "Who has made man's mouth? Who makes him dumb, or deaf, or seeing, or blind? Is it not I, the LORD? ¹² Now therefore go, and I will be with your mouth and teach you what you shall speak." ¹³ But he said, "Oh, my Lord, send, I pray, some other person." ¹⁴ Then the anger of the LORD was kindled against Moses and he said, "Is there not Aaron, your brother, the Levite? I know that he can speak well; and behold, he is coming out to meet you, and when he sees you he will be glad in his heart. ¹⁵ And you shall speak to him and put the words in his mouth; and I will be with your mouth and with his mouth, and will teach you what you shall do. ¹⁶ He shall speak for you to the people; and he shall be a mouth for you, and you shall be to him as God. ¹⁷ And you shall take in your hand this rod, with which you shall do the signs."

18 Moses went back to Jethro his father-in-law and said to him, "Let me go back, I pray, to my kinsmen in Egypt and see whether they are still alive." And Jethro said to Moses, "Go in peace." ¹⁹ And the LORD said to Moses in Mid'ian, "Go back to Egypt; for all the men who were seeking your life are dead." ²⁰ So Moses took his wife and his sons and set them on an ass, and went back to the land of Egypt; and in his hand Moses took the rod of God.

21 And the LORD said to Moses, "When you go back to Egypt, see that you do before Pharaoh all the miracles which I have put in your power; but I will harden his heart, so that he will not let the people go. ²² And you shall say to Pharaoh, 'Thus says the LORD, Israel is my first-born son, ²³ and I say to you, "Let my son go that he may serve me"; if you refuse to let him go, behold, I will slay your first-born son.' "

27 The LORD said to Aaron, "Go into the wilderness to meet Moses." So he went, and met him at the mountain of God and kissed him. ²⁸ And Moses told Aaron all the words of the LORD with which he had sent him, and all the signs which he had charged him to do. ²⁹ Then Moses and Aaron went and gathered together all the elders of the people of Israel. ³⁰ And Aaron spoke all the words which the LORD had spoken to Moses, and did the signs in the sight of the people. ³¹ And the people believed; and when they heard that the LORD had visited the people of Israel and that he had seen their affliction, they bowed their heads and worshiped.

3:1–3 Since the fourth century the monks of the monastery of St. Catherine at Mt. Sinai have identified this bush with a blackberry bush that grows in the region. Many scholars think of it as a thorn bush, influenced perhaps by the Septuagint (Greek) translation of the Hebrew word as "a bramble thorn bush." **3:10** On this text William Booth (1829–1912) based his administrative policy of a strong central authority for the Salvation Army. "Had the children of Israel been managed by a committee," he said, "they would never have crossed the Red Sea." **3:14** Many translations and interpretations are given to the Hebrew words *Ehyeh-Asher-Ehyeh;* for example: "I am that I am," or "I will be what I will be." In order to preserve the ineffable quality of God's self-revelation to Moses and the mystical nature of Moses' encounter with God, the new Jewish Publication Society translation maintains the Hebrew without translating the words. **3:15** "LORD," is a translation of the word for the Hebrew letters YHWH. This substitute word Jews in prayer pronounce "Adonoy." The letters YHWH derive from the Hebrew rootword *"Hyh"* which means "to be." Biblical scholars identify YHWH as Yahweh, the Lord of the Exodus who was first introduced to the Semitic Hebrews by Moses and identified as the same God as El, the God of Abraham, Isaac and Jacob. Jewish tradition has never permitted these four letters to be pronounced. It was believed that the letters themselves were symbolic representation of the ineffable name, unknown and now forgotten. "Adonoy," itself a substitute, has become associated with such holiness that Orthodox Jews will only pronounce that word in prayer, otherwise reciting it as "Adoshem." In fact, Orthodox Jews will not spell out the name of the divinity in English. They write G-d. The pronunciation of God's name as "Jehovah" was popularized by Pope Leo X's confessor Peter Galatin about 1518. Correcting that error the new Catholic *Jerusalem Bible* of 1966 now uses the accepted scholarly rendering of the word "Yahweh." The new Jewish Publication Society translation of the Torah, in order to maintain the ineffable quality of the Name, spells it out in Hebrew letters; it does not translate or transliterate the Hebrew. **4:10** Many scholars believe that Moses' impediment was that of a stammerer. **4:22** In this passage, God for the first time refers to Israel as His first-born son. While the prophetic teachers will suggest that other nations are God's children too, Israel's responsibility as first-born is to assume the duties of the priest-nation through whom all others of God's children will be blessed.

Moses Returns to Egypt
Exodus 5:1–4, 6–14, 19–23; 6:1

5 Afterward Moses and Aaron went to Pharaoh and said, "Thus says the LORD, the God of Israel, 'Let my people go, that they may hold a feast to me in the wilderness.'" [2] But Pharaoh said, "Who is the

LORD, that I should heed his voice and let Israel go? I do not know the LORD, and moreover I will not let Israel go." ³Then they said, "The God of the Hebrews has met with us; let us go, we pray, a three days' journey into the wilderness, and sacrifice to the LORD our God, lest he fall upon us with pestilence or with the sword." ⁴But the king of Egypt said to them, "Moses and Aaron, why do you take the people away from their work? Get to your burdens."

6 The same day Pharaoh commanded the taskmasters of the people and their foremen, ⁷"You shall no longer give the people straw to make bricks, as heretofore; let them go and gather straw for themselves. ⁸But the number of bricks which they made heretofore you shall lay upon them, you shall by no means lessen it; for they are idle; therefore they cry, 'Let us go and offer sacrifice to our God.' ⁹Let heavier work be laid upon the men that they may labor at it and pay no regard to lying words."

10 So the taskmasters and the foremen of the people went out and said to the people, "Thus says Pharaoh, 'I will not give you straw. ¹¹Go yourselves, get your straw wherever you can find it; but your work will not be lessened in the least.'" ¹²So the people were scattered abroad throughout all the land of Egypt, to gather stubble for straw. ¹³The taskmasters were urgent, saying, "Complete your work, your daily task, as when there was straw." ¹⁴And the foremen of the people of Israel, whom Pharaoh's taskmasters had set over them, were beaten, and were asked, "Why have you not done all your task of making bricks today, as hitherto?"

19 The foremen of the people of Israel saw that they were in evil plight, when they said, "You shall by no means lessen your daily number of bricks." ²⁰They met Moses and Aaron, who were waiting for them as they came forth from Pharaoh; ²¹and they said to them, "The LORD look upon you and judge, because you have made us offensive in the sight of Pharaoh and his servants, and have put a sword in their hand to kill us."

22 Then Moses turned again to the LORD and said, "O LORD, why has thou done evil to this people? Why didst thou ever send me? ²³For since I came to Pharaoh to speak in thy name, he has done evil to this people, and thou has not delivered thy people at all."

6 But the LORD said to Moses, "Now you shall see what I will do to Pharaoh; for with a strong hand he will send them out, yea, with a strong hand he will drive them out of his land."

5:10 Bricks were made of sun-dried clay. Chopped straw formed a skeleton for the brick and prevented crumbling. Pharaoh withheld the straw, so the Jews had to gather it themselves and still maintain their production quota. **5:21** History records few incidents in which individuals or groups voluntarily gave up wealth, power or privilege. Liberty and freedom seem to come only at the price of blood and tears. Compare contemporary progress on elimination of racial discrimination in the United States, of economic caste groups in South America, Africa, Asia.

God Renews His Promise of Redemption
Exodus 6:2–13

2 And God said to Moses, "I am the LORD. ³I appeared to Abraham, to Isaac, and to Jacob, as God Almighty, but by my name the LORD I did not make myself known to them. ⁴I also established my covenant with them, to give them the land of Canaan, the land in which they dwelt as sojourners. ⁵Moreover I have heard the groaning of the people of Israel whom the Egyptians hold in bondage and I have remembered my covenant. ⁶Say therefore to the people of Israel, 'I am the LORD, and I will bring you out from under the burdens of the Egyptians, and I will deliver you from their bondage, and I will redeem you with an outstretched arm and with great acts of judgment, ⁷and I will take you for my people, and I will be your God; and you shall know that I am the LORD your God, who has brought you out from under the burdens of the Egyptians. ⁸And I will bring you into the land which I swore to give to Abraham, to Isaac, and to Jacob; I will give it to you for a possession. I am the LORD.' " ⁹Moses spoke thus to the people of Israel; but they did not listen to Moses, because of their broken spirit and their cruel bondage.

10 And the LORD said to Moses, ¹¹"Go in, tell Pharaoh king of Egypt to let the people of Israel go out of his land." ¹²But Moses said to the LORD, "Behold, the people of Israel have not listened to me; how then shall Pharaoh listen to me, who am a man of uncircumcised lips?" ¹³But the LORD spoke to Moses and Aaron, and gave them a charge to the people of Israel and to Pharaoh king of Egypt to bring the people of Israel out of the land of Egypt.

6:2–3 Some Bible scholars suggest that God was originally known to the Semitic tribes who journeyed to Palestine as El Shaddai, "God Almighty." Moses introduced the Hebrews of the Exodus to the God called YHWH translated Lord. In this passage the biblical author explains that the "Lord" and the "God Almighty" are identical. They are merely two names for the same God—the one God of all men. Other Bible scholars insist that the worship of YHWH extends back to the days even before the flood (cf. Genesis 4:26); thus, it is not exclusively through Moses that the Semites came to learn about the God, YHWH.

God Brings Ten Plagues upon the Egyptians

Ten plagues came upon the Egyptians before Pharaoh recognized that he must let the Israelites go. The plagues: water turned into blood, frogs, gnats, beetles, murrain or cattle disease, boils, hail, locust, darkness and slaying of the first born. During the Passover service, *Seder,* Jews recount these ten plagues; as they do, they spill out wine from the ceremonial cup. Since wine symbolizes joy in life, the Jews are forbidden to drink a full measure, recognizing that the Egyptians had to endure great suffering and loss, including the drowning of their troops. The delight of freedom is tempered with remorse at the tragic cost in acquiring that emancipation.

Exodus 11:1, 4–8, 10

11 The LORD said to Moses, "Yet one plague more I will bring upon Pharaoh and upon Egypt; afterwards he will let you go hence; when he lets you go, he will drive you away completely."

4 And Moses said, "Thus says the LORD: About midnight I will go forth in the midst of Egypt; ⁵and all the first-born in the land of Egypt shall die, from the first-born of Pharaoh who sits upon his throne, even to the first-born of the maidservant who is behind the mill; and all the first-born of the cattle. ⁶And there shall be a great cry throughout all the land of Egypt, such as there has never been, nor ever shall be again. ⁷But against any of the people of Israel, either man or beast, not a dog shall growl; that you may know that the LORD makes a distinction between the Egyptians and Israel. ⁸And all these your servants shall come down to me, and bow down to me, saying, 'Get you out, and all the people who follow you.' And after that I will go out." And he went out from Pharaoh in hot anger.

10 Moses and Aaron did all these wonders before Pharaoh; and the LORD hardened Pharaoh's heart, and he did not let the people of Israel go out of his land.

11:1 Some scholars point out that in the account of these plagues there is to be seen an attack on the Egyptian gods. The Egyptians worshipped the rich Nile; they also regarded fishes, frogs and locusts as totem animals. The plagues may be seen also as attacks on the Egyptian God of the earth, Seb; the god of heaven, Nut; and the sun God, Re or Hores.

God Institutes the Observance of Passover

These rites make up essential parts of the Passover service, celebrated annually in the homes of Jews. In contemporary Jewish homes the ceremony is called a *Seder*—which literally means "the order" of the service. That order of ritual, designed to recall the experience of slavery and emancipation, is contained in a prayer book called a

Haggadah. The dinner table is decorated with festive items that will stimulate questions and lead to a telling of the Passover account. These items include: salt water and greens to represent the life that comes forth at spring; a roasted bone to recall the Paschal lamb; unleavened bread or "matzos" which are eaten throughout the week-long observance; bitter herbs ("moror"), such as horse radish, to recall the bitterness of slavery; and haroseth, a sweet condiment made of apples, nuts and wine—in color made to look like the mortar of which bricks are made but sweet to the taste, to symbolize the hope of freedom that sweetens the taste of slavery. Children begin the narrative portion of the Passover service by asking four questions highlighting the differences between this night and all other nights:

1. On all other nights we can eat leavened bread or matzah, why on this night do we eat only matzos?

2. On all other nights we can eat any kind of herbs, why on this night do we eat only bitter herbs?

3. On all other nights we do not even dip once, why on this night do we dip greens into salt water, and bitter herbs into haroseth?

4. On all other nights we eat sitting erect or reclining, why on this night do we eat at the table reclining? (In ancient times a free man ate his dinner without haste reclining at the table.)

Exodus 12:1–17, 21–27, 29–39, 51

12 The LORD said to Moses and Aaron in the land of Egypt, ² "This months shall be for you the beginning of months; it shall be the first month of the year for you. ³ Tell all the congregation of Israel that on the tenth day of this month they shall take every man a lamb according to their fathers' houses, a lamb for a household; ⁴ and if the household is too small for a lamb, then a man and his neighbor next to his house shall take according to the number of persons; according to what each can eat you shall make your count for the lamb. ⁵ Your lamb shall be without blemish, a male a year old; you shall take it from the sheep or from the goats; ⁶ and you shall keep it until the fourteenth day of this month, when the whole assembly of the congregation of Israel shall kill their lambs in the evening. ⁷ Then they shall take some of the blood, and put it on the two doorposts and the lintel of the houses in which they eat them. ⁸ They shall eat the flesh that night, roasted; with unleavened bread and bitter herbs they shall eat it. ⁹ Do not eat any of it raw or boiled with water, but roasted, its head with its legs and its inner parts. ¹⁰ And you shall let none of it remain until the morning, anything that remains until the morning you shall burn. ¹¹ In this manner you shall eat it: your loins girded, your sandals on your feet, and your staff in your hand; and you shall eat it in haste. It is the LORD's passover. ¹² For I will pass through the land of Egypt that night, and I will smite all the first-born in the land of Egypt, both man and beast; and on all the gods of Egypt I will execute judgments: I am the LORD. [13] The blood shall be a sign for you, upon the houses where you are; and when I see the blood, I will pass over you, and no plague shall fall upon you to destroy you, when I smite the land of Egypt.

14 This day shall be for you a memorial day, and you shall keep it as a feast to the LORD; throughout your generations you shall observe it as an ordinance for ever. [15] Seven days you shall eat unleavened bread; on the first day you shall put away leaven out of your houses, for if any one eats what is leavened, from the first day until the seventh day, that person shall be cut off from Israel. [16] On the first day you shall hold a holy assembly, and on the seventh day a holy assembly; no work shall be done on those days; but what every one must eat, that only may be prepared by you. [17] And you shall observe the feast of unleavened bread, for on this very day I brought your hosts out of the land of Egypt: therefore you shall observe this day, throughout your generations, as an ordinance for ever."

21 Then Moses called all the elders of Israel, and said to them, "Select lambs for yourselves according to your families, and kill the passover lamb. [22] Take a bunch of hyssop and dip it in the blood which is in the basin, and touch the lintel and the two doorposts with the blood which is in the basin; and none of you shall go out of the door of his house until the morning. [23] For the LORD will pass through to slay the Egyptians; and when he sees the blood on the lintel and on the two doorposts, the LORD will pass over the door, and will not allow the destroyer to enter your houses to slay you. [24] You shall observe this rite as an ordinance for you and for your sons for ever. [25] And when you come to the land which the LORD will give you, as he has promised, you shall keep this service. [26] And when your children say to you, 'What do you mean by this service?' [27] you shall say, 'It is the sacrifice of the LORD'S passover, for he passed over the houses of the people of Israel in Egypt, when he slew the Egyptians but spared our houses.' " And the people bowed their heads and worshiped.

29 At midnight the LORD smote all the first-born in the land of Egypt, from the first-born of Pharaoh who sat on his throne to the first-born of the captive who was in the dungeon, and all the first-born of the cattle. [30] And Pharaoh rose up in the night, he, and all his servants, and all the Egyptians; and there was a great cry in Egypt, for there was not a house where one was not dead. [31] And he summoned Moses and Aaron by night, and said, "Rise up, go forth from among my people, both you and the people of Israel; and go, serve the LORD, as you have said. [32] Take your flocks and your herds, as you have said, and be gone; and bless me also!"

33 And the Egyptians were urgent with the people, to send them out of the land in haste; for they said, "We are all dead men." ³⁴ So the people took their dough before it was leavened, their kneading bowls being bound up in their mantles on their shoulders. ³⁵ The people of Israel had also done as Moses told them, for they had asked of the Egyptians jewelry of silver and of gold, and clothing; ³⁶ and the LORD had given the people favor in the sight of the Egyptians, so that they let them have what they asked. Thus they despoiled the Egyptians.

37 And the people of Israel journeyed from Ram′eses to Succoth, about six hundred thousand men on foot, besides women and children. ³⁸ A mixed multitude also went up with them, and very many cattle, both flocks and herds. ³⁹ And they baked unleavened cakes of the dough which they had brought out of Egypt, for it was not leavened, because they were thrust out of Egypt and could not tarry, neither had they prepared for themselves any provisions.

51 And on that very day the LORD brought the people of Israel out of the land of Egypt by their hosts.

12:5 Christians regard Jesus dying on Passover Day as the Paschal Lamb, "who takes away the sin of the world" (John 1:29). **12:11** *The Berkeley Version in Modern English* (1959, Zondervan), here reads: "Eat it this way, with your waist belted, your feet sandaled and your staff in hand; eat it in expectant haste, it is a Passover for the Lord." Compare this experience of the Hebrew slaves with the status of refugees who fled Italy's fascism, Germany's nazism, Cuba's communism. **12:21–22** Some scholars believe that the ancient Hebrews once observed a springtime pastoral festival that consisted of the sacrifice of a lamb. That shepherd holiday is now associated with the Exodus and invested with a new meaning by Moses. **12:23** The "destroyer" who killed the Egyptian first-born is an angel of death commissioned by God (cf. 2 Kings 19:35, and 2 Samuel 24:15). In Rabbinic writings it was believed that devotion to the study of Torah could shield a man from the angel of death, although man could never escape his mortality. The Talmud records also that once given permission to destroy—as in time of war—the angel of death makes no distinction between good and bad (*Babba Kamma* 60a). According to both Jewish and Christian thought the Messiah, upon his coming, will conquer death (*Pesikta Rabbah* 161b; 1 Corinthians 15:26).

God Guides Israel in the Flight from Egypt
Exodus 13:17–22

17 When Pharaoh let the people go, God did not lead them by way of the land of the Philistines, although that was near; for God said,

"Lest the people repent when they see war, and return to Egypt."
¹⁸ But God led the people round by the way of the wilderness toward
the Red Sea. And the people of Israel went up out of the land of
Egypt equipped for battle. ¹⁹ And Moses took the bones of Joseph
with him; for Joseph had solemnly sworn the people of Israel, saying,
"God will visit you; then you must carry my bones with you from
here." ²⁰ And they moved on from Succoth, and encamped at Etham,
on the edge of the wilderness. ²¹ And the LORD went before them by
day in a pillar of cloud to lead them along the way, and by night in a
pillar of fire to give them light, that they might travel by day and by
night; ²² the pillar of cloud by day and the pillar of fire by night did
not depart from before the people.

13:18 "Red Sea" is the traditional translation, but the Hebrew
means literally "sea of reeds." An Egyptian document of about 1100
B.C. refers to the marshes and lakes along the Mediterranean coast
as a sea of reeds; the route taken by the Israelites may have been
through that area.

The Egyptians Pursue
Exodus 14:5–14, 26–31

5 When the king of Egypt was told that the people had fled, the mind
of Pharaoh and his servants was changed toward the people, and
they said, "What is this we have done, that we have let Israel go
from serving us?" ⁶ So he made ready his chariot and took his army
with him, ⁷ and took six hundred picked chariots and all the other
chariots of Egypt with officers over all of them. ⁸ And the LORD
hardened the heart of Pharaoh king of Egypt and he pursued the
people of Israel as they went forth defiantly. ⁹ The Egyptians
pursued them, all Pharaoh's horses and chariots and his horsemen
and his army, and overtook them encamped at the sea, by Pi-
ha-hi'roth, in front of Ba'al-zephon.

10 When Pharaoh drew near, the people of Israel lifted up their
eyes, and behold, the Egyptians were marching after them; and they
were in great fear. And the people of Israel cried out to the LORD;
¹¹ and they said to Moses, "Is it because there are no graves in Egypt
that you have taken us away to die in the wilderness? What have you
done to us, in bringing us out of Egypt? ¹² Is not this what we said to
you in Egypt, 'Let us alone and let us serve the Egyptians'? For it
would have been better for us to serve the Egyptians than to die in
the wilderness." ¹³ And Moses said to the people, "Fear not, stand
firm, and see the salvation of the LORD, which he will work for you
today; for the Egyptians whom you see today, you shall never see
again. ¹⁴ The LORD will fight for you, and you have only to be still."

26 Then the LORD said to Moses, "Stretch out your hand over the sea, that the water may come back upon the Egyptians, upon their chariots, and upon their horsemen." [27] So Moses stretched forth his hand over the sea, and the sea returned to its wonted flow when the morning appeared; and the Egyptians fled into it, and the LORD routed the Egyptians in the midst of the sea. [28] The waters returned and covered the chariots and the horsemen and all the host of Pharaoh that had followed them into the sea; not so much as one of them remained. [29] But the people of Israel walked on dry ground through the sea, the waters being a wall to them on their right hand and on their left.

30 Thus the LORD saved Israel that day from the hand of the Egyptians; and Israel saw the Egyptians dead upon the seashore. [31] And Israel saw the great work which the LORD did against the Egyptians, and the people feared the LORD; and they believed in the LORD and in his servant Moses.

14:29 In one method of Biblical interpretation, known as typology, the passage of the Hebrew tribes through the Sea of Reeds is understood to be a pre-figuring for the Christian ceremony of Baptism (see 1 Corinthians 10:1).

Moses and Israel Praise God in Song
Exodus 15:1–13, 17–18, 20–21

15 Then Moses and the people of Israel sang this song to the LORD, saying,
"I will sing to the LORD, for he has triumphed gloriously;
the horse and his rider he has thrown into the sea.
[2] The LORD is my strength and my song,
and he has become my salvation;
this is my God, and I will praise him,
my father's God, and I will exalt him.
[3] The LORD is a man of war;
the LORD is his name.

[4] "Pharaoh's chariots and his host he cast into the sea;
and his picked officers are sunk in the Red Sea.
[5] The floods cover them;
they went down into the depths like a stone.
[6] Thy right hand, O LORD, glorious in power,
thy right hand, O LORD, shatters the enemy.
[7] In the greatness of thy majesty thou overthrowest thy adversaries;
thou sendest forth thy fury, it consumes them like stubble.

⁸At the blast of thy nostrils the waters piled up,
　　the floods stood up in a heap;
　　the deeps congealed in the heart of the sea.
⁹The enemy said, 'I will pursue, I will overtake,
　　I will divide the spoil, my desire shall have its fill of them.
　　I will draw my sword, my hand shall destroy them.'
¹⁰Thou didst blow with thy wind, the sea covered them;
　　they sank as lead in the mighty waters.

¹¹"Who is like thee, O LORD, among the gods?
　　Who is like thee, majestic in holiness,
　　terrible in glorious deeds, doing wonders?
¹²Thou didst stretch out thy right hand,
　　the earth swallowed them.

¹³"Thou hast led in thy steadfast love the people whom thou
　　　hast redeemed,
　　thou hast guided them by thy strength to thy holy abode.
¹⁷Thou wilt bring them in, and plant them on thy own mountain,
　　the place, O LORD, which thou hast made for thy abode,
　　the sanctuary, O LORD, which thy hands have established.
¹⁸The LORD will reign for ever and ever."

20 Then Miriam, the prophetess, the sister of Aaron, took a
timbrel in her hand; and all the women went out after her
with timbrels and dancing. ²¹And Miriam sang to them:
　　"Sing to the LORD, for he has triumphed gloriously;
　　the horse and his rider he has thrown into the sea."

15:11 When the Hebrew Bible was translated into Aramaic, the
very first translation of the Bible into another language, the rabbis
rendered this verse: "There is no one beside Thee, for Thou art God
alone." The rabbis would not countenance the suggestion that there
were other gods with whom the God of the Exodus could be
compared, an evidence of the development of a profounder monotheistic emphasis in Judaism. The new Jewish Publication Society
translation renders this verse "Who is like You, O Lord, among the
celestials?" **15:21** Many scholars believe this verse to be the extant
verse of a song originally composed by Miriam, and that the
preceding poem (1–19), based on it, was composed at a later date.
Note that verse 17 refers to a subsequent event, the building of the
temple of Mt. Zion.

God Gives Healing
Exodus 15:22–27

22 Then Moses led Israel onward from the Red Sea, and they went
into the wilderness of Shur; they went three days in the wilderness

and found no water. ²³ When they came to Marah, they could not drink the water of Marah because it was bitter; therefore it was named Marah. ²⁴ And the people murmured against Moses, saying, "What shall we drink?" ²⁵ And he cried to the LORD; and the LORD showed him a tree, and he threw it into the water, and the water became sweet.

There the LORD made for them a statute and an ordinance and there he proved them, ²⁶ saying, "If you will diligently hearken to the voice of the LORD your God, and do that which is right in his eyes, and give heed to his commandments and keep all his statutes, I will put none of the diseases upon you which I put upon the Egyptians; for I am the LORD, your healer."

27 Then they came to Elim, where there were twelve springs of water and seventy palm trees; and they encamped there by the water.

God Provides Manna and Quail

The miraculous quality of God's provision for and protection over Israel is here emphasized with the account of the rain of manna. No one knows what *manna* is. Manna is derived from the Hebrew words *man-hu,* meaning "What is it?" Some suggest a white resinous gum exuded by the tamarisk shrub. Quail (4:13) were also available at some seasons, as the Sinai desert was a resting place for birds in flight.

Each man was provided according to his need; there was neither rich nor poor.

The Hebrews at each moment of discomfort mutter and rumble; they remember the fleshpots of Egypt and forget the bitterness of their slavery. The true enslavement of the Israelites was that they had accepted slavery in their hearts.

Exodus 16:2–6, 13–31; 17:1–6

2 And the whole congregation of the people of Israel murmured against Moses and Aaron in the wilderness, ³ and said to them, "Would that we had died by the hand of the LORD in the land of Egypt, when we sat by the fleshpots and ate bread to the full; for you have brought us out into this wilderness to kill this whole assembly with hunger."

4 Then the LORD said to Moses, "Behold, I will rain bread from heaven for you; and the people shall go out and gather a day's portion every day, that I may prove them, whether they will walk in my law or not. ⁵ On the sixth day, when they prepare what they bring in, it will be twice as much as they gather daily." ⁶ So Moses and Aaron said to all the people of Israel, "At evening you shall

know that it was the LORD who brought you out of the land of Egypt."

13 In the evening quails came up and covered the camp: and in the morning dew lay round about the camp. ¹⁴ And when the dew had gone up, there was on the face of the wilderness a fine, flake-like thing, fine as hoarfrost on the ground. ¹⁵ When the people of Israel saw it, they said to one another, "What is it?" For they did not know what it was. And Moses said to them, "It is the bread which the LORD has given you to eat. ¹⁶ This is what the LORD has commanded: 'Gather of it, every man of you, as much as he can eat; you shall take an omer apiece, according to the number of the persons whom each of you has in his tent.' " ¹⁷ And the people of Israel did so; they gathered, some more, some less. ¹⁸ But when they measured it with an omer, he that gathered much had nothing over, and he that gathered little had no lack; each gathered according to what he could eat. ¹⁹ And Moses said to them, "Let no man leave any of it till the morning." ²⁰ But they did not listen to Moses; some left part of it till the morning, and it bred worms and became foul; and Moses was angry with them. ²¹ Morning by morning they gathered it, each as much as he could eat; but when the sun grew hot, it melted.

22 On the sixth day they gathered twice as much bread, two omers apiece; and when all the leaders of the congregation came and told Moses, ²³ he said to them, "This is what the LORD has commanded: 'Tomorrow is a day of solemn rest, a holy sabbath to the LORD; bake what you will bake and boil what you will boil, and all that is left over lay by to be kept till the morning.' " ²⁴ So they laid it by till the morning, as Moses bade them; and it did not become foul, and there were no worms in it. ²⁵ Moses said, "Eat it today, for today is a sabbath to the LORD; today you will not find it in the field. ²⁶ Six days you shall gather it; but on the seventh day, which is a sabbath, there will be none." ²⁷ On the seventh day some of the people went out to gather, and they found none. ²⁸ And the LORD said to Moses, "How long do you refuse to keep my commandments and my laws? ²⁹ See! The LORD has given you the sabbath, therefore on the sixth day he gives you bread for two days; remain every man of you in his place, let no man go out of his place on the seventh day." ³⁰ So the people rested on the seventh day.

31 Now the house of Israel called its name manna; it was like coriander seed, white, and the taste of it was like wafers made with honey.

17 All the congregation of the people of Israel moved on from the wilderness of Sin by stages, according to the commandment of the LORD, and camped at Reph'idim; but there was no water for the people to drink. [2] Therefore the people found fault with Moses, and said, "Give us water to drink." And Moses said to them, "Why do you find fault with me? Why do you put the LORD to the proof?" [3] But the people thirsted there for water, and the people murmured against Moses, and said, "Why did you bring us up out of Egypt, to kill us and our children and our cattle with thirst?" [4] So Moses cried to the LORD, "What shall I do with this people? They are almost ready to stone me." [5] And the LORD said to Moses, "Pass on before the people, taking with you some of the elders of Israel; and take in your hand the rod with which you struck the Nile, and go. [6] Behold, I will stand before you there on the rock at Horeb; and you shall strike the rock, and water shall come out of it, that the people may drink." And Moses did so, in the sight of the elders of Israel.

16:3 Enslaved men have no experience in being responsible for themselves. Is slavery with fat living more likely to bring happiness than freedom with the possibility of starvation? Voters still must sometimes make choices between freedom and its risks and what is sometimes promised to be a security at a price of regimentation. The American patriot Patrick Henry said, "Give me liberty or give me death." **16:4** In Christian tradition the manna foreshadows the Eucharist—the spiritual food of the Church. (Cf. John 6:26–58.) **17:1–6** Archaeologists have verified that there are limestone formations in the desert that have been known, when broken, to yield water. **17:6** This scene of Moses smiting the rock is portrayed in catacomb paintings of the early Christians more often than any other scene of the Old Testament. In 1 Corinthians 10:4, Paul provides a symbolic interpretation for this event, identifying the rock with the pre-existent Christ.

Amalek Attacks Israel
Exodus 17:8–16

8 Then came Am'alek and fought with Israel at Reph'idim. [9] And Moses said to Joshua, "Choose for us men, and go out, fight with Am'alek; tomorrow I will stand on the top of the hill with the rod of God in my hand." [10] So Joshua did as Moses told him, and fought with Am'alek; and Moses, Aaron, and Hur went up to the top of the hill. [11] Whenever Moses held up his hand, Israel prevailed; and whenever he lowered his hand, Am'alek prevailed. [12] But Moses' hands grew weary; so they took a stone and put it under him, and he sat upon it, and Aaron and Hur held up his hands, one on one side, and the other on the other side; so his hands were steady until the going down of the sun. [13] And Joshua mowed down Am'alek and his people with the edge of the sword.

14 And the LORD said to Moses, "Write this as a memorial in a

book and recite it in the ears of Joshua, that I will utterly blot out
the remembrance of Am'alek from under heaven." [15] And Moses
built an altar and called the name of it, The LORD is my banner,
[16] saying, "A hand upon the banner of the LORD! The LORD will have
war with Am'alek from generation to generation."

Jethro Instructs Moses in Judgment

The leader of the tribe dispensed judgment at the gate of the city.
Jethro convinces Moses to share the burdensome task. The
decentralization of power and authority in order to facilitate the
rendering of justice provided a more satisfactory social arrangement.
This important lesson in judicial administration was provided by a
Midianite chieftain; Moses was willing to adopt good ideas, even
though foreign.

Exodus 18 : 1, 6– 7, 13– 26

18 Jethro, the priest of Mid'ian, Moses' father-in-law, heard of all
that God had done for Moses and for Israel his people, how the LORD
had brought Israel out of Egypt.

6 And when one told Moses, "Lo, your father-in-law Jethro is
coming to you with your wife and her two sons with her," [7] Moses
went out to meet his father-in-law, and did obeisance and kissed him;
and they asked each other of their welfare, and went into the tent.

13 On the morrow Moses sat to judge the people, and the people
stood about Moses from morning till evening. [14] When Moses'
father-in-law saw all that he was doing for the people, he said,
"What is this that you are doing for the people? Why do you sit
alone, and all the people stand about you from morning till
evening?" [15] And Moses said to his father-in-law, "Because the
people come to me to inquire of God; [16] when they have a dispute,
they come to me and I decide between a man and his neighbor, and I
make them know the statutes of God and his decisions." [17] Moses'
father-in-law said to him, "What you are doing is not good. [18] You
and the people with you will wear yourselves out, for the thing is too
heavy for you; you are not able to perform it alone. [19] Listen now to
my voice; I will give you counsel, and God be with you! You shall
represent the people before God, and bring their cases to God; [20] and
you shall teach them the statutes and the decisions, and make them
know the way in which they must walk and what they must do.
[21] Moreover choose able men from all the people, such as fear God,
men who are trustworthy and who hate a bribe; and place such men
over the people as rulers of thousands, of hundreds, of fifties, and of
tens. [22] And let them judge the people at all times; every great matter
they shall bring to you, but any small matter they shall decide

themselves; so it will be easier for you, and they will bear the burden with you. [23] If you do this, and God so commands you, then you will be able to endure, and all this people also will go to their place in peace."

24 So Moses gave heed to the voice of his father-in-law and did all that he had said. [25] Moses chose able men out of all Israel, and made them heads over the people, rulers of thousands, of hundreds, of fifties, and of tens. [26] And they judged the people at all times; hard cases they brought to Moses, but any small matter they decided themselves.

18:21 Is there to be a rule of persons, or a rule of law? How can a king rule and insure justice beyond the limits of his personal sight, hearing, voice? Division of authority makes a code of laws necessary. Compare this history with the solution of the problem in other cultures, e.g., Persia, Rome. Note the development of a court of appellate jurisdiction in verse 26.

God Appoints Israel a Kingdom of Priests

This passage above all others defines God's special relationship to Israel and Israel's responsibility to God; to this day it determines the religious Jew's definition of himself. The obligation to be a "kingdom of priests" and a "holy nation" inspires Jewish commitment to a ceremonial regimen but even more to the performance of ethical ideals by which holiness is demonstrated in life. Note the use made of this passage in 1 Peter 2:9, where it is argued that those who accept Christianity become God's chosen people.

Exodus 19:2–8, 16–22

2 And when they set out from Reph'idim and came into the wilderness of Sinai, they encamped in the wilderness; and there Israel encamped before the mountain. [3] And Moses went up to God, and the LORD called to him out of the mountain, saying, "Thus you shall say to the house of Jacob, and tell the people of Israel: [4] You have seen what I did to the Egyptians, and how I bore you on eagles' wings and brought you to myself. [5] Now therefore, if you will obey my voice and keep my covenant, you shall be my own possession among all peoples; for all the earth is mine, [6] and you shall be to me a kingdom of priests and a holy nation. These are the words which you shall speak to the children of Israel."

7 So Moses came and called the elders of the people, and set before them all these words which the LORD had commanded him. [8] And all the people answered together and said, "All that the LORD has spoken we will do." And Moses reported the words of the people to the LORD.

16 On the morning of the third day there were thunders and lightnings, and a thick cloud upon the mountain, and a very loud trumpet blast, so that all the people who were in the camp trembled. [17] Then Moses brought the people out of the camp to meet God; and they took their stand at the foot of the mountain. [18] And Mount Sinai was wrapped in smoke, because the LORD descended upon it in fire; and the smoke of it went up like the smoke of a kiln, and the whole mountain quaked greatly. [19] And as the sound of the trumpet grew louder and louder, Moses spoke, and God answered him in thunder. [20] And the LORD came down upon Mount Sinai, to the top of the mountain; and the LORD called Moses to the top of the mountain, and Moses went up. [21] And the LORD said to Moses, "Go down and warn the people, lest they break through to the LORD to gaze and many of them perish. [22] And also let the priests who come near to the LORD concentrate themselves, lest the LORD break out upon them."

19:2 The *Midrash* provides the following Jewish interpretation: "If the Torah had been given in the land of Israel, Israel might have said to the nations of the world: 'you have no share in it.' Therefore the Torah was given in the wilderness, i.e., in public for all to see; and everyone who wishes to receive it let him come and receive it" (*Mekhilta*). 19:18 A tradition maintained by Christian pilgrims dating back to the fifth century A.D. equates Mt. Sinai with the granite mass of Jebel Musa (Arabic for Mountain of Moses) at the tip of the southern Sinai peninsula. Many scholars however see the reference in Deuteronomy 33:2 and Judges 5:4–5 mentioning Mount Paran and Seir as indicating that Mt. Sinai should not be located so far south; it is rather to be found somewhere near the Gulf of Aqaba and the Dead Sea. 19:20 Rabbinic writings reflect a conflict in Jewish tradition on the understanding of this verse. Rabbi Akiba adhered to a literal interpretation, believing that God actually appeared on the mountain. Rabbi Judah ha Nasi held that the passage must be understood in a spiritual sense. He countered: If the sun, one of the many servants of God, may remain in its place and be effective beyond it, how much more He by whose word the world came into being? (*Mekhilta*)

The Ten Commandments

Jewish teachers explain that God spoke the Ten Words in the open desert and declared it in the tongue of all nations. The Commandments were not made for Israel alone, but represent a summary of human duties binding on all men. While much of the Mosaic legislation draws upon the legal precedents to be found in the law codes of Near Eastern culture, scholars agree that the commandments as revealed in chapters 20–21, with the formula "Thou shalt" or "Thou shalt not" are unique to Hebraic thought.

Exodus 20 : 1–17

20 And God spoke all these words, saying, ² "I am the LORD your God, who brought you out of the land of Egypt, out of the house of bondage.

3 "You shall have no other gods before me.

4 "You shall not make for yourself a graven image, or any likeness of anything that is in heaven above, or that is in the earth beneath, or that is in the water under the earth; ⁵ you shall not bow down to them or serve them; for I the LORD your God am a jealous God, visiting the iniquity of the fathers upon the children to the third and the fourth generation of those who hate me, ⁶ but showing steadfast love to thousands of those who love me and keep my commandments.

7 "You shall not take the name of the LORD your God in vain; for the LORD will not hold him guiltless who takes his name in vain.

8 "Remember the sabbath day, to keep it holy. ⁹ Six days you shall labor, and do all your work; ¹⁰ but the seventh day is a sabbath to the LORD your God; in it you shall not do any work, you, or your son, or your daughter, your manservant, or your maidservant, or your cattle, or the sojourner who is within your gates; ¹¹ for in six days the LORD made heaven and earth, the sea, and all that is in them, and rested the seventh day; therefore the LORD blessed the sabbath day and hallowed it.

12 "Honor your father and your mother, that your days may be long in the land which the LORD your God gives you.

13 "You shall not kill.

14 "You shall not commit adultery.

15 "You shall not steal.

16 "You shall not bear false witness against your neighbor.

17 "You shall not covet your neighbor's house; you shall not covet your neighbor's wife, or his manservant, or his maidservant, or his ox, or his ass, or anything that is your neighbor's."

20:1 Traditionally in pictorial representations of the Tablets of the Law, the words are presented on two tablets with Commandments referring to God on one side, and those concerned with the duties of man to man on the other. America's religious groups maintain different traditions concerning the Commandments. e.g., since Hebrew is written from right to left, the Jewish tradition places the first commandments referring to God on the right side of the tablet. In the Jewish tradition five commandments are placed on both sides of the tablet; in the Catholic tradition the division is three and seven. **20:2** *I am the Lord your God.* In Jewish tradition this is the First Commandment. In some Protestant traditions, it is con-

THE TEN COMMANDMENTS

Episcopal	Catholic	Lutheran	Hebrew	Protestant (other)	
1			1	Preface	I am the Lord thy God who brought thee out of the house of bondage.
	1	1	2	1	THOU shalt not have other gods before Me.
2				2	THOU shalt not make unto thee any graven image.
3	2	2	3	3	THOU shalt not take the name of the Lord thy God in vain.
4	3	3	4	4	REMEMBER the Sabbath day to keep it holy.
5	4	4	5	5	HONOR thy father and thy mother.
6	5	5	6	6	THOU shalt not kill.
7	6	6	7	7	THOU shalt not commit adultery.
8	7	7	8	8	THOU shalt not steal.
9	8	8	9	9	THOU shalt not bear false witness against thy neighbor.
	10	9			THOU shalt not covet thy neighbor's house.
10	9	10	10	10	THOU shalt not covet thy neighbor's wife.

sidered the preface; in Episcopal, Lutheran and Catholic traditions it is joined to the next sentence (or sentences) to make up the First Commandment. **20:3–4** "You shall have no other gods before me" is considered by Jews to be the first part of the second Commandment. "You shall not make yourself a graven image" is considered by Jews to be the second part of the Second Commandment intended to forbid idolatry. In the Catholic and Lutheran traditions the verses were considered part of the First Commandment. But in some Protestant traditions the proscription against creating graven images was emphasized and considered the Second Commandment. The commandment has hindered at times the development of the plastic arts. On the other hand, it has preserved the realization that God is spirit, not corporeal. Jews and some Christian groups on the basis of this commandment forbid three-dimensional representations in their sanctuaries. In 787 the Second Council of Nicea (generally reckoned as the Seventh Ecumenical Council) declared against the Iconoclasts, decreeing the prohibition that "you shall not make to yourself a graven image" was proclaimed only to the Israelites. The phrase is one of about two dozen in the Bible authoritatively explained by the Catholic Church. **20:7** Jews understand this commandment, "You shall not take the name of the Lord your God in vain" to forbid both profane swearing and perjury. The new Jewish Publication Society translation of the Torah, emphasizing the latter interpretation renders this verse: "Ye shall not swear falsely by the name of the Lord your God." Some Christians, e.g., members of the Society of Friends, refuse to take any oath, on the basis of this passage. **20:8** Both Jews and Christians count the seventh day (Saturday) as the Sabbath. Most Christians, however, observe the first day on which Jesus rose from the dead—Sunday—as the Lord's Day. Some Christian Adventist and Baptist groups join the Jews in maintaining Saturday as a day of rest and worship. **20:9** A Jewish Midrash comments on this verse: "Rabbi Eliezer used to say 'Labor is great, for as Israel was commanded to keep the Sabbath so they were also commanded to labor.' As it is said 'six days you shall labor and do all your work.' " *(Abot de Rabbi Nathan.)* **20:12** *Honor your father and your mother.* In the Jewish view this is the Fifth Commandment and it is placed on the first tablet to indicate that parents stand in the place of God so far as children are concerned. **20:13** From *You shall not kill*, it has traditionally been understood that both murder and suicide are forbidden. There is division among religious leaders regarding the circumstances under which, for the sake of justice or in time of war, it is permitted to take life. See also Genesis 9:5–6. **20:14** In the tradition of that time, a husband was guilty of adultery when he had extra-marital relations with a married or betrothed woman (cf. Deuteronomy 22:23–27), but not for relations with an unbetrothed maiden (Deuteronomy 22:28) or harlot. A married woman was guilty of adultery if she had relations with any man except her husband. Both parties guilty of adultery, the man as well as the married woman, were to be stoned to death. A man who seduced an unbetrothed maiden, although technically not guilty of adultery, had to pay a fine, i.e., the customary marriage price of 50 shekels (cf. Exodus 22:16; Deuteronomy 22:28). The girl's father was not obliged to give the unmarried girl to the man as wife; on the other hand the man was obliged to marry her on demand and could never divorce her (Deuteronomy 22:29). Commonly in western law and Christian civilization adultery is any act of sexual intercourse between a married person and anyone not his or her spouse; in most Christian traditions the commandment is understood also to forbid sexual intercourse out of wedlock. The prophets frequently portrayed the Covenant between God and Israel as a marriage and character- ized Israel's idolatry as adultery (cf. Hosea 2:4; Jeremiah 2:2). **20:16** *You shall not bear false witness.* This commandment is understood to embrace all forms of slander, defamation and mis- representation, whether directed against an individual or a people, a race or a faith. **20:17** *You shall not covet.* This commandment reaches to the heart of evil action, i.e., to the impulses, appetites, and lusts. In Jewish law, while such impulses were considered sinful, they were not called crimes nor subject to legislation. Some sins were considered beyond the reach of human laws but subject to God's judgment. On October 1, 1567, Pope St. Pius V condemned an interpretation of this verse by Michael du Bay (Baius), who said that movements of concupiscence were prohibited by this verse, and therefore that if a man felt concupiscence he transgressed the precept, even if he did not consent to the concupiscence and even though the transgression would not be imputed to the man as a sin. The verse is one of the few in the Bible interpreted officially by the Catholic Church.

The Civil Legislation

Scholars have found and translated the codes of law of seven nations in the Near East. The most prominent are: the Sumerian (2050 B.C.), Akkadian (1925 B.C.), the Hamurabbi Code (1700 B.C.), Hittite (1450 B.C.) and Assyrian (1350 B.C.). These codes parallel each other in many ways. It appears that much of the case law in Exodus (21–24) draws upon and follows the pattern of law promulgated through the Mesopotamian world, reflecting in many cases, however, the profounder spiritual insights of the Hebrews. The absolute laws of "Thou shalt" and "Thou shalt not" as found in Exodus 20–21 are presumed to be of original Hebraic authorship.

Exodus 21:1–6, 12–13, 26–31, 33–34;
22:1–3, 15–27; 23:1–12, 14–17, 19–22

21 "Now these are the ordinances which you shall set before them. ²When you buy a Hebrew slave, he shall serve six years, and in the seventh he shall go out free, for nothing. ³ If he comes in single, he shall go out single; if he comes in married, then his wife shall go out with him. ⁴ If his master gives him a wife and she bears him sons or daughters, the wife and her children shall be her master's and he shall go out alone. ⁵ But if the slave plainly says, 'I love my master, my wife, and my children; I will not go out free,' ⁶ then his master shall bring him to God, and he shall bring him to the door or the doorpost; and his master shall bore his ear through with an awl; and he shall serve him for life.

12 "Whoever strikes a man so that he dies shall be put to death. ¹³ But if he did not lie in wait for him, but God let him fall into his hand, then I will appoint for you a place to which he may flee.

26 "When a man strikes the eye of his slave, male or female, and destroys it, he shall let the slave go free for the eye's sake. ²⁷ If he knocks out the tooth of his slave, male or female, he shall let the slave go free for the tooth's sake.

28 "When an ox gores a man or a woman to death, the ox shall be stoned, and its flesh shall not be eaten; but the owner of the ox shall be clear. ²⁹ But if the ox has been accustomed to gore in the past, and its owner has been warned but has not kept it in, and it kills a man or a woman, the ox shall be stoned, and its owner also shall be put to death. ³⁰ If a ransom is laid on him, then he shall give for the redemption of his life whatever is laid upon him. ³¹ If it gores a man's son or daughter, he shall be dealt with according to this same rule.

33 "When a man leaves a pit open, or when a man digs a pit and does not cover it, and an ox or an ass falls into it, ³⁴ the owner of the pit shall make it good; he shall give money to its owner, and the dead beast shall be his.

22 "If a man steals an ox or a sheep, and kills it or sells it, he shall pay five oxen for an ox, and four sheep for a sheep. He shall make restitution; if he has nothing, then he shall be sold for his theft.

2 "If a thief is found breaking in, and is struck so that he dies, there shall be no bloodguilt for him; ³ but if the sun has risen upon him, there shall be bloodguilt for him.

16 "If a man seduces a virgin who is not betrothed, and lies with her, he shall give the marriage present for her, and make her his wife. ¹⁷ If her father utterly refuses to give her to him, he shall pay money equivalent to the marriage present for virgins.

18 "You shall not permit a sorceress to live.

19 "Whoever lies with a beast shall be put to death.

20 "Whoever sacrifices to any god, save to the LORD only, shall be utterly destroyed.

21 "You shall not wrong a stranger or oppress him, for you were strangers in the land of Egypt. 22 You shall not afflict any widow or orphan. 23 If you do afflict them, and they cry out to me, I will surely hear their cry; 24 and my wrath will burn, and I will kill you with the sword, and your wives shall become widows and your children fatherless.

25 "If you lend money to any of my people with you who is poor, you shall not be to him as a creditor, and you shall not exact interest from him. 26 If ever you take your neighbor's garment in pledge, you shall restore it to him before the sun goes down; 27 for that is his only covering, it is his mantle for his body; in what else shall he sleep? And if he cries to me, I will hear, for I am compassionate.

23 "You shall not utter a false report. You shall not join hands with a wicked man, to be a malicious witness. You shall not follow a multitude to do evil; nor shall you bear witness in a suit, turning aside after a multitude, so as to pervert justice; 3 nor shall you be partial to a poor man in his suit.

4 "If you meet your enemy's ox or his ass going astray, you shall bring it back to him. 5 If you see the ass of one who hates you lying under its burden, you shall refrain from leaving him with it, you shall help him to lift it up.

6 "You shall not pervert the justice due to your poor in his suit. 7 Keep far from a false charge, and do not slay the innocent and righteous, for I will not acquit the wicked. 8 And you shall take no bribe, for a bribe blinds the officials, and subverts the cause of those who are in the right.

9 "You shall not oppress a stranger; you know the heart of a stranger, for you were strangers in the land of Egypt.

10 "For six years you shall sow your land and gather in its yield; 11 but the seventh year you shall let it rest and lie fallow, that the poor of your people may eat; and what they leave the wild beasts may eat. You shall do likewise with your vineyard, and with your olive orchard.

12 "Six days you shall do your work, but on the seventh day you shall rest; that your ox and your ass may have rest, and the son of your bondmaid, and the alien, may be refreshed.

14 "Three times in the year you shall keep a feast to me. 15 You shall keep the feast of unleavened bread; as I commanded you, you shall eat unleavened bread for seven days at the appointed time in the month of Abib, for in it you came out of Egypt. None shall appear before me empty-handed. 16 You shall keep the feast of harvest, of the first fruits of your labor, of what you sow in the field. You shall keep the feast of ingathering at the end of the year, when

you gather in from the field the fruit of your labor. [17] Three times in the year shall all your males appear before the Lord GOD.

19 "The first of the first fruits of your ground you shall bring into the house of the LORD your God.

"You shall not boil a kid in its mother's milk.

20 "Behold, I send an angel before you, to guard you on the way and to bring you to the place which I have prepared. [21] Give heed to him and hearken to his voice, do not rebel against him, for he will not pardon your transgression; for my name is in him.

22 "But if you hearken attentively to his voice and do all that I say, then I will be an enemy to your enemies and an adversary to your adversaries."

21:2 Compare indentured servants in the history of the United States who had terms of service similar to these. **21:6** In Babylonian law a runaway slave was punished by having his ear drilled through. In Hebrew law it is the slave who refused freedom who was punished. Rabbinical commentators expounded that the ear was selected because the ear of man had heard the divine utterance "for unto me the children of Israel are servants" (Leviticus 25:55). Yet this man had preferred to be a servant to a *human* master. **21:26** Although the Hebrew civilization had not yet arrived at a social and economic arrangement permitting abolition of slavery, they tried to civilize it. Slaves were not to be treated merely as chattel or property; they were persons and if mistreated they were awarded freedom. **21:31** In Babylonian law if an ox gored another man's son or daughter, it was required that the master's son or daughter be punished: a son for a son, a daughter for a daughter. The biblical law revokes that principle, making it possible for punishment to be fulfilled through payment of a fine or ransom. **22:18** Fanatics cited this passage when witches and sorcerers were burned at the stake in Colonial America. **22:25** These passages on the payment of interest for use of money were among those which led churches to prohibit usury and banking in the Middle Ages. Note distinctions between loans for necessity and loans for profits in commerce, as well as distinctions between lending inside and outside the nation. **22:28** This passage is interpreted in various ways, including a proscription against blasphemy; a command not to speak disrespectfully of the religious beliefs of the followers of other faiths; and a call to treat with respect the authorities of the state. **23:2** One with God and right are the true majority. This sentence is an appeal for honest individual judgment not related to the pressures of conformity. **23:3** Justice is impartial—each case must be tried on its merits. Neither the rich nor the poor, the mighty nor the weak should be judged on the basis of their station but rather by the righteousness of their cause. **23:4** One is required to aid even the dumb animals of his enemy; how much more is a man required to be just in all human dealings? **23:8** Compare present codes of ethics for civil officers and corporation purchasing agents. **23:9** Sometimes cited in discussions of immigration policy in the United States—all of whose citizens except "Indians" came by immigration in the past four centuries. **23:10–11** In the valley of the Nile River from which they were moving, floods of the Nile renewed soil fertility each year. This was not true of their new farm lands; it was necessary to legislate for crop rotation and soil conservation. Note also legislation for relief of the poor. **23:15** The celebration of the Passover. **23:16** The festival of the First Harvest. This holiday is given several names in Scriptures. See Numbers 28:26 where it is called *Yom Habikurim*, the day on which the first loaves were made from the new corn. In Deuteronomy 16:10 it is called *Shevuoth*, the Feast of Weeks, because it was observed seven complete weeks after the first day of Passover. The Feast of Weeks is rendered in the Greek as Pentecost (50th day). **23:16b** The pilgrimage festival known as *Sukkoth* the Feast of Booths or Tabernacles. **23:19b** On the basis of this sentence, Jews of strict observance will not mix dairy and meat products at one meal; the rabbinic law requires as well, two sets of dishes and silverware, one for milk and the other for meat dishes. Recent archaeological evidence indicates that this dish, "a kid seethed in its mother's milk," was served to the idol Baal; the proscription was perhaps intended to prevent idolatrous worship. **23:20** This passage includes the Epistle for the Mass on the Feast of the Guardian Angels, October 20. The gradual for the Mass is taken from Psalm 90: "God has given his angels charge over you to keep you in all your ways. . . ." The Bible does not speculate on the origins of angels. It accepts their function as agents of God and rarely provides them with an identity. When questioned, the angel, if he appears in human form, generally refuses to give his name (Genesis 32:30; Judges 13:18). Not until the Book of Zechariah and the Book of Daniel do angels appear in organized rank or have individual function. Finally in the Rabinnic period and in Christian literature angels were assigned a prominent place as heavenly creatures. The Sadducees, however, disputed the very existence of angels. In this biblical passage no particular form is ascribed to the angel.

God Instructs Israel in the Construction of the Sanctuary

With the exception of the incident of the golden calf, the remainder of the book of Exodus describes the construction of the sanctuary—considered a visible sign that God dwells among the people. The sanctuary was a portable tent with a wooden frame work to give it stability.

The entire sanctuary consisted of three parts:

1 An outer court enclosed by curtains supported on pillars. It was oblong in shape and the entrance was on the East side.

2 The altar of sacrifice was within the court, facing the entrance.

3 The tabernacle was located at the Western part of the court. The tabernacle was divided by a veil or hanging curtain into two chambers. The first chamber was called the Holy Place, it contained the table, candlestick and altar of incense. Only priests were allowed into this section. The second chamber was called the Holy of Holies; it contained the ark of the covenant. The High Priest entered this chamber only once a year on the Day of Atonement. The objects closest to the Holy of Holies were constructed of precious metals and cloths. Those farther off were made of bronze and ordinary woven materials. The entire tabernacle was covered by a tent and additional cloth covers.

Some of the routine described in these chapters were not instituted in practice until after the return from Babylonian exile in the late sixth century B.C. Thus some scholars believe that many of these regulations were written by the authors of the "P" source (see Appendix, "The Documentary Theory and the Hebrew Bible").

Moses Requests Free Will Offerings for the Tabernacle
Exodus 25:1–8

25 The LORD said to Moses, ²"Speak to the people of Israel, that they take for me an offering; from every man whose heart makes him willing you shall receive the offering for me. ³ And this is the offering which you shall receive from them: gold, silver, and bronze, ⁴ blue and purple and scarlet stuff and fine twined linen, goats' hair, ⁵ tanned rams' skins, goatskins, acacia wood, ⁶ oil for the lamps, spices for the anointing oil and for the fragrant incense, ⁷ onyx stones, and stones for setting, for the ephod and for the breastpiece." ⁸ And let them make me a sanctuary, that I may dwell in their midst.

The Ark of the Tabernacle

The purpose of the tabernacle was to house the Ark in which the tablets of the Ten Commandments were placed. It is not certain what the cherubim looked like; see note at Genesis 3:24.

Exodus 25:10–22

10 "They shall make an ark of acacia wood; two cubits and a half shall be its length, a cubit and a half its breadth, and a cubit and a half its height. ¹¹ And you shall overlay it with pure gold, within and without shall you overlay it, and you shall make upon it a molding of gold round about. ¹² And you shall cast four rings of gold for it and put them on its four feet, two rings on the one side of it, and two rings on the other side of it. ¹³ You shall make poles of acacia wood, and overlay them with gold. ¹⁴ And you shall put the poles into the rings on the sides of the ark, to carry the ark by them. ¹⁵ The poles

shall remain in the rings of the ark; they shall not be taken from it. [16] And you shall put into the ark the testimony which I shall give you. [17] Then you shall make a mercy seat of pure gold; two cubits and a half shall be its length, and a cut and a half its breadth. [18] And you shall make two cherubim of gold; of hammered work shall you make them, on the two ends of the mercy seat. [19] Make one cherub on the one end, and one cherub on the other end; of one piece with the mercy seat shall you make the cherubim on its two ends. [20] The cherubim shall spread out their wings above, overshadowing the mercy seat with their wings, their faces one to another; toward the mercy seat shall the faces of the cherubim be. [21] And you shall put the mercy seat on the top of the ark; and in the ark you shall put the testimony that I shall give you. [22] There I will meet with you, and from above the mercy seat, from between the two cherubim that are upon the ark of the testimony, I will speak with you of all that I will give you in commandment for the people of Israel."

Lamp Stand
Exodus 25:31–32

31 "And you shall make a lampstand of pure gold. The base and the shaft of the lampstand shall be made of hammered work; its cups, its capitals, and its flowers shall be of one piece with it; [32] and there shall be six branches going out of its sides, three branches of the lampstand out of one side of it and three branches of the lampstand out of the other side of it."

A Curtain Between the Holy and the Holy of Holies
Exodus 26:31–33

31 "And you shall make a veil of blue and purple and scarlet stuff and fine twined linen; in skilled work shall it be made, with cherubim; [32] and you shall hang it upon four pillars of acacia overlaid with gold, with hooks of gold, upon four bases of silver. [33] And you shall hang the veil from the clasps, and bring the ark of the testimony in thither within the veil; and the veil shall separate for you the holy place from the most holy."

The Altar of Burnt Offerings
Exodus 27:1–3

27 "You shall make the altar of acacia wood, five cubits long and five cubits broad; the altar shall be square, and its height shall be three cubits. [2] And you shall make horns for it on its four corners; its horns shall be of one piece with it, and you shall overlay it with

bronze. [3] You shall make pots for it to receive its ashes, and shovels and basins and forks and firepans; all its utensils you shall make of bronze."

27:2 The horns of the altar were considered particularly sacred. They were touched with the blood of the sacrifice (Exodus 29:12), and a guilty man whose crime was accidental could escape punishment by laying hold of the horns (1 Kings 1:50, 2:28).

The Perpetual Light

The Rabbis interpret the lamp as a symbol of Israel, whose mission it is to become "a light to the nations" (Isaiah 42:7). In the present day synagogue there are similar religious items. The ark is located on the East wall of the synagogue; it contains the Torah scrolls. Above the ark, an eternal lamp is kept burning. To the side of the ark a menorah or seven branched candelabra is placed.

Exodus 27:20–21

20 "And you shall command the people of Israel that they bring to you pure beaten olive oil for the light, that a lamp may be set up to burn continually. [21] In the tent of meeting, outside the veil which is before the testimony, Aaron and his sons shall tend it from evening to morning before the LORD. It shall be a statute for ever to be observed throughout their generations by the people of Israel.

Aaron's Vestments
Exodus 28:1–5

28 "Then bring near to you Aaron your brother, and his sons with him, from among the people of Israel, to serve me as priests—Aaron and Aaron's sons, Nadab and Abi'hu, Elea'zar and Ith'amar. [2] And you shall make holy garments for Aaron your brother, for glory and for beauty. [3] And you shall speak to all who have ability, whom I have endowed with an able mind, that they make Aaron's garments to consecrate him for my priesthood. [4] These are the garments which they shall make: a breastpiece, an ephod, a robe, a coat of checker work, a turban, and a girdle; they shall make holy garments for Aaron your brother and his sons to serve me as priests.

5 "They shall receive gold blue and purple and scarlet stuff, and fine twined linen. . . ."

28:1 Christian bishops' miters and priests' vestments in many respects are direct descendants of the garments described in this chapter.

Breastplate of Decision
Exodus 28 : 15, 17a, 21, 29–30

15 "And you shall make a breastpiece of judgment, in skilled work; like the work of the ephod you shall make it; of gold, blue and purple and scarlet stuff, and fine twined linen shall you make it. [17] And you shall set in it four rows of stones. [21] There shall be twelve stones with their names according to the names of the sons of Israel; they shall be like signets, each engraved with its name, for the twelve tribes. [29] So Aaron shall bear the names of the sons of Israel in the breastpiece of judgment upon his heart, when he goes into the holy place, to bring them to continual remembrance before the LORD. [30] And in the breastpiece of judgment you shall put the Urim and the Thummim, and they shall be upon Aaron's heart, when he goes in before the LORD; thus Aaron shall bear the judgment of the people of Israel upon his heart before the LORD continually.

28 : 30 It is not known for certain what the Urim and Thummim were. Considered a medium of divine communication, they were during periods of crisis consulted for information and guidance. (Cf. Numbers 27 : 21, 1 Samuel 28 : 6.)

The Ephod
Exodus 28 : 31–35

31 "And you shall make the robe of the ephod all of blue. [32] It shall have in it an opening for the head, with a woven binding around the opening, like the opening in a garment, that it may not be torn. [33] On its skirts you shall make pomegranates of blue and purple and scarlet stuff, around its skirts, with bells of gold between them, [34] a golden bell and a pomegranate, a golden bell and a pomegranate, round about on the skirts of the robe. [35] And it shall be upon Aaron when he ministers, and its sound shall be heard when he goes into the holy place before the LORD, and when he comes out, lest he die."

In this day the Torah scrolls of the synagogue are frequently wrapped in blue or purple velvet or silk cloths. A breast plate adorns the scroll, and a crown or coronets of silver and gold with tinkling bells are placed upon its rollers; these recall some of the items of dress of the High Priest.

Holy to the Lord
Exodus 28 : 36–38

36 "And you shall make a plate of pure gold, and engrave on it, like the engraving of a signet, 'Holy to the LORD.' [37] And you shall fasten it on the turban by a lace of blue; it shall be on the front of the

turban. [38] It shall be upon Aaron's forehead, and Aaron shall take upon himself any guilt incurred in the holy offering which the people of Israel hallow as their holy gifts; it shall always be upon his forehead, that they may be accepted before the LORD."

The Law of the Shekel

In ancient times the taking of the census was considered an act fraught with great danger. Hence the Bible requires the payment of half a shekel "to ransom the soul." The ransom of the soul was also required of soldiers before they went into battle. Although the soldier was not considered a murderer, nevertheless he would cause the loss of life of others. No matter how justified the battle, since war itself is inherently evil, the soldier must therefore make an atonement for his soul (cf. Numbers 31:52). This ransom was collected at the time of the mustering of the soldiers, that is, at the time of census. At the time of census it was only the men, capable of battle, from the age of twenty who were numbered.

Money thus acquired was used to aid the sanctuary. All of Israel participated in the support of the Holy Shrine. In later years a half shekel annual tax was instituted for this purpose. Jews outside the Holy Land also contributed the same amount. A collection of shekels now supports rabbinical academies in Palestine; it has also been adopted by the World Zionist Organization as a token of membership in the Jewish people's effort to assist the state of Israel.

Exodus 30:11–16

11 The LORD said to Moses, [12] "When you take the census of the people of Israel, then each shall give a ransom for himself to the LORD when you number them, that there be no plague among them when you number them. [13] Each who is numbered in the census shall give this: half a shekel according to the shekel of the sanctuary (the shekel is twenty gerahs), half a shekel as an offering to the LORD. [14] Every one who is numbered in the census, from twenty years old and upward, shall give the LORD's offering. [15] The rich shall not give more, and the poor shall not give less, than the half shekel, when you give the LORD's offering to make atonement for yourselves. [16] And you shall take the atonement money from the people of Israel, and shall appoint it for the service of the tent of meeting; that it may bring the people of Israel to remembrance before the LORD, so as to make atonement for yourselves."

The People Commit Idolatry with the Golden Calf
Exodus 32:1–14, 30–35

32 When the people saw that Moses delayed to come down from the mountain, the people gathered themselves together to Aaron, and

said to him, "Up, make us gods, who shall go before us; as for this Moses, the man who brought us up out of the land of Egypt, we do not know what has become of him." ²And Aaron said to them, "Take off the rings of gold which are in the ears of your wives, your sons, and your daughters, and bring them to me." ³So all the people took off the rings of gold which were in their ears, and brought them to Aaron. ⁴And he received the gold at their hand, and fashioned it with a graving tool, and made a molten calf; and they said, "These are your gods, O Israel, who brought you up out of the land of Egypt!" ⁵When Aaron saw this, he built an altar before it; and Aaron made proclamation and said, "Tomorrow shall be a feast to the LORD." ⁶And they rose up early on the morrow, and offered burnt offerings and brought peace offerings; and the people sat down to eat and drink, and rose up to play.

7 And the LORD said to Moses, "Go down; for your people, whom you brought up out of the land of Egypt, have corrupted themselves; ⁸they have turned aside quickly out of the way which I commanded them; they have made for themselves a molten calf, and have worshiped it and sacrificed to it, and said, 'These are your gods, O Israel, who brought you up out of the land of Egypt!' " ⁹And the LORD said to Moses, "I have seen this people, and behold, it is a stiff-necked people; ¹⁰now therefore let me alone, that my wrath may burn hot against them and I may consume them; but of you I will make a great nation."

11 But Moses besought the LORD his God, and said, "O LORD, why does thy wrath burn hot against thy people, whom thou hast brought forth out of the land of Egypt with great power and with a mighty hand? ¹²Why should the Egyptians say, 'With evil intent did he bring them forth, to slay them in the mountains, and to consume them from the face of the earth'? Turn from thy fierce wrath, and repent of this evil against thy people. ¹³Remember Abraham, Isaac, and Israel, thy servants, to whom thou didst swear by thine own self, and didst say to them, 'I will multiply your descendants as the stars of heaven, and all this land that I have promised I will give to your descendants, and they shall inherit it for ever.' " ¹⁴And the LORD repented of the evil which he thought to do to his people.

30 On the morrow Moses said to the people, "You have sinned a great sin. And now I will go up to the LORD; perhaps I can make atonement for your sin." ³¹So Moses returned to the LORD and said, "Alas, this people have sinned a great sin; they have made for themselves gods of gold. ³²But now, if thou wilt forgive their sin—and if not, blot me, I pray thee, out of thy book which thou hast written." ³³But the LORD said to Moses, "Whoever has sinned

against me, him will I blot out of my book. [34] But now go, lead the people to the place of which I have spoken to you; my angel shall go before you. Nevertheless, in the day when I visit, I will visit their sin upon them."

35 And the LORD sent a plague upon the people, because they made the calf which Aaron made.

32:11 ff. Throughout the journey in the wilderness Moses had to plead on behalf of the Israelites. His role as mediator is recollected by Jeremiah 15:1, Psalms 99:6, 106:23. Christian writings suggest that his intercession foreshadows a function assumed by Jesus. **32:33** According to an early biblical view God writes the names of all who are living on earth in a heavenly book. When a man dies his name is erased from the book; a long life was looked upon as a special reward from God, and premature death as punishment. Toward the end of the Old Testament period, the *Book of Life* received a messianic or eschatological coloring (Daniel 12:1). Daniel 7:10 suggests that men will be judged at the heavenly tribunal according to the deeds recorded in these books.

God Reveals His Goodness to Moses

Man cannot see God face to face. Though man cannot totally comprehend God, he can recognize manifestations and attributes of God in history.

Exodus 33:12–23; 34:1–4, 6–16, 28–35

12 Moses said to the LORD, "See, thou sayest to me, 'Bring up this people'; but thou hast not let me know whom thou wilt send with me. Yet thou hast said, 'I know you by name, and you have also found favor in my sight.' [13] Now therefore, I pray thee, if I have found favor in thy sight, show me now thy ways, that I may know thee and find favor in thy sight. Consider too that this nation is thy people." [14] And he said, "My presence will go with you, and I will give you rest." [15] And he said to him, "If thy presence will not go with me, do not carry us up from here. [16] For how shall it be known that I have found favor in thy sight, I and thy people? Is it not in thy going with us, so that we are distinct, I and thy people, from all other people that are upon the face of the earth?"

17 And the LORD said to Moses, "This very thing that you have spoken I will do; for you have found favor in my sight, and I know you by name." [18] Moses said, "I pray thee, show me thy glory." [19] And he said, "I will make all my goodness pass before you, and will proclaim before you my name 'The LORD'; and I will be gracious to whom I will be gracious, and will show mercy on whom I will show mercy. [20] But," he said, "you cannot see my face; for man shall not

see me and live." ²¹ And the LORD said, "Behold, there is a place by me where you shall stand upon the rock; ²² and while my glory passes by I will put you in a cleft of the rock, and I will cover you with my hand until I have passed by; ²³ then I will take away my hand, and you shall see my back; but my face shall not be seen."

34 The LORD said to Moses, "Cut two tables of stone like the first; and I will write upon the tables the words that were on the first tables, which you broke. ² Be ready in the morning, and come up in the morning to Mount Sinai, and present yourself there to me on the top of the mountain. ³ No man shall come up with you, and let no man be seen throughout all the mountain; let no flocks or herds feed before that mountain." ⁴ So Moses cut two tables of stone like the first; and he rose early in the morning and went up on Mount Sinai, as the LORD had commanded him, and took in his hand two tables of stone.

6 The LORD passed before him, and proclaimed, "The LORD, the LORD, a God merciful and gracious, slow to anger, and abounding in steadfast love and faithfulness, ⁷ keeping steadfast love for thousands, forgiving iniquity and transgression and sin, but who will by no means clear the guilty, visiting the iniquity of the fathers upon the children and the children's children, to the third and the fourth generation." ⁸ And Moses made haste to bow his head toward the earth, and worshiped. ⁹ And he said, "If now I have found favor in thy sight, O LORD, let the Lord, I pray thee, go in the midst of us, although it is a stiff-necked people; and pardon our iniquity and our sin, and take us for thy inheritance."

10 And he said, "Behold, I make a covenant. Before all your people I will do marvels, such as have not been wrought in all the earth or in any nation; and all the people among whom you are shall see the work of the LORD; for it is a terrible thing that I will do with you.

11 "Observe what I command you this day. Behold, I will drive out before you the Amorites, the Canaanites, the Hittites, the Per'izzites, the Hivites, and the Jeb'usites. ¹² Take heed to yourself, lest you make a covenant with the inhabitants of the land whither you go, lest it become a snare in the midst of you. ¹³ You shall tear down their altars, and break their pillars, and cut down their Ashe'rim ¹⁴ (for you shall worship no other god, for the LORD, whose name is Jealous, is a jealous God), ¹⁵ lest you make a covenant with the inhabitants of the land, and when they play the harlot after their gods and sacrifice to their gods and one invites you, you eat of his sacrifice, ¹⁶ and you take of their daughters for your sons, and their daughters play the harlot after their gods and make your sons play the harlot after their gods."

28 And he was there with the LORD forty days and forty nights; he neither ate bread nor drank water. And he wrote upon the tables the words of the covenant, the ten commandments.

29 When Moses came down from Mount Sinai, with the two tables of the testimony in his hand as he came down from the mountain, Moses did not know that the skin of his face shone because he had been talking with God. 30 And when Aaron and all the people of Israel saw Moses, behold, the skin of his face shone, and they were afraid to come near him. 31 But Moses called to them; and Aaron and all the leaders of the congregation returned to him, and Moses talked with them. 32 And afterward all the people of Israel came near, and he gave them in commandment all that the LORD had spoken with him in Mount Sinai. 33 And when Moses had finished speaking with them, he put a veil on his face; 34 whenever Moses went in before the LORD to speak with him, he took the veil off, until he came out; and when he came out, and told the people of Israel what he was commanded, 35 the people of Israel saw the face of Moses, that the skin of Moses' face shone; and Moses would put the veil upon his face again, until he went in to speak with him.

34:11–16 Those who believe that much of the Pentateuch was written long after Moses, at a time when the monarchy had been established but idolatrous practices were still widespread, see in these passages a stern pronouncement to the listeners of that period warning them that their prevailing idolatrous practices were forbidden by Mosaic Law. The sacred posts—the Asherah, for example—were symbols of the Canaanite goddess of love and fecundity encountered by the Hebrews after settling in Palestine. **34:16** The prohibition against mixed marriage given here was a preventive measure against the adoption of idolatrous customs (cf. Leviticus 18:2). Scripture records many Israelite marriages with non-Jews (Judges 3:6; 2 Samuel 3:3, 11:3; 1 Kings 7:14, 11:1, 14:21). **34:29** Rembrandt's painting of Moses holding the Tables of the Law above his head for the people to see (signed and dated 1659, now in the Berlin Museum) depicts the Ten Commandments engraved in gold letters on black stone, and a glowing radiance comes from Moses' face, in accordance with this verse. The Hebrew word "KRN" is translated here "shone" as with beams or rays of light. The word may also mean horns. It was this translation in the Latin Vulgate ("cornuta," horned) that led medieval artists like Michelangelo to represent Moses with animal horns protruding from his forehead. Michelangelo's statue (Church of St. Peter in Chains, Rome) is one of the world's masterpieces of art. It shows Moses seated; with one powerful hand he holds the Tables of the Law, and with the other he plays with his long beard; his pose denotes strength of will and the dignity of Israel's great lawgiver.

The Book of Leviticus

The third of the Five Books of Moses, Leviticus, was once known by the Hebrew title, *Torath Kohanim*, the Law of the Priests. It describes the functions of the ancient priesthood and the cultic duties of the priestly nation.

The present Hebrew name, *Vayikra* is taken from the opening word of the text. The English title, Leviticus, i.e. "with respect to the Levites," derives from the Septuagint, the Greek translation.

Although Leviticus describes the sacrificial system in great detail, the spiritual emphasis within the Hebrew cultic practice is evident throughout, thereby distinguishing Hebrew worship from similar patterns of worship that prevailed among their neighbors. Magic and incantation were banished. Everything thought to be idolatrous and unholy was forbidden. Through offering a sacrifice one could not achieve cleansing; repentance and restitution had to precede the ceremonial act.

The purpose of the priesthood and the sacrificial system is expressed in the Levitical command, "Ye shall be holy, for I the Lord your God am holy" (Leviticus 19:2). Holiness was understood as an active principle, disciplining all of human existence. As a holy people the Hebrews were provided with both *ethical laws* by which they were to guide their lives as well as *liturgical rites* by which to preserve their unique relationship with a Holy God.

With the destruction of the Temple in Jerusalem in 70 A.D. the rabbis enjoined that God will accept a contrite heart (Psalm 51:15) and prayer in the synagogue (Isaiah 66:20) as fitting offerings. They ruled also that students engaged anywhere in study of Torah were as dear to God as those who burned incense on the altar (*Menahot* 110a).

With the destruction of the Temple animal sacrifice ended. The contemporary rabbi is a teacher of his congregation, not a priest. Contemporary Jewish worship today no longer requires a sacrificial system, nor would most Jews wish to see such practices reinstated.

Christian tradition sees in this sacrificial ritual a foreshadowing of the redemptive sacrifice of Jesus and the institution of the sacraments of the Church (cf. Hebrews 8–10).

The Laws of Sacrifice

Chapters 1 to 5 form a manual of the sacrificial offerings, voluntary and private. These include:

The *burnt offering* (chapters 1, 2) brought whenever a man's conscience prompted him to seek a renewed dedication to God. Rabbinic commentators note that the Hebrew name for the burnt offering, *Olah*, signifies "that which ascends," symbolizing the ascent of the soul in worship to God.

The *peace offering* (chapter 3), an expression of gratitude for God's bounties and mercies.

The *sin offering* (chapters 4–5:13), an expression of sorrow at wrongdoing. Priest and layman, ruler and citizen, or the community in collective action—all were required to make this offering as an action of atonement and reconciliation.

Burnt Offering
Leviticus 1:1–9

1 The LORD called Moses, and spoke to him from the tent of meeting, saying, **2** "Speak to the people of Israel, and say to them, When any man of you brings an offering to the LORD, you shall bring your offering of cattle from the herd or from the flock.

3 "If his offering is a burnt offering from the herd, he shall offer a male without blemish; he shall offer it at the door of the tent of meeting, that he may be accepted before the LORD; **4** he shall lay his hand upon the head of the burnt offering, and it shall be accepted for him to make atonement for him. **5** Then he shall kill the bull before the LORD; and Aaron's sons the priests shall present the blood, and throw the blood round about against the altar that is at the door of the tent of meeting. **6** And he shall flay the burnt offering and cut it into pieces; **7** and the sons of Aaron the priest shall put fire on the altar, and lay wood in order upon the fire; **8** and Aaron's sons the priests shall lay the pieces, the head, and the fat, in order upon the wood that is on the fire upon the altar; **9** but its entrails and its legs he shall wash with water. And the priest shall burn the whole on the altar, as a burnt offering, an offering by fire, a pleasing odor to the LORD."

Peace Offering
Leviticus 3:1–5, 14–15, 17

3 "If a man's offering is a sacrifice of peace offering, if he offers an animal from the herd, male or female, he shall offer it without blemish before the LORD. **2** And he shall lay his hand upon the head of his offering and kill it at the door of the tent of meeting; and Aaron's sons the priests shall throw the blood against the altar round about. **3** And from the sacrifice of the peace offering, as an offering by fire to the LORD, he shall offer the fat covering the entrails and all the fat that is on the entrail, **4** and the two kidneys with the fat that is on them at the loins, and the appendage of the liver which he shall take away with the kidneys. **5** Then Aaron's sons shall burn it on the altar upon the burnt offering, which is upon the wood on the fire; it is an offering by fire, a pleasing odor to the LORD.

14 "If his offering to the LORD is a burnt offering of birds, then he shall bring his offering of turtledoves or of young pigeons. ¹⁵ And the priest shall bring it to the altar and wring off its head, and burn it on the altar; and its blood shall be drained out on the side of the altar; ¹⁷ he shall tear it by its wings, but shall not divide it asunder. And the priest shall burn it on the altar, upon the wood that is on the fire; it is a burnt offering, an offering by fire, a pleasing odor to the LORD."

3:17 Blood was considered symbolic of the life of the animal. Scripture prohibits the taking of a man's life; it also prohibits the eating of the blood of an animal. Observant Jews today prepare their meat in such fashion that the blood will have been thoroughly drained from it.

Sin Offering
Leviticus 4:1–3, 13–19, 22–23, 27–28

4 And the LORD said to Moses, ² "Say to the people of Israel, If any one sins unwittingly in any of the things which the LORD has commanded not to be done, and does any one of them, ³ if it is the anointed priest who sins, thus bringing guilt on the people, then let him offer for the sin which he has committed a young bull without blemish to the LORD for a sin offering.

13 "If the whole congregation of Israel commits a sin unwittingly and the thing is hidden from the eyes of the assembly, and they do any one of the things which the LORD has commanded not to be done and are guilty; ¹⁴ when the sin which they have committed becomes known, the assembly shall offer a young bull for a sin offering and bring it before the tent of meeting; ¹⁵ and the elders of the congregation shall lay their hands upon the head of the bull before the LORD, and the bull shall be killed before the LORD. ¹⁶ Then the anointed priest shall bring some of the blood of the bull to the tent of meeting, ¹⁷ and the priest shall dip his finger in the blood and sprinkle it seven times before the LORD in front of the veil. ¹⁸ And he shall put some of the blood on the horns of the altar which is in the tent of meeting before the LORD; and the rest of the blood he shall pour out at the base of the altar of burnt offering which is at the door of the tent of meeting. ¹⁹ And all its fat he shall take from it and burn upon the altar.

22 "When a ruler sins, doing unwittingly any one of all the things which the LORD his God has commanded not to be done, and is guilty, ²³ if the sin which he has committed is made known to him, he shall bring as his offering a goat, a male without blemish.

27 "If any one of the common people sins unwittingly in doing any one of the things which the LORD has commanded not to be done, and is guilty, [28] when the sin which he has committed is made known to him, he shall bring for his offering a goat, a female without blemish, for his sin which he has committed."

Restitution of Property
Leviticus 6:1–7

6 The LORD said to Moses, [2] "If any one sins and commits a breach of faith against the LORD by deceiving his neighbor in a matter of deposit or security, or through robbery, or if he has oppressed his neighbor [3] or has found what was lost and lied about it, swearing falsely—in any of all the things which men do and sin therein, [4] when one has sinned and become guilty, he shall restore what he took by robbery, or what he got by oppression, or the deposit which was committed to him, or the lost thing which he found, [5] or anything about which he has sworn falsely; he shall restore it in full, and shall add a fifth to it, and give it to him to whom it belongs, on the day of his guilt offering. [6] And he shall bring to the priest his guilt offering to the LORD, a ram without blemish out of the flock, valued by you at the price for a guilt offering; [7] and the priest shall make atonement for him before the LORD, and he shall be forgiven for any of the things which one may do and thereby become guilty."

A Manual of Directions for the Priests

Chapters 6 to 7 form a manual of instructions specifically directed to the priests. The passage rendered here describes a continual or a *perpetual burnt offering* brought every morning and evening in the name of the community (see also Exodus 29:38–42). In later times this perpetual sacrifice was regarded as a national institution. The Pharisees insisted that the entire people, not merely a few wealthy donors, pay for its upkeep. They arranged for the country to be divided into twenty-four watches. Priests from each part of the country presented themselves in turn at the Temple with a delegation of elders—a system that recognized the responsibility of the entire nation to make atonement.

The Law of the Perpetual Burnt Offering
Leviticus 6:8–13

8 The LORD said to Moses, [9] "Command Aaron and his sons, saying, This is the law of the burnt offering. The burnt offering shall be on the hearth upon the altar all night until the morning, and the fire of the altar shall be kept burning on it. [10] And the priest shall put on his linen garment, and put his linen breeches upon his body, and he shall take up the ashes to which the fire has consumed the burnt offering on the altar, and put them beside the altar. [11] Then he shall put off his garments, and put on other garments, and carry forth the ashes outside the camp to a clean place. [12] The fire on the altar shall be kept burning on it, it shall not go out; the priest shall burn wood on it every morning, and he shall lay the burnt offering in order upon it, and shall burn on it the fat of the peace offerings. [13] Fire shall be kept burning upon the altar continually; it shall not go out."

The Dietary Laws Are Promulgated

Chapters 9 to 16 deal with those laws that Jews hold enable man to attain holiness in all of his existence, from the food that he eats to the medical practices that govern health and welfare.

These laws were classified by the rabbis as belonging to a category called *Hukkim,* statutes—laws which must be obeyed even if the reasons for them are not clear. Some contemporary scholars explain these laws by virtue of their hygienic significance. Others consider them symbolic of man's need to discipline his instinctual life in utter surrender to God's will. *Reform* Jews do not regard the dietary laws as essential to the achievement of holiness; instead they emphasize the ethical teachings of Scripture as having primary authority. They point to prophetic teachings that suggest that cleanliness of heart and spirit is what God requires of man (cf. Isaiah 1:16; Psalm 51:10).

Leviticus 11:1–8, 12–20, 41, 44–45

11 And the LORD said to Moses and Aaron, [2] "Say to the people of Israel, These are the living things which you may eat among all the beasts that are on the earth. [3] Whatever parts the hoof and is cloven-footed and chews the cud, among the animals, you may eat. [4] Nevertheless among those that chew the cud or part the hoof, you shall not eat these: The camel, because it chews the cud but does not part the hoof, is unclean to you. [5] And the rock badger, because it chews the cud but does not part the hoof, is unclean to you. [6] And the hare, because it chews the cud but does not part the hoof, is unclean to you. [7] And the swine, because it parts the hoof and is cloven-footed but does not chew the cud, is unclean to you. [8] Of their flesh you shall not eat, and their carcasses you shall not touch; they are unclean to you.

12 "Everything in the waters that has not fins and scales is an abomination to you.

13 "And these you shall have in abomination among the birds, they shall not be eaten, they are an abomination: the eagle, the vulture, the osprey, [14] the kite, the falcon according to its kind, [15] every raven according to its kind, [16] the ostrich, the nighthawk, the sea gull, the hawk according to its kind, [17] the owl, the cormorant,

the ibis, [18] the water hen, the pelican, the carrion vulture, [19] the stork, the heron according to its kind, the hoopoe, and the bat.

20 "All winged insects that go upon all fours are an abomination to you.

41 "Every swarming thing that swarms upon the earth is an abomination; it shall not be eaten. [44] For I am the LORD your God; consecrate yourselves therefore, and be holy, for I am holy. You shall not defile yourselves with any swarming thing that crawls upon the earth. [45] For I am the LORD who brought you up out of the land of Egypt, to be your God; you shall therefore be holy, for I am holy."

Laws Are Established to Protect the Community Against Disease

Leprosy—now properly termed Hansen's disease—was prevalent in the Middle East. In pre-scientific days, a variety of diseases, not all of them incurable, were included in the broad term "leprosy." Some believe that more specific diagnoses—such as psoriasis—should now be used by translators in such contexts as this. In any case, the point here is that the afflicted or unclean person was separated.

Leviticus 13:1–3, 45–46; 15:1–3, 31–33

13 The LORD said to Moses and Aaron, [2] "When a man has on the skin of his body a swelling or an eruption or a spot, and it turns into a leprous disease on the skin of his body, then he shall be brought to Aaron the priest or to one of his sons the priests, [3] and the priest shall examine the diseased spot on the skin of his body; and if the hair in the diseased spot has turned white and the disease appears to be deeper than the skin of his body, it is a leprous disease; when the priest has examined him he shall pronounce him unclean.

45 "The leper who has the disease shall wear torn clothes and let the hair of his head hang loose, and he shall cover his upper lip and cry, 'Unclean, unclean.' [46] He shall remain unclean as long as he has the disease; he is unclean; he shall dwell alone in a habitation outside the camp."

15 The LORD said to Moses and Aaron, [2] "Say to the people of Israel, When any man has a discharge from his body, his discharge is unclean. [3] And this is the law of his uncleanness for a discharge: whether his body runs with his discharge, or his body is stopped from discharge, it is uncleanness in him.

31 "Thus you shall keep the people of Israel separate from their uncleanness, lest they die in their uncleanness by defiling my tabernacle that is in their midst."

32 This is the law for him who has a discharge and for him who has an emission of semen, becoming unclean thereby; [33] also for her

who is sick with her impurity; that is, for any one, male or female, who has a discharge, and for the man who lies with a woman who is unclean.

13:46 These early regulations represent ancient experience long pre-dating the modern knowledge of germs and viruses as carriers of communicable diseases; compare quarantine laws today.

Ritual Observances for the Day of Atonement

The Day of Atonement is the most holy of celebrations in the Jewish calendar. Only on that day did the High Priest, dressed in simple white breeches, enter the inner sanctuary, the Holy of Holies. This passage is read annually in synagogues on the Day of Atonement recalling the ancient rite of purification. The tragic word "scapegoat" has entered our language as a result of the ritual here described. The people placed their sins symbolically upon one goat; driving that goat into the wilderness they rid themselves of evil. Tyrants have used a scapegoat device; for example, wishing to distract the people from the shortcomings of his rule, Hitler blamed Jews for the evils in the Nazi nation. By persecuting the Jews his people presumed they would be purged from their distress.

Leviticus 16:2–6, 8–10, 17–22, 29–31, 34

2 And the LORD said to Moses, "Tell Aaron your brother not to come at all times into the holy place within the veil, before the mercy seat which is upon the ark, lest he die; for I will appear in the cloud upon the mercy seat. ³ But thus shall Aaron come into the holy place: with a young bull for a sin offering and a ram for a burnt offering. ⁴ He shall put on the holy linen coat, and shall have the linen breeches on his body, be girded with the linen girdle, and wear the linen turban; these are the holy garments. He shall bathe his body in water, and then put them on. ⁵ And he shall take from the congregation of the people of Israel two male goats for a sin offering, and one ram for a burnt offering.

6 "And Aaron shall offer the bull as a sin offering for himself, and shall make atonement for himself and for his house. ⁸ And Aaron shall cast lots upon the two goats, one lot for the LORD and the other lot for Aza'zel. ⁹ And Aaron shall present the goat on which the lot fell for the LORD, and offer it as a sin offering; ¹⁰ but the goat on which the lot fell for Aza'zel shall be presented alive before the LORD to make atonement over it, that it may be sent away into the wilderness to Aza'zel.

17 "There shall be no man in the tent of meeting when he enters to make atonement in the holy place until he comes out and has made atonement for himself and for his house and for all the

assembly of Israel. [18] Then he shall go out to the altar which is before the LORD and make atonement for it, and shall take some of the blood of the bull and of the blood of the goat, and put it on the horns of the altar round about. [19] And he shall sprinkle some of the blood upon it with his finger seven times, and cleanse it and hallow it from the uncleannesses of the people of Israel.

20 "And when he has made an end of atoning for the holy place and the tent of meeting and the altar, he shall present the live goat; [21] and Aaron shall lay both his hands upon the head of the live goat, and confess over him all the iniquities of the people of Israel, and all their transgressions, all their sins; and he shall put them upon the head of the goat, and send him away into the wilderness by the hand of a man who is in readiness. [22] The goat shall bear all their iniquities upon him to a solitary land; and he shall let the goat go in the wilderness.

29 "And it shall be a statute to you for ever that in the seventh month, on the tenth day of the month, you shall afflict yourselves, and shall do no work, either the native or the stranger who sojourns among you; [30] for on this day shall atonement be made for you, to cleanse you; from all your sins you shall be clean before the LORD. [31] It is a sabbath of solemn rest to you, and you shall afflict yourselves; it is a statute for ever.

34 "And this shall be an everlasting statute for you, that atonement may be made for the people of Israel once in the year because of all their sins." And Moses did as the LORD commanded him.

16:10 The Hebrew word *azazel* used here refers to the act of dismissing the goat into the wilderness. The word is also used as the name of a demon and as the name of a place somewhat akin to hell. Bible scholars consider this ceremony to be one of the very ancient rites that the Hebrews borrowed from the neighboring culture; but in their distinctive fashion they rid the ceremony of all demonology. While the goat is dedicated to "the demon," Azazel, the handing over of the animal and the rite of expiation are performed before the Lord (verse 10) and at the hands of the priest (verse 21). It is clear that the LORD rules over all forces and principalities; it is He who forgives transgressions and makes atonement.

A Restriction Against the Eating of Blood

The reason for this restriction against eating blood is not clarified. It has been suggested, since blood is a sign of life and life the gift of God, that biblical law reserved the blood to God. Jews were enjoined by rabbinic law to "Kosher" all their meat, draining away the blood by means of salting and washing. Such procedures are a significant part of Jewish dietary regulations. Charges once made against some

Jews that they slaughtered Gentile children in order to use their blood for ritual purposes were obviously made in ignorance of the Scriptures.

Leviticus 17:1–2, 10–14

17 And the LORD said to Moses, [2] "Say to Aaron and his sons, and to all the people of Israel, This is the thing which the LORD has commanded.

10 "If any man of the house of Israel or of the strangers that sojourn among them eats any blood, I will set my face against that person who eats blood, and will cut him off from among his people. [11] For the life of the flesh is in the blood; and I have given it for you upon the altar to make atonement for your souls; for it is the blood that makes atonement, by reason of the life. [12] Therefore I have said to the people of Israel, No person among you shall eat blood, neither shall any stranger who sojourns among you eat blood. [13] Any man also of the people of Israel, or of the strangers that sojourn among them, who takes in hunting any beast or bird that may be eaten shall pour out its blood and cover it with dust.

14 "For the life of every creature is the blood of it; therefore I have said to the people of Israel, You shall not eat the blood of any creature, for the life of every creature is its blood; whoever eats it shall be cut off."

God Warns Israel against Moral Uncleanness

Chapters 18 to 20 contain laws that are a foundation of holiness in the social order, including laws forbidding impurity in marriage, incestuous promiscuity, and other sexual and social abominations.

Leviticus 18:1–9, 19–23, 30

18 And the LORD said to Moses, [2] "Say to the people of Israel, I am the LORD your God. [3] You shall not do as they do in the land of Egypt, where you dwelt, and you shall not do as they do in the land of Canaan, to which I am bringing you. You shall not walk in their statutes. [4] You shall do my ordinances and keep my statutes and walk in them. I am the LORD your God. [5] You shall therefore keep my statutes and my ordinances, by doing which a man shall live: I am the LORD.

6 "None of you shall approach any one near of kin to him to uncover nakedness. I am the LORD. [7] You shall not uncover the nakedness of your father, which is the nakedness of your mother; she is your mother, you shall not uncover her nakedness. [8] You shall not uncover the nakedness of your father's wife; it is your father's nakedness. [9] You shall not uncover the nakedness of your sister, the

daughter of your father or the daughter of your mother, whether born at home or born abroad.

19 "You shall not approach a woman to uncover her nakedness while she is in her menstrual uncleanness. [20] And you shall not lie carnally with your neighbor's wife, and defile yourself with her. [21] You shall not give any of your children to devote them by fire to Molech, and so profane the name of your God: I am the LORD. [22] You shall not lie with a male as with a woman; it is an abomination. [23] And you shall not lie with any beast and defile yourself with it, neither shall any woman give herself to a beast to lie with it: it is perversion.

30 "So keep my charge never to practice any of these abominable customs which were practiced before you, and never to defile yourselves by them: I am the LORD your God."

18:5 By virtue of this sentence, that the laws were intended as something for men "*to live by*," the rabbis taught that most Mosaic legislative requirements could be held in abeyance during a period of physical crisis or for the sake of health and welfare. The law was something to live by, not an occasion for death. Thus the Sabbath laws could be broken in time of war or to preserve health. The degree to which this was allowed became a point of difference between Jesus and the Pharisees. The rabbis also derived a homiletic lesson from the phrase, "a *man* shall live," teaching: "A Gentile who engages in the Torah he is like a High Priest"; biblical ideals provide a sanctity to life that is meaningful not merely for Jews but for all human beings. *Any man* who lives by these ideals is holy. **18:19** In Jewish religious law, sexual contact is forbidden during a woman's menstrual period and for seven days thereafter. A procedure of ritual cleansing by immersion, *Mikveh*, is followed by most observant Jewish women. The effect of such legislation is to permit sexual relations only during that period of which is normally woman's greatest capacity for conception.

The Essentials of Ethical Behavior are Summarized

The following reading was considered by the rabbis to have summarized "the essentials of the Torah." It is read in the Reform synagogue on the Day of Atonement. The Lesson is unmistakable: cult purity and moral sanctity are directly related.

Leviticus 19:1–4, 9–18, 28–37; 22:31–33

19 And the LORD said to Moses, [2] "Say to all the congregation of the people of Israel, You shall be holy; for I the LORD your God am holy. [3] Every one of you shall revere his mother and his father, and you shall keep my sabbaths: I am the LORD your God. [4] Do not turn to idols or make for yourselves molten gods: I am the LORD your God.

9 "When you reap the harvest of your land, you shall not reap your field to its very border, neither shall you gather the gleanings after your harvest. ¹⁰ And you shall not strip your vineyard bare, neither shall you gather the fallen grapes of your vineyard; you shall leave them for the poor and for the sojourner: I am the LORD your God.

11 "You shall not steal, nor deal falsely, nor lie to one another. ¹² And you shall not swear by my name falsely, and so profane the name of your God: I am the LORD.

13 "You shall not oppress your neighbor or rob him. The wages of a hired servant shall not remain with you all night until the morning. ¹⁴ You shall not curse the deaf or put a stumbling block before the blind, but you shall fear your God: I am the LORD.

15 "You shall do no injustice in judgment; you shall not be partial to the poor or defer to the great, but in righteousness shall you judge your neighbor. ¹⁶ You shall not go up and down as a slanderer among your people, and you shall not stand forth against the life of your neighbor: I am the LORD.

17 "You shall not hate your brother in your heart, but you shall reason with your neighbor, lest you bear sin because of him. ¹⁸ You shall not take vengeance or bear any grudge against the sons of your own people, but you shall love your neighbor as yourself: I am the LORD.

28 "You shall not make any cuttings in your flesh on account of the dead or tattoo any marks upon you: I am the LORD.

29 "Do not profane your daughter by making her a harlot, lest the land fall into harlotry and the land become full of wickedness. ³⁰ You shall keep my sabbaths and reverence my sanctuary: I am the LORD.

31 "Do not turn to mediums or wizards; do not seek them out, to be defiled by them: I am the LORD your God.

32 "You shall rise up before the hoary head, and honor the face of an old man, and you shall fear your God: I am the LORD.

33 "When a stranger sojourns with you in your land, you shall not do him wrong. ³⁴ The stranger who sojourns with you shall be to you as the native among you, and you shall love him as yourself; for you were strangers in the land of Egypt: I am the LORD your God.

35 "You shall do no wrong in judgment, in measures of length or weight or quantity. ³⁶ You shall have just balances, just weights, a just ephah, and a just hin: I am the LORD your God, who brought you out of the land of Egypt. ³⁷ And you shall observe all my statutes and all my ordinances, and do them: I am the LORD."

22 ³¹ "So you shall keep my commandments and do them: I am the LORD. ³² And you shall not profane my holy name, but I will be

hallowed among the people of Israel; I am the LORD who sanctify you, [33] who brought you out of the land of Egypt to be your God: I am the LORD."

19:9-10 Practices of unemployment compensation and relief, social security and public works projects seek to achieve a similar end in contemporary society. **19:14** Handicapped people in some cultures are the butt of insults and practical jokes. Understood as a universal principle the law here affirms that it matters to God how you behave toward your neighbor. A deaf man cannot hear who curses him or a blind man see who tripped him; nevertheless God sees, and we are to act accordingly. **19:15** Consider "justice" today as meted out in the courts of your city, state, and nation. The ideal here expressed has not yet been realized. Can you recall cases in which the degree of punishment was correlated with class status or racial background, or the ability to pay for legal talent? **19:18, 19:34** These are sources for the high ethical teaching of love of neighbor. The Hebrews were required to recall the bitterness of their own slavery in Egypt so that they would do no wrong to their fellow man. They are also enjoined positively to love him. **19:33-34** Compare the laws of our country on the status of aliens and the naturalization of citizens. (Cf. also Leviticus 24:22.)

Fixed Times and Seasons

This chapter provides a comprehensive description of the Holy Days celebrated in the Jewish calendar. These portions are read in the synagogue on the Sabbath of each festival. Leviticus is concerned only with the sacrificial requirements, and does not fully describe the holidays as now observed. (For another description of these days see Numbers 28 and 29.) Both an agricultural and an historic reason are now attributed to these holidays. Thus *Passover* commemorates both the spring harvest and the emancipation of the Hebrews from slavery in Egypt. *Shavuoth* observes both the harvest of the first fruits and the revelation of the Commandments at Sinai. *Succoth* recalls both the fall harvest and the period when the Hebrews wandered in the desert after the Exodus, when God provided for each man according to his need.

Sabbath

Leviticus 23:1-3

23 The LORD said to Moses, [2]"Say to the people of Israel, The appointed feasts of the LORD which you shall proclaim as holy convocations, my appointed feasts, are these. [3] Six days shall work be done; but on the seventh day is a sabbath of solemn rest, a holy convocation; you shall do no work; it is a sabbath to the LORD in all your dwellings."

23:3 Sunday closing laws, where they exist in the United States, limit in some degree business on Sunday. The Supreme Court has ruled these laws constitutional, not on grounds that they encourage the observance of a religious holiday, but in that they fulfill a community need for rest and recreation.

Passover
Leviticus 23:5–8

5 "In the first month, on the fourteenth day of the month in the evening, is the LORD's passover. [6]And on the fifteenth day of the same month is the feast of unleavened bread to the LORD; seven days you shall eat unleavened bread. [7]On the first day you shall have a holy convocation; you shall do no laborious work. [8]But you shall present an offering by fire to the LORD seven days; on the seventh day is a holy convocation; you shall do no laborious work."

Feast of Weeks—Shavuoth (Pentecost)
Leviticus 23:10–17, 21

10 "Say to the people of Israel, When you come into the land which I give you and reap its harvest, you shall bring the sheaf of the first fruits of your harvest to the priest; [11]and he shall wave the sheaf before the LORD, that you may find acceptance; on the morrow after the sabbath the priest shall wave it. [12]And on the day when you wave the sheaf, you shall offer a male lamb a year old without blemish as a burnt offering to the LORD. [13]And the cereal offering with it shall be two tenths of an ephah of fine flour mixed with oil, to be offered by fire to the LORD, a pleasing odor; and the drink offering with it shall be of wine, a fourth of a hin. [14]And you shall eat neither bread nor grain parched or fresh until this same day, until you have brought the offering of your God: it is a statute for ever throughout your generations in all your dwellings.

15 "And you shall count from the morrow after the sabbath, from the day that you brought the sheaf of the wave offering; seven full weeks shall they be, [16]counting fifty days to the morrow after the seventh sabbath; then you shall present a cereal offering of new grain to the LORD. [17]You shall bring from your dwellings two loaves of bread to be waved, made of two tenths of an ephah; they shall be of fine flour, they shall be baked with leaven, as first fruits to the LORD.

21 "And you shall make proclamation on the same day; you shall hold a holy convocation; you shall do no laborious work: it is a statute for ever in all your dwellings throughout your generations."

Rosh Hashanah—Jewish New Year
Leviticus 23 : 24– 25

24 "Say to the people of Israel, In the seventh month, on the first day of the month, you shall observe a day of solemn rest, a memorial proclaimed with blast of trumpets, a holy convocation. 25 You shall do no laborious work; and you shall present an offering by fire to the LORD."

Yom Kippur—The Day of Atonement
Leviticus 23 : 26– 32

26 And the LORD said to Moses, 27 "On the tenth day of this seventh month is the day of atonement; it shall be for you a time of holy convocation, and you shall afflict yourselves and present an offering by fire to the LORD. 28 And you shall do no work on this same day; for it is a day of atonement, to make atonement for you before the LORD your God. 29 For whoever is not afflicted on this same day shall be cut off from his people. 30 And whoever does any work on this same day, that person I will destroy from among his people. 31 You shall do no work: it is a statute for ever throughout your generations in all your dwellings. 32 It shall be to you a sabbath of solemn rest, and you shall afflict yourselves; on the ninth day of the month beginning at evening, from evening to evening shall you keep your sabbath."

Feast of Booths—Succoth
Leviticus 23 : 39– 44

39 "On the fifteenth day of the seventh month, when you have gathered in the produce of the land, you shall keep the feast of the LORD seven days; on the first day shall be a solemn rest, and on the eighth day shall be a solemn rest. 40 And you shall take on the first day the fruit of goodly trees, branches of palm trees, and boughs of leafy trees, and willows of the brook; and you shall rejoice before the LORD your God seven days. 41 You shall keep it as a feast to the LORD seven days in the year; it is a statute for ever throughout your generations; you shall keep it in the seventh month. 42 You shall dwell in booths for seven days; all that are native in Israel shall dwell in booths, 43 that your generations may know that I made the people of Israel dwell in booths when I brought them out of the land of Egypt: I am the LORD your God."

44 Thus Moses declared to the people of Israel the appointed feasts of the LORD.

23:40 On the basis of this verse it was enjoined in the Talmudic period that the Hebrews were to carry in a procession on the festival of the Feast of Booths a *"Lulav,"* i.e., a bouquet consisting of a citron (*ethrog*), and a palm branch, two willow branches and three myrtle branches. During the procession the Levites intoned the opening verse of Psalm 118. Later rabbinical custom added to this eight-day celebration a ninth day, called *Simchat Torah,* on which the daily cycle of the readings from the Torah came to a close; and on the following Sabbath a new yearly cycle commenced.

The Perpetual Light and the Show Bread
Leviticus 24:1–9

24 The LORD said to Moses, [2]"Command the people of Israel to bring you pure oil from beaten olives for the lamp, that a light may be kept burning continually. [3]Outside the veil of the testimony, in the tent of meeting, Aaron shall keep it in order from evening to morning before the LORD continually; it shall be a statute for ever throughout your generations. [4]He shall keep the lamps in order upon the lampstand of pure gold before the LORD continually.

5 "And you shall take fine flour, and bake twelve cakes of it; two tenths of an ephah shall be in each cake. [6]And you shall set them in two rows, six in a row, upon the table of pure gold. [7]And you shall put pure frankincense with each row, that it may go with the bread as a memorial portion to be offered by fire to the LORD. [8]Every sabbath day Aaron shall set it in order before the LORD continually on behalf of the people of Israel as a covenant for ever. [9]And it shall be for Aaron and his sons, and they shall eat it in a holy place, since it is for him a most holy portion out of the offerings by fire to the LORD, a perpetual due."

24:2 Following this statute, a light is kept burning in contemporary synagogues before the Ark which contains the Torah scrolls.

The Penalty of Blasphemy

To blaspheme God was considered an unpardonable sin. Even strangers in the camp of the Hebrews were subject to this law. A stranger was not required to worship the God of Israel; but he was forbidden from reviling publicly the Holy Name. By rabbinic interpretation blasphemy included not only cursing God but attributing His powers to men. In the New Testament Jesus is accused of blasphemy because he claimed such divine powers. See Matthew 9:3 and John 10:33, 36.

Leviticus 24:15–16

15 "And say to the people of Israel, Whoever curses his God shall bear his sin. [16]He who blasphemes the name of the LORD shall be put

to death; all the congregation shall stone him; the sojourner as well as the native, when he blasphemes the Name, shall be put to death."

"Life for Life" Laws

This group of laws restrained unbridled vengeance, a common practice of that period (cf. Genesis 4 : 24). It sought a kind of justice. There is no biblical record that the laws were ever carried out literally. For example, compensation, generally of a monetary nature, was paid after judicial appraisal of an injury.

Leviticus 24 : 17–22

17 "He who kills a man shall be put to death. [18] He who kills a beast shall make it good, life for life. [19] When a man causes a disfigurement in his neighbor, as he has done it shall be done to him, [20] fracture for fracture, eye for eye, tooth for tooth; as he has disfigured a man, he shall be disfigured. [21] He who kills a beast shall make it good; and he who kills a man shall be put to death. [22] You shall have one law for the sojourner and for the native; for I am the LORD your God."

24:20 Code laws of the period contain similar statements of retributive justice, e.g. Hammurabi's Code. But these laws permitted harsher or lesser treatment to be determined by the social status of the persons involved. Not so biblical law, which judges all men equally. See Appendix. 24:22 Recalling the Hebrews' own harsh experiences as strangers in Egypt, Hebrew law provided firm measures for the stranger's protection and freedom. Non-Jews were included in the benefits of the biblical poor law (Deuteronomy 14 : 28; 26 : 11), and the Israelites were frequently enjoined to treat non-Jews with kindness (Jeremiah 7 : 6, 22 : 3; Ezekiel 22 : 7; Zechariah 7 : 10). On the other hand, it was expected that strangers who intended to make permanent residence in Palestine would forego worship of idols (Leviticus 20 : 2), the practice of incest and other abominations (Leviticus 18 : 26), eating blood (Leviticus 17 : 10), and working on Sabbath (Exodus 20 : 10, 23 : 12).

The Sabbatical Year

In order that the land not be exhausted, a *Sabbatical* Year was enjoined on the Hebrews; during this year the land lay fallow—a soil conservation practice. In Egypt, where floods annually deposited new soil, such a practice was unnecessary. Through this biblical injunction the rabbis underscored the teaching that the land was not the absolute possession of man; rather man is responsible to God for the use he will make of it. Alexander the Great and Julius Caesar refrained from exacting the tribute from Jews in the Seventh Year because they did not sow their fields and so would be poorer. The Roman historian Tacitus did not understand this unique law and accused the Jews of indolence. During the Sabbatical Year, when there was more leisure than usual, a nationwide effort was made to inform the population of the teachings of the Torah (cf. Deuteronomy 31:10 ff). This practice is still followed by observant Jewish farmers in the state of Israel.

Leviticus 25:1–7

25 The LORD said to Moses on Mount Sinai, ²"Say to the people of Israel, When you come into the land which I shall give you, the land shall keep a sabbath to the LORD. ³Six years you shall sow your field, and six years you shall prune your vineyard, and gather in its fruits; ⁴but in the seventh year there shall be a sabbath of solemn rest for the land, a sabbath to the LORD; you shall not sow your field or prune your vineyard. ⁵What grows of itself in your harvest you shall not reap, and the grapes of your undressed vine you shall not gather; it shall be a year of solemn rest for the land. ⁶The sabbath of the land shall provide food for you, for yourself and for your male and female slaves and for your hired servant and the sojourner who lives with you; ⁷for your cattle also and for the beasts that are in your land all its yield shall be for food."

The Jubilee Year

The word Jubilee came from the Hebrew word *Yoval*, the name of the horn sounded on the occasion of the Jubilee. Biblical legislation required that all land revert to its original owners in the fiftieth year. This law sought to prevent the accumulation of wealth in the hands of a few. Pauperism would then be prevented. Since "the earth is the Lord's," man could lease his property only until the fiftieth year when he or his descendants would then again regain possession of it. Property rights by this arrangement were not abolished but they were assigned a moral purpose. Scholars differ on the number of times that this Jubilee year was actually observed. Ezekiel refers to the lack of its observance as one of Israel's great sins. In 1 Maccabees 6:49–53 we find that an enemy takes advantage of Israel's weakness by virtue of her observance of the Sabbatical year. Verse 25:10 is inscribed on America's Liberty Bell in Independence Hall, Philadelphia.

Leviticus 25:8–17, 23–24

8 "And you shall count seven weeks of years, seven times seven years, so that the time of the seven weeks of years shall be to you forty-nine years. ⁹Then you shall send abroad the loud trumpet on the tenth day of the seventh month; on the day of atonement you shall send abroad the trumpet throughout all your land. ¹⁰And you shall hallow the fiftieth year, and proclaim liberty throughout the land to all its inhabitants; it shall be a jubilee for you, when each of you shall return to his property and each of you shall return to his family. ¹¹A jubilee shall that fiftieth year be to you; in it you shall neither sow, nor reap what grows of itself, nor gather the grapes from the undressed vines. ¹²For it is a jubilee; it shall be holy to you; you shall eat what it yields out of the field.

13 "In this year of jubilee each of you shall return to his property. ¹⁴And if you sell to your neighbor or buy from your neighbor, you shall not wrong one another. ¹⁵According to the number of years after the jubilee, you shall buy from your neighbor, and according to the number of years for crops he shall sell to you. ¹⁶If the years are many you shall increase the price, and if the years are few you shall diminish the price, for it is the number of the crops that he is selling to you. ¹⁷You shall not wrong one another, but you shall fear your God; for I am the LORD your God.

23 "The land shall not be sold in perpetuity, for the land is mine; for you are strangers and sojourners with me. ²⁴And in all the country you possess, you shall grant a redemption of the land."

25:8 ff. Consider how contemporary society tries to maintain some equality between social classes. What has occurred in societies where inequality became too huge?

The Book of Numbers

Fourth of the Five Books of Moses, Numbers is given its name because of the account contained within it of the numbering or census of the Israelites. Its Hebrew name, *Bamidbar*, "in the wilderness," is taken from the opening sentence, describing the time and events of the narrative. Numbers tells of the vicissitudes of the Israelites in the wanderings after the exodus until thirty-eight years later when they are about to enter the Promised Land.

Combining narrative with legislation, the text records the civil and political ordinances promulgated during or attributed later to that period. Its record of the spiritual trials of the Israelites demonstrates that God, who protects and preserves His people, deals severely with those who rebel against His will or threaten the unity of the faith.

God Commands a Numbering of the Israelites
Numbers 1:1–4, 17–19; 2:1–21, 32–34

1 The LORD spoke to Moses in the wilderness of Sinai, in the tent of meeting, on the first day of the second month, in the second year after they had come out of the land of Egypt, saying, ² "Take a census of all the congregation of the people of Israel, by families, by fathers' houses, according to the number of names, every male, head by head; ³ from twenty years old and upward, all in Israel who are able to go forth to war, you and Aaron shall number them, company by company. ⁴ And there shall be with you a man from each tribe, each man being the head of the house of his fathers."

17 Moses and Aaron took these men who have been named, ¹⁸ and on the first day of the second month, they assembled the whole congregation together, who registered themselves by families, by fathers' houses, according to the number of names from twenty years old and upward, head by head, ¹⁹ as the LORD commanded Moses. So he numbered them in the wilderness of Sinai.

2 The LORD said to Moses and Aaron, ² "The people of Israel shall encamp each by his own standard, with the ensigns of their fathers' houses; they shall encamp facing the tent of meeting on every side. ³ Those to encamp on the east side toward the sunrise shall be of the standard of the camp of Judah by their companies, the leader of the people of Judah being Nahshon the son of Ammin'adab, ⁴ his host as numbered being seventy-four thousand six hundred. ⁵ Those to encamp next to him shall be the tribe of Is'sachar, the leader of the people of Is'sachar being Nethan'el the son of Zu'ar, ⁶ his host as numbered being fifty-four thousand four hundred. ⁷ Then the tribe of Zeb'ulun, the leader of the people of Zeb'ulun being Eli'ab the son of Helon, [8] his host as numbered being fifty-seven thousand four hundred. [9] The whole number of the camp of Judah, by their companies, is a hundred and eighty-six thousand four hundred. They shall set out first on the march.

10 "On the south side shall be the standard of the camp of Reuben by their companies, the leader of the people of Reuben being Eli'zur the son of Shed'eur, [11] his host as numbered being forty-six thousand five hundred. [12] And those to encamp next to him shall be the tribe of Simeon, the leader of the people of Simeon being Shelu'mi-el the son of Zurishad'dai, [13] his host as numbered being fifty-nine thousand three hundred. [14] Then the tribe of Gad, the leader of the people of Gad being Eli'asaph the son of Reu'el, [15] his host as numbered being forty-five thousand six hundred and fifty. [16] The whole number of the camp of Reuben, by their companies, is a hundred and fifty-one thousand four hundred and fifty. They shall set out second.

17 "Then the tent of meeting shall set out, with the camp of the Levites in the midst of the camps; as they encamp, so shall they set out, each in position, standard by standard.

18 "On the west side shall be the standard of the camp of E'phraim by their companies, the leader of the people of E'phraim being Eli'shama the son of Ammi'hud, [19] his host as numbered being forty thousand five hundred. [20] And next to him shall be the tribe of Manas'seh, the leader of the people of Manas'seh being Gama'liel the son of Pedah'zur, [21] his host as numbered being thirty-two thousand two hundred."

32 These are the people of Israel as numbered by their fathers' houses; all in the camp who were numbered by their companies were six hundred and three thousand five hundred and fifty. [33] But the Levites were not numbered among the people of Israel, as the LORD commanded Moses.

34 Thus did the people of Israel. According to all that the LORD commanded Moses, so they encamped by their standards, and so they set out, every one in his family, according to his fathers' house.

1:2 In the United States it is the practice to take a census every ten years. Consider the uses of a census.

The Levites are Assigned Their Duties

The first born of each family was earlier entrusted with priestly functions for their household. Now God chooses the family of Levi as His first born. See also selection at Numbers 18.

Numbers 3:5–13, 44–51

5 And the LORD said to Moses, ⁶ "Bring the tribe of Levi near, and set them before Aaron the priest, that they may minister to him. ⁷ They shall perform duties for him and for the whole congregation before the tent of meeting, as they minister at the tabernacle; ⁸ they shall have charge of all the furnishings of the tent of meeting, and attend to the duties for the people of Israel as they minister at the tabernacle. ⁹ And you shall give the Levites to Aaron and his sons; they are wholly given to him from among the people of Israel. ¹⁰ And you shall appoint Aaron and his sons, and they shall attend to their priesthood; but if any one else comes near, he shall be put to death."

11 And the LORD said to Moses, ¹² "Behold, I have taken the Levites from among the people of Israel, instead of every first-born that opens the womb among the people of Israel. The Levites shall be mine, ¹³ for all the first-born are mine; on the day that I slew all the first-born in the land of Egypt, I consecrated for my own all the first-born in Israel, both of man and of beast; they shall be mine: I am the LORD."

44 And the LORD said to Moses, ⁴⁵ "Take the Levites instead of all the first-born among the people of Israel, and the cattle of the Levites instead of their cattle; and the Levites shall be mine: I am the LORD. ⁴⁶ And for the redemption of the two hundred and seventy-three of the first-born of the people of Israel, over and above the number of the male Levites, ⁴⁷ you shall take five shekels apiece; reckoning by the shekel of the sanctuary, the shekel of twenty gerahs, you shall take them, ⁴⁸ and give the money by which the excess number of them is redeemed to Aaron and his sons." ⁴⁹ So Moses took the redemption money from those who were over and above those redeemed by the Levites; ⁵⁰ from the first-born of the people of Israel he took the money, one thousand three hundred and sixty-five shekels, reckoned by the shekel of the sanctuary; ⁵¹ and Moses gave the redemption money to Aaron and his sons, according to the word of the LORD, as the LORD commanded Moses.

> **3:5** ff. The Levites participated in the Temple ritual as assistants to the priests, as gate-keepers and as musicians; the family of Aaron was lifted up from among the Levites to serve as the consecrated priests (Hebrew: *Kohen*). Observant Jews who are of "Kohen" (Cohen) descent today still follow the biblical restrictions placed on the Kohen (Leviticus 21)—e.g., they will not enter a cemetery nor marry a divorced woman, etc. **3:46–48** See note on Numbers 18:15–16.

The Law of the Nazirite

Israelites who for personal reasons elected to serve God with special dedication were called *Nazirites*. They would take vows which usually lasted for a minimum period of thirty days; some devoted their entire lives to this ascetic commitment (e.g., Jeremiah 35). Samson and probably Samuel and John the Baptist were consecrated at birth to the Nazirite way. The Hebrew word *Nazir* means one separated or consecrated.

Numbers 6:1–8

6 And the LORD said to Moses, [2] "Say to the people of Israel, When either a man or a woman makes a special vow, the vow of a Nazirite, to separate himself to the LORD, [3] he shall separate himself from wine and strong drink; he shall drink no vinegar made from wine or strong drink, and shall not drink any juice of grapes or eat grapes, fresh or dried. [4] All the days of his separation he shall eat nothing that is produced by the grapevine, not even the seeds or the skins.

[5] "All the days of his vow of separation no razor shall come upon his head; until the time is completed for which he separates himself to the LORD, he shall be holy; he shall let the locks of hair of his head grow long. [6] "All the days that he separates himself to the LORD he shall not go near a dead body. [7] Neither for his father nor for his mother, nor for brother or sister, if they die, shall he make himself unclean; because his separation to God is upon his head. [8] All the days of his separation he is holy to the LORD."

6:1 For Samson as a Nazirite, see Judges 13:5; for Samuel, 1 Samuel 1:11; for John the Baptist, Luke 1:15. See also Acts 21:26 for Paul. The observance of the Nazirite vow is recognized by Jewish scholars into the Middle Ages and then disappears. A treatise of the Mishna and Talmud is devoted to a discussion of the laws found in this scriptural passage. Recorded there is a minority rabbinic view that opposed asceticism, considering the Nazirites sinners. Said one rabbi: "The Nazirite has sinned by denying himself wine; and if one who denies himself wine, which is not absolutely necessary, is deemed a sinner, one who denies himself other things which are needful for the sustenance of life is a much greater sinner" (*Nazir* 19a). **6:3** ff. Some scholars have suggested the following interpretation in explanation of these three forms of self-denial: to abstain from wine (6:3) is to abandon a life of ease (cf. the Rechabites, Jeremiah 35:5–8); to allow the hair to grow (6:5) symbolically demonstrates the Nazirite's intention to allow God's powers of strength to act upon him; to stay apart from a dead body (6:6) is to become in that respect like a priest, dedicated in a special way to God (cf. Leviticus 21:1–2, 10–11; priests were forbidden to come near a corpse).

God Ordains the Priestly Blessing

According to rabbinic law these blessings were to be pronounced only by a priest while standing in the Temple with outspread arms and rendered in the Hebrew tongue. They were chanted every morning and evening. The blessings are still used as part of synagogue worship.

Rabbinic scholars interpret the words as follows:

"Bless you and keep you"—with life, health and prosperity.

"Face to shine upon you"—the gift of knowledge and moral insight.

"Give you peace"—the Hebrew word for peace, *Shalom*, means completeness or wholeness, not just the cessation of hostilities. It includes both a petition for personal wholeness as well as political and international harmony among nations. The Hebrew word translated "give you" (RSV) may be rendered "establish for thee." The rabbis understood this to mean that peace was not a gift granted and passively received; it was rather the climax of a process in which man was obliged to participate.

I will bless them (v. 27) Although the priest prays, it is the Lord who blesses.

The priestly blessing is also frequently used in Christian churches as the parting word of benediction.

Numbers 6:22–27

22 The LORD said to Moses, ²³ "Say to Aaron and his sons, Thus you shall bless the people of Israel: you shall say to them,

²⁴ The LORD bless you and keep you:

²⁵ The LORD make his face to shine upon you, and be gracious to you:

²⁶ The LORD lift up his countenance upon you, and give you peace.

27 "So shall they put my name upon the people of Israel, and I will bless them."

Term of Office for the Priests

Numbers 8:23–26

23 And the LORD said to Moses, ²⁴ "This is what pertains to the Levites: from twenty-five years old and upward they shall go in to perform the work in the service of the tent of meeting; ²⁵ and from the age of fifty years they shall withdraw from the work of the service and serve no more, ²⁶ but minister to their brethren in the tent of meeting, to keep the charge, and they shall do no service. Thus shall you do to the Levites in assigning their duties."

8:23 Many organizations have their own requirements about retirement. Enforced retirement is often subject to debate, however, by those who challenge its validity and social usefulness.

The Horns of Silver

The spiritual significance of the sounding of the horn is attested to also in 2 Chronicles 13:12–16, and 1 Maccabees 4:40; 5:33. The silver clarions were long and narrow with an expanded mouth. They differ from the Shofar, the ram's horn, which was sounded at the Jubilee Year and at the celebration of the Day of Atonement. The blast notes commanded here, however, are repeated in the Shofar service for the New Year celebration in contemporary synagogues. The Catholic liturgy in some countries allows the use of horns or silver trumpets, and they were for centuries heard at the most solemn part of the Mass celebrated by the Pope in St. Peter's Basilica.

Numbers 10:1–10

10 The LORD said to Moses, ²"Make two silver trumpets; of hammered work you shall make them; and you shall use them for summoning the congregation, and for breaking camp. ³And when both are blown all the congregation shall gather themselves to you at the entrance of the tent of meeting. ⁴But if they blow only one, then the leaders, the heads of the tribes of Israel, shall gather themselves to you. ⁵When you blow an alarm, the camps that are on the east side shall set out. ⁶And when you blow an alarm the second time, the camps that are on the south side shall set out. An alarm is to be blown whenever they are to set out. ⁷But when the assembly is to be gathered together, you shall blow, but you shall not sound an alarm. ⁸And the sons of Aaron, the priests, shall blow the trumpets. The trumpets shall be to you for a perpetual statute throughout your generations. ⁹And when you go to war in your land against the adversary who oppresses you, then you shall sound an alarm with the trumpets, that you may be remembered before the LORD your God, and you shall be saved from your enemies. ¹⁰On the day of your gladness also, and at your appointed feasts, and at the beginnings of your months, you shall blow the trumpets over your burnt offerings and over the sacrifices of your peace offerings; they shall serve you for remembrance before your God: I am the LORD your God."

10:10 Orchestras are used during the Mass especially in countries where the Baroque tradition prevails.

God Protects Israel in War

This passage describes how the Lord protected the Israelites on their journey by placing a cloud over them (cf. Psalm 115:39). The Israelites, when commencing a journey, placed the Ark of the Testimony before the camp in order to inspire themselves with confidence in God as their champion; at other times on the move, the ark was stationed in the middle of the line of march.

In the Hebrew text the last verses are bracketed, indicating that they were inserted from another source (possibly from a book called "The Book of the Wars of the Lord"). There were still other historical books in which the records of the Hebrews were kept, but these were not accepted into the canon of Scripture and unfortunately are no longer available to us. References to them are found in several places throughout Scripture. These verses are chanted in the synagogue service when the Torah scroll is removed from the Ark for the reading of Scripture.

Numbers 10:33–36

33 So they set out from the mount of the LORD three days' journey; and the ark of the covenant of the LORD went before them three days' journey, to seek out a resting place for them. ³⁴ And the cloud of the LORD was over them by day, whenever they set out from the camp.

35 And whenever the ark set out, Moses said, "Arise, O LORD, and let thy enemies be scattered; and let them that hate thee flee before thee." ³⁶ And when it rested, he said, "Return, O LORD, to the ten thousand thousands of Israel."

The People Murmur against the Lord

Chapters 11 to 14 record the murmurings and rebellion of the Hebrew people against the hardship of their journey and against the leadership of Moses. For this reason the generation is judged unworthy to enter the Promised Land. Enslaved spiritually, they were incapable of accepting the responsibilities and difficulties of freedom.

Numbers 11:1–17, 25–27, 31–33

11 And the people complained in the hearing of the LORD about their misfortunes; and when the LORD heard it, his anger was kindled, and the fire of the LORD burned among them, and consumed some outlying parts of the camp. ² Then the people cried to Moses; and Moses prayed to the LORD, and the fire abated. ³ So the name of that place was called Tab'erah, because the fire of the LORD burned among them.

4 Now the rabble that was among them had a strong craving; and the people of Israel also wept again, and said, "O that we had meat to eat! ⁵ We remember the fish we ate in Egypt for nothing, the cucumbers, the melons, the leeks, the onions, and the garlic; ⁶ but now our strength is dried up, and there is nothing at all but this manna to look at."

7 Now the manna was like coriander seed, and its appearance like that of bdellium. ⁸ The people went about and gathered it, and

ground it in mills or beat it in mortars, and boiled it in pots, and made cakes of it; and the taste of it was like the taste of cakes baked with oil. ⁹ When the dew fell upon the camp in the night, the manna fell with it.

10 Moses heard the people weeping throughout their families, every man at the door of his tent; and the anger of the LORD blazed hotly, and Moses was displeased. ¹¹ Moses said to the LORD, "Why hast thou dealt ill with thy servant? And why have I not found favor in thy sight, that thou dost lay the burden of all this people upon me? ¹² Did I conceive all this people? Did I bring them forth, that thou shouldst say to me, 'Carry them in your bosom, as a nurse carries the sucking child, to the land which thou didst swear to give their fathers?' ¹³ Where am I to get meat to give to all this people? For they weep before me and say, 'Give us meat, that we may eat.' ¹⁴ I am not able to carry all this people alone, the burden is too heavy for me. ¹⁵ If thou wilt deal thus with me, kill me at once, if I find favor in thy sight, that I may not see my wretchedness."

16 And the LORD said to Moses, "Gather for me seventy men of the elders of Israel, whom you know to be the elders of the people and officers over them; and bring them to the tent of meeting, and let them take their stand there with you. ¹⁷ And I will come down and talk with you there; and I will take some of the spirit which is upon you and put it upon them; and they shall bear the burden of the people with you, that you may not bear it yourself alone."

25 Then the LORD came down in the cloud and spoke to him, and took some of the spirit that was upon him and put it upon the seventy elders; and when the spirit rested upon them, they prophesied. But they did so no more.

26 Now two men remained in the camp, one named Eldad, and the other named Medad, and the spirit rested upon them; they were among those registered, but they had not gone out to the tent, and so they prophesied in the camp. ²⁷ And a young man ran and told Moses, "Eldad and Medad are prophesying in the camp."

31 And there went forth a wind from the LORD, and it brought quails from the sea, and let them fall beside the camp, about a day's journey on this side and a day's journey on the other side, round about the camp, and about two cubits above the face of the earth. ³² And the people rose all that day, and all night, and all the next day, and gathered the quails; he who gathered least gathered ten homers; and they spread them out for themselves all around the camp. ³³ While the meat was yet between their teeth, before it was consumed, the anger of the LORD was kindled against the people, and the LORD smote the people with a very great plague.

11:3 The Hebrew word *Taberah* means "burning."
11:7 See note preceding Exodus 16:2–6. **11:16** To aid Moses in the administration of justice seventy elders were chosen. God provided them with an experience of ecstasy so compelling that they were able to draw upon it throughout their careers. **11:26** The word "prophesied" does not mean the foretelling of future events, but rather describes the ability to speak inspired lessons of truth. This visitation of the spirit is similar to the transforming experience narrated in the New Testament in Acts 2:1–7. **11:31** In the fall of the year it sometimes happens that quail migrating from Europe to Arabia and Africa will stop for rest in the Sinai desert where they can easily be caught.

Moses Has Trouble in His Household

The Cushite woman is believed by some scholars to have been from an Ethiopian tribe; this interracial marriage with a woman of their former captors provoked Miriam and Aaron to speak evil against Moses. They also challenged his spiritual authority, claiming equality with him. God makes clear the unique place granted Moses.

Numbers 12:1–15

12 Miriam and Aaron spoke against Moses because of the Cushite woman whom he had married, for he had married a Cushite woman; ²and they said, "Has the LORD indeed spoken only through Moses? Has he not spoken through us also?" And the LORD heard it. ³Now the man Moses was very meek, more than all men that were on the face of the earth. ⁴And suddenly the LORD said to Moses and to Aaron and Miriam, "Come out, you three, to the tent of meeting." And the three of them came out. ⁵And the LORD came down in a pillar of cloud, and stood at the door of the tent, and called Aaron and Miriam; and they both came forward. ⁶And he said, "Hear my words: If there is a prophet among you, I the LORD make myself known to him in a vision, I speak with him in a dream. ⁷Not so with my servant Moses; he is entrusted with all my house. ⁸With him I speak mouth to mouth, clearly, and not in dark speech; and he beholds the form of the LORD. Why then were you not afraid to speak against my servant Moses?"

9 And the anger of the LORD was kindled against them, and he departed; ¹⁰and when the cloud removed from over the tent, behold, Miriam was leprous, as white as snow. And Aaron turned towards Miriam, and behold, she was leprous. ¹¹And Aaron said to Moses, "Oh, my lord, do not punish us because we have done foolishly and have sinned. ¹²Let her not be as one dead, of whom the flesh is half consumed when he comes out of his mother's womb." ¹³And Moses cried to the LORD, "Heal her, O God, I beseech thee." ¹⁴But the

LORD said to Moses, "If her father had but spit in her face, should she not be shamed seven days? Let her be shut up outside the camp seven days, and after that she may be brought in again." [15] So Miriam was shut up outside the camp seven days; and the people did not set out on the march till Miriam was brought in again.

Moses Spies Out the Promised Land

The Israelites had scored a military victory over the king of Arad in the extreme south of Canaan. Moses believed them ready to enter the Promised Land. Spies were sent to search it out. A pessimistic report and the fear and rebelliousness of the people demonstrated their inability to take possession of the land.

Numbers 13:1–3, 17–21, 23–33; 14:1–4, 10b–24

13 The LORD said to Moses, [2] "Send men to spy out the land of Canaan, which I give to the people of Israel; from each tribe of their fathers shall you send a man, every one a leader among them." [3] So Moses sent them from the wilderness of Paran, according to the command of the LORD, all of them men who were heads of the people of Israel.

17 Moses sent them to spy out the land of Canaan, and said to them, "Go up into the Negeb yonder, and go up into the hill country, [18] and see what the land is, and whether the people who dwell in it are strong or weak, whether they are few or many, [19] and whether the land that they dwell in is good or bad, and whether the cities that they dwell in are camps or strongholds, [20] and whether the land is rich or poor, and whether there is wood in it or not. Be of good courage, and bring some of the fruit of the land." Now the time was the season of the first ripe grapes.

21 So they went up and spied out the land from the wilderness of Zin to Rehob, near the entrance of Hamath.

23 And they came to the Valley of Eshcol, and cut down from there a branch with a single cluster of grapes, and they carried it on a pole between two of them; they brought also some pomegranates and figs. [24] That place was called the Valley of Eshcol, because of the cluster which the men of Israel cut down from there.

25 At the end of forty days they returned from spying out the land. [26] And they came to Moses and Aaron and to all the congregation of the people of Israel in the wilderness of Paran, at Kadesh; they brought back word to them and to all the congregation, and showed them the fruit of the land. [27] And they told him, "We came to the land to which you sent us; it flows with milk and honey, and this is its fruit. [28] Yet the people who dwell in the land are strong, and the cities are fortified and very large; and besides, we saw the descend-

ants of Anak there. ²⁹ The Amal'ekites dwell in the land of the Negeb; the Hittites, the Jeb'usites, and the Amorites dwell in the hill country; and the Canaanites dwell by the sea, and along the Jordan."

30 But Caleb quieted the people before Moses, and said, "Let us go up at once, and occupy it; for we are well able to overcome it." ³¹ Then the men who had gone up with him said, "We are not able to go up against the people; for they are stronger than we." ³² So they brought to the people of Israel an evil report of the land which they had spied out, saying, "The land, through which we have gone, to spy it out, is a land that devours its inhabitants; and all the people that we saw in it are men of great stature. ³³ And there we saw the Nephilim (the sons of Anak, who come from the Nephilim); and we seemed to ourselves like grasshoppers, and so we seemed to them."

14 Then all the congregation raised a loud cry; and the people wept that night. ² And all the people of Israel murmured against Moses and Aaron; the whole congregation said to them, "Would that we had died in the land of Egypt! Or would that we had died in this wilderness! ³ Why does the LORD bring us into this land, to fall by the sword? Our wives and our little ones will become a prey; would it not be better for us to go back to Egypt?"

4 And they said to one another, "Let us choose a captain, and go back to Egypt."

Then the glory of the LORD appeared at the tent of meeting to all the people of Israel. ¹¹ And the LORD said to Moses, "How long will this people despise me? And how long will they not believe in me, in spite of all the signs which I have wrought among them? ¹² I will strike them with the pestilence and disinherit them, and I will make of you a nation greater and mightier than they."

13 But Moses said to the LORD, "Then the Egyptians will hear of it, for thou didst bring up this people in thy might from among them, ¹⁴ and they will tell the inhabitants of this land. They have heard that thou, O LORD, art in the midst of this people; for thou, O LORD, art seen face to face, and thy cloud stands over them and thou goest before them, in a pillar of cloud by day and in a pillar of fire by night. ¹⁵ Now if thou dost kill this people as one man, then the nations who have heard thy fame will say, ¹⁶ 'Because the LORD was not able to bring this people into the land which he swore to give to them, therefore he has slain them in the wilderness.' ¹⁷ And now, I pray thee, let the power of the LORD be great as thou hast promised, saying, ¹⁸ 'The LORD is slow to anger, and abounding in steadfast love, forgiving iniquity and transgression, but he will by no means clear the guilty, visiting the iniquity of fathers upon children, upon

the third and upon the fourth generation.' ¹⁹ Pardon the iniquity of this people, I pray thee, according to the greatness of thy steadfast love, and according as thou hast forgiven this people, from Egypt even until now."

20 Then the LORD said, "I have pardoned, according to your word; ²¹ but truly, as I live, and as all the earth shall be filled with the glory of the LORD, ²² none of the men who have seen my glory and my signs which I wrought in Egypt and in the wilderness, and yet have put me to the proof these ten times and have not hearkened to my voice, ²³ shall see the land which I swore to give to their fathers; and none of those who despised me shall see it. ²⁴ But my servant Caleb, because he has a different spirit and has followed me fully, I will bring into the land into which he went, and his descendants shall possess it."

13:1 ff. Many countries today maintain intelligence services for self-defense and as an aid to shaping foreign policy.

Prayer Shawl
Numbers 15:37–41

37 The LORD said to Moses, ³⁸ "Speak to the people of Israel, and bid them to make tassels on the corners of their garments throughout their generations, and to put upon the tassel of each corner a cord of blue; ³⁹ and it shall be to you a tassel to look upon and remember all the commandments of the LORD, to do them, not to follow after your own heart and your own eyes, which you are inclined to go after wantonly. ⁴⁰ So you shall remember and do all my commandments, and be holy to your God. ⁴¹ I am the LORD your God, who brought you out of the land of Egypt, to be your God: I am the LORD your God."

15:37 To this day Jewish men adorn themselves with a prayer shawl (*tallith*) containing tassels, (*tzitzit*), when engaged in prayer at the morning service during weekdays, on sabbaths and holy days. The New Testament records Jesus adorned with *tallith* (Matthew 9:20), although he criticized the ostentation with which the garb was sometimes worn (Matthew 23:5). **15:38** The "cord of blue" was a sign of nobility. It demonstrated the Hebrew conviction that the LORD was their king and that by service to Him they assumed status as a priestly people.

God Ordains the Duties and Gifts of the Priests and Levites
Numbers 18:1–5, 8, 12–21

18 So the LORD said to Aaron, "You and your sons and your fathers' house with you shall bear iniquity in connection with the sanctuary;

and you and your sons with you shall bear iniquity in connection with your priesthood. [2] And with you bring your brethren also, the tribe of Levi, the tribe of your father, that they may join you, and minister to you while you and your sons with you are before the tent of the testimony. [3] They shall attend you and attend to all duties of the tent; but shall not come near to the vessels of the sanctuary or to the altar, lest they, and you, die. [4] They shall join you, and attend to the tent of the meeting, for all the service of the tent; and no one else shall come near you. [5] And you shall attend to the duties of the sanctuary and the duties of the altar, that there be wrath no more upon the people of Israel.

8 Then the LORD said to Aaron, "And behold, I have given you whatever is kept of the offerings made to me, all the consecrated things of the people of Israel; I have given them to you as a portion, and to your sons as a perpetual due.

12 "All the best of the oil, and all the best of the wine and of the grain, the first fruits of what they give to the LORD, I give to you. [13] The first ripe fruits of all that is in their land, which they bring to the LORD, shall be yours; every one who is clean in your house may eat of it. [14] Every devoted thing in Israel shall be yours. [15] Everything that opens the womb of all flesh, whether man or beast, which they offer to the LORD, shall be yours; nevertheless the first-born of man you shall redeem, and the firstling of unclean beasts you shall redeem. [16] And their redemption price (at a month old you shall redeem them) you shall fix at five shekels in silver, according to the shekel of the sanctuary, which is twenty gerahs. [17] But the firstling of a cow, or the firstling of a sheep, or the firstling of a goat, you shall not redeem; they are holy. You shall sprinkle their blood upon the altar, and shall burn their fat as an offering by fire, a pleasing odor to the LORD; [18] but their flesh shall be yours, as the breast that is waved and as the right thigh are yours. [19] All the holy offerings which the people of Israel present to the LORD I give to you, and to your sons and daughters with you, as a perpetual due; it is a covenant of salt for ever before the LORD for you and for your offspring with you." [20] And the LORD said to Aaron, "You shall have no inheritance in their land, neither shall you have any portion among them; I am your portion and your inheritance among the people of Israel.

21 "To the Levites I have given every tithe in Israel for an inheritance, in return for their service which they serve, their service in the tent of meeting."

18:2, 4 The Hebrew word *levi* means "to be joined." The biblical text here suggests that members of the tribe of Levi will be joined as assistants to the Kohanim, the priests of the family of Aaron, who alone were permitted to offer the sacrifices. Later Rabbinic literature in a more romantic vein suggests that even though they performed menial tasks at the sanctuary their service "joined the sons (the people of Israel) to their Father in Heaven" (*Genesis Rabbah*, 71:5). See Deuteronomy 33:8–10 for a scriptural account of the profound piety of the Levites. Separate functions were reserved for each of the Levitical families: The Kohathites cared for the furniture of the sanctuaries; the Gershonites its curtains; the Merarites its boards, pins and poles. The Levites were specifically forbidden to assume the priestly function of offering sacrifice reserved to Aaron and his sons (Numbers 4:19). In 1 Chronicles 23:26–28 we see the emergence of Levites as keepers of the sanctuary treasury and, in 1 Chronicles 25–26, as Temple singers. Some scholars believe that the priestly functions were limited to the Levitical tribe only after the reforms of King Josiah in 621 B.C. Before that time, as Scripture records, many persons—even slave peoples—performed these menial tasks at the sanctuary (cf. Joshua 9:23). With the final destruction of the Temple priestly functioning ceased in Judaism. The Catholic Church has maintained aspects of worship which embody in form some of the characteristics of the Old Testament priesthood. **18:15–16** To this day in observant Jewish homes the ceremony of "the redemption of the son" (called *Pidyon Haben*) is performed thirty days after the birth of the first son, if he is the first child born of the mother. The proud father will donate to the rabbi or to charity a gift worth at least five silver coins. **18:21** Israelites were also instructed to tithe for the sake of the poor (see Deuteronomy 14:22–29).

Moses Commits a Sin

In this tragic account a truth is imbedded: the greater the man, the stricter the standard by which he is judged and the more awful the consequences in punishment for his wrongdoing. Moses fails to trust in God's word, to simply *tell* the rock to produce water; instead he *strikes* upon the rock with his rod. For this reason Moses forfeits his right to enter the Promised Land.

Numbers 20:2–13

2 Now there was no water for the congregation; and they assembled themselves together against Moses and against Aaron. ³ And the people contended with Moses, and said, "Would that we had died when our brethren died before the LORD! ⁴ Why have you brought the assembly of the LORD into this wilderness, that we should die here, both we and our cattle? ⁵ And why have you made us come up out of Egypt, to bring us to this evil place? It is no place for grain, or figs, or vines, or pomegranates; and there is no water to drink." ⁶ Then Moses and Aaron went from the presence of the

assembly to the door of the tent of meeting, and fell on their faces. And the glory of the LORD appeared to them, [7] and the LORD said to Moses, [8] "Take the rod, and assemble the congregation, you and Aaron your brother, and tell the rock before their eyes to yield its water; so you shall bring water out of the rock for them; so you shall give drink to the congregation and their cattle." [9] And Moses took the rod from before the LORD, as he commanded him.

10 And Moses and Aaron gathered the assembly together before the rock, and he said to them, "Hear now, you rebels; shall we bring forth water for you out of this rock?" [11] And Moses lifted up his hand and struck the rock with his rod twice; and water came forth abundantly, and the congregation drank, and their cattle. [12] And the LORD said to Moses and Aaron, "Because you did not believe in me, to sanctify me in the eyes of the people of Israel, therefore you shall not bring this assembly into the land which I have given them." [13] These are the waters of Mer'ibah, where the people of Israel contended with the LORD, and he showed himself holy among them.

20:13 The Hebrew word *meribah* means "contention."

God Heals by the Bronze Serpent

The coiled serpent upon a standard has become a symbol of medicine. The rabbis were quick to observe, however, that the bronze serpent did not in itself have the power to heal. When later generations began to revere the serpent as an idol, King Hezekiah destroyed it (cf. 2 Kings 18:14).

Numbers 21:4–9

4 From Mount Hor they set out by the way to the Red Sea, to go around the land of Edom; and the people became impatient on the way. [5] And the people spoke against God and against Moses, "Why have you brought us up out of Egypt to die in the wilderness? For there is no food and no water, and we loathe this worthless food." [6] Then the LORD sent fiery serpents among the people, and they bit the people, so that many people of Israel died. [7] And the people came to Moses, and said, "We have sinned, for we have spoken against the LORD and against you; pray to the LORD, that he take away the serpents from us." So Moses prayed for the people. [8] And the LORD said to Moses, "Make a fiery serpent, and set it on a pole; and every one who is bitten, when he sees it, shall live." [9] So Moses made a bronze serpent, and set it on a pole; and if a serpent bit any man, he would look at the bronze serpent and live.

Balaam Praises Israel

The effort made by Balak, king of Moab, to enlist the aid of a far-famed soothsayer, Balaam, to *curse* the Israelites and to cast a spell over them is the last trial the Israelites must overcome before entering the Promised Land. Despite his intentions Balaam is compelled by a Higher Power to *bless* Israel. In poetic phrases he predicts the Israelites' glorious future.

Some biblical commentators, considering Balaam's evil intent against Israel regard him as a scoundrel. Others look upon him as one of the prophets among the nations who though unconnected with Israel affirmed their faith in the one true God, as did Melchizedek, Jethro, and Job.

Numbers 22:1–12, 15–35, 41; 23:5–13, 16, 20–21, 25–27; 24:2–3, 5–7, 9b–14, 17–19, 25

22 Then the people of Israel set out, and encamped in the plains of Moab beyond the Jordan at Jericho. ²And Balak the son of Zippor saw all that Israel had done to the Amorites. ³And Moab was in great dread of the people, because they were many; Moab was overcome with fear of the people of Israel. ⁴And Moab said to the elders of Mid′ian, "This horde will now lick up all that is round about us, as the ox licks up the grass of the field." So Balak the son of Zippor, who was king of Moab at that time, ⁵sent messengers to Balaam the son of Be′or at Pethor, which is near the River, in the land of Amaw to call him, saying, "Behold, a people has come out of Egypt; they cover the face of the earth, and they are dwelling opposite me. ⁶Come now, curse this people for me, since they are too mighty for me; perhaps I shall be able to defeat them and drive them from the land; for I know that he whom you bless is blessed, and he whom you curse is cursed."

7 So the elders of Moab and the elders of Mid′ian departed with the fees for divination in their hand; and they came to Balaam, and gave him Balak's message. ⁸And he said to them, "Lodge here this night, and I will bring back word to you, as the LORD speaks to me"; so the princes of Moab stayed with Balaam. ⁹And God came to Balaam and said, "Who are these men with you?" ¹⁰And Balaam said to God, "Balak the son of Zippor, king of Moab, has sent to me, saying, ¹¹'Behold, a people has come out of Egypt, and it covers the face of the earth; now come, curse them for me; perhaps I shall be able to fight against them and drive them out.'" ¹²God said to Balaam, "You shall not go with them; you shall not curse the people, for they are blessed."

15 Once again Balak sent princes, more in number and more honorable than they. ¹⁶And they came to Balaam and said to him,

"Thus says Balak the son of Zippor: 'Let nothing hinder you from coming to me; [17]for I will surely do you great honor, and whatever you say to me I will do; come, curse this people for me.'" [18]But Balaam answered and said to the servants of Balak, "Though Balak were to give me his house full of silver and gold, I could not go beyond the command of the LORD my God, to do less or more. [19]Pray, now, tarry here this night also, that I may know what more the LORD will say to me." [20]And God came to Balaam at night and said to him, "If the men have come to call you, rise, go with them; but only what I bid you that shall you do."

21 So Balaam rose in the morning, and saddled his ass, and went with the princes of Moab. [22]But God's anger was kindled because he went; and the angel of the LORD took his stand in the way as his adversary. Now he was riding on the ass, and his two servants were with him. [23]And the ass saw the angel of the LORD standing in the road, with a drawn sword in his hand; and the ass turned aside out of the road, and went into the field; and Balaam struck the ass, to turn her into the road. [24]Then the angel of the LORD stood in a narrow path between the vineyards, with a wall on either side. [25]And when the ass saw the angel of the LORD, she pushed against the wall, and pressed Balaam's foot against the wall; so he struck her again. [26]Then the angel of the LORD went ahead, and stood in a narrow place, where there was no way to turn either to the right or to the left. [27]When the ass saw the angel of the LORD, she lay down under Balaam; and Balaam's anger was kindled, and he struck the ass with his staff. [28]Then the LORD opened the mouth of the ass, and she said to Balaam, "What have I done to you, that you have struck me these three times?" [29]And Balaam said to the ass, "Because you have made sport of me. I wish I had a sword in my hand, for then I would kill you." [30]And the ass said to Balaam, "Am I not your ass, upon which you have ridden all your life long to this day? Was I ever accustomed to do so to you?" And he said, "No."

31 Then the LORD opened the eyes of Balaam, and he saw the angel of the LORD standing in the way, with his drawn sword in his hand; and he bowed his head, and fell on his face. [32]And the angel of the LORD said to him, "Why have you struck your ass these three times? Behold, I have come forth to withstand you, because your way is perverse before me; [33]and the ass saw me, and turned aside before me these three times. If she had not turned aside from me, surely just now I would have slain you and let her live." [34]Then Balaam said to the angel of the LORD, "I have sinned, for I did not know

that thou didst stand in the road against me. Now therefore, if it is evil in thy sight, I will go back again." [35] And the angel of the LORD said to Balaam, "Go with the men; but only the word which I bid you, that shall you speak." So Balaam went on with the princes of Balak.

41 And on the morrow Balak took Balaam and brought him up to Bamoth-ba'al; and from there he saw the nearest of the people.

23 [5] And the LORD put a word in Balaam's mouth, and said, "Return to Balak, and thus you shall speak." [6] And he returned to him, and lo, he and all the princes of Moab were standing beside his burnt offering. [7] And Balaam took up his discourse, and said,

> "From Aram Balak has brought me,
>   the king of Moab from the eastern mountains:
> 'Come, curse Jacob for me,
>   and come, denounce Israel!'
> [8] How can I curse whom God has not cursed?
>   How can I denounce whom the LORD has not denounced?
> [9] For from the top of the mountains I see him,
>   from the hills I behold him;
> lo, a people dwelling alone,
>   and not reckoning itself among the nations!
> [10] Who can count the dust of Jacob,
>   or number the fourth part of Israel?
> Let me die the death of the righteous,
>   and let my end be like his!"

11 And Balak said to Balaam, "what have you done to me? I took you to curse my enemies, and behold, you have done nothing but bless them." [12] And he answered, "Must I not take heed to speak what the LORD puts in my mouth?"

13 And Balak said to him, "Come with me to another place, from which you may see them; you shall see only the nearest of them, and shall not see them all; then curse them for me from there."

16 And the LORD met Balaam, and put a word in his mouth, and said, "Return to Balak, and thus shall you speak."

> [20] Behold, I received a command to bless:
>   he has blessed, and I cannot revoke it.
> [21] He has not beheld misfortune in Jacob;
>   nor has he seen trouble in Israel.
> The LORD their God is with them,
>   and the shout of a king is among them.

25 And Balak said to Balaam, "Neither curse them at all, nor bless them at all." [26] But Balaam answered Balak, "Did I not tell

you, 'All that the LORD says, that I must do'?" ²⁷ And Balak said to Balaam, "Come now, I will take you to another place; perhaps it will please God that you may curse them for me from there."

24 ² And Balaam lifted up his eyes, and saw Israel encamping tribe by tribe. And the Spirit of God came upon him, ³ and he took up his discourse, and said,

> "The oracle of Balaam the son of Be'or,
> > the oracle of the man whose eye is opened . . .
> ⁵ how fair are your tents, O Jacob,
> > your encampments, O Israel!
> ⁶ Like valleys that stretch afar,
> > like gardens beside a river,
> like aloes that the LORD has planted,
> > like cedar trees beside the waters.
> ⁷ Water shall flow from his buckets,
> > and his seed shall be in many waters,
> his king shall be higher than Agag,
> > and his kingdom shall be exalted.
> Blessed be every one who blesses you,
> > and cursed be every one who curses you."

10 And Balak's anger was kindled against Balaam, and he struck his hands together; and Balak said to Balaam, "I called you to curse my enemies, and behold, you have blessed them these three times. ¹¹ Therefore now flee to your place; I said, 'I will certainly honor you,' but the LORD has held you back from honor." ¹² And Balaam said to Balak, "Did I not tell your messengers whom you sent to me, ¹³ 'If Balak should give me his house full of silver and gold, I would not be able to go beyond the word of the LORD, to do either good or bad of my own will; what the LORD speaks, that will I speak'? ¹⁴ And now, behold, I am going to my people; come, I will let you know what this people will do to your people in the latter days."

> ¹⁷ "I see him, but not now;
> > I behold him, but not nigh:
> a star shall come forth out of Jacob,
> > and a scepter shall rise out of Israel;
> it shall crush the forehead of Moab,
> > and break down all the sons of Sheth.
> ¹⁸ Edom shall be dispossessed,
> > Se'ir also, his enemies, shall be dispossessed,
> > while Israel does valiantly.
> ¹⁹ By Jacob shall dominion be exercised,
> > and the survivors of cities be destroyed!"

25 Then Balaam rose, and went back to his place; and Balak also went his way.

22:6 In that period men believed in the efficacy of blessings and curses, which could not be revoked. See Genesis 27:33. **22:22** The blindness and obstinacy of Balaam is depicted in this delightful account where he is rebuked by a dumb animal. Brought to reason by this unforeseen hindrance, Balaam is spared dishonor. In Jewish tradition the story is both accepted literally and held to have only symbolic significance. Josephus said in regard to this matter that readers are free to think what they please. **24:5** This sentence is used in the opening prayer service in the synagogue. The rabbis interpret "tents" to mean the religious school and "encampments" (KJV—"dwelling place") to mean the synagogue. **24:17** The word "star" in Near Eastern languages referred symbolically to God-kings. The Hebraic understanding was that this verse expressed hope in the emergence of the Davidic dynasty, from which the Messiah was to come.

Moses Commissions Joshua
Numbers 27:15–23

15 Moses said to the LORD, 16 "Let the LORD, the God of the spirits of all flesh, appoint a man over the congregation, 17 who shall go out before them and come in before them, who shall lead them out and bring them in; that the congregation of the LORD may not be as sheep which have no shepherd." 18 And the LORD said to Moses, "Take Joshua the son of Nun, a man in whom is the spirit, and lay your hand upon him; 19 cause him to stand before Elea'zar the priest and all the congregation, and you shall commission him in their sight. 20 You shall invest him with some of your authority, that all the congregation of the people of Israel may obey. 21 And he shall stand before Elea'zar the priest, who shall inquire for him by the judgment of the Urim before the LORD; at his word they shall go out, and at his word they shall come in, both he and all the people of Israel with him, the whole congregation." 22 And Moses did as the LORD commanded him; he took Joshua and caused him to stand before Elea'zar the priest and the whole congregation, 23 and he laid his hands upon him, and commissioned him as the LORD directed through Moses.

27:15–23 Note the process of election and validation of leadership.

The Sacredness of Vows
Numbers 30:1–4

30 Moses said to the heads of the tribes of the people of Israel, "That is what the LORD has commanded. 2 When a man vows a vow to the

LORD, or swears an oath to bind himself by a pledge, he shall not break his word; he shall do according to all that proceeds out of his mouth. ³Or when a woman vows a vow to the LORD, and binds herself by a pledge, while within her father's house, in her youth, ⁴ and her father hears of her vow and of her pledge by which she has bound herself, and says nothing to her; then all her vows shall stand, and every pledge by which she has bound herself shall stand.

The Book of Deuteronomy

Deuteronomy was originally entitled in the Hebrew, *Mishneh Torah*, i.e., The Repetition of the Torah, a phrase based on verse 17:18. Greek speaking Jews called the book "Deuteronomian," i.e., the Second Law, by which title it came to us through the Latin. In present Jewish tradition it is called *Devorim*, i.e., "(These are) the words," taken from the opening phrase of the Hebrew text. Deuteronomy is the fifth of the Five Books of Moses.

At the point of entrance to the Promised Land, Moses in three discourses exhorts the Israelites. In his First Discourse chapters 1:6–4:40, Moses recounts the history of Israel's journey through the wilderness. In the Second and Third Discourses, 4:44–30:20, he reviews the principal laws that the people are to observe in the Promised Land. Finally, Moses delivers words of charge to Joshua and to the priests, and he warns the people in a benediction to serve God faithfully.

Deuteronomy combines the narrative, legislative, priestly and prophetic strains of Scripture into one magnificent oration. Its sentences flow with passion, denunciation and exhortation. Its affirmations: God is one, man must love God with all his heart and soul, man must be righteous in dealings with his fellow man. These have all been incorporated into the daily liturgy of Jewish prayer. Deuteronomy's influence on the Jewish religion "has never been exceeded by any other book in Scripture" (Hertz).

Many biblical scholars believe this—or a part of it—to be the "book of the Law" discovered during the reign of King Josiah in 621 B.C. Others believe Deuteronomy to have been written by prophetic historians for such an occasion—to spark a religious reform.

Deuteronomy summarized the Law as it had been preserved by the Hebrews. Jesus frequently quoted Deuteronomy.

Moses Delivers His First Discourse

Here Moses recounts the experience of the Israelites in the terrible wilderness through which they have just journeyed. As consequence of their complaints and rebelliousness, the people were consigned to wander until a new generation would be permitted to enter the Promised Land. Even Moses became entangled in the back-sliding of the people; and he was instructed to turn the leadership over to another when the ascent to Canaan was to be made. Despite this, God's watchfulness over Israel remained constant.

Now that they have crossed the brook Zered a new era begins. The dread of Israel falls upon the neighboring peoples. Sihon, king of the Amorites, and Og, king of Bashan, succumb. Their cities are taken and divided among the tribes of Reuben, Gad and half the tribe of Manasseh.

Much of this history has already been included in the selections from Exodus, Leviticus and Numbers. Here we repeat only those passages that reveal the unique character of the Deuteronomist.

Deuteronomy 1:1; 2:7, 9, 13–19, 24–25; 3:8–10, 18–22

1 "These are the words that Moses spoke to all Israel beyond the Jordan in the wilderness, in the Arabah over against Suph, between Paran and Tophel, Laban, Haze′roth, and Di′-zahab.

2 [7] "For the Lord your God has blessed you in all the work of your hands; he knows your going through this great wilderness; these forty years the Lord your God has been with you; you have lacked nothing.'

9 "And the Lord said to me, 'Do not harass Moab or contend with them in battle, for I will not give you any of their land for a possession, because I have given Ar to the sons of Lot for a possession.'

13 "'Now rise up, and go over the brook Zered.' So we went over the brook Zered. [14] And the time from our leaving Ka′desh-bar′nea until we crossed the brook Zered was thirty-eight years, until the entire generation, that is, the men of war, had perished from the camp, as the Lord had sworn to them. [15] For indeed the hand of the Lord was against them, to destroy them from the camp, until they had perished.

16 "So when all the men of war had perished and were dead from among the people, [17] the Lord said to me, [18] 'This day you are to pass over the boundary of Moab at Ar; [19] and when you approach the frontier of the sons of Ammon, do not harass them or contend with them, for I will not give you any of the land of the sons of Ammon as a possession, because I have given it to the sons of Lot for a possession.'

24 "'Rise up, take your journey, and go over the valley of the Arnon; behold, I have given into your hand Sihon the Amorite, king of Heshbon, and his land; begin to take possession, and contend with him in battle. [25] This day I will begin to put the dread and fear of you upon the peoples that are under the whole heaven, who shall hear the report of you and shall tremble and be in anguish because of you.'

3 [8] "So we took the land at that time out of the hand of the two kings of the Amorites who were beyond the Jordan, from the valley of the Arnon to Mount Hermon [9] (the Sido′nians call Hermon Sir′i-on, while the Amorites call it Senir), [10] all the cities of the tableland and all Gilead and all Bashan, as far as Sal'ecah and Ed're-i, cities of the kingdom of Og in Bashan.

18 "And I commanded you at that time, saying, 'The LORD your God has given you this land to possess; all your men of valor shall pass over armed before your brethren the people of Israel. ¹⁹ But your wives, your little ones, and your cattle (I know that you have many cattle) shall remain in the cities which I have given you, ²⁰ until the LORD gives rest to your brethren, as to you, and they also occupy the land which the LORD your God gives them beyond the Jordan; then you shall return every man to his possession which I have given you.' ²¹ And I commanded Joshua at that time, 'Your eyes have seen all that the LORD your God has done to these two kings; so will the LORD do to all the kingdoms into which you are going over. ²² You shall not fear them; for it is the LORD your God who fights for you.' "

Moses Pleads to Enter the Promised Land
Deuteronomy 3:23–28

23 "And I besought the LORD at that time, saying, ²⁴ 'O Lord GOD, thou hast only begun to show thy servant thy greatness and thy mighty hand; for what god is there in heaven or on earth who can do such works and mighty acts as thine? ²⁵ Let me go over, I pray, and see the good land beyond the Jordan, that goodly hill country, and Lebanon.' ²⁶ But the LORD was angry with me on your account, and would not hearken to me; and the LORD said to me, 'Let it suffice you; speak no more to me of this matter. ²⁷ Go up to the top of Pisgah, and lift up your eyes westward and northward and southward and eastward, and behold it with your eyes; for you shall not go over this Jordan. ²⁸ But charge Joshua, and encourage and strengthen him; for he shall go over at the head of this people, and he shall put them in possession of the land which you shall see.' "

    3:26 *Let it suffice you.* This statement has provoked much commentary from Jewish scholars, who see in it man's need to realize that all he can do is his part; this is enough. Man cannot ever hope to fulfill all his human wishes. He must accept whatever gratification comes from his particular role in the work of achieving God's will, even if he will not taste the fruit of his labor. Some commentators see also the truth that great leaders perform only limited functions in history. The warrior may achieve the revolution, but it is a statesman who is required to administer the country. Moses was the great legislator of his people; Joshua assumes the burden of the military conquest.

A Faithful Israel Will Abide in the Lord
Deuteronomy 4:1–2, 5–9, 23–31, 39–40

4 "And now, O Israel, give heed to the statutes and the ordinances which I teach you, and do them; that you may live, and go in and take possession of the land which the LORD, the God of your fathers, gives you. ²You shall not add to the word which I command you, nor take from it; that you may keep the commandments of the LORD your God which I command you.

5 "Behold, I have taught you statutes and ordinances, as the LORD my God commanded me, that you should do them in the land which you are entering to take possession of it. ⁶Keep them and do them; for that will be your wisdom and your understanding in the sight of the peoples, who, when they hear all these statutes, will say, 'Surely this great nation is a wise and understanding people.' ⁷For what great nation is there that has a god so near to it as the LORD our God is to us, whenever we call upon him? ⁸And what great nation is there, that has statutes and ordinances so righteous as all this law which I set before you this day?

9 "Only take heed, and keep your soul diligently, lest you forget the things which your eyes have seen, and lest they depart from your heart all the days of your life; make them known to your children and your children's children.

23 "Take heed to yourselves, lest you forget the covenant of the LORD your God, which he made with you, and make a graven image in the form of anything which the LORD your God has forbidden you. ²⁴For the LORD your God is a devouring fire, a jealous God.

25 "When you beget children and children's children, and have grown old in the land, if you act corruptly by making a graven image in the form of anything, and by doing what is evil in the sight of the LORD your God, so as to provoke him to anger. ²⁶I call heaven and earth to witness against you this day, that you will soon utterly perish from the land which you are going over the Jordan to possess; you will not live long upon it, but will be utterly destroyed. ²⁷And the LORD will scatter you among the peoples, and you will be left few in number among the nations where the LORD will drive you. ²⁸And there you will serve gods of wood and stone, the work of men's hands, that neither see, nor hear, nor eat, nor smell. ²⁹But from there you will seek the LORD your God, and you will find him, if you search after him with all your heart and with all your soul. ³⁰When you are in tribulation, and all these things come upon you in the latter days, you will return to the LORD your God and obey his voice. ³¹for the LORD your God is a merciful God; he will not fail you or

destroy you or forget the covenant with your fathers which he swore to them.

39 "Know therefore this day, and lay it to your heart, that the LORD is God in heaven above and on the earth beneath; there is no other. [40] Therefore you shall keep his statutes and his commandments, which I command you this day, that it may go well with you, and with your children after you, and that you may prolong your days in the land which the LORD your God gives you for ever."

> **4:39** This sentence has been incorporated into the Adoration, i.e., the closing prayer at every synagogue service. It summarizes the intent of Moses' First Oration.

Second Discourse

> The Second Discourse of Moses began with 4:44 and continues to the end of chapter 11. In it Moses reviews the Ten Commandments; there are slight textual variations between the Commandments as given in Exodus and as they are rendered here.

Deuteronomy 5:1–21

5 And Moses summoned all Israel, and said to them, "Hear, O Israel, the statutes and the ordinances which I speak in your hearing this day, and you shall learn them and be careful to do them. [2] The LORD our God made a covenant with us in Horeb. [3] Not with our fathers did the LORD make this covenant, but with us, who are all of us here alive this day. [4] The LORD spoke with you face to face at the mountain, out of the midst of the fire, [5] while I stood between the LORD and you at that time, to declare to you the word of the LORD; for you were afraid because of the fire, and you did not go up into the mountain. He said:

6 " 'I am the LORD your God, who brought you out of the land of Egypt, out of the house of bondage.

7 " 'You shall have no other gods before me.

8 " 'You shall not make for yourself a graven image, or any likeness of anything that is in heaven above, or that is on the earth beneath, or that is in the water under the earth; [9] you shall not bow down to them or serve them; for I the LORD your God am a jealous God, visiting the iniquity of the fathers upon the children to the third and fourth generation of those who hate me, [10] but showing steadfast love to thousands of those who love me and keep my commandments.

11 " 'You shall not take the name of the LORD your God in vain: for the LORD will not hold him guiltless who takes his name in vain.

12 " 'Observe the sabbath day, to keep it holy, as the LORD your

God commanded you. [13] Six days you shall labor, and do all your work; [14] but the seventh day is a sabbath to the LORD your God; in it you shall not do any work, you, or your son, or your daughter, or your manservant, or your maidservant, or your ox, or your ass, or any of your cattle, or the sojourner who is within your gates, that your manservant and your maidservant may rest as well as you. [15] You shall remember that you were a servant in the land of Egypt, and the LORD your God brought you out thence with a mighty hand and an outstretched arm; therefore the LORD your God commanded you to keep the sabbath day.

16 " 'Honor your father and your mother, as the LORD your God commanded you; that your days may be prolonged, and that it may go well with you, in the land which the LORD your God gives you.

17 " 'You shall not kill.

18 " 'Neither shall you commit adultery.

19 " 'Neither shall you steal.

20 " 'Neither shall you bear false witness against your neighbor.

21 " 'Neither shall you covet your neighbor's wife; and you shall not desire your neighbor's house, his field, or his manservant, or his maidservant, his ox, or his ass, or anything that is your neighbor's.' "

5:8 The restriction against idolatry is emphasized by adding the words "any manner of likeness" (KJV). **5:12** Exodus used the words "Remember the sabbath day" whereas here Moses emphasizing the sanctity of the day, commands "Observe the sabbath day." In Exodus the Sabbath commemorates creation; here Moses adds reference to Israel's enslavement in Egypt. As slaves in Egypt the Hebrews were given no rest. In their own land they are to avoid imposing on others what had been so bitter to them. **5:21** Moses distinguishes between coveting a neighbor's wife and desiring a neighbor's physical possessions. The new emphasis reflects the improved status of women. Deuteronomy also includes a specific reference to desiring a neighbor's field; upon their entrance to the Promised Land, the right of property takes on new significance.

The Shema: Hear O Israel

This prayer is called in Hebrew the "Shema" from the first word meaning "Hear"; it can be translated either to declare that God is one or that Israel serves God alone. Both thoughts are assumed when the declaration is made by observant Jews at least twice daily.

Deuteronomy 6:4–9 (JPS Torah)

4 Hear, O Israel! The LORD is our God, the LORD alone. [5] You must love the LORD your God with all your heart and with all your soul and with all your might. [6] Take to heart these words with which

I charge you this day. [7]Impress them upon your children. Recite them when you stay at home and when you are away, when you lie down and when you get up. [8]Bind them as a sign on your hand and let them serve as a symbol on your forehead; [9]inscribe them on the doorposts of your house and on your gates.

6:4 ff. Jews are enjoined by religious law to instruct a child in the Shema as his first lesson of faith, and it is the declaration every pious Jew would wish to recite upon his death. Its recitation twice daily is in fulfillment of Deuteronomy 6:7. In the synagogue liturgy the Shema now consists of three portions: Deuteronomy 6:4–9, 11:13–21; and Numbers 15:17–41; with benedictions preceding and following the Shema thought to have been composed by an Essene pietist during the period of the Second Temple. **6:4** Translated variously:

> The Lord our God, The Lord is one.
> The Lord is our God, The Lord is one.
> The Lord is our God, The Lord alone.
> The Lord our God is one Lord.

This monotheistic declaration distinguished the Jewish religion in the biblical period from the widespread belief of other peoples in many gods. Today Christians and Moslems join Jews in commitment to a monotheistic faith. **6:5** Quoting this passage Jesus declares it to be the greatest of all God's commandments (Matthew 22:37). **6:7** During the biblical period it was the duty of the father to provide religious and secular instruction for his sons. Prophets, priests and scribes offered public instruction in the religious law on the Sabbath, market days (Tuesdays and Thursdays), and holy days. The time of King Hezekiah was considered an exemplary period of universal literacy (*Sanhedrin* 49b). The existence in the biblical period of a group of professional teachers or tutors is evidenced from Proverbs 5:13, Psalm 119:99, Nehemiah 8:7, Ezra 8:16, Daniel 11:33, 35. The first evidence of formal state-supported educational system for all children is dated from the first century B.C. when the noted Rabbi Simon ben Shetah, president of the Sanhedrin, organized district schools for youths of sixteen to seventeen years of age. In A.D. 64 the High Priest, Joshua ben Gamala, established schools for boys six to seven years of age in all the cities of Palestine. One teacher was provided for twenty-one boys. "By the breath of the mouth of school children the world is sustained" (*Shabbat* 119b). **6:8** *Sign on your hand and . . . between your eyes.* Observant Jews adorn themselves at morning prayer with phylacteries (*tephillen*). These are small leather boxes to which leather straps are attached. One is worn on the left hand with the box directed toward the heart, the other is placed on the forehead. Within the phylacteries are four small sections of Scripture: Exodus 13:1–10; 11–16; Deuteronomy 6:4–9; 11:13–21. A meditation in the Prayer Book explains: "God commanded us to lay the Tephillen on the hand as a memorial of His outstretched arm . . . opposite the heart to indicate the duty of subjecting the longings and desires of our hearts to His service; and upon the forehead . . . thereby teaching that the mind . . . together with all senses and faculties is to be subjected to His service." **6:9** Observant Jews affix a *mezzuzah* at the righthand door post of every dwelling room in a house. The *mezzuzah* is a scroll of parchment in a metal or wood container. The scroll has this section of the Shema and other verses from Deuteronomy, 11:13–20. The word *Shaddai*, God Almighty, or the first letter of the word, is written on the back of the parchment and is visible by a small opening in the case.

God Chooses Israel

Deuteronomy 7:6–11

6 "For you are a people holy to the LORD your God; the LORD your God has chosen you to be a people for his own possession, out of all the peoples that are on the face of the earth. ⁷It was not because you were more in number than any other people that the LORD set his love upon you and chose you, for you were the fewest of all peoples; ⁸but it is because the LORD loves you, and is keeping the oath which he swore to your fathers, that the LORD has brought you out with a mighty hand, and redeemed you from the house of bondage, from the hand of Pharaoh king of Egypt. ⁹Know therefore that the LORD your God is God, the faithful God who keeps covenant and steadfast love with those who love him and keep his command- ments, to a thousand generations, ¹⁰and requites to their face those who hate him, by destroying them; he will not be slack with him who hates him, he will requite him to his face. ¹¹You shall therefore be careful to do the commandment, and the statutes, and the ordin- ances, which I command you this day."

God Tests Man's Faith

Moses interprets the adversity endured by the generation of the wilderness as a test of Israel. In adversity they would recognize their dependence on God. But also, if they withstood hardship without losing faith in God, they would demonstrate that their love had not been conditional upon good fortune. There is a danger in prosperity, Moses warns the people, for they may forget that it is God who provides.

Deuteronomy 8:1–14, 17–19

8 "All the commandment which I command you this day you shall be careful to do, that you may live and multiply, and go in and possess the land which the LORD swore to give to your fathers. ²And

you shall remember all the way which the LORD your God has led you these forty years in the wilderness, that he might humble you, testing you to know what was in your heart, whether you would keep his commandments, or not. ³ And he humbled you and let you hunger and fed you with manna, which you did not know, nor did your fathers know; that he might make you know that man does not live by bread alone, but that man lives by everything that proceeds out of the mouth of the LORD. ⁴ Your clothing did not wear out upon you, and your foot did not swell, these forty years. ⁵ Know then in your heart that, as a man disciplines his son, the LORD your God disciplines you. ⁶ So you shall keep the commandments of the LORD your God, by walking in his ways and by fearing him. ⁷ For the LORD your God is bringing you into a good land, a land of brooks of water, of fountains and springs, flowing forth in valleys and hills, ⁸ a land of wheat and barley, of vines and fig trees and pomegranates, a land of olive trees and honey, ⁹ a land in which you will eat bread without scarcity, in which you will lack nothing, a land whose stones are iron, and out of whose hills you can dig copper. ¹⁰ And you shall eat and be full, and you shall bless the LORD your God for the good land he has given you.

11 "Take heed lest you forget the LORD your God, by not keeping his commandments and his ordinances and his statutes, which I command you this day: ¹² lest, when you have eaten and are full, and have built goodly houses and live in them, ¹³ and when your herds and flocks multiply, and your silver and gold is multiplied, and all that you have is multiplied, ¹⁴ then your heart be lifted up, and you forget the LORD your God, who brought you out of the land of Egypt, out of the house of bondage. . . .

17 "Beware lest you say in your heart, 'My power and the might of my hand have gotten me this wealth.' ¹⁸ You shall remember the LORD your God, for it is he who gives you power to get wealth; that he may confirm his covenant which he swore to your fathers, as at this day. ¹⁹ And if you forget the LORD your God and go after other gods and serve them and worship them, I solemnly warn you this day that you shall surely perish."

8:3 Jesus quotes this famous verse, asserting, "Man shall not live by bread alone" (Matthew 4:4). **8:7–10** In the belief that these lines are applicable also to the people in the United States they are read as part of the Thanksgiving services in many Christian churches. **8:9** This verse refers to mines of iron and copper in the Holy Land. The desolate nature of present day Palestine led many to question this reference. In his explorations, the archaeologist Nelson Glueck has discovered remains of copper mines in the desert regions of Wadi

Ribah, and uncovered the ancient city of Ezion-Geber on the Gulf of Aqaba, a port developed by King Solomon. **8:10** This sentence led the Rabbis to institute a service of grace before and after each meal, a custom also maintained in the Christian tradition. On the Sabbath and festive occasions table hymns or "Zemiroth," are sung in Jewish homes, to make of the holiday meal a festive occasion of rejoicing and worship. The singing of the Mass derives from the chanting of the hymns and Psalms by the early Christians at the festive meal on the Lord's Day, the first day of the week.

Moses Concludes His Second Exhortation
Deuteronomy 10:12–22

12 "And now, Israel, what does the LORD your God require of you, but to fear the LORD your God, to walk in all his ways, to love him, to serve the LORD your God with all your heart and with all your soul, [13] and to keep the commandments and statutes of the LORD, which I command you this day for your good? [14] Behold, to the LORD your God belong heaven and the heaven of heavens, the earth with all that is in it; [15] yet the LORD set his heart in love upon your fathers and chose their descendants after them, you above all peoples, as at this day. [16] Circumcise therefore the foreskin of your heart, and be no longer stubborn. [17] For the LORD your God is God of gods and Lord of lords, the great, the mighty, and the terrible God, who is not partial and takes no bribe. [18] He executes justice for the fatherless and the widow, and loves the sojourner, giving him food and clothing. [19] Love the sojourner therefore; for you were sojourners in the land of Egypt. [20] You shall fear the LORD your God; you shall serve him and cleave to him, and by his name you shall swear. [21] He is your praise; he is your God, who has done for you these great and terrible things which your eyes have seen. [22] Your fathers went down to Egypt seventy persons; and now the LORD your God has made you as the stars of heaven for multitude."

The Third Discourse

Chapters 12–26 specify the laws and precepts that are to govern the lives of the Hebrews in the Promised Land. The laws in chapters 12–14 deal with the worship of God, expanding on the First Commandment. The laws found in chapter 15–16:7 enumerate the holy festivals in the spirit of the Fourth Commandment. Chapters 16–18 touch upon the civil and religious government which plays a part in the national life much like that of parents in the life of the family. The remainder of the section deals with the relationship of man to fellow man, as do the last five commandments.

The Central Sanctuary and Worship
Deuteronomy 12:1–5, 29–31

12 "These are the statutes and ordinances which you shall be careful to do in the land which the LORD, the God of your fathers, has given you to possess, all the days that you live upon the earth. [2] You shall surely destroy all the places where the nations whom you shall dispossess served their gods, upon the high mountains and upon the hills and under every green tree; [3] you shall tear down their altars, and dash in pieces their pillars, and burn their Ashe′rim with fire; you shall hew down the graven images of their gods, and destroy their name out of that place. [4] You shall not do so to the LORD your God. [5] But you shall seek the place which the LORD your God will choose out of all your tribes to put his name and make his habitation there; thither you shall go. . . .

[29] "When the LORD your God cuts off before you the nations whom you go in to dispossess, and you dispossess them and dwell in their land, [30] take heed that you be not ensnared to follow them, after they have been destroyed before you, and that you do not inquire about their gods, saying, 'How did these nations serve their gods?—that I also may do likewise.' [31] You shall not do so to the LORD your God; for every abominable thing which the LORD hates they have done for their gods; for they even burn their sons and their daughters in the fire to their gods."

12:5 The centralization of worship in one place, at the sanctuary in Jerusalem, was a revolutionary change. It was initiated by King Josiah after 621 B.C. in an effort to abolish idolatrous practices that had been incorporated in Jewish worship under the influence of the neighboring Canaanites (cf. Judges 6:28, 1 Kings 3:4). For an account of Josiah's reform see 2 Kings 23.

Do Not Add to the Law
Deuteronomy 12:32

[32] "Everything that I command you you shall be careful to do; you shall not add to it or take from it."

12:32 In the Hebrew Bible this verse begins chapter 13. Its immediate specific reference may be to false prophets who by adding to the Law attempted to seduce the people into idolatrous ways. In general the purity of the faith could be maintained only if the revealed Word were followed rigorously without deviation "to the right or left." In later generations, however, new conditions demanded that the law be reinterpreted, so the rabbis developed methods by which the scriptural Law could be expanded to deal with new situations, just as the U.S. Supreme Court makes rulings concerning the constitutionality of legislation that at the same time remains true to the spirit of the Constitution and permits the law to grow. At all times in Jewish life there were and are "liberals" and "conservatives" on the question of how Scripture should be interpreted in the light of later circumstances. In the days of Jesus, for example, the Sadducees refused to accept Pharisaic reinterpretations; they defended arrangements that favored long-standing vested interests. Jesus, still further reinterpreted the law and so incurred the anger of both. Today Orthodox Jews most rigorously uphold biblical law as developed and expanded through Talmudic (rabbinic) interpretation. Reform Jews have abandoned many of the rabbinic laws; but they believe that by the practices they have maintained or instituted they come closer to the original spiritual intent of the biblical word.

The Tithes
Deuteronomy 14:22–29

22 "You shall tithe all the yield of your seed, which comes forth from the field year by year. 23 And before the LORD your God, in the place which he will choose, to make his name dwell there, you shall eat the tithe of your grain, of your wine, and of your oil, and the firstlings of your herd and flock; that you may learn to fear the LORD your God always. 24 And if the way is too long for you, so that you are not able to bring the tithe, when the LORD your God blesses you, because the place is too far from you, which the LORD your God chooses, to set his name there, 25 then you shall turn it into money, and bind up the money in your hand, and go to the place which the LORD your God chooses, 26 and spend the money for whatever you desire, oxen, or sheep, or wine or strong drink, whatever your appetite craves; and you shall eat there before the LORD your God and rejoice, you and your household. 27 And you shall not forsake the Levite who is within your towns, for he has no portion or inheritance with you.

28 "At the end of every three years you shall bring forth all the tithe of your produce in the same year, and lay it up within your towns; 29 and the Levite, because he has no portion or inheritance with you, and the sojourner, the fatherless, and the widow, who are within your towns, shall come and eat and be filled; that the LORD your God may bless you in all the work of your hands that you do."

14:22 There are three tithes mentioned in Scriptures (cf. Leviticus 27:30–33 and Numbers 18:21–23): (1) a tithe for the maintenance of the Levites; (2) a tithe to be taken to the sanctuary and enjoyed there in celebrations of thanksgiving (Numbers 18:26 f.); (3) a tithe for the poor due in the third and sixth year of every seven year period instead of the second tithe. This tithe, or its monetary equivalent, was to be used in assistance to the poor. See Deuteronomy 26:1–13. **14:28–29** Compare the proportions of national incomes now devoted to charities, voluntary and tax-supported.

The Remission of Debts
Deuteronomy 15:1–11

15 "At the end of every seven years you shall grant a release. ²And this is the manner of the release: every creditor shall release what he has lent to his neighbor; he shall not exact it of his neighbor, his brother, because the LORD's release has been proclaimed. ³Of a foreigner you may exact it; but whatever of yours is with your brother your hand shall release. ⁴But there will be no poor among you (for the LORD will bless you in the land which the LORD your God gives you for an inheritance to possess), ⁵if only you will obey the voice of the LORD your God, being careful to do all this commandment which I command you this day. ⁶For the LORD your God will bless you, as he promised you, and you shall lend to many nations, but you shall not borrow; and you shall rule over many nations, but they shall not rule over you.

7 "If there is among you a poor man, one of your brethren, in any of your towns within your land which the LORD your God gives you, you shall not harden your heart or shut your hand against your poor brother, ⁸but you shall open your hand to him, and lend him sufficient for his need, whatever it may be. ⁹Take heed lest there be a base thought in your heart, and you say, 'The seventh year, the year of release is near,' and your eye be hostile to your poor brother, and you give him nothing, and he cry to the LORD against you, and it be sin in you. ¹⁰You shall give to him freely, and your heart shall not be grudging when you give to him; because for this the LORD your God will bless you in all your work and in all that you undertake. ¹¹For the poor will never cease out of the land; therefore I command you, You shall open wide your hand to your brother, to the needy and to the poor, in the land."

15:1–11 Compare bankruptcy laws now in effect in the United States. **15:3** "Foreigners" refers to a non-Canaanite resident who visited Canaan only for business and did not himself practice remission of debts. From such a foreigner the debt may be collected. The text does not say "must"; this collection of debt was not obligatory. **15:11** The Rabbis suggested that the promise that there will never be any poor in the land (15:4) was an ideal achievable only by the condition set forth in 15:5: "if only you will obey the voice of the Lord your God."

Courts of Justice
Deuteronomy 16:18–20

18 "You shall appoint judges and officers in all your towns which the LORD your God gives you, according to your tribes; and they shall judge the people with righteous judgment. [19] You shall not pervert justice; you shall not show partiality; and you shall not take a bribe, for a bribe blinds the eyes of the wise and subverts the cause of the righteous. [20] Justice, and only justice, you shall follow, that you may live and inherit the land which the LORD your God gives you."

16:18 Compare practices of election and appointment of civic officers today.

The King Is Bound by the Law
Deuteronomy 17:14–20

14 "When you come to the land which the LORD your God gives you, and you possess it and dwell in it, and then say, 'I will set a king over me, like all the nations that are round about me'; [15] you may indeed set as king over you him whom the LORD your God will choose. One from among your brethren you shall set as king over you; you may not put a foreigner over you, who is not your brother. [16] Only he must not multiply horses for himself, or cause the people to return to Egypt in order to multiply horses, since the LORD has said to you, 'You shall never return that way again.' [17] And he shall not multiply wives for himself, lest his heart turn away; nor shall he greatly multiply for himself silver and gold.

18 "And when he sits on the throne of his kingdom, he shall write for himself in a book a copy of this law, from that which is in charge of the Levitical priests; [19] and it shall be with him, and he shall read in it all the days of his life, that he may learn to fear the LORD his God, by keeping all the words of this law and these statutes, and doing them; [20] that his heart may not be lifted up above his brethren, and that he may not turn aside from the commandment, either to the right hand or to the left; so that he may continue long in his kingdom, he and his children, in Israel."

17:14 Those who believe that Deuteronomy was written in the seventh century B.C. see in these verses an image of a king quite contrary to the exploitative monarchs the Hebrews had already experienced. Some suggest that verse 17 is a veiled allusion to King Solomon (cf. 1 Kings 4:26; 5:16–18). **17:18–19** Compare rule by persons and rule by law. In effect, this would provide a written constitution to be administered by the king.

Respect for Another's Property
Deuteronomy 19 : 14

14 "In the inheritance which you will hold in the land that the LORD your God gives you to possess, you shall not remove your neighbor's landmark, which the men of old have set."

Rules of Evidence
Deuteronomy 19 : 15–20

15 "A single witness shall not prevail against a man for any crime or for any wrong in connection with any offence that he has committed; only on the evidence of two witnesses, or of three witnesses, shall a charge be sustained. [16] If a malicious witness rises against any man to accuse him of wrongdoing, [17] then both parties to the dispute shall appear before the LORD, before the priests and the judges who are in office in those days; [18] the judges shall inquire diligently, and if the witness is a false witness and has accused his brother falsely, [19] then you shall do to him as he had meant to do to his brother; so you shall purge the evil from the midst of you. [20] And the rest shall hear, and fear, and shall never again commit any such evil among you."

19 : 18–19 Compare penalties for perjury today.

The Laws of Warfare
Deuteronomy 20 : 1–13, 19–20; 21 : 10–14

20 "When you go forth to war against your enemies, and see horses and chariots and an army larger than your own, you shall not be afraid of them; for the LORD your God is with you, who brought you up out of the land of Egypt. [2] And when you draw near to the battle, the priest shall come forward and speak to the people, [3] and shall say to them, 'Hear, O Israel, you draw near this day to battle against your enemies: let not your heart faint; do not fear, or tremble, or be in dread of them; [4] for the LORD your God is he that goes with you, to fight for you against your enemies, to give you the victory.' [5] Then the officers shall speak to the people, saying, 'What man is there that has built a new house and has not dedicated it? Let him go back to his house, lest he die in the battle and another man dedicate it. [6] And what man is there that has planted a vineyard and has not enjoyed its fruit? Let him go back to his house, lest he die in the battle and another man enjoy its fruit. [7] And what man is there that has betrothed a wife and has not taken her? Let him go back to his house, lest he die in the battle and another man take her.' [8] And the officers shall speak further to the people, and say, 'What man is there that is fearful and fainthearted? Let him go back to his house,

lest the heart of his fellows melt as his heart.' [9] And when the officers have made an end of speaking to the people, then commanders shall be appointed at the head of the people.

10 "When you draw near to a city to fight against it, offer terms of peace to it. [11] And if its answer to you is peace and it opens to you, then all the people who are found in it shall do forced labor for you and shall serve you. [12] But if it makes no peace with you, but makes war against you, then you shall besiege it; [13] and when the LORD your God gives it into your hand you shall put all its males to the sword.

19 "When you besiege a city for a long time, making war against it in order to take it, you shall not destroy its trees by wielding an axe against them; for you may eat of them, but you shall not cut them down. Are the trees in the field men that they should be besieged by you? [20] Only the trees which you know are not trees for food you may destroy and cut down that you may build siegeworks against the city that makes war with you, until it falls.

21 [10] "When you go forth to war against your enemies, and the LORD your God gives them into your hands, and you take them captive, [11] and see among the captives a beautiful woman, and you have desire for her and would take her for yourself as wife, [12] then you shall bring her home to your house, and she shall shave her head and pare her nails. [13] And she shall put off her captive's garb, and shall remain in your house and bewail her father and her mother a full month; after that you may go in to her, and be her husband, and she shall be your wife. [14] Then, if you have no delight in her, you shall let her go where she will; but you shall not sell her for money, you shall not treat her as a slave, since you have humiliated her."

20:1 ff. Compare the popular saying "Might makes right," and the history of church-state relations during modern wars. **20:5–8** Compare present practices of exemption from compulsory military service. Evidence that these regulations were practiced may be seen in 1 Maccabees 3:56. Rabbinic law required that in besieging a city the troops had to leave one side free so that any who wished might escape, the object being the defeat of the city not the death of the population.

Death for the Disobedient Son

There is no record that this law was enforced, but it served as a warning. Parents did not have the right to execute their rebellious son; punishment of such extremity had to be administered by a proper judicial or communal authority.

Deuteronomy 21:18—21

18 "If a man has a stubborn and rebellious son, who will not obey
the voice of his father or the voice of his mother, and, though they
chastise him, will not give heed to them, [19] then his father and his
mother shall take hold of him and bring him out to the elders of his
city at the gate of the place where he lives, [20] and they shall say to the
elders of his city, 'This our son is stubborn and rebellious, he will not
obey our voice; he is a glutton and a drunkard.' [21] Then all the men
of the city shall stone him to death with stones; so you shall purge
the evil from your midst; and all Israel shall hear, and fear."

Bury the Dead

Capital punishment among the Israelites included stoning, burning,
the sword and strangulation. Crucifixion was a Roman form of
punishment. In the Jewish community the dead are buried as quickly
as possible.

Deuteronomy 21:22—23

22 "And if a man has committed a crime punishable by death and he
is put to death, and you hang him on a tree, [23] his body shall not
remain all night upon the tree, but you shall bury him the same day,
for a hanged man is accursed by God; you shall not defile your land
which the LORD your God gives you for an inheritance."

Laws of Kindness and Purity
*Deuteronomy 22:1—11, 22, 28—29; 23:15—16, 19—25;
24:1—4, 6, 10—18; 25:4, 13—16*

22 "You shall not see your brother's ox or his sheep go astray, and
withhold your help from them; you shall take them back to your
brother. [2] And if he is not near you, or if you do not know him, you
shall bring it home to your house, and it shall be with you until your
brother seeks it; then you shall restore it to him. [3] And so you shall
do with his ass; so you shall do with his garment; so you shall do
with any lost thing of your brother's, which he loses and you find;
you may not withhold your help. [4] You shall not see your brother's
ass or his ox fallen down by the way, and withhold your help from
them; you shall help him to lift them up again.

5 "A woman shall not wear anything that pertains to a man, nor
shall a man put on a woman's garment; for whoever does these
things is an abomination to the LORD your God.

6 "If you chance to come upon a bird's nest, in any tree or on the
ground, with young ones or eggs and the mother sitting upon the
young or upon the eggs, you shall not take the mother with the

young; [7] you shall let the mother go, but the young you may take to yourself; that it may go well with you, and that you may live long.

8 "When you build a new house, you shall make a parapet for your roof, that you may not bring the guilt of blood upon your house, if any one fall from it.

9 "You shall not sow your vineyard with two kinds of seed, lest the whole yield be forfeited to the sanctuary, the crop which you have sown and the yield of the vineyard. [10] You shall not plow with an ox and an ass together. [11] You shall not wear a mingled stuff, wool and linen together.

22 "If a man is found lying with the wife of another man, both of them shall die, the man who lay with the woman, and the woman; so you shall purge the evil from Israel.

28 "If a man meets a virgin who is not betrothed, and seizes her and lies with her, and they are found, [29] then the man who lay with her shall give to the father of the young woman fifty shekels of silver, and she shall be his wife, because he has violated her; he may not put her away all his days.

23 [15] "You shall not give up to his master a slave who has escaped from his master to you; [16] he shall dwell with you, in your midst, in the place which he shall choose within one of your towns, where it pleases him best; you shall not oppress him.

19 "You shall not lend upon interest to your brother, interest on money, interest on victuals, interest on anything that is lent for interest. [20] To a foreigner you may lend upon interest, but to your brother you shall not lend upon interest; that the LORD your God may bless you in all that you undertake in the land which you are entering to take possession of it.

21 "When you make a vow to the LORD your God, you shall not be slack to pay it; for the LORD your God will surely require it of you, and it would be sin in you. [22] But if you refrain from vowing, it shall be no sin in you. [23] You shall be careful to perform what has passed your lips, for you have voluntarily vowed to the LORD your God what you have promised with your mouth.

24 "When you go into your neighbor's vineyard, you may eat your fill of grapes, as many as you wish, but you shall not put any in your vessel. [25] When you go into your neighbor's standing grain, you may pluck the ears with your hand, but you shall not put a sickle to your neighbor's standing grain.

24 "When a man takes a wife and marries her, if then she finds no favor in his eyes because he has found some indecency in her, and he writes her a bill of divorce and puts it in her hand and sends her out of his house, and she departs out of his house, [2] and if she goes and

becomes another man's wife, ³and the latter husband dislikes her and writes her a bill of divorce and puts it in her hand and sends her out of his house, or if the latter husband dies, who took her to be his wife, ⁴then her former husband, who sent her away, may not take her again to be his wife, after she has been defiled.

6 "No man shall take a mill or an upper millstone in pledge; for he would be taking a life in pledge.

10 "When you make your neighbor a loan of any sort, you shall not go into his house to fetch his pledge. ¹¹You shall stand outside, and the man to whom you make the loan shall bring the pledge out to you. ¹²And if he is a poor man, you shall not sleep in his pledge; ¹³when the sun goes down, you shall restore to him the pledge that he may sleep in his cloak and bless you; and it shall be righteousness to you before the LORD your God.

14 "You shall not oppress a hired servant who is poor and needy, whether he is one of your brethren or one of the sojourners who are in your land within your towns; ¹⁵you shall give him his hire on the day he earns it, before the sun goes down (for he is poor, and sets his heart upon it); lest he cry against you to the LORD, and it be sin in you.

16 "The fathers shall not be put to death for the children, nor shall the children be put to death for the fathers; every man shall be put to death for his own sin.

17 "You shall not pervert the justice due to the sojourner or to the fatherless, or take a widow's garment in pledge; ¹⁸but you shall remember that you were a slave in Egypt and the LORD your God redeemed you from there; therefore I command you to do this.

25 ⁴"You shall not muzzle an ox when it treads out the grain.

13 "You shall not have in your bag two kinds of weights, a large and a small. ¹⁴You shall not have in your house two kinds of measures, a large and a small. ¹⁵A full and just weight you shall have, a full and just measure you shall have; that your days may be prolonged in the land which the LORD your God gives you. ¹⁶For all who do such things, all who act dishonestly, are an abomination to the LORD your God."

22:3 Compare the popular saying, "Finders keepers!" 22:5 This is an attack on heathen rites that had led to gross immoralities. 22:11 This prohibition is one of the laws for which the rabbis offer no explanation. Although it has become increasingly difficult in modern times, Orthodox Jews still observe this rule. 22:22 Compare single and double standards of sex morality. 23:15 Compare the history of the "Underground Railroad" in the United States. 23:21–23 This law underlies customs of requiring oaths for witnesses and officers, and the distinctions made by some people between what is said under oath and without it. **24:1** One school of rabbis (the school of Shammai) permitted divorce only in case of unchastity; the prevailing view accepted other grounds. All agreed that this law prevented a man from putting his wife away at will; the bill of divorce obligated him to pay alimony. **24:6** The millstone was required for making bread, the basic food. To take it away denied a man his life. **24:16** This law abrogated the shepherd code of Hammurabi where the family of a man might legally suffer punishment with him or in his stead. This is the first clear biblical assertion that each man is responsible for his own sinfulness. Cf. Exodus 20:5, 34:7. **25:4** Kindness to animals played such an important part in Jewish tradition that to this day Jews generally are disinterested in hunting. Not until the middle of the nineteenth century was legislation adopted in our civilization forbidding cruelty to animals.

The Rites of the First Fruit

Deuteronomy 26:1–13

26 "When you come into the land which the LORD your God gives you for an inheritance, and have taken possession of it, and live in it, [2] you shall take some of the first of all the fruit of the ground, which you harvest from your land that the LORD your God gives you, and you shall put it in a basket, and you shall go to the place which the LORD your God will choose, to make his name to dwell there. [3] And you shall go to the priest who is in office at that time, and say to him, 'I declare this day to the LORD your God that I have come into the land which the LORD swore to our fathers to give us.' [4] Then the priest shall take the basket from your hand, and set it down before the altar of the LORD your God.

5 "And you shall make response before the LORD your God, 'A wandering Aramean was my father; and he went down into Egypt and sojourned there, few in number; and there he became a nation, great, mighty, and populous. [6] And the Egyptians treated us harshly, and afflicted us, and laid upon us hard bondage. [7] Then we cried to the LORD the God of our fathers, and the LORD heard our voice, and saw our affliction, our toil, and our oppression; [8] and the LORD brought us out of Egypt with a mighty hand and an outstretched arm, with great terror, with signs and wonders; [9] and he brought us into this place and gave us this land, a land flowing with milk and honey. [10] And behold, now I bring the first of the fruit of the ground, which thou, O LORD, hast given me.' And you shall set it down before the LORD your God, and worship before the LORD your God; [11] and you shall rejoice in all the good which the LORD your God has given to you and to your house, you, and the Levite, and the sojourner who is among you.

12 "When you have finished paying all the tithe of your produce in the third year, which is the year of tithing, giving it to the Levite, the sojourner, the fatherless, and the widow, that they may eat within your town and be filled, [13] then you shall say before the LORD your God, 'I have removed the sacred portion out of my house, and moreover I have given it to the Levite, the sojourner, the fatherless, and the widow, according to all thy commandment which thou hast commanded me; I have not transgressed any of thy commandments, neither have I forgotten them.' "

26:12 See note on Deuteronomy 14:22.

Choose Life, Not Death
Deuteronomy 29:10–15, 29; 30:11–20

10 "You stand this day all of you before the LORD your God; the heads of your tribes, your elders, and your officers, all the men of Israel, [11] your little ones, your wives, and the sojourner who is in your camp, both he who hews your wood and he who draws your water, [12] that you may enter into the sworn covenant of the LORD your God, which the LORD your God makes with you this day; [13] that he may establish you this day as his people, and that he may be your God, as he promised you, and as he swore to your fathers, to Abraham, to Isaac, and to Jacob. [14] Nor is it with you only that I make this sworn covenant, [15] but with him who is not here with us this day as well as with him who stands here with us this day before the LORD our God. [29] The secret things belong to the LORD our God; but the things that are revealed belong to us and to our children for ever, that we may do all the words of this law.

30 [11] "For this commandment which I command you this day is not too hard for you, neither is it far off. [12] It is not in heaven, that you should say, 'Who will go up for us to heaven, and bring it to us, that we may hear it and do it?' [13] Neither is it beyond the sea, that you should say, 'Who will go over the sea for us, and bring it to us, that we may hear it and do it?' [14] But the word is very near you; it is in your mouth and in your heart, so that you can do it.

15 "See, I have set before you this day life and good, death and evil. [16] If you obey the commandments of the LORD God which I command you this day, by loving the LORD your God, by walking in his ways, and by keeping his commandments and his statutes and his ordinances, then you shall live and multiply, and the LORD your God will bless you in the land which you are entering to take possession of it. [17] But if your heart turns away, and you will not hear, but are drawn away to worship other gods and serve them, [18] I declare to you

this day, that you shall perish; you shall not live long in the land which you are going over the Jordan to enter and possess. [19] I call heaven and earth to witness against you this day, that I have set before you life and death, blessing and curse; therefore choose life, that you and your descendants may live, [20] loving the LORD your God, obeying his voice, and cleaving to him; for that means life to you and length of days, that you may dwell in the land which the LORD swore to your fathers, to Abraham, to Isaac, and to Jacob, to give them."

29:10 This passage is read in the synagogue as part of the scriptural lesson on the high holy days. **29:29** This is one of the fifteen passages in Hebrew Scriptures designated by special dotted markings to call attention to their homiletical significance and difficulty of interpretation. The concept expressed here is subject to many interpretations: e.g., that there are certain aspects of man's behavior, his inner life and his conscience, that are subject to God's discipline alone. Man is obliged to observe God's revealed law, and the secular court has authority only over man's public behavior. Freedom of conscience is here asserted, as well as limitation of civil authority. **30:19–20** Does man have free will, or is his behavior determined alone by environmental forces? Moses invites man to "choose," respecting man as made in the image of God.

The Last Days of Moses
Deuteronomy 31:1–3, 7–20; 34:1, 4–12

31 So Moses continued to speak these words to all Israel. [2] And he said to them, "I am a hundred and twenty years old this day; I am no longer able to go out and come in. The LORD has said to me, 'You shall not go over this Jordan.' [3] The LORD your God himself will go over before you; he will destroy these nations before you, so that you shall dispossess them; and Joshua will go over at your head, as the LORD has spoken."

7 Then Moses summoned Joshua, and said to him in the sight of all Israel, "Be strong and of good courage; for you shall go with this people into the land which the LORD has sworn to their fathers to give them; and you shall put them in possession of it. [8] It is the LORD who goes before you; he will be with you, he will not fail you or forsake you; do not fear or be dismayed."

9 And Moses wrote this law, and gave it to the priests the sons of Levi, who carried the ark of the covenant of the LORD, and to all the elders of Israel. [10] And Moses commanded them, "At the end of every seven years, at the set time of the year of release, at the feast of booths, [11] when all Israel comes to appear before the LORD your God at the place which he will choose, you shall read this law before all

Israel in their hearing. ¹²Assemble the people, men, women, and little ones, and the sojourner within your towns, that they may hear and learn to fear the LORD your God, and be careful to do all the words of this law, ¹³and that their children, who have not known it, may hear and learn to fear the LORD your God, as long as you live in the land which you are going over the Jordan to possess."

14 And the LORD said to Moses, "Behold, the days approach when you must die; call Joshua, and present yourselves in the tent of meeting, that I may commission him." And Moses and Joshua went and presented themselves in the tent of meeting. ¹⁵And the LORD appeared in the tent in a pillar of cloud; and the pillar of cloud stood by the door of the tent.

16 And the LORD said to Moses, "Behold, you are about to sleep with your fathers; then this people will rise and play the harlot after the strange gods of the land, where they go to be among them, and they will forsake me and break my covenant which I have made with them. ¹⁷Then my anger will be kindled against them in that day, and I will forsake them and hide my face from them, and they will be devoured; and many evils and troubles will come upon them, so that they will say in that day, 'Have not these evils come upon us because our God is not among us?' ¹⁸And I will surely hide my face in that day on account of all the evil which they have done, because they have turned to other gods. ¹⁹Now therefore write this song, and teach it to the people of Israel; put it in their mouths, that this song may be a witness for me against the people of Israel. ²⁰For when I have brought them into the land flowing with milk and honey, which I swore to give to their fathers, and they have eaten and are full and grown fat, they will turn to other gods and serve them, and despise me and break my covenant."

34 And Moses went up from the plains of Moab to Mount Nebo, to the top of Pisgah, which is opposite Jericho. And the LORD showed him all the land, Gilead as far as Dan.

4 And the LORD said to him, "This is the land of which I swore to Abraham, to Isaac, and to Jacob, 'I will give it to your descendants.' I have let you see it with your eyes, but you shall not go over there." ⁵So Moses the servant of the LORD died there in the land of Moab, according to the word of the LORD, ⁶and he buried him in the valley in the land of Moab opposite Beth-pe′or; but no man knows the place of his burial to this day. ⁷Moses was a hundred and twenty years old when he died; his eye was not dim, nor his natural force abated. ⁸And the people of Israel wept for Moses in the plains of Moab thirty days; then the days of weeping and mourning for Moses were ended.

9 And Joshua the son of Nun was full of the spirit of wisdom, for

Moses had laid his hands upon him; so the people of Israel obeyed him, and did as the LORD had commanded Moses. [10] And there has not arisen a prophet since in Israel like Moses, whom the LORD knew face to face, [11] none like him for all the signs and the wonders which the LORD sent him to do in the land of Egypt, to Pharaoh and to all his servants and to all his land, [12] and for all the mighty power and all the great and terrible deeds which Moses wrought in the sight of all Israel.

34:12 When the reading of any book of the Pentateuch is completed, it is the custom in the synagogue for all to exclaim, *Chazak, chazak, v'nitchazeyk,* "Be strong, be strong and let us strengthen one another." (Be strong, i.e., to observe the teachings in this book just completed.) On the Festival of "Simhath Torah," these last verses of the Torah are read and then immediately the reading is begun again at Genesis, to indicate a never-ending obligation to study the Word and to find in it wisdom and instruction, consolation and encouragement.

The Book of Joshua

The Book of Joshua continues the narrative begun in the Five Books of Moses. It recounts the conquest of Canaan, the land promised to Abraham (Genesis 13:14), Isaac (Genesis 25:3), Jacob (Genesis 28:13) and to the Hebrew nation (Exodus 6:8). The military engagement is understood by the author to be a sacred task. The Promised Land is now available to the Hebrews only because of the spiritual depravity of its inhabitants. By virtue of their immorality and idolatry the Canaanites have lost their right to the land. The agricultural peoples of Canaan worshiped the idol Baal and the goddess Asherah, before whom they engaged in magical rites, including mutilation of the body, human sacrifices and sexual orgies. In contrast, the Hebrews renew their covenant with God before entering the Promised Land. Their possession of the land obliges them to establish justice in society and to live by God's law.

Israel's collective history is seen as dependent on the individual's free-will acceptance of God and His Law. When one man sins, as in the account of Achan (7:11 ff.) the entire people suffer. Finally Joshua reminds the people at the end of his career: their own survival in the land will be determined by their spiritual worthiness and their faithfulness to God.

In Hebraic tradition, the book is the first of a series designated "The Former Prophets" (including the book of Judges, the two books of Samuel and the two books of Kings). Its designation as prophecy underscores the fact that events in history are presented in the Bible to illuminate spiritual truths rather than to record the chronological sequence of occurrences.

Joshua has already appeared in heroic proportions in earlier biblical books (cf. Exodus 17:9 ff.; Exodus 24:13; Numbers 27:18, 22). Chapters 1–12 describe the conquest of Canaan; chapters 23 and 24 contain Joshua's farewell to his people; the remaining section consists of geographical notes regarding the distribution of the land among the tribes.

The dating of the events in the book of Joshua is difficult, possibly because there seem to have been several invasions of Canaan in the period 1440–1200 B.C. The book may thus be a compilation of various invasion tales—personified in the leadership given by Joshua.

In ancient ruins called Tel el-Amarna, about two hundred miles south of Cairo, an Egyptian woman uncovered a cache of about 300 clay tablets written in cuneiform. When these were finally translated, scholars found them to be reports from the Canaanites who were then under Egyptian control. Written to the Pharaohs Amenhotep III (1412–1375 B.C.) and Amenhotep IV (1375–1366 B.C.), these letters refer constantly to an invading people called Habiru who were attempting to wrest control of the land from the inhabitant Canaanites.

Christian scholars observe that Joshua and Jesus both carry names in the Hebrew that mean "savior." For the Church Fathers, Joshua was a foreshadowing of Jesus (cf. 1 Corinthians 10:1): "Both led their followers through the waters (one the Jordan, the other of Baptism) to a Promised Land; while the conquest and the division of the territory are an image of the progressive expansion of the Church" (*Jerusalem Bible*, p. 269).

Joshua Commands the People
Joshua 1:1–11; 3:7–13; 4:1–7

1 After the death of Moses the servant of the LORD, the LORD said to Joshua the son of Nun, Moses' minister, ²"Moses my servant is dead; now therefore arise, go over this Jordan, you and all this people, into the land which I am giving to them, to the people of Israel. ³Every place that the sole of your foot will tread upon I have given to you, as I promised to Moses. ⁴From the wilderness and this Lebanon as far as the great river, the river Eu-phra′tes, all the land of the Hittites to the Great Sea toward the going down of the sun shall be your territory. ⁵No man shall be able to stand before you all the days of your life; as I was with Moses, so I will be with you; I will not fail you or forsake you. ⁶Be strong and of good courage; for you shall cause this people to inherit the land which I swore to their fathers to give them. ⁷Only be strong and very courageous, being careful to do according to all the law which Moses my servant commanded you; turn not from it to the right hand or to the left, that you may have good success wherever you go. ⁸This book of the law shall not depart out of your mouth, but you shall meditate on it day and night, that you may be careful to do according to all that is written in it; for then you shall make your way prosperous, and then you shall have good success. ⁹Have I not commanded you? Be strong and of good courage; be not frightened, neither be dismayed; for the LORD your God is with you wherever you go."

10 Then Joshua commanded the officers of the people, ¹¹"Pass through the camp, and command the people, 'Prepare your provisions; for within three days you are to pass over this Jordan, to go in to take possession of the land which the LORD your God gives you to possess.'"

3 ⁷And the LORD said to Joshua, "This day I will begin to exalt you in the sight of all Israel, that they may know that, as I was with Moses, so I will be with you. ⁸And you shall command the priests who bear the ark of the covenant, 'When you come to the brink of the waters of the Jordan, you shall stand still in the Jordan.' " ⁹And Joshua said to the people of Israel, "Come hither, and hear the words of the LORD your God." ¹⁰And Joshua said, "Hereby you shall know that the living God is among you, and that he will without fail drive out from before you the Canaanites, the Hittites, the Hivites, the Per'iz-zites, the Gir'gashites, the Amorites, and the Jeb'usites. ¹¹Behold, the ark of the covenant of the Lord of all the earth is to pass over before you into the Jordan. ¹²Now therefore take twelve men from the tribes of Israel, from each tribe a man. ¹³And when the soles of the feet of the priests who bear the ark of the LORD, the Lord of all the earth, shall rest in the waters of the Jordan, the waters of the Jordan shall be stopped from flowing, and the waters coming down from above shall stand in one heap."

4 When all the nation had finished passing over the Jordan, the LORD said to Joshua, ²"Take twelve men from the people, from each tribe a man, ³and command them. 'Take twelve stones from here out of the midst of the Jordan, from the very place where the priests' feet stood, and carry them over with you, and lay them down in the place where you lodge tonight.' " ⁴Then Joshua called the twelve men from the people of Israel, whom he had appointed, a man from each tribe; ⁵and Joshua said to them, "Pass on before the ark of the LORD your God into the midst of the Jordan, and take up each of you a stone upon his shoulder, according to the number of the tribes of the people of Israel, ⁶that this may be a sign among you, when your children ask in time to come, 'What do those stones mean to you?' ⁷Then you shall tell them that the waters of the Jordan were cut off before the ark of the covenant of the LORD; when it passed over the Jordan, the waters of the Jordan were cut off. So these stones shall be to the people of Israel a memorial for ever."

1:4 An empire of such extent, including Palestine, Transjordan and Syria, was achieved not in Joshua's days but for a brief period in the tenth century during the reigns of King David and Solomon. This fact suggests to some scholars that the book of Joshua was edited in that monarchial period. **3:7** Bible scholars observe that the account of Joshua's entrance into Canaan parallels in many ways the exodus of the Hebrews from Egypt under Moses' leadership: God stays the Jordan waters (3:7–4:18) just as he dried up the Sea of Reeds (Exodus 14:5–31); the Ark of God leads the Israelites (3:6–17) just as they had been earlier led by the pillar of cloud or fire (Exodus 13:21–22); the Passover is observed (5:10) just as it had been celebrated in Egypt before the first Exodus (Exodus 12:1–28). **3:10** The most numerous of these peoples were the Canaanites from whom the land at first received its name. The Jebusites lived within the walled city of Jerusalem. The Ammonites were confronted by the Hebrews at the southern tip of the Jordan Valley (Numbers 21:12–30). The Canaanites, Jebusites and Ammonites were Semitic peoples, as were the Hebrews. The Hittites were a non-Semitic people who had ruled Asia-Minor between 1900–1200 B.C. The Hivites are identified by the scholars with the Hurrians—enemies of the Hittites. It is not known for certain who the Perizzites and Girgashites were. (See Appendix.)

Joshua Takes Jericho

Joshua 5:1–5, 8, 10–15; 6:1–7, 11, 14–16, 20–21, 27

5 When all the kings of the Amorites that were beyond the Jordan to the west, and all the kings of the Canaanites that were by the sea, heard that the LORD had dried up the waters of the Jordan for the people of Israel until they had crossed over, their heart melted, and there was no longer any spirit in them, because of the people of Israel.

2 At that time the LORD said to Joshua, "Make flint knives and circumcise the people of Israel again the second time." ³ So Joshua made flint knives, and circumcised the people of Israel at Gibeath-haaraloth. ⁴ And this is the reason why Joshua circumcised them: all the males of the people who came out of Egypt, all the men of war, had died on the way in the wilderness after they had come out of Egypt. ⁵ Though all the people who came out had been circumcised, yet all the people that were born on the way in the wilderness after they had come out of Egypt, had not been circumcised.

8 When the circumcising of all the nation was done, they remained in their places in the camp till they were healed.

10 While the people of Israel were encamped in Gilgal they kept the passover on the fourteenth day of the month at evening in the plains of Jericho. ¹¹ And on the morrow after the passover, on that very day, they ate of the produce of the land, unleavened cakes and parched grain. ¹² And the manna ceased on the morrow, when they ate of the produce of the land; and the people of Israel had manna no more, but ate of the fruit of the land of Canaan that year.

13 When Joshua was by Jericho, he lifted up his eyes and looked, and behold, a man stood before him with his drawn sword in his hand; and Joshua went to him and said to him, "Are you for us, or for our adversaries?" ¹⁴ And he said, "No; but as commander of the army of the LORD I have now come." And Joshua fell on his face to the earth, and worshiped, and said to him, "What does my lord bid his servant?" ¹⁵ And the commander of the LORD'S army said to Joshua, "Put off your shoes from your feet; for the place where you stand is holy." And Joshua did so.

6 Now Jericho was shut up from within and from without because of the people of Israel; none went out, and none came in. ²And the LORD said to Joshua, "See, I have given into your hand Jericho, with its king and mighty men of valor. ³You shall march around the city, all the men of war going around the city once. Thus shall you do for six days. ⁴And seven priests shall bear seven trumpets of rams' horns before the ark; and on the seventh day you shall march around the city seven times, the priests blowing the trumpets. ⁵And when they make a long blast with the ram's horn, as soon as you hear the sound of the trumpet, then all the people shall shout with a great shout; and the wall of the city will fall down flat, and the people shall go up every man straight before him." ⁶So Joshua the son of Nun called the priests and said to them, "Take up the ark of the covenant, and let seven priests bear seven trumpets of rams' horns before the ark of the LORD." ⁷And he said to the people, "Go forward; march around the city, and let the armed men pass on before the ark of the LORD."

11 So he caused the ark of the LORD to compass the city, going about it once; and they came into the camp, and spent the night in the camp.

14 And the second day they marched around the city once, and returned into the camp. So they did for six days.

15 On the seventh day they rose early at the dawn of day, and marched around the city in the same manner seven times: it was only on that day that they marched around the city seven times. ¹⁶And at the seventh time, when the priests had blown the trumpets, Joshua said to the people, "Shout; for the LORD has given you the city."

20 So the people shouted, and the trumpets were blown. As soon as the people heard the sound of the trumpet, the people raised a great shout, and the wall fell down flat, so that the people went up into the city, every man straight before him, and they took the city. ²¹Then they utterly destroyed all in the city, both men and women, young and old, oxen, sheep, and asses, with the edge of the sword.

27 So the LORD was with Joshua; and his fame was in all the land.

5:2 The rite of circumcision symbolized the renewal of the covenant between the Hebrew people and God. **5:3** *Gibeath-haaraloth* means "the hill of the foreskins." **5:10** Because of this reference to an observance of Passover, Joshua 5:2–6:1, 27 has been selected for reading as the prophetic lesson in the Synagogue on the first day of Passover. **5:13** The account of Joshua's meeting with the "Commander of the army of the Lord" demonstrates the holiness of this mission and the sanctity of the land. It recalls also Moses' encounter with God at the burning bush. **6:1** ff. Jericho has been uncovered and researched by many teams of archaeologists over the years. It is believed to be the oldest known city in the world, dating back at least to 8,000 B.C.

Israel is Defeated at Ai

Through the defeat at Ai, the important Hebraic concept of man's collective responsibility found a dramatic demonstration.

Joshua 7:1–5, 10–12, 14–26; 8:1–2, 30–35

7 But the people of Israel broke faith in regard to the devoted things; for Achan the son of Carmi, son of Zabdi, son of Zerah, of the tribe of Judah, took some of the devoted things; and the anger of the LORD burned against the people of Israel.

2 Joshua sent men from Jericho to Ai, which is near Bethaven, east of Bethel, and said to them, "Go up and spy out the land." And the men went up and spied out Ai. ³And they returned to Joshua, and said to him, "Let not all the people go up, but let about two or three thousand men go up and attack Ai; do not make the whole people toil up there, for they are but few." ⁴So about three thousand went up there from the people; and they fled before the men of Ai, ⁵and the men of Ai killed about thirty-six men of them, and chased them before the gate as far as Sheb'arim, and slew them at the descent. And the hearts of the people melted, and became as water.

10 The LORD said to Joshua, "Arise, why have you thus fallen upon your face? ¹¹Israel has sinned; they have transgressed my covenant which I commanded them; they have taken some of the devoted things; they have stolen, and lied, and put them among their own stuff. ¹²Therefore the people of Israel cannot stand before their enemies; they turn their backs before their enemies, because they have become a thing for destruction. I will be with you no more, unless you destroy the devoted things from among you.

14 "In the morning therefore you shall be brought near by your tribes; and the tribe which the LORD takes shall come near by families; and the family which the LORD takes shall come near by households; and the household which the LORD takes shall come near man by man. ¹⁵And he who is taken with the devoted things shall be burned with fire, he and all that he has, because he has transgressed the covenant of the LORD, and because he has done a shameful thing in Israel."

16 So Joshua rose early in the morning, and brought Israel near tribe by tribe, and the tribe of Judah was taken; ¹⁷and he brought near the families of Judah, and the family of the Zer'ahites was taken; and he brought near the family of the Zer'ahites man by man, and Zabdi was taken; ¹⁸and he brought near his household man by man, and Achan the son of Carmi, son of Zabdi, son of Zerah, of the

tribe of Judah, was taken. [19] Then Joshua said to Achan, "My son, give glory to the LORD God of Israel, and render praise to him; and tell me now what you have done; do not hide it from me." [20] And Achan answered Joshua, "Of a truth I have sinned against the LORD God of Israel, and this is what I did: [21] when I saw among the spoil a beautiful mantle from Shinar, and two hundred shekels of silver, and a bar of gold weighing fifty shekels, then I coveted them, and took them; and behold, they are hidden in the earth inside my tent, with the silver underneath."

22 So Joshua sent messengers, and they ran to the tent; and behold, it was hidden in his tent with the silver underneath. [23] And they took them out of the tent and brought them to Joshua and all the people of Israel; and they laid them down before the LORD. [24] And Joshua and all Israel with him took Achan the son of Zerah, and the silver and the mantle and the bar of gold, and his sons and daughters, and his oxen and asses and sheep, and his tent, and all that he had; and they brought them up to the Valley of Achor. [25] And Joshua said, "Why did you bring trouble on us? The LORD brings trouble on you today." And all Israel stoned him with stones; they burned them with fire, and stoned them with stones. [26] And they raised over him a great heap of stones that remains to this day; then the LORD turned from his burning anger. Therefore to this day the name of that place is called the Valley of Achor.

8 And the LORD said to Joshua, "Do not fear or be dismayed; take all the fighting men with you, and arise, go up to Ai; see, I have given into your hand the king of Ai, and his people, his city, and his land; [2] and you shall do to Ai and its king as you did to Jericho and its king; only its spoil and its cattle you shall take as booty for yourselves; lay an ambush against the city, behind it."

30 Then Joshua built an altar in Mount Ebal to the LORD, the God of Israel, [31] as Moses the servant of the LORD had commanded the people of Israel, as it is written in the book of the law of Moses, "an altar of unhewn stones, upon which no man has lifted an iron tool"; and they offered on it burnt offerings to the LORD, and sacrificed peace offerings. [32] And there, in the presence of the people of Israel, he wrote upon the stones a copy of the law of Moses, which he had written. [33] And all Israel, sojourner as well as homeborn, with their elders and officers and their judges, stood on opposite sides of the ark before the Levitical priests who carried the ark of the covenant of the LORD, half of them in front of Mount Ger'izim and half of them in front of Mount Ebal, as Moses the servant of the LORD had commanded at the first, that they should bless the people of Israel. [34] And afterward he read all the words of the law, the blessing and the curse, according to all

that is written in the book of the law. [35] There was not a word of all that Moses commanded which Joshua did not read before all the assembly of Israel, and the women, and the little ones, and the sojourners who lived among them.

7:26 *Achor* means "trouble." **8:2** Archaeologists, puzzled by the fact that Ai had been destroyed many centuries earlier, suggest that the city here described may have been Beth-El which is less than two miles to the west of Ai. In 1934 Professor W. F. Albright excavated Bethel and disclosed it to have been ruined in the thirteenth century B.C. by violence such as the Scripture describes in this account.

The Gibeonites Become Hewers of Wood and Drawers of Water
Joshua 9: 3–6, 15–17, 22, 24–27

3 But when the inhabitants of Gibeon heard what Joshua had done to Jericho and to Ai, [4] they on their part acted with cunning, and went and made ready provisions, and took worn-out sacks upon their asses, and wineskins, worn-out and torn and mended, [5] with worn-out, patched sandals on their feet, and worn-out clothes; and all their provisions were dry and moldy. [6] And they went to Joshua in the camp at Gilgal, and said to him and to the men of Israel, "We have come from a far country; so now make a covenant with us."

15 And Joshua made peace with them, and made a covenant with them, to let them live; and the leaders of the congregation swore to them.

16 At the end of three days after they had made a covenant with them, they heard that they were their neighbors, and that they dwelt among them. [17] And the people of Israel set out and reached their cities on the third day. Now their cities were Gibeon, Chephi′rah, Be-er′oth, and Kir′iath-je′arim.

22 Joshua summoned them, and he said to them, "Why did you deceive us, saying, 'We are very far from you,' when you dwell among us?"

24 They answered Joshua, "Because it was told to your servants for a certainty that the LORD your God had commanded his servant Moses to give you all the land, and to destroy all the inhabitants of the land from before you; so we feared greatly for our lives because of you, and did this thing. [25] And now, behold, we are in your hand: do as it seems good and right in your sight to do to us." [26] So he did to them, and delivered them out of the hand of the people of Israel; and they did not kill them. [27] But Joshua made them that day hewers of wood and drawers of water for the congregation and for the altar

of the LORD, to continue to this day, in the place which he should choose.

9:27 The equivalent of slave labor, cf. Deuteronomy 29:10.

The Sun Stands Still: Israelites Win a Victory

Chapters 10 and 11 are considered by many Bible scholars to be a summary statement of the extended conquest—as personalized in the figure of Joshua. Many scholars believe Joshua to have been the commander of the Joseph tribes in the South. So brilliant were his feats, however, that later historians, in writing a unified history of the conquest of the land, felt free to place Joshua in charge of the nationwide effort. Thus contemporary Bible scholars suggest that this book was written not by Joshua but contains evidences of a process of historical writing found also in the Pentateuch (see Appendix, page 943), and this history is based on records maintained in the traditions of the various Israelite tribes (cf. 10:14).

Joshua 10:5–14, 20–21

5 Then the five kings of the Amorites, the king of Jerusalem, the king of Hebron, the king of Jarmuth, the king of Lachish, and the king of Eglon, gathered their forces, and went up with all their armies and encamped against Gibeon, and made war against it.

6 And the men of Gibeon sent to Joshua at the camp in Gilgal, saying, "Do not relax your hand from your servants; come up to us quickly, and save us, and help us; for all the kings of the Amorites that dwell in the hill country are gathered against us." ⁷ So Joshua went up from Gilgal, he and all the people of war with him, and all the mighty men of valor. ⁸ And the LORD said to Joshua, "Do not fear them, for I have given them into your hands; there shall not a man of them stand before you." ⁹ So Joshua came upon them suddenly, having marched up all night from Gilgal. ¹⁰ And the LORD threw them into a panic before Israel, who slew them with a great slaughter at Gibeon, and chased them by the way of the ascent of Beth-horon, and smote them as far as Aze'kah and Makkedah. ¹¹ And as they fled before Israel, while they were going down the ascent of Beth-horon, the LORD threw down great stones from heaven upon them as far as Aze'kah, and they died; there were more who died because of the hailstones than the men of Israel killed with the sword.

12 Then spoke Joshua to the LORD in the day when the LORD gave the Amorites over to the men of Israel; and he said in the sight of Israel,

  "Sun, stand thou still at Gibeon,
   and thou Moon in the valley of Ai'jalon."

¹³ And the sun stood still, and the moon stayed,
    until the nation took vengeance on their enemies.
Is this not written in the Book of Jashar? The sun stayed in the midst
of heaven, and did not hasten to go down for about a whole day.
¹⁴ There has been no day like it before or since, when the LORD
hearkened to the voice of a man; for the LORD fought for Israel.

20 When Joshua and the men of Israel had finished slaying them
with a very great slaughter, until they were wiped out, and when the
remnant which remained of them had entered into the fortified
cities, ²¹ all the people returned safe to Joshua in the camp at
Makke′dah; not a man moved his tongue against any of the people of
Israel.

> **10:14** This passage discloses the fact that there were other
> historical records dealing with the life of the Hebrews that have not
> become part of Scripture, and which are now lost to us. Compare 2
> Samuel 1:18 and Numbers 21:14.

The Land Is Conquered and Divided
*Joshua 11:1–9, 15–23; 13:1–8, 14; 17:14–18; 18:1; 19:49–51;
20:1–6*

11 When Jabin king of Hazor heard of this, he sent to Jobab king
of Madon, and to the king of Shimron, and to the king of
Ach′shaph, ² and to the kings who were in the northern hill
country, and in the Arabah south of Chin′neroth, and in the
lowland, and in Naphoth-dor on the west, ³ to the Canaanites in
the east and the west, the Amorites, the Hittites, the Per′izzites,
and the Jeb′usites in the hill country, and the Hivites under
Hermon in the land of Mizpah. ⁴ And they came out, with all
their troops, a great host, in number like the sand that is upon
the seashore, with very many horses and chariots. ⁵ And all these
kings joined their forces, and came and encamped together at the
waters of Merom, to fight with Israel.

6 And the LORD said to Joshua, "Do not be afraid of them, for
tomorrow at this time I will give over all of them, slain, to Israel; you
shall hamstring their horses, and burn their chariots with fire." ⁷ So
Joshua came suddenly upon them with all his people of war, by the
waters of Merom, and fell upon them. ⁸ And the LORD gave them into
the hand of Israel, who smote them and chased them as far as Great
Sidon and Mis′rephothma′im, and eastward as far as the valley of
Mizpeh; and they smote them, until they left none remaining. ⁹ And
Joshua did to them as the LORD bade him; he hamstrung their
horses, and burned their chariots with fire.

15 As the LORD had commanded Moses his servant, so Moses

commanded Joshua, and so Joshua did; he left nothing undone of all that the LORD had commanded Moses.

16 So Joshua took all that land, the hill country and all the Negeb and all the land of Goshen and the lowland and the Arabah and the hill country of Israel and its lowland [17] from Mount Halak, that rises toward Se'ir, as far as Ba'al-gad in the valley of Lebanon below Mount Hermon. And he took all their kings, and smote them, and put them to death. [18] Joshua made war a long time with all those kings. [19] There was not a city that made peace with the people of Israel, except the Hivites, the inhabitants of Gibeon; they took all in battle. [20] For it was the LORD'S doing to harden their hearts that they should come against Israel in battle, in order that they should be utterly destroyed, and should receive no mercy but be exterminated, as the LORD commanded Moses.

21 And Joshua came at that time, and wiped out the Anakim from the hill country, from Hebron, from Debir, from Anab, and from all the hill country of Judah, and from all the hill country of Israel; Joshua utterly destroyed them with their cities. [22] There was none of the Anakim left in the land of the people of Israel; only in Gaza, in Gath, and in Ashdod, did some remain. [23] So Joshua took the whole land, according to all that the LORD had spoken to Moses; and Joshua gave it for an inheritance to Israel according to their tribal allotments. And the land had rest from war.

13 Now Joshua was old and advanced in years; and the LORD said to him, "You are old and advanced in years, and there remains yet very much land to be possessed. [2] This is the land that yet remains: all the regions of the Philistines, and all those of the Gesh'urites [3] (from the Shihor, which is east of Egypt, northward to the boundary of Ekron, it is reckoned as Canaanite; there are five rulers of the Philistines, those of Gaza, Ashdod, Ash'kelon, Gath, and Ekron), and those of the Avvim, [4] in the south, all the land of the Canaanites, and Me-ar'ah which belongs to the Sido'nians, to Aphek, to the boundary of the Amorites, [5] and the land of the Geb'alites, and all Lebanon, toward the sunrising, from Ba'algad below Mount Hermon to the entrance of Hamath, [6] all the inhabitants of the hill country from Lebanon to Mis'rephothma'im, even all the Sido'nians. I will myself drive them out from before the people of Israel; only allot the land to Israel for an inheritance, as I have commanded you. [7] Now therefore divide this land for an inheritance to the nine tribes and half the tribe of Manas'seh."

8 With the other half of the tribe of Manas'seh the Reubenites and the Gadites received their inheritance, which Moses gave them, beyond the Jordan eastward, as Moses the servant of the LORD gave them:

14 To the tribe of Levi alone Moses gave no inheritance; the
offerings by fire to the LORD God of Israel are their inheritance, as
he said to him.

17 ¹⁴ And the tribe of Joseph spoke to Joshua, saying, "Why have
you given me but one lot and one portion as an inheritance,
although I am a numerous people, since hitherto the LORD has
blessed me?" ¹⁵ And Joshua said to them, "If you are a numerous
people, go up to the forest, and there clear ground for yourselves
in the land of the Per'izzites and the Reph'aim, since the hill country
of E'phraim is too narrow for you." ¹⁶ The tribe of Joseph said, "The
hill country is not enough for us; yet all the Canaanites who dwell in
the plain have chariots of iron, both those in Beth-she'an and its
villages and those in the Valley of Jezreel." ¹⁷ Then Joshua said to
the house of Joseph, to E'phraim and Manas'seh, "You are a
numerous people, and have great power; you shall not have one lot
only, ¹⁸ but the hill country shall be yours, for though it is a forest,
you shall clear it and possess it to its farthest borders; for you shall
drive out the Canaanites, though they have chariots of iron, and
though they are strong."

18 Then the whole congregation of the people of Israel assembled at
Shiloh, and set up the tent of meeting there; the land lay subdued
before them.

19 ⁴⁹ When they had finished distributing the several territories of
the land as inheritances, the people of Israel gave an inheritance
among them to Joshua the son of Nun. ⁵⁰ By command of the LORD
they gave him the city which he asked, Tim'nath-se'rah in the hill
country of E'phraim; and he rebuilt the city, and settled in it.

51 These are the inheritances which Elea'zar the priest and Joshua
the son of Nun and the heads of the fathers' houses of the tribes of
the people of Israel distributed by lot at Shiloh before the LORD, at
the door of the tent of meeting. So they finished dividing the land.

20 Then the LORD said to Joshua, ² "Say to the people of Israel,
'Appoint the cities of refuge, of which I spoke to you through Moses,
³ that the manslayer who kills any person without intent or unwittingly may flee there; they shall be for you a refuge from the
avenger of blood. ⁴ He shall flee to one of these cities and shall stand
at the entrance of the gate of the city, and explain his case to the
elders of that city; then they shall take him into the city, and give
him a place, and he shall remain with them. ⁵ And if the avenger of
blood pursues him, they shall not give up the slayer into his hand;
because he killed his neighbor unwittingly, having had no enmity
against him in times past. ⁶ And he shall remain in that city until he
has stood before the congregation for judgment, until the death of

him who is high priest at the time: then the slayer may go again to his own town and his own home, to the town from which he fled.' "

11:23 This verse exaggerates the extent of Joshua's conquests as seen by the more accurate description in 13:1–7.

Joshua Makes a Covenant with the People
Joshua 23:1–3, 14–16; 24:16–26, 29–30

23 A long time afterward, when the LORD had given rest to Israel from all their enemies round about, and Joshua was old and well advanced in years, ² Joshua summoned all Israel, their elders and heads, their judges and officers, and said to them, "I am now old and well advanced in years; ³ and you have seen all that the LORD your God has done to all these nations for your sake, for it is the LORD your God who has fought for you.

14 "And now I am about to go the way of all the earth, and you know in your hearts and souls, all of you, that not one thing has failed of all the good things which the LORD your God promised concerning you; all have come to pass for you, not one of them has failed. ¹⁵ But just as all the good things which the LORD your God promised concerning you have been fulfilled for you, so the LORD will bring upon you all the evil things, until he have destroyed you from off this good land which the LORD your God has given you, ¹⁶ if you transgress the covenant of the LORD your God, which he commanded you, and go and serve other gods and bow down to them. Then the anger of the LORD will be kindled against you, and you shall perish quickly from off the good land which he has given to you."

24 ¹⁶ Then the people answered, "Far be it from us that we should forsake the LORD, to serve other gods; ¹⁷ for it is the LORD our God who brought us and our fathers up from the land of Egypt, out of the house of bondage, and who did those great signs in our sight, and preserved us in all the way that we went, and among all the peoples through whom we passed; ¹⁸ and the LORD drove out before us all the peoples, the Amorites who lived in the land; therefore we also will serve the LORD, for he is our God."

19 But Joshua said to the people, "You cannot serve the LORD; for he is a holy God; he is a jealous God; he will not forgive your transgressions or your sins. ²⁰ If you forsake the LORD and serve foreign gods, then he will turn and do you harm, and consume you, after having done you good." ²¹ And the people said to Joshua, "Nay; but we will serve the LORD." ²² Then Joshua said to the people, "You are witnesses against yourselves that you have chosen

the LORD, to serve him." And they said, "We are witnesses." [23]He
said, "Then put away the foreign gods which are among you, and
incline your heart to the LORD, the God of Israel." [24]And the people
said to Joshua, "The LORD our God we will serve, and his voice we
will obey." [25]So Joshua made a covenant with the people that day,
and made statutes and ordinances for them at Shechem. [26]And
Joshua wrote these words in the book of the law of God; and he took
a great stone, and set it up there under the oak in the sanctuary of
the LORD.

29 After these things Joshua the son of Nun, the servant of the
LORD, died, being a hundred and ten years old. [30]And they buried
him in his own inheritance at Tim'nath-se'rah, which is in the hill
country of E'phraim, north of the mountain of Ga'ash.

23:1 ff. It is in the style of several biblical books to include such a
statement of final testimony. The author thereby summarizes his
life's teachings; he emphasizes the significance and purpose of the
book itself. (Cf. the last discourse of Moses, Deuteronomy 31; the
farewell of Samuel, 1 Samuel 12; David's testament, 1 Kings
2:1–9.) This speech is a kind of Hexateuch in miniature. **24:25** For
similar ceremonies see Genesis 28:18, Exodus 24:4 and Joshua 4:3.
Shechem. The Tel el-Amarna letters written by the Canaanites to
their overlords about the fifteenth century B.C. (at least a century
before the Exodus) mention that the city of Shechem had been
captured by the "Habiru." It has been suggested that the inhabitants
of Shechem are those Hebrews who came into Palestine with the
Patriarchs and who never went to Egypt, or those who left Egypt
earlier than Moses. By this ceremony Joshua brings them into the
covenant with Yahweh (YHWH) made by Moses; thus gradually the
Semitic tribes are joined into one people sharing together the
memory of a common history.

The Book of Judges

This book continues the account of Israel's growth into nationhood after the death of Joshua. Its title in the Hebrew, *Shofetim*, refers to "Judges" who ruled over the Hebrew people in those days and who, in times of emergency, defended them against their enemies.

Much of the writing in Judges reflects an immediacy of a contemporaneous account, although many scholars believe that it was written or edited at a later date. Judges brings the various tribal accounts together into one integrated text. Like other biblical books, it communicates a religious purpose in the historical writing. The authors describe the efforts of the Hebrews to consolidate the conquests made under Joshua, to defend themselves from continuous attack, to extend their gains. The book shows the transition of a nomadic people to a settled life of agriculture. It also reflects the conflict between individual tribal loyalties and the requirements of the nation at large—all as backdrop for this test: Will Israel remain firm in devotion to the God of Abraham, Isaac and Jacob, to the God who led them from slavery out of Egypt and was revealed at Sinai? Or will the Hebrew people succumb to idol worship? Will the Hebrews remain a separate people for God or lose themselves in the licentious ways of the Canaanites? Can the Hebrew tribes defend their freedom separately, or must they join together and appoint one king to rule over a united nation?

Of the twelve Judges in the book, representatives are selected.

A period of some 410 years is covered, if the dating in this book be regarded as consecutive. Most scholars suggest, however, that many of these accounts overlap each other in time, and rounded numbers may be approximate rather than exact, to give a 300-year period from about 1300 to 1000 B.C. According to the text, not all the judges lived exemplary lives. Even so the impact of their rule was to direct the hearts of people to the worship of God. The judges strengthened Hebrew resistance to idolatrous ways, and it is for this reason that their deeds were remembered and recorded.

The Lord Raised Up Judges
Judges 2:6–7, 10–16, 18–23

2 ⁶ When Joshua dismissed the people, the people of Israel went each to his inheritance to take possession of the land. ⁷ And the people served the LORD all the days of Joshua, and all the days of the elders who outlived Joshua, who had seen all the great work which the LORD had done for Israel.

10 And all that generation also were gathered to their fathers; and

there arose another generation after them, who did not know the LORD or the work which he had done for Israel.

11 And the people of Israel did what was evil in the sight of the LORD and served the Ba'als; ¹²and they forsook the LORD, the God of their fathers, who had brought them out of the land of Egypt; they went after other gods, from among the gods of the peoples who were round about them, and bowed down to them; and they provoked the LORD to anger. ¹³They forsook the LORD, and served the Ba'als and the Ash'taroth. ¹⁴So the anger of the LORD was kindled against Israel, and he gave them over to plunderers, who plundered them; and he sold them into the power of their enemies round about, so that they could no longer withstand their enemies. ¹⁵Whenever they marched out, the hand of the LORD was against them for evil, as the LORD had warned, and as the LORD had sworn to them; and they were in sore straits.

16 Then the LORD raised up judges, who saved them out of the power of those who plundered them.

18 Whenever the LORD raised up judges for them, the LORD was with the judge, and he saved them from the hand of their enemies all the days of the judge; for the LORD was moved to pity by their groaning because of those who afflicted and oppressed them. ¹⁹But whenever the judge died, they turned back and behaved worse than their fathers, going after other gods, serving them and bowing down to them; they did not drop any of their practices or their stubborn ways. ²⁰So the anger of the LORD was kindled against Israel; and he said, "Because this people have transgressed my covenant which I commanded their fathers, and have not obeyed my voice, ²¹I will not henceforth drive out before them any of the nations that Joshua left when he died, ²²that by them I may test Israel, whether they will take care to walk in the way of the LORD as their fathers did, or not." ²³So the LORD left those nations, not driving them out at once, and he did not give them into the power of Joshua.

2:10 *another generation:* demonstrates the difficulty in passing on a religious heritage. **2:11** Baals (in Hebrew *Baalim,* "nature gods"): the worship of Baal generally included human sacrifice and other immoralities such as ritual prostitution. **2:14** These sentences express the writer's view that sin was the cause of the nation's defeat and discomfort (see also Joshua 7:12, Leviticus 26:36 f., Numbers 14:42 ff.). **2:22–3** The author provides here a religious significance for Joshua's failure to drive out the former inhabitants. Scripture offers other explanations in addition: to provide Israel experience in warfare (Judges 3:2); to keep the land from desolation until Israel's numbers were sufficient (Exodus 23:29); and that the Hebrews could not drive them out because of their "walled cities" and "chariots of iron" (Judges 1:19).

The Song of Deborah

Language studies suggest that this may be the oldest poem preserved in the Bible.

Judges 5:1, 3, 6–9, 12–31

5 Then sang Deb'orah and Barak the son of Abin'o-am on that day:
> ³ "Hear, O kings; give ear, O princes;
>   to the LORD I will sing,
>   I will make melody to the LORD, the God of Israel.
>
> ⁶ "In the days of Shamgar, son of Anath,
>   in the day of Ja'el, caravans ceased
>   and travelers kept to the byways.
> ⁷ The peasantry ceased in Israel, they ceased
>   until you arose, Deb'orah,
>   arose as a mother in Israel.
> ⁸ When new gods were chosen,
>   then war was in the gates.
>   Was shield or spear to be seen
>   among forty thousand in Israel?
> ⁹ My heart goes out to the commanders of Israel
>   who offered themselves willingly among the people.
>   Bless the LORD.
>
> ¹² "Awake, awake, Deb'orah!
>   Awake, awake, utter a song!
>   Arise, Barak, lead away our captives,
>   O son of Abin'o-am.
> ¹³ Then down marched the remnant of the noble;
>   the people of the LORD marched down for him against the
>   mighty.
> ¹⁴ From E'phraim they set out thither into the valley
>   following you, Benjamin, with your kinsmen;
>   from Machir marched down the commanders,
>   and from Zeb'ulun those who bear the marshal's staff;
> ¹⁵ the princes of Is'sachar came with Deb'orah,
>   and Is'sachar faithful to Barak;
>   into the valley they rushed forth at his heels.
>   Among the clans of Reuben
>   there were great searchings of heart.

¹⁶ Why did you tarry among the sheepfolds,
    to hear the piping for the flocks?
  Among the clans of Reuben
    there were great searchings of heart.
¹⁷ Gilead stayed beyond the Jordan;
    and Dan, why did he abide with the ships?
  Asher sat still at the coast of the sea,
    settling down by his landings.
¹⁸ Zeb'ulun is a people that jeoparded their lives to the death;
    Naph'tali too, on the heights of the field.

¹⁹ "The kings came, they fought;
    then fought the kings of Canaan,
  at Ta'anach, by the waters of Megid'do;
    they got no spoils of silver.
²⁰ From heaven fought the stars,
    from their courses they fought against Sis'era.
²¹ The torrent Kishon swept them away,
    the onrushing torrent, the torrent Kishon.
    March on, my soul, with might!

²² "Then loud beat the horses' hoofs
    with the galloping, galloping of his steeds.

²³ "Curse Meroz, says the angel of the LORD,
    curse bitterly its inhabitants,
  because they came not to the help of the LORD,
    to the help of the LORD against the mighty.

²⁴ "Most blessed of women be Ja'el,
    the wife of Heber the Ken'ite,
    of tent-dwelling women most blessed.
²⁵ He asked water and she gave him milk,
    she brought him curds in a lordly bowl.
²⁶ She put her hand to the tent peg
    and her right hand to the workmen's mallet;
  she struck Sis'era a blow,
    she crushed his head,
    she shattered and pierced his temple.
²⁷ He sank, he fell,
    he lay still at her feet;
  at her feet he sank, he fell;
    where he sank, there he fell dead.

²⁸ "Out of the window she peered,
    the mother of Sis'era gazed through the lattice:
     'Why is his chariot so long in coming?
    Why tarry the hoofbeats of his chariots?'
²⁹ Her wisest ladies make answer,
    nay, she gives answer to herself,
³⁰ 'Are they not finding and dividing the spoil?—
    A maiden or two for every man;
   spoil of dyed stuffs for Sis'era,
    spoil of dyed stuffs embroidered,
    two pieces of dyed work embroidered for my neck as spoil?'

³¹ "So perish all thine enemies, O Lᴏʀᴅ!
    But thy friends be like the sun as he rises in his might."

And the land had rest for forty years.

5:6 Deborah was the only woman among the Judges. Until she began to rule, it was unsafe to travel in Israel. **5:9** ff. Deborah offers thanks to the Hebrew tribes who fought beside Barak: Zebulun, Naphtali, Ephraim, Benjamin and Issachar. Deborah taunts Reuben, Dan and Asher for their failure to give aid. Scholars note that Deborah does not mention the Southern tribes of Judah, Simon and Levi. They suggest: (1) either these tribes were too far removed and too hemmed in by Canaanites to have come to her assistance; or (2) this account may refer to an earlier period before the southern tribes had consolidated their possession of the southern area. **5:19** Archaeological work at Megiddo dates this battle at about 1125 B.C.

Gideon Rescues Israel from the Midianites

Judges 6:1–4, 7–8a, 11–16, 25–40; 7:2–7, 9, 16–22; 8:22–28

6 The people of Israel did what was evil in the sight of the Lᴏʀᴅ; and the Lᴏʀᴅ gave them into the hand of Mid'ian seven years. ² And the hand of Mid'ian prevailed over Israel; and because of Mid'ian the people of Israel made for themselves the dens which are in the mountains, and the caves and the strongholds. ³ For whenever the Israelites put in seed the Mid'ianites and the Amal'ekites and the people of the East would come up and attack them; ⁴ they would encamp against them and destroy the produce of the land, as far as the neighborhood of Gaza, and leave no sustenance in Israel, and no sheep or ox or ass.

7 When the people of Israel cried to the Lᴏʀᴅ on account of the Mid'ianites, ⁸ the Lᴏʀᴅ sent a prophet to the people of Israel.

11 Now the angel of the Lᴏʀᴅ came and sat under the oak at

Ophrah, which belonged to Jo'ash the Abiez'rite, as his son Gideon was beating out wheat in the wine press, to hide it from the Mid'ianites. ¹²And the angel of the LORD appeared to him and said to him, "The LORD is with you, you mighty man of valor." ¹³And Gideon said to him, "Pray, sir, if the LORD is with us, why then has all this befallen us? And where are all his wonderful deeds which our fathers recounted to us, saying, 'Did not the LORD bring us up from Egypt?' But now the LORD has cast us off, and given us into the hand of Mid'ian." ¹⁴And the LORD turned to him and said, "Go in this might of yours and deliver Israel from the hand of Mid'ian; do not I send you?" ¹⁵And he said to him, "Pray, Lord, how can I deliver Israel? Behold, my clan is the weakest in Manas'seh, and I am the least in my family." ¹⁶And the LORD said to him, "But I will be with you, and you shall smite the Mid'ianites as one man."

25 That night the LORD said to him, "Take your father's bull, the second bull seven years old, and pull down the altar of Ba'al which your father has, and cut down the Ashe'rah that is beside it; ²⁶and build an altar to the LORD your God on the top of the stronghold here, with stones laid in due order; then take the second bull, and offer it as a burnt offering with the wood of the Ashe'rah which you shall cut down." ²⁷So Gideon took ten men of his servants, and did as the LORD had told him; but because he was too afraid of his family and the men of the town to do it by day, he did it by night.

28 When the men of the town rose early in the morning, behold, the altar of Ba'al was broken down, and the Ashe'rah beside it was cut down, and the second bull was offered upon the altar which had been built. ²⁹And they said to one another, "Who has done this thing?"And after they had made search and inquired, they said, "Gideon the son of Jo'ash has done this thing." ³⁰Then the men of the town said to Jo'ash, "Bring out your son, that he may die, for he has pulled down the altar of Ba'al and cut down the Ashe'rah beside it." ³¹But Jo'ash said to all who were arrayed against him, "Will you contend for Ba'al? Or will you defend his cause? Whoever contends for him shall be put to death by morning. If he is a god, let him contend for himself, because his altar has been pulled down." ³²Therefore on that day he was called Jerubba'al, that is to say, "Let Ba'al contend against him," because he pulled down his altar.

33 Then all the Mid'ianites and the Amal'ekites and the people of the East came together, and crossing the Jordan they encamped in the Valley of Jezreel. ³⁴But the Spirit of the LORD took possession of Gideon; and he sounded the trumpet, and the Abiez'rites were called out to follow him. ³⁵And he sent messengers throughout all Manas'seh; and they too were called out to follow him. And he sent

messengers to Asher, Zeb'ulun, and Naph'tali; and they went up to meet them.

36 Then Gideon said to God, "If thou wilt deliver Israel by my hand, as thou hast said, ³⁷ behold, I am laying a fleece of wool on the threshing floor; if there is dew on the fleece alone, and it is dry on all the ground, then I shall know that thou wilt deliver Israel by my hand, as thou hast said." ³⁸ And it was so. When he rose early next morning and squeezed the fleece, he wrung enough dew from the fleece to fill a bowl with water. ³⁹ Then Gideon said to God, "Let not thy anger burn against me, let me speak but this once; pray, let me make trial only this once with the fleece; pray, let it be dry only on the fleece, and on all the ground let there be dew." ⁴⁰ And God did so that night; for it was dry on the fleece only, and on all the ground there was dew.

7 ² The LORD said to Gideon, "The people with you are too many for me to give the Mid'ianites into their hand, lest Israel vaunt themselves against me, saying, 'My own hand has delivered me.' ³ Now therefore proclaim in the ears of the people, saying, 'Whoever is fearful and trembling, let him return home.'" And Gideon tested them; twenty-two thousand returned, and ten thousand remained.

4 And the LORD said to Gideon, "The people are still too many; take them down to the water and I will test them for you there; and he of whom I say to you, 'This man shall go with you,' shall go with you; and any of whom I say to you, 'This man shall not go with you,' shall not go." ⁵ So he brought the people down to the water; and the LORD said to Gideon, "Every one that laps the water with his tongue, as a dog laps, you shall set by himself; likewise every one that kneels down to drink." ⁶ And the number of those that lapped, putting their hands to their mouths, was three hundred men; but all the rest of the people knelt down to drink water. ⁷ And the LORD said to Gideon, "With the three hundred men that lapped I will deliver you, and give the Mid'ianites into your hand; and let all the others go every man to his home."

9 That same night the LORD said to him, "Arise, go down against the camp; for I have given it into your hand."

16 And he divided the three hundred men into three companies, and put trumpets into the hands of all of them and empty jars, with torches inside the jars. ¹⁷ And he said to them, "Look at me, and do likewise; when I come to the outskirts of the camp, do as I do. ¹⁸ When I blow the trumpet, I and all who are with me, then blow the trumpets also on every side of all the camp, and shout, 'For the LORD and for Gideon.'"

19 So Gideon and the hundred men who were with him came to

the outskirts of the camp at the beginning of the middle watch, when they had just set the watch; and they blew the trumpets and smashed the jars that were in their hands. ²⁰And the three companies blew the trumpets and broke the jars, holding in their left hands the torches, and in their right hands the trumpets to blow; and they cried, "A sword for the LORD and for Gideon!" ²¹They stood every man in his place round about the camp, and all the army ran; they cried out and fled. ²²When they blew the three hundred trumpets, the LORD set every man's sword against his fellow and against all the army; and the army fled as far as Beth-shit'tah toward Zer'erah, as far as the border of A'bel-meho'lah, by Tabbath.

8 ²²Then the men of Israel said to Gideon, "Rule over us, you and your son and your grandson also; for you have delivered us out of the hand of Mid'ian." ²³Gideon said to them, "I will not rule over you, and my son will not rule over you; the LORD will rule over you." ²⁴And Gideon said to them, "Let me make a request of you; give me every man of you the earrings of his spoil." (For they had golden earrings, because they were Ish'maelites.) ²⁵And they answered, "We will willingly give them." And they spread a garment, and every man cast in it the earrings of his spoil. ²⁶And the weight of the golden earrings that he requested was one thousand seven hundred shekels of gold; besides the crescents and the pendants and the purple garments worn by the kings of Mid'ian, and besides the collars that were about the necks of their camels. ²⁷And Gideon made an ephod of it and put it in his city, in Ophrah; and all Israel played the harlot after it there, and it became a snare to Gideon and to his family. ²⁸So Mid'ian was subdued before the people of Israel, and they lifted up their heads no more. And the land had rest forty years in the days of Gideon.

6:2 Evidence of the meager foothold the Hebrew tribes had in some parts of Canaan. **6:36** f. Moses also had asked for a sign from God to verify that a genuine call to leadership had been given, Exodus 3:12, 4:1. (See also 1 Samuel 10:7.) **7:1** This incident is recalled in debates on the comparative effectiveness of volunteer and conscripted armies. **8:22** The emerging desire of Israel for a king who would wield the tribes together for protection and support is here indicated. **8:23** The Gideon Bible Society organized in 1899 places Bibles in hotels and hospitals. The name recalls the zeal with which Gideon fought "for the glory of God." **8:27** See Judges 17:5, 18:14; Hosea 3:4.

Abimelech Rules by Violence

The judge Gideon also known as Jerub-baal, had many wives and seventy sons. After his death, Abimelech, son of Gideon by a concubine in Shechem, killed all his brothers except the youngest, Jotham, who had been in hiding. Abimelech and his "worthless and reckless fellows" succeeded in persuading the people of Shechem to crown him king. Jotham then proclaims this parable of the crowning of the bramble bush.

Judges 9:6–15, 19–23, 56–57

9 ⁶And all the citizens of Shechem came together, and all Beth-millo, and they went and made Abim'elech king, by the oak of the pillar at Shechem.

7 When it was told to Jotham, he went and stood on the top of Mount Ger'izim, and cried aloud and said to them, "Listen to me, you men of Shechem, that God may listen to you. ⁸The trees once went forth to anoint a king over them; and they said to the olive tree, 'Reign over us.' ⁹But the olive tree said to them, 'Shall I leave my fatness, by which gods and men are honored, and go to sway over the trees?' ¹⁰And the trees said to the fig tree. 'Come you, and reign over us.' ¹¹But the fig tree said to them, 'Shall I leave my sweetness and my good fruit, and go to sway over the trees?' ¹²And the trees said to the vine, 'Come you, and reign over us.' ¹³But the vine said to them, 'Shall I leave my wine which cheers gods and men, and go to sway over the trees?' ¹⁴Then all the trees said to the bramble, 'Come you, and reign over us.' ¹⁵And the bramble said to the trees, 'If in good faith you are anointing me king over you, then come and take refuge in my shade; but if not, let fire come out of the bramble and devour the cedars of Lebanon.'

19 If you then have acted in good faith and honor with Jerubba'al and with his house this day, then rejoice in Abim'elech, and let him also rejoice in you; ²⁰but if not, let fire come out from Abim'elech, and devour the citizens of Shechem, and Beth-millo; and let fire come out from the citizens of Shechem, and from Beth-millo, and devour Abim'elech." ²¹And Jotham ran away and fled, and went to Beer and dwelt there, for fear of Abim'elech his brother.

22 Abim'elech ruled over Israel three years. ²³And God sent an evil spirit between Abim'elech and the men of Shechem; and the men of Shechem dealt treacherously with Abim'elech;

56 Thus God requited the crime of Abim'elech, which he committed against his father in killing his seventy brothers; ⁵⁷and God also made all the wickedness of the men of Shechem fall back upon their heads, and upon them came the curse of Jotham the son of Jerubba'al.

9:8 The parable implies that when business, financial and social leaders neglect civic duties, crooked politics takes over with disastrous results.

Jephthah Utters a Hasty Vow

This tragic tale recounts the defeat of the Ammonites at the hands of Jephthah, who was made judge over Gilead. As Jephthah went into battle he made a hasty and foolish vow. Vows were a serious matter. Even so, according to Jewish law, Jephthah's vow could have been annulled if he had gone to the High Priest. Neither ruler nor priest acted to save the life of the girl. According to rabbinic accounts, therefore, both men were punished for their pride: leprosy struck Jephthah, and the Divine Presence departed from the priest Phineas. The story remains for literature a classic account of the conflict between love and duty.

Judges 11:29–40

29 Then the Spirit of the LORD came upon Jephthah, and he passed through Gilead and Manas′seh, and passed on to Mizpah of Gilead, and from Mizpah of Gilead he passed on to the Ammonites. ³⁰ And Jephthah made a vow to the LORD, and said, "If thou wilt give the Ammonites into my hand, ³¹ then whoever comes forth from the doors of my house to meet me, when I return victorious from the Ammonites, shall be the LORD'S, and I will offer him up for a burnt offering." ³² So Jephthah crossed over to the Ammonites to fight against them; and the LORD gave them into his hand. ³³ And he smote them from Aro′er to the neighborhood of Minnith, twenty cities, and as far as Abel–keramim, with a very great slaughter. So the Ammonites were subdued before the people of Israel.

34 Then Jephthah came to his home at Mizpah; and behold, his daugher came out to meet him with timbrels and with dances; she was his only child; beside her he had neither son nor daughter. ³⁵ And when he saw her, he rent his clothes, and said, "Alas, my daughter! you have brought me very low, and you have become the cause of great trouble to me; for I have opened my mouth to the LORD, and I cannot take back my vow." ³⁶ And she said to him, "My father, if you have opened your mouth to the LORD, do to me according to what has gone forth from your mouth, now that the LORD has avenged you on your enemies, on the Ammonites." ³⁷ And she said to her father, "Let this thing be done for me; let me alone two months, that I may go and wander on the mountains, and bewail my virginity, I and my companions." ³⁸ And he said, "Go." And he sent her away for two months; and she departed, she and her companions, and bewailed her virginity upon the mountains. ³⁹ And at the end of two months, she returned to her father, who did with her according to his vow which he had made. She had never known a man. And it became a custom in Israel ⁴⁰ that the daughters of Israel went year by year to lament the daughter of Jephthah the Gileadite four days in the year.

11:35 Human sacrifice was forbidden by Jewish law; that Jephthah would consider making the sacrifice indicates the degree of Canaanite influence that existed, even for a "Judge" in Israel (cf. Leviticus 18:21). **11:36** A vow was held to be irrevocable (see Numbers 30:3).

Gilead Wars with Ephraim

This account of civil war depicts the uneasy situation among the tribes of Israel. The powerful tribe of Ephraim is offended that Jephthah had not called them to aid him in his battle against the Ammonites. This quarrel eventually results in a battle among the tribes. Gilead is victor over the bully tribe. The fleeing Ephraimites are detected and caught by a tribal peculiarity in pronunciation.

Judges 12:1–6

12 The men of E'phraim were called to arms, and they crossed to Zaphon and said to Jephthah, "Why did you cross over to fight against the Ammonites, and did not call us to go with you? We will burn your house over you with fire." ²And Jephthah said to them, "I and my people had a great feud with the Ammonites; and when I called you, you did not deliver me from their hand. ³And when I saw that you would not deliver me, I took my life in my hand, and crossed over against the Ammonites, and the LORD gave them into my hand; why then have you come up to me this day, to fight against me?" ⁴Then Jephthah gathered all the men of Gilead and fought with E'phraim; and the men of Gilead smote E'phraim, because they said, "You are fugitives of E'phraim, you Gileadites, in the midst of E'phraim and Manas'seh." ⁵And the Gileadites took the fords of the Jordan against the E'phraimites. And when any of the fugitives of E'phraim said, "Let me go over," the men of Gilead said to him, "Are you an E'phraimite?" When he said, "No," ⁶they said to him, "Then say Shibboleth," and he said, "Sibboleth," for he could not pronounce it right; then they seized him and slew him at the fords of the Jordan. And there fell at that time forty-two thousand of the E'phraimites.

Samson Saves Israel from the Philistines
Judges 13:1–5, 24; 14:1–20; 15:1, 4–16; 16:4–31

13 And the people of Israel again did what was evil in the sight of the LORD; and the LORD gave them into the hand of the Philistines for forty years.

2 And there was a certain man of Zorah, of the tribe of the Danites, whose name was Mano'ah; and his wife was barren and had no children. ³And the angel of the LORD appeared to the woman and

said to her, "Behold, you are barren and have no children; but you shall conceive and bear a son. ⁴Therefore beware, and drink no wine or strong drink, and eat nothing unclean, ⁵for lo, you shall conceive and bear a son. No razor shall come upon his head, for the boy shall be a Nazirite to God from birth; and he shall begin to deliver Israel from the hand of the Philistines."

24 And the woman bore a son, and called his name Samson; and the boy grew, and the LORD blessed him.

14 Samson went down to Timnah, and at Timnah he saw one of the daughters of the Philistines. ²Then he came up, and told his father and mother, "I saw one of the daughters of the Philistines at Timnah; now get her for me as my wife." ³But his father and mother said to him, "Is there not a woman among the daughters of your kinsmen, or among all our people, that you must go to take a wife from the uncircumcised Philistines?" But Samson said to his father, "Get her for me; for she pleases me well."

4 His father and mother did not know that it was from the LORD; for he was seeking an occasion against the Philistines. At that time the Philistines had dominion over Israel.

5 Then Samson went down with his father and mother to Timnah, and he came to the vineyards of Timnah. And behold, a young lion roared against him; ⁶and the Spirit of the LORD came mightily upon him, and he tore the lion asunder as one tears a kid; and he had nothing in his hand. But he did not tell his father or his mother what he had done. ⁷Then he went down and talked with the woman; and she pleased Samson well. ⁸And after a while he returned to take her; and he turned aside to see the carcass of the lion, and behold, there was a swarm of bees in the body of the lion, and honey. ⁹He scraped it out into his hands, and went on, eating as he went; and he came to his father and mother, and gave some to them, and they ate. But he did not tell them that he had taken the honey from the carcass of the lion.

10 And his father went down to the woman, and Samson made a feast there; for so the young men used to do. ¹¹And when the people saw him, they brought thirty companions to be with him. ¹²And Samson said to them, "Let me now put a riddle to you; if you can tell me what it is, within the seven days of the feast, and find it out, then I will give you thirty linen garments and thirty festal garments; ¹³but if you cannot tell me what it is, then you shall give me thirty linen garments and thirty festal garments." And they said to him, "Put your riddle, that we may hear it." ¹⁴And he said to them,

"Out of the eater came something to eat.
Out of the strong came something sweet."

And they could not in three days tell what the riddle was.

15 On the fourth day they said to Samson's wife, "Entice your husband to tell us what the riddle is, lest we burn you and your father's house with fire. Have you invited us here to impoverish us?" ¹⁶ And Samson's wife wept before him, and said, "You only hate me, you do not love me; you have put a riddle to my countrymen, and you have not told me what it is." And he said to her, "Behold, I have not told my father nor my mother, and shall I tell you?" ¹⁷ She wept before him the seven days that their feast lasted; and on the seventh day he told her, because she pressed him hard. Then she told the riddle to her countrymen. ¹⁸ And the men of the city said to him on the seventh day before the sun went down,

"What is sweeter than honey?
What is stronger than a lion?"
And he said to them,
"If you had not plowed with my heifer,
you would not have found out my riddle."
¹⁹ And the Spirit of the LORD came mightily upon him, and he went down to Ash'kelon and killed thirty men of the town, and took their spoil and gave the festal garments to those who had told the riddle. In hot anger he went back to his father's house. ²⁰ And Samson's wife was given to his companion, who had been his best man.

15 After a while, at the time of wheat harvest, Samson went to visit his wife with a kid; and he said, "I will go in to my wife in the chamber." But her father would not allow him to go in.

4 So Samson went and caught three hundred foxes, and took torches; and he turned them tail to tail, and put a torch between each pair of tails. ⁵ And when he had set fire to the torches, he let the foxes go into the standing grain of the Philistines, and burned up the shocks and the standing grain, as well as the olive orchards. ⁶ Then the Philistines said, "Who has done this?" And they said, "Samson, the son-in-law of the Timnite, because he has taken his wife and given her to his companion." And the Philistines came up, and burned her and her father with fire. ⁷ And Samson said to them, "If this is what you do I swear I will be avenged upon you, and after that I will quit." ⁸ And he smote them hip and thigh with great slaughter; and he went down and stayed in the cleft of the rock of Etam.

9 Then the Philistines came up and encamped in Judah, and made a raid on Lehi. ¹⁰ And the men of Judah said, "Why have you come up against us?" They said, "We have come up to bind Samson to do to him as he did to us." ¹¹ Then three thousand men of Judah went down to the cleft of the rock of Etam, and said to Samson, "Do you not know that the Philistines are rulers over us? What then is this

that you have done to us?" And he said to them, "As they did to me, so have I done to them." ¹²And they said to him, "We have come down to bind you, that we may give you into the hands of the Philistines." And Samson said to them, "Swear to me that you will not fall upon me yourselves." ¹³They said to him, "No; we will only bind you and give you into their hands; we will not kill you." So they bound him with two new ropes, and brought him up from the rock.

14 When he came to Lehi, the Philistines came shouting to meet him; and the Spirit of the LORD came mightily upon him, and the ropes which were on his arms became as flax that has caught fire, and his bonds melted off his hands. ¹⁵And he found a fresh jawbone of an ass, and put out his hand and seized it, and with it he slew a thousand men. ¹⁶And Samson said,

"With the jawbone of an ass,
heaps upon heaps,
with the jawbone of an ass
have I slain a thousand men."

16 ⁴After this he loved a woman in the valley of Sorek, whose name was Deli′lah. ⁵And the lords of the Philistines came to her and said to her, "Entice him, and see wherein his great strength lies, and by what means we may overpower him, that we may bind him to subdue him; and we will each give you eleven hundred pieces of silver." ⁶And Deli′lah said to Samson "Please tell me wherein your great strength lies, and how you might be bound, that one could subdue you." ⁷And Samson said to her, "If they bind me with seven fresh bowstrings which have not been dried, then I shall become weak, and be like any other man." ⁸Then the lords of the Philistines brought her seven fresh bowstrings which had not been dried, and she bound him with them. ⁹Now she had men lying in wait in an inner chamber. And she said to him, "The Philistines are upon you, Samson!" But he snapped the bowstrings, as a string of tow snaps when it touches the fire. So the secret of his strength was not known.

10 And Deli′lah said to Samson, "Behold, you have mocked me, and told me lies; please tell me how you might be bound." ¹¹And he said to her, "If they bind me with new ropes that have not been used, then I shall become weak, and be like any other man." ¹²So Deli′lah took new ropes and bound him with them, and said to him, "The Philistines are upon you, Samson!" And the men lying in wait were in an inner chamber. But he snapped the ropes off his arms like a thread.

13 And Deli′lah said to Samson, "Until now you have mocked me, and told me lies; tell me how you might be bound." And he said to her, "If you weave the seven locks of my head with the web and

make it tight with the pin, then I shall become weak, and be like any other man." [14] So while he slept, Deli'lah took the seven locks of his head and wove them into the web. And she made them tight with the pin, and said to him, "The Philistines are upon you, Samson!" But he awoke from his sleep, and pulled away the pin, the loom, and the web.

15 And she said to him, "How can you say, 'I love you,' when your heart is not with me? You have mocked me these three times, and you have not told me wherein your great strength lies." [16] And when she pressed him hard with her words day after day, and urged him, his soul was vexed to death. [17] And he told her all his mind, and said to her, "A razor has never come upon my head; for I have been a Nazirite to God from my mother's womb. If I be shaved, then my strength will leave me, and I shall become weak, and be like any other man."

18 When Deli'lah saw that he had told her all his mind, she sent and called the lords of the Philistines, saying, "Come up this once, for he has told me all his mind." Then the lords of the Philistines came up to her, and brought the money in their hands. [19] She made him sleep upon her knees; and she called a man, and had him shave off the seven locks of his head. Then she began to torment him, and his strength left him. [20] And she said, "The Philistines are upon you, Samson!" And he awoke from his sleep, and said, "I will go out as at other times, and shake myself free." And he did not know that the LORD had left him. [21] And the Philistines seized him and gouged out his eyes, and brought him down to Gaza, and bound him with bronze fetters; and he ground at the mill in the prison. [22] But the hair of his head began to grow again after it had been shaved.

23 Now the lords of the Philistines gathered to offer a great sacrifice to Dagon their god, and to rejoice; for they said, "Our god has given Samson our enemy into our hand." [24] And when the people saw him, they praised their god; for they said, "Our god has given our enemy into our hand, the ravager of our country, who has slain many of us." [25] And when their hearts were merry, they said, "Call Samson, that he may make sport for us." So they called Samson out of the prison, and he made sport before them. They made him stand between the pillars; [26] and Samson said to the lad who held him by the hand, "Let me feel the pillars on which the house rests, that I may lean against them." [27] Now the house was full of men and women; all the lords of the Philistines were there, and on the roof there were about three thousand men and women, who looked on while Samson made sport.

28 Then Samson called to the LORD and said, "O Lord GOD,

remember me, I pray thee, and strengthen me, I pray thee, only this once, O God, that I may be avenged upon the Philistines for one of my two eyes." [29] And Samson grasped the two middle pillars upon which the house rested, and he leaned his weight upon them, his right hand on the one and his left hand on the other. [30] And Samson said, "Let me die with the Philistines." Then he bowed with all his might; and the house fell upon the lords and upon all the people that were in it. So the dead whom he slew at his death were more than those whom he had slain during his life. [31] Then his brothers and all his family came down and took him and brought him up and buried him between Zorah and Esh'ta-ol in the tomb of Mano'ah his father. He had judged Israel twenty years.

13:1 The Philistines invaded Canaan shortly after the time of Joshua. An Aegean people, they possessed military superiority by virtue of their knowledge of the use of iron, a harder metal than that available to the Canaanites and the Hebrews (cf. 1 Samuel 13:19–22). "Palestine," as the name of the land, is derived from "Philistines," and was first used by the Greek historian, Herodotus, in the fifth century B.C. **13:3** Like some other noted biblical personalities Samson is miraculously born of a woman apparently barren. **13:5** Nazirite: see Numbers 6:3 ff. **13:24** The pranks and adventures of Samson have inspired many great works of music and literature, e.g., the oratorio "Samson" by Handel, the opera, "Samson and Delilah" by Saint-Saens and the poem "Samson Agonistes" by Milton. Some scholars believe that these tales about Samson .are folk legends, like the German Til Eulenspiegel or America's Paul Bunyan. Although based on historical persons, the stories grew in time with the telling. **14:2** Marriage was negotiated by the parents, especially the father (cf. Genesis 21:21; 24:4; 34:8; Exodus 21:9). **14:12** The recitation of a riddle was a source of entertainment that dates far back in history. For other accounts of the use of riddles in Scripture see 1 Kings 10:1, Ezekiel 17:2; 14:18. In this riddle, Samson's reference to his wife as a "heifer" is scornful. As a result of her betrayal, Samson divorces her. **15:16** There is an ironical word play here in the Hebrew. The word *chamor* means "heap," and it also means an ass.

The Book of Ruth

Originally preserved upon a parchment scroll, this book is known in the Hebrew as "*Megillath* Ruth"—the Scroll of Ruth. It is one of the Five Scrolls included in the Hebrew canon, and like the others it appears in the section known as Writings (Hebrew, *Ketubim*)—the third major division of Hebrew Scriptures. In the Septuagint (the Greek translation of the Bible) and in all Christian translations, this book immediately follows the book of Judges, since its story is placed "in the days when the Judges judged," about 1100 B.C. Scholars disagree whether this book is based on an historic account and written during the 300-year period when Israel was ruled by judges, or at a later time.

Some scholars suggest that the book was a novel of protest written much later in reaction against Ezra's rule prohibiting mixed marriage, about 450 B.C. Ruth's faith and devotion to the Hebrew people are offered as dramatic testimony that God's law can and does command the heart of foreigners. Ruth, a Moabite, from a people generally so detested that they were forbidden to enter the assembly of the Lord (see Deuteronomy 23:4), becomes an ancestor of David. Thus the family tree of David, king of Israel, and of the Messiah, includes the union of Jew and Gentile.

The book of Ruth is part of the liturgy for Shavuoth or Pentecost for these reasons: 1. Shavuoth is celebrated as a festival of first fruits; and the Harvest Festival figures prominently in Ruth; 2. Shavuoth commemorates the revelation at Sinai, and the book of Ruth recounts the devotion of Ruth to the Law and her faithfulness despite privation and suffering. Converts to the Jewish faith are often given the name Ruth in recollection of the heroine of this book.

"Whither Thou Goest I Will Go"
Ruth 1:1–11, 16–18

1 In the days when the judges ruled there was a famine in the land, and a certain man of Bethlehem in Judah went to sojourn in the country of Moab, he and his wife and his two sons. ² The name of the man was Elim'elech and the name of his wife Na'omi, and the names of his two sons were Mahlon and Chil'ion; they were Eph'rathites from Bethlehem in Judah. They went into the country of Moab and remained there. ³ But Elim'elech, the husband of Na'omi, died, and she was left with her two sons. ⁴ These took Moabite wives; the name of the one was Orpah and the name of the other Ruth. They lived there about ten years; ⁵ and both Mahlon and Chil'ion died, so that the woman was bereft of her two sons and her husband.

6 Then she started with her daughters-in-law to return from the country of Moab, for she had heard in the country of Moab that the LORD had visited his people and given them food. [7] So she set out from the place where she was, with her two daughters-in-law, and they went on the way to return to the land of Judah. [8] But Na'omi said to her two daughters-in-law, "Go, return each of you to her mother's house. May the LORD deal kindly with you, as you have dealt with the dead and with me. [9] The LORD grant that you may find a home, each of you in the house of her husband!" Then she kissed them, and they lifted up their voices and wept. [10] And they said to her, "No, we will return with you to your people." [11] But Na'omi said, "Turn back, my daughters, why will you go with me? Have I yet sons in my womb that they may become your husbands?"

16 But Ruth said, "Entreat me not to leave you or to return from following you; for where you go I will go, and where you lodge I will lodge; your people shall be my people, and your God my God; [17] where you die I will die, and there will I be buried. May the LORD do so to me and more also if even death parts me from you." [18] And when Na'omi saw that she was determined to go with her, she said no more.

1:2 The names of the chief characters indicate their fates: the two sons who die young are called Mahlon, meaning in Hebrew "sickness," and Chilion, meaning "pining away." Orpah, meaning "she turns away," is the daughter-in-law who leaves Naomi; and Ruth means "beloved."

Ruth Gleans in the Field of Boaz
Ruth 1:22; 2:1–8, 14–16, 23

22 So Na'omi returned, and Ruth the Moabitess her daughter-in-law with her, who returned from the country of Moab. And they came to Bethlehem at the beginning of barley harvest.
2 Now Na'omi had a kinsman of her husband's, a man of wealth, of the family of Elim'elech, whose name was Bo'az. [2] And Ruth the Moabitess said to Na'omi, "Let me go to the field, and glean among the ears of grain after him in whose sight I shall find favor." And she said to her. "Go, my daughter." [3] So she set forth and went and gleaned in the field after the reapers; and she happened to come to the part of the field belonging to Bo'az, who was of the family of Elim'elech. [4] And behold, Bo'az came from Bethlehem; and he said to the reapers, "The LORD be with you!" And they answered, "The LORD bless you." [5] Then Bo'az said to his servant who was in charge of the reapers, "Whose maiden is this?" [6] And the servant who was in charge of the reapers answered, "It is the Moabite maiden, who

came back with Na'omi from the country of Moab. [7]She said, 'Pray, let me glean and gather among the sheaves after the reapers.' So she came, and she has continued from early morning until now, without resting even for a moment."

8 Then Bo'az said to Ruth, "Now, listen, my daughter, do not go to glean in another field or leave this one, but keep close to my maidens."

14 And at mealtime Bo'az said to her, "Come here, and eat some bread, and dip your morsel in the wine." So she sat beside the reapers, and he passed to her parched grain; and she ate until she was satisfied, and she had some left over. [15]When she rose to glean, Bo'az instructed his young men, saying, "Let her glean even among the sheaves, and do not reproach her. [16]And also pull out some from the bundles for her, and leave it for her to glean, and do not rebuke her."

23 So she kept close to the maidens of Bo'az, gleaning until the end of the barley and wheat harvests; and she lived with her mother-in-law.

> **2:2** The poor were entitled by law to gather produce from the corners of the field and the gleanings that had fallen from the hands of the reapers (cf. Leviticus 19:9, 23:22; Deuteronomy 24:19).
> **2:23** The harvesting period lasted three months.

Ruth Seeks Betrothal with Boaz
Ruth 3:1–13

3 Then Na'omi her mother-in-law said to her, "My daughter, should I not seek a home for you, that it may be well with you? [2]Now is not Bo'az our kinsman, with whose maidens you were? See, he is winnowing barley tonight at the threshing floor. [3]Wash therefore and anoint yourself, and put on your best clothes and go down to the threshing floor; but do not make yourself known to the man until he has finished eating and drinking. [4]But when he lies down, observe the place where he lies; then, go and uncover his feet and lie down; and he will tell you what to do." [5]And she replied, "All that you say I will do."

6 So she went down to the threshing floor and did just as her mother-in-law had told her. [7]And when Bo'az had eaten and drunk, and his heart was merry, he went to lie down at the end of the heap of grain. Then she came softly, and uncovered his feet, and lay down. [8]At midnight the man was startled, and turned over, and behold, a woman lay at his feet! [9]He said, "Who are you?" And she answered, "I am Ruth, your maidservant; spread your skirt over your maidservant, for you are next of kin." [10]And he said, "May you

be blessed by the LORD, my daughter; you have made this last kindness greater than the first, in that you have not gone after young men, whether poor or rich. ¹¹ And now, my daughter, do not fear, I will do for you all that you ask, for all my fellow townsmen know that you are a woman of worth. ¹² And now it is true that I am a near kinsman, yet there is a kinsman nearer than I. ¹³ Remain this night, and in the morning, if he will do the part of the next of kin for you, well; let him do it; but if he is not willing to do the part of the next of kin for you, then, as the LORD lives, I will do the part of the next of kin for you. Lie down until the morning."

3:1 Naomi sought to fulfill the responsibility of a parent for the marriage of a child. **3:9** According to biblical law (Deuteronomy 25:5–6) it was the duty of the nearest kinsman of the deceased husband, if there were no children in the marriage, to assume responsibility for the widow and thus assure the name and heritage of the deceased husband. **3:10** According to Hebrew tradition, Boaz was old—eighty years of age—and so he was impressed by this act of love on the part of a young widow.

Boaz Marries Ruth
Ruth 4:1–11, 13–17

4 And Bo'az went up to the gate and sat down there; and behold, the next of kin, of whom Bo'az had spoken, came by. So Bo'az said, "Turn aside, friend; sit down here"; and he turned aside and sat down. ² And he took ten men of the elders of the city, and said, "Sit down here"; so they sat down. ³ Then he said to the next of kin, "Na'omi, who has come back from the country of Moab, is selling the parcel of land which belonged to our kinsman Elim'elech. ⁴ So I thought I would tell you of it, and say, Buy it in the presence of those sitting here, and in the presence of the elders of my people. If you will redeem it, redeem it; but if you will not, tell me, that I may know, for there is no one besides you to redeem it, and I come after you." And he said, "I will redeem it." ⁵ Then Bo'az said, "The day you buy the field from the hand of Na'omi, you are also buying Ruth the Moabitess, the widow of the dead, in order to restore the name of the dead to his inheritance." ⁶ Then the next of kin said, "I cannot redeem it for myself, lest I impair my own inheritance. Take my right of redemption yourself, for I cannot redeem it."

7 Now this was the custom in former times in Israel concerning redeeming and exchanging: to confirm a transaction, the one drew off his sandal and gave it to the other, and this was the manner of attesting in Israel. ⁸ So when the next of kin said to Bo'az, "Buy it for yourself," he drew off his sandal. ⁹ Then Bo'az said to the elders

and all the people, "You are witnesses this day that I have bought from the hand of Na'omi all that belonged to Elim'elech and all that belonged the Chil'ion and to Mahlon. [10] Also Ruth the Moabitess, the widow of Mahlon, I have bought to be my wife, to perpetuate the name of the dead in his inheritance, that the name of the dead may not be cut off from among his own brethren and from the gate of his native place; you are witnesses this day." [11] Then all the people who were at the gate, and the elders, said, "We are witnesses. May the LORD make the woman, who is coming into your house, like Rachel and Leah, who together built up the house of Israel. May you prosper in Eph'rathah and be renowned in Bethlehem."

13 So Bo'az took Ruth and she became his wife; and he went in to her, and the LORD gave her conception, and she bore a son. [14] Then the women said to Na'omi, "Blessed be the LORD, who has not left you this day without next of kin; and may his name be renowned in Israel! [15] He shall be to you a restorer of life and a nourisher of your old age; for your daughter-in-law who loves you, who is more to you than seven sons, has borne him." [16] Then Na'omi took the child and laid him in her bosom, and became his nurse. [17] And the women of the neighborhood gave him a name, saying, "A son has been born to Na'omi." They named him Obed; he was the father of Jesse, the father of David.

4:13 Rabbinic tradition reads into the phrase, "the Lord gave her conception," a miraculous occurence, in that the aged Boaz was fertile, and Ruth, who could have no children by her former husband Mahlon, was now able to conceive.

The Books of Samuel

Although the prophet Samuel is the principal personality only in the early chapters of the first of the two books bearing his name, his involvement in the selection of the first two Hebrew kings, Saul and David, decisively shaped that important period in Jewish history. Appropriately therefore, the accounts of these events carry his name.

First and Second Samuel continue the history begun in Joshua and Judges. They cover a period from about 1050 B.C. to 960 B.C. They narrate the consolidation of the tribes of Israel into one nation under monarchical rule and the dramatic experiences of Saul and David as they sought to maintain control over the nation and to protect it from its enemies. Individual character, seen in terms of fidelity to God and to His Law, is presented as decisive in their public record as leaders of the community.

Earliest Hebrew tradition regarded these two books as one. It was not until the appearance of the Hebrew Bible printed by Daniel Bomberg in 1516, influenced by the order maintained in the Latin Vulgate, that a two-part division of Samuel became acceptable. Traditional belief ascribed the authorship of the first part of this book to Samuel himself and the remainder to the prophet Nathan and the seer Gad. Many biblical scholars believe instead that the book was written after the division of the kingdom and after the death of King Solomon (See references to the kings of Judah in 1 Samuel 27:6). If that were so, the immediacy and vividness of the writing would suggest that the author must have used earlier written state papers and histories, including records that may have been written by Samuel, Nathan and Gad (see 1 Chronicles 29:29), or by one or more members of the court.

The monarchy established in Israel was from the first limited in authority (10:25). Although the biblical text suggests a divine right to the throne in the case of both Saul and David, the elders occasionally met in a council of state (1 Samuel 22:6) and joined into a covenant with the king (2 Samuel 5:3), wherein rights and responsibilities were clearly defined. But most decisive in disciplining the authoritarian nature of the monarchy was the moral instruction of the prophet. Recognizing that the prophet spoke not for himself but in the name of God, the king accepted his instruction. Samuel, the first of such prophets, set an example by the rigor of his morality and his courage in holding the monarch to righteous behavior. He organized schools of prophets (19:20) and thereby laid the groundwork for development of a spiritual institution that has influenced the history of Western civilization. By personal example he demonstrated that prophetic religion must stand free above all insitutions of man, judging even the king by the standards of God's Word.

THE FIRST BOOK OF SAMUEL

The first several chapters recount the birth of Samuel and his emergence as a prophet through whom God is revealed to His people (4:1) and by whom they are encouraged to make reconciliation with the Lord (7:3–4). The challenge of the Philistines to the scattered tribes is too severe, however, and the people plead with Samuel to appoint a king who can unite them into one nation and champion them in war (8:5). Samuel resists such a course. He warns of the despotic ways of kings and argues that God is King over Israel; but the people are not to be dissuaded. By inspiration Samuel selects Saul, a Benjamite (9:20) as king. The rest of the book records the life of Saul as ruler in Israel.

Hannah Prays for a Son
1 Samuel 1:1–18, 20, 24–28

1 There was a certain man of Ramatha′im-zo′phim of the hill country of E′phraim, whose name was Elka′nah the son of Jero′ham, son of Eli′hu, son of Tohu, son of Zuph, an E′phraimite. ²He had two wives; the name of the one was Hannah, and the name of the other Penin′nah. And Penin′nah had children, but Hannah had no children.

3 Now this man used to go up year by year from his city to worship and to sacrifice to the LORD of hosts at Shiloh, where the two sons of Eli, Hophni and Phin′ehas, were priests of the LORD. ⁴On the day when Elka′nah sacrificed, he would give portions to Penin′nah his wife and to all her sons and daughters; ⁵and, although he loved Hannah, he would give Hannah only one portion, because the LORD had closed her womb. ⁶And her rival used to provoke her sorely, to irritate her, because the LORD had closed her womb. ⁷So it went on year by year; as often as she went up to the house of the LORD, she used to provoke her. Therefore Hannah wept and would not eat. ⁸And Elka′nah, her husband, said to her, "Hannah, why do you weep? And why do you not eat? And why is your heart sad? Am I not more to you than ten sons?"

9 After they had eaten and drunk in Shiloh, Hannah rose. Now Eli the priest was sitting on the seat beside the doorpost of the temple of the LORD. ¹⁰She was deeply distressed and prayed to the LORD, and wept bitterly. ¹¹And she vowed a vow and said, "O LORD of hosts, if thou wilt indeed look on the affliction of thy maidservant, but wilt give to thy maidservant a son, then I will give him to the LORD all the days of his life, and no razor shall touch his head."

12 As she continued praying before the LORD, Eli observed her mouth. [13] Hannah was speaking in her heart; only her lips moved, and her voice was not heard; therefore Eli took her to be a drunken woman. [14] And Eli said to her, "How long will you be drunken? Put away your wine from you." [15] But Hannah answered, "No, my lord, I am a woman sorely troubled; I have drunk neither wine nor strong drink, but I have been pouring out my soul before the LORD. [16] Do not regard your maidservant as a base woman, for all along I have been speaking out of my great anxiety and vexation." [17] Then Eli answered, "Go in peace, and the God of Israel grant your petition which you have made to him." [18] And she said, "Let your maidservant find favor in your eyes." Then the woman went her way and ate, and her countenance was no longer sad.

20 And in due time Hannah conceived and bore a son, and she called his name Samuel, for she said, "I have asked him of the LORD."

24 And when she had weaned him, she took him up with her, along with a three-year-old bull, an ephah of flour, and a skin of wine; and she brought him to the house of the LORD at Shiloh; and the child was young. [25] Then they slew the bull, and they brought the child to Eli. [26] And she said, "Oh, my lord! As you live, my lord, I am the woman who was standing here in your presence, praying to the LORD. [27] For this child I prayed; and the LORD has granted me my petition which I made to him. [28] Therefore I have lent him to the LORD; as long as he lives, he is lent to the LORD."

And they worshiped the LORD there.

1:3 Biblical law required a pilgrimage on each of the harvest festivals (Exodus 34:23). Here is evidence that a pious man such as Elkanah came to Jerusalem at least once a year in fulfillment of that law. *Lord of hosts*, here used for the first time became popular in Israel. It may refer both to the concept of God as Lord of the hosts of Heaven and to His role as protector over the armies of Israel (17:45). Joshua (18:1) had first placed the Tabernacle in Shiloh, which is now identified by archeologists with the modern Seilun, 10 miles north of Beth-el. Its destruction by the Philistines later in biblical history is remembered as a national calamity (Jeremiah 7:12). **1:11** The Nazirite vow (Numbers 6:5).

Hannah Offers Thanksgiving

Hannah recognizes in her happy change of fortune the rule of God over all of life. Her prayer of thanksgiving is included in the prophetic reading for the first day of the Rosh Hashanah or Jewish New Year. It follows a reading of the announcement of the birth of Isaac to Sarah (Genesis 21:1−34). In both cases a barren woman is miraculously made to bear a child through whom the heritage of Israel is maintained and communicated. Some Christians consider this psalm to be the direct model for Mary's "Magnificat" (Luke 1:46–55).

1 Samuel 2:1–11
(Jewish Publication Society)

[1] And Hannah prayed, and said:
   My heart exulteth in the LORD,
   My horn is exalted in the LORD;
   My mouth is enlarged over mine enemies;
   Because I rejoice in Thy salvation.

[2] There is none holy as the LORD;
   For there is none beside Thee;
   Neither is there any rock like our God.

[3] Multiply not exceeding proud talk;
   Let not arrogancy come out of your mouth;
   For the LORD is a God of knowledge,
   And by Him actions are weighed.

[4] The bows of the mighty men are broken,
   And they that stumbled are girded with strength

[5] They that were full have hired out themselves for bread;
   And they that were hungry have ceased;
   While the barren hath borne seven,
   She that had many children hath languished.

[6] The LORD killeth, and maketh alive;
   He bringeth down to the grave, and bringeth up.

[7] The LORD maketh poor and maketh rich;
   He bringeth low, He also lifteth up.

[8] He raiseth up the poor out of the dust,
   He lifteth up the needy from the dung-hill,
   To make them sit with princes,
   And inherit the throne of glory;
   For the pillars of the earth are the LORD's.
   And he hath set the world upon them.

[9] He will keep the feet of His holy ones,
   But the wicked shall be put to silence in darkness;
   For not by strength shall man prevail.

[10] They that strive with the LORD shall be broken to pieces
Against them will He thunder in heaven;
The LORD will judge the ends of the earth;
And He will give strength unto His king,
And exalt the horn of His anointed.

[11] And Elkanah went to Ramah to his house. And the child did minister unto the LORD before Eli the priest.

2:6 Rabbinic authorities in the first Christian era, those who followed Rabbi Shammai, found in this passage and in Zechariah 13:9 confirmation for their belief in a purgatory within Sheol or Gehenna. There the souls of those not completely wicked or righteous were purified. The rabbinical followers of Rabbi Hillel, on the other hand, citing Exodus 34:6, denied the experience of purgatory. They suggested that God's mercy inclined to those who had some good in them, and that their souls ascended straightway to heaven. The followers of Shammai explained that a soul would be purified in purgatory for no more than 12 months. If the soul remained evil, however, then the memory of the person and his identity would be blotted out completely. And if the person had been an exceptionally cruel and violent man, he would be compelled to endure bodily tortures without cessation (Isaiah 66:24). Both in the church and later in the synagogue there were developed prayers in behalf of those souls under judgment in purgatory—the Mass for the Dead and the Kaddish. It is customary in the synagogue for a son to recite the Kaddish for his deceased father or mother for only 11 months: it is not to be presumed that one's relative would need to endure a purification in purgatory for the entire period of 12 months. Contemporary Jews no longer believe in eternal damnation, and many still agree with Hillel, rejecting the concept of a purgatory. Either a man's memory is blotted out, if he is evil, or his name is linked with God, if he has some righteousness in his being.

God Appears to Samuel in Shiloh

Hophni and Phineas, the sons of Eli, abused their priestly office. They expropriated the sacrifices of the people for their own use and engaged in other immoralities. Because of their sins and his own failure to discipline them, Eli and his house were punished by God. The priest Zadok and his family were later chosen to the office of High Priest, and they held that office from the reign of Solomon until the destruction of the First Temple.

1 Samuel 2:12, 3:1–21

12 Now the sons of Eli were worthless men; they had no regard for the LORD.

3 Now the boy Samuel was ministering to the LORD under Eli. And the word of the LORD was rare in those days; there was no frequent vision.

2 At that time Eli, whose eyesight had begun to grow dim, so that he could not see, was lying down in his own place; ³ the lamp of God had not yet gone out, and Samuel was lying down within the temple of the LORD, where the ark of God was. ⁴ Then the LORD called, "Samuel! Samuel!" and he said, "Here I am!" ⁵ and ran to Eli, and said, "Here I am, for you called me." But he said, "I did not call; lie down again." So he went and lay down. ⁶ And the LORD called again, "Samuel!" And Samuel arose and went to Eli, and said, "Here I am, for you called me." But he said, "I did not call, my son; lie down again." ⁷ Now Samuel did not yet know the LORD, and the word of the LORD had not yet been revealed to him. ⁸ And the LORD called Samuel again the third time. And he arose and went to Eli, and said, "Here I am, for you called me." Then Eli perceived that the LORD was calling the boy. ⁹ Therefore Eli said to Samuel, "Go, lie down; and if he calls you, you shall say, 'Speak, LORD, for thy servant hears.' " So Samuel went and lay down in his place.

10 And the LORD came and stood forth, calling as at other times, "Samuel! Samuel!" And Samuel said, "Speak, for thy servant hears." ¹¹ Then the LORD said to Samuel, "Behold, I am about to do a thing in Israel, at which the two ears of every one that hears it will tingle. ¹² On that day I will fulfil against Eli all that I have spoken concerning his house, from beginning to end. ¹³ And I tell him that I am about to punish his house for ever, for the iniquity which he knew, because his sons were blaspheming God, and he did not restrain them. ¹⁴ Therefore I swear to the house of Eli that the iniquity of Eli's house shall not be expiated by sacrifice or offering for ever."

15 Samuel lay until morning; then he opened the doors of the house of the LORD. And Samuel was afraid to tell the vision to Eli. ¹⁶ But Eli called Samuel and said, "Samuel, my son." And he said, "Here I am." ¹⁷ And Eli said, "What was it that he told you? Do not hide it from me. May God do so to you and more also, if you hide anything from me of all that he told you." ¹⁸ So Samuel told him everything and hid nothing from him. And he said, "It is the LORD; let him do what seems good to him."

19 And Samuel grew, and the LORD was with him and let none of his words fall to the ground. ²⁰ And all Israel from Dan to Beer-sheba knew that Samuel was established as a prophet of the LORD. ²¹ And to the LORD appeared again at Shiloh, for the LORD revealed himself to Samuel at Shiloh by the word of the LORD.

3:1 Jewish tradition as preserved by Josephus (*Antiquities*, Book V) suggests that Samuel had just completed his twelfth year when God appeared to him. **3:13** The Rabbis were reluctant to permit even a description of such a blasphemous act to be written into Holy Scripture. Thus the Hebrew euphemistically says "his sons were cursing *themselves.*' **3:15** *Opening the doors of the house* was part of his duties as a "helper to the Levites" (cf. 1 Chronicles 15:18, 23). **3:21** There is a difference of opinion, evident in the differing translations of Scriptures, over whether this verse should conclude chapter 3, as in the Latin Vulgate from which it was introduced into the Hebrew text in the sixteenth century, or should be the first sentence of the narrative starting in chapter 4, as given in the earliest Hebrew texts. If the latter reading is followed, then the battle with the Philistines is acknowledged as a decision deriving from the revelation of God through Samuel.

The Philistines Capture the Ark of the Lord
1 Samuel 4:1, 4–11; 5:1–7; 6:11–12; 7:1

4 And the word of Samuel came to all Israel.

Now Israel went out to battle against the Philistines; they encamped at Ebene'zer, and the Philistines encamped at Aphek.

4 So the people sent to Shiloh, and brought from there the ark of the covenant of the LORD of hosts, who is enthroned on the cherubim; and the two sons of Eli, Hophni and Phin'ehas, were there with the ark of the covenant of God.

5 When the ark of the covenant of the LORD came into the camp, all Israel gave a mighty shout, so that the earth resounded. [6] And when the Philistines heard the noise of the shouting, they said, "What does this great shouting in the camp of the Hebrews mean?" And when they learned that the ark of the LORD had come to the camp, [7] the Philistines were afraid; for they said, "A god has come into the camp." And they said, "Woe to us! For nothing like this has happened before. [8] Woe to us! Who can deliver us from the power of these mighty gods? These are the gods who smote the Egyptians with every sort of plague in the wilderness. [9] Take courage, and acquit yourselves like men, O Philistines, lest you become slaves to the Hebrews as they have been to you; acquit yourselves like men and fight."

10 So the Philistines fought, and Israel was defeated, and they fled, every man to his home; and there was a very great slaughter, for there fell of Israel thirty thousand foot soldiers. [11] And the ark of God was captured; and the two sons of Eli, Hophni and Phin'ehas, were slain.

5 When the Philistines captured the ark of God, they carried it from

Ebene'zer to Ashdod; ²then the Philistines took the ark of God and brought it into the house of Dagon and set it up beside Dagon. ³And when the people of Ashdod rose early the next day, behold, Dagon had fallen face downward on the ground before the ark of the LORD. So they took Dagon and put him back in his place. ⁴But when they rose early on the next morning, behold, Dagon had fallen face downward on the ground before the ark of the LORD, and the head of Dagon and both his hands were lying cut off upon the threshold; only the trunk of Dagon was left to him. ⁵This is why the priests of Dagon and all who enter the house of Dagon do not tread on the threshold of Dagon in Ashdod to this day.

6 The hand of the LORD was heavy upon the people of Ashdod, and he terrified and afflicted them with tumors, both Ashdod and its territory. ⁷And when the men of Ashdod saw how things were, they said, "The ark of the God of Israel must not remain with us; for his hand is heavy upon us and upon Dagon our god."

6 ¹¹And they put the ark of the LORD on the cart, and the box with the golden mice and the images of their tumors. ¹²And the cows went straight in the direction of Beth-she'mesh along one highway, lowing as they went; they turned neither to the right nor to the left, and the lords of the Philistines went after them as far as the border of Beth-she'mesh.

7 And the men of Kir'iath-je'arim came and took up the ark of the LORD, and brought it to the house of Abin'adab on the hill; and they consecrated his son, Elea'zar, to have charge of the ark of the LORD.

4:1 The Philistines were an Aegean people that had earlier developed an advanced civilization in Crete, Asia Minor and the Greek mainland. Their discovery of iron weapons gave them a military superiority over peoples still using bronze. They were organized into a loose confederation of five city states: Gath, Gaza, Ashdod, Askelon and Ekron. They sought at this time to extend their control over all of Canaan. In the battle against the Philistines the Hebrew tribes were fused into one nation. It was this threat, in fact, that stimulated the desire for a monarchy and centralized authority. For many years the Hebrew people remained completely under the domination of the Philistines; the issue was finally decided only when King David defeated the Philistine enemies (2 Samuel 5:17 ff.). **4:4** The ruling elders hoped that the presence of the Ark would inspire the army and that God, present within the sacred objects, would protect Israel. The Ark had similarly been placed before the troops upon the invasion of Canaan (Joshua 3:6) and at the siege of Jericho (Joshua 6:6). **5:2** Dagon was the national god of the Philistines. His name may be derived from the Hebrew word *dag* meaning fish. Assyrian art pictures a god with the hands and face of a human and the body of a fish. Hebrew tradition accepts this interpretation. A temple to this god was said to be existing in Ashdod in the time of the Maccabees (1 Maccabee 10:83 f.). **5:6** It has been suggested that this affliction transmitted by rats was the bubonic plague, of which boils are a symptom. **6:11** By these gifts the Philistines acknowledged their conviction that their troubles had been the consequence of their possession of the Ark of the Hebrew God. **6:12** The cows had been separated from their calves who were left behind. The fact that they went forward, therefore, indicated that they were being led by divine intervention. **7:1** The men of Bethshemesh had treated the Ark with irreverence (6:19). The plague spread among the surrounding Hebrews, and 5,070 men died. The people of Kiriathjearim volunteered to guard and protect the Ark; the sanctuary remained there for many years, until David brought the tabernacle to his new capital city, Jerusalem.

The People Demand a King

The corruption of Samuel's two sons, Joel and Abijah, strengthened the elders of Israel in their conviction that they ought to institute another form of government. A pressing reason was their desire to establish a central authority capable of welding the tribes into a unified effective fighting force against the threat of the Philistines (8:20).

1 Samuel 8:1–22a

8 When Samuel became old, he made his sons judges over Israel. ²The name of his first-born son was Jo'el, and the name of his second, Abi'jah; they were judges in Beer-sheba. ³Yet his sons did not walk in his ways, but turned aside after gain; they took bribes and perverted justice.

4 Then all the elders of Israel gathered together and came to Samuel at Ramah, ⁵and said to him, "Behold, you are old and your sons do not walk in your ways; now appoint for us a king to govern us like all nations." ⁶But the thing displeased Samuel when they said, "Give us a king to govern us." And Samuel prayed to the LORD. ⁷And the LORD said to Samuel, "Hearken to the voice of the people in all that they say to you; for they have not rejected you, but they have rejected me from being king over them. ⁸According to all the deeds which they have done to me, from the day I brought them up out of Egypt even to this day, forsaking me and serving other gods, so they are also doing to you. ⁹Now then, hearken to their voice; only, you shall solemnly warn them, and show them the ways of the king who shall reign over them."

10 So Samuel told all the words of the LORD to the people who were asking a king from him. ¹¹He said, "These will be the ways of

the king who will reign over you: he will take your sons and appoint them to his chariots and to be his horsemen, and to run before his chariots; [12] and he will appoint himself commanders of thousands and commanders of fifties, and some to plow his ground and to reap his harvest, and to make his implements of war and the equipment of his chariots. [13] He will take your daughters to be perfumers and cooks and bakers. [14] He will take the best of your fields and vineyards and olive orchards and give them to his servants. [15] He will take the tenth of your grain and of your vineyards and give it to his officers and to his servants. [16] He will take your menservants and maidservants, and the best of your cattle and your asses, and put them to his work. [17] He will take the tenth of your flocks, and you shall be his slaves. [18] And in that day you will cry out because of your king, whom you have chosen for yourselves; but the LORD will not answer you in that day."

19 But the people refused to listen to the voice of Samuel; and they said, "No! but we will have a king over us, [20] that we also may be like all the nations, and that our king may govern us and go out before us and fight our battles." [21] And when Samuel had heard all the words of the people, he repeated them in the ears of the LORD. [22] And the LORD said to Samuel, "Hearken to their voice, and make them a king."

8:11 Some scholars suggest that this passage was written after Israel endured some unhappy experiences with kings. For a similar passage see Deuteronomy 17:14–20. The pro-royalist position is voiced in chapters 9–10.

Samuel Anoints Saul
1 Samuel 9:1–2, 15–17; 10:1, 5–7, 9

9 There was a man of Benjamin whose name was Kish, the son of Abi'el, son of Zeror, son of Beco'rath, son of Aphi'ah, a Benjaminite, a man of wealth; [2] and he had a son whose name was Saul, a handsome young man. There was not a man among the people of Israel more handsome than he; from his shoulders upward he was taller than any of the people.

15 Now the day before Saul came, the LORD had revealed to Samuel: [16] "Tomorrow about this time I will send to you a man from the land of Benjamin, and you shall anoint him to be prince over my people Israel. He shall save my people from the hand of the Philistines; for I have seen the affliction of my people, because their cry has come to me." [17] When Samuel saw Saul, the LORD told him, "Here is the man of whom I spoke to you! He it is who shall rule over my people."

10 Then Samuel took a vial of oil and poured it on his head, and kissed him and said, "Has not the LORD anointed you to be prince over his people Israel? And you shall reign over the people of the LORD and you will save them from the hand of their enemies round about. And this shall be the sign to you that the LORD has anointed you to be prince over his heritage.

5 "After that you shall come to Gib′e-ath-elohim, where there is a garrison of the Philistines; and there, as you come to the city, you will meet a band of prophets coming down from the high place with harp, tambourine, flute, and lyre before them, prophesying. ⁶Then the spirit of the LORD will come mightily upon you, and you shall prophesy with them and be turned into another man. ⁷Now when these signs meet you, do whatever your hand finds to do, for God is with you."

9 When he turned his back to leave Samuel, God gave him another heart; and all these signs came to pass that day.

> **10:1** After anointing Saul, a visible sign of his endowment with God's spirit, Samuel gave him three signs by which he will know that his call to the kingship is from God: (1) he will meet two men who will tell him that his father has located the asses and is now anxious over his missing son; (2) he will meet three men on their way to worship God at Beth-el; they will salute him and give him two cakes of bread; (3) he will meet a band of prophets. **10:1–9** Contrast with 10:17–27. Here we have two versions of the selection of Saul as king. In the first the prophet Samuel willingly and privately anoints Saul. In 10:17–27 the king is chosen publicly by the people over Samuel's protest. Some scholars hold that 10:1–9 is a relic from an earlier version, the second the product of later rewriting and editing of the history of the period. **10:5** In this period prophets were holy men who induced ecstatic states by various practices. Their status was not high. Only later, when prophecy was related to moral conviction rather than to mystical or ecstatic experience, did prophecy emerge as a major institution in biblical religion.

The People Elect Saul Their King
1 Samuel 10:17–25; 11:1–7, 9, 11, 14–15; 14:47–52

17 Now Samuel called the people together to the LORD at Mizpah; ¹⁸ and he said to the people of Israel, "Thus says the LORD, the God of Israel, 'I brought up Israel out of Egypt, and I delivered you from the hand of the Egyptians and from the hand of all the kingdoms that were oppressing you.' ¹⁹But you have this day rejected your God, who saves you from all your calamities and your distresses; and you have said, 'No! but set a king over us.' Now therefore present yourselves before the LORD by your tribes and by your thousands."

20 Then Samuel brought all the tribes of Israel near, and the tribe of Benjamin was taken by lot. ²¹ He brought the tribe of Benjamin near by its families, and the family of the Matrites was taken by lot; finally he brought the family of the Matrites near man by man, and Saul the son of Kish was taken by lot. But when they sought him, he could not be found. ²² So they inquired again of the LORD, "Did the man come hither?" and the LORD said, "Behold, he has hidden himself among the baggage." ²³ Then they ran and fetched him from there; and when he stood among the people, he was taller than any of the people from his shoulders upward. ²⁴ And Samuel said to all the people, "Do you see him whom the LORD has chosen? There is none like him among all the people." And all the people shouted, "Long live the king!"

25 Then Samuel told the people the rights and duties of the kingship; and he wrote them in a book and laid it up before the LORD. Then Samuel sent all the people away, each one to his home.

11 Then Nahash the Ammonite went up and besieged Ja′besh-gil′ead; and all the men of Jabesh said to Nahash, "Make a treaty with us, and we will serve you." ² But Nahash the Ammonite said to them, "On this condition I will make a treaty with you, that I gouge out all your right eyes, and thus put disgrace upon all Israel." ³ The elders of Jabesh said to him, "Give us seven days respite that we may send messengers through all the territory of Israel. Then, if there is no one to save us, we will give ourselves up to you." ⁴ When the messengers came to Gib′e-ah of Saul, they reported the matter in the ears of the people; and all the people wept aloud.

5 Now Saul was coming from the field behind the oxen; and Saul said, "What ails the people, that they are weeping?" So they told him the tidings of the men of Jabesh. ⁶ And the spirit of God came mightily upon Saul when he heard these words, and his anger was greatly kindled. ⁷ He took a yoke of oxen, and cut them in pieces and sent them throughout all the territory of Israel by the hand of messengers, saying, "Whoever does not come out after Saul and Samuel, so shall it be done to his oxen!" Then the dread of the LORD fell upon the people, and they came out as one man.

9 And they said to the messengers who had come, "Thus shall you say to the men of Ja′besh-gil′ead: 'Tomorrow, by the time the sun is hot, you shall have deliverance.' " When the messengers came and told the men of Jabesh, they were glad.

11 And on the morrow Saul put the people in three companies; and they came into the midst of the camp in the morning watch, and cut down the Ammonites until the heat of the day; and those who survived were scattered, so that no two of them were left together.

14 Then Samuel said to the people, "Come, let us go to Gilgal and there renew the kingdom." ¹⁵ So all the people went to Gilgal, and there they made Saul king before the LORD in Gilgal. There they sacrificed peace offerings before the LORD, and there Saul and all the men of Israel rejoiced greatly.

14 ⁴⁷ When Saul had taken the kingship over Israel, he fought against all his enemies on every side, against Moab, against the Ammonites, against Edom, against the kings of Zobah, and against the Philistines; wherever he turned he put them to the worse. ⁴⁸ And he did valiantly, and smote the Amal'ekites, and delivered Israel out of the hands of those who plundered them.

49 Now the sons of Saul were Jonathan, Ishvi, and Mal'chishu'a; and the names of his two daughters were these: the name of the first-born was Merab, and the name of the younger Michal; ⁵⁰ and the name of Saul's wife was Ahin'o-am the daughter of Ahim'a-az. And the name of the commander of his army was Abner the son of Ner, Saul's uncle; ⁵¹ Kish was the father of Saul, and Ner the father of Abner was the son of Abi'el.

52 There was hard fighting against the Philistines all the days of Saul; and when Saul saw any strong man, or any valiant man, he attached him to himself.

10:22 Saul's modesty, revealed here, reassured the elders that their desire to establish a monarchical system, despite Samuel's speech, was a wise one. **10:25** Samuel not only chose the king but established the constitutional form by which this new form of government was to be regulated. Scholars believe that Saul ruled over the Israelites between approximately 1030–1010 B.C. **11:14** Whereas Saul had been elected king earlier at Mizpah, his authority had not been accepted by all the people. Now with his victory at Jabesh, all the tribes with great rejoicing confirmed his election at Gilgal. **14:47–52** A summary is inserted here, recapitulating the achievements of Saul's rule over Israel and providing personal data on his family. **14:52** We see here evidence of the development of the first professional army in Hebrew history.

Saul Sins against God in a War with Amalek
1 Samuel 15:1–3, 7–11, 13–16, 22–28

15 And Samuel said to Saul, "The LORD sent me to anoint you king over his people Israel; now therefore hearken to the words of the LORD. ² Thus says the LORD of hosts, 'I will punish what Am'alek did to Israel in opposing them on the way, when they came up out of Egypt. ³ Now go and smite Am'alek, and utterly destroy all that they have; do not spare them, but kill both man and woman, infant and suckling, ox and sheep, camel and ass.' "

7 And Saul defeated the Amal'ekites, from Hav'ilah as far as Shur, which is east of Egypt. ⁸And he took Agag the king of the Amal'ekites alive, and utterly destroyed all the people with the edge of the sword. ⁹But Saul and the people spared Agag, and the best of the sheep and of the oxen and of the fatlings, and the lambs, and all that was good, and would not utterly destroy them; all that was despised and worthless they utterly destroyed.

10 The word of the LORD came to Samuel: ¹¹"I repent that I have made Saul king; for he has turned back from following me, and has not performed my commandments." And Samuel was angry; and he cried to the LORD all night.

13 And Samuel came to Saul, and Saul said to him, "Blessed be you to the LORD; I have performed the commandment of the LORD." ¹⁴And Samuel said, "What then is this bleating of the sheep in my ears, and the lowing of the oxen which I hear?" ¹⁵Saul said, "They have brought them from the Amal'ekites; for the people spared the best of the sheep and of the oxen, to sacrifice to the LORD your God; and the rest we have utterly destroyed." ¹⁶Then Samuel said to Saul, "Stop! I will tell you what the LORD said to me this night." And he said to him, "Say on."

22 And Samuel said,

"Has the LORD as great delight in burnt offerings and sacrifices,
    as in obeying the voice of the LORD?
Behold, to obey is better than sacrifice,
    and to hearken than the fat of rams.
²³For rebellion is as the sin of divination,
    and stubbornness is as iniquity and idolatry.
Because you have rejected the word of the LORD,
    he has also rejected you from being king."

24 And Saul said to Samuel, "I have sinned; for I have transgressed the commandment of the LORD and your words, because I feared the people and obeyed their voice. ²⁵Now therefore, I pray, pardon my sin, and return with me, that I may worship the LORD." ²⁶And Samuel said to Saul, "I will not return with you; for you have rejected the word of the LORD, and the LORD has rejected you from being king over Israel." ²⁷As Samuel turned to go away, Saul laid hold upon the skirt of his robe, and it tore. ²⁸And Samuel said to him, "The LORD has torn the kingdom of Israel from you this day, and has given it to a neighbor of yours, who is better than you."

15:1-2 The Amalekites were a nomadic people who had been among the first to attack the Israelites on their way from Egypt to the Promised Land (Exodus 17:8). Their harassment of the Hebrews was continual (cf. Judges 3:13, 6:3). Their ultimate destruction, therefore, was called for (Exodus 17:16, Deuteronomy 25:19). The religious significance of this war is demonstrated by the renunciation of any profit from the victory. All spoil had to be destroyed (cf. Leviticus 27:28 f., Deuteronomy 13:16 ff.). The Amalekites were not utterly destroyed, however, and they continued to wage warfare against the Hebrews as reported in 1 Samuel 27:8; 30:1; 2 Samuel 8:12. **15:22** This classic statement of prophetic criticism of the sacrificial system is rendered in characteristic Hebrew rhythmical form, and in poetic parallelism. The prophet does not condemn the sacrificial system so much as its misuse. He points to the priority of man's faithfulness, as evidenced in righteous behavior, over a hypocritical display of ceremonial religiosity.

Samuel Anoints David King
1 Samuel 16:1, 4–7, 10–17, 21

16 The LORD said to Samuel, "How long will you grieve over Saul, seeing I have rejected him from being king over Israel? Fill your horn with oil, and go; I will send you to Jesse the Bethlehemite, for I have provided for myself a king among his sons."

4 Samuel did what the LORD commanded, and came to Bethlehem. The elders of the city came to meet him trembling, and said, "Do you come peaceably?" ?[5] And he said, "Peaceably; I have come to sacrifice to the LORD; consecrate yourselves, and come with me to the sacrifice." And he consecrated Jesse and his sons, and invited them to the sacrifice.

6 When they came, he looked on Eli′ab and thought, "Surely the LORD's anointed is before him." [7] But the LORD said to Samuel, "Do not look on his appearance or on the height of his stature, because I have rejected him; for the LORD sees not as man sees; man looks on the outward appearance, but the LORD looks on the heart."

10 And Jesse made seven of his sons pass before Samuel. And Samuel said to Jesse, "The LORD has not chosen these." [11] And Samuel said to Jesse, "Are all your sons here?" And he said, "There remains yet the youngest, but behold, he is keeping the sheep." And Samuel said to Jesse, "Send and fetch him; for we will not sit down till he comes here." [12] And he sent, and brought him in. Now he was ruddy, and had beautiful eyes, and was handsome. And the LORD said, "Arise, anoint him; for this is he." [13] Then Samuel took the horn of oil, and anointed him in the midst of his brothers; and the Spirit of the LORD came mightily upon David from that day forward. And Samuel rose up, and went to Ramah.

14 Now the Spirit of the LORD departed from Saul, and an evil spirit from the LORD tormented him. [15] And Saul's servants said to him, "Behold now, an evil spirit from God is tormenting you. [16] Let

our lord now command your servants, who are before you, to seek out a man who is skilful in playing the lyre; and when the evil spirit from God is upon you, he will play it, and you will be well." [17] So Saul said to his servants, "Provide for me a man who can play well, and bring him to me."

21 And David came to Saul, and entered his service. And Saul loved him greatly, and he became his armor-bearer.

> **16:1** For other accounts of David's anointing by the men of Judah see 2 Samuel 2:4 and by the elders of Israel 2 Samuel 5:3. This anointing by the prophet establishes that David's rule is in accordance with divine will. God selects the king over the Hebrews. Other kings would not meet with God's approval (see Hosea 8:4). **16:14** Saul suffers a form of insanity that manifests itself in fits of terror and violence. In ancient times such mental illness was understood to be the work of an evil spirit. In Hebrew belief, however, God was responsible for both good and evil. Thus the evil spirit was regarded as sent by God in consequence of Saul's sinfulness and rejection of God. Robert Browning in his poem "Saul" vividly describes Saul's melancholy and fitful rages. **16:21** There appear to be two biblical versions explaining how David came into Saul's service. In this account David enters Saul's coterie as a musician and armor bearer (16:14–23). But in another account David is an unknown shepherd lad visiting his brothers during the battle with Goliath (17:12–30); then Saul invites the young hero to his service (17:55–18:2).

David Slays Goliath
1 Samuel 17:1, 3–11, 16, 32–40, 48–51, 55–58

17 Now the Philistines gathered their armies for battle; and they were gathered at Soco, which belongs to Judah, and encamped between Soco and Aze'kah, in E'phesdam'mim.

3 And the Philistines stood on the mountain on the one side, and Israel stood on the mountain on the other side, with a valley between them. [4] And there came out from the camp of the Philistines a champion named Goliath, of Gath, whose height was six cubits and a span. [5] He had a helmet of bronze on his head, and he was armed with a coat of mail, and the weight of the coat was five thousand shekels of bronze. [6] And he had greaves of bronze upon his legs, and a javelin of bronze slung between his shoulders. [7] And the shaft of his spear was like a weaver's beam, and his spear's head weighed six hundred shekels of iron; and his shield-bearer went before him. [8] He stood and shouted to the ranks of Israel, "Why have you come out to draw up for battle? Am I not a Philistine, and are you not servants of Saul? Choose a man for yourselves, and let him come down to me. [9] If he is able to fight with me and kill me, then we will be your

servants; but if I prevail against him and kill him, then you shall be our servants and serve us." [10] And the Philistine said, "I defy the ranks of Israel this day; give me a man, that we may fight together." [11] When Saul and all Israel heard these words of the Philistine, they were dismayed and greatly afraid.

16 For forty days the Philistine came forward and took his stand, morning and evening.

32 And David said to Saul, "Let no man's heart fail because of him; your servant will go and fight with this Philistine." [33] And Saul said to David, "You are not able to go against this Philistine to fight with him; for you are but a youth, and he has been a man of war from his youth." [34] But David said to Saul, "Your servant used to keep sheep for his father; and when there came a lion, or a bear, and took a lamb from the flock, [35] I went after him and smote him and delivered it out of his mouth; and if he arose against me, I caught him by his beard, and smote him and killed him. [36] Your servant has killed both lions and bears; and this uncircumcised Philistine shall be like one of them, seeing he has defied the armies of the living God." [37] And David said, "The LORD who delivered me from the paw of the lion and from the paw of the bear, will deliver me from the hand of this Philistine." And Saul said to David, "Go, and the LORD be with you!" [38] Then Saul clothed David with his armor; he put a helmet of bronze on his head, and clothed him with a coat of mail. [39] And David girded his sword over his armor, and he tried in vain to go, for he was not used to them. Then David said to Saul, "I cannot go with these; for I am not used to them." And David put them off. [40] Then he took his staff in his hand, and chose five smooth stones from the brook, and put them in his shepherd's bag or wallet; his sling was in his hand, and he drew near to the Philistine.

48 When the Philistine arose and came and drew near to meet David, David ran quickly toward the battle line to meet the Philistine. [49] And David put his hand in his bag and took out a stone, and slung it, and struck the Philistine on his forehead; the stone sank into his forehead, and he fell on his face to the ground.

50 So David prevailed over the Philistine with a sling and with a stone, and struck the Philistine, and killed him; there was no sword in the hand of David. [51] Then David ran and stood over the Philistine, and took his sword and drew it out of its sheath, and killed him, and cut off his head with it. When the Philistines saw that their champion was dead, they fled.

55 When Saul saw David go forth against the Philistine, he said to Abner, the commander of the army, "Abner, whose son is this

youth?" And Abner said, "As your soul lives, O king, I cannot tell."
⁵⁶ And the king said, "Inquire whose son the stripling is." ⁵⁷ And as
David returned from the slaughter of the Philistine, Abner took him,
and brought him before Saul with the head of the Philistine in his
hand. ⁵⁸ And Saul said to him, "Whose son are you, young man?"
And David answered, "I am the son of your servant Jesse the
Bethlehemite."

> **17:5** *bronze* is a compound of copper and tin known to the
> ancients; *brass* (copper and zinc; the word "brass" was used in
> earlier English translations) was yet unkown. Goliath's defensive
> weapons were of bronze, whereas his spear was of iron. **17:8** ff.
> Greek literature describes a similar challenge to decide the Trojan
> War through individual combat (Paris vs. Menelaus). **17:40** Judges
> 20:16 describes the accuracy of the Benjamites in the use of this
> weapon. Archeologists have uncovered a relief depicting a slinger of a
> period contemporaneous with David. The weapon consisted of a sling
> strap made of leather or cloth. Whirling two thongs attached to the
> strap the slinger projected a missile of stone or lead with stunning
> velocity.

Jonathan and David Become Friends
1 Samuel 18:1–9

18 When he had finished speaking to Saul, the soul of Jonathan was
knit to the soul of David, and Jonathan loved him as his own soul.
² And Saul took him that day, and would not let him return to his
father's house. ³ Then Jonathan made a covenant with David,
because he loved him as his own soul. ⁴ And Jonathan stripped
himself of the robe that was upon him, and gave it to David, and his
armor, and even his sword and his bow and his girdle. ⁵ And David
went out and was successful wherever Saul sent him; so that Saul set
him over the men of war. And this was good in the sight of all the
people and also in the sight of Saul's servants.

6 As they were coming home, when David returned from slaying
the Philistine, the women came out of all the cities of Israel, singing
and dancing, to meet King Saul, with timbrels, with songs of joy,
and with instruments of music. ⁷ And the women sang to one another
as they made merry,

"Saul has slain his thousands,
　and David his ten thousands."

8 And Saul was very angry, and this saying displeased him; he
said, "They have ascribed to David ten thousands, and to me they
have ascribed thousands; and what more can he have but the
kingdom?" ⁹ And Saul eyed David from that day on.

Saul Seeks to Kill David

King Saul, jealous of David, seeks to be rid of him. He appoints
David first to a difficult military position; then he offers his daughter
Michal in marriage if David will personally slaughter 100 Philistines,
a test which he did not believe David would fulfill. David is successful
in all these trials. His popularity with the people increases as he
repeatedly defeats the Philistine enemies. Saul is now so incensed
that he decides to kill David directly.

1 Samuel 19:1–2, 4, 6–7, 9–19

19 And Saul spoke to Jonathan his son and to all his servants, that
they should kill David. But Jonathan, Saul's son, delighted much in
David. ²And Jonathan told David, "Saul my father seeks to kill you;
therefore take heed to yourself in the morning, stay in a secret place
and hide yourself."

4 And Jonathan spoke well of David to Saul his father, and said to
him, "Let not the king sin against his servant David; because he has
not sinned against you, and because his deeds have been of good
service to you."

6 And Saul hearkened to the voice of Jonathan; Saul swore, "As
the LORD lives, he shall not be put to death." ⁷And Jonathan called
David, and Jonathan showed him all these things. And Jonathan
brought David to Saul, and he was in his presence as before.

9 Then an evil spirit from the LORD came upon Saul, as he sat in
his house with his spear in his hand; and David was playing the lyre.
¹⁰And Saul sought to pin David to the wall with the spear; but he
eluded Saul, so that he struck the spear into the wall. And David
fled, and escaped.

11 That night Saul sent messengers to David's house to watch
him, that he might kill him in the morning. But Michal, David's
wife, told him, "If you do not save your life tonight, tomorrow you
will be killed." ¹²So Michal let David down through the window;
and he fled away and escaped. ¹³Michal took an image and laid it on
the bed and put a pillow of goats' hair at its head, and covered it
with the clothes. ¹⁴And when Saul sent messengers to take David,
she said, "He is sick." ¹⁵Then Saul sent the messengers to see David,
saying, "Bring him up to me in the bed, that I may kill him." ¹⁶And
when the messengers came in, behold, the image was in the bed, with
the pillow of goats' hair at its head. ¹⁷Saul said to Michal, "Why
have you deceived me thus, and let my enemy go, so that he has
escaped?" And Michal answered Saul, "He said to me, 'Let me go;
why should I kill you?'"

18 Now David fled and escaped, and he came to Samuel at

Ramah, and told him all that Saul had done to him. And he and Samuel went and dwelt at Nai′oth. ¹⁹ And it was told Saul, "Behold, David is at Nai′oth in Ramah."

19:13 The presence of household gods, known as *teraphim*, in David's home reveals that worship of the God of Abraham and some forms of idolatry existed side by side. Rabbinic scholars, in respect for David's stature as a man faithful to God, suggest that the teraphim belonged to Michal, who was then barren and intended through superstitious folk methods to treat her difficulty.

Jonathan Saves David's Life
1 Samuel 20 : 1–3, 16–25, 35–37, 39–42

20 Then David fled from Nai′oth in Ramah, and came and said before Jonathan, "What have I done? What is my guilt? And what is my sin before your father, that he seeks my life?" ² And he said to him, "Far from it! You shall not die. Behold, my father does nothing either great or small without disclosing it to me; and why should my father hide this from me? It is not so." ³ But David replied, "Your father knows well that I have found favor in your eyes; and he thinks, 'Let not Jonathan know this, lest he be grieved.' But truly, as the LORD lives and as your soul lives, there is but a step between me and death."

16 "Let not the name of Jonathan be cut off from the house of David. And may the LORD take vengeance on David's enemies." ¹⁷ And Jonathan made David swear again by his love for him; for he loved him as he loved his own soul.

18 Then Jonathan said to him, "Tomorrow is the new moon; and you will be missed, because your seat will be empty. ¹⁹ And on the third day you will be greatly missed; then go to the place where you hid yourself when the matter was in hand, and remain beside yonder stone heap. ²⁰ And I will shoot three arrows to the side of it, as though I shot at a mark. ²¹ And behold, I will send the lad, saying, 'Go, find the arrows.' If I say to the lad, 'Look, the arrows are on this side of you, take them,' then you are to come, for, as the LORD lives, it is safe for you and there is no danger. ²² But if I say to the youth, 'Look, the arrows are beyond you,' then go; for the LORD has sent you away. ²³ And as for the matter of which you and I have spoken, behold, the LORD is between you and me for ever."

24 So David hid himself in the field; and when the new moon came, the king sat down to eat food. ²⁵ The king sat upon his seat, as at other times, upon the seat by the wall; Jonathan sat opposite, and Abner sat by Saul's side, but David's place was empty.

35 In the morning Jonathan went out into the field to the

appointment with David, and with him a little lad. ³⁶ And he said to his lad, "Run and find the arrows which I shoot." As the lad ran, he shot an arrow beyond him. ³⁷ And when the lad came to the place of the arrow which Jonathan had shot, Jonathan called after the lad and said, "Is not the arrow beyond you?"

39 But the lad knew nothing; only Jonathan and David knew the matter. ⁴⁰ And Jonathan gave his weapons to his lad, and said to him, "Go and carry them to the city." ⁴¹ And as soon as the lad had gone, David rose from beside the stone heap and fell on his face to the ground, and bowed three times; and they kissed one another, and wept with one another, until David recovered himself. ⁴² Then Jonathan said to David, "Go in peace, forasmuch as we have sworn both of us in the LORD, saying, 'The LORD shall be between me and you, and between my descendants and your descendants, for ever.' " And he rose and departed; and Jonathan went into the city.

20:1 This chapter provides evidence for some contemporary biblical students that this book, like many other books in the Bible, joins together several historic accounts which sometimes offer differing interpretations or understandings of the events of history. At a later date, an editor tries to harmonize these varying records into one integrated book; but rough edges sometimes remain. This may be the case with the two tales describing how David spared Saul's life (chapters 24 and 26). In the case before us, chapter 20 seems to suggest that Jonathan is unaware that his father intends to kill David (20:2), and Saul himself is forgetful of his past attempts on David's life (20:26); whereas in chapter 19 Jonathan had warned David against his father's effort to kill him (19:2). The essential truth remains: Saul in his sickness attempted to kill David; Jonathan remained faithful to his friend and helped him escape. **20:18** A celebration at the time of the new moon was observed during this period as a day of rest (Amos 8:5) and an occasion for worship and religious instruction (2 Kings 4:23). Evidently on that occasion King Saul also gathered his family and the favorite members of his court for a festive meal. King Saul maintained his court at Gibeah, the first capital city of Israel. The noted archaeologist and Bible scholar, Professor W. F. Albright, in a series of excavations between 1922 and 1933 uncovered this ancient capital about three miles north of Jerusalem at Tel el-Ful, the highest hill in the area, 2,754 feet above sea level. Archaeologists believe they have uncovered the building that King Saul had used as his palace.

In Flight David Eats of Holy Bread
1 Samuel 21:1–15

21 Then came David to Nob to Ahim′elech the priest; and Ahim′elech came to meet David trembling, and said to him, "Why are you alone, and no one with you?" [2] And David said to Ahim'elech the priest, "The king has charged me with a matter, and said to me, 'Let no one know anything of the matter about which I send you, and with which I have charged you.' I have made an appointment with the young men for such and such a place. [3] Now then, what have you at hand? Give me five loaves of bread, or whatever is here." [4] And the priest answered David, "I have no common bread at hand, but there is holy bread; if only the young men have kept themselves from women." [5] And David answered the priest, "Of a truth women have been kept from us as always when I go on an expedition; the vessels of the young men are holy, even when it is a common journey; how much more today will their vessels be holy?" [6] So the priest gave him the holy bread; for there was no bread there but the bread of the Presence, which is removed from before the LORD, to be replaced by hot bread on the day it is taken away.

7 Now a certain man of the servants of Saul was there that day, detained before the LORD; his name was Do'eg the Edomite, the chief of Saul's herdsmen.

8 And David said to Ahim'elech, "And have you not here a spear or a sword at hand? For I have brought neither my sword nor my weapons with me, because the king's business required haste." [9] And the priest said, "The sword of Goliath the Philistine, whom you killed in the valley of Elah, behold, it is here wrapped in a cloth behind the ephod; if you will take that, take it, for there is none but that here." And David said, "There is none like that; give it to me."

10 And David rose and fled that day from Saul, and went to A'chish the king of Gath. [11] And the servants of A'chish said to him, "Is not this David the king of the land? Did they not sing to one another of him in dances,

'Saul has slain his thousands,
and David his ten thousands'?"

12 And David took these words to heart, and was much afraid of A'chish the king of Gath. [13] So he changed his behavior before them, and feigned himself mad in their hands, and made marks on the doors of the gate, and let his spittle run down his beard. [14] Then said A'chish to his servants, "Lo, you see the man is mad; why then have you brought him to me? [15] Do I lack madmen, that you have brought this fellow to play the madman in my presence? Shall this fellow come into my house?"

21:6 In later years both the Pharisees and Jesus were to cite this act of David's eating bread, reserved only for priests, in development of the principle that a ceremonial law may be set aside when life itself is at stake (see note on Matthew 12:3-4).

David Gathers a Following
1 Samuel 22:1–2; 23:1–2, 5, 13–18

22 David departed from there and escaped to the cave of Adullam; and when his brothers and all his father's house heard it, they went down there to him. ²And every one who was in distress, and every one who was in debt, and every one who was discontented, gathered to him; and he became captain over them. And there were with him about four hundred men.

23 Now they told David, "Behold, the Philistines are fighting against Kei'lah, and are robbing the threshing floors." ²Therefore David inquired of the LORD, "Shall I go and attack these Philistines?" And the LORD said to David, "Go and attack the Philistines and save Kei'lah."

5 And David and his men went to Kei'lah, and fought with the Philistines, and brought away their cattle, and made a great slaughter among them. So David delivered the inhabitants of Kei'lah.

13 Then David and his men, who were about six hundred, arose and departed from Kei'lah, and they went wherever they could go. When Saul was told that David had escaped from Kei'lah, he gave up the expedition. ¹⁴And David remained in the strongholds in the wilderness, in the hill country of the Wilderness of Ziph. And Saul sought him every day, but God did not gave him into his hand.

15 And David was afraid because Saul had come out to seek his life. David was in the Wilderness of Ziph at Horesh. ¹⁶And Jonathan, Saul's son, rose, and went to David at Horesh, and strengthened his hand in God. ¹⁷And he said to him, "Fear not; for the hand of Saul my father shall not find you; you shall be king over Israel, and I shall be next to you; Saul my father also knows this." ¹⁸And the two of them made a covenant before the LORD; David remained at Horesh, and Jonathan went home.

> **22:2** In those days anyone in debt faced the danger of being sold into slavery by his creditors (see 2 Kings 4:1). *400 men* The number increased quickly (23:12) to 600 hardened, desperate men, providing David a powerful following (see 25:13; 27:2; 30:10). **23:1** The fact that the people turn to David rather than King Saul to protect them demonstrates that David retained his popularity, even though he was an outlaw in the eyes of Saul.

David Renders Good to Saul
1 Samuel 24:1–22

24 When Saul returned from following the Philistines, he was told, "Behold, David is in the wilderness of Enge'di." ²Then Saul took three thousand chosen men out of all Israel, and went to seek

David and his men in front of the Wildgoats' Rocks. ³ And he came to the sheepfolds by the way, where there was a cave; and Saul went in to relieve himself. Now David and his men were sitting in the innermost parts of the cave. ⁴ And the men of David said to him, "Here is the day of which the LORD said to you, 'Behold, I will give your enemy into your hand, and you shall do to him as it shall seem good to you.' " Then David arose and stealthily cut off the skirt of Saul's robe. ⁵ And afterward David's heart smote him, because he had cut off Saul's skirt. ⁶ He said to his men, "The LORD forbid that I should do this thing to my lord, the LORD's annointed, to put forth my hand against him, seeing he is the LORD's anointed." ⁷ So David persuaded his men with these words, and did not permit them to attack Saul. And Saul rose up and left the cave, and went upon his way.

8 Afterward David also arose, and went out of the cave, and called after Saul, "My lord the king!" And when Saul looked behind him, David bowed with his face to the earth, and did obeisance. ⁹ And David said to Saul, "Why do you listen to the words of men who say, 'Behold, David seeks your hurt'? ¹⁰ Lo, this day your eyes have seen how the LORD gave you today into my hand in the cave; and some bade me kill you, but I spared you. I said, 'I will not put forth my hand against my lord; for he is the LORD's anointed.' ¹¹ See, my father, see the skirt of your robe in my hand; for by the fact that I cut off the skirt of your robe, and did not kill you, you may know and see that there is no wrong or treason in my hands. I have not sinned against you, though you hunt my life to take it.¹² May the LORD judge between me and you, may the LORD avenge me upon you; but my hand shall not be against you. ¹³ As the proverb of the ancient says, 'Out of the wicked comes forth wickedness'; but my hand shall not be against you. ¹⁴ After whom has the king of Israel come out? After whom do you pursue? After a dead dog! After a flea! ¹⁵ May the LORD therefore be judge, and give sentence between me and you, and see to it, and plead my cause, and deliver me from your hand."

16 When David had finished speaking these words to Saul, Saul said, "Is this your voice, my son David?" And Saul lifted up his voice and wept. ¹⁷ He said to David, "You are more righteous than I; for you have repaid me good, whereas I have repaid you evil. ¹⁸ And you have declared this day how you have dealt well with me, in that you did not kill me when the LORD put me into your hands. ¹⁹ For if a man finds his enemy, will he let him go away safe? So may the LORD reward you with good for what you have done to me this day. ²⁰ And now, behold, I know that you shall surely be king, and that the

kingdom of Israel shall be established in your hand. ²¹Swear to me therefore by the LORD that you will not cut off my descendants after me, and that you will not destroy my name out of my father's house." ²²And David swore this to Saul. Then Saul went home; but David and his men went up to the stronghold.

24:3 *To relieve himself:* The Hebrew text here uses a euphemism, "to cover his feet." **24:21** 2 Samuel 9:1–13 records how David kept his promise.

Saul Visits a Witch at Endor
1 Samuel 28:3–8, 11–17, 19–20

28 ³Now Samuel had died, and all Israel had mourned for him and buried him in Ramah, his own city. And Saul had put the mediums and the wizards out of the land. ⁴The Philistines assembled, and came and encamped at Shunem; and Saul gathered all Israel, and they encamped at Gilbo′a. ⁵When Saul saw the army of the Philistines, he was afraid, and his heart trembled greatly. ⁶And when Saul inquired of the LORD, the LORD did not answer him, either by dreams, or by Urim, or by prophets. ⁷Then Saul said to his servants, "Seek out for me a woman who is a medium, that I may go to her and inquire of her." And his servants said to him, "Behold, there is a medium at Endor."

8 So Saul disguised himself and put on other garments, and went, he and two men with him; and they came to the woman by night. And he said, "Divine for me by a spirit, and bring up for me whomever I shall name to you."

11 Then the woman said, "Whom shall I bring up for you?" He said, "Bring up Samuel for me." ¹²When the woman saw Samuel, she cried out with a loud voice; and the woman said to Saul, "Why have you deceived me? You are Saul." ¹³The king said to her, "Have no fear; what do you see?" And the woman said to Saul, "I see a god coming up out of the earth." ¹⁴He said to her, "What is his appearance?" And she said, "An old man is coming up; and he is wrapped in a robe." And Saul knew that it was Samuel, and he bowed with his face to the ground, and did obeisance.

15 Then Samuel said to Saul, "Why have you disturbed me by bringing me up?" Saul answered, "I am in great distress; for the Philistines are warring against me, and God has turned away from me and answers me no more, either by prophets or by dreams; therefore I have summoned you to tell me what I shall do." ¹⁶And Samuel said, "Why then do you ask me, since the LORD has turned from you and become your enemy? ¹⁷The LORD has done to you as

he spoke by me; for the LORD has torn the kingdom out of your hand, and given it to your neighbor, David.

19 "Moreover the LORD will give Israel also with you into the hand of the Philistines; and tomorrow you and your sons shall be with me; the LORD will give the army of Israel also into the hand of the Philistines."

20 Then Saul fell at once full length upon the ground, filled with fear because of the words of Samuel; and there was no strength in him, for he had eaten nothing all day and all night.

28:3 According to the biblical prohibition (Leviticus 20:27; Deuteronomy 28:11) Saul had put an end to all diviners and witches. But with Samuel's death, Saul reverts to the forbidden superstition in a desperate effort to obtain some reassurance. 28:6 Listed here are the common methods by which the early Hebrews consulted the will of God. Eventually direct revelation of God's Word through inspired prophets was considered most reliable. Occult "sciences" were forbidden.

Saul Dies in Battle
1 Samuel 31:1–7, 11–13

31 Now the Philistines fought against Israel; and the men of Israel fled before the Philistines, and fell slain on Mount Gilbo'a. ² And the Philistines overtook Saul and his sons; and the Philistines slew Jonathan and Abin'adab and Mal'chishu'a, the sons of Saul. ³ The battle pressed hard upon Saul, and the archers found him; and he was badly wounded by the archers. ⁴ Then Saul said to his armorbearer, "Draw your sword, and thrust me through with it, lest these uncircumcised come and thrust me through, and make sport of me." But his armor-bearer would not; for he feared greatly. Therefore Saul took his own sword, and fell upon it. ⁵ And when his armorbearer saw that Saul was dead, he also fell upon his sword, and died with him. ⁶ Thus Saul died, and his three sons, and his armor-bearer, and all his men, on the same day together. ⁷ And when the men of Israel who were on the other side of the valley and those beyond the Jordan saw that the men of Israel had fled and that Saul and his sons were dead, they forsook their cities and fled; and the Philistines came and dwelt in them.

11 But when the inhabitants of Ja'besh–gil'ead heard what the Philistines had done to Saul, ¹² all the valiant men arose, and went all night, and took the body of Saul and the bodies of his sons from the wall of Bethshan; and they came to Jabesh and burnt them there. ¹³ And they took their bones and buried them under the tamarisk tree in Jabesh, and fasted seven days.

31:11 Jabesh-gilead was the first city saved by Saul in the earliest day of his rule. The gratitude of the citizens is expressed by the rescue of the bodies of Saul and his sons. The Philistines upon discovering the deceased royal family, had fastened their bodies to the city wall as a humiliation. The loyal citizens of Jabesh-gilead, upon rescuing the bodies, cremated them. Cremation was not a Hebrew practice, but these bodies may by then have been so badly decomposed that they were not fit for burial. A traditional seven-day period of mourning was then observed. To this day Jews continue to mourn their deceased for such a period.

THE SECOND BOOK OF SAMUEL

This book opens with a lament by David over Saul and Jonathan. David is then anointed king by the people of Judah, but so is Ish-bosheth, Saul's son, by the late king's followers among the other tribes. Civil war breaks out and David is victorious. His rule is accepted by all of Israel. David captures Jerusalem, the fortified city long held by the Jebusites as an enclave within the tribal territory of Judah. David brings the Ark there, and establishes this city as the political and spiritual capital of the united nation.

David subdues many peoples, and extends the boundary of the Israelite nation to its farthest point in biblical history. Then David sins with Bathsheba, wife of Uriah. The prophet Nathan condemns David, warning him that now the sword will never depart from his house.

In apparent fulfillment of that prophecy, David's sons quarrel among themselves, and one of them, Absalom, leads a rebellion against his father, forcing the king to flee Jerusalem. In a battle between their respective forces Absalom is killed after an accident. And then as David prepares to return to his throne, jealousy breaks out between the northern ten tribes of Israel and the southern tribe of Judah. A schism develops in the nation. David is plagued till the end of his days with revolt, famine, and Philistine attacks. Yet the Lord assures David that his house will endure for ever. In later years, Israel will pray that the Messiah come from the "house of David."

Near its end 2 Samuel includes two psalms expressing David's thanksgiving to the Lord. Through David's words Israel affirms her own hope:

> For an everlasting covenent He hath made with me,
> Ordered in all things, and sure;
> For all my salvation and my desire,
> Will He not make it to grow?

David ruled over the Israelites from about 1010 to 970 B.C.

David Is Crowned King at Hebron
2 Samuel 3:1; 5:1–7, 9–11, 17–25

3 There was a long war between the house of Saul and the house of David; and David grew stronger and stronger, while the house of Saul became weaker and weaker.

5 Then all the tribes of Israel came to David at Hebron, and said, "Behold, we are your bone and flesh. ²In times past, when Saul was king over us, it was you that led out and brought in Israel; and the LORD said to you, 'You shall be shepherd of my people Israel, and you shall be prince over Israel.' " ³ So all the elders of Israel came to the king at Hebron; and King David made a covenant with them at Hebron before the LORD, and they anointed David king over Israel. ⁴ David was thirty years old when he began to reign, and he reigned forty years. ⁵ At Hebron he reigned over Judah seven years and six months; and at Jerusalem he reigned over all Israel and Judah thirty-three years.

6 And the king and his men went to Jerusalem against the Jeb′usites, the inhabitants of the land, who said to David, "You will not come in here, but the blind and the lame will ward you off"—thinking, "David cannot come in here." ⁷ Nevertheless David took the stronghold of Zion, that is, the city of David.

9 And David dwelt in the stronghold, and called it the city of David. And David built the city round about from the Millo inward. ¹⁰ And David became greater and greater, for the LORD, the God of hosts, was with him.

11 And Hiram king of Tyre sent messengers to David, and cedar trees, also carpenters and masons who built David a house.

17 When the Philistines heard that David had been anointed king over Israel, all the Philistines went up in search of David; but David heard of it and went down to the stronghold. ¹⁸ Now the Philistines had come and spread out in the valley of Reph′aim. ¹⁹ And David inquired of the LORD, "Shall I go up against the Philistines? wilt thou give them into my hand?" And the LORD said to David, "Go up; for I will certainly give the Philistines into your hand." ²⁰ And David came to Ba′al-pera′zim, and David defeated them there; and he said, "The LORD has broken through my enemies before me, like a bursting flood." Therefore the name of that place is called Ba′al-pera′zim. ²¹ And the Philistines left their idols there, and David and his men carried them away.

22 And the Philistines came up yet again, and spread out in the valley of Reph′aim. ²³ And when David inquired of the LORD, he said, "You shall not go up; go around to their rear, and come upon them opposite the balsam trees. ²⁴ And when you hear the sound of marching in the tops of the balsam trees, then bestir yourself; for then the LORD has gone out before you to smite the army of the Philistines." ²⁵ And David did as the LORD commanded him, and smote the Philistines from Geba to Gezer.

3:1 Some commentators suggest that five years elapsed from the death of Saul until the elders of Israel chose David to serve as their king (and not merely king of Judah). Israel needed his help to throw off the Philistines. During that period David successfully fought off attack from loyal followers of the household of King Saul. **5:2** The elders acknowledge here that David's right to rule is derived from his election by God. **5:3** The covenant established both the rights and the duties of the monarchy, which from its beginning was limited by such constitutional regulation. In biblical tradition, therefore, the divine right of the king to rule was not absolute; it was limited by the requirement of consultation and agreement with the elders of the people. **5:6** The tribes of Israel had failed in attempts to capture this proud city (Judges 1:8, 21). The Jebusites were confident that their city was impregnable; they boasted it could be defended even by the blind and the lame. **5:7** As the capital city of David's rule Jerusalem eventually became a symbol of the Hebrew people, Ezekiel 23, Isaiah 62; it also became viewed as the future meeting place of all the nations in the messianic era; Isaiah 2:1–5; 60. For its significance in New Testament see Revelation 21 f. **5:17** David's defeat of the Philistines freed the country finally from the dreaded enemy and reduced them to a minor power. **5:21** This same account is recorded in 1 Chronicles 14:12. There it is explained that the Philistines had "abandoned their gods," i.e., idols that they carried into war. David not only carried the idols away, but he burned them in accordance with Scriptural command (Deuteronomy 7:5, 25).

David Brings the Ark into Jerusalem
2 Samuel 6:1–2, 5, 14–15, 17

6 David again gathered all the chosen men of Israel, thirty thousand. ² And David arose and went with all the people who were with him from Ba'ale-judah, to bring up from there the ark of God, which is called by the name of the LORD of hosts who sits enthroned on the cherubim.

5 And David and all the house of Israel were making merry before the LORD with all their might, with songs and lyres and harps and tambourines and castanets and cymbals.

14 And David danced before the LORD with all his might; and David was girded with a linen ephod. ¹⁵ So David and all the house of Israel brought up the ark of the LORD with shouting, and with the sound of the horn.

17 And they brought in the ark of the LORD, and set it in its place, inside the tent which David had pitched for it; and David offered burnt offerings and peace offerings before the LORD.

6:2 This is the city also called Kiriath-jearim, where the Ark had been brought after its return from the Philistines (1 Samuel 7:1). Having successfully defeated the Philistines, David is now able to regain possession of the Ark, and he locates it in Jerusalem. He makes that city his political center and also the religious center of the nation.

David Desires to Build a Temple

2 Samuel 7:1–2, 4, 8–10, 12–13, 16

7 Now when the king dwelt in his house, and the LORD had given him rest from all his enemies round about, ²the king said to Nathan the prophet, "See now, I dwell in a house of cedar, but the ark of God dwells in a tent."

4 But that same night the word of the LORD came to Nathan.

8 "Now therefore thus you shall say to my servant David, 'Thus says the LORD of hosts, I took you from the pasture, from following the sheep, that you should be prince over my people Israel; ⁹and I have been with you wherever you went, and have cut off all your enemies from before you; and I will make for you a great name, like the name of the great ones of the earth. ¹⁰And I will appoint a place for my people Israel, and will plant them, that they may dwell in their own place, and be disturbed no more; and violent men shall afflict them no more, as formerly.

12 "'When your days are fulfilled and you lie down with your fathers, I will raise up your offspring after you, who shall come forth from your body, and I will establish his kingdom. ¹³He shall build a house for my name, and I will establish the throne of his kingdom for ever.

16 "'And your house and your kingdom shall be made sure for ever before me; your throne shall be established for ever.'"

> **7:13** Compare 1 Kings 5:17, 1 Chronicles 22:8, 28:3. **7:16** This promise to David assumed great significance in Hebraic thought, and provided the seedbed from which the messianic hope drew sustenance. For New Testament reference to this text as applying to Jesus, see Acts 2:30.

David Sins with Bathsheba

> The Bible heroes are human beings capable at one moment of their lives of great nobility and at another moment subject to temptation and sinfulness. The prophet addresses the conscience of the king and calls him to account.

2 Samuel 11:1–17, 26–27; 12:1–7, 9–10, 13–14, 24

11 In the spring of the year, the time when kings go forth to battle, David sent Jo'ab, and his servants with him, and all Israel; and they ravaged the Ammonites, and besieged Rabbah. But David remained at Jerusalem.

2 It happened, late one afternoon, when David arose from his couch and was walking upon the roof of the king's house, that he saw from the roof a woman bathing; and the woman was very

beautiful. ³ And David sent and inquired about the woman. And one said, "Is not this Bathshe′ba, the daughter of Eli′am, the wife of Uri′ah the Hittite?" ⁴ So David sent messengers, and took her; and she came to him, and he lay with her. (Now she was purifying herself from her uncleanness.) Then she returned to her house. ⁵ And the woman conceived; and she sent and told David, "I am with child."

6 So David sent word to Jo′ab, "Send me Uri′ah the Hittite." And Jo′ab sent Uri′ah to David. ⁷ When Uri′ah came to him, David asked how Jo′ab was doing, and how the people fared, and how the war prospered. ⁸ Then David said to Uri′ah, "Go down to your house, and wash your feet." And Uri′ah went out of the king's house, and there followed him a present from the king. ⁹ But Uri′ah slept at the door of the king's house with all the servants of his lord, and did not go down to his house. ¹⁰ When they told David, "Uri′ah did not go down to his house," David said to Uri′ah, "Have you not come from a journey? Why did you not go down to your house?" ¹¹ Uri′ah said to David, "The ark and Israel and Judah dwell in booths; and my lord Jo′ab and the servants of my lord are camping in the open field; shall I then go to my house, to eat and to drink, and to lie with my wife? As you live, and as your soul lives, I will not do this thing." ¹² Then David said to Uri′ah, "Remain here today also, and tomorrow I will let you depart." So Uri′ah remained in Jerusalem that day, and the next. ¹³ And David invited him, and he ate in his presence and drank, so that he made him drunk; and in the evening he went out to lie on his couch with the servants of his lord, but he did not go down to his house.

14 In the morning David wrote a letter to Jo′ab, and sent it by the hand of Uri′ah. ¹⁵ In the letter he wrote, "Set Uri′ah in the forefront of the hardest fighting, and then draw back from him, that he may be struck down, and die." ¹⁶ And as Jo′ab was besieging the city, he assigned Uri′ah to the place where he knew there were valiant men. ¹⁷ And the men of the city came out and fought with Jo′ab; and some of the servants of David among the people fell. Uri′ah the Hittite was slain also.

26 When the wife of Uri′ah heard that Uri′ah her husband was dead, she made lamentation for her husband. ²⁷ And when the mourning was over, David sent and brought her to his house, and she became his wife, and bore him a son. But the thing that David had done displeased the LORD,

12 And the LORD sent Nathan to David. He came to him, and said to him, "There were two men in a certain city, the one rich and the other poor. ² The rich man had very many flocks and herds; ³ but the poor man had nothing but one little ewe lamb, which he had bought.

And he brought it up, and it grew up with him and with his children; it used to eat of his morsel, and drink from his cup, and lie in his bosom, and was like a daughter to him. ⁴Now there came a traveler to the rich man, and he was unwilling to take one of his own flock or herd to prepare for the wayfarer who had come to him, but he took the poor man's lamb, and prepared it for the man who had come to him." ⁵Then David's anger was greatly kindled against the man; and he said to Nathan, "As the LORD lives, the man who has done this deserves to die; ⁶and he shall restore the lamb fourfold, because he did this thing, and because he had no pity."

7 Nathan said to David, "You are the man. Thus says the LORD, the God of Israel, 'I anointed you king over Israel, and I delivered you out of the hand of Saul.

9 " 'Why have you despised the word of the LORD, to do what is evil in his sight? You have smitten Uri′ah the Hittite with the sword, and have taken his wife to be your wife, and have slain him with the sword of the Ammonites. ¹⁰Now therefore the sword shall never depart from your house, because you have despised me, and have taken the wife of Uri′ah the Hittite to be your wife.' "

13 David said to Nathan, "I have sinned against the LORD." And Nathan said to David, "The LORD also has put away your sin; you shall not die. ¹⁴Nevertheless, because by this deed you have utterly scorned the LORD, the child that is born to you shall die."

24 Then David comforted his wife, Bathshe′ba, and went in to her, and lay with her; and she bore a son, and he called his name Solomon.

11:9 Uriah's refusal to go home to his wife leads David at last to plot his murder, then to take Bathsheba as his own wife. Otherwise Bathsheba's infidelity would have been discovered and biblical law would have required that she be put to death as an adulteress. Uriah, in his refusal, may have been complying with a customary military regulation forbidding marital relations during battle (1 Samuel 21:5); or, as some literary scholars suggest, he may have learned of his wife's indiscretions through gossip and sought to avoid encounter with David. **11:11** An indication that the Ark accompanied David's armies into battle. **12:10** A prophesy fulfilled within David's household. His son Absalom murdered his brother Amnon (13:29); then Absalom himself is killed after an unsuccessful rebellion against his father (18:15). Finally David's son Adonijah is executed (1 Kings 2:25). **12:13** David's prayer of repentance is repeated in Psalm 51.

"O Absalom, My Son, My Son"

Chapters 13–20 center upon the rebellion of Absalom, David's son. A series of family crises: David's own infidelity with Bathsheba, the loss of her first child, the rivalry between David's sons—all these are not unrelated to the social discontent that is also stirring in the country. For the biblical author personal immorality must have a social consequence. Absalom takes advantage of the continued rivalry between the northern and southern tribes to make his thrust for power. Supported chiefly by the northern tribe he forces his aging father to flee the throne.

The Bible describes Absalom as the most handsome man in the land: "From the sole of his foot to the crown of his head there was no blemish in him." (14:25 ff.). For years he had lived the life of an heir-apparent, without authority but with increasing popularity among the people. Riding through the woods during the battle, his neck was caught in the forked branch of an oak tree and he was left dangling, there to be finished off by David's soldiers. When the news of his death reached the king, David, to the surprise of many of his followers, burst out in a mournful cry, the classic utterance of a father's grief over his lost son.

2 Samuel 19:1–15

19 It was told Jo'ab, "Behold, the king is weeping and mourning for Ab'salom." ²So the victory that day was turned into mourning for all the people; for the people heard that day, "The king is grieving for his son." ³And the people stole into the city that day as people steal in who are ashamed when they flee in battle. ⁴The king covered his face, and the king cried with a loud voice, "O my son Ab'salom, O Ab'salom, my son, my son!" ⁵Then Jo'ab came into the house to the king, and said, "You have today covered with shame the faces of all your servants, who have this day saved your life, and the lives of your sons and your daughters, and the lives of your wives and your concubines, ⁶because you love those who hate you and hate those who love you. For you have made it clear today that commanders and servants are nothing to you; for today I perceive that if Ab'salom were alive and all of us were dead today, then you would be pleased. ⁷Now therefore arise, go out and speak kindly to your servants; for I swear by the LORD, if you do not go, not a man will stay with you this night; and this will be worse for you than all the evil that has come upon you from your youth until now." ⁸Then the king arose, and took his seat in the gate. And the people were all told, "Behold, the king is sitting in the gate"; and all the people came before the king.

Now Israel had fled every man to his own home. ⁹And all the people were at strife throughout all the tribes of Israel, saying, "The king delivered us from the hand of our enemies, and saved us from the hand of the Philistines; and now he has fled out of the land from Ab'salom. ¹⁰But Ab'salom, whom we anointed over us, is dead in battle. Now therefore why do you say nothing about bringing the king back?"

11 And King David sent this message to Zadok and Abi'athar the priests, "Say to the elders of Judah, 'Why should you be the last to bring the king back to his house, when the word of all Israel has come to the king? ¹² You are my kinsmen, you are my bone and my flesh; why then should you be the last to bring back the king?' ¹³ And say to Ama'sa, 'Are you not my bone and my flesh? God do so to me, and more also, if you are not commander of my army henceforth in place of Jo'ab.' " ¹⁴ And he swayed the heart of all the men of Judah as one man; so that they sent word to the king, "Return, both you and all your servants." ¹⁵ So the king came back to the Jordan; and Judah came to Gilgal to meet the king and to bring the king over the Jordan.

David Composes a Psalm of Thanksgiving

This psalm of thanksgiving was evidently composed shortly after David's victorious battles over the enemies of Israel. There is no hint here of the civil wars that were to divide his kingdom (22:44); there is also a proud boast of integrity (22:22–25). Much of this psalm has been embodied in the Psalter as Psalm 18. Variations in the reading suggest to some scholars that this is an earlier version and that the Psalm in the Psalter received editorial revision and polishing up at a later date. This chapter is read in the synagogue as the prophetic portion for the seventh day of Passover.

2 Samuel 22:1–8, 17–25, 44–51 (Jewish Publication Society)

¹ And David spoke unto the LORD the words of this song in the day that the Lord delivered him out of the hand of all his enemies, and out of the hand of Saul; ² and he said:

The LORD is my rock, and my fortress, and my deliverer;
³ The god who is my rock, in Him I take refuge;
My shield, and my horn of salvation,
My high tower, and my refuge;
My saviour, Thou savest me from violence.
⁴ Praised, I cry, is the LORD.
And I am saved from mine enemies.
⁵ For the waves of Death compassed me.
The floods of Belial assailed me;
⁶ The cords of Sheol surrounded me;
The snares of Death confronted me.
⁷ In my distress I called upon the LORD,
Yea, I called unto my God;
And out of His temple He heard my voice,
And my cry did enter into His ears.

⁸ Then the earth did shake and quake,
  The foundations of heaven did tremble;
  They were shaken, because He was wroth.
¹⁷ He sent from on high, He took me;
  He drew me out of many waters;
¹⁸ He delivered me from mine enemy most strong,
  From them that hated me, for they were too mighty for me.
¹⁹ They confronted me in the day of my calamity;
  But the Lord was a stay unto me.
²⁰ He brought me forth also into a large place;
  He delivered me, because He delighted in me,
²¹ The Lord rewarded me according to my righteousness;
  According to the cleanness of my hands hath He recompensed
    me.
²² For I have kept the ways of the Lord,
  And have not wickedly departed from my God.
²³ For all His ordinances were before me;
  And as for His statutes, I did not depart from them.
²⁴ And I was single-hearted toward Him
  And I kept myself from mine iniquity.
²⁵ Therefore hath the Lord recompensed me according to my
    righteousness,
  According to my cleanness in His eyes.
⁴⁴ Thou also hast delivered me from the contentions of my people;
  Thou hast kept me to be the head of the nations;
  A people whom I have not known serve me.
⁴⁵ The sons of the stranger dwindle away before me;
  As soon as they hear of me, they obey me;
  The sons of the stranger fade away,
  And come halting out of their close places.
⁴⁷ The Lord liveth, and blessed be my Rock;
  And exalted by the God, my Rock of salvation;
⁴⁸ Even the God that executeth vengeance for me;
  And bringeth down peoples under me,
⁴⁹ And that bringeth me forth from mine enemies;
  Yea, Thou liftest me up above them that rise up against me;
  Thou deliverest me from the violent man.
⁵⁰ Therefore I will give thanks unto Thee, O Lord, among the
    nations,
  And will sing praises unto Thy name.
⁵¹ A tower of salvation is He to His king;
  And showeth mercy to His anointed,
  To David and to his seed, for evermore.

David's Last Psalm

2 Samuel 23:1–7 (Jewish Publication Society)

¹Now these are the last words of David:
  The saying of David the son of Jesse,
  And the saying of the man raised on high,
  The anointed of the God of Jacob,
  And the sweet singer of Israel:
²The spirit of the LORD spoke by me,
  And His word was upon my tongue.
³The God of Israel said,
  The Rock of Israel spoke to me:
"Ruler over men shall be
  The righteous, even he that ruleth in the fear of God,
⁴And as the light of the morning when the sun riseth,
  A morning without clouds;
  When through clear shining after rain,
  The tender grass springeth out of the earth."
⁵For is not my house established with God?
  For an everlasting covenent He hath made with me,
  Ordered in all things, and sure;
  For all my salvation, and all my desire,
  Will He not make it to grow?
⁶But the ungodly, they are as thorns thrust away, all of them,
  For they cannot be taken with the hand;
⁷But the man that toucheth them
  Must be armed with iron and the staff of a spear;
  And they shall be utterly burned with fire in their place.

The Books of the Kings

In the Hebrew arrangement of Scripture the original Book of Kings was the last book of the Former Prophets. It was divided by the translators of the Septuagint into two books; that division was then adopted with the printing of a Hebrew Bible in 1518.

The two books continue the historic narrative of the monarchy from the last days of King David about 970 B.C. to the Babylonian captivity starting in 586 B.C. The first volume records the glory and decline of King Solomon. With his death the Hebrew people divide into two kingdoms: a Northern Kingdom, Israel, consisting of ten tribes, and a Southern Kingdom, Judah, comprised of the tribes of Judah and Benjamin. The second volume tells how, after two hundred years of existence the Northern Kingdom, Israel, is overrun by Assyria, and the people are taken into captivity, never to return. One hundred and thirty-five years later Judah succumbs to the power of Nebuchadnezzar, and its leaders are taken into exile in Babylonia.

As the text reports, much in these books is taken from historic collections now lost, such as the "Book of the Acts of Solomon" (1 Kings 11:41), the "Book of Chronicles of the Kings of Judah" (1 Kings 14:29) mentioned fifteen times, and the "Book of the Chronicles of Kings of Israel," mentioned eighteen times (cf. 2 Kings 21:25). It is traditionally held that the prophet Jeremiah edited and completed Kings. Some critics feel that Jeremiah's literary hand is to be seen, but they prefer a theory that accepts multiple authorship. Other scholars believe that its first edition may have been written shortly after the reformation of King Josiah in 621 B.C. Since 2 Kings does not record the return of the Exiles from Babylonia there is some agreement that it was probably written or edited between 550–536 B.C.

The Hebrew religious historian evaluated the monarchs and their achievements by the criterion of their devotion to God (cf. 2 Kings 2:1–4). Thus not all historic events are noted; the spiritual condition of a king's reign receives the major attention. Records of other nations found by archaeologists now disclose to us important events in the history of Israel and Judah that have been omitted in the Books of Kings. On the other hand, while the biblical text rushes on to make its moral point, it is accurate on the events reported. Recent excavations, for example, have uncovered the chariot cities and stables at Megiddo (1 Kings 10:26), remains of Solomon's copper industry and his shipbuilding facilities at the southern port of Ezion-Geber (1 Kings 9:26) both of which are mentioned in the text. A cuneiform inscription (in the British Museum) describes King Ahab's war with other Syrian kings against the Assyrian ruler

Shalmaneser III. In fact, the tablet provides scholars with the first biblical date that can be checked by reference to extra biblical records: the battle in June 853 B.C. at Karkar.

A black obelisk in the British Museum (the only representation available anywhere depicting an Israelite king) pictures the Hebrew monarch Jehu prostrate before the Assyrian king.

The author or compiler of this history is not interested in describing the might or glory of Israel and Judah, or her rulers, but rather their moral stature. For example, a Moabite stone discovered in 1868 refers to King Omri as a conqueror of Moab. Omri reigned over Israel twelve years, 887–876 B.C. He was a mighty king, yet the text dismisses him in five sentences (16:23–27); he "did what was evil in the sight of the LORD," and the text refers the reader to the "Chronicles of the Kings of Israel" for further details of his military exploits. On the other hand, King Hezekiah, no warrior, was the most respected of all the kings. He repaired the temple, organized the services of the priests and the Levites, destroyed the bronze serpent, restored the Law to its central place. He is given several chapters within Kings.

The selections sample the lives of some of the kings.

THE FIRST BOOK OF THE KINGS

David Selects Solomon as His Successor

1 Kings 1:1a, 28–35, 38–40; 2:1–4, 10, 12

1 Now King David was old and advanced in years. . . .

28 Then King David [said], "Call Bathshe′ba to me." So she came into the king's presence, and stood before the king. ²⁹ And the king swore, saying, "As the LORD lives, who has redeemed my soul out of every adversity, ³⁰ as I swore to you by the LORD, the God of Israel, saying, 'Solomon your son shall reign after me, and he shall sit upon my throne in my stead'; even so will I do this day." ³¹ Then Bathshe′ba bowed with her face to the ground, and did obeisance to the king, and said, "May my lord King David live for ever!"

32 King David said, "Call to me Zadok the priest, Nathan the prophet, and Benai′ah the son of Jehoi′ada." So they came before the king. ³³ And the king said to them, "Take with you the servants of your lord, and cause Solomon my son to ride on my own mule, and bring him down to Gihon; ³⁴ and let Zadok the priest and Nathan the prophet there anoint him king over Israel; then blow the trumpet, and say, 'Long live King Solomon!' ³⁵ You shall then come up after him, and he shall come and sit upon my throne; for he shall be king in my stead; and I have appointed him to be ruler over Israel and over Judah."

38 So Zadok the priest, Nathan the prophet, and Benai′ah the son of Jehoi′ada, and the Cher′ethites and the Pel′ethites, went down and caused Solomon to ride on King David's mule, and brought him to Gihon. ³⁹ There Zadok the priest took the horn of oil from the tent, and anointed Solomon. Then they blew the trumpet; and all the people said, "Long live King Solomon!" ⁴⁰ And all the people went up after him, playing on pipes, and rejoicing with great joy, so that the earth was split by their noise.

2 When David's time to die drew near, he charged Solomon his son, saying, ²"I am about to go the way of all the earth. Be strong, and show yourself a man, ³ and keep the charge of the LORD your God, walking in his ways and keeping his statutes, his commandments, his ordinances, and his testimonies, as it is written in the law of Moses, that you may prosper in all that you do and wherever you turn; ⁴ that the LORD may establish his word which he spoke concerning me, saying, 'If your sons take heed to their way, to walk before me in faithfulness with all their heart and with all their soul, there shall not fail you a man on the throne of Israel.'"

10 Then David slept with his fathers, and was buried in the city of David.

12 So Solomon sat upon the throne of David his father; and his kingdom was firmly established.

2:10 The term, "slept with his fathers," earlier meant that the deceased was buried in a family sepulchre; but now it is used in a general sense, signifying death.

Solomon Requests an Understanding Heart
1 Kings 3:1–14

3 Solomon made a marriage alliance with Pharaoh king of Egypt; he took Pharaoh's daughter, and brought her into the city of David, until he had finished building his own house and the house of the LORD and the wall around Jerusalem. [2] The people were sacrificing at the high places, however, because no house had yet been built for the name of the LORD.

3 Solomon loved the LORD, walking in the statutes of David his father; only, he sacrificed and burnt incense at the high places. [4] And the king went to Gibeon to sacrifice there, for that was the great high place; Solomon used to offer a thousand burnt offerings upon that altar. [5] At Gibeon the LORD appeared to Solomon in a dream by night; and God said, "Ask what I shall give you." [6] And Solomon said, "Thou hast shown great and steadfast love to thy servant David my father, because he walked before thee in faithfulness, in righteousness, and in uprightness of heart toward thee; and thou hast kept for him this great and steadfast love, and hast given him a son to sit on his throne this day. [7] And now, O LORD my God, thou hast made thy servant king in place of David my father, although I am but a little child; I do not know how to go out or come in. [8] And thy servant is in the midst of thy people whom thou hast chosen, a great people, that cannot be numbered or counted for multitude. [9] Give thy servant therefore an understanding mind to govern thy people, that I may discern between good and evil; for who is able to govern this thy great people?"

10 It pleased the Lord that Solomon had asked this. [11] And God said to him, "Because you have asked this, and have not asked for yourself long life or riches or the life of your enemies, but have asked for yourself understanding to discern what is right, [12] behold, I now do according to your word. Behold, I give you a wise and discerning mind, so that none like you has been before you and none like you shall arise after you. [13] I give you also what you have not asked, both riches and honor, so that no other king shall compare with you, all your days. [14] And if you will walk in my ways, keeping my statutes

and my commandments, as your father David walked, then I will lengthen your days."

Solomon Judges between the Mothers
1 Kings 3:16–28

16 Then two harlots came to the king, and stood before him. [17] The one woman said, "Oh, my lord, this woman and I dwell in the same house; and I gave birth to a child while she was in the house. [18] Then on the third day after I was delivered, this woman also gave birth; and we were alone; there was no one else with us in the house, only we two were in the house. [19] And this woman's son died in the night, because she lay on it. [20] And she arose at midnight, and took my son from beside me, while your maidservant slept, and laid it in her bosom, and laid her dead son in my bosom. [21] When I rose in the morning to nurse my child, behold, it was dead; but when I looked at it closely in the morning, behold, it was not the child that I had borne." [22] But the other woman said, "No, the living child is mine, and the dead child is yours." The first said, "No, the dead child is yours, and the living child is mine." Thus they spoke before the king.

23 Then the king said, "The one says, 'This is my son that is alive, and your son is dead'; and the other says, 'No; but your son is dead, and my son is the living one.'" [24] And the king said, "Bring me a sword." So a sword was brought before the king. [25] And the king said, "Divide the living child in two, and give half to the one, and half to the other." [26] Then the woman whose son was alive said to the king, because her heart yearned for her son, "Oh, my lord, give her the living child, and by no means slay it." But the other said, "It shall be neither mine nor yours; divide it." [27] Then the king answered and said, "Give the living child to the first woman, and by no means slay it; she is its mother." [28] And all Israel heard of the judgment which the king had rendered; and they stood in awe of the king, because they perceived that the wisdom of God was in him, to render justice.

The Grandeur of Solomon's Reign
1 Kings 4:1, 20–34; 5:1–18

4 King Solomon was king over all Israel.

20 Judah and Israel were as many as the sand by the sea; they ate and drank and were happy. [21] Solomon ruled over all the kingdoms from the Eu-phra'tes to the land of the Philistines and to the border of Egypt; they brought tribute and served Solomon all the days of his life.

22 Solomon's provision for one day was thirty cors of fine flour,

and sixty ears cors of meal, ^{23} ten fat oxen, and twenty pasture-fed cattle, a hundred sheep, besides harts, gazelles, roebucks, and fatted fowl. ^{24} For he had dominion over all the region west of the Eu-phra'tes from Tiphsah to Gaza, over all the kings west of the Eu-phra'tes; and he had peace on all sides round about him. ^{25} And Judah and Israel dwelt in safety, from Dan even to Beersheba, every man under his vine and under his fig tree, all the days of Solomon. ^{26} Solomon also had forty thousand stalls of horses for his chariots, and twelve thousand horsemen. ^{27} And those officers supplied provisions for King Solomon, and for all who came to King Solomon's table, each one in his month; they let nothing be lacking. ^{28} Barley also and straw for the horses and swift steeds they brought to the place where it was required, each according to his charge.

29 And God gave Solomon wisdom and understanding beyond measure, and largeness of mind like the sand on the seashore, ^{30} so that Solomon's wisdom surpassed the wisdom of all the people of the east, and all the wisdom of Egypt. ^{31} For he was wiser than all other men, wiser than Ethan the Ez'rahite, and Heman, Calcol, and Darda, the sons of Mahol; and his fame was in all the nations round about. ^{32} He also uttered three thousand proverbs; and his songs were a thousand and five. ^{33} He spoke of trees, from the cedar that is in Lebanon to the hyssop that grows out of the wall; he spoke also of beasts, and of birds, and of reptiles, and of fish. ^{34} And men came from all peoples to hear the wisdom of Solomon, and from all the kings of the earth, who had heard of his wisdom.

5 Now Hiram king of Tyre sent his servants to Solomon, when he heard that they had anointed him king in place of his father; for Hiram always loved David. ^{2} And Solomon sent word to Hiram, ^{3} "You know that David my father could not build a house for the name of the LORD his God because of the warfare with which his enemies surrounded him, until the LORD put them under the soles of his feet. ^{4} But now the LORD my God has given me rest on every side; there is neither adversary nor misfortune. ^{5} And so I purpose to build a house for the name of the LORD my God, as the LORD said to David my father, 'Your son, whom I will set upon your throne in your place, shall build the house for my name.' ^{6} Now therefore command that cedars of Lebanon be cut for me; and my servants will join your servants, and I will pay you for your servants such wages as you set; for you know that there is no one among us who knows how to cut timber like the Sido'nians."

7 When Hiram heard the words of Solomon, he rejoiced greatly, and said, "Blessed be the LORD this day, who has given to David a wise son to be over this great people." ⁸ And Hiram sent to Solomon, saying, "I have heard the message which you have sent to me; I am ready to do all you desire in the matter of cedar and cypress timber. ⁹ My servants shall bring it down to the sea from Lebanon; and I will make it into rafts to go by sea to the place you direct, and I will have them broken up there, and you shall receive it; and you shall meet my wishes by providing food for my household." ¹⁰ So Hiram supplied Solomon with all the timber of cedar and cypress that he desired, ¹¹ while Solomon gave Hiram twenty thousand cors of wheat as food for his household, and twenty thousand cors of beaten oil. Solomon gave this to Hiram year by year. ¹² And the LORD gave Solomon wisdom, as he promised him; and there was peace between Hiram and Solomon; and the two of them made a treaty.

13 King Solomon raised a levy of forced labor out of all Israel; and the levy numbered thirty thousand men. ¹⁴ And he sent them to Lebanon, ten thousand a month in relays; they would be a month in Lebanon and two months at home; Adoni'ram was in charge of the levy. ¹⁵ Solomon also had seventy thousand burden-bearers and eighty thousand hewers of stone in the hill country, ¹⁶ besides Solomon's three thousand three hundred chief officers who were over the work, who had charge of the people who carried on the work. ¹⁷ At the king's command, they quarried out great, costly stones in order to lay the foundation of the house with dressed stones. ¹⁸ So Solomon's builders and Hiram's builders and the men of Gebal did the hewing and prepared the timber and the stone to build the house.

4:21 Solomon's kingdom was the largest in the history of Israel. He ruled around 970–931 B.C. **4:32** Some of these may be preserved in the Book of Proverbs. It is traditionally held that the Song of Songs was another of Solomon's creative literary efforts.

Solomon Builds a House to God

1 Kings 6:1–2, 7, 11–14, 18–19, 22; 8:1–15, 27–34, 41–43; 9:25

6 In the four hundred and eightieth year after the people of Israel came out of the land of Egypt, in the fourth year of Solomon's reign over Israel, in the month of Zith, which is the second month, he began to build the house of the LORD. ² The house which King Solomon built for the LORD was sixty cubits long, twenty cubits wide, and thirty cubits high.

7 When the house was built, it was with stone prepared at the

quarry; so that neither hammer nor axe nor any tool of iron was heard in the temple, while it was being built.

11 Now the word of the LORD came to Solomon, ¹² "Concerning this house which you are building, if you will walk in my statutes and obey my ordinances and keep all my commandments and walk in them, then I will establish my word with you, which I spoke to David your father. ¹³ And I will dwell among the children of Israel, and will not forsake my people Israel."

14 So Solomon built the house, and finished it.

18 The cedar within the house was carved in the form of gourds and open flowers; all was cedar, no stone was seen. ¹⁹ The inner sanctuary he prepared in the innermost part of the house, to set there the ark of the covenant of the LORD.

22 And he overlaid the whole house with gold, until all the house was finished. Also the whole altar that belonged to the inner sanctuary he overlaid with gold.

8 Then Solomon assembled the elders of Israel and all the heads of the tribes, the leaders of the fathers' houses of the people of Israel, before King Solomon in Jerusalem, to bring up the ark of the covenant of the LORD out of the city of David, which is Zion. ² And all the men of Israel assembled to King Solomon at the feast in the month Eth'anim, which is the seventh month. ³ And all the elders of Israel came, and the priests took up the ark. ⁴ And they brought up the ark of the LORD, the tent of meeting, and all the holy vessels that were in the tent; the priests and the Levites brought them up. ⁵ And King Solomon and all the congregation of Israel, who had assembled before him, were with him before the ark, sacrificing so many sheep and oxen that they could not be counted or numbered. ⁶ Then the priests brought the ark of the covenant of the LORD to its place, in the inner sanctuary of the house, in the most holy place, underneath the wings of the cherubim. ⁷ For the cherubim spread out their wings over the place of the ark, so that the cherubim made a covering above the ark and its poles. ⁸ And the poles were so long that the ends of the poles were seen from the holy place before the inner sanctuary; but they could not be seen from outside; and they are there to this day. ⁹ There was nothing in the ark except the two tables of stone which Moses put there at Horeb, where the LORD made a covenant with the people of Israel, when they came out of the land of Egypt. ¹⁰ And when the priests came out of the holy place, a cloud filled the house of the LORD, ¹¹ so that the priests could not stand to minister because of the cloud; for the glory of the LORD filled the house of the LORD.

12 Then Solomon said,

"The LORD has set the sun in the heavens,
　　but has said that he would dwell in thick darkness.
[13] I have built thee an exalted house,
　　a place for thee to dwell in for ever."

14 Then the king faced about, and blessed all the assembly of Israel, while all the assembly of Israel stood. [15] And he said, "Blessed be the LORD, the God of Israel, who with his hand has fulfilled what he promised with his mouth to David my father.

27 "But will God indeed dwell on the earth? Behold, heaven and the highest heaven cannot contain thee; how much less this house which I have built! [28] Yet have regard to the prayer of thy servant and to his supplication, O LORD my God, hearkening to the cry and to the prayer which thy servant prays before thee this day; [29] that thy eyes may be open night and day toward this house, the place of which thou hast said, 'My name shall be there,' that thou mayest hearken to the prayer which thy servant offers toward this place. [30] And hearken thou to the supplication of thy servant and of thy people Israel, when they pray toward this place; yea, hear thou in heaven thy dwelling place; and when thou hearest, forgive.

31 "If a man sins against his neighbor and is made to take an oath, and comes and swears his oath before thine altar in this house, [32] then hear thou in heaven, and act, and judge thy servants, condemning the guilty by bringing his conduct upon his own head, and vindicating the righteous by rewarding him according to his righteousness.

33 "When thy people Israel are defeated before the enemy because they have sinned against thee, if they turn again to thee, and acknowledge thy name, and pray and make supplication to thee in this house; [34] then hear thou in heaven, and forgive the sin of thy people Israel, and bring them again to the land which thou gavest to their fathers.

41 "Likewise when a foreigner, who is not of thy people Israel, comes from a far country for thy name's sake [42] (for they shall hear of thy great name, and thy mighty hand, and of thy outstretched arm), when he comes and prays toward this house, [43] hear thou in heaven thy dwelling place, and do according to all for which the foreigner calls to thee; in order that all the peoples of the earth may know thy name and fear thee, as do thy people Israel, and that they may know that this house which I have built is called by thy name."

9 [25] Three times a year Solomon used to offer up burnt offerings and peace offerings upon the altar which he built to the LORD, burning incense before the LORD. So he finished the house.

6:1–2 The Temple built by Solomon consisted of (*a*) the *house*, or main chamber, rectangular in shape, 60 cubits in length from east to west, and 20 cubits from north to south, and 30 cubits in height, a cubit being about 18 inches; (*b*) a *porch* or entrance on the east side, extending from north to south along the whole width of the house; (*c*) *side chambers* in three stories built along the northwest and south sides. The *main chamber* itself was divided into two portions: the inner chamber known as the Sanctuary or holy of holies, was 20 cubits square; the outer portion, known as the Temple, was 40 by 20 cubits. A large court surrounded the entire structure. **6:7** Rabbinic commentators suggest that since the Temple symbolized peace, tools of iron, the metal used in warfare, were not to be used in the construction of the temple. It took seven years and six months to build. **8:2** The feast described here is Succoth (Tabernacles). Verses 8:2–21 are read in the synagogue on the second day of Succoth. **8:6** The Ark of the Covenant is never again mentioned in Scriptures and no other record of it has yet been discovered.

The Queen of Sheba Tests Solomon
1 Kings 9:26–28; 10:1–3, 6–7, 10, 13–15, 22–29

26 King Solomon built a fleet of ships at E′zion-ge′ber, which is near Eloth on the shore of the Red Sea, in the land of Edom. ²⁷ And Hiram sent with the fleet his servants, seamen who were familiar with the sea, together with the servants of Solomon; ²⁸ and they went to Ophir, and brought from there gold, to the amount of four hundred and twenty talents; and they brought it to King Solomon.
10 Now when the queen of Sheba heard of the fame of Solomon concerning the name of the LORD, she came to test him with hard questions. ²She came to Jerusalem with a very great retinue, with camels bearing spices, and very much gold, and precious stones; and when she came to Solomon, she told him all that was on her mind. ³And Solomon answered all her questions; there was nothing hidden from the king which he could not explain to her.

6 And she said to the king, "The report was true which I heard in my own land of your affairs and of your wisdom, ⁷but I did not believe the reports until I came and my own eyes had seen it; and, behold, the half was not told me; your wisdom and prosperity surpass the report which I heard."

10 Then she gave the king a hundred and twenty talents of gold, and a very great quantity of spices, and precious stones; never again came such an abundance of spices as these which the queen of Sheba gave to King Solomon.

13 And King Solomon gave to the queen of Sheba all that she desired, whatever she asked besides what was given her by the

bounty of King Solomon. So she turned and went back to her own land, with her servants.

14 Now the weight of gold that came to Solomon in one year was six hundred and sixty-six talents of gold, ¹⁵ besides that which came from the traders and from the traffic of the merchants, and from all the kings of Arabia and from the governors of the land.

22 For the king had a fleet of ships of Tarshish at sea with the fleet of Hiram. Once every three years the fleet of ships of Tarshish used to come bringing gold, silver, ivory, apes, and peacocks.

23 Thus King Solomon excelled all the kings of the earth in riches and in wisdom. ²⁴ And the whole earth sought the presence of Solomon to hear his wisdom, which God had put into his mind. ²⁵ Every one of them brought his present, articles of silver and gold, garments, myrrh, spices, horses, and mules, so much year by year.

26 And Solomon gathered together chariots and horsemen; he had fourteen hundred chariots and twelve thousand horsemen, whom he stationed in the chariot cities and with the king in Jerusalem. ²⁷ And the king made silver as common in Jerusalem as stone, and he made cedar as plentiful as the sycamore of the Shephe'lah. ²⁸ And Solomon's import of horses was from Egypt and Ku'e, and the king's traders received them from Ku'e at a price. ²⁹ A chariot could be imported from Egypt for six hundred shekels of silver, and a horse for a hundred and fifty; and so through the king's traders they were exported to all the kings of the Hittites and the kings of Syria.

9:26 The new State of Israel has built a port city at the site of Elath, near ancient Ezion-Geber. 10:1 Two operas stimulated by this account of the meeting between the beautiful queen and the wise king are Goldmark's and Gounod's "The Queen of Sheba." 10:1–13 The Queen of Sheba's visit undoubtedly had commercial as well as political significance. This short account of riddles and answers has stimulated Hebraic and Arabic folklore. 10:13 The Queen of Sheba ruled a domain in the southwest portion of the Arabian peninsula. The king of modern-day Ethiopia bears the honorific title "Lion of Judah" as a descendant of Solomon and the Queen of Sheba. 10:14 A talent of gold equals $30,000. Solomon's annual income in gold alone approached twenty million dollars. 10:26–29 The number of Solomon's chariots and horsemen were long questioned. Excavations at Megiddo in 1928, however, showed that they could be true; at Megiddo alone archaeologists have uncovered stables for 450 horses and rooms for 150 chariots. Scholars today interpret verse 29 to be a record of the price for which Solomon sold horses and chariots to the Hittites.

Solomon Is Seduced into Idolatry

The Law warned against foreign marriages (cf. Deuteronomy 7:3 ff., Joshua 23:7 ff.). It was the manner of oriental kings to maintain a large harem and to use marriage as a means of confirming political and economic transactions. In the process Solomon was led to give financial support to the foreign worship of his wives. The people resented taxation and labor conscription to maintain idolatrous establishments. After Solomon died the people revolted, and Jeroboam was supported in his rebellion by the prophet Ahijah.

1 Kings 11:1–4, 11–13, 20, 40–43

11 Now King Solomon loved many foreign women: the daughter of Pharaoh, and Moabite, Ammonite, Edomite, Sido'nian, and Hittite women, ² from the nations concerning which the LORD had said to the people of Israel, "You shall not enter into marriage with them, neither shall they with you, for surely they will turn away your heart after their gods"; Solomon clung to these in love. ³ He had seven hundred wives, princesses, and three hundred concubines; and his wives turned away his heart. ⁴ For when Solomon was old his wives turned away his heart after other gods; and his heart was not wholly true to the LORD his God, as was the heart of David his father.

11 Therefore the LORD said to Solomon, "Since this has been your mind and you have not kept my covenant and my statutes which I have commanded you, I will surely tear the kingdom from you and will give it to your servant. ¹² Yet for the sake of David your father I will not do it in your days, but I will tear it out of the hand of your son. ¹³ However I will not tear away all the kingdom; but I will give one tribe to your son, for the sake of David my servant and for the sake of Jerusalem which I have chosen."

20 And the sister of Tah'penes bore him Genu'bath his son, whom Tah'penes weaned in Pharaoh's house; and Genu'bath was in Pharaoh's house among the sons of Pharaoh.

40 Solomon sought therefore to kill Jerobo'am; but Jerobo'am arose and fled into Egypt, to Shishak king of Egypt, and was in Egypt until the death of Solomon.

41 Now the rest of the acts of Solomon, and all that he did, and his wisdom, are they not written in the book of the acts of Solomon? ⁴² And the time that Solomon reigned in Jerusalem over all Israel was forty years. ⁴³ And Solomon slept with his fathers, and was buried in the city of David his father; and Rehobo'am his son reigned in his stead.

The Kingdom Is Split

An old division among the Hebrew tribes is reasserted. Jeroboam, as his first act of apostasy, restores the sanctuaries of former worship. Both Israel and Judah lapse into sin. The prophets warn to no avail.

1 Kings 12:1–14, 16–17, 20, 25–31; 14: 19–27, 29–31

12 Rehobo'am went to Shechem, for all Israel had come to Shechem to make him king. ² And when Jerobo'am the son of Nebat heard of it (for he was still in Egypt, whither he had fled from King Solomon), then Jerobo'am returned from Egypt. ³ And they sent and called him; and Jerobo'am and all the assembly of Israel came and said to Rehobo'am, ⁴ "Your father made our yoke heavy. Now therefore lighten the hard service of your father and his heavy yoke upon us, and we will serve you." ⁵ He said to them, "Depart for three days, then come again to me." So the people went away.

6 Then King Rehobo'am took counsel with the old men, who had stood before Solomon his father while he was yet alive, saying, "How do you advise me to answer this people?" ⁷ And they said to him, "If you will be a servant to this people today and serve them, and speak good words to them when you answer them, then they will be your servants for ever." ⁸ But he forsook the counsel which the old men gave him, and took counsel with the young men who had grown up with him and stood before him. ⁹ And he said to them, "What do you advise that we answer this people who have said to me, 'Lighten the yoke that your father put upon us'?" ¹⁰ And the young men who had grown up with him said to him, "Thus shall you speak to this people who said to you, 'Your father made our yoke heavy, but do you lighten it for us'; thus shall you you say to them, 'My little finger is thicker than my father's loins. ¹¹ And now, whereas my father laid upon you a heavy yoke, I will add to your yoke. My father chastised you with whips, but I will chastise you with scorpions.' "

12 So Jerobo'am and all the people came to Rehobo'am the third day, as the king said, "Come to me again the third day." ¹³ And the king answered the people harshly, and forsaking the counsel which the old men had given him, ¹⁴ he spoke to them according to the counsel of the young men, saying, "My father made your yoke heavy, but I will add to your yoke; my father chastised you with whips, but I will chastise you with scorpions."

16 And when all Israel saw that the king did not hearken to them, the people answered the king,

"What portion have we in David?
We have no inheritance in the son of Jesse.
To your tents, O Israel!
Look now to your own house, David."

So Israel departed to their tents. [17] But Rehobo'am reigned over the people of Israel who dwelt in the cities of Judah.

20 And when all Israel heard that Jerobo'am had returned, they sent and called him to the assembly and made him king over all Israel. There was none that followed the house of David, but the tribe of Judah only.

25 Then Jerobo'am built Shechem in the hill country of E'phraim, and dwelt there; and he went out from there and built Penu'el. [26] And Jerobo'am said in his heart, "Now the kingdom will turn back to the house of David; [27] if this people go up to offer sacrifices in the house of the LORD at Jerusalem, then the heart of this people will turn again to their lord, to Rehobo'am the king of Judah, and they will kill me and return to Rehobo'am king of Judah." [28] So the king took counsel, and made two calves of gold. And he said to the people, "You have gone up to Jerusalem long enough. Behold your gods, O Israel, who brought you up out of the land of Egypt." [29] And he set one in Bethel, and the other he put in Dan. [30] And this thing became a sin, for the people went to the one at Bethel and to the other as far as Dan. [31] He also made houses on high places, and appointed priests from among all the people, who were not of the Levites.

14 [19] Now the rest of the acts of Jerobo'am, how he warred and how he reigned, behold, they are written in the Book of the Chronicles of the Kings of Israel. [20] And the time that Jerobo'am reigned was twenty-two years; and he slept with his fathers, and Nadab his son reigned in his stead.

21 Now Rehobo'am the son of Solomon reigned in Judah. Rehobo'am was forty-one years old when he began to reign, and he reigned seventeen years in Jerusalem, the city which the LORD had chosen out of all the tribes of Israel, to put his name there. His mother's name was Na'amah the Ammonitess. [22] And Judah did what was evil in the sight of the LORD, and they provoked him to jealousy with their sins which they committed, more than all that their fathers had done. [23] For they also built for themselves high places, and pillars, and Ashe'rim on every high hill and under every green tree; [24] and there were also male cult prostitutes in the land. They did according to all the abominations of the nations which the LORD drove out before the people of Israel.

25 In the fifth year of King Rehobo'am, Shishak king of Egypt

came up against Jerusalem; ²⁶ he took away the treasures of the house of the LORD and the treasures of the king's house; he took away everything. He also took away all the shields of gold which Solomon had made; ²⁷ and King Rehobo'am made in their stead shields of bronze, and committed them to the hands of the officers of the guard, who kept the door of the king's house.

29 Now the rest of the acts of Rehobo'am, and all that he did, are they not written in the Book of the Chronicles of the Kings of Judah? ³⁰ And there was war between Rehobo'am and Jerobo'am continually. ³¹ And Rehobo'am slept with his fathers and was buried with his fathers in the city of David. His mother's name was Na'amah the Ammonitess. And Abi'jam his son reigned in his stead.

12:25 The Northern Kingdom of Israel is frequently referred to as Ephraim, after the tribe from which Jeroboam, the first king of Israel, is descended. It is sometimes also called Samaria, the name of its capital city.

Elijah Battles against Baal Worship
1 Kings 16:29–32; 17:1–24; 18:1–8, 17–40

29 In the thirty-eighth year of Asa king of Judah, Ahab the son of Omri began to reign over Israel, and Ahab the son of Omri reigned over Israel in Samar'ia twenty-two years. ³⁰ And Ahab the son of Omri did evil in the sight of the LORD more than all that were before him. ³¹ And as if it had been a light thing for him to walk in the sins of Jerobo'am the son of Nebat, he took for wife Jez'ebel the daughter of Ethba'al king of the Sido'nians, and went and served Ba'al, and worshiped him. ³² He erected an altar for Ba'al in the house of Ba'al, which he built in Samar'ia.

17 Now Eli'jah the Tishbite, of Tishbe in Gilead, said to Ahab, "As the LORD the God of Israel lives, before whom I stand, there shall be neither dew nor rain these years, except by my word." ² And the word of the LORD came to him, ³ "Depart from here and turn eastward, and hide yourself by the brook Cherith, that is east of the Jordan. ⁴ You shall drink from the brook, and I have commanded the ravens to feed you there." ⁵ So he went and did according to the word of the LORD; he went and dwelt by the brook Cherith that is east of the Jordan. ⁶ And the ravens brought him bread and meat in the morning, and bread and meat in the evening; and he drank from the brook. ⁷ And after a while the brook dried up, because there was no rain in the the the land.

8 Then the word of the LORD came to him, ⁹ "Arise, go to Zar'ephath, which belongs to Sidon, and dwell there. Behold, I have commanded a widow there to feed you." ¹⁰ So he arose and went to

Zar'ephath; and when he came to the gate of the city, behold, a widow was there gathering sticks; and he called to her and said, "Bring me a little water in a vessel, that I may drink." ¹¹ And as she was going to bring it, he called to her and said, "Bring me a morsel of bread in your hand." ¹² And she said, "As the LORD your God lives, I have nothing baked, only a handful of meal in a jar, and a little oil in a cruse; and now, I am gathering a couple of sticks, that I may go in and prepare it for myself and my son, that we may eat it, and die." ¹³ And Eli'jah said to her, "Fear not; go and do as you have said; but first make me a little cake of it and bring it to me, and afterward make for yourself and your son. ¹⁴ For thus says the LORD the God of Israel, 'The jar of meal shall not be spent, and the cruse of oil shall not fail, until the day that the LORD sends rain upon the earth.' " ¹⁵ And she went and did as Eli'jah said; and she, and he, and her household ate for many days. ¹⁶ The jar of meal was not spent, neither did the cruse of oil fail, according to the word of the LORD which he spoke by Eli'jah.

17 After this the son of the woman, the mistress of the house, became ill; and his illness was so severe that there was no breath left in him. ¹⁸ And she said to Eli'jah, "What have you against me, O man of God? You have come to me to bring my sin to remembrance, and to cause the death of my son!" ¹⁹ And he said to her, "Give me your son." And he took him from her bosom, and carried him up into the upper chamber, where he lodged, and laid him upon his own bed. ²⁰ And he cried to the LORD, "O LORD my God, hast thou brought calamity even upon the widow with whom I sojourn, by slaying her son?" ²¹ Then he stretched himself upon the child three times, and cried to the LORD, "O LORD my God, let this child's soul come into him again." ²² And the LORD hearkened to the voice of Eli'jah; and the soul of the child came into him again, and he revived. ²³ And Eli'jah took the child, and brought him down from the upper chamber into the house, and delivered him to his mother; and Eli'jah said, "See, your son lives." ²⁴ And the woman said to Eli'jah, "Now I know that you are a man of God, and that the word of the LORD in your mouth is truth."

18 After many days the word of the LORD came to Eli'jah, in the third year, saying, "Go, show yourself to Ahab; and I will send rain upon the earth." ² So Eli'jah went to show himself to Ahab. Now the famine was severe in Samar'ia. ³ And Ahab called Obadi'ah, who was over the household. (Now Obadi'ah revered the LORD greatly; ⁴ and when Jez'ebel cut off the prophets of the LORD, Obadi'ah took a hundred prophets and hid them by fifties in a cave, and fed them with bread and water.) ⁵ And Ahab said to Obadi'ah, "Go through

the land to all the springs of water and to all the valleys; perhaps we may find grass and save the horses and mules alive, and not lose some of the animals." ⁶ So they divided the land between them to pass through it; Ahab went in one direction by himself, and Obadi'ah went in another direction by himself.

7 And as Obadi'ah was on the way, behold, Eli'jah met him; and Obadi'ah recognized him, and fell on his face, and said, "Is it you, my lord Eli'jah?" ⁸ And he answered him, "It is I. Go, tell your lord, 'Behold, Eli'jah is here.' "

17 When Ahab saw Eli'jah, Ahab said to him, "Is it you, you troubler of Israel?" ¹⁸ And he answered, "I have not troubled Israel; but you have, and your father's house, because you have forsaken the commandments of the LORD and followed the Ba'als. ¹⁹ Now therefore send and gather all Israel to me at Mount Car'mel, and the four hundred and fifty prophets of Ba'al and the four hundred prophets of Ashe'rah, who eat at Jez'ebel's table."

20 So Ahab sent to all the people of Israel, and gathered the prophets together at Mount Car'mel. ²¹ And Eli'jah came near to all the people, and said, "How long will you go limping with two different opinions? If the LORD is God, follow him; but if Ba'al, then follow him." And the people did not answer him a word. ²² Then Eli'jah said to the people, "I, even I only am left a prophet of the LORD; but Ba'al's prophets are four hundred and fifty men. ²³ Let two bulls be given to us; and let them choose one bull for themselves, and cut it in pieces and lay it on the wood, but put no fire to it; and I will prepare the other bull and lay it on the wood, and put no fire to it. ²⁴ And you call on the name of your god and I will call on the name of the LORD; and the God who answers by fire, he is God." And all the people answered, "It is well spoken." ²⁵ Then Eli'jah said to the prophets of Ba'al, "Choose for yourselves one bull and prepare it first, for you are many; and call on the name of your god, but put no fire to it." ²⁶ And they took the bull which was given them, and they prepared it, and called on the name of Ba'al from morning until noon, saying, "O Ba'al, answer us!" But there was no voice, and no one answered. And they limped about the altar which they had made. ²⁷ And at noon Eli'jah mocked them, saying, "Cry aloud, for he is a god; either he is musing, or he has gone aside, or he is on a journey, or perhaps he is asleep and must be awakened." ²⁸ And they cried aloud, and cut themselves after their custom with swords and lances, until the blood gushed out upon them. ²⁹ And as midday passed, they raved on until the time of the offering of the oblation, but there was no voice; no one answered, no one heeded.

30 Then Eli'jah said to all the people, "Come near to me"; and all

the people came near to him. And he repaired the altar of the LORD that had been thrown down; [31] Eli'jah took twelve stones, according to the number of the tribes of the sons of Jacob, to whom the word of the LORD came, saying, "Israel shall be your name"; [32] and with the stones he built an altar in the name of the LORD. And he made a trench about the altar, as great as would contain two measures of seed. [33] And he put the wood in order, and cut the bull in pieces and laid it on the wood. And he said, "Fill four jars with water, and pour it on the burnt offering, and on the wood." [34] And he said, "Do it a second time"; and they did it a second time. And he said, "Do it a third time"; and they did it a third time. [35] And the water ran round about the altar, and filled the trench also with water.

36 And at the time of the offering of the oblation, Eli'jah the prophet came near and said, "O LORD, God of Abraham, Isaac, and Israel, let it be known this day that thou art God in Israel, and that I am thy servant, and that I have done all these things at thy word. [37] Answer me, O LORD, answer me, that this people may know that thou, O LORD, art God, and that thou hast turned their hearts back." [38] Then the fire of the LORD fell, and consumed the burnt offering, and the wood, and the stones, and the dust, and licked up the water that was in the trench. [39] And when all the people saw it, they fell on their faces; and they said, "The LORD, he is God; the LORD, he is God." [40] And Eli'jah said to them, "Seize the prophets of Ba'al; let not one of them escape." And they seized them; and Eli'jah brought them down to the brook Kishon, and killed them there.

17:1 Regarded as the messenger of good tidings, Elijah is glorified in Jewish legend. Since he will announce the coming of the Messiah and the age of redemption, many Jewish ceremonies developed around his name: for example, when a Jewish child is circumcised, he is placed on "the chair of Elijah"; a place is set for Elijah at the Passover Seder (Jews hope that each child may be God's agent of redemption and that each Passover ceremony, celebrating emancipation from an ancient slavery may be the occasion for Elijah to proclaim man's ultimate redemption). Elijah is also pictured in heaven recording all marriages, and he is alert to lead the righteous into their place in Paradise. Folk-lore also recounts his continual reappearance on earth in various guises as he brings help and comfort to needy individuals. Critical scholars suggest that the miracle stories about Elijah and Elisha are a unique type of literary form and are not meant to be understood as history. The stories duplicate each other, in some points even contradict each other: Contrast 1 Kings 19:15 ff., where Elijah is commissioned to appoint Kings Hazael and Jehu, and 2 Kings 8:7 ff.; 9:1 ff. where Elisha does the anointing. It is agreed that the episode on Mount Carmel, however, refers to an extraordinary event. **18:38** *The Lord He is God* is the confession of faith recited seven times at the climax of the day-long services on the Day of Atonement. It is part of the confession of faith made when a Jew is about to die. **18:40** Mendelssohn's oratorio Elijah reaches its climax as it recalls this contest between the prophet and the priests of Baal.

The Lord Speaks to Elijah in a Still Small Voice
Kings 19:1–21

19 Ahab told Jez′ebel all that Eli′jah had done, and how he had slain all the prophets with the sword. ²Then Jez′ebel sent a messenger to Eli′jah, saying, "So may the gods do to me, and more also, if I do not make your life as the life of one of them by this time tomorrow." ³Then he was afraid, and he arose and went for his life, and came to Beer-sheba, which belongs to Judah, and left his servant there.

4 But he himself went a day's journey into the wilderness, and came and sat down under a broom tree; and he asked that he might die, saying, "It is enough; now, O LORD, take away my life; for I am no better than my fathers." ⁵And he lay down and slept under a broom tree; and behold, an angel touched him, and said to him, "Arise and eat." ⁶And he looked, and behold, there was at his head a cake baked on hot stones and a jar of water. And he ate and drank, and lay down again. ⁷And the angel of the LORD came again a second time, and touched him, and said, "Arise and eat, else the journey will be too great for you." ⁸And he arose, and ate and drank, and went in the strength of that food forty days and forty nights to Horeb the mount of God.

9 And there he came to a cave, and lodged there; and behold, the word of the LORD came to him, and he said to him, "What are you doing here, Eli′jah?" ¹⁰He said, "I have been very jealous for the LORD, the God of hosts; for the people of Israel have forsaken thy covenant, thrown down thy altars, and slain thy prophets with the sword; and I, even I only, am left; and they seek my life, to take it away." ¹¹And he said, "Go forth, and stand upon the mount before the LORD." And behold, the LORD passed by, and a great and strong wind rent the mountains, and broke in pieces the rocks before the LORD, but the LORD was not in the wind; and after the wind an earthquake, but the LORD was not in the earthquake; ¹²and after the earthquake a fire, but the LORD was not in the fire; and after the fire a still small voice. ¹³And when Eli′jah heard it, he wrapped his face in his mantle and went out and stood at the entrance of the cave. And behold, there came a voice to him, and said, "What are you doing here, Eli′jah?" ¹⁴He said, "I have been very jealous for the

LORD, the God of hosts; for the people of Israel have forsaken thy covenant, thrown down thy altars, and slain thy prophets with the sword; and I, even I only, am left; and they seek my life, to take it away." ¹⁵ And the LORD said to him, "Go, return on your way to the wilderness of Damascus; and when you arrive, you shall anoint Haz′ael to be king over Syria; ¹⁶ and Jehu the son of Nimshi you shall anoint to be king over Israel; and Eli′sha the son of Shaphat of A′bel-meho′lah you shall anoint to be prophet in your place. ¹⁷ And him who escapes from the sword of Haz′ael shall Jehu slay; and him who escapes from the sword of Jehu shall Eli′sha slay. ¹⁸ Yet I will leave seven thousand in Israel, all the knees that have not bowed to Ba′al, and every mouth that has not kissed him."

19 So he departed from there, and found Eli′sha the son of Shaphat, who was plowing, with twelve yoke of oxen before him, and he was with the twelfth. Eli′jah passed by him and cast his mantle upon him. ²⁰ And he left the oxen, and ran after Eli′jah, and said, "Let me kiss my father and my mother, and then I will follow you." And he said to him, "Go back again; for what have I done to you?" ²¹ And he returned from following him, and took the yoke of oxen, and slew them, and boiled their flesh with the yokes of the oxen, and gave it to the people, and they ate. Then he arose and went after Eli′jah, and ministered to him.

19:8 Compare Moses and his fast, Exodus 34:28.

Ahab Steals the Vineyard of Naboth
1 Kings 21:1–10, 15–19, 27–29

21 Now Naboth the Jezreelite had a vineyard in Jezreel, beside the palace of Ahab king of Samar′ia. ² And after this Ahab said to Naboth, "Give me your vineyard, that I may have it for a vegetable garden, because it is near my house; and I will give you a better vineyard for it; or if it seems good to you, I will give you its value in money." ³ But Naboth said to Ahab, "The LORD forbid that I should give you the inheritance of my fathers." ⁴ And Ahab went into his house vexed and sullen because of what Naboth the Jezreelite had said to him; for he had said, "I will not give you the inheritance of my fathers." And he lay down on his bed, and turned away his face, and would eat no food.

5 But Jez′ebel his wife came to him, and said to him, "Why is your spirit so vexed that you eat no food?" ⁶ And he said to her, "Because I spoke to Naboth the Jezreelite, and said to him, 'Give me your vineyard for money; or else, if it please you, I will give you another vineyard for it'; and he answered, 'I will not give you my vineyard.'" ⁷ And Jez′ebel his wife said to him, "Do you now govern

Israel? Arise, and eat bread, and let your heart be cheerful; I will give you the vineyard of Naboth the Jezreelite."

8 So she wrote letters in Ahab's name and sealed them with his seal, and she sent the letters to the elders and the nobles who dwelt with Naboth in his city. ⁹And she wrote in the letters, "Proclaim a fast, and set Naboth on high among the people; ¹⁰and set two base fellows opposite him, and let them bring a charge against him, saying, 'You have cursed God and the king.' Then take him out, and stone him to death."

15 As soon as Jez'ebel heard that Naboth had been stoned and was dead, Jez'ebel said to Ahab, "Arise, take possession of the vineyard of Naboth the Jezreelite, which he refused to give you for money; for Naboth is not alive, but dead." ¹⁶And as soon as Ahab heard that Naboth was dead, Ahab arose to go down to the vineyard of Naboth the Jezreelite, to take possession of it.

17 Then the word of the LORD came to Eli'jah the Tishbite, saying, ¹⁸"Arise, go down to meet Ahab king of Israel, who is in Samar'ia; behold, he is in the vineyard of Naboth, where he has gone to take possession. ¹⁹And you shall say to him, 'Thus says the LORD, "Have you killed, and also taken possession?" ' And you shall say to him, 'Thus says the LORD: "In the place where dogs licked up the blood of Naboth shall dogs lick your own blood." ' "

27 And when Ahab heard those words, he rent his clothes, and put sackcloth upon his flesh, and fasted and lay in sackcloth, and went about dejectedly. ²⁸And the word of the LORD came to Eli'jah the Tishbite, saying, ²⁹"Have you seen how Ahab has humbled himself before me? Because he has humbled himself before me, I will not bring the evil in his days; but in his son's days I will bring the evil upon his house."

21:5 Jezebel's name remains to this day a by-word of evil.

THE SECOND BOOK OF THE KINGS

The Spirit of Elijah Rests on Elisha

2 Kings 2:1–15

2 Now when the LORD was about to take Eli′jah up to heaven by a whirlwind, Eli′jah and Eli′sha were on their way from Gilgal. ²And Eli′jah said to Eli′sha, "Tarry here, I pray you; for the LORD has sent me as far as Bethel." But Eli′sha said, "As the LORD lives, and as you yourself live, I will not leave you." So they went down to Bethel. ³And the sons of the prophets who were in Bethel came out to Eli′sha, and said to him, "Do you know that today the LORD will take away your master from over you?" And he said, "Yes, I know it; hold your peace."

4 Eli′jah said to him, "Eli′sha, tarry here, I pray you; for the LORD has sent me to Jericho." But he said, "As the LORD lives, and as you yourself live, I will not leave you." So they came to Jericho. ⁵The sons of the prophets who were at Jericho drew near to Eli′sha, and said to him, "Do you know that today the LORD will take away your master from over you?" And he answered, "Yes, I know it; hold your peace."

6 Then Eli′jah said to him, "Tarry here, I pray you; for the LORD has sent me to the Jordan." But he said, "As the LORD lives, and as you yourself live, I will not leave you." So the two of them went on. ⁷Fifty men of the sons of the prophets also went, and stood at some distance from them, as they both were standing by the Jordan. ⁸Then Eli′jah took his mantle, and rolled it up, and struck the water, and the water was parted to the one side and to the other, till the two of them could go over on dry ground.

9 When they had crossed, Eli′jah said to Eli′sha, "Ask what I shall do for you, before I am taken from you." And Eli′sha said, "I pray you, let me inherit a double share of your spirit." ¹⁰And he said, "You have asked a hard thing; yet, if you see me as I am being taken from you, it shall be so for you; but if you do not see me, it shall not be so." ¹¹And as they still went on and talked, behold, a chariot of fire and horses of fire separated the two of them. And Eli′jah went up by a whirlwind into heaven. ¹²And Eli′sha saw it and he cried, "My father, my father! the chariots of Israel and its horsemen!" And he saw him no more.

Then he took hold of his own clothes and rent them in two pieces. ¹³And he took up the mantle of Eli′jah that had fallen from him, and went back and stood on the bank of the Jordan. ¹⁴Then he took the mantle of Eli′jah that had fallen from him, and struck the water, saying, "Where is the LORD, the God of Eli′jah?" And when he had struck the water, the water was parted to the one side and to the other; and Eli′sha went over.

15 Now when the sons of the prophets who were at Jericho saw him over against them, they said, "The spirit of Eli′jah rests on Eli′sha." And they came to meet him, and bowed to the ground before him.

> **2:11** This account of Elijah's bodily ascension to heaven has inspired a Jewish belief that Elijah can and does return to earth to protect the helpless and that he will return to announce the coming of the Messiah. Cf. Malachi 4:5 ff. and Matthew 11:14. **2:12** Rabbinic law requires that clothing be torn in two as a sign of mourning. (*Babba Metziah* 25.)

Elisha Counsels the Defeat of Moab

This selection records one of the few instances during this period of division when Israel and Judah join together to resist a common foe.

2 Kings 3:1–27

3 In the eighteenth year of Jehosh′aphat king of Judah, Jeho′ram the son of Ahab became king over Israel in Samar′ia, and he reigned twelve years. ²He did what was evil in the sight of the LORD, though not like his father and mother, for he put away the pillar of Ba′al which his father had made. ³Nevertheless he clung to the sin of Jerobo′am the son of Nebat, which he made Israel to sin; he did not depart from it.

4 Now Mesha king of Moab was a sheep breeder; and he had to deliver annually to the king of Israel a hundred thousand lambs, and the wool of a hundred thousand rams. ⁵But when Ahab died, the king of Moab rebelled against the king of Israel. ⁶So King Jeho′ram marched out of Samar′ia at that time and mustered all Israel. ⁷And he went and sent word to Jehosh′aphat king of Judah, "The king of Moab has rebelled against me; will you go with me to battle against Moab?" And he said, "I will go; I am as you are, my people as your people, my horses as your horses." ⁸Then he said, "By which way shall we march?" Jeho′ram answered, "By the way of the wilderness of Edom."

9 So the king of Israel went with the king of Judah and the king of Edom. And when they had made a circuitous march of seven days, there was no water for the army or for the beasts which followed them. ¹⁰Then the king of Israel said, "Alas! The LORD has called these three kings to give them into the hand of Moab." ¹¹And

Jehosh′aphat said, "Is there no prophet of the LORD here, through whom we may inquire of the LORD?" Then one of the king of Israel's servants answered, "Eli′sha the son of Shaphat is here, who poured water on the hands of Eli′jah." ¹² And Jehosh′aphat said, "The word of the LORD is with him." So the king of Israel and Jehosh′aphat and the king of Edom went down to him.

13 And Eli′sha said to the king of Israel, "What have I to do with you? Go to the prophets of your father and the prophets of your mother." But the king of Israel said to him, "No; it is the LORD who has called these three kings to give them into the hand of Moab." ¹⁴ And Eli′sha said, "As the LORD of hosts lives, whom I serve, were it not that I have regard for Jehosh′aphat the king of Judah, I would neither look at you, nor see you. ¹⁵ But now bring me a minstrel." And when the minstrel played, the power of the LORD came upon him. ¹⁶ And he said, "Thus says the LORD, 'I will make this dry stream-bed full of pools.' ¹⁷ For thus says the LORD, 'You shall not see wind or rain, but that stream-bed shall be filled with water, so that you shall drink, you, your cattle, and your beasts.' ¹⁸ This is a light thing in the sight of the LORD; he will also give the Moabites into your hand, ¹⁹ and you shall conquer every fortified city, and every choice city, and shall fell every good tree, and stop up all springs of water, and ruin every good piece of land with stones." ²⁰ The next morning, about the time of offering the sacrifice, behold, water came from the direction of Edom, till the country was filled with water.

21 When all the Moabites heard that the kings had come up to fight against them, all who were able to put on armor, from the youngest to the oldest, were called out, and were drawn up at the frontier. ²² And when they rose early in the morning, and the sun shone upon the water, the Moabites saw the water opposite them as red as blood. ²³ And they said, "This is blood; the kings have surely fought together, and slain one another. Now then, Moab, to the spoil!" ²⁴ But when they came to the camp of Israel, the Israelites rose and attacked the Moabites, till they fled before them; and they went forward, slaughtering the Moabites as they went. ²⁵ And they overthrew the cities, and on every good piece of land every man threw a stone, until it was covered; they stopped every spring of water, and felled all the good trees; till only its stones were left in Kir-har′eseth, and the slingers surrounded and conquered it. ²⁶ When the king of Moab saw that the battle was going against him, he took with him seven hundred swordsmen to break through, opposite the king of Edom; but they could not. ²⁷ Then he took his eldest son who was to reign in his stead, and offered him for a burnt offering upon

the wall. And there came great wrath upon Israel; and they withdrew from him and returned to their own land.

3:14 f. In anger Elisha could not prophesy. He needed to be soothed first with music. Rabbinic legend moralizes: God's spirit rests only upon those who are in a peaceful and joyful mood (*Pesahim* 66a). **3:27** The Bible says that the Hebrew forces "withdrew," the implication being that God brought "wrath" upon the land as consequence of the Moabite sacrifice of a human being and that the Israelite forces retreated without having been defeated. A Moabite stone uncovered by archaeologists in 1868 at Dibon describes the military strategy by which the Moabite army claims to have driven the Israelites back. The Hebrews would not have wished to acknowledge a Moabite victory following upon such a scandalous human sacrifice.

Elisha Works Miracles
2 Kings 4:1–7; 5:1–3, 9–17

4 Now the wife of one of the sons of the prophets cried to Eli'sha, "Your servant my husband is dead; and you know that your servant feared the LORD, but the creditor has come to take my two children to be his slaves." ²And Eli'sha said to her, "What shall I do for you? Tell me; what have you in the house?" And she said, "Your maidservant has nothing in the house, except a jar of oil." ³Then he said, "Go outside, borrow vessels of all your neighbors, empty vessels and not too few. ⁴Then go in, and shut the door upon yourself and your sons, and pour into all these vessels; and when one is full, set it aside." ⁵So she went from him and shut the door upon herself and her sons; and as she poured they brought the vessels to her. ⁶When the vessels were full, she said to her son, "Bring me another vessel." And he said to her, "There is not another." Then the oil stopped flowing. ⁷She came and told the man of God, and he said, "Go, sell the oil and pay your debts, and you and your sons can live on the rest."

5 Na'aman, commander of the army of the king of Syria, was a great man with his master and in high favor, because by him the LORD had given victory to Syria. He was a mighty man of valor, but he was a leper. ²Now the Syrians on one of their raids had carried off a little maid from the land of Israel, and she waited on Na'aman's wife. ³She said to her mistress, "Would that my lord were with the prophet who is in Samar'ia! He would cure him of his leprosy."

⁹So Na'aman came with his horses and chariots, and halted at the door of Eli'sha's house. ¹⁰And Eli'sha sent a messenger to him, saying, "Go and wash in the Jordan seven times, and your flesh shall

be restored, and you shall be clean." ¹¹ But Na'aman was angry, and
went away, saying, "Behold, I thought that he would surely come
out to me, and stand, and call on the name of the LORD his God, and
wave his hand over the place, and cure the leper. ¹² Are not Aba'na
and Pharpar, the rivers of Damascus, better than all the waters of
Israel? Could I not wash in them, and be clean?" So he turned and
went away in a rage. ¹³ But his servants came near and said to him,
"My father, if the prophet had commanded you to do some great
thing, would you not have done it? How much rather, then, when he
says to you, 'Wash, and be clean'?" ¹⁴ So he went down and dipped
himself seven times in the Jordan, according to the word of the man
of God; and his flesh was restored like the flesh of a little child, and
he was clean.

15 Then he returned to the man of God, he and all his company,
and he came and stood before him; and he said, "Behold, I know
that there is no God in all the earth but in Israel; so accept now a
present from your servant." ¹⁶ But he said, "As the LORD lives,
whom I serve, I will receive none." And he urged him to take it, but
he refused. ¹⁷ Then Na'aman said, "If not, I pray you, let there be
given to your servant two mules' burden of earth; for henceforth
your servant will not offer burnt offering or sacrifice to any god but
the LORD."

    5:17 Note here the primitive idea that a god could be worshiped
only in his own land. Thus Naaman believes he must take soil from
Israel back to his own country if he is to worship the God of Elisha.

Syria Endangers Israel and Judah
2 Kings 12:17–18; 13:1–9

17 At that time Haz'ael king of Syria went up and fought against
Gath, and took it. But when Haz'ael set his face to go up against
Jerusalem, ¹⁸ Jeho'ash king of Judah took all the votive gifts that
Jehosh'aphat and Jeho'ram and Ahazi'ah, his fathers, the kings of
Judah, had dedicated, and his own votive gifts, and all the gold that
was found in the treasuries of the house of the LORD and of the
king's house, and sent these to Haz'ael king of Syria. Then Haz'ael
went away from Jerusalem.

13 In the twenty-third year of Jo'ash the son of Ahazi'ah, king of
Judah, Jeho'ahaz the son of Jehu began to reign over Israel in
Samar'ia, and he reigned seventeen years. ² He did what was evil in
the sight of the LORD, and followed the sins of Jerobo'am the son of
Nebat, which he made Israel to sin; he did not depart from them.
³ And the anger of the LORD was kindled against Israel, and he gave
them continually into the hand of Haz'ael king of Syria and into the

hand of Ben-ha'dad the son of Haz'ael. ⁴Then Jeho'ahaz besought the LORD, and the LORD hearkened to him; for he saw the oppression of Israel, how the king of Syria oppressed them. ⁵(Therefore the LORD gave Israel a savior, so that they escaped from the hand of the Syrians; and the people of Israel dwelt in their homes as formerly. ⁶Nevertheless they did not depart from the sins of the house of Jerobo'am, which he made Israel to sin, but walked in them; and the Ashe'rah also remained in Samar'ia.) ⁷For there was not left to Jeho'ahaz an army of more than fifty horsemen and ten chariots and ten thousand footmen; for the king of Syria had destroyed them and made them like the dust at threshing. ⁸Now the rest of the acts of Jeho'ahaz and all that he did, and his might, are they not written in the Book of the Chronicles of the Kings of Israel? ⁹So Jeho'ahaz slept with his fathers, and they buried him in Samar'ia; and Jo'ash his son reigned in his stead.

12:17 These passages record the emergence of the Syrians (or Arameans) as a power dominant over both Israel and Judah. Syria earlier had been conquered by King David, who placed garrisons in the capital city, Damascus. Then Rezon, an Israelite enemy to King Solomon, became king over the Syrians and led them in war. The Syrians now succeeded in their forays against the Hebrews; they overwhelmed the Northern Kingdom and received booty from Judah. Soon a new power, Assyria, emerged and threatened both Syria and the Hebrews. Thus in 853 B.C. Syria and Israel joined forces to block Assyria. A century later Syria and Israel tried to compel Judah to join them in a new coalition against Assyria. King Ahaz of Judah instead chose an alliance with Tiglath-Pileser III, king of Assyria, at the cost of his nation's independence (16:8). In 732 B.C. the Assyrians routed the Syrians. They captured Damascus and exiled many of her inhabitants into her inner provinces (16:9).

Elisha Performs Miracles Even in Death
2 Kings 13:14–25

14 Now when Eli'sha had fallen sick with the illness of which he was to die, Jo'ash king of Israel went down to him, and wept before him, crying, "My father, my father! The chariots of Israel and its horsemen!" ¹⁵And Eli'sha said to him, "Take a bow and arrows"; so he took a bow and arrows. ¹⁶Then he said to the king of Israel, "Draw the bow"; and he drew it. And Eli'sha laid his hands upon the king's hands. ¹⁷And he said, "Open the window eastward"; and he opened it. Then Eli'sha said, "Shoot"; and he shot. And he said, "The LORD's arrow of victory, the arrow of victory over Syria! For you shall fight the Syrians in Aphek until you have made an end of them." ¹⁸And he said, "Take the arrows"; and he took them. And he

said to the king of Israel, "Strike the ground with them"; and he struck three times, and stopped. [19] Then the man of God was angry with him, and said, "You should have struck five or six times; then you would have struck down Syria until you had made an end of it, but now you will strike down Syria only three times."

20 So Eli′sha died, and they buried him. Now bands of Moabites used to invade the land in the spring of the year. [21] And as a man was being buried, lo, a marauding band was seen and the man was cast into the grave of Eli′sha; and as soon as the man touched the bones of Eli′sha, he revived, and stood on his feet.

22 Now Haz′ael king of Syria oppressed Israel all the days of Jeho′ahaz. [23] But the LORD was gracious to them and had compassion on them, and he turned toward them, because of his covenant with Abraham, Isaac, and Jacob, and would not destroy them; nor has he cast them from his presence until now.

24 When Haz′ael king of Syria died, Ben-ha′dad his son became king in his stead. [25] Then Jeho′ash the son of Jeho′ahaz took again from Ben-ha′dad the son of Haz′ael the cities which he had taken from Jeho′ahaz his father in war. Three times Jo′ash defeated him and recovered the cities of Israel.

Israel Falls into the Hands of Spoilers

This account records the final defeat of the Northern Kingdom and the dispersal of the people by the Assyrians. The siege of Samaria, capital city of the Hebrew Northern Kingdom, was started by Shalmaneser V, and the task was completed by Sargon II, in 720 B.C. According to Assyrian records, 27,290 of the Hebrew inhabitants were carried away, and a governor was set over the remainder. The dispersed people never returned to their land and are known as the Ten Lost Tribes. Those who remained mingled with captives of other nations who were brought to Israel and became known as Samaritans. Scripture offers a religious interpretation of Israel's defeat: having turned to idolatry, they were punished by God.

2 Kings 17:1–18, 20, 23b

17 In the twelfth year of Ahaz king of Judah Hoshe′a the son of Elah began to reign in Samar′ia over Israel, and he reigned nine years. [2] And he did what was evil in the sight of the LORD, yet not as the kings of Israel who were before him. [3] Against him came up Shalmane′ser king of Assyria; and Hoshe′a became his vassal, and paid him tribute. [4] But the king of Assyria found treachery in Hoshe′a; for he had sent messengers to So, king of Egypt, and offered no tribute to the king of Assyria, as he had done year by

year; therefore the king of Assyria shut him up, and bound him in prison. ⁵Then the king of Assyria invaded all the land and came to Samar'ia, and for three years he besieged it. ⁶In the ninth year of Hoshe'a the king of Assyria captured Samar'ia, and he carried the Israelites away to Assyria, and placed them in Halah, and on the Habor, the river of Gozan, and in the cities of the Medes.

7 And this was so, because the people of Israel had sinned against the LORD their God, who had brought them up out of the land of Egypt from under the hand of Pharaoh king of Egypt, and had feared other gods and walked in the customs of the nations whom the LORD drove out before the people of Israel, and in the customs which the kings of Israel had introduced. ⁹And the people of Israel did secretly against the LORD their God things that were not right. They built for themselves high places at all their towns, from watch tower to fortified city; ¹⁰they set up for themselves pillars and Ashe'rim on every high hill and under every green tree; ¹¹and there they burned incense on all the high places, as the nations did whom the LORD carried away before them. And they did wicked things, provoking the LORD to anger, ¹²and they served idols, of which the LORD had said to them, "You shall not do this." ¹³Yet the LORD warned Israel and Judah by every prophet and every seer, saying, "Turn from your evil ways and keep my commandments and my statutes, in accordance with all the law which I commanded your fathers, and which I sent to you by my servants the prophets." ¹⁴But they would not listen, but were stubborn, as their fathers had been, who did not believe in the LORD their God. ¹⁵They despised his statutes, and his covenant that he made with their fathers, and the warnings which he gave them. They went after false idols, and became false, and they followed the nations that were round about them, concerning whom the LORD had commanded them that they should not do like them. ¹⁶And they forsook all the commandments of the LORD their God, and made for themselves molten images of two calves; and they made an Ashe'rah, and worshiped all the host of heaven, and served Ba'al. ¹⁷And they burned their sons and their daughters as offerings, and used divination and sorcery, and sold themselves to do evil in the sight of the LORD, provoking him to anger. ¹⁸Therefore the LORD was very angry with Israel, and removed them out of his sight; none was left but the tribe of Judah only.

20 And the LORD rejected all the descendants of Israel, and afflicted them, and gave them into the hand of spoilers, until he had cast them out of his sight.

23 So Israel was exiled from their own land to Assyria until this day.

Hezekiah Cleaves to the Lord

Judah is stirred to repentance after the fall of Israel. The prophet Isaiah calls the people back to the service of the Lord. The new King Hezekiah uproots idolatry; he does "that which is right." Additional accounts of his rule (720–692 B.C.) are to be found in 2 Chronicles 29–32 and Isaiah 36–39.

2 Kings 18:1–8

18 In the third year of Hoshe'a son of Elah, king of Israel, Hezeki'ah the son of Ahaz, king of Judah, began to reign. [2] He was twenty-five years old when he began to reign, and he reigned twenty-nine years in Jerusalem. His mother's name was Abi the daughter of Zechari'ah. [3] And he did what was right in the eyes of the LORD, according to all that David his father had done. [4] He removed the high places, and broke the pillars, and cut down the Ashe'rah. And he broke in pieces the bronze serpent that Moses had made, for until those days the people of Israel had burned incense to it; it was called Nehush'tan. [5] He trusted in the LORD the God of Israel; so that there was none like him among all the kings of Judah after him, nor among those who were before him. [6] For he held fast to the LORD; he did not depart from following him, but kept the commandments which the LORD commanded Moses. [7] And the LORD was with him; wherever he went forth, he prospered. He rebelled against the king of Assyria, and would not serve him. [8] He smote the Philistines as far as Gaza and its territory, from watchtower to fortified city.

Isaiah Predicts the Defeat of Sennacherib

Sennacherib, king of Assyria, and conqueror of Israel, attacks Judah and Egypt. He overwhelms the fortified cities in Judah and sets siege to Jerusalem in 701 B.C. King Hezekiah, who had done no evil before the Lord, pleads now for God's intervention as a sign of favor and receives assurance that the city will be spared.

2 Kings 19:20–21a, 22, 28, 32–36

20 Then Isaiah the son of Amoz sent to Hezeki'ah, saying, "Thus says the LORD, the God of Israel: Your prayer to me about Sennach'erib king of Assyria I have heard. [21] This is the word that the LORD has spoken concerning him:

> [22] "Whom have you mocked and reviled?
>> Against whom have you raised your voice
>> and haughtily lifted your eyes?
>> Against the Holy One of Israel!

[28] Because you have raged against me
  and your arrogance has come into my ears,
I will put my hook in your nose
  and my bit in your mouth,
and I will turn you back on the way
  by which you came.

32 "Therefore thus says the LORD concerning the king of Assyria, He shall not come into this city or shoot an arrow there, or come before it with a shield or cast up a siege mound against it. [33] By the way that he came, by the same he shall return, and he shall not come into this city, says the LORD. [34] For I will defend this city to save it, for my own sake and for the sake of my servant David."

35 And that night the angel of the LORD went forth, and slew a hundred and eighty-five thousand in the camp of the Assyrians; and when men arose early in the morning, behold, these were all dead bodies. [36] Then Sennach'erib king of Assyria departed, and went home, and dwelt at Nin'eveh.

> **19:20** A prism of Sennacherib; uncovered by archaeologists and now located in the Oriental Museum of the University of Chicago, confirms the biblical account that King Hezekiah earlier had to pay Sennacherib a ransom of thirty talents of gold—about 2,250 pounds of gold (2 Kings 18:14), in current value a ransom of nearly one million dollars. Royal records of Sennacherib's court also describe how he besieged forty-six Judaean cities and contained Hezekiah in Jerusalem, a prisoner like "a bird in a cage." **19:35** A passage in Herodotus offers a natural explanation for this miracle. He describes swarms of mice that destroyed the weapons of the Assyrians. Some interpret this reference to mice, plague-carrying rodents, to mean that the event was an outbreak of bubonic plague.

Manasseh Violates Judah

Although Judah had been spared conquest by Assyria, the new King Manasseh curried Assyria's favor by introducing Assyrian ancestral worship and idolatrous practices. Manasseh's reign lasted fifty-five years, the longest of all kings in Judah and Israel. According to the biblical historian, however, his wicked rule ultimately brought about Jerusalem's exposure to invasion and conquest.

2 Kings 20:21; 21:12, 16–18

21 And Hezeki'ah slept with his fathers; and Manas'seh his son reigned in his stead.

21 [12] Therefore thus says the LORD, the God of Israel, Behold, I am bringing upon Jerusalem and Judah such evil that the ears of every one who hears of it will tingle.

16 Moreover Manas'seh shed very much innocent blood, till he had filled Jerusalem from one end to another, besides the sin which he made Judah to sin so that they did what was evil in the sight of the LORD.

17 Now the rest of the acts of Manas'seh, and all that he did, and the sin that he committed, are they not written in the Book of the Chronicles of the Kings of Judah? ¹⁸ And Manas'seh slept with his fathers, and was buried in the garden of his house, in the garden of Uzza; and Amon his son reigned in his stead.

Josiah Attempts a Reform

In the reign of Josiah, 637–608 B.C. the discovery in the Temple of a book of the Law (thought to be the Book of Deuteronomy) sparked a reform of the idolatrous practices that had been introduced by Josiah's grandfather, Manasseh. But the reform was not far-reaching enough and Judah's destruction is confirmed.

2 Kings 22:1a, 2, 8, 10–13; 23:1–14, 21–30

22 Josi'ah was eight years old when he began to reign, and he reigned thirty-one years in Jerusalem.

2 And he did what was right in the eyes of the LORD, and walked in all the way of David his father, and he did not turn aside to the right hand or to the left.

8 And Hilki'ah the high priest said to Shaphan the secretary, "I have found the book of the law in the house of the LORD." And Hilki'ah gave the book to Shaphan, and he read it.

10 Then Shaphan the secretary told the king, "Hilki'ah the priest has given me a book." And Shaphan read it before the king.

11 And when the king heard the words of the book of the law, he rent his clothes. ¹² And the king commanded Hilki'ah the priest, and Ahi'kam the son of Shaphan, and Achbor the son of Micai'ah, and Shaphan the secretary, and Asai'ah the king's servant, saying, ¹³ "Go, inquire of the LORD for me, and for the people, and for all Judah, concerning the words of this book that has been found; for great is the wrath of the LORD that is kindled against us, because our fathers have not obeyed the words of this book, to do according to all that is written concerning us."

23 Then the king sent, and all the elders of Judah and Jerusalem were gathered to him. ² And the king went up to the house of the LORD, and with him all the men of Judah and all the inhabitants of Jerusalem, and the priests and the prophets, all the people, both small and great; and he read in their hearing all the words of the book of the covenant which had been found in the house of the LORD. ³ And the king stood by the pillar and made a covenant before

the LORD, to walk after the LORD and to keep his commandments and his testimonies and his statutes, with all his heart and all his soul, to perform the words of this covenant that were written in this book; and all the people joined in the covenant.

4 And the king commanded Hilki'ah, the high priest, and the priests of the second order, and the keepers of the threshold, to bring out of the temple of the LORD all the vessels made for Ba'al, for Ashe'rah, and for all the host of heaven; he burned them outside Jerusalem in the fields of the Kidron, and carried their ashes to Bethel. ⁵ And he deposed the idolatrous priests whom the kings of Judah had ordained to burn incense in the high places at the cities of Judah and round about Jerusalem; those also who burned incense to Ba'al, to the sun, and the moon, and the constellations, and all the host of the heavens. ⁶ And he brought out the Ashe'rah from the house of the LORD, outside Jerusalem, to the brook Kidron, and burned it at the brook Kidron, and beat it to dust and cast the dust of it upon the graves of the common people. ⁷ And he broke down the houses of the male cult prostitutes which were in the house of the LORD, where the women wove hangings for the Ashe'rah. ⁸ And he brought all the priests out of the cities of Judah, and defiled the high places where the priests had burned incense, from Geba to Beer-sheba; and he broke down the high places of the gates that were at the entrance of the gate of Joshua the governor of the city, which were on one's left at the gate of the city. ⁹ However, the priests of the high places did not come up to the altar of the LORD in Jerusalem, but they ate unleavened bread among their brethren. ¹⁰ And he defiled To'pheth, which is in the valley of the sons of Hinnom, that no one might burn his son or his daughter as an offering to Molech. ¹¹ And he removed the horses that the kings of Judah had dedicated to the sun, at the entrance to the house of the LORD, by the chamber of Nathan-melech the chamberlain, which was in the precincts; and he burned the chariots of the sun with fire. ¹² And the altars on the roof of the upper chamber of Ahaz, which the kings of Judah had made, and the altars which Manas'seh had made in the two courts of the house of the LORD, he pulled down and broke in pieces, and cast the dust of them into the brook Kidron. ¹³ And the king defiled the high places that were east of Jerusalem, to the south of the mount of corruption, which Solomon the king of Israel had built for Ash'toreth the abomination of the Sido'nians, and for Chemosh the abomination of Moab, and for Milcom the abomination of the Ammonites. ¹⁴ And he broke in pieces the pillars, and cut down the Ashe'rim, and filled their places with the bones of men.

21 And the king commanded all the people, "Keep the passover to

the LORD your God, as it is written in this book of the covenant."
²² For no such passover had been kept since the days of the judges
who judged Israel, or during all the days of the kings of Israel or of
the kings of Judah; ²³ but in the eighteenth year of King Josi'ah this
passover was kept to the LORD in Jerusalem.

24 Moreover Josi'ah put away the mediums and the wizards and
the teraphim and the idols and all the abominations that were seen
in the land of Judah and in Jerusalem, that he might establish the
words of the law which were written in the book that Hilki'ah the
priest found in the house of the LORD. ²⁵ Before him there was no
king like him, who turned to the LORD with all his heart and with all
his soul and with all his might, according to all the law of Moses; nor
did any like him arise after him.

26 Still the LORD did not turn from the fierceness of his great
wrath, by which his anger was kindled against Judah, because of all
the provocations with which Manas'seh had provoked him. ²⁷ And
the LORD said, "I will remove Judah also out of my sight, as I have
removed Israel, and I will cast off this city which I have chosen,
Jerusalem, and the house of which I said, My name shall be there."

28 Now the rest of the acts of Josi'ah, and all that he did, are they
not written in the Book of the Chronicles of the Kings of Judah? ²⁹ In
his days Pharaoh Neco king of Egypt went up to the king of Assyria
to the river Eu-phra'tes. King Josi'ah went to meet him; and
Pharaoh Neco slew him at Megid'do, when he saw him. ³⁰ And his
servants carried him dead in a chariot from Megid'do, and brought
him to Jerusalem, and buried him in his own tomb. And the people
of the land took Jeho'ahaz the son of Josi'ah, and anointed him, and
made him king in his father's stead.

22:10 Mosaic Law had been little regarded for many years. The
young king, upon hearing these words, particularly Deuteronomy 28,
decides upon a reformation. **23:4–5** The last great Assyrian
monarch died in 626 B.C. and the empire began to crumble. Thus
Josiah could dare to destroy the Assyrian altar with some sense of
immunity. **23:21** Because of the celebration of the Passover
recounted here, this portion (23:1–9, 21–25) is recited in synagogues throughout the world on the second day of Passover.

Jerusalem Falls

2 Kings 23:36–37; 24:1–6, 10–14, 17–20; 25:1–12, 22, 25–30

23 ³⁶ Jehoi'akim was twenty-five years old when he began to reign,
and he reigned eleven years in Jerusalem. His mother's name was
Zebi'dah the daughter of Pedai'ah of Rumah. ³⁷ And he did what was
evil in the sight of the LORD, according to all that his father had
done.

24 In his days Nebuchadnez′zar king of Babylon came up, and Jehoi′akim became his servant three years; then he turned and rebelled against him. ²And the LORD sent against him bands of the Chalde′ans, and bands of the Syrians, and bands of the Moabites, and bands of the Ammonites, and sent them against Judah to destroy it, according to the word of the LORD which he spoke by his servants the prophets. ³Surely this came upon Judah at the command of the LORD, to remove them out of his sight, for the sins of Manas′seh, according to all that he had done, ⁴and also for the innocent blood that he had shed; for he filled Jerusalem with innocent blood, and the LORD would not pardon. ⁵Now the rest of the deeds of Jehoi′akim, and all that he did, are they not written in the Book of the Chronicles of the Kings of Judah? ⁶So Jehoi′akim slept with his fathers, and Jehoi′achin his son reigned in his stead.

10 At that time the servants of Nebuchadnez′zar king of Babylon came up to Jerusalem, and the city was besieged. ¹¹And Nebuchadnez′zar king of Babylon came to the city, while his servants were besieging it; ¹²and Jehoi′achin the king of Judah gave himself up to the king of Babylon, himself, and his mother, and his servants, and his princes, and his palace officials. The king of Babylon took him prisoner in the eighth year of his reign, ¹³and carried off all the treasures of the house of the LORD, and the treasures of the king's house, and cut in pieces all the vessels of gold in the temple of the LORD, which Solomon king of Israel had made, as the LORD had foretold. ¹⁴He carried away all Jerusalem, and all the princes, and all the mighty men of valor, ten thousand captives, and all the craftsmen and the smiths; none remained, except the poorest people of the land.

17 And the king of Babylon made Mattani′ah, Jehoi′achin's uncle, king in his stead, and changed his name to Zedeki′ah.

18 Zedeki′ah was twenty-one years old when he became king, and he reigned eleven years in Jerusalem. His mother's name was Hamu′tal the daughter of Jeremiah of Libnah. ¹⁹And he did what was evil in the sight of the LORD, according to all that Jehoi′akim had done. ²⁰For because of the anger of the LORD it came to the point in Jerusalem and Judah that he cast them out from his presence.

And Zedeki′ah rebelled against the king of Babylon.

25 And in the ninth year of his reign, in the tenth month, on the tenth day of the month, Nebuchadnez′zar king of Babylon came with all his army against Jerusalem, and laid siege to it; and they built siegeworks against it round about. ²So the city was besieged till the eleventh year of King Zedeki′ah. ³On the ninth day of the fourth month the famine was so severe in the city that there was no food for the people of the land. ⁴ Then a breach was made in the city; the king with all the men of war fled by night by the way of the gate between the two walls, by the king's garden, though the Chalde′ans were around the city. And they went in the direction of the Arabah. ⁵ But the army of the Chalde′ans pursued the king, and overtook him in the plains of Jericho; and all his army was scattered from him. ⁶ Then they captured the king, and brought him up to the king of Babylon at Riblah, who passed sentence upon him. ⁷ They slew the sons of Zedeki′ah before his eyes, and put out the eyes of Zedeki′ah, and bound him in fetters, and took him to Babylon.

8 In the fifth month, on the seventh day of the month—which was the nineteenth year of King Nebuchadnez′zar, king of Babylon—Nebu′zarad′an, the captain of the bodyguard, a servant of the king of Babylon, came to Jerusalem. ⁹ And he burned the house of the LORD, and the king's house and all the houses of Jerusalem; every great house he burned down. ¹⁰ And all the army of the Chalde′ans, who were with the captain of the guard, broke down the walls around Jerusalem. ¹¹ And the rest of the people who were left in the city and the deserters who had deserted to the king of Babylon, together with the rest of the multitude, Nebu′zarad′an the captain of the guard carried into exile. ¹² But the captain of the guard left some of the poorest of the land to be vinedressers and plowmen.

22 And over the people who remained in the land of Judah, whom Nebuchadnez′zar king of Babylon had left, he appointed Gedali′ah the son of Ahi′kam, son of Shaphan, governor.

25 But in the seventh month, Ishmael the son of Nethani′ah, son of Eli′shama, of the royal family, came with ten men, and attacked and killed Gedali′ah and the Jews and the Chalde′ans who were with him at Mizpah. ²⁶ Then all the people, both small and great, and the captains of the forces arose, and went to Egypt; for they were afraid of the Chalde′ans.

27 And in the thirty-seventh year of the exile of Jehoi′achin king of Judah, in the twelfth month, on the twenty-seventh day of the month, Evil-mero′dach king of Babylon, in the year that he began to reign, graciously freed Jehoi′achin king of Judah from prison; ²⁸ and he spoke kindly to him, and gave him a seat above the seats of the kings who were with him in Babylon. ²⁹ So Jehoi′achin put off his prison garments. And every day of his life he dined regularly at the king's table; ³⁰ and for his allowance, a regular allowance was given him by the king, every day a portion, as long as he lived.

24:1 Nebuchadnezzar is also commonly known as Nebuchadrezzar; the latter spelling is closer to the Babylonian pronunciation. Both the prophet Jeremiah and Ezekiel, contemporary with this period, counseled against resistance to the Babylonians. They believed that, were Judah to remain a vassal state instead of a rebellious one, and to place her trust in God instead of arms, she would survive unscathed. **24:12** 598 B.C. **25:8** 586 B.C. The Syrian Royal Documents now preserved at the Oriental Institute in Chicago confirm this imprisonment of King Jehoiachin. They offer the added information, however, that a quota of oil was provided the prisoner from the royal treasury indicating that Jehoiachin was treated in his captivity with some deference. **25:27** Jehoiachin was the last surviving monarch of Judah. With these final four sentences the historic account of the Books of Kings ends on a hopeful note. The pardon granted the captive king portends a brighter future for the Hebrew people, the end of the exile and the restoration of the Davidic monarchy. The date of his pardon is estimated to be 562 B.C., twenty-six years after the fall of Jerusalem. The Second Book of Chronicles, which reviews much of the same material contained in this Book of Kings, but was written later, concludes with the announcement of Cyrus' decree in 538 B.C. that the exiles may return to their land.

The Books of the Chronicles

The Hebrew title for these two books is *Dibre Hayammim,* figuratively "the events of the times." The book received its English name from the title in the Vulgate: *Liber Chronicorum,* and its division into two books from the Greek translation. Noting that the closing verses of Chronicles are repeated in Ezra 1, some scholars believe the books of Chronicles and Ezra-Nehemiah were once integrated.

In the Greek and Latin translations Chronicles is placed directly after the books of Kings, since it is a supplementary account of that same era. In the Hebrew canon, Chronicles is included among the Writings, usually as the last book of Scripture; thus the Hebraic tradition emphasizes its literary rather than its historical character. The book reinterprets national events in such a way as to demonstrate that all history reflects the consequences of moral behavior. It also underscores the significance for Jewish history of the Davidic dynasty—the house from which the Redeemer will appear.

Some scholars think the book was written about 300 B.C. by a priest-author who drew from old historical records. According to Rabbinic tradition, however, it was begun by Ezra and concluded by Nehemiah, which would date its authorship about 450 B.C. The book is concerned with genealogies, Temple ritual and the Davidic dynasty. The language shows evidence of Aramaic influence on the Hebrew tongue. Not too long afterwards, Aramaic became the everyday language of the Hebrew people.

THE FIRST BOOK OF THE CHRONICLES

Chapter 1 traces the genealogy of the Hebrews from Adam through the patriarchs, with a list of the kings of Edom appended. Chapters 2 to 8 recount the genealogies of the Twelve Tribes with greater attention given to the tribes of Judah and Benjamin than to the northern tribes. Chapters 10–29 describe the reign of David with emphasis on matters that touch the priesthood and the services of the Temple.

Genealogies of Israel
1 Chronicles 9:1; 10:1–7, 13–14; 11:1–9

9 So all Israel was enrolled by genealogies; and these are written in the Book of the Kings of Israel. And Judah was taken into exile in Babylon because of their unfaithfulness.

10 Now the Philistines fought against Israel; and the men of Israel fled before the Philistines, and fell slain on Mount Gilbo'a. ²And the Philistines overtook Saul and his sons; and the Philistines slew Jonathan and Abin'adab and Mal'chishu'a, the sons of Saul. ³The battle pressed hard upon Saul, and the archers found him; and he was wounded by the archers. ⁴Then Saul said to his armor-bearer, "Draw your sword, and thrust me through with it, lest these uncircumcised come and make sport of me." But his armor-bearer would not; for he feared greatly. Therefore Saul took his own sword, and fell upon it. ⁵And when his armor-bearer saw that Saul was dead, he also fell upon his sword, and died. ⁶Thus Saul died; he and his three sons and all his house died together. ⁷And when all the men of Israel who were in the valley saw that the army had fled and that Saul and his sons were dead, they forsook their cities and fled; and the Philistines came and dwelt in them.

13 So Saul died for his unfaithfulness; he was unfaithful to the LORD in that he did not keep the command of the LORD, and also consulted a medium, seeking guidance, ¹⁴and did not seek guidance from the LORD. Therefore the LORD slew him, and turned the kingdom over to David the son of Jesse.

11 Then all Israel gathered together to David at Hebron, and said, "Behold, we are your bone and flesh. ²In times past, even when Saul was king, it was you that led out and brought in Israel; and the LORD your God said to you, 'You shall be shepherd of my people Israel, and you shall be prince over my people Israel.' " ³So all the elders of Israel came to the king at Hebron; and David made a covenant with them at Hebron before the LORD, and they anointed David king over Israel, according to the word of the LORD by Samuel.

4 And David and all Israel went to Jerusalem, that is Jebus, where the Jeb'usites were, the inhabitants of the land. ⁵ The inhabitants of Jebus said to David, "You will not come in here." Nevertheless David took the stronghold of Zion, that is, the city of David. ⁶ David said, "Whoever shall smite the Jeb'usites first shall be chief and commander." And Jo'ab the son of Zeru'iah went up first, so he became chief. ⁷ And David dwelt in the stronghold; therefore it was called the city of David. ⁸ And he built the city round about from the Millo in complete circuit; and Jo'ab repaired the rest of the city. ⁹ And David became greater and greater, for the LORD of hosts was with him.

10:13 These moral reflections on the violent death of Saul are not found in 1 Samuel. They are characteristic of this book.

David Gives Thanks to the Lord

David's skill as a composer of psalms is here illustrated. Verses in this hymn of thanksgiving make use of portions of Psalms 105, 96 and 106. Further chapters continue the account of David's life. Derogatory references to David, however, are omitted in the Book of Chronicles. His rivalry with Saul is minimized; the incident with Bath-sheba is overlooked, and the story of Absalom's rebellion is ignored.

1 Chronicles 16 : 1–26

16 And they brought in the ark of God, and set it inside the tent which David had pitched for it; and they offered burnt offerings and peace offerings before God. ² And when David had finished offering the burnt offerings and the peace offerings, he blessed the people in the name of the LORD, ³ and distributed to all Israel, both men and women, to each a loaf of bread, a portion of meat, and a cake of raisins.

4 Moreover he appointed certain of the Levites as ministers before the ark of the LORD, to invoke, to thank, and to praise the LORD, the God of Israel. ⁵ Asaph was the chief, and second to him were Zechari'ah, Je-i'el, Shemiramoth, Jehi'el, Mattithi'ah, Eli'ab, Benai'ah, O'bed-e'dom, and Je-i'el, who were to play harps and lyres; Asaph was to sound the cymbals, ⁶ and Benai'ah and Jaha'ziel the priests were to blow trumpets continually, before the ark of the covenant of God.

7 Then on that day David first appointed that thanksgiving be sung to the LORD by Asaph and his brethren.

⁸ O give thanks to the LORD, call on his name,
    make known his deeds among the peoples!
⁹ Sing to him, sing praises to him,
    tell of all his wonderful works!
¹⁰ Glory in his holy name;
    let the hearts of those who seek the LORD rejoice!
¹¹ Seek the LORD and his strength,
    seek his presence continually!
¹² Remember the wonderful works that he has done,
    the wonders he wrought, the judgments he uttered,
¹³ O offspring of Abraham his servant,
    sons of Jacob, his chosen ones!

¹⁴ He is the LORD our God;
    his judgments are in all the earth.
¹⁵ He is mindful of his covenant for ever,
    of the word that he commanded, for a thousand genera-
    tions,
¹⁶ the covenant which he made with Abraham,
    his sworn promise to Isaac,
¹⁷ which he confirmed as a statute to Jacob,
    as an everlasting covenant to Israel,
¹⁸ saying, "To you I will give the land of Canaan,
    as your portion for an inheritance."

¹⁹ When they were few in number,
    and of little account, and sojourners in it,
²⁰ wandering from nation to nation,
    from one kingdom to another people,
²¹ he allowed no one to oppress them;
    he rebuked kings on their account,
²² saying, "Touch not my anointed ones,
    do my prophets no harm!"

²³ Sing to the LORD, all the earth!
    Tell of his salvation from day to day.
²⁴ Declare his glory among the nations,
    his marvelous works among all the peoples!
²⁵ For great is the LORD, and greatly to be praised,
    and he is to be held in awe above all gods.
²⁶ For all the gods of the peoples are idols;
    but the LORD made the heavens.

David Instructs Solomon
1 Chronicles 22 : 7 – 16; 29 : 26 – 30

7 David said to Solomon, "My son, I had it in my heart to build a house to the name of the LORD my God. ⁸ But the word of the LORD came to me, saying, 'You have shed much blood and have waged great wars; you shall not build a house to my name, because you have shed so much blood before me upon the earth. ⁹ Behold, a son shall be born to you; he shall be a man of peace. I will give him peace from all his enemies round about; for his name shall be Solomon, and I will give peace and quiet to Israel in his days. ¹⁰ He shall build a house for my name. He shall be my son, and I will be his father, and I will establish his royal throne in Israel for ever.' ¹¹ Now, my son, the LORD be with you, so that you may succeed in building the house of the LORD your God, as he has spoken concerning you. ¹² Only, may the LORD grant you discretion and understanding, that when he gives you charge over Israel you may keep the law of the LORD your God. ¹³ Then you will prosper if you are careful to observe the statutes and the ordinances which the LORD commanded Moses for Israel. Be strong, and of good courage. Fear not; be not dismayed. ¹⁴ With great pains I have provided for the house of the LORD a hundred thousand talents of gold, a million talents of silver, and bronze and iron beyond weighing, for there is so much of it; timber and stone too I have provided. To these you must add. ¹⁵ You have an abundance of workmen: stonecutters, masons, carpenters, and all kinds of craftsmen without number, skilled in working ¹⁶ gold, silver, bronze, and iron. Arise and be doing! The LORD be with you!"

26 Thus David the son of Jesse reigned over all Israel. ²⁷ The time that he reigned over Israel was forty years; he reigned seven years in Hebron, and thirty-three years in Jerusalem. ²⁸ Then he died in a good old age, full of days, riches, and honor; and Solomon his son reigned in his stead. ²⁹ Now the acts of King David, from first to last, are written in the Chronicles of Samuel the seer, and in the Chronicles of Nathan the prophet, and in the Chronicles of Gad the seer, ³⁰ with accounts of all his rule and his might and of the circumstances that came upon him and upon Israel, and upon all the kingdoms of the countries.

THE SECOND BOOK OF THE CHRONICLES

2 Chronicles, in its first ten chapters, discusses the reign of Solomon and deals particularly with the building and furnishing of the Temple, its personnel and the organization of its services. The last sixteen chapters review the lives of the monarchs of the divided kingdom of Judah. (The books of Chronicles omit any mention of the Northern Kingdom.) It extends the historical account about thirty years beyond the book of Kings and concludes with the proclamation of Cyrus (538 B.C.) permitting the Babylonian exiles to return to their homeland.

God Is with a Righteous King

The book of Kings gives only sixteen verses to King Asa (914–874 B.C.), whereas the Chronicler devotes three chapters to him. The passage below illustrates well the didactic purpose of this historical account in seeking to inspire the readers' faith.

2 Chronicles 15:1–13

15 The Spirit of God came upon Azari′ah the son of Oded, ²and he went out to meet Asa, and said to him, "Hear me, Asa, and all Judah and Benjamin: The LORD is with you, while you are with him. If you seek him, he will be found by you, but if you forsake him, he will forsake you. ³For a long time Israel was without the true God, and without a teaching priest, and without law; ⁴but when in their distress they turned to the LORD, the God of Israel, and sought him, he was found by them. ⁵In those times there was no peace to him who went out or to him who came in, for great disturbances afflicted all the inhabitants of the lands. ⁶They were broken in pieces, nation against nation and city against city, for God troubled them with every sort of distress. ⁷But you, take courage! Do not let your hands be weak, for your work shall be rewarded."

8 When Asa heard these words, the prophecy of Azari′ah the son of Oded, he took courage, and put away the abominable idols from all the land of Judah and Benjamin and from the cities which he had taken in the hill country of E′phraim, and he repaired the altar of the LORD that was in front of the vestibule of the house of the LORD. ⁹And he gathered all Judah and Benjamin, and those from E′phraim, Manas′seh, and Simeon who were sojourning with them, for great numbers had deserted to him from Israel when they saw that the LORD his God was with him. ¹⁰They were gathered at Jerusalem in the third month of the fifteenth year of the reign of Asa. ¹¹They sacrificed to the LORD on that day, from the spoil which

they had brought, seven hundred oxen and seven thousand sheep.
¹²And they entered into a covenant to seek the LORD, the God of
their fathers, with all their heart and with all their soul; ¹³and that
whoever would not seek the LORD, the God of Israel, should be put to
death, whether young or old, man or woman.

15:3–6 Refers to the period of Judges. 15:6 For accounts of
intertribal wars see Judges 9:26 ff.; 12:1 ff.; 20:12 ff.

Jehoshaphat Is Delivered from Moab and Ammon
2 Chronicles 17:1–6; 19:4–11; 20:1–4, 13–23, 35–37

17 Jehosh'aphat his son reigned in his stead, and strengthened
himself against Israel. ²He placed forces in all the fortified cities of
Judah, and set garrisons in the land of Judah, and in the cities of
E'phraim which Asa his father had taken. ³The LORD was with
Jehosh'aphat, because he walked in the earlier ways of his father; he
did not seek the Ba'als, ⁴but sought the God of his father and
walked in his commandments, and not according to the ways of
Israel. ⁵Therefore the LORD established the kingdom in his hand;
and all Judah brought tribute to Jehosh'aphat; and he had great
riches and honor. ⁶His heart was courageous in the ways of the
LORD; and furthermore he took the high places and the Ashe'rim
out of Judah.

19 ⁴Jehosh'aphat dwelt at Jerusalem; and he went out again among
the people, from Beer-sheba to the hill country of E'phraim, and
brought them back to the LORD, the God of their fathers. ⁵He
appointed judges in the land in all the fortified cities of Judah, city
by city, ⁶and said to the judges, "Consider what you do, for you
judge not for man but for the LORD; he is with you in giving
judgment. ⁷Now then, let the fear of the LORD be upon you; take
heed what you do, for there is no perversion of justice with the LORD
our God, or partiality, or taking bribes."

8 Moreover in Jerusalem Jehosh'aphat appointed certain Levites
and priests and heads of families of Israel, to give judgment for the
LORD and to decide disputed cases. They had their seat at Jerusalem.
⁹And he charged them: "Thus you shall do in the fear of the LORD,
in faithfulness, and with your whole heart: ¹⁰whenever a case comes
to you from your brethren who live in their cities, concerning
bloodshed, law or commandment, statutes or ordinances, then you
shall instruct them, that they may not incur guilt before the LORD
and wrath may not come upon you and your brethren. Thus you
shall do, and you will not incur guilt. ¹¹And behold, Amari'ah the
chief priest is over you in all matters of the LORD; and Zebadi'ah the
son of Ish'mael, the governor of the house of Judah, in all the king's

matters; and the Levites will serve you as officers. Deal courageously, and may the LORD be with the upright!"

20 After this the Moabites and Ammonites, and with them some of the Me-u′nites, came against Jehosh′aphat for battle. [2] Some men came and told Jehosh′aphat, "A great multitude is coming against you from Edom, from beyond the sea; and, behold, they are in Haz′azon-ta′mar" (that is, En-ge′di). [3] Then Jehosh′aphat feared, and set himself to seek the LORD, and proclaimed a fast throughout all Judah. [4] And Judah assembled to seek help from the LORD; from all the cities of Judah they came to seek the LORD.

13 Meanwhile all the men of Judah stood before the LORD, with their little ones, their wives, and their children. [14] And the Spirit of the LORD came upon Jaha′ziel the son of Zechari′ah, son of Benai′ah, son of Je-i′el, son of Mattani′ah, a Levite of the sons of Asaph, in the midst of the assembly. [15] And he said, "Hearken, all Judah and inhabitants of Jerusalem, and King Jehosh′aphat: Thus says the LORD to you, 'Fear not, and be not dismayed at this great multitude; for the battle is not yours but God's. [16] Tomorrow go down against them; behold, they will come up by the ascent of Ziz; you will find them at the end of the valley, east of the wilderness of Jeru′el. [17] You will not need to fight in this battle; take your position, stand still, and see the victory of the LORD on your behalf, O Judah and Jerusalem.' Fear not, and be not dismayed; tomorrow go out against them, and the LORD will be with you."

18 Then Jehosh′aphat bowed his head with his face to the ground, and all Judah and the inhabitants of Jerusalem fell down before the LORD, worshiping the LORD. [19] And the Levites, of the Ko′hathites and the Kor′ahites, stood up to praise the LORD, the God of Israel, with a very loud voice.

20 And they rose early in the morning and went out into the wilderness of Teko′a; and as they went out, Jehosh′aphat stood and said, "Hear me, Judah and inhabitants of Jerusalem! Believe in the LORD your God, and you will be established; believe his prophets, and you will succeed." [21] And when he had taken counsel with the people, he appointed those who were to sing to the LORD and praise him in holy array, as they went before the army, and say,

"Give thanks to the LORD,
    for his steadfast love endures for ever."

[22] And when they began to sing and praise, the LORD set an ambush against the men of Ammon, Moab, and Mount Se′ir, who had come against Judah, so that they were routed. [23] For the men of Ammon and Moab rose against the inhabitants of Mount Se′ir, destroying

them utterly, and when they had made an end of the inhabitants of Se'ir, they all helped to destroy one another.

35 After this Jehosh'aphat king of Judah joined with Ahazi'ah king of Israel, who did wickedly. ³⁶ He joined him in building ships to go to Tarshish, and they built the ships in E'zion-ge'ber. ³⁷ Then Elie'zer the son of Dodav'ahu of Mare'-shah prophesied against Jehosh'aphat, saying, "Because you have joined with Ahazi'ah, the LORD will destroy what you have made." And the ships were wrecked and were not able to go to Tarshish.

19:5 This is a rare account of a king establishing a judiciary in accordance with biblical law. **19:11** Although all Hebraic litigation was to be decided according to the law of the Torah, a distinction is made between matters of the Lord over which the High Priest has authority, and matters of the king—that is, civil cases—over which the king's appointed judge has authority. **20:3** It was customary to declare a fast at a time of crisis (see Joel 2:15, Jonah 3:5, Esther 4:16). **20:14** This inspired Levitical musician is not mentioned elsewhere in Scripture. **20:17** Reliance on God alone is a central theme in Chronicles. **20:22** At a critical moment, men in the area living thereabout attacked the invading force, confused and routed them. The Chronicler believed God, directly intervening, turned danger away from Judah. **20:37** This is the only account in Scripture of this prophet.

The Chronicler Ends His History on a Happy Note
2 Chronicles 36:22–23

22 Now in the first year of Cyrus king of Persia, that the word of the LORD by the mouth of Jeremiah might be accomplished, the LORD stirred up the spirit of Cyrus king of Persia so that he made a proclamation throughout all his kingdom and also put it in writing: ²³ "Thus says Cyrus king of Persia, 'The LORD, the God of heaven, has given me all the kingdoms of the earth, and he has charged me to build him a house at Jerusalem, which is in Judah. Whoever is among you of all his people, may the LORD his God be with him. Let him go up.' "

36:22 These verses also form the beginning of the Book of Ezra suggesting to some scholars a common editor for both books. Note that the Chronicler interprets Cyrus' declaration of freedom for the Israelites to be a fulfillment of Jeremiah's prophecies, compare Jeremiah 29:10.

The Book of Ezra

Tracing his descent from Aaron the High Priest and a disciple of the scribe of Jeremiah, Ezra was given authority over all Jewish religious matters by the Persian King Artaxerxes I in 458 B.C.

Eighty years earlier, 538 B.C., the Israelites had been given permission to return to their homeland by Cyrus, king of the Medes and Persians. Responding to the appeals of the prophets Haggai and Zechariah, the exiles restored the Temple in Jerusalem and dedicated it in 516 B.C. Then a silence of sixty years intervenes in our historical records. During that time, evidently, a period of deterioration set in.

Ezra's arrival kindled a new wave of religious and national enthusiasm. His most significant reform was the establishment of a body known as "The Men of the Great Synagogue." This group arranged and canonized Israel's holy writings. It also made the Holy Word available to the people through the institution of schools and the use of public occasions as an opportunity for adult education. According to Rabbinic tradition the custom of inviting three men to read from the Torah scroll at the morning prayer service on Mondays and Thursdays was instituted by Ezra (*Babba Kamma* 82b). Thus Ezra began the process that transformed Judaism into the religion of an entire people.

Jewish tradition credits Ezra himself with the writing of this book, about 450 B.C. Obviously he drew upon official records and civic lists, as well as his own personal correspondence. Some biblical scholars hold that the book was edited at a later date. It has been suggested that the books of Ezra and Nehemiah, 1 and 2 Chronicles were once joined together in a single long work by a priest-editor about 300 B.C. In the Hebrew canon it is included in that section known as Writings, between Daniel and Nehemiah. Considerable portions of the book (14:8–6, 18 and 7:12–26) are in Aramaic, reflecting the bilingual character of fourth-century Jews. The use of words of Akkadian and Persian origin testify to Ezra's contacts with other nations.

The Greek rendering of Ezra's name is Esdras.

The Jews Return to Jerusalem
Ezra 1:1–7

1 In the first year of Cyrus king of Persia, that the word of the LORD by the mouth of Jeremiah might be accomplished, the LORD stirred up the spirit of Cyrus king of Persia so that he made a proclamation throughout all his kingdom and also put it in writing:

2 "Thus says Cyrus king of Persia: The LORD, the God of heaven,

has given me all the kingdoms of the earth, and he has charged me to build him a house at Jerusalem, which is in Judah. ³ Whoever is among you of all his people, may his God be with him, and let him go up to Jerusalem, which is in Judah, and rebuild the house of the LORD, the God of Israel—he is the God who is in Jerusalem; ⁴ and let each survivor, in whatever place he sojourns, be assisted by the men of his place with silver and gold, with goods and with beasts, besides freewill offerings for the house of God which is in Jerusalem."

5 Then rose up the heads of the fathers' houses of Judah and Benjamin, and the priests and the Levites, everyone whose spirit God had stirred to go up to rebuild the house of the LORD which is in Jerusalem; ⁶ and all who were about them aided them with vessels of silver, with gold, with goods, with beasts, and with costly wares, besides all that was freely offered. ⁷ Cyrus the king also brought out the vessels of the house of the LORD which Nebuchadnez'zar had carried away from Jerusalem and placed in the house of his gods.

1:1 See Jeremiah 29:10. Allusions to Cyrus also appear in the writing of Isaiah (44:28; 45:1). The historian Josephus suggests that Cyrus may have known of these writings and may have received aid from the Jewish exiles. **1:3** Since Jerusalem is located on the crests of hills, the expression "to go up to Jerusalem" contains in Jewish tradition both a spiritual and a geographical significance. King Cyrus reversed the policy of the Babylonian kings who had forcibly removed the leaders of conquered nations from their homes and transplanted them to desolate regions or restricted them within the walls of Babylon. Thus at one stroke Cyrus removed malcontent peoples from the heart of his empire and curried the affection of grateful subjects in every quarter of his dominion. For the biblical historians the policy was fulfillment of the will of the Lord.

A Foundation Is Laid for the Temple
Ezra 3:1–13

3 When the seventh month came, and the sons of Israel were in the towns, the people gathered as one man to Jerusalem. ² Then arose Jeshua the son of Jo'zadak, with his fellow priests, and Zerub'babel the son of She-al'ti-el with his kinsmen, and they built the altar of the God of Israel, to offer burnt offerings upon it, as it is written in the law of Moses the man of God. ³ They set the altar in its place, for fear was upon them because of the peoples of the lands, and they offered burnt offerings upon it to the LORD, burnt offerings morning and evening. ⁴ And they kept the feast of booths, as it is written, and offered the daily burnt offerings by number according to the

ordinance, as each day required, [5] and after that the continual burnt offerings, the offerings at the new moon and at all the appointed feasts of the LORD, and the offerings of every one who made a freewill offering to the LORD. [6] From the first day of the seventh month they began to offer burnt offerings to the LORD. But the foundation of the temple of the LORD was not yet laid. [7] So they gave money to the masons and the carpenters, and food, drink, and oil to the Sido'nians and the Tyrians to bring cedar trees from Lebanon to the sea, to Joppa, according to the grant which they had from Cyrus king of Persia.

8 Now in the second year of their coming to the house of God at Jerusalem, in the second month, Zerub'babel the son of She-al'ti-el and Jeshua the son of Jo'zadak made a beginning, together with the rest of their brethren, the priests and the Levites and all who had come to Jerusalem from the captivity. They appointed the Levites, from twenty years old and upward, to have the oversight of the work of the house of the LORD. [9] And Jeshua with his sons and his kinsmen, and Kad'mi-el and his sons, the sons of Judah, together took the oversight of the workmen in the house of God, along with the sons of Hen'adad and the Levites, their sons and kinsmen.

10 And when the builders laid the foundation of the temple of the LORD, the priests in their vestments came forward with trumpets, and the Levites, the sons of Asaph, with cymbals, to praise the LORD, according to the directions of David king of Israel; [11] and they sang responsively, praising and giving thanks to the LORD,

"For he is good,
    for his steadfast love endures for ever toward Israel."
And all the people shouted with a great shout, when they praised the LORD, because the foundation of the house of the LORD was laid. [12] But many of the priests and Levites and heads of fathers' houses, old men who had seen the first house, wept with a loud voice when they saw the foundation of this house being laid, though many shouted aloud for joy; [13] so that the people could not distinguish the sound of the joyful shout from the sound of the people's weeping, for the people shouted with a great shout, and the sound was heard afar.

> **3:8** It is characteristic of the Chronicler's history to record the central role of the Levites in the reconstruction of the Jewish religion.

The Samaritans Interfere with the Work on the Temple
Ezra 4:1–5; 5:1–2; 6:14–16, 19–22

4 Now when the adversaries of Judah and Benjamin heard that the returned exiles were building a temple to the LORD, the God of

Israel, ²they approached Zerub'babel and the heads of fathers' houses and said to them, "Let us build with you; for we worship your God as you do, and we have been sacrificing to him ever since the days of E'sar-had'don king of Assyria who brought us here." ³But Zerub'babel, Jeshua, and the rest of the heads of fathers' houses in Israel said to them, "You have nothing to do with us in building a house to our God; but we alone will build to the Lord, the God of Israel, as King Cyrus the king of Persia has commanded us."

4 Then the people of the land discouraged the people of Judah, and made them afraid to build, ⁵and hired counselors against them to frustrate their purpose, all the days of Cyrus king of Persia, even until the reign of Darius king of Persia.

5 Now the prophets, Hag'gai and Zechari'ah the son of Iddo, prophesied to the Jews who were in Judah and Jerusalem, in the name of the God of Israel who was over them. ²Then Zerub'babel the son of She-al'ti-el and Jeshua the son of Jo'zadak arose and began to rebuild the house of God which is in Jerusalem; and with them were the prophets of God, helping them.

14 And the elders of the Jews built and prospered, through the prophesying of Haggai the prophet and Zechari'ah the son of Iddo. They finished their building by command of the God of Israel and by decree of Cyrus and Darius and Ar-ta-xerx'es king of Persia; ¹⁵and this house was finished on the third day of the month of Adar, in the sixth year of the reign of Darius the king.

16 And the people of Israel, the priests and the Levites, and the rest of the returned exiles, celebrated the dedication of this house of God with joy.

19 On the fourteenth day of the first month the returned exiles kept the passover. ²⁰For the priests and the Levites had purified themselves together; all of them were clean. So they killed the passover lamb for all the returned exiles, for their fellow priests, and for themselves; ²¹it was eaten by the people of Israel who had returned from exile, and also by every one who had joined them and separated himself from the pollutions of the the peoples of the land to worship the Lord, the God of Israel. ²²And they kept the feast of unleavened bread seven days with joy; for the Lord had made them joyful, and had turned the heart of the king of Assyria to them, so that he aided them in the work of the house of God, the God of Israel.

4:1 The Samaritans were the chief "adversaries." They were foreign colonists who had been brought in from Babylon and elsewhere by the king of Assyria. They had intermingled with remnants of the Northern Kingdom of Israel (cf. 2 Kings 17:24 ff.)

and they worshiped both the Israelite God and graven idols. The returning exiles rejected their offer of help, wishing to preserve the distinctive religious purity of their community. The Samaritans thereupon became enemies of the Hebrews; by overt attack and diplomatic intervention they succeeded in halting work on the Temple for more than nine years. (Note that the Chronicler blames the Samaritans for the delay in building the Temple whereas Haggai 1:2 criticizes the indifference of the Jews.) Later the Samaritans erected their own Temple on Mt. Gerizim. In 128 B.C. John Hyrcanus destroyed their shrine but the Samaritans maintained their distinctiveness. Jesus comments on the unfriendly relations between the Jews and Samaritans. There are Samaritans still in modern Israel. **6:15** The actual building of the Temple took four and a half years, around 520–515 B.C. **6:19** The celebration of Passover is similarly recalled at other great moments in the national life of Israel (see Numbers 9:5; Joshua 5:10; 2 Kings 23:21; 1 Chronicles 30:1 ff., 35:1 ff.).

Ezra Returns to the Holy Land
Ezra 7:1, 6, 10–20, 25–28; 8:15–23

7 Now after this, in the reign of Ar-ta-xerx′es king of Persia, Ezra the son of Serai′ah, son of Azari′ah, son of Hilki′ah,

6 this Ezra went up from Babylonia. He was a scribe skilled in the law of Moses which the LORD the God of Israel had given; and the king granted him all that he asked, for the hand of the LORD his God was upon him.

10 For Ezra had set his heart to study the law of the LORD, and to do it, and to teach his statutes and ordinances in Israel.

11 This is a copy of the letter which King Ar-ta-xerx′es gave to Ezra the priest, the scribe, learned in matters of the commandments of the LORD and his statutes for Israel: [12]"Ar-ta-xerx′es, king of kings, to Ezra the priest, the scribe of the law of the God of heaven. And now [13]I make a decree that any one of the people of Israel or their priests or Levites in my kingdom, who freely offer to go to Jerusalem, may go with you. [14]For you are sent by the king and his seven counselors to make inquiries about Judah and Jerusalem according to the law of your God, which is in your hand, [15]and also to convey the silver and gold which the king and his counselors have freely offered to the God of Israel, whose dwelling is in Jerusalem, [16]with all the silver and gold which you shall find in the whole province of Babylonia, and with the freewill offerings of the people and the priests, vowed willingly for the house of their God which is in Jerusalem. [17]With this money, then, you shall with all diligence buy bulls, rams, and lambs, with their cereal offerings and their

drink offerings, and you shall offer them upon the altar of the house of your God which is in Jerusalem. [18]Whatever seems good to you and your brethren to do with the rest of the silver and gold, you may do, according to the will of your God. [19]The vessels that have been given you for the service of the house of your God, you shall deliver before the God of Jerusalem. [20]And whatever else is required for the house of your God, which you have occasion to provide, you may provide it out of the king's treasury.

25 "And you, Ezra, according to the wisdom of your God which is in your hand, appoint magistrates and judges who may judge all the people in the province Beyond the River, all such as know the laws of your God; and those who do not know them, you shall teach. [26]Whoever will not obey the law of your God and the law of the king, let judgment be strictly executed upon him, whether for death or for banishment or for confiscation of his goods or for imprisonment."

27 Blessed be the LORD, the God of our fathers, who put such a thing as this into the heart of the king, to beautify the house of the LORD which is in Jerusalem, [28]and who extended to me his steadfast love before the king and his counselors, and before all the king's mighty officers. I took courage, for the hand of the LORD my God was upon me, and I gathered leading men from Israel to go up with me.

8 [15]I gathered them to the river that runs to Aha'va, and there we encamped three days. As I reviewed the people and the priests, I found there none of the sons of Levi. [16]Then I sent for Elie'zer, Ar'i-el, Shemai'ah, Elna'than, Jarib, Elna'than, Nathan, Zechari'ah, and Meshul'lam, leading men, and for Joi'arib and Elna'than, who were men of insight, [17]and sent them to Iddo, the leading man at the place Casiphi'a, telling them what to say to Iddo and his brethren the temple servants at the place Casiphi'a, namely, to send us ministers for the house of our God. [18]And by the good hand of our God upon us, they brought us a man of discretion, of the sons of Mahli the son of Levi, son of Israel, namely Sherebi'ah with his sons and kinsmen, eighteen; [19]also Hashabi'ah and with him Jeshai'ah of the sons of Merar'i, with his kinsmen and their sons, twenty; [20]besides two hundred and twenty of the temple servants, whom David and his officials had set apart to attend the Levites. These were all mentioned by name.

21 Then I proclaimed a fast there, at the river Aha'va, that we might humble ourselves before our God, to seek from him a straight way for ourselves, our children, and all our goods. [22]For I was ashamed to ask the king for a band of soldiers and horsemen to protect us against the enemy on our way; since we had told the king,

"The hand of our God is for good upon all that seek him, and the power of his wrath is against all that forsake him." [23]So we fasted and besought our God for this, and he listened to our entreaty.

7:6 In 2 Samuel 20:25 the term "scribe" refers to the state secretary. Later it was applied to those who studied, interpreted and copied Scriptures (cf. Jeremiah 8:8). Finally the scribes succeeded the prophets as spiritual leaders of the Israelites. **7:13** It has become customary to refer to a threefold division of the Hebrews: priests, Levites, and the people of Israel, rather than division by tribal inheritance; the custom continues today among Orthodox and Conservative Jews. **7:26** The Law of Moses is given civil status as the law of the land, supported by Persian authority. **8:15** ff. It is estimated that about 5,000 men, women and children returned with Ezra. Note the importance he places upon having Levites accompany the pilgrimage.

The Israelites Put Away Their Foreign Wives
Ezra 9:1–3; 10:9–17

9 After these things had been done, the officials approached me and said, "The people of Israel and the priests and the Levites have not separated themselves from the peoples of the lands with their abominations, from the Canaanites, the Hittites, the Per'izzites, the Jeb'usites, the Ammonites, the Moabites, the Egyptians, and the Amorites. [2]For they have taken some of their daughters to be wives for themselves and for their sons; so that the holy race has mixed itself with the peoples of the lands. And in this faithlessness the hand of the officials and chief men has been foremost." [3]When I heard this, I rent my garments and my mantle, and pulled hair from my head and beard, and sat appalled.

10 [9]Then all the men of Judah and Benjamin assembled at Jerusalem within the three days; it was the ninth month, on the twentieth day of the month. And all the people sat in the open square before the house of God, trembling because of this matter and because of the heavy rain. [10]And Ezra the priest stood up and said to them, "You have trespassed and married foreign women and so increased the guilt of Israel. [11]Now then make confession to the LORD the God of your fathers, and do his will; separate yourselves from the peoples of the land and from the foreign wives." [12]Then all the assembly answered with a loud voice, "It is so; we must do as you have said. [13]But the people are many, and it is a time of heavy rain; we cannot stand in the open. Nor is this a work for one day or two; for we have greatly transgressed in this matter. [14]Let our officials stand for the whole assembly; let all in our cities who have taken foreign wives come at appointed times, and with them the elders and judges of every city, till the fierce wrath of our God over this matter be averted from us." [15]Only Jonathan the son of As'ahel and Jahzei'ah the son of Tikvah opposed this, and Meshul'lam and Shab'bethai the Levite supported them.

16 Then the returned exiles did so. Ezra the priest selected men, heads of fathers' houses, according to their fathers' houses, each of them designated by name. On the first day of the tenth month they sat down to examine the matter; [17]and by the first day of the first month they had come to the end of all the men who had married foreign women.

9:1 In the reference to mixed marriages, the concern is spiritual, not racial. The Jews themselves were of mixed racial background. Marriage with these foreign wives introduced idolatrous practices and values alien to the Jewish tradition. Ezra's concern therefore was for the religious purity of his people. Other nations of this period similarly maintained severe restrictions against mixed marriage. Roman law forbade patricians to marry plebeians; in Athens there were regulations forbidding marriage to outsiders. The religious law prohibited mixed marriage (Deuteronomy 7:3), but it also provided a procedure for divorce respecting the right of the wife to support and to alimony (Deuteronomy 24:1 ff.). Despite the Deuteronomic prohibition on mixed marriage, Scripture recollects such marriages many times. **10:16–17** This commission was in session for three months. The text later records (10:18–44) that 113 men had taken foreign wives. These included seventeen priests and ten Levites. In Nehemiah (13:23) there is an intimation that some of these men remarried their wives after having divorced them under Ezra's pressure.

The Book of Nehemiah

This book was originally included in the Book of Ezra. The Church Father Origen (died A.D. 253) was apparently the first authority to call Nehemiah "The Second Book of Ezra."

According to Jewish tradition Ezra wrote this book, drawing upon the contemporary records of Nehemiah, probably about 424 B.C. Some biblical scholars hold, however, that Nehemiah preceded Ezra, others suggest that the books of Ezra, Nehemiah and Chronicles were all the work of historians about 300 B.C. In any case, this book supplements information on the period after the return of the exiles from Babylonia and the building of the Second Temple.

While Ezra concerned himself chiefly with religious matters, and the communication of the Holy Word, Nehemiah is entrusted with authority over the political and social situation in Judah. Under his inspiration the walls of Jerusalem were rebuilt and the desolate capital repopulated.

Centuries later Ben Sirach numbered Nehemiah as one of the famous men of the past whose "memorial is great" (Ecclesiasticus 44:13).

Nehemiah Requests Permission to Visit Jerusalem
Nehemiah 1:1–4; 2:1–6, 8b, 11, 13, 16–18

1 The words of Nehemi'ah the son of Hacali'ah.

Now it happened in the month of Chislev, in the twentieth year, as I was in Susa the capital, ²that Hana'ni, one of my brethren, came with certain men out of Judah; and I asked them concerning the Jews that survived, who had escaped exile, and concerning Jerusalem. ³And they said to me, "The survivors there in the province who escaped exile are in great trouble and shame; the wall of Jerusalem is broken down, and its gates are destroyed by fire."

4 When I heard these words I sat down and wept, and mourned for days; and I continued fasting and praying before the God of heaven.

2 In the month of Nisan, in the twentieth year of King Ar-ta-xerx'es, when wine was before him, I took up the wine and gave it to the king. Now I had not been sad in his presence. ²And the king said to me, "Why is your face sad, seeing you are not sick? This is nothing else but sadness of the heart." Then I was very much afraid. ³I said to the king, "Let the king live for ever! Why should not my face be sad, when the city, the place of my fathers' sepulchres lies waste, and its gates have been destroyed by fire?" ⁴Then the king said to me, "For what do you make request?" So I prayed to the God of heaven.

⁵ And I said to the king, "If it pleases the king, and if your servant has found favor in your sight, that you send me to Judah, to the city of my fathers' sepulchres, that I may rebuild it." ⁶ And the king said to me (the queen sitting beside him), "How long will you be gone, and when will you return?" So it pleased the king to send me; and I set him a time.

8b And the king granted me what I asked, for the good hand of my God was upon me.

11 So I came to Jerusalem and was there three days.

13 I went out by night by the Valley Gate to the Jackal's Well and to the Dung Gate, and I inspected the walls of Jerusalem which were broken down and its gates which had been destroyed by fire.

16 And the officials did not know where I had gone or what I was doing; and I had not yet told the Jews, the priests, the nobles, the officials, and the rest that were to do the work.

17 Then I said to them, "You see the trouble we are in, how Jerusalem lies in ruins with its gates burned. Come, let us build the wall of Jerusalem, that we may no longer suffer disgrace." ¹⁸ And I told them of the hand of my God which had been upon me for good, and also of the words which the king had spoken to me. And they said, "Let us rise up and build." So they strengthened their hands for the good work.

2:1 According to tradition, 444 B.C.

The Walls of Jerusalem Are Repaired
Nehemiah 4:1–2, 6–11, 21–23; 6:15–16

4 Now when Sanbal'lat heard that we were building the wall, he was angry and greatly enraged, and he ridiculed the Jews. ² And he said in the presence of his brethren and of the army of Samar'ia, "What are these feeble Jews doing? Will they restore things? Will they sacrifice? Will they finish up in a day? Will they revive the stones out of the heaps of rubbish, and burned ones at that?"

6 So we built the wall; and all the wall was joined together to half its height. For the people had a mind to work.

7 But when Sanbal'lat and Tobi'ah and the Arabs and the Ammonites and the Ash'dodites heard that the repairing of the walls of Jerusalem was going forward and that the breaches were beginning to be closed, they were very angry; ⁸ and they all plotted together to come and fight against Jerusalem and to cause confusion in it. ⁹ And we prayed to our God, and set a guard as a protection against them day and night.

10 But Judah said, "The strength of the burden-bearers is failing, and there is much rubbish; we are not able to work on the wall."

¹¹ And our enemies said, "They will not know or see till we come into the midst of them and kill them and stop the work."

21 So we labored at the work, and half of them held the spears from the break of dawn till the stars came out. ²² I also said to the people at that time, "Let every man and his servant pass the night within Jerusalem, that they may be a guard for us by night and may labor by day." ²³ So neither I nor my brethren nor my servants nor the men of the guard who followed me, none of us took off our clothes; each kept his weapon in his hand.

6 ¹⁵ So the wall was finished on the twenty-fifth day of the month Elul, in fifty-two days. ¹⁶ And when all our enemies heard of it, all the nations round about us were afraid and fell greatly in their own esteem; for they perceived that this work had been accomplished with the help of our God.

> **6:15** Josephus records that the rebuilding and repair of the entire wall around Jerusalem took two years and four months.

Nehemiah Achieves a Social Reform

Nehemiah 5:1–13

5 Now there arose a great outcry of the people and of their wives against their Jewish brethren. ² For there were those who said, "With our sons and our daughters, we are many; let us get grain, that we may eat and keep alive." ³ There were also those who said, "We are mortgaging our fields, our vineyards, and our houses to get grain because of the famine." ⁴ And there were those who said, "We have borrowed money for the king's tax upon our fields and our vineyards. ⁵ Now our flesh is as the flesh of our brethren, our children are as their children; yet we are forcing our sons and our daughters to be slaves, and some of our daughters have already been enslaved; but it is not in our power to help it, for other men have our fields and our vineyards."

6 I was very angry when I heard their outcry and these words. ⁷ I took counsel with myself, and I brought charges against the nobles and the officials. I said to them, "You are exacting interest, each from his brother." And I held a great assembly against them, ⁸ and said to them, "We, as far as we are able, have bought back our Jewish brethren who have been sold to the nations; but you even sell your brethren that they may be sold to us!" They were silent, and could not find a word to say. ⁹ So I said, "The thing that you are doing is not good. Ought you not to walk in the fear of our God to prevent the taunts of the nations our enemies? ¹⁰ Moreover I and my brethren and my servants are lending them money and grain. Let us leave off this interest. ¹¹ Return to them this very day their fields,

their vineyards, their olive orchards, and their houses, and the hundredth of money, grain, wine and oil which you have been exacting of them." ¹²Then they said, "We will restore these and require nothing from them. We will do as you say." And I called the priests, and took an oath of them to do as they had promised. ¹³I also shook out my lap and said, "So may God shake out every man from his house and from his labor who does not perform this promise. So may he be shaken out and emptied." And all the assembly said "Amen" and praised the LORD. And the people did as they had promised.

Nehemiah Supports the Religious Revival
Nehemiah 8:1–18

8 And all the people gathered as one man into the square before the Water Gate; and they told Ezra the scribe to bring the book of the law of Moses which the LORD had given to Israel. ²And Ezra the priest brought the law before the assembly, both men and women and all who could hear with understanding, on the first day of the seventh month. ³And he read from it facing the square before the Water Gate from early morning until midday, in the presence of the men and the women and those who could understand; and the ears of all the people were attentive to the book of the law. ⁴And Ezra the scribe stood on a wooden pulpit which they had made for the purpose; and beside him stood Mat-ti-thi′ah, Shema, Anai′ah, Uri′ah, Hilki′ah, and Ma-asei′ah on his right hand; and Pedai′ah, Mish′a-el, Malachi′jah, Hashum, Hash-bad′danah, Zechari′ah, and Meshul′lam on his left hand. ⁵And Ezra opened the book in the sight of all the people, for he was above all the people; and when he opened it all the people stood. ⁶And Ezra blessed the LORD, the great God; and all the people answered, "Amen, Amen," lifting up their hands; and they bowed their heads and worshiped the LORD with their faces to the ground. ⁷Also Jeshua, Bani, Sherebi′ah, Jamin, Akkub, Shab′bethai, Hodi′ah, Ma-asei′ah, Keli′ta, Azari′ah, Jo′zabad, Hanan, Pelai′ah, the Levites, helped the people to understand the law, while the people remained in their places. ⁸And they read from the book, from the law of God, clearly; and they gave the sense, so that the people understood the reading.

9 And Nehemi′ah, who was the governor, and Ezra the priest and scribe, and the Levites who taught the people said to all the people, "This day is holy to the LORD your God; do not mourn or weep." For all the people wept when they heard the words of the law. ¹⁰Then he said to them, "Go your way, eat the fat and drink sweet

wine and send portions to him for whom nothing is prepared; for this day is holy to our Lord; and do not be grieved, for the joy of the LORD is your strength." [11] So the Levites stilled all the people, saying, "Be quiet, for this day is holy; do not be grieved." [12] And all the people went their way to eat and drink and to send portions and to make great rejoicing, because they had understood the words that were declared to them.

13 On the second day the heads of fathers' houses of all the people, with the priests and the Levites, came together to Ezra the scribe in order to study the words of the law. [14] And they found it written in the law that the LORD had commanded by Moses that the people of Israel should dwell in booths during the feast of the seventh month, [15] and that they should publish and proclaim in all their towns and in Jerusalem, "Go out to the hills and bring branches of olive, wild olive, myrtle, palm, and other leafy trees to make booths, as it is written." [16] So the people went out and brought them and made booths for themselves, each on his roof, and in their courts and in the courts of the house of God, and in the square at the Water Gate and in the square at the Gate of E'phraim. [17] And all the assembly of those who had returned from the captivity made booths and dwelt in the booths; for from the days of Jeshua the son of Nun to that day the people of Israel had not done so. And there was very great rejoicing. [18] And day by day, from the first day to the last day, he read from the book of the law of God. They kept the feast seven days; and on the eighth day there was a solemn assembly, according to the ordinance.

8:2 The Jewish holy day observed on the first day of the seventh month is Rosh Hashanah, the Jewish New Year. With the city wall restored, the people feel secure and attend to their religious obligations. 8:5 The rabbis instituted a regulation that the congregation must rise at the presence of the Scroll, a practice followed to this day. 8:6 To this day a benediction is recited before the reading of each portion of the Scriptural lesson in the synagogue. 8:8 Ezra read the text; then interpreters explained it. Many scholars believe that the language used in interpreting the biblical text was Aramaic. The very first translation of the Hebrew Bible into another language was in Aramaic. Such a Bible is known as a Targum. In attempting to determine the exact rendering or meaning of a biblical word as understood by the Jews in the pre-Christian era, scholars find it valuable to consult the most famous of the Aramaic translations, the Targum by Onkelos. 8:14 In celebration of the biblical festival Succoth. (Cf. Exodus 23:16, Leviticus 23:34 ff., Numbers 29:12 ff., Deuteronomy 16:13 ff.).

The People Renew Their Covenant with God

Nehemiah 9:1–3, 6a, 34–38; 10:28–33, 35–37; 11:1–2

9 Now on the twenty-fourth day of this month the people of Israel were assembled with fasting and in sackcloth, and with earth upon their heads. ²And the Israelites separated themselves from all foreigners, and stood and confessed their sins and the iniquities of their fathers. ³And they stood up in their place and read from the book of the law of the LORD their God for a fourth of the day; for another fourth of it they made confession and worshiped the LORD their God.

6 And Ezra said: "Thou art the LORD, thou alone; thou hast made heaven, the heaven of heavens, with all their host, the earth and all that is on it, the seas and all that is in them. . . .

34 "Our kings, our princes, our priests, and our fathers have not kept thy law or heeded thy commandments and thy warnings which thou didst give them. ³⁵They did not serve thee in their kingdom, and in thy great goodness which thou gavest them, and in the large and rich land which thou didst set before them; and they did not turn from their wicked works. ³⁶Behold, we are slaves this day; in the land that thou gavest to our fathers to enjoy its fruit and its good gifts, behold, we are slaves. ³⁷And its rich yield goes to the kings whom thou has set over us because of our sins; they have power also over our bodies and over our cattle at their pleasure, and we are in great distress."

38 Because of all this we make a firm covenant and write it, and our princes, our Levites, and our priests set their seal to it.

10 ²⁸The rest of the people, the priests, the Levites, the gatekeepers, the singers, the temple servants, and all who have separated themselves from the peoples of the lands to the law of God, their wives, their sons, their daughters, all who have knowledge and understanding, ²⁹join with their brethren, their nobles, and enter into a curse and an oath to walk in God's law which was given by Moses the servant of God, and to observe and do all the commandments of the LORD our Lord and his ordinances and his statutes. ³⁰We will not give our daughters to the peoples of the land or take their daughters for our sons; ³¹and if the peoples of the land bring in wares or any grain on the sabbath day to sell, we will not buy from them on the sabbath or on a holy day; and we will forego the crops of the seventh year and the exaction of every debt.

32 We also lay upon ourselves the obligation to charge ourselves yearly with the third part of a shekel for the service of the house of our God: ³³for the showbread, the continual cereal offering, the

continual burnt offering, the sabbaths, the new moons, the appointed feasts, the holy things, and the sin offerings to make atonement for Israel, and for all the work of the house of our God.

35 We obligate ourselves to bring the first fruits of our ground and the first fruits of all fruit of every tree, year by year, to the house of the LORD; [36] also to bring to the house of our God, to the priests who minister in the house of our God, the first-born of our sons and of our cattle, as it is written in the law, and the firstlings of our herds and of our flocks; [37] and to bring the first of our coarse meal, and our contributions, the fruit of every tree, the wine and the oil, to the priests, to the chambers of the house of our God; and to bring to the Levites the tithes from our ground, for it is the Levites who collect the tithes in all our rural towns.

11 Now the leaders of the people lived in Jerusalem; and the rest of the people cast lots to bring one out of ten to live in Jerusalem the holy city, while nine tenths remained in the other towns. [2] And the people blessed all the men who willingly offered to live in Jerusalem.

9:3 Jewish scholars believe that during this generation under Ezra and Nehemiah there was organized a Great Synagogue (or assembly) that included priests, the secular leaders of the Israelites, and the prophets. This legislative body authorized the social reforms of the hour (see Nehemiah 5:7). It instituted some significant patterns of Jewish worship. It regulated the prayer liturgy still observed by Jews in their synagogues to this day. It accepted into the Canon certain Scriptural books that had been written outside of Palestine, and it organized the book of the twelve minor prophets. **9:38** In the Hebrew Bible this verse commences chapter 10. **10:31** For the earlier legislation regarding the prohibition of soil cultivation in the Sabbatical year, see Exodus 23:1–11, Leviticus 25:2 ff. Regarding the exaction of every debt, see Deuteronomy 15:2. **10:32** In addition to the half shekel already required by Mosaic law (Exodus 30:13 ff.), the people agreed to pay a third part of a shekel for the maintenance of the Temple service. **10:33** Twelve cakes of fine flour were laid on the golden table each Sabbath in two rows of six as the show bread. **10:35** Regarding the first fruits, see Exodus 23:19; 34:26; Deuteronomy 26:2 ff. **10:36** The first born sons were to be redeemed in a religious ceremony and the money given to the priests. See Exodus 13:3, Numbers 18:15 ff. **11:1** Defense of the city required that it be populated. Volunteers and conscripts chosen by lot were selected for this purpose. In contemporary Israel similar efforts are made to establish villages along border areas as a means of settling the land and also securing it against infiltration and attack.

The Book of Esther

The Book of Esther is one of five scrolls, or *megilloth*, a Hebrew word, plural form; singular, *megillah*, designating a book that was preserved originally on one wooden roller. In the Hebrew Bible the five scrolls are included in the collection of biblical books known as Writings. They are placed in the order in which they are read in the synagogue: Song of Songs is read at the Passover (usually in April); Ruth at the Festival of Pentecost (in June); Lamentations at the Fast of the Ninth of Av (in August); Ecclesiastes at the Festival of Tabernacles (in September); and the Scroll of Esther is read during the celebration of the holiday Purim (in March). The public reading of the Book of Esther achieved such a prominent place in Jewish religious practice that the word "megillah" is now almost exclusively identified with the Scroll of Esther.

The Book of Esther recalls the defeat of the tyrant Haman, who would have murdered all the Jews, and the victory of the heroine Esther and her uncle Mordecai.

When the scroll is read it is customary to drown out the name of Haman with noisemakers (*greggers*). Thus Jews impose on Haman the worst curse that they believe can be invoked upon a man— blotting out his name or soul from memory.

Haman became the prototype of every enemy of Israel. The recalling of his defeat provided the Jewish people in every generation with an assurance that God would protect and preserve them. At least twenty-five Jewish communities throughout the world observe their own particular "Purim," recalling, in ceremonies similar to the Purim celebration, their own unique deliverance from a tyrant. Accompanying the reading of the scroll in the Jewish celebration of Purim, there are carnivals, plays, songs and dances, the giving of gifts, costume parties, and other manifestations of joy.

Jewish tradition itself cannot agree on the authorship of this book, nor do scholars agree that the book necessarily describes an historical event. It has been proposed by some that this book was written as a novel in order to encourage the faith of Hebrew people suffering under an alien oppression, perhaps that of Antiochus Epiphanes (reference to the observance of a "Day of Mordecai" is to be found in 2 Maccabees 15:36) or, at a later date, that of Rome. Some suggest that it provided an historic explanation for a festival observed by Eastern Jews and by this account commended to the Greek-speaking Jews. Scholars also suggest that the Ahasuerus of this account may have been modeled after Xerxes I, who ruled Persia from 485–464 B.C.

Ahasuerus Removes Vashti as Queen

Esther 1:1–4, 10–13, 15–17, 19–22

(Jewish Publication Society)

1 Now it came to pass in the days of Ahasuerus—this is Ahasuerus who reigned, from India even unto Ethiopia, over a hundred and seven and twenty provinces—²that in those days, when the king Ahasuerus sat on the throne of his kingdom, which was in Shushan the castle, ³in the third year of his reign, he made a feast unto all his princes and his servants; the army of Persia and Media, the nobles and princes of the provinces, being before him; ⁴when he showed the riches of his glorious kingdom and the honor of his excellent majesty, many days, even a hundred and fourscore days.

10 On the seventh day, when the heart of the king was merry with wine, he commanded Mehuman, Bizzetha, Harbona, Bigtha, and Abagtha, Zethar, and Carcas, the seven chamberlains that ministered in the presence of Ahasuerus the king, ¹¹to bring Vashti the queen before the king with the crown royal, to show the peoples and the princes her beauty; for she was fair to look on. ¹²But the queen Vashti refused to come at the king's commandment by the chamberlains; therefore was the king very wroth, and his anger burned in him.

13 Then the king said to the wise men, who knew the times—for so was the king's manner toward all that knew law and judgment: ¹⁵"What shall we do unto the queen Vashti according to law, forasmuch as she hath not done the bidding of the king Ahasuerus by the chamberlains?"

16 And Memucan answered before the king and the princes: "Vashti the queen hath not done wrong to the king only, but also to all the princes, and to all the peoples, that are in all the provinces of the king Ahasuerus. ¹⁷For this deed of the queen will come abroad unto all women, to make their husbands contemptible in their eyes, when it will be said: The king Ahasuerus commanded Vashti the queen to be brought in before him but she came not. ¹⁹If it please the king, let there go forth a royal commandment from him, and let it be written among the laws of the Persians and the Medes, that it be not altered, that Vashti come no more before king Ahasuerus, and that the king give her royal estate unto another that is better than she. ²⁰And when the king's decree which he shall make shall be published throughout all his kingdom, great though it be, all the wives will give to their husbands honour, both to great and small." ²¹And the word pleased the king and the princes; and the king did according to the word of Memucan; ²²for he sent letters into all the king's provinces,

into every province according to the writing thereof, and to every people after their language, that every man should bear rule in his own house, and speak according to the language of his people.

Ahasuerus Makes Esther Queen

Esther 2:2–10, 17

(Jewish Publication Society)

2 Then said the king's servants that ministered unto him: "Let there be sought for the king young virgins fair to look on; ³ and let the king appoint officers in all the provinces of his kingdom, that they may gather together all the fair young virgins unto Shushan the castle, to the house of the women, unto the custody of Hegai the king's chamberlain, keeper of the women; and let their ointments be given them; ⁴ and let the maiden that pleaseth the king be queen instead of Vashti." And the thing pleased the king; and he did so.

5 There was a certain Jew in Shushan the castle, whose name was Mordecai the son of Jair the son of Shimei the son of Kish, a Benjamite, ⁶ who had been carried away from Jerusalem with the captives that had been carried away with Jeconiah king of Judah, whom Nebuchadnezzar the king of Babylon had carried away. ⁷ And he brought up Hadassah, that is, Esther, his uncle's daughter; for she had neither father nor mother, and the maiden was of beautiful form and fair to look on; and when her father and mother were dead, Mordecai took her for his own daughter.

8 And so it came to pass, when the king's commandment and his decree was published, and when many maidens were gathered together unto Shushan the castle, to the custody of Hegai, that Esther was taken into the king's house, to the custody of Hegai, keeper of the women. ⁹ And the maiden pleased him, and she obtained kindness of him, and he speedily gave her ointments, with her portions, and seven maidens, who were meet to be given her out of the king's house; and he advanced her and her maidens to the best place in the house of the women. ¹⁰ Esther had not made known her people nor her kindred; for Mordecai had charged her that she should not tell it. ¹⁷ And the king loved Esther above all the women, and she obtained grace and favour in his sight more than all the virgins; so that he set the royal crown upon her head, and made her queen instead of Vashti.

2:5 The Hebrew word *yehudi*, translated "Jew," originally designated a man from the tribe of Judah. After the Babylonian exile it came to be the generic term for all Hebrews. 2:6–7 Mordecai is not a Hebrew name. Some suggest that it derives from the Babylonian god "Marduk"; it is explained that Mordecai must have been born in captivity. Similarly Esther may be derived from the Persian word "stara" or from the name of the Babylonian goddess "Ishtar." Her Hebrew name was Hadassah. To this day all Jewish children are assigned a Hebrew name in addition to their given public name. **2:7** Handel's oratorio, *Esther,* sings the praises of the Jewish heroine. **2:10** This is one of the controversial sentences in the book: why did Mordecai tell Esther not to reveal her kindred or religion? The Greek translation, with which the rabbinic tradition agrees, adds the information that Esther did not change her way of life religiously while in the king's harem; Esther followed the Mosaic commandments just as she did when she lived with Mordecai.

Haman Plots to Kill the Jews
Esther 2:21–23; 3:1–2, 5–11, 13
(Jewish Publication Society)

21 In those days, while Mordecai sat in the kings' gate two of the king's chamberlains, Bigthan and Teresh, of those that kept the door, were wroth, and sought to lay hands on the king Ahasuerus. ²² And the thing became known to Mordecai, who told it unto Esther the queen; and Esther told the king thereof in Mordecai's name. ²³ And when inquisition was made of the matter, and it was found to be so, they were both hanged on a tree; and it was written in the book of the chronicles before the king. **3** After these things did king Ahasuerus promote Haman the son of Hammedatha the Agagite, and advanced him, and set his seat above all the princes that were with him. ² And all the king's servants, that were in the king's gate, bowed down, and prostrated themselves before Haman; for the king had so commanded concerning him. But Mordecai bowed not down, nor prostrated himself before him. ⁵ And when Haman saw that Mordecai bowed not down, nor prostrated himself before him, then was Haman full of wrath. ⁶ But it seemed contemptible in his eyes to lay hands on Mordecai alone; for they had made known to him the people of Mordecai; wherefore Haman sought to destroy all the Jews that were throughout the whole kingdom of Ahasuerus, even the people of Mordecai. ⁷ In the first month, which is the month Nisan, in the twelfth year of king Ahasuerus, they cast pur, that is, the lot, before Haman from day to day, and from month to month to the twelfth month, which is the month Adar. 8 And Haman said unto king Ahasuerus: "There is a certain people scattered abroad and dispersed among the peoples in all the provinces of thy kingdom; and their laws are diverse from those of every people; neither keep they the king's laws; therefore it profiteth not the king to suffer them. ⁹ If it please the king, let it be written

that they be destroyed; and I will pay ten thousand talents of silver
into the hands of those that have the charge of the king's business, to
bring it into the king's treasures." [10] And the king took his ring from
his hand, and gave it unto Haman the son of Hammedatha the
Agagite, the Jews' enemy. [11] And the king said unto Haman: "The
silver is given to thee, the people also, to do with them as it seemeth
good to thee." [13] And letters were sent by posts into all the king's
provinces, to destroy, to slay, and to cause to perish, all Jews, both
young and old, little children and women, in one day, even upon the
thirteenth day of the twelfth month, which is the month Adar, and
to take the spoil of them for a prey.

3:1 There is no record of a country "Agag." The name, however,
is that of the king of the hated Amelekites conquered by Saul (see I
Samuel 15:7–9). The fact that Mordecai is related to King Saul—
that is, a descendant of Kish and a Benjamite—emphasizes the enmity
between Mordecai and Haman but intimates the ultimate Hebrew
victory. 3:2 The Greek translation has a prayer by Mordecai to God,
in which he makes it clear that his refusal to bow down to Haman was
motivated not by personal vainglory or pride; Mordecai refused to bow
down to anyone but God in order not to place the glory of man above
God's. 3:5–11 These few sentences reveal the psychology of the
hatemonger and have been the subject of many synagogue sermons.
Haman holds a personal grudge, but he generalizes from his individual
experience and hates the entire Jewish people. He then justifies his
hatred by the innuendo that their religious difference is a sign of
political disloyalty. Only recently in history have we achieved the kind
of a pluralistic society where we assume a citizen's political loyalty
without regard to his religious persuasion. Finally, Haman bribes the
king with a promise of rich financial reward from this persecution and
plunder of the Jews. 3:7 *Pur* were large marked stones, rectangular
prisms with numbers 1, 2, 5, 6 engraved on them, used as a device for
arriving at decisions. Several have been uncovered at Susa (Shushan).
The Jewish holiday derives its name Purim from this reference. 3:10
In the Persian empire official documents were sealed with a signet ring
if written on papyrus, or with a cylinder seal if written on clay tablets.
Archaeologists have uncovered such rings and seals belonging to King
Xerxes. 3:13 Posts or stations were established at marked distances,
and relays of horses and men carried the message from one end of the
kingdom to another.

Mordecai Requests Esther's Help
Esther 4:1–5, 7–16
(Jewish Publication Society)

4 Now when Mordecai knew all that was done, Mordecai rent his
clothes, and put on sackcloth with ashes, and went out into the midst

of the city and cried with a loud and a bitter cry; [2] and he came even before the king's gate; for none might enter within the king's gate clothed with sackcloth. [3] And in every province, whithersoever the king's commandment and his decree came, there was great mourning among the Jews, and fasting, and weeping, and wailing; and many lay in sackcloth and ashes.

4 And Esther's maidens and her chamberlains came and told it her; and the queen was exceedingly pained; and she sent raiment to clothe Mordecai, and to take his sackcloth from off him; but he accepted it not. [5] Then called Esther for Hathach, one of the king's chamberlains, whom he had appointed to attend upon her, and charged him to go to Mordecai, to know what this was, and why it was.

7 And Mordecai told him of all that had happened unto him, and the exact sum of the money that Haman had promised to pay to the king's treasuries for the Jews, to destroy them. [8] Also he gave him the copy of the writing of the decree and that was given out in Shushan to destroy them, to show it unto Esther, and to declare it unto her; and to charge her that she should go in unto the king. To make supplication unto him, and to make request before him, for her people.

9 And Hathach came and told Esther the words of Mordecai. [10] Then Esther spoke unto Hathach, and gave him a message unto Mordecai: [11] All the king's servants, and the people of the king's provinces, do know, that whosoever, whether man or woman, shall come unto the king into the inner court, who is not called, there is one law for him, that he be put to death, except such to whom the king shall hold out the golden sceptre, that he may live; but I have not been called to come in unto the king these thirty days.

12 And they told to Mordecai Esther's words.

13 Then Mordecai bade them return answer unto Esther: Think not with thyself that thou shalt escape in the king's house, more than all the Jews. [14] For if thou altogether holdest thy peace at this time, then will relief and deliverance arise to the Jews from another place, but thou and thy father's house will perish; and who knoweth whether thou art not come to royal estate for such a time as this? [15] Then Esther bade them return answer unto Mordecai: [16] Go, gather together all the Jews that are present in Shushan, and fast ye for me, and neither eat nor drink three days, night or day; I also and my maidens will fast in like manner; and so will I go in unto the king, which is not according to the law; and if I perish, I perish."

4:1 Rending of clothes is a sign of grief (see Genesis 37:34). Adornment with sackcloth and ashes is a sign of repentance (see Jonah 3:6). **4:13–14** Jewish tradition teaches the interdependence of individual and community. Mordecai intimates that even if she fails in her responsibility, relief and deliverance will nevertheless arise from another place; the Rabbis interpret this as a veiled reference to God. The word "God" is not once mentioned in the Hebrew text.

Esther Plans to Help her People

Esther 5:1–14

(Jewish Publication Society)

5 Now it came to pass on the third day, that Esther put on her royal apparel, and stood in the inner court of the king's house, over against the king's house; and the king sat upon his throne in the royal house, over against the entrance of the house. ² And it was so, when the king saw Esther the queen standing in the court, that she obtained favour in his sight; and the king held out to Esther the golden sceptre that was in his hand. So Esther drew near, and touched the top of the sceptre. ³ Then said the king unto her: "What wilt thou, queen Esther? for whatever thy request, even to the half of the kingdom, it shall be given thee." ⁴ And Esther said: "If it seem good unto the king, let the king and Haman come this day unto the banquet that I have prepared for him." ⁵ Then the king said: "Cause Haman to make haste, that it may be done as Esther hath said." So the king and Haman came to the banquet that Esther had prepared. ⁶ And the king said unto Esther at the banquet of wine: "Whatever thy petition, it shall be granted thee; and whatever thy request, even to the half of the kingdom, it shall be performed." ⁷ Then answered Esther, and said: "My petition and my request is—⁸ if I have found favour in the sight of the king, and if it please the king to grant my petition, and to perform my request—let the king and Haman come to the banquet that I shall prepare for them, and I will do to-morrow as the king hath said."

9 Then went Haman forth that day joyful and glad of heart; but when Haman saw Mordecai in the king's gate, that he stood not up nor moved for him, Haman was filled with wrath against Mordecai. ¹⁰ Nevertheless Haman refrained himself, and went home; and he sent and fetched his friends and Zeresh his wife. ¹¹ And Haman recounted unto them the glory of his riches, and the multitude of his children, and everything as to how the king had promoted him, and how he had advanced him above the princes and servants of the king. ¹² Haman said moreover: "Yes Esther the queen did let no man

come in with the king unto the banquet that she had prepared but myself; and to-morrow also am I invited by her together with the king. ¹³ Yet all this availeth me nothing, so long as I see Mordecai the Jew sitting at the king's gate." ¹⁴ Then said Zeresh his wife and all his friends unto him: "Let a gallows be made of fifty cubits high, and in the morning speak thou unto the king that Mordecai may be hanged thereon; then go thou in merrily with the king unto the banquet." And the thing pleased Haman; and he caused the gallows to be made.

The King Honors Mordecai

Esther 6:1–11

(Jewish Publication Society)

6 On that night could not the king sleep; and he commanded to bring the book of records of the chronicles; and they were read before the king. ² And it was found written, that Mordecai had told of Bigthana and Teresh, two of the king's chamberlains, of those that kept the door, who had sought to lay hands on the king Ahasuerus. ³ And the king said: "What honor and dignity hath been done to Mordecai for this?" Then said the king's servants that ministered unto him: "There is nothing done for him." ⁴ And the king said: "Who is in the court?"—Now Haman was come into the outer court of the king's house, to speak unto the king to hang Mordecai on the gallows that he had prepared for him.—⁵ And the king's servants said unto him: "Behold, Haman standeth in the court." And the king said: "Let him come in." ⁶ So Haman came in. And the king said unto him: "What shall be done unto the man whom the king delighteth to honor?"—Now Haman said in his heart: "Whom would the king delight to honor besides myself?"—⁷ And Haman said unto the king: "For the man whom the king delighteth to honor, ⁸ let royal apparel be brought which the king useth to wear, and the horse that the king rideth upon, and on whose head a crown royal is set; ⁹ and let the apparel and the horse be delivered to the hand of one of the king's most noble princes, that they may array the man therewith whom the king delighteth to honor, and cause him to ride on horseback through the street of the city, and proclaim before him: Thus shall it be done to the man whom the king delighteth to honor." ¹⁰ Then the king said to Haman: "Make haste, and take the apparel and the horse, as thou hast said, and do even so to Mordecai the Jew, that sitteth at the king's gate; let nothing fail of all that thou hast spoken." ¹¹ Then took Haman the apparel and the horse, and arrayed Mordecai, and caused him to ride through the street of the city, and proclaimed before him:

"Thus shall it be done unto the man whom the king delighteth to honor."

Esther Accuses Haman
Esther 7:1–10

7 So the king and Ha'man went in to feast with Queen Esther. ² And on the second day, as they were drinking wine, the king again said to Esther, "What is your petition, Queen Esther? It shall be granted you. And what is your request? Even to the half of my kingdom, it shall be fulfilled." ³ Then Queen Esther answered; "If I have found favor in your sight, O king, and if it please the king, let my life be given me at my petition, and my people at my request. ⁴ For we are sold, I and my people, to be destroyed, to be slain, and to be annihilated. If we had been sold merely as slaves, men and women, I would have held my peace; for our affliction is not to be compared with the loss to the king." ⁵ Then King A·has'u-e'rus said to Queen Esther, "Who is he, and where is he, that would presume to do this?" ⁶ And Esther said, "A foe and enemy! This wicked Ha'man!" Then Haman was in terror before the king and the queen. ⁷ And the king rose from the feast in wrath and went into the palace garden; but Ha'man stayed to beg his life from Queen Esther, for he saw that evil was determined against him by the king. ⁸ And the king returned from the palace garden to the place where they were drinking wine, as Ha'man was falling on the couch where Esther was; and the king said, "Will he even assault the queen in my presence, in my own house?" As the words left the mouth of the king, they covered Haman's face. ⁹ Then said Har·bo'na, one of the eunuchs in attendance on the king, "Moreover, the gallows which Ha'man has prepared for Mor'de·cai, whose word saved the king, is standing in Haman's house, fifty cubits high." ¹⁰ And the king said, "Hang him on that." So they hanged Ha'man on the gallows which he had prepared for Mordecai.

The Jews Celebrate Purim
Esther 8:7–8, 10–11; 9:5, 17–19, 26–28
(Jewish Publication Society)

7 Then the king Ahasuerus said unto Esther the queen and to Mordecai the Jew: "Behold, I have given Esther the house of Haman, and him they have hanged upon the gallows, because he laid his hand upon the Jews. ⁸ Write ye also concerning the Jews, as it liketh you, in the king's name, and, seal it with the king's ring; for the writing which is written in the king's name, and sealed with the king's ring, may no man reverse." ¹⁰ And they wrote in the name of king

Ahasuerus, and sealed it with the king's ring, and sent letters by posts on horseback, riding on swift steeds that were used in the king's service, bred of the stud; [11] that the king had granted the Jews that were in every city to gather themselves together, and to stand for their life, to destroy, and to slay, and to cause to perish, all the forces of the people and province that would assault them, for little ones and women, and to take the spoil of them for a prey.

9 [5] And the Jews smote all their enemies with the stroke of the sword, and with slaughter and destruction, and did what they would unto them that hated them. [17] On the thirteenth day of the month Adar, and on the fourteenth day of the same they rested, and made it a day of feasting and gladness.

18 But the Jews that were in Shushan assembled together on the thirteenth day thereof, and on the fourteenth thereof; and on the fifteenth day of the same they rested, and made it a day of feasting and gladness. [19] Therefore do the Jews of the villages, that dwell in the unwalled towns, make the fourteenth day of the month Adar a day of gladness and feasting, and a good day, and of sending portions one to another. [26] Wherefore they called these days Purim, after the name of pur. Therefore because of all the words of this letter, and of that which they had seen concerning this matter, and that which had come unto them, [27] the Jews ordained . . . [28] that these days should be remembered and kept throughout every generation, every family, every province, and every city; and that these days of Purim should not fail from among the Jews, nor the memorial of them perish from their seed.

The Book of Job

Job, the central personality in this biblical book, is catapulted from wealth to poverty, from health to sickness, from happiness in family life to near total bereavement. His condition raises the problem of evil and invokes questions about man's reward or punishment on this earth.

Job's sudden turn of fortune challenged the prevailing opinion of his time, that man is rewarded with good for his righteousness and with evil for iniquity. Job had been a righteous man. Now in misery, Job discovers that even his good friends turn on him and rebuke him. "Search your way," they demand, "and discover wherein you have sinned, in that you now endure such misfortune." Job's protestations of innocence only infuriate his friends. Job will not be crushed by their various arguments, neither will he curse the God who has afflicted him. Daring to voice fearless questions in an effort to obtain insight into God's justice, Job presses at the boundaries of theological understanding; yet heroically, in spite of all his tragedy, he keeps his faith intact declaring: "I know that my Redeemer lives" (19:25) and "I hold fast my righteousness and will not let it go" (27:6).

Job has been enacted on the stage in many forms and variations. There is a prose prologue; the conversations take place in three cycles; toward the end of the book God appears through a whirlwind; and finally there is a prose epilogue. But unlike a stage drama, the theme is not developed through the action of the players, nor do ideas flow in a sequential order. The movement is in the intensity of feeling.

The Book of Job offers in the end no final answer to the questions raised, but it sets the issues before us.

In the prologue it would appear that Job's faith is being put to a test, just as Abraham had been tried by God's demand that he sacrifice his son Isaac. But the problem of evil in life is more complicated than that. Many, indeed, suffer because they are wicked and deserving of punishment. The prophets, in fact, had interpreted the rise and fall of empires in such fashion. No one doubts that evil corrupts society and results inevitably in its destruction. But what of the individual? Are his sufferings always the direct result of his sinfulness? Is it not a fact that sometimes in life it appears that the wicked are rewarded and the righteous suffer?

Job's three friends reject Job's questions. If man suffers, they insist, it is because he has sinned. When Elihu enters the conversation, he points to the significance of suffering. It provides man with insight, with understanding for the plight of others. Elihu argues, in effect, that one must not question suffering, but rather use it constructively. Finally God speaks to Job out of a whirlwind. God does not answer Job's questions. God does not define His behavior nor justify it. He merely proclaims His grandeur. Yet God's response provides an answer for Job. The assurance that there is a God enables man to rise above suffering and maintain, even in pain, confidence that there is purpose and meaning in a righteous life.

Other answers continue to be given to the problem of suffering. A rabbinic idea that the righteous endure trial, not for their own sins but as atonement for the sins of others (*Shabbas* 33b), is also a central concept in Christian thought. The Book of Job appears to have been written before the Hebrews developed any clear idea of life after death, although it is intimated at points in this text. For this reason scholars date the writing of this book around the year 400 B.C.; but for that reason, also, there is lacking in this book the consolation now maintained by many religions that man is rewarded for his righteousness not in this world, but in the life to come.

Traditional Jewish thought ascribes the authorship of this book to Moses. Most biblical scholars of today, however, agree that the author of this book expresses thoughts of such sophistication that they could have been composed only at a much later date. The prose prologue and epilogue probably are considerably older than the dramatic poem; together they comprise a short folk-tale that the poet-philosopher found useful as a framework for his own composition. The beginning and end of the book seem to differ in form and content from what lies between them.

Not all rabbis believed that a Job ever existed; one distinguished rabbi, Simeon ben Lakish, insisting that there was such a person, agreed nevertheless that the narratives and dialogues were creative literary inventions (*Genesis Rabbah* 57). Some rabbis also considered Job to be one of the prophets among the Gentiles, thus acknowledging the wisdom available by God's graciousness to all of mankind.

Throughout literary history authors have created novels and plays that build upon the themes in this book, e.g. Archibald MacLeish's Broadway play *J.B.*, Mark Twain's *The Mysterious Stranger*, H. G. Wells's *The Undying Fire*, and Robert Frost's *The Masque of Reason*.

Prologue

Implicit in the prologue are older biblical assumptions: that a righteous man is rewarded with prosperity, that misfortune may be imposed upon a man as a test of his faith, and that the faithful man accepts nobly the judgments of God. The action in these first two chapters moves from heaven to earth in five scenes and sets the stage for the discussion that follows.

Job 1:1–22; 2:1–13

1 There was a man in the land of Uz, whose name was Job; and that man was blameless and upright, one who feared God, and turned away from evil. ²There were born to him seven sons and three daughters. ³He had seven thousand sheep, three thousand camels, five hundred yoke of oxen, and five hundred she-asses, and very many servants; so that this man was the greatest of all the people of the east. ⁴His sons used to go and hold a feast in the house of each on his day; and they would send and invite their three sisters to eat and drink with them. ⁵And when the days of the feast had run their course, Job would send and sanctify them, and he would rise early in the morning and offer burnt offerings according to the number of them all; for Job said, "It may be that my sons have sinned, and cursed God in their hearts." Thus Job did continually.

6 Now there was a day when the sons of God came to present themselves before the LORD, and Satan also came among them. ⁷The LORD said to Satan, "Whence have you come?" Satan answered the LORD, "From going to and fro on the earth, and from walking up and down on it." ⁸And the LORD said to Satan, "Have you considered my servant Job, that there is none like him on earth, a blameless and upright man, who fears God and turns away from evil?" ⁹Then Satan answered the LORD. "Does Job fear God for nought? ¹⁰Hast thou not put a hedge about him and his house and all that he has, on every side? Thou hast blessed the work of his hands, and his possessions have increased in the land. ¹¹But put forth thy hand now, and touch all that he has, and he will curse thee to thy face." ¹²And the LORD said to Satan, "Behold, all that he has is in your power; only upon himself do not put forth your hand." So Satan went forth from the presence of the LORD.

13 Now there was a day when his sons and daughters were eating and drinking wine in their eldest brother's house; ¹⁴and there came a messenger to Job, and said, "The oxen were plowing and the asses feeding beside them; ¹⁵and the Sabe'ans fell upon them and took them, and slew the servants with the edge of the sword; and I alone have escaped to tell you." ¹⁶While he was yet speaking, there came another, and said, "The fire of God fell from heaven and burned up the sheep and the servants, and consumed them; and I alone have escaped to tell you." ¹⁷While he was yet speaking, there came another, and said, "The Chalde'ans formed three companies, and made a raid upon the camels and took them, and slew the servants with the edge of the sword; and I alone have escaped to tell you." ¹⁸While he was yet speaking, there came another, and said, "Your sons and daughters were eating and drinking wine in their eldest brother's house; ¹⁹and behold, a great wind came across the wilderness, and struck the four corners of the house, and it fell upon the young people, and they are dead; and I alone have escaped to tell you."

20 Then Job arose, and rent his robe, and shaved his head, and fell upon the ground, and worshiped. ²¹And he said, "Naked I came from my mother's womb, and naked shall I return; the LORD gave, and the LORD has taken away; blessed be the name of the LORD."

22 In all this Job did not sin or charge God with wrong.

2 Again there was a day when the sons of God came to present themselves before the LORD, and Satan also came among them to present himself before the LORD. ²And the LORD said to Satan, "Whence have you come?" Satan answered the LORD, "From going to and fro on the earth, and from walking up and down on it." ³And the LORD said to Satan, "Have you considered my servant Job, that there is none like him on the earth, a blameless and upright man, who fears God and turns away from evil? He still holds fast his integrity, although you moved me against him, to destroy him without cause." ⁴Then Satan answered the LORD, "Skin for skin! All that a man has he will give for his life. ⁵But put forth thy hand now, and touch his bone and his flesh, and he will curse thee to thy face." ⁶And the LORD said to Satan, "Behold, he is in your power; only spare his life."

7 So Satan went forth from the presence of the LORD, and afflicted Job with loathsome sores from the sole of his foot to the crown of his head. ⁸And he took a potsherd with which to scrape himself, and sat among the ashes.

9 Then his wife said to him, "Do you still hold fast your integrity? Curse God, and die." ¹⁰But he said to her, "You speak as one of the foolish women would speak. Shall we receive good at the hand of God, and shall we not receive evil?" In all this Job did not sin with his lips.

11 Now when Job's three friends heard of all this evil that had come upon him, they came each from his own place, Eli'phaz the Te'manite, Bildad the Shuhite, and Zophar the Na'amathite. They made an appointment together to come to condole with him and comfort him. ¹²And when they saw him from afar, they did not recognize him; and they raised their voices and wept; and they rent their robes and sprinkled dust upon their heads toward heaven. ¹³And they sat with him on the ground seven days and seven nights, and no one spoke a word to him, for they saw that his suffering was very great.

1:1 The land of Uz is mentioned in Lamentations 4:21; it may refer to a country east of Palestine. Job is probably a non-Israelite. A reference to a Job in Ezekiel 14:4 leads traditional Jewish commentators to believe he may have been a historical person. There is no agreement as to when he lived, if he is an historical personality. **1:5** Burnt offerings may be sacrificed as an atonement for evil thoughts of the heart (Leviticus 1). Job is presented as a man, perfect in spirit, who takes care to maintain the religious devotion of his entire household. The rabbis found it objectionable to use the words "curse God" in such an outright fashion; the Hebrew Bible avoids it by use of euphemism. **1:6** Jewish tradition suggests that the "day" was the Day of Judgment—that is, Yom Kippur. "Sons of God" refers to the angels, the Heavenly Hosts, who sing the praises of God (Psalm 29:9) and serve as God's messengers (Psalm 103:20). Reference to "Satan" in this text, as in Zechariah 3:1, is preceded in the Hebrew by a definite article, meaning "the adversary." The appellation, therefore, refers to the function of one of the angels who serves as a "hindrance," a "block" (cf. Numbers 22:22), an "adversary to man" (Psalm 109:6), "the prosecuting attorney" as it were, who marks out man's shortcomings and failures. Only later did religious literature develop a concept of Satan, personified, as a source of evil in the world (see Luke 10:19); this view is rejected by contemporary Judaism. **1:14** The impact of the tragedy accumulates as four messengers appear in successive order, each bearing a tale of woe. **1:20** Rending the cloak as a sign of mourning is still observed in Jewish tradition. As the garment is torn, the contemporary Jew recites this phrase from Job: "The Lord giveth and the Lord hath taken away. Blessed be the name of the Lord." **2:11** Wise men were thought to live in the East. These three cities situated in Edomite territory were considered a center for such men of wisdom. See 1 Kings 4:30–31. **2:12–13** The three friends share Job's grief in the traditional manner. In the rabbinic tradition, visitors to a bereaved person are counseled not to speak until the mourner himself opens his mouth.

Job Curses the Day of His Birth
Job 3:1–4, 11–17, 20–26

3 After this Job opened his mouth and cursed the day of his birth. ²And Job said:

³ "Let the day perish wherein I was born,
   and the night which said,
      'A man-child is conceived.'
⁴ Let that day be darkness!
   May God above not seek it,
      or light shine upon it.

¹¹ "Why did I not die at birth,
      come forth from the womb and expire?
¹² Why did the knees receive me?
      Or why the breasts, that I should suck?

¹³ For then I should have lain down and been quiet;
   I should have slept; then I should have been at rest,
¹⁴ with kings and counselors of the earth
   who rebuilt ruins for themselves,
¹⁵ or with princes who had gold,
   who filled their houses with silver.
¹⁶ Or why was I not as a hidden untimely birth,
   as infants that never see the light?
¹⁷ There the wicked cease from troubling,
   and there the weary are at rest.

²⁰ "Why is light given to him that is in misery,
   and life to the bitter in soul,
²¹ who long for death, but it comes not,
   and dig for it more than for hid treasures;
²² who rejoice exceedingly,
   and are glad, when they find the grave?
²³ Why is light given to a man whose way is hid,
   whom God has hedged in?
²⁴ For my sighing comes as my bread,
   and my groanings are poured out like water.
²⁵ For the thing that I fear comes upon me,
   and what I dread befalls me.
²⁶ I am not at ease, nor am I quiet;
   I have no rest; but trouble comes."

3:16–17 Job believes in the existence of a nether world, Sheol, where the souls of all the deceased find their rest. See Numbers 16:33; 1 Samuel 28:19; Psalm 89:48. In Sheol may be found both the wicked and righteous alike. It is clear from this passage that Job has no conception of a reward or punishment in a life after death. See also Job 10:21–22; 14:7–14.

Job's Friends Respond to His Grief

With this speech by Eliphaz, three cycles of debate commence in which three of Job's acquaintances argue against him, Job answering each in turn. (In the third cycle Zophar's speech is missing, and there is an extra speech by Job.) The first cycle extends from chapters 4 to 14.

Job 4:1–9, 12–17; 5:6–7, 17–19, 26–27

4 Then Eli′phaz the Te′manite answered:
   ² "If one ventures a word with you, will you be offended?
      Yet who can keep from speaking?
   ³ Behold, you have instructed many,
      and you have strengthened the weak hands.

⁴ Your words have upheld him who was stumbling,
   and you have made firm the feeble knees.
⁵ But now it has come to you, and you are impatient;
   it touches you, and you are dismayed.
⁶ Is not your fear of God your confidence,
   and the integrity of your ways your hope?

⁷ "Think now, who that was innocent ever perished?
   Or where were the upright cut off?
⁸ As I have seen, those who plow iniquity
   and sow trouble reap the same.
⁹ By the breath of God they perish,
   and by the blast of his anger they are consumed.

¹² "Now a word was brought to me stealthily,
   my ear received the whisper of it.
¹³ Amid thoughts from visions of the night,
   when deep sleep falls on men,
¹⁴ dread came upon me, and trembling,
   which made all my bones shake.
¹⁵ A spirit glided past my face;
   the hair of my flesh stood up.
¹⁶ It stood still,
   but I could not discern its appearance.
   A form was before my eyes;
   there was silence, then I heard a voice:
¹⁷ 'Can mortal man be righteous before God?
   Can a man be pure before his Maker?

5 ⁶ "For affliction does not come from the dust,
   nor does trouble sprout from the ground;
 ⁷ but man is born to trouble
   as the sparks fly upward.

¹⁷ "Behold, happy is the man whom God reproves;
   therefore despise not the chastening of the Almighty.
¹⁸ For he wounds, but he binds up;
   he smites, but his hands heal.
¹⁹ He will deliver you from six troubles;
   in seven there shall no evil touch you.
²⁶ You shall come to your grave in ripe old age,
   as a shock of grain comes up to the threshing floor in its
   season.
²⁷ Lo, this we have searched out; it is true.
   Hear, and know it for your good."

4:3 Eliphaz, recalling to Job his former serenity and confidence, encourages Job to renew his faith. Since it is only the wicked who will perish and the upright have nothing to fear, Job need not be so bitter. **4:8** A statement of the classic doctrine that man is rewarded and punished in life according to his deeds. **4:12–17** On the basis of a revelation from God in a dream, Eliphaz justifies his conviction that no man can think of himself as free from sin. Using the style of proverbial wisdom literature (see Proverbs 6:16–19; 30:15 f.), Eliphaz goes on to describe the traditional signs of a man under God's providence: he is safe from any harm or misfortune, blessed with many children and grandchildren, and privileged to live to an old age. **5:6** Eliphaz reassures Job that suffering must come to all men since no man is free from sinfulness. **5:17–18** Rejoice therefore, says Eliphaz to Job, that you have been given the opportunity to be corrected and cleansed. There is no cause for bitterness.

Job Answers Eliphaz

Job responds in anger to Eliphaz's calm and seemingly reasonable words of consolation. Compared to his sinfulness, asserts Job, his misfortunes are heavy.

Job 6:1–4, 8–10, 24–25; 7:9–11, 17–21

6 Then Job answered:
> [2] "O that my vexation were weighed,
>   and all my calamity laid in the balances!
> [3] For then it would be heavier than the sand of the sea;
>   therefore my words have been rash.
> [4] For the arrows of the Almighty are in me;
>   my spirit drinks their poison;
>   the terrors of God are arrayed against me.

> [8] "O that I might have my request,
>   and that God would grant my desire;
> [9] that it would please God to crush me,
>   that he would let loose his hand and cut me off!
> [10] This would be my consolation;
>   I would even exult in pain unsparing;
>   for I have not denied the words of the Holy One.

> [24] "Teach me, and I will be silent;
>   make me understand how I have erred.
> [25] How forceful are honest words!
>   But what does reproof from you reprove?

7[9] "As the cloud fades and vanishes,
>   so he who goes down to Sheol does not come up;

¹⁰ he returns no more to his house,
    nor does his place know him any more.

¹¹ "Therefore I will not restrain my mouth;
    I will speak in the anguish of my spirit;
    I will complain in the bitterness of my soul.
  Let me alone, for my days are a breath.

¹⁷ "What is man, that thou dost make so much of him,
    and that thou dost set thy mind upon him,
¹⁸ dost visit him every morning,
    and test him every moment?
¹⁹ How long wilt thou not look away from me,
    nor let me alone till I swallow my spittle?
²⁰ If I sin, what do I do to thee, thou watcher of men?
  Why hast thou made me thy mark?
  Why have I become a burden to thee?
²¹ Why dost thou not pardon my transgression
    and take away my iniquity?
  For now I shall lie in the earth;
    thou wilt seek me, but I shall not be."

6:10 If Job could only know that he were soon to die, he would exult in his sufferings; for despite his pain he has not blasphemed God. **6:24–30** If you say that I sinned, Job asserts, then tell me where! He accuses his friends of callousness. **7:9–11** Job expresses here the belief that there is no life after death. Since his life is soon to ebb away and his bitterness is so great, he turns directly to God and announces that he will speak his mind. Job complains that God appears to have particularly marked him out for suffering (7:20); he pleads for pardon or for death (7:21). **7:17** In Psalm 8 the identical question, "What is man that Thou art mindful of him?" offers occasion to praise God's care and solicitude. Here Job sees God as a hostile, inscrutable tester of men. Job rejects such a God and seeks to experience God in His aspect of mercy. In Rabbinic thought, it is in such an expression of anger at his condition that Job reveals his human frailty.

Bildad Scolds Job

Eliphaz had earlier defended the ways of God on the basis of a knowledge revealed to him in a vision. Bildad now appeals to human experience: all the wisdom of former ages verifies that God will not permit the wicked to flourish, nor will He cast off the innocent.

Job 8:1–10, 20

8 Then Bildad the Shuhite answered:

² "How long will you say these things,
      and the words of your mouth be a great wind?
³ Does God pervert justice?
      Or does the Almighty pervert the right?
⁴ If your children have sinned against him,
      he has delivered them into the power of their transgression.
⁵ If you will seek God
      and make supplication to the Almighty,
⁶ if you are pure and upright,
      surely then he will rouse himself for you
      and reward you with a rightful habitation.
⁷ And though your beginning was small,
      your latter days will be very great.

⁸ "For inquire, I pray you, of bygone ages,
      and consider what the fathers have found;
⁹ for we are but of yesterday, and know nothing,
      for our days on earth are a shadow.
¹⁰ Will they not teach you, and tell you,
      and utter words out of their understanding?

²⁰ "Behold, God will not reject a blameless man,
      nor take the hand of evildoers."

Job: "God Is Not a Man That I Can Answer Him"

Job answers the argument of Bildad. First he agrees: of course it is foolish to try to argue against God. But then Job continues, it is foolish, not because God's ways are certain as Eliphaz and Bildad had suggested, but rather because God dwarfs man in every way. Recognizing this, Job turns to God (10:2) and pleads that God make known his transgressions or at least release him by death (10:18–22).

Job 9:1–4, 14–16, 20–22, 32–35; 10:1–2, 18–22

9 Then Job answered:
      ² "Truly I know that it is so:
            But how can a man be just before God?
      ³ If one wished to contend with him,
            one could not answer him once in a thousand times.
      ⁴ He is wise in heart, and mighty in strength
            —who has hardened himself against him, and succeeded?—
      ¹⁴ How then can I answer him,
            choosing my words with him?
      ¹⁵ Though I am innocent, I cannot answer him;
            I must appeal for mercy to my accuser.

¹⁶ If I summoned him and he answered me,
  I would not believe that he was listening to my voice.
²⁰ Though I am innocent, my own mouth would condemn me;
  though I am blameless, he would prove me perverse.
²¹ I am blameless; I regard not myself;
  I loathe my life.
²² It is all one; therefore I say,
  he destroys both the blameless and the wicked.

³² "For he is not a man, as I am, that I might answer him,
  that we should come to trial together.
³³ There is no umpire between us,
  who might lay his hand upon us both.
³⁴ Let him take his rod away from me,
  and let not dread of him terrify me.
³⁵ Then I would speak without fear of him,
  for I am not so in myself.

10 "I loathe my life;
  I will give free utterance to my complaint;
  I will speak in the bitterness of my soul.
² I will say to God, Do not condemn me;
  let me know why thou dost contend against me.

¹⁸ "Why didst thou bring me forth from the womb?
  Would that I had died before any eye had seen me,
¹⁹ and were as though I had not been,
  carried from the womb to the grave.
²⁰ Are not the days of my life few?
  Let me alone, that I may find a little comfort
²¹ before I go whence I shall not return,
  to the land of gloom and deep darkness,
²² the land of gloom and chaos,
  where light is as darkness."

Zophar Accuses Job of Evil
Job 11 : 1– 11, 13–18

11 Then Zophar the Na'amathite answered:
² "Should a multitude of words go unanswered,
  and a man full of talk be vindicated?
³ Should your babble silence men,
  and when you mock, shall no one shame you?
⁴ For you say, 'My doctrine is pure,
  and I am clean in God's eyes.'

⁵ But oh, that God would speak,
    and open his lips to you,
⁶ and that he would tell you the secrets of wisdom!
    For he is manifold in understanding.
Know then that God exacts of you less than your guilt deserves.

⁷ "Can you find out the deep things of God?
    Can you find out the limit of the Almighty?
⁸ It is higher than heaven—what can you do?
    Deeper than Sheol—what can you know?
⁹ Its measure is longer than the earth,
    and broader than the sea.
¹⁰ If he passes through, and imprisons,
    and calls to judgment, who can hinder him?
¹¹ For he knows worthless men;
    when he sees iniquity, will he not consider it?

¹³ "If you set your heart aright,
    you will stretch out your hands toward him.
¹⁴ If iniquity is in your hand, put it far away,
    and let not wickedness dwell in your tents.
¹⁵ Surely then you will lift up your face without blemish;
    you will be secure, and will not fear.
¹⁶ You will forget your misery;
    you will remember it as waters that have passed away.
¹⁷ And your life will be brighter than the noonday;
    its darkness will be like the morning.
¹⁸ And you will have confidence, because there is hope;
    you will be protected and take your rest in safety.

Job Answers
Job 13 : 1– 5, 13, 15– 18; 14 : 1– 2, 7– 14; 19 : 23– 29

13 "Lo, my eye has seen all this,
    my ear has heard and understood it.
² What you know, I also know;
    I am not inferior to you.
³ But I would speak to the Almighty,
    and I desire to argue my case with God.
⁴ As for you, you whitewash with lies;
    worthless physicians are you all.
⁵ Oh that you would keep silent,
    and it would be your wisdom!

¹³ "Let me have silence, and I will speak,
    and let come on me what may.

¹⁵ Behold, he will slay me; I have no hope;
    yet I will defend my ways to his face.
¹⁶ This will be my salvation,
    that a godless man shall not come before him.
¹⁷ Listen carefully to my words,
    and let my declaration be in your ears.
¹⁸ Behold, I have prepared my case;
    I know that I shall be vindicated.

14 "Man that is born of a woman
    is of few days, and full of trouble.
² He comes forth like a flower, and withers;
    he flees like a shadow, and continues not.

⁷ "For there is hope for a tree,
    if it be cut down, that it will sprout again,
    and that its shoots will not cease.
⁸ Though its root grow old in the earth,
    and its stump die in the ground,
⁹ yet at the scent of water it will bud
    and put forth branches like a young plant.
¹⁰ But man dies, and is laid low;
    man breathes his last, and where is he?
¹¹ As waters fail from a lake,
    and a river wastes away and dries up,
¹² so man lies down and rises not again;
    till the heavens are no more he will not awake,
    or be roused out of his sleep.
¹³ Oh that thou wouldest hide me in Sheol,
    that thou wouldest conceal me until thy wrath be past,
    that thou wouldest appoint me a set time, and remember me!
¹⁴ If a man die, shall he live again?
    All the days of my service I would wait,
    till my release should come.

19 ²³"Oh that my words were written!
    Oh that they were inscribed in a book!
²⁴ Oh that with an iron pen and lead
    they were graven in the rock for ever!
²⁵ For I know that my Redeemer lives,
    and at last he will stand upon the earth;
²⁶ and after my skin has been thus destroyed,
    then from my flesh I shall see God,

²⁷ whom I shall see on my side,
and my eyes shall behold, and not another.
My heart faints within me!
²⁸ If you say, 'How we will pursue him!'
and, 'The root of the matter is found in him';
²⁹ be afraid of the sword,
for wrath brings the punishment of the sword,
that you may know there is a judgment."

13:15 The translation of the Jewish Publication Society, "Though He slay me, Yet will I trust in Him," has been frequently quoted as an expression of unswerving faith. **14:13** Job hopes that Sheol may not really mark the end of man; he longs for a hiding place where he may live until God's wrath has passed over. **19:25–26** Some commentators on this passage see Job expressing a conviction in the immortality of the soul and in a justification that will come after life has ended. Then he will behold his "Redeemer" and know that his false friends have been punished. Some Christians believe that Job prophetically anticipates the risen Christ. Jewish commentators do not accept this interpretation, holding that Job did not have a conception of another life to come (see 16:22). They suggest that he was expressing here confidence that God would be his blood-avenger (see Numbers 35:19). The Hebrew *Goel*, translated "redeemer," is understood in the sense of "vindicator." Job dared hope that he might experience this justification before his death, even if he were at the terminal stages of his disease, that is, even after his flesh is falling away from his bones; or he may actually hope to be raised from death—but for a moment—to see his vindication. See 1 Samuel 2:6 and 1 Kings 17:17–24 for expressions of biblical conviction that God can renew the dead. This deeply held trust in God's justice eventually motivated the development of a fuller conception of resurrection (see 2 Maccabees 7:9).

The Second Cycle

The second cycle of speeches (of which but a very brief selection is given) extends from chapters 15 to 21. Few new arguments are set forth in this series of speeches. There is now an overlapping of arguments; each friend repeats something of the others' arguments. Job begins to feel himself more and more alone, having to reject his friends consolations. They not only accuse him of sin but suggest that his stubborn refusal to acknowledge guilt is, in itself, harmful to a true faith in God. Job vigorously repeats his observation that wicked men frequently do flourish (chapter 21). His suffering, therefore, is not necessarily related either to his righteousness or iniquity. Challenging God's righteousness in permitting him to suffer, Job paradoxically calls upon Heaven itself to witness to the justice of his cause. Thus like Abraham before him (Genesis 18:25) Job appeals from God's actions, which are beyond understanding, to God's justice of which he is by faith convinced

Job Pleads for God's Justice and the Pity of Friends
Job 16:19–22; 19:21–22

16 ¹⁹ "Even now, behold, my witness is in heaven,
and he that vouches for me is on high.
²⁰ My friends scorn me;
my eye pours out tears to God,
²¹ that he would maintain the right of a man with God
like that of a man with his neighbor.
²² For when a few years have come
I shall go the way whence I shall not return.

19 ²¹ "Have pity on me, have pity on me, O you my friends,
for the hand of God has touched me!
²² Why do you, like God, pursue me?
Why are you not satisfied with my flesh?"

The Third Cycle

The third cycle is incomplete and varies in syle from earlier portions. It extends from chapter 22 to 31. It begins with a long speech by Eliphaz followed by Job's response. But then Bildad's speech in chapter 25 has only six verses, obviously incomplete, whereas Job's answer comprises six entire chapters, 26 to 31, obviously too lengthy. There is no speech at all by Zophar. Confusing too is the fact that in his six-chapter address, Job expresses ideas that one would judge were more sympathetic to the arguments of his three friends than to his own position (e.g. 27:7–23). This has led many to believe that parts of the addresses of Bildad and Zophar have been incorporated into Job's speech by accident or perhaps by design (to reveal Job in the end as repentant and traditional in viewpoint). The headings of chapter 27 and chapter 29 begin with an unusual formulation: "And Job *again* took up his discourse and said," whereas all of the other speeches begin: "And Job answered and said." Some scholars feel that here is verification that the editor himself was aware that these chapters were additions to the original speeches of Job.

In his third address, chapter 22, Eliphaz unleashes his most bitter attack on Job. He accuses him now specifically of robbing the poor, withholding aid to the needy, and acting like a tyrant (22:5–9). Job does not defend himself, but rather he addresses himself again to God: "Oh that I knew where I might find Him . . . I would order my cause before Him" (23:3–4). He again describes the ways of the wicked and repeats his complaint that God does not seem to take account of nor punish the evil-doers (chapter 24).

My Righteousness I Hold Fast

In this short selection Job reaffirms his righteousness even as he acknowledges God's power over the wicked.

Job 27:1–6

27 And Job again took up his discourse, and said:
² "As God lives, who has taken away my right,
and the Almighty, who has made my soul bitter;
³ as long as my breath is in me,
and the spirit of God is in my nostrils;
⁴ my lips will not speak falsehood,
and my tongue will not utter deceit.
⁵ Far be it from me to say that you are right;
till I die I will not put away my integrity from me
⁶ I hold fast my righteousness, and will not let it go;
my heart does not reproach me for any of my days."

The Fear of the Lord is Wisdom

This poetic passage, defining "wisdom" as the fear of the Lord and "understanding" as separation from evil, expresses the biblical view on the moral purpose of life. This God-rooted conception of wisdom distinguished the biblical wisdom literature from the humanistic, practical wisdom of Israel's neighbors. Scholars are sharply divided as to whether this passage was originally part of the drama and whether it is in its proper place. One theory holds that it was a late editorial insertion that had never been part of the original book. Another theory maintains that it belongs in the book, but that it ought to have been the climax of God's address from the whirlwind. In effect, God would be telling man that, although he has but little knowledge of the mysteries of the universe, he does have this assurance: wisdom is to revere God and to live a righteous life. A third theory suggests that this was a part of Job's speech, a powerful expression that his conscience is clear and that his love for God remains unshaken.

Job 28:1–2, 12–28

(Revised Version, 1885)

Surely there is a mine for silver, and a place for gold which they refine.

2 Iron is taken out of the earth, and brass is molten out of the stone.

12 But where shall wisdom be found? and where is the place of understanding?

13 Man knoweth not the price thereof; neither is it found in the land of the living.

14 The deep saith, It is not in me: and the sea saith, It is not with me.

15 It cannot be gotten for gold, neither shall silver be weighed for the price thereof.

16 It cannot be valued with the gold of Ophir, with the precious onyx, or the sapphire.

17 Gold and glass cannot equal it: neither shall the exchange thereof be jewels of fine gold.

18 No mention shall be made of coral or of crystal: yea, the price of wisdom is above rubies.

19 The topaz of Ethiopia shall not equal it, neither shall it be valued with pure gold.

20 Whence then cometh wisdom? and where is the place of understanding?

21 Seeing it is hid from the eyes of all living, and kept close from the fowls of the air.

22 Destruction and Death say, We have heard a rumour thereof with our ears.

23 God understandeth the way thereof, and he knoweth the place thereof.

24 For he looketh to the ends of the earth, and seeth under the whole heaven;

25 To make a weight for the wind; yea, he meteth out the waters by measure.

26 When he made a decree for the rain, and a way for the lightning of the thunder:

27 Then did he see it, and declare it; he established it, yea, and searched it out.

28 And unto man he said, Behold, the fear of the Lord, that is wisdom; and to depart from evil is understanding.

28:1–2 No matter to what depths man may dig, and regardless of what precious metals he may discover, wisdom, the most precious of all possessions, will not be found in a physical place. **28:28** See Psalm 111:10; Proverbs 8:13; Ecclesiastes 12:13.

Job Concludes

As the climax of his self-defense Job makes a series of vows before God and man that he is not guilty of wrong-doing; the calamities that befell him were in no way related to the question of reward or punishment for behavior.

Job 31:5–12, 16–35, 40b

5 "If I have walked with falsehood,
   and my foot has hastened to deceit;

6 (Let me be weighed in a just balance,
 and let God know my integrity!)
7 if my step has turned aside from the way,
 and my heart has gone after my eyes,
 and if any spot has cleaved to my hands;
8 then let me sow, and another eat;
 and let what grows for me be rooted out.
9 "If my heart has been enticed to a woman,
 and I have lain in wait at my neighbor's door;
10 then let my wife grind for another,
 and let others bow down upon her.
11 For that would be a heinous crime;
 that would be an iniquity to be punished by the judges;
12 for that would be a fire which consumes unto Abaddon,
 and it would burn to the root all my increase.

16 "If I have withheld anything that the poor desired,
 or have caused the eyes of the widow to fail,
17 or have eaten my morsel alone,
 and the fatherless has not eaten of it
18 (for from his youth I reared him as a father,
 and from his mother's womb I guided him);
19 if I have seen any one perish for lack of clothing,
 or a poor man without covering;
20 if his loins have not blessed me,
 and if he was not warmed with the fleece of my sheep;
21 if I have raised my hand against the fatherless,
 because I saw help in the gate;
22 then let my shoulder blade fall from my shoulder,
 and let my arm be broken from its socket.
23 For I was in terror of calamity from God,
 and I could not have faced his majesty.

24 "If I have made gold my trust,
 or called fine gold my confidence;
25 if I have rejoiced because my wealth was great,
 or because my hand had gotten much;
26 if I have looked at the sun when it shone,
 or the moon moving in splendor,
27 and my heart has been secretly enticed,
 and my mouth has kissed my hand;
28 this also would be an iniquity to be punished by the judges,
 for I should have been false to God above.

²⁹ "If I have rejoiced at the ruin of him that hated me,
    or exulted when evil overtook him

³⁰ (I have not let my mouth sin
    by asking for his life with a curse);

³¹ if the men of my tent have not said,
    'Who is there that has not been filled with his meat?'

³² (the sojourner has not lodged in the street;
    I have opened my doors to the wayfarer);

³³ if I have concealed my transgressions from men,
    by hiding my iniquity in my bosom,

³⁴ because I stood in great fear of the multitude,
    and the contempt of families terrified me,
    so that I kept silence, and did not go out of doors—

³⁵ Oh, that I had one to hear me!
    (Here is my signature! let the Almighty answer me!)
    Oh, that I had the indictment written by my adversary!"

⁴⁰ The words of Job are ended.

31:40b This formulaic ending suggests that the chapters that follow may have been additions of later editors.

Elihu Enters the Debate

In the next chapters, 32–37 a new character, Elihu, enters the debate. Many biblical scholars believe that these speeches are an addition to the original text. They point to the fact that the Hebrew here—unlike that in the earlier chapters—reflects the later impact of the Aramaic language. Also Elihu refers frequently to statements made both by Job and his friends as though his address was intended specifically to be a response to arguments already given and well known. Traditional Bible scholars retort that this is exactly what the original author had in mind. Job had effectively silenced and answered his three friends; therefore a new attack on the problem had to be made. Elihu has no patience with the viewpoint held by the three acquaintances, i.e., that suffering is a direct consequence of sin; he rebukes them for having condemned Job. On the other hand, he asserts, there is a purifying, refining purpose in suffering. Suffering has meaning and value for man beyond the question of reward and punishment.

Elihu objects to Job's strictures against God. The Lord is not as distant or as unconcerned with man as Job intimates. God reveals himself to man in many ways; suffering, in fact, is one of them. Elihu calls on Job to halt his cries that God takes no account of righteousness or wickedness. He suggests that Job remain patient, "The case is before Him; therefore wait thou for Him" (35:14).

Job 32 : 1 – 10; 33 : 8 – 22, 29 – 30

32 So these three men ceased to answer Job, because he was righteous in his own eyes. ²Then Eli'hu the son of Bar'achel the Buzite, of the family of Ram, became angry. He was angry at Job because he justified himself rather than God; ³he was angry also at Job's three friends because they had found no answer, although they had declared Job to be in the wrong. ⁴Now Elihu had waited to speak to Job because they were older than he. ⁵And when Eli'hu saw that there was no answer in the mouth of these three men, he became angry.

6 And Eli'hu the son of Bar'achel the Buzite answered:

"I am young in years,
    and you are aged;
  therefore I was timid and afraid
    to declare my opinion to you.
⁷I said, 'Let days speak,
    and many years teach wisdom.'
⁸But it is the spirit in a man,
    the breath of the Almighty, that makes him understand.
⁹It is not the old that are wise,
    nor the aged that understand what is right.
¹⁰Therefore I say, 'Listen to me;
    let me also declare my opinion.'

33⁸"Surely, you have spoken in my hearing,
    and I have heard the sound of your words.
⁹You say, 'I am clean, without transgression;
    I am pure, and there is no iniquity in me.
¹⁰Behold, he finds occasions against me,
    he counts me as his enemy;
¹¹he puts my feet in the stocks,
    and watches all my paths.'

¹²"Behold, in this you are not right. I will answer you.
    God is greater than man.
¹³Why do you contend against him,
    saying, 'He will answer none of my words'?
¹⁴For God speaks in one way,
    and in two, though man does not perceive it.
¹⁵In a dream, in a vision of the night,
    when deep sleep falls upon men,
    while they slumber on their beds,
¹⁶then he opens the ears of men,
    and terrifies them with warnings,

¹⁷ that he may turn man aside from his deed,
  and cut off pride from man;
¹⁸ he keeps back his soul from the Pit,
  his life from perishing by the sword.

¹⁹ "Man is also chastened with pain upon his bed,
  and with continual strife in his bones;
²⁰ so that his life loathes bread,
  and his appetite dainty food.
²¹ His flesh is so wasted away that it cannot be seen;
  and his bones which were not seen stick out.
²² His soul draws near the Pit,
  and his life to those who bring death.
²⁹ "Behold, God does all these things,
  twice, three times, with a man,
³⁰ to bring back his soul from the Pit,
  that he may see the light of life."

33:8–11 Elihu first restates Job's arguments drawn directly from Job's remarks in 13:24, 27. **33:12–18** Elihu points out that God speaks to man at least in two ways: through dreams, a commonly held idea (cf. Numbers 12:6 ff.); and—a new thought—through man's sufferings, providing men thereby with wisdom and a perspective from which to make those decisions in life that might save his soul.

God Answers Job Out of the Whirlwind

God's answers do not seem to be answers. He never refers to Elihu. He rebukes the three friends but does not condemn their thesis. He recites an account of His majesty, and Job, acknowledging his own finitude, repents: but the issue of Job's innocence and his questioning of God's ways remain. Many scholars consider this exactly to be the mystery and the greatness of this book. It is not a logical presentation of ideas. It is a series of emotional reactions, all of which are partially true and sometimes false in explaining the condition of man. God's apparently irrelevant response to Job's questions is in fact an answer. Man, humbled before the majesty of God, is assured of God's existence; in that experience man can find a justification for a life of reverence and righteousness. Men can have faith in God even without fully comprehending God's ways, no matter what the pain or injustice man may have to endure.

Job 38:1–15, 22–24, 28–38

38 Then the LORD answered Job out of the whirlwind:
  ² "Who is this that darkens counsel by words without knowledge?
   ³ Gird up your loins like a man,
    I will question you, and you shall declare to me.

4 "Where were you when I laid the foundation of the earth?
   Tell me, if you have understanding.
5 Who determined its measurements—surely you know!
   Or who stretched the line upon it?
6 On what were its bases sunk
   or who laid its cornerstone,
7 when the morning stars sang together,
   and all the sons of God shouted for joy?

8 "Or who shut in the sea with doors,
   when it burst forth from the womb;
9 when I made clouds its garment,
   and thick darkness its swaddling band,
10 and prescribed bounds for it,
   and set bars and doors,
11 and said, 'Thus far shall you come, and no farther,
   and here shall your proud waves be stayed'?

12 "Have you commanded the morning since your days began,
   and caused the dawn to know its place,
13 that it might take hold of the skirts of the earth,
   and the wicked be shaken out of it?
14 It is changed like clay under the seal,
   and it is dyed like a garment.
15 From the wicked their light is withheld,
   and their uplifted arm is broken.

22 "Have you entered the storehouses of the snow,
   or have you seen the storehouses of the hail,
23 which I have reserved for the time of trouble,
   for the day of battle and war?
24 What is the way to the place where the light is distributed,
   or where the east wind is scattered upon the earth?

28 "Has the rain a father,
   or who has begotten the drops of dew?
29 From whose womb did the ice come forth,
   and who has given birth to the hoarfrost of heaven?
30 The waters become hard like stone,
   and the face of the deep is frozen.

31 "Can you bind the chains of the Plei'ades,
   or loose the cords of Orion?
32 Can you lead forth the Maz'zaroth in their season,
   or can you guide the Bear with its children?

³³ Do you know the ordinances of the heavens?
     Can you establish their rule on the earth?

³⁴ "Can you lift up your voice to the clouds,
     that a flood of waters may cover you?
³⁵ Can you send forth lightnings, that they may go
     and say to you, 'Here we are'?
³⁶ Who has put wisdom in the clouds,
     or given understanding to the mists?
³⁷ Who can number the clouds by wisdom?
     Or who can tilt the waterskins of the heavens,
³⁸ when the dust runs into a mass
     and the clods cleave fast together?"

38:1 A Jewish midrash recalls that God smote Job with a whirlwind (1:19). He now heals him from the whirlwind. See also Ezekiel 1:4.

Job Repents
Job 42:1–6

42 Then Job answered the Lord:
² "I know that thou canst do all things,
     and that no purpose of thine can be thwarted.
³ 'Who is this that hides counsel without knowledge?'
     Therefore I have uttered what I did not understand,
     things too wonderful for me, which I did not know.
⁴ 'Hear, and I will speak;
     I will question you, and you declare to me.'
⁵ I had heard of thee by the hearing of the ear,
     but now my eye sees thee;
⁶ therefore I despise myself,
     and repent in dust and ashes."

Epilogue
Job 42:7–17

7 After the Lord had spoken these words to Job, the Lord said to Eli′phaz the Te′manite: "My wrath is kindled against you and against your two friends; for you have not spoken of me what is right, as my servant Job has. ⁸ Now therefore take seven bulls and seven rams, and go to my servant Job, and offer up for yourselves a burnt offering; and my servant Job shall pray for you, for I will accept his prayer not to deal with you according to your folly; for you have not spoken of me what is right, as my servant Job has."

⁹ So Eli'phaz the Te'manite and Bildad the Shuhite and Zophar the Na'amathite went and did what the LORD had told them; and the LORD accepted Job's prayer.

10 And the LORD restored the fortunes of Job, when he had prayed for his friends; and the LORD gave Job twice as much as he had before. ¹¹ Then came to him all his brothers and sisters and all who had known him before, and ate bread with him in his house; and they showed him sympathy and comforted him for all the evil that the LORD had brought upon him; and each of them gave him a piece of money and a ring of gold. ¹² And the LORD blessed the latter days of Job more than his beginning; and he had fourteen thousand sheep, six thousand camels, a thousand yoke of oxen, and a thousand she-asses. ¹³ He had also seven sons and three daughters. ¹⁴ And he called the name of the first Jemi'mah; and the name of the second Kezi'ah; and the name of the third Ker'en-hap'puch. ¹⁵ And in all the land there were no women so fair as Job's daughters; and their father gave them inheritance among their brothers. ¹⁶ And after this Job lived a hundred and forty years, and saw his sons, and his sons' sons, four generations. ¹⁷ And Job died, an old man, and full of days.

42:8 By virtue of his righteousness and suffering, Job is given spiritual power. He can intercede by prayer in behalf of his friends. For other biblical examples of intercession by saintly men see: Genesis 18:22–32; 20:7; Exodus 32:11; 1 Samuel 7:5; 12:19; Amos 7:2–6; Jeremiah 11:14, 37:3.

The Psalms

Andrew Fletcher, who devoted himself to protecting the civil and religious liberties of seventeenth century Scotland, said: "Give me the making of the songs of a nation, and I care not who makes its laws." The Book of Psalms is the song book of the Hebrew people. It is in large measure a song book of humanity.

Worship in synagogue or church without the use of a Psalm is almost unthinkable. Copies of the New Testament are often bound up with the Psalms. In the daily public prayer of the Roman Catholic Church particular psalms are recited at certain hours of the day, and the entire book is covered in the course of a week.

The Psalms are associated with the name of David. 1 Samuel 16:23 tells how, when melancholia came upon King Saul, the youthful "David took the lyre and played it with his hand; so Saul was refreshed, and was well, and the evil spirit departed from him." 2 Samuel 23:1 refers to David as "the sweet psalmist of Israel."

As the name of Moses personified law and that of Solomon personified wisdom, so the name of David was synonymous with song. As later ages paid tribute to Solomon by naming wisdom works for him, so psalms, whenever they originated, would be spoken of as "Psalms of David." That David himself did not write all the psalms is clear, for example, from Psalm 30, which carries the title, "A Psalm of David, a song at the Dedication of the Temple." David not only did not live to see the dedication of the Temple, but was specifically forbidden to build it. Rabbinic tradition identifies this psalm with the rebuilding of the Temple under Ezra.

The psalms were written by many men in many ages. Titles at Psalms 1, 42, 73, 90 and 107 reveal that the Psalter is a collection of books. The second book concludes with the words, "The prayers of David . . . are ended" (Psalm 72:20). Materials within the psalms themselves suggest that some were composed in the time of Israel's first confrontation with the Canaanites, others as late as the Maccabean era, a span of nearly a thousand years. Whenever and by whomever composed, the Psalms run the gamut of human emotions and recapitulate the human story.

Jesus was fond of the Psalms. His ministry began with Psalm 2:7, and he died with Psalm 22 on his lips. Of Old Testament quotations found in the New, forty percent are from the Psalms.

Some Psalms are of a personal character. Psalm 4 is the song of a troubled man laying down to rest at night. Psalm 5 is the prayer of the same man arising in the morning to face another day. Psalm 30 sings the gratitude of one who is recovering from serious illness. Psalms 42 and 43 express the feelings of the homesick man. Psalm 91 is often on the lips of those facing separation from loved ones. Psalm 103 is pure thanksgiving for joys already received.

Some of the Psalms (8, 19, 29, 65, 104, 107, and 148) celebrate God's sovereignty over the natural world; some (78, 105, 106, 114, 136) interpret the history of Israel. Psalm 2 may be a wedding or coronation hymn for a king. Psalms 35, 59, 83 and 109 denounce foes, not personal enemies but those who would destroy the nation and its witness to the living God.

The Psalms follow Hebrew literary style in that the words do not rhyme and metered measure is found only occasionally. Their poetic form is free verse, with a generous and creative use of parallelisms. A Psalm is generally a series of couplets with each phrase in the couplet restating the thesis or antithetical to it. Sometimes the couplets are climaxed by an extra verse, and there are multiple variations on this form. An example:

(a) What is man that thou are mindful of him?
(b) and the son of man that thou dost care for him?
(c) Yet thou hast made him little less than God,
(d) and dost crown him with glory and honor. (8:4–5)

Or an antithetical parallelism:

(a) For the Lord knows the way of the righteous:
(b) but the way of the wicked will perish. (1:6)

It was customary in the Temple worship for the Psalms to be chanted by cantor and priestly chorus. Rabbinic tradition recalls that twelve adult Levites constituted the minimum membership of the chorus. Boys were later included in order to extend the vocal range of the choir. Members of the chorus accompanied their chanting by playing on musical instruments: nine played a kinor—according to Josephus, a ten-stringed instrument (see Psalm 112:3); two played on the nebel—a twelve-note stringed instrument with a membranous diaphragm attached to provide a resonant effect; one played the cymbals. The sounding of the flute was added to the orchestration on Holy Days.

Scholars also suggest that the Psalms used in the early synagogue were chanted antiphonally. Reciting the word "Halleluyah"—praise God—the cantor invited the congregation to respond as the chorus sang verses from this book.

Since the chanting of Psalms is such a central part of religious worship, many composers of note have set the psalms to music. Among the well-known works are Honegger's "King David," Stravinsky's "Symphony of Psalms," and Dello Joio's choral rendering "Psalm of David." Ernest Bloch's settings of Psalms 22, 114, 137 are frequently performed in American synagogues.

The Psalms have had a conspicuous place in the life of America. The first book published in the new world was *The Whole Book of Psalms Faithfully Translated into English.* When President Nathan A. Pusey was installed at Harvard, the assembled company sang

Jeremy Belknap's metrical version of Psalm 78, always used on ceremonial occasions at Harvard. During World War II a member of the U.S. Signal Corps carried with him a pocket edition of the Psalms. He spent his leisure turning them into blank verse. His title, "The Unquenched Cup," is derived from Psalm 23 : 5. The brimming cup there referred to, he says, "must continue to flow in all ages for those who seek its source."

Psalm 1

1 Blessed is the man
    who walks not in the counsel of the wicked,
  nor stands in the way of sinners,
    nor sits in the seat of scoffers;
  ² but his delight is in the law of the LORD,
    and on his law he meditates day and night.
  ³ He is like a tree
    planted by streams of water,
  that yields its fruit in its season,
    and its leaf does not wither.
  In all that he does, he prospers.
  ⁴ The wicked are not so,
    but are like chaff which the wind drives away.
  ⁵ Therefore the wicked will not stand in the judgment,
    nor sinners in the congregation of the righteous;
  ⁶ for the LORD knows the way of the righteous,
    but the way of the wicked will perish.

1:3, 6 Stated here is the simple conviction of reward and punishment maintained in the early biblical period: Those who observe God's law will prosper; those who oppose God's law will perish; and the reward and punishment is this-worldly. See books of Job and Ecclesiastes where this formula of reward and punishment is questioned, evidence of an awareness in the later biblical period that the problem of evil is more complicated. See also Psalms 18, 37, 49, 73.

Psalm 2

Jewish Publication Society

  Why are the nations in an uproar?
  And why do the peoples mutter in vain?
  ² The kings of the earth stand up,
  And the rulers take counsel together,
  Against the LORD, and against His anointed:
  ³ Let us break their bands asunder,
  And cast away their cords from us.

⁴ He that sitteth in heaven laugheth,
  The Lᴏʀᴅ hath them in derision.
⁵ Then will He speak unto them in His wrath,
  And affright them in His sore displeasure:
⁶ "Truly it is I that have established My king
  Upon Zion, My holy mountain."

⁷ I will tell of the decree:
  The Lᴏʀᴅ said unto me: "Thou art My son,
  This day have I begotten thee.
⁸ Ask of Me, and I will give the nations for thine inheritance,
  And the ends of the earth for thy possession.
⁹ Thou shalt break them with a rod iron;
  Thou shalt dash them in pieces like a potter's vessel."

¹⁰ Now therefore, O ye kings, be wise;
   Be admonished, ye judges of the earth.
¹¹ Serve the Lᴏʀᴅ with fear,
   And rejoice with trembling.
¹² Do homage in purity, lest He be angry, and ye perish in the
   way,
   When suddenly His wrath is kindled.

Happy are all they that take refuge in Him.

2:7 Jewish commentators point to Exodus 4:22: "Israel is my
son, my first born." Christian commentators have often seen this
Psalm as referring to Jesus. Some translate verse 12 to read "Kiss the
Son . . ." (as in KJV). RSV reads "Kiss his feet." The midnight Mass
of Christmas begins with the recitation of verse 7. **2:12** Jewish
commentators understand this verse to refer to the personified
people, Israel, whose priestly function will be acknowledged in the
time of the Messiah.

Psalm 8
Coverdale Bible

O Lᴏʀᴅ our Governor, how excellent is thy Name in all the
world; thou hast set thy glory above the heavens!
² Out of the mouth of very babes and sucklings hast thou
ordained strength, because of thine enemies, that thou mightest
still the enemy and the avenger.
³ When I consider thy heavens, even the work of thy fingers; the
moon and the stars which thou hast ordained;
⁴ What is man, that thou art mindful of him? and the son of man,
that thou visitest him?
⁵ Thou madest him lower than the angels, to crown him with
glory and worship.

[6] Thou makest him to have dominion of the works of thy hands;
and thou hast put all things in subjection under his feet:

[7] All sheep and oxen; yea, and the beasts of the field;

[8] The fowls of the air, and the fishes of the sea; and whatsoever
walketh through the paths of the seas.

[9] O Lord our Governor, how excellent is thy Name in all the
world!

8:2 The Catholic liturgy makes use of this passage for the Feast of
Holy Innocents, commemorating the murder of children in
Bethlehem by King Herod. See Matthew 2:16. **8:4** This questioning
of man's significance when contrasted with the grandeur of the
heavens is recalled in the liturgy of the Jewish Memorial Service. The
fact of death stimulates questions concerning the meaning of life and
the values by which a man is to be judged.

Psalm 14

14 The fool says in his heart,
"There is no God."
They are corrupt, they do abominable deeds,
there is none that does good.

[2] The Lord looks down from heaven upon the children
of men,
to see if there are any that act wisely,
that seek after God.

[3] They have all gone astray, they are all alike corrupt;
there is none that does good,
no, not one.

[4] Have they no knowledge, all the evildoers
who eat up my people as they eat bread,
and do not call upon the Lord?

[5] There they shall be in great terror,
for God is with the generation of the righteous.

[6] You would confound the plans of the poor,
but the Lord is his refuge.

[7] O that deliverance for Israel would come out of Zion!
When the Lord restores the fortunes of his people,
Jacob shall rejoice, Israel shall be glad.

Psalm 19

19 The heavens are telling the glory of God;
and the firmament proclaims his handiwork.

² Day to day pours forth speech,
   and night to night declares knowledge.
³ There is no speech, nor are there words;
   their voice is not heard;
⁴ yet their voice goes out through all the earth,
   and their words to the end of the world.

In them he has set a tent for the sun,
⁵ which comes forth like a bridegroom leaving
      his chamber,
   and like a strong man runs its course with joy.

⁶ Its rising is from the end of the heavens,
   and its circuit to the end of them;
   and there is nothing hid from its heat.

⁷ The law of the LORD is perfect,
   reviving the soul;
 the testimony of the LORD is sure,
   making wise the simple;
⁸ the precepts of the LORD are right,
   rejoicing the heart;
 the commandment of the LORD is pure,
   enlightening the eyes;
⁹ the fear of the LORD is clean,
   enduring for ever;
 the ordinances of the LORD are true,
   and righteous altogether.
¹⁰ More to be desired are they than gold,
   even much fine gold;
 sweeter also than honey
   and drippings of the honeycomb.

¹¹ Moreover by them is thy servant warned;
   in keeping them there is great reward.
¹² But who can discern his errors?
   Clear thou me from hidden faults.
¹³ Keep back thy servant also from presumptuous sins;
   let them not have dominion over me!
 Then I shall be blameless,
   and innocent of great transgression.

¹⁴ Let the words of my mouth and the meditation of
      my heart
   be acceptable in thy sight,
   O LORD, my rock and my redeemer.

19:5 In the prophetic imagery, the sun symbolized righteousness. See Malachi 4:2. Thus the Psalmist recognizes a unity between God's work in the heavens and His revelation of the law of truth on earth. **19:7–9** These phrases are recited in the Reform synagogue when the Torah (Scroll of the Law) is returned to the Ark. **19:14** This phrase concludes the period of silent meditation in the Reform synagogue service. It is also used as an invocation in Protestant and Catholic worship. The Hebrew word Goel translated here "Redeemer" originally meant one who avenges a slain innocent; see Numbers 35:19. In prophetic writing it referred to God who rescues His people and saves them from death. See Isaiah 41:14; 44:6. See discussion at Job 19:25.

Psalm 22

CCD

My God, my God, why have you forsaken me, far from my prayer, from the words of my cry? O my God, I cry out by day, and you answer not; by night, and there is no relief for me. Yet you are enthroned in the holy place, O glory of Israel! In you our fathers trusted; they trusted, and you delivered them. To you they cried, and they escaped; in you they trusted, and they were not put to shame.

But I am a worm, not a man; the scorn of men, despised by the people. All who see me scoff at me; they mock me with parted lips, they wag their heads: "He relied on the Lord; let him deliver him, let him rescue him, if he loves him." You have been my guide since I was first formed, my security at my mother's breast. To you I was committed at birth, from my mother's womb you are my God.

Be not far from me, for I am in distress; be near, for I have no one to help me. Many bullocks surround me; the strong bulls of Basan encircle me. They open their mouths against me like ravening and roaring lions.

I am like water poured out; all my bones are racked. My heart has become like wax melting away within my bosom. My throat is dried up like baked clay, my tongue cleaves to my jaws; to the dust of death you have brought me down.

Indeed, many dogs surround me, a pack of evildoers closes in upon me; they have pierced my hands and my feet; I can count all my bones. They look on and gloat over me; they divide my garments among them, and for my vesture they cast lots.

But you, O Lord, be not far from me; O my help, hasten to aid me. Rescue my soul from the sword, my loneliness from the grip of the dog. Save me from the lion's mouth; from the horns of the wild bulls, my wretched life.

I will proclaim your name to my brethren; in the midst of the assembly I will praise you: "You who fear the Lord, praise him; all you descendants of Jacob, give glory to him; revere him, all you descendants of Israel! For he has not spurned nor disdained the wretched man in his misery, nor did he turn his face away from him, but when he cried out to him, he heard him." So by your gift will I utter praise in the vast assembly; I will fulfill my vows before those who fear him. The lowly shall eat their fill; they who seek the Lord shall praise him: "May your hearts be ever merry!"

All the ends of the earth shall remember and turn to the Lord; all the families of the nations shall bow down before him. For dominion is the Lord's, and he rules the nations. To him alone shall bow down all who sleep in the earth; before him shall bend all who go down into the dust. And to him my soul shall live; my descendants shall serve him. Let the coming generation be told of the Lord that they may proclaim to a people yet to be born the justice he has shown.

22:1 Not a cry of despair, this Psalm praises God for deliverance from enemies. The grateful Psalmist prays that the account of God's deliverance will be heard in all the ends of the earth and will inspire all men to turn to the Lord. Mark 15:34 and Matthew 27:46 report that its phrases were on Jesus' lips as he hung on the Cross. **22:7–8, 18** The early Hebrew-Christians saw in these verses a premonition of events in the life of Jesus.

Psalm 23

23The LORD is my shepherd,
　　I shall not want;
² he makes me lie down in green pastures.
　　He leads me beside still waters;
³　　he restores my soul.
　　He leads me in paths of righteousness
　　　for his name's sake.

⁴ Even though I walk through the valley of the shadow of death,
　　I fear no evil;
　for thou art with me;
　　thy rod and thy staff,
　　they comfort me.

⁵ Thou preparest a table before me in the presence of my
　　　enemies;
　thou anointest my head with oil,
　　my cup overflows.

⁶ Surely goodness and mercy shall follow me
    all the days of my life;
  and I shall dwell in the house of the LORD
    for ever.

Psalm 23

Indian Version

The Great Father above a Shepherd Chief is, I am His and with Him I want not.

He throws out to me a rope, and the name of the rope is Love, and He draws me, and He draws me, and He draws me to where the grass is green and the water not dangerous, and I eat and lie down satisfied.

Sometimes my heart is very weak and falls down, but He lifts it up again and draws me into a good road. His name is wonderful.

Sometime, it may be very soon, it may be longer, it may be long, long time, He will draw me into a place between mountains. It is dark there, but I'll draw back not, I'll be afraid not, for it is in there between those mountains that the Shepherd Chief wills me, and the hunger I have felt in my heart all through this life will be satisfied. Sometimes He makes the rope into a whip, but afterwards He gives me a staff to lean on.

He spreads a table before me with all kinds of food. He puts His hand upon my head, and all the "tired" is gone. My cup he fills till it runs over.

What I tell you is true. I lie not. These roads that are "away ahead" will stay with me through this life, and afterward I will go to live in the "Big Tepee" and sit down with the Shepherd Chief forever.

23:1 This well-known and beautiful Psalm is frequently recited at the funeral services of Jew and Christian; in its own context it is a prayer of thanksgiving for God's graciousness to the psalmist in life.

Psalm 24

Jewish Publication Society

The earth is the LORD's and the fulness thereof;
  The world, and they that dwell therein.
² For He hath founded it upon the seas.
  And established it upon the floods.
³ Who shall ascend into the mountain of the LORD?
  And who shall stand in His holy place?

⁴ He that hath clean hands, and a pure heart;
  Who hath not taken My name in vain,
  And hath not sworn deceitfully.
⁵ He shall receive a blessing from the LORD,
  And righteousness from the God of his salvation.
⁶ Such is the generation of them that seek after Him,
  That seek Thy face, even Jacob.   *Selah*
⁷ Lift up your heads, O ye gates,
  And be ye lifted up, ye everlasting doors;
  That the King of glory may come in.
⁸ 'Who is the King of glory?'
  'The LORD strong and mighty,
  The LORD mighty in battle.'
⁹ Lift up your heads, O ye gates,
  Yea, lift them up, ye everlasting doors;
  That the King of glory may come in.
¹⁰ 'Who then is the King of glory?'
  'The LORD of Hosts;
  He is the king of glory.'   *Selah*

24:1 This Psalm may have been composed by David to celebrate the occasion when the Ark was brought to Jerusalem and to Mount Zion (2 Samuel 6:12–16). It describes the virtue of a man worthy to stand in God's presence. Its pattern of questions and answers suggest an antiphonal response by two groups in the procession. It was sung by the Levites in the Temple on the first day of the week (Sunday) and it is still the selection for use on that day in synagogue worship. Verses 2–6 and 7–10 are also recited as part of the prayer service when the Torah scroll is taken from the Ark in preparation for the scriptural lesson in the synagogue. **24:1** In context this phrase may suggest that although the Ark is to be brought to the sanctuary, God's presence is everywhere (see Isaiah 66:1). It has also been quoted in religious teachings that stress that worldly possessions are but lent to man. The earth is the Lord's; therefore man must account for his use of God's possessions. The use of personal property stands under the judgment of God. **24:2** In the view of the times, the earth was a flat surface supported by a deep, i.e., water under the earth. See Exodus 20:4. **24:3–6** This is a description of the kind of person deserving to stand before the Lord. (See also Psalm 15.) It is customary for the Catholic mother, after the birth of a baby, to go to the church with the child as soon as possible for a ceremony called "The Churching of Women." (Episcopalians in a similar service recite Psalm 116.) The ceremony consists of a special blessing for woman who comes in gladness to God's temple. Psalm 24 is recited first while the woman holds a lighted candle in her hand. This Psalm is also read at the Catholic burial for a young child. **24:10** The

phrase Lord of Hosts referred to God as a champion of Israel's army
(see 1 Samuel 17:45). Later the verse came to define God as the Lord
of all the heavenly hosts (see 29:1; 82:1; 89:6; Job 1:6).

Psalm 26

26 Vindicate me, O Lord,
    for I have walked in my integrity,
    and I have trusted in the Lord without wavering.
² Prove me, O Lord, and try me;
    test my heart and my mind.
³ For thy steadfast love is before my eyes,
    and I walk in faithfulness to thee.

⁴ I do not sit with false men,
    nor do I consort with dissemblers;
⁵ I hate the company of evildoers,
    and I will not sit with the wicked.

⁶ I wash my hands in innocence,
    and go about thy altar, O Lord,
⁷ singing aloud a song of thanksgiving,
    and telling all thy wondrous deeds.

⁸ O Lord, I love the habitation of thy house,
    and the place where thy glory dwells.
⁹ Sweep me not away with sinners,
    nor my life with bloodthirsty men,
¹⁰ men in whose hands are evil devices,
    and whose right hands are full of bribes.

¹¹ But as for me, I walk in my integrity;
    redeem me, and be gracious to me.
¹² My foot stands on level ground;
    in the great congregation I will bless the Lord.

26:2 In older translations the Hebrew words were translated
literally, "Test my veins (kidneys) and my heart." In popular biblical
usage the kidneys were considered the source of emotions and the
heart the source of thought. **26:6–12** In ancient days the Levitical
priests washed their hands before offering sacrifice. To this day
orthodox Jews wash hands before reciting the blessing over bread at
the daily meal. The Catholic priest recites these verses every day in
the Mass when he goes to the right side of the altar and washes his
hands in preparation for the most solemn part of the sacrificial
ceremony. See Deuteronomy 21:6–7 for ceremony of washing hands
as purification from guilt. **26:10** Rabbinic tradition uses this verse as a
reference to games of dice or other forms of gambling. The rabbis
enacted stringent regulations against such games. They considered it a

form of robbery and disqualified the professional gambler from testifying as a witness in court—he was not to be trusted even under oath. On the other hand, the Hebrews did not frown upon relaxing games of amusement such as: target shooting, 1 Samuel 20:20; weight-lifting, Zechariah 12:3; foot-racing, Psalm 19:5–6; guessing games and riddles, Judges 14:14, 1 Kings 10:1–3.

Psalm 29

Jewish Publication Society

Ascribe unto the LORD, O ye sons of might,
Ascribe unto the LORD glory and strength.
² Ascribe unto the LORD the glory due unto His name;
Worship the LORD in the beauty of holiness.

³ The voice of the LORD is upon the waters;
The God of glory thundereth,
Even the LORD upon many waters.
⁴ The voice of the LORD is powerful;
The voice of the LORD is full of majesty.
⁵ The voice of the LORD breaketh the cedars;
Yea, the LORD breaketh in pieces the cedars of Lebanon.
⁶ He maketh them also to skip like a calf;
Lebanon and Sirion like a young wild-ox.
⁷ The voice of the LORD heweth out flames of fire.
⁸ The voice of the LORD shaketh the wilderness;
The LORD shaketh the wilderness of Kadesh.
⁹ The voice of the LORD maketh the hinds to calve,
And strippeth the forests bare;
And in His temple all say: 'Glory.'

¹⁰ The LORD sat enthroned at the flood;
Yea, the LORD sitteth as King for ever.
¹¹ The LORD will give strength unto His people;
The LORD will bless His people with peace.

29:1 A nature Psalm describing God's might as manifested in a storm. A recently found Canaanite text suggests that the Hebrews borrowed this psalm, eliminated references to the Canaanite deities, and praised instead YHWH as the Lord of glory and strength. God's power assures peace for His chosen people. **29:11** This verse is used frequently as a benediction, closing religious services in the synagogue.

Psalm 33

33 Rejoice in the LORD, O you righteous!
Praise befits the upright.

3 Praise the LORD with the lyre,
   make melody to him with the harp of ten strings!
3 Sing to him a new song,
   play skilfully on the strings, with loud shouts.

4 For the word of the LORD is upright;
   and all his work is done in faithfulness.
5 He loves righteousness and justice;
   the earth is full of the steadfast love of the LORD.

6 By the word of the LORD the heavens were made,
   and all their host by the breath of his mouth.
7 He gathered the waters of the sea as in a bottle;
   he put the deeps in storehouses.
8 Let all the earth fear the LORD,
   let all the inhabitants of the world stand in awe of him!
9 For he spoke, and it came to be;
   he commanded, and it stood forth.

10 The LORD brings the counsel of the nations to nought;
   he frustrates the plans of the peoples.
11 The counsel of the LORD stands for ever,
   the thoughts of his heart to all generations.
12 Blessed is the nation whose God is the LORD,
   the people whom he has chosen as his heritage!

13 The LORD looks down from heaven,
   he sees all the sons of men;
14 from where he sits enthroned he looks forth
   on all the inhabitants of the earth,
15 he who fashions the hearts of them all,
   and observes all their deeds.

16 A king is not saved by his great army;
   a warrior is not delivered by his great strength.
17 The war horse is a vain hope for victory,
   and by its great might it cannot save.

18 Behold, the eye of the LORD is on those who fear him,
   on those who hope in his steadfast love,
19 that he may deliver their soul from death,
   and keep them alive in famine.

20 Our soul waits for the LORD;
   he is our help and shield.
21 Yea, our heart is glad in him,
   because we trust in his holy name.

²² Let thy steadfast love, O LORD, be upon us,
  even as we hope in thee.

33:1 This Psalm, celebrating God's role as creator of the universe and ruler over men and nations, is recited on Sabbath mornings in Jewish worship. **33:2** John Calvin (1509– 1564) held that music in the church should be confined to unison congregational singing of metrical versions of the Psalms and Canticles. Andreas Carlstadt (1480?–1541), friend and colleague of Luther, said; "Relegate organs, trumpets and flutes to the theatre." Luther, however, believed that art and music, like the sacraments, were appropriate expressions of religion. **33:16–17** In the prophetic period both Israel and Judah were tempted to make alliances with other nations in order to secure peace. The prophets warned against such entanglements, fearing that it would lead to the introduction of idolatry. They counseled the nation to place its full trust in God. Consider in our day whether military might is a means of national security.

Psalm 34

Jewish Publication Society

34 ² I will bless the LORD at all times;
  His praise shall continually be in my mouth.
³ My soul shall glory in the LORD;
  The humble shall hear thereof, and be glad.
⁴ O magnify the LORD with me,
  And let us exalt His name together.
⁵ I sought the LORD, and He answered me,
  And delivered me from all my fears.
⁶ They looked unto Him, and were radiant;
  And their faces shall never be abashed.
⁷ This poor man cried, and the LORD heard
  And saved him out of all his troubles.
⁸ The angel of the LORD encampeth round about them that fear
    Him.
  And delivereth them.
⁹ O consider and see that the LORD is good;
  Happy is the man that taketh refuge in Him.
¹⁰ O fear the LORD, ye His holy ones;
  For there is no want to them that fear Him.
¹¹ The young lions do lack, and suffer hunger;
  But they that seek the LORD want not any good thing.
¹² Come, ye children, hearken unto me;
  I will teach you the fear of the LORD.
¹³ Who is the man that desireth life,
  And loveth days, that he may see good therein?

¹⁴ Keep thy tongue from evil,
   And thy lips from speaking guile.
¹⁵ Depart from evil, and do good;
   Seek peace, and pursue it.
¹⁶ The eyes of the LORD are toward the righteous,
   And His ears are open unto their cry.
¹⁷ The face of the LORD is against them that do evil,
   To cut off the remembrance of them from the earth.
¹⁸ They cried, and the LORD heard
   And delivered them out of all their troubles.
¹⁹ The LORD is nigh unto them that are of a broken heart,
   And saveth such as are of a contrite spirit.
²⁰ Many are the ills of the righteous,
   But the LORD delivereth him out of them all.
²¹ He keepeth all his bones;
   Not one of them is broken.
²² Evil shall kill the wicked;
   And they that hate the righteous shall be held guilty.
²³ The LORD redeemeth the soul of His servants;
   And none of them that take refuge in Him shall be desolate.

34:1 The Jewish translation counts the inscription to this Psalm as the first verse (it is here omitted). Other translations do not number the inscription. Thus the Jewish text numbers as verse 2 the sentence which is verse 1 in Christian texts.
34:2 Composed as an acrostic, the first letter of each verse in the Hebrew follows the alphabetical order. (Other acrostic psalms include Psalms 25, 34, 37, 111, 112, 119, 145.) Some scholars suggest that these alphabetical Psalms were also used for the purpose of ethical instruction since students could easily memorize the verse. **34:10** Irwin Shaw wrote a famous novel about the fate of wartime soldiers, the title of which, *The Young Lions,* was drawn from this reference. See also 104:21. **34:15** The rabbinic tradition warns against a compulsive attention to iniquity emphasizing the latter part of this sentence: "Do good." This is the antidote to evil. Similarly, those versed in homiletics note that peace is not easily obtained; it must be pursued. **34:18–19** The Psalmist here acknowledges that piety and faithfulness to God's law do not in themselves save a man from affliction. But the Psalmist has confidence that God will deliver the righteous man from all his troubles, enabling the faithful to see his problems in their spiritual significance.

Psalm 46

46 God is our refuge and strength,
   a very present help in trouble.

² Therefore we will not fear though the earth should change,
    though the mountains shake in the heart of the sea;
³ though its waters roar and foam,
    though the mountains tremble with its tumult.   *Selah*

⁴ There is a river whose streams make glad the city of God,
    the holy habitation of the Most High.
⁵ God is in the midst of her, she shall not be moved;
    God will help her right early.
⁶ The nations rage, the kingdoms totter;
    he utters his voice, the earth melts.
⁷ The LORD of hosts is with us;
    the God of Jacob is our refuge.   *Selah*

⁸ Come, behold the works of the LORD,
    how he has wrought desolations in the earth.
⁹ He makes wars cease to the end of the earth;
    he breaks the bow, and shatters the spear,
    he burns the chariots with fire!
¹⁰ "Be still, and know that I am God.
    I am exalted among the nations,
    I am exalted in the earth!"
¹¹ The LORD of hosts is with us;
    the God of Jacob is our refuge.   *Selah*

46:1 This Psalm, chosen by President Dwight D. Eisenhower to be read at pre-inaugural worship on January 20, 1957, had earlier been the inspiration of what has been called "the greatest hymn of the greatest man in the greatest period in German history." The reference is to Martin Luther's "A mighty fortress is our God," a paraphrase of this Psalm. **46:8, 9** Sennacherib's attack upon Jerusalem may have provided the occasion of the writing of this Psalm (see 2 Kings 18:13–19:36). Herodotus tells how a plague of mice cut the Assyrian bow strings and spread disease among the invaders. **46:9** This is a favorite passage among advocates of world peace. **46:10** The author, rebuking man's pride and self-dependence, seems to be saying: "Give in! Admit that I am God!"

Psalm 47

47 Clap your hands, all peoples!
    Shout to God with loud songs of joy!
² For the LORD, the Most High, is terrible,
    a great king over all the earth.
³ He subdued peoples under us,
    and nations under our feet.

⁴ He chose our heritage for us,
    the pride of Jacob whom he loves.   *Selah*

⁵ God has gone up with a shout,
    the LORD with the sound of a trumpet.
⁶ Sing praises to God, sing praises!
    Sing praises to our King, sing praises!
⁷ For God is the king of all the earth;
    sing praises with a psalm!

⁸ God reigns over the nations;
    God sits on his holy throne.
⁹ The princes of the peoples gather
    as the people of the God of Abraham.
For the shields of the earth belong to God;
    he is highly exalted!

47:1 First of the "Psalms of Kingship," this hymn expresses hope for a time when the princes of all people will acknowledge God. Since this Psalm refers to the sounding of a horn (verse 5), it is recited in the synagogue at the service for the Shofar (Ram's Horn) on the Jewish New Year (Rosh Hashanah) which usually falls in September. In the Catholic liturgy this Psalm is sung during the distribution of palms on Palm Sunday. **47:9** In the Messianic era all nations that accept God's rule will be included in the blessings of the covenant that God made with Abraham.

Psalm 51

51 Have mercy on me, O God, according to thy steadfast love;
    according to thy abundant mercy blot out my transgressions.
² Wash me thoroughly from my iniquity,
    and cleanse me from my sin!

³ For I know my transgressions,
    and my sin is ever before me.
⁴ Against thee, thee only, have I sinned,
    and done that which is evil in thy sight,
so that thou art justified in thy sentence
    and blameless in thy judgment.
⁵ Behold, I was brought forth in iniquity,
    and in sin did my mother conceive me.

⁶ Behold, thou desirest truth in the inward being;
    therefore teach me wisdom in my secret heart.
⁷ Purge me with hyssop, and I shall be clean;
    wash me, and I shall be whiter than snow.

⁸ Fill me with joy and gladness;
    let the bones which thou hast broken rejoice.
⁹ Hide thy face from my sins,
    and blot out all my iniquities.

¹⁰ Create in me a clean heart, O God,
    and put a new and right spirit within me.
¹¹ Cast me not away from thy presence,
    and take not thy holy Spirit from me.
¹² Restore to me the joy of thy salvation,
    and uphold me with a willing spirit.

¹³ Then I will teach transgressors thy ways,
    and sinners will return to thee.
¹⁴ Deliver me from bloodguiltiness, O God,
    thou God of my salvation,
    and my tongue will sing aloud of thy deliverance.

¹⁵ O Lord, open thou my lips,
    and my mouth shall show forth thy praise.
¹⁶ For thou hast no delight in sacrifice;
    were I to give a burnt offering, thou wouldst not be pleased.
¹⁷ The sacrifice acceptable to God is a broken spirit;
    a broken and contrite heart, O God, thou wilt not despise.

¹⁸ Do good to Zion in thy good pleasure;
    rebuild the walls of Jerusalem,
¹⁹ then wilt thou delight in right sacrifices,
    in burnt offerings and whole burnt offerings;
    then bulls will be offered on thy altar.

51:1 One of the seven "Penitential Psalms" (others are Psalms 6, 32, 38, 102, 143, 151), the Psalmist pleads for God's forgiveness for a sin committed against Him. **51:1–2, 10** These verses are part of the Methodist Covenant Service, originated by John Wesley in 1755. **51:5** Jewish scholars do not see this verse as a reference to original sin. They contend that what the Psalmist means is that "from his birth man has been prone to sin," rather than born in sin as a consequence of Adam's corruption. Jews and Christians all agree, however, that there is a tendency on man's part to evil, Genesis 8:21; Job 14:4; Proverbs 20:9. For elaboration of the Christian concept of original sin see Romans 5:12–21. See also discussion on original sin at Genesis 3. **51:7** The hyssop is a plant used in biblical purification rites. See Leviticus 14:4 f.; Numbers 19:6, 18. **51:10–6** These verses along with verses 17–19 and Psalm 116:12, 13, 18 are used by the Lutheran Church in America at the Offertory in the Communion. **51:11** In this context the "holy Spirit" is that insight provided man by God that enables him to know God's will. See Psalm 143:10, Isaiah 63:11, Nehemiah 9:20, Haggai 2:5. **51:16–17** The prophetic view is here invoked. See Isaiah 57:15, 66:2. The Psalmist recognizes that God prefers a man's sincere repentance to sacrifices that are offered without a genuine turning of the heart. Note, however, that the Psalmist does not wish to eliminate the Temple sacrificial offerings altogether.

Psalm 84

CCD

2.3　How lovely is your dwelling place, O Lord of hosts! | My soul yearns and pines for the courts of the Lord. My heart 4 and my flesh cry out for the living God. | Even the sparrow finds a home, and the swallow a nest in which she puts her young—your altars, O Lord of hosts, my king and my God!

5　Happy they who dwell in your house! continually they 6 praise you. | Happy the men whose strength you are! their 7 hearts are set upon the pilgrimage: | when they pass through the arid valley, they make a spring of it; the early rain 8 clothes it with generous growth. | They go from strength to strength; they shall see the God of gods in Sion.

9　O Lord of hosts, hear my prayer; hearken, O God of 10 Jacob! | O God, behold our shield, and look upon the face of 11 your anointed. | I had rather one day in your courts than a thousand elsewhere; I had rather lie at the threshold of the 12 house of my God than dwell in the tents of the wicked. | For a sun and a shield is the Lord God; grace and glory he bestows; the Lord withholds no good thing from those who 13 walk in sincerity. | O Lord of hosts, happy the men who trust in you!

84:4 This passage begins the Afternoon Service in the synagogue, the opening prayer of which takes its name from the Hebrew word "ashrey," which literally means "happy are they." **84:6** The Hebrew text adds the words "to Zion," clarifying the destination of the pilgrimage. The Greek text uses the word "ascents," referring to the pilgrims' upward climb to the mount of the Temple on one of the highest hills of Jerusalem. See Psalm 120 f. **85:7** "May you go from strength to strength" is a favorite benediction and blessing among Jews to this day.

Psalm 89

89 I will sing of thy steadfast love, O Lord, for ever;
　　　with my mouth I will proclaim thy faithfulness to all generations.

2 For thy steadfast love was established for ever,
  thy faithfulness is firm as the heavens.
3 Thou hast said, "I have made a covenant with my chosen one,
  I have sworn to David my servant:
4 'I will establish your descendants for ever,
  and build your throne for all generations.' "   *Selah*
5 Let the heavens praise thy wonders, O LORD,
  thy faithfulness in the assembly of the holy ones!
6 For who in the skies can be compared to the LORD?
  Who among the heavenly beings is like the LORD,
7 a God feared in the council of the holy ones,
  great and terrible above all that are round about him?
8 O LORD God of hosts,
  who is mighty as thou art, O LORD,
  with thy faithfulness round about thee?
9 Thou dost rule the raging of the sea;
  when its waves rise, thou stillest them.
10 Thou didst crush Rahab like a carcass,
  thou didst scatter thy enemies with thy mighty arm.
11 The heavens are thine, the earth also is thine;
  the world and all that is in it, thou hast founded them.
12 The north and the south, thou hast created them;
  Tabor and Hermon joyously praise thy name.
13 Thou hast a mighty arm;
  strong is thy hand, high thy right hand.
14 Righteousness and justice are the foundation of thy throne;
  steadfast love and faithfulness go before thee.
15 Blessed are the people who know the festal shout,
  who walk, O LORD, in the light of thy countenance,
16 who exult in thy name all the day,
  and extol thy righteousness.
17 For thou art the glory of their strength;
  by thy favor our horn is exalted.
18 For our shield belongs to the LORD,
  our king to the Holy One of Israel.
19 Of old thou didst speak in a vision
  to thy faithful one, and say:
"I have set the crown upon one who is mighty,
  I have exalted one chosen from the people.
20 I have found David, my servant;
  with my holy oil I have anointed him;
21 so that my hand shall ever abide with him,
  my arm also shall strengthen him.

22 The enemy shall not outwit him,
   the wicked shall not humble him.
23 I will crush his foes before him
   and strike down those who hate him.
24 My faithfulness and my steadfast love shall be with him,
   and in my name shall his horn be exalted.
25 I will set his hand on the sea
   and his right hand on the rivers.
26 He shall cry to me, 'Thou art my Father,
   my God, and the Rock of my salvation.'
27 And I will make him the first-born,
   the highest of the kings of the earth.
28 My steadfast love I will keep for him for ever,
   and my covenant will stand firm for him.
29 I will establish his line for ever
   and his throne as the days of the heavens.
30 If his children forsake my law
   and do not walk according to my ordinances,
31 if they violate my statutes
   and do not keep my commandments,
32 then I will punish their transgression with the rod
   and their iniquity with scourges;
33 but I will not remove from him my steadfast love,
   or be false to my faithfulness.
34 I will not violate my covenant,
   or alter the word that went forth from my lips.
35 Once for all I have sworn by my holiness;
   I will not lie to David.
36 His line shall endure for ever,
   his throne as long as the sun before me.
37 Like the moon it shall be established for ever;
   it shall stand firm while the skies endure."   *Selah*

38 But now thou hast cast off and rejected,
   thou art full of wrath against thy anointed.
39 Thou hast renounced the covenant with thy servant;
   thou hast defiled his crown in the dust.
40 Thou hast breached all his walls;
   thou hast laid his strongholds in ruins.
41 All that pass by despoil him;
   he has become the scorn of his neighbors.
42 Thou hast exalted the right hand of his foes;
   thou hast made all his enemies rejoice.

⁴³ Yea, thou hast turned back the edge of his sword,
      and thou hast not made him stand in battle.
⁴⁴ Thou hast removed the scepter from his hand,
      and cast his throne to the ground.
⁴⁵ Thou hast cut short the days of his youth;
      thou hast covered him with shame.   *Selah*

⁴⁶ How long, O LORD? Wilt thou hide thyself for ever?
      How long will thy wrath burn like fire?
⁴⁷ Remember, O Lord, what the measure of life is,
      for what vanity thou hast created all the sons of men!
⁴⁸ What man can live and never see death?
      Who can deliver his soul from the power of Sheol?   *Selah*

⁴⁹ Lord, where is thy steadfast love of old,
      which by thy faithfulness thou didst swear to David?
⁵⁰ Remember, O Lord, how thy servant is scorned;
      how I bear in my bosom the insults of the peoples,
⁵¹ with which thy enemies taunt, O LORD,
      with which they mock the footsteps of thy anointed.

⁵² Blessed be the LORD for ever!
      Amen and Amen.

89:1 This Psalm is considered by Jews to be a classic statement of
God's fidelity to the Hebrew people. He will establish them forever
(verse 4). The passage 19–29 alludes to the fact that the House of
David is the "first born" of God. If Israel transgresses, God will
punish; but He will not violate his Covenant (verses 30–37). He will
not reject Israel nor remove them from their election. On that faith the
psalmist pleads for God's mercy to Israel during a time of punishment.
89:4 See 2 Samuel 7:8–16 for first reference to God's promise to the
House of David. **89:10** Rahab can refer to the sea monster of the
primeval chaos. See Job 7:12 and index for fuller discussion. The
name "Rahab" can also be applied to Egypt. See Psalm 87:4.

Psalm 90

90 Lord, thou hast been our dwelling place in all generations.
² Before the mountains were brought forth,
      or ever thou hadst formed the earth and the world
      from everlasting to everlasting thou art God.

³ Thou turnest man back to the dust,
      and sayest, "Turn back, O children of men!"
⁴ For a thousand years in thy sight
      are but as yesterday when it is past,
      or as a watch in the night.

⁵ Thou dost sweep men away; they are like a dream,
     like grass which is renewed in the morning:
⁶ in the morning it flourishes and is renewed;
     in the evening it fades and withers.

⁷ For we are consumed by thy anger;
     by thy wrath we are overwhelmed.
⁸ Thou hast set our iniquities before thee
     our secret sins in the light of thy countenance.

⁹ For all our days pass away under thy wrath,
     our years come to an end like a sigh.
¹⁰ The years of our life are threescore and ten,
     or even by reason of strength fourscore;
    yet their span is but toil and trouble;
     they are soon gone, and we fly away.

¹¹ Who considers the power of thy anger,
     and thy wrath according to the fear of thee?
¹² So teach us to number our days
     that we may get a heart of wisdom.

¹³ Return, O LORD! How long?
     Have pity on thy servants!
¹⁴ Satisfy us in the morning with thy steadfast love,
     that we may rejoice and be glad all our days.
¹⁵ Make us glad as many days as thou hast afflicted us,
     and as many years as we have seen evil,
¹⁶ Let thy work be manifest to thy servants,
     and thy glorious power to their children.
¹⁷ Let the favor of the Lord our God be upon us,
     and establish thou the work of our hands upon us,
     yea, the work of our hands establish thou it.

90:1 Psalms 90 and 91 are recited at the Saturday morning prayer service in the synagogue. They are also used frequently at Jewish memorial services as a warning to the listeners and as inspiration to the bereaved. This Psalm is the source of Isaac Watt's famous Hymn "O God Our Help in Ages Past." It is used in the burial service in the Book of Common Prayer of the Protestant Episcopal church.

Psalm 91

91 He who dwells in the shelter of the Most High,
     who abides in the shadow of the Almighty,
² will say to the LORD, "My refuge and my fortress;
     my God, in whom I trust."

³ For he will deliver you from the snare of the fowler
     and from the deadly pestilence;
⁴ he will cover you with his pinions,
     and under his wings you will find refuge;
     his faithfulness is a shield and buckler.
⁵ You will not fear the terror of the night,
     nor the arrow that flies by day,
⁶ nor the pestilence that stalks in darkness,
     nor the destruction that wastes at noonday.

⁷ A thousand may fall at your side,
     ten thousand at your right hand;
     but it will not come near you.
⁸ You will only look with your eyes
     and see the recompense of the wicked.

⁹ Because you have made the LORD your refuge,
     the Most High your habitation,
¹⁰ no evil shall befall you,
     no scourge come near your tent.

¹¹ For he will give his angels charge of you
     to guard you in all your ways.
¹² On their hands they will bear you up,
     lest you dash your foot against a stone.
¹³ You will tread on the lion and the adder,
     the young lion and the serpent you will trample under foot.
¹⁴ Because he cleaves to me in love, I will deliver him;
     I will protect him, because he knows my name.
¹⁵ When he calls to me, I will answer him;
     I will be with him in trouble,
     I will rescue him and honor him.
¹⁶ With long life I will satisfy him,
     and show him my salvation.

91:1–2 Four prominent names for the Divine are here invoked in one passage: *Elyon*—Most High; *Shaddai*—Almighty; YHWH (Adonai)—Lord; Elohim—God.

Psalm 92

92 It is good to give thanks to the LORD,
     to sing praises to thy name, O Most High;
² to declare thy steadfast love in the morning,
     and thy faithfulness by night,
³ to the music of the lute and the harp,
     to the melody of the lyre.

⁴ For thou, O LORD, hast made me glad by thy work;
　　at the works of thy hands I sing for joy.

⁵ How great are thy works, O LORD!
　　Thy thoughts are very deep!
⁶ The dull man cannot know,
　　the stupid cannot understand this:
⁷ that, though the wicked sprout like grass
　　and all evildoers flourish,
　they are doomed to destruction for ever,
⁸　　but thou, O LORD, art on high for ever.
⁹ For, lo, thy enemies, O LORD,
　　for, lo, thy enemies shall perish;
　　all evildoers shall be scattered.

¹⁰ But thou has exalted my horn like that of the wild ox;
　　thou hast poured over me fresh oil.
¹¹ My eyes have seen the downfall of my enemies,
　　my ears have heard the doom of my evil assailants.

¹² The righteous flourish like the palm tree,
　　and grow like a cedar in Lebanon.
¹³ They are planted in the house of the LORD,
　　they flourish in the courts of our God.
¹⁴ They still bring forth fruit in old age,
　　they are ever full of sap and green,
¹⁵ to show that the LORD is upright;
　　he is my rock, and there is no unrighteousness in him.

92 : 1 This psalm is a favorite hymn in Jewish Sabbath worship. It also has a place in the daily evening prayer in the Protestant Episcopal church.

Psalm 95

Coverdale Bible

95 O come, let us sing unto the LORD; let us heartily rejoice in the strength of our salvation.

² Let us come before his presence with thanksgiving; and show ourselves glad in him with psalms.

³ For the LORD is a great God; and a great King above all gods.

⁴ In his hand are all the corners of the earth; and the strength of the hills is his also.

⁵ The sea is his, and he made it; and his hands prepared the dry land.

⁶ O come, let us worship and fall down, and kneel before the LORD our Maker.

⁷ For he is the LORD our God; and we are the people of his pasture, and the sheep of his hand.

⁸ To-day if ye will hear his voice, harden not your hearts as in the provocation, and as in the day of temptation in the wilderness;

⁹ When your fathers tempted me, proved me, and saw my works.

¹⁰ Forty years long was I grieved with this generation, and said, It is a people that do err in their hearts, for they have not known my ways:

¹¹ Unto whom I sware in my wrath, that they should not enter into my rest.

95:1 Psalms 95–100 emphasize God as king over the earth. They are called by modern commentators the "theocratic Psalms." Jewish commentators interpret these psalms as referring to a messianic time. They are recited on Friday evenings in the synagogue. On the Sabbath the Jew is to live as though to experience a foretaste of that time-to-come when all the world will be in peace.

The Prayer Book of the Church of England took its Psalter from the translation of Myles Coverdale, 1539. Under the title "Venite, exultemus Domino," the Book of Common Prayer of the Protestant Episcopal Church in the United States of America uses Psalm 95:1–7 in daily morning prayer. **95:6** Jews gave up kneeling at their prayer services when that tradition was widely adopted by the Christians. Jews now stand at attention at the holiest parts of their services. It is still the custom in the synagogue, however, for Jews to kneel or prostrate themselves on the Day of Atonement, at that part of the service which recalls a similar act by the High Priest in the Temple at Jerusalem.

Psalm 100

100 Make a joyful noise to the LORD, all the lands!

² Serve the LORD with gladness!
    Come into his presence with singing!

³ Know that the LORD is God!
    It is he that made us, and we are his;
    we are his people, and the sheep of his pasture.

⁴ Enter his gates with thanksgiving,
    and his courts with praise!
    Give thanks to him, bless his name!

⁵ For the LORD is good;
    his steadfast love endures for ever,
    and his faithfulness to all generations.

100:1 This psalm, used in the daily morning service in the synagogue, and in the Order for Daily Morning Worship in the Protestant Episcopal church has inspired many Christian hymns. The translation of Farrar Fenton, an English business man, published in 1903, here reads:

Hurrah to the Lord of all the Earth;
Serve the Lord with delight;
Come into His Presence with cheering.

Psalm 104

CCD

1 Bless the Lord, O my soul! O Lord, my God, you are great
2 indeed! You are clothed with majesty and glory, | robed in
light as with a cloak. You have spread out the heavens like a
3 tent-cloth; | you have constructed your palace upon the
waters. You make the clouds your chariot; you travel on the
4 wings of the wind. | You make the winds your messengers,
and flaming fire your ministers.

5 You fixed the earth upon its foundation, not to be moved
6 forever; | with the ocean, as with a garment, you covered it;
7 above the mountains the waters stood. | At your rebuke they
8 fled, at the sound of your thunder they took to flight; | as the
mountains rose, they went down the valleys to the place you
9 had fixed for them. | You set a limit they may not pass, nor
shall they cover the earth again.

10 You send forth springs into the watercourses that wind
11 among the mountains, | and give drink to every beast of the
12 field, till the wild asses quench their thirst. | Beside them the
birds of heaven dwell; from among the branches they send
13 forth their song. | You water the mountains from your
14 palace; the earth is replete with the fruit of your works. | You
raise grass for the cattle, and vegetation for men's use,
15 producing bread from the earth, | and wine to gladden men's
hearts, so that their faces gleam with oil, and bread fortifies
16 the hearts of men. | Well watered are the trees of the Lord,
17 the cedars of Lebanon, which he planted; | in them the birds
18 build their nests; fir trees are the home of the stork. | The high
mountains are for wild goats; the cliffs are a refuge for
rock-badgers.

19 You made the moon to mark the seasons; the sun knows
20 the hour of its setting. | You bring darkness, and it is night;
21 then all the beasts of the forest roam about; | young lions roar
22 for the prey and seek their food from God. | When the sun

²³ rises, they withdraw and couch in their dens. | Man goes
forth to his work and to his tillage till the evening.

²⁴   How manifold are your works, O Lord! In wisdom you
have wrought them all—the earth is full of your creatures;
²⁵ | the sea also, great and wide, in which are schools without
²⁶ number of living things both small and great, | and where
ships move about with Leviathan, which you formed to make
sport of it.

²⁷·²⁸   They all look to you to give them food in due time. | When
you give it to them, they gather it; when you open your
²⁹ hand, they are filled with good things. | If you hide your face,
they are dismayed; if you take away their breath, they perish
³⁰ and return to their dust. | When you send forth your spirit,
they are created, and you renew the face of the earth.

³¹   May the glory of the Lord endure forever; may the Lord
³² be glad in his works! | He who looks upon the earth, and it
³³ trembles; who touches the mountains, and they smoke! | I will
sing to the Lord all my life; I will sing praise to my God
³⁴ while I live. | Pleasing to him be my theme; I will be glad in
³⁵ the Lord. | May sinners cease from the earth, and may the
wicked be no more. Bless the Lord, O my soul! Alleluia.

104:1 Referring to God's creation of the universe, this psalm is
recited in the synagogue on Sabbath afternoons during the winter
months and is part of the morning service at the celebration of the
beginning of each month. **104:15** In the Bible, wine drunk in
moderation is accepted as a festive stimulant. See Ecclesiastes 10:17
and Proverbs 31:4 ff., however, for criticism of a nation's leaders who
waste themselves in carousing and drinking. See also Jeremiah 35 for
praise of the Rechabites who eschewed any alcoholic beverage altogether. **104:24** Parallel poetic descriptions have been uncovered in a
song of praise to the Sun-God composed by Pharaoh Ikhnaton (1375–
1358 B.C.). **104:30** The word "Spirit" when capitalized expresses the
personified aspect of God's influence. Jews translating the Hebrew
Bible, however, will render the Hebrew word "ruach" as "breath" or
"spirit" uncapitalized. The new Catholic "Jerusalem Bible" following
the Hebrew translates this verse: "You give *breath*, fresh life begins,
you keep renewing the world." See discussion at 51:11.

Psalm 113

113 Praise the Lord!
    Praise, O servants of the Lord,
        praise the name of the Lord!

² Blessed be the name of the Lord
        from this time forth and for evermore!

³ From the rising of the sun to its setting
    the name of the LORD is to be praised!
⁴ The LORD is high above all nations,
    and his glory above the heavens!

⁵ Who is like the LORD our God,
    who is seated on high,
⁶ who looks far down
    upon the heavens and the earth?
⁷ He raises the poor from the dust,
    and lifts the needy from the ash heap,
⁸ to make them sit with princes,
    with the princes of his people.
⁹ He gives the barren woman a home,
    making her the joyous mother of children.
    Praise the LORD!

113:1 The first of the Hallel, or Praise, Psalms, this psalm and its companions 114–118 are recited as one unit in the synagogue particularly during important festivals, such as Passover, Shavuoth, Succoth and Hanukkah. It is believed that Psalms 115–118 are the "hymns" recited by the disciples of Jesus after the Last Supper (Mark 14:26 and Matthew 26:30). **113:9** See these verses: Sarah, Genesis 17:15–21; Hannah, 1 Samuel 1–2.

Psalm 118
Jewish Publication Society

"O give thanks unto the LORD for He is good.
    For His mercy endureth for ever.'
² So let Israel now say,
    For His mercy endureth for ever.
    So let the house of Aaron now say,
    For His mercy endureth for ever.
⁴ So let them now that fear the LORD say,
    For His mercy endureth for ever.
⁵ Out of my straits I called upon the LORD;
    He answered me with great enlargement.
⁶ The LORD is for me; I will not fear;
    What can man do unto me?
⁷ The LORD is for me as my helper;
    And I shall gaze upon them that hate me.
⁸ It is better to take refuge in the LORD
    Than to trust in man.
⁹ It is better to take refuge in the LORD
    Than to trust in princes.

¹⁰ All nations compass me about;
Verily, in the name of the LORD I will cut them off.
¹¹ They compass me about, yea, they compass me about;
Verily, in the name of the LORD I will cut them off.
¹² They compass me about like bees;
They are quenched as the fire of thorns;
Verily, in the name of the LORD I will cut them off.
¹³ Thou didst thrust sore at me that I might fall;
But the LORD helped me.
¹⁴ The LORD is my strength and song;
And He is become my salvation.
¹⁵ The voice of rejoicing and salvation is in the tents of the
righteous;
The right hand of the LORD doeth valiantly.
¹⁶ The right hand of the LORD is exalted;
The right hand of the LORD doeth valiantly.
¹⁷ I shall not die, but live,
And declare the works of the LORD
¹⁸ The LORD hath chastened me sore;
But He hath not given me over unto death.
¹⁹ Open to me the gates of righteousness;
I will enter into them, I will give thanks unto the LORD.
²⁰ This is the gate of the LORD
The righteous shall enter into it.
²¹ I will give thanks unto Thee, for Thou has answered me,
And art become my salvation.
²² The stone which the builders rejected
Is become the chief corner-stone.
²³ This is the LORD's doing;
It is marvellous in our eyes.
²⁴ This is the day which the LORD hath made;
We will rejoice and be glad in it.
²⁵ We beseech Thee, O LORD, save now!
We beseech Thee, O LORD, make us now to prosper!
²⁶ Blessed be he that cometh in the name of the LORD;
We bless you out of the house of the LORD
²⁷ The LORD is God, and hath given us light;
Order the festival procession with boughs, even unto the horns
of the altar.
²⁸ Thou art my God, and I will give thanks unto Thee;
Thou art my God, I will exalt Thee.
²⁹ O give thanks unto the LORD, for He is good,
For His mercy endureth for ever.

118:1 Scholars believe that this Psalm was composed after the exile of the Hebrews into Babylonia and their return to Jerusalem. God had punished His people but would not utterly destroy them. He has now opened the gates of salvation to His people. It has been suggested that this Psalm was composed for the Succoth celebration at the dedication of the Temple in 516 B.C. See Nehemiah 8:13–18. **118:2–4** The Israelites were called upon first to express their thanksgiving, then the priestly house of Aaron, and finally the proselytes, i.e., the Gentile converts who joined Israel and were known as "those who fear (revere) the Lord." **118:5** Martin Luther (1483–1546), Protestant Reformation leader, regarded the Psalms as a "little Bible." Of man he said: "Thou must learn to cry. Come now, thou lazy rascal, fall down upon thy knees, and set forth thy need with tears before God." **118:22** Jewish commentators interpreted this verse as referring to Israel, scorned of nations but central in God's plan of history. Jesus quotes this verse when he confronts the chief priests and elders in the Temple (Matthew 21:42). **118:25** This refrain is repeated in the special litany for the Succoth, Feast of Tabernacles, celebrated in the synagogue. The congregants parade around the sanctuary holding clusters of Lulav (bound stalks of palm, willow and myrtle leaves) as they sing this refrain. **118:26** Jewish Midrash suggests that Verse 26 was composed when David became King. It will be recited again when the Messiah appears. The multitude greeted Jesus with these verses when he entered Jerusalem (Matthew 21:9; Mark 11:9; Luke 19:38; John 12:13).

Psalm 119:1–16, 97–105

CCD

Aleph

1   Happy are they whose way is blameless, who walk in the
2 law of the Lord.|Happy are they who observe his decrees, who
3 seek him with all their heart,|and do no wrong, but walk in his
4 ways.|You have commanded that your precepts be diligently
5 kept.| Oh, that I might be firm in the ways of keeping your
6 statutes!|Then should I not be put to shame when I beheld all
7 your commands.| I will give you thanks with an upright heart,
8 when I have learned your just ordinances. | I will keep your
statutes; do not utterly forsake me.

Beth

9   How shall a young man be faultless in his way? By
10 keeping to your words.| With all my heart I seek you; let me
11 not stray from your commands.| Within my heart I treasure
12 your promise, that I may not sin against you.| Blessed are
13 you, O Lord; teach me your statutes.| With my lips I declare

14 all the ordinances of your mouth. | In the way of your decrees
15 I rejoice, as much as in all riches. | I will meditate on your
16 precepts and consider your ways. | In your statutes I will
delight; I will not forget your words.

Mem

97 How I love your law, O Lord! It is my meditation all the
98 day. | Your command has made me wiser than my enemies,
99 for it is ever with me. | I have more understanding than all
100 my teachers when your decrees are my meditation. | I have
more discernment than the elders, because I observe your
101 precepts. | From every evil way I withhold my feet, that I may
102 keep your words. | From your ordinances I turn not away, for
103 you have instructed me. | How sweet to my palate are your
104 promises, sweeter than honey to my mouth! | Through your
precepts I gain discernment; therefore I hate every false way.

Nun

105 A lamp to my feet is your word, a light to my path.

119:1 This is the longest psalm in the psalter, 176 verses; and it is
the largest chapter in the Bible. A hymn of praise for God's law, it is
an octuple acrostic: there are eight verses beginning with the first
letter of the Hebrew alphabet, then eight beginning with the second
letter, etc. We give here the first two of the selections, verses 1–16,
and then a series of verses that express the psalmist's delight in God's
commandments. This Psalm is read in the Divine Office of the
Catholic Church on all Sundays and major feasts. The first sixteen
verses of this Psalm are also sung or recited in a Catholic Church
when the body of a little child is brought for the burial service.

Psalm 121

121 I lift up my eyes to the hills.
   From whence does my help come?
2 My help comes from the LORD,
   who made heaven and earth.

3 He will not let your foot be moved,
   he who keeps you will not slumber.
4 Behold, he who keeps Israel
   will neither slumber nor sleep.

5 The LORD is your keeper;
   the LORD is your shade
   on your right hand.
6 The sun shall not smite you by day,
   nor the moon by night.

⁷ The LORD will keep you from all evil;
    he will keep your life.
⁸ The LORD will keep
    your going out and your coming in
    from this time forth and for evermore.

121:1 This psalm, praising God as the guardian of Israel, is part of the collection known as the Song of Ascents (Psalms 120–134), thought by some to be marching songs of pilgrims climbing up the hills to Jerusalem for the biblical festivals. Others hold that they were chanted by Levites stationed at the fifteen steps in the Temple leading from the court of women to the court of men.

Psalm 122

122 I was glad when they said to me,
    "Let us go to the house of the LORD!"
² Our feet have been standing
    within your gates, O Jerusalem!

³ Jerusalem, built as a city
    which is bound firmly together,
⁴ to which the tribes go up,
    the tribes of the LORD,
  as was decreed for Israel,
    to give thanks to the name of the LORD.
⁵ There thrones for judgment were set,
    the thrones of the house of David.

⁶ Pray for the peace of Jerusalem!
    "May they prosper who love you!
⁷ Peace be within your walls,
    and security within your towers!"
⁸ For my brethren and companions' sake
    I will say, "Peace be within you!"
⁹ For the sake of the house of the LORD our God,
    I will seek your good.

122:2 Pope Paul VI, first pope to visit the Holy Land, chose this psalm for recitation upon his arrival at Jerusalem's Damascus Gate on January 4, 1964.

Psalm 130

130 Out of the depths I cry to thee, O LORD!
    Lord, hear my voice!
  Let thy ears be attentive
    to the voice of my supplications!

³ If thou, O LORD, shouldst mark iniquities,
   Lord, who could stand?
⁴ But there is forgiveness with thee,
   that thou mayest be feared.

⁵ I wait for the LORD, my soul waits,
   and in his word I hope;
⁶ my soul waits for the LORD
   more than watchmen for the morning,
   more than watchmen for the morning.

⁷ O Israel, hope in the LORD!
   For with the LORD there is steadfast love,
   and with him is plenteous redemption.
⁸ And he will redeem Israel
   from all his iniquities.

130:1 Not a lament, this psalm ends with an affirmative expression of hope. There is plenteous redemption with God. He will redeem and forgive. Because of its contemplative nature, this Psalm is the final prayer of the day in many monasteries, convents and seminaries. It is usually recited privately while a bell tolls slowly. The same rite is observed at the moment a member of a religious community dies. The priest recites this Psalm when he meets the body at the beginning of the burial service. It is included in the Order for the Burial of the Dead in the Book of Common Prayer of the Protestant Episcopal Church and in the Service Book of the Lutheran Church in America.

Psalm 136

Jewish Publication Society

O give thanks unto the LORD, for He is good,
   For His mercy endureth for ever.
² O give thanks unto the God of gods,
   For His mercy endureth for ever.
³ O give thanks unto the Lord of lords,
   For His mercy endureth for ever.

⁴ To Him who alone doeth great wonders,
   For His mercy endureth for ever.
⁵ To Him that by understanding made the heavens,
   For His mercy endureth for ever.
⁶ To Him that spread forth the earth above the waters,
   For His mercy endureth for ever.
⁷ To Him that made great lights,
   For His mercy endureth for ever;

⁸ The sun to rule by day,
   For His mercy endureth for ever.
⁹ The moon and stars to rule by night,
   For His mercy endureth for ever.

¹⁰ To Him that smote Egypt in their first-born,
   For His mercy endureth for ever;
¹¹ And brought out Israel from among them,
   For His mercy endureth for ever;
¹² With a strong hand, and with an outstretched arm,
   For His mercy endureth for ever.
¹³ To Him who divided the Red Sea in sunder,
   For His mercy endureth for ever;
¹⁴ And made Israel to pass through the midst of it,
   For His mercy endureth for ever;
¹⁵ But overthrew Pharaoh and his host in the Red Sea,
   For His mercy endureth for ever.
¹⁶ To Him that led His people through the wilderness,
   For His mercy endureth for ever.

¹⁷ To Him that smote great kings;
   For His mercy endureth for ever;
¹⁸ And slew mighty kings,
   For His mercy endureth for ever;
¹⁹ Sihon king of the Amorites,
   For His mercy endureth for ever.
²⁰ And Og king of Bashan,
   For His mercy endureth for ever.
²¹ And gave their land for a heritage,
   For His mercy endureth for ever.
²² Even a heritage unto Israel His servant,
   For His mercy endureth for ever.

²³ Who remembered us in our low estate,
   For His mercy endureth for ever;
²⁴ And hath delivered us from our adversaries,
   For His mercy endureth for ever.
²⁵ Who giveth food to all flesh,
   For His mercy endureth for ever.
²⁶ O give thanks unto the God of heaven,
   For His mercy endureth for ever.

136:1 This psalm is known in Jewish tradition as "The Great Hallel." It praises God as creator of the universe and as author of history. It is unique in the use of the refrain "O give thanks," following each line; it must have been recited as a responsive reading or chant (See Ezra 3:11). It is used in the Jewish Passover service following the Hallel prayers (Psalms 113–118) at the close of the Seder meal.

Psalm 137

Jewish Publication Society

By the rivers of Babylon,
There we sat down, yes, we wept,
When we remembered Zion.
² Upon the willows in the midst thereof
We hanged up our harps.
³ For there they that led us captive asked of us words of song,
And our tormentors asked of us mirth:
'Sing us one of the songs of Zion.'

⁴ How shall we sing the LORD's song
In a foreign land?
⁵ If I forget thee, O Jerusalem,
Let my right hand forget her cunning.
⁶ Let my tongue cleave to the roof of my mouth,
If I remember thee not;
If I set not Jerusalem
Above my chiefest joy.

⁷ Remember, O LORD, against the children of Edom
The day of Jerusalem;
Who said: 'Rase it, rase it,
Even to the foundation thereof.'
⁸ O daughter of Babylon, that art to be destroyed;
Happy shall he be, that repayeth thee
As thou hast served us.
⁹ Happy shall he be, that taketh and dasheth thy little ones
Against the rock.

137:1 A beautiful dirge, this Psalm expresses the spiritual plight of the Judean exiles in Babylonia; they would rather hang up their harps than sing the revered Temple songs and be mocked by their captors. Some suggest that the Levites at that time believed they could worship God properly only in the Holy Land. The vow to remember Jerusalem became a slogan during the modern Zionist awakening. Verses 7–9 of this Psalm, making it the most shocking of imprecatory Psalms, are no longer used in Jewish liturgy, but beautiful Hebrew hymns have been composed of the earlier verses. In a time when there was no belief in a life after death, the call for vengeance over enemies was also an affirmation of confidence in God's justice. Later in the rabbinic period, the rabbis were to instruct Jews to hate

wickedness, not the wicked. And in the Hassidic period pious leaders
taught that it is a lack of love that turns a man toward evil. For a
Christian view, see Matthew 5:43–48.

Psalm 139

139 O Lord, thou hast searched me and known me!
    ² Thou knowest when I sit down and when I rise up;
        thou discernest my thoughts from afar.
    ³ Thou searchest out my path and my lying down,
        and art acquainted with all my ways.
    ⁴ Even before a word is on my tongue,
        lo, O Lord, thou knowest it altogether.
    ⁵ Thou dost beset me behind and before,
        and layest thy hand upon me.
    ⁶ Such knowledge is too wonderful for me;
        it is high, I cannot attain it.

    ⁷ Whither shall I go from thy Spirit?
        Or whither shall I flee from thy presence?
    ⁸ If I ascend to heaven, thou art there!
        If I make my bed in Sheol, thou art there!
    ⁹ If I take the wings of the morning
        and dwell in the uttermost parts of the sea,
    ¹⁰ even there thy hand shall lead me,
        and thy right hand shall hold me.
    ¹¹ If I say, "Let only darkness cover me,
        and the light about me be night,"
    ¹² even the darkness is not dark to thee,
        the night is bright as the day;
        for darkness is as light with thee.

    ¹³ For thou didst form my inward parts,
        thou didst knit me together in my mother's womb.
    ¹⁴ I praise thee, for thou art fearful and wonderful.
        Wonderful are thy works!
    Thou knowest me right well;
    ¹⁵   my frame was not hidden from thee,
    when I was being made in secret,
        intricately wrought in the depths of the earth.
    ¹⁶ Thy eyes beheld my unformed substance;
        in thy book were written, every one of them,
    the days that were formed for me,
        when as yet there was none of them.
    ¹⁷ How precious to me are thy thoughts, O God!
        How vast is the sum of them!

¹⁸ If I would count them, they are more than the sand.
When I awake, I am still with thee.

139 : 18 The Mass of Easter Sunday begins with the second part of this verse but in this form: *Resurrexi, et adhuc tecum sum* (usually translated: "I have risen and am still with you").

Psalm 145

Jewish Publication Society

I will extol Thee, my God, O King;
And I will bless Thy name for ever and ever.
² Every day will I bless Thee;
And I will praise Thy name for ever and ever.
³ Great is the LORD, and highly to be praised;
And His greatness is unsearchable.
⁴ One generation shall laud Thy works to another,
And shall declare Thy mighty acts.
⁵ The glorious splendour of Thy majesty,
And Thy wondrous works, will I rehearse.
⁶ And men shall speak of the might of Thy tremendous acts;
And I will tell of Thy greatness.
⁷ They shall utter the fame of Thy great goodness,
And shall sing of Thy righteousness.
⁸ The LORD is gracious, and full of compassion;
Slow to anger, and of great mercy.
⁹ The LORD is good to all;
And His tender mercies are over all His works.
¹⁰ All Thy works shall praise Thee, O LORD;
And Thy saints shall bless Thee.
¹¹ They shall speak of the glory of Thy kingdom.
And talk of Thy might;
¹² To make known to the sons of men His mighty acts,
And the glory of the majesty of His kingdom.
¹³ Thy kingdom is a kingdom for all ages,
And Thy dominion endureth throughout all generations.
¹⁴ The LORD upholdeth all that fall,
And raiseth up all those that are bowed down.
¹⁵ The eyes of all wait for Thee,
And Thou givest them their food in due season.
¹⁶ Thou openest Thy hand,
And satisfiest every living thing with favour.
¹⁷ The LORD is righteous in all His ways,
And gracious in all His works.

¹⁸ The LORD is nigh unto all them that call upon Him,
　　To all that call upon Him in truth.
¹⁹ He will fulfil the desire of them that fear Him;
　　He also will hear their cry, and will save them.
²⁰ The LORD preserveth all them that love Him;
　　But all the wicked will He destroy.
²¹ My mouth shall speak the praise of the LORD;
　　And let all flesh bless His holy name for ever and ever.

This Psalm in praise of God is recited three times a day in the synagogue. In the morning service it is joined with Psalms 146–150, all of which begin and end Halleluyah, "Praise ye the Lord." This Psalm is another of the acrostic Psalms. However, the verse for the Hebrew letter "Nun," is missing between verses 13–14. The Talmud explains that it had been an ominous phrase taken from Amos 3 "Fallen (*Naflah*) is the virgin of Israel, she shall no more rise." Because of the sad nature of this sentence it was excised from this Psalm. In the Greek translation, the Septuagint, another sentence was added: "Faithful (*Ne'eman*) is the Lord in all His works."

Psalm 150

150 Praise the LORD!
　　Praise God in his sanctuary;
　　　　praise him in his mighty firmament!
² Praise him for his mighty deeds;
　　praise him according to his exceeding greatness!

³ Praise him with trumpet sound;
　　praise him with lute and harp!
⁴ Praise him with timbrel and dance;
　　praise him with strings and pipe!
⁵ Praise him with sounding cymbals;
　　praise him with loud clashing cymbals!
⁶ Let everything that breathes praise the LORD!
　　Praise the LORD!

150:1 The last psalm in the psalter, this psalm serves as a doxology to the entire book. From the Hebrew words *Hallelu-yah*—Praise the Lord—comes the Hebrew title for the Book of Psalms, *Tehillim*—it is a book of praises to God.

The Proverbs

The Book of Proverbs is today commonly divided into thirty-one chapters, a pattern set by medieval arrangers. Chapters 1 to 24 are ascribed to King Solomon as author. Chapters 25 to 29 are said to have been edited by the "men of Hezekiah." Agur Bin Jakeh is traditionally credited with chapter 30, and a King Lemuel with the last chapter. Biblical books were often ascribed to great men. Most biblical scholars today agree that the Book of Proverbs derives from a long period of Hebraic experience, from the days of Solomon in the tenth century to the second century B.C., and that they were attributed to Solomon, famed for his wisdom, in order to win acceptance. Solomon may have collected proverbs that formed a nucleus for later additions.

Unlike the writings of the prophets, which resound with denunciation of personal and national unrighteousness, pleadings for justice and consoling visions of Israel's future glory, the Book of Proverbs provides nothing more than practical, this-worldly wisdom. The rabbis, nevertheless, likened the value of a proverb to "a king who has lost a piece of gold or a pearl, but by means of a wick, which is worth but a trifle, was able to find it again" (*Midrash Canticles* 1b). Each proverb is a shaft of light illuminating an aspect of truth. A basic theme is that all of man's life is under the judgment of God.

Proverbial literature allows for no gray area of good and evil. All behavior is either wise or foolish; it is in accordance with God's will or it is rebellious.

In the prophetic literature the wisdom of wise men was often scathingly repudiated. The wise had rejected the word of God (see Jeremiah 8:9, 9:23; Ezekiel 7:26). In the Book of Proverbs, however, Wisdom becomes the highest expression of God's will. The Hebrew author accepts man's ability, through conscience, without need of angel or mediator, to know God's way. Reward and punishment for conduct are this-worldly. Wickedness leads to a premature death (5:5; 9:18), while Wisdom confers long life (3:16). Although the ethical system is frequently utilitarian and materialistic, the ultimate purpose is man's achievement of a happy life and spiritual contentment (3:13–18).

The book's influence and popularity is reflected by its frequent use in the New Testament, in which at least 14 quotations and about 20 allusions are drawn from the Book of Proverbs.

The proverbs are not arranged by subject matter. It appears that separate collections of proverbs were merely joined together and the inscription of 1:1 added.

Some proverbs reflect the wisdom derived from experience: e.g., Do not rejoice when your enemy falls / And let not your heart be glad when he stumbleth (24:17). Others are folk sayings using idiomatic language and imagery of peasant origin: e.g., "A whip for the horses, a bridle for the ass / and a rod for the back of fools" (26:3).

The proverbs are written in verse form and show three types of parallelisms: *Synonymous:* The thought of the first verse is extended in different words by the second verse: e.g., My son, do not despise the Lord's discipline / or be weary of his reproof (3:11). *Antithetic:* The two verses contrast with each other: e.g., "Righteousness exalts a nation, / but sin is a reproach to any people" (14:34). *Synthetic:* The second verse is the conclusion of the first: e.g., "Do not withhold good from those to whom it is due, / when it is in your power to do it". (3:27).

Lessons are also drawn from the natural world: e.g., although ants were considered a lowly insect, the author in one series of selections describes their industriousness and then moralizes that the sluggard had better learn ants' ways (6:11–19). Lists of virtues or vices are also a feature: e.g., "There are six things which the Lord hateth,/seven which are an abomination to him." (6:16–19).

The Fear of the Lord is the Beginning of Knowledge

Chapters 1 to 9 offers a series of discourses in which Wisdom, seen as a knowledge of God's ways, is contrasted with the seductions of Immorality and Folly, all personified. Wisdom is conceived as the very first of God's works; God, with Wisdom present, formed and shaped the world.

Proverbs 1:1–9; 3:1–2, 5–7, 11–18, 27–32;
6:6–11, 16–19, 23, 27–35

1 The proverbs of Solomon, son of David, king of Israel:

² That men may know wisdom and instruction,
    understand words of insight,
³ receive instruction in wise dealing,
    righteousness, justice, and equity;
⁴ that prudence may be given to the simple,
    knowledge and discretion to the youth—
⁵ the wise man also may hear and increase in learning,
    and the man of understanding acquiring skill,
⁶ to understand a proverb and a figure,
    the words of the wise and their riddles.

⁷ The fear of the LORD is the beginning of knowledge;
    fools despise wisdom and instruction.

⁸ Hear, my son, your father's instruction,
    and reject not your mother's teaching;

⁹ for they are a fair garland for your head,
    and pendants for your neck.

3 My son, do not forget my teaching,
    but let your heart keep my commandments;
² for length of days and years of life
    and abundant welfare will they give you.

⁵ Trust in the LORD with all your heart,
    and do not rely on your own insight.
⁶ In all your ways acknowledge him,
    and he will make straight your paths.
⁷ Be not wise in your own eyes;
    fear the LORD, and turn away from evil.

¹¹ My son, do not despise the LORD's discipline
    or be weary of his reproof,
¹² for the LORD reproves him whom he loves,
    as a father the son in whom he delights.

¹³ Happy is the man who finds wisdom,
    and the man who gets understanding,
¹⁴ for the gain from it is better than gain from silver
    and its profit better than gold.
¹⁵ She is more precious than jewels,
    and nothing you desire can compare with her.
¹⁶ Long life is in her right hand;
    in her left hand are riches and honor.
¹⁷ Her ways are ways of pleasantness,
    and all her paths are peace.
¹⁸ She is a tree of life to those who lay hold of her;
    those who fold her fast are called happy.

²⁷ Do not withhold good from those to whom it is due,
    when it is in your power to do it.

²⁸ Do not say to your neighbor, "Go, and come again,
    tomorrow I will give it"—when you have it with you.
²⁹ Do not plan evil against your neighbor
    who dwells trustingly beside you.
³⁰ Do not contend with a man for no reason,
    when he has done you no harm.
³¹ Do not envy a man of violence
    and do not choose any of his ways;
³² for the perverse man is an abomination to the LORD,
    but the upright are in his confidence.

6 ⁶ Go to the ant, O sluggard;
    consider her ways, and be wise.
⁷ Without having any chief,
    officer or ruler,
⁸ she prepares her food in summer,
    and gathers her sustenance in harvest.
⁹ How long will you lie there, O sluggard?
    When will you arise from your sleep?
¹⁰ A little sleep, a little slumber,
    a little folding of the hands to rest,
¹¹ and poverty will come upon you like a vagabond,
    and want like an armed man.

¹⁶ There are six things which the LORD hates,
    seven which are an abomination to him;
¹⁷ haughty eyes, a lying tongue,
    and hands that shed innocent blood,
¹⁸ a heart that devises wicked plans,
    feet that make haste to run to evil,
¹⁹ a false witness who breathes out lies,
    and a man who sows discord among brothers.

²³ For the commandment is a lamp and the teaching a light,
    and the reproofs of discipline are the way of life,
²⁷ Can a man carry fire in his bosom
    and his clothes not be burned?
²⁸ Or can one walk upon hot coals
    and his feet not be scorched?
²⁹ So is he who goes in to his neighbor's wife;
    none who touches her will go unpunished.
³⁰ Do not men despise a thief if he steals
    to satisfy his appetite when he is hungry?
³¹ And if he is caught, he will pay sevenfold;
    he will give all the goods of his house.
³² He who commits adultery has no sense;
    he who does it destroys himself.
³³ Wounds and dishonour will he get,
    and his disgrace will not be wiped away.
³⁴ For jealousy makes a man furious,
    and he will not spare when he takes revenge.
³⁵ He will accept no compensation,
    nor be appeased though you multiply gifts.

1:1 According to 1 Kings 4:32, Solomon spoke three thousand proverbs. **3:2** Note that Proverbs promises to the faithful "length of days." When this was written the Hebrews had not yet developed a concept of reward in a life to come. **3:6** The eminent Orthodox rabbi, Samson Raphael Hirsch, cited this phrase to justify the pursuit of secular knowledge "so that one might know God in all ways." **3:17–18** With the chanting of these verses Jews return the Torah Scroll to the Ark after its reading as part of the Sabbath service.

Wisdom is the First of God's Works

In these verses Wisdom is personified and has a meaning larger than that of plain common sense. Reflecting perhaps the influence of Greek thought upon the Hebrews, Wisdom (*Logos*) is identified with Torah (Law), which the rabbis taught had also existed before creation and from which God drew His plans for the shaping of earth. John 1:1 identifies the God incarnate in Jesus with *Logos*, thus attributing to Jesus a significance that Jews had accepted in Torah. (See also Matthew 11:19; Luke 11:49; John 6:35.)

Proverbs 8:1–4, 10–11, 15–36

8 Does not wisdom call,
    does not understanding raise her voice?
²On the heights beside the way,
    in the paths she takes her stand;
³beside the gates in front of the town,
    at the entrance of the portals she cries aloud:
⁴"To you, O men, I call,
    and my cry is to the sons of men.

¹⁰Take my instruction instead of silver,
    and knowledge rather than choice gold;
¹¹for wisdom is better than jewels,
    and all that you may desire cannot compare with her.

¹⁵By me kings reign,
    and rulers decree what is just;
¹⁶by me princes rule,
    and nobles govern the earth.
¹⁷I love those who love me,
    and those who seek me diligently find me.
¹⁸Riches and honor are with me,
    enduring wealth and prosperity.
¹⁹My fruit is better than gold, even fine gold,
    and my yield than choice silver.

²⁰ I walk in the way of righteousness,
    in the paths of justice,
²¹ endowing with wealth those who love me,
    and filling their treasuries.

²² The LORD created me at the beginning of his work,
    the first of his acts of old.
²³ Ages ago I was set up,
    at the first, before the beginning of the earth.
²⁴ When there were no depths I was brought forth,
    when there were no springs abounding with water.
²⁵ Before the mountains had been shaped,
    before the hills, I was brought forth;
²⁶ before he had made the earth with its fields,
    or the first of the dust of the world.
²⁷ When he established the heavens, I was there,
    when he drew a circle on the face of the deep,
²⁸ when he made firm the skies above,
    when he established the fountains of the deep,
²⁹ when he assigned to the sea its limit,
    so that the waters might not transgress his command,
when he marked out the foundations of the earth,
³⁰   then I was beside him, like a master workman;
and I was daily his delight,
    rejoicing before him always,
³¹ rejoicing in his inhabited world
    and delighting in the sons of men.

³² And now, my sons, listen to me:
    happy are those who keep my ways.
³³ Hear instruction and be wise,
    and do not neglect it.
³⁴ Happy is the man who listens to me,
    watching daily at my gates,
    waiting beside my doors.
³⁵ For he who finds me finds life
    and obtains favor from the LORD;
³⁶ but he who misses me injures himself;
    all who hate me love death."

8:22 Verses 22–35 have long been used in liturgies of Christian churches, with application to the Virgin Mary, in the Mass on the Feast of the Immaculate Conception, December 8, a holy day of obligation on which American Catholics honor the saint to whose care they specially entrust their country.

Treasures of Wickedness Profit Not

Chapters 10 through 22 contain a large selection of unconnected pithy statements usually expressed in antithetical parallelisms. These are generally considered the core of the collection and the oldest of the proverbs, some perhaps dating back to King Solomon.

Proverbs 10:1–2, 11–12, 27–30; 11:1, 4, 14, 22; 12:4, 9, 18; 13:11–12, 20, 24; 14:29–34; 15:1, 13, 16–17, 22–23, 27; 16:2, 8–9, 18, 32; 17:1, 17, 22, 28; 18:2, 22, 24; 20:1, 9, 11–12, 17, 19–22; 21:2–3, 9, 13–15; 22:1–2, 6–7

10 A wise son makes a glad father,
    but a foolish son is a sorrow to his mother.
² Treasures gained by wickedness do not profit,
    but righteousness delivers from death.
¹¹ The mouth of the righteous is a fountain of life,
    but the mouth of the wicked conceals violence.
¹² Hatred stirs up strike,
    but love covers all offenses.
²⁷ The fear of the LORD prolongs life,
    but the years of the wicked will be short.
²⁸ The hope of the righteous ends in gladness,
    but the expectation of the wicked comes to nought.
²⁹ The LORD is a stronghold to him whose way is upright,
    but destruction to evildoers.
³⁰ The righteous will never be removed,
    but the wicked will not dwell in the land.

11 A false balance is an abomination to the LORD,
    but a just weight is his delight.
⁴ Riches do not profit in the day of wrath,
    but righteousness delivers from death.
¹⁴ Where there is no guidance, a people falls;
    but in an abundance of counselors there is safety.
²² Like a gold ring in a swine's snout
    is a beautiful woman without discretion.

12 ⁴ A good wife is the crown of her husband,
    but she who brings shame is like rottenness in his bones.
⁹ Better is a man of humble standing who works for himself
    than one who plays the great man but lacks bread.
¹⁸ There is one whose rash words are like sword thrusts,
    but the tongue of the wise brings healing.

13 ¹¹ Wealth hastily gotten will dwindle,
    but he who gathers little by little will increase it.

¹² Hope deferred makes the heart sick,
   but a desire fulfilled is a tree of life.
²⁰ He who walks with wise men becomes wise,
   but the companion of fools will suffer harm.
²⁴ He who spares the rod hates his son,
   but he who loves him is diligent to discipline him.
14 ²⁹ He who is slow to anger has great understanding,
   but he who has a hasty temper exalts folly.
³⁰ A tranquil mind gives life to the flesh,
   but passion makes the bones rot.
³¹ He who oppresses a poor man insults his Maker,
   but he who is kind to the needy honors him.
³² The wicked is overthrown through his evil-doing,
   but the righteous finds refuge through his integrity.
³³ Wisdom abides in the mind of a man of understanding,
   but it is not known in the heart of fools.
³⁴ Righteousness exalts a nation,
   but sin is a reproach to any people.
15 A soft answer turns away wrath,
   but a harsh word stirs up anger.
¹³ A glad heart makes a cheerful countenance,
   but by sorrow of heart the spirit is broken.
¹⁶ Better is a little with the fear of the Lord
   than great treasure and trouble with it.
¹⁷ Better is a dinner of herbs where love is
   than a fatted ox and hatred with it.
²² Without counsel plans go wrong,
   but with many advisers they succeed.
²³ To make an apt answer is a joy to a man,
   and a word in season, how good it is!
²⁷ He who is greedy for unjust gain makes trouble for his
     household,
   but he who hates bribes will live.
16 ² All the ways of a man are pure in his own eyes,
   but the Lord weighs the spirit.
⁸ Better is a little with righteousness
   than great revenues with injustice.
⁹ A man's mind plans his way,
   but the Lord directs his steps.
¹⁸ Pride goes before destruction,
   and a haughty spirit before a fall.
³² He who is slow to anger is better than the mighty,
   and he who rules his spirit than he who takes a city.

17 Better is a dry morsel with quiet
     than a house full of feasting with strife.
^{17} A friend loves at all times,
     and a brother is born for adversity.
^{22} A cheerful heart is a good medicine,
     but a downcast spirit dries up the bones.
^{28} Even a fool who keeps silent is considered wise;
     when he closes his lips, he is deemed intelligent.

18 ^{2} A fool takes no pleasure in understanding,
     but only in expressing his opinion.
^{22} He who finds a wife finds a good thing,
     and obtains favor from the LORD.
^{24} There are friends who pretend to be friends,
     but there is a friend who sticks closer than a brother.

20 Wine is a mocker, strong drink a brawler;
     and whoever is led astray by it is not wise.
^{9} Who can say, "I have made my heart clean;
     I am pure from my sin"?
^{11} Even a child makes himself known by his acts,
     whether what he does is pure and right.
^{12} The hearing ear and the seeing eye,
     the LORD has made them both.
^{17} Bread gained by deceit is sweet to a man,
     but afterward his mouth will be full of gravel.
^{19} He who goes about gossiping reveals secrets;
     therefore do not associate with one who speaks foolishly.
^{20} If one curses his father or his mother,
     his lamp will be put out in utter darkness.
^{21} An inheritance gotten hastily in the beginning
     will in the end not be blessed.
^{22} Do not say, "I will repay evil";
     wait for the LORD, and he will help you.

21 ^{22} Every way of a man is right in his own eyes,
     but the LORD weighs the heart.
^{3} To do righteousness and justice
     is more acceptable to the LORD than sacrifice.
^{9} It is better to live in a corner of the housetop
     than in a house shared with a contentious woman.
^{13} He who closes his ear to the cry of the poor
     will himself cry out and not be heard.
^{14} A gift in secret averts anger;
     and a bribe in the bosom, strong wrath.

¹⁵ When justice is done, it is a joy to the righteous,
  but dismay to evildoers.
22 A good name is to be chosen rather than great riches,
  and favor is better than silver or gold.
² The rich and the poor meet together;
  the LORD is the maker of them all.
⁶ Train up a child in the way he should go,
  and when he is old he will not depart from it.
⁷ The rich rules over the poor,
  and the borrower is the slave of the lender.

12:9 A difference in translation provides another meaning to this verse: e.g., "He that is despised and hath a servant is better than he that honoreth himself and lacketh bread" (KJV). **15:17** This selection of various translations of this verse, taken from *The Interpreter's Bible*, Volume 1, page 102, demonstrates the development of the English tongue and of the art of translation.

Proverbs 15:17

First Wycliffite Bible (ca. 1382)	Betere is to be clepid to wrtis with charitie, than to a fat calf with hate.
Second Wycliffite Bible (ca. 1400)	It is betere to be clepid to wortis with charitie, than with hatrede to a calf maad fat.
Coverdale Bible (1535)	Better is a meace of potage with loue, then a fat oxe with euell will.
Matthew Bible 1537)	Better is a messe of potage with loue, than a fat oxe with euyl wyll.
Taverner Bible (1539)	Better is a messe of potage with loue, than a fat oxe with euyl wyll.
Great Bible (1539)	Better is a measse of potage with loue, than a fat oxe with euell will.
Geneva Bible (1560)	Better is a dinner of grene herbes where loue is, than a stalled oxe and hatred therewith.
Bishops' Bible (1568)	Better is a dynner of hearbes with loue, than a fat oxe with euyll wyll.
Reims-Douay Bible (1609–10)	It is better to be called to herbes with charitie, than to an fatted calfe with hatred.

King James Version (1611)	Better is a dinner of herbes where loue is, than a stalled oxe and hatred therewith.
Revised Version English and American (1881–1885, 1901)	Better is a dinner of herbs where love is, than a stalled ox and hatred therewith.
Moffatt Old Testament (1924)	Better a dish of vegetables, with love, than the best beef served with hatred.
American Translation Old Testament (1931)	Better a dish of herbs, where love is, Than a fatted ox, and hatred with it.
Revised Standard Version (1946–52)	Better is a dinner of herbs where love is than a fatted ox and hatred with it.

Through Wisdom a House Is Built

The passage 22:17–24, a distinct unit in content and style, projects a form of teacher-pupil communication unlike the more dogmatic statements of earlier sections. These proverbs parallel sayings of an Egyptian teacher, Amen-em-ope, a contemporary of Jeremiah (600 B.C.), and both may have come from one source.

Proverbs 22:22–23, 28, 29; 23:29–34; 24:3–5, 29

22 ²² Do not rob the poor, because he is poor,
    or crush the afflicted at the gate;
  ²³ for the LORD will plead their cause
    and despoil of life those who despoil them.
  ²⁸ Remove not the ancient landmark
    which your fathers have set.
  ²⁹ Do you see a man skilful in his work?
    he will stand before kings;
    he will not stand before obscure men.
23 ²⁹ Who has woe? Who has sorrow?
    Who has strife? Who has complaining?
  Who has wounds without cause?
    Who has redness of eyes?
  ³⁰ Those who tarry long over wine,
    those who go to try mixed wine.
  ³¹ Do not look at wine when it is red,
    when it sparkles in the cup
    and goes down smoothly.
  ³² At the last it bites like a serpent,
    and stings like an adder.

³³ Your eyes will see strange things,
  and your mind utter perverse things.
³⁴ You will be like one who lies down in the midst of the sea,
  like one who lies on the top of a mast.

24 ³ By wisdom a house is built,
  and by understanding it is established;
⁴ by knowledge the rooms are filled
  with all precious and pleasant riches.
⁵ A wise man is mightier than a strong man;
  and a man of knowledge than he who has strength;
²⁹ Do not say, "I will do to him as he has done to me;
  I will pay the man back for what he has done."

24:29 This proverb and 25:21 provide scriptural background for
the teachings of Jesus in the Golden Rule (Matthew 7:12) and "Love
your enemies . . . do good to them that hate you" (Matthew 5:44).

Proverbs that "the Men of Hezekiah Copied"

The proverbs found today in chapters 25–29 were compiled (and
perhaps some were composed) during the reign of King Hezekiah of
Judah 720–692 B.C. Israel's defeat by Assyria in 721 stimulated a
religious revival among the people. The Talmud records that "the
men of Hezekiah" also edited the works of Isaiah, the Song of Songs,
and Ecclesiastes, but the latter two are probably much later. Many of
the sayings contained in Proverbs 25 to 29 have a folk quality about
them. The teacher-student style is dropped; the proverbs are
delivered more simply.

Proverbs 25:1, 16–18, 21–22, 28; 26:4–5; 27:2, 10;
28:1, 23, 26, 28

25 These also are proverbs of Solomon which the men of Hezekiah
king of Judah copied.
¹⁶ If you have found honey, eat only enough for you,
  lest you be sated with it and vomit it.
¹⁷ Let your foot be seldom in your neighbor's house,
  lest he become weary of you and hate you.
¹⁸ A man who bears false witness against his neighbor
  is like a war club, or a sword, or a sharp arrow.
²¹ If your enemy is hungry, give him bread to eat;
  and if he is thirsty, give him water to drink;
²² for you will heap coals of fire on his head,
  and the LORD will reward you.
²⁸ A man without self-control
  is like a city broken into and left without walls.

26 ⁴ Answer not a fool according to his folly,
    lest you be like him yourself.
  ⁵ Answer a fool according to his folly,
    lest he be wise in his own eyes.
27 ² Let another praise you, and not your own mouth;
    a stranger, and not your own lips.
  ¹⁰ Your friend, and your father's friend, do not forsake;
    and do not go to your brother's house in the day
      of your calamity.
  Better is a neighbor who is near
    than a brother who is far away.
28 The wicked flee when no one pursues,
    but the righteous are bold as a lion.
  ²³ He who rebukes a man will afterward find more favor
    than he who flatters with his tongue.
  ²⁶ He who trusts in his own mind is a fool;
    but he who walks in wisdom will be delivered.
  ²⁸ When the wicked rise, men hide themselves,
    but when they perish, the righteous increase.

26:4–5 These proverbs are obviously contradictory. The Rabbis were so troubled by such contradictions within the Book of Proverbs that they considered rejecting it from the canon. In this case, they decided that verse 24 is to be applied to secular matters, where silence is advisable; but verse 25 refers to religious matters: when a matter of spiritual principle is concerned one should speak up.

The Words of Agur

Some scholars believe that Agur and King Lemuel (31:1) were wise men of Edom or Arabia. Their sayings are preserved as separate collections within Proverbs. It is generally held that throughout the book there are to be found proverbs and sayings gathered from many nations in the Near East. Proverbs has been characterized as "a collection of collections."

Proverbs 30:5–9, 18–19, 21–28

30 ⁵ Every word of God proves true;
    he is a shield to those who take refuge in him.
  ⁶ Do not add to his words,
    lest he rebuke you, and you be found a liar.

  ⁷ Two things I ask of thee;
    deny them not to me before I die:
  ⁸ Remove far from me falsehood and lying;
    give me neither poverty nor riches;
    feed me with the food that is needful for me,

⁹lest I be full, and deny thee,
     and say, "Who is the LORD?"
or lest I be poor, and steal,
     and profane the name of my God.

¹⁸Three things are too wonderful for me;
     four I do not understand:
¹⁹the way of an eagle in the sky,
     the way of a serpent on a rock,
the way of a ship on the high seas,
     and the way of a man with a maiden.

²¹Under three things the earth trembles;
     under four it cannot bear up:
²²a slave when he becomes king,
     and a fool when he is filled with food;
²³an unloved woman when she gets a husband,
     and a maid when she succeeds her mistress.

²⁴Four things on earth are small,
     but they are exceedingly wise:
²⁵the ants are a people not strong,
     yet they provide their food in the summer;
²⁶the badgers are a people not mighty,
     yet they make their homes in the rocks;
²⁷the locusts have no king,
     yet all of them march in rank;
²⁸the lizard you can take in your hands,
     yet it is in kings' palaces.

A Woman of Valor

The Book of Proverbs comes to an end with this poem in praise of a virtuous woman. It consists of 22 verses in an alphabetic acrostic form: i.e., each line starts with a Hebrew letter in alphabetical order. This poem is still recited by husband and children in Jewish homes on Friday evening before the Sabbath meal. Portions are also recited at the funeral service for a worthy woman. Christian preachers have for centuries quoted phrases from it in praise of a woman or of wives in general. The Catholic Church uses the whole passage in the Mass of a woman who is canonized saint but not a virgin or martyr.

Proverbs 31:10–31

31¹⁰A good wife who can find?
     She is far more precious than jewels.

¹¹ The heart of her husband trusts in her,
    and he will have no lack of gain.
¹² She does him good, and not harm,
    all the days of her life.
¹³ She seeks wool and flax,
    and works with willing hands.
¹⁴ She is like the ships of the merchant,
    she brings her food from afar.
¹⁵ She rises while it is yet night
    and provides food for her household
    and tasks for her maidens.
¹⁶ She considers a field and buys it;
    with the fruit of her hands she plants a vineyard.
¹⁷ She girds her loins with strength
    and makes her arms strong.
¹⁸ She perceives that her merchandise is profitable.
    Her lamp does not go out at night.
¹⁹ She puts her hands to the distaff,
    and her hands hold the spindle.
²⁰ She opens her hand to the poor,
    and reaches out her hands to the needy.
²¹ She is not afraid of snow for her household,
    for all her household are clothed in scarlet.
²² She makes herself coverings;
    her clothing is fine linen and purple.
²³ Her husband is known in the gates,
    when he sits among the elders of the land.
²⁴ She makes linen garments and sells them;
    she delivers girdles to the merchant.
²⁵ Strength and dignity are her clothing,
    and she laughs at the time to come.
²⁵ She opens her mouth with wisdom,
    and the teaching of kindness is on her tongue.
²⁷ She looks well to the ways of her household,
    and does not eat the bread of idleness.
²⁸ Her children rise up and call her blessed;
    her husband also, and he praises her:
²⁹ "Many women have done excellently,
    but you surpass them all."
³⁰ Charm is deceitful and beauty is vain,
    but a woman who fears the LORD is to be praised.
³¹ Give her the fruit of her hands,
    and let her works praise her in the gates.

31:10 The Douay versions reads here: "Who shall find a valiant woman? Far and from the uttermost coasts is the price of her." *Valiant woman* is a translation for *mulier fortis*, the Latin words in the Vulgate text upon which the Douay translation is based.

Ecclesiastes

This book with its melancholy refrain, "vanity of vanities, all is vanity," is read in synagogues on Succoth, the Festival of Tabernacles, when Jews are commanded to rejoice. A contrasting note of skepticism about the durability of life's physical pleasures is thereby injected into a celebration of the harvest and the abundance of earth's produce.

The book itself expresses a contradictory mood of faith and futility. In one breath the author exalts the beauty of life and in the next expresses dejection at the sham, hypocrisy, injustice and vanity prevailing everywhere. Talmudic literature records that some rabbis wished "to hide this book," i.e., to exclude it from the canon. The majority view prevailed; the rabbis recognized that the preacher was honestly and courageously seeking life's meaning; and that finally after having measured all of life's philosophies, he had affirmed the quiet dignity of a life of reverence and obedience to God's Law.

Traditionally this book has been ascribed to King Solomon. Most biblical students today suggest, however, that the philosophical tone of the writing, the use of Persian words, and the evidence of grammatical forms prevalent in later Aramaic (all of these influencing later Hebrew biblical writings) point to an authorship at a later period, somewhere between 300 and 100 B.C.

This book is the fourth of the five *megilloth* or scrolls that are to be found in that section of the Hebrew Bible known as Writings.

All Is Vanity
Ecclesiastes 1:1–18

1 The words of the Preacher, the son of David,
  king in Jerusalem.
2 Vanity of vanities, says the Preacher,
  vanity of vanities! All is vanity.
3 What does man gain by all the toil
  at which he toils under the sun?
4 A generation goes, and a generation comes,
  but the earth remains for ever.
5 The sun rises and the sun goes down,
  and hastens to the place where it rises.
6 The wind blows to the south,
  and goes round to the north;
round and round goes the wind,
  and on its circuits the wind returns.

⁷ All streams run to the sea,
    but the sea is not full;
to the place where streams flow,
    there they flow again.
⁸ All things are full of weariness;
    a man cannot utter it;
the eye is not satisfied with seeing,
    nor the ear filled with hearing.
⁹ What has been is what will be,
    and what has been done is what will be done;
    and there is nothing new under the sun.
¹⁰ Is there a thing of which it is said,
    "See, this is new"?
It has been already,
    in the ages before us.
¹¹ There is no remembrance of former things,
    nor will there by any remembrance
of later things yet to happen
    among those who come after.

12 I the Preacher have been king over Israel in Jerusalem. ¹³ And I applied my mind to seek and to search out by wisdom all that is done under heaven; it is an unhappy business that God has given to the sons of men to be busy with. ¹⁴ I have seen everything that is done under the sun; and behold, all is vanity and a striving after wind.

¹⁵ What is crooked cannot be made straight,
    and what is lacking cannot be numbered.

16 I said to myself, "I have acquired great wisdom, surpassing all who were over Jerusalem before me; and my mind has had great experience of wisdom and knowledge." ¹⁷ And I applied my mind to know wisdom and to know madness and folly. I perceived that this also is but a striving after wind.

¹⁸ For in much wisdom is much vexation,
    and he who increases knowledge increases sorrow.

1:1 The Hebrew word *koheleth* may describe the function of one who addresses a congregation (Hebrew, *kahal*; Greek, *ekklesia*). Thus the word "preacher" and the title of this book are taken from the Greek "Ecclesiastes." An allusion in 1 Kings 8:1, where King Solomon is said to have gathered an assembly, is cited by those who think Solomon the author. **1:2** *Vanity of vanities:* The double use of this word in Hebrew expresses the superlative degree. Counting the plural as two, the rabbis note that the word "vanity" is used seven times in this sentence. This number has inspired many ideas: Koheleth was expressing a judgment on each day of creation; Koheleth was referring to seven stages in the growth and development of man, etc. **1:3** Gain, also translated "profit," occurs ten times in the book, but nowhere else in the Bible. Drawing upon a standard derived from a commercial value system, Koheleth asks at the beginning of this book, "What profit is there in life?" At the conclusion he recognizes that the worth of life is not to be measured by commercial standards. **1:10** A similar view was expressed by the Roman Emperor and stoic, Marcus Aurelius, who wrote: "They that come after us will see nothing new, and they who went before us saw nothing more than we have seen."

There Is a Time for Everything

Ecclesiastes 3:1–14, 16–17

3 For everything there is a season, and a time for every matter under heaven:

² a time to be born, and a time to die;

a time to plant, and a time to pluck up what is planted;

³ a time to kill, and a time to heal;

a time to break down, and a time to build up;

⁴ a time to weep, and a time to laugh;

a time to mourn, and a time to dance;

⁵ a time to cast away stones, and a time to gather
     stones together;

a time to embrace, and a time to refrain from embracing;

⁶ a time to seek, and a time to lose;

a time to keep, and a time to cast away;

⁷ a time to rend, and a time to sew;

a time to keep silence, and a time to speak;

⁸ a time to love, and a time to hate;

a time for war, and a time for peace.

⁹ What gain has the worker from his toil?

10 I have seen the business that God has given to the sons of men to be busy with. ¹¹ He has made everything beautiful in its time; also he has put eternity into man's mind, yet so that he cannot find out what God has done from the beginning to the end. ¹² I know that there is nothing better for them than to be happy and enjoy themselves as long as they live; ¹³ also that it is God's gift to man that everyone should eat and drink and take pleasure in all his toil. ¹⁴ I know that whatever God does endures for ever; nothing can be added to it, nor anything taken from it; God has made it so, in order that men should fear before him.

16 Moreover I saw under the sun that in the place of justice, even there was wickedness, and in the place of righteousness, even there was wickedness. ¹⁷ I said in my heart, God will judge the righteous and the wicked, for he has appointed a time for every matter, and for every work.

3:1 While most of the nation watched on television, verses 1–8 were read by a bishop at the funeral of John F. Kennedy, November 25, 1963, in Washington, D.C., because the passage had been one of the assassinated President's favorites from Scripture. **3:17** The Jewish Publication Society translation renders this verse: "I said in my heart: 'The righteous and the wicked God will judge; for there is a time *there* for every purpose and for every work.' " Some Jewish scholars in the post biblical period found in the word "there" an allusion to judgment after death.

There Is No Wisdom in the Grave
Ecclesiastes 9:1–12; 10:8; 11:1–2, 6–10

9 But all this I laid to heart, examining it all, how the righteous and the wise and their deeds are in the hand of God; whether it is love or hate man does not know. Everything before them is vanity, ²since one fate comes to all, to the righteous and the wicked, to the good and the evil, to the clean and the unclean, to him who sacrifices and him who does not sacrifice. As is the good man, so is the sinner; and he who swears is as he who shuns an oath. ³This is an evil in all that is done under the sun, that one fate comes to all; also the hearts of men are full of evil, and madness is in their hearts while they live, and after that they go to the dead. ⁴But he who is joined with all the living has hope, for a living dog is better than a dead lion. ⁵For the living know that they will die, but the dead know nothing, and they have no more reward; but the memory of them is lost. ⁶Their love and their hate and their envy have already perished, and they have no more for ever any share in all that is done under the sun.

7 Go, eat your bread with enjoyment, and drink your wine with a merry heart; for God has already approved what you do.

8 Let your garments be always white; let not oil be lacking on your head.

9 Enjoy life with the wife whom you love, all the days of your vain life which he has given you under the sun, because that is your portion in life and in your toil at which you toil under the sun. ¹⁰Whatever your hand finds to do, do it with your might; for there is no work or thought or knowledge or wisdom in Sheol, to which you are going.

11 Again I saw that under the sun the race is not to the swift, nor the battle to the strong, nor bread to the wise, nor riches to the intelligent, nor favor to the men of skill; but time and chance happen to them all. ¹²For man does not know his time. Like fish which are taken in an evil net, and like birds which are caught in a snare, so the sons of men are snared at an evil time, when it suddenly falls upon them.

10 [8] He who digs a pit will fall into it;
    and a serpent will bite him who breaks through a wall.

11 Cast you bread upon the waters,
    for you will find it after many days.
  [2] Give a portion to seven, or even to eight,
    for you know not what evil may happen on earth.

6 In the morning sow your seed, and at evening withhold not your hand; for you do not know which will prosper, this or that, or whether both alike will be good.

7 Light is sweet, and it is pleasant for the eyes to behold the sun.

8 For if a man lives many years, let him rejoice in them all; but let him remember that the days of darkness will be many. All that comes is vanity.

9 Rejoice, O young man, in your youth, and let your heart cheer you in the days of your youth; walk in the ways of your heart and the sight of your eyes. But know that for all these things God will bring you into judgment.

10 Remove vexation from your mind, and put away pain from your body; for youth and the dawn of life are vanity.

9:5 The Preacher's strong words here provide evidence that a concept of life after death was not part of the Hebrew faith until quite late in the biblical period—at least not until after 300 B.C.; its development, in fact, may have been due to the kinds of questions raised by Koheleth and Job. **11:9** Compare Numbers 15:39.

The End of the Matter: Fear God
Ecclesiastes 12:1–14

12 Remember also your Creator in the days of your youth, before the evil days come, and the years draw nigh, when you will say, "I have no pleasure in them"; [2] before the sun and the light and the moon and the stars are darkened and the clouds return after the rain; [3] in the day when the keepers of the house tremble, and the strong men are bent, and the grinders cease because they are few, and those that look through the windows are dimmed, [4] and the doors on the street are shut; when the sound of the grinding is low, and one rises up at the voice of a bird, and all the daughters of song are brought low; [5] they are afraid also of what is high, and terrors are in the way; the almond tree blossoms, the grasshopper drags itself along and desire fails; because man goes to his eternal home, and the mourners go about the streets; [6] before the silver cord is snapped, or the golden bowl is broken, or the pitcher is broken at the fountain, or the wheel broken at the cistern, [7] and the dust returns to the earth as it was, and the spirit returns to God who gave it. [8] Vanity of vanities, says the Preacher; all is vanity.

9 Besides being wise, the Preacher also taught the people knowledge, weighing and studying and arranging proverbs with great care. [10] The Preacher sought to find pleasing words, and uprightly he wrote words of truth.

11 The sayings of the wise are like goads, and like nails firmly fixed are the collected sayings which are given by one Shepherd. [12] My son, beware of anything beyond these. Of making many books there is no end, and much study is a weariness of the flesh.

13 The end of the matter; all has been heard. Fear God, and keep his commandments; for this is the whole duty of man. [14] For God will bring every deed into judgment, with every secret thing, whether good or evil.

Ecclesiastes 12:1–7
(David Macrae Translation, 1799)

Remember thy Creator in the days of youth, before the days of affliction come, and the years of old age approach, when thou shalt say, I have no pleasure in them. **2** Before the sun, and the light, and the moon, and the stars, become dark to thee, and the cloud return after rain, or one trouble come upon another. **3** When (the arms) the keepers of the (corporeal) house shall shake, and the strong ones (the limbs) be feeble, and (the teeth) the grinders shall cease, as being few (and unfit for use); and they that look out of the windows (the optic nerves of the eyes) become dim. **4** And the doors be shut in the streets (the lips fall in, the teeth being gone), and the sounding of the grinding (in eating) be low; and they shall rise up at the sounding of the bird (sleep being diminished and easily broken); and all the daughters of music (the accents of the voice, and the acuteness of the ear) fail. **5** They shall be afraid of (ascending) the place which is nigh (being weak and breathless); and fears (of stumbling) shall be in their way; and (gray hairs like) the almond tree's leaves shall flourish; and the grasshopper shall be a burden (small matters being troublesome, as being crooked and fretful); and the desire of enjoyment shall fail; for man goeth to his long home, and the mourners go about the streets. **6** Before the silver cord (the marrow of the backbone, with its roots and branches) be contracted; or the golden vial (the brain's membranes) be cracked, or the pitcher be broken at the fountain (the cavities and conveyers of the blood from the heart), or the wheel be broken at the cistern (the returns of it from the lungs, head, hands and feet); the double, yea, quadruple circulation be repeated, be interrupted and cease. **7**

Then shall the dust return to the earth as it was; and the spirit shall return to God who gave it.

12:1 David Macrae was a Scottish Presbyterian who included a commentary with his translation of the whole Bible. His commentary, as this selection indicates, was concise and was inserted directly into the text, within parenthesis. **12:2−7** Many interpretations are given to this passage where Koheleth describes the days of darkness. As the Macrae commentary suggests, Koheleth may be referring to the weakened powers of the organs of the body in old age. Another interpretation: this is the mood and feeling of one who experiences the diminution of his life force, here expressed in the figure of a gathering of a storm. **12:9−14** These verses serve as an epilogue. Some biblical critics believe that this conclusion was added to the original text by one who wanted to insure the book's inclusion in the canon.

The Song of Solomon

Many interpretations have been given to this book. It is considered by some scholars to be an ode composed on the wedding of King Solomon to one of his queens; by others, a collection of wedding songs for use at any wedding feast. Still other scholars consider it to be an allegorical expression of God's love for Israel or (by Christian scholars) God's love for the Church. And mystics have seen in this book the outpouring of an individual soul in love with God.

The scroll seems to describe the experiences of a beautiful shepherd maiden who has fallen in love with a shepherd of the same village. Her brothers disapprove of her choice and transfer her from her work in the pasture to the vineyard, hoping thereby to prevent further meetings with the shepherd. The king happens to meet the maiden and is smitten with her beauty. He tempts her with his love and wealth and seeks her hand. The ladies at the king's court, to which the maiden has been brought, taunt her for fidelity to her shepherd lover. The maiden dreams only of him; she imagines that he will rescue her. Impressed finally by her constancy, the king dismisses the maiden and she rejoins her beloved.

Whether this book should be included in the biblical canon was debated; many rabbis were critical of its attention to physical manifestations of love. Rabbi Akiba in the second century argued that the book should be interpreted in an allegorical sense as referring to the love between God and Israel. Such an interpretation was in keeping with a literary tradition used by several prophets who had similarly described the relation between Israel and God in terms of a bride and groom, or likened waywardness of Israel to marital infidelity, e.g., Hosea 2:4. 21; Isaiah 62:5; Jeremiah 2:2.

In Talmudic tradition it was held that "he who recites any of these verses as a wine song at a feast brings evil into the world" (*Sanhedrin* 10a). Similarly in the Christian tradition a church council in 553 banned a work of Bishop Theodore of Mopsuestia (360–429) that had offered a literal interpretation of this book.

Some noted personalities (e.g., the Church Father Origen in the third century and the German poet Goethe) have suggested that the Song of Songs is a collection of wedding songs. Although passages of this book are frequently still recited at weddings, its use in the Jewish and Christian traditions is based chiefly on its allegorical interpretation and message. Jews, for example, identify themselves with the Shulamite maiden and are encouraged in the reading to maintain their fidelity to God. No matter what dangers they may endure or how much they are tempted by the nations among whom they reside, they are inspired to remain faithful to God and His word, just as this maiden remained true to her shepherd lover.

Song of Songs is read on Passover in the synagogue. The book's authorship is traditionally ascribed to King Solomon, but there is no agreement on this point. Based on the language and how the text is interpreted many Bible students suggest a later date ranging from the fifth to the second centuries B.C. Various sections of the book appear to be disjointed, without logical sequence. Parts of it slip from imaginary conversation to actual dialogue, and the reading requires careful attention. Attempting to meet this difficulty some modern translations have taken liberties with the text, arranging it in dramatic form.

This book is the first of five scrolls or *megilloth* that are to be found in the section of the Hebrew Bible known as Writings. Since it was attributed to King Solomon it was located in the Greek Bible after Ecclesiastes, another book attributed to him.

The Maiden Is Like a Lily Among Thorns
Song of Solomon 1 : 1, 5–7; 2 : 1–7

1 The Song of Songs, which is Solomon's.
⁵ I am very dark, but comely,
  O daughters of Jerusalem,
 like the tents of Kedar,
  like the curtains of Solomon.
⁶ Do not gaze at me because I am swarthy,
  because the sun has scorched me.
 My mother's sons were angry with me,
  they made me keeper of the vineyards;
  but, my own vineyard I have not kept!
⁷ Tell me, you whom my soul loves,
  where you pasture your flock,
  where you make it lie down at noon;
 for why should I be like one who wanders
  beside the flocks of your companions?
2 I am a rose of Sharon,
  a lily of the valleys.
² As a lily among brambles,
  so is my love among maidens.
³ As an apple tree among the trees of the wood
  so is my beloved among young men.
 With great delight I sat in his shadow,
  and his fruit was sweet to my taste.
⁴ He brought me to the banqueting house,
  and his banner over me was love.
⁵ Sustain me with raisins,
  refresh me with apples;
  for I am sick with love.

⁶ O that his left hand were under my head,
    and that his right hand embraced me!
⁷ I adjure you, O daughters of Jerusalem,
    by the gazelles or the hinds of the field,
    that you stir not up nor awaken love
    until it please.

1:1 The repetition of the Hebrew word "song" (*Shir Hashirim*) is the biblical way of saying that this is the best of the songs composed by Solomon. Another example: *most* holy is rendered in Hebrew *Kodesh hakodashim*, "Holy of Holies"—the name given to the inner room of the Sanctuary in Jerusalem. **2:1** The maiden earlier (1:16) had described her shepherd lover as "fair and pleasant"; she speaks of herself in humble terms as only like a desert flower. The king compliments her (2:2): "If you are only a lily," he says, "compared to the women of Jerusalem you are like a lily among thorns." **2:3 ff.** The maiden pays no heed to the king's compliment and continues in a description of her lover; she cries out her need for his comfort and embrace. **2:5** In the Jewish allegorical interpretation of this verse it is suggested that the sickness (i.e., sufferings of Israel) results from love of God. A Midrash on this verse explains: The Congregation of Israel said to the Holy One, Blessed be He: "Master of the Universe, all the ills you bring upon me are to bring me to love you more." Another interpretation was offered: The congregation of Israel said to the Holy One, Blessed be He: "Master of the Universe, all the ills that the nations of the world bring upon me are because I love you." **2:7** The maiden pleads with the women of the court not to tempt her, to allow her to express her love to whomever her heart freely would choose. This refrain also serves as a literary device to mark the close of various sections (see 3:5). In the Hebrew a play of words suggests the seriousness of this adjuration. The Hebrew words *ayaloth* (gazelles) and *sebaoth* (hinds) evoke *Elohey Sebaoth* ("God of Hosts").

Arise My Love and Come Away

The maiden anticipates the arrival of her beloved. However, he cannot enter the wall of the building in which she is confined. He calls out to her, beseeching the sound of her voice. In love she responds in song, believed by some scholars to be excerpts of an old vineyard song.

Song of Solomon 2:8–3:5

2 ⁸ The voice of my beloved!
    Behold, he comes,
    leaping upon the mountains,
    bounding over the hills.

⁹ My beloved is like a gazelle,
    or a young stag.
Behold, there he stands
    behind our wall,
gazing in at the windows,
    looking through the lattice.
¹⁰ My beloved speaks and says to me:
"Arise, my love, my fair one,
    and come away;
¹¹ for lo, the winter is past,
    the rain is over and gone.
¹² The flowers appear on the earth,
    the time of singing has come,
and the voice of the turtledove
    is heard in our land.
¹³ The fig tree puts forth its figs,
    and the vines are in blossom;
    they give forth fragrance.
Arise, my love, my fair one,
    and come away.
¹⁴ O my dove, in the clefts of the rock,
    in the covert of the cliff,
let me see your face,
    let me hear your voice,
for your voice is sweet,
    and your face is comely.
¹⁵ Catch us the foxes,
    the little foxes,
that spoil the vineyards,
    for our vineyards are in blossom."

¹⁶ My beloved is mine and I am his,
    he pastures his flock among the lilies.
¹⁷ Until the day breathes
    and the shadows flee,
turn, my beloved, be like a gazelle,
    or a young stag upon rugged mountains.

3 Upon my bed by night
    I sought him whom my soul loves;
I sought him, but found him not;
    I called him, but he gave no answer.
² "I will rise now and go about the city,
    in the streets and in the squares;

I will seek him whom my soul loves."
  I sought him, but found him not.
³ The watchmen found me,
  as they went about in the city.
"Have you seen him whom my soul loves?"
⁴ Scarcely had I passed them,
  when I found him whom my soul loves.
I held him, and would not let him go
until I had brought him into my mother's house,
  and into the chamber of her that conceived me.
⁵ I adjure you, O daughters of Jerusalem,
  by the gazelles or the hinds of the field,
that you stir not up nor awaken love until it please.

2:15 The maiden comparing herself to a "vineyard" may be warning her lover of the danger in which she finds herself from the "little foxes," that is, from the ladies at court who seek to spoil her love. **2:16** She turns to the ladies and assures them that she is her beloved's. He will not be separated from her, nor can these women separate her from him. Among modern Jews this phrase (or others such as 7:10) is carved into the wedding band and embossed on marriage contracts.

The Lover Praises the Beauty of His Maiden

Song of Solomon 4:1–6, 9–12, 16

4 Behold, you are beautiful, my love,
  behold, you are beautiful!
Your eyes are doves
  behind your veil.
Your hair is like a flock of goats,
  moving down the slopes of Gilead.
² Your teeth are like a flock of shorn ewes
  that have come up from the washing,
all of which bear twins,
  and not one among them is bereaved.
³ Your lips are like a scarlet thread,
  and your mouth is lovely.
Your cheeks are like halves of a pomegranate
  behind your veil.
⁴ Your neck is like the tower of David,
  built for an arsenal,
whereon hang a thousand bucklers,
  all of them shields of warriors.

⁵ Your two breasts are like two fawns,
    twins of a gazelle,
    that feed among the lilies.
⁶ Until the day breathes
    and the shadows flee,
 I will hie me to the mountain of myrrh
    and the hill of frankincense.
⁷ You are all fair, my love;
    there is no flaw in you.

⁹ You have ravished my heart, my sister, my bride,
    you have ravished my heart with a glance of your eyes,
    with one jewel of your necklace.
¹⁰ How sweet is your love, my sister, my bride!
    how much better is your love than wine,
    and the fragrance of your oils than any spice!
¹¹ Your lips distil nectar, my bride;
    honey and milk are under your tongue;
    the scent of your garments is like the scent of Lebanon.
¹² A garden locked is my sister, my bride,
    a garden locked, a fountain sealed.

¹⁶ Awake, O north wind,
    and come, O south wind!
Blow upon my garden,
    let its fragrance be wafted abroad.
Let my beloved come to his garden,
    and eat its choicest fruits.

4:6 The maiden interrupts the praises of her beloved and promises to meet him at eventide. Delighted he continues with his song of praise (4:7–15). **4:7** In the Catholic liturgy this verse is used in reference to the Immaculate Conception. **4:16** The maiden pining for her beloved responds to his song of praise.

The Maiden Describes Her Beloved

The maiden is haunted by a bad dream: she cannot find her lover and she pleads with the ladies at the court, should they see him, to tell him that she longs for him (5:8). The ladies taunt her (5:9). "What is so special about your beloved?" they ask. The maiden answers with a vivid account of his handsome features (5:10–16).

Song of Solomon 5:5–6, 8–16

⁵ I arose to open to my beloved,
    and my hands dripped with myrrh,
my fingers with liquid myrrh,
    upon the handles of the bolt.

⁶ I opened to my beloved,
    but my beloved had turned and gone.
My soul failed me when he spoke.
I sought him, but found him not;
    I called him, but he gave no answer.
⁸ I adjure you, O daughters of Jerusalem,
    if you find my beloved,
that you tell him
    I am sick with love.

⁹ What is your beloved more than another beloved,
    O fairest among women?
What is your beloved more than another beloved,
    that you thus adjure us?

¹⁰ My beloved is all radiant and ruddy,
    distinguished among ten thousand.
¹¹ His head is the finest gold;
    his locks are wavy,
    black as a raven.
¹² His eyes are like doves
    beside springs of water,
bathed in milk,
    fitly set.
¹³ His cheeks are like beds of spices,
    yielding fragrance.
His lips are lilies,
    distilling liquid myrrh.
¹⁴ His arms are rounded gold,
    set with jewels.
His body is ivory work,
    encrusted with sapphires.
¹⁵ His legs are alabaster columns,
    set upon bases of gold.
His appearance is like Lebanon,
    choice as the cedars.
¹⁶ His speech is most sweet,
    and he is altogether desirable.
This is my beloved and this is my friend,
    O daughters of Jerusalem.

Love Is Strong as Death

The maiden is again wooed by the king (7:1–9), but her love for the
shepherd is faithful and enduring. She rejects the royal suitor (7:10);
then she calls upon her beloved (7:11–12) to take her back to their

village, to the vineyard, the place of their original meeting and there
to marry her. She recalls that her brothers were worried about her in
her youth and wished to protect her (8:8). They promised that if she
were like a "wall," i.e., maintained her virtue, they would reward
her; but if she were like a "door," that is promiscuous, they would
punish her. She boasts that she is now a woman and ready for
marriage; that she has been both faithful to her love and virtuous.
Her brothers are content and she is at peace.

Song of Solomon 7:6–12; 8:6–10

⁶ How fair and pleasant you are,
   O loved one, delectable maiden!
⁷ You are stately as a palm tree,
   and your breasts are like its clusters.
⁸ I say I will climb the palm tree
   and lay hold of its branches.
 Oh, may your breasts be like clusters of the vine,
   And the scent of your breath like apples,
⁹ and your kisses like the best wine
   that goes down smoothly,
   gliding over lips and teeth.

¹⁰ I am my beloved's,
   and his desire is for me.
¹¹ Come, my beloved,
   let us go forth into the fields,
   and lodge in the villages;
¹² let us go out early to the vineyards,
   and see whether the vines have budded,
 whether the grape blossoms have opened
   and the pomegranates are in bloom.
 There I will give you my love.

8 ⁶ Set me as a seal upon your heart,
   as a seal upon your arm;
 for love is strong as death,
   jealousy is cruel as the grave.
 Its flashes are flashes of fire,
   a most vehement flame.
⁷ Many waters cannot quench love,
   neither can floods drown it.
 If a man offered for love
   all the wealth of his house,
   it would be utterly scorned.

⁸ We have a little sister,
  and she has no breasts.
 What shall we do for our sister,
  on the day when she is spoken for?
⁹ If she is a wall,
  we will build upon her a battlement of silver;
 but if she is a door,
  we will enclose her with boards of cedar.
¹⁰ I was a wall,
  and my breasts were like towers;
 then I was in his eyes
  as one who brings peace.

The Book of Isaiah

According to Jewish tradition, Isaiah is second only to Moses in greatness. A life-long resident of Jerusalem he was qualified by birth and education to serve as a counselor to kings. Influenced as a young man by the earlier prophets, Amos and Hosea, Isaiah prophesied in Judah from the closing year in the reign of Uzziah, 740 B.C. through the successive rule of Jotham, Ahaz, and Hezekiah. Later Jewish tradition holds that he was put to death by King Manasseh.

The book of Isaiah consists of 66 chapters. These may be divided into three parts on the basis of their varying historical contexts and literary styles. Chapters 1 to 39 deal with the historical problems of Judah between 740 and 701 B.C. Chapters 40 to 55 pertain to the time when Judah was in captivity (between 587–538 B.C.). Chapters 56 to 66 speak of the situation of the exiles who returned from Babylonia to Palestine (between 538–400 B.C.). Many scholars today hold that the latter two collections of oracles were written by separate and unknown authors whose works were then bound up with the historical Isaiah of the earlier period. More conservative Jewish and Christian scholars state that the entire book is the work of one inspired author who was given the vision and power to speak of far-ranging events.

Like most prophets, Isaiah spoke his prophesies. Later they were recorded in scroll form by devoted followers. This book contains oratory of prophetic and poetic magnificence; understandably, therefore, passage after passage has found its way into the liturgy of church and synagogue.

Isaiah's first task was to warn his people against foreign alliances. He urged them to place their complete trust in God alone. Ultimately Isaiah's personal experience of God's presence led him to a ministry that went far beyond such offering of political counsel. God for Isaiah was "the Holy God." Isaiah taught that man by his unrighteousness and sinfulness had separated himself from God. Isaiah pleaded with his people to renew their holiness by a change of heart. He inveighed against the false piety that characterized Hebrew worship and he called the people to a service of justice.

Despite the eloquence of his scathing pronouncements the prophet is remembered best in Jewish tradition for his magnificent declarations of consolation. He promised his people that at some future time their enemies would be subdued, and Jerusalem restored. God, Isaiah promised, will blot out the sins of His people. He will reestablish His covenant with them forever.

The prophet brilliantly envisioned a Messianic era when men would live in peace and God's children rule to the ends of the earth. He encouraged the Hebrews to accept converts to the faith, and he invoked that time when all men will worship before the Lord: "I am coming to gather all nations and tongues; and they shall come and see my glory."

A copy of the Book of Isaiah has been discovered among the Dead Sea Scrolls. It is the oldest complete text of a biblical book now available in the ancient Hebrew, dated from the first century. Its language is almost identical with that preserved by the Jewish copyists (Masoretes), the Hebrew text still used in the synagogues.

ISAIAH 1–39

Ah! Sinful Nation Laden with Wickedness

Logically the Book of Isaiah should begin with chapter 6, where the prophet receives his call and commission. The opening chapter, however, serves as an introduction to the burden of Isaiah's ministry: Judah suffers misfortune because she has rebelled against the Lord. Were it not that God had protected a remnant of the nation, Judah would be utterly destroyed like Sodom and Gomorrah. Isaiah warns the nation: sacrifices and burnt offerings will be of no avail in making amends; God demands not a public display of religiosity, but moral reformation.

Chapter 1 is read as the prophetic portion in the synagogue on the Sabbath before the "Fast of the Ninth Day of Ab" (falling in late July or early August), commemorating the destruction of the Second Temple and the exile of the Hebrew people in A.D. 70.

Isaiah 1:1–20, 27–28

1 The vision of Isaiah the son of Amoz, which he saw concerning Judah and Jerusalem in the days of Uzzi'ah, Jotham, Ahaz, and Hezeki'ah, kings of Judah.
> ² Hear, O heavens, and give ear, O earth;
>> for the LORD has spoken:
> "Sons have I reared and brought up,
>> but they have rebelled against me.
> ³ The ox knows its owner,
>> and the ass its master's crib;
> but Israel does not know,
>> my people does not understand."
>
> ⁴ Ah, sinful nation,
>> a people laden with iniquity,
> offspring of evildoers,
>> sons who deal corruptly!
> They have forsaken the LORD,
>> they have despised the Holy One of Israel,
>> they are utterly estranged.

⁵ Why will you still be smitten,
    that you continue to rebel?
The whole head is sick,
    and the whole heart faint.
⁶ From the sole of the foot even to the head,
    there is no soundness in it,
but bruises and sores
    and bleeding wounds;
they are not pressed out, or bound up,
    or softened with oil.

⁷ Your country lies desolate,
    your cities are burned with fire;
in your very presence
    aliens devour your land;
    it is desolate, as overthrown by aliens.
⁸ And the daughter of Zion is left
    like a booth in a vineyard,
like a lodge in a cucumber field,
    like a besieged city.

⁹ If the LORD of hosts
    had not left us a few survivors,
we should have been like Sodom,
    and become like Gomor'rah.

¹⁰ Hear the word of the LORD,
    you rulers of Sodom!
Give ear to the teaching of our God,
    you people of Gomor'rah!
¹¹ "What to me is the multitude of your sacrifices?
    says the LORD;
I have had enough of burnt offerings of rams
    and the fat of fed beasts;
I do not delight in the blood of bulls,
    or of lambs, or of he-goats.

¹² "When you come to appear before me,
    who requires of you
    this trampling of my courts?
¹³ Bring no more vain offerings;
    incense is an abomination to me.
New moon and sabbath and the calling of assemblies—
    I cannot endure iniquity and solemn assembly.

14 Your new moons and your appointed feasts
        my soul hates;
they have become a burden to me,
        I am weary of bearing them.
15 When you spread forth your hands,
        I will hide my eyes from you;
even though you make many prayers,
        I will not listen;
        your hands are full of blood.
16 Wash yourselves; make yourselves clean;
        remove the evil of your doings
        from before my eyes;
cease to do evil,
17   learn to do good;
seek justice,
        correct oppression;
defend the fatherless,
        plead for the widow.
18 "Come now, let us reason together,
        says the LORD:
though your sins are like scarlet,
        they shall be as white as now;
though they are red like crimson,
        they shall become like wool.
19 If you are willing and obedient,
        you shall eat the good of the land;
20 But if you refuse and rebel,
        you shall be devoured by the sword;
        for the mouth of the LORD has spoken."

27 Zion shall be redeemed by justice,
        and those in her who repent, by righteousness.
28 But rebels and sinners shall be destroyed together,
        and those who forsake the LORD shall be consumed.

1:5–9 Isaiah used the occasion of a military defeat by Judah to associate that "punishment" with the nation's ethical immoralities and religious apostasy. Verse 6 has been adopted by the Christian Church in its liturgy to describe the suffering Messiah. **1:10–17** The performance of religious ritual without a corresponding commitment to social righteousness is attacked by many of the Hebrew prophets as false religion. See also Hosea 6:6; Amos 5:21; Micah 6:6–8; Jeremiah 6:20.

Nor Shall They Learn War Anymore

This is the first of Isaiah's messianic visions, i.e., a vision of a time to come when all nations will accept the law of God and not make war any more. Isaiah hopes to arouse the people to a moral and spiritual reformation. This prophesy is often read in Reform synagogues in the service introductory to the reading of the Scriptural lesson.

Isaiah 2:1–5

2 The word which Isaiah the son of Amoz saw concerning Judah and Jerusalem.

2 It shall come to pass in the latter days
    that the mountain of the house of the LORD
shall be established as the highest of the mountains,
    and shall be raised above the hills;
and all the nations shall flow to it,
3   and many peoples shall come, and say:
"Come, let us go up to the mountain of the LORD,
    to the house of the God of Jacob;
that he may teach us his ways
    and that we may walk in his paths."
For out of Zion shall go forth the law,
    and the word of the LORD from Jerusalem.
4 He shall judge between the nations,
    and shall decide for many peoples;
and they shall beat their swords into plowshares,
    and their spears into pruning hooks;
nation shall not lift up sword against nation,
    neither shall they learn war any more.

5 O house of Jacob,
    come, let us walk
    in the light of the LORD.

2:3 Characteristic of the Hebrew prophet is this conviction that the attainment of an era of universal peace will be accompanied by the acknowledgement of Israel's central role as a source of spiritual instruction for mankind.

The Lord Judges the Daughters of Zion

Isaiah 3:13–4:1

3 13 The LORD has taken his place to contend,
    he stands to judge his people.

¹⁴ The LORD enters into judgment
    with the elders and princes of his people:
"It is you who have devoured the vineyard,
    the spoil of the poor is in your houses.
¹⁵ What do you mean by crushing my people,
    by grinding the face of the poor?"
      says the Lord GOD of hosts.
¹⁶ The LORD said:
Because the daughters of Zion are haughty
    and walk with outstretched necks,
    glancing wantonly with their eyes,
mincing along as they go,
    tinkling with their feet;
¹⁷ the Lord will smite with a scab
    the heads of the daughters of Zion,
    and the LORD will lay bare their secret parts.

18 In that day the Lord will take away the finery of the anklets, the headbands, and the crescents; ¹⁹ the pendants, the bracelets, and the scarfs; ²⁰ the headdresses, the armlets, the sashes, the perfume boxes, and the amulets; ²¹ the signet rings and nose rings; ²² the festal robes, the mantles, the cloaks, and the handbags; ²³ the garments of gauze, the linen garments, the turbans, and the veils.

²⁴ Instead of perfume there will be rottenness;
    and instead of a girdle, a rope;
and instead of well-set hair, baldness;
    and instead of a rich robe, a girding of sackcloth;
    instead of beauty, shame.
²⁵ Your men shall fall by the sword
    and your mighty men in battle.
²⁶ And her gates shall lament and mourn;
    ravaged, she shall sit upon the ground.

4 And seven women shall take hold of one man in that day, saying, "We will eat our own bread and wear our own clothes, only let us be called by your name; take away our reproach."

The Parable of the Vineyard

The farmers must have nodded their heads in approval as Isaiah described the care with which a farmer tended this field which kept reverting to a wild state. How justified was the farmer to let this difficult land lie waste! Then the prophet brought his listeners up short. In a like manner, God had cared for Israel; but instead of justice he saw violence, theft, drunkenness, bribery, chicanery. Therefore a mighty military power (probably referring to the Assyrians) will invade the land and carry Israel into exile. Isaiah here defends God's justice and holiness in bringing such retribution upon his chosen people; a just and holy God will not forever protect an unrighteous people.

Isaiah 5:1–9, 11–13, 15–16, 20–30

5 Let me sing for my beloved
    a love song concerning his vineyard:
My beloved had a vineyard
    on a very fertile hill.
² He digged it and cleared it of stones,
    and planted it with choice vines;
he built a watchtower in the midst of it,
    and hewed out a wine vat in it;
and he looked for it to yield grapes,
    but it yielded wild grapes.

³ And now, O inhabitants of Jerusalem
    and men of Judah,
judge, I pray you, between me
    and my vineyard.
⁴ What more was there to do for my vineyard,
    that I have not done in it?
When I looked for it to yield grapes,
    why did it yield wild grapes?
⁵ And now I will tell you
    what I will do to my vineyard.
I will remove its hedge,
    and it shall be devoured;
I will break down its wall,
    and it shall be trampled down.
⁶ I will make it a waste;
    it shall not be pruned or hoed,
    and briers and thorns shall grow up;
I will also command the clouds
    that they rain no rain upon it.

⁷ For the vineyard of the LORD of hosts
    is the house of Israel,
and the men of Judah
    are his pleasant planting;
and he looked for justice,
    but behold, bloodshed;
for righteousness,
    but behold, a cry!

8 Woe to those who join house to house,
  who add field to field,
until there is no more room,
  and you are made to dwell alone
  in the midst of the land
9 The LORD of hosts has sworn in my hearing:
"Surely many houses shall be desolate,
  large and beautiful houses, without inhabitant."

11 Woe to those who rise early in the morning,
  that they may run after strong drink,
who tarry late into the evening
  till wine inflames them!
12 They have lyre and harp,
  timbrel and flute and wine at their feasts;
but they do not regard the deeds of the LORD,
  or see the work of his hands.

13 Therefore my people go into exile
  for want of knowledge;.
their honored men are dying of hunger,
  and their multitude is parched with thirst.
15 Man is bowed down, and men are brought low,
  and the eyes of the haughty are humbled.
16 But the LORD of hosts is exalted in justice,
  and the Holy God shows himself holy in righteousness.

20 Woe to those who call evil good
  and good evil,
who put darkness for light
  and light for darkness,
who put bitter for sweet
  and sweet for bitter!
21 Woe to those who are wise in their own eyes,
  and shrewd in their own sight!
22 Woe to those who are heroes at drinking wine,
  and valiant men in mixing strong drink,
23 who acquit the guilty for a bribe,
  and deprive the innocent of his right!

24 Therefore, as the tongue of fire devours the stubble,
  and as dry grass sinks down in the flame,
so their root will be as rottenness,
  and their blossom go up like dust;

for they have rejected the law of the LORD of hosts,
    and have despised the word of the Holy One of Israel.
[25] Therefore the anger of the LORD was kindled
      against his people,
  and he stretched out his hand against them and smote them,
    and the mountains quaked;
and their corpses were as refuse
  in the midst of the streets.
For all this his anger is not turned away
  and his hand is stretched out still.

[26] He will raise a signal for a nation afar off,
    and whistle for it from the ends of the earth;
  and lo, swiftly, speedily it comes!
[27] None is weary, none stumbles,
    none slumbers or sleeps,
not a waistcloth is loose,
    not a sandal-thong broken;
[28] their arrows are sharp,
    all their bows bent,
their horses' hoofs seem like flint,
    and their wheels like the whirlwind.
[29] Their roaring is like a lion,
    like young lions they roar;
they growl and seize their prey,
    they carry it off, and none can rescue.
[30] They will growl over it on that day,
    like the roaring of the sea.
And if one look to the land,
  behold, darkness and distress;
and the light is darkened by its clouds.

5:1 ff. The image of Israel as a vine was popular among the prophets. See Hosea 10:1; Jeremiah 2:21; 5:10; 6:9; 12:10; Ezekiel 13:1–8; 17:3–10; 19:10–14. **5:8** ff. The remainder of this selection contains a series of maledications directed against those sins that the prophet considered most venal: the corrupt concentration of economic power in the hands of a few; debauchery; the taking of bribes and the perversion of justice. Above all, Isaiah attacked those who were so insensitive to such immorality that they complacently considered their way of life sweet and good.

Holy, Holy, Holy Is the Lord of Hosts

This vision, initiating Isaiah into the calling of prophecy, occurred about 740 B.C., after the death of Uzziah under whose rule Judah

had prospered. Isaiah realized that the people had lapsed back
into injustice. They misused their prosperity. He attempted to
call them to righteousness. God warns the prophet: the people
will not comprehend his message until they have endured suffering or punishment for their sinfulness. But after Israel and
Judah have been devoured (verse 13), a holy seed will remain,
from whose indestructible stock the tree of Israel will again
spring to life. Like other prophets touched by God's presence
(e.g., Amos 3:8), Isaiah knew he could do no other than speak
the Lord's word. In poetic imagery Isaiah envisions *seraphim*
calling to each other, "Holy, holy, holy." This graphic vision has
inspired religious mystics, artists and musicians, both Jewish and
Christian.

Isaiah 6:1–13

6 In the year that King Uzzi'ah died I saw the Lord sitting upon a
throne, high and lifted up; and his train filled the temple. ²Above
him stood the seraphim; each had six wings: with two he covered his
face, and with two he covered his feet, and with two he flew. ³And
one called to another and said:

"Holy, holy, holy is the LORD of hosts;
   the whole earth is full of his glory."
⁴And the foundations of the thresholds shook at the voice of him
who called, and the house was filled with smoke. ⁵And I said: "Woe
is me! For I am lost; for I am a man of unclean lips, and I dwell in
the midst of a people of unclean lips; for my eyes have seen the King,
the LORD of hosts!"

6 Then flew one of the seraphim to me, having in his hand a
burning coal which he had taken with tongs from the altar. ⁷And he
touched my mouth, and said: "Behold, this has touched your lips;
your guilt is taken away, and your sin forgiven." ⁸And I heard the
voice of the Lord saying, "Whom shall I send, and who will go for
us?" Then I said, "Here am I! Send me." ⁹And he said, "Go, and say
to this people:

'Hear and hear, but do not understand;
   see and see, but do not perceive.'
¹⁰Make the heart of this people fat,
      and their ears heavy,
      and shut their eyes;
   lest they see with their eyes,
      and hear with their ears,
   and understand with their hearts,
      and turn and be healed."
¹¹Then I said, "How long, O Lord?" And he said:

"Until cities lie waste
  without inhabitant,
and houses without men,
  and the land is utterly desolate,
12 and the LORD removes men far away,
  and the forsaken places are many in the midst
    of the land.
13 And though a tenth remain in it,
  it will be burned again,
like a terebinth or an oak,
  whose stump remains standing
  when it is felled."
The holy seed is its stump.

6:3 This verse, recited while standing, is incorporated in the morning service in the synagogue known as the *Kedushah* or Sanctification. This theme that God is Holy is a central affirmation in Isaiah's ministry. The prophet interpreted this to mean that man in similar fashion must try to make himself holy (Leviticus 17:1 ff.), by avoiding all immorality (6:5–7) and most particularly by involving himself in every effort to establish God's justice (1:26; 5:16): "The Lord of hosts is exalted in justice and the Holy God shows himself holy in righteousness." The concept of "holiness" in the biblical tradition does not require of the individual an ascetic withdrawal from the world of men or a severe disciplined pattern of liturgical performances. It does require that man involve himself in the effort to secure a just and peaceful society.

The Lord Whistles for the Fly . . .
and for the Bee

Here we see Isaiah in his role as a counselor to kings. King Ahaz was panic-stricken when in 735 B.C. the combined powers, Syria and Ephraim (Israel), angered by Judah's refusal to join them in an alliance against Assyria, launched an attack on Judah. Isaiah assured King Ahaz that Judah would survive, whereas both Syria and Ephraim would fall to Assyria. Damascus, capital of Syria, was captured three years later, in 732, and Samaria, capital of Israel, experienced a similar fate in 722 (see 2 Kings 15:29–16:9). Isaiah warned Ahaz, however, that Assyria ("the bee") and Egypt ("the fly") would contend over Judah, lying on the natural caravan route between these mighty powers. Isaiah predicted that Assyria would win; he advised the king not to resist Assyria's might, but to trust the Lord to save Judah. Ahaz did not accept assurance easily, so God sent him a sign: A young woman will conceive and bear a son, Immanuel. Before the child is mature, he will have to eat of the natural produce of the field (honey) and of the flocks (curd), for the cultivated land will have been laid waste by Assyria's armies.

Isaiah 7: 1–19

7 In the days of Ahaz the son of Jotham, son of Uzzi'ah, king of Judah, Rezin the king of Syria and Pekah the son of Remali'ah the king of Israel came up to Jerusalem to wage war against it, but they could not conquer it. ² When the house of David was told, "Syria is in league with E'phraim," his heart and the heart of his people shook as the trees of the forest shake before the wind.

3 And the LORD said to Isaiah, "Go forth to meet Ahaz, you and She'ar-jash'ub your son, at the end of the conduit of the upper pool on the highway to the Fuller's Field, ⁴ and say to him, 'Take heed, be quiet, do not fear, and do not let your heart be faint because of these two smoldering stumps of firebrands, at the fierce anger of Rezin and Syria and the son of Remali'ah. ⁵ Because Syria, with E'phraim and the son of Remali'ah, has devised evil against you, saying, ⁶ "Let us go up against Judah and terrify it, and let us conquer it for ourselves, and set up the son of Ta'be-el as king in the midst of it," ⁷ thus says the Lord GOD:

It shall not stand,
and it shall not come to pass.
⁸ For the head of Syria is Damascus,
and the head of Damascus is Rezin.

(Within sixty-five years E'phraim will be broken to pieces so that it will no longer be a people.)

⁹ And the head of E'phraim is Samar'ia,
and the head of Samar'ia is the son of Remali'ah.

If you will not believe,
surely you shall not be established.' "

10 Again the LORD spoke to Ahaz, ¹¹ "Ask a sign of the LORD your God; let it be deep as Sheol or high as heaven." ¹² But Ahaz said, "I will not ask, and I will not put the LORD to the test." ¹³ And he said, "Hear then, O house of David! Is it too little for you to weary men, that you weary my God also? ¹⁴ Therefore the Lord himself will give you a sign. Behold, a young woman shall conceive and bear a son, and shall call his name Imman'u-el. ¹⁵ He shall eat curds and honey when he knows how to refuse the evil and choose the good. ¹⁶ For before the child knows how to refuse the evil and choose the good, the land before whose two kings you are in dread will be deserted. ¹⁷ The LORD will bring upon you and upon your people and upon your father's house such days as

have not come since the day that E'phraim departed from
Judah—the king of Assyria."

18 In that day the LORD will whistle for the fly which is at the
sources of the streams of Egypt, and for the bee which is in the land
of Assyria. ¹⁹ And they will all come and settle in the steep ravines,
and in the clefts of the rocks, and on all the thornbushes, and on all
the pastures.

> **7:3** Communities of Jewish exiles in later generations named their
> congregations *Shearit Yisrael,* the remnant of Israel. This was the
> name given the oldest synagogue in New York, founded in America's
> colonial period. These earliest Jews to come to the American con-
> tinent were remnants of Spanish Jews who had survived the In-
> quisition. This conviction that God would never permit Israel to be
> utterly destroyed has provided Jews with hope during every dark
> period in their history. **7:14** Some commentators suggest: Isaiah was
> here intending to warn King Ahaz that the next monarch, Hezekiah,
> would taste the bitterness of a land ravaged by the Assyrians even
> though he would be a monarch righteous in the eyes of the Lord.
> Hezekiah, in fact, did institute significant religious reforms. He
> campaigned against idolatry, and thought of himself as a pious man.
> But eventually he was made to pay tribute to Sennacherib, king of
> the Assyrians. Others interpret this passage to have a meaning far
> beyond the immediate moment: they see in it a prophecy of a
> Messiah-Redeemer. For centuries, many Christians (following the
> Septuagint) translated the Hebrew word *almah* as "virgin" and
> discerned in this verse a Messianic prophecy about Jesus and his
> mother, Mary. Though most Christian scholars now agree that the
> word means "maiden" or "young woman," the Church, following
> Matthew 1:23, which quotes the Septuagint, continues to apply the
> verse to Mary and her child Jesus, especially in the liturgy (e.g.,
> in the Mass of the Blessed Virgin Mary on Saturdays in Advent).

The Prophet Gives His Son a Name
Isaiah 8:1–8

8 Then the LORD said to me, "Take a large tablet and write upon it
in common characters, 'Belonging to Ma'her-shal'al-hash'-baz.' "
² And I got reliable witnesses, Uri'ah the priest and Zechari'ah the
son of Jeberechi'ah, to attest for me. ³ And I went to the
prophetess, and she conceived and bore a son. Then the LORD said
to me, "Call his name Ma'her-shal'al-hash'-baz; ⁴ for before the
child knows how to cry 'My father' or 'My mother,' the wealth of
Damascus and the spoil of Samar'ia will be carried away before the
king of Assyria."

5 The LORD spoke to me again: ⁶ "Because this people have

refused the waters of Shilo'ah that flow gently, and melt in fear before Rezin and the son of Remali'ah; [7] therefore, behold, the Lord is bringing up against them the waters of the River, mighty and many, the king of Assyria and all his glory; and it will rise over all its channels and go over all its banks; [8] and it will sweep on into Judah, it will overflow and pass on, reaching even to the neck; and its outspread wings will fill the breadth of your land, O Imman'u-el."

8:3 Isaiah gives his newly born son the name "Maher-Shalal-Hash-Baz" which means "Spoil speeds, Prey hastes," an ominous message referring to the riches of Syria and of Israel, soon to be carried off to Assyria. Lacking faith King Ahaz failed to follow Isaiah's advice. He turned to Assyria for help against Judah and Syria; and he lived to rue his decision (see 2 Kings 16:7–9). Isaiah was not the first to dramatize his prophetic message through the names given his children; see Hosea 1:4, 6, 9. **8:6** The *waters of Shiloah* refer to Jerusalem's only spring (see 2 Kings 20:20). Here it is a symbol of the silent, unobtrusive power of God, as the river Euphrates is a symbol of the power of Assyria in verse 7.

A Light Shines

Hebrew commentators understand Isaiah 9:2–5 as an account of the joy of the population when they will see the fall of Assyria, the verbs being in the prophetic perfect, best translated in the future tense. Verses 6–7 to these commentators are a contemporary reassertion of Hezekiah's dynastic claims and the Hebrew hope for a reunion of the divided kingdom, under the righteous Hezekiah. (For a fuller account of his reign, see 2 Kings 18–19.) Christians have traditionally read verses 6–7 as an allusion to the birth of Jesus and the peace that will come only in the Messianic era. Hence the verses are used as the opening prayer of the second and third Masses on Christmas Day (each priest is privileged to celebrate three Masses that day), and on the Octave Day, which commemorates the circumcision of Jesus. In Handel's oratorio, *The Messiah*, verses 6–7 are the climactic lines in the Christmas portion.

Isaiah 9:2–7

[2] The people who walked in darkness
    have seen a great light;
  those who dwelt in a land of deep darkness,
    on them has light shined.
[3] Thou has multiplied the nation,
    thou has increased its joy;
  they rejoice before thee
    as with joy at the harvest,
    as men rejoice when they divide the spoil.

⁴ For the yoke of his burden,
and the staff for his shoulder,
the rod of his oppressor,
thou hast broken as on the day of Mid′i·an.
⁵ For every boot of the tramping warrior
in battle tumult
and every garment rolled in blood
will be burned as fuel for the fire.
⁶ For to us a child is born,
to us a son is given;
and the government will be upon his shoulder,
and his name will be called
"Wonderful Counselor, Mighty God,
Everlasting Father, Prince of Peace."
⁷ Of the increase of his government and of peace
there will be no end,
upon the throne of David, and over his kingdom,
to establish it, and to uphold it
with justice and with righteousness
from this time forth and for evermore.

Woe to Assyria!

Isaiah had interpreted Assyria's attack on Israel and then Judah as
God's punishment of Hebrew sinfulness. God is the author of history.
But Assyria does not recognize that she is the rod of God's anger; the
king boasts of his own power. Isaiah therefore predicts that Assyria
herself will be cut down. It is Isaiah's insight from God that
arrogance and tyranny inevitably lead to self-destruction. After
Assyria's downfall, he predicts, a remnant of Israel will return in
faithfulness to God. Thus the wheel of history will have turned full
circle. To symbolize this view Isaiah had given his son (7:3) the
name "Shear-Yashub," "a remnant will return." Sennacherib, king
of Assyria, invaded Judah in 701 B.C.

Isaiah 10:5–21

⁵ Ah, Assyria, the rod of my anger,
the staff of my fury!
⁶ Against a godless nation I send him,
and against the people of my wrath I command him,
to take spoil and seize plunder,
and to tread them down like the mire of the streets.
⁷ But he does not so intend,
and his mind does not so think;
but it is in his mind to destroy,
and to cut off nations not a few;

⁸ for he says:
"Are not my commanders all kings?
⁹ Is not Calno like Car′chemish?
    Is not Hamath like Arpad?
    Is not Samar′ia like Damascus?
¹⁰ As my hand has reached to the kingdoms of the idols
    whose graven images were greater than
        those of Jerusalem and Samar′ia,
¹¹ shall I not do to Jerusalem and her idols
    as I have done to Samar′ia and her images?"

12 When the Lord has finished all his work on Mount Zion and on
Jerusalem he will punish the arrogant boasting of the king of Assyria
and his haughty pride. ¹³ For he says:

"By the strength of my hand I have done it,
    and by my wisdom, for I have understanding;
I have removed the boundaries of peoples,
    and have plundered their treasures;
    like a bull I have brought down those who sat on thrones.
¹⁴ My hand has found like a nest
    the wealth of the peoples;
and as men gather eggs that have been forsaken
    so I have gathered all the earth;
and there was none that moved a wing,
    or opened the mouth, or chirped."

¹⁵ Shall the ax vaunt itself over him who hews with it,
    or the saw magnify itself against him who wields it?
As if a rod should wield him who lifts it,
    or as if a staff should lift him who is not wood!
¹⁶ Therefore the Lord, the LORD of hosts,
    will send wasting sickness among his stout warriors,
and under his glory a burning will be kindled,
    like the burning of fire.
¹⁷ The light of Israel will become a fire,
    and his Holy One a flame;
and it will burn and devour
    his thorns and briers in one day.
¹⁸ The glory of his forest and of his fruitful land
    the LORD will destroy, both soul and body,
    and it will be as when a sick man wastes away.
¹⁹ The remnant of the trees of his forest will be so few
    that a child can write them down.

20 In that day the remnant of Israel and the survivors of the house of Jacob will no more lean upon him that smote them, but will lean upon the LORD, the Holy One of Israel, in truth. ²¹ A remnant will return, the remnant of Jacob, to the mighty God.

10:9 Calno, Carchemish, Hamath, Arpad were Assyrian cities destroyed by Assyrian kings between 738–717 B.C. In similar fashion, says Isaiah, because of the idolatry of her people, Jerusalem will also be punished.

Isaiah Describes the Messianic Age

This poetic description of the messianic age climaxes Isaiah's word of hope for the remnant of Israel. From the House of David will come a righteous leader who will rule in a period of universal peace; nature itself will be transformed. Then God will restore all the exiles from the far corners of the earth and Israel will once again be re-established in the Holy Land. This graphic picture of universal peace and the transformation of nature has stimulated many a poet and artist. It is included in the scriptural lesson recited in the synagogue on the concluding day of Passover.

Isaiah 11:1–9, 12

11 There shall come forth a shoot from the stump of Jesse,
    and a branch shall grow out of his roots.
² And the Spirit of the LORD shall rest upon him,
    the spirit of wisdom and understanding,
    the spirit of counsel and might,
    the spirit of knowledge and the fear of the LORD.
³ And his delight shall be in the fear of the LORD.

He shall not judge by what his eyes see,
    or decide by what his ears hear;
⁴ but with righteousness he shall judge the poor,
    and decide with equity for the meek of the earth;
and he shall smite the earth with the rod of his mouth,
    and with the breath of his lips he shall slay the wicked.
⁵ Righteousness shall be the girdle of his waist,
    and faithfulness the girdle of his loins.

⁶ The wolf shall dwell with the lamb,
    and the leopard shall lie down with the kid,
and the calf and the lion and the fatling together,
    and a little child shall lead them.
⁷ The cow and the bear shall feed;
    their young shall lie down together;
    and the lion shall eat straw like the ox.

⁸ The sucking child shall play over the hole of the asp,
  and the weaned child shall put his hand on the adder's den.
⁹ They shall not hurt or destroy
  in all my holy mountain;
 for the earth shall be full of the knowledge
   of the LORD
  as the waters cover the sea.

¹² He will raise an ensign for the nations,
  and will assemble the outcasts of Israel,
 and gather the dispersed of Judah
  from the four corners of the earth.

11:2 Christian tradition finds here the source of its teaching of "The Seven Gifts of the Holy Spirit." The Septuagint and Latin Vulgate add "piety" to the list enumerated here. **11:12** The prophet combines both a nationalistic and universalistic concern in his vision of the Messianic era: the scattered tribes of Israel will be reunited *and* an era of universal peace will be ushered in.

Isaiah Denounces Judah's Alliance with Egypt

Caught between Assyria and Egypt, King Hezekiah of Judah chose to reject Assyria's demands and ally himself with the new powerful Ethiopian ruler in Egypt about 703 B.C. Hezekiah thereby—like his father Ahaz before him—rejected the counsel of Isaiah, who had warned that the nation should place its confidence in the Lord only.

Isaiah 30:1–5, 8–16, 18

30 "Woe to the rebellious children," says the LORD,
  "who carry out a plan, but not mine;
 and who make a league, but not of my spirit,
   that they may add sin to sin;
² who set out to go down to Egypt,
  without asking for my counsel,
 to take refuge in the protection of Pharaoh,
   and to seek shelter in the shadow of Egypt!

³ Therefore shall the protection of Pharaoh turn to your shame,
  and the shelter in the shadow of Egypt to your humiliation.
⁴ For though his officials are at Zo'an
  and his envoys reach Ha'nes,
⁵ every one comes to shame
  through a people that cannot profit them,
 that brings neither help nor profit,
  but shame and disgrace."

[8] And now, go, write it before them on a tablet,
    and inscribe it in a book,
that it may be for the time to come
    as a witness for ever.

[9] For they are a rebellious people,
    lying sons,
sons who will not hear
    the instruction of the LORD;

[10] who say to the seers, "See not";
    and to the prophets,
      "Prophesy not to us what is right;
speak to us smooth things,
    prophesy illusions,

[11] leave the way, turn aside from the path,
    let us hear no more of the Holy One of Israel."

[12] Therefore thus says the Holy One of Israel,
"Because you despise this word,
    and trust in oppression and perverseness,
    and rely on them;

[13] therefore this iniquity shall be to you
    like a break in a high wall, bulging out,
      and about to collapse,
    whose crash comes suddenly, in an instant;

[14] and its breaking is like that of a potter's vessel
    which is smashed so ruthlessly
that among its fragments not a sherd is found
    with which to take fire from the hearth,
    or to dip up water out of the cistern."

[15] For thus said the Lord GOD, the Holy One of Israel,
    "In returning and rest you shall be saved;
    in quietness and in trust shall be your strength."
And you would not, [16] but you said,
"No! We will speed upon horses,"
    therefore you shall speed away;
and, "We will ride upon swift steeds,"
    therefore your pursuers shall be swift.

[18] Therefore the LORD waits to be gracious to you;
    therefore he exalts himself to show mercy to you.
For the LORD is a God of justice;
    blessed are all those who wait for him.

30:8 Isaiah, like the prophet Amos before him, now writes his prophecy in a book so that it may be preserved as a testimony of his counsel and as a witness against the policy followed by the frightened king.

God Delivers Jerusalem from Assyria

Despite Isaiah's anger at Hezekiah for his alliance with Egypt, he remained a friend to the king. Concerned for Judah's fate when Sennacherib in 701 besieged Jerusalem, Isaiah assured Hezekiah that the city would be saved by God's intervention. Compare 2 Kings 19:35 and note there.

Isaiah 33:1–2, 7–17; 37:33–37

33 Woe to you, destroyer,
    who yourself have not been destroyed;
you treacherous one,
    with whom none has dealt treacherously!
When you have ceased to destroy,
    you will be destroyed;
and when you have made an end of dealing treacherously,
    you will be dealt with treacherously.

² O LORD, be gracious to us; we wait for thee.
Be our arm every morning,
    our salvation in the time of trouble.

⁷ Behold the valiant ones cry without;
    the envoys of peace weep bitterly.
⁸ The highways lie waste,
    the wayfaring man ceases.
Covenants are broken,
    witnesses are despised,
    there is no regard for man.
⁹ The land mourns and languishes;
    Lebanon is confounded and withers away;
Sharon is like a desert;
    and Bashan and Carmel shake off their leaves.

¹⁰ "Now I will arise," says the LORD,
    "now I will lift myself up;
    now I will be exalted.
¹¹ You conceive chaff, you bring forth stubble;
    your breath is a fire that will consume you.
¹² And the people will be as if burned to lime,
    like thorns cut down, that are burned in the fire."

^{13} Hear, you who are far off, what I have done;
    and you who are near, acknowledge my might.
^{14} The sinners in Zion are afraid;
    trembling has seized the godless:
"Who among us can dwell with the devouring fire?
    Who among us can dwell with everlasting burnings?"
^{15} He who walks righteously and speaks uprightly,
    who despises the gain of oppressions,
who shakes his hands, lest they hold a bribe,
    who stops his ears from hearing of bloodshed
    and shuts his eyes from looking upon evil,
^{16} he will dwell on the heights;
    his place of defense will be the fortresses of rocks;
    his bread will be given him, his water will be sure.

^{17} Your eyes will see the king in his beauty;
    they will behold a land that stretches afar.

37 ^{33} "Therefore thus says the LORD concerning the king of Assyria: He shall not come into this city, or shoot an arrow there, or come before it with a shield, or cast up a siege mound against it. ^{34} By the way that he came, by the same he shall return, and he shall not come into this city, says the LORD. ^{35} For I will defend this city to save it, for my own sake and for the sake of my servant David."

36 And the angel of the LORD went forth, and slew a hundred and eighty-five thousand in the camp of the Assyrians; and when men arose early in the morning, behold, these were all dead bodies. ^{37} Then Sennach'erib king of Assyria departed, and went home and dwelt at Nin'eveh.

ISAIAH 40– 55

Speak Tenderly to Jerusalem

With this chapter the Book of Isaiah introduces prophecies directed to the exiles in Babylonia, announcing the end of the exile.

Isaiah 40 : 1-31

40 Comfort, comfort my people,
    says your God.
^{2} Speak tenderly to Jerusalem,
    and cry to her
that her warfare is ended,
    that her iniquity is pardoned,
that she has received from the LORD's hand
    double for all her sins.

³ A voice cries:
"In the wilderness prepare the way of the LORD.
　　make straight in the desert a highway for our God.
⁴ Every valley shall be lifted up,
　　and every mountain and hill be made low;
　the uneven ground shall become level,
　　and the rough places a plain.
⁵ And the glory of the LORD shall be revealed,
　　and all flesh shall see it together,
　　for the mouth of the LORD has spoken."

⁶ A voice says, "Cry!"
　　And I said, "What shall I cry?"
　All flesh is grass,
　　and all its beauty is like the flower of the field.
⁷ The grass withers, the flower fades,
　　when the breath of the LORD blows upon it;
　　surely the people is grass.
⁸ The grass withers, the flower fades;
　　but the word of our God will stand for ever.

⁹ Get you up to a high mountain,
　　O Zion, herald of good tidings;
　lift up your voice with strength,
　　O Jerusalem, herald of good tidings,
　　lift it up, fear not;
　say to the cities of Judah,
　　"Behold your God!"
¹⁰ Behold, the Lord GOD comes with might,
　　and his arm rules for him;
　behold, his reward is with him,
　　and his recompense before him.
¹¹ He will feed his flock like a shepherd,
　　he will gather the lambs in his arms,
　he will carry them in his bosom,
　　and gently lead those that are with young.

¹² Who has measured the waters in the hollow of his hand
　　and marked off the heavens with a span,
　enclosed the dust of the earth in a measure
　　and weighed the mountains in scales
　　and the hills in a balance?
¹³ Who has directed the Spirit of the LORD,
　　or as his counselor has instructed him?

¹⁴ Whom did he consult for his enlightenment,
and who taught him the path of justice,
and taught him knowledge,
and showed him the way of understanding?
¹⁵ Behold, the nations are like a drop from a bucket,
and are accounted as the dust on the scales;
behold, he takes up the isles like fine dust.
¹⁶ Lebanon would not suffice for fuel,
nor are its beasts enough for a burnt offering.
¹⁷ All the nations are as nothing before him,
they are accounted by him as less than
nothing and emptiness.

¹⁸ To whom then will you liken God,
or what likeness compare with him?
¹⁹ The idol! a workman casts it,
and a goldsmith overlays it with gold,
and casts for it silver chains.
²⁰ He who is impoverished chooses for an offering
wood that will not rot;
he seeks out a skilful craftsman
to set up an image that will not move.

²¹ Have you not known? Have you not heard?
Has it not been told you from the beginning?
Have you not understood from the foundations of
the earth?
²² It is he who sits above the circle of the earth,
and its inhabitants are like grasshoppers;
who stretches out the heavens like a curtain,
and spreads them like a tent to dwell in;
²³ who brings princes to nought,
and makes the rulers of the earth as nothing.

²⁴ Scarcely are they planted, scarcely sown,
scarcely has their stem taken root in the earth,
when he blows upon them, and they wither,
and the tempest carries them off like stubble.

²⁵ To whom then will you compare me,
that I should be like him? says the Holy One.
²⁶ Lift up your eyes on high and see:
who created these?
He who brings out their host by number,
calling them all by name;

by the greatness of his might,
    and because he is strong in power
    not one is missing.

²⁷ Why do you say, O Jacob,
    and speak, O Israel,
"My way is hid from the LORD,
    and my right is disregarded by my God"?
²⁸ Have you not known? Have you not heard?
The LORD is the everlasting God,
    the Creator of the ends of the earth.
He does not faint or grow weary,
    his understanding is unsearchable.
²⁹ He gives power to the faint,
    and to him who has no might he increases strength.

³⁰ Even youths shall faint and be weary,
    and young men shall fall exhausted;
³¹ but they who wait for the LORD shall renew
      their strength,
    they shall mount up with wings like eagles,
they shall run and not be weary,
    they shall walk and not faint.

40:3 The Latin text translates the Hebrew thus: *vox clamantis in deserto*, "a voice crying in the wilderness," now considered by Bible scholars to be a misreading, corrected in the RSV and other modern translations. It is the motto of Dartmouth College. In the New Testament this passage is quoted by John the Baptist, who called on the faithful to prepare for the Messiah's coming (Matthew 3:3). **40:18** Paul Tillich (1886–1965), a German-American philosopher-theologian, argued that no definition of God devised by human mind could adequately encompass and describe the whole nature of God.

My Servant Will Bring Forth Justice

This message is repeated several times in Isaiah 40–55; see 50:4–9; 52:13–15. Citing 41:8; 49:3 Jews hold that the Hebrew nation is personified in these "servant psalms." Christians interpret these passages as a reference to the sacrificial ministry of Jesus. (See Matthew 3:17; Luke 17–21; Acts 3:13.)

Isaiah 41:8–13; 42:1–9; 49:1–6

⁸ But you, Israel, my servant,
    Jacob, whom I have chosen,
    the offspring of Abraham, my friend;

⁹ you whom I took from the ends of the earth,
    and called from its farthest corners,
        saying to you, "You are my servant,
    I have chosen you and not cast you off";
¹⁰ fear not, for I am with you,
    be not dismayed, for I am your God;
I will strengthen you, I will help you,
    I will uphold you with my victorious right hand.

¹¹ Behold, all who are incensed against you
    shall be put to shame and confounded;
those who strive against you
    shall be as nothing and shall perish.
¹² You shall seek those who contend with you,
    but you shall not find them;
those who war against you
    shall be as nothing at all.
¹³ For I, the LORD your God,
    hold your right hand;
it is I who say to you, "Fear not,
    I will help you."

42 Behold my servant, whom I uphold,
    my chosen, in whom my soul delights;
I have put my Spirit upon him,
    he will bring forth justice to the nations,
² He will not cry or lift up his voice,
    or make it heard in the street;
³ a bruised reed he will not break,
    and a dimly burning wick he will not quench;
    he will faithfully bring forth justice.
⁴ He will not fail or be discouraged
    till he has established justice in the earth;
    and the coastlands wait for his law.

⁵ Thus says God, the LORD,
    who created the heavens and stretched them out,
    who spread forth the earth and what comes from it,
who gives breath to the people upon it
    and spirit to those who walk in it:
⁶ "I am the LORD, I have called you in righteousness,
    I have taken you by the hand and kept you;
I have given you as a covenant to the people,
    a light to the nations,

7 to open the eyes that are blind,
to bring out the prisoners from the dungeon,
from the prison those who sit in darkness.
8 I am the LORD, that is my name;
    my glory I give to no other,
    nor my praise to graven images.
9 Behold, the former things have come to pass,
    and new things I now declare;
before they spring forth
    I tell you of them."

49 Listen to me, O coastlands,
    and hearken, you people from afar.
The LORD called me from the womb,
    from the body of my mother he named my name.
2 He made my mouth like a sharp sword,
    in the shadow of his hand he hid me;
he made me a polished arrow,
    in his quiver he hid me away.
3 And he said to me, "You are my servant,
    Israel, in whom I will be glorified."
4 But I said, "I have labored in vain,
    I have spent my strength for nothing and vanity;
yet surely my right is with the LORD,
    and my recompense with my God."

5 And now the LORD says,
    who formed me from the womb to be his servant,
to bring Jacob back to him,
    and that Israel might be gathered to him,
for I am honored in the eyes of the LORD,
    and my God has become my strength—
6 he says:
"It is too light a thing that you should be my servant
    to raise up the tribes of Jacob
    and to restore the preserved of Israel;
    I will give you as a light to the nations,
    that my salvation may reach to the end of the earth."

42:4 On the basis of this and similar passages (such as Isaiah
11:11; 23:2; 24:15) the Baptist William Carey (1761–1834), an
English cobbler, developed a great interest in "the isles" of the seas
(as rendered in the KJV). Even pin-point dottings of the ocean were
precious in his sight; he was always eager to see God's justice
established through the globe. Ultimately Carey himself went to

India; he was one of the founders of the modern Protestant missionary enterprise.

Fear Not, for I have Redeemed Thee

The prophet again assures Israel: God loves His people and He will spare them. He will blot out the memory of their sins. Then exposing the foolishness of idols, the prophet urges the people to abandon paganism for the worship of the one God.

Isaiah 43 : 1–3a, 5–7, 10–11, 25; 44 : 1–2, 6b–22

43 But now thus says the LORD, he who created you, O Jacob,
    he who formed you, O Israel:
"Fear not, for I have redeemed you;
    I have called you by name, you are mine.
² When you pass through the waters I will be with you;
    and through the rivers, they shall not overwhelm you;
when you walk through fire you shall not be burned,
    and the flame shall not consume you.
³ For I am the LORD your God,
    the holy One of Israel, your Savior.
⁵ Fear not, for I am with you;
    I will bring your offspring from the east,
    and from the west I will gather you;
⁶ I will say to the north, Give up,
    and to the south, Do not withhold;
bring my sons from afar
    and my daughters from the end of the earth,
⁷ every one who is called by my name,
    whom I created for my glory,
    whom I formed and made."

¹⁰ "You are my witnesses," says the LORD,
    "and my servant whom I have chosen,
that you may know and believe me
    and understand that I am He.
Before me no god was formed,
    nor shall there be any after me.
¹¹ I, I am the LORD.
    and besides me there is no savior.

44 "But now hear, O Jacob my servant,
    Israel whom I have chosen!
² Thus says the LORD who made you,
    who formed you from the womb and will help you:

⁶ "I am the first and I am the last;
    besides me there is no god.
⁷ Who is like me? Let him proclaim it,
    let him declare and set it forth before me.
Who has announced from of old the things to come?
    Let them tell us what is yet to be.
⁸ Fear not, nor be afraid;
    have I not told you from of old and declared it?
And you are my witnesses!
Is there a God besides me?
    There is no Rock; I know not any."

9 All who make idols are nothing, and the things they delight in do not profit; their witnesses neither see nor know, that they may be put to shame. ¹⁰ Who fashions a god or casts an image, that is profitable for nothing? ¹¹ Behold, all his fellows shall be put to shame, and the craftsmen are but men; let them all assemble, let them stand forth, they shall be terrified, they shall be put to shame together.

12 The ironsmith fashions it and works it over the coals; he shapes it with hammers, and forges it with his strong arm; he becomes hungry and his strength fails, he drinks no water and is faint. ¹³ The carpenter stretches a line, he marks it out with a pencil; he fashions it with planes, and marks it with a compass; he shapes it into the figure of a man, with the beauty of a man, to dwell in a house. ¹⁴ He cuts down cedars; or he chooses a holm tree or an oak and lets it grow strong among the trees of the forest; he plants a cedar and the rain nourishes it. ¹⁵ Then it becomes fuel for a man; he takes a part of it and warms himself, he kindles a fire and bakes bread; also he makes a god and worships it, he makes it a graven image and falls down before it. ¹⁶ Half of it he burns in the fire; over the half he eats flesh, he roasts meat and is satisfied; also he warms himself and says, "Aha, I am warm, I have seen the fire!" ¹⁷ And the rest of it he makes into a god, his idol; and falls down to it and worships it; he prays to it and says, "Deliver me, for thou art my god!"

18 They know not, nor do they discern; for he has shut their eyes, so that they cannot see, and their minds, so that they cannot understand. ¹⁹ No one considers, nor is there knowledge or discernment to say, "Half of it I burned in the fire, I also baked bread on its coals, I roasted flesh and have eaten; and shall I make the residue of it an abomination? Shall I fall down before a block of wood?" ²⁰ He feeds on ashes; a deluded mind has led him astray, and he cannot deliver himself or say, "Is there not a lie in my right hand?"

²¹ Remember these things, O Jacob,
    and Israel, for you are my servant;
I formed you, you are my servant;
    O Israel, you will not be forgotten by me.
²² I have swept away your transgressions like a cloud,
    and your sins like mist;
return to me, for I have redeemed you.

43:10 An inclusive statement of monotheism, this theme is repeated many times in Isaiah 40–55. God is conceived as spirit transcending time and space.

Cyrus Is God's Anointed

The prophet declares that Cyrus, king of the Persians and Medes, victor over Babylonia, has been appointed by God to free the Hebrews. In time all people, in all the ends of the earth, will recognize through this deliverance of the Hebrews that there is only one God and that He is the author of history.

Isaiah 45:1–8, 22–23

45 Thus says the LORD to his anointed, to Cyrus,
    whose right hand I have grasped,
to subdue nations before him
    and ungird the loins of kings,
to open doors before him
    that gates may not be closed:
² "I will go before you
    and level the mountains,
I will break in pieces the doors of bronze
    and cut asunder the bars of iron,
³ I will give you the treasures of darkness
    and the hoards in secret places,
that you may know that it is I, the LORD,
    the God of Israel, who call you by your name.
⁴ For the sake of my servant Jacob,
    and Israel my chosen,
I call you by your name,
    I surname you, though you do not know me.
⁵ I am the LORD, and there is no other,
    besides me there is no God;
I gird you, though you do not know me,
⁶ that men may know, from the rising of the sun
    and from the west, that there is none besides me;
I am the LORD, and there is no other.

⁷ I form light and create darkness,
     I make weal and create woe,
     I am the LORD, who do all these things.

⁸ "Shower, O heavens, from above,
     and let the skies rain down righteousness;
   let the earth open, that salvation may sprout forth,
     and let it cause righteousness to spring up also;
     I the LORD have created it.

²² "Turn to me and be saved,
     all the ends of the earth!
   For I am God, and there is no other.
²³ By myself I have sworn,
     from my mouth has gone forth in righteousness
     a word that shall not return:
 'To me every knee shall bow,
     every tongue shall swear.' "

45:7 "I form the light, and create darkness: I make peace and create evil" (Jewish Publication Society). To assure that no one will mistakenly read this text literally and attribute to God evil purposes and motivations, the Hebrew prayer book has translated the words to read: "I make peace and create all things." The one God's responsibility for both light and darkness, peace and woe was strongly asserted in contrast to dualistic Persian beliefs that the world was ruled by Ahura Mazda, the god of light, and Ahrimon, the god of darkness. In the prophetic view whatever evil a nation suffered was not the result of arbitrary caprice by God, nor the work of a god of darkness, but rather the just consequence of their own sinfulness. **45:8** The Latin Vulgate renders the Hebrew word *Tzedek* ("righteousness") as "the Righteous One," thereby giving a messianic meaning to this text. For that reason this verse is included by Catholics in the Advent Liturgy. **45:22** A magnificent offer of salvation to the whole world. This prophetic call to "all the ends of the earth" (i.e., to the gentile nations) to turn to God and to be saved, was quoted in justification by those early Christians who argued that gentiles be converted to Christianity without the requirement of observance of Jewish law (cf. Acts 15:1 ff.). **45:23** The climactic Adoration Prayer recited at every service in the synagogue reads: "Fervently we pray that the day may come . . . when all who dwell on earth shall know that to Thee alone every knee must bend and every tongue give homage."

Where Is the Bill of Divorce?

The Hebrew exiles in Babylonia were afraid that their covenant relationship with God had been broken by the punishment of exile. The prophet reassures them: they are still God's people. Then he

comforts them: the exiles will return to their land, and there will be a
time of gladness and salvation.

Isaiah 50:1; 52:1−2, 7−10

50 Thus says the LORD:
  "Where is your mother's bill of divorce,
      with which I put her away?
  Or which of my creditors is it
      to whom I have sold you?
  Behold, for your iniquities you were sold,
      and for your transgressions your mother was put away."

52 Awake, awake,
      put on your strength, O Zion;
  put on your beautiful garments,
      O Jerusalem, the holy city;
  for there shall no more come into you
      the uncircumcised and the unclean.
  ² Shake yourself from the dust, arise,
      O captive Jerusalem;
  loose the bonds from your neck,
      O captive daughter of Zion.
  ⁷ How beautiful upon the mountains
      are the feet of him who brings good tidings,
  who publishes peace, who brings good tidings of good,
      who publishes salvation,
      who says to Zion, "Your God reigns."
  ⁸ Hark, your watchmen lift up their voice,
      together they sing for joy;
  for eye to eye they see
      the return of the LORD to Zion.
  ⁹ Break forth together into singing,
      you waste places of Jerusalem;
  for the LORD has comforted his people,
      he has redeemed Jerusalem.
  ¹⁰ The LORD has bared his holy arm
      before the eyes of all the nations;
  and all the ends of the earth shall see
      the salvation of our God.

50:1 See also Hosea 2:4−9 where Israel is first pictured in
prophetic literature as a faithless wife. A bill of divorcement would be
required to set aside a wife (Deuteronomy 24:1). Isaiah assures his
listeners: the marriage between God and Israel has not been broken.

The Suffering Servant Bears the Sins of Many

Some commentators suggest that this prophecy is a personification of the sufferings of the dispersed Hebrew people, soon to be gloriously rewarded by the ending of the exile and the restoration of Zion. Others suggest that it is a description of the hardships endured by a prophet of the exile, and the promise of glory that will be his and his people's, in return for his sacrificial service to men and God. Christians have traditionally seen in it a description of the sufferings of Jesus.

Isaiah 52:13–15; 53:1–12

13 Behold, my servant shall prosper,
    he shall be exalted and lifted up,
    and shall be very high.
14 As many were astonished at him—
    his appearance was so marred, beyond human semblance,
    and his form beyond that of the sons of men—
15 so shall he startle many nations;
    kings shall shut their mouths because of him;
for that which has not been told them they shall see,
    and that which they have not heard they shall understand.

53 Who has believed what we have heard?
    And to whom has the arm of the LORD been revealed?
2 For he grew up before him like a young plant,
    and like a root out of dry ground;
he had no form or comeliness that we should look at him,
    and no beauty that we should desire him.
3 He was despised and rejected by men;
    a man of sorrows, and acquainted with grief;
and as one from whom men hide their faces
    he was despised, and we esteemed him not.

4 Surely he has borne our griefs
    and carried our sorrows,
yet we esteemed him stricken,
    smitten by God, and afflicted.
5 But he was wounded for our transgressions,
    he was bruised for our iniquities;
upon him was the chastisement that made us whole,
    and with his stripes we are healed.
6 All we like sheep have gone astray;
    we have turned every one to his own way;
and the LORD has laid on him
    the iniquity of us all.

⁷ He was oppressed, and he was afflicted,
    yet he opened not his mouth;
like a lamb that is led to the slaughter,
    and like a sheep that before its shearers is dumb,
    so he opened not his mouth.
⁸ By oppression and judgment he was taken away;
    and as for his generation, who considered
that he was cut off out of the land of the living,
    stricken for the transgression of my people?
⁹ And they made his grave with the wicked
    and with a rich man in his death,
although he had done no violence,
    and there was no deceit in his mouth.

¹⁰ Yet it was the will of the LORD to bruise him;
    he has put him to grief;
when he makes himself an offering for sin,
    he shall see his offspring, he shall prolong his days;
the will of the LORD shall prosper in his hand;
¹¹   he shall see the fruit of the travail of his soul and be satisfied;
by his knowledge shall the righteous one, my servant,
    make many to be accounted righteous;
    and he shall bear their iniquities.
¹² Therefore I will divide him a portion with the great,
    and he shall divide the spoil with the strong;
because he poured out his soul to death,
    and was numbered with the transgressors;
yet he bore the sin of many,
    and made intercession for the transgressors.

53:1–12 This passage is read in the Mass on Wednesday of Holy Week just before the reading of Luke's Passion account (Luke 22:39 ff.). The Catholic liturgy for Lent, using both Old and New Testaments, draws a parallel between the teaching of the Evangelists and St. Paul on Jesus' sufferings and the prophecies of Isaiah, Jeremiah, Jonah and Daniel. **53:5–12** Paul quotes these verses (1 Corinthians 15:3) to justify from Scripture the fact that the Messiah could be crucified and that his death was an atonement for the sin of men.

Seek the Lord While He May Be Found

The people's return to God evokes a promise of the fulfillment of the Davidic dynasty and a renewal of the everlasting covenant between God and Israel.

Isaiah 55:1–13

"Ho, every one who thirsts,
 come to the waters;
and he who has no money,
 come, buy, and eat!
Come, buy wine and milk
 without money and without price.
2 Why do you spend your money for that which is not bread,
 and your labor for that which does not satisfy?
Hearken diligently to me, and eat what is good,
 and delight yourselves in fatness.
3 Incline your ear, and come to me;
 hear, that your soul may live;
and I will make with you an everlasting covenant,
 my steadfast, sure love for David.
4 Behold, I made him a witness to the peoples,
 a leader and commander for the peoples.
5 Behold, you shall call nations that you know not,
 and nations that knew you not shall run to you,
because of the LORD your God, and of the Holy One of Israel,
 for he has glorified you.

6 "Seek the LORD while he may be found,
 call upon him while he is near;
7 let the wicked forsake his way,
 and the unrighteous man his thoughts;
let him return to the LORD, that he may have mercy on him,
 and to our God, for he will abundantly pardon.
8 For my thoughts are not your thoughts,
 neither are your ways my ways, says the LORD.
9 For as the heavens are higher than the earth,
 so are my ways higher than your ways
 and my thoughts than your thoughts.

10 "For as the rain and the snow come down from heaven,
 and return not thither but water the earth,
making it bring forth and sprout,
 giving seed to the sower and bread to the eater,
11 so shall my word be that goes forth from my mouth;
 it shall not return to me empty,
but it shall accomplish that which I purpose,
 and prosper in the thing for which I sent it.

¹² "For you shall go out in joy,
    and be led forth in peace;
the mountains and the hills before you
    shall break forth into singing,
    and all the trees of the field shall clap their hands.
¹³ Instead of the thorn shall come up the cypress;
    instead of the brier shall come up the myrtle;
and it shall be to the LORD for a memorial,
    for an everlasting sign which shall not be cut off."

55:8−9 There have been philosophers in all times who have sought, through their philosophies, to make the nature of God comprehensible to man. Other Christian theologians have contended that such an effort was a hopeless enterprise. Søren Kierkegaard (1813−1855), the Danish thinker, argued: "The gulf is unbridgeable. God the unsearchable is not man. God is God and world is world." Similarly German theologian Karl Barth (1886−1968) insisted that we cannot speak of God merely by speaking of man in a loud tone of voice.

God Welcomes Converts in Israel

Isaiah 56−66

Many scholars believe that this passage introduces the writings of a third Isaiah. The historical context of this passage may be that post-exilic period when Ezra and Nehemiah, in an effort to maintain religious purity, compelled the Judeans to set aside their foreign wives. There was much resistance. Some scholars believe that the Book of Jonah (describing the merit of despised Ninevites who repented of their evil ways) and the Book of Ruth (pointing to the beloved Ruth, a Moabite, as a model convert) were short stories written in protest to the official harsh policy. In a spirit similarly critical of Ezra's edict Isaiah would here be suggesting that if foreigners observed the Jewish religious laws they should certainly be made welcome into the Jewish faith.

Isaiah 56:1−8

56 Thus says the LORD:
    "Keep justice, and do righteousness,
    for soon my salvation will come,
        and my deliverance be revealed.
² Blessed is the man who does this,
    and the son of man who holds it fast,
who keeps the sabbath, not profaning it,
    and keeps his hand from doing any evil."

³ Let not the foreigner who has joined himself to the LORD say,
   "The LORD will surely separate me from his people";
and let not the eunuch say,
   "Behold, I am a dry tree."
⁴ For thus says the LORD:
"To the eunuchs who keep my sabbaths,
   who choose the things that please me
   and hold fast my covenant,
⁵ I will give in my house and within my walls
   a monument and a name
   better than sons and daughters;
I will give them an everlasting name
   which shall not be cut off.

⁶ "And the foreigners who join themselves to the LORD,
   to minister to him, to love the name of the LORD,
   and to be his servants,
every one who keeps the sabbath, and does not profane it,
   and holds fast my covenant—
⁷ these I will bring to my holy mountain,
   and make them joyful in my house of prayer;
their burnt offerings and their sacrifices
   will be accepted on my altar;
for my house shall be called a house of prayer
   for all peoples.
⁸ Thus says the Lord GOD,
   who gathers the outcasts of Israel,
I will gather yet others to him
   besides those already gathered."

The Fasting That God Wishes

Penitence, the prophet warns Israel, will not be achieved by fasting
apart from a sincere turning of the heart. God desires that man act
justly toward his fellow man in accordance with God's Law. This
selection is recited in the synagogue at the morning service on
the Day of Atonement, a day when Jews observe a fast before the
Lord as a sign of their penitence. The Christian liturgy also makes
use of this proclamation at the beginning of Lent.

Isaiah 58:1–14

58 "Cry aloud, spare not,
   lift up your voice like a trumpet;
declare to my people their transgression,
   to the house of Jacob their sins.

² Yet they seek me daily,
 and delight to know my ways,
as if they were a nation that did righteousness
 and did not forsake the ordinance of their God;
they ask of me righteous judgments,
 they delight to draw near to God.
³ 'Why have we fasted, and thou seest it not?
 Why have we humbled ourselves, and thou takest no
  knowledge of it?'
Behold, in the day of your fast you seek your own pleasure,
 and oppress all your workers.
⁴ Behold, you fast only to quarrel and to fight
 and to hit with wicked fist.
Fasting like yours this day
 will not make your voice to be heard on high.
⁵ Is such the fast that I choose,
 a day for a man to humble himself?
Is it to bow down his head like a rush,
 and to spread sackcloth and ashes under him?
Will you call this a fast,
 and a day acceptable to the LORD?

⁶ "Is not this the fast that I choose:
 to loose the bonds of wickedness,
 to undo the thongs of the yoke,
to let the oppressed go free,
 and to break every yoke?
⁷ Is it not to share your bread with the hungry,
 and bring the homeless poor into your house;
when you see the naked, to cover him,
 and not to hide yourself from your own flesh?
⁸ Then shall your light break forth like the dawn,
 and your healing shall spring up speedily;
your righteousness shall go before you,
 the glory of the LORD shall be your rear guard.
⁹ Then you shall call, and the LORD will answer;
 you shall cry, and he will say, Here I am.

"If you take away from the midst of you the yoke,
 the pointing of the finger, and speaking wickedness,
¹⁰ if you pour yourself out for the hungry
 and satisfy the desire of the afflicted,
then shall your light rise in the darkness
 and your gloom be as the noonday.

[11] And the LORD will guide you continually,
>and satisfy your desire with good things,
>and make your bones strong;
>and you shall be like a watered garden,
>>like a spring of water,
>>whose waters fail not.

[12] And your ancient ruins shall be rebuilt;
>you shall raise up the foundations of many generations;
>you shall be called the repairer of the breach,
>>the restorer of streets to dwell in.

[13] "If you turn back your foot from the sabbath,
>from doing your pleasure on my holy day,
>and call the sabbath a delight
>and the holy day of the LORD honorable;
>if you honor it, not going your own ways,
>or seeking your own pleasure, or talking idly;

[14] then you shall take delight in the LORD,
>and I will make you ride upon the heights of the earth;
>I will feed you with the heritage of Jacob your father,
>>for the mouth of the LORD has spoken."

58:12–14 Those scholars who believe that this chapter speaks to the situation of the exiles upon their return from Babylonia to Jerusalem see in these verses references to the repair of the city walls and the effort made by Ezra and Nehemiah to strengthen observance of the Sabbath.

God's Covenant with Israel

God is here described as a warrior in a garb of righteousness who will requite His foes and reward the righteous; His spirit will never depart from Israel.

Isaiah 59:1–4, 9, 15b–21

[59] Behold, the LORD's hand is not shortened, that it cannot save,
>or his ear dull, that it cannot hear;

[2] but your iniquities have made a separation
>between you and your God,
>and your sins have hid his face from you
>so that he does not hear.

[3] For your hands are defiled with blood
>and your fingers with iniquity;
>your lips have spoken lies,
>>your tongue mutters wickedness.

⁴No one enters suit justly,
    no one goes to law honestly;
they rely on empty pleas, they speak lies,
    they conceive mischief and bring forth iniquity.
⁹Therefore justice is far from us,
    and righteousness does not overtake us;
we look for light, and behold, darkness,
    and for brightness, but we walk in gloom.

¹⁵The LORD saw it, and it displeased him
    that there was no justice.
¹⁶He saw that there was no man,
    and wondered that there was no one to intervene;
then his own arm brought him victory,
    and his righteousness upheld him.
¹⁷He put on righteousness as a breastplate,
    and a helmet of salvation upon his head;
he put on garments of vengeance for clothing,
    and wrapped himself in fury as a mantle.
¹⁸According to their deeds, so will he repay,
    wrath to his adversaries, requital to his enemies;
    to the coastlands he will render requital.
¹⁹So they shall fear the name of the LORD from the west,
    and his glory from the rising of the sun;
for he will come like a rushing stream,
    which the wind of the LORD drives.

²⁰"And he will come to Zion as Redeemer,
    to those in Jacob who turn from transgression, says the
    LORD.

²¹"And as for me, this is my covenant with them, says the LORD: my spirit which is upon you, and my words which I have put in your mouth, shall not depart out of your mouth, or out of the mouth of your children, or out of the mouth of your children's children, says the LORD, from this time forth and for evermore."

59:2 Believers in God of all faiths find here an admirable definition of sin and its consequences: sin separates man from God. **59:18** An affirmation of the biblical conviction: God will reward and punish man in accordance with the righteousness of his deeds.

"Nations Shall Come to Your Light"

This poem on the glory of Jerusalem has traditionally been interpreted by Christians as addressed to the heavenly Jerusalem. It is read on the Feast of the Epiphany (i.e., "manifestation" of Jesus to the Gentiles) together with Matthew's account of wise men from the East coming to worship the child Jesus, because Christians believe that it was on the day of the Epiphany that the movement of the nations toward the Church began, and that admission to the Church is a way of entering into the heavenly Jerusalem. Jews understand this passage to refer to the glory of the Hebrew nation in a time to come.

Isaiah 60 : 1–7

60 Arise, shine; for your light has come,
and the glory of the LORD has risen upon you.
² For behold, darkness shall cover the earth,
and thick darkness the peoples;
but the LORD will arise upon you,
and his glory will be seen upon you.
³ And nations shall come to your light,
and kings to the brightness of your rising.

⁴ Lift up your eyes round about, and see;
they all gather together, they come to you;
your sons shall come from far,
and your daughters shall be carried in the arms.
⁵ Then you shall see and be radiant,
your heart shall thrill and rejoice;
because the abundance of the sea shall be turned to you,
the wealth of the nations shall come to you.
⁶ A multitude of camels shall cover you,
the young camels of Mid′ian and Ephah;
all those from Sheba shall come.
They shall bring gold and frankincense,
and shall proclaim the praise of the LORD.
⁷ All the flocks of Kedar shall be gathered to you,
the rams of Nebai′oth shall minister to you;
they shall come up with acceptance on my altar,
and I will glorify my glorious house.

They Are a People Whom the Lord Has Blessed
Isaiah 61 : 1–9; 62 : 1–4, 31–32

61 The Spirit of the Lord God is upon me,
because the LORD has anointed me
to bring good tidings to the afflicted;
he has sent me to bind up the brokenhearted,
to proclaim liberty to the captives,
and the opening of the prison to those who are bound;

^{2} to proclaim the year of the L<small>ORD</small>'s favor,
     and the day of vengeance of our God;
     to comfort all who mourn;

^{3} to grant to those who mourn in Zion—
     to give them a garland instead of ashes,
the oil of gladness instead of mourning,
     the mantle of praise instead of a faint spirit;
that they may be called oaks of righteousness,
     the planting of the L<small>ORD</small>, that he may be glorified.
^{4} They shall build up the ancient ruins,
     they shall raise up the former devastations;
they shall repair the ruined cities,
     the devastations of many generations.

^{5} Aliens shall stand and feed your flocks,
     foreigners shall be your plowmen and vine-dressers;
^{6} but you shall be called the priests of the L<small>ORD</small>,
     men shall speak of you as the ministers of our God;
you shall eat the wealth of the nations,
     and in their riches you shall glory.
^{7} Instead of your shame you shall have a double portion,
     instead of dishonor you shall rejoice in your lot;
therefore in your land you shall possess a double portion;
     yours shall be everlasting joy.

^{8} For I the L<small>ORD</small> love justice,
     I hate robbery and wrong;
I will faithfully give them their recompense,
     and I will make an everlasting covenant with them.
^{9} Their descendants shall be known among the nations,
     and their offspring in the midst of the peoples;
all who see them shall acknowledge them,
     that they are a people whom the L<small>ORD</small> has blessed.

62 For Zion's sake I will not keep silent,
     and for Jerusalem's sake I will not rest,
until her vindication goes forth as brightness,
     and her salvation as a burning torch.
^{2} The nations shall see your vindication,
     and all the kings your glory;
and you shall be called by a new name
     which the mouth of the L<small>ORD</small> will give.
^{3} You shall be a crown of beauty in the hand of the L<small>ORD</small>,
     and a royal diadem in the hand of your God.

⁴ You shall no more be termed Forsaken,
    and your land shall no more be termed Desolate;
but you shall be called My delight is in her,
    and your land Married;
for the L<small>ORD</small> delights in you,
    and your land shall be married.

³¹ Behold, the L<small>ORD</small> has proclaimed
    to the end of the earth:
Say to the daughter of Zion,
    "Behold, your salvation comes;
behold, his reward is with him,
    and his recompense before him."
³² And they shall be called The holy people,
    The redeemed of the L<small>ORD</small>;
and you shall be called Sought out,
    a city not forsaken.

61:1–2 This was the portion read by Jesus at the Synagogue in Nazareth (Luke 4:16 ff.).

I Will Rejoice in Jerusalem

The Book of Isaiah ends with an apocalyptic vision. The Hebrews who had returned from exile may have been disappointed that the messianic expectations they had thought would follow on their return to Palestine and the building of the Second Temple had not been realized. Isaiah reassures them. God *will* create a new heaven and a new earth. In time God will bring a final retribution to those who rebel against Him. Faithful Israel will endure forever and all men will worship God. His presence will fill all the earth.

Isaiah 65:17–25; 66:1–2, 22–23

65 ¹⁷ "For behold, I create new heavens
    and a new earth;
and the former things shall not be remembered
    or come into mind.
¹⁸ But be glad and rejoice for ever
    in that which I create;
for behold, I create Jerusalem a rejoicing,
    and her people a joy.
¹⁹ I will rejoice in Jerusalem,
    and be glad in my people;
no more shall be heard in it the sound of weeping
    and the cry of distress.

²⁰ No more shall there be in it
> an infant that lives but a few days,
> or an old man who does not fill out his days,
> for the child shall die a hundred years old,
> and the sinner a hundred years old shall be accursed.
²¹ They shall build houses and inhabit them;
> they shall plant vineyards and eat their fruit.
²² They shall not build and another inhabit;
> they shall not plant and another eat;
> for like the days of a tree shall the days of my people be,
> and my chosen shall long enjoy the work of their hands.
²³ They shall not labor in vain,
> or bear children for calamity;
> for they shall be the offspring of the blessed of the Lord,
> and their children with them.
²⁴ Before they call I will answer,
> while they are yet speaking I will hear.
²⁵ The wolf and the lamb shall feed together,
> the lion shall eat straw like the ox;
> and dust shall be the serpent's food.
> They shall not hurt or destroy
> in all my holy mountain,
>   says the Lord."

66 Thus says the Lord:
> "Heaven is my throne
> and the earth is my footstool;
> what is the house which you would build for me,
> and what is the place of my rest?
² All these things my hand has made,
> and so all these things are mine,
>   says the Lord.
> But this is the man to whom I will look,
> he that is humble and contrite in spirit,
> and trembles at my word.

²² "For as the new heavens and the new earth
> which I will make
> shall remain before me, says the Lord;
> so shall your descendants and your name remain.
²³ From new moon to new moon,
> and from sabbath to sabbath,
> all flesh shall come to worship before me,
> says the Lord.

The Book of Jeremiah

More is known of the inner life and feelings of Jeremiah than of any other prophet. Jeremiah, son of Hilkiah, of a priestly family in Anathoth in Benjamin, born just over a century after Isaiah, lived in a bitter and tragic period of Jewish history. Not only did he have to rebuke his people, but he lived long enough to witness their humiliation and destruction as a nation. Despite his sincerity, he was mocked by the people; prophets and priests plotted against his life; the rulers of the nation charged him with sedition. He described himself as a "gentle lamb led to the slaughter" (11:19). Jeremiah nevertheless refused to withdraw from his mission. Sharing the grief of his people, he consoled them with assurance that God would not reject them for ever.

Jeremiah's ministry ranged over forty years, from the thirteenth year of the reign of King Josiah, 626 B.C. until after the destruction of the Temple and the overthrow of Judah in 586 B.C. King Josiah came to the throne when but a child of eight, succeeding his brother Amnon, who had been assassinated after only two years of rule. Judah was under the control of Assyria, and the Mosaic religion had been severely compromised by accommodation to the Baal nature worship of the Canaanites and to the astral cult of Mesopotamia. The former king of Judah, Manasseh, grandfather of Josiah, had even caused his sons to pass through fire, one of the barbaric pagan practices in honor of the god Moloch.

In the eighteenth year of Josiah's reign, 621 B.C., while the Temple was undergoing repairs, a copy of "the book of the law" was discovered by the High Priest Hilkiah. (Scholars believe that it was a large part of the Book of Deuteronomy.) Its public reading shook the nation and stirred it to repentance (2 Kings 22–23). The people recognized how far they had departed from the laws of their God, and vigorous religious reform was instituted. Idols were destroyed, rural sanctuaries dismantled, superstitious practices forbidden. Jeremiah assisted the king in his efforts to win the hearts of the people for God.

Unfortunately Josiah was mortally wounded in battle against the Egyptians in 609 B.C. (2 Kings 23:29). His defeat served to undermine the impact of the religious reform, for the people interpreted his death as the vengeance of the idolatrous foreign gods. Egypt had at that time joined arms with Assyria in an effort to defeat a new power on the world stage, Babylonia. Josiah had hoped to secure the independence of Judah by aligning himself with Babylonia. At Megiddo he unsuccessfully attempted to cut off the advance of Egyptian troops into Syria and Mesopotamia via the age-old route up the coast of Palestine. With Josiah's defeat the idolatries of Egypt and Assyria were resumed, and the revived enthusiasm for the moral discipline of Mosaic law soon ended in disillusionment. Josiah's son, Jehoahaz, was elected to the throne by the people, but after only three months he was deposed by Pharaoh Necho and exiled to Egypt where he died. His brother Jehoiakim, who reigned from 609 to 598, was appointed in his stead, perhaps because he was pro-Egyptian. His reign, however, was troubled by constant attacks from surrounding nations (2 Kings 24:2).

During this period of upheaval Jeremiah sought to sustain the people in their faith and to discourage backsliding in religious practice and ethical behavior, but to no avail. He warned those who felt that Jerusalem was secure by virtue of the Temple that the mere existence of the Holy Sanctuary would offer no certain protection, and that a national calamity was sure to occur should the people not repent of their unrighteousness. Such charges infuriated the priestly classes, and they plotted against Jeremiah's life. The prophet made himself even more vulnerable to attack when he hailed the emergence of Babylonia and its new king Nebuchadrezzar. King Jehoiakim of Judah, torn between his allegiance to Egypt and his nationalistic aspirations for independence, fought a war in 598 B.C. against armies aligned with Babylonia in which he was killed. His son Jehoiachin continued the war for three months, only at last to be decisively defeated by Nebuchadrezzar. Judah's royal house and 7,000 leading families were taken into exile to Babylonia (2 Kings 24:10 ff.).

Zedekiah (598–586), another son of Jehoiakim, assumed the throne after subjecting himself to Babylonia. Deluded by a false prophetic group within the court, he joined an anti-Babylonian coalition consisting of Edom, Ammon, Moab, Tyre, Sidon and Judah. In vain Jeremiah implored the king to keep aloof from such entanglements. Nebuchadrezzar laid siege to Jerusalem in the winter of 588-87, and then lifted the siege temporarily to fight off an Egyptian attack. During this period of respite Jeremiah left Jerusalem for his home in Anathoth, where he was arrested for desertion. The king secretly visited the prophet in prison; Jeremiah pleaded with him to surrender Jerusalem and save the city. But it was too late for the king to reverse his policy. In 586 Nebuchadrezzar, having disposed of the Egyptian threat, breached the city wall, and a month later his commander-in-chief, Nebuzaradan, razed the Temple and exiled another large part of the population. King Zedekiah was compelled to watch the murder of his sons, then was blinded, put in chains and taken into captivity (2 Kings 25).

The few remaining Jews were placed under the authority of Gedaliah, son of Ahikam and grandson of Shaphan the scribe. An anti-Babylonian group aligned with Ballis, king of Ammon, arranged to assassinate Gedaliah. The rebellion failed. Fearing the wrath of Babylonia, the leaders fled to Egypt, forcing Jeremiah to accompany them despite his protestations. With this third exile no hope remained for any autonomous community in Judah. According to post-biblical legend Jeremiah was stoned to death by refugees in Egypt who—even then—refused to heed his prophetic call to return to faith.

The writing of Jeremiah consists both of prose and poetry. Despite the vigor of his denunciations, the sorrow he felt for his people emerges compellingly.

The prophecies are arranged roughly in a chronological order, interrupted by insertions of different dates. Chapters 1–45 contain much that deals with historic events and the political and religious life of Judah; chapters 46–51 contain Jeremiah's oracles against the foreign nations; chapter 53 is a supplementary historical appendix by a later writer recounting the collapse of Judah. The book ends with a message of comfort, recalling that the exiled King Jehoiachin was freed from prison in the thirty-seventh year of his captivity and shown favor by the ruling king of Babylonia.

One of the difficult tasks of Bible scholars is deciding which of the variant texts of the biblical books in existence is the oldest or the truest to the original. The Book of Jeremiah illustrates this difficulty. The Hebrew book of Jeremiah differs markedly, for example, from the text that has been preserved in the Greek translation, the Septuagint. Thus the question is asked: Is the text in the Hebrew Bible nearest to the original, or the Hebrew scroll used for the translation into the Greek? The Greek text is shorter by 2,700 words and includes concepts not to be found in the Hebrew text. Scholars only recently have had an opportunity to study the most ancient extant biblical manuscripts yet discovered—those that were included among the famous Dead Sea Scrolls. To their delight they discovered, among the Qumran collection, two scrolls of Jeremiah both written in Hebrew. But then to their bewilderment the scholars ascertained that one scroll followed the text preserved in the Greek translation and the other was closer to the Masoretic Hebrew text.

God Places His Words in the Mouth of the Prophet

The opening ten verses are introductory. Describing the religious experience that led to Jeremiah's mission as a prophet, they outline the theme of his ministry.

Jeremiah 1:1–10

1 The words of Jeremiah, the son of Hilki′ah, of the priests who were in An′athoth in the land of Benjamin, ²to whom the word of the LORD came in the days of Josi′ah the son of Amon, king of Judah, in the thirteenth year of his reign. ³It came also in the days of Jehoi′akim the son of Josi′ah, king of Judah, and until the end of the eleventh year of Zedeki′ah, the son of Josi′ah, king of Judah, until the captivity of Jerusalem in the fifth month.

4 Now the word of the LORD came to me saying,

5 "Before I formed you in the womb I knew you,
  and before you were born I consecrated you;
  I appointed you a prophet to the nations."

6 Then I said, "Ah, Lord GOD! Behold, I do not know how to speak, for I am only a youth." 7 But the LORD said to me,

"Do not say, 'I am only a youth';
  for to all to whom I send you you shall go,
  and whatever I command you you shall speak.

8 Be not afraid of them,
  for I am with you to deliver you,

                                        says the LORD."

9 Then the LORD put forth his hand and touched my mouth; and the LORD said to me,

"Behold, I have put my words in your mouth.

10 See, I have set you this day over nations and over kingdoms,
  to pluck up and to break down,
  to destroy and to overthrow,
  to build and to plant."

1:1 Anathoth, one of the cities set aside for residence by the Levites and the Priests (cf. Joshua 21), is located about three miles northeast of Jerusalem. **1:2** Note the custom of dating events from the beginning of the rule of the reigning king. Josiah came to the throne in 639 B.C., so Jeremiah began his ministry about 626 B.C. **1:3** The "carrying away of Jerusalem" was in 586 B.C. (See 2 Kings 25:8 f.) **1:5** In this verse Hebrew prophecy is understood to be relevant not only for Israel but for all people. **1:9** Isaiah had a similar experience (Isaiah 6:7). Later Jewish tradition, rejecting anthropomorphism, interpreted this verse symbolically, as an expression of Jeremiah's conviction that he spoke with an authority given him by God—a conviction rooted in a mystical religious experience. **1:10** A proclamation of the destruction of the old order and a reconciling promise that there will be a new order. Both are within Jeremiah's responsibility—a two-fold obligation similar to that given other prophets.

The Lord Accuses Israel of Infidelity

This first group of prophecies of Jeremiah extends from chapter 2 to the end of chapter 6. Written before the reforms made by King Josiah in 621 B.C., these prophecies contrast the former devotion of Israel to God in the early days of their national existence with the people's present wickedness.

Jeremiah 2:1–13, 18–19; 3:20; 4:1–4

2 The word of the LORD came to me, saying, 2 "Go and proclaim in the hearing of Jerusalem, Thus says the LORD,

I remember the devotion of your youth,
   your love as a bride,
how you followed me in the wilderness,
   in a land not sown.
³ Israel was holy to the LORD,
   the first fruits of his harvest.
All who ate of it became guilty;
   evil came upon them,
                     says the LORD."

4 Hear the word of the LORD, O house of Jacob, and all the families of the house of Israel. ⁵ Thus says the LORD:
"What wrong did your fathers find in me
   that they went far from me,
and went after worthlessness, and became worthless?
⁶ They did not say, 'Where is the LORD
   who brought us up from the land of Egypt,
who led us in the wilderness,
   in a land of deserts and pits,
in a land of drought and deep darkness,
   in a land that none passes through,
   where no man dwells?'
⁷ And I brought you into a plentiful land
   to enjoy its fruits and its good things.
But when you came in you defiled my land,
   and made my heritage an abomination.
⁸ The priests did not say, 'Where is the LORD?'
   Those who handle the law did not know me;
the rulers transgressed against me;
   the prophets prophesied by Ba'al,
   and went after things that do not profit.
⁹ "Therefore I still contend with you,
                     says the LORD,
   and with your children's children I will contend.
¹⁰ For cross to the coasts of Cyprus and see,
   or send to Kedar and examine with care;
   see if there has been such a thing.
¹¹ Has a nation changed its gods,
   even though they are no gods?
But my people have changed their glory
   for that which does not profit.
¹² Be appalled, O heavens, at this,
   be shocked, be utterly desolate,
                     says the LORD,

¹³ for my people have committed two evils:
    they have forsaken me,
  the fountain of living waters,
    and hewed out cisterns for themselves,
  broken cisterns,
    that can hold no water.
¹⁸ And now what do you gain by going to Egypt,
    to drink the waters of the Nile?
Or what do you gain by going to Assyria,
    to drink the waters of the Eu-phra′tes?
¹⁹ Your wickedness will chasten you,
    and your apostasy will reprove you.
Know and see that it is evil and bitter
    for you to forsake the LORD your God;
    the fear of me is not in you,
                says the Lord GOD of hosts.

3 ²⁰ " 'Surely, as a faithless wife leaves her husband,
    so you have been faithless to me, O house of Israel,
              says the LORD.' "

4 "If you return, O Israel,
         says the LORD,
  to me you should return.
If you remove your abominations from my presence,
    and do not waver,
² and if you swear, 'As the LORD lives,'
    in truth, in justice, and in uprightness,
then nations shall bless themselves in him,
    and in him shall they glory."

3 For thus says the LORD to the men of Judah and to the inhabitants of Jerusalem:
"Break up your fallow ground,
    and sow not among thorns.
⁴ Circumcise yourselves to the LORD,
    remove the foreskin of your hearts,
    O men of Judah and inhabitants of Jerusalem;
  lest my wrath go forth like fire,
    and burn with none to quench it,
    because of the evil of your doings."

2:2 The Hebrew word *chesed*, translated here as "devotion," is expressive of a mutuality of feeling. It refers, therefore, both to God's intimate love for Israel and Israel's love for God. The language evokes the imagery of a bride, Israel, who leaves her home in order to

follow her husband, God, to a strange land. **2:3** Just as the first
fruits of the field were sacred and were offered to God in a sacrifice of
thanksgiving, so Israel was considered by God to be "the first fruits
of humanity" (Philo). **2:4** The kingdom of Israel had come to the
end of its existence a century earlier. Jeremiah addresses Judah as the
heir, the representative of the entire nation. **2:8** Jeremiah's fearless-
ness is seen in this sweeping indictment of the priests, prophets and
rulers of the people. **2:10** The sense of the verse is: neither in the
west nor in the east has any other people been so unfaithful to their
God. *Kedar* denotes Arabia. **2:18** The plight of a small nation
caught between two large powers, Assyria and Egypt, is here
depicted. The prophet denounces any alliance, considering both these
nations "broken cisterns." He calls upon the nation to place its trust
in God; the political game of foreign alliances is fruitless. **4:1–4** God
offers to restore Israel to her former glory if only the nation will truly
repent, put away idolatrous practices and restore truth, justice and
uprightness in the national life. Using the imagery of agriculture,
Jeremiah warns the citizenry that in order to achieve this reformation they will have to plow up the hard soil around the heart, v. 3 (cf.
Hosea 10:12). They will have to circumcise their hearts in a renewal
of the Covenant, v. 4 (cf. Deuteronomy 10:16; 30:6). Paul in the
New Testament similarly invokes this concept: the true circumcision
is that of the heart (Romans 2:25–29).

Jeremiah Warns of Invasion and of Desolation
Jeremiah 4:5–8, 13–14, 18–20a, 23–28

4 ⁵ Declare in Judah, and proclaim in Jerusalem, and say,
  "Blow the trumpet through the land;
    cry aloud and say,
   'Assemble, and let us go
    into the fortified cities!'
⁶ Raise a standard toward Zion,
    flee for safety, stay not,
  for I bring evil from the north,
    and great destruction.
⁷ A lion has gone up from his thicket,
    a destroyer of nations has set out;
    he has gone forth from his place
  to make your land a waste;
    your cities will be ruins
    without inhabitant.
⁸ For this gird you with sackcloth,
    lament and wail;
  for the fierce anger of the LORD
    has not turned back from us."

¹³ Behold, he comes up like clouds,
 his chariots like the whirlwind;
his horses are swifter than eagles—
 woe to us, for we are ruined!
¹⁴ O Jerusalem, wash your heart from wickedness,
 that you may be saved.
How long shall your evil thoughts
 lodge within you?

¹⁸ "Your ways and your doings
 have brought this upon you.
This is your doom, and it is bitter;
 it has reached your very heart."
¹⁹ My anguish, my anguish! I writhe in pain!
 Oh, the walls of my heart!
My heart is beating wildly;
 I cannot keep silent;
for I hear the sound of the trumpet,
 the alarm of war.
²⁰ Disaster follows hard on disaster,
 the whole land is laid waste.

²³ I looked on the earth, and lo, it was waste and void;
 and to the heavens, and they had no light.
²⁴ I looked on the mountains, and lo, they were quaking,
 and all the hills moved to and fro.
²⁵ I looked, and lo, there was no man,
 and all the birds of the air had fled.
²⁶ I looked, and lo, the fruitful land was a desert,
 and all its cities were laid in ruins
 before the Lord, before his fierce anger.

27 For thus says the Lord, "The whole land shall be a desolation;
yet I will not make a full end.
²⁸ For this the earth shall mourn,
 and the heavens above be black;
for I have spoken, I have purposed;
 I have not relented nor will I turn back."

4:7 *Lion* is a figure either for the Scythians who overran western
Asia in 625 B.C.; or, if the passage is later, for Nebuchadrezzar, king
of Babylon. **4:19** Jeremiah suffers anguish at the agonies of his
people. This outburst is representative of the emotional quality of his
writing. **4:23–28** Jeremiah evokes an image of the physical universe
returning to its primeval condition, a waste and void (cf. Genesis
1:2) as a result of the iniquity of Israel and the punishment she is

sure to receive. This is the only instance in Jeremiah of portrayal of cosmic destruction.

The Lord Will Take Vengeance on Israel
Jeremiah 5:1–3, 20–31; 6:13–15, 19–20

5 Run to and fro through the streets of Jerusalem,
  look and take note!
 Search her squares to see
  if you can find a man,
 one who does justice
  and seeks truth;
 that I may pardon her.
² Though they say, "As the LORD lives,"
  yet they swear falsely.
³ O LORD, do not thy eyes look for truth?
 Thou hast smitten them,
  but they felt no anguish;
 thou hast consumed them,
  but they refused to take correction.
 They have made their faces harder than rock;
  they have refused to repent.

²⁰ Declare this in the house of Jacob,
  proclaim it in Judah:
²¹ "Hear this, O foolish and senseless people,
  who have eyes, but see not,
  who have ears, but hear not.
²² Do you not fear me? says the LORD;
  Do you not tremble before me?
 I placed the sand as the bound for the sea,
  a perpetual barrier which it cannot pass;
 though the waves toss, they cannot prevail,
  though they roar, they cannot pass over it.
²³ But this people has a stubborn and rebellious heart;
  they have turned aside and gone away.
²⁴ They do not say in their hearts,
  'Let us fear the LORD our God,
 who gives the rain in its season,
  the autumn rain and the spring rain,
 and keeps for us
  the weeks appointed for the harvest.'
²⁵ Your iniquities have turned these away,
  and your sins have kept good from you.

²⁶ For wicked men are found among my people;
    they lurk like fowlers lying in wait.
They set a trap;
    they catch men.
²⁷ Like a basket full of birds,
    their houses are full of treachery;
therefore they have become great and rich,
²⁸   they have grown fat and sleek.
They know no bounds in deeds of wickedness;
    they judge not with justice
the cause of the fatherless, to make it prosper,
    and they do not defend the rights of the needy.
²⁹ Shall I not punish them for these things?
                              says the LORD.

    and shall I not avenge myself
    on a nation such as this?"

³⁰ An appalling and horrible thing
    has happened in the land:
³¹ the prophets prophesy falsely,
    and the priests rule at their direction;
my people love to have it so,
    but what will you do when the end comes?

6 ¹³ "For from the least to the greatest of them,
    every one is greedy for unjust gain;
and from prophet to priest,
    every one deals falsely.
¹⁴ They have healed the wound of my people lightly,
    saying, 'Peace, peace,'
when there is no peace.
¹⁵ Were they ashamed when they committed abomination?
    No, they were not at all ashamed;
    they did not know how to blush.
Therefore they shall fall among those who fall;
    at the time that I punish them, they shall be overthrown,"
says the LORD.

¹⁹ "Hear, O earth; behold, I am bringing evil upon this people,
    the fruit of their devices,
because they have not given heed to my words;
    and as for my law, they have rejected it.

²⁰ To what purpose does frankincense come to me from Sheba,
   or sweet cane from a distant land?
Your burnt offerings are not acceptable,
   nor your sacrifices pleasing to me."

5:1 Compare the Greek philosopher Diogenes (*c.* 412–323 B.C.),
who walked the streets of Athens carrying a lighted lantern in search
of one honest man. **5:21** Paul in Romans 11:8 finds in this "spirit of
stupor" an explanation for Israel's failure to recognize Jesus as the
Christ. **6:20** Sacrifice without good deeds in unacceptable to God.
Jeremiah repeats the classic prophetic criticism of formal religiosity
uninformed by genuine religious spirit. See Amos 5:21 ff.; Hosea
6:6; Isaiah 1:11 ff.; Micah 6:6 ff.

Jeremiah Calls the People to Repentance

Chapter 7 opens with an address delivered at the Temple gates in a
time of national crisis, perhaps early in the reign of Jehoiakim
(608–597 B.C.). Jeremiah poses the question: What gives men
security? Jeremiah warns the people that the existence of the Holy
Temple is not the answer.

Jeremiah 7:1–15; 8:4–9, 10b–11, 22; 9:1, 23–24

7 The word that came to Jeremiah from the LORD: ² "Stand in the
gate of the LORD's house, and proclaim there this word, and say,
Hear the word of the LORD, all you men of Judah who enter these
gates to worship the LORD. ³ Thus says the LORD of hosts, the God of
Israel, Amend your ways and your doings, and I will let you dwell in
this place. ⁴ Do not trust in these deceptive words: 'This is the temple
of the LORD, the temple of the LORD, the temple of the LORD.'

5 "For if you truly amend your ways and your doings, if you truly
execute justice one with another, ⁶ if you do not oppress the alien,
the fatherless or the widow, or shed innocent blood in this place, and
if you do not go after other gods to your own hurt, ⁷ then I will let
you dwell in this place, in the land that I gave of old to your fathers
for ever.

8 "Behold, you trust in deceptive words to no avail. ⁹ Will you
steal, murder, commit adultery, swear falsely, burn incense to Ba'al,
and go after other gods that you have not known, ¹⁰ and then come
and stand before me in this house, which is called by my name, and
say, 'We are delivered!'—only to go on doing all these abominations?
¹¹ Has this house, which is called by my name, become a den of
robbers in your eyes? Behold, I myself have seen it, says the LORD.
¹² Go now to my place that was in Shiloh, where I made my name
dwell at first, and see what I did to it for the wickedness of my people
Israel. ¹³ And now, because you have done all these things, says the

LORD, and when I spoke to you persistently you did not listen, and when I called you, you did not answer, [14] therefore I will do to the house which is called by my name, and in which you trust, and to the place which I gave to you and to your fathers, as I did to Shiloh. [15] And I will cast you out of my sight, as I cast out all your kinsmen, all the offspring of E′phraim.

8 [4] "You shall say to them, Thus says the LORD:

When men fall, do they not rise again?
  If one turns away, does he not return?
[5] Why then has this people turned away
  in perpetual backsliding?
They hold fast to deceit,
  they refuse to return.
[6] I have given heed and listened,
  but they have not spoken aright;
no man repents of his wickedness,
  saying, 'What have I done?'
Every one turns to his own course,
  like a horse plunging headlong into battle.
[7] Even the stork in the heavens
  knows her times;
and the turtledove, swallow, and crane
  keep the time of their coming;
but my people know not
  the ordinance of the LORD.

[8] "How can you say, 'We are wise,
  and the law of the LORD is with us'?
But, behold, the false pen of the scribes
  has made it into a lie.
[9] The wise men shall be put to shame,
  they shall be dismayed and taken;
lo, they have rejected the word of the LORD,
  and what wisdom is in them?
from prophet to priest
  every one deals falsely.
[11] They have healed the wound of my people lightly,
  saying, 'Peace, peace,'
  when there is no peace.

[22] "Is there no balm in Gilead?
  Is there no physician there?
Why then has the health of the daughter of my people
  not been restored?

9 O that my head were waters,
  and my eyes a fountain of tears,
  that I might weep day and night
  for the slain of the daughter of my people!"

23 Thus says the LORD; "Let not the wise man glory in his wisdom, let not the mighty man glory in his might, let not the rich man glory in his riches; ²⁴ but let him who glories glory in this, that he understands and knows me, that I am the LORD who practice steadfast love, justice, and righteousness in the earth; for in these things I delight, says the LORD."

7:4 There was a popular belief in the inviolability of the Temple. In 701 King Sennacherib of Assyria miraculously had been denied entrance to the Temple walls (2 Kings 19:32–34). Jeremiah warns the people that they ought not expect another such stroke of good fortune. **7:12** Once before in Israel's history the people had presumed that the Tabernacle would save them from their enemies. Hoping to shake them out of their complacency, Jeremiah recalls that event: the destruction by the Philistines of Shiloh where the Ark had been located in the days of Eli and Samuel (cf. Samuel 4:1 ff.). The entire address infuriated the leaders, and they sought Jeremiah's life (cf. 25:7–15). **7:15** Ephraim, a figure for the Northern Kingdom, had been destroyed as punishment for similar wickedness a century earlier. **8:8** The people evidently denied Jeremiah's charges, asserting that they lived by the Mosaic Law. Jeremiah retorts that the leaders destroy that law in a greedy effort to obtain gain. **8:22** The prophet evidently means to ask: "Is there no prophet or leader who can inspire the people to heal their spiritual sickness?" He invokes the image of a medicine produced in Gilead from the gum of the mastic tree or of the styrax, famous for its healing powers (cf. Genesis 37:25). The famous Negro spiritual "There is a Balm in Gilead" represents a Christian folk response to the tragedy elucidated in this text.

Jeremiah Attacks Idolatry
Jeremiah 10:1–11, 15–16

10 Hear the word which the LORD speaks to you, O house of Israel. ² Thus says the LORD:
  "Learn not the way of the nations,
    nor be dismayed at the signs of the heavens
    because the nations are dismayed at them,
  ³ for the customs of the peoples are false.
  A tree from the forest is cut down,
    and worked with an axe by the hands of a craftsman.

⁴ Men deck it with silver and gold;
    they fasten it with hammers and nails
      so that it cannot move.
⁵ Their idols are like scarecrows in a cucumber field,
    and they cannot speak;
  they have to be carried,
    for they cannot walk.
  Be not afraid of them,
    for they cannot do evil,
      neither is it in them to do good.''

⁶ There is none like thee, O LORD;
    thou art great, and thy name is great in might.
⁷ Who would not fear thee, O King of the nations?
    For this is thy due;
  for among all the wise ones of the nations
    and in all their kingdoms
      there is none like thee.
⁸ They are both stupid and foolish;
    the instruction of idols is but wood!
⁹ Beaten silver is brought from Tarshish,
    and gold from Uphaz.
  They are the work of the craftsmen and of the hands of the
      goldsmith;
    their clothing is violet and purple;
    they are all the work of skilled men.
¹⁰ But the LORD is the true God;
    he is the living God and the everlasting King.
  At his wrath the earth quakes,
    and the nations cannot endure his indignation.

11 Thus shall you say to them: "The gods who did not make the
heavens and the earth shall perish from the earth and from under
the heavens.''

¹⁵ They are worthless, a work of delusion;
    at the time of their punishment they shall perish.
¹⁶ Not like these is he who is the portion of Jacob,
    for he is the one who formed all things,
  and Israel is the tribe of his inheritance;
    the LORD of hosts is his name.

10:1 This passage is similar in content to Isaiah's blistering attack
on idolatry. See Isaiah 40:20 ff. and 42:8 ff.

Jeremiah's Self-denial Is a Warning to Israel

Jeremiah 16 : 1–13

16 The word of the Lord came to me: [2] "You shall not take a wife, nor shall you have sons or daughters in this place. [3] For thus says the Lord concerning the sons and daughters who are born in this place, and concerning the mothers who bore them and the fathers who begot them in this land: [4] They shall die of deadly diseases. They shall not be lamented, nor shall they be buried; they shall be as dung on the surface of the ground. They shall perish by the sword and by famine, and their dead bodies shall be food for the birds of the air and for the beasts of the earth.

5 "For thus says the Lord: Do not enter the house of mourning, or go to lament, or bemoan them; for I have taken away my peace from this people, says the Lord, my steadfast love and mercy. [6] Both great and small shall die in this land; they shall not be buried, and no one shall lament for them or cut himself or make himself bald for them. [7] No one shall break bread for the mourner, to comfort him for the dead; nor shall any one give him the cup of consolation to drink for his father or his mother. [8] You shall not go into the house of feasting to sit with them, to eat and drink. [9] For thus says the Lord of hosts, the God of Israel: Behold, I will make to cease from this place, before your eyes and in your days, the voice of mirth and the voice of gladness, the voice of the bridegroom and the voice of the bride.

10 "And when you tell this people all these words, and they say to you, 'Why has the Lord pronounced all this great evil against us? What is our iniquity? What is the sin that we have committed against the Lord our God?' [11] then you shall say to them: 'Because your fathers have forsaken me, says the Lord, and have gone after other gods and have served and worshiped them, and have forsaken me and have not kept my law, [12] and because you have done worse than your fathers, for behold, every one of you follows his stubborn evil will, refusing to listen to me; [13] therefore I will hurl you out of this land into a land which neither you nor your fathers have known, and there you shall serve other gods day and night, for I will show you no favor.' "

16:6 It was forbidden in Scripture to cut oneself or to shave the head as a sign of mourning (cf. Leviticus 19:28; Deuteronomy 14:1). Here is evidence that these practices were widespread, a sign of the people's assimilation to idolatrous practices. **16:7** It was customary, and still is, among Jews and some Christians for the friends to provide mourners their first meal after the funeral (cf. 2 Samuel 3:25; Ezekiel 24:17; Isaiah 9:4).

Jeremiah Laments His Vocation

The Book of Jeremiah is unique among the prophetic writings in the number of times it contains intimate autobiographical references to the feelings of the prophet. See also 11:18; 12:5; 15:10–21; 17:14–18; 18:18–23. The account at 15:10–21 contains a rebuke of the prophet; God warns Jeremiah that he has no choice but to speak God's word if he wishes to be worthy of being a prophet: "If you utter what is precious and not what is worthless, you shall be as my mouth."

Jeremiah 20:1–9, 14

20 Now Pashhur the priest, the son of Immer, who was chief officer in the house of the LORD, heard Jeremiah prophesying these things. ² Then Pashhur beat Jeremiah the prophet, and put him in the stocks that were in the upper Benjamin Gate of the house of the LORD. ³ On the morrow, when Pashhur released Jeremiah from the stocks, Jeremiah said to him, "The LORD does not call your name Pashhur, but Terror on every side. ⁴ For thus says the LORD: Behold, I will make you a terror to yourself and to all your friends. They shall fall by the sword of their enemies while you look on. And I will give all Judah into the hand of the king of Babylon; he shall carry them captive to Babylon, and shall slay them with the sword. ⁵ Moreover, I will give all the wealth of the city, all its gains, all its prized belongings, and all the treasures of the kings of Judah into the hand of their enemies, who shall plunder them, and seize them, and carry them to Babylon. ⁶ And you, Pashhur, and all who dwell in your house, shall go into captivity; to Babylon you shall go; and there you shall die, and there you shall be buried, you and all your friends, to whom you have prophesied falsely."

⁷ O LORD, thou hast deceived me,
    and I was deceived;
thou art stronger than I,
    and thou hast prevailed.
I have become a laughingstock all the day;
    every one mocks me.
⁸ For whenever I speak, I cry out,
    I shout, "Violence and destruction!"
For the word of the LORD has become for me
    a reproach and derision all day long.
⁹ If I say, "I will not mention him,
    or speak any more in his name,"
there is in my heart as it were a burning fire
    shut up in my bones,
and I am weary with holding it in,
    and I cannot.

¹⁴Cursed be the day
    on which I was born!
The day when my mother bore me,
    let it not be blessed!

20:3 The Hebrew words *Magor-Missabib*, translated "Terror on every side," are an epithet coined by Jeremiah to express his attitude toward Passhur, chief of the Temple police. Passhur, then, would have been a leader of the pro-Egyptian faction in the nation's political life, who were saying that trust in Egypt would obviate any fear of the Babylonians. In his epithet Jeremiah is predicting that Passhur will himself become *terror* personified, full of fear and radiating it in all directions when the Babylonians close in. The prophet had earlier suggested that the rise of Babylon was in accordance with God's purpose, and would result in Judah's freedom from the bondage of Egypt and Assyria. The nation rejected Jeremiah's counsel and did indeed suffer "terror on every side" when Babylonia invaded the land. In Ezra 2:37 and 10:20 there is reference to a family named Pashhur in the captivity. **20:7 ff.** In this black hour of despair Jeremiah bewails his lot (cf. 15:10–11). There is no ray of light, no sign of hope within him. Here is the saddest and gloomiest of his several "confessions" within his book. Jeremiah mercilessly exposes his mental state—the lot of a rejected prophet. See also Job 3:3–6. **20:7** The Hebrew word *pathoth* has been translated in various ways: "enticed me" in Jewish Publication Society; "persuaded me" by Leeser and Moffatt; "duped me" in the American Translation. The Hebrew is a strong word, used for seducing a virgin. **20:9** The word of God is an objective reality to Jeremiah, compelling utterance, no matter at what cost.

Jeremiah Pronounces God's Judgment upon the Kings of Judah

Chapters 22–23:8 are a collection of Jeremiah's judgments upon the kings of Judah and upon the false prophets, uttered at different times.

Jeremiah 22:1–5, 10–19; 23:5–6

22 Thus says the LORD: "Go down to the house of the king of Judah, and speak there this word, ²and say, 'Hear the word of the LORD, O King of Judah, who sit on the throne of David, you, and your servants, and your people who enter these gates. ³Thus says the LORD: Do justice and righteousness, and deliver from the hand of the oppressor him who has been robbed. And do no wrong or violence to the alien, the fatherless, and the widow, nor shed innocent blood in this place. ⁴For if you will indeed obey this word, then there shall enter the gates of this house kings who sit on the throne of David, riding in chariots and on horses, they, and their servants, and their people. ⁵But if you will not heed these words, I swear by myself, says the LORD, that this house shall become a desolation.' "

¹⁰ Weep not for him who is dead,
  nor bemoan him;
but weep bitterly for him who goes away,
  for he shall return no more
  to see his native land.

11 For thus says the LORD concerning Shallum the son of Josi'ah, king of Judah, who reigned instead of Josi'ah his father, and who went away from this place: "He shall return here no more, ¹²but in the place where they have carried him captive, there shall he die, and he shall never see this land again."

¹³ "Woe to him who builds his house by unrighteousness,
  and his upper rooms by injustice;
who makes his neighbor serve him for nothing,
  and does not give him his wages;
¹⁴ who says, 'I will build myself a great house
  with spacious upper rooms,'
and cuts out windows for it,
  paneling it with cedar,
  and painting it with vermilion.
¹⁵ Do you think you are a king
  because you compete in cedar?
Did not your father eat and drink
  and do justice and righteousness?
  Then it was well with him.
¹⁶ He judged the cause of the poor and needy;
  then it was well.
Is not this to know me?
                    says the LORD.
¹⁷ But you have eyes and heart
  only for your dishonest gain,
for shedding innocent blood,
  and for practicing oppression and violence."

18 Therefore thus says the LORD concerning Jehoi'akim the son of Josi'ah, king of Judah:
"They shall not lament for him, saying,
  'Ah my brother!' or 'Ah sister!'
They shall not lament for him, saying,
  'Ah lord!' or 'Ah his majesty!'
¹⁹ With the burial of an ass he shall be buried,
  dragged and cast forth beyond the gates of Jerusalem."

23 ⁵ "Behold, the days are coming, says the LORD, when I will raise up for David a righteous Branch, and he shall reign as king and deal wisely, and shall execute justice and righteousness in the land. ⁶ In his days Judah will be saved, and Israel will dwell securely. And this is the name by which he will be called: 'The LORD is our righteousness.' "

22:10 King Josiah was slain at the battle of Megiddo. His son Shallum, also known as Jehoahaz (cf. 2 Kings 23:30 ff.) reigned only three months and was then taken into captivity to Egypt, where he died. **22:13–19** A denunciation of Jehoiakim, another son of Josiah, who was placed on the throne by Pharoah as an Egyptian puppet. Jeremiah's life was particularly difficult during his eleven-year reign. Jeremiah accuses Jehoiakim of using forced labor (v. 13) and condemning innocent people (v. 17) in order to appropriate their property and make himself powerful. When Jehoiakim died he did not receive a burial, but was left to rot—like the "burial of an ass." **23:5–6** Here we have Jeremiah's description of an ideal ruler; by such passages did the prophets stimulate the people's hope for the future. In verse 6 we again find the prophetic promise that in the messianic era there will be a reunion of Judah and a restored Israel (cf. Ezekiel 37:19).

Nebuchadrezzar Is a Servant of God

The fairly precise dating of verse 1 indicates that Jeremiah's conviction that Nebuchadrezzar was the servant appointed by God to discipline the nations was written in 605 or 604 B.C., after the Babylonians had defeated Pharaoh Necho, king of Egypt, at Carchemish. Jeremiah counseled the people to submit to the conqueror and to mend their ways. He points out that he has been prophesying for some twenty-three years, but the people have refused to hearken. The prophet gloomily proclaims seventy years of subjugation for Judah.

Jeremiah 25:1–16

25 The word that came to Jeremiah concerning all the people of Judah, in the fourth year of Jehoi′akim the son of Josi′ah, king of Judah (that was the first year of Nebuchadrez′zar king of Babylon), ² which Jeremiah the prophet spoke to all the people of Judah and all the inhabitants of Jerusalem: ³ "For twenty-three years, from the thirteenth year of Josi′ah the son of Amon, king of Judah, to this day, the word of the LORD has come to me, and I have spoken persistently to you, but you have not listened. ⁴ You have neither listened nor inclined your ears to hear, although the LORD persistently sent to you all his servants the prophets, ⁵ saying, 'Turn now, every one of you, from his evil way and wrong doing, and dwell upon the land which the LORD has given to you and your fathers from old and for ever; ⁶ do not go after other gods to serve and worship them, or provoke me to anger with the work of your hands. Then I will do you no harm.' ⁷ Yet you have not listened to me, says the LORD, that you might provoke me to anger with the work of your hands to your own harm.

8 "Therefore thus says the LORD of hosts: Because you have not obeyed my words, ⁹ behold, I will send for all the tribes of the north, says the LORD, and for Nebuchadrez'zar the king of Babylon, my servant, and I will bring them against this land and its inhabitants, and against all these nations round about; I will utterly destroy them, and make them a horror, a hissing, and an everlasting reproach. ¹⁰ Moreover, I will banish from them the voice of mirth and the voice of gladness, the voice of the bridegroom and the voice of the bride, the grinding of the millstones and the light of the lamp. ¹¹ This whole land shall become a ruin and a waste, and these nations shall serve the king of Babylon seventy years. ¹² Then after seventy years are completed, I will punish the king of Babylon and that nation, the land of the Chalde'ans, for their iniquity, says the LORD, making the land an everlasting waste. ¹³ I will bring upon that land all the words which I have uttered against it, everything written in this book, which Jeremiah prophesied against all the nations. ¹⁴ For many nations and great kings shall make slaves even of them; and I will recompense them according to their deeds and the work of their hands."

15 Thus the LORD, the God of Israel, said to me: "Take from my hand this cup of the wine of wrath, and make all the nations to whom I send you drink it. ¹⁶ They shall drink and stagger and be crazed because of the sword which I am sending among them."

25:12–14 This passage, probably later, provides reassurance to Judah that the exile will eventually come to an end through Babylon's collapse (cf. 29:10). Not Judah alone, but any and all nations who violate God's laws of righteousness must drink from the cup of disaster. **25:15** The cup of wine symbolizing disaster is also used in Isaiah 51:17, 11.

Jeremiah Counsels the Exiles in Babylonia

Several years after Nebuchadrezzar had carried away King Jehoiakim in 597 B.C. Jeremiah wrote to the exiles. He repudiated the false prophets who predicted that the exile would soon come to an end. Warning that it would last at least seventy years, Jeremiah pleaded with the exiles to build a community for themselves in Babylonia and to repent of their sins before God; thus, he says, they may eventually merit restoration. He introduced a radical idea: God could be worshiped in Babylonia. The Deity was not confined to any one land or territory.

Jeremiah 29 : 1, 4–14

29 These are the words of the letter which Jeremiah the prophet sent from Jerusalem to the elders of the exiles, and to the priests, the prophets, and all the people, whom Nebuchadnez'zar had taken into exile from Jerusalem to Babylon.

4 "Thus says the LORD of hosts, the God of Israel, to all the exiles whom I have sent into exile from Jerusalem to Babylon: ⁵Build houses and live in them; plant gardens and eat their produce. ⁶Take wives and have sons and daughters; take wives for your sons, and give your daughters in marriage, that they may bear sons and daughters; multiply there, and do not decrease. ⁷But seek the welfare of the city where I have sent you into exile, and pray to the LORD on its behalf, for in its welfare you will find your welfare. ⁸For thus says the LORD of hosts, the God of Israel: Do not let your prophets and your diviners who are among you deceive you, and do not listen to the dreams which they dream, ⁹for it is a lie which they are prophesying to you in my name; I did not send them, says the LORD.

10 "For thus says the LORD: When seventy years are completed for Babylon, I will visit you, and I will fulfil to you my promise and bring you back to this place. ¹¹For I know the plans I have for you, says the LORD, plans for welfare and not for evil, to give you a future and a hope. ¹²Then you will call upon me and come and pray to me, and I will hear you. ¹³You will seek me and find me; when you seek me with all your heart, ¹⁴I will be found by you, says the LORD, and I will restore your fortunes and gather you from all the nations and all the places where I have driven you, says the LORD, and I will bring you back to the place from which I sent you into exile."

29:4–7 Although the Jewish Prayerbook contains the hope that Jews be reunited as one people in the land of Israel, the attitude of Jews in exile towards the land of their residence has been controlled by these passages. **29:5** Jewish scholars point out that the Jews were encouraged by Jeremiah to engage in agriculture, not in commerce. Large-scale Jewish participation in commercial enterprises is a consequence of modern history, when Christian Europe, under the influence of anti-Semitism, denied Jews the right to own land. **29:7** To this day a prayer for the head of the state is included as a part of the Jewish prayer service on the Sabbath and festival days. **29:13** This sentence is a key passage in the biblical tradition, expressing the power of repentance and the essential requirement: that man must first seek the Lord. God assures man that He may be found.

God Will Make a New Covenant with Israel

Chapters 30–31 comprise a separate little book of consolation addressed by Jeremiah to exiles. It describes in idyllic terms the ultimate restoration of Israel to her land, the rebuilding of Jerusalem and the new covenant that God will make with His people. The optimistic note sounded here partly balances the sorrowful refrain found so often in Jeremiah's writings.

Jeremiah 30 : 1–3, 8–11, 15–22; 31 : 5–9, 15–17, 27–37

30 The word that came to Jeremiah from the LORD: ² "Thus says the LORD, the God of Israel: Write in a book all the words that I have spoken to you. ³ For behold, days are coming, says the LORD, when I will restore the fortunes of my people, Israel and Judah, says the LORD, and I will bring them back to the land which I gave to their fathers, and they shall take possession of it."

8 "And it shall come to pass in that day, says the LORD of hosts, that I will break the yoke from off their neck, and I will burst their bonds, and strangers shall no more make servants of them. ⁹ But they shall serve the LORD their God and David their king, whom I will raise up for them.

¹⁰ "Then fear not, O Jacob my servant, says the LORD,
    nor be dismayed, O Israel;
  for lo, I will save you from afar,
    and your offspring from the land of their captivity.
  Jacob shall return and have quiet and ease,
    and none shall make him afraid.
¹¹ For I am with you to save you,
                says the LORD;
  I will make a full end of all the nations
    among whom I scattered you,
    but of you I will not make a full end.
  I will chasten you in just measure,
    and I will by no means leave you unpunished.

¹⁵ "Why do you cry out over your hurt?
    Your pain is incurable.
  Because your guilt is great,
    because your sins are flagrant,
    I have done these things to you.
¹⁶ Therefore all who devour you shall be devoured,
    and all your foes, every one of them, shall go into captivity;
  those who despoil you shall become a spoil,
    and all who prey on you I will make a prey.

¹⁷ For I will restore health to you,
    and your wounds I will heal,

says the LORD,

because they have called you an outcast:
    'It is Zion, for whom no one cares!'

¹⁸ "Thus says the LORD:

Behold, I will restore the fortunes of the tents of Jacob,
    and have compassion on his dwellings;
the city shall be rebuilt upon its mound,
    and the palace shall stand where it used to be.
¹⁹ Out of them shall come songs of thanksgiving,
    and the voices of those who make merry.
I will multiply them, and they shall not be few;
    I will make them honored, and they shall not be small.
²⁰ Their children shall be as they were of old,
    and their congregation shall be established before me;
    and I will punish all who oppress them.
²¹ Their prince shall be one of themselves,
    their ruler shall come forth from their midst;
I will make him draw near, and he shall approach me,
    for who would dare of himself to approach me?

says the LORD.

²² And you shall be my people,
    and I will be your God."

31 ⁵ "Again you shall plant vineyards
    upon the mountains of Samar′ia;
the planters shall plant,
    and shall enjoy the fruit.
⁶ For there shall be a day when watchmen will call
    in the hill country of E′phraim:
'Arise, and let us go up to Zion,
    to the LORD our God.' "

⁷ For thus says the LORD:
"Sing aloud with gladness for Jacob,
    and raise shouts for the chief of the nations;
proclaim, give praise, and say,
    'The LORD has saved his people,
    the remnant of Israel.'
⁸ Behold, I will bring them from the north country,
    and gather them from the farthest parts of the earth,

    among them the blind and the lame,
       the woman with child and her who is in travail, together;
      a great company, they shall return here.
9 With weeping they shall come,
      and with consolations I will lead them back,
    I will make them walk by brooks of water,
      in a straight path in which they shall not stumble,
    for I am a father to Israel,
      and E'phraim is my first-born."

15 Thus says the LORD:
"A voice is heard in Ramah,
    lamentation and bitter weeping.
Rachel is weeping for her children;
    she refuses to be comforted for her children,
    because they are not."

16 Thus says the LORD:
"Keep your voice from weeping,
    and your eyes from tears;
for your work shall be rewarded,
                says the LORD,
and they shall come back from the land of the enemy.
17 There is hope for your future,
               says the LORD,
and your children shall come back to their own country."

27 "Behold, the days are coming, says the LORD, when I will sow the house of Israel and the house of Judah with the seed of man and the seed of beast. 28 And it shall come to pass that as I have watched over them to pluck up and break down, to overthrow, destroy, and bring evil, so I will watch over them to build and to plant, says the LORD. 29 In those days they shall no longer say:

    'The fathers have eaten sour grapes,
      and the children's teeth are set on edge.'

30 But every one shall die for his own sin; each man who eats sour grapes, his teeth shall be set on edge.

31 "Behold, the days are coming, says the LORD, when I will make a new covenant with the house of Israel and the house of Judah, 32 not like the covenant which I made with their fathers when I took them by the hand to bring them out of the land of Egypt, my covenant which they broke, though I was their husband, says the LORD. 33 But this is the covenant which I will make with the house of Israel after those days, says the LORD: I will put my law within them,

and I will write it upon their hearts; and I will be their God, and they shall be my people. ³⁴ And no longer shall each man teach his neighbor and each his brother, saying, 'Know the LORD,' for they shall all know me, from the least of them to the greatest, says the LORD; for I will forgive their iniquity, and I will remember their sin no more."

³⁵ Thus says the LORD,
who gives the sun for light by day
and the fixed order of the moon and the stars for light by night,
who stirs up the sea so that its waves roar—
the LORD of hosts is his name:
³⁶ "If this fixed order departs
from before me, says the LORD,
then shall the descendants of Israel cease
from being a nation before me for ever."

³⁷ Thus says the LORD:
"If the heavens above can be measured,
and the foundations of the earth below can be explored
then I will cast off all the descendants of Israel
for all that they have done,
says the LORD."

30:8–10 During King Josiah's reign Judah was able to undertake the reconquest of Samaria and Galilee (2 Kings 23:15–19; 2 Chronicles 35:18). This excited the hope that the exiles of the Northern Kingdom might also be restored from captivity and all the Hebrews once again reunited around the religious center in Jerusalem (31:16). The regathering of the scattered nation became a central hope of the prophetic tradition (see Isaiah 43:5; 49:5–6; 18–23; Ezekiel 11:17; 20:34; 28:25; 34:12–13) and an integral part of Jewish messianic expectation. **30:11b** *I will chasten you*: a central idea of Jeremiah's is that the suffering of the exile will be a form of cleansing and purification for the nation. **30:17** Beneath the English translation there is a play on the Hebrew word *Tziyon* meaning "Zion." Israel's ill-wishers pronounced the word *Tziyah*, meaning "a desert," the kind of land (as verse 17 says) for which no one would care. But, as Jeremiah says, God cares. **30:18** A city was frequently built on a mound, known in the Hebrew as *tel*. On higher ground they would be better protected from attack. Many cities in the Bible carry the word *tel* in their name: for example, Tel-Assar, 2 Kings 19:12; Tel-Abib, Ezekiel, 3:15, etc. A tel is now the name given to a mound built even higher by the accumulation of debris from a series of destructions. Archaeologists digging in such a tel can trace the history of a city over the centuries with considerable accuracy. This prophecy, therefore, may be suggesting that Jerusalem or Samaria will be rebuilt on the very spot of its former ruins. **31:1–19** The entire passage, only parts of which are printed here, is the prophetic portion assigned for reading in the synagogue on the second day of Rosh Hashonah, the New Year. **31:15–17** Ramah, in the vicinity of Rachel's tomb, is on the highway five miles north of Jerusalem and would be on the route of those taken off to exile. This image of Rachel, wife of the patriarch Jacob, weeping and interceding for her people has inspired poetic and artistic creations in the Jewish community. **31:29** Jeremiah here initiates a revision in the traditional concept of collective guilt and punishment. It is one of the most important passages in his book. Ezekiel 18:2–4 will firmly reiterate this teaching of individual responsibility. **31:31–33** The new covenant will endure, since it will be written into the hearts of the people. For Jeremiah it is new in that it will confer a new, inward power for fulfilling the Law. Christian students of the Hebrew text and Jewish scholars are in agreement: insofar as Jeremiah's prophecy is concerned, this new covenant is made by God with the nation Israel. As the next sentences proclaim, the survival of Israel is as certain as the order of nature. Christians find in this verse a prediction of the new covenant mediated by Jesus.

Jeremiah Dictates His Prophecies to Baruch
Jeremiah 36:1–10, 21–32

36 In the fourth year of Jehoi'akim the son of Josi'ah, king of Judah, this word came to Jeremiah from the LORD: ² "Take a scroll and write on it all the words that I have spoken to you against Israel and Judah and all the nations, from the day I spoke to you, from the days of Josi'ah until today. ³ It may be that the house of Judah will hear all the evil which I intend to do to them, so that every one may turn from his evil way, and that I may forgive their iniquity and their sin."

4 Then Jeremiah called Baruch the son of Neri'ah, and Baruch wrote upon a scroll at the dictation of Jeremiah all the words of the LORD which he had spoken to him. ⁵ And Jeremiah ordered Baruch, saying, "I am debarred from going to the house of the LORD; ⁶ so you are to go, and on a fast day in the hearing of all the people in the LORD's house you shall read the words of the LORD from the scroll which you have written at my dictation. You shall read them also in the hearing of all the men of Judah who come out of their cities. ⁷ It may be that their supplication will come before the LORD, and that every one will turn from his evil way, for great is the anger and wrath that the LORD has pronounced against this people." ⁸ And Baruch the son of Neri'ah did all that Jeremiah the prophet ordered

him about reading from the scroll the words of the LORD in the LORD'S house.

9 In the fifth year of Jehoi'akim the son of Josi'ah, king of Judah, in the ninth month, all the people in Jerusalem and all the people who came from the cities of Judah to Jerusalem proclaimed a fast before the LORD. ¹⁰ Then, in the hearing of all the people, Baruch read the words of Jeremiah from the scroll, in the house of the LORD, in the chamber of Gemari'ah the son of Shaphan the secretary, which was in the upper court, at the entry of the New Gate of the LORD'S house.

21 Then the king sent Jehu'di to get the scroll, and he took it from the chamber of Eli'shama the secretary; and Jehu'di read it to the king and all the princes who stood beside the king. ²² It was the ninth month, and the king was sitting in the winter house and there was a fire burning in the brazier before him. ²³ As Jehu'di read three or four columns, the king would cut them off with a penknife and throw them into the fire in the brazier, until the entire scroll was consumed in the fire that was in the brazier. ²⁴ Yet neither the king, nor any of his servants who heard all these words, was afraid, nor did they rend their garments. ²⁵ Even when Elna'than and Delai'ah and Gemari'ah urged the king not to burn the scroll, he would not listen to them. ²⁶ And the king commanded Jerah'meel the king's son and Serai'ah the son of Az'ri-el and Shelemi'ah the son of Abdeel to seize Baruch the secretary and Jeremiah the prophet, but the LORD hid them.

27 Now, after the king had burned the scroll with the words which Baruch wrote at Jeremiah's dictation, the word of the LORD came to Jeremiah: ²⁸ "Take another scroll and write on it all the former words that were in the first scroll, which Jehoi'akim the king of Judah has burned. ²⁹ And concerning Jehoi'akim king of Judah you shall say, 'Thus says the LORD, You have burned this scroll, saying, "Why have you written in it that the king of Babylon will certainly come and destroy this land, and will cut off from it man and beast?" ³⁰ Therefore thus says the LORD concerning Jehoi'akim king of Judah, He shall have none to sit upon the throne of David, and his dead body shall be cast out to the heat by day and the frost by night. ³¹ And I will punish him and his offspring and his servants for their iniquity; I will bring upon them, and upon the inhabitants of Jerusalem, and upon the men of Judah, all the evil that I have pronounced against them, but they would not hear.' "

32 Then Jeremiah took another scroll and gave it to Baruch the scribe, the son of Neri'ah, who wrote on it at the dictation of Jeremiah all the words of the scroll which Jehoi'akim king of

Judah had burned in the fire; and many similar words were added to them.

Jeremiah Is Cast into Prison
Jeremiah 37:1–21; 38:1–13; 39:1–2, 8–18

37 Zedeki'ah the son of Josi'ah, whom Nebuchadrez'zar king of Babylon made king in the land of Judah, reigned instead of Coni'ah the son of Jehoi'akim. ²But neither he nor his servants nor the people of the land listened to the words of the LORD which he spoke through Jeremiah the prophet.

3 King Zedeki'ah sent Jehu'cal the son of Shelemi'ah, and Zephani'ah the priest, the son of Ma-asei'ah, to Jeremiah the prophet, saying, "Pray for us to the LORD our God." ⁴Now Jeremiah was still going in and out among the people, for he had not yet been put in prison. ⁵The army of Pharaoh had come out of Egypt; and when the Chalde'ans who were besieging Jerusalem heard news of them, they withdrew from Jerusalem.

6 Then the word of the LORD came to Jeremiah the prophet: ⁷"Thus says the LORD, God of Israel: Thus shall you say to the king of Judah who sent you to me to inquire of me, 'Behold, Pharaoh's army which came to help you is about to return to Egypt, to its own land. ⁸And the Chalde'ans shall come back and fight against this city; they shall take it and burn it with fire. ⁹Thus says the LORD, Do not deceive yourselves, saying, "The Chalde'ans will surely stay away from us," for they will not stay away. ¹⁰For even if you should defeat the whole army of Chalde'ans who are fighting against you, and there remained of them only wounded men, every man in his tent, they would rise up and burn this city with fire.'"

11 Now when the Chalde'an army had withdrawn from Jerusalem at the approach of Pharaoh's army, ¹²Jeremiah set out from Jerusalem to go to the land of Benjamin to receive his portion there among the people. ¹³When he was at the Benjamin Gate, a sentry there named Iri'jah the son of Shelemi'ah, son of Hanani'ah, seized Jeremiah the prophet, saying, "You are deserting to the Chalde'ans." ¹⁴And Jeremiah said, "It is false; I am not deserting to the Chalde'ans." But Iri'jah would not listen to him, and seized Jeremiah and brought him to the princes. ¹⁵And the princes were enraged at Jeremiah, and they beat him and imprisoned him in the house of Jonathan the secretary, for it had been made a prison.

16 When Jeremiah had come to the dungeon cells, and remained there many days, ¹⁷King Zedeki'ah sent for him, and received him. The king questioned him secretly in his house, and said, "Is there any word from the LORD?" Jeremiah said, "There is." Then he said,

"You shall be delivered into the hand of the king of Babylon."
[18] Jeremiah also said to King Zedeki'ah, "What wrong have I done to
you or your servants or this people, that you have put me in prison?
[19] Where are your prophets who prophesied to you, saying, 'The king
of Babylon will not come against you and against this land'? [20] Now
hear, I pray you, O my lord the king: let my humble plea come
before you, and do not send me back to the house of Jonathan the
secretary, lest I die there." [21] So King Zedeki'ah gave orders, and
they committed Jeremiah to the court of the guard; and a loaf of
bread was given him daily from the bakers' street, until all the bread
of the city was gone. So Jeremiah remained in the court of the guard.
38 Now Shephati'ah the son of Mattan, Gedali'ah the son of
Pashhur, Jucal the son of Shelemi'ah, and Pashhur the son of
Malchi'ah heard the words that Jeremiah was saying to all the
people, [2] "Thus says the LORD, He who stays in this city shall die
by the sword, by famine, and by pestilence; but he who goes out
to the Chalde'ans shall live; he shall have his life as a prize of
war, and live. [3] Thus says the LORD, This city shall surely be
given into the hand of the army of the king of Babylon and be
taken." [4] Then the princes said to the king, "Let this man be put
to death, for he is weakening the hands of the soldiers who are
left in this city, and the hands of all the people, by speaking such
words to them. For this man is not seeking the welfare of this
people, but their harm." [5] King Zedeki'ah said, "Behold, he is in
your hands; for the king can do nothing against you." [6] So they
took Jeremiah and cast him into the cistern of Malchi'ah, the
king's son, which was in the court of the guard, letting Jeremiah
down by ropes. And there was no water in the cistern, but only
mire, and Jeremiah sank in the mire.

7 When E'bed-mel'ech the Ethiopian, a eunuch, who was in the
king's house, heard that they had put Jeremiah into the cistern—the
king was sitting in the Benjamin Gate—[8] E'bed-mel'ech went from
the king's house and said to the king, [9] "My lord the king, these men
have done evil in all that they did to Jeremiah the prophet by casting
him into the cistern; and he will die there of hunger, for there is no
bread left in the city." [10] Then the king commanded E'bed-mel'ech,
the Ethiopian, "Take three men with you from here, and lift Jeremiah
the prophet out of the cistern before he dies." [11] So E'bed-mel'ech took
the men with him and went to the house of the king, to a wardrobe of
the storehouse, and took from there old rags and worn-out clothes,
which he let down to Jeremiah in the cistern by ropes. [12] Then
E'bed-mel'ech the Ethiopian said to Jeremiah, "Put the rags and
clothes between your armpits and the ropes." Jeremiah did so. [13] Then

they drew Jeremiah up with ropes and lifted him out of the cistern. And Jeremiah remained in the court of the guard.

39 In the ninth year of Zedeki'ah king of Judah, in the tenth month, Nebuchadrez'zar king of Babylon and all his army came against Jerusalem and besieged it; ² in the eleventh year of Zedeki'ah, in the fourth month, on the ninth day of the month, a breach was made in the city.

8 The Chalde'ans burned the king's house and the house of the people, and broke down the walls of Jerusalem. ⁹ Then Nebu'zarad'an, the captain of the guard, carried into exile to Babylon the rest of the people who were left in the city, those who had deserted to him, and the people who remained. ¹⁰ Nebu'zarad'an, the captain of the guard, left in the land of Judah some of the poor people who owned nothing, and gave them vineyards and fields at the same time.

11 Nebuchadrez'zar king of Babylon gave command concerning Jeremiah through Nebu'zarad'an, the captain of the guard, saying, ¹² "Take him, look after him well and do him no harm, but deal with him as he tells you." ¹³ So Nebu'zarad'an the captain of the guard, Nebushaz'ban the Rab'saris, Ner'gal-share'zer the Rabmag, and all the chief officers of the king of Babylon ¹⁴ sent and took Jeremiah from the court of the guard. They entrusted him to Gedali'ah the son of Ahi'kam, son of Shaphan, that he should take him home. So he dwelt among the people.

15 The word of the LORD came to Jeremiah while he was shut up in the court of the guard: ¹⁶ "Go, and say to E'bed-mel'ech the Ethiopian, 'Thus says the LORD of hosts, the God of Israel: Behold, I will fulfil my words against this city for evil and not for good, and they shall be accomplished before you on that day. ¹⁷ But I will deliver you on that day, says the LORD, and you shall not be given into the hand of the men of whom you are afraid. ¹⁸ For I will surely save you, and you shall not fall by the sword; but you shall have your life as a prize of war, because you have put your trust in me, says the LORD.' "

37:3 A fulfillment of Jeremiah's prophecy at 15:11. There he warned that even though the false prophets mocked at his gloomy predictions, the day would come when the rulers would realize that only Jeremiah had spoken the true word. Then they would ask him to intercede for them. For other similar petitions for intercession see 21:1 ff. and 42:1 ff. **37:5** Pharaoh Hophra (cf. 44:30) who ruled from 590 to 571 B.C. and who was an ally of Judah, may have been defeated in this battle (cf. Ezekiel 30:31). Despite his promises he offered Judah no significant assistance.

Jeremiah Chooses to Remain in Jerusalem

Chapters 40–44 narrate incidents in Jeremiah's life after the fall of Jerusalem.

Jeremiah 40 : 1–6

40 The word that came to Jeremiah from the LORD after Nebu'zarad'an the captain of the guard had let him go from Ramah, when he took him bound in chains along with all the captives of Jerusalem and Judah who were being exiled to Babylon. ² The captain of the guard took Jeremiah and said to him, "The LORD your God pronounced this evil against this place; ³ the LORD has brought it about, and has done as he said. Because you sinned against the LORD, and did not obey his voice, this thing has come upon you. ⁴ Now, behold, I release you today from the chains on your hands. If it seems good to you to come with me to Babylon, come, and I will look after you well; but if it seems wrong to you to come with me to Babylon, do not come. See, the whole land is before you; go wherever you think it good and right to go. ⁵ If you remain, then return to Gedali'ah the son of Ahi'kam, son of Shaphan, whom the king of Babylon appointed governor of the cities of Judah, and dwell with him among the people; or go wherever you think it right to go." So the captain of the guard gave him an allowance of food and a present, and let him go. ⁶ Then Jeremiah went to Gedali'ah the son of Ahi'kam, at Mizpah, and dwelt with him among the people who were left in the land.

40:5 An impression of what may have been the seal of Gedaliah, appointed governor over Judea, has been found in excavations at Lachish.

Jeremiah Cautions against Flight to Egypt

Gedaliah, the appointed governor of Judea, was senselessly murdered. The people, fearful that Nebuchadrezzar would wreak vengeance upon them, consult Jeremiah. He urges them to stay. But they reject his counsel. They decide to flee to Egypt and they carry Jeremiah away with them. Even there, despite his old age, Jeremiah is not still. He castigates the Egyptian Jews for their idolatrous worship of the "queen of heaven," and he predicts that with the defeat of Pharaoh Hophra their last refuge will be destroyed.

Jeremiah 42:7–16; 43:1–4, 7; 44:1, 13–14

7 At the end of ten days the word of the LORD came to Jeremiah. ⁸ Then he summoned Joha'nan the son of Kare'ah and all the commanders of the forces who were with him, and all the people from the least to the greatest, ⁹ and said to them, "Thus says the LORD, the

God of. Israel, to whom you sent me to present your supplication before him: [10] If you will remain in this land, then I will build you up and not pull you down; I will plant you, and not pluck you up; for I repent of the evil which I did to you. [11] Do not fear the king of Babylon, of whom you are afraid; do not fear him, says the LORD, for I am with you, to save you and to deliver you from his hand. [12] I will grant you mercy, that he may have mercy on you and let you remain in your own land. [13] But if you say, 'We will not remain in this land,' disobeying the voice of the LORD your God [14] and saying, 'No, we will go to the land of Egypt, where we shall not see war, or hear the sound of the trumpet, or be hungry for bread, and we will dwell there,' [15] then hear the word of the LORD, O remnant of Judah. Thus says the LORD of hosts, the God of Israel: If you set your faces to enter Egypt and go to live there, [16] then the sword which you fear shall overtake you there in the land of Egypt; and the famine of which you are afraid shall follow hard after you to Egypt; and there you shall die.

43 When Jeremiah finished speaking to all the people all these words of the LORD their God, with which the LORD their God had sent him to them, [2] Azari'ah the son of Hoshai'ah and Joha'nan the son of Kare'ah and all the insolent men said to Jeremiah, "You are telling a lie. The LORD our God did not send you to say, 'Do not go to Egypt to live there'; [3] but Baruch the son of Neri'ah has set you against us, to deliver us into the hand of the Chalde'ans, that they may kill us or take us into exile in Babylon." [4] So Joha'nan the son of Kare'ah and all the commanders of the forces and all the people did not obey the voice of the LORD, to remain in the land of Judah.

7 And they came into the land of Egypt, for they did not obey the voice of the LORD. And they arrived at Tah'panhes.

44 The word that came to Jeremiah concerning all the Jews that dwelt in the land of Egypt, at Migdol, at Tah'panhes, at Memphis, and in the land of Pathros.

13 I will punish those who dwell in the land of Egypt, as I have punished Jerusalem, with the sword, with famine, and with pestilence, [14] so that none of the remnant of Judah who have come to live in the land of Egypt shall escape or survive or return to the land of Judah, to which they desire to return to dwell there; for they shall not return, except some fugitives."

The Book Concludes on a Note of Hope

Jeremiah's book concludes with a detailed account of Nebuchadrezzar's destruction of Jerusalem. But lest it end on a sad note, the historian records that the exiled King Jehoiachin, in the thirty-seventh year of his captivity, was released from prison and set above all other captive kings. Thus the book closes with an expression of confidence that God has not rejected His people entirely. Even in the exile He watches over them.

Jeremiah 52:12–16, 28–34

12 In the fifth month, on the tenth day of the month—which was the nineteenth year of King Nebuchadrez'zar, king of Babylon— Nebu'zarad'an the captain of the bodyguard who served the king of Babylon, entered Jerusalem. ¹³ And he burned the house of the LORD, and the king's house and all the houses of Jerusalem; every great house he burned down. ¹⁴ And all the army of the Chalde'ans, who were with the captain of the guard, broke down all the walls round about Jerusalem. ¹⁵ And Nebu'zarad'an the captain of the guard carried away captive some of the poorest of the people and the rest of the people who were left in the city and the deserters who had deserted to the king of Babylon, together with the rest of the artisans. ¹⁶ But Nebu'zarad'an the captain of the guard left some of the poorest of the land to be vinedressers and plowmen.

28 This is the number of the people whom Nebuchadrez'zar carried away captive: in the seventh year, three thousand and twenty-three Jews; ²⁹ in the eighteenth year of Nebuchadrez'zar he carried away captive from Jerusalem eight hundred and thirty-two persons; ³⁰ in the twenty-third year of Nebuchadrez'zar, Nebu'zarad'an the captain of the guard carried away captive of the Jews seven hundred and forty-five persons; all the persons were four thousand and six hundred.

31 And in the thirty-seventh year of the captivity of Jehoi'achin king of Judah, in the twelfth month, on the twenty-fifth day of the month, E'vil-mer'odach king of Babylon, in the year that he became king, lifted up the head of Jehoi'achin king of Judah and brought him out of prison; ³² and he spoke kindly to him, and gave him a seat above the seats of the kings who were with him in Babylon. ³³ So Jehoi'achin put off his prison garments. And every day of his life he dined regularly at the king's table; ³⁴ as for his allowance, a regular allowance was given him by the king according to his daily need, until the day of his death as long as he lived.

The Lamentations of Jeremiah

Traditionally it has been held that Lamentations, the third of the Five Scrolls in the Hebrew Bible, was written by the prophet Jeremiah who experienced the calamity of his people in the destruction of Jerusalem in 586 B.C. It was first ascribed to him in the Greek translation, probably on the basis of 3:1, in a prose introduction to that version. Many modern scholars, however, feel that were it truly by Jeremiah it would bear a greater resemblance to that prophet's own thought and style. They attribute Lamentations instead to an unknown poet of the Exile who had experienced the horrors of the first days of captivity—perhaps as a member of King Zedekiah's party.

The book consists of five chapters, each a complete poem in itself, unrelieved in its repetition of lament. In each there is a description of the sufferings of the people and a prayerful plea that God accept the repentance of the nation.

The poet uses an alphabetic acrostic form in the first four lamentations: each verse starts with a new letter of the alphabet in order. The author has also employed the characteristic Hebrew lamentation metre known as the "elegiac metre," that evokes the sound of sobbing. In the Hebrew text a three-beat first line is followed by a two-beat second line.

This book is read in the synagogue at the service commemorating the tragic destruction of the temples of Jerusalem, the first in 586 B.C., the second in A.D. 70. That day falls on the ninth day of the Hebrew month Av (July or August) and is observed by Orthodox Jews as a fast day. In some synagogues the sanctuaries are darkened and, by candlelight, congregants chant to a mournful tune the verses of this book.

The Poet Laments Over Jerusalem
Lamentations 1:1–3, 10–12

1 How lonely sits the city
   that was full of people!
How like a widow has she become,
   she that was great among the nations!
She that was a princess among the cities
   has become a vassal.

² She weeps bitterly in the night,
   tears on her cheeks;

among all her lovers
    she has none to comfort her;
all her friends have dealt treacherously with her,
    they have become her enemies.

³ Judah has gone into exile because of affliction
    and hard servitude;
she dwells now among the nations,
    but finds no resting place;
her pursuers have all overtaken her
    in the midst of her distress.

¹⁰ The enemy has stretched out his hands
    over all her precious things;
yea, she has seen the nations
    invade her sanctuary,
those whom thou didst forbid
    to enter thy congregation.

¹¹ All her people groan
    as they search for bread;
they trade their treasures for food
    to revive their strength.
"Look, O LORD, and behold,
    for I am despised."

¹² "Is it nothing to you, all you who pass by?
    Look and see
if there is any sorrow like my sorrow
    which was brought upon me,
which the LORD inflicted
    on the day of his fierce anger."

1:10 For description of Jerusalem's sack see 2 Kings 24:13. For the biblical law prohibiting pagans to enter the sanctuary see Deuteronomy 23:4.

Prayer for the Lord's Forgiveness
Lamentations 5:1–22

5 Remember, O LORD, what has befallen us;
    behold, and see our disgrace!
² Our inheritance has been turned over to strangers,
    our homes to aliens.
³ We have become orphans, fatherless;
    our mothers are like widows.

⁴ We must pay for the water we drink,
    the wood we get must be bought.
⁵ With a yoke on our necks we are hard driven;
    we are weary, we are given no rest.
⁶ We have given the hand to Egypt,
    and to Assyria, to get bread enough.
⁷ Our fathers sinned, and are no more;
    and we bear their iniquities.
⁸ Slaves rule over us;
    there is none to deliver us from their hand.
⁹ We get our bread at the peril of our lives,
    because of the sword in the wilderness.
¹⁰ Our skin is hot as an oven
    with the burning heat of famine.
¹¹ Women are ravished in Zion,
    virgins in the towns of Judah.
¹² Princes are hung up by their hands;
    no respect is shown to the elders.
¹³ Young men are compelled to grind at the mill;
    and boys stagger under loads of wood.
¹⁴ The old men have quit the city gate,
    the young men their music.
¹⁵ The joy of our hearts has ceased;
    our dancing has been turned to mourning.
¹⁶ The crown has fallen from our head;
    woe to us, for we have sinned!
¹⁷ For this our heart has become sick,
    for these things our eyes have grown dim,
¹⁸ for Mount Zion which lies desolate;
    jackals prowl over it.

¹⁹ But thou, O LORD, dost reign for ever;
    thy throne endures to all generations.
²⁰ Why dost thou forget us for ever,
    why dost thou so long forsake us?
²¹ Restore us to thyself, O LORD, that we may be restored!
    Renew our days as of old!
²² Or hast thou utterly rejected us?
    Art thou exceedingly angry with us?

5:7 The poet interprets the disaster to be a judgment on the entire society because of the sins of the fathers. In contrast, the prophet Ezekiel later emphasized the concept of individual retribution (Ezekiel 18:2 ff.). **5:21** This verse is recited in the synagogue as the concluding hymn, when after the scriptural lesson the Torah Scroll is returned to the Ark. **5:22** According to Jewish custom it is not fitting to conclude a biblical book on a sad note. Thus verse 21 is repeated after verse 22 in the Hebrew Bible. A similar repetition occurs at the end of Isaiah, Malachi and Ecclesiastes.

The Book of Ezekiel

Ezekiel, who prophecied among the Hebrew exiles in Babylon, is the only prophet in Scripture whose mission took place almost completely outside the land of Israel. He lived in Tel Abib on the banks of the river Chebar in Babylonia, an area of settlement for the exiles. His activity may be dated 593–571 B.C.

The superscription to the book (1:1–3) recounts that Ezekiel was the son of Buzi, a Jerusalem priest. Like Jeremiah before him, therefore, Ezekiel was both a priest and a prophet.

Ezekiel was moved to prophesy in the fifth year of King Jehoiachin's captivity, that is, 593 B.C. Undoubtedly he was aware of a plot being prepared jointly by patriots in Jerusalem and the exiles in Babylon to overthrow Babylonian domination. Like Jeremiah, Ezekiel protested against such a rebellion. He interpreted Judah's subjugation to Babylonia as a discipline of God, a consequence of the Hebrew people's idolatry and unrighteousness.

Like Jeremiah, Ezekiel attacked the complacency of Judah's leaders; they believed that the existence of the sanctuary in Jerusalem would assure them of protection against the enemy. Ezekiel joined Jeremiah in stressing that the iniquities of Judah would have to be punished. He warned of the imminent destruction of Jerusalem and pleaded with the people to see in the collapse of the state a moral lesson that should lead them to repentance. The first twenty-four chapters of this book (written 593-586 B.C.) are on this theme.

Like the other prophets, Ezekiel combined both judgment and consolation in his message. Chapters 25–32 are oracles against foreign nations; 33–39 promise restoration to the penitent exiles in a time to come; 40–48 provide a vision of the new Jerusalem. His priestly background is evidenced as Ezekiel provides a blueprint for a restored Temple and suggests new procedures to be followed by the chastened community. In Ezekiel's view the culminating expression of a revitalized religious life would be one that was both ethically upright and liturgically informed, demonstrating thereby proper reverence for God and His Law.

Ezekiel's prophetic ministry covered about twenty years. Although no exact date is given for his death, tradition holds that he died in Babylon during the reign of Nebuchadrezzar and was buried at Kefil near Birs Nimrud. For many centuries Jews and Moslems made pilgrimages to the tomb there and to a nearby synagogue named after him.

Unlike most of the prophets, Ezekiel's writing does not often burst into poetry. He is distinguished, however, by his frequent use of allegory and symbol, and particularly by the performance of elaborate symbolic actions as a form of instruction. In his mystic visions, he describes the divine throne-chariot; these stimulated esoteric groups among the Jews who engaged in mystic study. One of these, a poet and liturgist, Eliezar Kalir, drew upon Ezekiel's visions to create prayers and hymns that are still recited in synagogues on the Sabbath and on the Day of Atonement. Several Negro spirituals such as "Ezekiel Saw the Wheels" (1:16) and "Dry Bones" (37:7) magnify these most provocative visions in the life of this important prophet.

Ezekiel Experiences a Vision of the Divine Chariot

Ezekiel's "visions of God" and particularly his vision of the Divine Throne stimulated the development in Judaism of groups of mystics who sought by ablutions, fasts, prayers and incantations to stimulate ecstatic states whereby they might similarly see such visions. Such persons frequently experienced hallucinations and believed in the reality of their visions. Fearful of such mysticism, the rabbis, early in the Talmudic period, ruled that knowledge of the Divine Throne should not be taught to anyone "except he be wise" (*Hagigah* 2:1). Some rabbis even suggested that this chapter of Ezekiel should not be read by anyone younger than thirty years of age.

The Jewish translator, Abraham Harkavy, distinguishes words he has placed into the text for literary style from the exact and literal rendering of the Hebrew language. The inserted English words, intended to make the translation intelligible, are in italics.

Ezekiel 1:1–20, 26–28

Harkavy Translation

1 Now it came to pass in the thirtieth year, in the fourth *month*, in the fifth *day* of the month, as I *was* among the captives by the river of Chebar, *that* the heavens were opened, and I saw visions of God.

2 In the fifth *day* of the month (it *was* the fifth year of king Jehoiachin's captivity).

3 The word of the Lord came expressly unto Ezekiel the priest, the son of Buzi, in the land of the Chaldeans by the river Chebar; and the hand of the Lord was there upon him.

4 And I looked, and, behold, a whirlwind came out of the north, a great cloud, and a fire infolding itself, and a brightness *was* about it, and out of the midst thereof as the colour of amber, out of the midst of fire.

5 Also out of the midst thereof *came* the likeness of four living creatures. And this *was* their appearance; they had the likeness of a man.

6 And every one had four faces, and every one had four wings.

7 And their feet *were* straight feet; and the sole of their feet *was*

like the sole of a calf's foot: and they sparkled like the colour of burnished brass.

8 And *they had* the hands of a man under their wings on their four sides; and they four had their faces and their wings.

9 Their wings *were* joined one to another; they turned not when they went; they went every one straight forward.

10 As for the likeness of their faces, they four had the face of a man, and the face of a lion, on the right side: and they four had the face of an ox on the left side; they four also had the face of an eagle.

11 Thus *were* their faces: and their wings *were* stretched upward; two *wings* of every one were joined one to another, and two covered their bodies.

12 And they went every one straight forward: whither the spirit was to go, they went; and they turned not when they went.

13 As for the likeness of the living creatures, their appearance *was* like burning coals of fire, *and* like the appearance of torches: it went up and down among the living creatures; and the fire was bright, and out of the fire went forth lightning.

14 And the living creatures ran and returned as the appearance of a flash of lightning.

15 Now as I beheld the living creatures, behold one wheel upon the earth by the living creatures, at each of their four faces.

16 The appearance of the wheels and their work *was* like unto the colour of a beryl; and they four had one likeness: and their appearance and their work *was* as it were a wheel in the middle of a wheel.

17 When they went, they went upon their four sides: *and* they turned not when they went.

18 As for their rings, they were so high that they were dreadful; and their rings *were* full of eyes round about them four.

19 And when the living creatures went, the wheels went by them: and when the living creatures were lifted up from the earth, the wheels were lifted up.

20 Whithersoever the spirit was to go, they went, thither *was their* spirit to go; and the wheels were lifted up over against them: for the spirit of the living creature *was* in the wheels.

26 And above the firmament that *was* over their heads *was* the likeness of a throne, as the appearance of a sapphire stone: and upon the likeness of the throne *was* the likeness as the appearance of a man above upon it.

27 And I saw the colour of amber, as the appearance of fire round about within it, from the appearance of his loins even upward, and

from the appearance of his loins even downward, I saw as it were the appearance of fire, and it had brightness round about.

28 As the appearance of the bow that is in the cloud in the day of rain, so *was* the appearance of the brightness round about. This *was* the appearance of the likeness of the glory of the Lord. And when I saw *it*, I fell upon my face, and I heard a voice of one that spake.

1:1 The first chapter of Ezekiel is recited in the synagogue as the prophetic portion on the first day of Shavuoth, Pentecost, celebrating the revelation of the Ten Commandments at Sinai. **1:10** The Assyrians had created a servant creature for their gods known as Karibu which was stationed at the gates of their Temple. It contained the head of a man, the body of a lion, the hooves of a bull and the wings of an eagle. Some scholars suggest that the biblical cherubim are reminiscent of these Karibu (see Exodus 25:18). God's transcendent majesty over all creation and His authority over all gods is manifest in that He sits above these creatures. The characteristics of the four creatures described in Ezekiel's vision were used in the New Testament to describe that which is noblest, strongest, most productive and swiftest among God's creations. (See Relevation 4:7–8.) **1:26–28** Jewish scholars, fearful that it be presumed that Ezekiel actually saw God in the appearance of a man, emphasize that all Ezekiel saw was the *glory* of the Lord, not the Lord Himself. Judaism rejects the idea that God has shape or form like a man.

The Lord Commissions Ezekiel as His Prophet
Ezekiel 2:1–6, 9–10; 3:1–4

2 And he said to me, "Son of man, stand upon your feet, and I will speak with you." [2] And when he spoke to me, the Spirit entered into me and set me upon my feet; and I heard him speaking to me. [3] And he said to me, "Son of man, I send you to the people of Israel, to a nation of rebels, who have rebelled against me; they and their fathers have transgressed against me to this very day. [4] The people also are impudent and stubborn: I send you to them; and you shall say to them, 'Thus says the Lord God.' [5] And whether they hear or refuse to hear (for they are a rebellious house) they will know that there has been a prophet among them. [6] And you, son of man, be not afraid of them, nor be afraid of their words, though briers and thorns are with you and you sit upon scorpions; be not afraid of their words, nor be dismayed at their looks, for they are a rebellious house.

9 And when I looked, behold, a hand was stretched out to me, and, lo, a written scroll was in it; [10] and he spread it before me; and it had writing on the front and on the back, and there were written on it words of lamentation and mourning and woe.

3 And he said to me, "Son of man, eat what is offered to you; eat this scroll, and go, speak to the house of Israel." [2] So I opened my mouth, and he gave me the scroll to eat. [3] And he said to me, "Son of man, eat this scroll that I give to you and fill your stomach with it." Then I ate it; and it was in my mouth as sweet as honey.

4 And he said to me, "Son of man, go, get you to the house of Israel, and speak with my words to them."

> **2:1** Jewish tradition does not interpret the words "son of man" to mean that Ezekiel was of a divine nature; to the contrary, although he was privileged to experience a vision of the divine chariot, he was only a human being. Such a similar emphasis is given to the word "man" in describing Moses, even though Moses spoke to God "mouth to mouth" (cf. Numbers 12:3, 8). Christian scholars also view the appellation as God's usual address to Ezekiel, expressing creaturely weakness. In later literature, however, the words were given a messianic significance (cf. Enoch 1:15). They were adopted by the Gospel writers as a messianic title. **3:1** Compare Isaiah 6:5–7, Jeremiah 1:9.

Ezekiel Is Charged to be a Watchman
Ezekiel 3:17–21

3 [17] "Son of man, I have made you a watchman for the house of Israel; whenever you hear a word from my mouth, you shall give them a warning from me. [18] If I say to the wicked, 'You shall surely die,' and you give him no warning, nor speak to warn the wicked from his wicked way, in order to save his life, that wicked man shall die in his iniquity; but his blood I will require at your hand. [19] But if you warn the wicked, and he does not turn from his wickedness, or from his wicked way, he shall die in his iniquity; but you will have saved your life. [20] Again, if a righteous man turns from his righteousness and commits iniquity, and I lay a stumbling block before him, he shall die; because you have not warned him, he shall die for his sin, and his righteous deeds which he has done shall not be remembered; but his blood I will require at your hand. [21] Nevertheless if you warn the righteous man not to sin, and he does not sin, he shall surely live, because he took warning; and you will have saved your life."

Ezekiel Performs Acts Symbolic of Jerusalem's Destruction

Chapter 4 through chapter 5:4 record four symbolic acts by which Ezekiel instructed the people about the fate of Jerusalem. In the selection given here the prophet is instructed to inscribe a plan of the siege of the city on a slab of clay. He also mimes the rebelliousness of Israel, the famine to be endured during the siege, and the tragic fate awaiting the population of the doomed city. Verses 5:5–12 then provide a clear explanation of these symbolic acts and God's intent for Jerusalem.

Ezekiel 4:1–3; 5:5–8

4 "And you, O son of man, take a brick and lay it before you, and portray upon it a city, even Jerusalem; ² and put siegeworks against it, and build a siege wall against it, and cast up a mound against it; set camps also against it, and plant battering rams against it round about. ³ And take an iron plate, and place it as an iron wall between you and the city; and set your face toward it, and let it be a state of siege, and press the siege against it. This is a sign for the house of Israel.

5 ⁵ "Thus says the Lord GOD: This is Jerusalem; I have set her in the center of the nations, with countries round about her. ⁶ And she has wickedly rebelled against my ordinances more than the nations, and against my statutes more than the countries round about her, by rejecting my ordinances and not walking in my statutes. ⁷ Therefore thus says the Lord GOD: Because you are more turbulent than the nations that are round about you, and have not walked in my statutes or kept my ordinances, but have acted according to the ordinances of the nations that are round about you; ⁸ therefore thus says the Lord GOD: Behold, I, even I, am against you; and I will execute judgments in the midst of you in the sight of the nations."

4:1 It was common in Assyria and Babylonia to write upon a softened slab of clay, which was then hardened by exposure to the sun. **4:2** Assyrian bas-reliefs depicts such towers manned by archers (cf. 2 Kings 25:1).

Make Yourselves a New Heart and a New Spirit

Some of the exiles, touched by Ezekiel's teaching, must have given vent to a sense of hopelessness. They argued that their punishment was after all a consequence of the sins of their fathers. Such was the interpretation made by the author of Lamentations 5:7. Of what value, then, their own remorse if they would have to endure punishment for the iniquity of former generations? Moses had described God as visiting the iniquity of the fathers upon the children until the fourth generation (cf. Exodus 20:5). Ezekiel teaches (18:2–4) that each individual is immediately related to God; He deals with everyone directly; *only* the soul that sins dies. The theme of this chapter is repeated again in chapter 33:10–20.

Ezekiel 18:1–32

18 The word of the LORD came to me again: ² "What do you mean by repeating this proverb concerning the land of Israel. 'The fathers have eaten sour grapes, and the children's teeth are on edge'? ³ As I live, says the Lord GOD, this proverb shall no more be used by you in Israel. [4] Behold, all souls are mine; the soul of the father as well as the soul of the son is mine: the soul that sins shall die.

5 "If a man is righteous and does what is lawful and right—[6] if he does not eat upon the mountains or lift up his eyes to the idols of the house of Israel, does not defile his neighbor's wife or approach a woman in her time of impurity, [7] does not oppress any one, but restores to the debtor his pledge, commits no robbery, gives his bread to the hungry and covers the naked with a garment, [8] does not lend at interest or take any increase, withholds his hand from iniquity, executes true justice between man and man, [9] walks in my statutes, and is careful to observe my ordinances—he is righteous, he shall surely live, says the Lord GOD.

10 "If he begets a son who is a robber, a shedder of blood, [11] who does none of these duties, but eats upon the mountains, defiles his neighbor's wife, [12] oppresses the poor and needy, commits robbery, does not restore the pledge, lifts up his eyes to the idols, commits abomination, [13] lends at interest, and takes increase; shall he then live? He shall not live. He has done all these abominable things; he shall surely die; his blood shall be upon himself.

14 "But if this man begets a son who sees all the sins which his father has done, and fears, and does not do likewise, [15] who does not eat upon the mountains or lift up his eyes to the idols of the house of Israel, does not defile his neighbor's wife, [16] does not wrong any one, exacts no pledge, commits no robbery, but gives his bread to the hungry and covers the naked with a garment, [17] withholds his hand from iniquity, takes no interest or increase, observes my ordinances, and walks in my statutes; he shall not die for his father's iniquity; he shall surely live. [18] As for his father, because he practiced extortion, robbed his brother, and did what is not good among his people, behold, he shall die for his iniquity.

19 "Yet you say, 'Why should not the son suffer for the iniquity of the father?' When the son has done what is lawful and right, and has been careful to observe all my statutes, he shall surely live. [20] The soul that sins shall die. The son shall not suffer for the iniquity of the father, nor the father suffer for the iniquity of the son; the righteousness of the righteous shall be upon himself, and the wickedness of the wicked shall be upon himself.

21 "But if a wicked man turns away from all his sins which he has committed and keeps all my statutes and does what is lawful and right, he shall surely live; he shall not die. [22] None of the transgressions which he has committed shall be remembered against him; for the righteousness which he has done he shall live. [23] Have I any

pleasure in the death of the wicked, says the Lord GOD, and not rather that he should turn from his way and live? [24]But when a righteous man turns away from his righteousness and commits iniquity and does the same abominable things that the wicked man does, shall he live? None of the righteous deeds which he has done shall be remembered; for the treachery of which he is guilty and the sin he has committed, he shall die.

25 "Yet you say, 'The way of the Lord is not just.' Hear now, O house of Israel: Is my way not just? Is it not your ways that are not just? [26]When a righteous man turns away from his righteousness and commits iniquity, he shall die for it; for the iniquity which he has committed he shall die. [27]Again, when a wicked man turns away from the wickedness he has committed and does what is lawful and right, he shall save his life. [28]Because he considered and turned away from all the transgressions which he had committed, he shall surely live, he shall not die. [29]Yet the house of Israel says, 'The way of the Lord is not just.' O house of Israel, are my ways not just? Is it not your ways that are not just?

30 "Therefore I will judge you, O house of Israel, every one according to his ways, says the Lord GOD. Repent and turn from all your transgressions, lest iniquity be your ruin. [31]Cast away from you all the transgressions which you have committed against me, and get yourselves a new heart and a new spirit! Why will you die, O house of Israel? [32]For I have no pleasure in the death of any one, says the Lord GOD; so turn, and live."

18:5–9 These verses provide a description of a righteous man in Ezekiel's time. 18:6 Idols were detestably worshipped by eating a ceremonial meal at a sanctuary upon one of the high places. 18:21–29 Jewish tradition reasons: If an individual is not punished for his own sins after he repents, how much less should he be punished for the sins of others? 18:21 The Rabbis point to the key verbs in this verse as defining two stages of repentance: man must *turn* away from his evil; he must then *keep* the law of God.

The Prophet Predicts a Messianic Ruler

As preparation for the restoration, Ezekiel exhorts the exiles to remove their false leaders, i.e., shepherds who feed themselves instead of their flock. He seeks to inspire the people with a description of an ideal ruler who will be established by God as a blessing to Israel and all nations.

Ezekiel 34:1–5, 23–31

34 The word of the LORD came to me: [2]"Son of man, prophesy against the shepherds of Israel, prophesy, and say to them, even to the shepherds, Thus says the Lord GOD: Ho, shepherds of Israel who have been feeding yourselves! Should not shepherds feed the sheep? ³ You eat the fat, you clothe yourselves with the wool, you slaughter the fatlings; but you do not feed the sheep. ⁴ The weak you have not strengthened, the sick you have not healed, the crippled you have not bound up, the strayed you have not brought back, the lost you have not sought, and with force and harshness you have ruled them. ⁵ So they were scattered, because there was no shepherd; and they became food for all the wild beasts.

23 And I will set up over them one shepherd, my servant David, and he shall feed them: he shall feed them and be their shepherd. ²⁴ And I, the LORD, will be their God, and my servant David shall be prince among them; I, the LORD, have spoken.

25 "I will make with them a covenant of peace and banish wild beasts from the land, so that they may dwell securely in the wilderness and sleep in the woods. ²⁶ And I will make them and the places round about my hill a blessing; and I will send down the showers in their season; they shall be showers of blessing. ²⁷ And the trees in the field shall yield their fruit, and the earth shall yield its increase, and they shall be secure in their land; and they shall know that I am the LORD, when I break the bars of their yoke, and deliver them from the hand of those who enslaved them. ²⁸ They shall no more be a prey to the nations, nor shall the beasts of the land devour them; they shall dwell securely, and none shall make them afraid. ²⁹ And I will provide for them prosperous plantations so that they shall no more be consumed with hunger in the land, and no longer suffer the reproach of the nations. ³⁰ And they shall know that I, the LORD their God, am with them, and that they, the house of Israel, are my people, says the Lord GOD. ³¹ And you are my sheep, the sheep of my pasture, and I am your God, says the Lord GOD."

34:23 The prophet Jeremiah had earlier envisioned a time when God would give his people new shepherds to lead them in righteousness. See Jeremiah 3:15; 23:4–6. Some Christians find this passage a source for the New Testament figure of the Good Shepherd, John 10:11–18, claiming that Jesus is the Messiah here predicted.

God Will Restore Israel for His Own Sake
Ezekiel 36:6–11, 22–28

36 ⁶ Therefore prophesy concerning the land of Israel, and say to the mountains and hills, to the ravines and valleys, Thus says the Lord GOD: Behold, I speak in my jealous wrath, because you have suffered the reproach of the nations; ⁷ therefore thus says the Lord GOD: I swear that the nations that are round about you shall themselves suffer reproach.

8 "But you, O mountains of Israel, shall shoot forth your branches, and yield your fruit to my people Israel; for they will soon come home. [9] For, behold, I am for you, and I will turn to you, and you shall be tilled and sown; [10] and I will multiply men upon you, the whole house of Israel, all of it; the cities shall be inhabited and the waste places rebuilt; [11] and I will multiply upon you man and beast; and they shall increase and be fruitful; and I will cause you to be inhabited as in your former times, and will do more good to you than ever before. Then you will know that I am the LORD.

22 "Therefore say to the house of Israel, Thus says the Lord GOD: It is not for your sake, O house of Israel, that I am about to act, but for the sake of my holy name, which you have profaned among the nations to which you came. [23] And I will vindicate the holiness of my great name, which has been profaned among the nations, and which you have profaned among them; and the nations will know that I am the LORD, says the Lord GOD, when through you I vindicate my holiness before their eyes. [24] For I will take you from the nations, and gather you from all the countries, and bring you into your own land. [25] I will sprinkle clean water upon you, and you shall be clean from all your uncleannesses, and from all your idols I will cleanse you. [26] A new heart I will give you, and a new spirit I will put within you; and I will take out of your flesh the heart of stone and give you a heart of flesh. [27] And I will put my spirit within you, and cause you to walk in my statutes and be careful to observe my ordinances. [28] You shall dwell in the land which I gave to your fathers; and you shall be my people, and I will be your God.

> **36:10** The "whole house of Israel" is an allusion to the eventual restoration in the messianic period of both Hebrew kingdoms, Judah and Israel—a common prophetic theme. **36:25** Sprinkling is a biblical method of purification from uncleanness due to sin. In the New Testament the "rebirth" of man through water and the spirit of God is seen as necessary to enter the kingdom of God. See John 3:5.

Israel Will Be Resurrected

In this vision of the Valley of Dry Bones, the prophet gave dramatic expression to his conviction that Israel will be restored in her own land as a nation under God. Its powerful image captured the hearts of his listeners and encouraged them. A painting of this vision (c. 245 A.D.) has been found on the walls of a ruined synagogue in Dura-Europos. This passage is read in the synagogue on the Sabbath during the week-long Passover celebration.

Ezekiel 37:1–14

37 The hand of the LORD was upon me, and he brought me out by the Spirit of the LORD, and set me down in the midst of the valley; it was full of bones. ²And he led me round among them; and behold, there were very many upon the valley, and lo, they were very dry. ³And he said to me, "Son of man, can these bones live?" And I answered, "O Lord GOD, thou knowest." ⁴Again he said to me, "Prophesy to these bones and say to them, O dry bones, hear the word of the LORD. ⁵Thus says the Lord GOD to these bones: Behold, I will cause breath to enter you, and you shall live. ⁶And I will lay sinews upon you, and will cause flesh to come upon you, and cover you with skin, and put breath in you, and you shall live; and you shall know that I am the LORD."

7 So I prophesied as I was commanded; and as I prophesied there was a noise, and behold, a rattling; and the bones came together, bone to its bone. ⁸And as I looked, there were sinews on them, and flesh had come upon them, and skin had covered them; but there was no breath in them. ⁹Then he said to me, "Prophesy to the breath, prophesy, son of man, and say to the breath, Thus says the Lord GOD: Come from the four winds, O breath, and breathe upon these slain, that they may live." ¹⁰So I prophesied as he commanded me, and the breath came into them, and they lived, and stood upon their feet, an exceedingly great host.

11 Then he said to me, "Son of man, these bones are the whole house of Israel. Behold, they say, 'Our bones are dried up, and our hope is lost; we are clean cut off.' ¹²Therefore prophesy, and say to them, Thus says the Lord GOD: Behold, I will open your graves, and raise you from your graves, O my people; and I will bring you home into the land of Israel. ¹³And you shall know that I am the LORD, when I open your graves, and raise you from your graves, O my people. ¹⁴And I will put my Spirit within you, and you shall live, and I will place you in your own land; then you shall know that I, the LORD, have spoken, and I have done it, says the LORD."

37:12 The "graves" are the foreign countries in which Israel has been dispersed.

Ezekiel Prophesies against Gog of Magog
Ezekiel 38:1–3, 14–23
Leeser Translation

¹And the word of the LORD came unto me, saying,

²Son of man, direct thy face against Gog of the land of Magog, the prince of Rosh, Meshech and Thubal, and prophesy against him.

³ And say, Thus hath said the LORD Eternal, Behold, I will be against thee, O Gog, the prince of Rosh, Meshech and Thubal.

¹⁴ Therefore, prophesy, son of man, and say unto Gog, Thus hath said the LORD Eternal, Behold, on the day when my people of Israel dwelleth in safety, shalt thou know (my power).

¹⁵ And thou wilt come from thy place out of the farthest ends of the north, thou, and many people with thee, all of them riding upon horses, a great assemblage, and a mighty army;

¹⁶ And thou wilt come up against my people of Israel, like a cloud to cover the land; in the latter days this will be, and I will bring thee over my land, in order that the nations may know me, when I am sanctified on thee, before their eyes, O Gog.

¹⁷ Thus hath said the LORD Eternal, Art thou (not) he of whom I have spoken in ancient days through means of my servants the prophets of Israel, who prophesied in those days (many) years, that I would bring thee against them?

¹⁸ And it shall come to pass at the same time, on the day of God's coming over the land of Israel, saith the LORD Eternal, that my fury shall be kindled in my nose.

¹⁹ And in my zealousness, in the fire of my wrath, have I spoken, Surely on that day there shall be a great earthquake in the country of Israel;

²⁰ And there shall quake at my presence the fishes of the sea, and the fowls of the heaven, and the beasts of the field, and every creeping thing that creepeth upon the earth, and the mountains shall be thrown down, and the cliffs shall fall, and every wall fall to the ground.

²¹ And I will call against him throughout all my mountains for the sword, saith the LORD Eternal: every man's sword shall be against his brother.

²² And I will hold judgment over him with pestilence and with blood (-shedding); and an overflowing rain, and great hailstones, fire, and sulphur will I let rain over him and his armies, and over the many people that are with him.

²³ Thus will I magnify myself, and sanctify myself, and make myself known before the eyes of many nations: and they shall know that I am the LORD.

38:2 Biblical scholars offer many theories concerning this chapter. Some hold that Ezekiel was its author; some that it was written later by another; still others who see two hands in it. Gog is sometimes identified as a veiled reference to a particular great power that the Hebrews hoped would be destroyed. For example,

Babylonia (Dr. Louis Finkelstein, chancellor of the Jewish Theological Seminary in America ingeniously suggests that if one writes Magog backward and substitutes for each Hebrew letter the one preceding it in the Hebrew alphabet it becomes Babel, i.e., Babylonia); or the empire of Alexander the Great; or Antiochus Epiphanes, etc. But most scholars hold that Gog is an eschatological reference, i.e., refers to an event in end-time and not to any specific historic period. In Revelation 20:8 Gog and Magog are understood as *two* persons. **38:17** Predictions of such a worldwide battle, ushering in the new age, have been made by other prophets (e.g., Zephaniah 1:14 ff., Jeremiah 4–6). But Ezekiel is the first to use Gog as the subject of these prophesies. Zechariah 14 will later use the same theme. **38:18** Here starts the prophetic portion (ending at 39:16), read in the synagogue on the Sabbath during the week-long Succoth celebration.

Ezekiel Describes the Restored Temple

In the concluding chapters 40 to 48, Ezekiel provides direction for the new Temple to be erected when the Hebrews will at last be restored to their land. He envisions a temple so protected from idolatrous defilements, so purified that it will merit the return of the Divine Presence in the chariot, which in the beginning of his career he saw leaving the Temple.

These chapters provide difficulty for Talmudic scholars in that new laws are promulgated and practices are described for which there is no scriptural precedent. By tradition (Shabbat 104a) a prophet had no authority to make such innovations. For example, Ezekiel introduced new festivals not mentioned in Leviticus 23. He added the sin and trespass offerings to the ancient sacrifices of the burnt offerings and peace offerings. He restricted non-Jews from the Temple court and replaced the gentile workers at the Temple with Levitical labor. He reserved the priesthood to a single family, the sons of Zadok; allowed the priests to serve as judges; imposed marriage restrictions on the priests (44:22) more stringent than those found in Scripture (Leviticus 21:7–14). He assigned to the Levites, who had heretofore served as priests, menial responsibilities as assistants to the priests of the family of Zadok. Some of Ezekiel's suggestions were adopted into practice, others were never acted upon. Orthodox Jews believe that all will be explained in the Messianic era by the prophet Elijah. These chapters challenge liberal Jews who no longer believe that a sacrificial ritual is required. They would affirm the spirit here expressed rather than the literal text, i.e., that the profoundest expression of man's reverence for God will be demonstrated both by man's righteous behavior toward his fellow man and through ceremonies of prayer and thanksgiving before the LORD. Ezekiel emphasizes God's holiness and His presence among a redeemed people.

Ezekiel   40:1–4;   43:1–12;   44:9–15a,   20–31;   46:16–18;
                    48:30–35

40 In the twenty-fifth year of our exile, at the beginning of the year,
on the tenth day of the month, in the fourteenth year after the city
was conquered, on that very day, the hand of the LORD was upon
me, ² and brought me in the visions of God into the land of Israel,
and set me down upon a very high mountain, on which was a
structure like a city opposite me. ³ When he brought me there,
behold, there was a man, whose appearance was like bronze, with a
line of flax and a measuring reed in his hand; and he was standing in
the gateway. ⁴ And the man said to me, "Son of man, look with your
eyes, and hear with your ears, and set your mind upon all that I shall
show you, for you were brought here in order that I might show it to
you; declare all that you see to the house of Israel."

43 Afterward he brought me to the gate, the gate facing east. ² And
behold, the glory of the God of Israel came from the east; and the
sound of his coming was like the sound of many waters; and the
earth shone with his glory. ³ And the vision I saw was like the vision
which I had seen when he came to destroy the city, and like the
vision which I had seen by the river Chebar; and I fell upon my face.
⁴ As the glory of the LORD entered the temple by the gate facing east,
⁵ the Spirit lifted me up, and brought me into the inner court; and
behold, the glory of the LORD filled the temple.

6 While the man was standing beside me, I heard one speaking to
me out of the temple; ⁷ and he said to me, "Son of man, this is the
place of my throne and the place of the soles of my feet, where I will
dwell in the midst of the people of Israel for ever. And the house of
Israel shall no more defile my holy name, neither they, nor their
kings, by their harlotry, and by the dead bodies of their kings, ⁸ by
setting their threshold by my threshold and their doorposts beside
my doorposts, with only a wall between me and them. They have
defiled my holy name by their abominations which they have
committed, so I have consumed them in my anger. ⁹ Now let them
put away their idolatry and the dead bodies of their kings far from
me, and I will dwell in in their midst for ever.

10 "And you, son of man, describe to the house of Israel the
temple and its appearance and plan, that they may be ashamed of
their iniquities. ¹¹ And if they are ashamed of all that they have done,
portray the temple, its arrangement, its exits and its entrances,
and its whole form; and make known to them all its ordinances
and all its laws; and write down in their sight, so that they may
observe and perform all its laws and all its ordinances. ¹² This is
the law of the temple: the whole territory round about upon the

top of the mountain shall be most holy. Behold, this is the law of the temple."

44 [9] "Therefore thus says the Lord GOD: No foreigner, uncircumcised in heart and flesh, of all the foreigners who are among the people of Israel, shall enter my sanctuary. [10] But the Levites who went far from me, going astray from me after their idols when Israel went astray, shall bear their punishment. [11] They shall be ministers in my sanctuary, having oversight at the gates of the temple, and serving in the temple; they shall slay the burnt offering and the sacrifice for the people, and they shall attend on the people, to serve them. [12] Because they ministered to them before their idols and became a stumbling block of iniquity to the house of Israel, therefore I have sworn concerning them, says the Lord GOD, that they shall bear their punishment. [13] They shall not come near to me, to serve me as priest, nor come near any of my sacred things and the things that are most sacred; but they shall bear their shame, because of the abominations which they have committed. [14] Yet I will appoint them to keep charge of the temple, to do all its service and all that is to be done in it.

[15] "But the Levitical priests, the sons of Zadok, who kept the charge of my sanctuary when the people of Israel went astray from me, shall come near to me to minister to me . . . [20] They shall not shave their heads or let their locks grow long; they shall only trim the hair of their heads. [21] No priest shall drink wine, when he enters the inner court. [22] They shall not marry a widow, or a divorced woman, but only a virgin of the stock of the house of Israel, or a widow who is the widow of a priest. [23] They shall teach my people the difference between the holy and the common, and show them how to distinguish between the unclean and the clean. [24] In a controversy they shall act as judges, and they shall judge it according to my judgments. They shall keep my laws and my statutes in all my appointed feasts, and they shall keep my sabbaths holy. [25] They shall not defile themselves by going near to a dead person; however, for father or mother, for son or daughter, for brother or unmarried sister they may defile themselves. [26] After he is defiled, he shall count for himself seven days, and than he shall be clean. [27] And on the day that he goes into the holy place, into the inner court, to minister in the holy place, he shall offer his sin offering, says the Lord GOD.

[28] "They shall have no inheritance; I am their inheritance: and you shall give them no possession in Israel; I am their possession. [29] They shall eat the cereal offering, the sin offering, and the guilt offering; and every devoted thing in Israel shall be theirs. [30] And the first of all the first fruits of all kinds, and every offering of all kinds

from all your offerings, shall belong to the priests; you shall also give
to the priests the first of your coarse meal, that a blessing may rest
on your house. [31] The priests shall not eat of anything, whether bird
or beast, that has died of itself or is torn."

46 [16] "Thus says the Lord GOD: If the prince makes a gift to any of
his sons out of his inheritance, it shall belong to his sons, it is their
property by inheritance. [17] But if he makes a gift out of his
inheritance to one of his servants, it shall be his to the year of
liberty; then it shall revert to the prince; only his sons may keep a
gift from his inheritance. [18] The prince shall not take any of the
inheritance of the people, thrusting them out of their property; he
shall give his sons their inheritance out of his own property, so that
none of my people shall be dispossessed of his property."

48 [30] "These shall be the exits of the city: On the north side, which is
to be four thousand five hundred cubits by measure, [31] three gates,
the gate of Reuben, the gate of Judah, and the gate of Levi, the gates
of the city being named after the tribes of Israel. [32] On the east side,
which is to be four thousand five hundred cubits, three gates, the gate
of Joseph, the gate of Benjamin, and the gate of Dan. [33] On the south
side, which is to be four thousand five hundred cubits by measure,
three gates, the gate of Simeon, the gate of Is'sachar, and the gate of
Zeb'ulun. [34] On the west side, which is to be four thousand five
hundred cubits, three gates, the gate of Gad, the gate of Asher, and
the gate of Naph'tali. [35] The circumference of the city shall be
eighteen thousand cubits. And the name of the city henceforth shall
be, The LORD is there."

40:1 According to Jewish tradition, Ezekiel had this vision in the
year 572 B.C. on the Day of Atonement. **40:2** The prophet was
transported in a vision to a very high mountain, probably an allusion
to the Temple Mount as described in Isaiah 2:2 as "top of the
mountain." **40:4** Verses following this provide a description and an
accurate measurement of the physical outline of the Temple. **43:2**
The Divine Spirit had departed from the East (10:19) and consequently returned from that direction. **43:7** The former Temple
was only God's "footstool," His throne being in heaven (see Isaiah
60:13). It is promised here that the new Temple will be the abode of
the Divine Presence in a complete way. **43:8** The palace of David
had heretofore joined the Temple, see 1 Kings 7:8. In the restored
city the new Temple will occupy the entire site and the palace of the
king will be placed in another part of the city. **44:9** A stone with a
Greek inscription warning Gentiles against entering the sanctuary
was discovered in 1870; it is now in a museum in Constantinople.
This passage may also refer to those priests who were alien to God by
virtue of their wicked deeds. **44:10-14** Menial work heretofore

performed by strangers (Joshua 9:27; Deuteronomy 29:10) will now be the obligation of these Levites as punishment of their past sins. **44:15** Zadok was the first high priest of King Solomon's Temple (1 Kings 2:2–35) and was rewarded with a promise of everlasting priesthood. Ezekiel himself was of the family of Zadok. **44:20–31** Many of these rules are still observed by Orthodox Jews who consider themselves descendants of the Kohen lineage. **44:20** Shaving the head bald or permitting the hair to grow long were heathen practices forbidden to priests (cf. Leviticus 21:5, 10). **46:16–18** In the new era, the head of the state will be permitted no rights over property belonging to others. This is an effort to correct a severe abuse in former times (e.g., 1 Kings 21). **48:30–35** The book concludes with a description of the gates of Jerusalem; they are twelve in all, three on each side, named after the twelve tribes. The prophet assures Israel that God will remain forever in Jerusalem; the name of the city itself will be changed to express that fact. Revelation 21:12–13 adopts this picture of the Holy City.

The Book of Daniel

When the Syrians were oppressing them in the second century B.C., the Hebrews were encouraged to remain faithful to their religion by this series of dramatic narratives having to do with Daniel and his three young friends during the Babylonian exile. Chapters 1 to 6 are about Daniel; chapters 7 to 12 purport to be by him. The book is in two languages (2:4–6 through 7:28 is in Aramaic, the remainder in Hebrew) and appears to have been drawn from several sources. Until the discovery of the Dead Sea Scrolls, the Book of Daniel was the oldest complete Hebrew text in existence, a manuscript edited by Ben Asher in the tenth century A.D.

Probably these stories—appearing in the Hebrew canon not among the Prophets but among the Writings—were collected when the Maccabean revolt was at its height and the issue was still unresolved. Confidence in God enabled Daniel, Hananiah, Mishael and Azariah to triumph in every adversity. So, too, would those persecuted by the Syrian king Antiochus IV (who is spoken of in veiled language) be delivered if they would stand fast. The book has inspired courage in the persecuted of every age.

That the stories grew up in an age later than the assigned setting is suggested by the indifference of the stories to historical accuracy about past events. Daniel is pictured as adviser to Belshazzar, described here as the son of Nebuchadrezzar; to Darius the Mede, and to Cyrus, king of the Medes and Persians. Extra-biblical history does not recognize the king Darius pictured here, and cuneiform documents discovered in 1924 identify Belshazzar as the son of King Nabonidus, not Nebuchadrezzar. As did the authors of Ruth, Esther, and Judith, so apparently the writer of Daniel used historical romance to glorify God. These stories of heroism center about Daniel, a name drawn perhaps from Ezekiel, where Daniel is a wise man (28:3; cf. 14:14, 20). (In Ugaritic literature there is a King Daniel noted for insisting upon justice for widows and orphans.)

In spite of these difficulties, some consider that Daniel is a continuation of the history in the Books of Kings. This view is supported by a tradition that Daniel was accepted as canonical by the men of the great Synagogue organized by Ezra about 450 B.C.

Daniel is one of the earliest examples of a type of literature known as apocalyptic. Under the guise of unveiling the future (the word apocalypse means "unveiling" or "revelation"), it uses picturesque imagery to portray the ever-recurring conflict between good and evil. Daniel became the model for Enoch and for Revelation, the last book in the New Testament and the best Christian example of this Hebrew literary form, in which the present is dealt with as if it were the future (see Revelation 1 : 1, 3).

"The abomination that makes desolate" (Daniel 12 : 11; see Mark 13 : 14) probably referred originally to the defilement wrought by Antiochus when he had pigs slaughtered on the Temple altar in Jerusalem; in Mark it appears to have been the Roman tyranny.

Daniel Is Taken into Captivity

Daniel 1 : 1– 15, 17, 20

1 In the third year of the reign of Jehoi'akim king of Judah, Nebuchadnez'zar king of Babylon came to Jerusalem and besieged it. ² And the Lord gave Jehoi'akim king of Judah into his hand, with some of the vessels of the house of God; and he brought them to the land of Shinar, to the house of his god, and placed the vessels in the treasury of his god. ³ Then the king commanded Ash'penaz, his chief eunuch, to bring some of the people of Isaael, both of the royal family and of the nobility, ⁴ youths without blemish, handsome and skilful in all wisdom, endowed with knowledge, understanding learning, and competent to serve in the king's palace, and to teach them the letters and language of the Chalde'ans. ⁵ The king assigned them a daily portion of the rich food which the king ate, and of the wine which he drank. They were to be educated for three years, and at the end of that time they were to stand before the king. ⁶ Among these were Daniel, Hanani'ah, Mish'a-el, and Azari'ah of the tribe of Judah. ⁷ And the chief of the eunuchs gave them names: Daniel he called Belteshaz'zar, Hanani'ah he called Shadrach, Mish'a-el he called Meshach, and Azari'ah he called Abed'nego.

8 But Daniel resolved that he would not defile himself with the king's rich food, or with the wine which he drank; therefore he asked the chief of the eunuchs to allow him not to defile himself. ⁹ And God gave Daniel favor and compassion in the sight of the chief of the eunuchs; ¹⁰ and the chief of the eunuchs said to Daniel, "I fear lest my lord the king, who appointed your food and your drink, should see that you were in poorer condition than the youths who are of your own age. So you would endanger my head with the king." ¹¹ Then Daniel said to the steward whom the chief of the eunuchs had appointed over Daniel, Hanani'ah, Mish'a-el, and Azari'ah; ¹² "Test your servants for ten days; let us be given vegetables to eat and water to drink. ¹³ Then let our appearance and the appearance of the youths who eat the king's rich food be observed by you, and according to what you see deal with your servants." ¹⁴ So he hearkened to them in this matter, and tested them for ten days.

¹⁵ At the end of ten days it was seen that they were better in appearance and fatter in flesh than all the youths who ate the king's rich food.

17 As for these four youths, God gave them learning and skill in all letters and wisdom; and Daniel had understanding in all visions and dreams.

20 And in every matter of wisdom and understanding concerning which the king inquired of them, he found them ten times better than all the magicians and enchanters that were in all his kingdom.

> **1:2** Shinar is another name for Babylon. **1:5** The rank and file of Babylonians spoke one language, Babylonian; the Chaldean tongue was the language of the scholars and learned classes. Chaldean learning included astrology and divinations of all sorts. **1:16** A vegetarian diet is permitted in Mosaic Law. Obviously the king's food contained forbidden meat or animal fat. See Leviticus 11. Those scholars who suggest that this book was intended to support the faith of Jews against the attacks of Antiochus IV Epiphanes in the second century B.C. point to this passage. Antiochus as part of his deliberate policy of hellenization tried to dissuade Jews from maintaining the dietary laws. See 2 Maccabees 6:18; 7:42.

Daniel Reveals the Dream of King Nebuchadrezzar

Nebuchadrezzar in his own inscriptions is named *Nabu-kudurri-usur*. This is correctly given as Nebuchadrezzar in Jeremiah and Ezekiel. The later form, substituting *n* for *r*, has crept into 2 Kings and is widely used in Ezra, Chronicles and Esther. It is the only form found in Daniel Mss., and is therefore used here by RSV.

Daniel 2:1–12, 19–23, 26–49

2 In the second year of the reign of Nebuchadnez'zar, Nebuchadnez'zar had dreams; and his spirit was troubled, and his sleep left him. ² Then the king commanded that the magicians, the enchanters, the sorcerers, and the Chalde'ans be summoned, to tell the king his dreams. So they came in and stood before the king. ³ And the king said to them, "I had a dream, and my spirit is troubled to know the dream." ⁴ Then the Chalde'ans said to the king, "O king, live for ever! Tell your servants the dream, and we will show the interpretation." ⁵ The king answered the Chalde'ans, "The word from me is sure: if you do not make known to me the dream and its interpretation, you shall be torn limb from limb, and your houses shall be laid in ruins. ⁶ But if you show the dream and its interpretation, you shall receive from me gifts and rewards and great honor. Therefore show me the dream and its interpretation." ⁷ They answered a second time, "Let the king tell his servants the dream,

and we will show its interpretation." [8] The king answered, "I know with certainty that you are trying to gain time, because you see that the word from me is sure [9] that if you do not make the dream known to me, there is but one sentence for you. You have agreed to speak lying and corrupt words before me till the times change. Therefore tell me the dream, and I shall know that you can show me its interpretation." [10] The Chalde′ans answered the king, "There is not a man on earth who can meet the king's demand; for no great and powerful king has asked such a thing of any magician or enchanter or Chalde′an. [11] The thing that the kings asks is difficult, and none can show it to the king except the gods, whose dwelling is not with flesh."

12 Because of this the king was angry and very furious, and commanded that all the wise men of Babylon be destroyed.

19 Then the mystery was revealed to Daniel in a vision of the night. Then Daniel blessed the God of heaven. [20] Daniel said:

"Blessed be the name of God for ever and ever,
    to whom belong wisdom and might.
[21] He changes times and seasons;
    he removes kings and sets up kings;
  he gives wisdom to the wise
    and knowledge to those who have understanding;
[22] he reveals deep and mysterious things;
    he knows what is in the darkness,
    and the light dwells with him.
[23] To thee, O God of my fathers,
    I give thanks and praise,
  for thou hast given me wisdom and strength,
    and hast now made known to me what we asked of thee,
    for thou hast made known to us the king's matter."

26 The king said to Daniel, whose name was Belteshaz′zar, "Are you able to make known to me the dream that I have seen and its interpretation?" [27] Daniel answered the king, "No wise men, enchanters, magicians, or astrologers can show to the king the mystery which the king has asked, [28] but there is a God in heaven who reveals mysteries, and he has made known to King Nebuchadnez′zar what will be in the latter days. Your dream and the visions of your head as you lay in bed are these: [29] To you, O king, as you lay in bed came thoughts of what would be hereafter, and he who reveals mysteries made known to you what is to be. [30] But as for me, not because of any wisdom that I have more than all the living has this mystery been revealed to me, but in order that the interpretation may be made known to the king, and that you may know the thoughts of your mind.

31 "You saw, O king, and behold, a great image. This image, mighty and of exceeding brightness, stood before you, and its appearance was frightening. [32] The head of this image was of fine gold, its breast and arms of silver, its belly and thighs of bronze, [33] its legs of iron, its feet partly of iron and partly of clay. [34] As you looked, a stone was cut out by no human hand, and it smote the image on its feet of iron and clay, and broke them in pieces; [35] then the iron, the clay, the bronze, the silver, and the gold, all together were broken in pieces, and became like the chaff of the summer threshing floors; and the wind carried them away, so that not a trace of them could be found. But the stone that struck the image became a great mountain and filled the whole earth.

36 "This was the dream; now we will tell the king its interpretation. [37] You, O king, the king of kings, to whom the God of heaven has given the kingdom, the power, and the might, and the glory, [38] and into whose hand he has given, wherever they dwell, the sons of men, the beasts of the field, and the birds of the air, making you rule over them all—you are the head of gold. [39] After you shall arise another kingdom inferior to you, and yet a third kingdom of bronze, which shall rule over all the earth. [40] And there shall be a fourth kingdom, strong as iron, because iron breaks to pieces and shatters all things; and like iron which crushes, it shall break and crush all these. [41] And as you saw the feet and toes partly of potter's clay and partly of iron, it shall be a divided kingdom; but some of the firmness of iron shall be in it, just as you saw iron mixed with the miry clay. [42] And as the toes of the feet were partly iron and partly clay, so the kingdom shall be partly strong and partly brittle. [43] As you saw the iron mixed with miry clay, so they will mix with one another in marriage, but they will not hold together, just as iron does not mix with clay. [44] And in the days of those kings the God of heaven will set up a kingdom which shall never be destroyed, nor shall its sovereignty be left to another people. It shall break in pieces all these kingdoms and bring them to an end, and it shall stand for ever; [45] just as you saw that a stone was cut from a mountain by no human hand, and that it broke in pieces the iron, the bronze, the clay, the silver, and the gold. A great God has made known to the king what shall be hereafter. The dream is certain, and its interpretation sure."

46 Then King Nebuchadnez'zar fell upon his face, and did homage to Daniel, and commanded that an offering and incense be offered up to him. [47] The king said to Daniel, "Truly, your God is God of gods and Lord of kings, and a revealer of mysteries, for you have been able to reveal this mystery." [48] Then the king gave Daniel

high honors and many great gifts, and made him ruler over the whole province of Babylon, and chief prefect over all the wise men of Babylon. [49] Daniel made request of the king, and he appointed Shadrach, Meshach, and Abed'nego over the affairs of the province of Babylon; but Daniel remained at the king's court.

2:12 Daniel and his companions, who were included in the king's threat, would have been put to death by this decree. Thus their lives, as well as that of the Chaldeans, were spared by God's revelation to Daniel. **2:22** Reference to God surrounded by light, or as light Himself, is an image frequently used in prophetic writings. See for example Exodus 24:17, Isaiah 60:19 f., Ezekiel 1:27. This idea is also to be found in New Testament writings, for example, 1 John 1:5–7; 1 Timothy 6:16; James 1:17. **2:39** According to some scholars "another kingdom" is that of the Medes; it was joined to the empire of Persia under Cyrus in 550 B.C. The third kingdom was that of the Persians. It extended from India to Ethiopia and was defeated by Alexander the Great in 331 B.C. The fourth kingdom (verse 40) is Alexander's, which became a divided kingdom after his death. **2:44** Later Jewish tradition applied this verse to the kings who would reign during the long exile of the Jews after the fall of Jerusalem to Rome in A.D. 70. Most contemporary Bible scholars, however, find here is a reference to Antiochus IV Epiphanes and the rise of the Maccabean dynasty. **2:45** In prophetic writings references to such a stone and to the shattering of the enemy have a messianic significance. See Zechariah 3:9, 4:7. The Gospel of Luke 20:18, in an obvious allusion to this passage, claims Jesus to be that stone.

God Protects the Faithful from the Fiery Furnace
Daniel 3:1, 8–29; 4:3

3 King Nebuchadnez'zar made an image of gold, whose height was sixty cubits and its breadth six cubits. He set it up on the plain of Dura, in the province of Babylon.

8 Therefore at that time certain Chalde'ans came forward and maliciously accused the Jews. [9] They said to King Nebuchadnez'zar, "O king, live for ever! [10] You, O king, have made a decree, that every man who hears the sound of the horn, pipe, lyre, trigon, harp, bagpipe, and every kind of music, shall fall down and worship the golden image; [11] and whoever does not fall down and worship shall be cast into a burning fiery furnace. [12] There are certain Jews whom you have appointed over the affairs of the province of Babylon: Shad'rach, Me'shach, and Abed'nego. These men, O king, pay no heed to you; they do not serve your gods or worship the golden image which you have set up."

13 Then Nebuchadnez'zar in furious rage commanded that

Shad'rach, Me'shach, and Abed'nego be brought. Then they brought these men before the king. ¹⁴Nebuchadnez'zar said to them, "Is it true, O Shad'rach, Me'shach, and Abed'nego, that you do not serve my gods or worship the golden image which I have set up? ¹⁵Now if you are ready when you hear the sound of the horn, pipe, lyre, trigon, harp, bagpipe, and every kind of music, to fall down and worship the image which I have made, well and good; but if you do not worship, you shall immediately be cast into a burning fiery furnace; and who is the god that will deliver you out of my hands?"

16 Shad'rach, Me'shach, and Abed'nego answered the king, "O Nebuchadnez'zar, we have no need to answer you in this matter. ¹⁷If it be so, our God whom we serve is able to deliver us from the burning fiery furnace; and he will deliver us out of your hand, O king. ¹⁸But if not, be it known to you, O king, that we will not serve your gods or worship the golden image which you have set up."

19 Then Nebuchadnez'zar was full of fury, and the expression of his face was changed against Shad'rach, Me'shach, and Abed'nego. He ordered the furnace heated seven times more than it was wont to be heated. ²⁰And he ordered certain mighty men of his army to bind Shad'rach, Me'shach, and Abed'nego, and to cast them into the burning fiery furnace. ²¹Then these men were bound in their mantles, their tunics, their hats, and their other garments, and they were cast into the burning fiery furnace. ²²Because the king's order was strict and the furnace very hot, the flame of the fire slew those men who took up Shad'rach, Me'shach, and Abed'nego. ²³And these three men, Shad'rach, Me'shach, and Abed'nego, fell bound into the burning fiery furnace.

24 Then King Nebuchadnez'zar was astonished and rose up in haste. He said to his counselors, "Did we not cast three men bound into the fire?" They answered the king, "True, O king." ²⁵He answered, "But I see four men loose, walking in the midst of the fire, and they are not hurt; and the appearance of the fourth is like a son of the gods."

26 Then Nebuchadnez'zar came near to the door of the burning fiery furnace and said, "Shad'rach, Me'shach, and Abed'nego, servants of the Most High God, come forth, and come here!" Then Shad'rach, Me'shach, and Abed'nego came out from the fire. ²⁷And the satraps, the prefects, the governors, and the king's counselors gathered together and saw that the fire had not had any power over the bodies of those men; the hair of their heads was not singed, their mantles were not harmed, and no smell of fire had come upon them. ²⁸Nebuchadnez'zar said, "Blessed be the God of Shad'rach,

Me'shach, and Abed'nego, who has sent his angel and delivered his servants, who trusted in him, and set at nought the king's command, and yielded up their bodies rather than serve and worship any god except their own God. [29] Therefore I make a decree: Any people, nation, or language that speaks anything against the God of Shad'rach, Me'shach, and Abed'nego shall be torn limb from limb, and their houses laid in ruins; for there is no other god who is able to deliver in this way."

4 [3] How great are his signs,
   how mighty his wonders!
His kingdom is an everlasting kingdom,
   and his dominion is from generation to generation.

3:25 Rabbinic tradition suggests that the fourth man was the angel Gabriel, sent to protect Shadrach, Meshach, and Abednego. Gabriel is also the angel who explains to Daniel his visions in 8:16–26; 9:21–27. According to Jewish tradition Gabriel was one of the three angels who announced to Abraham the birth of Isaac (Genesis 18). In the New Testament he announces to Mary that she is about to have a son, Jesus (Luke 1:19–31). In both Jewish and Christian mystic literature Gabriel is the angel who greets righteous souls at the gates of Heaven. **4:1–3** In the Hebrew Bible these verses are included in chapter three, thus concluding the narration with a hymn of praise of God.

Daniel Interprets the Writing on the Wall
Daniel 5:1–9, 13–17, 25–31

5 King Belshaz'zar made a great feast for a thousand of his lords, and drank wine in front of the thousand.

2 Belshaz'zar, when he tasted the wine, commanded that the vessels of gold and of silver which Nebuchadnez'zar his father had taken out of the temple in Jerusalem be brought, that the king and his lords, his wives, and his concubines might drink from them. [3] Then they brought in the golden and silver vessels which had been taken out of the temple, the house of God in Jerusalem; and the king and his lords, his wives, and his concubines drank from them. [4] They drank wine, and praised the gods of gold and silver, bronze, iron, wood, and stone.

5 Immediately the fingers of a man's hand appeared and wrote on the plaster of the wall of the king's palace, opposite the lampstand; and the king saw the hand as it wrote. [6] Then the king's color changed, and his thoughts alarmed him; his limbs gave way, and his knees knocked together. [7] The king cried aloud to bring in the enchanters, the Chalde'ans, and the astrologers. The king said to the

wise men of Babylon, "Whoever reads this writing, and shows me its interpretation, shall be clothed with purple, and have a chain of gold about his neck, and shall be the third ruler in the kingdom." [8] Then all the king's wise men came in, but they could not read the writing or make known to the king the interpretation. [9] Then the King Belshaz'zar was grealy alarmed, and his color changed; and his lords were perplexed.

13 Then Daniel was brought in before the king. The king said to Daniel, "You are that Daniel, one of the exiles of Judah, whom the king my father brought from Judah. [14] I have heard of you that the spirit of the holy gods is in you, and that light and understanding and excellent wisdom are found in you. [15] Now the wise men, the enchanters, have been brought in before me to read this writing and make known to me its interpretation; but they could not show the interpretation of the matter. [16] But I have heard that you can give interpretations and solve problems. Now if you can read the writing and make known to me its interpretation, you shall be clothed with purple, and have a chain of gold about your neck, and shall be the third ruler in the kingdom."

17 Then Daniel answered before the king, "Let your gifts be for yourself, and give your rewards to another; nevertheless I will read the writing to the king and make known to him the interpretation.

25 "And this is the writing that was inscribed: MENE, MENE, TEKEL, and PARSIN. [26] This is the interpretation of the matter: MENE, God has numbered the days of your kingdom and brought it to an end; [27] TEKEL, you have been weighted in the balances and found wanting; [28] PERES, your kingdom is divided and given to the Medes and Persians."

29 Then Belshaz'zar commanded, and Daniel was clothed with purple, a chain of gold was put about his neck, and proclamation was made concerning him, that he should be the third ruler in the kingdom.

30 That very night Belshaz'zar the Chalde'an king was slain. [31] And Darius the Mede received the kingdom, being about sixty-two years old.

5:1 The drama of the events recorded here have stimulated the creation of such choral works as Handel's oratorio *Belshazzar* and Walton's *Belshazzar's Feast.* 5:4 The Babylonians desecrated the holy vessels by such folly, and they used them while indulging in idolatrous worship. For such a disregard of God, Belshazzar and his empire would be destroyed. 5:5 Excavations in Babylon have uncovered a room with white plastered walls of a kind to reflect the lights of the candelabra. 5:25 According to Jewish tradition the writing was in Hebrew letters which the Chaldeans could read but which they could not understand, since it was written in the form of an anagram, that is, the writing followed the Hebrew in going from right to left, but the words had to be read by reading downwards. Each word itself had a double meaning:

```
S  U  T  M  M
I  P  K  N  N
N  R  L  A  A
```

Mene: a coin (a *mina*), worth sixty shekels, and also the verb "to count." *Tekel:* Aramic for the Hebrew coin "shekel," and also the verb "to weigh." *Parsin:* dual or plural form of the word *peres,* a half mina, and also the verb "to divide." The usual interpretation is that Nebuchadrezzar was worth a mina, Belshazzar only a shekel, and his successors a half mina—a form of belittlement, with a play on words based on the alternative meanings of the three words. **5:31** There is no historic record of "Darius, the Mede." It was Cyrus, king of Persia who overthrew Babylon, *after* conquering the Medes. The possession of the Chaldean empire by the Medes *before* Persian supremacy, however, had been forecast in the prophetic writings of Isaiah (13:17) and Jeremiah (51:11, 28). The Book of Daniel may have drawn upon this prophetic tradition.

God Rescues Daniel from the Lions' Den
Daniel 6:1–28

6 It pleased Darius to set over the kingdom a hundred and twenty satraps, to be throughout the whole kingdom; ² and over them three presidents, of whom Daniel was one, to whom these satraps should give account, so that the king might suffer no loss. ³ Then this Daniel became distinguished above all the other presidents and satraps, because an excellent spirit was in him; and the king planned to set him over the whole kingdom. ⁴ Then the presidents and the satraps sought to find a ground for complaint against Daniel with regard to the kingdom; but they could find no ground for complaint or any fault, because he was faithful, and no error or fault was found in him. ⁵ Then these men said, "We shall not find any ground for complaint against this Daniel unless we find it in connection with the law of his God."

6 Then these presidents and satraps came by agreement to the king and said to him, "O King Darius, live for ever! ⁷ All the presidents of the kingdom, the prefects and the satraps, the counselors and the governors are agreed that the king should establish an ordinance and enforce an interdict, that whoever makes petition to any god or man for thirty days, except to you, O king, shall be cast into the den of lions. ⁸ Now, O king, establish the interdict and sign

the document, so that it cannot be changed, according to the law of the Medes and the Persians, which cannot be revoked." ⁹ Therefore King Darius signed the document and interdict.

10 When Daniel knew that the document had been signed, he went to his house where he had windows in his upper chamber open toward Jerusalem; and he got down upon his knees three times a day and prayed and gave thanks before his God, as he had done previously. ¹¹ Then these men came by agreement and found Daniel making petition and supplication before his God. ¹² Then they came near and said before the king, concerning the interdict, "O king! Did you not sign an interdict, that any man who makes petition to any god or man within thirty days except to you, O king, shall be cast into the den of lions?" The king answered, "The thing stands fast, according to the law of the Medes and Persians, which cannot be revoked." ¹³ Then they answered before the king, "That Daniel, who is one of the exiles from Judah, pays no heed to you, O king, or the interdict you have signed, but makes his petition three times a day."

14 Then the king, when he heard these words, was much distressed, and set his mind to deliver Daniel; and he labored till the sun went down to rescue him. ¹⁵ Then these men came by agreement to the king, and said to the king, "Know, O king, that it is a law of the Medes and Persians that no interdict or ordinance which the king establishes can be changed."

16 Then the king commanded, and Daniel was brought and cast into the den of lions. The king said to Daniel, "May your God, whom you serve continually, deliver you!" ¹⁷ And a stone was brought and laid upon the mouth of the den, and the king sealed it with his own signet and with the signet of his lords, that nothing might be changed concerning Daniel. ¹⁸ Then the king went to his palace, and spent the night fasting; no diversions were brought to him, and sleep fled from him.

19 Then, at break of day, the king arose and went in haste to the den of lions. ²⁰ When he came near to the den where Daniel was he cried out in a tone of anguish and said to Daniel, "O Daniel, servant of the living God, has your God, whom you serve continually, been able to deliver you from the lions?" ²¹ Then Daniel said to the king, "O king, live for ever! ²² My God sent his angel and shut the lions' mouths, and they have not hurt me, because I was found blameless before him; and also before you, O king, I have done no wrong." ²³ Then the king was exceedingly glad, and commanded that Daniel be taken up out of the den. So Daniel was taken up out of the den, and no kind of hurt was found upon him, because he had trusted in his God. ²⁴ And the king commanded, and those men who had

accused Daniel were brought and cast into the den of lions—they, their children, and their wives; and before they reached the bottom of the den the lions overpowered them and broke all their bones in pieces.

25 Then King Darius wrote to all the peoples, nations, and languages that dwell in all the earth: "Peace be multiplied to you. 26 I make a decree, that in all my royal dominion men tremble and fear before the God of Daniel,

> for he is the living God,
>   enduring for ever;
> his kingdom shall never be destroyed,
>   and his dominion shall be to the end.
> 27 He delivers and rescues,
>   he works signs and wonders
>   in heaven and on earth,
> he who has saved Daniel
>   from the power of the lions."

28 So this Daniel prospered during the reign of Darius and the reign of Cyrus the Persian.

6:8 The immutability of Persian royal decrees is also described in Esther 8:8. **6:10** Jews to this day face toward Jerusalem as they recite their prayers, and Orthodox Jews engage in three prayer services each day—morning, afternoon and evening. The posture of kneeling, however, is reserved only for the holiest of prayers in the synagogue on the Day of Atonement.

Daniel Has Visions

There follows a series of four apocalyptic visions, which have been subject to many interpretations relating figures such as a winged lion to Babylon, a bear to Media, a leopard to Persia, ten horns to ten rulers of Syria. This would provide the text with a political significance. Others, however, wish to see here in the text an end-time, messianic hope. At the end of "a season and a time," "one like unto a son of man" shall be given dominion over all the earth. ". . . the saints of the Most High shall receive the kingdom, and possess the kingdom for ever. . . ." (Daniel 7:18.) The book concludes with the following passage.

At That Time the People Shall Be Delivered
Daniel 12:1–10, 13

12 "At that time shall arise Michael, the great prince who has charge of your people. And there shall be a time of trouble, such as never has been since there was a nation till that time; but at that time your people shall be delivered, every one whose name shall be found written in the book. 2 And many of those who sleep in the dust of the

earth shall awake, some to everlasting life, and some to shame and everlasting contempt. [3] And those who are wise shall shine like the brightness of the firmament; and those who turn many to righteousness, like the stars for ever and ever. [4] But you, Daniel, shut up the words, and seal the book, until the time of the end. Many shall run to and fro, and knowledge shall increase."

5 Then I Daniel looked, and behold, two others stood, one on this bank of the stream and one on that bank of the stream. [6] And I said to the man clothed in linen, who was above the waters of the stream, "How long shall it be till the end of these wonders?" [7] The man clothed in linen, who was above the waters of the stream, raised his right hand and his left hand toward heaven; and I heard him swear by him who lives for ever that it would be for a time, two times, and half a time; and that when the shattering of the power of the holy people comes to an end all these things would be accomplished. [8] I heard, but I did not understand. Then I said, "O my lord, what shall be the issue of these things?" [9] He said, "Go your way, Daniel, for the words are shut up and sealed until the time of the end. [10] Many shall purify themselves, and make themselves white, and be refined; but the wicked shall do wickedly; and none of the wicked shall understand; but those who are wise shall understand.

13 "But go your way till the end; and you shall rest, and shall stand in your allotted place at the end of the days."

12:1 Angels, referred to on several occasions in Scripture, are considered agents of God and assume whatever form is required by their particular mission. In the Book of Daniel for the first time they are named. Rabbinic tradition acknowledges that the names of the angels were brought from Babylon (*Genesis Rabbah* 48:9). Michael is regarded as the guardian angel of Israel. Thus he is pictured in Rabbinic literature as the angel who rescued Lot at the destruction of Sodom, prevented Laban from harming Jacob, and served as Moses' instructor. He destroyed the army of Sennacherib and rescued Esther. In time some Jews addressed prayers to Michael as an intercessor to God. This led the Rabbis to enjoin: "When a man is in need he must pray directly to God and neither to Michael or Gabriel" (*Yer. Ber.* 9:13). Michael is considered by Jewish tradition to be the greatest of the angels. **12:2** Some scholars believe that this passage intimates a new Hebrew doctrine of life after death, resurrection, and eternal punishment. The book of Daniel, therefore, marks a transition from biblical Judaism to the religious concepts of rabbinic Judaism and of early Christianity.

The Twelve

Jewish tradition as early as 400 B.C. collected twelve small prophetic books into one scroll, probably because they conveniently filled a single papyrus scroll. The traditional Jewish arrangement of the books followed here, however, is not necessarily chronological, and some appear to have been written quite late in Jewish history.

The first six prophets—Amos, Hosea and Micah—belonged to the eighth century B.C. Zephaniah, Nahum and Habakkuk probably prophesied in the seventh century; Haggai, Zechariah, Obadiah, Malachi and Joel during the Persian period, 539–333 B.C. The story about Jonah may belong in the later Greek period, and some scholars assign Zechariah 9–14 to this era also. Lack of sufficient information makes exact dating of each book impossible.

The Christian Church speaks of this collection as "The Minor Prophets," minor only in their size.

The student will find here selections to illustrate the following prophetic ideals. The prophet speaks not only to the Hebrew nation. His concern is universal and he addresses all the nations. He declares that God is Lord over all nations, and His graciousness extends to the ends of the earth: Amos 1; 9:7; Jonah; Zephaniah 3:9; Habakkuk 1:5 ff. But God requires of men that they live according to His law of righteousness. Societies built upon corruption and violence will not long endure.

Israel, God's chosen people, is also required to live by God's law. Their election assures them no special favor from God; to the contrary, it places upon them a special moral responsibility. See Amos 3; 5:14; Micah 6:8; Zechariah 8:16–17.

The prophets denounce Israel for her faithlessness in following the ways of idolatry, Hosea 1:2; for placing her trust in the might of idolatrous nations, Hosea 8:9–10, 14; 10:13–15; for perverting justice, Malachi 3:5. Fearlessly they attacked the rich and powerful, Amos 8:4–12; Micah 2:1–3; the rulers of society, Micah 3:1–2; false prophets, Micah 3:5–8; even the priests of the religion, Malachi 1:6–13; 2:13; 2:1–2.

Most powerfully the prophets denounce those who believed they had fulfilled their obligations to God by the offering of sacrifices and faithful performance of the Temple ritual. God hates false piety, proclaim the prophets. He desires love, not sacrifices; knowledge of God, not burnt offerings; justice in relations among men, not a hypocritical show of faith (Amos 5:21–24; Micah 6:6–8).

If Israel persists in her evil ways, the prophets declare, she will suffer the wrath of God. The Hebrew people believed in a "Day of the Lord," ultimately to come, when they will be vindicated over their enemies and the nation re-established in integrity and power. In such a time, men will live in abundance and an era of peace will be initiated. But the prophets warn, the Day of the Lord may not be a day of joy but a day of gloom and darkness, punishment and suffering (Joel 2:1–2; Amos 2:4–6; 5:18–20; Malachi 4:1).

God, the prophets taught, was faithful, even as He was compassionate. He will not utterly destroy his people (Hosea 11:8–9; Amos 9:13–15; Micah 4:1–5; 7:18–20). By their suffering the Hebrew people will be purified, and a remnant will be saved for the time to come (Amos 5:15; Zephaniah 3:12 ff.). A repentant Israel will once again enjoy the favors of God (Hosea 2:13–23; 14:1–2; Joel 2:28–29). The prophets who returned with the exiles and witnessed the building of the Second Temple even dared hope that the messianic era was soon to be experienced: Haggai 2:6 ff.; Zechariah 8:20–23.

This messianic era which was awaited eagerly, particularly by the Hebrew people in the post-exilic era, was understood to be a time of judgment. The enemies of God and of God's people would receive their just retribution (Joel 3:1–2; 9–12; Obadiah; Nahum 1; Zephaniah 1:14–18; Zechariah 14:1–3, 12–13). But some of the prophets, in a more humanitarian vein, also envisioned a time when many of these peoples would repent of their ways and accept God as their Lord. These prophets longed not for the destruction of their enemies but rather for their conversion (Jonah; Habakkuk 1:5 ff.; Zephaniah 3:9; Zechariah 14:9).

A prophet can do no other than proclaim the word, even if the proclamation places him in mortal danger as it frequently did. He is God's messenger (Amos 3:8; 7:15; Micah 3:8).

Prophetic instruction took place not only through the declaration of words but also through symbolic action. The prophet gave his children names that proclaimed his message. He interpreted the experiences of his life in terms of its prophetic meaning. He performed deeds that would arouse the curiosity of the people and shock them to an understanding of his ministry (Hosea 2:2; Micah 1:8).

The Book of Hosea

Hosea lived and taught during the forty years before the fall of Samaria, capital of the Northern Kingdom. He exercised an active prophetic ministry during the short reigns of the last kings of Israel, Menahem (743–738), Pekahiah (738–737), Pekah (737–732) and Hoshea (732–724). The Temple was still standing in Jerusalem; the people of both kingdoms were independent in their own land and felt secure. But Hosea realized that injustice and moral transgression threatened to bring about a collapse of the society. The prophet Amos, a native of the Southern Kingdom, had already spoken of the stern requirements of justice; Hosea repeats that message but he reveals a more compassionate spirit, likening God's relation to Israel as that of a loving husband toward a wayward wife. Israel had been unfaithful. The people had broken God's laws; priests and rulers had been ensnared in political and religious alliances with idolatrous nations. Hosea also warned: the officious performance of the rituals of religion was not enough; God demanded obedience to Himself and righteousness between man and man. Should the people repent, Hosea assured them, God, like a long suffering husband, would receive them back in love and forgiveness.

Hosea does not provide enough historical references to enable us to date his various prophecies. It is likely that Hosea's last prophecies were delivered when neighboring Syria had already fallen to Assyria and Israel itself was near collapse in 721 B.C.

The Prophet Takes a Wife
Hosea 1:1–9

1 The word of the Lord that came to Hose'a the son of Be-e'ri, in the days of Uzzi'ah, Jotham, Ahaz, and Hezeki'ah, kings of Judah, and in the days of Jerobo'am the son of Jo'ash, king of Israel.

2 When the Lord first spoke through Hose'a, the Lord said to Hose'a, "Go, take to yourself a wife of harlotry and have children of harlotry, for the land commits great harlotry by forsaking the Lord." ³ So he went and took Gomer the daughter of Dibla'im, and she conceived and bore him a son.

4 And the Lord said to him, "Call his name Jezreel; for yet a little while, and I will punish the house of Jehu for the blood of Jezreel, and I will put an end to the kingdom of the house of Israel. ⁵ And on that day, I will break the bow of Israel in the valley of Jezreel."

6 She conceived again and bore a daughter. And the Lord said to him, "Call her name Not pitied, for I will no more have pity on the house of Israel, to forgive them at all. ⁷ But I will have pity on the

house of Judah, and I will deliver them by the LORD their God; I will not deliver them by bow, nor by sword, nor by war, nor by horses, nor by horsemen."

8 When she had weaned Not pitied, she conceived and bore a son. ⁹ And the LORD said, "Call his name Not my people, for you are not my people and I am not your God."

1:1 The opening verses set the date of Hosea's ministry. Uzziah reigned from 781–740 B.C. and Hezekiah came to the throne of Judah in 720 B.C. Hosea probably did not start his prophesying until late in Uzziah's reign. Although he preached chiefly to the kingdom of Israel he sometimes made reference to Judah. Jeroboam II reigned over Israel from about 783 to 743 B.C.

1:2 Hosea understood that his marriage to an unfaithful wife was symbolic of Israel's relation to God. Comparison of God's relations to Israel as that of a marriage was also evoked by other prophets. See Isaiah 1:21–26; Jeremiah 2:2; 3:1, 6–12; Ezekiel 16, 23. **1:4** The children bear names that symbolize Hosea's message to the people. A similar device was used by the prophet Isaiah; see Isaiah 1:26 ff. *Jezreel* was the residence of the Israelite kings where Jehu murdered the descendants of the former king Ahab. The dynasty of Jehu came to an end with the assassination of King Zechariah in 743. It was evidently in that same Valley of Jezreel at Megiddo that Israel lost a major battle to the Assyrian power. **1:7** See 2 Kings 19:35. The Greek historian Herodotus (II, 141) attributes the defeat of Sennacherib's army, besieging Jerusalem, to a plague of field mice, which might have borne bubonic plague.

Hosea Warns and Cajoles Israel

In this typical passage Hosea expresses both the lover's anger at betrayal and his deeper wish that there be reconciliation. The prophet here denounces the prevalence of the idolatrous ˙Baal worship and warns of the misfortune that will follow upon such infidelity. But he holds out hope also for a new covenant between God and the Hebrew people.

Hosea 2:2–7, 13–23

2 ² "Plead with your mother, plead—
for she is not my wife,
and I am not her husband—
that she put away her harlotry from her face,
and her adultery from between her breasts;
³ lest I strip her naked
and make her as in the day she was born,
and make her like a wilderness,
and set her like a parched land,
and slay her with thirst.

⁴ Upon her children also I will have no pity,
　　because they are children of harlotry.
⁵ For their mother has played the harlot;
　　she that conceived them has acted shamefully.
　For she said, 'I will go after my lovers,
　　who give me my bread and my water,
　　my wool and my flax, my oil and my drink.'
⁶ Therefore I will hedge up her way with thorns;
　　and I will build a wall against her,
　　so that she cannot find her paths.
⁷ She shall pursue her lovers,
　　but not overtake them;
　and she shall seek them,
　　but shall not find them.
　Then she shall say, 'I will go
　　and return to my first husband,
　　for it was better with me then than now.'
¹³ And I will punish her for the feast days of the Ba'als
　　when she burned incense to them
　and decked herself with her ring and jewelry,
　　and went after her lovers,
　　and forgot me, says the LORD.
¹⁴ "Therefore, behold, I will allure her,
　　and bring her into the wilderness,
　　and speak tenderly to her.
¹⁵ And there I will give her her vineyards,
　　and make the Valley of Achor a door of hope.
　And there shall answer as in the days of her youth,
　　as at the time when she came out of the land of Egypt.

16 "And in that day, says the LORD, you will call me, 'My husband,' and no longer will you call me, 'My Ba'al.' ¹⁷ For I will remove the names of the Ba'als from her mouth, and they shall be mentioned by name no more. ¹⁸ And I will make for you a covenant on that day with the beasts of the field, the birds of the air, and the creeping things of the ground; and I will abolish the bow, the sword, and war from the land; and I will make you lie down in safety. ¹⁹ And I will betroth you to me for ever; I will betroth you to me in righteousness and in justice, in steadfast love, and in mercy. ²⁰ I will betroth you to me in faithfulness; and you shall know the LORD.

²¹ "And in that day, says the LORD,
　　I will answer the heavens
　　and they shall answer the earth;

²² and the earth shall answer the grain, the wine, and the oil,
    and they shall answer Jezreel;
²³   and I will sow him for myself in the land.
    And I will have pity on Not pitied,
        and I will say to Not my people, 'You are my people';
        and he shall say, 'Thou art my God.' ''

2:5 Adultery destroyed the marriage bond, and an adulteress was
to be punished (cf. Deuteronomy 22:22 and Ezekiel 16:39). Hosea
warned that by her pagan ways Israel had broken her vow to God and
her land would be stripped bare as punishment. **2:17** Many Biblical
persons were given names compounded with "Baal" (e.g., Meri-baal,
Jerub-baal). The association of the name with the Canaanite gods,
however, made it disreputable, and Hosea now forbade the use of that
name. **2:18** ff. Here is a characteristic prophetic vision of the nature of
the messianic era: there will be no more war, men will live in security,
the love of God will be in their hearts, the earth will produce abundantly. Nature and history will be in harmony. **2:19–20** The Jewish
worshipper recites these verses as he puts on the phylacteries at the
morning prayer service. The leather thongs are wrapped around the
fingers as though a marriage ring.

God Loves Israel Like a Father

Characteristically of the early prophets, Hosea cannot long describe
God's anger at Israel without also testifying to God's love. Here he
evokes the image of God as a father, whose anger is not intended to
destroy but rather to discipline, purify and rehabilitate.

Hosea 11:1–9

11 When Israel was a child, I loved him, .
    and out of Egypt I called my son.
² The more I called them,
    the more they went from me;
  they kept sacrificing to the Ba'als,
    and burning incense to idols.

³ Yet it was I who taught E'phraim to walk,
    I took them up in my arms;
    but they did not know that I healed them.
⁴ I led them with cords of compassion,
    with the bands of love,
  and I became to them as one
    who eases the yoke on their jaws,
    and I bent down to them and fed them.

⁵ They shall return to the land of Egypt,
    and Assyria shall be their king,
    because they have refused to return to me.
⁶ The sword shall rage against their cities,
    consume the bars of their gates,
    and devour them in their fortresses.
⁷ My people are bent on turning away from me;
    so they are appointed to the yoke,
    and none shall remove it.

⁸ How can I give you up, O E'phraim!
    How can I hand you over, O Israel!
How can I make you like Admah!
    How can I treat you like Zeboi'im!
My heart recoils within me,
    my compassion grows warm and tender.
⁹ I will not execute my fierce anger,
    I will not again destroy E'phraim;
for I am God and not man,
    the Holy One in your midst,
    and I will not come to destroy.

11:8 Admah and Zeboim were cities of the plain that were overthrown with Sodom and Gomorrah.

The Prophet Calls for Repentance

This last utterance of Hosea, a heartfelt appeal to Israel to repent, is recited in synagogues on the first Sabbath of the Jewish New Year between the holidays of Rosh Hashanah and Yom Kippur, a period of penitence.

Hosea 14:2–10
Jewish Publication Society

14 ² Return, O Israel, unto the LORD thy God;
    For thou hast stumbled in thine iniquity.
³ Take with you words,
    And return unto the LORD;
    Say unto Him: "Forgive all iniquity,
    And accept that which is good;
    So will we render for bullocks the offering of our lips
⁴ Asshur shall not save us;
    We will not ride upon horses;
    Neither will we call any more the work of our hands our gods;
    For in Thee the fatherless findeth mercy."

⁵ I will heal their backsliding,
  I will love them freely;
  For Mine anger is turned away from him.
⁶ I will be as the dew unto Israel;
  He shall blossom as the lily,
  And cast forth his roots as Lebanon.
  His branches shall spread,
  And his beauty shall be as the olive-tree,
  And his fragrance as Lebanon.
⁸ They that dwell under his shadow shall again
  Make corn to grow,
  And shall blossom as the vine;
  The scent thereof shall be as the wine of Lebanon.
⁹ Ephraim (shall say):
  "What have I to do any more with idols?"
  As for Me, I respond and look on him;
  I am like a leafy cypress-tree;
  From Me is thy fruit found.

¹⁰ Whoso is wise, let him understand these things,
  Whoso is prudent, let him know them.
  For the ways of the LORD are right,
  And the just do walk in them;
  But transgressors do stumble therein

14:9 This passage of reconciliation climaxes with the promise that Ephraim will recognize that it is from God that fruit (goodness) is found. In the Hebrew there is a play on words: the word "Ephraim" includes the Hebrew word *pri*, meaning fruit.

The Book of Joel

This book of only three chapters is usually placed between Hosea and Amos, prophets of the eighth century. Tradition suggests, therefore, that Joel was a prophet of that period. Scholars today, however, tend to place Joel's vividly written prophecy in the fourth century. The book contains no allusions to the Northern Kingdom, nor does Joel mention a king or princes. Instead "elders" are referred to, and Temple sacrifices are viewed as indispensable, in striking contrast to the more critical attitude of the great pre-exilic prophets. Also Jews are in dispersion (3:2), and Greeks are mentioned (3:6). Hence 400-350 B.C. is offered by many as the period of its writing.

Except for the prophet's name and that of his father, nothing is known about Joel. The book considers an invasion of locusts to be a punishment from God. The priests call the people to a solemn assembly of fasting and prayer. They repent and God forgives them.

In the Christian tradition Joel's call to fasting and penance makes his book fitting for use in the Lenten liturgy. Joel's vision of an outpouring of God's spirit on His people (3:1-5) is understood to have been fulfilled in the Pentecostal experience (Acts 2:16-21) by Christians.

The Locusts Invade the Land
Joel 1: 1-7, 15

1 The word of the LORD that came to Joel, the son of Pethu'el:

² Hear this, you aged men,
　　give ear, all inhabitants of the land!
Has such a thing happened in your days,
　　or in the days of your fathers?
³ Tell your children of it,
　　and let your children tell their children,
　　and their children another generation.

⁴ What the cutting locust left,
　　the swarming locust has eaten.
What the swarming locust left,
　　the hopping locust has eaten,
and what the hopping locust left,
　　the destroying locust has eaten.

⁵ Awake, you drunkards, and weep;
　　and wail, all you drinkers of wine,
because of the sweet wine,
　　for it is cut off from your mouth.

⁶ For a nation has come up against my land,
    powerful and without number;
its teeth are lions' teeth,
    and it has the fangs of a lioness.
⁷ It has laid waste my vines,
    and splintered my fig trees;
it has stripped off their bark and thrown it down;
    their branches are made white.

¹⁵ Alas for the day!
For the day of the LORD is near,
    and as destruction from the Almighty it comes.

Rend Your Heart, Not Your Garments

Will "the Day of the Lord" be a day of triumph and joy, or a time of punishment and retribution (cf. Amos 8:9–12 and Zephaniah 1:14–18)? Joel answers: the Day of the Lord will be a time of punishment for Israel (2:1–2); but if Israel repents it will be a day of spiritual renewal (2:28–29) and the punishment of enemies (3:1–2).

Joel 2:1–2, 12–13, 15–19, 21–22, 28–29; 3:1–2

2 Blow the trumpet in Zion;
    sound the alarm on my holy mountain!
Let all the inhabitants of the land tremble,
    for the day of the LORD is coming, it is near,
² a day of darkness and gloom,
    a day of clouds and thick darkness!
Like blackness there is spread upon the mountains
    a great and powerful people;
their like has never been from of old,
    nor will be again after them
    through the years of all generations.

¹² "Yet even now," says the LORD,
    "return to me with all your heart,
with fasting, with weeping, and with mourning;
¹³   and rend your hearts and not your garments."
Return to the LORD, your God,
    for he is gracious and merciful,
slow to anger, and abounding in steadfast love,
    and repents of evil.

¹⁵ Blow the trumpet in Zion;
    sanctify a fast;
call a solemn assembly;

¹⁶   gather the people.
Sanctify the congregation;
   assemble the elders;
gather the children,
   even nursing infants.
Let the bridegroom leave his room,
   and the bride her chamber.

¹⁷ Between the vestibule and the altar
   let the priests, the ministers of the LORD, weep
and say, "Spare thy people, O LORD,
   and make not thy heritage a reproach,
   a byword among the nations.
Why should they say among the peoples,
   'Where is their God?'"

¹⁸ Then the LORD became jealous for his land,
   and had pity on his people.
¹⁹ The LORD answered and said to his people,
"Behold, I am sending to you
   grain, wine, and oil,
   and you will be satisfied;
and I will no more make you
   a reproach among the nations.

²¹ "Fear not, O land;
   be glad and rejoice,
   for the LORD has done great things!
²² Fear not, you beasts of the field,
   for the pastures of the wilderness are green;
the tree bears its fruit,
   the fig tree and vine give their full yield.

²⁸ "And it shall come to pass afterward,
   that I will pour out my spirit on all flesh;
your sons and your daughters shall prophesy,
   your old men shall dream dreams,
   and your young men shall see visions.
²⁹ Even upon the menservants and maidservants
   in those days, I will pour out my spirit."

3 "For behold, in those days and at that time, when I restore the
fortunes of Judah and Jerusalem, ² I will gather all the nations and
bring them down to the valley of Jehosh'aphat, and I will enter into
judgment with them there, on account of my people and my heritage

Israel, because they have scattered them among the nations, and have divided up my land. . . ."

2:13 Tearing the garments is a sign of grief in Jewish tradition (cf. Joshua 7:16; 1 Samuel 4:12). **2:15–17** These sentences (along with Hosea 14:2–10) are read in the synagogue service on the Sabbath between the New Year and the Day of Atonement. They are also read in the Catholic liturgy on Ash Wednesday, the first day of the annual penitential season called Lent. **2:28** Peter identifies the miracle of the Pentecost with this prophecy (Acts 2:16–21). Pentecostal Christians find in these verses a source for their conviction that true believers, when filled with God's spirit, will prophesy, that is, speak in tongues. Jews connecting these verses with the prediction of judgment upon the enemies of Israel, see in the text a classic statement of end-time hope: it combines a promise of physical well-being and spiritual renewal.

God Brings Judgment upon the Nations
Joel 3:9–12, 14, 16–17, 20–21

3 ⁹ Proclaim this among the nations:
 Prepare war,
  stir up the mighty men.
 Let all the men of war draw near,
  let them come up.
¹⁰ Beat your plowshares into swords,
  and your pruning hooks into spears;
  let the weak say, "I am a warrior."

¹¹ Hasten and come,
  all you nations round about,
  gather yourselves there.
 Bring down thy warriors, O Lord.
¹² Let the nations bestir themselves,
  and come up to the valley of Jehosh′aphat;
 for there I will sit to judge
  all the nations round about.

¹⁴ Multitudes, multitudes,
  in the valley of decision!
 For the day of the Lord is near
  in the valley of decision.

¹⁶ And the Lord roars from Zion,
  and utters his voice from Jerusalem,
  and the heavens and the earth shake.
 But the Lord is a refuge to his people,
  a stronghold to the people of Israel.

¹⁷ "So you shall know that I am the Lord your God,
    who dwell in Zion, my holy mountain.
And Jerusalem shall be holy
    and strangers shall never again pass through it.

²⁰ . . . Judah shall be inhabited for ever,
    and Jerusalem to all generations.
²¹ I will avenge their blood, and I will not clear the guilty,
    for the Lord dwells in Zion."

The Book of Amos

Amos, the first literary prophet, was a herdsman among the shepherds of Tekoa, a hill town at the edge of the desert in Judah, twelve miles south of Jerusalem. About 750 B.C. he felt himself called by God to preach to the Northern Kingdom, then at the height of its power and wealth. He journeyed to Samaria and Bethel, two cities in Israel which were centers of moral corruption and idolatrous worship. By his emphasis on social justice as the true measure of religious devotion Amos is know as a pioneer in ethical religion, and as a social reformer.

Amos's powerful message inspired other prophets. His influence on Jeremiah is particularly marked. He was first among the prophets to warn Israel that it could expect no special favors from God by virtue of her election. The "day of the Lord," he also warned, will not be a time of vindication and delight, as the people anticipated; if they do not repent of their evil ways it will be a time of darkness and punishment. But then Amos, like other prophets to follow him, tempered his harsh prophecy with a word of consolation: a remnant of the House of Israel will be worthy of redemption.

God Judges All Nations
Amos 1:1–5, 9–12; 2:4–8, 12–16

1 The words of Amos, who was among the shepherds of Teko'a, which he saw concerning Israel in the days of Uzzi'ah king of Judah and in the days of Jerobo'am the son of Jo'ash, king of Israel, two years before the earthquake. ² And he said:

"The LORD roars from Zion,
    and utters his voice from Jerusalem;
the pastures of the shepherds mourn,
    and the top of Carmel withers."

³ Thus says the LORD:
"For three transgressions of Damascus,
    and for four, I will not revoke the punishment;
because they have threshed Gilead
    with threshing sledges of iron.
⁴ So I will send a fire upon the house of Haz'ael,
    and it shall devour the strongholds of Ben-ha'dad.
⁵ I will break the bar of Damascus,
    and cut off the inhabitants from the Valley of Aven,
and him that holds the scepter from Beth-eden;
    and the people of Syria shall go into exile to Kir."
                      says the LORD.

⁹ Thus says the LORD:
"For three trangressions of Tyre,
    and for four, I will not revoke the punishment;
because they delivered up a whole people to Edom,
    and did not remember the covenant of brotherhood.
¹⁰ So I will send a fire upon the wall of Tyre,
    and it shall devour her strongholds."

¹¹ Thus says the LORD:
"For three trangressions of Edom,
    and for four, I will not revoke the punishment;
because he pursued his brother with the sword,
    and cast off all pity,
and his anger tore perpetually,
    and he kept his wrath for ever.
¹² So I will send a fire upon Teman,
    and it shall devour the strongholds of Bozrah."

2 ⁴ Thus says the LORD:
"For three transgressions of Judah,
    and for four, I will not revoke the punishment;
because they have rejected the law of the LORD,
    and have not kept his statutes,
but their lies have led them astray,
    after which their father walked.
⁵ So I will send a fire upon Judah,
    and it shall devour the strongholds of Jerusalem."

⁶ Thus says the LORD:
"For three transgressions of Israel,
    and for four, I will not revoke the punishment;
because they sell the righteous for silver,
    and the needy for a pair of shoes—
⁷ they that trample the head of the poor into the dust of the
      earth,
    and turn aside the way of the afflicted;
a man and his father go in to the same maiden,
    so that my holy name is profaned;
⁸ they lay themselves down beside every altar
    upon garments taken in pledge;
and in the house of their God they drink
    the wine of those who have been fined.

¹² "But you made the Nazirites drink wine,
    and commanded the prophets
    saying, 'You shall not prophesy.'

¹³ "Behold, I will press you down in your place,
    as a cart full of sheaves presses down.
¹⁴ Flight shall perish from the swift,
    and the strong shall not retain his strength,
    nor shall the mighty save his life;
¹⁵ he who handles the bow shall not stand,
    and he who is swift of foot shall not save himself,
    nor shall he who rides the horse save his life;
¹⁶ and he who is stout of heart among the mighty
    shall flee away naked in that day,"

says the LORD.

1:1 The earthquake is historical. Some writers attributed it to the fact that Uzziah, king of Judah, usurped the function of the priest and entered the Temple to burn incense (cf. 2 Chronicles 26:16 and Zechariah 14:5). **1:3** The Syrian kings Hazael and Ben-Hadad were hated enemies of both Israel and Judah. Hazael received tribute from Jehu, king of Israel, and he abandoned an attack on Jerusalem only after receiving a gift of gold from Jehoash, king of Judah. Ben-Hadad also attacked Israel during the reign of Jehoahaz (2 Kings 13:3; 6:24). **1:5** *Valley of Aven* and *Beth-eden* are derogatory references, the Hebrew meaning "Valley of Wickedness" and "House of Evil." See 2 Kings 16:9 for reference to Assyria's defeat of Damascus whose people were taken captive to Kir. The Syrian King Rezin was also put to death. **1:11** The Israelites had been commanded (Deuteronomy 2:4) not to attack the Edomites, descendants of Esau, but the Edomites persisted in enmity (cf. 1 Samuel 14:27). **2:5** The Babylonians destroyed Jerusalem (cf. 2 Kings 25:8–10). **2:7** The second half of this verse refers to sexual immoralities associated with the worship of the goddess Ashtoreth (cf. Deuteronomy 23:17). **2:8** Retaining a garment pledged by the poor as security for a loan was contrary to the biblical law of Exodus 22:25.

God's Favors Bring Responsibilities

The people found it difficult to accept Amos's word of doom. After all, were they not God's favored people? Just so, warned Amos; their intimacy with God *obliges* them to be more holy and righteous than other nations.

Amos 3:1–8

3 Hear this word that the LORD has spoken against you, O people of Israel, against the whole family which I brought up out of the land of Egypt:
    ² "You only have I known
        of all the families of the earth;

    therefore I will punish you
       for all your iniquities.

³ "Do two walk together,
    unless they have made an appointment?
⁴ Does a lion roar in the forest,
    when he has no prey?
Does a young lion cry out from his den,
    if he has taken nothing?
⁵ Does a bird fall in a snare on the earth,
    when there is no trap for it?
Does a snare spring up from the ground,
    when it has taken nothing?
⁶ Is a trumpet blown in a city,
    and the people are not afraid?
Does evil befall a city,
    unless the LORD has done it?
⁷ Surely the Lord GOD does nothing,
    without revealing his secret
    to his servants the prophets.
⁸ The lion has roared;
    who will not fear?
The Lord GOD has spoken;
    who can but prophesy?"

3:8 Amos here and in 7:14 describes the compelling demand on conscience that led him to his vocation. God has spoken to the prophet. He can do no other but declare God's word. See also Jeremiah 20:7–10.

Hate Evil and Love Good
Amos 5:4–5, 10–15, 18–24

5 ⁴ For thus says the LORD to the house of Israel:
"Seek me and live;
⁵   but do not seek Bethel,
and do not enter into Gilgal
    or cross over to Beer-sheba;
for Gilgal shall surely go into exile,
    and Bethel shall come to nought."

¹⁰ They hate him who reproves in the gate,
    and they abhor him who speaks the truth.
¹¹ Therefore because you trample upon the poor
    and take from him exactions of wheat,

you have built houses of hewn stone,
>   but you shall not dwell in them;
you have planted pleasant vineyards,
>   but you shall not drink their wine.
12 For I know how many are your transgressions,
>   and how great are your sins—
you who afflict the righteous, who take a bribe,
>   and turn aside the needy in the gate.
13 Therefore he who is prudent will keep silent in such a time;
>   for it is an evil time.

14 Seek good, and not evil,
>   that you may live;
and so the LORD, the God of hosts, will be with you,
>   as you have said.
15 Hate evil, and love good,
>   and establish justice in the gate;
it may be that the LORD, the God of hosts,
>   will be gracious to the remnant of Joseph.
18 Woe to you who desire the day of the LORD!
>   Why would you have the day of the LORD?
It is darkness, and not light;
19   as if a man fled from a lion,
>   and a bear met him;
or went into the house and leaned with his hand against the
>   wall,
>   and a serpent bit him.
20 Is not the day of the LORD darkness, and not light,
>   and gloom with no brightness in it?

21 "I hate, I despise your feasts,
>   and I take no delight in your solemn assemblies.
22 Even though you offer me your burnt offerings and cereal
>   offerings,
>   I will not accept them,
and the peace offerings of your fatted beasts
>   I will not look upon.
23 Take away from me the noise of your songs;
>   to the melody of your harps I will not listen.
24 But let justice roll down like waters,
>   and righteousness like an ever-flowing stream.

5:4 The phrase "Seek me and live" was considered by one of the great rabbis, Simlai, as an expression of the single basic commandment of the Hebrew Scriptures. **5:18** The prevailing opinion was that "the

Day of the Lord" would be a time of victory and rejoicing. Amos warns: if Israel will not mend her ways the Day of the Lord will be a time of gloom and punishment. See also Joel 2:1–2; Zephaniah 1:14–18; Isaiah 2:6–22. **5:21** ff. This attack on the hypocrisy of formalized religious practice unaccompanied by genuine spiritual renewal is characteristic of prophetic teaching: See also 1 Samuel 15:22; Isaiah 1:10–16; 29:13–14; 58:1–8; Hosea 6:6; Micah 6:5–8; Jeremiah 6:20. See also the same emphasis in the New Testament: Luke 11:4–42; Matthew 7:21; John 4:21–24.

God Provides Amos with Visions

In chapters 7–9 Amos records five visions that communicate moral truths, one of a plumbline. This idea is used elsewhere, e.g., 2 Kings 11:13; Isaiah 28:17; 34:11; Lamentations 2:8.

Amos 7:7–15

7 ⁷ He showed me: behold, the Lord was standing beside a wall built with a plumb line, with a plumb line in his hand. ⁸ And the LORD said to me, "Amos, what do you see?" And I said, "A plumb line." Then the Lord said,

"Behold, I am setting a plumb line
in the midst of my people Israel;
I will never again pass by them;
⁹ the high places of Isaac shall be made desolate,
and the sanctuaries of Israel shall be laid waste,
and I will rise against the house of Jerobo′am with the sword."

10 Then Amazi′ah the priest of Bethel sent to Jerobo′am king of Israel, saying, "Amos has conspired against you in the midst of the house of Israel; the land is not able to bear all his words. ¹¹ For thus Amos has said,

'Jerobo′am shall die by the sword,
and Israel must go into exile
away from his land.' "

12 And Amazi′ah said to Amos, "O seer, go, flee away to the land of Judah, and eat bread there, and prophesy there; ¹³ but never again prophesy at Bethel, for it is the king's sanctuary, and it is a temple of the kingdom."

14 Then Amos answered Amazi′ah, "I am no prophet, nor a prophet's son; but I am a herdsman, and a dresser of sycamore trees, ¹⁵ and the LORD took me from following the flock, and the LORD said to me, 'Go, prophesy to my people Israel.' "

7:14 Amos is the first prophet to write down his prophetic proclamations.

Amos Denounces the Hypocrisy of the Rich

Amos scores the contradiction between an alleged public piety and
personal immorality and warns that it will surely lead to the ruin of
the nation.

Amos 8:4–8

8 4 Hear this, you who trample upon the needy,
and bring the poor of the land to an end,
5 saying, "When will the new moon be over,
that we may sell grain?
And the sabbath,
that we may offer wheat for sale,
that we may make the ephah small and the shekel great,
and deal deceitfully with false balances,
6 that we may buy the poor for silver
and the needy for a pair of sandals,
and sell the refuse of the wheat?"

7 The LORD has sworn by the pride of Jacob:
"Surely I will never forget any of their deeds.
8 Shall not the land tremble on this account,
and every one mourn who dwells in it,
and all of it rise like the Nile,
and be tossed about and sink again, like the Nile of Egypt?"

God Pronounces Judgment upon Israel

The prophet teaches that God is a universal Lord. Just as He had
once rescued Israel from slavery in Egypt, so He redeemed the
Philistines from Caphtor and Syrians from Kir. Israel cannot expect,
on account of God's past graciousness, that He will now overlook
their evil. The wicked will perish, but the righteous will survive.

Amos 9:1, 7–15

9 I saw the LORD standing beside the altar, and he said:
"Smite the capitals until the thresholds shake,
and shatter them on the heads of all the people;
and what are left of them I will slay with the sword;
not one of them shall flee away,
not one of them shall escape.

7 "Are you not like the Ethiopians to me,
O people of Israel?" says the LORD.
"Did I not bring up Israel from the land of Egypt,
and the Philistines from Caphtor and the Syrians from Kir?

⁸ Behold, the eyes of the Lord GOD are upon the sinful kingdom,
    and I will destroy it from the surface of the ground;
    except that I will not utterly destroy the house of Jacob,"
                    says the LORD.

⁹ "For lo, I will command,
    and shake the house of Israel among all the nations
as one shakes with a sieve,
    but no pebble shall fall upon the earth.
¹⁰ All the sinners of my people shall die by the sword,
    who say, 'Evil shall not overtake or meet us.'

¹¹ "In that day I will raise up
    the booth of David that is fallen
and repair its breaches,
    and raise up its ruins,
    and rebuild it as in the days of old;
¹² that they may possess the remnant of Edom
    and all the nations who are called by my name,"
    says the LORD who does this.

¹³ "Behold, the days are coming," says the LORD,
    "when the plowman shall overtake the reaper
    and the treader of grapes him who sows the seed;
the mountains shall drip sweet wine,
    and all the hills shall flow with it.
¹⁴ I will restore the fortunes of my people Israel,
    and they shall rebuild the ruined cities and inhabit them;
they shall plant vineyards and drink their wine,
    and they shall make gardens and eat their fruit.
¹⁵ I will plant them upon their land,
    and they shall never again be plucked up
    out of the land which I have given them,"
                    says the LORD your God.

9:13 See note at Hosea 2:18. The prophetic vision of a time of redemption includes both spiritual and physical dimensions. **9:14** Compare this verse with 5:11. This optimistic vision, when contrasted to the thrust of the dire predictions of the rest of Amos's book suggests to some that verses 8b–15 are an appendix added by an exilic or later prophet, who thus made the book speak more directly to the needs of another generation.

The Book of Obadiah

This book, only one chapter, is the shortest of the prophetic books. It is a denunciation of the neighboring country Edom and is intensely nationalistic in tone.

Almost every period in Hebrew history witnessed hostilities between Edom and Israel, or at least rivalry over southern trade routes. The Rabbis later used the name Edom to denote any nation of evil, e.g., Rome, so that this book of denunciation became at many times in Jewish history an appropriate prophetic reading. Tradition ascribes this book to an Obadiah who lived in the reign of King Ahab (1 Kings 18:3 ff.). Most scholars, however, believe that verses 11–14 refer to the sack of Jerusalem by Nebuchadrezzar in 586 B.C., a calamity in which the Edomites joined. They point out also that there are striking similarities between Jeremiah 49:14–16 and 9–10a and Obadiah 1–4 and 5–6. Thus they date Obadiah in the period just prior to or shortly after exile. In 312 B.C. Edom was itself conquered by the Nabateans.

Obadiah's words have become the prototype of the cry of vengeance of a suppressed people. The book concludes with an expression of hope for the time of the Messiah: enemy nations will then be placed under judgment, Israel will be restored in her integrity, and God's rule over history will be acknowledged.

The Prophet Condemns Edom
Obadiah 1:1, 10–18, 21

1 The vision of Obadi'ah.

Thus says the Lord GOD concerning Edom:
We have heard tidings from the LORD,
    and a messenger has been sent among the nations:
"Rise up! let us rise against her for battle!"
¹⁰ For the violence done to your brother Jacob,
    shame shall cover you,
    and you shall be cut off for ever.
¹¹ On the day that you stood aloof,
    on the day that strangers carried off his wealth,
  and foreigners entered his gates
    and cast lots for Jerusalem,
    you were like one of them.
¹² But you should not have gloated over the day of your brother
    in the day of his misfortune;
  you should not have rejoiced over the people of Judah
    in the day of their ruin;

you should not have boasted
  in the day of distress.
¹³ You should not have entered the gate of my people
  in the day of his calamity;
you should not have gloated over his disaster
  in the day of his calamity;
you should not have looted his goods
  in the day of his calamity.
¹⁴ You should not have stood at the parting of the ways
  to cut off his fugitives;
you should not have delivered up his survivors
  in the day of distress.

¹⁵ For the day of the LORD is near upon all the nations.
  As you have done, it shall be done to you,
    your deeds shall return on your own head.
¹⁶ For as you have drunk upon my holy mountain,
  all the nations round about shall drink;
they shall drink, and stagger,
  and shall be as though they had not been.
¹⁷ But in Mount Zion there shall be those that escape,
  and it shall be holy;
and the house of Jacob shall possess their own possessions.
¹⁸ The house of Jacob shall be a fire,
  and the house of Joseph a flame,
  and the house of Esau stubble;
they shall burn them and consume them,
  and there shall be no survivor to the house of Esau;
                              for the LORD has spoken.
²¹ Saviors shall go up to Mount Zion
  to rule Mount Esau;
  and the kingdom shall be the LORD'S.

The Book of Jonah

Preoccupation with the symbol of the whale and disputes over whether this book is history or fiction have obscured the central message of Jonah. This book teaches that God is Lord over Gentiles as well as Jews, and that God prefers man's repentance to his destruction.

Jonah, son of Amittai, is mentioned in 2 Kings 14:25—the only such historical reference to a Jonah in Scripture. He was a prophet who lived in the reign of Jeroboam II (783–743 B.C.). Some commentators suggest, therefore, that this book records historic events of that century when Assyria was the leading world power. Others contend that the language points to a sixth-century date about the time of Judah's captivity to Babylonia. The later author may have selected the name of the earlier prophet because the Hebrew word "Yonah," dove, had become a symbolic name for Israel (Hosea 11:11), and Nineveh, capital of Assyria, had become a symbol of the hated enemy. If this latter interpretation is accepted, then the author is telling the people not to hate the Babylonians, even though Babylonia took Judah into exile, but instead to view them as a nation also capable of faith in God.

Still other scholars suggest that the book was written upon the return of the exiles in the days of Ezra and Nehemiah. Placing a messianic significance on their return, the people anticipated the ultimate defeat of their enemies (see Psalms 22:27 ff.; 103:19; 145:11–13). The short story about Jonah explains, therefore, that all nations are within God's concern. God will not so easily destroy His creations, even if men and nations are evil. He prefers their repentance and conversion. From this perspective the book of Jonah is to be seen in relation to the book of Ruth. Jonah dramatizes God's compassion toward other nations; Ruth demonstrates that among even a hated enemy there are persons who will seek the Living God.

The Book of Jonah has stimulated the creative imagination of artists, poets and songwriters. It is the scriptural reading for the afternoon service on the Day of Atonement, the most sacred day in the Jewish calendar.

Jonah Refuses God's Commission

Jonah shared the popular hatred of the Ninevites; he did not wish them to avoid the punishment he thought was their due. Jonah presumed God's Word could not reach him outside his own country, but, as the story reveals, God is present no matter where man flees.

Jonah 1 : 1–16

1 Now the word of the LORD came to Jonah the son of Amit'tai, saying, ² "Arise, go to Nin'eveh, that great city, and cry against it; for their wickedness has come up before me." ³ But Jonah rose to flee to Tarshish from the presence of the LORD. He went down to Joppa and found a ship going to Tarshish; so he paid the fare, and went on board, to go with them to Tarshish, away from the presence of the LORD.

4 But the LORD hurled a great wind upon the sea, and there was a mighty tempest on the sea, so that the ship threatened to break up. ⁵ Then the mariners were afraid, and each cried to his god; and they threw the wares that were in the ship into the sea, to lighten it for them. But Jonah had gone down into the inner part of the ship and had lain down, and was fast asleep. ⁶ So the captain came and said to him, "What do you mean, you sleeper? Arise, call upon your god! Perhaps the god will give a thought to us, that we do not perish."

7 And they said to one another, "Come, let us cast lots, that we may know on whose account this evil has come upon us." So they cast lots, and the lot fell upon Jonah. ⁸ Then they said to him, "Tell us, on whose account this evil has come upon us? What is your occupation? And whence do you come? What is your country? And of what people are you?" ⁹ And he said to them, "I am a Hebrew; and I fear the LORD, the God of heaven, who made the sea and the dry land." ¹⁰ Then the men were exceedingly afraid, and said to him, "What is this that you have done!" For the men knew that he was fleeing from the presence of the LORD, because he had told them.

11 Then they said to him, "What shall we do to you, that the sea may quiet down for us?" For the sea grew more and more tempestuous. ¹² He said to them, "Take me up and throw me into the sea; then the sea will quiet down for you; for I know it is because of me that this great tempest has come upon you." ¹³ Nevertheless the men rowed hard to bring the ship back to land, but they could not, for the sea grew more and more tempestuous against them. ¹⁴ Therefore they cried to the LORD, "We beseech thee, O LORD, let us not perish for this man's life, and lay not on us innocent blood; for thou, O LORD, hast done as it pleased thee." ¹⁵ So they took up Jonah and threw him into the sea; and the sea ceased from its raging. ¹⁶ Then the men feared the LORD exceedingly, and they offered a sacrifice to the LORD and made vows.

Jonah Is Swallowed by a Large Fish
Jonah 1 : 17; 2 : 1–10

1 ¹⁷ And the LORD appointed a great fish to swallow up Jonah; and Jonah was in the belly of the fish three days and three nights.
2 Then Jonah prayed to the LORD his God from the belly of the fish. . . .

> and he answered me;
> out of the belly of Sheol I cried,
>   and thou didst hear my voice.
> ³ For thou didst cast me into the deep,
>   into the heart of the seas,
>   and the flood was round about me;
> all thy waves and thy billows
>   passed over me.
> ⁴ Then I said, 'I am cast out
>   from thy presence;
> how shall I again look
>   upon thy holy temple?'
> ⁵ The waters closed in over me,
>   the deep was round about me;
> weeds were wrapped about my head
> ⁶   at the roots of the mountains.
> I went down to the land
>   whose bars closed upon me for ever;
> yet thou didst bring up my life from the Pit,
>   O LORD my God.
> ⁷ When my soul fainted within me,
>   I remembered the LORD;
> and my prayer came to thee,
>   into thy holy temple.
> ⁸ Those who pay regard to vain idols
>   forsake their true loyalty.
> ⁹ But I with the voice of thanksgiving
>   will sacrifice to thee;
> what I have vowed I will pay.

10 And the LORD spoke to the fish, and it vomited out Jonah upon the dry land.

The Ninevites Repent
Jonah 3 : 1–10

3 Then the word of the LORD came to Jonah the second time, saying, ² "Arise, go to Nin'eveh, that great city, and proclaim to it the message that I tell you." ³So Jonah arose and went to Nin'eveh, according to the word of the LORD. Now Nin'eveh was an exceedingly great city, three days' journey in breadth. ⁴Jonah began to go into the city, going a day's journey. And he cried, "Yet forty days, and Nin'eveh shall be overthrown!" ⁵And the people of Nin'eveh believed God; they proclaimed a fast, and put on sackcloth, from the greatest of them to the least of them.

6 Then tidings reached the king of Nin'eveh, and he arose from his throne, removed his robe, and covered himself with sackcloth, and sat in ashes. ⁷And he made proclamation and published through Nin'eveh, "By the decree of the king and his nobles: Let neither man nor beast, herd nor flock, taste anything; let them not feed, or drink water, ⁸but let man and beast be covered with sackcloth, and let them cry mightily to God; yea, let every one turn from his evil way and from the violence which is in his hands. ⁹Who knows, God may yet repent and turn from his fierce anger, so that we perish not?"

10 When God saw what they did, how they turned from their evil way, God repented of the evil which he had said he would do to them; and he did not do it.

God Instructs Jonah in Compassion
Jonah 4:1–11

4 But it displeased Jonah exceedingly, and he was angry. ²And he prayed to the LORD and said, "I pray thee, LORD, is not this what I said when I was yet in my country? That is why I made haste to flee to Tarshish; for I knew that thou art a gracious God and merciful, slow to anger, and abounding in steadfast love, and repentest of evil. ³Therefore now, O LORD, take my life from me, I beseech thee, for it is better for me to die than to live." ⁴And the LORD said, "Do you do well to be angry?" ⁵Then Jonah went out of the city and sat to the east of the city, and made a booth for himself there. He sat under it in the shade, till he should see what would become of the city.

6 And the LORD God appointed a plant, and made it come up over Jonah, that it might be a shade over his head, to save him from his discomfort. So Jonah was exceedingly glad because of the plant. ⁷But when dawn came up the next day, God appointed a worm which attacked the plant, so that it withered. ⁸When the sun rose, God appointed a sultry east wind, and the sun beat upon the head of Jonah so that he was faint; and he asked that he might die, and said, "It is better for me to die than to live." ⁹But God said to Jonah, "Do you do well to be angry for the plant?" And he said, "I do well to be angry, angry enough to die." ¹⁰And the LORD said, "You pity the

plant, for which you did not labor, nor did you make it grow, which came into being in a night, and perished in a night. [11] And should not I pity Nin'eveh, that great city, in which there are more than a hundred and twenty thousand persons who do not know their right hand from their left, and also much cattle?''

The Book of Micah

Micah was a younger contemporary of Hosea and Isaiah, and his teachings have much in common with theirs. He prophesied in Judah during the reigns of Jotham, Ahaz and Hezekiah, 740 to 693 B.C.

Both Israel in the north, under Jeroboam II, and Judah to the south, under King Uzziah, had achieved prosperity. Extremes of wealth and poverty appeared that had never before existed in the rural economy governed by biblical laws of tithing, land tenure, and remission of debt.

Micah was a country man. Like Amos he was shocked at the corruption he saw. He warned the leaders that a society breeding such inequality could not long endure; prosperity was not to be interpreted as a sign of God's favor, for the powerful by greed and inhumanity had corrupted God's gifts.

Like Hosea Micah concluded that God would not utterly abandon his people. At the end-time there will be a saving remnant who will be restored; God's law will be observed throughout the world, and there will be peace among the nations.

In chapter 5 (not included in this *Bible Reader*) Micah envisions a "ruler in Israel" who will emerge from the tribe of Bethlehem and usher in the era of peace. "He shall be great to the ends of the earth." The New Testament invokes that chapter, attributing Micah's words to Jesus (Matthew 2:6; John 7:42).

Micah Denounces Both Israel and Judah
Micah 1:1–2, 5–7, 15–16

1 The word of the LORD that came to Micah of Mo'resheth in the days of Jotham, Ahaz, and Hezeki'ah, kings of Judah, which he saw concerning Samar'ia and Jerusalem.

² Hear, you peoples, all of you;
    hearken, O earth, and all that is in it;
and let the LORD God be a witness against you,
    the Lord from his holy temple.
⁵ All this is for the transgression of Jacob
    and for the sins of the house of Israel.
What is the transgression of Jacob?
    Is it not Samar'ia?
And what is the sin of the house of Judah?
    Is it not Jerusalem?
⁶ Therefore I will make Samar'ia a heap in the open country,
    a place for planting vineyards;
and I will pour down her stones into the valley,
    and uncover her foundations.

⁷ All her images shall be beaten to pieces,
   all her hires shall be burned with fire,
   and all her idols I will lay waste;
for from the hire of a harlot she gathered them,
   and to the hire of a harlot they shall return.

15 I will again bring a conqueror upon you,
   inhabitants of Mare′shah;
the glory of Israel
   shall come to Adullam.
¹⁶ Make yourselves bald and cut off your hair,
   for the children of your delight;
make yourselves as bald as the eagle,
   for they shall go from you into exile.

1:5 The prophet here refers to the idolatries practised in Samaria, capital city of Israel, and in Jerusalem, capital city of Judah, and to the ethical and social corruption of the whole society. **1:6** In this context shaving the head is a sign of mourning.

The Leaders Fail Their People
Micah 2:1–3; 3:1–2, 5–8

2 Woe to those who devise wickedness
   and work evil upon their beds!
When the morning dawns, they perform it,
   because it is in the power of their hand.
² They covet fields, and seize them;
   and houses, and take them away;
they oppress a man and his house,
   a man and his inheritance.
³ Therefore thus says the LORD:
Behold, against this family I am devising evil,
   from which you cannot remove your necks;
and you shall not walk haughtily,
   for it will be an evil time.

3 And I said:
Hear, you heads of Jacob
   and rulers of the house of Israel!
Is it not for you to know justice?—
²   you who hate the good and love the evil,
who tear the skin from off my people,
   and their flesh from off their bones;

⁵ Thus says the LORD concerning the prophets
   who lead my people astray,

who cry "Peace"
    when they have something to eat,
but declare war against him
    who puts nothing into their mouths.
⁶ Therefore it shall be night to you, without vision,
    and darkness to you, without divination.
The sun shall go down upon the prophets,
    and the day shall be black over them;
⁷ the seers shall be disgraced,
    and the diviners put to shame;
they shall all cover their lips,
    for there is no answer from God.
⁸ But as for me, I am filled with power,
    with the Spirit of the LORD,
    and with justice and might,
to declare to Jacob his transgression
    and to Israel his sin.

3:5–8 Verse 8 contrasts a prophet of the Lord—one who is filled with God's spirit and committed to justice—with those bands of diviners who traveled the land and sold visions and fortunes for a price.

A Vision of the Days to Come

Micah 4:1–5

4 It shall come to pass in the latter days
    that the mountain of the house of the LORD
shall be established as the highest of the mountains,
    and shall be raised up above the hills;
and peoples shall flow to it,
²   and many nations shall come, and say:
"Come, let us go up to the mountain of the LORD,
    to the house of the God of Jacob;
that he may teach us his ways
    and we may walk in his paths."
For out of Zion shall go forth the law,
    and the word of the LORD from Jerusalem.
³ He shall judge between many peoples,
    and shall decide for strong nations afar off;
and they shall beat their swords into plowshares,
    and their spears into pruning hooks;
nation shall not lift up sword against nation,
    neither shall they learn war any more;

⁴but they shall sit every man under his vine and under his fig
    tree,
    and none shall make them afraid;
    for the mouth of the LORD of hosts has spoken

⁵For all the peoples walk
    each in the name of its god,
    but we will walk in the name of the LORD our God
    for ever and ever.

4:3 This dream of peace has inspired poets, e.g., Tennyson's
"Locksley Hall." Many artists and sculptors have depicted man
converting his spear into a pruning-hook. This passage referring to
"latter days" evokes questions concerning man's ability to achieve
peace through his own devices, even as it inspires further efforts for
peace. Compare Isaiah 2:2 ff. **4:5** This passage is a great scriptural
expression of religious tolerance.

God's Controversy with Israel
Micah 6:1–4, 6–8

6 Hear what the LORD says:
    Arise, plead your case before the mountains,
    and let the hills hear your voice.
²Hear, you mountains, the controversy of the LORD,
    and you enduring foundations of the earth;
    for the LORD has a controversy with his people,
    and he will contend with Israel.

³"O my people, what have I done to you?
    In what have I wearied you? Answer me!
⁴For I brought you up from the land of Egypt,
    and redeemed you from the house of bondage;
    and I sent before you Moses,
    Aaron, and Miriam."

⁶"With what shall I come before the LORD,
    and bow myself before God on high?
    Shall I come before him with burnt offerings,
    with calves a year old?
⁷Will the LORD be pleased with thousands of rams,
    with ten thousands of rivers of oil?
    Shall I give my first-born for my transgression,
    the fruit of my body for the sin of my soul?"

8 He has showed you, O man, what is good;
    and what does the LORD require of you
but to do justice, and to love kindness,
    and to walk humbly with your God?"

6:8 The priority of righteous behavior in the service of God is given its classic expression in this verse.

Micah Appeals to God for Guidance

Micah ends his prophecy with an appeal to God to pardon and forgive. This passage is part of the prophetic reading in the synagogue on the Sabbath between the New Year and the Day of Atonement, and it is recited also following the reading of the book of Jonah at the afternoon service on the Day of Atonement.

Micah 7:18−20

7 18 Who is a God like thee, pardoning iniquity
    and passing over transgression
    for the remnant of his inheritance?
He does not retain his anger for ever
    because he delights in steadfast love.
19 He will again have compassion upon us,
    he will tread our iniquities under foot.
Thou wilt cast all our sins
    into the depths of the sea.
20 Thou wilt show faithfulness to Jacob
    and steadfast love to Abraham,
as thou hast sworn to our fathers
    from the days of old.

7:19 This verse is the source of the ceremony of *Tashlich* observed by Orthodox Jews, who journey to a body of water on the Jewish New Year; there, reciting these verses they confidently cast their sins, as it were, into the depths of the sea.

The Book of Nahum

This three-chapter book provides scant knowledge of the prophet's personal life. When Assurbanipal, a cruel conqueror, died in 626 B.C. Assyrian power deteriorated rapidly, subject nations seized their opportunity, and Nineveh fell in 612 B.C. under the combined attack of the Medes and Babylonians. Nahum foresaw the city's fate and in unforgettable style he passionately and realistically described what would happen. Assyria had formerly been viewed as God's instrument in the disciplining of Judah. Now Assyria in turn will be censured by a just God for her cruelty.

God Brings Vengeance on His Enemies
Nahum 1:1−3, 6−8; 2:1, 8−10, 13

1 An oracle concerning Nin'eveh. The book of the vision of Nahum of Elkosh.

²The LORD is a jealous God and avenging,
   the LORD is avenging and wrathful;
 the LORD takes vengeance on his adversaries
   and keeps wrath for his enemies.
³The LORD is slow to anger and of great might,
   and the LORD will by no means clear the guilty.

⁶Who can stand before his indignation?
   Who can endure the heat of his anger?
 His wrath is poured out like fire,
   and the rocks are broken asunder by him.
⁷The LORD is good,
   a stronghold in the day of trouble;
   he knows those who take refuge in him.
⁸But with an overflowing flood
   he will make a full end of his adversaries,
   and will pursue his enemies into darkness.

2 The shatterer has come up against you.
   Man the ramparts;
   watch the road;
 gird your loins;
   collect all your strength.

⁸Nin'e·veh is like a pool
   whose waters run away.
 "Halt! Halt!" they cry;
   but none turns back.

⁹ Plunder the silver,
    plunder the gold!
There is no end of treasure,
    or wealth of every precious thing.
¹⁰ Desolate! Desolation and ruin!
    Hearts faint and knees tremble,
anguish is on all loins,
    all faces grow pale!

13 Behold, I am against you, says the LORD of hosts, and I will
burn your chariots in smoke, and the sword shall devour your young
lions; I will cut off your prey from the earth, and the voice of your
messengers shall no more be heard.

Nineveh Is Destroyed
Nahum 3:1–4, 18–19

3 Woe to the bloody city,
    all full of lies and booty—
        no end to the plunder!
² The crack of whip, and rumble of wheel,
    galloping horse and bounding chariot!
³ Horsemen charging,
    flashing sword and glittering spear,
hosts of slain,
    heaps of corpses,
dead bodies without end—
    they stumble over the bodies!
⁴ And all for the countless harlotries of the harlot,
    graceful and of deadly charms,
who betrays nations with her harlotries,
    and peoples with her charms.

¹⁸ Your shepherds are asleep,
    O king of Assyria;
    your nobles slumber.
Your people are scattered on the mountains
    with none to gather them.
¹⁹ There is no assuaging your hurt,
    your wound is grievous.
All who hear the news of you
    clap their hands over you.
For upon whom has not come
    your unceasing evil?

3:4 The prophet here attacks the idolatrous cult that the Assyrians had thought to be their strength and protection.

The Book of Habakkuk

Other prophets denounced the sins of the Hebrews and suggested that their enemies were divinely appointed instruments of retribution. But Habakkuk asks: How can a just God give these sinful nations a victory? Why do the innocent suffer and the wicked prosper? Habakkuk's answer is that the wicked only flourish for a moment and then they too will be betrayed by their own unrighteousness. Habakkuk tells Israel: be strong in faith: for the righteous will be justified.

This short prophecy offers little information about the prophet. His name is not Hebrew, but may be derived from an Assyrian word. Could his ministry therefore have taken place during the Exile, say in 550 B.C.? Yet the context of his writings suggests events between the battle of Carchemish in 605 B.C. and the fall of Jerusalem in 586 B.C., so a date in this earlier period is proposed by other scholars.

The third chapter of Habakkuk, written in the poetic style of a psalm, describes God's deliverance of his people and the prophet's joy in the Lord. Some think it to be a later addition to Habukkuk's writings. Among the Dead Sea Scrolls is a commentary on Habukkuk that stops at the end of chapter 2. Chapter 3 is read in synagogues on Shavuoth, the festival of Pentecost.

The Prophet Reasons with God on His Justice
Habakkuk 1:1–6; 2:2–4, 6b, 14, 18–20, 3:16b–19

1 The oracle of God which Habak'kuk the prophet saw.
[2] O LORD, how long shall I cry for help,
and thou wilt not hear?
Or cry to thee "Violence!"
and thou wilt not save?
[3] Why dost thou make me see wrongs
and look upon trouble?
Destruction and violence are before me;
strife and contention arise.
[4] So the law is slacked
and justice never goes forth.
For the wicked surround the righteous,
so justice goes forth perverted.

[5] Look among the nations, and see;
wonder and be astounded.
For I am doing a work in your days
that you would not believe if told.

⁶ For lo, I am rousing the Chalde′ans,
    that bitter and hasty nation,
who march through the breadth of the earth,
    to seize habitations not their own.
2 ² And the Lord answered me:
"Write the vision;
    make it plain upon tablets,
    so he may run who reads it.
³ For still the vision awaits its time;
    it hastens to the end—it will not lie.
If it seem slow, wait for it;
    it will surely come, it will not delay.
⁴ Behold, he whose soul is not upright in him shall fail,
    but the righteous shall live by his faith.

⁶ "Woe to him who heaps up what is not his own—
    for how long?—
    and loads himself with pledges!"
¹⁴ For the earth will be filled
    with the knowledge of the glory of the Lord,
    as the waters cover the sea.

¹⁸ What profit is an idol
    when its maker has shaped it,
    a metal image, a teacher of lies?
For the workman trusts in his own creation
    when he makes dumb idols!
¹⁹ Woe to him who says to a wooden thing, Awake;
    to a dumb stone, Arise!
    Can this give revelation?
Behold, it is overlaid with gold and silver,
    and there is no breath at all in it.

²⁰ But the Lord is in his holy temple;
    let all the earth keep silence before him.

3 ¹⁶ I will quietly wait for the day of trouble
    to come upon people who invade us.

¹⁷ Though the fig tree do not blossom,
    nor the fruit be on the vines,
the produce of the olive fail
    and the fields yield no food,
the flock be cut off from the fold
    and there be no herd in the stalls,

¹⁸ yet I will rejoice in the LORD,
    I will joy in the God of my salvation.
¹⁹ GOD, the Lord, is my strength;
    he makes my feet like hinds' feet,
    he makes me tread upon my high places.

2:3 Christian liturgy during the Advent makes use of this passage to express conviction in the coming of the Messiah (see Hebrews 10:37). **2:4** "Faith" may also be translated "faithfulness." In the later controversy between Paul and the Pharisees over faithfulness to the observance of the Law as the essential Jewish obligation this verse was cited by both, each within his own understanding. This verse is quoted in Hebrews 10:36 f., in justification of this doctrine: the single sacrifice of Jesus "perfected for all time those who were sanctified." **2:20** This verse, set to music in many forms, frequently opens worship services in synagogues and churches. **3:16b–19** This passage follows an account of the destruction of the enemy nation. Although the war may have ravaged the land, the prophet rejoices because Judah will have been saved. God's harvest will be realized in a time-to-come.

The Book of Zephaniah

The prophet Zephaniah dreamed that, after retribution, a purified remnant among the Hebrews would be reestablished in Zion; the exiles would be gathered together and all men live harmoniously in an era of peace and tranquility.

Mention of Zephaniah's lineage in 1:1 suggests that he was from a distinguished family. It is generally accepted that he prophesied during the early days of King Josiah's reign (638–609 B.C.) before the reformation by that king of the religious life of the nation (621 B.C.). If so, Zephaniah, a contemporary of Jeremiah, may be credited with influencing the political and religious direction of the young king. Zephaniah interpreted the emergence of the Scythian nations then invading Western Asia (cf. Jeremiah 4:6) as a portent that God's judgment would soon be brought upon tyrannical nations.

The Latin rendering of his poem found in 1:14–18 became one of the most famous hymns of the Middle Ages, the *"Dies irae, dies illa."*

The Day of the Lord's Wrath
Zephaniah 1:1, 14–18

1 The word of the LORD which came to Zephani'ah the son of Cushi, son of Gedali'ah, son of Amari'ah, son of Hezeki'ah, in the days of Josi'ah the son of Amon, king of Judah.

¹⁴ The great day of the LORD is near,
    near and hastening fast;
the sound of the day of the LORD is bitter,
    the mighty man cries aloud there.
¹⁵ A day of wrath is that day,
    a day of distress and anguish,
a day of ruin and devastation,
    a day of darkness and gloom,
a day of clouds and thick darkness,
¹⁶   a day of trumpet blast and battle cry
against the fortified cities
    and against the lofty battlements.

¹⁷ I will bring distress on men,
    so that they shall walk like the blind,
    because they have sinned against the LORD;
their blood shall be poured out like dust,
    and their flesh like dung.

¹⁸Neither their silver nor their gold
  shall be able to deliver them
  on the day of the wrath of the LORD.
 In the fire of his jealous wrath,
  all the earth shall be consumed;
 for a full, yea, sudden end
  he will make of all the inhabitants of the earth.

Zephaniah Encourages the Faithful
Zephaniah 3 : 8–9, 12–15, 17–20

3 ⁸ "Therefore wait for me," says the LORD,
  "for the day when I arise as a witness.
 For my decision is to gather nations,
  to assemble kingdoms,
 to pour out upon them my indignation,
  all the heat of my anger;
 for in the fire of my jealous wrath
  all the earth shall be consumed.

⁹ "Yea, at that time I will change the speech of the peoples
  to a pure speech,
 that all of them may call on the name of the LORD
  and serve him with one accord.
¹² For I will leave in the midst of you
  a people humble and lowly.
 They shall seek refuge in the name of the LORD,
¹³ those who are left in Israel;
 they shall do no wrong
  and utter no lies,
 nor shall there be found in their mouth
  a deceitful tongue.
 For they shall pasture and lie down,
  and none shall make them afraid."

¹⁴ Sing aloud, O daughter of Zion;
  shout, O Israel!
 Rejoice and exult with all your heart,
  O daughter of Jerusalem!
¹⁵ The LORD has taken away the judgments against you,
  he has cast out your enemies.
 The King of Israel, the LORD, is in your midst;
  you shall fear evil no more.
¹⁷ The LORD, your God, is in your midst,
  a warrior who gives victory;

> he will rejoice over you with gladness,
> he will renew you in his love;
> he will exult over you with loud singing
> ¹⁸   as on a day of festival.
> "I will remove disaster from you,
> so that you will not bear reproach for it.
> ¹⁹ Behold, at that time I will deal
> with all your oppressors.
> And I will save the lame
> and gather the outcast,
> and I will change their shame into praise
> and renown in all the earth.
> ²⁰ At that time I will bring you home,
> at the time when I gather you together;
> yea, I will make you renowned and praised
> among all the peoples of the earth,
> when I restore your fortunes
> before your eyes," says the LORD.

3:9 The ecumenical movement in Christianity, when expressing its hope for harmonious relations among men in the future, frequently invokes this sentence. **3:20** A native of Israel today, reading such a passage, would be moved by the significance of Israel's establishment and the ingathering of the exiles.

The Book of Haggai

References within this short book enable us to place Haggai in a firm historical context. He was among the Judeans who returned from exile in Babylonia after 538 B.C., probably in 521. He was the earliest of the post-exilic prophets (Haggai, Zechariah and Malachi) all of whom concerned themselves with restoration of the Second Temple and the problems of the new community. A summary of that period may be found in the writings of Ezra and Nehemiah.

If Haggai remembered the First Temple (2:3) he must have been an old man during the short ministry recorded here. He and the young prophet Zechariah, who returned to Jerusalem shortly after Haggai, encouraged the exiles to restore the Temple. The Second Temple was dedicated at joyous ceremonies in 516 B.C. Did Haggai live to see it? Tradition holds that he did.

Several psalms bear superscriptions attributing them to Haggai, for example Psalm 38.

According to Jewish tradition, Haggai, Zechariah and Malachi served as the prophets in an essemblage of Jewish leaders known as the Great Synagogue. That assembly established the pattern of Jewish worship—followed to this day in the synagogue—and accepted into the canon a number of biblical books, providing the Hebrew Bible with its essential form.

The Prophet Appeals for Rebuilding the Temple
Haggai 1:1–10; 2:1–9, 20–23

1 In the second year of Darius the king, in the sixth month, on the first day of the month, the word of the LORD came by Haggai the prophet to Zerub'babel the son of She-al'ti-el, governor of Judah, and to Joshua the son of Jehoz'adak, the high priest, ² "Thus says the LORD of hosts: This people say the time has not yet come to rebuild the house of the LORD." ³ Then the word of the LORD came by Haggai the prophet, ⁴ "Is it a time for you yourselves to dwell in your paneled houses, while this house lies in ruins? ⁵ Now therefore thus says the LORD of hosts: Consider how you have fared. ⁶ You have sown much, and harvested little; you eat, but you never have enough; you drink, but you never have your fill; you clothe yourselves, but no one is warm, and he who earns wages earns wages to put them into a bag with holes.

⁷ "Thus says the LORD of hosts: Consider how you have fared. ⁸ Go up to the hills and bring wood and build the house, that I may take pleasure in it and that I may appear in my glory, says the LORD. ⁹ You have have looked for much, and, lo, it came to little; and when

you brought it home, I blew it away. Why? says the LORD of hosts. Because of my house that lies in ruins, while you busy yourselves each with his own house. ¹⁰ Therefore the heavens above you have withheld the dew, and the earth has withheld its produce.

2 In the second year of Darius the king, ¹ in the seventh month, on the twenty-first day of the month, the word of the LORD came by Haggai the prophet, ² "Speak now to Zerub′babel the son of She-al′ti-el, governor of Judah, and to Joshua the son of Jehoz′adak, the high priest, and to all the remnant of the people, and say, ³ 'Who is left among you that saw this house in its former glory? How do you see it now? Is it not in your sight as nothing? ⁴ Yet now take courage, O Zerub′babel, says the LORD, take courage, O Joshua, son of Jehoz′adak, the high priest; take courage, all you people of the land, says the LORD; work, for I am with you, says the LORD of hosts, ⁵ according to the promise that I made you when you came out of Egypt. My Spirit abides among you; fear not. ⁶ For thus says the LORD of hosts:Once again, in a little while, I will shake the heavens and the earth and the sea and the dry land; ⁷ and I will shake all nations, so that the treasures of all nations shall come in, and I will fill this house with splendor, says the LORD of hosts. ⁸ The silver is mine, and the gold is mine, says the LORD of hosts. ⁹ The latter splendor of this house shall be greater than the former, says the LORD of hosts; and in this place I will give prosperity, says the LORD of hosts.' "

20 The word of the LORD came a second time to Haggai on the twenty-fourth day of the month, ²¹ "Speak to Zerub′babel, governor of Judah, saying, I am about to shake the heavens and the earth, ²² and to overthrow the throne of kingdoms; I am about to destroy the strength of the kingdoms of the nations, and overthrow the chariots and their riders; and the horses and their riders shall go down, every one by the sword of his fellow. ²³ On that day, says the LORD of hosts, I will take you, O Zerub′babel my servant, the son of She-al′ti-el, says the LORD, and make you like a signet ring; for I have chosen you, says the LORD of hosts."

1:1 From this text scholars deduce that Haggai began his ministry in the autumn of 520 B.C. He addressed the people on the first day of a new moon, when a large gathering would be in Jerusalem to observe that festival (see 2 Kings 4:23). **1:10** Note that the prophet interprets the drought as a punishment because of the failure of the Judeans to start work on the Temple. In biblical writing a man's individual and social behavior is understood to have a consequence even on the order of nature. **2:7** The prophet interpreted the far-off rumblings of revolt in the Persian empire as a sign that a new day was at hand; the glory of the Second Temple would be greater than that of the First Temple, and the Lord would bring peace to Jerusalem. The Latin Vulgate translation used in the Catholic Church says: "And the Desired of all nations will come," a messianic reference. Thus this passage is used in the prayers during Advent.

2:20 ff. The messianic significance given to the building of the Second Temple is here well expressed. Later the Hebrews were to experience a period of disillusionment as the high hopes attached to the building of the Temple were not realized.

The Book of Zechariah

Zechariah, priest and younger contemporary of the prophet Haggai, was of a family that had returned from exile in Babylonia in one of the contingents starting in 536 B.C. For sixteen years the people had done nothing to restore the Temple. Then they were awakened to responsibility by the prophet Haggai. Zechariah joined him in urging the restoration of the sanctuary. The Temple, Zechariah taught, must not become merely a symbol of outward religious conformity; worship there must be accompanied by holiness of life.

Biblical scholars, noting in the latter half of the book a shift in the historical situation, the content of the messages, and the style of writing suggest that chapters 9–14 were composed in a much later period by another author.

Call to Repentance

Zechariah 1:1–6

1 In the eight month, in the second year of Darius, the word of the LORD came to Zechari′ah the son of Berechi′ah, son of Iddo, the prophet, saying, ²"The LORD was very angry with your fathers. ³Therefore say to them, Thus says the LORD of hosts: Return to me, says the LORD of hosts, and I will return to you, says the LORD of hosts. Be not like your fathers, to whom the former prophets cried out, 'Thus says the LORD of hosts, Return from your evil ways and from your evil deeds.' But they did not hear or heed me, says the LORD. ⁵Your fathers, where are they? And the prophets, do they live for ever? ⁶But my words and my statutes, which I commanded my servants the prophets, did they not overtake your fathers? So they repented and said, As the LORD of hosts purposed to deal with us for our ways and deeds, so has he dealt with us."

The Vision of the Four Horsemen

This selection is the first of a series of eight visions by which the prophet communicates his conviction. In this one the report of the horsemen that the world is now tranquil justifies the prophet's conviction that the time is appropriate for the restoration of the Temple.

Zechariah 1:7–17

1 ⁷On the twenty-fourth day of the eleventh month which is the month of Shebat, in the second year of Darius, the word of the LORD came to Zechari′ah the son of Berechi′ah, son of Iddo, the prophet; and Zechari′ah said, ⁸"I saw in the night, and behold, a man riding upon a red horse! He was standing among the myrtle trees in the glen; and behind him were red, sorrel, and white horses. ⁹Then I said, 'What are these, my lord?' The angel who talked with me said to me, 'I will show you what they are.' ¹⁰So the man who was standing among the myrtle trees answered, 'These are they whom the LORD has sent to patrol the earth.' ¹¹And they answered the angel of the LORD who was standing among the myrtle trees, 'We have patrolled the earth, and behold, all the earth remains at rest.' ¹²Then the angel of the LORD said, 'O LORD of hosts, how long wilt thou have no mercy on Jerusalem and the cities of Judah, against which thou hast had indignation these seventy years?' ¹³And the LORD answered gracious and comforting words to the angel who talked with me. ¹⁴So the angel who talked with me said to me, 'Cry out, Thus says the LORD of hosts: I am exceedingly jealous for Jerusalem and for Zion. ¹⁵And I am very angry with the nations that are at ease; for while I was angry but a little they furthered the disaster. ¹⁶Therefore, thus says the LORD, I have returned to Jerusalem with compassion; my house shall be built in it, says the LORD of hosts, and the measuring line shall be stretched out over Jerusalem. ¹⁷Cry again, Thus says the LORD of hosts: My cities shall again overflow with prosperity, and the LORD will again comfort Zion and again choose Jerusalem.' "

1:9 An angel interprets the vision to Zechariah. This revelation is not direct from God to man. Rabbinical scholars interpreted this as a sign that the skill of prophecy was waning in Israel. **1:11** Under the rule of Darius I (520) the Near Eastern world enjoyed a rare period of comparative tranquillity.

The Vision of the Golden Lamp

The seven-branched candlestick, the menorah, symbolized the restored Jewish state, which is sustained by divine grace through both its civic and religious leaders. The menorah in this vision is kept lit perpetually without human effort, through oil conveyed by the olive tree to the lamps. The ruler Zerubbabel is thus warned that the success of his kingdom will depend not on force of arms or military might but on rule by the Divine Spirit. This portion is recited in the synagogue on the first Sabbath during the Hanukkah celebration, because of its reference to the vision of the menorah. The phrase "Not by might . . ." modifies the celebration of the military prowess of the Maccabees.

Zechariah 4:1–6

4 And the angel who talked with me came again, and waked me, like a man that is wakened out of his sleep. ²And he said to me, "What do you see?" I said, "I see, and behold, a lampstand all of gold, with a bowl on the top of it, and seven lamps on it, with seven lips on each of the lamps which are on the top of it. ³ And there are two olive trees by it, one on the right of the bowl and the other on its left." ⁴ And I said to the angel who talked with me, "What are these, my lord?" ⁵ Then the angel who talked with me answered me, "Do you not know what these are?" I said, "No, my lord." ⁶ Then he said to me, "This is the word of the LORD to Zerub'babel: Not by might, nor by power, but by my Spirit, says the LORD of hosts.

4:6 Compare Kipling's "Recessional."

God Assures Jerusalem

Ten divine messages are introduced by the formula: "Thus says the Lord of Hosts." The messages describing Jerusalem in a future period of glory encouraged the newly returned exiles.

Zechariah 8:4–8, 14–17, 20–23

8 ⁴ Thus says the LORD of hosts: Old men and old women shall again sit in the streets of Jerusalem, each with staff in hand for very age. ⁵ And the streets of the city shall be full of boys and girls playing in its streets. ⁶ Thus says the LORD of hosts: If it is marvelous in the sight of the remnant of this people in these days, should it also be marvelous in my sight, says the LORD of hosts? ⁷ Thus says the LORD of hosts: Behold, I will save my people from the east country and from the west country; ⁸ and I will bring them to dwell in the midst of Jerusalem; and they shall be my people and I will be their God, in faithfulness and in righteousness."

14 For thus says the LORD of hosts: "As I purposed to do evil to you, when your fathers provoked me to wrath, and I did not relent, says the LORD of hosts, ¹⁵ so again have I purposed in these days to do good to Jerusalem and to the house of Judah; fear not. ¹⁶ These are the things that you shall do: Speak the truth to one another, render in your gates judgments that are true and make for peace, ¹⁷ do not devise evil in your hearts against one another, and love no false oath, for all these things I hate, says the LORD."

20 "Thus says the LORD of hosts: Peoples shall yet come, even the inhabitants of many cities; ²¹ the inhabitants of one city shall go to another, saying, 'Let us go at once to entreat the favor of the LORD, and to seek the LORD of hosts; I am going.' ²² Many peoples and strong nations shall come to seek the LORD of hosts in Jerusalem, and to entreat the favor of the LORD. ²³ Thus says the LORD of hosts: In those days ten men from the nations of every tongue shall take hold of the robe of a Jew, saying, 'Let us go with you, for we have heard that God is with you.' "

The Rule of the King of Peace

Zechariah's dream for Jerusalem will be climaxed when the king-Messiah rules over her. War will cease from the land; imprisoned exiles will be restored to their homes; the Hebrews will receive a double portion of goodness in return for all their sufferings.

Some biblical commentators, seeing no messianic significance in this passage, suggest that—if it is viewed in its entirety, including the references in verse 13—the prophet was merely predicting Judah Maccabee's imminent victory over the Greek Syrians in the second century B.C.

Zechariah 9:9–13, 16–17

9 ⁹ Rejoice greatly, O daughter of Zion!
Shout aloud, O daughter of Jerusalem!
Lo, your king comes to you;
triumphant and victorious is he,
humble and riding on an ass,
on a colt the foal of an ass.
¹⁰ I will cut off the chariot from E′phraim
and the war horse from Jerusalem;
and the battle bow shall be cut off,
and he shall command peace to the nations;
his dominion shall be from sea to sea,
and from the River to the ends of the earth.
¹¹ As for you also, because of the blood of my covenant with you,
I will set your captives free from the waterless pit.
¹² Return to your stronghold, O prisoners of hope;
today I declare that I will restore to you double.
¹³ For I have bent Judah as my bow;
I have made E′phraim its arrow.
I will brandish your sons, O Zion,
over your sons, O Greece,
and wield you like a warrior's sword.
¹⁶ On that day the LORD their God will save them
for they are the flock of his people;
for like the jewels of a crown
they shall shine on his land.
¹⁷ Yea, how good and how fair it shall be!
Grain shall make the young men flourish,
and new wine the maidens.

9:9 The king comes not as a proud warrior as in former times (compare 1 Kings 1:5 with 1 Kings 1:38), but he rides on a peaceful animal. The JPS translation reads: "Behold thy king cometh unto thee. He is triumphant and victorious. . . ." Douay: "See your king shall come to you, a just Saviour is he. . . ." **9:10** An aspect of the messianic dream of the Hebrews was the reuniting of the Northern and Southern Kingdoms. Ephraim is another name for Israel, the Northern Kingdom. See Jeremiah 3:18.

The Universal Feast of Booths

In this oracle about "a day of the Lord," wicked nations will be destroyed; others will recognize that God is one and that He is King over all the earth. Then all nations will offer thanksgiving to God by celebrating the Feast of Booths (14:16). (In some translations it is called Feast of Tabernacles.) This feast is called Sukkoth in the Hebrew (from a word meaning booth, tabernacle or tent). The feast is the third of the three annual pilgrimage festivals and a time of thanksgiving for the harvest. During this eight-day festival, sacrifices were brought to the Temple on behalf of the nations of the world. This passage is recited in the synagogue on the first Sabbath of the Sukkoth celebration. When the Pilgrim Fathers established their new homes in the "promised land" of America, they celebrated a Thanksgiving inspired by the biblical account of the Sukkoth festival.

Zechariah 14:1–3, 6–9, 12–13, 16

14 Behold, a day of the LORD is coming, when the spoil taken from you will be divided in the midst of you. ²For I will gather all the nations against Jerusalem to battle, and the city shall be taken and the houses plundered and the women ravished; half of the city shall go into exile, but the rest of the people shall not be cut off from the city. ³Then the LORD will go forth and fight against those nations as when he fights on a day of battle.

6 On that day there shall be neither cold nor frost. ⁷And there shall be continuous day (it is known to the LORD), not day and not night, for at evening time there shall be light.

8 On that day living waters shall flow out from Jerusalem, half of them to the eastern sea and half of them to the western sea; it shall continue in summer as in winter.

9 And the LORD will become king over all the earth; on that day the LORD will be one and his name one.

12 And this shall be the plague with which the LORD will smite all the peoples that wage war against Jerusalem: their flesh shall rot while they are still on their feet, their eyes shall rot in their sockets, and their tongues shall rot in their mouths. ¹³And on that day a great panic from the LORD shall fall on them, so that each will lay hold on the hand of his fellow, and the hand of the one will be raised against the hand of the other;

16 Then every one that survives of all the nations that have come against Jerusalem shall go up year after year to worship the King, the LORD of hosts, and to keep the feast of booths.

14:9 This verse climaxes the adoration prayer that concludes the daily Jewish worship service. See also Zephaniah 3:9, Malachi 1:11 for the prophetic view that in the messianic era all nations will serve God as the One.

The Book of Malachi

This book is the last of the twelve minor prophets in their traditional order of presentation. Most scholars place Malachi's ministry in Judah around 460–450 B.C. some sixty years after the building of the Second Temple. The community's condition was generally wretched. The hopes aroused in the people by the messianic-type promises (Haggai 2:9; Zechariah 8–9) connected with the re-establishment of the sanctuary remained unfulfilled. Consequently the priests and people tended to become careless. Malachi tried to arouse the people to rededicate themselves to their religion. Advocating the restoration of Temple ritual, he emphasized that inner commitment must accompany religious rites. Like other prophets, Malachi asserts the belief that there will be a "day of the Lord" when Israel will be purified by God's judgment and a saving remnant will survive to witness the messianic era.

Malachi occasionally expresses a magnanimous view of the nations and their religions (1:11, 14) and reflects the universal monotheism of Isaiah 40–55.

Malachi communicates his message through a dialectic process: statement of a truth; posing of a question to that thesis; a final demonstration of the valdidity of his thesis. The method heightened interest among a depressed and skeptical audience, who probably shared the doubts voiced in Malachi's questions. This method of question and answer was later adopted by Jewish scholars in the Rabbinic period as *the* method of instruction. Christians from early times have used a like method of question and answer in catechisms.

According to one Jewish tradition, the spirit of prophecy departed from Israel with the death of Malachi, called the last of the prophets (*Sotah* 48b). We know nothing about his life. Some think his book was originally anonymous and that a later editor supplied a name by transforming *malakhi,* meaning "my messenger," into a proper name so that all of the books of The Twelve would bear names of authors.

Malachi Rebukes the Priests
Malachi 1:1; 6–12; 2:1–2

1 The oracle of the word of the LORD to Israel by Mal'achi.

6 "A son honors his father, and a servant his master. If then I am a father, where is my honor? And if I am a master, where is my fear? says the LORD of hosts to you, O priests, who despise my name. You say, 'How have we despised thy name?' 7 By offering polluted food upon my altar. And you say, 'How have we polluted it?' By thinking

that the LORD's table may be despised. [8] When you offer blind animals in sacrifice, is that no evil? And when you offer those that are lame or sick, is that no evil? Present that to your governor; will he be pleased with you or show you favor? says the LORD of hosts. [9] And now entreat the favor of God, that he may be gracious to us. With such a gift from your hand, will he show favor to any of you? says the LORD of hosts. [10] Oh, that there were one among you who would shut the doors, that you might not kindle fire upon my altar in vain! I have no pleasure in you, says the LORD of hosts, and I will not accept an offering from your hand. [11] For from the rising of the sun to its setting my name is great among the nations, and in every place incense is offered to my name, and a pure offering; for my name is great among the nations, says the LORD of hosts. [12] But you profane it when you say that the LORD's table is polluted, and the food for it may be despised.

2 "And now, O priests, this command is for you. [2] If you will not listen, if you will not lay it to heart to give glory to my name, says the LORD of hosts, then I will send the curse upon you and I will curse your blessings; indeed I have already cursed them, because you do not lay it to heart.

> **1:11** Malachi cites the devotion of other nations as a rebuke to Israel. Significant for later religious thought is Malachi's contention that the intent at heart, when heathens bring sincere offerings to their gods, renders their act acceptable to the one true God. God judges people by the devotion of their hearts, though not everywhere do they yet know Him by name. The Council of Trent interpreted this text to refer to the perfect sacrifice that will be offered in the messianic age.

The Prophet Censures Divorce and Intermarriage

Intermarriage historically led the Hebrews to idolatrous ways; the inherent danger of divorce threatened home life and vows were treated lightly. Malachi asserts a moral lesson: social ills weaken the moral strength of the community, and pave the way for its destruction.

Malachi 2:10–16

2 [10] Have we not all one father? Has not one God created us? Why then are we faithless to one another, profaning the covenant of our fathers? [11] Judah has been faithless, and abomination has been committed in Israel and in Jerusalem; for Judah has profaned the sanctuary of the LORD, which he loves, and has married the daughter of a foreign god. [12] May the LORD cut off from the tents of Jacob, for the man who does this, any to witness or answer, or to bring an offering to the LORD of hosts!

13 And this again you do. You cover the LORD's altar with tears, with weeping and groaning because he no longer regards the offering or accepts it with favor at your hand. ¹⁴ You ask, "Why does he not?" Because the LORD was witness to the covenant between you and the wife of your youth, to whom you have been faithless, though she is your companion and your wife by covenant. ¹⁵ Has not the one God made and sustained for us the spirit of life? And what does he desire? Godly offspring. So take heed to yourselves, and let none be faithless to the wife of his youth. ¹⁶ "For I hate divorce, says the LORD the God of Israel, and covering one's garment with violence, says the LORD of hosts. So take heed to yourselves and do not be faithless."

2:10 The first half of this verse, taken out of context—the question reflects the prophet's concern for the sanctity of family relationship in Israel—has been used to express man's brotherhood under the fatherhood of God: man's moral obligations to deal justly with his brother is based upon his relation to God by virtue of creation.

Malachi Speaks to the Doubting Mind

The people asked: what was the point of fulfilling religious obligations when all round them wicked men were prospering? Malachi answers that there will come a day—some hold this to be a messianic vision—when God will suddenly appear and bring a blessing to the nation.

Malachi 2:17–4:6

2 ¹⁷ You have wearied the LORD with your words. Yet you say, "How have we wearied him?" By saying, "Every one who does evil is good in the sight of the LORD, and he delights in them." Or by asking, "Where is the God of justice?"

3 "Behold, I send my messenger to prepare the way before me, and the Lord whom you seek will suddenly come to his temple; the messenger of the covenant in whom you delight, behold, he is coming, says the LORD of hosts. ² But who can endure the day of his coming, and who can stand when he appears?

"For he is like a refiner's fire and like fullers' soap; ³ he will sit as a refiner and purifier of silver, and he will purify the sons of Levi and refine them like gold and silver, till they present right offerings to the LORD. ⁴ Then the offering of Judah and Jerusalem will be pleasing to the LORD as in the days of old and as in former years.

5 "Then I will draw near to you for judgment; I will be a swift witness against the sorcerers, against the adulterers, against those

who swear falsely, against those who oppress the hireling in his wages, the widow and the orphan, against those who thrust aside the sojourner, and do not fear me, says the LORD of hosts.

6 "For I the LORD do not change; therefore you, O sons of Jacob, are not consumed. 7 From the days of your fathers you have turned aside from my statutes and have not kept them. Return to me, and I will return to you, says the LORD of hosts. But you say, 'How shall we return?' 8 Will man rob God? Yet you are robbing me. But you say, 'How are we robbing thee?' In your tithes and offerings. 9 You are cursed with a curse, for you are robbing me; the whole nation of you. 10 Bring the full tithes into the storehouse, that there may be food in my house; and thereby put me to the test, says the LORD of hosts, if I will not open the windows of heaven for you and pour down for you an overflowing blessing. 11 I will rebuke the devourer for you, so that it will not destroy the fruits of your soil; and your vine in the field shall not fail to bear, says the LORD of hosts. 12 Then all nations will call you blessed, for you will be a land of delight, says the LORD of hosts.

13 "Your words have been stout against me, says the LORD. Yet you say, 'How have we spoken against thee?' 14 You have said, 'It is vain to serve God. What is the good of our keeping his charge or of walking as in mourning before the LORD of hosts? 15 Henceforth we deem the arrogant blessed; evildoers not only prosper but when they put God to the test they escape.' "

16 Then those who feared the LORD spoke with one another; the LORD heeded and heard them, and a book of remembrance was written before him of those who feared the LORD and thought on his name. 17 "They shall be mine, says the LORD of hosts, my special possession on the day when I act, and I will spare them as a man spares his son who serves him. 18 Then once more you shall distinguish between the righteous and the wicked, between one who serves God and one who does not serve him.

4 "For behold, the day comes, burning like an oven, when all the arrogant and all evildoers will be stubble; the day that comes shall burn them up, says the LORD of hosts, so that it will leave them neither root nor branch. 2 But for you who fear my name the sun of righteousness shall rise, with healing in its wings. You shall go forth leaping like calves from the stall. 3 And you shall tread down the wicked, for they will be ashes under the soles of your feet, on the day when I act, says the LORD of hosts.

4 "Remember the law of my servant Moses, the statutes and ordinances that I commanded him at Horeb for all Israel.

5 "Behold, I will send you Eli'jah the prophet before the great and

terrible day of the LORD comes. ⁶And he will turn the hearts of fathers to their children and the hearts of children to their fathers, lest I come and smite the land with a curse."

3:16 Such a "book of remembrance" constantly opened before God is also alluded to in Exodus 32:32, Isaiah 4:3 and Psalms 69:29 and 134:16. This image is also invoked by Jews during the ten days of penitence when their prayers call upon God to forgive them their sins and to inscribe their names within a book of life for the forthcoming year. **4:1** For other prophetic references to the fire on the "day of the Lord," see Isaiah 10:16 f.; 30:27; Zephaniah 1:18; 3:8; Jeremiah 21:14. **4:5** Malachi gives expression to a dream long to be cherished by the Jews, that in a time to come Elijah the prophet will appear and announce the period of Messianic reconciliation. In Matthew 11:14 this verse is quoted. Jesus identified John the Baptist with the expected Elijah. **4:6b** It is against Jewish law to conclude a book with a word of doom such as the last phrase of 4:6b: "lest I come and smite the land with a curse." The prior verse, 4:5, therefore, is repeated in Hebrew Bibles. Similar repetitions are found at the end of the book of Isaiah, Lamentations and Ecclesiastes.

The Apocrypha (Deutero-canonical Books)

Introduction

American Protestant churches circulated a leaflet entitled "Hands." It pictured men's hands laying brick, sorting mail, using mortar and pestle, giving a patient a hypodermic injection; women's hands peeling potatoes, playing the piano, taking notes in shorthand, guiding the hand of a child. All these hands, says the brochure, are praying hands. The point is clinched with reference to the words of a Jewish sage who lived and wrote in the time between the Old and New Testaments: "Their prayer is in the practice of their trade."

An American firm's house organ published this advice for dinner guests: "Leave in good season and do not be the last; go home quickly, and do not linger."

In 1941 James Agee, then a writer for *Time* and *Fortune,* published a novel about the depression entitled *Let Us Now Praise Famous Men.*

Here are three contemporary quotations from a collection of writings, together known as the Apocrypha or the deutero-canonical books. The Roman Catholic Church prefers the latter designation (*deutero* meaning "second" or "later"), for it reserves the word "Apocrypha" for those works outside any biblical canon that are known to Protestant scholars as pseudepigrapha (later writings attributed to earlier biblical characters).

What, then, are the Apocrypha? The word itself is from the Greek, meaning "kept secret" or "hidden." The application of the word has had a curious history. Some scholars hold that "Apocrypha" was the term used to translate the Hebrew word *Genuzim*, i.e., repositories for writings stored away or withdrawn from use. It was customary to remove worn-out scrolls to a *Genizah*. The same fate occasionally overtook books whose connection with the sacred writings was not too securely established. Even some books that did finally get included in the canon were at one time under criticism: Proverbs because of its numerous contradictions, the Song of Solomon because of its secular character, Ecclesiastes because of its "heretical" ideas.

This theory that the word "Apocrypha" refers to books "stored away" is, however, opposed by other scholars, who point out that the regular rabbinical designation for the extra-canonical books is *Sefarim Hitzonim*, "outside books." To these scholars "Apocrypha" clearly refers to those books "outside" the canon. It is a plural noun.

Whatever the word meant originally, the Apocrypha consist of fifteen books, as counted in the Revised Standard Version. (There are other ways of reckoning the number.) All are anonymous, and nothing precise has been determined about their authorship or date. It is known, however, that they came into being between the close of the Old Testament and the beginning of the New. Therefore they have also been called the Intermediate Testament.

Two books of this collection—1 and 2 Maccabees—are invaluable to historians of the second century B.C. They deal with the resistance movement known as the Maccabean War, an insurrection inspired by the aged priest Mattathias and led by his five sons, of whom Judas Maccabeus is the best known.

In these books we find the origin and meaning of "the feast of the Dedication at Jerusalem" (John 10:22), better known as Hanukkah, which has ever since been a holy day. It commemorates the crowning exploit of the Maccabean heroes. Howard Fast tells their story in fictionalized form in *My Glorious Brothers*.

Ecclesiasticus is one of two wisdom books in this collection; its alternative name is Wisdom of Jesus son of Sirach. The other book is Wisdom of Solomon. Both sparkle with the same wit and paradox as the wisdom books of the Hebrew Bible.

Some of the books are supplementary to Hebrew scriptures. 1 Esdras is an extension of the book of Ezra. There are also additions to the Book of Esther that were inserted in the Septuagint at various points. Baruch was Jeremiah's companion and secretary, and a book bearing his name, included in the Apocrypha, contains a confession of the nation's guilt and words of comfort and hope for the exiles. To this is appended a letter reported to have been sent by Jeremiah himself to his fellow countrymen who had been carried away captive to Babylon.

2 Chronicles 33:11–13 tells how King Manasseh, Judah's wicked king, went through a period of great distress, "entreated the favor of the Lord his God and . . . prayed to him," but it does not tell us what the prayer was. The Prayer of Manasseh, composed probably at a later time, records that fervent petition of penitence. Daniel 3:23 tells how Shadrach, Meshach and Abednego "fell bound into the burning fiery furnace." Additions to the book of Daniel—including the Prayer of Azariah and the Song of the Three Young Men—tell us what they did there, not cringing in terror before the flames but calling upon the whole creation to join in hymns of adoration.

At least three twentieth-century Bible translators—Ronald Knox, James Moffatt and Edgar J. Goodspeed—have written detective stories. This may be because of their familiarity with the early examples of this *genre* in the Apocrypha. The pure religion of the Hebrews pitted them in unending struggle against idolators. Bel and the Dragon is the story of how Daniel outwitted the priests of Bel and brought about the overthrow of a great idol. Susanna pictures Daniel's ingenuity in tracking down a guilty party. Deeds such as these account for Shakespeare's words, "A Daniel come to judgment!"

Shakespeare had two daughters, Susanna and Judith. As the name of the one commemorated the charming woman whose honor was preserved by Daniel, so the name of the other recalls a Hebrew heroine who ranks with Deborah and Esther. By the use of feminine wiles, Judith delivered her people from the cruel invaders captained by Holofernes. The book about Judith is a kind of novella. So also is Tobit, which recounts the story of what happened to a dutiful son who went on a long journey to recover money belonging to his father. Both Judith and Tobit are replete with illustrations of Hebrew piety.

The remaining book in the Apocrypha, 2 Esdras, helps us to understand that form of literature known as apocalyptic, of which Daniel and Revelation are examples.

The books above enumerated represent, in general, writings in the Alexandrian canon that were not accepted in the Jerusalem canon. Though some of the books called Apocrypha were written in Hebrew, the popular version was in Greek, and they were included in the Septuagint, the Greek translation of the Hebrew Scriptures made in Alexandria in the third century B.C.

Because of his close association with the Hebrew canon, Jerome rejected the authority given to the Apocrypha in Alexandria. His view has prevailed in the Protestant church. Luther separated the Apocryphal books from the strictly canonical ones, putting them into a section by themselves, as Jerome had done. The Roman Catholic Church, at the Council of Trent, in 1546, affirmed the inspiration and full scriptural authority of eleven books of the Apocrypha. In the Vulgate, the other three—the Prayer of Manasseh and 1 and 2 Esdras—appear after the New Testament. The Thirty-Nine Articles of the Anglican Church lists the canonical books of the Old Testament and the names of fourteen apocryphal works, with this introduction: "And the other Books (as Hierome saith) the Church doth read for example of life and instruction of manners; but yet it doth not apply them to establish any doctrine." The (Presbyterian) Westminster Confession, 1647, states: "The books commonly called Apocrypha, not being of divine inspiration, are no part of the canon of the Scripture, and therefore are of no authority in the Church of God nor to be any otherwise approved, or made use of, than other human writings."

The Apocryphal books have been in all authorized English Bibles. It was more than 200 years after its publication in 1611 that editions of the King James Version appeared without the Apocrypha. In 1827 the British and Foreign Bible Society decided to omit them. The American Bible Society followed suit, as did private publishers, who were quick to discern in their omission a lowered cost of printing. The Revised Standard Version prints the Apocrypha *after* the Old and New Testaments.

If we ask why the Apocrypha were dropped from the King James Version, the answer seems to be that the Puritans, following the Reformers, regarded those books as containing false doctrine. 2 Maccabees 15:14 pictures Judas Maccabaeus as undergoing a kind of transfiguration experience. He communes with Onias, the former high priest, and with Jeremiah, the prophet of God, "who loves the brethren, and prays much for the people and the holy city." Origen, on the other hand, used this as a proof text for the intercession of the saints. A passage (2 Maccabees 12:43–45) about making atonement for the dead has been cited in support of the Requiem Mass.

The Apocrypha are important for understanding the development of religious ideas in the time between the Testaments. The concept of angels and demons becomes explicit in these books, as does that of personal immortality. In contrast with Job 14:7, 10, the Wisdom of Solomon affirms that "The souls of the righteous are in the hands of God." Knowledge of the Apocrypha is presupposed in many New Testament passages. When the Sadducees pose for Jesus the question of the resurrection status of one woman married successively to seven brothers (Mark 12:20–23), they may not have contrived the incident. The woman loved by Tobias, in the book of Tobit, has been married to seven men in succession.

The Song of the Three Young Men has made its way into Christian liturgy as *Benedicite*, and the Apocrypha have in many ways entered into our history and culture. 2 Esdras 6:42 relates that at the creation God commanded "the waters to be gathered together in the seventh part of the earth," the remaining six-sevenths being available for cultivation. On the basis of this verse Columbus believed that six-sevenths of the earth was dry land, and no great amount of ocean could separate him from the wealth of India and Cathay. Scientists now affirm that more than 70 per cent of the earth's surface is ocean.

The facade of the New York Public Library bears the inscription: "But above all things Truth beareth away the victory." A quotation from 1 Esdras 4:35, this is the prize-winning answer in an Apocryphal forerunner of a modern quiz program. The 64,000 drachma question was: "What one thing is strongest?" Wine, women and the king have their advocates, but the conclusion is, "Truth is great, and stronger than all things."

Over the entrance to the Columbia-Presbyterian hospital in New York are the words, "Of the Most High Cometh Healing," a quotation from Ecclesiasticus, which also affirms: "The Lord created medicines from the earth, and a sensible man will not despise them."

Many works of art capture dramatic moments out of the Apocrypha: "Judith," by Allori; "Tobias and the Angel" by Raphael; "Susanna and the Elders" by Guido Reni; "Heliodorus Driven from the Temple" by Raphael. Handel's oratorio, "Judas Maccabaeus" was the big hit of the Lenten season of 1747 in

London, after the defeat of Bonnie Prince Charlie. It contains the chorus, "See, the conquering hero comes." A recent opera of Carlisle Floyd, an American composer, is entitled "Susannah." Its libretto begins in the Apocrypha.

God's concern for all human kind is given eloquent expression in the Apocrypha. For example, Wisdom of Solomon 6:7 says:

For the LORD of all will not stand in awe of anyone,
nor show deference to greatness;
because he himself made both small and great,
and he takes thought for all alike.

The Book of Tobit

The book of Tobit is a novella which combines two favorite themes of ancient literature: the Grateful Dead and the Dangerous Bride. From 1:1 through 3:6 it tells the story of Tobit a man exiled from his homeland, who tried to be faithful to his religion, wherever he was. Taken from Thisbe, in Galilee, during the invasion of the Assyrians, Tobit walked "in the ways of truth and righteousness," even in captivity in Nineveh. He gave bread to the hungry and clothing to the naked, and was especially careful to see that all the poor among his people received decent interment. One evening, while he was sleeping "by the wall of the courtyard," bird droppings fell into his eyes and blinded him.

Far away at Ecbatana in Media, on the same day, a young woman, Sarah, daughter of Raguel, a kinsman of Tobit, felt that her life was no longer worth living. Her seven husbands had successively been slain on the wedding night by Asmodeus, a jealous demon. Both Tobit and Sarah, unknown to each other, pray to God for relief. Their prayer is heard and the angel Raphael is dispatched "to heal the two of them."

Tobit, remembering a sum of money he had earlier left in Media, sends his son Tobias to collect it. Tobias is accompanied by the angel Raphael, disguised as a guide and interpreter, using the name Azarias.

In Media, Tobias meets Sarah. He falls in love with her and asks to marry her. On their wedding night Raphael, still in the guise of Azarias, gives Tobias the heart and liver of a fish, instructing him to place them upon ashes of incense in order to drive away the demon. Tobias survives the ordeal, and he and Sarah are happily married. Returning to his home with his bride, Tobias finds that the gill of the same fish will cure his father's blindness. Tobit lives to be 158 years old.

Through the ministry of Raphael the story emphasizes a point made in Ecclesiasticus 38:2, that "healing comes from the Most High." It demonstrates also that God's divine providence may be with man each day. The story provides a picture of Judaism in the Diaspora (dispersion). Before he was carried away from home, Tobit had given three-tenths of his income to good causes; in exile he continued to perform acts of charity, to refrain from eating forbidden foods, and to preserve ritual cleanliness. The prayers include one in which Tobit confesses his nation's sinfulness but expresses confidence in its ultimate redemption in a messianic period. Sarah similarly acknowledges her dependence upon God.

There are differences among scholars as to whether this book was written in Egypt, Palestine, or Babylonia, and on the date of its writing. It is clear, however, that the novella Tobit must have been written to encourage the Jews to remain true to their faith and to the Mosiac Law, even under conditions of oppression.

Tobit Sends Tobias on a Journey

Tobit 4:1–16

4 On that day Tobit remembered the money which he had left in trust with Gabael at Rages in Media, and he said to himself: ² "I have asked for death. Why do I not call my son Tobias so that I may explain to him about the money before I die?" ³ So he called him and said, "My son, when I die, bury me, and do not neglect your mother. Honor her all the days of your life; do what is pleasing to her, and do not grieve her. ⁴ Remember, my son, that she faced many dangers for you while you were yet unborn. When she dies, bury her beside me in the same grave.

5 "Remember the LORD our God all your days, my son, and refuse to sin or to transgress his commandments. Live uprightly all the days of your life, and do not walk in the ways of wrongdoing. ⁶ For if you do what is true, your ways will prosper through your deeds. ⁷ Give alms from your possessions to all who live uprightly, and do not let your eye begrudge the gift when you make it. Do not turn your face away from any poor man, and the face of God will not be turned away from you. ⁸ If you have many possessions, make your gift from them in proportion; if few, do not be afraid to give according to the little you have. ⁹ So you will be laying up a good treasure for yourself against the day of necessity. ¹⁰ For charity delivers from death and keeps you from entering the darkness; ¹¹ and for all who practice it charity is an excellent offering in the presence of the Most High.

12 "Beware, my son, of all immorality. First of all take a wife from among the descendants of your father and do not marry a foreign woman, who is not of your father's tribe; for we are the sons of the prophets. Remember, my son, that Noah, Abraham, Isaac, and Jacob, our fathers of old, all took wives from among their brethren. They were blessed in their children, and their posterity will inherit the land. ¹³ So now, my son, love your brethren, and in your heart do not disdain your brethren and the sons and daughters of your people by refusing to take a wife for yourself from among them. For in pride there is ruin and great confusion; and in shiftlessness there is loss and great want, because shiftlessness is the mother of famine. ¹⁴ Do not hold over till the next day the wages of any man who works for you, but pay him at once; and if you serve God you will receive payment.

"Watch yourself, my son, in everything you do, and be disciplined in all your conduct. [15] And what you hate, do not do to any one. Do not drink wine to excess or let drunkenness go with you on your way. [16] Give of your bread to the hungry, and of your clothing to the naked. Give all your surplus to charity, and do not let your eye begrudge the gift when you make it.

4:3 It was a tragic matter not to be buried; cf. Psalm 79:3; Jeremiah 2:19. **4:4** Cf. Genesis 25:10. Placing a wife next to her mate is a practice still followed in the Jewish religion. **4:6** In the biblical period the reward promised for virtuous behavior was this-worldly: prosperity and long life. The spiritual crisis evoked when the righteous did not always enjoy such material favor is to be seen in the questions raised by the Book of Job and Psalms 37, 49, 73. **4:11** Cf. Proverbs 21:3. The Talmud records: "Greater is the act of one who gives alms than all the sacrifices" (*Sukkah* 49b). **4:12** Tobit summarizes here the Jew's proud sense of his mission and destiny. Sons of prophets, who spoke eloquently the word of God, the Hebrews are to maintain the purity of their religious commitments. Thus they are discouraged from entering into mixed marriages. In the biblical experience mixed marriage was accompanied by the introduction of idolatrous ways into Judaism. See criticism of King Solomon on this account, 1 Kings 11 and the legislation enacted by Ezra and Nehemiah, who compelled Judeans to set aside their foreign wives after the exile from Babylonia, Ezra 10; Nehemiah 13:23–27. To this day mixed marriage is avoided in the Jewish religion, and most rabbis require conversion to the Jewish faith before they will sanctify the marriage. **4:14** A restatement of the humanitarian direction to employers found in Deuteronomy 24:14, 15. **4:15** A negative statement of what, put positively (Matthew 7:12), has come to be called the Golden Rule.

Tobit and Tobias Rejoice in the Goodness of God
Tobit 12:1–21

12 Tobit then called his son Tobias and said to him, "My son, see to the wages of the man who went with you; and he must also be given more." [2] He replied, "Father, it would do me no harm to give him half of what I have brought back. [3] For he has led me back to you safely, he cured my wife, he obtained the money for me, and he also healed you." [4] The old man said, "He deserves it." [5] So he called the angel and said to him, "Take half of all that you two have brought back."

[6] Then the angel called the two of them privately and said to them: "Praise God and give thanks to him; exalt him and give thanks to him in the presence of all the living for what he has done for you. It is good to praise God and to exalt his name, worthily

declaring the works of God. Do not be slow to give him thanks. [7] It is good to guard the secret of a king, but gloriously to reveal the works of God. Do good, and evil will not overtake you. [8] Prayer is good when accompanied by fasting, almsgiving, and righteousness. A little with righteousness is better than much with wrongdoing. It is better to give alms than to treasure up gold. [9] For almsgiving delivers from death, and it will purge away every sin. Those who perform deeds of charity and of righteousness will have fulness of life; [10] but those who commit sins are the enemies of their own lives.

11 "I will not conceal anything from you. I have said, 'It is good to guard the secret of a king, but gloriously to reveal the works of God.' [12] And so, when you and your daughter-in-law Sarah prayed, I brought a reminder of your prayer before the Holy One; and when you buried the dead, I was likewise present with you. [13] When you did not hesitate to rise and leave your dinner in order to go and lay out the dead, your good dead was not hidden from me, but I was with you. [14] So now God sent me to heal you and your daughter-in-law Sarah. [15] I am Raphael, one of the seven holy angels who present the prayers of the saints and enter into the presence of the glory of the Holy One."

16 They were both alarmed; and they fell upon their faces, for they were afraid. [17] But he said to them, "Do not be afraid; you will be safe. But praise God for ever. [18] For I did not come as a favor on my part, but by the will of our God. Therefore praise him for ever. [19] All these days I merely appeared to you and did not eat or drink, but you were seeing a vision. [20] And now give thanks to God, for I am ascending to him who sent me. Write in a book everything that has happened." [21] Then they stood up; but they saw him no more.

12:12 In the Book of Common Prayer (1549) Tobias and Sarah, rather than Abraham and Sarah (as now), were mentioned as the ideal married couple. **12:14** The name Raphael, meaning "God heals," is aptly applied to one who "is set over all the diseases and all the wounds of the children of men" (Enoch 4:9). **12:15** In Rabbinical thought Raphael was one of seven archangels (cf. Revelation 8:12), the others being Uriel, Raquel, Michael, Sarakiel, Gabriel and Jeremiel. Jewish tradition held that Raphael was the angel who imparted to Sarah "power to conceive" (Hebrew 11:11; cf. Genesis 18:1–15) and also that, after the flood, God sent Raphael to instruct Noah in the use of curative plants and roots. Among many artistic representations of Tobias and the Angel are those of Salvatore Rose (the Louvre), F. Lippi (National Gallery, Washington, D.C.) and Ghirlandaio (Metropolitan Museum, New York).

Tobit Offers a Prayer of Thanksgiving
Tobit 13:1-6; 14:3-7

13 Then Tobit wrote a prayer of rejoicing, and said:
"Blessed is God who lives for ever,
 and blessed is his kingdom.
 ² For he afflicts, and he shows mercy;
  he leads down to Hades, and brings up again,
  and there is no one who can escape his hand.
 ³ Acknowledge him before the nations,
  O sons of Israel;
  for he has scattered us among them.
 ⁴ Make his greatness known there,
  and exalt him in the presence of all the living;
 because he is our Lord and God,
  he is our Father for ever.
 ⁵ He will afflict us for our iniquities;
  and again he will show mercy,
 and will gather us from all the nations
  among whom you have been scattered.
 ⁶ If you turn to him with all your heart
  and with all your soul,
  to do what is true before him,
 then he will turn to you
  and will not hide his face from you.
 But see what he will do with you;
  give thanks to him with your full voice.
 Praise the Lord of righteousness,
  and exalt the King of the ages.
 I give him thanks in the land of my captivity,
  and I show his power and majesty
   to a nation of sinners.
 Turn back, you sinners, and do right before him;
  who knows if he will accept you
   and have mercy on you?

14 ³ When Tobit had grown very old he called his son and grandsons, and said to him, "My son, take your sons; behold, I have grown old and am about to depart this life. ⁴ Go to Media, my son, for I fully believe what Jonah the prophet said about Nineveh, that it will be overthrown. But in Media there will be peace for a time. Our brethren will be scattered over the earth from the good land, and Jerusalem will be desolate. The house of God in it will be burned down and will be in ruins for a time. ⁵ But God will again have mercy on them, and bring them back into their land; and they will rebuild the house of God, though it will not be like the former one until the times of the age are completed. After this they will return from the places of their captivity, and will rebuild Jerusalem in splendor. And the house of God will be rebuilt there with a glorious building for all generations for ever, just as the prophets said of it. ⁶Then all the Gentiles will turn to fear the Lord God in truth, and will bury their idols. ⁷All the Gentiles will praise the Lord, and his people will give thanks to God, and the Lord will exalt his people. And all who love the Lord God in truth and righteousness will rejoice, showing mercy to our brethren.

13:2 *Hades* literally means "unseen place." The Greeks spoke of Hades as god of the underworld, even as Poseidon was god of the sea, Uranus god of the heaven, and Ge goddess of the earth. **13:3** In latter Rabbinic thought Jews understood their dispersion throughout the world in exactly this sense: it provided an opportunity to acknowledge God before all nations. **13:5** Tobit summarizes the teachings of many prophets. The Hebrew nation has been humiliated because of its unrighteousness; but after a period of purification, when they shall have repented, God will restore His people. In verses 15–18 Tobit climaxes this hope with a vision of Jerusalem built with sapphires and emeralds. See Isaiah 54:11, 60:17. The hearts of all Jews were quickened in recent years when the city of Jerusalem was reunited and the ancient wall of the Temple restored for use by pious Jews who there pronounce prayers. Most Jews, however, no longer hope for the restoration of the sacrificial system in a renewed Jerusalem.

The Book of Judith

Judith takes her place in the Bible with Jael, Deborah and Esther, heroic women who periodically saved the Jewish people. This romantic story, set in the days of Nebuchadrezzar, represents the Hebrews as having returned from exile (a deliverance not historically effected until after the time of Nebuchadrezzar).

Assyrian armies, under Holofernes, Nebuchadrezzar's "chief general," have subdued the regions of Mesopotamia, the cities of Damascus, the coastal towns of Tyre and Sidon. They turn now toward the Hebrews. The frightened people of Israel clamor to surrender, but their king urges them to hold out another five days. Meanwhile Judith and her servant make their way into the enemy lines and attract the attention of Holofernes. He stages a great banquet and asks to be left alone with Judith. But he has drunk too much, and while he is in his stupor Judith decapitates him with his own sword. His troops, terrified at the murder of their leader, flee in disarray. Israel is saved and Judith is hailed (15:9) as "the exaltation of Jerusalem ... the great glory of Israel ... the great pride of our nation."

The book has been variously interpreted. Jerome thought of it as an allegory depicting the way the Church gets the better of the devil. Martin Luther thought it a holy parable describing how the Jews, through divine intervention, triumphed over their enemies. Others consider it a kind of passion play in which God's victory over evil is acted out.

Some in our modern world would question the morality of a story in which Judith uses deceit and her seductive powers to bring down an enemy. The story breathes the kind of patriotism which assumes that "all is fair in love and war."

The story appears to have been written about 150 B.C., in the days of the Maccabees; it was intended to encourage those suffering under the Syrian tyrant Antiochus IV by recalling heroic days of old.

Thomas A. Arne's oratorio, *Judith, a Sacred Drama*, was the first oratorio in which female voices were introduced into the choruses. Sir C. Hubert H. Parry's oratorio *Judith, or the Regeneration of Manasseh*, treats this as a historical event in the reign of King Manasseh.

Holofernes Wages War against Judea
Judith 2:1–6; 4:1–9

2 In the eighteenth year, on the twenty-second day of the first month, there was talk in the palace of Nebuchadnezzar king of the Assyrians about carrying out his revenge on the whole region, just as he had said. ²He called together all his officers and all his nobles and set forth to them his secret plan and recounted fully, with his own lips, all the wickedness of the region; ³and it was decided that every one who had not obeyed his command should be destroyed. ⁴When he had finished setting forth his plan, Nebuchadnezzar king of the Assyrians called Holofernes, the chief general of his army, second only to himself, and said to him,

5 "Thus says the Great King, the lord of the whole earth: When you leave my presence, take with you men confident in their strength, to the number of one hundred and twenty thousand foot soldiers and twelve thousand cavalry. ⁶Go and attack the whole west country, because they disobeyed my orders.

4 By this time the people of Israel living in Judea heard of everything that Holofernes, the general of Nebuchadnezzar the king of the Assyrians, had done to the nations, and how he had plundered and destroyed all their temples; ²they were therefore very greatly terrified at his approach, and were alarmed both for Jerusalem and for the temple of the Lord their God. ³For they had only recently returned from the captivity, and all the people of Judea were newly gathered together, and the sacred vessels and the altar and the temple had been consecrated after their profanation. ⁴So they sent to every district of Samaria, and to Kona and Beth-horon and Belmain and Jericho and to Choba and Aesora and the valley of Salem, ⁵and immediately seized all the high hilltops and fortified the villages on them and stored up food in preparation for war—since their fields had recently been harvested. ⁶And Joakim, the high priest, who was in Jerusalem at that time, wrote to the people of Bethulia and Betomesthaim, which faces Esdraelon opposite the plain near Dothan, ⁷ordering them to seize the passes up into the hills, since by them Judea could be invaded, and it was easy to stop any who tried to enter, for the approach was narrow, only wide enough for two men at the most.

8 So the Israelites did as Joakim the high priest and the senate of the whole people of Israel, in session at Jerusalem, had given order. ⁹And every man of Israel cried out to God with great fervor, and they humbled themselves with much fasting.

> **2:1** Nebuchadrezzar was king of Babylon not Assyria. In this case and in many others, this book takes liberties with historic facts. Scholars see in this evidence that the author did not intend to write history, but through the telling of ancient events (that happened possibly 400 years earlier) encourage the faith of his own generation. Nebuchadrezzar, then, is pictured as prototype of Israel's enemy. His general Holofernes is the embodiment of evil. Judith, the Jewess,

devout in her faith, is victorious. **4:8** Josephus recalls that a senate or Sanhedrin existed in the time of Antiochus the Great, and it appears to have been known to the Chronicler (2 Chronicles 19:8) about 250 B.C. The kind of influence here ascribed to the senate would seem to date the writing in the time of the Maccabees.

Judith Makes Herself Enticing

Judith 10:1–4

10 When Judith had ceased crying out to the God of Israel, and had ended all these words, ²she rose from where she lay prostrate and called her maid and went down into the house where she lived on sabbaths and on her feast days; ³and she removed the sackcloth which she had been wearing, and took off her widow's garments, and bathed her body with water, and anointed herself with precious ointment, and combed her hair and put on a tiara, and arrayed herself in her gayest apparel, which she used to wear while her husband Manasseh was living. ⁴And she put sandals on her feet, and put on her anklets and bracelets and rings, and her earrings and all her ornaments, and made herself very beautiful, to entice the eyes of all men who might see her.

Judith Visits Holofernes

Judith 10:18–23; 11:1–5, 8, 10–19, 21

18 There was great excitement in the whole camp, for her arrival was reported from tent to tent, and they came and stood around her as she waited outside the tent of Holofernes while they told him about her. ¹⁹And they marveled at her beauty, and admired the Israelites, judging them by her, and every one said to his neighbor, "Who can despise these people, who have women like this among them? Surely not a man of them had better be left alive, for if we let them go they will be able to ensnare the whole world!"

20 Then Holofernes' companions and all his servants came out and led her into the tent. ²¹Holofernes was resting on his bed, under a canopy which was woven with purple and gold and emeralds and precious stones. ²²When they told him of her he came forward to the front of the tent, with silver lamps carried before him. ²³And when Judith came into the presence of Holofernes and his servants, they all marveled at the beauty of her face; and she prostrated herself and made obeisance to him, and his slaves raised her up.

11 Then Holofernes said to her, "Take courage, woman, and do not be afraid in your heart, for I have never hurt any one who chose to serve Nebuchadnezzar, the king of all the earth. ²And even now, if your people who live in the hill country had not slighted me, I would

never have lifted my spear against them; but they have brought all
this on themselves. ³ And now tell me why you have fled from them
and have come over to us—since you have come to safety. ⁴ Have
courage; you will live, tonight and from now on. No one will hurt
you, but all will treat you well, as they do the servants of my lord
King Nebuchadnezzar."

5 Judith replied to him, "Accept the words of your servant, and
let your maidservant speak in your presence, and I will tell nothing
false to my lord this night. ⁸ For we have heard of your wisdom and
skill, and it is reported throughout the whole world that you are the
one good man in the whole kingdom, thoroughly informed and
marvelous in military strategy.

10 "Therefore, my lord and master, do not disregard what he
[A'-chi-or] said, but keep it in your mind, for it is true: our nation
cannot be punished, nor can the sword prevail against them, unless
they sin against their God. ¹¹ "And now, in order that my lord may
not be defeated and his purpose frustrated, death will fall upon
them, for a sin has overtaken them by which they are about to
provoke their God to anger when they do what is wrong. ¹² Since
their food supply is exhausted and their water has almost given out,
they have planned to kill their cattle and have determined to use all
that God by his laws has forbidden them to eat. ¹³ They have decided
to consume the first fruits of the grain and the tithes of the wine and
oil, which they had consecrated and set aside for the priests who
minister in the presence of our God at Jerusalem—although it is not
lawful for any of the people so much as to touch these things with
their hands. ¹⁴ They have sent men to Jerusalem, because even the
people living there have been doing this, to bring back to them
permission from the senate. ¹⁵ When the word reaches them and they
proceed to do this, on that very day they will be handed over to you
to be destroyed.

16 "Therefore, when I, your servant, learned all this, I fled from
them; and God has sent me to accomplish with you things that will
astonish the whole world, as many as shall hear about them. ¹⁷ For
your servant is religious, and serves the God of heaven day and
night; therefore, my lord, I will remain with you, and every night
your servant will go out into the valley, and I will pray to God and
he will tell me when they have committed their sins. ¹⁸ And I will
come and tell you, and then you shall go out with your whole army,
and not one of them will withstand you. ¹⁹ Then I will lead you
through the middle of Judea, till you come to Jerusalem; and I will
set your throne in the midst of it; and you will lead them like sheep
that have no shepherd, and not a dog will so much as open its mouth

to growl at you. For this has been told me, by my foreknowledge; it was announced to me, and I was sent to tell you."

21 "There is not such a woman from one end of the earth to the other, either for beauty of face or wisdom of speech!"

11:19 "Sheep that have no shepherd" is a phrase echoed in Mark 6:34 and Matthew 9:36.

The Lord Smites Holofernes by the Hand of a Woman
Judith 12:10–13:20

On the fourth day Holofernes held a banquet for his slaves only, and did not invite any of his officers. ¹¹ And he said to Bagoas, the eunuch who had charge of all his personal affairs, "Go now and persuade the Hebrew woman who is in your care to join us and eat and drink with us. ¹² For it will be a disgrace if we let such a woman go without enjoying her company, for if we do not embrace her she will laugh at us." ¹³ So Bagoas went out from the presence of Holofernes, and approached her and said, "This beautiful maidservant will please come to my lord and be honored in his presence, and drink wine and be merry with us, and become today like one of the daughters of the Assyrians who serve in the house of Nebuchadnezzar." ¹⁴ And Judith said, "Who am I, to refuse my lord? Surely whatever pleases him I will do at once, and it will be a joy to me until the day of my death!" ¹⁵ So she got up and arrayed herself in all her woman's finery, and her maid went and spread on the ground for her before Holofernes the soft fleeces which she had received from Bagoas for her daily use, so that she might recline on them when she ate.

16 Then Judith came in and lay down, and Holofernes' heart was ravished with her and he was moved with great desire to possess her; for he had been waiting for an opportunity to deceive her, ever since the day he first saw her. ¹⁷ So Holofernes said to her, "Drink now, and be merry with us!" ¹⁸ Judith said, "I will drink now, my lord, because my life means more to me today than in all the days since I was born." ¹⁹ Then she took and ate and drank before him what her maid had prepared. ²⁰ And Holofernes was greatly pleased with her, and drank a great quantity of wine, much more than he had ever drunk in any one day since he was born.

13 When evening came, his slaves quickly withdrew, and Bagoas closed the tent from outside and shut out the attendants from his master's presence; and they went to bed, for they all were weary because the banquet had lasted long. ² So Judith was left alone in the tent, with Holofernes stretched out on his bed, for he was overcome with wine.

3 Now Judith had told her maid to stand outside the bedchamber and to wait for her to come out, as she did every day; for she said she

would be going out for her prayers. And she had said the same thing to Bagoas. ⁴So every one went out, and no one, either small or great, was left in the bedchamber. Then Judith, standing beside his bed, said in her heart, "O Lord God of all might, look in this hour upon the work of my hands for the exaltation of Jerusalem. ⁵For now is the time to help thy inheritance, and to carry out my undertaking for the destruction of the enemies who have risen up against us."

6 She went up to the post at the end of the bed, above Holofernes' head, and took down his sword that hung there. ⁷She came close to his bed and took hold of the hair of his head, and said, "Give me strength this day, O Lord God of Israel!" ⁸And she struck his neck twice with all her might, and severed his head from his body. ⁹Then she tumbled his body off the bed and pulled down the canopy from the posts; after a moment she went out, and gave Holofernes' head to her maid, ¹⁰who placed it in her food bag.

Then the two of them went out together, as they were accustomed to go for prayer; and they passed through the camp and circled around the valley and went up the mountain to Bethulia and came to its gates. ¹¹Judith called out from afar to the watchmen at the gates, "Open, open the gate! God, our God, is still with us, to show his power in Israel, and his strength against our enemies, even as he has done this day!"

12 When the men of her city heard her voice, they hurried down to the city gate and called together the elders of the city. ¹³They all ran together, both small and great, for it was unbelievable that she had returned; they opened the gate and admitted them, and they kindled a fire for light, and gathered around them. ¹⁴Then she said to them with a loud voice, "Praise God, O praise him! Praise God, who has not withdrawn his mercy from the house of Israel, but has destroyed our enemies by my hand this very night!"

15 Then she took the head out of the bag and showed it to them, and said, "See, here is the head of Holofernes, the commander of the Assyrian army, and here is the canopy beneath which he lay in his drunken stupor. The Lord has struck him down by the hand of a woman. ¹⁶As the Lord lives, who has protected me in the way I went, it was my face that tricked him to his destruction, and yet he committed no act of sin with me, to defile and shame me."

17 All the people were greatly astonished, and bowed down and worshiped God, and said with one accord, "Blessed art thou, our God, who hast brought into contempt this day the enemies of thy people."

18 And Uzziah said to her, "O daughter, you are blessed by the Most High God above all women on earth; and blessed be the Lord God, who created the heavens and the earth, who has guided you to strike the head of the leader of our enemies. ¹⁹Your hope will never

depart from the hearts of men, as they remember the power of God. ²⁰ May God grant this to be a perpetual honor to you, and may he visit you with blessings, because you did not spare your own life when our nation was brought low, but have avenged our ruin, walking in the straight path before our God." And all the people said, "So be it, so be it!"

> **13:8** Judith holding the head of Holofernes has been a common theme of artists; examples are Allori's "Judith," in the Uffizi Gallery, Florence; Michelangelo's "Judith with the Head of Holofernes," in the Sistine Chapel; Botticelli, Titian, Cranach, and Matteo di Giovanni produced works with the same title; these are located, respectively in the Cincinnati Art Museum, the Detroit Institute of Arts, the New York Metropolitan Museum, and the National Gallery in Washington, D.C. In English literature, Holofernes and Judith are depicted in Chaucer's *Canterbury Tales.*

The Hebrews Rejoice over Judith's Victory
Judith 15:1–4, 9–10

15 When the men in the tents heard it, they were amazed at what had happened. ² Fear and trembling came over them, so that they did not wait for one another, but with one impulse all rushed out and fled by every path across the plain and through the hill country. ³ Those who had camped in the hills around Bethulia also took to flight. Then the men of Israel, every one that was a soldier, rushed out upon them. ⁴ And Uzziah sent men to Betomasthaim and Bebai and Choba and Kola, and to all the frontiers of Israel, to tell what had taken place and to urge all to rush out upon their enemies to destroy them.

9 And when they met her they all blessed her with one accord and said to her, "You are the exaltation of Jerusalem, you are the great glory of Israel, you are the great pride of our nation! ¹⁰ You have done all this singlehanded; you have done great good to Israel, and God is well pleased with it. May the Almighty Lord bless you for ever!" And all the people said, "So be it!"

The Wisdom of Solomon

The wise man, like the priest and the prophet, had a recognized position in Hebrew society. The works of some of these creative religious thinkers became part of a body of biblical literature known as Writings.

Just as the Law was associated with Moses and the Psalms with David, so the wisdom writing came to be associated with King Solomon. In some passages in this book (e.g., 1:1; 7:7, 17–20; 8:12; 9:1–18) Solomon, who lived in the tenth century B.C., is represented as speaking. But some of the ideas and vocabulary, as well as the structural unity, suggest that the book was composed or edited in Greek in the second century B.C. The author several times quotes biblical passages drawn from the Septuagint, a Greek translation of the Old Testament begun in the third century B.C., and differing at points from the Hebrew. In fact some scholars date the writing of the book so late as to make possible either a Christian origin or Christian interpolations, attributing its authorship to Apollos, a learned and eloquent Jewish convert of Alexandria.

From his panegyric on wisdom the author deduces truths about the greatness of God (He has "power over life and death"); the mercy of God ("He watches over His holy ones"); the equality of all men (God "takes thought for all alike"); the folly of fear ("nothing but surrender of the helps that come from reason"). Many phrases in the book are quoted or alluded to in the New Testament.

Various motives are attributed to the author of this text. His book may have been aimed at keeping the dispersed Jews loyal to their ancestral beliefs and practices or intended to convince pagans of the folly of their polytheism and idolatry.

The influence of Greek thought is seen in the allegorical interpretation of scriptural references, i.e., a procedure whereby universal Greek philosophic concepts are read into the concrete symbols and events of the Bible. e.g.: 10:7, the pillar of salt represents incredulity; 16:28, the manna stands for prayer; 17:1, the Egyptian darkness is equivalent to hell; 18:24, Aaron's ephod represents the whole world.

In this book we also find acceptance of such Greek ideas as the following: an evil nature attaches to the human body (1:4); the body is a temporary prisonhouse of a pre-existent soul (9:15). Such thoughts are not found in the Hebrew Bible and were rejected by Jewish theology. In the Hebraic view both the soul and the body, creations of God, are good and sacred. The body would be considered not the prisonhouse of the soul, but the temple in which the soul resides.

Reflected here also is the idea of the immortality of the soul (1:12 f. and 3:1), an idea accepted by the Pharisees but rejected by the Sadducees. Pharisees, needing a scriptural source for this doctrine, suggested that it was earlier derived from Deuteronomy 31:16, "And this people will rise up"; from Isaiah 26:19, "Thy dead shall live"; and from Daniel 12:12, "And many of them that sleep in the dust of the earth shall awake soon to everlasting life." The Greek concept of resurrection was also accepted by the Pharisees and rejected by the Sadducees. As their scriptural source, the Pharisees pointed to Ezekiel's vision of the Valley of the Dry Bones, chapter 37 (ignoring, however, Job 7:9, "He who goes down to the grave shall come up no more"). One of the earliest prayers of Jewish liturgy, introduced at the beginning of the Eighteen Benedictions, described God in his power to resurrect (bring to life) the dead.

Perverse Thoughts Separate Man from God
Wisdom of Solomon 1:1–7, 9, 12–15

1 Love righteousness, you rulers of the earth,
   think of the Lord with uprightness,
   and seek him with sincerity of heart;
2 because he is found by those who do not put him to the test,
   and manifests himself to those who do not distrust him.
3 For perverse thoughts separate men from God,
   and when his power is tested, it convicts the foolish;
4 because wisdom will not enter a deceitful soul,
   nor dwell in a body enslaved to sin.
5 For a holy and disciplined spirit will flee from deceit,
   and will rise and depart from foolish thoughts,
   and will be ashamed at the approach of unrighteousness.

6 For wisdom is a kindly spirit and
   will not free a blasphemer from the guilt of his words;
   because God is witness of his inmost feelings,
   and a true observer of his heart, and a hearer of his tongue.
7 Because the Spirit of the Lord has filled the world,
   and that which holds all things together knows what is said;

9 For inquiry will be made into the counsels of an ungodly man,
   and a report of his words will come to the Lord,
   to convict him of his lawless deeds.

12 Do not invite death by the error of your life,
   nor bring on destruction by the works of your hands;
13 because God did not make death,
   and he does not delight in the death of the living.
14 For he created all things that they might exist,
   and the generative forces of the world are wholesome,
   and there is no destructive poison in them;
   and the dominion of Hades is not on earth.
15 For righteousness is immortal.

1:3 Judaism accepted the idea that sin separates man from God. But the rabbis divided on whether perverse thoughts were, in themselves, sinful or whether man had to act upon his thoughts and thus by his evil *deeds* turn his back on God. See verse 12. **1:4** Some scholars see in this verse an expression of the idea that both the body and the soul are prone to sin. In 9:15, however, corruption is ascribed to the body alone, where it is called "that loathsome prisonhouse"; Jewish theology rejected that idea. **1:6** In biblical psychology the kidneys—the word used in the original text—were thought to be the source of feelings; the heart was the source of thoughts and ideas. Together they connote all of men's inner resources. See Psalms 7:9; 26:2; Jeremiah 11:20; 17:10; 20:12. In Colossians 1:17 Paul applies this idea to Jesus. **1:9** The report of the deeds of men were recorded in a Book of Remembrance. See Malachi 3:16. The Book of Jubilees 3:20 ff. speaks of two heavenly books, a Book of Life for the righteous and a Book of Death for the wicked. When one contrives evil against his fellow men his name is erased from the Book of Remembrance and placed in the Book of Death. Such imagery has been accepted into the liturgy of the synagogue and is evoked on the High Holy days, Rosh Hashanah and Yom Kippur. **1:13, 15** The author here repeats a biblical idea that death entered the world with the sin of man. See discussion of Original Sin at the opening of Genesis 3. The Hebrew Bible throughout understood that death would come as a punishment for sin and wrongdoing; the Hebrews considered long life the reward of a virtuous man. But the author here adds a new note (verse 15). By his virtue a man can escape death, spiritually achieving immortality. The spiritual death imposed on the wicked, therefore, is not God's doing but the inevitable consequence of iniquity. See also 4:7–9 where the author explains that man must not measure his days by their length, but rather by the quality of life lived in the time allotted.

The Impious Are Led Astray by Their Foolishness

Verses 1–20 place into the mouth of an impious man many of the tenets of the Epicureans. In making his critical response the author of this book, unlike the author of Ecclesiastes, has the assurance that comes from a belief in reward and punishment in the afterlife.

Wisdom of Solomon 2:1–15, 21–24

2 For they reasoned unsoundly, saying to themselves,
  "Short and sorrowful is our life,
    and there is no remedy when a man comes to his end,
    and no one has been known to return from Hades.
 ² Because we were born by mere chance,
    and hereafter we shall be as though we had never been;
    because the breath in our nostrils is smoke,
    and reason is a spark kindled by the beating of our hearts.

³ When it is extinguished, the body will turn to ashes,
and the spirit will dissolve like empty air.
⁴ Our name will be forgotten in time,
and no one will remember our works;
our life will pass away like the traces of a cloud,
and be scattered like mist
that is chased by the rays of the sun
and overcome by its heat.
⁵ For our allotted time is the passing of a shadow,
and there is no return from our death,
because it is sealed up and no one turns back.
⁶ "Come, therefore, let us enjoy the good things that exist,
and make use of the creation to the full as in youth.
⁷ Let us take our fill of costly wine and perfumes,
and let no flower of spring pass by us.
⁸ Let us crown ourselves with rosebuds before they wither.
⁹ Let none of us fail to share in our revelry,
everywhere let us leave signs of enjoyment,
because this is our portion, and this our lot.
¹⁰ Let us oppress the righteous poor man;
let us not spare the widow
nor regard the gray hairs of the aged.
¹¹ But let our might be our law of right,
for what is weak proves itself to be useless.
¹² "Let us lie in wait for the righteous man,
because he is inconvenient to us and opposes our actions;
he reproaches us for sins against the law,
and accuses us of sins against our training.
¹³ He professes to have knowledge of God,
and calls himself a child of the Lord.
¹⁴ He became to us a reproof of our thoughts;
¹⁵ the very sight of him is a burden to us,
because his manner of life is unlike that of others,
and his ways are strange."
²¹ Thus they reasoned, but they were led astray,
for their wickedness blinded them,
²² and they did not know the secret purposes of God,
nor hope for the wages of holiness,
nor discern the prize for blameless souls;
²³ for God created man for incorruption,
and made him in the image of his own eternity,
²⁴ but through the devil's envy death entered the world,
and those who belong to his party experience it.

2:1 *Short and sorrowful:* see Ecclesiastes 2:23; *no remedy:* see Jeremiah 14:19; Nahum 3:19; Job 7:9. **2:2** *Smoke . . . spark.* In Greek philosophy it was widely held that fire was the origin of all things. The Greeks had no knowledge of the brain as the seat of thought, believing its source was in the heart. **2:3** Cf. Psalm 144:4 and Job 7:7. **2:4** Cf. Ecclesiastes 2:16; 9:5–6. **2:5** Cf. Ecclesiastes 8:13; Job 8:9. **2:6** Cf. Ecclesiastes 2:24; 3:12; 9:7. **2:8** *Rosebuds:* a pagan custom adopted by the Hellenistic Jews; cf. Isaiah 28:1; Ezekiel 23:42. Plutarch, explaining this practice, wrote: "Warm flowers opened the pores and provided an exit for the spirit and vapor of the wine." **2:10** In the view of the author of Wisdom, the philosophy heretofore described can lead only to unrighteousness. Koheleth, the author of Ecclesiastes, also held that oppression was abhorrent. See Ecclesiastes 4:1. There is irony in the Epicurean's voice, for Scripture had promised that righteous men would not be poor or forsaken. See Psalm 37:25; 112:3; Proverbs 3:9–10; 12:21. **2:11** The whole force of Scripture is a repudiation of the view that might makes right or that in God's eyes that which is weak is useless. **2:22** *Secret purposes of God:* a phrase open to much interpretation, it is most frequently understood to mean God's ways of dealing with man, i.e., rewarding and punishing him in the afterlife. **2:24** *Devil's envy:* scholars differ over whether this text means to imply that death entered the world with the sin of Adam, the snake being identified with Satan, or by the sinfulness of Cain's murder of his brother Abel, i.e., out of envy. The cosmic power of the Devil as described here extends the power of Satan as an adversary of man (cf. Psalm 109:6) beyond the point Old Testament authors were prepared to go. Judaism denied such cosmic power to a devil, and some commentators believe this last sentence to be an interpolation.

The Souls of the Righteous Are in the Hand of God
Wisdom of Solomon 3:1–9

3 But the souls of the righteous are in the hand of God,
   and no torment will ever touch them.
² In the eyes of the foolish they seemed to have died,
   and their departure was thought to be an affliction,
³ and their going from us to be their destruction;
   but they are at peace.
⁴ For though in the sight of men they were punished,
   their hope is full of immortality.
⁵ Having been disciplined a little, they will receive great good,
   because God tested them and found them worthy of himself;
⁶ like gold in the furnace he tried them,
   and like a sacrificial burnt offering he accepted them.

⁷ In the time of their visitation they will shine forth,
   and will run like sparks through the stubble.
⁸ They will govern nations and rule over peoples,
   and the Lord will reign over them for ever.
⁹ Those who trust in him will understand truth,
   and the faithful will abide with him in love,
   because grace and mercy are upon his elect,
   and he watches over his holy ones.

3:1 ff. This passage, set to music by T. Tertius Noble, often read at burial services, is one of the earliest explicit statements of the doctrine of personal immortality. Compare Wisdom 5:15:

> But the righteous live forever,
> and their reward is with the Lord;
> the Most High takes care of them;

And Wisdom 15:3:

> For to know thee is complete righteousness,
> and to know thy power is the root of immortality.

The Catholic Church applies verses 1–8 to those who gave their lives in witness to the faith in a Mass for Martyrs. **3:1** This expressed the Greek belief in the immortality of the soul, an idea accepted in the Rabbinic tradition: "The souls of the righteous are concealed under the throne of glory" (*Shabbat* 152b). The Greek idea of torment for the wicked after death was also accepted into Judaism. It conflicted, however, with the popularly held prophetic view that the wicked suffered their punishments in life, or that in after life they were annihilated. Both views were held together in various vague conceptions of the nature of judgment in the life to come. **3:4** The old idea that tormented Job—that suffering was an indication of God's punishment for evil-doing—is here dismissed. Instead, this author teaches that while righteous men may appear to have been punished "in the sight of men," their suffering was in God's purpose to benefit them. The word "immortality" here appears for the first time in Scripture. **3:5** *Tested them:* cf. Genesis 22:1; Psalm 26:2; 66:10; 118:75; Proverbs 3:11–12. **3:7** Hebrew Scripture projected a time when the people of Israel would triumph over enemies who would perish like stubble in a fire. See Jeremiah 5:14; Zechariah 12:6; Malachi 3:19. 1 Peter 1:7 applies the same figure of speech to believers undergoing persecution. **3:9** Compare Proverbs 28:5 and Psalm 111:10.

God Loves the Man Who Lives with Wisdom

Wisdom of Solomon 7:1–6, 15–28

7 I also am mortal, like all men,
   a descendant of the first-formed child of earth;
   and in the womb of a mother I was molded into flesh,

² within the period of ten months, compacted with blood,
  from the seed of a man and the pleasure of marriage.
³ And when I was born, I began to breathe the common air,
  and fell upon the kindred earth,
  and my first sound was a cry, like that of all.
⁴ I was nursed with care in swaddling cloths.
⁵ For no king has had a different beginning of existence;
⁶ there is for all mankind one entrance into life, and a common
  departure.

¹⁵ May God grant that I speak with judgment
  and have thoughts worthy of what I have received,
  for he is the guide even of wisdom
  and the corrector of the wise.
¹⁶ For both we and our words are in his hand,
  as are all understanding and skill in crafts.
¹⁷ For it is he who gave me unerring knowledge of what exists,
  to know the structure of the world and the activity of the
  elements;
¹⁸ the beginning and end and middle of times,
  the alternations of the solstices and the changes of the seasons,
¹⁹ the cycles of the year and the constellations of the stars,
²⁰ the natures of animals and the tempers of wild beasts,
  the powers of spirits and the reasonings of men,
  the varieties of plants and the virtues of roots;
²¹ I learned both what is secret and what is manifest,
²² for wisdom, the fashioner of all things, taught me.
  For in her there is a spirit that is intelligent, holy,
  unique, manifold, subtle,
  mobile, clear, unpolluted,
  distinct, invulnerable, loving the good, keen, irresistible,
²³ beneficent, humane, steadfast, sure, free from anxiety, all-
  powerful, overseeing all,
  and penetrating through all spirits
  that are intelligent and pure and most subtle.
²⁴ For wisdom is more mobile than any motion;
  because of her pureness she pervades and penetrates all things.
²⁵ For she is a breath of the power of God,
  and a pure emanation of the glory of the Almighty;
  therefore nothing defiled gains entrance into her.
²⁶ For she is a reflection of eternal light,
  a spotless mirror of the working of God,
  and an image of his goodness.

²⁷ Though she is but one, she can do all things,
    and while remaining in herself, she renews all things;
    in every generation she passes into holy souls
    and makes them friends of God, and prophets;
²⁸ for God loves nothing so much as the man who lives with
    wisdom.

7:1–6 Solomon declares that his birth was precisely like that of all the children of men. All men, therefore, are similarly capable of exercising wisdom. **7:17 f.** The passage which follows expresses the conviction that the pursuit of scientific knowledge is a religious pursuit, in that all knowledge is a gift of God. **7:26** *Eternal light:* The significance of God's light is expressed in Isaiah 60:19 f.; Psalms 50:3; 104:1–2. It is also given elaboration in the New Testament; see John 8:12; 1 John 1:5 and James 1:7. **7:26** *Mirror:* Hebrews 1:3 applies the same figure of speech to Christ.

Wisdom Steers the Course
Wisdom of Solomon 14:1–7

14 Again, one preparing to sail and about to voyage over raging
    waves
    calls upon a piece of wood more fragile than the ship which
    carries him.
² For it was desire for gain that planned that vessel,
    and wisdom was the craftsman who built it;
³ but it is thy providence, O Father, that steers its course,
    because thou hast given it a path in the sea,
    and a safe way through the waves,
⁴ showing that thou canst save from every danger,
    so that even if a man lacks skill, he may put to sea.
⁵ It is thy will that the works of thy wisdom should not be
    without effect;
    therefore men trust their lives even to the smallest piece of wood,
    and passing through the billows on a raft they come safely to land.
⁶ For even in the beginning, when arrogant giants were perishing,
    the hope of the world took refuge on a raft,
    and guided by thy hand left to the world the seed of a new
    generation.
⁷ For blessed is the wood by which righteousness comes.

14:3 The word *providence*, taken from the Greek, is used here for the first time in Scripture. For its counterpart concept in Hebrew Scripture, see Psalm 145:8, 9, 15, 16; 147:9. **14:6** The raft referred to here is Noah's ark. **14:7** The Church Fathers interpreted this verse to apply to the cross.

Ecclesiasticus, or The Wisdom of Jesus the Son of Sirach

Longest of the wisdom books is Ecclesiasticus, or the Wisdom of Jesus the Son of Sirach. The alternative titles are derived, respectively, from the Greek (Septuagint) and Hebrew versions. The word "Ecclesiasticus," based on the Greek word for "church," intimates that of all the books in the Apocrypha this is pre-eminently the one which "the Church doth read for example of life and instruction of manners."

"Jesus" is the Greek form of the Hebrew "Joshua." This Jesus identifies himself as the son of Sirach, who, in 50:27, is identified as "son of Eleazar of Jerusalem." "Son of Sirach" is English for Ben Sira, a Hebrew phrase by which the author is often referred to.

The book was a Greek translation of an original Hebrew work of the translator's grandfather, Jesus. Although the grandson has devoted "diligent labor" to his task, he admits that he may have "rendered some phrases imperfectly." His problem will be recognized by anyone who has ever tried to take a piece of literature out of one tongue and put it into another. "For what was originally expressed in Hebrew," he says, "does not have exactly the same sense when translated into another language." The grandfather was born about 250 B.C.; the grandson's translation was made 190–180 B.C.

Wisdom, represented here as "the fear of the Lord," manifests itself in the way a man meets prosperity and adversity; in what he decides is worth working for in life; in the delight a wise man has in a good wife; in the discipline he imposes upon his household; in friendship and duty; in the obligation of magistrates to instruct their people. The volume is a kind of handbook of good manners.

The man who fears the Lord, teaches Ben Sira,
> will find gladness and a crown of rejoicing,
> and will acquire an everlasting name.

This "everlasting name," however, does not involve personal immortality. It is to be won through the institutions to which the individual gives himself and through the offspring he trains wisely.

This book forms a bridge between the Testaments. The author knew the threefold Old Testament canon of "the law and the prophets and the others that followed them." His own literary style owes much to Proverbs, Psalms, and Job; he praises, too, Jeremiah, Ezekiel, and "the twelve prophets." Ben Sira seems to have given St. Paul such phrases as "weep with those who weep," "all things hold together," and "if you have a servant, treat him like a brother."

Many passages have special significance in the twentieth century, not least the following:

> What race is worthy of honor? The human race.
> What race is unworthy of honor? Those who transgress the
> commandments (10:19).

This book was a favorite of Jewish religious teachers. Until at least
the tenth century there was known to be a Hebrew text available to
Jewish scholars. It is quoted in the Talmud. It was translated into
Aramaic so that it could be read widely by the Palestinian Jews. It is
cited in the *Ethics of the Fathers,* a post-biblical book of maxims and
sayings read regularly on Sabbath afternoons in the synagogue. Next
to the Psalms, it is the most frequently quoted book in the Catholic
liturgy.

The Fear of the Lord Is Wisdom

Ecclesiasticus 1:1–11, 18, 20

1 All wisdom comes from the Lord
   and is with him forever.
² The sand of the sea, the drops of rain,
   and the days of eternity—who can count them?
³ The height of heaven, the breadth of the earth,
   the abyss, and wisdom—who can search them out?
⁴ Wisdom was created before all things,
   and prudent understanding from eternity.
⁶ The root of wisdom—to whom has it been revealed?
   Her clever devices—who knows them?
⁸ There is One who is wise, greatly to be feared,
   sitting upon his throne.
⁹ The Lord himself created wisdom;
   he saw her and apportioned her,
   he poured her out upon all his works.
¹⁰ She dwells with all flesh according to his gift,
   and he supplied her to those who love him.

¹¹ The fear of the Lord is glory and exultation,
   and gladness and a crown of rejoicing.
¹⁸ The fear of the Lord is the crown of wisdom,
   making peace and perfect health to flourish.
²⁰ To fear the Lord is the root of wisdom,
   and her branches are long life.

1:1 Compare Job 12:13; Proverbs 8:22–23, 30; John 1:1–2.
1:4 In the Talmud it is asserted: "The Torah [wisdom] was in
existence 2,000 years before creation." **1:18** Here the reward of
wisdom is not life eternal but peace, health, and a prolonged life on
earth. The concept of immortal life had not yet taken hold in the
Jewish tradition. In contrast Wisdom of Solomon 3 held that

righteous men, whose death may have appeared to be a destruction, are in reality brought into the protecting care of God. See also 2 Maccabees 7.

Be Steadfast in Trial
Ecclesiasticus 2:1–6

2 My son, if you come forward to serve the Lord,
    prepare yourself for temptation.
² Set your heart right and be steadfast,
    and do not be hasty in time of calamity.
³ Cleave to him and do not depart,
    that you may be honored at the end of your life.
⁴ Accept whatever is brought upon you,
    and in changes that humble you be patient.
⁵ For gold is tested in the fire,
    and acceptable men in the furnace of humiliation.
⁶ Trust in him, and he will help you;
    make your ways straight and hope in him.

2:1 The word *temptation* may also be translated "trials." The author is encouraging his people not to be tempted in any way to forego their faith during a time of persecution or calamity.

Honor Your Parents
Ecclesiasticus 3:1–9, 16

3 Listen to me your father, O children;
    and act accordingly, that you may be kept in safety.
² For the Lord honored the father above the children,
    and he confirmed the right of the mother over her sons.
³ Whoever honors his father atones for sins,
⁴   and whoever glorifies his mother is like one who lays up treasure.
⁵ Whoever honors his father will be gladdened by his own children,
    and when he prays he will be heard.
⁶ Whoever glorifies his father will have long life,
    and whoever obeys the Lord will refresh his mother;
⁷   he will serve his parents as his masters.
⁸ Honor your father by word and deed,
    that a blessing from him may come upon you.
⁹ For a father's blessing strengthens the houses of the children,
    but a mother's curse uproots their foundations.

¹⁶ Whoever forsakes his father is like a blasphemer,
    and whoever angers his mother is cursed by the Lord.

3:1 According to the understanding of that time, to be kept in safety (saved) meant to enjoy a goodly life in this world; cf. 5:16. On the subject of this passage Ecclesiasticus 7:28 reads: Remember that through your parents you were born; and what can you give back to them that equals their gift to you?

Value Your Friend
Ecclesiasticus 6:15–17

¹⁵ There is nothing so precious as a faithful friend,
   and no scales can measure his excellence.
¹⁶ A faithful friend is an elixir of life;
   and those who fear the Lord will find him.
¹⁷ Whoever fears the Lord directs his friendship aright,
   for as he is, so is his neighbor also.

Justice Is a Nation's Security
Ecclesiasticus 10:1–8, 12, 19

10 A wise magistrate will educate his people,
   and the rule of an understanding man will be well ordered.
² Like the magistrate of the people, so are his officials;
   and like the ruler of the city, so are all its inhabitants.
³ An undisciplined king will ruin his people,
   but a city will grow through the understanding of its rulers.
⁴ The government of the earth is in the hands of the Lord,
   and over it he will raise up the right man for the time.
⁵ The success of a man is in the hands of the Lord,
   and he confers his honor upon the person of the scribe.

⁶ Do not be angry with your neighbor for any injury,
   and do not attempt anything by acts of insolence.
⁷ Arrogance is hateful before the Lord and before men,
   and injustice is outrageous to both.
⁸ Sovereignty passes from nation to nation
   on account of injustice and insolence and wealth.
¹² The beginning of man's pride is to depart from the Lord;
   his heart has forsaken his Maker.

¹⁹ What race is worthy of honor? The human race.
   What race is worthy of honor? Those who fear the Lord.
   What race is unworthy of honor? The human race.
   What race is unworthy of honor? Those who transgress the
      commandments.

10:1 f. These words were written in a society governed by kings; they have perhaps even more point in a democracy. **10:3** This translation here follows the Hebrew, "undisciplined." The Greek word used here is "uneducated." **10:4** This passage is cited by those who would argue that both Church and State are under authority of God. **10:8** Consider in our day how political parties, kings and rulers fare by virtue of the justice they achieve, the injustice they fail to correct, and the prosperity of the people.

Moral Maxims
Ecclesiasticus 11:2–3, 7–9, 28; 12:1–3; 14:11–14

² Do not praise a man for his good looks,
  nor loathe a man because of his appearance.
³ The bee is small among flying creatures,
  but her product is the best of sweet things.
⁷ Do not find fault before you investigate;
  first consider, and then reprove.
⁸ Do not answer before you have heard,
  nor interrupt a speaker in the midst of his words.
⁹ Do not argue about a matter which does not concern you,
  nor sit with sinners when they judge a case.

²⁸ Call no one happy before his death;
  a man will be known through his children.

12 If you do a kindness, know to whom you do it,
  and you will be thanked for your good deeds.
² Do good to a godly man, and you will be repaid—
  if not by him, certainly by the Most High.
³ No good will come to the man who persists in evil
  or to him who does not give alms.

14 ¹¹ My son, treat yourself well, according to your means,
  and present worthy offerings to the Lord.
¹² Remember that death will not delay,
  and the decree of Hades has not been shown to you.
¹³ Do good to a friend before you die,
  and reach out and give to him as much as you can.
¹⁴ Do not deprive yourself of a happy day;
  let not your share of desired good pass by you.

Flee from Sin
Ecclesiasticus 21:1–3, 10, 14, 19, 21, 26

21 Have you sinned, my son?
  Do so no more,
    but pray about your former sins.

² Flee from sin as from a snake;
 for if you approach sin, it will bite you.
Its teeth are lion's teeth,
 and destroy the souls of men.

³ All lawlessness is like a two-edged sword;
 there is no healing for its wound.

¹⁰ The way of sinners is smoothly paved with stones,
 but at its end is the pit of Hades.

¹⁴ The mind of a fool is like a broken jar;
 it will hold no knowledge.

¹⁹ To a senseless man education is fetters on his feet,
 and like manacles on his right hand.

²¹ To a sensible man education is like a golden ornament,
 and like a bracelet on the right arm.

²⁶ The mind of fools is in their mouth,
 but the mouth of wise men is in their mind.

A Good Wife Is a Blessing
Ecclesiasticus 25 : 1; 26 : 1–4, 13–18

25 My soul takes pleasure in three things,
 and they are beautiful in the sight of the Lord and of men:
agreement between brothers, friendship between neighbors,
 and a wife and husband who live in harmony.
26 Happy is the husband of a good wife;
 the number of his days will be doubled.
 ² A loyal wife rejoices her husband,
 and he will complete his years in peace.
 ³ A good wife is a great blessing;
 she will be granted among the blessings of the man who fears
  the Lord.
 ⁴ Whether rich or poor, his heart is glad,
 and at all times his face is cheerful.
¹³ A wife's charm delights her husband,
 and her skill puts fat on his bones.
¹⁴ A silent wife is a gift of the Lord,
 and there is nothing so precious as a disciplined soul.
¹⁵ A modest wife adds charm to charm,
 and no balance can weigh the value of a chaste soul.
¹⁶ Like the sun rising in the heights of the Lord,
 so is the beauty of a good wife in her well-ordered home.

¹⁷ Like the shining lamp on the holy lampstand,
  so is a beautiful face on a stately figure.
¹⁸ Like pillars of gold on a base of silver,
  so are beautiful feet with a steadfast heart.

26:1 Compare Proverbs 31. **26:13** Through providing a scientifically planned diet, such as may be learned in home economics courses, a wife may now do better things for her husband than put "fat on his bones."

Discipline Your Son
Ecclesiasticus 30:1–6, 14–23

30 He who loves his son will whip him often,
  in order that he may rejoice at the way he turns out.
² He who disciplines his son will profit by him,
  and will boast of him among acquaintances.
³ He who teaches his son will make his enemies envious,
  and will glory in him in the presence of friends.
⁴ The father may die, and yet he is not dead,
  for he has left behind him one like himself;
⁵ while alive he saw and rejoiced,
  and when he died he was not grieved;
⁶ he has left behind him an avenger against his enemies,
  and one to repay the kindness of his friends.

¹⁴ Better off is a poor man who is well and strong in constitution
  than a rich man who is severely afflicted in body.
¹⁵ Health and soundness are better than all gold,
  and a robust body than countless riches.
¹⁶ There is no wealth better than health of body,
  and there is no gladness above joy of heart.
¹⁷ Death is better than a miserable life,
  and eternal rest than chronic sickness.
¹⁸ Good things poured out upon a mouth that is closed
  are like offerings of food placed upon a grave.
¹⁹ Of what use to an idol is an offering of fruit?
  For it can neither eat nor smell.
  So is he who is afflicted by the Lord;
²⁰ he sees with his eyes and groans,
  like a eunuch who embraces a maiden and groans.

²¹ Do not give yourself over to sorrow,
  and do not afflict yourself deliberately.
²² Gladness of heart is the life of man,
  and the rejoicing of a man is length of days.

²³ Delight your soul and comfort your heart,
    and remove sorrow far from you.

30:1–6 Compare Proverbs 13:24; 23:13, 14; 29:15. Consider methods for maintaining discipline in this day and age.

Guide to Good Manners
Ecclesiasticus 31:12–15, 18, 25–31; 32:3, 7–8, 11–13

¹² Are you seated at the table of a great man?
    Do not be greedy at it,
    and do not say, "There is certainly much upon it!"
¹³ Remember that a greedy eye is a bad thing.
    What has been created more greedy than the eye?
    Therefore it sheds tears from every face.
¹⁴ Do not reach out your hand for everything you see,
    and do not crowd your neighbor at the dish.
¹⁵ Judge your neighbor's feelings by your own,
    and in every matter be thoughtful.
¹⁸ If you are seated among many persons,
    do not reach out your hand before they do.

²⁵ Do not aim to be valiant over wine,
    for wine has destroyed many.
²⁶ Fire and water prove the temper of steel,
    so wine tests hearts in the strife of the proud.
²⁷ Wine is like life to men,
    if you drink it in moderation.
    What is life to a man who is without wine?
    It has been created to make men glad.
²⁸ Wine drunk in season and temperately
    is rejoicing of heart and gladness of soul.
²⁹ Wine drunk to excess is bitterness of soul,
    with provocation and stumbling.
³⁰ Drunkenness increases the anger of a fool to his injury,
    reducing his strength and adding wounds.
³¹ Do not reprove your neighbor at a banquet of wine,
    and do not despise him in his merrymaking;
    speak no word of reproach to him,
    and do not afflict him by making demands of him.

32 ³ Speak, you who are older, for it is fitting that you should,
    but with accurate knowledge, and do not interrupt the
    music.
    ⁷ Speak, young man, if there is need of you,
    but no more than twice, and only if asked.

⁸ Speak concisely, say much in few words;
    be as one who knows and yet holds his tongue.
¹¹ Leave in good time and do not be the last;
    go home quickly and do not linger.
¹² Amuse yourself there, and do what you have in mind,
    but do not sin through proud speech.
¹³ And for these things bless him who made you
    and satisfies you with his good gifts.

31:12 ff. How does this compare with books of etiquette designed for the twentieth century? See Proverbs 23 : 1–3, 6–8. **31:13** *Greedy eye:* to be envious and begrudging. In the biblical period the eye was considered a main source of sin. See Numbers 15 : 38 f.; Job 31 : 1. **31:15** A Golden Rule for etiquette on social occasions. **31:25** See Proverbs 20 : 1; 23 : 20–21, 29–35; 31 : 4–7.

The Lord Will Heal
Ecclesiasticus 38 : 1–9, 12–14, 24–34

38 Honor the physician with the honor due him, according to your
       need of him,
    for the Lord created him;
² for healing comes from the Most High,
    and he will receive a gift from the king.
³ The skill of the physician lifts up his head,
    and in the presence of great men he is admired.
⁴ The Lord created medicines from the earth,
    and a sensible man will not despise them.
⁵ Was not water made sweet with a tree
    in order that his power might be known?
⁶ And he gave skill to men
    that he might be glorified in his marvelous works.
⁷ By them he heals and takes away pain;
⁸   the pharmacist makes of them a compound.
His works will never be finished;
    and from him health is upon the face of the earth.

⁹ My son, when you are sick do not be negligent,
    but pray to the Lord, and he will heal you.
¹² And give the physician his place, for the Lord created him;
    let him not leave you, for there is need of him.
¹³ There is a time when success lies in the hands of physicians,
¹⁴   for they too will pray to the Lord
that he should grant them success in diagnosis
    and in healing, for the sake of preserving life.

24 The wisdom of the scribe depends on the opportunity of leisure;
  and he who has little business may become wise.
25 How can he become wise who handles the plow,
  and who glories in the shaft of a goad,
 who drives oxen and is occupied with their work,
  and whose talk is about bulls?
26 He sets his heart on plowing furrows,
  and he is careful about fodder for the heifers.
27 So too is every craftsman and master workman
  who labors by night as well as by day;
 those who cut the signets of seals,
  each is diligent in making a great variety;
 he sets his heart on painting a lifelike image,
  and he is careful to finish his work.
28 So too is the smith sitting by the anvil,
  intent upon his handiwork in iron;
 the breath of the fire melts his flesh,
  and he wastes away in the heat of the furnace;
 he inclines his ear to the sound of the hammer,
  and his eyes are on the pattern of the object.
 He sets his heart on finishing his handiwork,
  and he is careful to complete its decoration.
29 So too is the potter sitting at his work
  and turning the wheel with his feet;
 he is always deeply concerned over his work,
  and all his output is by number.
30 He moulds the clay with his arm
  and makes it pliable with his feet;
 he sets his heart to finish the glazing,
  and he is careful to clean the furnace.

31 All these rely upon their hands,
  and each is skilful in his own work.
32 Without them a city cannot be established,
  and men can neither sojourn nor live there.
33 Yet they are not sought out for the council of the people,
  nor do they attain eminence in the public assembly.
 They do not sit in the judge's seat,
  nor do they understand the sentence of judgment;
 they cannot expound discipline or judgment,
  and they are not found using proverbs.
34 But they keep stable the fabric of the world,
  and their prayer is in the practice of their trade.

38:1 There is a Midrashic saying: "Honor thy physician before thou hast need of him." **38:2** The words *healing comes from the Most High* are sometimes inscribed over hospital entrances, as at the Presbyterian Hospital in New York. **38:34** Compare the saying, "*Laborare est orare*" (To work is to pray).

Do Not Fear Death

Ecclesiasticus 41:1–4, 11–13

41 O death, how bitter is the reminder of you
    to one who lives at peace among his possessions,
  to a man without distractions, who is prosperous in everything,
    and who still has the vigor to enjoy his food!
² O death, how welcome is your sentence
    to one who is in need and is failing in strength,
  very old and distracted over everything;
    to one who is contrary, and has lost his patience!
³ Do not fear the sentence of death;
    remember your former days and the end of life;
  this is the decree from the Lord for all flesh,
⁴   and how can you reject the good pleasure of the Most High?
Whether life is for ten or a hundred or a thousand years,
    there is no inquiry about it in Hades.
¹¹ The mourning of men is about their bodies,
    but the evil name of sinners will be blotted out.
¹² Have regard for your name, since it will remain for you
    longer than a thousand great stores of gold.
¹³ The days of a good life are numbered,
    but a good name endures for ever.

41:3 Jerusalem Bible: "Remember those who came before you and those who will come after."

Praise Famous Men

This passage is often read at funerals and at community gatherings on Memorial Day.

Ecclesiasticus 44:1–15

44 Let us now praise famous men,
    and our fathers in their generations.
² The Lord apportioned to them great glory,
    his majesty from the beginning.
³ There were those who ruled in their kingdoms,
    and were men renowned for their power,

giving counsel by their understanding,
  and proclaiming prophecies;
⁴ leaders of the people in their deliberations
  and in understanding of learning for the people,
  wise in their words of instruction;
⁵ those who composed musical tunes,
  and set forth verses in writing;
⁶ rich men furnished with resources,
  living peaceably in their habitations—
⁷ all these were honored in their generations,
  and were the glory of their times.
⁸ There are some of them who have left a name,
  so that men declare their praise.
⁹ And there are some who have no memorial,
  who have perished as though they had not lived;
they have become as though they had not been born,
  and so have their children after them.
¹⁰ But these were men of mercy,
  whose righteous deeds have not been forgotten;
¹¹ their prosperity will remain with their descendants,
  and their inheritance to their children's children.
¹² Their descendants stand by the covenants;
  their children also, for their sake.
¹³ Their posterity will continue for ever,
  and their glory will not be blotted out.
¹⁴ Their bodies were buried in peace,
  and their name lives to all generations.
¹⁵ Peoples will declare their wisdom,
  and the congregation proclaims their praise.

44:1 The word here translated "famous," follows the Greek; the Hebrew (*hesed*), however, is rendered "pious men." This passage (extending to chapter 50) reviews Jewish history from the perspective of a pious man. Several similar historical reviews appear in the Old Testament, such as Psalms 78, 105, 106, 135, 136, and Ezekiel 20. The author's purpose is to demonstrate that God's glory was revealed in its highest form among Israel's leaders. The author reveals a bias for the cultic as an expression of Israel's greatest religious achievement. Thus he subordinates Moses to Aaron, and he praises David for his Temple music and the writing of psalms. Biblical scholars have made use of the names mentioned in these six chapters in efforts to determine when the Hebrew Bible was canonized. Ben Sira knows of the Law (Pentateuch) and the Prophets (including Joshua, Judges, Samuel, and Kings). He refers also to Chronicles, Nehemiah, Psalms, Proverbs, Job, and Ecclesiastes. Missing, however, is any reference to

Daniel, Ruth, Lamentations, and Song of Songs—perhaps not yet canonized. On the basis of this, scholars suggest that the Law and the Prophets were canonized at least by 200 B.C., but that the Writings had not yet taken final form.

First Book of Maccabees

The background for the events celebrated by the Feast of Dedication, commonly known in the Jewish tradition as Hanukkah, is recorded in 1 Maccabees. Following the death of Alexander the Great, the far-flung Greek empire was divided four ways (see note on Daniel 8:1–8). In Syria the ruling dynasty took its name from Seleucus, one of Alexander's generals, and in 175 B.C. the most famous of the Seleucid rulers, Antiochus IV, came to the throne. He arrogated to himself the surname "Epiphanes," proclaiming himself thereby to be "god manifest"; his enemies nicknamed him Epimanes, or "mad man." Antiochus undertook to unify the disparate cultures and peoples in his realm by imposing Hellenism upon them; he demanded that they serve him faithfully as a god. There was resistance to such a policy from the Jewish people. Antiochus exploited the fact that the Hebrew high priesthood had been corrupted, and in return for a large sum of money placed Jason in that office on condition that Jason further the cause of Hellenization.

With the assistance of the vassal priests Antiochus forced certain Greek customs upon the Jews. He introduced athletic contests in honor of the pagan gods. He robbed the Temple treasure in Jerusalem and turned the altar into a place for sacrificing pigs to Zeus. He forbade circumcision. When the Jews of the resistance movement, in accordance with custom immemorial, would not go out to fight on the Sabbath, Antiochus slaughtered them. Daniel 11:31 refers to "the abomination that makes desolate," and Mark 13:11 to "the desolating sacrilege set up where it ought not to be." These terms depict the horror and revulsion that Antiochus provoked.

Mattathias, an aged priest of the village of Modein, and his five sons gave leadership to a Jewish resistance movement. These "glorious brothers," called Maccabeus from the Hebrew word for "hammer" bestowed as an epithet upon one of them, summoned the people to revolt. They were victorious, emancipating the sanctuary in Jerusalem. After the defilement had been cleansed, there was a feast of dedication (1 Maccabees 4:5–58), lasting eight days.

The historical events in this book cover a period between 175–135 B.C. It was probably written not long after, in the last quarter of the second century. The author is not identified. Scholars believe that he was a Hebrew of Palestine. He was well acquainted with the topography of the land. He appears to have some personal knowledge of the events he describes. Students consider this book to be the best history we have of the period. The author, at times breaking out into poetic strain, reveals his deep concern for the fate of his people in an otherwise straightforward presentation of historical events. Unlike the prophetic historians of the Old Testament, however, the author of 1 Maccabees does not directly mention God by name, and he seems reluctant to interpret the deeds of men as reflections of God's intervention in history, although there is no doubt that the author believes in an all-seeing Providence who helps those who are worthy.

Luther, noting that in style and vocabulary 1 Maccabees resembled "the rest of the books of Holy Scripture," said that it "would not have been unworthy to be reckoned among them, because it is a very necessary and useful book for the understanding of the eleventh chapter of the prophet Daniel."

Antiochus Denies Religious Freedom to Israel
1 Maccabees 1:1–17, 20–30, 41–53, 56–57, 62–64

1 After Alexander son of Philip, the Macedonian, who came from the land of Kittim, had defeated Darius, king of the Persians and the Medes, he succeeded him as king. (He had previously become king of Greece.) ² He fought many battles, conquered strongholds, and put to death the kings of the earth. ³ He advanced to the ends of the earth, and plundered many nations. When the earth became quiet before him, he was exalted, and his heart was lifted up. ⁴ He gathered a very strong army and ruled over countries, nations, and princes, and they became tributary to him.

5 After this he fell sick and perceived that he was dying. ⁶ So he summoned his most honored officers, who had been brought up with him from youth, and divided his kingdom among them while he was still alive. ⁷ And after Alexander had reigned twelve years, he died.

8 Then his officers began to rule, each in his own place. ⁹ They all put on crowns after his death, and so did their sons after them for many years; and they caused many evils on the earth.

10 From them came forth a sinful root, Antiochus Epiphanes, son of Antiochus the king; he had been a hostage in Rome. He began to reign in the one hundred and thirty-seventh year of the kingdom of the Greeks.

11 In those days lawless men came forth from Israel, and misled many, saying, "Let us go and make a covenant with the Gentiles round about us, for since we separated from them many evils have come upon us." ¹² This proposal pleased them, ¹³ and some of the people eagerly went to the king. He authorized them to observe the ordinances of the Gentiles. ¹⁴ So they built a gymnasium in Jerusalem, according to Gentile custom, ¹⁵ and removed the marks of circumcision, and abandoned the holy covenant. They joined with the Gentiles and sold themselves to do evil.

16 When Antiochus saw that his kingdom was established, he determined to become king of the land of Egypt, that he might reign

over both kingdoms. ¹⁷ So he invaded Egypt with a strong force, with chariots and elephants and cavalry and with a large fleet.

20 After subduing Egypt, Antiochus returned in the one hundred and forty-third year. He went up against Israel and came to Jerusalem with a strong force. ²¹ He arrogantly entered the sanctuary and took the golden altar, the lampstand for the light, and all its utensils. ²² He took also the table for the bread of the Presence, the cups for drink offerings, the bowls, the golden censers, the curtain, the crowns, and the gold decoration on the front of the temple; he stripped it all off. ²³ He took the silver and the gold, and the costly vessels; he took also the hidden treasures which he found. ²⁴ Taking them all, he departed to his own land.

> He committed deeds of murder,
>> and spoke with great arrogance.
> ²⁵ Israel mourned deeply in every community,
> ²⁶   rulers and elders groaned,
> maidens and young men became faint,
>> the beauty of the women faded.
> ²⁷ Every bridegroom took up the lament;
>> she who sat in the bridal chamber was mourning.
> ²⁸ Even the land shook for its inhabitants,
>> and all the house of Jacob was clothed with shame.

29 Two years later the king sent to the cities of Judah a chief collector of tribute, and he came to Jerusalem with a large force. ³⁰ Deceitfully he spoke peaceable words to them, and they believed him; but he suddenly fell upon the city, dealt it a severe blow, and destroyed many people of Israel.

41 Then the king wrote to his whole kingdom that all should be one people, ⁴² and that each should give up his customs. ⁴³ All the Gentiles accepted the command of the king. Many even from Israel gladly adopted his religion; they sacrificed to idols and profaned the sabbath. ⁴⁴ And the king sent letters by messengers to Jerusalem and the cities of Judah; he directed them to follow customs strange to the land, ⁴⁵ to forbid burnt offerings and sacrifices and drink offerings in the sanctuary, to profane sabbaths and feasts, ⁴⁶ to defile the sanctuary and the priests, ⁴⁷ to build altars and sacred precincts and shrines for idols, to sacrifice swine and unclean animals, ⁴⁸ and to leave their sons uncircumcised. They were to make themselves abominable by everything unclean and profane, ⁴⁹ so that they should forget the law and change all the ordinances. ⁵⁰ "And whoever does not obey the command of the king shall die."

51 In such words he wrote to his whole kingdom. And he appointed inspectors over all the people and commanded the cities of

Judah to offer sacrifice, city by city. [52] Many of the people, every one who forsook the law, joined them, and they did evil in the land; [53] they drove Israel into hiding in every place of refuge they had.

[56] The books of the law which they found they tore to pieces and burned with fire. [57] Where the book of the covenant was found in the possession of any one, or if any one adhered to the law, the decree of the king condemned him to death.

62 But many in Israel stood firm and were resolved in their hearts not to eat unclean food. [63] They chose to die rather than to be defiled by food or to profane the holy covenant; and they did die. [64] And very great wrath came upon Israel.

1:1 Alexander lived from 356 to 323 B.C. The Kittim mentioned here are the Macedonians. **1:3** *Ends of the earth:* Alexander conquered most of the known world from the Balkan peninsula to the subcontinent of India. **1:8** Alexander (died 323 B.C.) divided his kingdom into four parts, each ruled by one of his generals: Macedonia was entrusted to Cassander; Thrace and Asia Minor to Lysimachus; Syria with Babylonia and the East to Seleucus; Egypt to Ptolemy. **1:10** Antiochus, following the murder of his brother Seleucus IV, succeeded to the Syrian throne in 175 B.C. **1:11** These men were not "lawless" in the sense that they were criminals. Rather, they were violators of the Mosaic Law who had accepted the pagan practices of the Hellenic culture. **1:21** *Golden altar,* cf. Exodus 30:1-6; *lampstand,* cf. Exodus 25:31; *bread of the Presence,* cf. Exodus 25:23-30. **1:41** It was customary to believe that conformity in religious practice was required of *one people.* The Hebrews would have accepted political domination but not religious suppression. The Maccabean revolt, therefore, was at first a battle for religious freedom. Only in recent history have we come to realize that a nation can be *one people* even though the people worship God in different ways. Such religious diversity within political unity has been a contribution of the democratic system, with its guarantee of freedom. **1:47** The pig was holy to the Syrian goddess Astarte. **1:56** It is the way of tyrants in every age to burn books that contain ideas contradictory to their oppressive ways.

Mattathias Resists the Oppression
1 Maccabees 2:1-6, 15-25, 42-48

2 In those days Mattathias the son of John, son of Simeon, a priest of the sons of Joarib, moved from Jerusalem and settled in Modein. [2] He had five sons, John surnamed Gaddi, [3] Simon called Thassi, [4] Judas called Maccabeus, [5] Eleazar called Avaran, and Jonathan called Apphus. [6] He saw the blasphemies being committed in Judah and Jerusalem.

15 Then the king's officers who were enforcing the apostasy came to the city of Modein to make them offer sacrifice. [16] Many from Israel came to them; and Mattathias and his sons were assembled. [17] Then the king's officers spoke to Mattathias as follows: "You are a leader, honored and great in this city, and supported by sons and brothers. [18] Now be the first to come and do what the king commands, as all the Gentiles and the men of Judah and those that are left in Jerusalem have done. Then you and your sons will be numbered among the friends of the king, and you and your sons will be honored with silver and gold and many gifts."

19 But Mattathias answered and said in a loud voice: "Even if all the nations that live under the rule of the king obey him, and have chosen to do his commandments, departing each one from the religion of his fathers, [20] yet I and my sons and my brothers will live by the covenant of our fathers. [21] Far be it from us to desert the law and the ordinances. [22] We will not obey the king's words by turning aside from our religion to the right or to the left."

23 When he had finished speaking these words, a Jew came forward in the sight of all to offer sacrifice upon the altar in Modein, according to the king's command. [24] When Mattathias saw it, he burned with zeal and his heart was stirred. He gave vent to righteous anger; he ran and killed him upon the altar. [25] At the same time he killed the king's officer who was forcing them to sacrifice, and he tore down the altar.

42 Then there united with them a company of Hasideans, mighty warriors of Israel, every one who offered himself willingly for the law. [43] And all who became fugitives to escape their troubles joined them and reinforced them. [44] They organized an army, and struck down sinners in their anger and lawless men in their wrath; the survivors fled to the Gentiles for safety. [45] And Mattathias and his friends went about and tore down the altars; [46] they forcibly circumcised all the uncircumcised boys that they found within the borders of Israel. [47] They hunted down the arrogant men, and the work prospered in their hands. [48] They rescued the law out of the hands of the Gentiles and kings, and they never let the sinner gain the upper hand.

2:1 From the Greek of Simeon came the name Hasmonean, by which the Maccabee family and dynasty later came to be known. Modein is a mountain village between Jerusalem and the sea. 2:2–5 The surnames mean, respectively, *Gaddi:* fortunate; *Thassi:* zealous; *Maccabeus:* hammer; *Avaran:* alert; *Apphus:* cunning or favored. 2:24 *Heart:* literally the word here is "kidney." In Hebraic psychology the kidneys were the source of emotion; cf. Psalm 73:21.

2:42 *Hasideans,* "pious ones." Their attitude is summed up in Daniel 3:17–18; the Pharisees are their heirs. Believing that men ought to rely only on divine help the Hasideans at first mistrusted the Maccabees. Later they not only gave Judas their support but also consented to fight in self-defense on the Sabbath. The Book of Enoch, symbolically describing this change, says that "horns grew on the little lambs."

The Hasideans distinguished themselves by fidelity to the Law, rejecting the assimilation to Greek custom adopted by Hellenistic Jews. They are mentioned in several of the Psalms: 30:4; 31:23; 37:28; 149:6–9. 1 Maccabees 7 indicates that the Hasideans were not so much interested in a political victory as in achieving religious freedom. The Syrians were not content to provide this religious freedom. They continued their effort to suppress the Jews completely and were, themselves, at last defeated. For the first time in four hundred years an independent Jewish state emerged.

Judas Takes Command
1 Maccabees 3:1–3, 13–27

3 Then Judas his son, who was called Maccabeus, took command in his place. ²All his brothers and all who had joined his father helped him; they gladly fought for Israel.

³He extended the glory of his people.

Like a giant he put on his breastplate;

he girded on his armor of war and waged battles,

protecting the host by his sword.

13 Now when Seron, the commander of the Syrian army, heard that Judas had gathered a large company, including a body of faithful men who stayed with him and went out to battle, ¹⁴he said, "I will make a name for myself and win honor in the kingdom. I will make war on Judas and his companions, who scorn the king's command." ¹⁵And again a strong army of ungodly men went up with him to help him, to take vengeance on the sons of Israel.

16 When he approached the ascent of Beth-horon, Judas went out to meet him with a small company. ¹⁷But when they saw the army coming to meet them, they said to Judas, "How can we, few as we are, fight against so great and strong a multitude? And we are faint, for we have eaten nothing today." ¹⁸Judas replied, "It is easy for many to be hemmed in by few, for in the sight of Heaven there is no difference between saving by many or by few. ¹⁹It is not on the size of the army that victory in battle depends, but strength comes from Heaven. ²⁰They come against us in great pride and lawlessness to destroy us and our wives and our children, and to despoil us; ²¹but we fight for our lives and our laws. ²²He himself will crush them before us; as for you, do not be afraid of them."

23 When he finished speaking, he rushed suddenly against Seron and his army, and they were crushed before him. ²⁴They pursued them down the descent of Beth-horon to the plain; eight hundred of them fell, and the rest fled into the land of the Philistines. ²⁵Then Judas and his brothers began to be feared, and terror fell upon the Gentiles round about them. ²⁶His fame reached the king, and the Gentiles talked of the battles of Judas.

27 When King Antiochus heard these reports, he was greatly angered; and he sent and gathered all the forces of his kingdom, a very strong army.

3:1 Mattathias died 167 or 166 B.C. and was buried in Modein.
3:20 *Heaven:* Other varying texts make it clear that what is meant here is the "God of heaven" or "Him that dwelleth in heaven." The Jews during this period tended to refrain from invoking directly the name of God. See also verse 22 and verse 60.

The Temple Is Rededicated

Under the leadership of Judas and his brothers, the Jews maintained the independence of the nation through several desperate campaigns, with many deeds of heroism against great odds. At last a respite in the battles gave them a chance to repair their sanctuary.

1 Maccabees 4:36, 42–43, 47–48, 52, 54–56, 59

36 Then said Judas and his brothers, "Behold, our enemies are crushed; let us go up to cleanse the sanctuary and dedicate it."

42 He chose blameless priests devoted to the law, ⁴³and they cleansed the sanctuary and removed the defiled stones to an unclean place.

47 Then they took unhewn stones, as the law directs, and built a new altar like the former one. ⁴⁸They also rebuilt the sanctuary and the interior of the temple, and consecrated the courts.

52 Early in the morning on the twenty-fifth day of the ninth month, which is the month of Chislev, in the one hundred and forty-eighth year.

54 At the very season and on the very day that the Gentiles had profaned it, it was dedicated with songs and harps and lutes and cymbals. ⁵⁵All the people fell on their faces and worshiped and blessed Heaven, who had prospered them. ⁵⁶So they celebrated the dedication of the altar for eight days, and offered burnt offerings with gladness; they offered a sacrifice of deliverance and praise.

59 Then Judas and his brothers and all the asembly of Israel determined that every year at that season the days of the dedication of the altar should be observed with gladness and joy for eight days, beginning with the twenty-fifth day of the month of Chislev.

4:36 The Hebrew word for *cleanse* signifies ritual cleansing, i.e., the removing of the idolatrous images. **4:47** *As the law directs:* cf. Exodus 20:25; Deuteronomy 27:6. **4:52** ff. *Kislev (Chislev)*, a Hebrew month that usually falls in December. The event is celebrated by Jews for an eight-day period known as Hanukkah. On each evening of the festival the Jewish family kindles the lights of a Menorah, a nine-branch candelabra; one light, plus a helper candle (Shammus), is kindled successively on each night until the eighth night when nine candles are lit altogether. According to 2 Maccabees 1:18 and 10:6–7 the eight-day festival may have served to celebrate the Feast of Tabernacles, which had evidently gone unobserved when the Temple had been desecrated. Talmudic records recall the miracle of a cruse of holy oil, used in lighting the eternal lamp before the Ark. Although there was only enough holy oil for a one-day period, it lasted miraculously eight days until the Jews were able to prepare additional oil. In the early history of Christianity, the Maccabeans were canonized and accorded a yearly festival August 1 in Greek and Latin churches.

Judas Makes an Alliance with Rome

After the victory at Jerusalem Judas Maccabeus was called upon several time to defend the Hebrew people against the continued attacks of the Syrians. About 162 B.C. Judas confronted an army of 100,000 foot soldiers, 20,000 cavalry and 32 elephants led by King Antiochus V. The enemy besieged Jerusalem; but they turned aside at the last moment when Antioch, the Syrian capital, found itself under attack from a traitor to King Antiochus V.

Later another contender to the Syrian throne, Demetrius I, killed Antiochus. Then pretending to offer peace to the Judeans, Demetrius sent a force of men under Bacchides and Alcimus, a renegade Hebrew priest of the house of Aaron. The pious Hasideans were willing to accept peace with Alcimus as high priest; but Bacchides foolishly and treacherously slew sixty of their number seeking complete domination of the country. The people under Judas again rose to the occasion. This time with only 3,000 men Judas overcame a huge army led by Nicanor. Thereupon to secure the political freedom he had at last won for the Jewish people, Judas made a treaty with Rome, then emerging as an effective power against the Greeks. Later, in 63 B.C., the Romans succeeded the Greeks in dominating Judea.

1 Maccabees 8:1–4, 12–29

8 Now Judas heard of the fame of the Romans, that they were very strong and were well-disposed toward all who made an alliance with them, that they pledged friendship to those who came to them, ²and that they were very strong. Men told him of their wars and of the brave deeds which they were doing among the Gauls, how they had defeated them and forced them to pay tribute, ³ and what they had done in the land of Spain to get control of the silver and gold mines there, ⁴ and how they had gained control of the whole region by their planning and patience, even though the place was far distant from them. They also subdued the kings who came against them from the ends of the earth, until they crushed them and inflicted great disaster upon them; the rest paid them tribute every year. . . . ¹² but with their friends and those who rely on them they have kept friendship. They have subdued kings far and near, and as many as have heard of their fame have feared them. ¹³ Those whom they wish to help and to make kings, they make kings, and those whom they wish they depose; and they have been greatly exalted. ¹⁴ Yet for all this not one of them has put on a crown or worn purple as a mark of pride. ¹⁵ but they have built for themselves a senate chamber, and every day three hundred and twenty senators constantly deliberate concerning the people, to govern them well. ¹⁶ They trust one man each year to rule over them and to control all their land; they all heed the one man, and there is no envy or jealousy among them.

17 So Judas chose Eupolemus the son of John, son of Accos, and Jason the son of Eleazar, and sent them to Rome to establish friendship and alliance, ¹⁸ and to free themselves from the yoke; for they saw that the kingdom of the Greeks was completely enslaving Israel. ¹⁹ They went to Rome, a very long journey; and they entered the senate chamber and spoke as follows: ²⁰ "Judas, who is also called Maccabeus, and his brothers and the people of the Jews have sent us to you to establish alliance and peace with you, that we may be enrolled as your allies and friends." ²¹ The proposal pleased them, ²² and this is a copy of the letter which they wrote in reply, on bronze tablets, and sent to Jerusalem to remain with them there as a memorial of peace and alliance:

23 "May all go well with the Romans and with the nation of the Jews at sea and on land for ever, and may sword and enemy be far from them. ²⁴ If war comes first to Rome or to any of their allies in all their dominion, ²⁵ the nation of the Jews shall act as their allies wholeheartedly, as the occasion may indicate to them. ²⁶ And to the enemy who makes war they shall not give or supply grain, arms, money, or ships, as Rome has decided; and they shall keep their obligations without receiving any return. ²⁷ In the same way, if war comes first to the nation of the Jews, the Romans shall willingly act as their allies, as the occasion may indicate to them. ²⁸ And to the enemy allies shall be given no grain, arms, money, or ships, as Rome has decided; and they shall keep these obligations and do so without deceit. ²⁹ Thus on these terms the Romans make a treaty with the Jewish people."

8:16 *One man each year:* Historically there were two consuls each year. **8:22** *On bronze tablets,* a method by which such treaties could be kept as a permanent record.

Simon Wins Political Freedom

Judas Maccabeus died courageously in 160 B.C. in battle against the Syrian general Bacchides and the traitor-priest Acimus. He was succeeded by his brother Jonathan (160-142 B.C.), who by skillful political maneuver maintained both a political and spiritual authority until murdered by the traitor Trypho. Whereupon Jonathan's brother Simon (142-134 B.C.) succeeded to the authority.

1 Maccabees 13:41–42; 14:4–15

41 In the one hundred and seventieth year the yoke of the Gentiles was removed from Israel, ⁴² and the people began to write in their documents and contracts, "In the first year of Simon the great high priest and commander and leader of the Jews."

14 ⁴ The land had rest all the days of Simon.
> He sought the good of his nation;
> > his rule was pleasing to them,
> > > as was the honor shown him, all his days.

⁵ To crown all his honors he took Joppa for a harbor,
> and opened a way to the isles of the sea.

⁶ He extended the borders of his nation,
> and gained full control of the country.

⁷ He gathered a host of captives;
> he ruled over Gazara and Beth-zur and the citadel,
> > and he removed its uncleanliness from it;
> > and there was none to oppose him.

⁸ They tilled their land in peace;
> the ground gave its increase,
> and the trees of the plains their fruit.

⁹ Old men sat in the streets;
> they all talked together of good things;
> and the youths donned the glories and garments of war.

¹⁰ He supplied the cities with food,
> and furnished them with the means of defense,
> till his renown spread to the ends of the earth.

¹¹ He established peace in the land,
> and Israel rejoiced with great joy.

¹² Each man sat under his vine and his fig tree,
> and there was none to make them afraid.

¹³ No one was left in the land to fight them,
> and the kings were crushed in those days.

¹⁴ He strengthened all the humble of his people;
 he sought out the law,
 and did away with every lawless and wicked man.
¹⁵ He made the sanctuary glorious,
 and added to the vessels of the sanctuary.

13:41 *In the one hundred and seventieth year,* i.e., 143–142 B.C., Simon Maccabee finally achieved political freedom for the Jews. This is noted by the fact that the Jewish calendar begins to record the date of the year according to the years of his rule. Note also that in his reign the high priesthood is now merged with the political head of the state and made one office. The Rabbis were later to look upon this mingling of church and state hierarchy in one person as a tragedy.

Second Book of Maccabees

1 Maccabees is a restrained historical narrative setting forth the facts and circumstances of the Maccabean revolt. 2 Maccabees is a romantic elaboration. 1 Maccabees is inhibited in invoking God's help as explanation for historical events. 2 Maccabees is much less reserved. 1 Maccabees covers the years 175–134 B.C. 2 Maccabees is concerned only with the period 175 to 160 B.C. The author tells us that he has attempted "to condense into a single book" the five-volume work of Jason of Cyrene (otherwise unknown).

The historical embellishment is prefaced by two letters, one from Jerusalem Jews to Egyptian Jews, the other from Judean Jews and Aristobulus, "teacher of Ptolemy the king, to the Jews in Egypt." These letters summarize the efforts of the Maccabees to purify the Temple from its pagan defilements. Through descriptions of a frustrated would-be Temple robber, a "golden-clad horseman" who led the Hebrew armies, and the incurable disease that inflicted Antiochus, the author stresses the divine help which was always near when most needed.

This book, unlike 1 Maccabees, contains theological concepts current among Alexandrian or Greek-speaking Jews, which concepts were significant in the early development of Christian thought: prayers for the dead (12:43, 45); the intercession of saints (15:11–16); the belief that the righteous will be resurrected after death to life eternal, perhaps in a messianic kingdom on earth (7:11–37, 14:26).

Author's Preface
2 Maccabees 2:19–32

19 The story of Judas Maccabeus and his brothers, and the purification of the great temple, and the dedication of the altar, [20] and further the wars against Antiochus Epiphanes and his son Eupator, [21] and the appearances which came from heaven to those who strove zealously on behalf of Judaism, so that though few in number they seized the whole land and pursued the barbarian hordes, [22] and recovered the temple famous throughout the world and freed the city and restored the laws that were about to be abolished, while the Lord with great kindness became gracious to them— [23] all this, which has been set forth by Jason of Cyrene in five volumes, we shall attempt to condense into a single book. [24] For considering the flood of numbers involved and the difficulty there is for those who wish to enter upon the narratives of history because of

the mass of material, ²⁵ we have aimed to please those who wish to read, to make it easy for those who are inclined to memorize, and to profit all readers. ²⁶ For us who have undertaken the toil of abbreviating, it is no light matter but calls for sweat and loss of sleep, ²⁷ just as it is not easy for one who prepares a banquet and seeks the benefit of others. However, to secure the gratitude of many we will gladly endure the uncomfortable toil, ²⁸ leaving the responsibility for exact details to the compiler, while devoting our effort to arriving at the outlines of the condensation. ²⁹ For as the master builder of a new house must be concerned with the whole construction, while the one who undertakes its painting and decoration has to consider only what is suitable for its adornment, such in my judgment is the case with us. ³⁰ It is the duty of the original historian to occupy the ground and to discuss matters from every side and to take trouble with details, ³¹ but the one who recasts the narrative should be allowed to strive for brevity of expression and to forego exhaustive treatment. ³² At this point therefore let us begin our narrative, adding only so much to what has already been said; for it is foolish to lengthen the preface while cutting short the history itself.

The Priesthood Is Corrupted
2 Maccabees 4:7–10, 12–17, 23–27

7 When Seleucus died and Antiochus who was called Epiphanes succeeded to the kingdom, Jason the brother of Onias obtained the high priesthood by corruption, ⁸ promising the king at an interview three hundred and sixty talents of silver and, from another source of revenue, eighty talents. ⁹ In addition to this he promised to pay one hundred and fifty more if permission were given to establish by his authority a gymnasium and a body of youth for it, and to enrol the men of Jerusalem as citizens of Antioch. ¹⁰ When the king assented and Jason came to office, he at once shifted his countrymen over to the Greek way of life.

12 For with alacrity he founded a gymnasium right under the citadel, and he induced the noblest of the young men to wear the Greek hat. ¹³ There was such an extreme of Hellenization and increase in the adoption of foreign ways because of the surpassing wickedness of Jason, who was ungodly and no high priest, ¹⁴ that the priests were no longer intent upon their service at the altar. Despising the sanctuary and neglecting the sacrifices, they hastened to take part in the unlawful proceedings in the wrestling arena after the call to the discus, ¹⁵ disdaining the honors prized by their fathers and putting the highest value upon Greek forms of prestige. ¹⁶ For this

reason heavy disaster overtook them, and those whose ways of living they admired and wished to imitate completely became their enemies and punished them. [17] For it is no light thing to show irreverence to the divine laws—a fact which later events will make clear.

23 After a period of three years Jason sent Menelaus, the brother of the previously mentioned Simon, to carry the money to the king and to complete the records of essential business. [24] But he, when presented to the king, extolled him with an air of authority, and secured the high priesthood for himself, outbidding Jason by three hundred talents of silver. [25] After receiving the king's orders he returned, possessing no qualification for the high priesthood, but having the hot temper of a cruel tyrant and the rage of a savage wild beast. [26] So Jason, who after supplanting his own brother was supplanted by another man, was driven as a fugitive into the land of Ammon. [27] And Menelaus held the office, but he did not pay regularly any of the money promised to the king.

> **4:9** *Enrol the men of Jerusalem as citizens of Antioch:* i.e., form them into a city within a city, bestowing on them certain civic rights; see Philippians 3:20. **4:12** *Greek hat:* a broad-brimmed felt headpiece, mark of the adolescent. **4:14** The Greek games included dedications and honors to the pagan gods, making participation in these activities particularly blasphemous to religious Jews.

Menelaus and Antiochus Corrupt the Temple
2 Maccabees 5:11–17, 19–20; 6:1–2

11 When news of what had happened reached the king, he took it to mean that Judea was in revolt. So, raging inwardly, he left Egypt and took the city by storm. [12] And he commanded his soldiers to cut down relentlessly every one they met and to slay those who went into the houses. [13] Then there was killing of young and old, destruction of boys, women and children, and slaughter of virgins and infants. [14] Within the total of three days eighty thousand were destroyed, forty thousand in hand-to-hand fighting; and as many were sold into slavery as were slain.

15 Not content with this, Antiochus dared to enter the most holy temple in all the world, guided by Menelaus, who had become a traitor both to the laws and to his country. [16] He took the holy vessels with his polluted hands, and swept away with profane hands the votive offerings which other kings had made to enhance the glory and honor of the place. [17] Antiochus was elated in spirit, and did not perceive that the Lord was angered for a little while because of the sins of those who dwelt in the city, and that therefore he was disregarding the holy place.

19 But the Lord did not choose the nation for the sake of the holy place, but the place for the sake of the nation. ²⁰ Therefore the place itself shared in the misfortunes that befell the nation and afterward participated in its benefits; and what was forsaken in the wrath of the Almighty was restored again in all its glory when the great Lord became reconciled.

6 Not long after this, the king sent an Athenian senator to compel the Jews to forsake the laws of their fathers and cease to live by the laws of God, ² and also to pollute the temple in Jerusalem and call it the temple of Olympian Zeus, and to call the one in Gerizim the temple of Zeus the Friend of Strangers, as did the people who dwelt in that place.

> **6 : 1** Antiochus thought that uniformity of religious practice would demonstrate a uniformity of political allegiance. But the idolatry he introduced into the Temple area only aroused Jewish opposition. In addition Antiochus forbade circumcision, the observance of the Sabbath and compelled Jews to eat forbidden meat. Rebellion followed. **6 : 2** The Greeks represented Mount Olympus as the home of the gods; Zeus, founder of kingly power, originator of law and order, was supreme over the Greek gods.

Hannah and Her Seven Sons Die Martyrs
2 Maccabees 7 : 1–6, 20–41

7 It happened also that seven brothers and their mother were arrested and were being compelled by the king, under torture with whips and cords, to partake of unlawful swine's flesh. ² One of them, acting as their spokesman, said, "What do you intend to ask and learn from us? For we are ready to die rather than transgress the laws of our fathers."

3 The king fell into a rage, and gave orders that pans and caldrons be heated. ⁴ These were heated immediately, and he commanded that the tongue of their spokesman be cut out and that they scalp him and cut off his hands and feet, while the rest of the brothers and the mother looked on. ⁵ When he was utterly helpless, the king ordered them to take him to the fire, still breathing, and to fry him in a pan. The smoke from the pan spread widely, but the brothers and their mother encouraged one another to die nobly, saying, ⁶ "The Lord God is watching over us and in truth has compassion on us, as Moses declared in his song which bore witness against the people to their faces, when he said, 'And he will have compassion on his servants.'"

20 The mother was especially admirable and worthy of honorable memory. Though she saw her seven sons perish within a single day, she bore it with good courage because of her hope in the Lord.

²¹ She encouraged each of them in the language of their fathers. Filled with a noble spirit, she fired her woman's reasoning with a man's courage, and said to them, ²² "I do not know how you came into being in my womb. It was not I who gave you life and breath, nor I who set in order the elements within each of you. ²³ Therefore the Creator of the world, who shaped the beginning of man and devised the origin of all things, will in his mercy give life and breath back to you again, since you now forget yourselves for the sake of his laws."

24 Antiochus felt that he was being treated with contempt, and he was suspicious of her reproachful tone. The youngest brother being still alive, Antiochus not only appealed to him in words, but promised with oaths that he would make him rich and enviable if he would turn from the ways of his fathers, and that he would take him for his friend and entrust him with public affairs. ²⁵ Since the young man would not listen to him at all, the king called the mother to him and urged her to advise the youth to save himself. ²⁶ After much urging on his part, she undertook to persuade her son. ²⁷ But, leaning close to him, she spoke in their native tongue as follows, deriding the cruel tyrant: "My son, have pity on me. I carried you nine months in my womb, and nursed you for three years, and have reared you and brought you up to this point in your life, and have taken care of you. ²⁸ I beseech you, my child, to look at the heaven and the earth and see everything that is in them, and recognize that God did not make them out of things that existed. Thus also mankind comes into being. ²⁹ Do not fear this butcher, but prove worthy of your brothers. Accept death, so that in God's mercy I may get you back again with your brothers."

30 While she was still speaking, the young man said, "What are you waiting for? I will not obey the king's command, but I obey the command of the law that was given to our fathers through Moses. ³¹ But you, who have contrived all sorts of evil against the Hebrews, will certainly not escape the hands of God. ³² For we are suffering because of our own sins. ³³ And if our living Lord is angry for a little while, to rebuke and discipline us, he will again be reconciled with his own servants. ³⁴ But you, unholy wretch, you most defiled of all men, do not be elated in vain and puffed up by uncertain hopes, when you raise your hand against the children of heaven. ³⁵ You have not yet escaped the judgment of the almighty, all-seeing God. ³⁶ For our brothers after enduring a brief suffering have drunk of everflowing life under God's covenant; but you, by the judgment of God, will receive just punishment for your arrogance. ³⁷ I, like my brothers, give up body and life for the laws of our fathers, appealing

to God to show mercy soon to our nation and by afflictions and plagues to make you confess that he alone is God, [38] and through me and my brothers to bring to an end the wrath of the Almighty which has justly fallen on our whole nation."

39 The king fell into a rage, and handled him worse than the others, being exasperated at his scorn. [40] So he died in his integrity, putting his whole trust in the Lord.

41 Last of all, the mother died, after her sons.

> **7:1** The Calendar of Martyrs of the Syrian Church gives the mother the name of Shamuni. The Eastern Orthodox Church calls the mother Solomonis. She and her sons are commemorated on August 1. The names of the sons are given as Abion, Antonius, Gourias, Eleazar, Eusebonas, Alim, and Marcellus. Relics of the family are said to be preserved in the Church of St. Peter ad Vincula in Rome and at Cologne in a convent dedicated to the Maccabees. Churches in Antioch, Lyons and Vienna have also been dedicated to these seven martyrs. This is one of the several incidents from the Maccabean uprising depicted in Henry Wadsworth Longfellow's poetic dramatization, "Judas Maccabeus." Anton Rubinstein composed a lengthy opera, *The Maccabees,* with libretto by H. S. von Mosenthal. Handel's oratorio, *Judas Maccabaeus,* written to celebrate the English victory after the Scottish Highlanders rose under the leadership of Bonnie Prince Charlie, re-established his reputation after the failure of his operatic enterprises. More martial in tone than *Messiah,* it has for its hero not the Lamb of God but a Lion of Judah. In addition to the chorus, "See the conquering hero comes," it also contains "Sion now her head shall raise," the last great chorus he composed. **7:6** See Deuteronomy 32:36. **7:8** *The language of his fathers:* English uses a different idiom, "mother tongue." **7:9** This is the first and clearest expression of the doctrine of bodily resurrection, only hinted at in Isaiah 26:19 and Job 19:26–27. **7:29** This passage reflects the view that the righteous are reunited in another life after their life on earth. Verse 33 hints at the possibility of a messianic kingdom on earth for the righteous, whereas the evil will suffer torments and plagues. And verse 36 intimates immortality of the soul. Both a conviction of immortality and resurrection are here expressed. **7:38** The seventh son here invokes the hope that his own martyrdom and that of his brothers will serve as a reconciling sacrifice for his people and thus bring an end to God's anger at the nation.

Judas Maccabeus Routs Nicanor
2 Maccabees 8:16–19a, 22–29

16 But Maccabeus gathered his men together, to the number of six thousand, and exhorted them not to be frightened by the enemy and

not to fear the great multitude of Gentiles who were wickedly coming against them, but to fight nobly, [17] keeping before their eyes the lawless outrage which the Gentiles had committed against the holy place, and the torture of the derided city, and besides, the overthrow of their ancestral way of life. [18] "For they trust to arms and acts of daring," he said, "but we trust in the Almighty God, who is able with a single nod to strike down those who are coming against us and even the whole world."

19 Moreover he told them of the times when help came to their ancestors;

22 He appointed his brothers also, Simon and Joseph and Jonathan, each to command a division, putting fifteen hundred men under each. [23] Besides, he appointed Eleazar to read aloud from the holy book, and gave the watchword, "God's help"; then, leading the first division himself, he joined battle with Nicanor.

24 With the Almighty as their ally, they slew more than nine thousand of the enemy, and wounded and disabled most of Nicanor's army, and forced them all to flee. [25] They captured the money of those who had come to buy them as slaves. After pursuing them for some distance, they were obliged to return because the hour was late. [26] For it was the day before the sabbath, and for that reason they did not continue their pursuit. [27] And when they had collected the arms of the enemy and stripped them of their spoils, they kept the sabbath, giving great praise and thanks to the Lord, who had preserved them for that day and allotted it to them as the beginning of mercy. [28] After the sabbath they gave some of the spoils to those who had been tortured and to the widows and orphans, and distributed the rest among themselves and their children. [29] When they had done this, they made common supplication and besought the merciful Lord to be wholly reconciled with his servants.

8:16 Nicanor was sent by the king with a troop of 20,000 men to exterminate the entire population. He intended, however, to sell them into slavery. He called upon Phoenician slave traders to be present at the battle in order to receive their booty. 8:18 Judas' appeal is to faith as power. In the synagogue during the celebration of Hanukkah, the military significance of the event is minimized and the slogan or motto for the Hanukkah celebration is the text: "Not by might, nor by power, but by my spirit, says the Lord of hosts."

The Celebration of Hanukkah Is Instituted
2 Maccabees 10:1–8

10 Now Maccabeus and his followers, the Lord leading them on, recovered the temple and the city; [2] and they tore down the altars

which had been built in the public square by the foreigners, and also destroyed the sacred precincts. ³ They purified the sanctuary, and made another altar of sacrifice; then, striking fire out of flint, they offered sacrifices, after a lapse of two years, and they burned incense and lighted lamps and set out the bread of the Presence. ⁴ And when they had done this, they fell prostrate and besought the Lord that they might never again fall into such misfortunes, but that, if they should ever sin, they might be disciplined by him with forbearance and not be handed over to blasphemous and barbarous nations. ⁵ It happened that on the same day on which the sanctuary had been profaned by the foreigners, the purification of the sanctuary took place, that is, on the twenty-fifth day of the same month, which was Chislev. ⁶ And they celebrated it for eight days with rejoicing, in the manner of the feast of booths, remembering how not long before, during the feast of booths, they had been wandering in the mountains and caves like wild animals. ⁷ Therefore bearing ivy-wreathed wands and beautiful branches and also fronds of palm, they offered hymns of thanksgiving to him who had given success to the purifying of his own holy place. ⁸ They decreed by public ordinance and vote that the whole nation of the Jews should observe these days every year.

10:3 *After a lapse of two years:* the actual time was three years.
10:6 See discussion of Hanukkah at 1 Maccabees 4:52 ff. One of the purposes of 2 Maccabees may have been to impress on Jews the duty to celebrate this feast.

Judas Intercedes for the Fallen Sinners
2 Maccabees 12:32–45

32 After the feast called Pentecost, they hastened against Gorgias, the governor of Idumea. ³³ And he came out with three thousand infantry and four hundred cavalry. ³⁴ When they joined battle, it happened that a few of the Jews fell. ³⁵ But a certain Dositheus, one of Bacenor's men, who was on horseback and was a strong man, caught hold of Gorgias, and grasping his cloak was dragging him off by main strength, wishing to take the accursed man alive, when one of the Thracian horsemen bore down upon him and cut off his arm; so Gorgias escaped and reached Marisa.

36 As Esdris and his men had been fighting for a long time and were weary, Judas called upon the Lord to show himself their ally and leader in the battle. ³⁷ In the language of their fathers he raised the battle cry, with hymns; then he charged against Gorgias' men when they were not expecting it, and put them to flight.

38 Then Judas assembled his army and went to the city of

Adullam. As the seventh day was coming on, they purified themselves according to the custom, and they kept the sabbath there.

39 On the next day, as by that time it had become necessary, Judas and his men went to take up the bodies of the fallen and to bring them back to lie with their kinsmen in the sepulchres of their fathers. [40] Then under the tunic of every one of the dead they found sacred tokens of the idols of Jamnia, which the law forbids the Jews to wear. And it became clear to all that this was why these men had fallen. [41] So they all blessed the ways of the Lord, the righteous Judge, who reveals the things that are hidden; [42] and they turned to prayer, beseeching that the sin which had been committed might be wholly blotted out. And the noble Judas exhorted the people to keep themselves free from sin, for they had seen with their own eyes what had happened because of the sin of those who had fallen. [43] He also took up a collection, man by man, to the amount of two thousand drachmas of silver, and sent it to Jerusalem to provide for a sin offering. In doing this he acted very well and honorably, taking account of the resurrection. [44] For if he were not expecting that those who had fallen would rise again, it would have been superfluous and foolish to pray for the dead. [45] But if he was looking to the splendid reward that is laid up for those who fall asleep in godliness, it was a holy and pious thought. Therefore he made atonement for the dead, that they might be delivered from their sin.

12:40 It was forbidden to wear amulets or to worship idols in any way; cf. Deuteronomy 7:26. 12:42 This is the earliest and clearest expression in biblical literature of the idea that the souls of men undergo a period of purification, and that the prayers of friends and relatives can serve an expiatory purpose. 12:43–45 This passage is the basis for Mass on behalf of the dead; one musical setting for this Mass is Brahms' *German Requiem*.

Judas Defeats Antiochus Eupator
2 Maccabees 13:1–17

13 In the one hundred and forty-ninth year word came to Judas and his men that Anti'ochus Eu'pator was coming with a great army aginst Jude'a, [2] and with him Lys'ias, his guardian, who had charge of the government. Each of them had a Greek force of one hundred and ten thousand infantry, five thousand three hundred cavalry, twenty-two elephants, and three hundred chariots armed with scythes.

3 Men·e·la'us also joined them and with utter hypocrisy urged An·ti'o-chus on, not for the sake of his country's welfare, but because he thought that he would be established in office. [4] But the

King of kings aroused the anger of An·ti'o·chus against the scoundrel; and when Lys'i·as informed him that this man was to blame for all the trouble, he ordered them to take him to Be·roe'a and to put him to death by the method which is the custom in that place. ⁵ For there is a tower in that place, fifty cubits high, full of ashes, and it has a rim running around it which on all sides inclines precipitously into the ashes. ⁶ There they all push to destruction any man guilty of sacrilege or notorious for other crimes. ⁷ By such a fate it came about that Men·e·la'us the lawbreaker died, without even burial in the earth. ⁸ And this was eminently just; because he had committed many sins against the altar whose fire and ashes were holy, he met his death in ashes.

9 The king with barbarous arrogance was coming to show to the Jews things far worse than those that had been done in his father's time. ¹⁰ But when Judas heard of this, he ordered the people to call upon the Lord day and night, now if ever to help those who were on the point of being deprived of the law and their country and the holy temple, ¹¹ and not to let the people who had just begun to revive fall into the hands of the blasphemous Gentiles. ¹² When they had all joined in the same petition and had besought the merciful Lord with weeping and fasting and lying prostrate for three days without ceasing, Judas exhorted them and ordered them to stand ready.

13 After consulting privately with the elders, he determined to march out and decide the matter by the help of God before the king's army could enter Ju·de'a and get possession of the city. ¹⁴ So, committing the decision to the Creator of the world and exhorting his men to fight nobly to the death for the laws, temple, city, country, and commonwealth, he pitched his camp near Mo'dein. ¹⁵ He gave his men the watchword, "God's victory," and with a picked force of the bravest young men, he attacked the king's pavilion at night and slew as many as two thousand men in the camp. He stabbed the leading elephant and its rider. ¹⁶ In the end they filled the camp with terror and confusion and withdrew in triumph. ¹⁷ This happened, just as day was dawning, because the Lord's help protected him.

THE NEW TESTAMENT

Introduction

The New Testament is a library of twenty-seven books. In length, they are like pamphlets and letters. They tell about Jesus Christ and his teaching, his suffering, death and resurrection, the church he founded and the experiences of his early disciples. Christians who live by the New Testament believe its message to be relevant for all time.

The literature of the New Testament is varied and unusual in form, deserving study in any survey of Western literature. Its translations have influenced the prose and poetry and common speech of the past five hundred years. Its stories have inspired creative artists and musicians, and their works have contributed to the rich fullness of our culture.

In a pluralistic society it is important, also, to know something about the varied uses made of the Bible by the different religious groups. We gain thereby in appreciation of the common heritage shared by all in the Bible, and we are enriched by an understanding of the reasons and the meaning for the differences in interpretation preserved by each group.

Finally, the New Testament is a source of concepts that have influenced our social behavior and the institutional forms of our society. Here the reader will find ideas that have shaped our society and our understandings of democracy, freedom and justice. Attitudes towards birth, sex, marriage, life and death have sources here. We live more intelligently in our society when we are aware of these influences on man's strivings.

The title, "New" Testament, reveals that it builds upon and complements an earlier or "Old" Testament. The Latin word *Testament* means "covenant." The New Testament is understood only if seen in the context of God's covenant with Israel recorded in the Hebrew Bible. Jesus, Paul and other early disciples of Jesus were Jews. The Christian Church was organized in the Jewish synagogue. Holy Scripture for the early Christians was the Law, the Prophets and the Writings of the Jews. Throughout the New Testament Christian concepts are seen to be rooted within, and to be extensions of, Hebraic thought. The followers of Jesus believed that Jesus had fulfilled the Law and that Christians did not need to become Jews by the flesh; the Jews who became Christians felt they remained Israel in spirit.

Jews who rejected the claim that Jesus was the Messiah resented Christian assertions that God had established a New Covenant with a New Israel, the Church, through Christ, His son. A record of the conflict as seen from a Christian point of view is preserved in the Acts of the Apostles (chapter 15) and in Paul's Letter to the Galatians. So sharp is the discussion at some points that it requires effort to keep before us the large area of practices and ideals shared together by synagogue and church. It is easy to come away with distorted conceptions of the Jews and the value of the Mosaic Law to which Jews remained faithful. Exactly this happened in early Church history; Church fathers were compelled to condemn a movement to separate the Old from the New Testament. Both collections of books are now part of Sacred Literature for the Christian.

In recent years some Jews have come to appreciate how well the Church nurtured within its New Testament many precious ideals of Judaism. Just as Christians cannot fully understand their faith without a knowledge of the Hebrew Bible, so Jews without a knowledge of the Christian Bible will fail to appreciate how much of the Hebraic component in Western civilization is transmitted through the New Testament.

The milieu of the New Testament, however, is different from that of the Hebrew Bible. One, composed in classic Hebrew over a period of a thousand years, includes history, codes of law, prophetic orations, poetry and reflective literature; it is the spiritual record of a people and God's dealings with them. The other, composed in popular Greek, written within a period of one hundred years, less than one-third in size, centers upon the life and significance of one person. Together, Christians believe, they reveal God's word to mankind and set forth ideals upon which our civilization endures.

The Gospels

The word "gospel" is an Old English term for "glad tidings" or "good news." The Gospels are the books that tell the good news about Jesus, "Son of God" and "Son of Man." The four Gospels, at the beginning of the New Testament, each stress certain aspects of Jesus' life and teaching. The Christian Church considered these gospels as inspired (coming from God as their principal author) and belonging to the canon (authorized collection) of the New Testament. Other so-called gospels have come down from ancient times—e.g., the Gospel of Thomas, the Gospel of James—but they have never been included in the canon.

Originally the gospel was not a book but an announcement, a message that was proclaimed and preached. From the Greek word for the gospel or good news, *euangelion,* come our words evangelism, evangelist and evangelical. The gospel was a presentation of what Jesus preached, together with the testimony of his apostles speaking after his death. At first this message was spoken, not written down. Eventually, at various times and in different places in the first century, it was written down in the four presentations we know as the Four Gospels.

The Synoptic Gospels

The first three Gospels are called "synoptic" Gospels because they follow the same general arrangement. If placed in parallel columns, so that they can be "seen together" (the meaning of the Greek word *synoptic*) they present a common view. In this synoptic pattern the outline of Mark, taken over by Matthew and Luke, appears to be basic. There is also a body of material not found in Mark but common to Matthew and Luke which presupposes still another source. Furthermore, Matthew and Luke each make distinctive additions. Even when presenting the same episode in much the same way, Matthew, Mark and Luke reveal differences that show the individuality of the human authors.

The Gospel according to Matthew

The name "Matthew" in Hebrew means "the gift of the Lord." The person to whom this Gospel is traditionally attributed was also called Levi. He was a publican, that is a tax collector or customs official, until Jesus called him to join the group of apostles.

An old tradition says that Matthew died a martyr in Ethiopia for his beliefs. According to tradition, he wrote his Gospel in Hebrew (which would mean Aramaic, the language spoken by the people in Jesus' time and region) around the year A.D. 60. The Aramaic text has not been preserved. According to tradition, it was soon translated into the Greek that has come to us in the various English translations. Some modern scholars challenge the attribution to the disciple, and contend from internal evidence that this Gospel should be dated about A.D. 85.

The Gospel according to Matthew appropriately comes first in the New Testament: it links the new message with Jewish traditions. It had the greatest influence in the early Church. It is the fullest of the synoptic Gospels. We present Matthew's account, therefore, more fully than those of Mark and Luke.

The Gospel according to Matthew gathers sayings of Jesus into five great sermons or collections. The first of these is the Sermon on the Mount, a summary of the religious and ethical teachings of Jesus. There is a theory that the five collections were intended to parallel the five books of Moses. Matthew's Gospel regards Jesus as the royal Messiah promised to the Jewish people, and the Church that Jesus founded as heir to the covenant promises that God made to Israel.

Prologue: Family Tree

Matthew traces Jesus' lineage back to King David because he regards Jesus as the son of David in whom God's promise of a messianic king is realized, and back to Abraham, the patriarch, because he regards Jesus as the "seed of Abraham" through whom God's blessings will come to all nations. Matthew seeks to establish Jesus' right to "the throne of David."

In Christian art, St. Matthew is sometimes represented by the symbol of an animal with a human face. The prophet Ezekiel saw four symbolic animals in a vision. Early Christians saw them as types of the four evangelists. Matthew is connected with the animal of the human face because he begins his Gospel by tracing the human descent of Jesus.

The liturgies of the churches generally turn to Luke's fuller account of the birth and childhood of Jesus for Christmas readings.

Verses 1–16 of Matthew's first chapter are used for the Feast of the Nativity of the Blessed Virgin Mary (September 8).

Matthew 1:1–6, 12–17

1 The book of the genealogy of Jesus Christ, the son of David, the son of Abraham.

2 Abraham was the father of Isaac, and Isaac the father of Jacob, and Jacob the father of Judah and his brothers, and Judah the father of Perez and Zerah by Tamar, and Perez the father of Hezron, and Hezron the father of Ram, ⁴ and Ram the father of Ammin′adab, and Ammin′adab the father of Nahshon, and Nahshon the father of Salmon, ⁵ and Salmon the father of Bo′az by Rahab, and Bo′az the father of Obed by Ruth, and Obed the father of Jesse, ⁶ and Jesse the father of David the king.

12 And after the deportation to Babylon: Jechoni′ah was the father of She-al′ti-el, and She-al′ti-el the father of Zerub′babel, ¹³ and Zerub′babel the father of Abi′ud, and Abi′ud the father of Eli′akim, and Eli′akim the father of Azor, ¹⁴ and Azor the father of Zadok, and Zadok the father of Achim, and Achim the father of Eli′ud, ¹⁵ and Eli′ud the father of Elea′zar, and Elea′zar the father of Matthan, and Matthan the father of Jacob, ¹⁶ and Jacob the father of Joseph the husband of Mary, of whom Jesus was born, who is called Christ.

17 So all the generations from Abraham to David were fourteen generations, and from David to the deportation to Babylon fourteen generations, and from the deportation to Babylon to the Christ fourteen generations.

1:12 The word "Jesus" is Greek (and Latin) for the Hebrew "Joshua," meaning "the Lord is salvation," or "the Lord will save." "Christ" is Greek for the Hebrew *Moshiah,* meaning "Messiah," or "anointed one." From early Christian times to the present, the monogram ☧ (often X) has been used in art, on altars and vestments. X and P are the first two letters of the name of Christ in Greek, *chi* and *rho,* so the symbol is often called the Chi Rho. The Emperor Constantine put the symbol on his new standard when Christianity became the official religion of the Roman Empire. The monogram IHS represents the first three letters in the Greek spelling of Jesus. **1:16** Matthew's genealogy, like Luke's, traces Jesus' ancestry through Joseph, who, from the legal point of view, stood *in loco parentis.*

The Child Is Born
Matthew 1:18–25

18 Now the birth of Jesus Christ took place in this way. When his mother Mary had been betrothed to Joseph, before they came

together she was found to be with child of the Holy Spirit; [19] and her husband Joseph, being a just man and unwilling to put her to shame, resolved to divorce her quietly. [20] But as he considered this, behold, an angel of the Lord appeared to him in a dream, saying, "Joseph, son of David, do not fear to take Mary your wife, for that which is conceived in her is of the Holy Spirit; [21] she will bear a son, and you shall call his name Jesus, for he will save his people from their sins." [22] All this took place to fulfil what the Lord had spoken by the Prophet:

[23] "Behold, a virgin shall conceive and bear a son,
and his name shall be called Emman'uel"

(which means, God with us). [24] When Joseph woke from sleep, he did as the angel of the Lord commanded him; he took his wife, [25] but knew her not until she had borne a son; and he called his name Jesus.

1:18 Verses 18–21 are read on the Vigil of Christmas (December 24), and the Feast of St. Joseph (March 19). The special veneration of Joseph in the Catholic Church is founded largely on this Gospel passage. Catholics have felt that, by his marriage with the Virgin Mary, Joseph had certain rights over the child Jesus and his position of dignity called for special veneration. In 1621, Pope Gregory XV extended the Feast of St. Joseph to the whole Church. In 1870 Pope Pius IX proclaimed Joseph "Protector of the Universal Church." Pope John XXIII entrusted the Second Vatican Council to Joseph's patronage and inserted into the most sacred part of the Mass a reference to "blessed Joseph, spouse of the Virgin Mary." St. Joseph has long been considered patron of the dying, because he is presumed to have died a happy death in the arms of Jesus and Mary, and patron of contemplative souls, because of his close union with the holiest of persons. **1:23** Isaiah 7:14. **1:25** "Know" in the Bible often means, as here, "to have sexual intercourse." Many Christians take this verse (and others that we shall see) as evidence that Mary had other children by Joseph; others hold that Mary always remained a virgin.

Wise Men Visit the Infant
Matthew 2:1–12

2 Now when Jesus was born in Bethlehem of Judea in the days of Herod the king, behold, wise men from the East came to Jerusalem, saying, [2] "Where is he who has been born king of the Jews? For we have seen his star in the East, and have come to worship him." [3] When Herod the king heard this, he was troubled, and all Jerusalem with him; [4] and assembling all the chief priests and scribes of the people, he inquired of them where the Christ was to be born.

⁵ They told him, "In Bethlehem of Judea; for so it is written by the prophet:

⁶ 'And you, O Bethlehem, in the land of Judah,
   are by no means least among the rulers of Judah;
   for from you shall come a ruler
   who will govern my people Israel.' "

7 Then Herod summoned the wise men secretly and ascertained from them what time the star appeared; ⁸ and he sent them to Bethlehem, saying, "Go and search diligently for the child, and when you have found him bring me word, that I too may come and worship him." ⁹ When they had heard the king they went their way; and lo, the star which they had seen in the East went before them, till it came to rest over the place where the child was. ¹⁰ When they saw the star, they rejoiced exceedingly with great joy; ¹¹ and going into the house they saw the child with Mary his mother, and they fell down and worshiped him. Then, opening their treasures, they offered him gifts, gold and frankincense and myrrh. ¹² And being warned in a dream not to return to Herod, they departed to their own country by another way.

2:1 This section of Matthew's Gospel is the foundation of the Feast of the Epiphany (i.e., manifestation or showing forth of a king to the people; in this case, Christ revealing himself to Gentiles, members of the non-Jewish world). The Bible account does not say there were three wise men; devout imagination has added such details as that they were kings, that their names were Casper (Gaspar), Melchior and Balthasar, that one had a long beard, one a short beard and one no beard, and that they represented different branches of the human family; black, white, brown. Matthew simply calls them "magi" (learned men, members of a class that originated in ancient Persia). Attempts have been made to identify the guiding star of the magi with some known comet or conjunction of stars. Many people put a star at the top of their Christmas tree, to represent the star of Bethlehem, as it has come to be called. The poinsettia is a popular flower at Christmas time because it looks like a flaming red star and is thus reminiscent of the star of Bethlehem. In the churches of the East, the visit of the magi is celebrated with Christmas (December 25); Epiphany (January 6) is observed there as the great feast of Christ's baptism (hence the ceremony of diving for a cross thrown into the water on that day). The gifts brought by the wise men have been regarded as symbolic: gold denoting kingship; frankincense denoting divinity; myrrh (a burial spice) denoting that the child was marked to die. **2:2** Some Rabbinic scholars have seen in this reference a homiletical illustration of Numbers 24:17, "There shall come a star out of Jacob," which passage was understood by some to be a messianic reference (*Midrash Lekach Tov*). **2:6** Micah 5:2.

The Holy Family Escapes the Wrath of Herod
Matthew 2:13–23

13 Now when they had departed, behold, an angel of the Lord appeared to Joseph in a dream and said, "Rise, take the child and his mother, and flee to Egypt, and remain there till I tell you; for Herod is about to search for the child, to destroy him." [14] And he rose and took the child and his mother by night, and departed to Egypt, [15] and remained there until the death of Herod. This was to fulfil what the Lord had spoken by the prophet, "Out of Egypt have I called my son."

16 Then Herod, when he saw that he had been tricked by the wise men, was in a furious rage, and he sent and killed all the male children in Bethlehem and in all that region who were two years old or under, according to the time which he had ascertained from the wise men. [17] Then was fulfilled what was spoken by the prophet Jeremiah:
[18] "A voice was heard in Ramah,
     wailing and loud lamentation,
     Rachel weeping for her children;
     she refused to be consoled,
     because they were no more."

19 But when Herod died, behold, an angel of the Lord appeared in a dream to Joseph in Egypt, saying, [20] "Rise, take the child and his mother, and go to the land of Israel, for those who sought the child's life are dead." [21] And he rose and took the child and his mother, and went to the land of Israel. [22] But when he heard that Archela'us reigned over Judea in place of his father Herod, he was afraid to go there, and being warned in a dream he withdrew to the district of Galilee. [23] And he went and dwelt in a city called Nazareth, that what was spoken by the prophets might be fulfilled, "He shall be called a Nazarene."

2:15 Hosea 11:1; cf. Exodus 4:22.
2:16 Holy Innocents Day (December 28) commemorates the event described here. Ramah, north of Jerusalem, was a transit point for Jews being deported into exile, as in the days of Jeremiah. The prophet records that mother Rachel, who had died in childbirth and was buried in Ramah, wept for Jewish exiles. God was so moved by her prayers that He assured the Hebrews that the exiled would one day be restored. Matthew invokes this tradition of Rachel, as the sorrowing mother (Jeremiah 31:15), and applies Jeremiah's verses about her to the innocents slaughtered in the time of Herod. **2:19** By modern calculations Herod died in 4 B.C.; Jesus would therefore be born about 6 B.C. Our calendars follow the calculation of a monk (about A.D. 500) whose sources were less complete than ours.

John the Baptist Preaches Repentance
Matthew 3:1–6

3 In those days came John the Baptist, preaching in the wilderness of Judea, ²"Repent, for the kingdom of heaven is at hand." ³For this is he who was spoken of by the prophet Isaiah when he said,
"The voice of one crying in the wilderness:
Prepare the way of the Lord,
make his paths straight."
⁴Now John wore a garment of camel's hair; and a leather girdle around his waist; and his food was locusts and wild honey. ⁵Then went out to him Jerusalem and all Judea and all the region about the Jordan, ⁶and they were baptized by him in the river Jordan, confessing their sins.

· **3:1** Of the four Gospel writers, Luke makes the most serious attempt to place his narration in historic context. In his account of this event (Luke 3:1) he explains the phrase "in those days" to mean in the fifteenth year of the reign of Tiberius Caesar, who reigned from A.D. 14–37. Luke also mentions the ruling governors of Judea and the nearby regions. John is called the Baptist because he baptized (i.e., used water as a sign of purification or cleansing). **3:2** John held that the end-time spoken of by the prophets was near at hand. In describing this, Matthew uses the Hebraic formula "kingdom of heaven," following the pattern of Jewish reticence in the use of the name God (the other Gospels use "kingdom of God"). The prophetic tradition had emphasized the power of repentance in achieving Israel's reconciliation with God. The Talmud preserved that religious conviction: "If Israel were to repent they would straightway be redeemed" (*Sanhedrin* 97b). "Great is repentance which hastens the redemption" (*Yoma* 86b). John here applies the concept to the individual, promising the Kingdom to those who repent. **3:3** Isaiah 40:3, 3:4; 2 Kings 1:8.

John Baptizes Jesus
Matthew 3:11–17

11 "I baptize you with water for repentance, but he who is coming after me is mightier than I, whose sandals I am not worthy to carry; he will baptize you with the Holy Spirit and with fire. ¹²His winnowing fork is in his hand, and he will clear his threshing floor and gather his wheat into the granary, but the chaff he will burn with unquenchable fire."

13 Then Jesus came from Galilee to the Jordan to John, to be baptized by him. ¹⁴John would have prevented him, saying, "I need to be baptized by you, and do you come to me?" ¹⁵But Jesus answered him, "Let it be so now; for thus it is fitting for us to fulfil all righteousness." Then he consented. [16] And when Jesus was baptized, he went up immediately from the water, and behold, the heavens were opened and he saw the Spirit of God descending like a dove, and alighting on him; [17] and lo, a voice from heaven, saying, "This is my beloved Son, with whom I am well pleased."

3:11 Both sprinkling with water and immersion were scripturally enjoined methods for cleansing from sin. The Jews required baptism of prospective converts. The Talmud describes those who undergo baptism "as children newly born" (*Yebamoth* 22a). **3:16** Paintings of this scene often represent the Father by a hand reaching down from the clouds. This seems to be the earliest symbolic representation of the First Person of the Trinity in Christian art. The dove is a traditional symbol for the Holy Spirit, Third Person of the Trinity. This first appearance of Jesus as an adult has attracted the attention of artists from early times. Controversy about the personal appearance of Jesus had a very important influence on the art of the East and the West. In the West a tradition developed that Jesus was the "fairest of the children of men" and he was frequently depicted as light haired. In the East, Byzantine Greeks held that Jesus was not handsome. This disagreement largely explains the difference between Byzantine and Western treatment of sacred subjects. In the West, paintings of Jesus have now become more and more realistic; he is often made to look like a fellow-countryman of the artist. In the East to this day, however, Jesus is represented in the conventional severe dignity developed by early Byzantine artists. **3:16–17** The symbolism of the dove for the spirit of God was current among Jews. In explaining the words for Genesis 1:2, "The spirit of God hovered over the face of the waters," the Rabbis taught: God's spirit was "like a dove brooding over her young, partly touching them and partly not touching them" (*Chagigah* 15a). Similarly since the dove is a most faithful bird that never abandons her mate, the Rabbis also evoked it as an image of the Congregation of Israel which never betrays its God (*Song of Songs Rabbah* 1).

Jesus Meets Temptation

As he considered the kind of ministry his would be, Jesus—like Moses and Elijah before him—"fasted forty days and forty nights." Tempted with physical security—to assuage his hunger by turning stones into bread—Jesus quotes Deuteronomy 8:3. Tempted with the possibility of popular favor by resorting to spectacular achievement—to leap from the pinnacle of the Temple—Jesus refrains from invoking God's powers for such a mundane purpose, quoting Deuteronomy 6:16. Tempted with political power—to win "all the kingdoms of the world"—Jesus quotes Deuteronomy 6:13. His life would be dedicated to God alone. He would seek neither material riches, popular esteem, nor worldly power.

Jesus acts upon a principle enunciated by the Rabbis that evil is to be met by confronting it with the word of God. Theologians have discussed what the temptation shows about Christ's human nature; Hebrews 4:15 refers to him as "one who in every respect has been tempted as we are, yet without sinning." Young people deciding upon a career, must, like Jesus, face the question of what is worth living for.

Matthew 4:1–17

4 Then Jesus was led up by the Spirit into the wilderness to be tempted by the devil. [2] And he fasted forty days and forty nights, and afterward he was hungry. [3] And the tempter came and said to him, "If you are the Son of God, command these stones to become loaves of bread." [4] But he answered, "It is written,

'Man shall not live by bread alone,
but by every word that proceeds from the mouth of God.' "
[5] Then the devil took him to the holy city, and set him on the pinnacle of the temple, [6] and said to him, "If you are the Son of God, throw yourself down; for it is written,

'He will give his angels charge of you,'
and
'On their hands they will bear you up,
lest you strike your foot against a stone.' "
[7] Jesus said to him, "Again it is written, 'You shall not tempt the Lord your God.' " [8] Again, the devil took him to a very high mountain, and showed him all the kingdoms of the world and the glory of them; [9] and he said to him, "All these I will give you, if you will fall down and worship me." [10] Then Jesus said to him, "Begone, Satan! for it is written,

'You shall worship the Lord your God
and him only shall you serve.' "
[11] Then the devil left him, and behold, angels came and ministered to him.

12 Now when he heard that John had been arrested, he withdrew into Galilee; [13] and leaving Nazareth he went and dwelt in Caper'na-um by the sea, in the territory of Zeb'ulun and Naph'tali, [14] that what was spoken by the prophet Isaiah might be fulfilled:

[15] "The land of Zeb'ulun and the land of Naph'tali,
toward the sea, across the Jordan,
Galilee of the Gentiles—
[16] the people who sat in darkness
have seen a great light,
and for those who sat in the region and shadow of death light has dawned."

¹⁷ From that time Jesus began to preach, saying, "Repent, for the kingdom of heaven is at hand."

4:1 On the devil, see note on Job 1:6. This section (verses 1–11) is read on the first Sunday of Lent. Originally the forty days of Lent were counted from this Sunday. **4:13** A synagogue dating from the end of the second century A.D. has been excavated in the city of Capernaum and reconstructed by the Franciscan Fathers. It is a favorite visiting place in the modern state of Israel. **4:15** Isaiah 9:1–2.

Jesus Calls His First Disciples
Matthew 4:18–25

18 As he walked by the Sea of Galilee, he saw two brothers, Simon who is called Peter and Andrew his brother, casting a net into the sea; for they were fishermen. ¹⁹ And he said to them, "Follow me, and I will make you fishers of men." ²⁰ Immediately they left their nets and followed him. ²¹ And going on from there he saw two other brothers, James the son of Zeb'edee and John his brother, in the boat with Zeb'edee their father, mending their nets, and he called them. ²² Immediately they left the boat and their father, and followed him.

23 And he went about all Galilee, teaching in their synagogues and preaching the gospel of the kingdom and healing every disease and every infirmity among the people. ²⁴ So his fame spread throughout all Syria, and they brought him all the sick, those afflicted with various diseases and pains, demoniacs, epileptics, and paralytics, and he healed them. ²⁵ And great crowds followed him from Galilee and the Decap'olis and Jerusalem and Judea and from beyond the Jordan.

4:18 Verses 18–22 are read on the Feast of St. Andrew (November 30). Andrew is said to have died, in Greece, on the special form of cross (x-shaped) which is named after him. He is the patron saint of Scotland. **4:23** In such passages one finds scriptural motivation for churches and church members in sponsoring hospitals and medical care plans. **4:24** *Demoniacs:* persons regarded as controlled, dominated or "possessed" by evil forces (demons).

The Sermon on the Mount
Matthew 5:1–48; 6:1–8

5 Seeing the crowds, he went up on the mountain, and when he sat down his disciples came to him. ² And he opened his mouth and taught them, saying:

3 "Blessed are the poor in spirit, for theirs is the kingdom of heaven.

4 "Blessed are those who mourn, for they shall be comforted.

5 "Blessed are the meek, for they shall inherit the earth.

6 "Blessed are those who hunger and thirst for righteousness, for they shall be satisfied.

7 "Blessed are the merciful, for they shall obtain mercy.

8 "Blessed are the pure in heart, for they shall see God.

9 "Blessed are the peacemakers, for they shall be called sons of God.

10 "Blessed are those who are persecuted for righteousness' sake, for theirs is the kingdom of heaven.

11 "Blessed are you when men revile you and persecute you and utter all kinds of evil against you falsely on my account. 12 Rejoice and be glad, for your reward is great in heaven, for so men persecuted the prophets who were before you.

13 "You are the salt of the earth; but if salt has lost its taste, how shall its saltness be restored? It is no longer good for anything except to be thrown out and trodden under foot by men.

14 "You are the light of the world. A city set on a hill cannot be hid. 15 Nor do men light a lamp and put it under a bushel, but on a stand, and it gives light to all in the house. 16 Let your light so shine before men, that they may see your good works and give glory to your Father who is in heaven.

17 "Think not that I have come to abolish the law and the prophets; I have come not to abolish them but to fulfil them. 18 For truly, I say to you, till heaven and earth pass away, not an iota, not a dot, will pass from the law until all is accomplished. 19 Whoever then relaxes one of the least of these commandments and teaches men so, shall be called least in the kingdom of heaven; but he who does them and teaches them shall be called great in the kingdom of heaven. 20 For I tell you, unless your righteousness exceeds that of the scribes and Pharisees, you will never enter the kingdom of heaven.

21 "You have heard that it was said to the men of old, 'You shall not kill; and whoever kills shall be liable to judgment.' 22 But I say to you that every one who is angry with his brother shall be liable to judgment; whoever insults his brother shall be liable to the council, and whoever says, 'You fool!' shall be liable to the hell of fire. 23 So if you are offering your gift at the altar, and there remember that your brother has something against you, 24 leave your gift there before the altar and go; first be reconciled to your brother, and then come and offer your gift. 25 Make friends quickly with your accuser, while you are going with him to court, lest your accuser hand you over to the judge, and the judge to the guard, and you be put in

prison; [26] truly, I say to you, you will never get out till you have paid the last penny.

27 "You have heard that it was said, 'You shall not commit adultery.' [28] But I say to you that every one who looks at a woman lustfully has already committed adultery with her in his heart. [29] If your right eye causes you to sin, pluck it out and throw it away; it is better that you lose one of your members than that your whole body be thrown into hell. [30] And if your right hand causes you to sin, cut it off and throw it away; it is better that you lose one of your members than that your whole body go into hell.

31 "It was also said, 'Whoever divorces his wife, let him give her a certificate of divorce.' [32] But I say to you that every one who divorces his wife, except on the ground of unchastity, makes her an adulteress; and whoever marries a divorced woman commits adultery.

33 "Again you have heard that it was said to the men of old, 'You shall not swear falsely, but shall perform to the Lord what you have sworn.' [34] But I say to you, Do not swear at all, either by heaven, for it is the throne of God, [35] or by the earth, for it is his footstool, or by Jerusalem, for it is the city of the great King. [36] And do not swear by your head, for you cannot make one hair white or black. [37] Let what you say be simply 'Yes' or 'No'; anything more than this comes from evil.

38 "You have heard that it was said, 'An eye for an eye and a tooth for a tooth.' [39] But I say to you, Do not resist one who is evil. But if any one strikes you on the right cheek, turn to him the other also; [40] and if any one would sue you and take your coat, let him have your cloak as well; [41] and if any one forces you to go one mile, go with him two miles. [42] Give to him who begs from you, and do not refuse him who would borrow from you.

43 "You have heard that it was said, 'You shall love your neighbor and hate your enemy.' [44] But I say to you, Love your enemies and pray for those who persecute you, [45] so that you may be sons of your Father who is in heaven; for he makes his sun rise on the evil and on the good, and sends rain on the just and on the unjust. [46] For if you love those who love you, what reward have you? Do not even the tax collectors do the same? [47] And if you salute only your brethren, what more are you doing than others? Do not even the Gentiles do the same? [48] You, therefore, must be perfect, as your heavenly Father is perfect.

6 "Beware of practicing your piety before men in order to be seen by them; for then you will have no reward from your Father who is in heaven.

2 "Thus when you give alms, sound no trumpet before you, as the hypocrites do in the synagogues and in the streets, that they may be praised by men. Truly, I say to you, they have their reward. ³ But when you give alms, do not let your left hand know what your right hand is doing, ⁴ so that your alms may be in secret; and your Father who sees in secret will reward you.

5 "And when you pray, you must not be like the hypocrites; for they love to stand and pray in the synagogues and at the street corners, that they may be seen by men. Truly, I say to you, they have their reward. ⁶ But when you pray, go into your room and shut the door and pray to your Father who is in secret; and your Father who sees in secret will reward you.

7 "And in praying do not heap up empty phrases as the Gentiles do; for they think that they will be heard for their many words. ⁸ Do not be like them, for your Father knows what you need before you ask him.

5:1 Matthew describes Jesus as speaking from a "mountain," perhaps to suggest Jesus' authority as lawgiver, in an image associated by Jews with Moses (cf. Exodus 19:3). Verses 1–12 form the Gospel for the Feast of All Saints (November 1). 5:3 The blessings which Jesus speaks are commonly called the Beatitudes ("beatitude" is perfect blessedness or happiness). These sayings, paralleled in the Old Testament, indicate Jesus' mastery of the Scriptures. *Poor in spirit.* Compare Isaiah 66:2, "But this is the man to whom I will look. He that is humble and contrite in spirit and trembles at my work." *Kingdom of heaven.* Compare Daniel 2:44. Matthew, whose Jewishness led him to avoid mention of the divine name, uses *kingdom of heaven* where the other evangelists use *kingdom of God*." In Christian use the *kingdom of God* seems to represent God's reign over freely surrendered hearts. The Hebrew concept of the kingdom includes a national restoration and material blessings for the faithful. Jesus' emphasis is upon the individual's ability to achieve the kingdom through faith, a spiritual concept. 5:4 *Comforted:* compare Psalm 23:4, "Even though I walk through the valley of the shadow of death. . . . Thy rod and Thy staff they comfort me." 5:5 *Meek:* compare Psalm 37:11, "But the meek shall possess the land. . . ." 5:7 *Merciful:* compare the Talmudic teaching: "He who has compassion upon men, upon him God has compassion. And upon him who has no compassion, upon him God has no compassion" (*Sabbath* 151b). 5:8 *Pure in heart:* compare Psalm 73:1, "Truly God is good to the upright and to those who are pure in heart." 5:9 *Peacemaker:* compare Psalm 34:14, "Depart from evil and do good. Seek peace and pursue it." Whom would we consider peacemakers in our society? 5:10–11 *Persecuted for righteousness' sake:* compare Isaiah 51:7–8, "Fear not the reproach of men and be not dismayed at their revilings." **5:12** *Reward is great in Heaven:* The concept of a reward for the righteous in an afterlife fully emerged in Jewish religious thought only after the canon of the Hebrew Bible had been established. Some Rabbinic teachers, contemporaneous with Jesus, believed the righteous receive a reward in heaven. Seeking to locate that view within Scripture—just as the Gospel writers sought to justify their conviction that Jesus was the Christ from within Old Testament prophecy—the Rabbis elaborated on the verse "The commandment which I bid you do this day" (Deuteronomy 7:11): "It is inscribed 'To do' this day; but not 'to receive your reward this day.' So says David: 'How great is the reward which thou hast stored away (in an afterlife) for them that fear Thee.' " **5:13** Verses 13–19 make up the Gospel in the Mass of a Doctor of the Church. The Doctors (great teachers of the Church) include such well-known saints as Augustine, Ambrose, John Chrysostom, and Thomas Aquinas. **5:17** The statement of Jesus here and in verses 23–24 was based on the Jewish ritual law observed to this day in the synagogue: a man will not be forgiven his sins unless he first seeks reconciliation with the one he has aggrieved.

The Law and the Prophets, referring to the first two divisions of the Hebrew canon, was a common way of describing the Hebrew Scriptures. In saying that he came "Not to abolish" (that is, do away with) these "but to fulfill them" (that is, round them out, complete them), Jesus asserts that by his perfect obedience the will and purpose of God are exemplified. He is a law-abiding Jew; his freedom to criticize particularly rigid regulations was within the accepted tradition. His additional claim is that he fulfills messianic expectations by making them come true; on this claim Jews and Christians disagree to this day. **5:18** In other translations: "not one jot or one tittle," referring to the smallest letter of the Hebrew alphabet *(yod)* and one of the little parts or hooks of a Hebrew letter. **5:20** "Righteousness" (usually "justice" in Catholic translations) is, basically, conformity to God's will. The Scribes copied out and interpreted the sacred books. The Pharisees were members of a group who distinguished themselves by their religious devotion to the Law (see Index). Verses 20–24 are the Gospel for the Fifth Sunday after Pentecost. The liturgy of that Sunday stresses forgiveness. **5:12** The literary style used in these sentences is paralleled by Rabbinic interpretations of the Bible text. The Talmud includes a formula whereby the rabbi would quote a verse of Scripture, introducing it with the words—"I have *heard* it to mean . . ." offering the verse's literal meaning; then the rabbi would supplement or revise the literal sense of the first verse by contrasting it with a second verse; he would introduce the second verse with the Hebrew word *Amar,* "to say." For example: Commenting on the verse "And the Lord came down on Mt. Sinai" (Exodus 19:20), Rabbi Judah ha Nasi explains: "I might *hear* this according to its literal meaning; but thou must *say,*

"If the sun, one of the many servants of God may remain in its place, and nevertheless be effective beyond it, how much more He, by whose word the world came into being" *(Mekhilta)*. It is according to such a rabbinic formula: ye have *heard* . . . but I *say* (explicating a profounder understanding of Scripture) that Jesus teaches here. **5:21–26** *Angry . . . insults* Compare Proverbs 10:12. A parallel view is to be found in Talmudic literature: "All the divisions of hell rule over the angry man" *(Nedarim* 22a). **5:22** In 1755 John Wesley published *The New Testament with Notes, for Plain Unlettered Men who know only their Mother Tongue.* He stated in the 'preface: "The alterations are few and seemingly small: but they may be of considerable importance." One of the most significant of these "alterations" was at this verse which, in the King James Version, reads in part: 'Whosoever is angry with his brother without a cause shall be in danger of the judgment." Wesley recognized "without a cause" as the insertion of a copyist. His rendering anticipates the Revised Standard Version: "Whosoever is angry with his brother shall be liable to the judgment." Wesley added in a note: "Which of the prophets ever spake thus?" The council referred to here is the Sanhedrin, supreme court of Judea and final court of appeal for questions connected with the Mosaic Law. Some translations (e.g., Confraternity) have "Gehenna" for "hell." Gehenna is an English form of the Greek word used here. The Greek is, in turn, from the Hebrew for "Valley (Ge) of Hinnom," a valley to the south of Jerusalem, a sinister place because it was the site of earlier human sacrifice to Moloch, probably a common burial pit for criminals, and probably including a city dump with fires and smoke. Thus it became a symbol of eternal punishment in Jewish apocalyptic literature (e.g., Henoch, chapters 26–27) and, as here, in Christian books. **5:27–30** In traditional Jewish legal opinion a man is to be judged by what he does rather than by what he thinks. Jewish religious leaders were not unconcerned, however, with the inner life of a man. Thus two opinions are to be found in Talmudic literature. The traditional view: "Rabbi Nehamia said, if a man purposes to commit a sin God does not reckon it to him until he has done it. But if he purposes to fulfill a command, and although he has no opportunity to do it, God writes down to his credit at once, as if he did it" (Midrash on Psalm 30). Another view: "Immoral thoughts are worse than immoral deeds" *(Yoma* 29a). "He also is an adulterer who lusts with his eyes." *(Pes. Rabbah* 124b.) **5:32** Some Christians understand this verse to mean that adultery is legitimate grounds for a divorce. To others (Catholics especially) it means only that unfaithfulness justifies separation from bed and board, or that Christ is talking about divorce being permitted for a man and woman who are living in an invalid union (i.e., not a true marriage to begin with). **5:33–37** *Do not swear at all:* In this command Jesus went beyond Pharisaic opinion; his viewpoint is paralleled by that held by the Essenes.

Compare Ecclesiasticus 23:9: "Accustom not thy mouth to swearing.' To the degree that Jesus was warning men to speak truthfully, the Pharisaic tradition would agree: "Do not speak with your mouth what you do not mean in your heart . . . let your nay and yea be both righteous" (*Babba Bathra* 49a). **5:34** Some who interpret this verse strictly refuse to take an oath even in a court of justice; by laws of the United States they are permitted to make an "affirmation" instead. **5:37** Older translations: yea, yea; nay, nay. **5:38** Strict adherence to verses 38–39 and 44 has led some persons to register as "conscientious objectors" to military service. Laws of some countries respect freedom of conscience, permitting such objectors noncombatant or civilian public service. *Eye for an eye:* The Pharisees contemporary with Jesus had legislated that the Scriptural text, an eye for an eye, means "payment for money" (*Babba Kama* 83b). The Sadducees who denied the oral law and held to the literal word of the Bible may have been the subject of this criticism by Jesus. **5:39** *Do not resist . . . evil.* Among Jews, the Essenes were closest to this viewpoint, while the Zealots who sought to achieve the Kingdom through violence were furthest removed. Compare Proverbs 20:22. Verses 39–40 are paralleled by the Talmudic expression: "A righteous man must be among those who are insulted but do not insult, who hear themselves reviled without answering" (*Gittin* 36b). **5:41** Soldiers in the Roman army of occupation could require citizens to carry their pack a distance of one mile, just as today the police have authority to commandeer an automobile needed to discharge their duties. **5:43** Exodus 12:49 directs that "There shall be one law for the native and for the stranger who sojourns among you." A command to "hate your enemy" is found nowhere in Hebrew law. See also Leviticus 19:18. (In Exodus 23:4–5, a man was bidden to lift his enemy's ass if it is lying under a burden, and to return a lost ass to the owner. The Rabbis deduced that if a man is required to be kind to the dumb animal of his enemy he must certainly also be respectful of the dignity of the person. See also Proverbs 25:21.) Perhaps Jesus was mindful of the enmity expressed in Psalm 137:7–9; or perhaps the matter has been clarified by the recent discovery of the Dead Sea Scrolls, documents revealing the life of a separatist sect contemporary with Jesus and the New Testament. One of these documents, *The Manual of Discipline*, requires all adherents "to love all the children of light . . . and to hate all the children of darkness"; "to bear unremitting hatred towards all men of ill repute," and "to keep in seclusion from them." **5:48** King James Version: Be ye therefore perfect, even as your Father which is in heaven is perfect. **6:2** Alms . . . in secret. A parallel view is to be found in Talmudic literature. "He who gives alms in secret is greater than Moses" (*Babba Bathra* 9b). "Do not put a poor man to shame by giving him your gift in public" (*Chagiga* 5a). What procedures do we follow in our society to aid the poor and spare them embarrassment in receiving charity? **6:5** In this attack on hypocrites in the synagogue Jesus is not attacking all the Jews of his day and certainly not all Jews of this day. His criticism, like that of rabbis contemporary with him, is directed against those kinds of persons— found in all religions—who misuse religion to serve themselves. Many Pharisees also had no patience with hypocrites. Rabbi Jeremiah said: "Four classes of men do not receive the face of the Shekinah (presence of God): the mocker, the hypocrite, the liars and slanderers" (*Sota* 42b). The Rabbis similarly held that sincerity in prayer was required if it was to be efficacious (cf. Psalm 145:8: "The Lord is near to all that call, to all that call upon him in truth"). However, they did not encourage prayer in secret. A more common emphasis among Jews is that placed upon the communality of prayer; if at all possible, a Jew is encouraged to join his personal prayers to those of the community through participation in a *minyan,* a prayer service that consists of at least ten men.

Our Father
Matthew 6:9–13

⁹ Pray then like this:
Our Father who art in heaven,
Hallowed be thy name.
¹⁰ Thy kingdom come,
Thy will be done,
On earth as it is in heaven.
¹¹ Give us this day our daily bread;
¹² And forgive us our debts,
As we also have forgiven our debtors;
¹³ And lead us not into temptation,
But deliver us from evil.

6:9 The Lord's Prayer or "Pater Noster" (Latin for "Our Father") is the most widely used Christian prayer, a key element in the liturgies of the churches. Different versions of this prayer are in common use. Protestants and others who say "trespasses" and "those who trespass against us" follow the usage of the Book of Common Prayer of the Anglican Church; those who say "debts" and "debtors" follow the rendering in the King James and later versions. Elements of the prayer are Jewish. Two of the prayers used in the regular liturgy of the synagogue particularly provide parallel concepts: (1) The *Kaddish,* a doxology written in Aramaic and recited by a rabbinic teacher at the close of his class. Excerpts include the following: "Magnified and sanctified (hallowed) be His great name. . . . May He establish His kingdom during your lifetime and during your days . . . and speedily and at a near time. . . ." (2) "The Eighteen Benedictions," known in the Hebrew as *Shmoneh Esreh* or

Amidah, a most reverent prayer which all read silently: "Forgive us O Father for we have sinned . . . Bless this year unto us, O Lord our God, together with every kind of produce thereof for our welfare; Give a blessing upon the face of the earth . . . Lead us not into sin, or transgression, iniquity, temptation or shame . . . for the Kingdom is Thine and to all eternity and Thou will reign in glory."

In the year 899 there died the only king to whom his countrymen have ever given the title of "The Great"—Alfred, ruler of the West Saxons. Although only a few portions of the Bible had then been translated in English, Alfred wished that "all the free born youth of his kingdom should employ themselves on nothing till they could first read well the English Scriptures." The Lord's Prayer in the time of Alfred read in what we now call old English, as follows:

Uren Fader dhic art in heofnas,
Sic gehalged dhin noma,
To cymedh dhin ric,
Sic dhin uuilla sue is in heofnas and in eardho,
Uren hlaf ofer uuirthe sel us to daeg,
And forgef us scylda urna
Sue uue forgefan sculdgun urum,
And no inlead uridk in costnung,
Afdgerrig urich from ifle.

6:10 The "Social Gospel" movement finds its charter here. It seeks to change social structures in order to achieve justice and peace for men, the realization of God's kingdom on earth. **6:12** The first part of verse 12 is one of some two dozen biblical verses that the Catholic Church has explained with a decree of her fullest authority. Pope Zozimus and the Council of Carthage (A.D. 418) declared positively that "forgive us our debts" can truly be said even by saints. The decree quotes the Letter to James 3:2 and many verses of the Old Testament to prove the point. **6:13** To these words the Church early added what has become known as the Doxology to the Lord's Prayer: "For thine is the kingdom and the power and the glory for ever." Not found in the best Greek texts nor in the Vulgate, these words occur in some translations based on late manuscripts. They appear to be derived from the prayer of David in 1 Chronicles 29. Here is evidence of the way in which the early church used the Old Testament in worship, and of the ease with which it moved from Jewish liturgy to Christian.

Jesus Teaches with Authority
Matthew 6:14–34; 7:1–29

14 For if you forgive men their trespasses, your heavenly Father also will forgive you; ¹⁵ but if you do not forgive men their trespasses, neither will your Father forgive your trespasses.

16 "And when you fast, do not look dismal, like the hypocrites,

for they disfigure their faces that their fasting may be seen by men. Truly, I say to you, they have their reward. [17] But when you fast, anoint your head and wash your face, [18] that your fasting may not be seen by men but by your Father who is in secret; and your Father who sees in secret will reward you.

19 "Do not lay up for yourselves treasures on earth, where moth and rust consume and where thieves break in and steal, but lay up for yourself treasures in heaven, where neither moth nor rust consumes and where thieves do not break in and steal. For where your treasure is, there will your heart be also.

22 "The eye is the lamp of the body. So, if your eye is sound, your whole body will be full of light; [23] but if your eye is not sound, your whole body will be full of darkness. If then the light in you is darkness, how great is the darkness!

24 "No one can serve two masters; for either he will hate the one and love the other, or he will be devoted to the one and despise the other. You cannot serve God and mammon.

25 "Therefore I tell you, do not be anxious about your life, what you shall eat or what you shall drink, nor about your body, what you shall put on. Is not life more than food, and the body more than clothing? [26] Look at the birds of the air: they neither sow nor reap nor gather into barns, and yet your heavenly Father feeds them. Are you not of more value than they? [27] And which of you by being anxious can add one cubit to his span of life? [28] And why are you anxious about clothing? Consider the lilies of the field, how they grow; they neither toil nor spin; [29] yet I tell you, even Solomon in all his glory was not arrayed like one of these. [30] But if God so clothes the grass of the field, which today is alive and tomorrow is thrown into the oven, will he not much more clothe you, O men of little faith? [31] Therefore do not be anxious, saying, 'What shall we eat?' or 'What shall we drink?' or 'What shall we wear?' [32] For the Gentiles seek all these things; and your heavenly Father knows that you need them all. [33] But seek first his kingdom and his righteousness, and all these things shall be yours as well.

34 "Therefore do not be anxious about tomorrow, for tomorrow will be anxious for itself. Let the day's own trouble be sufficient for the day.

7 "Judge not, that you be not judged. [2] For with the judgment you pronounce you will be judged, and the measure you give will be the measure you get. [3] Why do you see the speck that is in your brother's eye, but do not notice the log that is in your own eye? [4] Or how can you say to your brother, 'Let me take the speck out of your eye,' when there is the log in your own eye? [5] You hypocrite, first take the

log out of your own eye, and then you will see clearly to take the speck out of your brother's eye.

6 "Do not give dogs what is holy; and do not throw your pearls before swine, lest they trample them under foot and turn to attack you.

7 "Ask, and it will be given you; seek, and you will find; knock, and it will be opened to you. [8] For every one who asks receives, and he who seeks finds, and to him who knocks it will be opened. [9] Or what man of you, if his son asks him for bread, will give him a stone? [10] Or if he asks for a fish, will give him a serpent? [11] If you then, who are evil, know how to give good gifts to your children, how much more will your Father who is in heaven give good things to those who ask him! [12] So whatever you wish that men would do to you, do so to them; for this is the law and the prophets.

13 "Enter by the narrow gate; for the gate is wide and the way is easy, that leads to destruction, and those who enter by it are many. [14] For the gate is narrow and the way is hard, that leads to life, and those who find it are few.

15 "Beware of false prophets, who come to you in sheep's clothing but inwardly are ravenous wolves. [16] You will know them by their fruits. Are grapes gathered from thorns, or figs from thistles? [17] So, every sound tree bears good fruit, but the bad tree bears evil fruit. [18] A sound tree cannot bear evil fruit, nor can a bad tree bear good fruit. [19] Every tree that does not bear good fruit is cut down and thrown into the fire. [20] Thus you will know them by their fruits.

21 "Not every one who says to me, 'Lord, Lord,' shall enter the kingdom of heaven, but he who does the will of my Father who is in heaven. [22] On that day many will say to me, 'Lord, Lord, did we not prophesy in your name, and cast out demons in your name, and do many mighty works in your name?' [23] And then will I declare to them, 'I never knew you; depart from me, you evildoers.'

24 "Every one then who hears these words of mine and does them will be like a wise man who built his house upon the rock; [25] and the rain fell, and the floods came, and the winds blew and beat upon that house, but it did not fall, because it had been founded on the rock. [26] And every one who hears these words of mine and does not do them will be like a foolish man who built his house upon the sand; [27] and the rain fell, and the floods came, and the winds blew and beat against that house, and it fell; and great was the fall of it."

28 And when Jesus finished these sayings, the crowds were astonished at his teaching, [29] for he taught them as one who had authority, and not as their scribes.

6:19–22 Judaism joins Christianity in emphasizing that the doing of righteousness is more important than acquiring money. The following legend taken from the Talmud parallels the sentiments here expressed by Jesus: "Monobaz distributed all his treasures to the poor in the year of trouble (famine). His brothers sent to him and said: 'Our fathers gathered treasures and added to those of their fathers and you have dispersed yours and theirs.' He said to them: 'Our fathers gathered treasures for below and I have gathered treasure for above. They stored treasures in a place over which the hand of man cannot rule. Our fathers collected treasures which bear no fruit (interest), but I have gathered treasures which do bear fruit. Our fathers gathered treasures of money (mammon), I have gathered treasures in souls" (*Rabbinic Anthology*, pages 211, 212). Judaism does not deprecate wealth for its own sake. All things of the flesh were to be hallowed, i.e., to be used for God's purpose, rather than rejected, repressed or denied. **6:24** *Mammon:* an Aramaic word meaning money or wealth. **6:25** Verses 25–34 are the Gospel for the Fourteenth Sunday after Pentecost, in late August or early September. Jesus does not condemn hard work, thrift or prudence, but he does warn against anxiety and preoccupation with material things. **6:27** *Cubit:* about eighteen inches. **6:28** Toyohiko Kagawa (1888–1960), Japanese Christian, reports that he was won to the Gospel when he found that Jesus, too, loved the lilies and the grass of the field. "O God," he prayed, "make me like Christ." Kagawa undertook a ministry of reconciliation between social classes in Japan and between warring nations in the Orient. From the hundred books he wrote he received royalties totalling more than $100,000, which he devoted to improving the lot of the poor in his native land. **6:34** Tyndale: for the daye present hath ever enough of his awne trouble. Rheims: Sufficient for the day is the evil thereof. Confraternity: Sufficient for the day is its own trouble. King James Version: Sufficient unto the day is the evil thereof. Some persons hear this passage as forbidding participation in plans of insurance and social security; others interpret it as saying that if we do well the work of each day, we thereby shape the future. **7:1** *Judge not:* Rabbi Hillel, a contemporary of Jesus said, "Judge not thy neighbor until thou art come unto his place" (*Abot* 2:5). Rabbi Tarphon said, "I wonder if there be a man of this generation that will allow himself to be reproved. If someone says to his fellow, 'cast out the mote of thine eye,' he will retort 'cast out the beam of thine own eye' " (*Babba Bathra* 15b). Charles B. Williams' "The New Testament in the Language of the People," (see essay, "The Bible in English Translation") here reads: "Stop criticising others, so that you may not be criticised yourselves. For exactly as you criticise others, you will be criticised, and in accordance with the measure that you give to others, it will be measured back to you." **7:4** Older translations have "mote" for *speck* and "beam" for *log*. **7:12** This sentence has traditionally been called the Golden Rule. Rabbi Hillel said: "What is hateful to you, do not do unto thy neighbor. This is the whole Law, the rest is commentary. Go and study" *(Shabbat* 31a). **7:13** King James Version: "Enter ye in at the strait gate: for wide is the gate and broad is the way, that leadeth to destruction, and many there be which go in thereat." Compare Psalm 117:20, "This is the gate of the Lord, the righteous shall enter through it." A similar reference is also to be found in the Talmud, "The pious of all people will enjoy the bliss of the world to come" *(Sanhedrin* 105a). **7:24** A parable is a story pointing to a moral. Jesus taught in the Jewish tradition when he held that a man must demonstrate through his deeds his religious convictions. The Talmud put it this way: "A man who has good works and has learnt much Torah, to what may he be likened? To a man who builds below with stones and above with clay; and when much water comes and surrounds it the stones are not moved from their place. But a man who has no good works and learns Torah to what may he be likened? To a man who builds first with clay and then with stones: And when even small streams come they are immediately toppled over" *(Abot D'Rab Nathan).* **7:28** These or similar words are used as a formula in concluding each of the five major discourses in Matthew's Gospel. In each case, a narrative section follows. **7:29** Jesus astonished his listeners because he taught the Law on his own authority. The Pharisees would have invoked devices by which the biblical Law could be reinterpreted and new law developed. Their method of teaching was to give expression to a consensus in which they demonstrated the biblical source text and then the legitimacy of the new interpretation. Jesus neither spoke in the name of the Rabbis nor did he cite precedents in the Law for his views. The Pharisees may not have disagreed with what Jesus taught so much as his method. By assuming authority in his own right to change the Law he was undermining the procedures they felt were required for an orderly society. They did not see Jesus as the Messiah with the power and authority to legislate new law.

A Roman Soldier Asks Jesus' Help

In chapters 8 and 9 Matthew gathers ten miracle stories, events that were scattered through the period of Jesus' journeys in Galilee. He first recounts the cure of a leper. Then comes the story of the centurion and his servant.

Matthew 8:5–13

5 As he entered Caper'na-um, a centurion came forward to him, beseeching him [6] and saying, "Lord, my servant is lying paralyzed at home, in terrible distress." [7] And he said to him, "I will come and heal him." [8] But the centurion answered him, "Lord, I am not worthy to have you come under my roof; but only say the word, and

my servant will be healed. ⁹For I am a man under authority, with soldiers under me; and I say to one, 'Go,' and he goes, and to another, 'Come,' and he comes, and to my slave, 'Do this,' and he does it." ¹⁰When Jesus heard him, he marveled, and said to those who followed him, "Truly, I say to you, not even in Israel have I found such faith. ¹¹I tell you, many will come from east and west and sit at table with Abraham, Isaac, and Jacob in the kingdom of heaven, ¹²while the sons of the kingdom will be thrown into the outer darkness; there men will weep and gnash their teeth." ¹³And to the centurion Jesus said, "Go; be it done for you as you have believed." And the servant was healed at that very moment.

8:5 Both stories in this section are contained in the Gospel for the Third Sunday after Epiphany, the season when the Church teaches that Jesus is King over both Jews and Gentiles (the leper was a Jew, the centurion a Gentile). This section is also the Gospel of the Mass for the Sick and the Mass for a Dying Person. **8:8** Before the Communion in every Mass, the priest says three times (in an adaptation of verse 8 here): *Domine non sum dignus* . . . ("Lord, I am not worthy to have you come under my roof; but only say the word, and my soul will be healed"). **8:10–12** This verse is cited by Christians seeking to prove that persons who serve the right as they know it may find salvation. Compare Luke 13:29, Matthew 11:27. See also discussion in note at Luke 1:71. Jews traditionally anticipated that in the messianic era the exiled and dispersed Hebrew tribes would be gathered from all corners of the globe (see Isaiah 49:12). Jesus here suggests that those who will join the patriarchs in the time to come will be the righteous of all nations.

Jesus Calms a Storm

Matthew recounts the cure of Peter's mother-in-law (from a fever) and other sick people. These things, Matthew says, fulfilled the prophecy of Isaiah: "He took our infirmities and bore our diseases." There follows some advice Jesus gave His disciples, and then this story.

Matthew 8:23–27

23 And when he got into the boat, his disciples followed him. ²⁴And behold, there arose a great storm on the sea, so that the boat was being swamped by the waves; but he was asleep. ²⁵And they went and woke him, saying, "Save, Lord; we are perishing." ²⁶And he said to them, "Why are you afraid, O men of little faith?" Then he rose and rebuked the winds and the sea; and there was a great calm. ²⁷And the men marveled, saying, "What sort of man is this, that even winds and sea obey him?"

8:23–27 This story is the Gospel for the Fourth Sunday after Epiphany, the liturgical season with special stress on the divinity and kingship of Jesus. Gospel episodes about ships resulted in the ship becoming a symbol of the Church (hence such expressions as "the bark of Peter," meaning the Church of Rome). A ship is the symbol of the ecumenical movement, seeking closer relations between the churches. There are many representations in early Christian art of ships with Jesus or Peter as helmsman. The word "nave" (main body of a church) comes from the Latin word *navis*, meaning "ship." This usage may allude to Noah's ark, the first ship of salvation. **8:26** King James Version: Why are ye fearful, O ye of little faith?

Jesus Heals a Paralytic
Matthew 9:1–8

9 And getting into a boat he crossed over and came to his own city. [2] And behold, they brought to him a paralytic, lying on his bed; and when Jesus saw their faith he said to the paralytic, "Take heart, my son; your sins are forgiven." [3] And behold, some of the scribes said to themselves, "This man is blaspheming." [4] But Jesus, knowing their thoughts, said, "Why do you think evil in your hearts? [5] For which is easier, to say, 'Your sins are forgiven,' or to say, 'Rise and walk'? [6] But that you may know that the Son of man has authority on earth to forgive sins"—he then said to the paralytic—"Rise, take up your bed and go home." [7] And he rose and went home. [8] When the crowds saw it, they were afraid, and they glorified God, who had given such authority to men.

9:1 This story of the favor granted the paralytic ("one sick of the palsy," in other translations) is the Gospel for the Eighteenth Sunday after Pentecost. In Matthew's account, the man's physical cure is a symbol of the unseen forgiveness of his sins. **9:3** For the first time in Matthew's Gospel, we are shown opposition to Jesus by some Jewish leaders. It arises from his claim to forgive sins, a power reserved in their opinion to God alone. **9:2** Tyndale: sonne be of good chere. Geneva Bible: Sonne, be of good comfort. Rheims: have a good hart sonne. King James Version: Son, be of good cheer. **9:6** The designation "Son of man" was Jesus' favorite way of describing himself. It occurs 69 times in the synoptic Gospels. An Old Testament term, it refers both to the people Israel and the long-awaited Messiah. See note at Daniel 7:13 for other Old Testament reference; see also Psalm 2:7, Ezekiel 24:2, Daniel 8:17.

Jesus Chooses Matthew
Matthew 9:9–17

9 As Jesus passed on from there, he saw a man called Matthew sitting at the tax office; and he said to him, "Follow me." And he rose and followed him.

10 And as he sat at table in the house, behold, many tax collectors and sinners came and sat down with Jesus and his disciples. [11] And when the Pharisees saw this, they said to his disciples, "Why does your teacher eat with tax collectors and sinners?" [12] But when he heard it, he said, "Those who are well have no need of a physician, but those who are sick. [13] Go and learn what this means, 'I desire mercy, and not sacrifice.' For I came not to call the righteous, but sinners."

14 Then the disciples of John came to him, saying, "Why do we and the Pharisees fast, but your disciples do not fast?" [15] And Jesus said to them, "Can the wedding guests mourn as long as the bridegroom is with them? The days will come, when the bridegroom is taken away from them, and then they will fast. [16] And no one puts a piece of unshrunk cloth on an old garment, for the patch tears away from the garment, and a worse tear is made. [17] Neither is new wine put into old wineskins; if it is, the skins burst, and the wine is spilled, and the skins are destroyed; but new wine is put into fresh wineskins, and so both are preserved."

9:9 This passage is the Gospel for the Feast of St. Matthew, Apostle and Evangelist (September 21). **9:14** This passage provides authority for those Christians who maintain periods of fasting, e.g., Ember Days. **9:15** Jesus answers the question according to Jewish law: it was forbidden those tending the bridegroom to engage in mourning. He hints (verses 16–17) that he not only brings a new teaching (new wine) but a new religion (fresh wineskins).

Missionary Discourse

The second great sermon, or collection of statements by Jesus, is presented as instruction to the disciples before they set out on a missionary journey among their own. It was only after His resurrection that Jesus announced their mission to the Gentiles.

Matthew 10:1–11:1

10 And he called to him his twelve disciples and gave them authority over unclean spirits, to cast them out, and to heal every disease and every infirmity. [2] The names of the twelve apostles are these: first, Simon, who is called Peter, and Andrew his brother; James the son of Zeb'edee, and John his brother; [3] Philip and Bartholomew; Thomas and Matthew the tax collector; James the son of Alphaeus, and Thaddaeus; [4] Simon the Cananaean, and Judas Iscariot, who betrayed him.

5 These twelve Jesus sent out, charging them, "Go nowhere among the Gentiles, and enter no town of the Samaritans, [6] but go rather to the lost sheep of the house of Israel. [7] And preach as you go,

saying, 'The kingdom of heaven is at hand.' ⁸ Heal the sick, raise the dead, cleanse lepers, cast out demons. You received without pay, give without pay. ⁹ Take no gold, nor silver, nor copper in your belts, ¹⁰ no bag for your journey, nor two tunics, nor sandals, nor a staff; for the laborer deserves his food. ¹¹ And whatever town or village you enter, find out who is worthy in it, and stay with him until you depart. ¹² As you enter the house, salute it. ¹³ And if the house is worthy, let your peace come upon it; but if it is not worthy, let your peace return to you. ¹⁴ And if any one will not receive you or listen to your words, shake off the dust from your feet as you leave that house or town. ¹⁵ Truly, I say to you, it shall be more tolerable on the day of judgment for the land of Sodom and Gomor'rah than for that town.

16 "Behold, I send you out as sheep in the midst of wolves; so be wise as serpents and innocent as doves. ¹⁷ Beware of men; for they will deliver you up to councils, and flog you in their synagogues, ¹⁸ and you will be dragged before governors and kings for my sake, to bear testimony before them and the Gentiles. ¹⁹ When they deliver you up, do not be anxious how you are to speak or what you are to say; for what you are to say will be given to you in that hour; ²⁰ for it is not you who speak, but the Spirit of your Father speaking through you. ²¹ Brother will deliver up brother to death, and the father his child, and children will rise against parents and have them put to death; ²² and you will be hated by all for my name's sake. But he who endures to the end will be saved. ²³ When they persecute you in one town, flee to the next; for truly, I say to you, you will not have gone through all the towns of Israel, before the Son of man comes.

24 "A disciple is not above his teacher, nor a servant above his master; ²⁵ it is enough for the disciple to be like his teacher, and the servant like his master. If they have called the master of the house Be-el'zebul, how much more will they malign those of his household.

26 "So have no fear of them; for nothing is covered that will not be revealed, or hidden that will not be known. ²⁷ What I tell you in the dark, utter in the light; and what you hear whispered, proclaim upon the housetops. ²⁸ And do not fear those who kill the body but cannot kill the soul; rather fear him who can destroy both soul and body in hell. ²⁹ Are not two sparrows sold for a penny? And not one of them will fall to the ground without your Father's will. ³⁰ But even the hairs of your head are all numbered. ³¹ Fear not, therefore; you are of more value than many sparrows. ³² So every one who acknowledges me before men, I also will acknowledge before my Father who is in heaven; ³³ but whoever denies me before men, I also will deny before my Father who is in heaven.

34 "Do not think that I have come to bring peace on earth; I have not come to bring peace, but a sword. [35] For I have come to set a man against his father, and a daughter against her mother, and a daughter-in-law against her mother-in-law; [36] and a man's foes will be those of his own household. [37] He who loves father or mother more than me is not worthy of me; and he who loves son or daughter more than me is not worthy of me; [38] and he who does not take his cross and follow me is not worthy of me. [39] He who finds his life will lose it, and he who loses his life for my sake will find it.

40 "He who receives you receives me, and he who receives me receives him who sent me. [41] He who receives a prophet because he is a prophet shall receive a prophet's reward, and he who receives a righteous man because he is a righteous man shall receive a righteous man's reward. [42] And whoever gives to one of these little ones even a cup of cold water because he is a disciple, truly, I say to you, he shall not lose his reward."

11 And when Jesus had finished instructing his twelve disciples, he went on from there to teach and preach in their cities.

10:7 The Catholic Church uses verse 7:14 as the Gospel of the Mass for Pilgrims and Travelers. "The kingdom of heaven is at hand" summarizes views appearing in many parts of the New Testament that seem to suggest that the world was about to come to its end. To understand this phrase, certain things must be kept in mind: (a) Impatient with the teaching of the prophets regarding end-time redemption, some Old Testament writers known as apocalyptists (from a Greek word meaning "unveiling") proclaimed that things were so bad God would soon have to make an end of everything; many New Testament writers employ this apocalyptic imagery. (b) Side by side with passages which seem to expect a quick end of everything are passages which suggest a long period of the kind of growth which cannot be hurried: see such parables as Mark 4:26–29 and Matthew 13:24–30. In 1 Thessalonians Paul expects that "the day of the Lord will come like a thief in the night" (5:2), and "we who are alive . . . shall be caught up . . . in the clouds to meet the Lord in the air" (4:17); in Philippians 1:23, however, he says: "My desire is to depart and be with Christ." (c) Jerusalem was destroyed by the Romans in A.D. 70; it is argued by some that everything Jesus said about the coming end was fulfilled at that time. For the Hebrews it was the end of an age; the loss of their homeland meant that they became a nation without a country, a condition which prevailed to the middle of the twentieth century. (d) Still another interpretation holds that in the person of Jesus a new age did begin for all humanity (Old Testament apocalyptists spoke of the present evil age and of the glorious age to come). This interpretation holds that in Christ the glorious age to come had already come; in his own person the kingdom was at hand for all with the faith to recognize it. **10:15** See Genesis 18 for the story of these two towns destroyed by God for their wickedness. **10:16** In verses 16–26 the sermon clearly looks forward to something beyond what the disciples will find in the villages on this journey. Jesus foretells the sufferings and struggles of the apostolic Church. **10:18–19** From this passage E. Stanley Jones (b.1884), Methodist minister and author, reports he derived the courage to undertake a ministry to the educated and governing classes of India. **10:25** Older translations have *Beelzebub* ("lord of filth"), which they understood as derived from *Baalzebub* ("lord of flies"), a derogatory reference by the Hebrews in place of the word *Baalzebul* ("lord of the lofty dwelling"), which has been found in ancient tablets, referring to the "great god Baal" of Syria. **10:26** Verses 26–32 are used by the Catholic Church in the second of her masses for martyrs (witnesses to the faith by death) who were not bishops. Verses 34–42 are used in the first of the masses for martyrs who were not bishops, e.g., St. Valentine (February 14), St. Christopher (July 25), St. Thomas More (July 6). **10:32–33** These verses have been cited by some Christian writers as evidence that those who do not accept the claims of Jesus will not be saved. Compare Matthew 7:21. Other Christian writers teach that a desire to do what is right before God ("baptism of desire," as some have called it) will include Jews and others in the acknowledgment Jesus makes before the Father in heaven (cf. John 10:16; 1 Timothy 2–4). **10:34b** This verse is often cited by Christians maintaining the rightness of military service and method. (Cf. Matthew 5:38–39). Others hear it as saying that important issues of faith divide even families. **10:38** The cross was a Roman instrument of execution, often carried by the condemned man to the scene of his death. Jesus means that following him leads to a kind of death in the sacrifices made for love of him, even a person's rejection of involvement in the ways of sin. **10:39** There is a Talmudic legend, according to which Alexander the Great asked the Elders of Africa "What shall a man do that he may live?" They answered: "Let him kill himself." Then the king asked: "And what shall a man do that he may die?" To which the Elders replied: "Let him keep himself alive" (*Taanit* 32a). In this Talmudic legend, as in the biblical text, the words are not meant to be read literally, i.e., to kill one's self means to die, in a moral and spiritual sense, to the influences of the sinful world and thus to gain life eternal.

"Take My Yoke upon You"
Matthew 11:2–30

2 Now when John heard in prison about the deeds of the Christ, he sent word by his disciples ³ and said to him, "Are you he who is to come, or shall we look for another?" ⁴ And Jesus answered them,

"Go and tell John what you hear and see: ⁵the blind receive their sight and the lame walk, lepers are cleansed and the deaf hear, and the dead are raised up, and the poor have good news preached to them. ⁶And blessed is he who takes no offense at me.''

7 As they went away, Jesus began to speak to the crowds concerning John: "What did you go out into the wilderness to behold? A reed shaken by the wind? ⁸Why then did you go out? To see a man clothed in soft raiment? Behold, those who wear soft raiment are in kings' houses. ⁹Why then did you go out? To see a prophet? Yes, I tell you, and more than a prophet. ¹⁰This is he of whom it is written,

'Behold, I send my messenger before thy face,
who shall prepare thy way before thee.'

11 Truly, I say to you, among those born of women there has risen no one greater than John the Baptist; yet he who is least in the kingdom of heaven is greater than he. ¹²From the days of John the Baptist until now the kingdom of heaven has suffered violence and men of violence take it by force. ¹³For all the prophets and the law prophesied until John; ¹⁴and if you are willing to accept it, he is Eli'jah who is to come. ¹⁵He who has ears to hear, let him hear.

16 "But to what shall I compare this generation? It is like children sitting in the market places and calling to their playmates,

¹⁷ 'We piped to you, and you did not dance;
we wailed, and you did not mourn.'

18 For John came neither eating nor drinking, and they say, 'He has a demon'; ¹⁹the Son of man came eating and drinking, and they say, 'Behold, a glutton and a drunkard, a friend of tax collectors and sinners!' Yet wisdom is justified by her deeds.''

20 Then he began to upbraid the cities where most his mighty works had been done, because they did not repent. ²¹"Woe to you, Chora'zin! woe to you, Beth-sa'ida! for if the mighty works done in you had been done in Tyre and Sidon, they would have repented long ago in sackcloth and ashes. ²²But I tell you, it shall be more tolerable on the day of judgment for Tyre and Sidon than for you. ²³And you, Caper'na-um, will you be exalted in heaven? You shall be brought down to Hades. For if the mighty works done in you had been done in Sodom, it would have remained until this day. ²⁴But I tell you that it shall be more tolerable on the day of judgment for the land of Sodom than for you.''

25 At that time Jesus declared, "I thank thee, father, Lord of heaven and earth, that thou hast hidden these things from the wise and understanding and revealed them to babes; ²⁶yea, Father, for such was thy gracious will. ²⁷All things have been delivered to me by

my Father; and no one knows the Son except the Father, and no one knows the Father except the Son and any one to whom the Son chooses to reveal him. [28] Come to me, all who labor and are heavy laden, and I will give you rest. [29] Take my yoke upon you, and learn from me; for I am gentle and lowly in heart, and you will find rest for your souls. [30] For my yoke is easy, and my burden is light."

11:2 Verses 2–10 from the Gospel for the second Sunday of Advent; in preparing for Christmas, the Church recalls John's preparation for Jesus' coming. **11:6** Tyndale: happy is he that is not offended by me. Rheims: blessed is he that shall not be scandalized in me. **11:10** Malachi 3:1. **11:14** Malachi 4:5–6: "Behold, I will send you Elijah the prophet before the great and terrible day of the Lord comes. And he will turn the hearts of fathers to their children and the hearts of children to their fathers, lest I come and smite the land with a curse." Ecclesiasticus has a similar sentence (84:10). Matthew represents Jesus as convinced that John the Baptist fulfilled this prophecy. **11:25** Verses 25–30 are the Gospel of the Mass for the Feast of St. Francis of Assisi (October 4) and St. Paul, the first hermit (January 15). It is a key passage in Catholic devotion to the Sacred Heart. **11:27** This verse is cited by Christians seeking to prove that no one can be saved except through the Christ. Compare Luke 13:29, Matthew 8:10–12. **11:28** Tyndale: Come unto me all ye that laboure and are laden and I will ease you. Rheims: Come ye to me all that labour, and are burdened, and I will refresh you. King James Version: Come unto me, all ye that labour and are heavy laden, and I will give you rest.

A Dispute about the Sabbath
Matthew 12:1–8

12 At that time Jesus went through the grainfields on the sabbath; his disciples were hungry, and they began to pluck ears of grain and to eat. [2] But when the Pharisees saw it, they said to him, "Look, your disciples are doing what is not lawful to do on the sabbath." [3] He said to them, "Have you not read what David did, when he was hungry, and those who were with him: [4] how he entered the house of God and ate the bread of the Presence, which it was not lawful for him to eat nor for those who were with him, but only for the priests? [5] Or have you not read in the law how on the sabbath the priests in the temple profane the sabbath, and are guiltless? [6] I tell you, something greater than the temple is here. [7] And if you had known what this means, 'I desire mercy, and not sacrifice,' you would not have condemned the guiltless. [8] For the Son of man is lord of the sabbath."

12:1 Compare Mark 2:23–28 and note there. **12:8** Rabbinic authorities agreed that the preservation of human life is more significant than the strict observance of the Sabbath. The rabbis also cited the precedent of David's eating of the altar bread (1 Samuel 21:1–6). They concluded "the needs of life override Sabbath restrictions." The issue between Jesus and the Pharisees therefore was on the strictness of this principle's application. Was there really a question of life or death here, necessitating a violation of the holy Sabbath? The rabbis were also angered at the fact that Jesus on his own authority felt free to reinterpret the Law. His contention that he was "Lord of the Sabbath" sounded like blasphemy to the rabbis. Matthew already has reported that Jesus' method of teaching astonished the people, 7:28–29.

Jesus Heals on the Sabbath
Matthew 12:9–21, 46–50

9 And he went on from there, and entered their synagogue. ¹⁰ And behold, there was a man with a withered hand. And they asked him, "Is it lawful to heal on the sabbath?" so that they might accuse him. ¹¹ He said to them, "What man of you, if he has one sheep and it falls into a pit on the sabbath, will not lay hold of it and lift it out? ¹² Of how much more value is a man than a sheep! So it is lawful to do good on the sabbath." ¹³ Then he said to the man, "Stretch out your hand." And the man stretched it out, and it was restored, whole like the other. ¹⁴ But the Pharisees went out and took counsel against him, how to destroy him.

15 Jesus, aware of this, withdrew from there. And many followed him, and he healed them all, ¹⁶ and ordered them not to make him known. ¹⁷ This was to fulfil what was spoken by the prophet Isaiah:
¹⁸ "Behold, my servant whom I have chosen,
my beloved with whom my soul is well pleased.
I will put my Spirit upon him,
and he shall proclaim justice to the Gentiles.
¹⁹ He will not wrangle or cry aloud,
nor will any one hear his voice in the streets;
²⁰ he will not break a bruised reed
or quench a smoldering wick,
till he brings justice to victory;
²¹   and in his name will the Gentiles hope."
46 While he was still speaking to the people, behold, his mother and his brothers stood outside, asking to speak to him. ⁴⁸ But he replied to the man who told him, "Who is my mother, and who are my brothers?" ⁴⁹ And stretching out his hand toward his

disciples, he said, "Here are my mother and my brothers! ⁵⁰For whoever does the will of my Father in heaven is my brother, and sister, and mother."

12:18–21 See Isaiah 42:1–4. **12:46–50** This passage is often cited to prove Jesus had brothers, and therefore that Mary did not remain a virgin after Jesus' birth. Catholics and Orthodox hold that, since Hebrew and Aramaic used the same word for brother, cousin and uncle, the word "brothers" here means only "relatives."

Parables of the Kingdom

The third great discourse in Matthew's Gospel is this collection of parables. Each parable is a story that illustrates an aspect of Jesus' teaching.

The Sower
Matthew 13:1–23

13 That same day Jesus went out of the house and sat beside the sea. ²And great crowds gathered about him, so that he got into a boat and sat there; and the whole crowd stood on the beach. ³And he told them many things in parables, saying: "A sower went out to sow. ⁴And as he sowed, some seeds fell along the path, and the birds came and devoured them. ⁵Other seeds fell on rocky ground, where they had not much soil, and immediately they sprang up, since they had no depth of soil, ⁶but when the sun rose they were scorched; and since they had no root they withered away. ⁷Other seeds fell upon thorns, and the thorns grew up and choked them. ⁸Other seeds fell on good soil and brought forth grain, some a hundredfold, some sixty, some thirty. ⁹He who has ears, let him hear.

10 Then the disciples came and said to him, "Why do you speak to them in parables?" ¹¹And he answered them, "To you it has been given to know the secrets of the kingdom of heaven, but to them it has not been given. ¹²For to him who has will more be given, and he will have abundance; but from him who has not, even what he has will be taken away. ¹³This is why I speak to them in parables, because seeing they do not see, and hearing they do not hear, nor do they understand. ¹⁴With them indeed is fulfilled the prophecy of Isaiah which says:

'You shall indeed hear but never understand,
    and you shall indeed see but never perceive.
¹⁵For this people's heart has grown dull,
    and their ears are heavy of hearing,
    and their eyes they have closed,

lest they should perceive with their eyes,
    and hear with their ears,
  and understand with their heart,
    and turn for me to heal them.'

16 But blessed are your eyes, for they see, and your ears, for they hear. [17] Truly, I say to you, many prophets and righteous men longed to see what you see, and did not see it, and to hear what you hear, and did not hear it.

18 "Hear then the parable of the sower. [19] When any one hears the word of the kingdom and does not understand it, the evil one comes and snatches away what is sown in his heart; this is what was sown along the path. [20] As for what was sown on rocky ground, this is he who hears the word and immediately receives it with joy; [21] yet he has no root in himself, but endures for a while, and when tribulation or persecution arises on account of the word, immediately he falls away. [22] As for what was sown among thorns, this is he who hears the word, but the cares of the world and the delight in riches choke the word, and it proves unfruitful. [23] As for what was sown on good soil, this is he who hears the word and understands it; he indeed bears fruit, and yields, in one case a hundredfold, in another sixty, and in another thirty."

13:14–15 See Isaiah 6:9–10.

The Weeds
Matthew 13:24–30

24 Another parable he put before them, saying, "The kingdom of heaven may be compared to a man who sowed good seed in his field; [25] but while men were sleeping, his enemy came and sowed weeds among the wheat, and went away. [26] So when the plants came up and bore grain, then the weeds appeared also. [27] And the servants of the householder came and said to him, 'Sir, did you not sow good seed in your field? How then has it weeds?' [28] He said to them, 'An enemy has done this.' The servants said to him, 'Then do you want us to go and gather them?' [29] But he said, 'No; lest in gathering the weeds you root up the wheat along with them. [30] Let both grow together until the harvest; and at harvest time I will tell the reapers, Gather the weeds first and bind them in bundles to be burned, but gather the wheat into my barn.' "

13:24 This is the Gospel for the Fifth Sunday after Epiphany. Christians have traditionally understood this passage to mean that God allows good and evil to exist together until the time of final judgment. The Parable of the Tares (older translations had "tares" or "cockle" for "weeds") has been applied in Christian writings since

the time of St. Augustine to justify tolerance and religious freedom.
13:24 ff. In using these parables regarding the harvest as a metaphor
for describing the ultimate fate of men of faith, Jesus evoked an
image popular among Rabbinic teachers. The Midrash, for example,
includes this tale in explanation of the Hebrew words *Nakshu-Bar*
(Psalm 2:12), which can be translated "kiss the wheat" (the Hebrew
is unclear and the phrase has been variously translated): "The Straw
and Chaff are arguing. Each maintains that, for its own sake alone,
the field was sown and ploughed. Thereupon the wheat said 'Wait
until the harvest comes and we shall know for what purpose the field
was sown.' When the harvest came and the work of threshing began,
the chaff was scattered to the wind, the stem was burned in the
flames, and the wheat was carefully gathered. In like manner, the
heathens say: 'It is for our sakes the world was created.' Israel
responds: 'Wait for Judgment Day when the chaff will be eliminated,
and the wheat will be kissed.' "

The Mustard Seed
Matthew 13:31–35

31 Another parable he put before them, saying, "The kingdom of
heaven is like a grain of mustard seed which a man took and sowed
in his field; ³²It is the smallest of all seeds, but when it has grown it
is the greatest of shrubs and becomes a tree, so that the birds of the
air come and make nests in its branches."

33 He told them another parable. "The kingdom of heaven is like
leaven which a woman took and hid in three measures of meal, till it
was all leavened."

34 All this Jesus said to the crowds in parables; indeed he said
nothing to them without a parable. ³⁵This was to fulfil what was
spoken by the prophet.

"I will open my mouth in parables,
  I will utter what has been hidden since the foundation of the
  world."

13:31 This is the Gospel for the Sixth Sunday after Epiphany.
13:35 See Psalm 78:2.

Treasure, Pearl, Net
Matthew 13:44–50

44 "The kingdom of heaven is like treasure hidden in a field, which a
man found and covered up; then in his joy he goes and sells all that
he has and buys that field.

45 "Again, the kingdom of heaven is like a merchant in search of
fine pearls, ⁴⁶who, on finding one pearl of great value, went and sold
all that he had and bought it.

47 "Again, the kingdom of heaven is like a net which was thrown into the sea and gathered fish of every kind; 48 when it was full, men drew it ashore and sat down and sorted the good into vessels but threw away the bad. 49 So it will be at the close of the age. The angels will come out and separate the evil from the righteous, 50 and throw them into the furnace of fire; there men will weep and gnash their teeth.

13:44 These verses are read in masses of virgins and women martyrs, as well as in the Mass of a holy woman who was neither virgin nor martyr, for example, St. Monica, mother of St. Augustine (May 4) and St. Anne, mother of the Virgin Mary (July 26).

"A Prophet Is Not Without Honor . . ."
Matthew 13:53–58

53 And when Jesus had finished these parables, he went away from there, 54 and coming to his own country he taught them in their synagogue, so that they were astonished, and said, "Where did this man get this wisdom and these mighty works? 55 Is not this the carpenter's son? Is not his mother called Mary? And are not his brothers James and Joseph and Simon and Judas? 56 And are not all his sisters with us? Where then did this man get all this?" 57 And they took offense at him. But Jesus said to them, "A prophet is not without honor except in his own country and in his own house." 58 And he did not do many mighty works there, because of their unbelief.

13:55–56 Compare note at 12:46.

Herod Beheads John
Matthew 14:1–12

14 At that time Herod the tetrarch heard about the fame of Jesus; 2 and he said to his servants, "This is John the Baptist, he has been raised from the dead; that is why these powers are at work in him." 3 For Herod had seized John and bound him and put him in prison, for the sake of Hero'di-as, his brother Philip's wife, because John said to him, "It is not lawful for you to have her." 5 And though he wanted to put him to death, he feared the people, because they held him to be a prophet. 6 But when Herod's birthday came, the daughter of Hero'di-as danced before the company, and pleased Herod, 7 so that he promised with an oath to give her whatever she might ask. 8 Prompted by her mother, she said, "Give me the head of John the Baptist here on a platter." 9 And the king was sorry; but because of his oaths and his guests he commanded it to be given; 10 he sent and had John beheaded in the prison, 11 and his head was brought on a platter and given to the girl, and she brought it to her mother. [12] And his disciples came and took the body and buried it; and they went and told Jesus.

14:1 The scene described here has been depicted by artists and in the opera *Salome*, by Richard Strauss. **14:4** John invoked biblical law, Leviticus 18:16.

Jesus Feeds Five Thousand
Matthew 14:13–21

13 Now when Jesus heard this, he withdrew from there in a boat to a lonely place apart. But when the crowds heard it, they followed him on foot from the towns. [14] As he went ashore he saw a great throng; and he had compassion on them, and healed their sick. [15] When it was evening, the disciples came to him and said, "This is a lonely place, and the day is now over; send the crowds away to go into the villages and buy food for themselves." [15] Jesus said, "They need not go away; you give them something to eat." [17] They said to him, "We have only five loaves here and two fish." [18] And he said, "Bring them here to me." [19] Then he ordered the crowds to sit down on the grass; and taking the five loaves and the two fish he looked up to heaven, and blessed, and broke and gave the loaves to the disciples, and the disciples gave them to the crowds. [20] And they all ate and were satisfied. And they took up twelve baskets full of the broken pieces left over. [21] And those who ate were about five thousand men, besides women and children.

14:19 This is the only miracle recounted by all four Gospels. John's account of it is the Gospel for the Fourth Sunday in Lent. The Catholic liturgy at that time is occupied with the recollection of Moses, and Catholic commentators have for centuries seen a parallel between Jesus and Moses, between the manna in the desert and the bread of the Eucharist. They take this miracle as a prophetic act, foreshadowing the Eucharist. In every Mass, before the priest blesses and consecrates the bread, he is instructed by the book before him to "raise his eyes to heaven," as Jesus does in this account.

What Defiles a Man?
Matthew 15:1–2; 10–20

15 Then Pharisees and scribes came to Jesus from Jerusalem and said, [2] "Why do your disciples transgress the tradition of the elders? For they do not wash their hands when they eat."

10 And he called the people to him and said to them, "Hear and understand: [11] not what goes into the mouth defiles a man, but what comes out of the mouth, this defiles a man." [12] Then the disciples

came and said to him, "Do you know that the Pharisees were offended when they heard this saying?" [13] He answered, "Every plant which my heavenly Father has not planted will be rooted up. [14] Let them alone; they are blind guides. And if a blind man leads a blind man, both will fall into a pit." [15] But Peter said to him, "Explain the parable to us." [16] And he said, "Are you also still without understanding? [17] Do you not see that whatever goes into the mouth passes into the stomach, and so passes on? [18] But what comes out of the mouth proceeds from the heart, and this defiles a man. [19] For out of the heart come evil thoughts, murder, adultery, fornication, theft, false witness, slander. [20] These are what defile a man; but to eat with unwashed hands does not defile a man."

15 : 1 ff. Some scholars point out that this New Testament account utilizes a technical Jewish literary device intended to teach a new ethical insight. Rabbinic writings contemporaneous with the New Testament for example, describe several such disputations: (1) An outsider puts a question to the law; (2) a retort is made that satisfies the outsider but seems to lack profundity; (3) the disciples of the rabbi request a further elucidation; (4) the rabbi provides his disciples in private with a profound insight. The Talmud records, for example, that a pagan asked Rabbi Johanan ben Zaccai whether it was not witchcraft to purify a person who had been defiled by contact with a corpse merely by sprinkling the person with water containing the ashes of a red heifer (Numbers 19 : 2). Rabbi Johanan asked the pagan: How do you cure a man possessing demons? The idolator explained it was customary to burn roots under the man and then sprinkle the water upon the smoke, the demon, as it flies into the air. Rabbi Johanan responded: In exactly like spirit we cleanse a person of the spirit of uncleanness by sprinkling upon him the water of purification. When the idolater left, the disciples queried their master: Master, this man you put off with a make-shift answer, but what explanation will you give us? Rabbi Johanan revealed to his disciples that in truth neither did contact with the dead defile, nor water purify. Since God established this ritual in the law, however, the observance had to be accepted as God's will even though there was no rational explanation. (For another example of such a disputation see note on Genesis 1 : 26).

Jesus Heals a Canaanite
Matthew 15 : 21–28

21 And Jesus went away from there and withdrew to the district of Tyre and Sidon. [22] And behold, a Canaanite woman from that region came out and cried, "Have mercy on me, O Lord, Son of David; my daughter is severely possessed by a demon." [23] But he did not answer her a word. And his disciples came and begged him, saying, "Send

her away, for she is crying after us." ²⁴ He answered, "I was sent only to the lost sheep of the house of Israel." ²⁵ But she came and knelt before him, saying, "Lord, help me." ²⁶ And he answered, "It is not fair to take the children's bread and throw it to the dogs." ²⁷ She said, "Yes, Lord, yet even the dogs eat the crumbs that fall from their master's table." ²⁸ Then Jesus answered her, "O woman, great is your faith! Be it done for you as you desire." And her daughter was healed instantly.

"You Are the Christ"
Matthew 16:13–20

13 Now when Jesus came into the district of Caesare′a Philippi, he asked his disciples, "Who do men say that the Son of man is?" ¹⁴ And they said, "Some say John the Baptist, others say Eli′jah, and others Jeremiah or one of the prophets." ¹⁵ He said to them, "But who do you say that I am?" ¹⁶ Simon Peter replied, "You are the Christ, the Son of the living God." ¹⁷ And Jesus answered him, "Blessed are you, Simon Bar-Jona! For flesh and blood has not revealed this to you, but my Father who is in heaven. ¹⁸ And I tell you, you are Peter, and on this rock I will build my church, and the powers of death shall not prevail against it. ¹⁹ I will give you the keys of the kingdom of heaven, and whatever you bind on earth shall be bound in heaven, and whatever you loose on earth shall be loosed in heaven." ²⁰ Then he strictly charged the disciples to tell no one that he was the Christ.

16:13 ff. There is a play on two Greek words: *Petros* (Peter) and *petra* (rock). In Aramaic, the language Jesus spoke, the word for Peter and rock would be the same: "You are *Kepha,* and on this *kepha* ..." Catholics have understood this sentence to mean a promise of the conferring of primacy in Church jurisdiction upon Peter. The First Vatican Council, 1869–1870, declared that in these words the primacy was promised to Peter, thus making the verse one of the two dozen explained by the Church's highest authority. The verse (in Latin) is inscribed in giant letters around the inside of the dome of St. Peter's Basilica in Rome. This passage is the Gospel of the Mass on the Feast of Sts. Peter and Paul (June 29), and the Gospel of the Mass for a Pope who is a saint. Protestants have a different understanding of the passage. They note Matthew 16:21–23, in which Peter elicits from Jesus the stern rebuke: "Get behind me, Satan!" and Peter's three-fold denial of Christ in the critical hours before the Crucifixion (Matthew 26:69–75). They point out that, for Paul, it is not Peter but Christ upon whom the Church is built: "For no other foundation can any one lay than that which is laid, which is Jesus Christ" (1 Corinthians 3:11). They note that Paul did not recognize the primacy of Peter; compare Galatians 2:11. On this view, it is Peter's confession of faith, his recognition that Jesus is the Messiah, which constitutes the basis of the Church; the Church is built not upon Peter but upon Christ whose true identity Peter confessed. **16:18** The word *Petra,* meaning rock, is used by Rabbinic commentators to refer to Abraham. According to a Midrashic legend, God wondered how He could build His world seeing that there will be such wickedness perpetrated by men. However, when he perceived that there would rise an Abraham, God said, 'Behold I have found the rock upon which to build and lay foundations.' Therefore God called Abraham, "Rock," as it is said (Isaiah 51 : 1, 2) "Look unto the rock whence you are hewn . . . look unto Abraham your Father" (*Yalkut* 1). **16:19** Catholics regard this verse as a biblical basis for their doctrines of purgatory and indulgences. Protestants point out that purgatory is not a biblical word; that there is little in the Scriptures that can be cited in support of such a doctrine, and that the New Testament instances of dying men represent them as going immediately into the Father's presence: to the penitent thief on the cross, Jesus said: "Today you will be with me in Paradise"; the martyred Stephen saw "the heavens opened, and the Son of man standing at the right hand of God. . . . And he prayed, 'Lord Jesus, receive my spirit." (Acts 7 : 56, 59). With respect to the use of this passage as supporting the doctrine of indulgences, Protestants point out that the statement here regarding "the keys of the kingdom" must be interpreted by such passages as (*a*) Revelation 1 : 18 where it is the risen Christ who holds "the keys of death and Hades"; and (*b*) Matthew 18 : 15 – 20, where the power of decision is bestowed not upon an individual but upon the Church collectively: "where two or three are gathered in my name, there am I in the midst of them." Protestants hold, not that heaven is required to ratify the decisions of the Church, but rather that in the fellowship of good people there is granted a collective wisdom which enables the company of believers to make decisions which will be in accord with the mind and purpose of God.

What Will It Profit a Man?
Matthew 16:21–28

21 From that time Jesus began to show his disciples that he must go to Jerusalem and suffer many things from the elders and chief priests and scribes, and be killed, and on the third day be raised. [22] And Peter took him and began to rebuke him, saying, "God forbid, Lord! This shall never happen to you." [23] But he turned and said to Peter, "Get behind me, Satan! You are a hindrance to me; for you are not on the side of God, but of men."

24 Then Jesus told his disciples, "If any man would come after me, let him deny himself and take up his cross and follow me. [25] For whoever would save his life will lose it, and whoever loses his life for

my sake will find it. ²⁶ For what will it profit a man, if he gains the whole world and forfeits his life? Or what shall a man give in return for his life? ²⁷ For the Son of man is to come with his angels in the glory of his Father, and then he will repay every man for what he has done. ²⁸ Truly, I say to you, there are some standing here who will not taste death before they see the Son of man coming in his kingdom."

16:24 Verses 24–27 are the Gospel of the Catholic Church's second Mass for a martyr who was a bishop, for example, St. Blaise (February 3). The passage is also used in the Mass on the Feast of St. Joan of Arc (May 30).

Jesus Is Transfigured
Matthew 17:1–13

17 And after six days Jesus took with him Peter and James and John his brother, and led them up a high mountain apart. ² And he was transfigured before them, and his face shone like the sun, and his garments became white as light. ³ And behold, there appeared to them Moses and Eli'jah, talking with him. ⁴ And Peter said to Jesus, "Lord, it is well that we are here; if you wish, I will make three booths here, one for you and one for Moses and one for Eli'jah." ⁵ He was still speaking, when lo, a bright cloud overshadowed them, and a voice from the cloud said, "This is my beloved Son, with whom I am well pleased; listen to him." ⁶ When the disciples heard this, they fell on their faces, and were filled with awe. ⁷ But Jesus came and touched them, saying, "Rise, and have no fear." ⁸ And when they lifted up their eyes, they saw no one but Jesus only.

9 And as they were coming down the mountain, Jesus commanded them, "Tell no one the vision, until the Son of man is raised from the dead." ¹⁰ And the disciples asked him, "Then why do the scribes say that first Eli'jah must come?" ¹¹ He replied, "Eli'jah does come, and he is to restore all things; ¹² but I tell you that Eli'jah has already come, and they did not know him, but did to him whatever they pleased. So also the Son of man will suffer at their hands." ¹³ Then the disciples understood that he was speaking to them of John the Baptist.

17:1 In the Roman Catholic calendar, this event is commemorated on August 6. Verses 1–9 are also read on the Second Sunday of Lent. Tradition has assigned Mt. Tabor, highest peak of the Lower Galilee region, as the site of the Transfiguration. **17:2** The Transfiguration of Jesus is seen by many as a revelation of Jesus' divine majesty in anticipation of his resurrection (see also Acts 7:55). This passage parallels the account of the theophany on Mount Sinai

(Exodus 19:16–20, 24:15–18; 34:29–30). For Elijah, see 2 Kings 2:9–12. **17:4** Peter's idea of making booths (older translations: tabernacles) is derived from the Feast of Booths (Tents, Tabernacles—Succoth), the most joyful of Israel's feasts. (Zechariah 14:16 teaches that the Feast of Booths will be celebrated universally when the Messiah comes.)

Become like Children

The fourth sermon of Matthew's Gospel begins here. Jesus teaches here against ambition, on avoiding scandal, on fraternal correction and on the power of united prayer.

Matthew 18:1–20

18 At that time the disciples came to Jesus, saying, "Who is the greatest in the kingdom of heaven?" ² And calling to him a child, he put him in the midst of them, ³ and said, "Truly, I say to you, unless you turn and become like children, you will never enter the kingdom of heaven. ⁴ Whoever humbles himself like this child, he is the greatest in the kingdom of heaven.

5 "Whoever receives one such child in my name receives me; ⁶ but whoever causes one of these little ones who believe in me to sin, it would be better for him to have a great millstone fastened round his neck and to be drowned in the depth of the sea.

7 "Woe to the world for temptations to sin! For it is necessary that temptations come, but woe to the man by whom the temptation comes! ⁸ And if your hand or your foot causes you to sin, cut it off and throw it from you; it is better for you to enter life maimed or lame than with two hands or two feet to be thrown into the eternal fire. ⁹ And if your eye causes you to sin, pluck it out and throw it from you; it is better for you to enter life with one eye than with two eyes to be thrown into the hell of fire.

10 "See that you do not despise one of these little ones; for I tell you that in heaven their angels always behold the face of my Father who is in heaven. ¹² What do you think? If a man has a hundred sheep, and one of them has gone astray, does he not leave the ninety-nine on the hills and go in search of the one that went astray? ¹³ And if he finds it, truly, I say to you, he rejoices over it more than over the ninety-nine that never went astray. ¹⁴ So it is not the will of my Father who is in heaven that one of these little ones should perish.

15 "If your brother sins against you, go and tell him his fault, between you and him alone. If he listens to you, you have gained your brother. ¹⁶ But if he does not listen, take one or two others along with you, that every word may be confirmed by the evidence of

two or three witnesses. [17] If he refuses to listen to them, tell it to the church; and if he refuses to listen even to the church, let him be to you as a Gentile and a tax collector. [18] Truly, I say to you, whatever you bind on earth shall be bound in heaven, and whatever you loose on earth shall be loosed in heaven. [19] Again I say to you, if two of you agree on earth about anything they ask, it will be done for them by my Father in heaven. [20] For where two or three are gathered in my name, there am I in the midst of them."

18:1 The passage has been the basis of much theological writing: about angels (verses 1–10 are read in the Mass of the Holy Guardian Angels, October 2, the Feast of St. Michael Archangel, September 29, etc.); about God's universal will to save all men (verse 14); about ecclesiastical authority (verses 15–18). **18:5–10** From this passage Walter Rauschenbusch (1861–1918), pastor in a slum area of New York City known as "Hell's Kitchen," preached that sweatshops and the exploitation of child labor are sins. He wrote books such as *Christianizing the Social Order, A Theology for the Social Gospel* and *Christianity and the Social Crisis.* **18:18** This is one of the two dozen verses defined by the Catholic Church. The Council of Trent declared (14th session, November 25, 1551) that only bishops and priests are given the power of the keys, that is, the power to forgive sins; that a priest does not lose this power even if he is in sin; that the exercise of the power of the keys is more than simply preaching of the gospel; that a priest may impose a penance for sins in accordance with the power defined here. These Catholic definitions were a response to Protestant interpretations that all the faithful share in the power described in the verse. **18:20** Compare the Talmudic concept: "When three men sit together discussing words of Torah, the Shekinah (the Divine Presence) is in the midst of them."

The Parable of the Unmerciful Servant

This parable, which concludes the fourth discourse, is found only in Matthew's Gospel. The difference between talents and denarii in the story is like that between several million dollars and one hundred dollars.

Matthew 18:21–35

21 Then Peter came up and said to him, "Lord, how often shall my brother sin against me, and I forgive him? As many as seven times?" [22] Jesus said to him, "I do not say to you seven times, but seventy times seven.

23 "Therefore the kingdom of heaven may be compared to a king who wished to settle accounts with his servants. [24] When he began the reckoning, one was brought to him who owed him ten thousand

talents; ²⁵ and as he could not pay, his lord ordered him to be sold, with his wife and children and all that he had, and payment to be made. ²⁶ So the servant fell on his knees, imploring him, 'Lord, have patience with me, and I will pay you everything.' ²⁷ And out of pity for him the lord of that servant released him and forgave him the debt. ²⁸ But that same servant, as he went out, came upon one of his fellow servants who owed him a hundred denarii; and seizing him by the throat he said, 'Pay what you owe.' ²⁹ So his fellow servant fell down and besought him, 'Have patience with me, and I will pay you.' ³⁰ He refused and went and put him in prison till he should pay the debt. ³¹ When his fellow servants saw what had taken place, they were greatly distressed, and they went and reported to their lord all that had taken place. ³² Then his lord summoned him and said to him, 'You wicked servant! I forgave you all that debt because you besought me; ³³ and should not you have had mercy on your fellow servant, as I had mercy on you?' ³⁴ And in anger his lord delivered him to the jailers, till he should pay all his debt. ³⁵ So also my heavenly Father will do to every one of you, if you do not forgive your brother from your heart."

18:23–35 The parable is the Gospel for the Thirty-first Sunday after Pentecost.

The Two Shall Become One
Matthew 19:1–12

19 Now when Jesus had finished these sayings, he went away from Galilee and entered the region of Judea beyond the Jordan; ² and large crowds followed him, and he healed them there.

3 And Pharisees came up to him and tested him by asking, "Is it lawful to divorce one's wife for any cause?" ⁴ He answered, "Have you not read that he who made them from the beginning made them male and female, ⁵ and said, 'For this reason a man shall leave his father and mother and be joined to his wife, and the two shall become one'? ⁶ So they are no longer two but one. What therefore God has joined together, let no man put asunder." ⁷ They said to him, "Why then did Moses command one to give a certificate of divorce, and to put her away?" ⁸ He said to them, "For your hardness of heart Moses allowed you to divorce your wives, but from the beginning it was not so. ⁹ And I say to you; whoever divorces his wife, except for unchastity, and marries another, commits adultery."

10 The disciples said to him, "If such is the case of a man with his wife, it is not expedient to marry." ¹¹ But he said to them, "Not all men can receive this precept, but only those to whom it is given. ¹² For there are eunuchs who have been so from birth, and there are

eunuchs who have been made eunuchs by men, and there are eunuchs who have made themselves eunuchs for the sake of the kingdom of heaven. He who is able to receive this, let him receive it."

19:3 The Catholic Church uses verses 3–6 as the Gospel in the Nuptial (Wedding) Mass. **19:5** Tyndale: for this thinge, shall a man leve father and mother and cleve unto his wyfe, and they twayne shal be one flesshe. Geneva Bible: For this cause, shal a man leave father and mother, and cleve unto his wife, and they twaine shalbe one flesh. Rheims: and they two shal be in one flesh. King James Version: they twain shall be one flesh. **19:6, 9** Arguments over divorce laws sometimes cite these verses as well as 5:31–32. Compare *Deuteronomy* 24:1 ff. for a Jewish position. **19:8** Jesus suggests here that the Jewish Law made allowance for men's weakness; it was a Law of men. Under the New Covenant, however, the faithful would be capable of living according to a higher Law, the Law of God. Jewish scholars in another age also reasoned the same way about the Law, suggesting that its purpose was disciplinary and that in a new age the Law could and would be revised. Jews disagree with Christians and Christians still disagree among themselves, however, as to what laws should or should not be required of men who would be faithful to God. Jews, who do not believe that a redemption has yet visited the earth, believe that they are enjoined by God to remain as faithful as they can to the Mosaic Law, knowing that God will forgive their transgressions if they approach Him in penitence. **19:12** Verses 12 and 14 are cited in discussion about celibacy in the priesthood and religious orders.

Let the Children Come
Matthew 19:13–15

13 Then children were brought to him that he might lay his hands on them and pray. The disciples rebuked the people; [14] but Jesus said, "Let the children come to me, and do not hinder them; for to such belongs the kingdom of heaven." [15] And he laid his hands on them and went away.

What Must I Do to Have Eternal Life?
Matthew 19:16–30; 20:1–16

16 And behold, one came up to him, saying, "Teacher, what good deed must I do, to have eternal life?" [17] And he said to him, "Why do you ask me about what is good? One there is who is good. If you would enter life, keep the commandments." [18] He said to him, "Which?" And Jesus said, "You shall not kill, You shall not commit adultery, You shall not steal, You shall not bear false witness,

[19] Honor your father and mother, and, You shall love your neighbor as yourself." [20] The young man said to him, All these I have observed; what do I still lack?" [21] Jesus said to him, "If you would be perfect, go, sell what you possess and give to the poor, and you will have treasure in heaven; and come, follow me." [22] When the young man heard this he went away sorrowful; for he had great possessions.

23 And Jesus said to his disciples, "Truly, I say to you, it will be hard for a rich man to enter the kingdom of heaven. [24] Again I tell you, it is easier for a camel to go through the eye of a needle than for a rich man to enter the kingdom of God." [25] When the disciples heard this they were greatly astonished, saying, "Who then can be saved?" [26] But Jesus looked at them and said to them, "With men this is impossible, but with God all things are possible." [27] Then Peter said in reply, "Lo, we have left everything and followed you. What then shall we have?" [28] Jesus said to them, "Truly, I say to you, in the new world, when the Son of man shall sit on his glorious throne, you who have followed me will also sit on twelve thrones, judging the twelve tribes of Israel. [29] And every one who has left houses or brothers or sisters or father or mother or children or lands, for my name's sake, will receive a hundredfold, and inherit eternal life. [30] But many that are first will be last, and the last first.

20 "For the kingdom of heaven is like a householder who went out early in the morning to hire laborers for his vineyard. [2] After agreeing with the laborers for a denarius a day, he sent them into his vineyard. [3] And going out about the third hour he saw others standing idle in the market place; [4] and to them he said, 'You go into the vineyard too, and whatever is right I will give you.' So they went. [5] Going out again about the sixth hour and the ninth hour, he did the same. [6] And about the eleventh hour he went out and found others standing; and he said to them, 'Why do you stand here idle all day?' [7] They said to him, 'Because no one has hired us.' He said to them, 'You go into the vineyard too.' [8] And when evening came, the owner of the vineyard said to his steward, 'Call the laborers and pay them their wages, beginning with the last, up to the first.' [9] And when those hired about the eleventh hour came, each of them received a denarius. [10] Now when the first came, they thought they would receive more; but each of them also received a denarius. [11] And on receiving it they grumbled at the householder, [12] saying, 'These last worked only one hour, and you have made them equal to us who have borne the burden of the day and the scorching heat.' [13] But he replied to one of them, 'Friend, I am doing you no wrong; did you not agree with me for a denarius? [14] Take what belongs to you, and go; I choose to give to this last as I give to you. [15] Am I not allowed to do what I choose with what belongs to me? Or do you begrudge my generosity?' [16] So the last will be first, and the first last."

19:21 These words are taken literally by some Christians: Peter Waldo (died 1217) a wealthy merchant of Lyons, for example, gave away his property, about 1176. He preached poverty. He left a band of followers, the Waldenses; their headquarters are in the Italian Alps. They consider themselves Reformers before the Reformation. St. Francis of Assisi (1182–1226), son of a wealthy Italian merchant, became an itinerant preacher of humility. He found joy in absolute poverty and founded the Franciscan friars, an entirely new type of order in the church. In our day, Muriel Lester (1883–1968), a high-born Englishwoman, renounced her patrimony. She founded, in the East End of London, the Brethren of the Common Table, and worked for world peace through the Fellowship of Reconciliation. **19:24** Many regard this as an example of Jesus' use of hyperbole. The apostles are astonished (verse 25); it was commonly held that prosperity was a sign of God's favor. **19:27** Verses 27–29 are the Gospel in the Mass of a holy abbot. **20:1–16** This passage has sometimes been understood also to mean that people of the new (messianic) age enjoy the same status as good men who have lived before them; and that converts to Christianity from paganism are just as worthy as Jewish Christians. The parable is the Gospel for Septuagesima Sunday, which begins the first of the penitential seasons that prepare for Easter. **20:9** Earlier translations have "penny" for "denarius."

Jesus Enters Jerusalem
Matthew 21:1–27

21 And when they drew near to Jerusalem and came to Beth'phage, to the Mount of Olives, then Jesus sent two disciples, [2] saying to them, "Go into the village opposite you, and immediately you will find an ass tied, and a colt with her; untie them and bring them to me. [3] If any one says anything to you, you shall say, 'The Lord has need of them,' and he will send them immediately." [4] This took place to fulfil what was spoken by the prophet, saying,

[5] "Tell the daughter of Zion,
    Behold, your king is coming to you,
    humble, and mounted on an ass,
    and on a colt, the foal of an ass."

[6] The disciples went and did as Jesus had directed them; [7] they brought the ass and the colt, and put their garments on them, and he sat thereon. [8] Most of the crowd spread their garments on the road, and others cut branches from the trees and spread them on the road.

⁹ And the crowds that went before him and that followed him shouted, "Hosanna to the Son of David! Blessed is he who comes in the name of the Lord! Hosanna in the highest!" ¹⁰ And when he entered Jerusalem, all the city was stirred, saying, "Who is this?" ¹¹ And the crowds said, "This is the prophet Jesus from Nazareth of Galilee."

12 And Jesus entered the temple of God and drove out all who sold and bought in the temple, and he overturned the tables of the money-changers and the seats of those who sold pigeons. ¹³ He said to them, "It is written, 'My house shall be called a house of prayer'; but you make it a den of robbers."

14 And the blind and the lame came to him in the temple, and he healed them. ¹⁵ But when the chief priests and the scribes saw the wonderful things that he did, and the children crying out in the temple, "Hosanna to the Son of David!" they were indignant; ¹⁶ and they said to him, "Do you hear what these are saying?" And Jesus said to them, "Yes; have you never read,

'Out of the mouth of babes and sucklings
    thou hast brought perfect praise'?"

¹⁷ And leaving them, he went out of the city to Bethany and lodged there.

18 In the morning, as he was returning to the city, he was hungry. ¹⁹ And seeing a fig tree by the wayside he went to it, and found nothing on it but leaves only. And he said to it, "May no fruit ever come from you again!" And the fig tree withered at once. ²⁰ When the disciples saw it they marveled, saying, "How did the fig tree wither at once?" ²¹ And Jesus answered them, "Truly, I say to you, if you have faith and never doubt, you will not only do what has been done to the fig tree, but even if you say to this mountain, 'Be taken up and cast into the sea,' it will be done. ²² And whatever you ask in prayer, you will receive, if you have faith."

23 And when he entered the temple, the chief priests and the elders of the people came up to him as he was teaching, and said, "By what authority are you doing these things, and who gave you this authority?" ²⁴ Jesus answered them, "I also will ask you a question; and if you tell me the answer, then I also will tell you by what authority I do these things. ²⁵ The baptism of John, whence was it? From heaven or from men?" And they argued with one another, "If we say, 'From heaven,' he will say to us, 'Why then did you not believe him?' ²⁶ But if we say, 'From men,' we are afraid of the multitude; for all hold that John was a prophet." ²⁷ So they answered Jesus, "We do not know." And he said to them, "Neither will I tell you by what authority I do these things.

21:5 See Zechariah 9:9.

21:8 The scene described here is commemorated annually by Christians on Palm Sunday, which is the beginning of Holy Week, the final week of Lent. The liturgy (since the eighth century) calls for a blessing of palms (verses 1–9 here are read during the ceremony) and a procession. The people have a custom of keeping the palms in their homes during the rest of the year (hung on a wall or attached to a crucifix or holy picture). In South America a large palm bouquet is hung behind the front door. In Italy people offer a blessed palm as a sign that they wish to make up with someone after a quarrel. Ukrainians have a custom of striking each other with pussy-willow palms in imitation and remembrance of the scourging endured by Jesus. Poles have the same custom. **21:9** *Hosanna:* A Hebrew word meaning "save us, please!" Originally addressed to God, it came to be used as a cry of joy. **21:12** This passage has been used to justify every form of violence, up to and including the atomic bomb. If Jesus drove out the money-changers, the argument runs, then men and nations are entitled to use whatever force is necessary to rid themselves of evil-doers. Jerome says of Jesus on this occasion that "a fierce and starry light shone in his eyes," suggesting that the earnestness with which he went about purifying the place of worship so troubled the consciences of the merchandisers that they fled without bothering to retrieve their flying coins. Jesus did not cleanse the Temple the instant the abuse came to his attention. Mark 11:11 relates that Jesus entered Jerusalem, and went into the Temple; and "when he had looked round at everything," he went outside the city to spend the night. It was only on the next day that "he entered the temple and began to drive out those who sold and those who bought." The Talmud also records Pharisaic objections against trafficking in the Temple area. Justification for the money-changers was based on the Jewish Law that coins carrying the image of the Emperor were forbidden as donations to the Temple. The Temple and the priests also were supported in part through the tax levied on the money-changing procedure. But such activity could have taken place in a designated area well removed from the Temple courts. **21:13** Older translations have "thieves" for "robbers." **21:16** See Psalm 8:2.

The Parable of the Marriage Feast
Matthew 22:1–14

22 And again Jesus spoke to them in parables, saying, ²"The kingdom of heaven may be compared to a king who gave a marriage feast for his son, ³ and sent his servants to call those who were invited to the marriage feast; but they would not come. ⁴ Again he sent other servants, saying, 'Tell those who are invited, Behold, I have made ready my dinner, my oxen and my fat calves are killed, and everything is ready; come to the marriage feast.' ⁵But they made light of it and went off, one to his farm, another to his business, ⁶while the rest seized his servants, treated them shamefully, and killed them. ⁷The king was angry, and he sent his troops and destroyed those murderers and burned their city. ⁸Then he said to his servants, 'The wedding is ready, but those invited were not worthy. ⁹Go therefore to the thoroughfares, and invite to the marriage feast as many as you find.' ¹⁰And those servants went out into the streets and gathered all whom they found, both bad and good; so the wedding hall was filled with guests.

11 "But when the king came in to look at the guests, he saw there a man who had no wedding garment; ¹²and he said to him, 'Friend, how did you get in here without a wedding garment?' And he was speechless. ¹³Then the king said to the attendants, 'Bind him hand and foot, and cast him into the outer darkness; there men will weep and gnash their teeth.' ¹⁴For many are called, but few are chosen."

22:1 This parable is the Gospel for the Nineteenth Sunday after Pentecost. **22:9** Older translations have "highways" for "thoroughfares."

Render to Caesar the Things That Are Caesar's
Matthew 22:15–22

15 Then the Pharisees went and took counsel how to entangle him in his talk. ¹⁶And they sent their disciples to him, along with the Hero'di-ans, saying, "Teacher, we know that you are true, and teach the way of God truthfully, and care for no man; for you do not regard the position of men. ¹⁷Tell us, then, what you think. Is it lawful to pay taxes to Caesar, or not?" ¹⁸But Jesus, aware of their malice, said, "Why put me to the test, you hypocrites? ¹⁹Show me the money for the tax." And they brought him a coin. ²⁰And Jesus said to them, "Whose likeness and inscription is this?" ²¹They said, "Caesar's." Then he said to them, "Render therefore to Caesar the things that are Caesar's, and to God the things that are God's." ²²When they heard it, they marveled; and they left him and went away.

22:15 If Jesus answered that he was opposed to the payment of tribute to Rome, he would be in rebellion against the ruling power; if he favored the payment of the tribute, he would disappoint those Jews who believed that the Savior, predicted by the prophets, would restore the nation to its former independence. This passage is the Gospel for the Twenty-second Sunday after Pentecost. **22:21** This verse, interpreted variously, is often cited in discussions of church-state relations.

Jesus Teaches about Resurrection
Matthew 22:23–33

23 The same day Sad'ducees came to him, who say that there is no resurrection; and they asked him a question, ²⁴ saying, "Teacher, Moses said, 'If a man dies, having no children, his brother must marry the widow, and raise up children for his brother.' ²⁵ Now there were seven brothers among us; the first married, and died, and having no children left his wife to his brother. ²⁶ So too the second and third, down to the seventh. ²⁷ After them all, the woman died. ²⁸ In the resurrection, therefore, to which of the seven will she be wife? For they all had her."

29 But Jesus answered them, "You are wrong, because you know neither the scriptures nor the power of God. ³⁰ For in the resurrection they neither marry nor are given in marriage, but are like angels in heaven. ³¹ And as for the resurrection of the dead, have you not read what was said to you by God, ³² 'I am the God of Abraham, and the God of Isaac, and the God of Jacob'? He is not God of the dead, but of the living." ³³ And when the crowd heard it, they were astonished at his teaching.

22:23 Jesus had effectively answered the questions posed by the Pharisees. The Sadducees now put him to a test. Perhaps he would agree with them. But they were astonished. In expounding belief in a life after death, Jesus sided with the Pharisees. **22:30** Jesus' view of life after the resurrection, distinguishing the spiritual from a fleshly existence, has a parallel in the Talmud: "The world to come consists not in eating and drinking; the righteous sit with crowns on their heads and enjoy the brightness of the *Shekinah* (God's presence)" (*Berachoth* 17a).

The Great Commandment
Matthew 22:34–40

34 But when the Pharisees heard that he had silenced the Sad'ducees, they came together. ³⁵ And one of them, a lawyer, asked him a question, to test him. ³⁶ "Teacher, which is the great commandment in the law?" ³⁷ And he said to him, "You shall love the Lord your God with all your heart, and with all your soul, and with all your mind. ³⁸ This is the great and first commandment. ³⁹ And a second is like it, You shall love your neighbor as yourself. ⁴⁰ On these two commandments depend all the law and the prophets."

22:34 This is the first part of the Gospel for the Seventeenth Sunday after Pentecost. Both of these commandments are Old Testament teachings: Deuteronomy 6:5 and Leviticus 19:18.

Jesus Denounces False Religion
Matthew 23 : 1–13, 27–28, 37–39

23 Then said Jesus to the crowds and to his disciples, [2] "The scribes and the Pharisees sit on Moses' seat; [3] so practice and observe whatever they tell you, but not what they do; for they preach, but do not practice. [4] They bind heavy burdens, hard to bear, and lay them on men's shoulders; but they themselves will not move them with their finger. [5] They do all their deeds to be seen by men; for they make their phylacteries broad and their fringes long, [6] and they love the place of honor at feasts and the best seats in the synagogues, [7] and salutations in the market places, and being called rabbi by men. [8] But you are not to be called rabbi, for you have one teacher, and you are all brethren. [9] And call no man your father on earth, for you have one Father, who is in heaven. [10] Neither be called masters, for you have one master, the Christ. [11] He who is greatest among you shall be your servant; [12] whoever exalts himself will be humbled, and whoever humbles himself will be exalted.

[13] "But woe to you, scribes and Pharisees, hypocrites! because you shut the kingdom of heaven against men; for you neither enter yourselves, nor allow those who would enter to go in.

[27] "Woe to you, scribes and Pharisees, hypocrites! for you are like whitewashed tombs, which outwardly appear beautiful, but within they are full of dead men's bones and all uncleanness. [28] So you also outwardly appear righteous to men, but within you are full of hypocrisy and iniquity.

[37] "O Jerusalem, Jerusalem, killing the prophets and stoning those who are sent to you! How often would I have gathered your children together as a hen gathers her brood under her wings, and you would not! [38] Behold, your house is forsaken and desolate. [39] For I tell you, you will not see me again, until you say, 'Blessed is he who comes in the name of the Lord.' "

23 : 5 *Phylacteries:* little boxes containing texts of the Hebrew Bible. The very devout Jew wore these little boxes on his forehead and left arm when he prayed. See note on Exodus 13:9, Deuteronomy 6:80. **23 : 11** Compare other known standards of success. **23 : 13** Jewish scholars point out that many Pharisees shared Jesus' distaste for hypocrisy and for false overt manifestations of religiosity that mask any inner commitment or lack of it. Thus Rabbi Joshua Ben Hanania, himself a Pharisee, speaks of "the plagues of the Pharisees" (*Sotah* 3:4). A Rabbinic commentary on Ecclesiastes 4 : 5 states: "The hypocrites are supposed to know Bible and Midrash but they do not. They are covered with their praying shawls and wear the *tephillin* (phylacteries). God says of them: 'I must punish them, for it is said: cursed be he who does the work of the Lord deceitfully' " (*Ecclesiastes Rabbah*). Careful students today make distinctions between types of Pharisees and recognize the sin of hypocrisy as possible among all religions. Paul took pride in his training as a Pharisee (Acts 26:5). **23:37–39** Jewish tradition preserves a record of violent death suffered by many of the prophets. Men have often turned with hatred upon those sent by God to reprove them. Jewish and Christian religious tradition recognizes a pastoral responsibility for the sinful man and also identifies itself with the ideals for which noble men were martyred. Some have read verses 38–39 and Luke 21–24 to mean that Jerusalem will never again be restored until Jews accept Jesus as Christ. The establishment of the Jewish state in Israel was supported by Christian leaders in many parts of the world.

Jesus Speaks of the End of the Age

This is the fifth of the discourses in Matthew's Gospel. In the first two verses, Jesus foretells the destruction of the temple, which took place in A.D. 70. Interpreters differ about which of the verses in the rest of the speech refer to the destruction of Jerusalem and which to the end of the world.

Matthew 24:1–42

24 Jesus left the temple and was going away, when his disciples came to point out to him the buildings of the temple. ²But he answered them, "You see all these, do you not? Truly, I say to you, there will not be left here one stone upon another, that will not be thrown down."

3 As he sat on the Mount of Olives, the disciples came to him privately, saying, "Tell us, when will this be, and what will be the sign of your coming and of the close of the age?" ⁴And Jesus answered them, "Take heed that no one leads you astray. ⁵For many will come in my name, saying, 'I am the Christ,' and they will lead many astray. ⁶And you will hear of wars and rumors of wars; see that you are not alarmed; for this must take place, but the end is not yet. ⁷For nation will rise against nation, and kingdom against kingdom, and there will be famines and earthquakes in various places; ⁸all this is but the beginning of the sufferings.

9 "Then they will deliver you up to tribulation, and put you to death; and you will be hated by all nations for my name's sake. ¹⁰And then many will fall away, and betray one another, and hate one another. ¹¹And many false prophets will arise and lead many astray. ¹²And because wickedness is multiplied, most men's love will grow cold. ¹³But he who endures to the end will be saved. ¹⁴And this gospel of the kingdom will be preached throughout the whole world, as a testimony to all nations; and then the end will come.

15 "So when you see the desolating sacrilege spoken of by the prophet Daniel, standing in the holy place (let the reader understand), [16] then let those who are in Judea flee to the mountains; [17] let him who is on the housetop not go down to take what is in his house; [18] and let him who is in the field not turn back to take his mantle. [19] And alas for those who are with child and for those who give suck in those days! [20] Pray that your flight may not be in winter or on a sabbath. [21] For then there will be great tribulation, such as has not been from the beginning of the world until now, no, and never will be. [22] And if those days had not been shortened, no human being would be saved; but for the sake of the elect those days will be shortened. [23] Then if any one says to you, 'Lo, here is the Christ!' or 'There he is!' do not believe it. [24] For false Christs and false prophets will arise and show great signs and wonders, so as to lead astray, if possible, even the elect. [25] Lo, I have told you beforehand. [26] So, if they say to you, 'Lo, he is in the wilderness,' do not go out; if they say, 'Lo, he is in the inner rooms,' do not believe it. [27] For as the lightning comes from the east and shines as far as the west, so will be the coming of the Son of man. [28] Wherever the body is, there the eagles will be gathered together.

29 "Immediately after the tribulation of those days the sun will be darkened, and the moon will not give its light, and the stars will fall from heaven, and the powers of the heavens will be shaken; [30] then will appear the sign of the Son of man in heaven, and then all the tribes of the earth will mourn, and they will see the Son of man coming on the clouds of heaven with power and great glory; [31] and he will send out his angels with a loud trumpet call, and they will gather his elect from the four winds, from one end of heaven to the other.

32 "From the fig tree learn its lesson: as soon as its branch becomes tender and puts forth its leaves, you know that summer is near. [33] So also, when you see all these things, you know that he is near, at the very gates. [34] Truly, I say to you, this generation will not pass away till all these things take place. [35] Heaven and earth will pass away, but my words will not pass away.

36 "But of that day and hour no one knows, not even the angels of heaven, nor the Son, but the Father only. [37] As were the days of Noah, so will be the coming of the Son of man. [38] For as in those days before the flood they were eating and drinking, marrying and giving in marriage, until the day when Noah entered the ark, [39] and they did not know until the flood came and swept them all away, so will be the coming of the Son of man. [40] Then two men will be in the field; one is taken and one is left. [41] Two women will be grinding at

the mill; one is taken and one is left. [42] Watch therefore, for you do not know on what day your Lord is coming.

24:3 Verses 3–8 are in the Gospel in the Catholic Church's Mass in Time of War. 24:6 The "wars and rumors of wars" here predicted form part of the apocalyptic woes commonly associated with the expected end of the age. Other "signs" of its coming are depicted in 2 Esdras: "the sea of Sodom shall cast up fish ... and fire shall break out, and the wild beasts shall roam their haunts, and monstrous women shall bring forth monsters. And salt waters shall be found in the sweet ... then shall reason hide itself, and wisdom shall withdraw into its chamber." 24:15 Verses 15–35 are the Gospel for the Twenty-fourth and Last Sunday after Pentecost; the liturgical year closes with contemplation of what is regarded as a prophecy of the last judgment. The "abomination of Desolation" is an expression used in the Book of Daniel (9:27) and 1 Maccabees (1:54) in reference to a heathen altar built by the Syrian King Antiochus IV in the Temple precincts in 168 B.C. The expression may have had some special meaning for the readers of Mark's Gospel (a veiled reference to the Emperor Caligula in A.D. 40, or to Titus' invasion of the Holy Land in A.D. 68?). 24:36 This verse is cited by those who discount predictions of a stated date for the end of the world.

"You Know Neither the Day nor the Hour"
Matthew 25:1–13

25 "Then the kingdom of heaven shall be compared to ten maidens who took their lamps and went to meet the bridegroom. [2] Five of them were foolish, and five were wise. [3] For when the foolish took their lamps, they took no oil with them; [4] but the wise took flasks of oil with their lamps. [5] As the bridegroom was delayed, they all slumbered and slept. [6] But at midnight there was a cry, 'Behold, the bridegroom! Come out to meet him.' [7] Then all those maidens rose and trimmed their lamps. [8] And the foolish said to the wise, 'Give us some of your oil, for our lamps are going out.' [9] But the wise replied, 'Perhaps there will not be enough for us and for you; go rather to the dealers and buy for yourselves.' [10] And while they went to buy, the bridegroom came, and those who were ready went in with him to the marriage feast; and the door was shut. [11] Afterwards the other maidens came also, saying, 'Lord, lord, open to us.' [12] But he replied, 'Truly, I say to you, I do not know you.' [13] Watch therefore, for you know neither the day nor the hour.

25:1 The Catholic Church uses this section as the Gospel in the first Mass of a virgin martyr and the first Mass of a virgin not a martyr. Examples of the latter are St. Clare (August 13) and St. Teresa of Avila (September 15).

Parable of the Talents
Matthew 25 : 14–30

14 "For it will be as when a man going on a journey called his servants and entrusted to them his property; ¹⁵to one he gave five talents, to another two, to another one, to each according to his ability. Then he went away. ¹⁶He who had received the five talents went at once and traded with them; and he made five talents more. ¹⁷So also, he who had the two talents made two talents more. ¹⁸But he who had received the one talent went and dug in the ground and hid his master's money. ¹⁹Now after a long time the master of those servants came and settled accounts with them. ²⁰And he who had received the five talents came forward, bringing five talents more, saying, 'Master, you delivered to me five talents; here I have made five talents more.' ²¹His master said to him, 'Well done, good and faithful servant; you have been faithful over a little, I will set you over much; enter into the joy of your master.' ²²And he also who had the two talents came forward, saying, 'Master, you delivered to me two talents; here I have made two talents more.' ²³His master said to him, 'Well done, good and faithful servant; you have been faithful over a little, I will set you over much; enter into the joy of your master.' ²⁴He also who had received the one talent came forward, saying, 'Master, I knew you to be a hard man, reaping where you did not sow, and gathering where you did not winnow; ²⁵so I was afraid, and I went and hid your talent in the ground. Here you have what is yours.' ²⁶But his master answered him, 'You wicked and slothful servant! You knew that I reap where I have not sowed, and gather where I have not winnowed? ²⁷ Then you ought to have invested my money with the bankers, and at my coming I should have received what was my own with interest. ²⁸So take the talent from him, and give it to him who has the ten talents. ²⁹For to every one who has will more be given, and he will have abundance; but from him who has not, even what he has will be taken away. ³⁰And cast the worthless servant into the outer darkness; there men will weep and gnash their teeth.

25:14 Verses 14–23 are used in the Mass of a confessor who was a bishop, for example, St. Patrick, patron of Ireland (March 17). **25:15** *Talent:* the Greek *talanton* referred to a certain weight of silver whose value can now be roughly equated with a thousand dollars. The English word "talent," however, has come to mean any gift of personality which is made to serve a worthy purpose. It is an impressive illustration of how the Gospels have enriched our speech by adding a word to our language. The parable of the talents is cited by many persons who support education as a means by which each individual can make the most of his potentialities. **25:30** Older translations have: There shall be weeping and gnashing of teeth.

The Final Judgment
Matthew 25:31–46

31 "When the Son of man comes in his glory, and all the angels with him, then he will sit on his glorious throne. ³²Before him will be gathered all the nations, and he will separate them one from another as a shepherd separates the sheep from the goats, ³³and he will place the sheep at his right hand, but the goats at the left. ³⁴Then the King will say to those at his right hand, 'Come, O blessed of my Father, inherit the kingdom prepared for you from the foundation of the world; ³⁵for I was hungry and you gave me food, I was thirsty and you gave me drink, I was a stranger and you welcomed me, ³⁶I was naked and you clothed me, I was sick and you visited me, I was in prison and you came to me.' ³⁷Then the righteous will answer him, 'Lord, when did we see thee hungry and feed thee, or thirsty and give thee drink? ³⁸And when did we see thee a stranger and welcome thee, or naked and clothe thee? ³⁹And when did we see thee sick or in prison and visit thee?' ⁴⁰And the King will answer them, 'Truly, I say to you, as you did it to one of the least of these my brethren, you did it to me.' ⁴¹Then he will say to those at his left hand, 'Depart from me, you cursed, into the eternal fire prepared for the devil and his angels; ⁴²for I was hungry and you gave me no food, I was thirsty and you gave me no drink, ⁴³I was a stranger and you did not welcome me, naked and you did not clothe me, sick and in prison and you did not visit me.' ⁴⁴Then they also will answer, 'Lord, when did we see thee hungry or thirsty or a stranger or naked or sick or in prison, and did not minister to thee?' ⁴⁵Then he will answer them, 'Truly, I say to you, as you did it not to one of the least of these, you did it not to me.' ⁴⁶And they will go away into eternal punishment, but the righteous into eternal life."

25:31 The most famous depiction of this scene in art is Michelangelo's great painting in the Sistine Chapel of the Vatican, on the wall behind the altar. The great porch at the western end of most European cathedrals faces the setting sun. In the Middle Ages this fact led artists and people to think of the close of life, and therefore the west end of the cathedral became a conventional position for sculptures or paintings of the Last Judgment (Notre Dame in Paris, Rheims, Amiens). Also, the west doorway is the main portal of these and many other churches. Thus the church came to be regarded as a type or symbol of heaven, to be entered through a portal at which the Judge sits separating sheep from goats. Some cathedrals and large churches (Riverside Church, New York City) have an archangel on the easternmost pinnacle, facing the rising sun, to remind the people in the city below that all must die and face judgment. **26:35** Dietrich Bonhoeffer (1906-1945), whose opposition to the Hitler régime cost him his life, said: "When Christ calls a man, he bids him come and die." For his own part, he said, God had granted him what he called "costly grace"—that is, the privilege of taking the cross for others and of affirming his faith by martyrdom. **25:36** This passage has inspired many efforts to alleviate the plight of prisoners. Thus the Englishman John Howard (1729–1790) visited prisoners in England, Scotland, France, Holland, Germany, Spain, Italy, Russia, Turkey, bringing their plight to the attention of the public. His was the first statue admitted to London's St. Paul's Cathedral; unveiling it, Dean Milman said: "Perhaps no man has assuaged so much human misery as John Howard." **25:37-39** Sam Higginbotham (1874–1958) was a Christian missionary who founded the Allahabad agricultural project in India. Princeton University invented for him a new degree, "Doctor of Philanthropy." Explaining his work, he said: "At the judgment day, when some will not recall having fed or clothed their LORD, the answer will be: 'When you went to that little famine-cursed village that had been growing ten bushels of wheat per acre and taught it to grow twenty, you were helping to feed the hungry. When you went to that village that was growing sixty pounds of poor, short-staple cotton per acre and taught them to grow three hundred pounds per acre of good long-staple cotton, you were helping to clothe the naked. When you went to that village where the well had dried up and you sent a boring outfit, and bored down until you had secured an abundant supply of water, enough for man and beast and some over for irrigation, you were helping to give drink to the thirsty.' "

Jesus' Passion and Death

Matthew 26:1–16

26 When Jesus had finished all these sayings, he said to his disciples, ² "You know that after two days the Passover is coming, and the Son of man will be delivered up to be crucified."

3 Then the chief priests and the elders of the people gathered in the palace of the high priest, who was called Ca′iaphas, ⁴ and took counsel together in order to arrest Jesus by stealth and kill him. ⁵ But they said, "Not during the feast, lest there be a tumult among the people."

6 Now when Jesus was at Bethany in the house of Simon the leper, ⁷ a woman came up to him with an alabaster jar of very expensive ointment, and she poured it on his head, as he sat at table. ⁸ But when the disciples saw it, they were indignant, saying, "Why

this waste? ⁹ For this ointment might have been sold for a large sum, and given to the poor." ¹⁰ But Jesus, aware of this, said to them, "Why do you trouble the woman? For she has done a beautiful thing to me. ¹¹ For you always have the poor with you, but you will not always have me. ¹² In pouring this ointment on my body she has done it to prepare me for burial. ¹³ Truly, I say to you, wherever this gospel is preached in the whole world, what she has done will be told in memory of her."

14 Then one of the twelve, who was called Judas Iscariot, went to the chief priests ¹⁵ and said, "What will you give me if I deliver him to you?" And they paid him thirty pieces of silver. ¹⁶ And from that moment he sought an opportunity to betray him.

26:1 Matthew's account of the Passion (suffering) of Jesus is read or chanted (Gregorian chant) on Palm Sunday. Mark's account is similarly used on Tuesday of Holy Week, Luke's on Wednesday, John's on Friday (Good Friday). In most Catholic parish churches three priests or deacons chant John's account on Good Friday, one taking the narrative parts, another the part of Christ, the third singing the words of others in the drama (a choir may sing the words of the crowd). All four Gospel narratives of the Passion have been set to music by great composers, most notably Johann Sebastian Bach, whose *Saint Matthew Passion* (produced for the first time in 1729) and *Saint John Passion* are still popular. The latter part of Handel's *Messiah* deals with the crucifixion and resurrection. The words of Jesus on the cross have been set to music also (*Seven Last Words* by Haydn; *Seven Last Words* by Gounod). In many Protestant churches on Good Friday there is a service three hours in length, commemorating Jesus' three hours of agony on the Cross; at this service it is customary to have short discourses or sermons on each of the seven last words. The seven words are assembled from the four Gospel accounts of what was spoken from the cross.

In the anointing at Bethany Matthew senses a kind of symbolic preparation for the Crucifixion; the woman's lavish outpouring of affection prepares Christ's body beforehand for its entombment.

The New Testament writers also link Christ's death for the whole world with an earlier deliverance wrought for the Hebrew people. In Luke 9:31 Jesus speaks "of his departure which he was to accomplish at Jerusalem." The word translated "departure" is the Greek word *exodus;* it represents Jesus's impending death as another exodus in which the people of God are delivered from bondage to sin. In accord with this Matthew presents Jesus' Last Supper as a passover meal, in which the unleavened bread, reminder of the hasty exit from Egypt, becomes the symbol of Christ's body, soon to be broken on the cross; and the wine, reminder of the blood of the lamb, placed on the doorpost so the death angel would know to pass over, becomes the symbol of Christ's blood, soon to pour from his wounded side. Summing up what he regards as the historic link between the Exodus and the Atonement, Paul says, in 1 Corinthians 5:7: "For Christ, our paschal lamb, has been sacrificed." **26:11** Deuteronomy 15:4 pictures an expectation among the Hebrews of life in the promised land: "there will no poor among you." Reflecting the realities of a later age, however, Deuteronomy 15:11 says: "For the poor will never cease out of the land." The Rabbis interpreted the existence of poverty as consequence of society's failure to keep faith with God and provide instruments of justice (see note on Deuteronomy 15:11) Jesus' word, "For you always have the poor with you," was followed by the emphasis of the conclusion of the sentence: "you will not always have me." Most interpreters agree that good deeds to the impoverished are always in order; but the disciples are reminded that the opportunities to honor Jesus were few and fleeting. Some interpreters invoke the first phrase out of context in arguments against private and public programs of relief. **26:15** The value is uncertain, but if shekels are meant (and they *are* meant in the passage Matthew quotes in 27:9), at four denarii to the shekel, thirty pieces of silver would be 120 days' wages.

The Last Supper
Matthew 26:17–30

17 Now on the first day of Unleavened Bread the disciples came to Jesus, saying, "Where will you have us prepare for you to eat the passover?" [18] He said, "Go into the city to such a one, and say to him, 'The Teacher says, My time is at hand; I will keep the passover at your house with my disciples.' " [19] And the disciples did as Jesus had directed them, and they prepared the passover.

20 When it was evening, he sat at table with the twelve disciples; [21] and as they were eating, he said, "Truly, I say to you, one of you will betray me." [22] And they were very sorrowful, and began to say to him one after another, "Is it I, Lord?" [23] He answered, "He who has dipped his hand in the dish with me will betray me. [24] The Son of man goes as it is written of him, but woe to that man by whom the Son of man is betrayed! It would have been better for that man if he had not been born." [25] Judas, who betrayed him, said, "Is it I, Master?" He said to him, "You have said so."

26 Now as they were eating, Jesus took bread, and blessed, and broke it, and gave it to the disciples and said, "Take, eat; this is my body." [27] And he took a cup, and when he had given thanks he gave it to them, saying, "Drink of it, all of you; [28] for this is my blood of the covenant, which is poured out for many for the forgiveness of sins. [29] I tell you I shall not drink again of this fruit of the vine until that day when I drink it new with you in my Father's kingdom."

30 And when they had sung a hymn, they went out to the Mount of Olives.

26:18 Older translations have "master" for "teacher." **26:20** Christians have traditionally commemorated this event on Thursday of Holy Week, calling it Holy Thursday, Thursday of the Lord's Supper (in the Greek Church, Holy and Great Thursday of the Mystic Supper) or Maundy Thursday (cf. note on John 13:14–17 for Maundy). The most famous representation of the Last Supper in art is Leonardo da Vinci's painting in Milan, Italy, on the wall of a monastery. His painting does not illustrate the blessing of bread and cup, but, rather, the moment when Jesus said: "One of you will betray me" (Matthew 26:21). **26:26** All Christians regard verses 26–28 as an account of the institution of the Holy Eucharist and the source of their Communion service (although they understand Eucharist and Communion in many different ways). Catholics hold that the substance of bread and wine is changed into the substance of Christ's body and blood. They call the conversion transubstantiation. According to this teaching, only the "accidents" (color, etc.) of bread and wine remain after the Consecration of the Mass, when the priest does what Jesus is here described as doing. Verses 26–28 and the parallel passages (Mark 14:22–24, Luke 22:19, 1 Corinthians 11:23–25) are among the two dozen biblical verses officially defined by the Catholic Church. The Council of Trent (13th session, October 11, 1551) declared these verses mean that Christ really and substantially is contained under the appearance of sensible things in the sacrament of the Eucharist instituted at the Last Supper. Orthodox Churches hold essentially the same doctrine, but they contend that the Roman Church's use of unleavened bread is an eleventh-century innovation and that it was an innovation to regard consecration as taking place when the words "this is my body . . . this is my blood" are uttered. The Orthodox believe the consecration occurs after invocation of the Holy Spirit in a prayer called the *epiclesis* that follows the Consecration. The Orthodox long charged that "the Papal Church from the ninth century downwards has made an innovation in this rite also by depriving the laity of the holy chalice, contrary to the Lord's command and the universal practice of many ancient orthodox bishops of Rome." In 1963 the Second Vatican Council restored the ancient rite for certain solemn occasions (e.g., weddings). Among Protestants, various understandings prevail regarding "This is my body." It is believed that the doctrine of transubstantiation goes beyond the obvious meaning of the words. It is argued that when a man points to the picture on a dollar bill and says: "This is George Washinton," he does not imply that this is somehow the flesh and blood of America's first president, but only that the portrait brings him vividly to mind. Rejecting the doctrine of an invisible miracle,

Zwingli interpreted the Lord' Supper as a memorial meal. Lutherans hold that there is a change by which the body and blood of Christ join with the bread and wine in a way that makes real Christ's substantial presence; he is in, with, and under the bread and wine; this doctrine is called consubstantiation. Holding that "the so-called sacrifice of the Mass is most contradictory to Christ's own sacrifice, the only propitiation for all the sins of the elect," Calvinists teach that "Worthy receivers, outwardly partaking of the visible elements in this sacrament, do then also inwardly by faith, really and indeed, yet not carnally and corporally, but spiritually, receive and feed upon Christ crucified, and all benefits of his death." Colorful accounts of the cup or chalice Jesus used at the supper have enriched the world's literature, chiefly in stories about King Arthur and the Knights of the Round Table, based on the legend that Joseph of Arimathea took the cup to England. This Holy Grail legend (*grail* is from a medieval Latin word for cup) is best known from Malory's *Morte d'Arthur*, Tennyson's *Idylls of the King,* and Wagner's opera *Parsifal.* The "Chalice of Antioch," discovered in 1910 and now on display at the Cloisters in New York City, dates from the fourth or fifth century.

Agony in the Garden
Matthew 26:31–46

31 Then Jesus said to them, 'You will all fall away because of me this night; for it is written, 'I will strike the shepherd, and the sheep of the flock will be scattered.' [32] But after I am raised up, I will go before you to Galilee." [33] Peter declared to him, "Though they all fall away because of you, I will never fall away." [34] Jesus said to him, "Truly, I say to you, this very night, before the cock crows, you will deny me three times." [35] Peter said to him, "Even if I must die with you, I will not deny you." And so said all the disciples.

36 Then Jesus went with them to a place called Gethsem'ane, and he said to his disciples, "Sit here, while I go yonder and pray." [37] And taking with him Peter and the two sons of Zeb'edee, he began to be sorrowful and troubled. [38] Then he said to them, "My soul is very sorrowful, even to death; remain here, and watch with me." [39] And going a little farther he fell on his face and prayed, "My Father, if it be possible, let this cup pass from me; nevertheless, not as I will, but as thou wilt." [40] And he came to the disciples and found them sleeping; and he said to Peter, "So, could you not watch with me one hour? [41] Watch and pray that you may not enter into temptation; the spirit is willing, but the flesh is weak." [42] Again, for the second time, he went away and prayed, "My Father, if this cannot pass unless I drink it, thy will be done." [43] And again he came and found them sleeping, for their eyes were heavy. [44] So, leaving

them again, he went away and prayed for the third time, saying the same words. ⁴⁵ Then he came to the disciples and said to them, "Are you still sleeping and taking your rest? Behold, the hour is at hand, and the Son of man is betrayed into the hands of sinners. ⁴⁶ Rise, let us be going; see, my betrayer is at hand."

26:31 *Agony* (from the Greek word describing the tenseness which an athlete feels before a contest begins) is the word that Luke uses in describing this scene. In Catholic devotions the event is known as the first sorrowful mystery of the Rosary (a combination of vocal prayers and meditation on fifteen principal events or mysteries in the life of Jesus and Mary). Since the "Hail Mary" is said ten times during the contemplation of each event, the Rosary is known as a Marian devotion. It has been promoted for many centuries by the Dominicans (Order of Preachers). The frescoes (paintings on walls) in cell after cell of the Convent of San Marco, Florence (Italy), by Dominican Fra Angelico (1387–1455), are a most beautiful representation of the mysteries of the Rosary.

Jesus Is Arrested
Matthew 26:47–27:31

47 While he was still speaking, Judas came, one of the twelve, and with him a great crowd with swords and clubs, from the chief priests and the elders of the people. ⁴⁸ Now the betrayer had given them a sign, saying, "The one I shall kiss is the man; seize him." ⁴⁹ And he came up to Jesus at once and said, "Hail, Master!" And he kissed him. ⁵⁰ Jesus said to him, "Friend, why are you here?" Then they came up and laid hands on Jesus and seized him. ⁵¹ And behold, one of those who were with Jesus stretched out his hand and drew his sword, and struck the slave of the high priest, and cut off his ear. ⁵² Then Jesus said to him, "Put your sword back into its place; for all who take the sword will perish by the sword. ⁵³ Do you think that I cannot appeal to my Father, and he will at once send me more than twelve legions of angels? ⁵⁴ But how then should the scriptures be fulfilled, that it must be so?" ⁵⁵ At that hour Jesus said to the crowds, "Have you come out as against a robber, with swords and clubs to capture me? Day after day I sat in the temple teaching, and you did not seize me. ⁵⁶ But all this has taken place, that the scriptures of the prophets might be fulfilled." Then all the disciples forsook him and fled.

57 Then those who had seized Jesus led him to Ca′iaphas the high priest, where the scribes and the elders had gathered. ⁵⁸ But Peter followed him at a distance, as far as the courtyard of the high priest, and going inside he sat with the guards to see the end. ⁵⁹ Now the

chief priests and the whole council sought false testimony against Jesus that they might put him to death, ⁶⁰ but they found none, though many false witnesses came forward. At last two came forward ⁶¹ and said, "This fellow said, 'I am able to destroy the temple of God, and to build it in three days.'" ⁶² And the high priest stood up and said, "Have you no answer to make? What is it that these men testify against you?" ⁶³ But Jesus was silent. And the high priest said to him, "I adjure you by the living God, tell us if you are the Christ, the Son of God." ⁶⁴ Jesus said to him, "You have said so. But I tell you, hereafter you will see the Son of man seated at the right hand of Power, and coming on the clouds of heaven." ⁶⁵ Then the high priest tore his robes, and said, "He has uttered blasphemy. Why do we still need witnesses? You have now heard his blasphemy. ⁶⁶ What is your judgment?" They answered, "He deserves death." ⁶⁷ Then they spat in his face, and struck him; and some slapped him, ⁶⁸ saying, "Prophesy to us, you Christ! Who is it that struck you?"

69 Now Peter was sitting outside in the courtyard. And a maid came up to him, and said, "You also were with Jesus the Galilean." ⁷⁰ But he denied it before them all, saying, "I do not know what you mean." ⁷¹ And when he went out to the porch, another maid saw him, and she said to the bystanders, "This man was with Jesus of Nazareth." ⁷² And again he denied it with an oath, "I do not know the man." ⁷³ After a little while the bystanders came up and said to Peter, "Certainly you are also one of them, for your accent betrays you." ⁷⁴ Then he began to invoke a curse on himself and to swear, "I do not know the man." And immediately the cock crowed. ⁷⁵ And Peter remembered the saying of Jesus, "Before the cock crows, you will deny me three times." And he went out and wept bitterly.

27 When morning came, all the chief priests and the elders of the people took counsel against Jesus to put him to death; ² and they bound him and led him away and delivered him to Pilate the governor.

3 When Judas, his betrayer, saw that he was condemned, he repented and brought back the thirty pieces of silver to the chief priests and the elders, ⁴ saying, "I have sinned in betraying innocent blood." They said, "What is that to us? See to it yourself." ⁵ And throwing down the pieces of silver in the temple, he departed; and he went and hanged himself. ⁶ But the chief priests, taking the pieces of silver, said, "It is not lawful to put them into the treasury, since they are blood money." ⁷ So they took counsel, and bought with them the potter's field, to bury strangers in. ⁸ Therefore that field has been

called the Field of Blood to this day. ⁹ Then was fulfilled what had been spoken by the prophet Jeremiah, saying, "And they took the thirty pieces of silver, the price of him on whom a price had been set by some of the sons of Israel, ¹⁰ and they gave them for the potter's field, as the Lord directed me."

11 Now Jesus stood before the governor; and the governor asked him, "Are you the King of the Jews?" Jesus said to him, "You have said so." ¹² But when he was accused by the chief priests and elders, he made no answer. ¹³ Then Pilate said to him, "Do you not hear how many things they testify against you?" ¹⁴ But he gave him no answer, not even to a single charge; so that the governor wondered greatly.

15 Now at the feast the governor was accustomed to release for the crowd any one prisoner whom they wanted. ¹⁶ And they had then a notorious prisoner, called Barab'bas. ¹⁷ So when they had gathered, Pilate said to them, "Whom do you want me to release for you, Barab'bas or Jesus who is called Christ?" ¹⁸ For he knew that it was out of envy that they had delivered him up. ¹⁹ Besides, while he was sitting on the judgment seat, his wife sent word to him, "Have nothing to do with that righteous man, for I have suffered much over him today in a dream." ²⁰ Now the chief priests and the elders persuaded the people to ask for Barab'bas and destroy Jesus. ²¹ The governor again said to them, "Which of the two do you want me to release for you?" And they said, "Barab'bas." ²² Pilate said to them, "Then what shall I do with Jesus who is called Christ?" They all said, "Let him be crucified." ²³ And he said, "Why, what evil has he done?" But they shouted all the more, "Let him be crucified."

24 So when Pilate saw that he was gaining nothing, but rather that a riot was beginning, he took water and washed his hands before the crowd, saying, "I am innocent of this man's blood; see to it yourselves." ²⁵ And all the people answered, "His blood be on us and on our children!" ²⁶ Then he released for them Barab'bas, and having scourged Jesus, delivered him to be crucified.

27 Then the soldiers of the governor took Jesus into the praetorium, and they gathered the whole battalion before him. ²⁸ And they stripped him and put a scarlet robe upon him, ²⁹ and plaiting a crown of thorns they put it on his head, and put a reed in his right hand. And kneeling before him they mocked him, saying, "Hail, King of the Jews!" ³⁰ And they spat upon him, and took the reed and struck him on the head. ³¹ And when they had mocked him, they stripped him of the robe, and put his own clothes on him, and led him away to crucify him.

26:47 The Talmud preserves a street-song in which the Jews complain of the "staves" and the "clubs" of the Boethusian high priests, their sons and treasurers, the temple officers and their servants (*Pesachin* 57a). This reference provides evidence for those Jewish scholars who believe that it was the officers of a corrupt priesthood and the Sadducees, not the Pharisees, who were responsible for the arrest of Jesus. **26:49** Older translations have "Rabbi" for "Master." **26:59** The procedure of the trial as given in the Gospel violates prescribed regulations of Jewish Law. Jewish scholars suggest: (1) the Sanhedrin, at that time, was in the control of a corrupt priestly Sadducean group (cf. Acts 3:17 ff.). Jesus, therefore, was not tried by a court operating under the rules of the Pharisees; or (2) it was not a trial but a preliminary inquiry under the jurisdiction of Roman rule. The Jews at this time were by the Romans denied the power to put any man to death (cf. John 18:31); Talmudic sources record the fact that the "trial of capital cases was taken away from Israel" (*Jerusalem Sanhedrin* 1:1, 7:2). The priests, scribes and elders mentioned here, therefore, were not bound by rabbinic laws of procedure and could only make their preliminary findings known to the Roman ruler who was then obligated himself to conduct a trial, pass judgment, and execute the sentence. In this view, the real trial of Jesus took place in the chambers of Pontius Pilate (27:1 ff.). **26:64** Rending a garment in two, as a sign of mourning, is specifically enjoined in Jewish law when hearing an utterance of blasphemy. **27:2** *Pilate*. The governor. A Jewish historian, Philo of Alexandria, contemporaneous with Jesus, refers to "the crimes of Pilate, his rages, his greed, his injustices, his abuses, the citizens he put to death without trial, his intolerable cruelty," but he provides no documentation. The ambiguous role of Pilate recorded in the Gospel may reflect the fact that when the accounts were written it was important to the Christians not to offend Rome. **27:5** Compare also Acts 1:16–20. **27:22** Arguing that Jesus was fastened on a stake or pole," rather than nailed to a cross, the *New World Translation of the Christian Greek Scriptures* published in 1950 by the Watchtower Bible and Tract Society, here translates: "Pilate said to them: 'What then, shall I do with Jesus the so-called Christ?' They all said: 'Let him be impaled.' " Similarly in this translation Matthew 27:35 begins: "When they had impaled him." **27:25** "To read over the commentaries and interpretations to which this verse has been exposed in the past is a sad and terrible experience ... a collection of the most vitriolic opinions would be a veritable anthology of hate," wrote Father Gregory Baum, O.S.A., referring to the interpretation that this verse justifies or excuses anti-Semitism. Several important international church bodies have spoken to the subject: The third Assembly of the World Council of Churches held at New Delhi, India (November 19–December 5, 1961): "The Assembly urges its member churches to do all in their power to resist every form of anti-Semitism. In Christian teaching the historic events which led to the crucifixion should not be so presented as to fasten upon the Jewish people of today the responsibilities which belong to our corporate humanity, and not to one race or community. . . ." The consultation on "The Church and the Jewish People" of the Lutheran World Federation held at Logumkloster, Denmark (April 26–May 2, 1963); "Anti-Semitism is primarily a denial of the image of God in the Jew; it represents a demonic form of rebellion against the God of Abraham, Isaac and Jacob; and a rejection of Jesus, the Jew, directed upon his people. 'Christian' anti-Semitism is spiritual suicide. . . . Especially reprehensible are the notions that Jews, rather than all mankind, are responsible for the death of Jesus the Christ, and that God has for this reason rejected His covenant people." The Roman Catholic Vatican Council's Declaration on Non-Christian Religions promulgated at Rome, October 28, 1965: "True, authorities of the Jews and those who followed their lead pressed for the death of Christ (cf. John 19:6); still what happened in His passion cannot be blamed on all the Jews then living, without distinction, nor upon the Jews of today. Although the Church is the new people of God, the Jews should not be presented as repudiated or cursed by God, as if such views followed from the Holy Scriptures. . . . The Church repudiates all persecutions against any man. Moreover, mindful of her common patrimony with the Jews and motivated by the gospels spiritual love and by no political considerations, she deplores the hatred, persecutions and displays of anti-Semitism directed against the Jews at any time and from any source."

Jesus Is Crucified
Matthew 27:32–66

32 As they were marching out, they came upon a man of Cyre'ne, Simon by name; this man they compelled to carry his cross. [33] And when they came to a place called Gol'gotha (which means the place of a skull), [34] they offered him wine to drink, mingled with gall; but when he tasted it, he would not drink it. [35] And when they had crucified him, they divided his garments among them by casting lots; [36] then they sat down and kept watch over him there. [37] And over his head they put the charge against him, which read, "This is Jesus the King of the Jews." [38] Then two robbers were crucified with him, one on the right and one on the left. [39] And those who passed by derided him, wagging their heads [40] and saying, "You who would destroy the temple and build it in three days, save yourself! If you are the Son of God, come down from the cross." [41] So also the chief priests, with the scribes and elders, mocked him, saying, [42] "He saved others; he cannot save himself. He is the King of Israel; let him come

down now from the cross, and we will believe in him. [43] He trusts in God; let God deliver him now, if he desires him; for he said, 'I am the Son of God.' " [44] And the robbers who were crucified with him also reviled him in the same way.

45 Now from the sixth hour there was darkness over all the land until the ninth hour. [46] And about the ninth hour Jesus cried with a loud voice, "Eli, Eli, la'ma sabach-tha'ni?" that is, "My God, my God, why hast thou forsaken me?" [47] And some of the bystanders hearing it said, "This man is calling Eli'jah." [48] And one of them at once ran and took a sponge, filled it with vinegar, and put it on a reed, and gave it to him to drink. [49] But the others said, "Wait, let us see whether Eli'jah will come to save him." [50] And Jesus cried again with a loud voice and yielded up his spirit.

51 And behold, the curtain of the temple was torn in two, from top to bottom; and the earth shook, and the rocks were split; [52] the tombs also were opened, and many bodies of the saints who had fallen asleep were raised, [53] and coming out of the tombs after his resurrection they went into the holy city and appeared to many. [54] When the centurion and those who were with him, keeping watch over Jesus, saw the earthquake and what took place, they were filled with awe, and said, "Truly this was the Son of God!"

55 There were also many women there, looking on from afar, who had followed Jesus from Galilee, ministering to him; [56] among whom were Mary Mag'dalene, and Mary the mother of James and Joseph, and the mother of the sons of Zeb'edee.

57 When it was evening, there came a rich man from Arimathe'a, named Joseph, who also was a disciple of Jesus. [58] He went to Pilate and asked for the body of Jesus. Then Pilate ordered it to be given to him. [59] And Joseph took the body, and wrapped it in a clean linen shroud, [60] and laid it in his own new tomb, which he had hewn in the rock; and he rolled a great stone to the door of the tomb, and departed. [61] Mary Mag'dalene and the other Mary were there, sitting opposite the sepulchre.

62 Next day, that is, after the day of Preparation, the chief priests and the Pharisees gathered before Pilate [63] and said, "Sir, we remember how that impostor said, while he was still alive, 'After three days I will rise again.' [64] Therefore order the sepulchre to be made secure until the third day, lest his disciples go and steal him away, and tell the people, 'He has risen from the dead,' and the last fraud will be worse than the first." [65] Pilate said to them, "You have a guard of soldiers; go, make it as secure as you can." [66] So they went and made the sepulchre secure by sealing the stone and setting a guard.

27:31 The Way of the Cross, a devotion preached by Franciscan friars in the Middle Ages, became so popular among Catholics that churches have the fourteen "stations" along the walls (essentially, each station is a wooden cross, but paintings, statues or wood carvings illustrate each event). "Jesus carries the cross" is the title of the fourth sorrowful mystery of the Rosary. 27:33 Many authorities hold it is now "reasonably certain" that Golgotha was outside the city walls and within the area covered later by the Church of the Holy Sepulchre. 27:45 The death of Jesus is commemorated in the Christian calendar by Good Friday, called "Good" because Christians believe that by His death Jesus saved them from their sins. This is the one day in the year on which Mass is not celebrated by the Catholic Church (only a Communion service, using hosts consecrated the preceding day, and devotions in honor of the cross). It is a day of mourning, fasting and prayer. In some countries, especially Spain, there are processions and pageants presenting scenes from the Passion. The bare altars in the churches on this day represent the body of Christ stripped of garments. The death of Jesus is commemorated as the fifth (and final) sorrowful mystery of the Rosary. The cross has become the most important symbol of Christianity. A crucifix is a cross showing Christ's body hanging from it. On Good Friday afternoon, from twelve o'clock until three, in many countries it is customary for devout Christians to commemorate the hours Jesus hung upon the cross (the *Tre Ore*—Three Hours—devotion with sermons, often about the seven "words" or statements Jesus made during those hours). For many centuries, too, the ceremony of *Tenebrae* (literally: shadows or night), held on Wednesday, Thursday and Friday of Holy Week, was thought by the people to have special significance in its rites. (The candles put out one by one during the chanting symbolized the abandonment of Jesus by his disciples one by one; the noise made by the people hitting the benches or their books at the end of Tenebrae symbolized the earthquake mentioned here in Matthew 27:51.) 27:55 The best-known depiction of this scene is Michelangelo's sculpture entitled "Pietà" (in St. Peter's Basilica, Rome, loaned for exhibition at the 1964 New York World's Fair). Christ's rest in the tomb is commemorated on Holy Saturday. 27:59 Tyndale: a clene lynnen clooth. Great Bible: a cleane lynnen cloth. Geneva Bible: a cleane linnen cloth. Rheims: in cleane sinden. King James Version: in a clean linen cloth. A cloth kept in a shrine at the Cathedral of Turin, Italy, has long been venerated as the shroud of Christ.

He Is Risen!
Matthew 28: 1–15

28 Now after the sabbath, toward the dawn of the first day of the week, Mary Mag'dalene and the other Mary went to see the sepulchre. ²And behold, there was a great earthquake; for an angel of the Lord descended from heaven and came and rolled back the stone, and sat upon it. ³His appearance was like lightning, and his raiment white as snow. ⁴And for fear of him the guards trembled and became like dead men. ⁵But the angel said to the women, "Do not be afraid; for I know that you seek Jesus who was crucified. ⁶He is not here; for he has risen, as he said. Come, see the place where he lay. ⁷Then go quickly and tell his disciples that he has risen from the dead, and behold, he is going before you to Galilee; there you will see him. Lo, I have told you." ⁸So they departed quickly from the tomb with fear and great joy, and ran to tell his disciples. ⁹And behold, Jesus met them and said, "Hail!" And they came up and took hold of his feet and worshiped him. ¹⁰Then Jesus said to them, "Do not be afraid; go and tell my brethren to go to Galilee, and there they will see me."

11 While they were going, behold, some of the guard went into the city and told the chief priests all that had taken place. ¹²And when they had assembled with the elders and taken counsel, they gave a sum of money to the soldiers ¹³and said, "Tell people, 'His disciples came by night and stole him away while we were asleep.' ¹⁴And if this comes to the governor's ears, we will satisfy him and keep you out of trouble." ¹⁵So they took the money and did as they were directed; and this story has been spread among the Jews to this day.

28:1 Because the Gospel says the resurrection (rising from the dead) of Jesus took place on "the first day of the week" (Sunday), Christians soon came to regard it as the most important liturgical day, and every Sunday is for them a representation of the Easter Sunday described here. The word Easter and the feast come originally from the celebration of the spring sun rising in the East and bringing new life to the earth. This symbolism was transferred by the Christians to the risen Christ who brought light and new life to the world. Easter is often called "Pasch" (from the Greek and Latin *pascha*, which comes from the Hebrew *pesach*, meaning passover) because Jesus, dying on Passover Day, is regarded as the paschal lamb "who takes away the sin of the world" (John 1:29). The Catholic Church's official calendar announces Easter Sunday with the words: "This is the day which the Lord has made, the Feast of Feasts, and our Pasch: the Resurrection of our Saviour Jesus Christ according to the flesh." Verses 1–7 here are the Gospel of the Easter Vigil, a solemn ceremony that begins Holy Saturday night and stresses light (the paschal candle is a symbol of Christ), joy (especially in the ancient hymn "Exsultet") and baptism (the water for baptism is blessed). Newly baptized Christians in early centuries wore new, white linen garments for the occasion; thus developed a tradition of new clothes for Easter. Sunrise meetings on Easter morning are also traditional, notably among the Moravian brethren. A hymn in the Easter Mass, "Victimae Paschali Laudes" (Praise to the Paschal Victim), based on the Easter biblical story, is the source of the miracle plays and subsequent religious drama from the tenth century. The resurrection is the first of the glorious mysteries in the Rosary.

Go and Make Disciples

Matthew 28:16–20

16 Now the eleven disciples went to Galilee, to the mountain to which Jesus had directed them. [17] And when they saw him they worshiped him; but some doubted. [18] And Jesus came and said to them, "All authority in heaven and on earth has been given to me. [19] Go therefore and make disciples of all nations, baptizing them in the name of the Father and of the Son and of the Holy Spirit, [20] teaching them to observe all that I have commanded you; and lo, I am with you always, to the close of the age."

28:19 Christian theology finds here the teaching on the Holy Trinity, on the Church's mission (which Jesus here broadens to include Gentiles as well as Jews), and on the function of apostles and their successors (to baptize and to teach). Verses 18–20 are the Gospel for Trinity Sunday, the Sunday after Pentecost. Preachers and artists throughout the centuries have used various symbols to express the doctrine of the Trinity, for example, a triangle, the shamrock, clover and other trefoil plants, three circles intertwined. The formula of baptism given here in Matthew's Gospel has been used ever since in Christian rites of baptism (although churches differ on whether baptism is to be by immersion, dipping or having water poured on the forehead). "In the name of the Father . . ." soon became the way Christians began and ended prayers (the Mass begins and ends with this formula. Some believe that passages of this character were "read back" by the author (writing a generation later) into the time of Jesus as rationale for the later practices of the Church. **28:20** Tyndale: And lo I am with you all waye, even untyll the ende of the worlde. Great Bible: And lo I am wyth you allwaye, even untyll the ende of the worlde. Geneva Bible: And lo, I am with you alwaye, until the end of the worlde. Amen. Rheims: And behold I am with you al daies, even to the consummation of the world.

The Gospel according to Mark

Mark's Gospel, shortest of the four, most scholars regard as the earliest of the Gospels. The longer Gospels of Matthew and Luke follow its outline, tell the stories in much the same fashion, and in parallel passages employ identical words over half the time. Having used Matthew as our chief Gospel source in this *Bible Reader*, we present here only enough of Mark to reveal its particular and unique characteristics.

Traditionally Mark's Gospel has been regarded as a written version of Peter's teaching in Rome. If this is so Mark can be taken to be the disciple Peter refers to as "my son Mark" (1 Peter 5:13), identical with "John Mark," son of the Mary in whose house in Jerusalem many gathered for prayer (Acts 12:12) and where Peter came after his imprisonment. In this view the author can also be identified with Mark, the cousin of Barnabas, and therefore, a companion of St. Paul on Paul's first missionary voyage. St. Irenaeus, toward the end of the second century, noted that after the death of Peter and Paul, "Mark, disciple and interpreter of Peter, also transmitted to us in writings the things preached by Peter." But this traditional identification is full of difficulties for the modern biblical student: e.g., the author, for a Palestinian Jew, seems unfamiliar with Palestinian geography and with Jewish customs and legal procedures; furthermore Mark (Marcus) was a common name in Rome in the sixties of the first century, where Peter was martyred in A.D. 62 or 64.

Made up of vividly told episodes rather than of sustained teaching materials, this Gospel is concerned to present Jesus as Son of God and as Son of Man (cf. Daniel 7:13), a title which Mark used fourteen times (in contrast to none for Paul), always in the spoken words of Jesus. A feature of the work is the preservation and transmission to us, in seven different places, of Aramaic syllables used by Jesus (3:17; 5:41; 7:11, 34; 10:46; 14:36; 15:34). The versions transliterate, rather than translate, these Aramaic terms. Unique in biblical literature is our ability to hear the very sounds that Jesus uttered. Mark also reports the gestures and movements of Jesus.

So large a portion of the work is given over to the last week in Jesus' life that it has been called "a story of our Lord's Passion, with an introduction." Though five-sixths of Mark is reproduced in Matthew and Luke, his distinctive contributions are memorable: one parable (4:26–29); two miracles (7:31–37; 8:22–26), both including the charge to secrecy; three questions about the dullness of the disciples (8:17 f.); the question in dispute among the disciples (9:33); the glimpse of the young man who lost his clothes the night of Jesus' arrest (14:52); Pilate's questioning of the centurion (15:44).

Prologue

The first verse of the Gospel tells what Mark sets out to show, i.e., that Jesus is the Son of God. It perhaps originally served as a title or superscription to his manuscript. Mark begins this work with a brief account of the preaching of John. In Christian art St. Mark is often represented by the symbol of a lion (sometimes a winged lion), because the lion made the desert echo with its roaring—and Mark's Gospel begins with the preaching of John the Baptist, whose voice was heard in the desert (or "wilderness," verse 3).

Mark 1:1–8

1 The beginning of the gospel of Jesus Christ, the Son of God.
  2 As it is written in Isaiah the prophet,
     "Behold, I send my messenger before thy face,
       who shall prepare thy way;
  ³ the voice of one crying in the wilderness:
     Prepare the way of the Lord,
       make his paths straight—"
⁴ John the baptizer appeared in the wilderness, preaching a baptism of repentance for the forgiveness of sins. ⁵ And there went out to him all the country of Judea, and all the people of Jerusalem; and they were baptized by him in the river Jordan, confessing their sins. ⁶ Now John was clothed with camel's hair, and had a leather girdle around his waist, and ate locusts and wild honey. ⁷ And he preached, saying, "After me comes he who is mightier than I, the thong of whose sandals I am not worthy to stoop down and untie. ⁸ I have baptized you with water; but he will baptize you with the Holy Spirit."

1:2 Actually a combination of Malachi 3:1 and Isaiah 40:3.

1:7 Jewish law regarded the slave as a human being whose dignity had to be protected; it forbade a master from requiring of his slave certain intimate duties, such as removing his shoes or carrying his clothes to the bath house. A son or a disciple, however, could be required to perform such services; to the intimate friend it would not be considered degrading, but rather an act of honor (*Siphra* on Numbers 15:41 and *Mekhilta* on Exodus 21:2.) John the Baptist here would agree with the Rabbis that only a disciple was worthy of carrying his teacher's sandal. **1:8** Tyndale: holy goost. Great Bible: holy gost. Geneva Bible: holie Gost. Bishops' Bible: holy Ghost.

Rheims: holy Ghost. King James Version: Holy Ghost. RV and RSV: Holy Spirit.

John Hails the Messiah

Mark 1:9–15

9 In those days Jesus came from Nazareth of Galilee and was baptized by John in the Jordan. ¹⁰ And when he came up out of the water, immediately he saw the heavens opened and the Spirit descending upon him like a dove; ¹¹ and a voice came from heaven, "Thou art my beloved Son; with thee I am well pleased."

12 The Spirit immediately drove him out into the wilderness. ¹³ And he was in the wilderness forty days, tempted by Satan; and he was with the wild beasts; and the angels ministered to him.

14 Now after John was arrested, Jesus came into Galilee, preaching the gospel of God, ¹⁵ and saying, "The time is fulfilled, and the kingdom of God is at hand; repent, and believe in the gospel."

1:10 Rabbi Hillel, contemporaneous with Jesus, was leader of those Jews who favored and welcomed converts to the Jewish faith. He taught that through the rite of baptism a man *rose up* from the grave, i.e., from his former pagan status (*Taanit* 32a). Other Rabbis considered a convert, who had been baptized, to have achieved the status of a newborn child, i.e., cleansed of sin (*Yebamoth* 22a and 48b). Thus some scholars find a Rabbinic source for the Christian concept that man is reborn in faith and resurrected to new life in the baptismal ceremony.

Jesus Begins His Ministry

Mark considers that the miracles performed by Jesus prove that Jesus is "the Son of God." Mark sometimes gives details that the other Gospels do not report, as in the cure of Peter's mother-in-law.

Mark 1:16–45

16 And passing along by the Sea of Galilee, he saw Simon and Andrew the brother of Simon casting a net in the sea; for they were fishermen. ¹⁷ And Jesus said to them, "Follow me and I will make you become fishers of men." ¹⁸ And immediately they left their nets and followed him. ¹⁹ And going on a little farther, he saw James the son of Zeb'edee and John his brother, who were in their boat mending the nets. ²⁰ And immediately he called them; and they left their father Zeb'edee in the boat with the hired servants, and followed him.

21 And they went into Caper'na-um; and immediately on the sabbath he entered the synagogue and taught. ²² And they were astonished at his teaching, for he taught them as one who had

authority, and not as the scribes. [23] And immediately there was in their synagogue a man with an unclean spirit; [24] and he cried out, "What have you to do with us, Jesus of Nazareth? Have you come to destroy us? I know who you are, the Holy One of God." [25] But Jesus rebuked him, saying, "Be silent, and come out of him!" [26] And the unclean spirit, convulsing him and crying with a loud voice, came out of him. [27] And they were all amazed, so that they questioned among themselves, saying, "What is this? A new teaching! With authority he commands even the unclean spirits, and they obey him." [28] And at once his fame spread everywhere throughout all the surrounding region of Galilee.

[29] And immediately he left the synagogue, and entered the house of Simon and Andrew, with James and John. [30] Now Simon's mother-in-law lay sick with a fever, and immediately they told him of her. [31] And he came and took her by the hand and lifted her up, and the fever left her; and she served them.

[32] That evening, at sundown, they brought to him all who were sick or possessed with demons. [33] And the whole city was gathered together about the door. [34] And he healed many who were sick with various diseases, and cast out many demons; and he would not permit the demons to speak, because they knew him.

[35] And in the morning, a great while before day, he rose and went out to a lonely place, and there he prayed. [36] And Simon and those who were with him followed him, [37] and they found him and said to him, "Every one is searching for you." [38] And he said to them, "Let us go on to the next towns, that I may preach there also; for that is why I came out." [39] And he went throughout all Galilee, preaching in their synagogues and casting out demons.

[40] And a leper came to him beseeching him, and kneeling said to him, "If you will, you can make me clean." [41] Moved with pity, he stretched out his hand and touched him, and said to him, "I will; be clean." [42] And immediately the leprosy left him, and he was made clean. [43] And he sternly charged him, and sent him away at once, [44] and said to him, "See that you say nothing to any one; but go, show yourself to the priest, and offer for your cleansing what Moses commanded, for a proof to the people." [45] But he went out and began to talk freely about it, and to spread the news, so that Jesus could no longer openly enter a town, but was out in the country; and people came to him from every quarter.

The Sabbath Was Made for Man

In Mark's account, as in Matthew's (12:1–8), opposition mounts up against Jesus. In this case the difficulty is not over stealing: the Law

(Deuteronomy 23:25) allowed one to pick grain while going through a field. The complaint is that Jesus' disciples are working (reaping) on the Sabbath (against Exodus 34:21). Jesus holds that answering a human need must be regarded as lawful on the Sabbath. See discussion at note on Matthew 12:8.

Mark 2:23–28

23 One sabbath he was going through the grainfields; and as they made their way his disciples began to pluck ears of grain. ²⁴ And the Pharisees said to him, "Look, why are they doing what is not lawful on the sabbath?" ²⁵ And he said to them, "Have you never read what David did, when he was in need and was hungry, he and those who were with him: ²⁶ how he entered the house of God, when Abi′athar was high priest, and ate the bread of the Presence, which it is not lawful for any but the priests to eat, and also gave it to those who were with him?" ²⁷ And he said to them, "The sabbath was made for man, not man for the sabbath; ²⁸ so the Son of man is lord even of the sabbath."

With Many Parables He Spoke the Word
Mark 4:21–29, 33–34

21 And he said to them, "Is a lamp brought in to be put under a bushel, or under a bed, and not on a stand? ²² For there is nothing hid, except to be made manifest; nor is anything secret, except to come to light. ²³ If any man has ears to hear, let him hear." ²⁴ And he said to them, "Take heed what you hear; the measure you give will be the measure you get, and still more will be given you. ²⁵ For to him who has will more be given; and from him who has not, even what he has will be taken away."

26 And he said, "The kingdom of God is as if a man should scatter seed upon the ground, ²⁷ and should sleep and rise night and day, and the seed should sprout and grow, he knows not how. ²⁸ The earth produces of itself, first the blade, then the ear, then the full grain in the ear. ²⁹ But when the grain is ripe, at once he puts in the sickle, because the harvest has come."

33 With many such parables he spoke the word to them, as they were able to hear it; ³⁴ he did not speak to them without a parable, but privately to his own disciples he explained everything.

4:21 A one-sentence parable. A bushel was a container holding about two gallons. **4:24** In this Parable of the Measure, Jesus takes the idea (common even in those days) that "the rich get richer and the poor get poorer," and gives it a spiritual sense: those who accept his teaching will go from joy to joy, and those who do not will be all the more the losers. **4:26** Verses 26–29 constitute a parable reported only by Mark.

Even Wind and Sea Obey Him
Mark 4:35–40

35 On that day, when evening had come, he said to them, "Let us go across to the other side." ³⁶ And leaving the crowd, they took him with them, just as he was, in the boat. And other boats were with him. ³⁷ And a great storm of wind arose, and the waves beat into the boat, so that the boat was already filling. ³⁸ But he was in the stern, asleep on the cushion; and they woke him and said to him, "Teacher, do you not care if we perish?" ³⁹ And he awoke and rebuked the wind, and said to the sea, "Peace! Be still!" And the wind ceased, and there was a great calm. ⁴⁰ He said to them, "Why are you afraid? Have you no faith?"

John the Baptist Is Executed
Mark 6:12–29

12 So they went out and preached that men should repent. ¹³ And they cast out many demons, and anointed with oil many that were sick and healed them.

14 King Herod heard of it; for Jesus' name had become known. Some said, "John the baptizer has been raised from the dead; that is why these powers are at work in him." ¹⁵ But others said, "It is Eli'jah." And others said, "It is a prophet, like one of the prophets of old." ¹⁶ But when Herod heard of it he said, "John, whom I beheaded, has been raised." ¹⁷ For Herod had sent and seized John, and bound him in prison for the sake of Hero'di-as, his brother Philip's wife; because he had married her. ¹⁸ For John said to Herod, "It is not lawful for you to have your brother's wife." ¹⁹ And Hero'di-as had a grudge against him, and wanted to kill him. But she could not, ²⁰ for Herod feared John, knowing that he was a righteous and holy man, and kept him safe. When he heard him, he was much perplexed; and yet he heard him gladly. ²¹ But an opportunity came when Herod on his birthday gave a banquet for his courtiers and officers and the leading men of Galilee. ²² For when Hero'di-as' daughter came in and danced, she pleased Herod and his guests; and the king said to the girl, "Ask me for whatever you wish, and I will grant it." ²³ And he vowed to her, "Whatever you ask me, I will give you, even half of my kingdom." ²⁴ And she went out, and said to her mother, "What shall I ask?" And she said, "The head of John the baptizer." ²⁵ And she came in immediately with haste to the king, and asked, saying, "I want you to give me at once the head of John the Baptist on a platter." ²⁶ And the king was exceedingly sorry; but because of his oaths and his guests he did not want to break his word

to her. ²⁷ And immediately the king sent a soldier of the guard and gave orders to bring his head. He went and beheaded him in the prison, ²⁸ and brought his head on a platter, and gave it to the girl; and the girl gave it to her mother. ²⁹ When his disciples heard of it, they came and took his body, and laid it in a tomb.

6:17 The flashback inserted here is the only one in the Gospels. We know the name of Herod's daughter, Salome, from the Jewish historian Josephus. The opera *Salome,* by Richard Strauss, is based on this story. The Church commemorates the beheading of John the Baptist on August 29, and this passage is the Gospel of the Mass on that day.

Jesus Cures a Deaf Mute
Mark 7:31–37

31 Then he returned from the region of Tyre, and went through Sidon to the Sea of Galilee, through the region of the Decap'olis. ³² And they brought to him a man who was deaf and had an impediment in his speech; and they besought him to lay his hand upon him. ³³ And taking him aside from the multitude privately, he put his fingers into his ears, and he spat and touched his tongue; ³⁴ and looking up to heaven, he sighed, and said to him, "Eph'phatha," that is, "Be opened." ³⁵ And his ears were opened, his tongue was released, and he spoke plainly. ³⁶ And he charged them to tell no one; but the more he charged them, the more zealously they proclaimed it. ³⁷ And they were astonished beyond measure, saying, "He has done all things well; he even makes the deaf hear and the dumb speak."

7:31 This passage is the Gospel for the Eleventh Sunday after Pentecost. The liturgy of that day teaches that God gives divine aid to those who ask for it with confidence. What Jesus does in this story has become part of the full rite of baptism administered in a Catholic church. The priest says the word *Ephphatha* (v. 34, meaning "open your heart to the things of faith") and imitates Jesus' gestures.

Jesus Feeds Four Thousand
Mark 8:1–9

8 In those days, when again a great crowd had gathered, and they had nothing to eat, he called his disciples to him, and said to them, ² "I have compassion on the crowd, because they have been with me now three days, and have nothing to eat; ³ and if I send them away hungry to their homes, they will faint on the way; and some of them have come a long way." ⁴ And his disciples answered him, "How can one feed these men with bread here in the desert?" ⁵ And he asked

them, "How many loaves have you?" They said, "Seven." ⁶ And he commanded the crowd to sit down on the ground; and he took the seven loaves, and having given thanks he broke them and gave them to his disciples to set before the people; and they set them before the crowd. ⁷ And they had a few small fish; and having blessed them, he commanded that these also should be set before them. ⁸ And they ate, and were satisfied; and they took up the broken pieces left over, seven baskets full. ⁹ And there were about four thousand people.

8:1 This is the Gospel for the Sixth Sunday after Pentecost.

The Son of Man Must Suffer

Mark 8:27–38

27 And Jesus went on with his disciples, to the villages of Caesare'a Philippi; and on the way he asked his disciples, "Who do men say that I am?" ²⁸ And they told him, "John the Baptist; and others say, Eli'jah; and others one of the prophets." ²⁹ And he asked them, "But who do you say that I am?" Peter answered him, "You are the Christ." ³⁰ And he charged them to tell no one about him.

31 And he began to teach them that the Son of man must suffer many things, and be rejected by the elders and the chief priests and the scribes, and be killed, and after three days rise again. ³² And he said this plainly. And Peter took him, and began to rebuke him. ³³ But turning and seeing his disciples, he rebuked Peter, and said, "Get behind me, Satan! For you are not on the side of God, but of men."

34 And he called to him the multitude with his disciples, and said to them, "If any man would come after me, let him deny himself and take up his cross and follow me. ³⁵ For whoever would save his life will lose it; and whoever loses his life for my sake and the gospel's will save it. ³⁶ For what does it profit a man, to gain the whole world and forfeit his life? ³⁷ For what can a man give in return for his life? ³⁸ For whoever is ashamed of me and of my words in this adulterous and sinful generation, of him will the Son of man also be ashamed, when he comes in the glory of his Father with the holy angels."

8:27 This section is a turning point in Mark's Gospel. The idea that the Messiah had to suffer contradicted the expectation of many Jews who believed that with the coming of the Messiah Israel would triumph over her enemies and all men live in peace. Christians insist that the cross is a way of victory over sin and death. **8:33** Tyndale: Go after me Satan. For thou saverest not the thinges of God but the thinges of men. Rheims: Goe behind me Satan, because thou savourest not the things that are of God, but of men. King James Version: Get thee behind me, Satan: for thou savourest not the things that be of God, but the things that be of men. RV and RSV: Get thee behind me, Satan; for thou mindest not the things of God, but the things of men.

James and John Seek Honor
Mark 10:35-45

35 And James and John, the sons of Zeb'edee, came forward to him, and said to him, "Teacher, we want you to do for us whatever we ask of you." ³⁶ And he said to them, "What do you want me to do for you?" ³⁷ And they said to him, "Grant us to sit, one at your right hand and one at your left, in your glory." ³⁸ But Jesus said to them, "You do not know what you are asking. Are you able to drink the cup that I drink, or to be baptized with the baptism with which I am baptized?" ³⁹ And they said to him, "We are able." And Jesus said to them, "The cup that I drink you will drink; and with the baptism with which I am baptized, you will be baptized; ⁴⁰ but to sit at my right hand or at my left is not mine to grant, but it is for those for whom it has been prepared." ⁴¹ And when the ten heard it, they began to be indignant at James and John. ⁴² And Jesus called them to him and said to them, "You know that those who are supposed to rule over the Gentiles lord it over them, and their great men exercise authority over them. ⁴³ But it shall not be so among you; but whoever would be great among you must be your servant, ⁴⁴ and whoever would be first among you must be slave of all. ⁴⁵ For the Son of man also came not to be served but to serve, and to give his life as a ransom for many."

10:45 This verse (only in Mark) contains what Christians regard as a summary of their faith. 10:44 Tyndale: And whosoever wilbe chefe, shalbe servaunt unto all. Geneva Bible: And whosoever will be chief of you, shal be the servant of all. Bishops' Bible: but whosoever of you will be great among you, shall be your minister. Rheims: and whosoever wil be first among you, shal be the servant of al. King James Version: and whosoever of you will be the chiefest, shall be servant of all.

Faith Moves Mountains
Mark 11:22-25

22 And Jesus answered them, "Have faith in God. ²³ Truly, I say to you, whoever says to this mountain, 'Be taken up and cast into the sea,' and does not doubt in his heart, but believes that what he says will come to pass, it will be done for him. ²⁴ Therefore I tell you, whatever you ask in prayer, believe that you receive it, and you will. ²⁵ And whenever you stand praying, forgive, if you have anything

against any one; so that your Father also who is in heaven may forgive you your trespasses."

11:22 The Catholic Church uses this section as the Gospel in the Votive Mass for Any Necessity.

The Widow's Offering
Mark 12:41–44

41 And he sat down opposite the treasury, and watched the multitude putting money into the treasury. Many rich people put in large sums. ⁴²And a poor widow came, and put in two copper coins, which make a penny. ⁴³And he called his disciples to him, and said to them, "Truly, I say to you, this poor widow has put in more than all those who are contributing to the treasury. ⁴⁴For they all contributed out of their abundance; but she out of her poverty has put in everything she had, her whole living."

12:42 English translations, from Tyndale to our own times, had "mites" here to translate the Greek word *lepta*. A mite was worth about one twelfth of a cent. She put in two, but for centuries people have referred to "the widow's mite." In addition to a Temple tax collected annually, pilgrims could make donations to the Sanctuary. The Mishnah recalls thirteen chests, each shaped like a *shofar* (ram's horn). Six were designated for specific purposes, and six for free-will offerings. The *lepton* was the smallest denomination of money in circulation, the Hebrew *perutha*, a small bronze coin. In deference to Jewish objections, these coins did not display the head of the emperor and many were decorated with a palm branch.

The Empty Tomb
Mark 16:1–8

16 And when the sabbath was past, Mary Mag'dalene, Mary the mother of James, and Salo'me bought spices, so that they might go and anoint him. ²And very early on the first day of the week they went to the tomb when the sun had risen. ³And they were saying to one another, "Who will roll away the stone for us from the door of the tomb?" ⁴And looking up, they saw that the stone was rolled back; for it was very large. ⁵And entering the tomb, they saw a young man sitting on the right side, dressed in a white robe; and they were amazed. ⁶And he said to them, "Do not be amazed; you seek Jesus of Nazareth, who was crucified. He has risen, he is not here; see the place where they laid him. ⁷But go, tell his disciples and Peter that he is going before you to Galilee; there you will see him, as he told you." ⁸And they went out and fled from the tomb; for

trembling and astonishment had come upon them; and they said nothing to any one, for they were afraid.

16:1 This passage is the Gospel for Easter Sunday. Marks' account of Jesus' passion (suffering) and death is read on Tuesday of Holy Week. **16:8** It is evident that the Gospel of Mark originally ended at this point. There is speculation as to why it should have concluded so abruptly: perhaps the author wanted to leave his work unfinished, with the thought that succeeding ages would add chapters to the ongoing story of the church; perhaps Roman persecution intervened and the author was hauled off to prison before he could conclude; more prosaically, the manuscript may have become dog-eared from constant use and the end dropped off. In any case, the church, dissatisfied with so abrupt an ending, composed at least three different conclusions to the work. One succinctly summarized the apostolic ministry: "But they reported to Peter and those with him all that they had been told, and after this, Jesus himself sent out by means of them, from east to west, the sacred and imperishable proclamation of eternal salvation." Another ending is an expanded version of the conclusion which made its way into many translations from the medieval manuscripts, commonly known as Mark 16:9–20. This passage has occasioned much controversy. From verse 16—"He who believes and is baptized will be saved; but he who does not believe will be condemned"—has grown the idea that the intellectual rejection of ecclesiastical dogma is fraught with such dire consequences that it is a crime to be prevented by whatever means may be necessary. From verse 18—"they pick up serpents, and if they drink any deadly thing, it will not hurt them"—has developed the snake-handling and the "salvation cocktail," made of strychnine, which have been featured in some American cults. Several states have passed laws making it illegal to pick up snakes in public meeting.

Conclusion
Mark 16:9–20

Other texts and versions add as 16:9–20 the following passage:

9 Now when he rose early on the first day of the week, he appeared first to Mary Magdalene, from whom he had cast out seven demons. [10] She went and told those who had been with him, as they mourned and wept. [11] But when they heard that he was alive and had been seen by her, they would not believe it.

12 After this he appeared in another form to two of them, as they were walking into the country. [13] And they went back and told the rest, but they did not believe them.

14 Afterward he appeared to the eleven themselves as they sat at table; and he upbraided them for their unbelief and hardness of heart,

because they had not believed those who saw him after he had risen. [15] And he said to them, "Go into all the world and preach the gospel to the whole creation. [16] He who believes and is baptized will be saved; but he who does not believe will be condemned. [17] And these signs will accompany those who believe: in my name they will cast out demons; they will speak in new tongues; [18] they will pick up serpents, and if they drink any deadly thing, it will not hurt them; they will lay their hands on the sick, and they will recover."

19 So then the Lord Jesus, after he had spoken to them, was taken up into heaven, and sat down at the right hand of God. [20] And they went forth and preached everywhere, while the Lord worked with them and confirmed the message by the signs that attended it. Amen.

16:9 The fact is, the two oldest Greek manuscripts and some other authorities omit this concluding passage. Some manuscripts give a different conclusion of only three verses. This "longer ending" is often regarded (from a study of the Greek words used) as the work of another author who composed it from various sections of the other Gospels. At no time, however, has the Church viewed the passage as not inspired. Verses 14–20 are used as the Gospel for Ascension Thursday, a holy day of obligation in the Catholic Church.

The Gospel according to Luke

Luke sets out to proclaim the Gospel, the good news of Jesus' coming, dying and rising from the dead to bring new life to man. Although he uses Mark as a major source, here the stress in his book is on Jesus as serving, loving, forgiving, healing. In Luke's book more than in the others, Jesus is especially sensitive to the suffering of the people, compassionate and tenderly solicitous Luke gives us most of what we have received about the infancy and childhood of Jesus. Luke also gives us canticles (hymns) and parables that are not found in Matthew and Mark (e.g., Good Samaritan, Rich Fool, Pharisee and Publican). It is traditionally held that the author of this Gospel was the physician Luke, Gentile convert and friend of Paul ("Luke, our most dear physician," 2 Timothy 4:11). In the case of Luke only among the Gospels, the tradition is generally upheld by modern scholars.

Luke seems to have had in mind chiefly a reading audience of Gentiles (non-Jews). His concern with rich and poor, women and children; his compassion and broad humanitarian concerns make this a book of universal appeal. The author of Luke also wrote the book of Acts; indeed the two were once one unified two-part work, now separated by the Gospel of John. Both seem to have been written to help dispel any notion among Romans that Christianity was a subversive sect; on the contrary, Luke stresses that it was a world religion that knew no racial limitations.

Preface to Luke

This passage deserves study as a summary of the process that led to the writing of the Gospels: events (v. 1); oral tradition (v. 2); there have been other writings (v. 1, 3a); now an "orderly account" (3b–4). The Gospel writers had many sources that are now lost. Through the otherwise unknown Theophilus, probably a friendly Roman official, Luke addresses Gentiles, perhaps converts to Christianity. Luke wants to give them a substantial account of what the Christian faith is based on.

In Christian art, St. Luke is often represented by the symbol of an ox (sometimes a winged ox) because at the beginning of his Gospel he mentions the priesthood of Zechariah (Zachary) and the ox was usually the victim offered by the priest in the sacrifices of the Temple.

Luke 1:1–4

1 Inasmuch as many have undertaken to compile a narrative of the things which have been accomplished among us, ²just as they were delivered to us by those who from the beginning were eyewitnesses and ministers of the word, [3] it seemed good to me also, having followed all things closely for some time past, to write an orderly account for you, most excellent The-oph'ilus, [4] that you may know the truth concerning the things of which you have been informed.

John's Birth Is Announced

Luke 1:5–25

5 In the days of Herod, king of Judea, there was a priest named Zechari'ah, of the division of Abi'jah; and he had a wife of the daughters of Aaron, and her name was Elizabeth. [6] And they were both righteous before God, walking in all the commandments and ordinances of the Lord blameless. [7] But they had no child, because Elizabeth was barren, and both were advanced in years.

8 Now while he was serving as priest before God when his division was on duty, [9] according to the custom of the priesthood, it fell to him by lot to enter the temple of the Lord and burn incense. [10] And the whole multitude of the people were praying outside at the hour of incense. [11] And there appeared to him an angel of the Lord standing on the right side of the altar of incense. [12] And Zechari'ah was troubled when he saw him, and fear fell upon him. [13] But the angel said to him, "Do not be afraid, Zechari'ah, for your prayer is heard, and your wife Elizabeth will bear you a son, and you shall call his name John.

[14] And you will have joy and gladness,
   and many will rejoice at his birth;
[15] for he will be great before the Lord,
   and he shall drink no wine nor strong drink,
   and he will be filled with the Holy Spirit,
   even from his mother's womb.
[16] And he will turn many of the sons of Israel to the Lord their
   God,
[17] and he will go before him in the spirit and power of Eli'jah,
   to turn the hearts of the fathers to the children,
   and the disobedient to the wisdom of the just,
   to make ready for the Lord a people prepared."

[18] And Zechari'ah said to the angel, "How shall I know this? For I am an old man, and my wife is advanced in years." [19] And the angel answered him, "I am Gabriel, who stand in the presence of God; and I was sent to speak to you, and to bring you this good news. [20] And behold, you will be silent and unable to speak until the day that these things come to pass, because you did not believe my words, which will be fulfilled in their time." [21] And the people were waiting for

Zechari'ah, and they wondered at his delay in the temple. ²² And when he came out, he could not speak to them, and they perceived that he had seen a vision in the temple; and he made signs to them and remained dumb. ²³ And when his time of service was ended, he went to his home.

24 After these days his wife Elizabeth conceived, and for five months she hid herself, saying, ²⁵ "Thus the Lord has done to me in the days when he looked on me, to take away my reproach among men."

> **1:5** Earlier translations have Zachary, Zacharias, Zacharie. **1:25** Jews regarded it a sign of God's disfavor if a married woman did not have a baby. As in Old Testament accounts (e.g., Sarah and Hannah), so here, the fact that a barren woman conceives dramatizes the author's conviction regarding God's intervention in history.

Jesus' Coming Is Announced
Luke 1:26–38

26 In the sixth month the angel Gabriel was sent from God to a city of Galilee named Nazareth, ²⁷ to a virgin betrothed to a man whose name was Joseph, of the house of David; and the virgin's name was Mary. ²⁸ And he came to her and said, "Hail, O favored one, the Lord is with you!" ²⁹ But she was greatly troubled at the saying, and considered in her mind what sort of greeting this might be. ³⁰ And the angel said to her, "Do not be afraid, Mary, for you have found favor with God. ³¹ And behold, you will conceive in your womb and bear a son, and you shall call his name Jesus.
³² He will be great, and will be called the Son of the Most High;
and the Lord God will give to him the throne of his father David,
³³ and he will reign over the house of Jacob for ever;
and of his kingdom there will be no end."
³⁴ And Mary said to the angel, "How can this be, since I have no husband?" ³⁵ And the angel said to her,
"The Holy Spirit will come upon you,
and the power of the Most High will overshadow you;
therefore the child to be born will be called holy,
the Son of God.
³⁶ And behold, your kinswoman Elizabeth in her old age has also conceived a son; and this is the sixth month with her who was called barren. ³⁷ For with God nothing will be impossible." ³⁸ And Mary said, "Behold, I am the handmaid of the Lord; let it be to me according to your word." And the angel departed from her.

1:26 This scene, the Annunciation (from a Latin word meaning "announcement"), has inspired many painters, such as Fra Angelico, and has been the source of much devotional and liturgical practice. The "Hail Mary," a daily prayer of Catholics, begins with the latter part of verse 28 and continues with verse 42; it is recited on all the small beads of the Rosary, and is the prayer used in the Angelus (a summary of this passage recited in the morning, at noon and in the evening by monks, sisters and devout laymen). In Catholic countries church bells announce the Angelus. A famous painting by Millet shows a farmer and his wife in a field saying the Angelus with bowed heads, as if listening to the church bell in the distance. Musical compositions (e.g., Gounod's "Ave Maria") have made this section of Luke's Gospel especially well known. **1:28** On account of the phrase "favored one" ("full of grace"), verses 26–28 are the Gospel for the Feast of the Immaculate Conception (December 8). Catholics hold that from the moment Mary herself was conceived she was "full of grace" in the sense of being without any sin, even the state of original sin that Catholics hold all descendants of Adam have when they come into the world. The whole passage (26–38) is read on St. Gabriel's day (March 24) and the Feast of the Annunciation (March 25). Tyndale: Haile full of grace, the Lorde is with the: blessed arte thou amonge wemen. Geneva Bible: Haile thou (that art) freely beloved: the Lord (is) with thee. Bishops' Bible: Haile *thou that art* in high favour, the Lord is with thee. Rheims: Haile ful of grace, our Lord is with thee. King James Version: Hail, *thou that art* highly favoured, the Lord *is* with thee. ("Blessed art thou among women" is not given in all the ancient Greek manuscripts.) **1:34** Catholics and Orthodox argue from verse 34 that Mary had resolved to remain a virgin in her marriage and did so.

Mary Visits Elizabeth

Luke 1:39–56

39 In those days Mary arose and went with haste into the hill country, to a city of Judah, [40] and she entered the house of Zechari′ah and greeted Elizabeth. [41] And when Elizabeth heard the greeting of Mary, the babe leaped in her womb; and Elizabeth was filled with the Holy Spirit [42] and she exclaimed with a loud cry, "Blessed are you among women, and blessed is the fruit of your womb! [43] And why is this granted me, that the mother of my Lord should come to me? [44] For behold, when the voice of your greeting came to my ears, the babe in my womb leaped for joy. [45] And blessed is she who believed that there would be a fulfilment of what was spoken to her from the Lord." [46] And Mary said,

"My soul magnifies the Lord,
[47] and my spirit rejoices in God my Savior,

⁴⁸ for he has regarded the low estate of his handmaiden.

For behold, henceforth all generations will call me blessed;
⁴⁹ for he who is mighty has done great things for me,
and holy is his name.
⁵⁰ And his mercy is on those who fear him
from generation to generation.
⁵¹ He has shown strength with his arm,
he has scattered the proud in the imagination of their hearts,
⁵² he has put down the mighty from their thrones,
and exalted those of low degree;
⁵³ he has filled the hungry with good things,
and the rich he has sent empty away.
⁵⁴ He has helped his servant Israel,
in remembrance of his mercy,
⁵⁵ as he spoke to our fathers,
to Abraham and to his posterity for ever."
⁵⁶ And Mary remained with her about three months, and returned to her home.

1:39 The feast commemorating this event, the Visitation, is observed on July 2. The Visitation is also the second joyful mystery of the Rosary. Verses 41–50 are the Gospel for the Feast of the Assumption (August 15). The doctrine that Mary was assumed (taken up) body and soul into heaven was defined as an article of the Catholic faith in 1950. The Assumption is actually the most ancient and most solemn of all the feasts of Mary in both the Eastern and Western Church, dating back at least to the sixth century. Veneration of Mary existed in the early Church before any of her feasts was instituted. The Assumption was originally celebrated in the East and the West as "The Falling Asleep of the Mother of God" (and it is still called that in Byzantine rites). On the traditional date of Mary's "falling asleep" and "being taken up," there grew up customs of blessing farms, fishing boats, etc., and going into the water to preserve good health through her intercession. On her feast water and the elements of nature were to be blessed. This devotion and the related feasts are largely derived from verses 46–55 (a hymn known as the "Magnificat," from its first word in a Latin translation), as is much of the theology about Mary (Mariology). Catholics venerate Mary above all other saints (adoration they consider as the worship paid to God; veneration is the worship offered to saints). Her conception, for example, is the only conception of a saint that is commemorated in the liturgy of the Church. (That feast, like the other feasts of Mary, originated in the Eastern Church; it has been a holy day in the Greek churches since 1166, and since 1854 in the Latin Church.) The Magnificat is recited every day by all Catholic priests (and it is chanted by many religious orders) at the end of

Vespers, the evening prayer in the Divine Office. The Assumption is the fourth glorious mystery of the Rosary (Mary's coronation in heaven is the fifth mystery.)

Elizabeth Gives Birth to John
Luke 1:57–80

57 Now the time came for Elizabeth to be delivered, and she gave birth to a son. [58] And her neighbors and kinsfolk heard that the Lord had shown great mercy to her, and they rejoiced with her. [59] And on the eighth day they came to circumcise the child; and they would have named him Zechari'ah after his father, [60] but his mother said, "Not so; he shall be called John." [61] And they said to her, "None of your kindred is called by this name." [62] And they made signs to his father, inquiring what he would have him called. [63] And he asked for a writing tablet, and wrote, "His name is John." And they all marveled. [64] And immediately his mouth was opened and his tongue loosed, and he spoke, blessing God. [65] And fear came on all their neighbors. And all these things were talked about through all the hill country of Judea; [66] and all who heard them laid them up in their hearts, saying, "What then will this child be?" For the hand of the Lord was with him.

67 And his father Zechari'ah was filled with the Holy Spirit, and prophesied, saying,

[68] "Blessed be the Lord God of Israel,
   for he has visited and redeemed his people,
[69] and has raised up a horn of salvation for us
   in the house of his servant David,
[70] as he spoke by the mouth of his holy prophets from of old,
[71] that we should be saved from our enemies,
   and from the hand of all who hate us;
[72] to perform the mercy promised to our fathers,
   and to remember his holy covenant,
[73] the oath which he swore to our father Abraham, [74] to grant us
   that we, being delivered from the hand of our enemies,
   might serve him without fear,
[75] in holiness and righteousness before him all the days of our
   life.
[76] And you, child, will be called the prophet of the Most High;
   for you will go before the Lord to prepare his ways,
[77] to give knowledge of salvation to his people
   in the forgiveness of their sins,
[78] through the tender mercy of our God,
   when the day shall dawn upon us from on high

[79] to give light to those who sit in darkness and in the shadow of
      death,
      to guide our feet into the way of peace."
[80] And the child grew and became strong in spirit, and he was in the
wilderness till the day of his manifestation to Israel.

1:57 Verses 57–68 are, appropriately, the Gospel for the Feast of
the Nativity of St. John the Baptist (June 24). **1:68** Verses 68–79
are known in music as the Benedictus (from the first word of the
hymn). The prayer is recited (or chanted) every morning in the
Divine Office, the daily prayer of Catholic priests. It is also recited in
the burial service (cf. 1:79). **1:69** Horn was a symbol of strength,
frequently applied to a king in near Eastern literature. It evokes, too,
the image of the sounding of the *shofar*, announcing the coming of
the Davidic redeemer. **1:71** The concept of salvation—deliverance
from enemies—described here and in verse 74, re-echoes the Hebraic
concept of salvation as a national liberation from political foes
(Psalm 106:9–10). Christians take the words "people" and "we" in
a wider sense, to include all members of the Church, which they
regard as the "new Israel." This whole canticle of Zechariah
(Zachary), verses 68–69, is recited every day in that sense as the
conclusion of the main section (Matins, morning prayers) of the
Divine Office, official prayer of the Roman Catholic Church. More
frequently, the New Testament speaks of salvation as forgiveness of
sin (Luke 1:77) and as a means by which man is transferred from the
Kingdom of Death to the Heavenly Kingdom of God (2 Timothy
4:18).

Mary Gives Birth to Jesus
Luke 2:1–20

2 In those days a decree went out from Caesar Augustus that all the
world should be enrolled. [2] This was the first enrollment, when
Quirin'i-us was governor of Syria. [3] And all went to be enrolled, each
to his own city. [4] And Joseph also went up from Galilee, from the city
of Nazareth, to Judea, to the city of David, which is called
Bethlehem, because he was of the house and lineage of David, [5] to be
enrolled with Mary, his betrothed, who was with child. [6] And while
they were there, the time came for her to be delivered. [7] And she gave
birth to her first-born son and wrapped him in swaddling cloths, and
laid him in a manger, because there was no place for them in the inn.

8 And in that region there were shepherds out in the field, keeping
watch over their flock by night. [9] And an angel of the Lord appeared
to them, and the glory of the Lord shone around them, and they
were filled with fear. [10] And the angel said to them, "Be not afraid;
for behold, I bring you good news of a great joy which will come to

all the people; ¹¹for to you is born this day in the city of David a
Savior, who is Christ the Lord. ¹²And this will be a sign for you: you
will find a babe wrapped in swaddling cloths and lying in a manger."
¹³And suddenly there was with the angel a multitude of the heavenly
host praising God and saying,
    ¹⁴"Glory to God in the highest,
      and on earth peace among men with whom he is pleased!"
15 When the angels went away from them into heaven, the
shepherds said to one another, "Let us go over to Bethlehem and see
this thing that has happened, which the Lord has made known to
us." ¹⁶And they went with haste, and found Mary and Joseph, and
the babe lying in a manger. ¹⁷And when they saw it they made
known the saying which had been told them concerning this child;
¹⁸and all who heard it wondered at what the shepherds told them.
¹⁹But Mary kept all these things, pondering them in her heart.
²⁰And the shepherds returned, glorifying and praising God for all
they had heard and seen, as it had been told them.

2:1 Verses 1–14 are the Gospel for the first (Midnight) Mass of
Christmas. Verses 15–20 are the Gospel of the second Christmas
Mass (at dawn), as well as for the Mass of the Blessed Virgin which is
said on Saturdays between Christmas and the Feast of the Purification (February 2). The whole passage is the basis of the Nativity,
third joyful mystery of the Rosary. The word Christmas comes from
the eleventh-century expression *Christes Maesse,* based on the idea
that the Mass was the most important part of the celebration of
Christ's birth. Catholic priests are permitted to offer three Masses on
Christmas Day. The first Mass honors the eternal generation of the
Son from the Father; the second, His incarnation and birth into the
world; the third, His birth in the hearts of men through love and
grace. Thus, people came to call the first Mass "Angels' Mass," the
second "Shepherds' Mass," and the third "Mass of the Divine
Word." The Christmas crib or "crèche" is a portrayal of this Gospel
scene, and, from the walls of early Christian chambers in catacombs
to our own day, this is probably the most frequently chosen subject of
painters. St. Francis of Assisi is usually credited with the introduction of the custom of setting up the crib outside churches. The
Christmas tree is apparently a combination of the Paradise Tree
traditional in Germany as a symbol of the tree of life (see note on
Genesis 2:16) and the Christmas candle that traditionally
symbolized Jesus as the light of the world. The custom of setting up
the Christmas tree in public places originated in Boston, Mass., in
1912. Laurel, ancient symbol of triumph, was the first plant used as
Christmas decoration by early Christians at Rome (to symbolize
victory over sin and death by Christ's birth). Holly became popular
at Christmas time, too, because its prickly points and red berries (like

drops of blood) reminded the people that the child Jesus was destined to wear a crown of thorns. Christmas is a holy day of obligation for Catholics. The vestments of the Mass are white, for joy and consolation. **2:2** Scholars debate the dating of the census. Quirinus as a legate of Syria is known to have taken a census in A.D. 6 which the Hebrews violently opposed; the upsurge of the Zealots in Galilee is dated from that period. But if that is the date of the census, then the birth date of Jesus would need to be revised. Other scholars suggest that there was also a census in 6 B.C. which took place under Herod's management. **2:7** Many Protestants hold that "firstborn" means Mary subsequently had other children. Roman and Orthodox Catholics maintain her perpetual virginity, holding that among Jews this title belonged to an only son, marking his rights and duties under the Law (Exodus 13:2; Numbers 8:17), and that popular language also used the term, as shown by a Greek inscription on a Hebrew tomb of the period. **2:14** The words of the angels (verse 14) are said or sung in every Sunday Mass and on feast days in the Catholic Church. The song is known as the "Gloria" (from the first word of the Latin translation; the first phrase is: *Gloria in excelsis Deo*). This son, we might say, was the first Christmas carol; the Church elaborated it into a hymn for the Mass. **2:20** Martin Luther (1483–1546) found here his doctrine of Christian vocation, that God calls men to labor in life's common occupations, and one calling is not better than another. Shepherds, Luther saw, led a rough life, but after visiting the manger they went back to it.

Jesus Is Circumcised
Luke 2:21–40

21 And at the end of eight days, when he was circumcised, he was called Jesus, the name given by the angel before he was conceived in the womb.

22 And when the time came for their purification according to the law of Moses, they brought him up to Jerusalem to present him to the Lord ²³ (as it is written in the law of the Lord, "Every male that opens the womb shall be called holy to the Lord") ²⁴ and to offer a sacrifice according to what is said in the law of the Lord, "a pair of turtledoves, or two young pigeons." ²⁵ Now there was a man in Jerusalem, whose name was Simeon, and this man was righteous and devout, looking for the consolation of Israel, and the Holy Spirit was upon him. ²⁶ And it had been revealed to him by the Holy Spirit that he should not see death before he had seen the Lord's Christ. ²⁷ And inspired by the Spirit he came into the temple; and when the parents brought in the child Jesus, to do for him according to the custom of the law, ²⁸ he took him up in his arms and blessed God and said,

29 "Lord, now lettest thou thy servant depart in peace,
   according to thy word;
30 for mine eyes have seen thy salvation
31 which thou hast prepared in the presence of all peoples,
32 a light for revelation to the Gentiles,
   and for glory to thy people Israel."

33 And his father and his mother marveled at what was said about him; 34 and Simeon blessed them and said to Mary his mother,

"Behold, this child is set for the fall and rising of many in Israel,
   and for a sign that is spoken against
35 (and a sword will pierce through your own soul also),
   that thoughts out of many hearts may be revealed."

36 And there was a prophetess, Anna, the daughter of Phan'u-el, of the tribe of Asher; she was of a great age, having lived with her husband seven years from her virginity, 37 and as a widow till she was eighty-four. She did not depart from the temple, worshiping with fasting and prayer night and day. 38 And coming up at that very hour she gave thanks to God, and spoke of him to all who were looking for the redemption of Jerusalem.

39 And when they had performed everything according to the law of the Lord, they returned into Galilee, to their own city, Nazareth. 40 And the child grew and became strong, filled with wisdom; and the favor of God was upon him.

2:21 Circumcision marked Jesus as a Jew under the covenant (Genesis 17:12 and Leviticus 12:13). The circumcision of a Jewish male child on the eighth day was the ritual by which the child symbolically entered into the covenant of the Hebrew people with God. The circumcision was administered by the father of the household; today a professional *mohel* performs the operation. By New Testament times it was customary for Jews to provide the child his name at this ceremony. Later Paul taught that through faith in Christ circumcision as a ritual becomes superfluous for a Christian (Galatians 5:6, 6:15). The Council of the Apostles (Acts 15:1–20) upheld Paul's contention that circumcision was not to be imposed on gentile converts. As a hygienic measure circumcision is practiced in many hospitals. British Crown Prince Charles was circumcised by the Chief Mohel of England. Verse 21 is the Gospel for the Feast of the Circumcision (January 1), a holy day of obligation in the Catholic Church. All Eastern rites that celebrate the Nativity on December 25 also keep this Feast of the Circumcision on January 1. Because Jesus received His name at the time of His circumcision, special devotions in honor of "the Holy Name" developed in the Middle Ages. St. Bernard, especially, promoted the devotion with his famous hymn *Jesu dulcis memoria* ("Sweet is the memory of Jesus")

which is still used in the Divine Office. The Gospel for the Feast of the
Holy Name (January 2 or the Sunday between January 1 and January
6) is this same verse 21. **2:22** See Leviticus 12:2–8; Exodus 13:2,
12. Verses 22–32 are the Gospel for the Feast of the Purification of
the Blessed Virgin Mary (February 2), which was originally a festival
of the Lord (the Armenians call it "The Coming of the Son of God
into the Temple" and celebrate it on February 14; in the Egyptian
Coptic rite it is called "Presentation of the Lord in the Temple"; in
the Greek Church it also came to be known as "The Meeting of the
Lord," in commemoration of Jesus meeting Simeon and Anna, and
Russians and Ukrainians still call it that; Chaldaeans and Syrians
call it the Feast of Simeon the Old Man). The ceremony of blessing
candles on this day goes back to the end of the eighth century. **2:29**
Verses 29–32 (known as *Nunc Dimittis,* from the first words in Latin
translation) are said every night in Compline, the final part of the
Divine Office. **2:33** Verses 33–40 are the Gospel for the Sunday
after Christmas.

The Boy Jesus Visits the Temple
Luke 2:41–52

41 Now his parents went to Jerusalem every year at the feast of the
Passover. ⁴²And when he was twelve years old, they went up
according to custom; ⁴³and when the feast was ended, as they were
returning, the boy Jesus stayed behind in Jerusalem. His parents did
not know it, ⁴⁴but supposing him to be in the company they went a
day's journey, and they sought him among their kinsfolk and
acquaintances; ⁴⁵and when they did not find him, they returned to
Jerusalem, seeking him. ⁴⁶After three days they found him in the
temple, sitting among the teachers, listening to them and asking
them questions; ⁴⁷and all who heard him were amazed at his
understanding and his answers. ⁴⁸And when they saw him they were
astonished; and his mother said to him, "Son, why have you treated
us so? Behold, your father and I have been looking for you
anxiously." ⁴⁹And he said to them, "How is it that you sought me?
Did you not know that I must be in my Father's house?" ⁵⁰And they
did not understand the saying which he spoke to them. ⁵¹And he
went down with them and came to Nazareth, and was obedient to
them; and his mother kept all these things in her heart.

52 And Jesus increased in wisdom and in stature, and in favor
with God and man.

2:41 It was the custom of the Jews—still followed to this
day—for a boy at about age thirteen to enter the synagogue and read
a lesson from the Torah and the Prophets and expound on the text.
The boy is called a Bar Mitzvah (a "son of the Commandment").

The ceremony signifies that the lad is now capable of assuming his own responsibility for observing the sacred Law, and he is henceforth to be considered as an adult in the *Minyan*, a quorum of ten men required for a public prayer or service. This passage (verses 41–52) is the Gospel for the Feast of the Holy Family (Sunday after Epiphany), and for the Maternity of the Blessed Virgin Mary (October 11). The Finding in the Temple is the fifth joyful mystery of the Rosary.

Jesus Teaches in the Synagogue

After an account of John the Baptist's preaching, the baptism of Jesus (and a genealogy of Jesus which traces Him back to "Adam, the son of God"), and the temptations in the desert, Luke's story continues with Jesus visiting the synagogue in his home town.

Luke 4:14–30

14 And Jesus returned in the power of the Spirit into Galilee, and a report concerning him went out through all the surrounding country. ¹⁵ And he taught in their synagogues, being glorified by all.

16 And he came to Nazareth, where he had been brought up; and he went to the synagogue, as his custom was, on the sabbath day. And he stood up to read; ¹⁷ and there was given to him the book of the prophet Isaiah. He opened the book and found the place where it was written,

¹⁸ "The Spirit of the Lord is upon me,

because he has anointed me to preach good news to the poor.

He has sent me to proclaim release to the captives

and recovering of sight to the blind,

to set at liberty those who are oppressed,

¹⁹ to proclaim the acceptable year of the Lord."

²⁰ And he closed the book, and gave it back to the attendant, and sat down; and the eyes of all in the synagogue were fixed on him. ²¹ And he began to say to them, "Today this scripture has been fulfilled in your hearing." ²² And all spoke well of him, and wondered at the gracious words which proceeded out of his mouth; and they said, "Is not this Joseph's son?" ²³ And he said to them, "Doubtless you will quote to me this proverb, 'Physician, heal yourself; what we have heard you did at Caper'na-um, do here also in your own country.'"
²⁴ And he said, "Truly, I say to you, no prophet is acceptable in his own country. ²⁵ But in truth, I tell you, there were many widows in Israel in the days of Eli'jah, when the heaven was shut up three years and six months, when there came a great famine over all the land; ²⁶ and Eli'jah was sent to none of them but only to Zar'ephath, in the land of Sidon, to a woman who was a widow. ²⁷ And there were

many lepers in Israel in the time of the prophet Eli'sha; and none of
them was cleansed, but only Na'aman the Syrian." ²⁸ When they
heard this, all in the synagogue were filled with wrath. ²⁹ And they
rose up and put him out of the city, and led him to the brow of the
hill on which their city was built, that they might throw him down
headlong. ³⁰ But passing through the midst of them he went away.

> **4:17–18** Today in the synagogue specific passages are appointed
> for the prophetic reading each Sabbath. In those days Jesus may
> have been free to choose whatever text he wished. **4:18–19** From
> this passage the Methodist minister and author E. Stanley Jones
> (1884–19—) derived what he considered to be the program of the
> Christian Church: "good news to the poor (that is, the economically
> disinherited) . . . release to the captives (the socially and politically
> disinherited) . . . recovering of sight to the blind (the physically
> disinherited) . . . to set at liberty those who are oppressed (the
> morally and spiritually disinherited) . . . to proclaim the acceptable
> year of the Lord (a new beginning on a world scale)."

"God Has Visited His People"
Luke 6:6–49; 7:1–17, 36–50; 8:1–3

6 On another sabbath, when he entered the synagogue and taught,
a man was there whose right hand was withered. ⁷ And the scribes
and the Pharisees watched him, to see whether he would heal on
the sabbath, so that they might find an accusation against him.
⁸ But he knew their thoughts, and he said to the man who had the
withered hand, "Come and stand here." And he rose and stood
there. ⁹ And Jesus said to them, "I ask you, is it lawful on the
sabbath to do good or to do harm, to save life or to destroy it?"
¹⁰ And he looked around on them all, and said to him, "Stretch out
your hand." And he did so, and his hand was restored. ¹¹ But they
were filled with fury and discussed with one another what they
might do to Jesus.

12 In these days he went out into the hills to pray; and all night
he continued in prayer to God. ¹³ And when it was day, he called his
disciples, and chose from them twelve, whom he named apostles;
¹⁴ Simon, whom he named Peter, and Andrew his brother, and James
and John, and Philip, and Bartholomew, ¹⁵ and Matthew, and
Thomas, and James the son of Alphaeus, and Simon who was called
the Zealot, ¹⁶ and Judas the son of James, and Judas Iscariot, who
became a traitor.

17 And he came down with them and stood on a level place, with a
great crowd of his disciples and a great multitude of people from all
Judea and Jerusalem and the seacoast of Tyre and Sidon, who came

to hear him and to be healed of their diseases; [18] and those who were troubled with unclean spirits were cured. [19] And all the crowd sought to touch him, for power came forth from him and healed them all.

20 And he lifted up his eyes on his disciples, and said:

"Blessed are you poor, for yours is the kingdom of God.

21 "Blessed are you that hunger now, for you shall be satisfied.

"Blessed are you that weep now, for you shall laugh.

22 "Blessed are you when men hate you, and when they exclude you and revile you, and cast out your name as evil, on account of the Son of man! [23] Rejoice in that day, and leap for joy, for behold, your reward is great in heaven; for so their fathers did to the prophets.

24 "But woe to you that are rich, for you have received your consolation.

25 "Woe to you that are full now, for you shall hunger.

"Woe to you that laugh now, for you shall mourn and weep.

26 "Woe to you, when all men speak well of you, for so their fathers did to the false prophets.

27 "But I say to you that hear, Love your enemies, do good to those who hate you, [28] bless those who curse you, pray for those who abuse you. [29] To him who strikes you on the cheek, offer the other also; and from him who takes away your cloak do not withhold your coat as well. [30] Give to every one who begs from you; and of him who takes away your goods do not ask them again. [31] And as you wish that men would do to you, do so to them.

32 "If you love those who love you, what credit is that to you? For even sinners love those who love them. [33] And if you do good to those who do good to you, what credit is that to you? For even sinners do the same. [34] And if you lend to those from whom you hope to receive, what credit is that to you? Even sinners lend to sinners, to receive as much again. [35] But love your enemies, and do good, and lend, expecting nothing in return, and your reward will be great, and you will be sons of the Most High; for he is kind to the ungrateful and the selfish. [36] Be merciful, even as your Father is merciful.

37 "Judge not, and you will not be judged; condemn not, and you will not be condemned; forgive, and you will be forgiven; [38] give, and it will be given to you; good measure, pressed down, shaken together, running over, will be put into your lap. For the measure you give will be the measure you get back."

39 He also told them a parable: "Can a blind man lead a blind man? Will they not both fall into a pit? [40] A disciple is not above his teacher, but every one when he is fully taught will be like his teacher. [41] Why do you see the speck that is in your brother's eye, but do not notice the log that is in your own eye? [42] Or how can you say

to your brother, 'Brother, let me take out the speck that is in your eye,' when you yourself do not see the log that is in your own eye? You hypocrite, first take the log out of your own eye, and then you will see clearly to take out the speck that is in your brother's eye.

43 "For no good tree bears bad fruit, nor again does a bad tree bear good fruit; ⁴⁴for each tree is known by its own fruit. For figs are not gathered from thorns, nor are grapes picked from a bramble bush. ⁴⁵The good man out of the good treasure of his heart produces good, and the evil man out of his evil treasure produces evil; for out of the abundance of the heart his mouth speaks.

46 "Why do you call me 'Lord, Lord,' and not do what I tell you? ⁴⁷Every one who comes to me and hears my words and does them, I will show you what he is like: ⁴⁸he is like a man building a house, who dug deep, and laid the foundation upon rock; and when a flood arose, the stream broke against that house, and could not shake it, because it had been well built. ⁴⁹But he who hears and does not do them is like a man who built a house on the ground without a foundation; against which the stream broke, and immediately it fell, and the ruin of that house was great."

7 After he had ended all his sayings in the hearing of the people he entered Caper'na-um. ²Now a centurion had a slave who was dear to him, who was sick and at the point of death. ³When he heard of Jesus, he sent to him elders of the Jews, asking him to come and heal his slave. ⁴And when they came to Jesus, they besought him earnestly, saying, "He is worthy to have you do this for him, ⁵for he loves our nation, and he built us our synagogue." ⁶And Jesus went with them. When he was not far from the house, the centurion sent friends to him, saying to him, "Lord, do not trouble yourself, for I am not worthy to have you come under my roof; ⁷therefore I did not presume to come to you. But say the word, and let my servant be healed. ⁸For I am a man set under authority, with soldiers under me: and I say to one, 'Go,' and he goes; and to another, 'Come,' and he comes; and to my slave, 'Do this,' and he does it." ⁹When Jesus heard this he marveled at him, and turned and said to the multitude that followed him, "I tell you, not even in Israel have I found such faith." ¹⁰And when those who had been sent returned to the house, they found the slave well.

11 Soon afterward he went to a city called Na'in, and his disciples and a great crowd went with him. ¹²As he drew near to the gate of the city, behold, a man who had died was being carried out, the only son of his mother, and she was a widow; and a large crowd from the city was with her. ¹³And when the Lord saw her, he had compassion on her and said to her, "Do not weep." ¹⁴And he came and touched

the bier, and the bearers stood still. And he said, "Young man, I say to you, arise." [15] And the dead man sat up, and began to speak. And he gave him to his mother. [16] Fear seized them all; and they glorified God, saying, "A great prophet has arisen among us!" and "God has visited his people!" [17] And this report concerning him spread through the whole of Judea and all the surrounding country.

36 One of the Pharisees asked him to eat with him, and he went into the Pharisee's house, and sat at table. [37] And behold, a woman of the city, who was a sinner, when she learned that he was sitting at table in the Pharisee's house, brought an alabaster flask of ointment, [38] and standing behind him at his feet, weeping, she began to wet his feet with her tears, and wiped them with the hair of her head, and kissed his feet, and anointed them with the ointment. [39] Now when the Pharisee who had invited him saw it, he said to himself, "If this man were a prophet, he would have known who and what sort of woman this is who is touching him for she is a sinner." [40] And Jesus answering said to him, "Simon, I have something to say to you." And he answered, "What is it, Teacher?" [41] "A certain creditor had two debtors; one owed five hundred denarii, and the other fifty. [42] When they could not pay, he forgave them both. Now which of them will love him more?" [43] Simon answered, "The one, I suppose, to whom he forgave more." And he said to him, "You have judged rightly." [44] Then turning toward the woman he said to Simon, "Do you see this woman? I entered your house, you gave me no water for my feet, but she has wet my feet with her tears and wiped them with her hair. [45] You gave me no kiss, but from the time I came in she has not ceased to kiss my feet. [46] You did not anoint my head with oil, but she has anointed my feet with ointment. [47] Therefore I tell you, her sins, which are many, are forgiven, for she loved much; but he who is forgiven little, loves little." [48] And he said to her, "Your sins are forgiven." [49] Then those who were at table with him began to say among themselves, "Who is this, who even forgives sins?" [50] And he said to the woman, "Your faith has saved you; go in peace."

8 Soon afterward he went on through cities and villages, preaching and bringing the good news of the kingdom of God. And the twelve were with him, [2] and also some women who had been healed of evil spirits and infirmities: Mary, called Mag'dalene, from whom seven demons had gone out, [3] and Jo-an'na, the wife of Chu'za, Herod's steward, and Susanna, and many others, who provided for them out of their means.

7:11 Verses 11–17 are the Gospel for the Fifteenth Sunday after Pentecost. The passage is also used for the feast of a famous Christian mother, St. Monica (May 4), in application to the rising of her son Augustine from a life of sin to holiness, in answer to her prayers, as related in St. Augustine's *Confessions*. **7:37** Luke does not reveal the identity of the penitent woman, but the Roman Catholic Church uses the passage as the Gospel for the Feast of St. Mary Magdalen (July 20).

"Follow Me"
Luke 9:57–62

57 As they were going along the road, a man said to him, "I will follow you wherever you go." [58] And Jesus said to him, "Foxes have holes, and birds of the air have nests; but the Son of man has nowhere to lay his head." [59] To another he said, "Follow me." But he said, "Lord, let me first go and bury my father." [60] But he said to him, "Leave the dead to bury their own dead; but as for you, go and proclaim the kingdom of God." [61] Another said, "I will follow you, Lord; but let me first say farewell to those at my home." [62] Jesus said to him, "No one who puts his hand to the plow and looks back is fit for the kingdom of God."

Jesus Sends Seventy Disciples
Luke 10:1–24

10 After this the Lord appointed seventy others, and sent them on ahead of him, two by two, into every town and place where he himself was about to come. [2] And he said to them, "The harvest is plentiful, but the laborers are few; pray therefore the Lord of the harvest to send out laborers into his harvest. [3] Go your way; behold, I send you out as lambs in the midst of wolves. [4] Carry no purse, no bag, no sandals; and salute no one on the road. [5] Whatever house you enter, first say, 'Peace be to this house!' [6] And if a son of peace is there, your peace shall rest upon him; but if not, it shall return to you. [7] And remain in the same house, eating and drinking what they provide, for the laborer deserves his wages; do not go from house to house. [8] Whenever you enter a town and they receive you, eat what is set before you; [9] heal the sick in it and say to them, 'The kingdom of God has come near to you.' [10] But whenever you enter a town and they do not receive you, go into its streets and say, [11] 'Even the dust of your town that clings to our feet, we wipe off against you; nevertheless know this, that the kingdom of God has come near.' [12] I tell you, it shall be more tolerable on that day for Sodom than for that town.

13 "Woe to you, Chora′zin! woe to you, Beth-sa′ida! for if the mighty works done in you had been done in Tyre and Sidon, they would have repented long ago, sitting in sackcloth and ashes. [14] But

it shall be more tolerable in the judgment for Tyre and Sidon than for you. ¹⁵ And you, Caper′na-um, will you be exalted to heaven? You shall be brought down to Hades.

16 "He who hears you hears me, and he who rejects you rejects me, and he who rejects me rejects him who sent me."

17 The seventy returned with joy, saying, "Lord, even the demons are subject to us in your name!" ¹⁸ And he said to them, "I saw Satan fall like lightning from heaven. ¹⁹ Behold, I have given you authority to tread upon serpents and scorpions, and over all the power of the enemy; and nothing shall hurt you. ²⁰ Nevertheless do not rejoice in this, that the spirits are subject to you; but rejoice that your names are written in heaven."

21 In that same hour he rejoiced in the Holy Spirit and said, "I thank thee, Father, Lord of heaven and earth, that thou hast hidden these things from the wise and understanding and revealed them to babes; yea, Father, for such was thy gracious will. ²² All things have been delivered to me by my Father; and no one knows who the Son is except the Father, or who the Father is except the Son and any one to whom the Son chooses to reveal him."

23 Then turning to the disciples he said privately, "Blessed are the eyes which see what you see! ²⁴ For I tell you that many prophets and kings desired to see what you see, and did not see it, and to hear what you hear, and did not hear it."

10:1 Other ancient authorities read "seventy-two" (thus the Rheims translation gives: other seventie too). It is probable that Jesus' hearers would here discern the kind of numerical symbolism of which the Hebrews were fond. Tradition had it that the Law was offered to the seventy nations which then existed; Moses was assisted by seventy elders (Numbers 11:16); sacrifices were offered during the week of Succoth, the Feast of Tabernacles, for seventy nations; the Septuagint derives its name from the fact that seventy (Latin *septuaginta*) men worked on the translation. When Jesus chose twelve disciples (Mark 3:14; Matthew 10:1–4; Luke 6:13–16), his contemporaries no doubt sensed a reference to the twelve tribes of Israel. Now that Jesus chooses seventy, the symbolism would not be lost: he is resolved now to take his message beyond the bounds of Judaism to all the seventy nations of mankind. Verses 1–9 are the Gospel for the Feast of St. Luke (October 18), St. Mark (April 25), St. Augustine of Canterbury (May 28), St. Vincent De Paul (July 19), St. Ignatius Loyola (July 31). **10:2** A portion of the Jewish *Ethics of the Fathers*, a book read on Sabbath afternoons in the synagogue, reads: "Rabbi Tarphon said: 'The day is short, the work is great, the laborers are slothful, the reward is much and the Master is urgent.' He added, 'It is not incumbent upon you to complete the work, but neither are you free to desist from it altogether'." **10:15** Traditionally, the translations give "hell" for "Hades." **10:21** Many scientists see in the natural workings of the universe evidence of a divine purpose. James Young Simpson (1873–1934), professor of Natural Science at New College, Edinburgh, said: "If Jesus Christ was right in addressing God as 'Lord of heaven and earth,' then there must be something about heaven and earth and the process by which they and we have come to be what they and we are, which is indicative or revelatory of Him in some degree."

The Good Samaritan
Luke 10:25–37

25 And behold, a lawyer stood up to put him to the test, saying, "Teacher, what shall I do to inherit eternal life?" 26 He said to him, "What is written in the law? How do you read?" 27 And he answered, "You shall love the Lord your God with all your heart, and with all your soul, and with all your strength, and with all your mind; and your neighbor as yourself." 28 And he said to him, "You have answered right; do this, and you will live."

29 But he, desiring to justify himself, said to Jesus, "And who is my neighbor?" 30 Jesus replied, "A man was going down from Jerusalem to Jericho, and he fell among robbers, who stripped him and beat him, and departed, leaving him half dead. 31 Now by chance a priest was going down that road; and when he saw him he passed by on the other side. 32 So likewise a Levite, when he came to the place and saw him, passed by on the other side. 33 But a Samaritan, as he journeyed, came to where he was; and when he saw him, he had compassion, 34 and went to him and bound up his wounds, pouring on oil and wine; then he set him on his own beast and brought him to an inn, and took care of him. 35 And the next day he took out two denarii and gave them to the innkeeper, saying, 'Take care of him; and whatever more you spend, I will repay you when I come back.' 36 Which of these three, do you think, proved neighbor to the man who fell among the robbers?" 37 He said, "The one who showed mercy on him." And Jesus said to him, "Go and do likewise."

10:25 This is the Gospel for the Twelfth Sunday after Pentecost. The "Priests" and "Levites," religious leaders of the community, should have shown compassion; instead it was a "Samaritan," an enemy of the Jews (2 Kings 17:29–34) who demonstrated good neighborliness. Verses 29–37 are the Gospel for the Feast of St. Peter Claver (September 9), patron of Catholic missionary work among Negroes. **10:27** Compare Deuteronomy 6:5; Leviticus 19:18. This verse sets forth an ideal that ought to be followed by all religious men. In all times men have fallen short. In the period of the Christian reformation Desiderius Erasmus (1466?–1536), Dutch scholar and humanist, declared that Christianity in his time had come to consist not in loving one's neighbor but in abstaining from butter and cheese during Lent. How would we live out, today, the principle of being a good neighbor?

Martha and Mary
Luke 10:38–42

38 Now as they went on their way, he entered a village; and a woman named Martha received him into her house. ³⁹ And she had a sister called Mary, who sat at the Lord's feet and listened to his teaching. ⁴⁰ But Martha was distracted with much serving; and she went to him and said, "Lord, do you not care that my sister has left me to serve alone? Tell her then to help me." ⁴¹ But the Lord answered her, "Martha, Martha, you are anxious and troubled about many things; ⁴² one thing is needful. Mary has chosen the good portion, which shall not be taken away from her."

10:38 The passage is the Gospel for the Feast of St. Martha (July 29).

Seek and You Will Find
Luke 11:1–13

11 He was praying in a certain place, and when he ceased, one of his disciples said to him, "Lord, teach us to pray, as John taught his disciples." ² And he said to them, "When you pray, say:
"Father, hallowed be thy name. Thy kingdom come. ³ Give us each day our daily bread, ⁴ and forgive us our sins, for we ourselves forgive every one who is indebted to us; and lead us not into temptation."
5 And he said to them, "Which of you who has a friend will go to him at midnight and say to him, 'Friend, lend me three loaves; ⁶ for a friend of mine has arrived on a journey, and I have nothing to set before him'; ⁷ and he will answer from within, 'Do not bother me; the door is now shut, and my children are with me in bed; I cannot get up and give you anything'? ⁸ I tell you, though he will not get up and give him anything because he is his friend, yet because of his importunity he will rise and give him whatever he needs. ⁹ And I tell you, Ask, and it will be given you; seek, and you will find; knock, and it will be opened to you. ¹⁰ For every one who asks receives, and he who seeks finds, and to him who knocks it will be opened. ¹¹ What father among you, if his son asks for a fish, will instead of a fish give him a serpent; ¹² or if he asks for an egg, will give him a

scorpion? [13] If you then, who are evil, know how to give good gifts to your children, how much more will the heavenly Father give the Holy Spirit to those who ask him!''

11:2 Luke gives only five petitions in the prayer which Jesus taught his disciples; Matthew gives seven (6:9–13). The early Christians preserved the prayer in different forms.

"Seek His Kingdom"
Luke 12:13–57

13 One of the multitude said to him, "Teacher, bid my brother divide the inheritance with me." [14] But he said to him, "Man, who made me a judge or divider over you?" [15] And he said to them, "Take heed, and beware of all covetousness; for a man's life does not consist in the abundance of his possessions." [16] And he told them a parable, saying, "The land of a rich man brought forth plentifully; [17] and he thought to himself, 'What shall I do, for I have nowhere to store my crops?' [18] And he said, 'I will do this: I will pull down my barns, and build larger ones; and there I will store all my grain and my goods. [19] And I will say to my soul, Soul, you have ample goods laid up for many years; take your ease, eat, drink, be merry.' [20] But God said to him, 'Fool! This night your soul is required of you; and the things you have prepared, whose will they be?' [21] So is he who lays up treasure for himself, and is not rich toward God.''

22 And he said to his disciples, "Therefore I tell you, do not be anxious about your life, what you shall eat, nor about your body, what you shall put on. [23] For life is more than food, and the body more than clothing. [24] Consider the ravens: they neither sow nor reap, they have neither storehouse nor barn, and yet God feeds them. Of how much more value are you than the birds! [25] And which of you by being anxious can add a cubit to his span of life? [26] If then you are not able to do as small a thing as that, why are you anxious about the rest? [27] Consider the lilies, how they grow; they neither toil nor spin; yet I tell you, even Solomon in all his glory was not arrayed like one of these. [28] But if God so clothes the grass which is alive in the field today and tomorrow is thrown into the oven, how much more will he clothe you, O men of little faith! [29] And do not seek what you are to eat and what you are to drink, nor be of anxious mind. [30] For all the nations of the world seek these things; and your Father knows that you need them. [31] Instead, seek his kingdom, and these things shall be yours as well.

32 "Fear not, little flock, for it is your Father's good pleasure to give you the kingdom. [33] Sell your possessions, and give alms;

provide yourselves with purses that do not grow old, with a treasure in the heavens that does not fail, where no thief approaches and no moth destroys. ³⁴ For where your treasure is, there will your heart be also.

35 "Let your loins be girded and your lamps burning, ³⁶ and be like men who are waiting for their master to come home from the marriage feast, so that they may open to him at once when he comes and knocks. ³⁷ Blessed are those servants whom the master finds awake when he comes; truly, I say to you, he will gird himself and have them sit at table, and he will come and serve them. ³⁸ If he comes in the second watch, or in the third, and finds them so, blessed are those servants! ³⁹ But know this, that if the householder had known at what hour the thief was coming, he would have been awake and would not have left his house to be broken into. ⁴⁰ You also must be ready; for the Son of man is coming at an hour you do not expect."

41 Peter said, "Lord, are you telling this parable for us or for all?" ⁴² And the Lord said, "Who then is the faithful and wise steward, whom his master will set over his household, to give them their portion of food at the proper time? ⁴³ Blessed is that servant whom his master when he comes will find so doing. ⁴⁴ Truly I tell you, he will set him over all his possessions. ⁴⁵ But if that servant says to himself, 'My master is delayed in coming,' and begins to beat the menservants and the maidservants, and to eat and drink and get drunk, ⁴⁶ the master of that servant will come on a day when he does not expect him and at an hour he does not know, and will punish him, and put him with the unfaithful. ⁴⁷ And that servant who knew his master's will, but did not make ready or act according to his will, shall receive a severe beating. ⁴⁸ But he who did not know, and did what deserved a beating, shall receive a light beating. Every one to whom much is given, of him will much be required; and of him to whom men commit much they will demand the more.

49 "I came to cast fire upon the earth; and would that it were already kindled! ⁵⁰ I have a baptism to be baptized with; and how I am constrained until it is accomplished! ⁵¹ Do you think that I have come to give peace on earth? No, I tell you, but rather division; ⁵² for henceforth in one house there will be five divided, three against two and two against three; ⁵³ they will be divided, father against son and son against father, mother against daughter and daughter against her mother, mother-in-law against her daughter-in-law and daughter-in-law against her mother-in-law."

54 He also said to the multitudes, "When you see a cloud rising in the west, you say at once, 'A shower is coming'; and so it happens.

[55] And when you see the south wind blowing, you say, 'There will be scorching heat'; and it happens. [56] You hypocrites! You know how to interpret the appearance of earth and sky; but why do you not know how to interpret the present time?

57 "And why do you not judge for yourselves what is right?"

12:19 Interesting attempts have been made to translate this soliloquy into contemporary idiom. In 1768, Edward Harwood, an English Unitarian, published *A Liberal Translation of the New Testament,* which rendered it: "I will say to my soul—happy soul! Distinguished in thy felicity! Come indulge thy soft envied repose—feast on the most delicious viands—taste the most exquisite liquors—traverse a circle of every amusement and joy." This may be set in contrast with the more succinct rendering of J. B. Phillips, whose *The New Testament in Modern English* was published in 1958: "I can say to my soul, Soul, you have plenty of good things stored up there for years to come. Relax! Eat, drink and have a good time!"

Judgment
Luke 13:22–35

22 He went on his way through towns and villages, teaching, and journeying toward Jerusalem. [23] And some one said to him, "Lord, will those who are saved be few?" And he said to them, [24] "Strive to enter by the narrow door; for many, I tell you, will seek to enter and will not be able. [25] When once the householder has risen up and shut the door, you will begin to stand outside and to knock at the door, saying, 'Lord, open to us.' He will answer you, 'I do not know where you come from.' [26] Then you will begin to say, 'We ate and drank in your presence, and you taught in our streets.' [27] But he will say, 'I tell you, I do not know where you come from; depart from me, all you workers of iniquity!' [28] There you will weep and gnash your teeth, when you see Abraham and Isaac and Jacob and all the prophets in the kingdom of God and you yourselves thrust out. [29] And men will come from east and west, and from north and south, and sit at table in the kingdom of God. [30] And behold, some are last who will be first, and some are first who will be last."

31 At that very hour some Pharisees came, and said to him, "Get away from here, for Herod wants to kill you." [32] And he said to them, "Go and tell that fox, 'Behold, I cast out demons and perform cures today and tomorrow, and the third day I finish my course. [33] Nevertheless I must go on my way today and tomorrow and the day following; for it cannot be that a prophet should perish away from Jerusalem.' [34] O Jerusalem, Jerusalem, killing the prophets and

stoning those who are sent to you! How often would I have gathered your children together as a hen gathers her brood under her wings, and you would not! [35] Behold, your house is forsaken. And I tell you, you will not see me until you say, 'Blessed is he who comes in the name of the Lord!' ''

13:29 This verse is cited by those Christians believing that persons who serve the right as it is known to them will find salvation. Compare Matthew 8:10–12; 11:27.

Parable of the Great Banquet
Luke 14:16–24

16 But he said to him, "A man once gave a great banquet, and invited many; [17] and at the time for the banquet he sent his servant to say to those who had been invited, 'Come; for all is now ready.' [18] But they all alike began to make excuses. The first said to him, 'I have bought a field, and I must go out and see it; I pray you, have me excused.' [19] And another said, 'I have bought five yoke of oxen, and I go to examine them; I pray you, have me excused.' [20] And another said, 'I have married a wife, and therefore I cannot come.' [21] So the servant came and reported this to his master. Then the householder in anger said to his servant, 'Go out quickly to the streets and lanes of the city, and bring in the poor and maimed and blind and lame.' [22] And the servant said, 'Sir, what you commanded has been done, and still there is room.' [23] And the master said to the servant, 'Go out to the highways and hedges, and compel people to come in, that my house may be filled. [24] For I tell you, none of those men who were invited shall taste my banquet.' ''

14:16 This section is the Gospel for the Second Sunday after Pentecost. Older translations have "supper" for "banquet."

The Prodigal Son

The parable is presented here in Wyclif's second version (completed in 1397 and attributed to Wyclif's secretary, John Purvey) and the Revised Standard Version (1946).

Luke 15:11–32

11 And he said, "There was a man who had two sons; [12] and the younger of them said to his father, 'Father, give me the share of property that falls to me.' And he divided his living between them. [13] Not many	11 And he seide, A man hadde twei sones; [12] and the ʒonger of hem seide to the fadir, Fadir, ʒyue me the porcioun of catel, that fallith to me. And he departide to hem the catel. [13] And not aftir many

days later, the younger son gathered all he had and took his journey into a far country, and there he squandered his property in loose living. ¹⁴And when he had spent everything, a great famine arose in that country, and he began to be in want. ¹⁵So he went and joined himself to one of the citizens of that country, who sent him into his fields to feed swine. ¹⁶And he would gladly have fed on the pods that the swine ate; and no one gave him anything. ¹⁷But when he came to himself he said, 'How many of my father's hired servants have bread enough and to spare, but I perish here with hunger! ¹⁸I will arise and go to my father, and I will say to him, "Father, I have sinned against heaven and before you; ¹⁹I am no longer worthy to be called your son; treat me as one of your hired servants." ' ²⁰And he arose and came to his father. But while he was yet at a distance, his father saw him and had compassion, and ran and embraced him and kissed him. ²¹And the son said to him, 'Father, I have sinned against heaven and before you; I am no longer worthy to be called your son.' ²²But the father said to his servants, 'Bring quickly the best robe, and put it on him; and put a ring on his hand, and shoes on his feet; ²³and bring the fatted calf and kill it, and let us eat and make merry;

daies, whanne alle thingis weren gederid togider, the ȝonger sone wente forth in pilgrymage in to a fer cuntre; and there he wastide hise goodis in lyuynge lecherously. ¹⁴And aftir that he hadde endid alle thingis, a strong hungre was maad in that cuntre, and he bigan to haue nede. ¹⁵And he wente, and drouȝ hym to oon of the citeseyns of that cuntre. And he sente hym in to his toun, to fede swyn. ¹⁶And he coueitide to fille his wombe of the coddis that the hoggis eeten, and no man ȝaf hym. ¹⁷And he turnede aȝen to hym silf, and seide, Hou many hirid men in my fadir hous han plente of looues; and Y perische here thorouȝ hungir. ¹⁸Y schal rise vp, and go to my fadir, and Y schal seie to hym, Fadir, Y haue synned in to heuene, and bifor thee; ¹⁹and now Y am not worthi to be clepid thi sone, make me as oon of thin hirid men. ²⁰And he roos vp, and cam to his fadir. And whanne he was ȝit afer, his fadir saiȝ hym, and was stirrid bi mercy. And he ran, and fel on his necke, and kisside hym. ²¹And the sone seide to hym, Fadir, Y haue synned in to heuene, and bifor thee; and now Y am not worthi to be clepid thi sone. ²²And the fadir seide to hise seruauntis, Swithe brynge ȝe forth the firste stoole, and clothe ȝe hym, and ȝyue ȝe a ryng in his hoond, ²³and schoon on his

24 for this my son was dead, and is alive again; he was lost, and is found.' And they began to make merry.

25 "Now his elder son was in the field; and as he came and drew near to the house, he heard music and dancing. 26 And he called one of the servants and asked what this meant. 27 And he said to him, 'Your brother has come, and your father has killed the fatted calf, because he has received him safe and sound.' 28 But he was angry and refused to go in. His father came out and entreated him, 29 but he answered his father, 'Lo, these many years I have served you, and I never disobeyed your command; yet you never gave me a kid, that I might make merry with my friends. 30 But when this son of yours came, who has devoured your living with harlots, you killed for him the fatted calf!' 31 And he said to him, 'Son, you are always with me, and all that is mine is yours. 32 It was fitting to make merry and be glad, for this your brother was dead, and is alive; he was lost, and is found.' "

feet; and brynge ȝe a fat calf, and sle ȝe, and ete we, and make we feeste. 24 For this my sone was deed, and hath lyued aȝen; he perischid, and is foundun. And alle men bigunnen to ete. 25 But his eldere sone was in the feeld; and whanne he cam, and neiȝede to the hous, he herde a symfonye and a croude. 26 And he clepide oon of the seruauntis, and axide, what these thingis weren. 27 And he seide to hym, Thi brother is comun, and thi fadir slewe a fat calf, for he resseyuede hym saaf. 28 And he was wrooth, and wolde not come in. Therfor his fadir wente out, and bigan to preye hym. 29 And he answerde to his fadir, and seide, Lo! so many ȝeeris Y serue thee, and Y neuer brak thi comaundement; and thou neuer ȝaf to me a kidde, that Y with my freendis schulde haue ete. 30 But aftir that this thi sone, that hath deuourid his substaunce with horis, cam, thou hast slayn to hym a fat calf. 31 And he seide to hym, Sone, thou art euer more with me, and alle my thingis ben thine. 32 But it bihofte for to make feeste, and to haue ioye; for this thi brother was deed, and lyuede aȝen; he perischide, and is foundun.

15: "Parable of the Prodigal Son," the column heading in some Bibles, is the title by which this story is generally known. Column headings represent editorial additions; they were not part of the original Scripture. Jesus nowhere calls the boy a prodigal, nor does the word "prodigal" occur in the story. The father is the principal character in the story, which might well be called "Parable of the Forgiving Father."

The Unjust Steward
Luke 16 : 1–13

16 He also said to the disciples, "There was a rich man who had a steward, and charges were brought to him that this man was wasting his goods. [2] And he called him and said to him, 'What is this that I hear about you? Turn in the account of your stewardship, for you can no longer be steward.' [3] And the steward said to himself, 'What shall I do, since my master is taking the stewardship away from me? I am not strong enough to dig, and I am ashamed to beg. [4] I have decided what to do, so that people may receive me into their houses when I am put out of the stewardship.' [5] So, summoning his master's debtors one by one, he said to the first, 'How much do you owe my master?' [6] He said, 'A hundred measures of oil.' And he said to him, 'Take your bill, and sit down quickly and write fifty.' [7] Then he said to another, 'And how much do you owe?' He said, 'A hundred measures of wheat.' He said to him, 'Take your bill, and write eighty.' [8] The master commended the dishonest steward for his prudence; for the sons of this world are wiser in their own generation than the sons of light. [9] And I tell you, make friends for yourselves by means of unrighteous mammon, so that when it fails they may receive you into the eternal habitations.

10 "He who is faithful in a very little is faithful also in much; and he who is dishonest in a very little is dishonest also in much. [11] If then you have not been faithful in the unrighteous mammon, who will entrust to you the true riches? [12] And if you have not been faithful in that which is another's, who will give you that which is your own? [13] No servant can serve two masters; for either he will hate the one and love the other, or he will be devoted to the one and despise the other. You cannot serve God and mammon."

16:11, 13 Compare Micah 6:8. Compare also the popular saying "Pride goes before a fall." Those who choose to consider themselves superior (e.g., racists) may according to this verse expect the consequences of their mistaken choices.

"They Have Moses and the Prophets"
Luke 16 : 19–31

19 "There was a rich man, who was clothed in purple and fine linen and who feasted sumptuously every day. [20] And at his gate lay a poor man named Laz′arus, full of sores, [21] who desired to be fed with

what fell from the rich man's table; moreover the dogs came and licked his sores. ²²The poor man died and was carried by the angels to Abraham's bosom. The rich man also died and was buried; ²³and in Hades, being in torment, he lifted up his eyes, and saw Abraham far off and Laz′arus in his bosom. ²⁴And he called out, 'Father Abraham, have mercy upon me, and send Laz′arus to dip the end of his finger in water and cool my tongue; for I am in anguish in this flame.' ²⁵But Abraham said, 'Son, remember that you in your lifetime received your good things, and Laz′arus in like manner evil things; but now he is comforted here, and you are in anguish. ²⁶And besides all this, between us and you a great chasm has been fixed, in order that those who would pass from here to you may not be able, and none may cross from there to us.' ²⁷And he said, 'Then I beg you, father, to send him to my father's house, ²⁸for I have five brothers, so that he may warn them, lest they also come into this place of torment.' ²⁹But Abraham said, 'They have Moses and the prophets; let them hear them.' ³⁰And he said, 'No, father Abraham; but if some one goes to them from the dead, they will repent.' ³¹He said to him, 'If they do not hear Moses and the prophets, neither will they be convinced if some one should rise from the dead.' "

16:19–21 When Albert Schweitzer (1875–1965), a foremost European theologian and expert on Bach, turned his back on careers in music and theology to become a missionary doctor in Gabon, he interpreted his renunciation in terms of this parable. He was the rich man, Africa the poor man. "Whatever benefits we confer upon the peoples of our colonies," he said, "is not beneficence but atonement for the terrible sufferings which we white people have been bringing upon them ever since the day on which the first of our ships found its way to their shores." **16:22** *Bosom* here denotes the place of honor when guests reclined (in ancient fashion) for dinner, at right or left (in front of the host).

The Grateful Samaritan
Luke 17:11–29

11 On the way to Jerusalem he was passing along between Samar′ia and Galilee. ¹²And as he entered a village, he was met by ten lepers, who stood at a distance ¹³and lifted up their voices and said, "Jesus, Master, have mercy on us." ¹⁴When he saw them he said to them, "Go and show yourselves to the priests." And as they went they were cleansed. ¹⁵Then one of them, when he saw that he was healed, turned back, praising God with a loud voice; ¹⁶and he fell on his face at Jesus' feet, giving him thanks. Now he was a Samaritan. ¹⁷Then said Jesus, "Were not ten cleansed? Where are the nine? ¹⁸Was no

one found to return and give praise to God except this foreigner?" ¹⁹ And he said to him, "Rise and go your way; your faith has made you well."

20 Being asked by the Pharisees when the kingdom of God was coming, he answered them, "The kingdom of God is not coming with signs to be observed; ²¹ nor will they say, 'Lo, here it is!' or 'There!' for behold, the kingdom of God is in the midst of you."

22 And he said to the disciples, "The days are coming when you will desire to see one of the days of the Son of man, and you will not see it. ²³ And they will say to you, 'Lo, there!' or 'Lo, here!' Do not go, do not follow them. ²⁴ For as the lightning flashes and lights up the sky from one side to the other, so will the Son of man be in his day. ²⁵ But first he must suffer many things and be rejected by this generation. ²⁶ As it was in the days of Noah, so will it be in the days of the Son of man. ²⁷ They ate, they drank, they married, they were given in marriage, until the day when Noah entered the ark, and the flood came and destroyed them all. ²⁸ Likewise as it was in the days of Lot—they ate, they drank, they bought, they sold, they planted, they built, ²⁹ but on the day when Lot went out from Sodom fire and brimstone rained from heaven and destroyed them all."

He Who Exalts Himself Will be Humbled
Luke 18 : 1–14

18 And he told them a parable, to the effect that they ought always to pray and not lose heart. ² He said, "In a certain city there was a judge who neither feared God nor regarded man; ³ and there was a widow in that city who kept coming to him and saying, 'Vindicate me against my adversary.' ⁴ For a while he refused; but afterward he said to himself, 'Though I neither fear God nor regard man, ⁵ yet because this widow bothers me, I will vindicate her, or she will wear me out by her continual coming.' " ⁶ And the Lord said, "hear what the unrighteous judge says. ⁷ And will not God vindicate his elect, who cry to him day and night? Will he delay long over them? ⁸ I tell you, he will vindicate them speedily. Nevertheless, when the Son of man comes, will he find faith on earth?"

9 He also told this parable to some who trusted in themselves that they were rightous and despised others: ¹⁰ "Two men went up into the temple to pray, one a Pharisee and the other a tax collector. ¹¹ The Pharisee stood and prayed thus with himself, 'God, I thank thee that I am not like other men, extortioners, unjust, adulterers, or even like this tax collector. ¹² I fast twice a week, I give tithes of all that I get.' ¹³ But the tax collector, standing far off, would not even lift up his eyes to heaven, but beat his breast, saying, 'God, be merciful to me a

sinner!' ¹⁴ I tell you, this man went down to his house justified rather than the other; for every one who exalts himself will be humbled, but he who humbles himself will be exalted."

18:6 In Rabbinical teaching there is a similar suggestion that insistent prayer has an influence on God. One rabbi describes the power of such prayer, "It is as if one seized hold of God and did not let him go until the request was granted" (*Berachot* 32a). **18:9** This story is the Gospel for the Tenth Sunday after Pentecost. **18:10** Older translations have "publican" for "tax collector."

The Blind Man at Jericho
Luke 18:31–43

31 And taking the twelve, he said to them, "Behold, we are going up to Jerusalem, and everything that is written of the Son of man by the prophets will be accomplished. ³² For he will be delivered to the Gentiles, and will be mocked and shamefully treated and spit upon; ³³ they will scourge him and kill him, and on the third day he will rise." ³⁴ But they understood none of these things; this saying was hid from them, and they did not grasp what was said.

35 As he drew near to Jericho, a blind man was sitting by the roadside begging; ³⁶ and hearing a multitude going by, he inquired what this meant. ³⁷ They told him, "Jesus of Nazareth is passing by." ³⁸ And he cried, "Jesus, Son of David, have mercy on me!" ³⁹ And those who were in front rebuked him, telling him to be silent; but he cried out all the more, "Son of David, have mercy on me!" ⁴⁰ And Jesus stopped, and commanded him to be brought to him; and when he came near, he asked him, ⁴¹ "What do you want me to do for you?" He said, "Lord, let me receive my sight." ⁴² And Jesus said to him, "Receive your sight; your faith has made you well." ⁴³ And immediately he received his sight and followed him, glorifying God; and all the people, when they saw it, gave praise to God.

18:31 This story is placed in Luke's Gospel right after Jesus has predicted his suffering, death and resurrection. St. Gregory comments that the blind man recovered his sight under the very eyes of the apostles in order that their faith might be strengthened. The passage is the Gospel for Quinquagesima Sunday, the Sunday before the beginning of Lent.

"Today Salvation Has Come to This House"
Luke 19:1–10

19 He entered Jericho and was passing through. ² And there was a man named Zacchae'us; he was a chief tax collector, and rich. ³ And he sought to see who Jesus was, but could not, on account of the crowd, because he was small of stature. [4] So he ran on ahead and climbed up into a sycamore tree to see him, for he was to pass that way. [5] And when Jesus came to the place, he looked up and said to him, "Zacchae'us, make haste and come down; for I must stay at your house today." [6] So he made haste and came down, and received him joyfully. [7] And when they saw it they all murmured, "He has gone in to be the guest of a man who is a sinner." [8] And Zacchae'us stood and said to the Lord, "Behold, Lord, the half of my goods I give to the poor; and if I have defrauded any one of anything, I restore it fourfold." [9] And Jesus said to him, "Today salvation has come to this house, since he also is a son of Abraham. [10] For the Son of man came to seek and to save the lost."

> **19:1** These verses are the Gospel in the Mass for the Dedication of a Church; the passage was chosen on account of the connections between Jesus and "house" (a church being regarded as the house of the Lord). **19:10** Is the Bible the account of man's effort to know God, or the record of God's effort to communicate with man? Upholding the latter view, the great Swiss theologian Karl Barth (1886–1968) asserted: "The Bible tells us not how man should talk with God, but what He says to us; not how we find the way to Him, but how He sought and found the way to us."

The Last Supper
Luke 22:14–30

14 And when the hour came, he sat at table, and the apostles with him. [15] And he said to them, "I have earnestly desired to eat this passover with you before I suffer; [16] for I tell you I shall not eat it until it is fulfilled in the kingdom of God." [17] And he took a cup, and when he had given thanks he said, "Take this, and divide it among yourselves; [18] for I tell you that from now on I shall not drink of the fruit of the vine until the kingdom of God comes." [19] And he took bread, and when he had given thanks he broke it and gave it to them, saying, "This is my body. [21] But behold the hand of him who betrays me is with me on the table. [22] For the Son of man goes as it has been determined; but woe to that man by whom he is betrayed!" [23] And they began to question one another, which of them it was that would do this.

24 A dispute also arose among them, which of them was to be regarded as the greatest. [25] And he said to them, "The kings of the Gentiles exercise lordship over them; and those in authority over them are called benefactors. [26] But not so with you; rather let the greatest among you become as the youngest, and the leader as one who serves. [27] For which is the greater, one who sits at table, or one

who serves? Is it not the one who sits at table? But I am among you
as one who serves.

28 "You are those who have continued with me in my trials; ²⁹ as
my Father appointed a kingdom for me, so do I appoint for you
³⁰ that you may eat and drink at my table in my kingdom, and sit on
thrones judging the twelve tribes of Israel."

22:19 From A.D. 1215 Catholic law has required that all
Catholics assist at the Lord's Supper (Mass) each Sunday. Protestants have differed as to the frequency with which the Lord's Supper
should be celebrated. Time was in the Church of Scotland when it
was celebrated only once or twice a year. The Disciples of Christ
celebrate it each Sunday. Lest the rite be cheapened, he thought, by
too frequent observance, the Protestant reformer John Calvin
(1509–1564) recommended that it be observed once a month.

Agony in the Garden
Luke 22:35–53

35 And he said to them, "When I sent you out with no purse or bag
or sandals, did you lack anything?" They said, "Nothing." ³⁶ He
said to them, "But now, let him who has a purse take it, and likewise
a bag. And let him who has no sword sell his mantle and buy one.
³⁷ For I tell you that this scripture must be fulfilled in me, 'And he
was reckoned with transgressors'; for what is written about me has
its fulfilment." ³⁸ And they said, "Look, Lord, here are two swords."
And he said to them, "It is enough."

39 And he came out, and went, as was his custom, to the Mount of
Olives; and the disciples followed him. ⁴⁰ And when he came to the
place he said to them, "Pray that you may not enter into temptation." ⁴¹ And he withdrew from them about a stone's throw, and
knelt down and prayed, ⁴² "Father, if thou art willing, remove this
cup from me; nevertheless not my will, but thine, be done." ⁴³ And
there appeared to him an angel from heaven, strengthening him.
⁴⁴ And being in an agony he prayed more earnestly; and his sweat
became like great drops of blood falling down upon the ground.
⁴⁵ And when he rose from prayer, he came to the disciples and found
them sleeping for sorrow, ⁴⁶ and he said to them, "Why do you sleep?
Rise and pray that you may not enter into temptation."

47 While he was still speaking, there came a crowd, and the man
called Judas, one of the twelve, was leading them. He drew near to
Jesus to kiss him; ⁴⁸ but Jesus said to him, "Judas, would you betray
the Son of man with a kiss?" ⁴⁹ And when those who were about him
saw what would follow, they said, "Lord, shall we strike with the
sword?" ⁵⁰ And one of them struck the slave of the high priest and

cut off his right ear. [51] But Jesus said, "No more of this!" And he touched his ear and healed him. [52] Then Jesus said to the chief priests and captains of the temple and elders, who had come out against him, "Have you come out as against a robber, with swords and clubs? [53] When I was with you day after day in the temple, you did not lay hands on me. But this is your hour, and the power of darkness."

22:36 Older translations have "wallet" for "purse," "scrip" for "bag." **22:42** Rheims has "chalice" for "cup."

Herod and Pilate Become Friends
Luke 23:1–12

23 Then the whole company of them arose, and brought him before Pilate. [2] And they began to accuse him, saying, "We found this man perverting our nation, and forbidding us to give tribute to Caesar, and saying that he himself is Christ a king." [3] And Pilate asked him, "Are you the King of the Jews?" And he answered him, "You have said so." [4] And Pilate said to the chief priests and the multitudes, "I find no crime in this man." [5] But they were urgent, saying, "He stirs up the people, teaching throughout all Judea, from Galilee even to this place."

6 When Pilate heard this, he asked whether the man was a Galilean. [7] And when he learned that he belonged to Herod's jurisdiction, he sent him over to Herod, who was himself in Jerusalem at that time. [8] When Herod saw Jesus, he was very glad, for he had long desired to see him, because he had heard about him, and he was hoping to see some sign done by him. [9] So he questioned him at some length; but he made no answer. [10] The chief priests and the scribes stood by, vehemently accusing him. [11] And Herod with his soldiers treated him with contempt and mocked him; then, arraying him in gorgeous apparel, he sent him back to Pilate. [12] And Herod and Pilate became friends with each other that very day, for before this they had been at enmity with each other.

"Weep for Yourselves"
Luke 23:26–31

26 And as they led him away, they seized one Simon of Cyre'ne, who was coming in from the country, and laid on him the cross, to carry it behind Jesus. [27] And there followed him a great multitude of the people, and of women who bewailed and lamented him. [28] But Jesus turning to them said, "Daughters of Jerusalem, do not weep for me, but weep for yourselves and for your children. [29] For behold, the days are coming when they will say, 'Blessed are the barren, and the wombs

that never bore, and the breasts that never gave suck!' [30] Then they will begin to say to the mountains, 'Fall on us'; and to the hills, 'Cover us.' [31] For if they do this when the wood is green, what will happen when it is dry?"

  23:31 Verse 31 is usually interpreted to mean: if innocent Jesus is so treated, what will happen to the guilty?

The Penitent Criminal
Luke 23 : 39–43

39 One of the criminals who were hanged railed at him, saying, "Are you not the Christ? Save yourself and us!" [40] But the other rebuked him, saying, "Do you not fear God, since you are under the same sentence of condemnation? [41] And we indeed justly; for we are receiving the due reward of our deeds; but this man has done nothing wrong." [42] And he said, "Jesus, remember me when you come in your kingly power." [43] And he said to him, "Truly, I say to you, today you will be with me in Paradise."

"You Are Witnesses of These Things"
Luke 24 : 13–53

13 That very day two of them were going to a village named Emma'us, about seven miles from Jerusalem, [14] and talking with each other about all these things that had happened. [15] While they were talking and discussing together, Jesus himself drew near and went with them. [16] But their eyes were kept from recognizing him. [17] And he said to them, "What is this conversation which you are holding with each other as you walk?" And they stood still, looking sad. [18] Then one of them, named Cle'opas, answered him, "Are you the only visitor to Jerusalem who does not know the things that have happened there in these days?" [19] And he said to them, "What things?" And they said to him, "Concerning Jesus of Nazareth, who was a prophet mighty in deed and word before God and all the people, [20] and how our chief priests and rulers delivered him up to be condemned to death, and crucified him. [21] But we had hoped that he was the one to redeem Israel. Yes, and besides all this, it is now the third day since this happened. [22] Moreover, some women of our company amazed us. They were at the tomb early in the morning [23] and did not find his body; and they came back saying that they had even seen a vision of angels, who said that he was alive. [24] Some of those who were with us went to the tomb, and found it just as the women had said; but him they did not see." [25] And he said to them, "O foolish men, and slow of heart to believe all that the prophets have spoken! [26] Was it not necessary that the Christ should suffer

these things and enter into his glory?" [27] And beginning with Moses and all the prophets, he interpreted to them in all the scriptures the things concerning himself.

28 So they drew near to the village to which they were going. He appeared to be going further, [29] but they constrained him, saying, "Stay with us, for it is toward evening and the day is now far spent." So he went in to stay with them. [30] When he was at table with them, he took the bread and blessed, and broke it, and gave it to them. [31] And their eyes were opened and they recognized him; and he vanished out of their sight. [32] They said to each other, "Did not our hearts burn within us while he talked to us on the road, while he opened to us the scriptures?" [33] And they rose that same hour and returned to Jerusalem; and they found the eleven gathered together and those who were with them, [34] who said, "The Lord has risen indeed, and has appeared to Simon!" [35] Then they told what had happened on the road, and how he was known to them in the breaking of the bread.

36 As they were saying this, Jesus himself stood among them. [37] But they were startled and frightened, and supposed that they saw a spirit. [38] And he said to them, "Why are you troubled, and why do questionings rise in your hearts? [39] See my hands and my feet, that it is I myself; handle me, and see; for a spirit has not flesh and bones as you see that I have." [41] And while they still disbelieved for joy, and wondered, he said to them, "Have you anything here to eat?" [42] They gave him a piece of broiled fish, [43] and he took it and ate before them.

44 Then he said to them, "These are my words which I spoke to you, while I was still with you, that everything written about me in the law of Moses and the prophets and the psalms must be fulfilled." [45] Then he opened their minds to understand the scriptures, [46] and said to them, "Thus it is written, that the Christ should suffer and on the third day rise from the dead, [47] and that repentance and forgiveness of sins should be preached in his name to all nations, beginning from Jerusalem. [48] You are witnesses of these things. [49] And behold, I send the promise of my Father upon you; but stay in the city, until you are clothed with power from on high."

50 Then he led them out as far as Bethany, and lifting up his hands he blessed them. [51] While he blessed them, he parted from them. [52] And they returned to Jerusalem with great joy, [53] and were continually in the temple blessing God.

24:52 Luke's Gospel ends on a note of joy and praise. Luke gave us the song of the angels at the beginning (2:13 f.). He often noted the joy of the people when they saw "the wonderful works" of Jesus (cf. 10:17; 13:17; 18:43).

The Gospel according to John

The Fourth Gospel differs from the three Synoptic Gospels. It begins with a prologue before time began, on the highest spiritual plane. That is why the symbol in art for the author of this book is the high flying eagle (fourth of the figures in Ezekiel's famous vision from which the symbols of the Gospel writers have been drawn).

The author of this book states plainly his purpose: ". . . these are written that you may believe that Jesus is the Christ, the Son of God, and that believing you may have life in his name" (20:31).

John does not mention some incidents narrated by other evangelists, such as the baptism of Jesus, and the transfiguration, but he gives us some that the others did not: the wedding at Cana, the raising of Lazarus from the dead, the washing of the feet at the Last Supper. One who has read the Synoptic Gospels will know that Jesus used things of everyday life to explain his teaching (bread, light, sheep and shepherds, etc.), but in this Gospel the terms often have additional symbolic meaning. What lies behind this use of some episodes in Jesus' life but not others, and the special use of symbols drawn from everyday life? John may have taken it for granted that his readers were already familiar with the three other Gospels and therefore he would fill in the account. On the other hand, John's purpose is more openly theological, rather than biographical.

In this Gospel we find a message that shows the result of some harsh experiences that the early Church had already encountered. Thus, for example, John seems to be refuting charges that Jesus' followers were victims of ignorant superstition. He is also zealous in his efforts to counter synagogue opposition to the Nazarene Christians; unlike the other Gospels, there are here frequent references to "the Jews." Another of the author's interests is in combating a form of religious thought called Gnosticism, which disparaged bodily life and denied the reality of the incarnation of Jesus Christ and his genuinely human nature. All of these characteristics argue for a date for this Gospel after the other three.

To the writer the main thing was that this Jesus lived, died, rose again from the dead, opening to man the possibility of new life. Who was the writer? From early Christian times it has been held that he was the apostle John, that he lived to a great age (till about A.D. 100), and that he produced his Gospel toward the end of the first century. Others attribute it to an "elder John." The Gospel itself gives evidence that, if the apostle was the original author, one of his disciples edited the material (see note at 12:44) or did for him what Mark reputedly did for Peter.

The Prologue

The first of the terms John uses as a symbol of Jesus is "Word" (then "light"). The concept of "Word" probably combines Jewish and Hellenistic elements (cf. Proverbs 8). By this John intended to express his belief that Jesus was always with God the Father, and has the same nature as God the Father but is distinct from the Father. According to John, it was a divine Person who became man in order to reveal God to us and to save us from our sins; obviously, it was the same God who had made the covenant with Abraham. The Old Testament describes the God who drew up the old covenant as "rich in kindness and fidelity" (Exodus 34:6; kind because he had chosen Israel, and faithful because he kept the promises he made). John uses the same expression in verse 14 (our translation has "full of grace and truth," but it could have been rendered "rich in kindness and fidelity").

John 1 : 1–18

1 In the beginning was the Word, and the Word was with God, and the Word was God. ²He was in the beginning with God; ³all things were made through him, and without him was not anything made that was made. ⁴In him was life, and the life was the light of men. ⁵The light shines in the darkness, and the darkness has not overcome it.

6 There was a man sent from God, whose name was John. ⁷He came for testimony, to bear witness to the light, that all might believe through him. ⁸He was not the light, but came to bear witness to the light.

9 The true light that enlightens every man was coming into the world. ¹⁰He was in the world, and the world was made through him, yet the world knew him not. ¹¹He came to his own home, and his own people received him not. ¹²But to all who received him, who believed in his name, he gave power to become children of God; ¹³who were born, not of blood nor of the will of the flesh nor of the will of man, but of God.

14 And the Word became flesh and dwelt among us, full of grace and truth; we have beheld his glory, glory as of the only Son from the Father. ¹⁵(John bore witness to him, and cried, "This was he of whom I said, 'He who comes after me ranks before me, for he was before me.'") ¹⁶And from his fulness have we all received, grace upon grace. ¹⁷For the law was given through Moses; grace and truth came through Jesus Christ. ¹⁸No one has ever seen God; the only Son, who is in the bosom of the Father, he has made him known.

1:1 The Greeks believed that the world was governed by a Higher Wisdom revealed to men in part through their minds and the use of reason. The Jews who lived among the Greeks suggested that this Higher Wisdom was "The Torah" (God's Law as revealed in Hebrew Scriptures). They also suggested that the Torah was pre-existent with God. John's formulation suggests that the Word was incarnate in Jesus. For the Christian, faith in Christ replaced the faith which the Jews placed in the Holy Law. Most of the Jews rejected the concept that the Messiah was a divine person or that he was pre-existent with God. Until the Second Vatican Council verses 1–14 were read at the end of every Mass every day in the Catholic Church and were thus known as the Last Gospel. The passage is the Gospel of the third Mass on Christmas Day.

John Gives Witness
John 1:19–34

19 And this is the testimony of John, when the Jews sent priests and Levites from Jerusalem to ask him, "Who are you?" [20] He confessed, he did not deny, but confessed, "I am not the Christ." [21] And they asked him, "What then? Are you Eli'jah?" He said, "I am not." "Are you the prophet?" And he answered, "No." [22] They said to him then, "Who are you? Let us have an answer for those who sent us. What do you say about yourself?" [23] He said, "I am the voice of one crying in the wilderness, 'Make straight the way of the Lord,' as the prophet Isaiah said."

24 Now they had been sent from the Pharisees. [25] They asked him, "Then why are you baptizing, if you are neither the Christ, nor Eli'jah, nor the prophet?" [26] John answered them, "I baptize with water; but among you stands one whom you do not know, [27] even he who comes after me, the thong of whose sandal I am not worthy to untie." [28] This took place in Bethany beyond the Jordan, where John was baptizing.

29 The next day he saw Jesus coming toward him, and said, "Behold, the Lamb of God, who takes away the sin of the world! [30] This is he of whom I said, 'After me comes a man who ranks before me, for he was before me.' [31] I myself did not know him; but for this I came baptizing with water, that he might be revealed to Israel." [32] And John bore witness, "I saw the Spirit descend as a dove from heaven, and it remained on him. [33] I myself did not know him; but he who sent me to baptize with water said to me, 'He on whom you see the Spirit descend and remain, this is he who baptizes with the Holy Spirit.' [34] And I have seen and have borne witness that this is the Son of God."

1:19 Each year, as the Catholic Church prepares liturgically for the coming of Jesus at Christmas, the testimony John gave is read on the Third Sunday of Advent. Many older translations (Tyndale, Great Bible, Geneva Bible, Bishops' Bible, King James Version) speak of the "record" of John; the Revised Version (ASV) reads, "witness"; the Rheims translation reads "testimonie." Whatever word is used, all biblical scholars agree it is the same thing. **1:29** The words of John the Baptist ("Behold, the Lamb of God, who takes away the sin of the world") are said by the Catholic priest when he faces the people with the bread in his hand before distribution of Holy Communion. In every Mass, shortly before he receives Communion himself, the priest calls three times upon the "Lamb of God, who takes away the sins of the world" and adds: "Have mercy on us." These three invocations are known to many as the *Agnus Dei* (Latin for "Lamb of God"), especially from hearing one of the Requiem Masses set to music (by Beethoven, Mozart, Fauré and many others). **1:33** The Society of Friends, which does not practice water baptism, believes that the one true baptism of Christ is a being baptized by the Holy Spirit. Their teaching is also founded upon Matthew 3:11; Acts 1:4–5; 11:16; Ephesians 1:14.

Nathanael Gives Witness

After an account of how Jesus gathered his disciples, there comes this episode.

John 1:47–51

47 Jesus saw Nathan'a-el coming to him, and said of him, "Behold, an Israelite indeed, in whom is no guile!" ⁴⁸ Nathan'a-el said to him, "How do you know me?" Jesus answered him, "Before Philip called you, when you were under the fig tree, I saw you." ⁴⁹ Nathan'a-el answered him, "Rabbi, you are the Son of God! You are the King of Israel!" ⁵⁰ Jesus answered him, "Because I said to you, I saw you under the fig tree, do you believe? You shall see greater things than these." ⁵¹ And he said to him, "Truly, truly, I say to you, you will see heaven opened, and the angels of God ascending and descending upon the Son of man."

1:47 The passage is the Gospel of the Votive Mass of the Holy Angels, and it is used by the Catholic Church in the Burial Mass for Little Children.

Wedding at Cana

John 2:1–11

2 On the third day there was a marriage at Cana in Galilee, and the mother of Jesus was there; ² Jesus also was invited to the marriage, with his disciples. ³ When the wine failed, the mother of Jesus said to

him, "They have no wine." ⁴And Jesus said to her, "O woman, what have you to do with me? My hour has not yet come." ⁵His mother said to the servants, "Do whatever he tells you." ⁶Now six stone jars were standing there, for the Jewish rites of purification, each holding twenty or thirty gallons. ⁷Jesus said to them, "Fill the jars with water." And they filled them up to the brim. ⁸He said to them, "Now draw some out, and take it to the steward of the feast." So they took it. ⁹When the steward of the feast tasted the water now become wine, and did not know where it came from (though the servants who had drawn the water knew), the steward of the feast called the bridegroom ¹⁰and said to him, "Every man serves the good wine first; and when men have drunk freely, then the poor wine; but you have kept the good wine until now." ¹¹This, the first of his signs, Jesus did at Cana in Galilee, and manifested his glory; and his disciples believed in him.

2:1 The miracle of Cana is the first of seven signs by which John shows forth the divinity of Jesus, and the Church uses the account for the same purpose on the Second Sunday after Epiphany. Roman Catholic and Orthodox Catholic writers have also appealed to the account to prove the power of Mary by virtue of her position as Mother of God. These writers, and many others who do not share this view of Mary, explain that Jesus was not rebuking his mother or being unkind to her in what he says at verse 4. They agree, generally, that the Greek word translated "woman" here (*gune*) was a respectful term (as if Jesus said, "My lady," whether solemnly or teasingly); but interpretations of the rest of the sentence vary considerably. The Greek says simply: "What to me and to you, woman?"

Nicodemus Comes to Jesus
John 3:1–21

3 Now there was a man of the Pharisees, named Nicode'mus, a ruler of the Jews. ²This man came to Jesus by night and said to him, "Rabbi, we know that you are a teacher come from God; for no one can do these signs that you do, unless God is with him." ³Jesus answered him, "Truly, truly, I say to you, unless one is born anew, he cannot see the kingdom of God." ⁴Nicode'mus said to him, "How can a man be born when he is old? Can he enter a second time into his mother's womb and be born?" ⁵Jesus answered, "Truly, truly, I say to you, unless one is born of water and the Spirit, he cannot enter the kingdom of God. ⁶That which is born of the flesh is flesh, and that which is born of the Spirit is spirit. ⁷Do not marvel that I said to you, 'You must be born anew.' ⁸The wind blows where it wills, and you hear the sound of it, but you do not know whence it comes or whither it goes; so it is with every one who is born of the Spirit." ⁹ Nicode'mus said to him, "How can this be?" ¹⁰ Jesus answered him, "Are you a teacher of Israel, and yet you do not understand this? ¹¹ Truly, truly, I say to you, we speak of what we know, and bear witness to what we have seen; but you do not receive our testimony. ¹² If I have told you earthly things and you do not believe, how can you believe if I tell you heavenly things? ¹³ No one has ascended into heaven but he who descended from heaven, the Son of man. ¹⁴ And as Moses lifted up the serpent in the wilderness, so must the Son of man be lifted up, ¹⁵ that whoever believes in him may have eternal life."

16 For God so loved the world that he gave his only Son, that whoever believes in him should not perish but have eternal life. ¹⁷ For God sent the Son into the world, not to condemn the world, but that the world might be saved through him. ¹⁸ He who believes in him is not condemned; he who does not believe is condemned already, because he has not believed in the name of the only Son of God. ¹⁹ And this is the judgment, that the light has come into the world, and men loved darkness rather than light, because their deeds were evil. ²⁰ For every one who does evil hates the light, and does not come to the light, lest his deeds should be exposed. ²¹ But he who does what is true comes to the light, that it may be clearly seen that his deeds have been wrought in God.

3:1 Nicodemus is a Pharisee. Impressed by the teachings of Jesus he also helps Joseph of Arimathea bury Jesus (19:39). Scholars point to Nicodemus, Joseph of Arimathea and Rabbi Gamaliel (Acts 5:33) as evidence that Jesus was not an enemy to all Pharisees. **3:3, 4** Rodolphus Dickinson, rector of St. Paul's parish, Pendleton, South Carolina, published in 1833 a translation of the New Testament which here read: "Except a man be reproduced, he cannot realize the reign of God. Nicodemus says to him, how can a man be produced when he is mature? Can he again pass into a state of embryo, and be produced?" **3:16** The use of this verse as a summary of the Christian religion has made it among the most quoted in the Bible. The Christian believes, as do Jews, that each person bears the image of God his Creator (see Genesis 1:27); Christians, in addition see in each person "a man for whom Christ died" (Romans 14:15)—a being of such infinite worth that God sent his Son to save him. Belief in the individual is reflected in the Declaration of Independence, and in the Bill of Rights which implements it.

Jesus Talks with the Samaritan Woman
John 4:1–42

4 Now when the Lord knew that the Pharisees had heard that Jesus was making and baptizing more disciples than John ² (although Jesus

himself did not baptize, but only his disciples), ³ he left Judea and departed again to Galilee. ⁴ He had to pass through Samar'ia. ⁵ So he came to a city of Samar'ia, called Sy'char, near the field that Jacob gave to his son Joseph. ⁶ Jacob's well was there, and so Jesus, wearied as he was with his journey, sat down beside the well. It was about the sixth hour.

7 There came a woman of Samar'ia to draw water. Jesus said to her, "Give me a drink." ⁸ For his disciples had gone away into the city to buy food. ⁹ The Samaritan woman said to him, "How is it that you, a Jew, ask a drink of me, a woman of Samar'ia?" For Jews have no dealings with Samaritans. ¹⁰ Jesus answered her, "If you knew the gift of God, and who it is that is saying to you, 'Give me a drink,' you would have asked him, and he would have given you living water." ¹¹ The woman said to him, "Sir, you have nothing to draw with, and the well is deep; where do you get that living water? ¹² Are you greater than our father Jacob, who gave us the well, and drank from it himself, and his sons, and his cattle?" ¹³ Jesus said to her, "Every one who drinks of this water will thirst again, ¹⁴ but whoever drinks of the water that I shall give him will never thirst; the water that I shall give him will become in him a spring of water welling up to eternal life." ¹⁵ The woman said to him, "Sir, give me this water, that I may not thirst, nor come here to draw."

16 Jesus said to her, "Go, call your husband, and come here." ¹⁷ The woman answered him, "I have no husband." Jesus said to her, "You are right in saying, 'I have no husband'; ¹⁸ for you have had five husbands, and he whom you now have is not your husband; this you said truly." ¹⁹ The woman said to him, "Sir, I perceive that you are a prophet. ²⁰ Our fathers worshiped on this mountain; and you say that in Jerusalem is the place where men ought to worship." ²¹ Jesus said to her, "Woman, believe me, the hour is coming when neither on this mountain nor in Jerusalem will you worship the Father. ²² You worship what you do not know; we worship what we know, for salvation is from the Jews. ²³ But the hour is coming, and now is, when the true worshipers will worship the Father in spirit and truth, for such the Father seeks to worship him. ²⁴ God is spirit, and those who worship him must worship in spirit and truth." ²⁵ The woman said to him, "I know that Messiah is coming (he who is called Christ); when he comes, he will show us all things." ²⁶ Jesus said to her, "I who speak to you am he."

27 Just then his disciples came. They marveled that he was talking with a woman, but none said, "What do you wish?" or, "Why are you talking with her?" ²⁸ So the woman left her water jar, and went away into the city, and said to the people, ²⁹ "Come, see a

man who told me all that I ever did. Can this be the Christ?" ³⁰ They went out of the city and were coming to him.

31 Meanwhile the disciples besought him, saying, "Rabbi, eat." ³² But he said to them, "I have food to eat of which you do not know." ³³ So the disciples said to one another, "Has any one brought him food?" ³⁴ Jesus said to them, "My food is to do the will of him who sent me, and to accomplish his work. ³⁵ Do you not say, 'There are yet four months, then comes the harvest'? I tell you, lift up your eyes, and see how the fields are already white for harvest. ³⁶ He who reaps receives wages, and gathers fruit for eternal life, so that sower and reaper may rejoice together. ³⁷ For here the saying holds true, 'One sows and another reaps.' ³⁸ I sent you to reap that for which you did not labor; others have labored, and you have entered into their labor."

39 Many Samaritans from that city believed in him because of the woman's testimony, "He told me all that I ever did." ⁴⁰ So when the Samaritans came to him, they asked him to stay with them; and he stayed there two days. ⁴¹ And many more believed because of his word. ⁴² They said to the woman, "It is no longer because of your words that we believe, for we have heard for ourselves, and we know that this is indeed the Savior of the world."

The Son Is Like the Father

In this passage, Jesus asserts an identity of will and action with the Father. He gives a glimpse into the life of the Trinity. In the first part Jesus says he gives life "to whom he will"; in the second part he speaks about future judgment and a life to be given on the last day. The passage is important in Christian theology, which combines the two parts and explains that the life of sanctifying grace we receive on earth is the beginning of the life to be possessed in heaven.

John 5:19–30

19 Jesus said to them, "Truly, truly, I say to you, the Son can do nothing of his own accord, but only what he sees the Father doing; for whatever he does, that the Son does likewise. ²⁰ For the Father loves the Son, and shows him all that he himself is doing; and greater works than these will he show him, that you may marvel. ²¹ For as the Father raises the dead and gives them life, so also the Son gives life to whom he will. ²² The Father judges no one, but has given all judgment to the Son, ²³ that all may honor the Son, even as they honor the Father. He who does not honor the Son does not honor the Father who sent him. ²⁴ Truly, truly, I say to you, he who hears my word and believes him who sent me has eternal life; he does not come into judgment, but has passed from death to life.

25 "Truly, truly, I say to you, the hour is coming, and now is, when the dead will hear the voice of the Son of God, and those who hear will live. [26] For as the Father has life in himself, so he has granted the Son also to have life in himself, [27] and has given him authority to execute judgment, because he is the Son of man. [28] Do not marvel at this; for the hour is coming when all who are in the tombs will hear his voice [29] and come forth, those who have done good, to the resurrection of life, and those who have done evil, to the resurrection of judgment.

30 "I can do nothing on my own authority; as I hear, I judge; and my judgment is just, because I seek not my own will but the will of him who sent me."

5:27 Verses 27–29 are the Gospel in the first Mass of All Souls Day (November 2), which is called officially in the liturgy the Commemoration of All the Faithful Departed. **5:29** John speaks of a "resurrection of life" and a "resurrection of judgment." Luke 14:14 speaks of a "resurrection of the just," and in Acts Paul expresses hope in a resurrection of "both the just and unjust." These views parallel the differing conceptions of resurrection to be found in rabbinic literature. According to some rabbis resurrection awaited only Israelites (*Genesis Rabbah* 13:4), according to R. Abbahu only the just (*Taanit* 7a). According to R. Jonathan the resurrection will be universal, but after judgment the wicked will die a second death and forever; whereas the just will be granted life everlasting (*Pirke R. Eleazar* 34).

"I Am the Bread of Life"

After recounting that Jesus fed five thousand people by multiplying barley loaves and fishes, and that he walked on the water during the night to reach his apostles, John gives us a great discourse in which Jesus says he is the "bread of life." Verse 59 locates this discourse in the synagogue at Capernaum. John does not give an account of the institution of the Holy Eucharist at the Last Supper; instead, he puts this teaching on the Bread of life into his Gospel.

John 6:28–70

28 Then they said to him, "What must we do, to be doing the works of God?" [29] Jesus answered them, "That is the work of God, that you believe in him whom he has sent." [30] So they said to him, "Then what sign do you do, that we may see, and believe you? What work do you perform? [31] Our fathers ate the manna in the wilderness; as it is written, 'He gave them bread from heaven to eat.' " [32] Jesus then said to them, "Truly, truly, I say to you, it was not Moses who gave you the bread from heaven; my Father gives you the true bread from

heaven. ³³ For the bread of God is that which comes down from heaven, and gives life to the world." ³⁴ They said to him, "Lord, give us this bread always."

35 Jesus said to them, "I am the bread of life; he who comes to me shall not hunger, and he who believes in me shall never thirst. ³⁶ But I said to you that you have seen me and yet do not believe. ³⁷ All that the Father gives me will come to me; and him who comes to me I will not cast out. ³⁸ For I have come down from heaven, not to do my own will, but the will of him who sent me; ³⁹ and this is the will of him who sent me, that I should lose nothing of all that he has given me, but raise it up at the last day. ⁴⁰ For this is the will of my Father, that every one who sees the Son and believes in him should have eternal life; and I will raise him up at the last day."

41 The Jews then murmured at him, because he said, "I am the bread which came down from heaven." ⁴² They said, "Is not this Jesus, the son of Joseph, whose father and mother we know? How does he now say, 'I have come down from heaven'?" ⁴³ Jesus answered them, "Do not murmur among yourselves. ⁴⁴ No one can come to me unless the Father who sent me draws him; and I will raise him up at the last day. ⁴⁵ It is written in the prophets, 'And they shall all be taught by God.' Every one who has heard and learned from the Father comes to me. ⁴⁶ Not that any one has seen the Father except him who is from God; he has seen the Father. ⁴⁷ Truly, truly, I say to you, he who believes has eternal life. ⁴⁸ I am the bread of life. ⁴⁹ Your fathers ate the manna in the wilderness, and they died. ⁵⁰ This is the bread which comes down from heaven, that a man may eat of it and not die. ⁵¹ I am the living bread which came down from heaven; if any one eats of this bread, he will live for ever; and the bread which I shall give for the life of the world is my flesh."

52 The Jews then disputed among themselves, saying, "How can this man give us his flesh to eat?" ⁵³ So Jesus said to them, "Truly, truly, I say to you, unless you eat the flesh of the Son of man and drink his blood, you have no life in you; ⁵⁴ he who eats my flesh and drinks my blood has eternal life, and I will raise him up at the last day. ⁵⁵ For my flesh is food indeed, and my blood is drink indeed. ⁵⁶ He who eats my flesh and drinks my blood abides in me, and I in him. ⁵⁷ As the living Father sent me, and I live because of the Father, so he who eats me will live because of me. ⁵⁸ This is the bread which came down from heaven, not such as the fathers ate and died; he who eats this bread will live for ever." ⁵⁹ This he said in the synagogue, as he taught at Caper'na-um.

60 Many of his disciples, when they heard it, said, "This is a hard saying; who can listen to it?" ⁶¹ But Jesus, knowing in himself that

his disciples murmured at it, said to them, "Do you take offense at this? ⁶²Then what if you were to see the Son of man ascending where he was before? ⁶³It is the spirit that gives life, the flesh is of no avail; the words that I have spoken to you are spirit and life. ⁶⁴But there are some of you that do not believe." For Jesus knew from the first who those were that did not believe, and who it was that should betray him. ⁶⁵And he said, "This is why I told you that no one can come to me unless it is granted him by the Father."

66 After this many of his disciples drew back and no longer went about with him. ⁶⁷Jesus said to the twelve, "Will you also go away?" ⁶⁸Simon Peter answered him, "Lord, to whom shall we go? You have the words of eternal life; ⁶⁹and we have believed, and have come to know, that you are the Holy One of God." ⁷⁰Jesus answered them, "Did I not choose you, the twelve, and one of you is a devil?" ⁷¹He spoke of Judas the son of Simon Iscariot, for he, one of the twelve, was to betray him.

6:27 Verses 37–40 are the Gospel for the Mass on the anniversary of death or burial; verses 51–55 are used in the daily Mass for the Dead. **6:56** The Catholic Church uses verses 56–59 as the Gospel for the Feast of Corpus Christi (Body of Christ), a day specially dedicated to the Blessed Sacrament (in some countries there are outdoor processions of the Blessed Sacrament on that day). The belief behind this devotion is that the Eucharist gives a share in that life which the Father shares with the Son.

Jesus Stays Away from a Test

John uses the term "Jew" over sixty times, usually to identify those he knew as opponents of Jesus. In 8:44 hostility to the Jews is most vigorously expressed, and it reaches a climax in 15:22–20. Jesus charges Jews present with being "children of the devil," leading some readers to call John's book the most anti-Jewish of all the New Testament accounts. Some of the heat of the first-century controversy in which the Hebrews and the Christians engaged is here reflected. The author is more concerned with "differences" from the Jews than with "continuities," that is, those aspects of Hebrew thought and life that are preserved, nourished and cherished within Christian faith. John's primary intent may have been thus to distinguish Christians from Jews. Bible scholars today are careful to note that John was really attacking those Jewish leaders and officials who placed themselves in direct opposition to the Church. He does not mean to condemn all Jews then living or those of this day.

John 7:1–9

7 After this Jesus went about in Galilee; he would not go about in Judea, because the Jews sought to kill him. ²Now the Jews' feast of

Tabernacles was at hand. ³ So his brothers said to him, "Leave here and go to Judea, that your disciples may see the works you are doing. ⁴ For no man works in secret if he seeks to be known openly. If you do these things, show yourself to the world." ⁵ For even his brothers did not believe in him. ⁶ Jesus said to them, "My time has not yet come, but your time is always here. ⁷ The world cannot hate you, but it hates me because I testify of it that its works are evil. ⁸ Go to the feast yourselves; I am not going up to this feast, for my time has not yet fully come." ⁹ So saying, he remained in Galilee.

"Let Him Come to Me and Drink"

It was on Succoth, the Feast of Tents (Booths or Tabernacles) that Jesus spoke the following words. As usual, the Evangelist provides an appropriate setting. During the week-long feast, the people lived in huts to recall their forefathers' years in the desert, and each day water was carried from the Pool of Siloe (Siloam) to the temple as a reminder of the water that came from the rock in the desert. Jesus may have pointed to the water carriers and then to himself as he spoke.

John 7:37–52

37 On the last day of the feast, the great day, Jesus stood up and proclaimed, "If any one thirst, let him come to me and drink. ³⁸ He who believes in me, as the scripture has said, 'Out of his heart shall flow rivers of living water.' " ³⁹ Now this he said about the Spirit, which those who believed in him were to receive; for as yet the Spirit had not been given, because Jesus was not yet glorified.

40 When they heard these words, some of the people said, "This is really the prophet." ⁴¹ Others said, "This is the Christ." But some said, "Is the Christ to come from Galilee? ⁴² Has not the scripture said that the Christ is descended from David, and comes from Bethlehem, the village where David was?" ⁴³ So there was a division among the people over him. ⁴ Some of them wanted to arrest him, but no one laid hands on him.

45 The officers then went back to the chief priests and Pharisees, who said to them, "Why did you not bring him?" ⁴⁶ The officers answered, "No man ever spoke like this man!" ⁴⁷ The Pharisees answered them, "Are you led astray, you also? ⁴⁸ Have any of the authorities or of the Pharisees believed in him? ⁴⁹ But this crowd, who do not know the law, are accursed." ⁵⁰ Nicode'mus, who had gone to him before, and who was one of them, said to them, ⁵¹ "Does our law judge a man without first giving him a hearing and learning what he does?" ⁵² They replied, "Are you from Galilee too? Search and you will see that no prophet is to rise from Galilee."

7:38 Tyndale to King James Version: "he that believeth on me," but Geneva Bible, Rheims: "in" me.

"Let Him without Sin Throw a Stone"

This episode is not found in the earliest Greek manuscripts. Scholars generally hold that the incident is an authentic one from the life of Jesus but that it did not originally belong to this Gospel. Some think the Greek style shows it belongs in Luke's Gospel (perhaps after Luke 21:38); others hold it may be one of John's stories put in here by another hand than the one that gave us the rest of the Gospel.

John 8:2–11

2 Early in the morning he came again to the temple; all the people came to him, and he sat down and taught them. ³The scribes and the Pharisees brought a woman who had been caught in adultery, and placing her in the midst ⁴they said to him, "Teacher, this woman has been caught in the act of adultery. ⁵Now in the law Moses commanded us to stone such. What do you say about her?" ⁶This they said to test him, that they might have some charge to bring against him. Jesus bent down and wrote with his finger on the ground. ⁷And as they continued to ask him, he stood up and said to them, "Let him who is without sin among you be the first to throw a stone at her." ⁸And once more he bent down and wrote with his finger on the ground. ⁹But when they heard it, they went away, one by one, beginning with the eldest, and Jesus was left alone with the woman standing before him. ¹⁰Jesus looked up and said to her, "Woman, where are they? Has no one condemned you?" ¹¹She said, "No one, Lord." And Jesus said, "Neither do I condemn you; go, and do not sin again."

"I Am the Light of the World"

John 8:12–18

12 Again Jesus spoke to them, saying, "I am the light of the world; he who follows me will not walk in darkness, but will have the light of life." ¹³The Pharisees then said to him, "You are bearing witness to yourself; your testimony is not true." ¹⁴Jesus answered, "Even if I do bear witness to myself, my testimony is true, for I know whence I have come and whither I am going, but you do not know whence I come or whither I am going. ¹⁵You judge according to the flesh, I judge no one. ¹⁶Yet even if I do judge, my judgment is true, for it is not I alone that judge, but I and he who sent me. ¹⁷In your law it is written that the testimony of two men is true; ¹⁸I bear witness to myself, and the Father who sent me bears witness to me."

8:12 We are told at verse 20 that Jesus spoke these words while he was teaching in the Temple, where he might have pointed to the great lamps as he spoke. In this passage Jesus bears testimony to himself, as with God. Such an identification of man with God would, in the rabbinic tradition, offend.

Jesus Opens the Eyes of the Blind

This ninth chapter of John's Gospel has often been regarded as a model short story. In the course of the story, we learn that Jesus refuses to attribute suffering and illness to sin. Most of his audience no doubt held the traditional belief that suffering and illness were always punishment for some transgressions. Jesus asserts that physical blindness is not caused by sin, but that spiritual blindness is.

John 9:1–41

9 As he passed by, he saw a man blind from his birth. ²And his disciples asked him, "Rabbi, who sinned, this man or his parents, that he was born blind?" ³Jesus answered, "It was not that this man sinned, or his parents, but that the works of God might be made manifest in him. ⁴We must work the works of him who sent me, while it is day; night comes, when no one can work. ⁵As long as I am in the world, I am the light of the world." ⁶As he said this, he spat on the ground and made clay of the spittle and anointed the man's eyes with the clay, ⁷saying to him, "Go, wash in the pool of Silo'am" (which means Sent). So he went and washed and came back seeing. ⁸The neighbors and those who had seen him before as a beggar, said, "Is not this the man who used to sit and beg?" ⁹Some said, "It is he"; others said, "No, but he is like him." He said, "I am the man." ¹⁰They said to him, "Then how were your eyes opened?" ¹¹He answered, "The man called Jesus made clay and anointed my eyes and said to me, 'Go to Silo'am and wash'; so I went and washed and received my sight." ¹²They said to him, "Where is he?" He said, "I do not know."

13 They brought to the Pharisees the man who had formerly been blind. ¹⁴Now it was a sabbath day when Jesus made the clay and opened his eyes. ¹⁵The Pharisees again asked him how he had received his sight. And he said to them, "He put clay on my eyes, and I washed, and I see." ¹⁶Some of the Pharisees said, "This man is not from God, for he does not keep the sabbath." But others said, "How can a man who is a sinner do such signs?" There was a division among them. ¹⁷So they again said to the blind man, "What do you say about him, since he has opened your eyes?" He said, "He is a prophet."

18 The Jews did not believe that he had been blind and had

received his sight, until they called the parents of the man who had received his sight, [19] and asked them, "Is this your son, who you say was born blind? How then does he now see?" [20] His parents answered, "We know that this is our son, and that he was born blind; [21] but how he now sees we do not know, nor do we know who opened his eyes. Ask him; he is of age, he will speak for himself." [22] His parents said this because they feared the Jews, for the Jews had already agreed that if any one should confess him to be Christ, he was to be put out of the synagogue. [23] Therefore his parents said, "He is of age, ask him."

24 So for the second time they called the man who had been blind, and said to him, "Give God the praise; we know that this man is a sinner." [25] He answered, "Whether he is a sinner, I do not know; one thing I know, that though I was blind, now I see." [26] They said to him, "What did he do to you? How did he open your eyes?" [27] He answered them, "I have told you already, and you would not listen. Why do you want to hear it again? Do you too want to become his disciples?" [28] And they reviled him, saying, "You are his disciple, but we are disciples of Moses. [29] We know that God has spoken to Moses, but as for this man, we do not know where he comes from." [30] The man answered, "Why, this is a marvel! You do not know where he comes from, and yet he opened my eyes. [31] We know that God does not listen to sinners, but if any one is a worshiper of God and does his will, God listens to him. [32] Never since the world began has it been heard that any one opened the eyes of a man born blind. [33] If this man were not from God, he could do nothing." [34] They answered him, "You were born in utter sin, and would you teach us?" And they cast him out.

35 Jesus heard that they had cast him out, and having found him he said, "Do you believe in the Son of man?" [36] He answered, "And who is he, sir, that I may believe in him?" [37] Jesus said to him, "You have seen him, and it is he who speaks to you." [38] He said, "Lord, I believe"; and he worshiped him. [39] Jesus said, "For judgment I came into this world, that those who do not see may see, and that those who see may become blind." [40] Some of the Pharisees near him heard this, and they said to him, "Are we also blind?" [41] Jesus said to them, "If you were blind, you would have no guilt; but now that you say, 'We see,' your guilt remains."

"I Am the Good Shepherd"
John 10:11–18

11 "I am the good shepherd. The good shepherd lays down his life for the sheep. [12] He who is a hireling and not a shepherd, whose own

the sheep are not, sees the wolf coming and leaves the sheep and flees; and the wolf snatches them and scatters them. [13] He flees because he is a hireling and cares nothing for the sheep. [14] I am the good shepherd; I know my own and my own know me, [15] as the Father knows me and I know the Father; and I lay down my life for the sheep. [16] And I have other sheep, that are not of this fold; I must bring them also, and they will heed my voice. So there shall be one flock, one shepherd. [17] For this reason the father loves me, because I lay down my life, that I may take it again. [18] No one takes it from me, but I lay it down of my own accord. I have power to lay it down, and I have power to take it again; this charge I have received from my Father."

10:11 The people were familiar with the idea of God being likened to a shepherd; it occurs frequently in Hebrew Scripture. Jesus emphasizes the idea of the shepherd laying down his life for his sheep. (Cf. 1 Samuel 17:33 ff. where David invokes the image of a brave shepherd who will risk his life to save his flock.) The passage is used as the Gospel for the Second Sunday after Easter, which is often called Good Shepherd Sunday. In early Christian centuries no representations of the crucifixion of Jesus are found in catacombs and cemeteries; the figure of the Good Shepherd carrying a sheep on his shoulders was preferred. The symbol was similar to the pagan figures of Hermes Kriophorus or Aristaeus (very much in vogue at that time). The Good Shepherd figure has endured as a symbol in art, liturgy and literature.

"I and the Father Are One"
John 10:22–38

Jesus here asserts identity between himself and the Father; some of his audience heard were offended, for Judaism taught that no man is identical with God.

22 It was the feast of the Dedication at Jerusalem; [23] it was winter, and Jesus was walking in the temple, in the portico of Solomon. [24] So the Jews gathered round him and said to him, "How long will you keep us in suspense? If you are the Christ, tell us plainly." [25] Jesus answered them, "I told you, and you do not believe. The works that I do in my Father's name, they bear witness to me; [26] but you do not believe, because you do not belong to my sheep. [27] My sheep hear my voice, and I know them, and they follow me; [28] and I give them eternal life, and they shall never perish, and no one shall snatch them out of my hand. [29] My Father, who has given them to me, is greater than all, and no one is able to snatch them out of the Father's hand. [30] I and the Father are one."

31 The Jews took up stones again to stone him. [32] Jesus answered them, "I have shown you many good works from the Father; for which of these do you stone me?" [33] The Jews answered him, "We stone you for no good work but for blasphemy; because you, being a man, make yourself God." [34] Jesus answered them, "Is it not written in your law, 'I said, you are gods'? [35] If he called them gods to whom the word of God came (and scripture cannot be broken), [36] do you say of him whom the Father consecrated and sent into the world, 'You are blaspheming,' because I said, 'I am the Son of God'? [37] If I am not doing the works of my Father, then do not believe me; [38] but if I do them, even though you do not believe me, believe the works, that you may know and understand that the Father is in me and I am in the Father."

10:22 The Feast of Dedication is Hanukkah, which comes late in December. See notes on 1 Maccabees and 2 Maccabees.

Jesus Raises Lazarus from the Dead

Word came to Jesus while he was on a trip beyond the Jordan that Lazarus, brother of Mary and Martha, was sick. Thomas (verse 16) foresees trouble if Jesus goes back to that part of Judea and raises a man from the dead.

John 11:17–53

17 Now when Jesus came, he found that Laz'arus had already been in the tomb four days. [18] Bethany was near Jerusalem, about two miles off, [19] and many of the Jews had come to Martha and Mary to console them concerning their brother. [20] When Martha heard that Jesus was coming, she went and met him, while Mary sat in the house. [21] Martha said to Jesus, "Lord, if you had been here, my brother would not have died. [22] And even now I know that whatever you ask from God, God will give you." [23] Jesus said to her, "Your brother will rise again." [24] Martha said to him, "I know that he will rise again in the resurrection at the last day." [25] Jesus said to her, "I am the resurrection and the life; he who believes in me, though he die, yet shall he live, [26] and whoever lives and believes in me shall never die. Do you believe this?" [27] She said to him, "Yes, Lord; I believe that you are the Christ, the Son of God, he who is coming into the world."

28 When she had said this, she went and called her sister Mary, saying quietly, "The Teacher is here and is calling for you." [29] And when she heard it, she rose quickly and went to him. [30] Now Jesus had not yet come to the village, but was still in the place where Martha had met him. [31] When the Jews who were with her in the

house, consoling her, saw Mary rise quickly and go out, they followed her, supposing that she was going to the tomb to weep there. [32] Then Mary, when she came where Jesus was and saw him, fell at his feet, saying to him, "Lord, if you had been here, my brother would not have died." [33] When Jesus saw her weeping, and the Jews who came with her also weeping, he was deeply moved in spirit and troubled; [34] and he said, "Where have you laid him?" They said to him, "Lord, come and see." [35] Jesus wept. [36] So the Jews said, "See how he loved him!" [37] But some of them said, "Could not he who opened the eyes of the blind man have kept this man from dying?"

38 Then Jesus, deeply moved again, came to the tomb; it was a cave, and a stone lay upon it. [39] Jesus said, "Take away the stone." Martha, the sister of the dead man, said to him, "Lord, by this time there will be an odor, for he has been dead four days." [40] Jesus said to her, "Did I not tell you that if you would believe you would see the glory of God?" [41] So they took away the stone. And Jesus lifted up his eyes and said, "Father, I thank thee that thou hast heard me. [42] I knew that thou hearest me always, but I have said this on account of the people standing by, that they may believe that thou didst send me." [43] When he had said this, he cried with a loud voice, "Laz'arus, come out." [44] The dead man came out, his hands and feet bound with bandages, and his face wrapped with a cloth. Jesus said to them, "Unbind him, and let him go."

45 Many of the Jews therefore, who had come with Mary and had seen what he did, believed in him; [46] but some of them went to the Pharisees and told them what Jesus had done. [47] So the chief priests and the Pharisees gathered the council, and said, "What are we to do? For this man performs many signs. [48] If we let him go on thus, every one will believe in him, and the Romans will come and destroy both our holy place and our nation." [49] But one of them, Ca'iaphas, who was high priest that year, said to them, "You know nothing at all; [50] you do not understand that it is expedient for you that one man should die for the people, and that the whole nation should not perish." [51] He did not say this of his own accord, but being high priest that year he prophesied that Jesus should die for the nation, [52] and not for the nation only, but to gather into one the children of God who are scattered abroad. [53] So from that day on they took counsel how to put him to death.

11:21 Verses 21–27 are the Gospel for the Mass on the day of burial or death.

Jesus Is Anointed at Bethany
John 12:1–8

12 Six days before the Passover, Jesus came to Bethany, where Laz'arus was, whom Jesus had raised from the dead. ²There they made him a supper; Martha served, and Laz'arus was one of those at table with him. ³Mary took a pound of costly ointment of pure nard and anointed the feet of Jesus and wiped his feet with her hair; and the house was filled with the fragrance of the ointment. ⁴But Judas Iscariot, one of his disciples (he who was to betray him), said, ⁵"Why was this ointment not sold for three hundred denarii and given to the poor?" ⁶This he said, not that he cared for the poor but because he was a thief, and as he had the money box he used to take what was put into it. ⁷Jesus said, "Let her alone, let her keep it for the day of my burial. ⁸The poor you always have with you, but you do not always have me."

> **12:1** Luke's Gospel (7:36–50) described a scene like this in Galilee, but that was an earlier event. The identification of Mary of Bethany with the sinful woman of Luke's episode (or with Mary Magdalene) is speculative.

"Believe in the Light"

> After describing Jesus' triumphal entry into Jerusalem, John gives us this account.

John 12:20–50

20 Now among those who went up to worship at the feast were some Greeks. ²¹So these came to Philip, who was from Beth-sa'ida in Galilee, and said to him, "Sir, we wish to see Jesus." ²²Philip went and told Andrew; Andrew went with Philip and they told Jesus. ²³And Jesus answered them, "The hour has come for the Son of man to be glorified. ²⁴Truly, truly, I say to you, unless a grain of wheat falls into the earth and dies, it remains alone; but if it dies, it bears much fruit. ²⁵He who loves his life loses it, and he who hates his life in this world will keep it for eternal life. ²⁶If any one serves me, he must follow me; and where I am, there shall my servant be also; if any one serves me, the Father will honor him.

27 "Now is my soul troubled. And what shall I say? 'Father, save me from this hour'? No, for this purpose I have come to this hour. ²⁸Father, glorify thy name." Then a voice came from heaven, "I have glorified it, and I will glorify it again." ²⁹The crowd standing by heard it and said that it had thundered. Others said, "An angel has spoken to him." ³⁰Jesus answered, "This voice has come for your sake, not for mine. ³¹Now is the judgment of this world, now shall the ruler of this world be cast out; [32] and I, when I am lifted up from the earth, will draw all men to myself." [33] He said this to show by what death he was to die. [34] The crowd answered him, "We have heard from the law that the Christ remains for ever. How can you say that the Son of man must be lifted up? Who is this Son of man?" [35] Jesus said to them, "The light is with you for a little longer. Walk while you have the light, lest the darkness overtake you; he who walks in the darkness does not know where he goes. [36] While you have the light, believe in the light, that you may become sons of light."

When Jesus had said this, he departed and hid himself from them. [37] Though he had done so many signs before them, yet they did not believe in him; [38] it was that the word spoken by the prophet Isaiah might be fulfilled:

"Lord, who has believed our report,
    and to whom has the arm of the Lord been revealed?"

[39] Therefore they could not believe. For Isaiah again said,

[40] "He has blinded their eyes and hardened their heart,
    lest they should see with their eyes and perceive with their
        heart,
    and turn for me to heal them."

[41] Isaiah said this because he saw his glory and spoke of him. [42] Nevertheless many even of the authorities believed in him, but for fear of the Pharisees they did not confess it, lest they should be put out of the synagogue: [43] for they loved the praise of men more than the praise of God.

44 And Jesus cried out and said, "He who believes in me, believes not in me but in him who sent me. [45] And he who sees me sees him who sent me. [46] I have come as light into the world, that whoever believes in me may not remain in darkness. [47] If any one hears my sayings and does not keep them, I do not judge him; for I did not come to judge the world but to save the world. [48] He who rejects me and does not receive my sayings has a judge; the word that I have spoken will be his judge on the last day. [49] For I have not spoken on my own authority; the Father who sent me has himself given me commandment what to say and what to speak. [50] And I know that his commandment is eternal life. What I say, therefore, I say as the Father has bidden me."

12:24 Martin Luther wrote: "If thou couldst understand a single grain of wheat, thou wouldst die for wonder." He believed that man "should see in the smallest and meanest flower God's omnipotent wisdom and goodness . . . every green tree is lovelier than gold and silver." **12:34** The disciple describes here a difficulty many Jews had in accepting a Messiah who would die. In the Hebrew messianic concept, the Christ glorious in victory would restore the Davidic kingdom, rule according to the Holy Law and reward all the faithful with abundance. That the Messiah was to be crucified was a scandal to such Jews and a stumbling block to their belief. **12:37** Verses 37–43 are reflections by the author of the Gospel. The origin of verse 38 is Isaiah 53:1; of verse 40, Isaiah 6:10. **12:44** Verses 44–50 were not spoken here by Jesus; from verse 36, we know he was in hiding at this time; the editor of the Gospel seems to have put this section in here out of its original order as a review of Jesus' teaching.

The Last Supper
Jesus Washes the Disciples' Feet
John 13:1–17

13 Now before the feast of the Passover, when Jesus knew that his hour had come to depart out of this world to the Father, having loved his own who were in the world, he loved them to the end. ²And during supper, when the devil had already put it into the heart of Judas Iscariot, Simon's son, to betray him, ³Jesus, knowing that the Father had given all things into his hands, and that he had come from God and was going to God, ⁴rose from supper, laid aside his garments, and girded himself with a towel. ⁵Then he poured water into a basin, and began to wash the disciples' feet, and to wipe them with the towel with which he was girded. ⁶He came to Simon Peter; and Peter said to him, "Lord, do you wash my feet?" ⁷Jesus answered him, "What I am doing you do not know now, but afterward you will understand." ⁸Peter said to him, "You shall never wash my feet." Jesus answered him, "If I do not wash you, you have no part in me." ⁹Simon Peter said to him, "Lord, not my feet only but also my hands and my head!" ¹⁰Jesus said to him, "He who has bathed does not need to wash, except for his feet, but he is clean all over; and you are clean, but not all of you." ¹¹For he knew who was to betray him; that was why he said, "You are not all clean."

12 When he had washed their feet, and taken his garments, and resumed his place, he said to them, "Do you know what I have done to you? ¹³You call me Teacher and Lord; and you are right, for so I am. ¹⁴If I then, your Lord and Teacher, have washed your feet, you also ought to wash one another's feet. ¹⁵For I have given you an example, that you also should do as I have done to you. ¹⁶Truly, truly, I say to you, a servant is not greater than his master; nor is he who is sent greater than he who sent him. ¹⁷If you know these things, blessed are you if you do them."

13:1 Verses 1–15 are the Gospel of the Mass for Holy Thursday, called in the liturgical calendar "Thursday of the Lord's Supper." For centuries people have also called it Maundy Thursday, from the word *mandatum* (commandment) in Latin translations of verse 34 (in following passage). The term *mandatum* (or maundy) was applied to the rite of washing the feet on this day, an ancient rite still practiced by the Pope and bishops (these verses are sung during the rite) and other Christians. **13:15** Martin Luther (1483–1546) believed that each Christian is called to be a Christ to other men. "I will give myself," he said, "as a sort of Christ to my neighbor as Christ gave himself to me."

"A New Commandment I Give to You"

After an account about Judas at the Last Supper (cf. Matthew 26:20–25), John gives us these lines.

John 13:31–35

31 When he had gone out, Jesus said, "Now is the Son of man glorified, and in him God is glorified; ³² if God is glorified in him, God will also glorify him in himself, and glorify him at once. ³³ Little children, yet a little while I am with you. You will seek me; and as I said to the Jews so now I say to you, 'Where I am going you cannot come.' ³⁴ A new commandment I give to you, that you love one another; even as I have loved you, that you also love one another. ³⁵ By this all men will know that you are my disciples, if you have love for one another."

13:34 See note on 13:1.

Father, Son and Holy Spirit

Chapters 14–17 are often called the Last Discourse or the Farewell Discourse. Like Matthew in the five discourses of the first Gospel, John has gathered things Jesus said on various occasions to make a sermon. At verse 31, Jesus says: "Rise, let us go hence"; what follows in the next three chapters was inserted from earlier occasions (unless one holds that Jesus spoke it all on the way to Gethsemane). The message appears to be addressed to persons who had made the choice to follow Jesus rather than to the public at large.

John 14:1–31

14 "Let not your hearts be troubled; believe in God, believe also in me. ² In my Father's house are many rooms; if it were not so, would I have told you that I go to prepare a place for you? ³ And when I go and prepare a place for you, I will come again and will take you to myself, that where I am you may be also. ⁴ And you know the way where I am going." ⁵ Thomas said to him, "Lord, we do not know

where you are going; how can we know the way?" ⁶ Jesus said to him, "I am the way, and the truth, and the life; no one comes to the Father, but by me. ⁷ If you had known me, you would have known my Father also; henceforth you know him and have seen him."

8 Philip said to him, "Lord, show us the Father, and we shall be satisfied." ⁹ Jesus said to him, "Have I been with you so long, and yet you do not know me, Philip? He who has seen me has seen the Father; how can you say, 'Show us the Father'? ¹⁰ Do you not believe that I am in the Father and the Father in me? The words that I say to you I do not speak on my own authority; but the Father who dwells in me does his works. ¹¹ Believe me that I am in the Father and the Father in me; or else believe me for the sake of the works themselves.

12 "Truly, truly, I say to you, he who believes in me will also do the works that I do; and greater works than these will he do, because I go to the Father. ¹³ Whatever you ask in my name, I will do it, that the Father may be glorified in the Son; ¹⁴ if you ask anything in my name, I will do it.

15 "If you love me, you will keep my commandments. ¹⁶ And I will pray the Father, and he will give you another Counselor, to be with you for ever, ¹⁷ even the Spirit of truth, whom the world cannot receive, because it neither sees him nor knows him; you know him, for he dwells with you, and will be in you.

18 "I will not leave you desolate; I will come to you. ¹⁹ Yet a little while, and the world will see me no more, but you will see me; because I live, you will live also. ²⁰ In that day you will know that I am in my Father, and you in me, and I in you. ²¹ He who has my commandments and keeps them, he it is who loves me; and he who loves me will be loved by my Father, and I will love him and manifest myself to him." ²² Judas (not Iscariot) said to him, "Lord, how is it that you will manifest yourself to us, and not to the world?" ²³ Jesus answered him, "If a man loves me, he will keep my word, and my Father will love him, and we will come to him and make our home with him. ²⁴ He who does not love me does not keep my words; and the word which you hear is not mine but the Father's who sent me.

25 "These things I have spoken to you, while I am still with you. ²⁶ But the Counselor, the Holy Spirit, whom the Father will send in my name, he will teach you all things, and bring to your remembrance all that I have said to you. ²⁷ Peace I leave with you; my peace I give to you; not as the world gives do I give to you. Let not your hearts be troubled, neither let them be afraid. ²⁸ You heard me say to you, 'I go away, and I will come to you.' If you loved me, you

would have rejoiced, because I go to the Father; for the Father is greater than I. ²⁹ And now I have told you before it takes place, so that when it does take place, you may believe. ³⁰ I will no longer talk much with you, for the ruler of this world is coming. He has no power over me; ³¹ but I do as the Father has commanded me, so that the world may know that I love the Father. Rise, let us go hence.''

14:1 Verses 1–3 are the Gospel for the Feast of St. Philip and James (May 11, formerly May 1). **14:2** Older translations have "mansions" (from a Latin word meaning "rooms"). **14:15** Verses 15–21 are the Gospel for the Vigil of Pentecost and the Votive Mass for the Election of a Pope. **14:16** From Tyndale to King James Version, RV and ASV: "comforter." Rheims: "paraclete." The same word is translated in all these versions of John 2:1 as "advocate." **14:23** Verses 23–31 are the Gospel for the Feast of Pentecost and for the Votive Mass of the Holy Spirit.

"I Am the Vine"
John 15:1–27

15 "I am the true vine, and my Father is the vinedresser. ² Every branch of mine that bears no fruit, he takes away, and every branch that does bear fruit he prunes, that it may bear more fruit. ³ You are already made clean by the word which I have spoken to you. ⁴ Abide in me, and I in you. As the branch cannot bear fruit by itself, unless it abides in the vine, neither can you, unless you abide in me. ⁵ I am the vine, you are the branches. He who abides in me, and I in him, he it is that bears much fruit, for apart from me you can do nothing. ⁶ If a man does not abide in me, he is cast forth as a branch and withers; and the branches are gathered, thrown into the fire and burned. ⁷ If you abide in me, and my words abide in you, ask whatever you will, and it shall be done for you. ⁸ By this my Father is glorified, that you bear much fruit, and so prove to be my disciples. ⁹ As the Father has loved me, so have I loved you; abide in my love. ¹⁰ If you keep my commandments, you will abide in my love, just as I have kept my Father's commandments and abide in his love. ¹¹ These things I have spoken to you, that my joy may be in you, and that your joy may be full.

12 "This is my commandment, that you love one another as I have loved you. ¹³ Greater love has no man than this, that a man lay down his life for his friends. ¹⁴ You are my friends if you do what I command you. ¹⁵ No longer do I call you servants, for the servant does not know what his master is doing; but I have called you friends, for all that I have heard from my Father I have made known to you. ¹⁶ You did not choose me, but I chose you and appointed you

that you should go and bear fruit and that your fruit should abide; so that whatever you ask the Father in my name, he may give it to you. ¹⁷ This I command you, to love one another.

18 "If the world hates you, know that it has hated me before it hated you. ¹⁹ If you were of the world, the world would love its own; but because you are not of the world, but I chose you out of the world, therefore the world hates you. ²⁰ Remember the word that I said to you, 'A servant is not greater than his master.' If they persecuted me, they will persecute you; if they kept my word, they will keep yours also. ²¹ But all this they will do to you on my account, because they do not know him who sent me. ²² If I had not come and spoken to them, they would not have sin; but now they have no excuse for their sin. ²³ He who hates me hates my Father also. ²⁴ If I had not done among them the works which no one else did, they would not have sin; but now they have seen and hated both me and my Father. ²⁵ It is to fulfil the word that is written in their law, 'They hated me without a cause.' ²⁶ But when the Counselor comes, whom I shall send to you from the Father, even the Spirit of truth, who proceeds from the Father, he will bear witness to me; ²⁷ and you also are witnesses, because you have been with me from the beginning."

15:1 Verses 1–7 are the Gospel for the Mass of a martyr during Paschaltide, e.g., St. George, patron of England (April 23), and 5–11 for the Mass of several martyrs during the same season. Verses 1–8 form the Scripture lesson provided in the Methodist Covenant Service. **15:12** Verses 12–16 are in the Mass for the Vigil of an Apostle; 15–21 are in the Mass for the Election of a Pope. **17–25** are used for the Feast of Sts. Simon and Jude (October 28).

"The Spirit of Truth Will Guide You"

Jesus predicts that the apostles will suffer persecution, but he outlines the role of the Holy Spirit (Comforter, Paraclete, Advocate). Much teaching about the Trinity is based on this passage.

John 16:1–33

16 "I have said all this to you to keep you from falling away. ² They will put you out of the synagogues; indeed, the hour is coming when whoever kills you will think he is offering service to God. ³ And they will do this because they have not known the Father, nor me. ⁴ But I have said these things to you, that when their hour comes you may remember that I told you of them.

"I did not say these things to you from the beginning, because I was with you. ⁵ But now I am going to him who sent me; yet none of you asks me, 'Where are you going?' ⁶ But because I have said these things to you, sorrow has filled your hearts. ⁷ Nevertheless I tell you the truth: it is to your advantage that I go away, for if I do not go away, the Counselor will not come to you; but if I go, I will send him to you. ⁸ And when he comes, he will convince the world of sin and of righteousness and of judgment: ⁹ of sin, because they do not believe in me; ¹⁰ of righteousness, because I go to the Father, and you will see me no more; ¹¹ of judgment, because the ruler of this world is judged.

12 "I have yet many things to say to you, but you cannot bear them now. ¹³ When the Spirit of truth comes, he will guide you into all the truth; for he will not speak on his own authority, but whatever he hears he will speak, and he will declare to you the things that are to come. ¹⁴ He will glorify me, for he will take what is mine and declare it to you. ¹⁵ All that the Father has is mine; therefore I said that he will take what is mine and declare it to you.

16 "A little while, and you will see me no more; again a little while, and you will see me." ¹⁷ Some of his disciples said to one another, "What is this that he says to us, 'A little while, and you will not see me, and again a little while, and you will see me'; and, 'because I go to the Father'?" ¹⁸ They said, "What does he mean by 'a little while'? We do not know what he means." ¹⁹ Jesus knew that they wanted to ask him; so he said to them, "Is this what you are asking yourselves, what I meant by saying, 'A little while, and you will not see me, and again a little while, and you will see me'? ²⁰ Truly, truly, I say to you, you will weep and lament, but the world will rejoice; you will be sorrowful, but your sorrow will turn into joy. ²¹ When a woman is in travail she has sorrow, because her hour has come; but when she is delivered of the child, she no longer remembers the anguish, for joy that a child is born into the world. ²² So you have sorrow now, but I will see you again and your hearts will rejoice, and no one will take your joy from you. ²³ In that day you will ask nothing of me. Truly, truly, I say to you, if you ask anything of the Father, he will give it to you in my name. ²⁴ Hitherto you have asked nothing in my name; ask, and you will receive, that your joy may be full.

25 "I have said this to you in figures; the hour is coming when I shall no longer speak to you in figures but tell you plainly of the Father. ²⁶ In that day you will ask in my name; and I do not say to you that I shall pray the Father for you; ²⁷ for the Father himself loves you, because you have loved me and have believed that I came from the Father. ²⁸ I came from the Father and have come into the world; again, I am leaving the world and going to the Father."

29 His disciples said, "Ah, now you are speaking plainly, not in any figure! ³⁰ Now we know that you know all things, and need

none to question you; by this we believe that you came from God." [31] Jesus answered them, "Do you now believe? [32] The hour is coming, indeed it has come, when you will be scattered, every man to his home, and will leave me alone; yet I am not alone, for the Father is with me. [33] I have said this to you, that in me you may have peace. In the world you have tribulation; but be of good cheer, I have overcome the world."

> **16:8** Tyndale: rebuke the world of synne. Geneva Bible: reprove the world of sin. RV (ASV): convict the world in respect of sin.
> **16:33** Rheims: have confidence, I have overcome the world.

Jesus Prays for the Unity of His Followers
John 17:1–26

17 When Jesus had spoken these words, he lifted up his eyes to heaven and said, "Father, the hour has come; glorify thy Son that the Son may glorify thee, [2] since thou hast given him power over all flesh, to give eternal life to all whom thou hast given him. [3] And this is eternal life, that they know thee the only true God, and Jesus Christ whom thou hast sent. [4] I glorified thee on earth, having accomplished the work which thou gavest me to do; [5] and now, Father, glorify thou me in thy own presence with the glory which I had with thee before the world was made.

6 "I have manifested thy name to the men whom thou gavest me out of the world; thine they were, and thou gavest them to me, and they have kept thy word. [7] Now they know that everything that thou hast given me is from thee; [8] for I have given them the words which thou gavest me, and they have received them and know in truth that I came from thee; and they have believed that thou didst send me. [9] I am praying for them; I am not praying for the world but for those whom thou hast given me, for they are thine; [10] all mine are thine, and thine are mine, and I am glorified in them. [11] And now I am no more in the world, but they are in the world, and I am coming to thee. Holy Father, keep them in thy name, which thou hast given me, that they may be one, even as we are one. [12] While I was with them, I kept them in thy name, which thou hast given me; I have guarded them, and none of them is lost but the son of perdition, that the scripture might be fulfilled. [13] But now I am coming to thee; and these things I speak in the world, that they may have my joy fulfilled in themselves. [14] I have given them thy word; and the world has hated them because they are not of the world, even as I am not of the world. [15] I do not pray that thou shouldst take them out of the world, but that thou shouldst keep them from the evil one. [16] They are not of the world, even as I

am not of the world. ¹⁷Sanctify them in the truth; thy word is truth. ¹⁸As thou didst send me into the world, so I have sent them into the world. ¹⁹And for their sake I consecrate myself, that they also may be consecrated in truth.

20 "I do not pray for these only, but also for those who believe in me through their word, ²¹that they may all be one; even as thou, Father, art in me, and I in thee, that they also may be in us, so that the world may believe that thou hast sent me. ²²The glory which thou hast given me I have given to them, that they may be one even as we are one, ²³I in them and thou in me, that they may become perfectly one, so that the world may know that thou hast sent me and hast loved them even as thou hast loved me. ²⁴Father, I desire that they also, whom thou hast given me, may be with me where I am, to behold my glory which thou hast given me in thy love for me before the foundation of the world. ²⁵O righteous Father, the world has not known thee, but I have known thee; and these know that thou hast sent me. ²⁶I made known to them thy name, and I will make it known, that the love with which thou hast loved me may be in them, and I in them."

17:1 Well known as the priestly prayer, or the High Priestly Prayer, this passage of John's Gospel has been the inspiration of churches, and of ecumenical councils in the Catholic Church (especially at Florence in the fifteenth century and at the Vatican in the twentieth century under Pope John XXIII). Both the Catholic Church and the World Council of Churches devote eight days of prayer that draw upon this passage during January every year (Church Unity Week, January 18–25). When Pope Paul VI and the Ecumenical Patriarch of Constantinople, Athenagoras I, met on the Mount of Olives, January 6, 1964, they recited the alternate verses of this passage, the Pope speaking in Latin and the Patriarch in Greek. It had been five centuries since the heads of the Roman and Orthodox Catholic Churches had met and prayed together.

Jesus Enters His Suffering

John gives an account of Jesus' arrest, Caiphas questioning Jesus, and Peter denying Jesus. Then, John says, the Jews brought Jesus to the pretorium (residence of the Roman governor).

John 18:29–19:16

29 So Pilate went out to them and said, "What accusation do you bring against this man?" ³⁰They answered him, "If this man were not an evildoer, we would not have handed him over." ³¹Pilate said to them, "Take him yourselves and judge him by your own law." The Jews said to him, "It is not lawful for us to put any man to

death." ³²This was to fulfil the word which Jesus had spoken to show by what death he was to die.

33 Pilate entered the praetorium again and called Jesus, and said to him, "Are you the King of the Jews?" ³⁴Jesus answered, "Do you say this of your own accord, or did others say it to you about me?" ³⁵Pilate answered, "Am I a Jew? Your own nation and the chief priests have handed you over to me; what have you done?" ³⁶Jesus answered, "My kingship is not of this world; if my kingship were of this world, my servants would fight, that I might not be handed over to the Jews; but my kingship is not from the world." ³⁷Pilate said to him, "So you are a king?" Jesus answered, "You say that I am a king. For this I was born, and for this I have come into the world, to bear witness to the truth. Every one who is of the truth hears my voice." ³⁸Pilate said to him, "What is truth?"

After he had said this, he went out to the Jews again, and told them, "I find no crime in him. ³⁹But you have a custom that I should release one man for you at the Passover; will you have me release for you the King of the Jews?" ⁴⁰They cried out again, "Not this man, but Barab′bas!" Now Barab′bas was a robber.

19 Then Pilate took Jesus and scourged him. ²And the soldiers plaited a crown of thorns, and put it on his head, and arrayed him in a purple robe; ³they came up to him, saying, "Hail, King of the Jews!" and struck him with their hands. ⁴Pilate went out again, and said to them, "Behold, I am bringing him out to you, that you may know that I find no crime in him." ⁵So Jesus came out, wearing the crown of thorns and the purple robe. Pilate said to them, "Here is the man!" ⁶When the chief priests and the officers saw him, they cried out, "Crucify him, crucify him!" Pilate said to them, "Take him yourselves and crucify him, for I find no crime in him." ⁷The Jews answered him, "We have a law, and by that law he ought to die, because he has made himself the Son of God." ⁸When Pilate heard these words, he was the more afraid; ⁹he entered the praetorium again and said to Jesus, "Where are you from?" But Jesus gave no answer. ¹⁰Pilate therefore said to him, "You will not speak to me? Do you not know that I have power to release you, and power to crucify you?" ¹¹Jesus answered him, "You would have no power over me unless it had been given you from above; therefore he who delivered me to you has the greater sin."

12 Upon this Pilate sought to release him, but the Jews cried out, "If you release this man, you are not Caesar's friend; every one who makes himself a king sets himself against Caesar." ¹³When Pilate heard these words, he brought Jesus out and sat down on the judgment seat at a place called The Pavement, and in Hebrew,

Gab'batha. ¹⁴ Now it was the day of Preparation of the Passover; it was about the sixth hour. He said to the Jews, "Here is your King!" ¹⁵ They cried out, "Away with him, away with him, crucify him!" Pilate said to them, "Shall I crucify your King?" The chief priests answered, "We have no king but Caesar." ¹⁶ Then he handed him over to them to be crucified.

18:28 This passage has sometimes been used to ask vengeance on Jews, charging them with the death of Jesus. This use overlooks a fundamental point in the teaching of John and the other apostles: it is not the Jews or Judas or Peter or Pilate or the Roman soldiers who are responsible for Jesus' death—these are representative of every known classification of men, Jewish, Christian, Gentile. It is rather *all* sinful men (which means *all* men) who are responsible. The sin of Adam and the continued transgressions of all men keep men from the divine life for which man had been created. According to the Christian faith, the Father decreed, therefore, that the Son should come into the world to give his life (cf. John 10:18) so that men may have the divine life restored to them. John and Jesus taught that the men participating that day were only the instruments for *all* men; all sinners brought Jesus to the cross and all can be redeemed by the death, resurrection and return of Jesus to the Father. It must always be remembered that Jesus was a Jew and that his earliest followers were Jews. Those who wept at his death on the cross were also Jews. It would be sinful to use the crucifixion account in order to foment hatred of Jews. Jesus' message is one of love and joy, not hate, precisely on account of his death and triumphant return to the Father. (For statements by the World Council of Churches and the Roman Catholic Church, cf. notes on Matthew 27:25.)

John's account of the Passion (suffering) is the one read on Good Friday (18:1–19:42). Verses 33–37 are the Gospel for the Feast of Christ the King (on the last Sunday in October).

Jesus Dies on the Cross
John 19:17–37

17 So they took Jesus, and he went out, bearing his own cross, to the place called the place of a skull, which is called in Hebrew Gol'gotha. ¹⁸ There they crucified him, and with him two others, one on either side, and Jesus between them. ¹⁹ Pilate also wrote a tile and put it on the cross; it read, "Jesus of Nazareth, the King of the Jews." ²⁰ Many of the Jews read this title, for the place where Jesus was crucified was near the city; and it was written in Hebrew, in Latin, and in Greek. ²¹ The chief priests of the Jews then said to Pilate, "Do not write, 'The King of the Jews,' but, 'This man said, I am King of the Jews.'" ²² Pilate answered "What I have written I have written."

23 When the soldiers had crucified Jesus they took his garments and made four parts, one for each soldier; also his tunic. But the tunic was without seam, woven from top to bottom; ²⁴ so they said to one another, "Let us not tear it, but cast lots for it to see whose it shall be." This was to fulfil the scripture,

"They parted my garments among them,
    and for my clothing they cast lots."

25 So the soldiers did this. But standing by the cross of Jesus were his mother, and his mother's sister, Mary the wife of Clopas, and Mary Mag′dalene. ²⁶ When Jesus saw his mother, and the disciple whom he loved standing near, he said to his mother, "Woman, behold, your son!" ²⁷ Then he said to the disciple, "Behold, your mother!" And from that hour the disciple took her to his own home.

28 After this Jesus, knowing that all was now finished, said (to fulfil the scripture), "I thirst." ²⁹ A bowl full of vinegar stood there; so they put a sponge full of the vinegar on hyssop and held it to his mouth. ³⁰ When Jesus had received the vinegar, he said, "It is finished"; and he bowed his head and gave up his spirit.

31 Since it was the day of preparation, in order to prevent the bodies from remaining on the cross on the sabbath (for that sabbath was a high day), the Jews asked Pilate that their legs might be broken, and that they might be taken away. ³² So the soldiers came and broke the legs of the first, and of the other who had been crucified with him; ³³ but when they came to Jesus and saw that he was already dead, they did not break his legs. ³⁴ But one of the soldiers pierced his side with a spear, and at once there came out blood and water. ³⁵ He who saw it has borne witness—his testimony is true, and he knows that he tells the truth—that you also may believe. ³⁶ For these things took place that the scripture might be fulfilled, "Not a bone of him shall be broken." ³⁷ And again another scripture says, "They shall look on him whom they have pierced."

19:24 See Psalm 22:18.

19:25 The words of Jesus on the cross have been put to music many times with powerful effect (by Haydn and many others). The scene of Jesus' mother at the foot of the cross is the subject of a famous medieval hymn, *Stabat Mater* (His Mother Stood by the Cross), which has been set to music also (by Rossini, Pergolesi, Palestrina and others). The crucifixion scene itself has been a constant theme of artists through the centuries, but perhaps no one has depicted it more powerfully than Grunewald (especially in his masterpiece in Colmar). **19:34** The piercing of Jesus' side is narrated only by John. Since the time of the Fathers of the Church, and perhaps even earlier, the blood and water have been symbols of the sacraments of baptism and the Eucharist, and of the birth of the

Church from the side of Christ. The opened side has been the inspiration of mystics. John's witness to Jesus as the paschal lamb (verse 36) and the Suffering Servant (verse 37) has also been a fruitful source of spiritual writing through the centuries. Verses 30–35 are the Gospel for the Feast of the Most Precious Blood (July 1) and 31–37 for the Feast of the Sacred heart of Jesus (a Friday in June).

Jesus Rises from the Dead
John 20:1–31

20 Now on the first day of the week Mary Mag'dalene came to the tomb early, while it was still dark, and saw that the stone had been taken away from the tomb. [2] So she ran, and went to Simon Peter and the other disciple, the one whom Jesus loved, and said to them, "They have taken the Lord out of the tomb, and we do not know where they have laid him." [3] Peter then came out with the other disciple, and they went toward the tomb. [4] They both ran, but the other disciple outran Peter and reached the tomb first; [5] and stooping to look in, he saw the linen cloths lying there, but he did not go in. [6] Then Simon Peter came, following him, and went into the tomb; he saw the linen cloths lying, [7] and the napkin, which had been on his head, not lying with the linen cloths but rolled up in a place by itself. [8] Then the other disciple, who reached the tomb first, also went in, and he saw and believed; [9] for as yet they did not know the scripture, that he must rise from the dead. [10] Then the disciples went back to their homes.

[11] But Mary stood weeping outside the tomb, and as she wept she stooped to look into the tomb; [12] and she saw two angels in white, sitting where the body of Jesus had lain, one at the head and one at the feet. [13] They said to her, "Woman, why are you weeping?" She said to them, "Because they have taken away my Lord, and I do not know where they have laid him." [14] Saying this, she turned round and saw Jesus standing, but she did not know that it was Jesus. [15] Jesus said to her, "Woman, why are you weeping? Whom do you seek?" Supposing him to be the gardener, she said to him, "Sir, if you have carried him away, tell me where you have laid him, and I will take him away." [16] Jesus said to her, "Mary." She turned and said to him in Hebrew, "Rab-bo'ni!" (which means Teacher). [17] Jesus said to her, "Do not hold me, for I have not yet ascended to the Father; but go to my brethren and say to them, I am ascending to my Father and your Father, to my God and your God." [18] Mary Mag'dalene went and said to the disciples, "I have seen the Lord"; and she told them that he had said these things to her.

19 On the evening of that day, the first day of the week, the doors being shut where the disciples were, for fear of the Jews, Jesus came and stood among them and said to them, "Peace be with you." ²⁰ When he had said this, he showed them his hands and his side. Then the disciples were glad when they saw the Lord. ²¹ Jesus said to them again, "Peace be with you. As the Father has sent me, even so I send you." ²² And when he had said this, be breathed on them, and said to them, "Receive the Holy Spirit. ²³ If you forgive the sins of any, they are forgiven; if you retain the sins of any, they are retained."

24 Now Thomas, one of the twelve, called the Twin, was not with them when Jesus came. ²⁵ So the other disciples told him, "We have seen the Lord." But he said to them, "Unless I see in his hands the print of the nails, and place my finger in the mark of the nails, and place my hand in his side, I will not believe."

26 Eight days later, his disciples were again in the house, and Thomas was with them. The doors were shut, but Jesus came and stood among them, and said, "Peace be with you." ²⁷ Then he said to Thomas, "Put your finger here, and see my hands; and put out your hand, and place it in my side; do not be faithless, but believing." ²⁸ Thomas answered him, "My Lord and my God!" ²⁹ Jesus said to him, "Have you believed because you have seen me? Blessed are those who have not seen and yet believe."

30 Now Jesus did many other signs in the presence of the disciples, which are not written in this book; ³¹ but these are written that you may believe that Jesus is the Christ, the Son of God, and that believing you may have life in his name.

20:17 John's account stresses the ascension of Jesus to the Father. In other words, the evangelist understood that man's salvation is achieved by the death, resurrection and ascension of Jesus—the ascension being the glorification of Jesus' humanity in the Father's presence. **20:19** The message of peace and forgiveness reported here (19–31) is used as the Gospel in the Catholic Church's Votive Mass for Peace. The passage is read to the people each year on Low Sunday (The Sunday after Easter). Verses 24–29 are the Gospel for the Feast of St. Thomas the Apostle (December 21). **20:22** The Catholic Church teaches that in verses 22–23 Jesus conferred on the apostles the power to forgive sins in the sacrament of penance, that this power was to pass on to their successors, and that the sole possessors of the power of absolution are the bishops and priests. When a priest is ordained, the bishop, in a special part of the ceremony, repeats the words of Jesus here and thus empowers the priest to hear confessions and give absolution. Protestants generally consider the teaching as addressed to the entire Church. **20:29** *The*

New Testament in Basic English uses a limited vocabulary of approximately one thousand words; an illustration of how it makes nouns do the work of verbs is its rendering of this passage: "Because you have seen me you have belief: a blessing will be on those who have belief though they have not seen me."

Epilogue

The last sentence of chapter 20 reads as if it were the ending of the book. John, or his disciple-editor (the Greek style here is quite different from the rest of the book, cf. verse 24), may have added this report about the risen Jesus in Galilee.

John 21:1–25

21 After this Jesus revealed himself again to the disciples by the Sea of Tibe'ri-as; and he revealed himself in this way. ²Simon Peter, Thomas called the Twin, Nathan'a-el of Cana in Galilee, the sons of Zeb'edee, and two others of his disciples were together. ³Simon Peter said to them, "I am going fishing." They said to him, "We will go with you." They went out and got into the boat; but that night they caught nothing.

4 Just as day was breaking, Jesus stood on the beach; yet the disciples did not know that it was Jesus. ⁵Jesus said to them, "Children, have you any fish?" They answered him, "No." ⁶He said to them, "Cast the net on the right side of the boat, and you will find some." So they cast it, and now they were not able to haul it in, for the quantity of fish. ⁷That disciple whom Jesus loved said to Peter, "It is the Lord!" When Simon Peter heard that it was the Lord, he put on his clothes, for he was stripped for work, and sprang into the sea. ⁸But the other disciples came in the boat, dragging the net full of fish, for they were not far from the land, but about a hundred yards off.

9 When they got out on land, they saw a charcoal fire there, with fish lying on it, and bread. ¹⁰Jesus said to them, "Bring some of the fish that you have just caught." ¹¹So Simon Peter went aboard and hauled the net ashore, full of large fish, a hundred and fifty-three of them; and although there were so many, the net was not torn. ¹²Jesus said to them, "Come and have breakfast." Now none of the disciples dared ask him, "Who are you?" They knew it was the Lord. ¹³Jesus came and took the bread and gave it to them, and so with the fish. ¹⁴This was now the third time that Jesus was revealed to the disciples after he was raised from the dead.

15 When they had finished breakfast, Jesus said to Simon Peter, "Simon, son of John, do you love me more than these?" He said to him, "Yes, Lord; you know that I love you." He said to him, "Feed

my lambs." [16] A second time he said to him, "Simon, son of John, do you love me?" He said to him, "Yes, Lord; you know that I love you." He said to him, "Tend my sheep." [17] He said to him the third time, "Simon, son of John, do you love me?" Peter was grieved because he said to him the third time, "Do you love me?" And he said to him, "Lord, you know everything; you know that I love you." Jesus said to him, "Feed my sheep. [18] Truly, truly, I say to you, when you were young, you girded yourself and walked where you would; but when you are old, you will stretch out your hands, and another will gird you and carry you where you do not wish to go." [19] (This he said to show by what death he was to glorify God.) And after this he said to him, "Follow me."

20 Peter turned and saw following them the disciple whom Jesus loved, who had lain close to his breast at the supper and had said, "Lord, who is it that is going to betray you?" [21] When Peter saw him, he said to Jesus, "Lord, what about this man?" [22] Jesus said to him, "If it is my will that he remain until I come, what is that to you? Follow me!" [23] The saying spread abroad among the brethren that this disciple was not to die; yet Jesus did not say to him that he was not to die, but, "If it is my will that he remain until I come, what is that to you?"

24 This is the disciple who is bearing witness to these things, and who has written these things; and we know that his testimony is true.

25 But there are also many other things which Jesus did; were every one of them to be written, I suppose that the world itself could not contain the books that would be written.

21:11 The number of fishes caught is probably symbolic (Greek zoologists thought there were just 153 kinds of fish). **21:15** In the threefold test of Peter many Fathers of the Church saw Jesus giving Peter a chance to make up for his three denials of his master the night Jesus was arrested. **21:19** Verses 19–24 are the Gospel for the Feast of St. John, Apostle and Evangelist (December 27).

The Acts of the Apostles

This is Luke's second volume (compare Acts 1:1 with Luke 1:1–4). It recounts the spread of the Christian message, from Jerusalem all the way to Rome, capital of the empire that ruled the Mediterranean world. The first part of the book is mostly about the apostle Peter, the second about the apostle Paul. Since the book does not tell all the acts of all the apostles, it is not a complete history of the early church. Luke chose details that confirm the realization of something Jesus had said (cf. Acts 1:8).

One convenient way to outline the book is to show its progress geographically: Jerusalem (chaps. 1–8:5), the seacoast (8:40), Damascus (9:10), Antioch and Cyprus (11:19), Asia Minor (13:13), Europe (16:11), Rome (28:16). This book also describes a great controversy. One group of apostles insisted on holding Gentile converts to the observance of the Mosaic Law (circumcision, dietary laws, etc.); another group opposed such requirements.

In this book there is frequent reference to the action of the Spirit. The book is therefore sometimes called the Gospel of the Holy Spirit. It shows us the essence of the apostles' preaching, with stress upon the resurrection of Jesus and on Jesus as the fulfillment of Old Testament prophecies. The sermons and speeches given in the book are summaries, not word-for-word transcriptions: the longest speech in the book would not have taken ten minutes to deliver.

Introduction
Acts 1:1–5

1 In the first book, O The-oph'ilus, I have dealt with all that Jesus began to do and teach, [2] until the day when he was taken up, after he had given commandment through the Holy Spirit to the apostles whom he had chosen. [3] To them he presented himself alive after his passion by many proofs, appearing to them during forty days, and speaking of the kingdom of God. [4] And while staying with them he charged them not to depart from Jerusalem, but to wait for the promise of the Father, which, he said, "you heard from me, [5] for John baptized with water, but before many days you shall be baptized with the Holy Spirit."

Jesus Ascends into Heaven
Acts 1:6–14

6 So when they had come together, they asked him, "Lord, will you at this time restore the kingdom to Israel?" [7] He said to them, "It is not for you to know times or seasons which the Father has fixed by

his own authority. [8] But you shall receive power when the Holy Spirit has come upon you; and you shall be my witnesses in Jerusalem and in all Judea and Samar'ia and to the end of the earth." [9] And when he had said this, as they were looking on, he was lifted up, and a cloud took him out of their sight. [10] And while they were gazing into heaven as he went, behold, two men stood by them in white robes, [11] and said, "Men of Galilee, why do you stand looking into heaven? This Jesus, who was taken up from you into heaven, will come in the same way as you saw him go into heaven."

12 Then they returned to Jerusalem from the mount called Olivet, which is near Jerusalem, a sabbath day's journey away; [13] and when they had entered, they went up to the upper room, where they were staying, Peter and John and James and Andrew, Philip and Thomas, Bartholomew and Matthew, James the son of Alphaeus and Simon the Zealot and Judas the son of James. [14] All these with one accord devoted themselves to prayer, together with the women and Mary the mother of Jesus, and with his brothers.

1:9 The event described here is commemorated in Christian churches each year on the Thursday of the sixth week after Easter. This Feast of the Ascension was celebrated throughout the Roman Empire by the fourth century; it has been a holy day of obligation in the Catholic Church from that time. The traditional Christian belief is that on this day Jesus took our human nature into heaven where it was enthroned above all the angels, taking with him the souls of all the just people who had died before he came into the world. The preface of the Mass on this day asserts that Jesus "was lifted up to heaven to make us sharers in his divinity." In the Byzantine Rite the feast is also called "Fulfilled Salvation" (*Episozomene),* meaning that man is saved by the suffering, death, resurrection and ascension of Jesus into heaven (thus the Ascension would be the consummation and fulfillment of all other feasts). In the Middle Ages it was a fairly general custom in European churches on this day to hoist a statue of Jesus up through an opening in the roof while the people stood stretching their arms out, praying and singing. The scene of Jesus rising into the sky from the top of Mount Olivet has been a theme for artists throughout the centuries, e.g., John LaFarge's painting in the Church of the Ascension on Fifth Avenue in New York City. The window depicting the Ascension in the Cathedral of Le Mans (France) is the oldest preserved stained glass in the world (eleventh century). **1:12** The Talmud sets forth the distance of a Sabbath's journey as 2000 cubits, or about two-thirds of a mile. It is derived from Exodus 16:29, where the Israelites were told to stay in their home on the Sabbath and not to go out to gather manna. A journey beyond the limit of the city therefore was defined as work and a violation of the Sabbath Law. **1:14** This verse is often regarded as the inspiration for the retreat movement, that is, the gathering of a group for several days of prayerful reflection on the mission of Jesus and its meaning in the lives of the members of the group.

The Holy Spirit Comes

After an account of the apostles electing a successor to Judas (a man named Matthias), Luke describes what happened on the day of Pentecost (a term based on the Greek word for fifty and meaning the fiftieth day after Easter).

Acts 2:1–13

2 When the day of Pentecost had come, they were all together in one place. ²And suddenly a sound came from heaven like the rush of a mighty wind, and it filled all the house where they were sitting. ³And there appeared to them tongues as of fire, distributed and resting on each one of them. ⁴And they were all filled with the Holy Spirit and began to speak in other tongues, as the Spirit gave them utterance.

5 Now there were dwelling in Jerusalem Jews, devout men from every nation under heaven. ⁶And at this sound the multitude came together, and they were bewildered, because each one heard them speaking in his own language. ⁷And they were amazed and wondered, saying, "Are not all these who are speaking Galileans? ⁸And how is it that we hear, each of us in his own native language? ⁹Par'thians and Medes and E'lamites and residents of Mesopota'mia, Judea and Cappado'cia, Pontus and Asia, ¹⁰Phryg'ia and Pamphyl'ia, Egypt and the parts of Libya belonging to Cyre'ne, and visitors from Rome, both Jews and proselytes, ¹¹Cretans and Arabians, we hear them telling in our own tongues the mighty works of God." ¹²And all were amazed and perplexed, saying to one another, "What does this mean?" ¹³But others mocking said, "They are filled with new wine."

2:1 When the apostles gathered on this day, they were celebrating Shevuoth, the Feast of First-Fruits (Exodus 23:16), also called the Feast of Weeks, because the Jews counted seven weeks or fifty days after the Passover meal (Leviticus 23:15–21). Jewish tradition also preserves a legend according to which the divine voice on that very festival of Shevuoth proclaimed the Law on Mount Sinai in seventy languages in order that the Law might be heard in all the ends of the earth and accepted by all men. The gift of tongues has been interpreted by Christians as a challenge to the apostles to spread the word to the ends of the earth through their missionary activities and thus remove the divisions of mankind which followed the confusion of languages at the Tower of Babel. The annual Christian commemoration of Pentecost ranks as one of the greatest liturgical feasts. In the Catholic Church, red vestments are used on this day, to symbolize the Holy

Spirit descending upon the apostles in the form of tongues of fire. The most common symbol of the Spirit in church art, from the earliest centuries of the Christian era, has been the dove (cf. Luke 3:21–22). In the Middle Ages in many French cathedrals pigeons were released in the church on this day. A very old Latin prayer that begins with the words *Veni Sancte Spiritus* ("Come, Holy Spirit") is still said or sung in the Mass on Pentecost Day and every day during the following week. Another old hymn used in the Divine Office, *Veni Creator Spiritus* ("Come, Creator Spirit"), in use for ten centuries, is the official opening prayer for Church councils and synods, the beginning of a school year, or other important events. That prayer is still used also in the Protestant Episcopal ordination service. **2:9–11** We find here an atlas of the countries in which Jews were dispersed. There was a synagogue in most of these communities. When Paul and the disciples began their missionary journeys, therefore, a congregation of Jews almost anywhere greeted them. Scholars estimate that five million Jews lived outside of Palestine and another two million in the Holy Land. The total population of the Roman Empire barely exceeded 60,000,000. Jews, therefore, were then a larger percentage of the world population, about eight per cent, than they are now. In the United States, where the Jewish community is larger than anywhere else in the world, they comprise $2\frac{1}{2}$ per cent of the population.

Peter Speaks to the People

Acts 2:14–36

14 But Peter, standing with the eleven, lifted up his voice and addressed them, "Men of Judea and all who dwell in Jerusalem, let this be known to you, and give ear to my words. ¹⁵ For these men are not drunk, as you suppose, since it is only the third hour of the day; ¹⁶ but this is what was spoken by the prophet Joel:
¹⁷ 'And in the last days it shall be, God declares,
  that I will pour out my Spirit upon all flesh,
  and your sons and your daughters shall prophesy,
  and your young men shall see visions,
  and your old men shall dream dreams;
¹⁸ yea, and on my menservants and my maidservants in those days
  I will pour out my Spirit; and they shall prophesy.
¹⁹ And I will show wonders in the heaven above
  and signs on the earth beneath,
  blood, and fire, and vapor of smoke;
²⁰ the sun shall be turned into darkness
  and the moon into blood,
  before the day of the Lord comes,
  the great and manifest day.

²¹ And it shall be that whoever calls on the name of the Lord shall
be saved.'

22 "Men of Israel, hear these words: Jesus of Nazareth, a man
attested to you by God with mighty works and wonders and signs
which God did through him in your midst, as you yourselves
know—²³ this Jesus, delivered up according to the definite plan and
foreknowledge of God, you crucified and killed by the hands of
lawless men. ²⁴ But God raised him up, having loosed the pangs of
death, because it was not possible for him to be held by it. ²⁵ For
David says concerning him,

'I saw the Lord always before me,
    for he is at my right hand that I may not be shaken;
²⁶ therefore my heart was glad, and my tongue rejoiced;
    moreover my flesh will dwell in hope.
²⁷ For thou wilt not abandon my soul to Hades,
    nor let thy Holy One see corruption.
²⁸ Thou hast made known to me the ways of life;
    thou wilt make me full of gladness with thy presence.'

29 "Brethren, I may say to you confidently of the patriarch David
that he both died and was buried, and his tomb is with us to this day.
³⁰ Being therefore a prophet, and knowing that God had sworn with
an oath to him that he would set one of his descendants upon his
throne, ³¹ he foresaw and spoke of the resurrection of the Christ, that
he was not abandoned to Hades, nor did his flesh see corruption.
³² This Jesus God raised up, and of that we all are witnesses. ³³ Being
therefore exalted at the right hand of God, and having received from
the Father the promise of the Holy Spirit, he has poured out this
which you see and hear. ³⁴ For David did not ascend into the
heavens; but he himself says,

'The Lord said to my Lord, Sit at my right hand,
³⁵ till I make thy enemies a stool for thy feet.'

³⁶ Let all the house of Israel therefore know assuredly that God has
made him both Lord and Christ, this Jesus whom you crucified."

2:16 The quotation that follows (verses 17–21) is from Joel
2:28–32.
    2:36 There is a vast difference between the understanding of
Jesus' mission manifested in this speech and the mentality of the
disciples noted in the first chapter. There (1:6), in accordance with
the traditional Jewish concern, they asked Jesus if he would "restore
the kingdom to Israel." Here, if Peter is regarded as speaking for
them, they profess that Jesus is the Christ (Messiah) and the
heavenly Lord.

Jesus' Followers Increase
Acts 2:37–47

37 Now when they heard this they were cut to the heart, and said to Peter and the rest of the apostles, "Brethren, what shall we do?" [38] And Peter said to them, "Repent, and be baptized every one of you in the name of Jesus Christ for the forgiveness of your sins; and you shall receive the gift of the Holy Spirit. [39] For the promise is to you and to your children and to all that are far off, every one whom the Lord our God calls to him." [40] And he testified with many other words and exhorted them, saying, "Save yourselves from this crooked generation." [41] So those who received his word were baptized, and there were added that day about three thousand souls. [42] And they devoted themselves to the apostles' teaching and fellowship, to the breaking of bread and the prayers.

43 And fear came upon every soul; and many wonders and signs were done through the apostles. [44] And all who believed were together and had all things in common; [45] and they sold their possessions and goods and distributed them to all, as any had need. [46] And day by day, attending the temple together and breaking bread in their homes, they partook of food with glad and generous hearts, [47] praising God and having favor with all the people. And the Lord added to their number day by day those who were being saved.

2:42 The passage (42–47) is important for the picture it gives of the way of life of the earliest Christians. At this stage, as Jews, they were still participating in the worship at the Temple. Many elements of the Temple worship were brought over into the Christian liturgy, such as the altar, lamps and candles, and reading of lessons from Scripture. The bishop's miter is derived from the High Priest's headcovering; the Catholic priest's vestments developed from the dress of Jewish priests. Simplified versions of these are worn by many Protestant ministers. In the "breaking of bread" many scholars see the re-enactment of what Jesus did with the bread at the Last Supper (cf. also Luke 24:30-31). This eating together and the celebration of the Eucharist were early practices in the development of Christian liturgy. **2:42–45** The pattern of organization described here is similar to the discipline exercised by the Qumran sect (Essenes) whose rules were discovered in the Dead Sea Scrolls.

Peter Performs a Miracle
Acts 3:1–26

3 Now Peter and John were going up to the temple at the hour of prayer, the ninth hour. [2] And a man lame from birth was being carried, whom they laid daily at that gate of the temple which is

called Beautiful to ask alms of those who entered the temple. ³ Seeing Peter and John about to go into the temple, he asked for alms. ⁴ And Peter directed his gaze at him, with John, and said, "Look at us." ⁵ And he fixed his attention upon them, expecting to receive something from them. ⁶ But Peter said, "I have no silver and gold, but I give you what I have; in the name of Jesus Christ of Nazareth, walk." ⁷ And he took him by the right hand and raised him up; and immediately his feet and ankles were made strong. ⁸ And leaping up he stood and walked and entered the temple with them, walking and leaping and praising God. ⁹ And all the people saw him walking and praising God, ¹⁰ and recognized him as the one who sat for alms at the Beautiful Gate of the temple; and they were filled with wonder and amazement at what had happened to him.

11 While he clung to Peter and John, all the people ran together to them in the portico called Solomon's, astounded. ¹² And when Peter saw it he addressed the people, "Men of Israel, why do you wonder at this, or why do you stare at us, as though by our own power or piety we had made him walk? ¹³ The God of Abraham and of Isaac and of Jacob, the God of our fathers, glorified his servant Jesus, whom you delivered up and denied in the presence of Pilate, when he had decided to release him. ¹⁴ But you denied the Holy and Righteous One, and asked for a murderer to be granted to you, ¹⁵ and killed the Author of life, whom God raised from the dead. To this we are witnesses. ¹⁶ And his name, by faith in his name, has made this man strong whom you see and know; and the faith which is through Jesus has given the man this perfect health in the presence of you all.

17 "And now, brethren, I know that you acted in ignorance, as did also your rulers. ¹⁸ But what God foretold by the mouth of all the prophets, that his Christ should suffer, he thus fulfilled. ¹⁹ Repent therefore, and turn again, that your sins may be blotted out, that times of refreshing may come from the presence of the Lord, ²⁰ and that he may send the Christ appointed for you, Jesus, ²¹ whom heaven must receive until the time for establishing all that God spoke by the mouth of his holy prophets from of old. ²² Moses said, 'The Lord God will raise up for you a prophet from your brethren as he raised me up. You shall listen to him in whatever he tells you. ²³ And it shall be that every soul that does not listen to that prophet shall be destroyed from the people.' ²⁴ And all the prophets who have spoken, from Samuel and those who came afterwards, also proclaimed these days. ²⁵ You are the sons of the prophets and of the covenant which God gave to your fathers, saying to Abraham, 'And in your posterity shall all the families of the earth be blessed.' ²⁶ God,

having raised up his servant, sent him to you first, to bless you in turning every one of you from your wickedness."

John and Peter Are Arrested and Freed
Acts 4:1–21

4 And as they were speaking to the people, the priests and the captain of the temple and the Sad'ducees came upon them, [2] annoyed because they were teaching the people and proclaiming in Jesus the resurrection from the dead. [3] And they arrested them and put them in custody until the morrow, for it was already evening. [4] But many of those who heard the word believed; and the number of the men came to about five thousand.

[5] On the morrow their rulers and elders and scribes were gathered together in Jerusalem, [6] with Annas the high priest and Ca'iaphas and John and Alexander, and all who were of the high-priestly family. [7] And when they had set them in the midst, they inquired, "By what power or by what name did you do this?" [8] Then Peter, filled with the Holy Spirit, said to them, "Rulers of the people and elders, [9] if we are being examined today concerning a good deed done to a cripple, by what means this man has been healed, [10] be it known to you all, and to all the people of Israel, that by the name of Jesus Christ of Nazareth, whom you crucified, whom God raised from the dead, by him this man is standing before you well. [11] This is the stone which was rejected by your builders, but which has become the head of the corner. [12] And there is salvation in no one else, for there is no other name under heaven given among men by which we must be saved."

[13] Now when they saw the boldness of Peter and John, and perceived that they were uneducated, common men, they wondered; and they recognized that they had been with Jesus. [14] But seeing the man that had been healed standing beside them, they had nothing to say in opposition. [15] But when they had commanded them to go aside out of the council, they conferred with one another, [16] saying, "What shall we do with these men? For that a notable sign has been performed through them is manifest to all the inhabitants of Jerusalem, and we cannot deny it. [17] But in order that it may spread no further among the people, let us warn them to speak no more to any one in this name." [18] So they called them and charged them not to speak or teach at all in the name of Jesus. [19] But Peter and John answered them, "Whether it is right in the sight of God to listen to you rather than to God, you must judge; [20] for we cannot but speak of what we have seen and heard." [21] And when they had further threatened them, they let them go, finding no way to punish them, because of the people; for all men praised God for what had happened.

4:13 *Uneducated* does not mean they were illiterate but that they had not attended rabbinical or adult academies.

The Christians Help Each Other

Acts 4:32–37; 5:1–11

32 Now the company of those who believed were of one heart and soul, and no one said that any of the things which he possessed was his own, but they had everything in common. ³³ And with great power the apostles gave their testimony to the resurrection of the Lord Jesus, and great grace was upon them all. ³⁴ There was not a needy person among them, for as many as were possessors of lands or houses sold them, and brought the proceeds of what was sold ³⁵ and laid it at the apostles' feet; and distribution was made to each as any had need. ³⁶ Thus Joseph who was surnamed by the apostles Barnabas (which means, Son of encouragement), a Levite, a native of Cyprus, ³⁷ sold a field which belonged to him, and brought the money and laid it at the apostles' feet.

5 But a man named Anani'as with his wife Sapphi'ra sold a piece of property, ² and with his wife's knowledge he kept back some of the proceeds, and brought only a part and laid it at the apostles' feet. ³ But Peter said, "Anani'as, why has Satan filled your heart to lie to the Holy Spirit and to keep back part of the proceeds of the land? ⁴ While it remained unsold, did it not remain your own? And after it was sold, was it not at your disposal? How is it that you have contrived this deed in your heart? You have not lied to men but to God." ⁵ When Anani'as heard these words, he fell down and died. And great fear came upon all who heard of it. ⁶ The young men rose and wrapped him up and carried him out and buried him.

7 After an interval of about three hours his wife came in, not knowing what had happened. ⁸ And Peter said to her, "Tell me whether you sold the land for so much." And she said, "Yes, for so much." ⁹ But Peter said to her, "How is it that you have agreed together to tempt the Spirit of the Lord? Hark, the feet of those that have buried your husband are at the door, and they will carry you out." ¹⁰ Immediately she fell down at his feet and died. When the young men came in they found her dead, and they carried her out and buried her beside her husband. ¹¹ And great fear came upon the whole church, and upon all who heard of these things.

4:36 Barnabas will be a companion of St. Paul on his missionary journeys. His exemplary conduct is contrasted here with that of Ananias and Sapphira, who pretended to be generous but actually were not.

The Apostles Are Arrested and Freed
Acts 5:12-42

12 Now many signs and wonders were done among the people by the hands of the apostles. And they were all together in Solomon's Portico. [13] None of the rest dared join them, but the people held them in high honor. [14] And more than ever believers were added to the Lord, multitudes both of men and women, [15] so that they even carried out the sick into the streets, and laid them on beds and pallets, that as Peter came by at least his shadow might fall on some of them. [16] The people also gathered from the towns around Jerusalem, bringing the sick and those afflicted with unclean spirits, and they were all healed.

17 But the high priest rose up and all who were with him, that is, the party of the Sad'ducees, and filled with jealousy [18] they arrested the apostles and put them in the common prison. [19] But at night an angel of the Lord opened the prison doors and brought them out and said, [20] "Go and stand in the temple and speak to the people all the words of this Life." [21] And when they heard this, they entered the temple at daybreak and taught.

Now the high priest came and those who were with him and called together the council and all the senate of Israel, and sent to the prison to have them brought. [22] But when the officers came, they did not find them in the prison, and they returned and reported, [23] "We found the prison securely locked and the sentries standing at the doors, but when we opened it we found no one inside." [24] Now when the captain of the temple and the chief priests heard these words, they were much perplexed about them, wondering what this would come to. [25] And some one came and told them, "The men whom you put in prison are standing in the temple and teaching the people." [26] Then the captain with the officers went and brought them, but without violence, for they were afraid of being stoned by the people.

27 And when they had brought them, they set them before the council. And the high priest questioned them, [28] saying, "We strictly charged you not to teach in this name, yet here you have filled Jerusalem with your teaching and you intend to bring this man's blood upon us." [29] But Peter and the apostles answered, "We must obey God rather than men. [30] The God of our fathers raised Jesus whom you killed by hanging him on a tree. [31] God exalted him at his right hand as Leader and Savior, to give repentance to Israel and forgiveness of sins. [32] And we are witnesses to these things, and so is the Holy Spirit whom God has given to those who obey him."

33 When they heard this they were enraged and wanted to kill

them. [34] But a Pharisee in the council named Gama'li-el, a teacher of the law, held in honor by all the people, stood up and ordered the men to be put outside for a while. [35] And he said to them, "Men of Israel, take care what you do with these men. [36] For before these days Theu'das arose, giving himself out to be somebody, and a number of men, about four hundred, joined him; but he was slain and all who followed him were dispersed and came to nothing. [37] After him Judas the Galilean arose in the days of the census and drew away some of the people after him; he also perished, and all who followed him were scattered. [38] So in the present case I tell you, keep away from these men and let them alone; for if this plan or this undertaking is of men, it will fail; [39] but if it is of God, you will not be able to overthrow them. You might even be found opposing God!"

40 So they took his advice, and when they had called in the apostles, they beat them and charged them not to speak in the name of Jesus, and let them go. [41] Then they left the presence of the council, rejoicing that they were counted worthy to suffer dishonor for the name. [42] And every day in the temple and at home they did not cease teaching and preaching Jesus as the Christ.

5:17 Paul's reference here to the High Priest and to the Sadducees provides verification for those scholars who contend that the court that placed Jesus on trial prior to the crucifixion was under the control of these same Sadducees, and that they violated rules laid down by the Pharisees. We see in 5:33 that a distinguished Pharisee, Rabbi Gamaliel, protested against the injustice that the Sadducees would have perpetrated. **5:29** The words of Peter in 29–32 are regarded as an outline of the basic Christian teaching (*catechesis*) he was using at the time. Verse 29 is cited by some who perform acts of civil disobedience for moral aims. Compare Matthew 22:21; Romans 13:1 ff. **5:29** When Reformation leaders were ordered to leave the city of Geneva in 1537, John Calvin said: "It is better to serve God than man. If we had sought to please men, we should have been badly rewarded, but we serve a higher Master." Ordered by the authorities to abjure the propositions he had advanced, Martin Luther said: "I do not accept the authority of popes and councils—my conscience is captive to the Word of God. I cannot and will not recant anything, for to go against conscience is neither right nor safe. God help me. Amen." Paston Martin Niemöller (1892–19—), a leader of the Confessing Church of Germany, imprisoned by the Nazis for defying the Hitler régime, wrote: "Do we want a Christianity which we can use to further our own plans and aims, or do we want the Lord Jesus Christ who reveals the plans and aims of God to us? Which is to be the criterion: our claim on God or God's claim on us? Is God's will to conform to our will, or is our will to conform to the will of God?" **5:33** Rabban Gamaliel, according to Jewish tradition, was a grandson of

Rabbi Hillel and one of the most renowned rabbis. Jews read his words on Sabbath afternoons in *The Ethics of the Fathers:* "All study of the Torah which is not supplemented by work must prove futile in the end, and may lead to iniquity." **5:34** The Gamaliel who gives such humane and liberal advice had among his students, as we shall see, the Saul who becomes St. Paul (Acts 22:3).

Seven Are Chosen to Serve

Acts 6:1–7

6 Now in these days when the disciples were increasing in number, the Hellenists murmured against the Hebrews because their widows were neglected in the daily distribution. ² And the twelve summoned the body of the disciples and said, "It is not right that we should give up preaching the word of God to serve tables. ³ Therefore, brethren, pick out from among you seven men of good repute, full of the Spirit and of wisdom, whom we may appoint to this duty. ⁴ But we will devote ourselves to prayer and to the ministry of the word." ⁵ And what they said pleased the whole multitude, and they chose Stephen, a man full of faith and of the Holy Spirit, and Philip, and Proch'orus, and Nica'nor, and Timon, and Par'menas, and Nicola'us, a proselyte of Antioch. ⁶ These they set before the apostles, and they prayed and laid their hands upon them.

7 And the word of God increased; and the number of the disciples multiplied greatly in Jerusalem, and a great many of the priests were obedient to the faith.

6:3 The seven are not called deacons here, but they have been traditionally regarded as the first seven deacons. They did not merely serve at table; they also taught.

Stephen Dies a Martyr

Stephen gives a speech reviewing Jewish history in the classic spirit of prophetic criticism. His prediction of the Temple's destruction infuriates his listeners. We present here the final lines of the speech, and the tragic result.

Acts 6:8–15; 7:1, 51–60; 8:1–3

8 And Stephen, full of grace and power, did great wonders and signs among the people. ⁹ Then some of those who belonged to the synagogue of the Freedmen (as it was called), and of the Cyre'nians, and of the Alexandrians, and of those from Cili'cia and Asia, arose and disputed with Stephen. ¹⁰ But they could not withstand the wisdom and the Spirit with which he spoke. ¹¹ Then they secretly instigated men, who said, "We have heard him speak blasphemous words against Moses and God." ¹² And they stirred up the people and the elders and

the scribes, and they came upon him and seized him and brought him before the council, [13] and set up false witnesses who said, "This man never ceases to speak words against this holy place and the law; [14] for we have heard him say that this Jesus of Nazareth will destroy this place, and will change the customs which Moses delivered to us." [15] And gazing at him, all who sat in the council saw that his face was like the face of an angel.

7 And the high priest said, "Is this so?"

51 "You stiff-necked people, uncircumcised in heart and ears, you always resist the Holy Spirit. As your fathers did, so do you. [52] Which of the prophets did not your fathers persecute? And they killed those who announced beforehand the coming of the Righteous One, whom you have now betrayed and murdered, [53] you who received the law as delivered by angels and did not keep it."

54 Now when they heard these things they were enraged, and they ground their teeth against him. [55] But he, full of the Holy Spirit, gazed into heaven and saw the glory of God, and Jesus standing at the right hand of God; [56] and he said, "Behold, I see the heavens opened, and the Son of man standing at the right hand of God." [57] But they cried out with a loud voice and stopped their ears and rushed together upon him. [58] Then they cast him out of the city and stoned him; and the witnesses laid down their garments at the feet of a young man named Saul. [59] And as they were stoning Stephen, he prayed, "Lord Jesus, receive my spirit." [60] And he knelt down and cried with a loud voice, "Lord, do not hold this sin against them." And when he had said this, he fell asleep.

8 And Saul was consenting to his death.

And on that day a great persecution arose against the church in Jerusalem; and they were all scattered throughout the region of Judea and Samar'ia, except the apostles. [2] Devout men buried Stephen, and made great lamentation over him. [3] But Saul laid waste the church, and entering house after house, he dragged off men and women and committed them to prison.

6:9 Scholars suggest that the synagogue, which had its beginnings as a meeting place for the Jews of the Exile, was only late established in Jerusalem, since the Holy Temple sufficed for the religious needs of the Jews. This synagogue in Jerusalem was made up of freed men, repatriated Jews from foreign lands, some of whom may have once been carried off as Roman slaves.

Philip Preaches the Gospel

Philip "went down to a city of Samaria, and proclaimed to them the Christ," Luke writes. Then comes the story of Simon the magician.

Acts 8:9–39

9 But there was a man named Simon who had previously practiced magic in the city and amazed the nation of Samar'ia, saying that he himself was somebody great. [10] They all gave heed to him, from the least to the greatest, saying, "This man is that power of God which is called Great." [11] And they gave heed to him, because for a long time he had amazed them with his magic. [12] But when they believed Philip as he preached good news about the kingdom of God and the name of Jesus Christ, they were baptized, both men and women. [13] Even Simon himself believed, and after being baptized he continued with Philip. And seeing signs and great miracles performed, he was amazed.

14 Now when the apostles at Jerusalem heard that Samar'ia had received the word of God, they sent to them Peter and John, [15] who came down and prayed for them that they might receive the Holy Spirit; [16] for it had not yet fallen on any of them, but they had only been baptized in the name of the Lord Jesus. [17] Then they laid their hands on them and they received the Holy Spirit. [18] Now when Simon saw that the Spirit was given through the laying on of the apostles' hands, he offered them money, [19] saying, "Give me also this power, that any one on whom I lay my hands may receive the Holy Spirit." [20] But Peter said to him, "Your silver perish with you, because you thought you could obtain the gift of God with money! [21] You have neither part nor lot in this matter, for your heart is not right before God. [22] Repent therefore of this wickedness of yours, and pray to the Lord that, if possible, the intent of your heart may be forgiven you. [23] For I see that you are in the gall of bitterness and in the bond of iniquity." [24] And Simon answered, "Pray for me to the Lord, that nothing of what you have said may come upon me."

25 Now when they had testified and spoken the word of the Lord, they returned to Jerusalem, preaching the gospel to many villages of the Samaritans.

26 But an angel of the Lord said to Philip, "Rise and go toward the south to the road that goes down from Jerusalem to Gaza." This is a desert road. [27] And he rose and went. And behold, an Ethiopian, a eunuch, a minister of Canda'ce the queen of the Ethiopians, in charge of all her treasure, had come to Jerusalem to worship [28] and was returning; seated in his chariot, he was reading the prophet Isaiah. [29] And the Spirit said to Philip, "Go up and join this chariot." [30] So Philip ran to him, and heard him reading Isaiah the prophet, and asked, "Do you understand what you are reading?" [31] And he said, "How can I, unless some one guides me?" And he

invited Philip to come up and sit with him. [32] Now the passage of the scripture which he was reading was this:

"As a sheep led to the slaughter
 or a lamb before its shearer is dumb,
  so he opens not his mouth.
[33] In his humiliation justice was denied him.
 Who can describe his generation?
 For his life is taken up from the earth."

[34] And the eunuch said to Philip, "About whom, pray, does the prophet say this, about himself or about some one else?" [35] Then Philip opened his mouth, and beginning with this scripture he told him the good news of Jesus. [36] And as they went along the road they came to some water, and the eunuch said, "See, here is water! What is to prevent my being baptized?" [38] And he commanded the chariot to stop, and they both went down into the water, Philip and the eunuch, and he baptized him. [39] And when they came up out of the water, the Spirit of the Lord caught up Philip; and the eunuch saw him no more, and went on his way rejoicing.

8:9 The word "simony," buying or selling spiritual things, such as church positions, comes from this episode. **8:17–18** The sentences about Peter and John transmitting the Spirit to the Samaritans through the laying on of their hands are regarded as the classic text for illustrating the sacrament of confirmation. (See Index for references to this ritual in Jewish traditions.) **8:37** Some ancient manuscripts add here: And Philip said: "If you believe with all your heart you may." And he replied: "I believe that Jesus Christ is the Son of God." (It is generally agreed by scholars that the addition is a very old one, that it was taken from a baptismal liturgy, that it was added here by someone who felt the Ethiopian's faith should be expressed in formal terms.)

Saul Becomes a Christian

Acts 9:1–31

9 But Saul, still breathing threats and murder against the disciples of the Lord, went to the high priest [2] and asked him for letters to the synagogues at Damascus, so that if he found any belonging to the Way, men or women, he might bring them bound to Jerusalem. [3] Now as he journeyed he approached Damascus, and suddenly a light from heaven flashed about him. [4] And he fell to the ground and heard a voice saying to him, "Saul, Saul, why do you persecute me?" [5] And he said, "Who are you, Lord?" And he said, "I am Jesus, whom you are persecuting; [6] but rise and enter the city, and you will be told what you are to do." [7] The men who were traveling with him stood speechless, hearing the voice but seeing no one. [8] Saul arose from the ground; and when his eyes were opened, he could see nothing; so they led him by the hand and brought him into Damascus. [9] And for three days he was without sight, and neither ate nor drank.

10 Now there was a disciple at Damascus named Anani′as. The Lord said to him in a vision, "Anani′as." And he said, "Here I am, Lord." [11] And the Lord said to him, "Rise and go to the street called Straight, and inquire in the house of Judas for a man of Tarsus named Saul; for behold, he is praying, [12] and he has seen a man named Anani′as come in and lay his hands on him so that he might regain his sight." [13] But Anani′as answered, "Lord, I have heard from many about this man, how much evil he has done to thy saints at Jerusalem; [14] and here he has authority from the chief priests to bind all who call upon thy name." [15] But the Lord said to him, "Go, for he is a chosen instrument of mine to carry my name before the Gentiles and kings and the sons of Israel; [16] for I will show him how much he must suffer for the sake of my name." [17] So Anani′as departed and entered the house. And laying his hands on him he said, "Brother Saul, the Lord Jesus, who appeared to you on the road by which you came, has sent me that you may regain your sight and be filled with the Holy Spirit." [18] And immediately something like scales fell from his eyes and he regained his sight. Then he rose and was baptized, [19] and took food and was strengthened.

For several days he was with the disciples at Damascus. [20] And in the synagogues immediately he proclaimed Jesus, saying, "He is the Son of God." [21] And all who heard him were amazed, and said, "Is not this the man who made havoc in Jerusalem of those who called on this name? And he has come here for this purpose, to bring them bound before the chief priests." [22] But Saul increased all the more in strength, and confounded the Jews who lived in Damascus by proving that Jesus was the Christ.

23 When many days had passed, the Jews plotted to kill him, [24] but their plot became known to Saul. They were watching the gates day and night, to kill him; [25] but his disciples took him by night and let him down over the wall, lowering him in a basket.

26 And when he had come to Jerusalem he attempted to join the disciples; and they were all afraid of him, for they did not believe that he was a disciple. [27] But Barnabas took him, and brought him to the apostles, and declared to them how on the road he had seen the Lord, who spoke to him, and how at Damascus he had preached boldly in the name of Jesus. [28] So he went in and out among them at Jerusalem, [29] preaching boldly in the name of the Lord. And he spoke

and disputed against the Hellenists; but they were seeking to kill him. [30] And when the brethren knew it, they brought him down to Caesare'a, and sent him off to Tarsus.

31 So the church throughout all Judea and Galilee and Samar'ia had peace and was built up; and walking in the fear of the Lord and in the comfort of the Holy Spirit it was multiplied.

9:1 The event on the road to Damascus is commonly known as the conversion of St. Paul. It has been a theme for painters throughout the centuries. As we shall see, Paul was born at Tarsus. **9:2** "The Way" was one of the earliest names for Christianity. It is also the term Jews use to refer to a religious life guided by rabbinic regulations considered to be the way of God. **9:11** Historians record that Damascus was rebuilt in the Hellenistic period according to principles set by a famous Greek town-planner, Hippidamus of Miletus, fifth century B.C. Straight streets crossed each other at right angles, and the longest of the East-West streets, "The Street called Straight," still serves as the main commercial thoroughfare for the Old City. **9:15** Older translations have "chosen vessel" or "vessel of election" for "chosen instrument."

Gentiles Receive the Holy Spirit

After recounting some miracles performed by Peter, including the raising of a woman from the dead, Luke comes to the story of Cornelius. When Peter has the vision that is described here, what bothers him is that the Jewish Law stated only animals chewing the cud and having cloven hoofs were permitted for food (Leviticus 11). In the plan of this book, Peter's vision and the conversion of Cornelius are a climax. As a result of the events described here, the Christians understand that their mission includes Gentiles who were not required to fulfill prescriptions of Jewish Law.

Acts 10:1–48; 11:1–4, 15–18

10 At Caesare'a there was a man named Cornelius, a centurion of what was known as the Italian Cohort, [2] a devout man who feared God with all his household, gave alms liberally to the people, and prayed constantly to God. [3] About the ninth hour of the day he saw clearly in a vision an angel of God coming in and saying to him, "Cornelius." [4] And he stared at him in terror, and said, "What is it, Lord?" And he said to him, "Your prayers and your alms have ascended as a memorial before God. [5] And now send men to Joppa, and bring one Simon who is called Peter; [6] he is lodging with Simon, a tanner, whose house is by the seaside." [7] When the angel who spoke to him had departed, he called two of his servants and a devout soldier from among those that waited on him, [8] and having related everything to them, he sent them to Joppa.

9 The next day, as they were on their journey and coming near the city, Peter went up on the housetop to pray, about the sixth hour. ¹⁰ And he became hungry and desired something to eat; but while they were preparing it, he fell into a trance ¹¹ and saw the heaven opened, and something descending, like a great sheet, let down by four corners upon the earth. ¹² In it were all kinds of animals and reptiles and birds of the air. ¹³ And there came a voice to him, "Rise, Peter; kill and eat." ¹⁴ But Peter said, "No, Lord; for I have never eaten anything that is common or unclean." ¹⁵ And the voice came to him again a second time, "What God has cleansed, you must not call common." ¹⁶ This happened three times, and the thing was taken up at once to heaven.

17 Now while Peter was inwardly perplexed as to what the vision which he had seen might mean, behold, the men that were sent by Cornelius, having made inquiry for Simon's house, stood before the gate ¹⁸ and called out to ask whether Simon who was called Peter was lodging there. ¹⁹ And while Peter was pondering the vision, the Spirit said to him, "Behold, three men are looking for you. ²⁰ Rise and go down, and accompany them without hesitation; for I have sent them." ²¹ And Peter went down to the men and said, "I am the one you are looking for; what is the reason for your coming?" ²² And they said, "Cornelius, a centurion, an upright and God-fearing man, who is well spoken of by the whole Jewish nation, was directed by a holy angel to send for you to come to his house, and to hear what you have to say." ²³ So he called them in to be his guests.

The next day he rose and went off with them, and some of the brethren from Joppa accompanied him. ²⁴ And on the following day they entered Caesare′a. Cornelius was expecting them and had called together his kinsmen and close friends. ²⁵ When Peter entered, Cornelius met him and fell down at his feet and worshiped him. ²⁶ But Peter lifted him up, saying, "Stand up; I too am a man." ²⁷ And as he talked with him, he went in and found many persons gathered; ²⁸ and he said to them, "You yourselves know how unlawful it is for a Jew to associate with or to visit any one of another nation; but God has shown me that I should not call any man common or unclean. ²⁹ So when I was sent for, I came without objection. I ask then why you sent for me."

30 And Cornelius said, "Four days ago, about this hour, I was keeping the ninth hour of prayer in my house; and behold, a man stood before me in bright apparel, ³¹ saying, 'Cornelius, your prayer has been heard and your alms have been remembered before God. ³² Send therefore to Joppa and ask for Simon who is called Peter; he is lodging in the house of Simon, a tanner, by the seaside.' ³³ So I

sent to you at once, and you have been kind enough to come. Now therefore we are all here present in the sight of God, to hear all that you have been commanded by the Lord."

34 And Peter opened his mouth and said: "Truly I perceive that God shows no partiality, [35] but in every nation any one who fears him and does what is right is acceptable to him. [36] You know the word which he sent to Israel, preaching good news of peace by Jesus Christ (he is Lord of all), [37] the word which was proclaimed throughout all Judea, beginning from Galilee after the baptism which John preached: [38] how God anointed Jesus of Nazareth with the Holy Spirit and with power; how he went about doing good and healing all that were oppressed by the devil, for God was with him. [39] And we are witnesses to all that he did both in the country of the Jews and in Jerusalem. They put him to death by hanging him on a tree; [40] but God raised him on the third day and made him manifest; [41] not to all the people but to us who were chosen by God as witnesses, who ate and drank with him after he rose from the dead. [42] And he commanded us to preach to the people, and to testify that he is the one ordained by God to be judge of the living and the dead. [43] To him all the prophets bear witness that every one who believes in him receives forgiveness of sins through his name."

44 While Peter was still saying this, the Holy Spirit fell on all who heard the word. [45] And the believers from among the circumcised who came with Peter were amazed, because the gift of the Holy Spirit had been poured out even on the Gentiles. [46] For they heard them speaking in tongues and extolling God. Then Peter declared, [47] "Can any one forbid water for baptizing these people who have received the Holy Spirit just as we have?" [48] And he commanded them to be baptized in the name of Jesus Christ. Then they asked him to remain for some days.

11 Now the apostles and the brethren who were in Judea heard that the Gentiles also had received the word of God. [2] So when Peter went up to Jerusalem, the circumcision party criticized him, [3] saying, "Why did you go to uncircumcised men and eat with them?" [4] But Peter began and explained to them in order:

15 "As I began to speak, the Holy Spirit fell on them just as on us at the beginning. [16] And I remembered the word of the Lord, how he said, 'John baptized with water, but you shall be baptized with the Holy Spirit.' [17] If then God gave the same gift to them as he gave to us when we believed in the Lord Jesus Christ, who was I that I could withstand God?" [18] When they heard this they were silenced. And they glorified God, saying, "Then to the Gentiles also God has granted repentance unto life."

10:36 Verses 36–43 are another important summary of early Christian doctrine.

Barnabas and Paul Teach in Antioch
Acts 11:19–30

19 Now those who were scattered because of the persecution that arose over Stephen traveled as far as Phoeni'cia and Cyprus and Antioch, speaking the word to none except Jews. [20] But there were some of them, men of Cyprus and Cyre'ne, who on coming to Antioch spoke to the Greeks also, preaching the Lord Jesus. [21] And the hand of the Lord was with them, and a great number that believed turned to the Lord. [22] News of this came to the ears of the church in Jerusalem, and they sent Barnabas to Antioch. [23] When he came and saw the grace of God, he was glad; and he exhorted them all to remain faithful to the Lord with steadfast purpose; [24] for he was a good man, full of the Holy Spirit and of faith. And a large company was added to the Lord. [25] So Barnabas went to Tarsus to look for Saul; [26] and when he had found him, he brought him to Antioch. For a whole year they met with the church, and taught a large company of people; and in Antioch the disciples were for the first time called Christians.

27 Now in these days prophets came down from Jerusalem to Antioch. [28] And one of them named Ag'abus stood up and foretold by the Spirit that there would be a great famine over all the world; and this took place in the days of Claudius. [29] And the disciples determined, every one according to his ability, to send relief to the brethren who lived in Judea; [30] and they did so, sending it to the elders by the hand of Barnabas and Saul.

11:30 On "elders" here, see the discussion at 14:23.

Peter in Chains Is Freed by an Angel
Acts 12:1–17

12 About that time Herod the king laid violent hands upon some who belonged to the church. [2] He killed James the brother of John with the sword; [3] and when he saw that it pleased the Jews, he proceeded to arrest Peter also. This was during the days of Unleavened Bread. [4] And when he had seized him, he put him in prison, and delivered him to four squads of soldiers to guard him, intending after the Passover to bring him out to the people. [5] So Peter was kept in prison; but earnest prayer for him was made to God by the church.

6 The very night when Herod was about to bring him out, Peter was sleeping between two soldiers, bound with two chains, and sentries before the door were guarding the prison; [7] and behold, an

angel of the Lord appeared, and a light shone in the cell; and he struck Peter on the side and woke him, saying, "Get up quickly." And the chains fell off his hands. [8] And the angel said to him, "Dress yourself and put on your sandals." And he did so. And he said to him, "Wrap your mantle around you and follow me." [9] And he went out and followed him; he did not know that what was done by the angel was real, but thought he was seeing a vision. [10] When they had passed the first and the second guard, they came to the iron gate leading into the city. It opened to them of its own accord, and they went out and passed on through one street; and immediately the angel left him. [11] And Peter came to himself, and said, "Now I am sure that the Lord has sent his angel and rescued me from the hand of Herod and from all that the Jewish people were expecting."

12 When he realized this, he went to the house of Mary, the mother of John whose other name was Mark, where many were gathered together and were praying. [13] And when he knocked at the door of the gateway, a maid named Rhoda came to answer. [14] Recognizing Peter's voice, in her joy she did not open the gate but ran in and told that Peter was standing at the gate. [15] They said to her, "You are mad." But she insisted that it was so. They said, "It is his angel!" [16] But Peter continued knocking; and when they opened, they saw him and were amazed. [17] But motioning to them with his hand to be silent, he described to them how the Lord had brought him out of the prison. And he said, "Tell this to James and to the brethren." Then he departed and went to another place.

Paul Goes to the Gentiles

Paul, Barnabas and a cousin of Barnabas (John, also called Mark) went to Cyprus and preached the message of Jesus there. Then they come back to the mainland. Paul and Barnabas journey to Antioch near Pisidia. Paul preaches in a synagogue, claiming that the promises of the Old Testament are fulfilled in Jesus, with the results that follow.

Acts 13:42–52; 14:8–18, 23

42 As they went out, the people begged that these things might be told them the next sabbath. [43] And when the meeting of the synagogue broke up, many Jews and devout converts to Judaism followed Paul and Barnabas, who spoke to them and urged them to continue in the grace of God.

44 The next sabbath almost the whole city gathered together to hear the word of God. [45] But when the Jews saw the multitudes, they were filled with jealousy, and contradicted what was spoken by Paul, and reviled him. [46] And Paul and Barnabas spoke out boldly, saying,

"It was necessary that the word of God should be spoken first to you. Since you thrust it from you, and judge yourselves unworthy of eternal life, behold, we turn to the Gentiles. [47] For so the Lord has commanded us, saying,

'I have set you to be a light for the Gentiles,
    that you may bring salvation to the uttermost parts of the earth.' "

48 And when the Gentiles heard this, they were glad and glorified the word of God; and as many as were ordained to eternal life believed. [49] And the word of the Lord spread throughout all the region. [50] But the Jews incited the devout women of high standing and the leading men of the city, and stirred up persecution against Paul and Barnabas, and drove them out of their district. [51] But they shook off the dust from their feet against them, and went to Ico'nium. [52] And the disciples were filled with joy and with the Holy Spirit.

14 [8] Now at Lystra there was a man sitting, who could not use his feet; he was a cripple from birth, who had never walked. [9] He listened to Paul speaking; and Paul, looking intently at him and seeing that he had faith to be made well, [10] said in a loud voice, "Stand upright on your feet." And he sprang up and walked. [11] And when the crowds saw what Paul had done, they lifted up their voices, saying in Lycao'nian, "The gods have come down to us in the likeness of men!" [12] Barnabas they called Zeus, and Paul, because he was the chief speaker, they called Hermes. [13] And the priest of Zeus, whose temple was in front of the city, brought oxen and garlands to the gates and wanted to offer sacrifice with the people. [14] But when the apostles Barnabas and Paul heard of it, they tore their garments and rushed out among the multitude, crying, [15] "Men, why are you doing this? We also are men, of like nature with you, and bring you good news, that you should turn from these vain things to a living God who made the heaven and the earth and the sea and all that is in them. [16] In past generations he allowed all the nations to walk in their own ways; [17] yet he did not leave himself without witness, for he did good and gave you from heaven rains and fruitful seasons, satisfying your hearts with food and gladness." [18] With these words they scarcely restrained the people from offering sacrifice to them.

23 And when they had appointed elders for them in every church, with prayer and fasting, they committed them to the Lord in whom they believed.

14:12–13 Greek literature contains many accounts of gods in human form performing miraculous deeds. The citizens of Lystra thought Barnabas, who appeared to be the elder, was a reincarnation of Zeus (Jupiter), chief deity of the Pantheon; whereas Paul, the spokesman, was considered a reincarnation of Hermes (Mercury), herald of the gods. The appearance of gods required a sacrifice of an animal. **14:23** This verse has been translated in different ways, depending on the translator's views. For example, Tyndale wanted to stress that the Church of his day was not like the Church of the first century, so he used the word "congregation." Another example: Catholic translators held that the sentence referred to sacramental ordination of priests, so they put "priests" or "presbyter" where Protestant translations used "elders." All of the translators, of course, were dealing with the same word in Greek: *presbuteroi,* which means, literally, older or elder ones. Nowadays, translators generally use the word "elders," although the churches continue to differ in their interpretation of what it means: Were the elders considered to be priests, or bishops (*episkopoi*), or forerunners of bishops, or was there no question of a sacramental ordination at all? Congregationalists, Presbyterians, Episcopalians and others indicate by the names they choose that they have different views on the subject.

A Council Is Held In Jerusalem

The decision reached at the Council of Jerusalem was that the Gentiles could become Christians without circumcision. The men who made the decision believed that God was guiding them (see verse 28: "It has seemed good to the Holy Spirit and to us . . .")

Acts 15:1–30

15 But some men came down from Judea and were teaching the brethren, "Unless you are circumcised according to the custom of Moses, you cannot be saved." ² And when Paul and Barnabas had no small dissension and debate with them, Paul and Barnabas and some of the others were appointed to go up to Jerusalem to the apostles and the elders about this question. ³ So, being sent on their way by the church, they passed through both Phoeni'cia and Samar'ia, reporting the conversion of the Gentiles, and they gave great joy to all the brethren. ⁴ When they came to Jerusalem, they were welcomed by the church and the apostles and the elders, and they declared all that God had done with them. ⁵ But some believers who belonged to the party of the Pharisees rose up, and said, "It is necessary to circumcise them, and to charge them to keep the law of Moses."

6 The apostles and the elders were gathered together to consider this matter. ⁷ And after there had been much debate, Peter rose and said to them, "Brethren, you know that in the early days God made choice among you, that by my mouth the Gentiles should hear the

word of the gospel and believe. [8] And God who knows the heart bore witness to them, giving them the Holy Spirit just as he did to us; [9] and he made no distinction between us and them, but cleansed their hearts by faith. [10] Now therefore why do you make trial of God by putting a yoke upon the neck of the disciples which neither our fathers nor we have been able to bear? [11] But we believe that we shall be saved through the grace of the Lord Jesus, just as they will."

12 And all the assembly kept silence; and they listened to Barnabas and Paul as they related what signs and wonders God had done through them among the Gentiles. [13] After they finished speaking, James replied, "Brethren, listen to me. [14] Symeon has related how God first visited the Gentiles, to take out of them a people for his name. [15] And with this the words of the prophets agree, as it is written,

[16] 'After this I will return,
  and I will rebuild the dwelling of David, which has fallen;
  I will rebuild its ruins,
  and I will set it up,
[17] that the rest of men may seek the Lord,
  and all the Gentiles who are called by my name,
[18] says the Lord, who has made these things known from of old.'

[19] Therefore my judgment is that we should not trouble those of the Gentiles who turn to God, [20] but should write to them to abstain from the pollutions of idols and from unchastity and from what is strangled and from blood. [21] For from early generations Moses has had in every city those who preach him, for he is read every sabbath in the synagogues."

22 Then it seemed good to the apostles and the elders, with the whole church, to choose men from among them and send them to Antioch with Paul and Barnabas. They sent Judas called Barsabbas, and Silas, leading men among the brethren, [23] with the following letter: "The brethren, both the apostles and the elders, to the brethren who are of the Gentiles in Antioch and Syria and Cili'cia, greeting. [24] Since we have heard that some persons from us have troubled you with words, unsettling your minds, although we gave them no instructions, [25] it has seemed good to us in assembly to choose men and send them to you with our beloved Barnabas and Paul, [26] men who have risked their lives for the sake of our Lord Jesus Christ. [27] We have therefore sent Judas and Silas, who themselves will tell you the same things by word of mouth. [28] For it has seemed good to the Holy Spirit and to us to lay upon you no greater burden than these necessary things: [29] that you abstain from what has been sacrificed to idols and from blood and from what is

strangled and from unchastity. If you keep yourselves from these, you will do well. Farewell."

30 So when they were sent off, they went down to Antioch; and having gathered the congregation together, they delivered the letter.

15:1 In the controversy among the early Christians over requiring converts from the pagan world to subscribe to Jewish ritual and law, the Nazarenes, or Hebrew-Christians, were in accord with the Pharisaic view: converts must observe the dietary laws and undergo circumcision. Paul may have been aware of minority opinion among the Pharisees that regarded baptism as more important than circumcision. There is an opinion in the name of Rabbi Joshua that "one who has performed the ritual ablution but has not been circumcised is still a proper proselyte." Reform Jews will today, in a special ceremony, accept a gentile convert, without baptism, and circumcision is optional. In Paul's day, the leaders of the synagogue were angered at a decision that enabled gentiles to consider themselves "Israel" without circumcision or the obligation to be disciplined by Jewish law.

Paul Starts His Second Journey

Acts 16:6–15

6 And they went through the region of Phry'gia and Galatia, having been forbidden by the Holy Spirit to speak the word in Asia. ⁷And when they had come opposite My'sia, they attempted to go into Bithyn'ia, but the Spirit of Jesus did not allow them; ⁸so, passing by My'sia, they went down to Tro'as. ⁹And a vision appeared to Paul in the night: a man of Macedo'nia was standing beseeching him and saying, "Come over to Macedo'nia and help us." ¹⁰And when he had seen the vision, immediately we sought to go on into Macedo'nia, concluding that God had called us to preach the gospel to them.

11 Setting sail therefore from Tro'as, we made a direct voyage to Sam'othrace, and the following day to Ne-ap'olis, ¹²and from there to Philippi, which is the leading city of the district of Macedo'nia, and a Roman colony. We remained in this city some days; ¹³and on the sabbath day we went outside the gate to the riverside, where we supposed there was a place of prayer; and we sat down and spoke to the women who had come together. ¹⁴One who heard us was a woman named Lydia, from the city of Thyati'ra, a seller of purple goods, who was a worshiper of God. The Lord opened her heart to give heed to what was said by Paul. ¹⁵And when she was baptized, with her household, she besought us, saying, "If you have judged me to be faithful to the Lord, come to my house and stay." And she prevailed upon us.

16:12 Philippi was the first place in Europe where the Christian gospel was preached. Gold mines nearby caused the city to prosper, although it was not the capital city. In 42 B.C. Mark Antony and Gaius Octavius, the future Caesar Augustus, had defeated Cassius and Brutus at Philippi. In gratitude, Augustus granted the city a privileged status as a Roman colony. **16:10** "We" suddenly becomes the subject of the narrative. Luke may be writing as an eyewitness, or he may be copying a diary of the trip written by someone else.

Paul Preaches at Athens

In Athens, intellectual and artistic capital of the Greek world, Paul met Epicureans. They held that everything, including gods and mind, was made of very tiny atoms that were destined to be scattered. Therefore, they held, there was no point in fearing the gods or worrying about survival—one should cultivate *ataraxia* (serenity) and pleasure. Paul also met Stoics. They believed there was a universal Mind and that all other minds would eventually be absorbed into that Mind. Therefore, they held, man should cultivate *apatheia* (impassivity). Paul attempts to speak to the Athenians after their own philosophical manner, and he quotes Greek writers; the reaction of his hearers is varied.

Acts 17:16–34

16 Now while Paul was waiting for them at Athens, his spirit was provoked within him as he saw that the city was full of idols. [17] So he argued in the synagogue with the Jews and the devout persons, and in the market place every day with those who chanced to be there. [18] Some also of the Epicurean and Stoic philosophers met him. And some said, "What would this babbler say?" Others said, "He seems to be a preacher of foreign divinities"—because he preached Jesus and the resurrection. [19] And they took hold of him and brought him to the Are-op′agus, saying, "May we know what this new teaching is which you present? [20] For you bring some strange things to our ears; we wish to know therefore what these things mean." [21] Now all the Athenians and the foreigners who lived there spent their time in nothing except telling or hearing something new.

22 So Paul, standing in the middle of the Are-op′agus, said: "Men of Athens, I perceive that in every way you are very religious. [23] For as I passed along and observed the objects of your worship, I found also an altar with this inscription, 'To an unknown god.' What therefore you worship as unknown, this I proclaim to you. [24] The God who made the world and everything in it, being Lord of heaven and earth, does not live in shrines made by man, [25] nor is he served by human hands, as though he needed anything, since he himself gives to all men life and breath and everything. [26] And he made from

one every nation of men to live on all the face of the earth, having determined allotted periods and the boundaries of their habitation, [27] that they should seek God, in the hope that they might feel after him and find him. Yet he is not far from each one of us, [28] for

'In him we live and move and have our being';
as even some of your poets have said,
'For we are indeed his offspring.'

[29] Being then God's offspring, we ought not to think that the Deity is like gold, or silver, or stone, a representation by the art and imagination of man. [30] The times of ignorance God overlooked, but now he commands all men everywhere to repent, [31] because he has fixed a day on which he will judge the world in righteousness by a man whom he has appointed, and of this he has given assurance to all men by raising him from the dead."

32 Now when they heard of the resurrection of the dead, some mocked; but others said, "We will hear you again about this." [33] So Paul went out from among them. [34] But some men joined him and believed, among them Dionys'ius the Are-op'agite and a woman named Dam'aris and others with them.

A Riotous Day in Ephesus

During the more than two years Paul spent in and around Ephesus, there was "no small commotion about the Way." Paul's preaching had begun to result in diminishing profits for businesses connected with the cult of the fertility goddess worshiped at Ephesus (the Greeks called her Artemis; the Romans called her Diana).

Acts 19:23–20:1

23 About that time there arose no little stir concerning the Way. [24] For a man named Deme'trius, a silversmith, who made silver shrines of Ar'temis, brought no little business to the craftsmen. [25] These he gathered together, with the workmen of like occupation, and said, "Men, you know that from this business we have our wealth. [26] And you see and hear that not only at Ephesus but almost throughout all Asia this Paul has persuaded and turned away a considerable company of people, saying that gods made with hands are not gods. [27] And there is danger not only that this trade of ours may come into disrepute but also that the temple of the great goddess Ar'temis may count for nothing, and that she may even be deposed from her magnificence, she whom all Asia and the world worship."

28 When they heard this they were enraged, and cried out, "Great is Ar'temis of the Ephesians!" [29] So the city was filled with the confusion; and they rushed together into the theater, dragging with them Ga'ius and Aristar'chus, Macedo'nians who were Paul's com-

panions in travel. ³⁰ Paul wished to go in among the crowd, but the disciples would not let him; ³¹ some of the A'si-archs also, who were friends of his, sent to him and begged him not to venture into the theater. ³² Now some cried one thing, some another; for the assembly was in confusion, and most of them did not know why they had come together. ³³ Some of the crowd prompted Alexander, whom the Jews had put forward. And Alexander motioned with his hand, wishing to make a defense to the people. ³⁴ But when they recognized that he was a Jew, for about two hours they all with one voice cried out, "Great is Ar'temis of the Ephesians!" ³⁵ And when the town clerk had quieted the crowd, he said, "Men of Ephesus, what man is there who does not know that the city of the Ephesians is temple keeper of the great Ar'temis, and of the sacred stone that fell from the sky? ³⁶ Seeing then that these things cannot be contradicted, you ought to be quiet and do nothing rash. ³⁷ For you have brought these men here who are neither sacrilegious nor blasphemers of our goddess. ³⁸ If therefore Deme'trius and the craftsmen with him have a complaint against any one, the courts are open, and there are proconsuls; let them bring charges against one another. ³⁹ But if you seek anything further, it shall be settled in the regular assembly. ⁴⁰ For we are in danger of being charged with rioting today, there being no cause that we can give to justify this commotion." ⁴¹ And when he had said this, he dismissed the assembly.

20 After the uproar ceased, Paul sent for the disciples and having exhorted them took leave of them and departed for Macedo'nia.

Paul's Third Journey

Paul spent over a year and a half at Corinth "teaching the word of God." Then he moved on to Ephesus, Caesarea, and finally back to Antioch. Then he set out again, to places in Galatia and Phrygia. Luke adds that a Jew named Apollos, a native of Alexandria (Egypt), came to Ephesus; he, too, was trying to prove to the Jews by Scripture that the promised Messiah was Jesus. Paul completes the conversion of disciples of John the Baptist.

Acts 19:1–7

19 While Apol'los was at Corinth, Paul passed through the upper country and came to Ephesus. There he found some disciples. ² And he said to them, "Did you receive the Holy Spirit when you believed?" And they said, "No, we have never even heard that there is a Holy Spirit." ³ And he said, "Into what then were you baptized?" They said, "Into John's baptism." ⁴ And Paul said, "John baptized with the baptism of repentance, telling the people to believe in the one who was to come after him, that is, Jesus." ⁵ On hearing this, they were baptized in the name of the Lord Jesus. ⁶ And when Paul had laid his hands upon them, the Holy Spirit came on them; and they spoke with tongues and prophesied. ⁷ There were about twelve of them in all.

19:28–39 Diana (or Artemis) of Ephesus was a popular goddess of fertility. Archaeologists have uncovered many statues showing her with arms outstretched, clad in a closely clinging dress and decorated with many breasts (or with ostrich eggs, also a symbol of fertility in the Greek world).

Paul Is Arrested in Jerusalem

Paul went again to Macedonia, then to Greece, then along the coast of Asia Minor, to the islands and finally to Jerusalem, where soldiers had to rescue him from irate followers of the Mosaic Law, who charged that he "brought Greeks into the Temple, and he has defiled this holy place." (In 1870 an inscription was uncovered by archaeologists warning non-Jews against entering the Temple. It reads: "Let no one of the Gentiles enter inside the barrier around the Sanctuary in this porch. If he transgresses he shall bear the blame himself for his consequent DEATH.") The commander of the soldiers allowed Paul to address the people.

Acts 22:1–29

22 "Brethren and fathers, hear the defense which I now make before you."

2 And when they heard that he addressed them in the Hebrew language, they were the more quiet. And he said:

3 "I am a Jew, born at Tarsus in Cili′cia, but brought up in this city at the feet of Gama′li-el, educated according to the strict manner of the law of our fathers, being zealous for God as you all are this day. ⁴ I persecuted this Way to the death, binding and delivering to prison both men and women, ⁵ as the high priest and the whole council of elders bear me witness. From them I received letters to the brethren, and I journeyed to Damascus to take those also who were there and bring them in bonds to Jerusalem to be punished.

6 "As I made my journey and drew near to Damascus, about noon a great light from heaven suddenly shone about me. ⁷ And I fell to the ground and heard a voice saying to me, 'Saul, Saul, why do you persecute me?' ⁸ And I answered, 'Who are you, Lord?' And he said to me, 'I am Jesus of Nazareth whom you are persecuting.' ⁹ Now those who were with me saw the light but did not hear the voice of the one who was speaking to me. ¹⁰ And I said, 'What shall I do, Lord?' And the Lord said to me, 'Rise, and go into Damascus, and there you will be told all that is appointed for you to do.' ¹⁴ And

when I could not see because of the brightness of that light, I was led by the hand by those who were with me, and came into Damascus.

12 "And one Anani'as, a devout man according to the law, well spoken of by all the Jews who lived there, [13] came to me, and standing by me said to me, 'Brother Saul, receive your sight.' And in that very hour I received my sight and saw him. [14] And he said, 'The God of our fathers appointed you to know his will, to see the Just One and to hear a voice from his mouth; [15] for you will be a witness for him to all men of what you have seen and heard. [16] And now why do you wait? Rise and be baptized, and wash away your sins, calling on his name.'

17 "When I had returned to Jerusalem and was praying in the temple, I fell into a trance [18] and saw him saying to me, 'Make haste and get quickly out of Jerusalem, because they will not accept your testimony about me.' [19] And I said, 'Lord, they themselves know that in every synagogue I imprisoned and beat those who believed in thee. [20] And when the blood of Stephen thy witness was shed, I also was standing by and approving, and keeping the garments of those who killed him.' [21] And he said to me, 'Depart; for I will send you far away to the Gentiles.' "

22 Up to this word they listened to him; then they lifted up their voices and said, "Away with such a fellow from the earth! For he ought not to live." [23] And as they cried out and waved their garments and threw dust into the air, [24] the tribune commanded him to be brought into the barracks, and ordered him to be examined by scourging, to find out why they shouted thus against him. [25] But when they had tied him up with the thongs, Paul said to the centurion who was standing by, "Is it lawful for you to scourge a man who is a Roman citizen, and uncondemned?" [26] When the centurion heard that, he went to the tribune and said to him, "What are you about to do? For this man is a Roman citizen." [27] So the tribune came and said to him, "Tell me, are you a Roman citizen?" And he said, "Yes." [28] The tribune answered, "I bought this citizenship for a large sum." Paul said, "But I was born a citizen." [29] So those who were about to examine him withdrew from him instantly; and the tribune also was afraid, for he realized that Paul was a Roman citizen and that he had bound him.

22:25 Compare rights of a citizen in the United States, by which trial and judgment of guilt are required before punishment.

Paul Defends Himself before the Governor

Paul was interrogated by the Sanhedrin, and then taken to the Roman governor's residence at Caesarea. The governor promised him a hearing when his accusers arrived from Jerusalem.

Acts 24 : 1–27

24 And after five days the high priest Anani'as came down with some elders and a spokesman, one Tertul'lus. They laid before the governor their case against Paul; ²and when he was called, Tertul'lus began to accuse him, saying:

"Since through you we enjoy much peace, and since by your provision, most excellent Felix, reforms are introduced on behalf of this nation, ³in every way and everywhere we accept this with all gratitude. ⁴But, to detain you no further, I beg you in your kindness to hear us briefly. ⁵For we have found this man a pestilent fellow, an agitator among all the Jews throughout the world, and a ringleader of the sect of the Nazarenes. ⁶He even tried to profane the temple, but we seized him. ⁸By examining him yourself you will be able to learn from him about everything of which we accuse him."

9 The Jews also joined in the charge, affirming that all this was so.

10 And when the governor had motioned to him to speak, Paul replied:

"Realizing that for many years you have been judge over this nation, I cheerfully make my defense. ¹¹As you may ascertain, it is not more than twelve days since I went up to worship at Jerusalem; ¹²and they did not find me disputing with any one or stirring up a crowd, either in the temple or in the synagogues, or in the city. ¹³Neither can they prove to you what they now bring up against me. ¹⁴But this I admit to you, that according to the Way, which they call a sect, I worship the God of our fathers, believing everything laid down by the law or written in the prophets, ¹⁵having a hope in God which these themselves accept, that there will be a resurrection of both the just and the unjust. ¹⁶So I always take pains to have a clear conscience toward God and toward men. ¹⁷Now after some years I came to bring to my nation alms and offerings. ¹⁸As I was doing this, they found me purified in the temple, without any crowd or tumult. But some Jews from Asia—¹⁹they ought to be here before you and to make an accusation, if they have anything against me. ²⁰Or else let these men themselves say what wrongdoing they found when I stood before the council, ²¹except this one thing which I cried out while standing among them, 'With respect to the resurrection of the dead I am on trial before you this day.' "

22 But Felix, having a rather accurate knowledge of the Way, put them off, saying, "When Lys'ias the tribune comes down, I will decide your case." ²³Then he gave orders to the centurion that he should be kept in custody but should have some liberty, and that none of his friends should be prevented from attending to his needs.

24 After some days Felix came with his wife Drusil′la, who was a Jewess; and he sent for Paul and heard him speak upon faith in Christ Jesus. ²⁵ And as he argued about justice and self-control and future judgment, Felix was alarmed and said, "Go away for the present; when I have an opportunity I will summon you." ²⁶ At the same time he hoped that money would be given him by Paul. So he sent for him often and conversed with him. ²⁷ But when two years had elapsed, Felix was succeeded by Porcius Festus; and desiring to do the Jews a favor, Felix left Paul in prison.

Paul's Case Is Heard by King Agrippa

Paul appealed his case to Caesar, and the new governor agreed that he should go to Caesar in Rome. Then the following episode took place.

Acts 25:13–26:32

13 Now when some days had passed, Agrippa the king and Berni′ce arrived at Caesare′a to welcome Festus. ¹⁴ And as they stayed there many days, Festus laid Paul's case before the king, saying, "There is a man left prisoner by Felix; ¹⁵ and when I was at Jerusalem, the chief priests and the elders of the Jews gave information about him, asking for sentence against him. ¹⁶ I answered them that it was not the custom of the Romans to give up any one before the accused met the accusers face to face, and had opportunity to make his defense concerning the charge laid against him. ¹⁷ When therefore they came together here, I made no delay, but on the next day took my seat on the tribunal and ordered the man to be brought in. ¹⁸ When the accusers stood up, they brought no charge in his case of such evils as I supposed; ¹⁹ but they had certain points of dispute with him about their own superstition and about one Jesus, who was dead, but whom Paul asserted to be alive. ²⁰ Being at a loss how to investigate these questions, I asked whether he wished to go to Jerusalem and be tried there regarding them. ²¹ But when Paul had appealed to be kept in custody for the decision of the emperor, I commanded him to be held until I could send him to Caesar." ²² And Agrippa said to Festus, "I should like to hear the man myself." "Tomorrow," said he, "you shall hear him."

23 So on the morrow Agrippa and Berni′ce came with great pomp, and they entered the audience hall with the military tribunes and the prominent men of the city. Then by command of Festus Paul was brought in. ²⁴ And Festus said, "King Agrippa and all who are present with us, you see this man about whom the whole Jewish people petitioned me, both at Jerusalem and here, shouting

that he ought not to live any longer. [25] But I found that he had done nothing deserving death; and as he himself appealed to the emperor, I decided to send him. [26] But I have nothing definite to write to my lord about him. Therefore I have brought him before you, and, especially before you, King Agrippa, that, after we have examined him, I may have something to write. [27] For it seems to me unreasonable, in sending a prisoner, not to indicate the charges against him."

26 Agrippa said to Paul, "You have permission to speak for yourself." Then Paul stretched out his hand and made his defense:

2 "I think myself fortunate that it is before you, King Agrippa, I am to make my defense today against all the accusations of the Jews, [3] because you are especially familiar with all customs and controversies of the Jews; therefore I beg you to listen to me patiently.

4 "My manner of life from my youth, spent from the beginning among my own nation and at Jerusalem, is known by all the Jews. [5] They have known for a long time, if they are willing to testify, that according to the strictest party of our religion I have lived as a Pharisee. [6] And now I stand here on trial for hope in the promise made by God to our fathers, [7] to which our twelve tribes hope to attain, as they earnestly worship night and day. And for this hope I am accused by Jews, O king! [8] Why is it thought incredible by any of you that God raises the dead?

9 "I myself was convinced that I ought to do many things in opposing the name of Jesus of Nazareth. [10] And I did so in Jerusalem; I not only shut up many of the saints in prison, by authority from the chief priests, but when they were put to death I cast my vote against them. [11] And I punished them often in all the synagogues and tried to make them blaspheme; and in raging fury against them, I persecuted them even to foreign cities.

12 "Thus I journeyed to Damascus with the authority and commission of the chief priests. [13] At midday, O king, I saw on the way a light from heaven, brighter than the sun, shining round me and those who journeyed with me. [14] And when we had all fallen to the ground, I heard a voice saying to me in the Hebrew language, 'Saul, Saul, why do you persecute me? It hurts you to kick against the goads.' [15] And I said, 'Who are you, Lord?' And the Lord said, 'I am Jesus whom you are persecuting. [16] But rise and stand upon your feet; for I have appeared to you for this purpose, to appoint you to serve and bear witness to the things in which you have seen me and to those in which I will appear to you, [17] delivering you from the people and from the Gentiles—to whom I send you [18] to open their eyes, that they may turn from darkness to light and from the power

of Satan to God, that they may receive forgiveness of sins and a place among those who are sanctified by faith in me.'

19 "Wherefore, O King Agrippa, I was not disobedient to the heavenly vision, [20] but declared first to those at Damascus, then at Jerusalem and throughout all the country of Judea, and also to the Gentiles, that they should repent and turn to God and perform deeds worthy of their repentance. [21] For this reason the Jews seized me in the temple and tried to kill me. [22] To this day I have had the help that comes from God, and so I stand here testifying both to small and great, saying nothing but what the prophets and Moses said would come to pass: [23] that the Christ must suffer, and that, by being the first to rise from the dead, he would proclaim light both to the people and to the Gentiles."

24 And as he thus made his defense, Festus said with a loud voice, "Paul, you are mad; your great learning is turning you mad." [25] But Paul said, "I am not mad, most excellent Festus, but I am speaking the sober truth. [26] For the king knows about these things, and to him I speak freely; for I am persuaded that none of these things has escaped his notice, for this was not done in a corner. [27] King Agrippa, do you believe the prophets? I know that you believe." [28] And Agrippa said to Paul, "In a short time you think to make me a Christian!" [29] And Paul said, "Whether short or long, I would to God that not only you but also all who hear me this day might become such as I am—except for these chains."

30 Then the king rose, and the governor and Berni'ce and those who were sitting with them; [31] and when they had withdrawn, they said to one another, "This man is doing nothing to deserve death or imprisonment." [32] And Agrippa said to Festus, "This man could have been set free if he had not appealed to Caesar."

Paul Comes to Rome

Paul was sent off to Italy by ship, but the ship was wrecked off the coast of Malta. The book ends with the following passage.

Acts 28:11–28, 30–31

11 After three months we set sail in a ship which had wintered in the island, a ship of Alexandria, with the Twin Brothers as figurehead. [12] Putting in at Syracuse, we stayed there for three days. [13] And from there we made a circuit and arrived at Rhe'gium; and after one day a south wind sprang up, and on the second day we came to Pute'oli. [14] There we found brethren, and were invited to stay with them for seven days. And so we came to Rome. [15] And the brethren there, when they heard of us, came as far as the Forum

of Ap'pius and Three Taverns to meet us. On seeing them Paul thanked God and took courage. ¹⁶ And when we came into Rome, Paul was allowed to stay by himself, with the soldier that guarded him.

17 After three days he called together the local leaders of the Jews; and when they had gathered, he said to them, "Brethren, though I had done nothing against the people or the customs of our fathers, yet I was delivered prisoner from Jerusalem into the hands of the Romans. ¹⁸ When they had examined me, they wished to set me at liberty, because there was no reason for the death penalty in my case. ¹⁹ But when the Jews objected, I was compelled to appeal to Caesar—though I had no charge to bring against my nation. ²⁰ For this reason therefore I have asked to see you and speak with you, since it is because of the hope of Israel that I am bound with this chain." ²¹ And they said to him, "We have received no letters from Judea about you, and none of the brethren coming here has reported or spoken any evil about you. ²² But we desire to hear from you what your views are; for with regard to this sect we know that everywhere it is spoken against."

23 When they had appointed a day for him, they came to him at his lodging in great numbers. And he expounded the matter to them from morning till evening, testifying to the kingdom of God and trying to convince them about Jesus both from the law of Moses and from the prophets. ²⁴ And some were convinced by what he said, while others disbelieve. ²⁵ So, as they disagreed among themselves, they departed, after Paul had made one statement: "The Holy Spirit was right in saying to your fathers through Isaiah the prophet:

²⁶ 'Go to this people, and say,
   You shall indeed hear but never understand,
   and you shall indeed see but never perceive.
²⁷ For this people's heart has grown dull,
   and their ears are heavy of hearing,
   and their eyes they have closed;
   lest they should perceive with their eyes,
   and hear with their ears,
   and understand with their heart,
   and turn for me to heal them.'

²⁸ Let it be known to you then that this salvation of God has been sent to the Gentiles; they will listen."

30 And he lived there two whole years at his own expense, and welcomed all who came to him, ³¹ preaching the kingdom of God and teaching about the Lord Jesus Christ quite openly and unhindered.

28:11 The twin brothers are Castor and Pollux, the patrons of pagan sailors. **28:30** Unlike the practice described below, the state assumes the costs of upkeep of prisoners in the United States and many other modern countries. Since Paul is said here to have preached for two whole years unhindered, we conclude that Nero's persecution of A.D. 64 had not yet begun. The story ends "up in the air," therefore, about A.D. 63. Was the book finished before Paul's trial in the court of Caesar? Did Luke plan another volume to continue the story? Did Luke deliberately decide not to end his book with an account of Paul's condemnation and execution?

The Letter of Paul to the Romans

Twenty-one of the twenty-seven books of the New Testament are letters or epistles. In modern English usage, an epistle is a public letter, intended for a wide audience. Most of Paul's writings, however, are private and informal letters written to a particular person or group for a specific purpose.

The order in which Paul's letters are found in the New Testament is not the order in which they were written. Though some have thought they were arranged according to the importance of the churches addressed or, roughly, according to length, Romans was probably placed first because it is the only formal theological treatise, and forms an introduction to—and summary of—all that Paul taught.

The Letter to the Romans is Paul's longest and some consider it his most important letter. From the details given at the end, scholars deduce that Paul wrote the letter in Corinth sometime between A.D. 54 and 58. This would have been toward the end of his third missionary journey, before he went to Jerusalem where he was arrested and imprisoned.

In this letter Paul deals with a vital religious question of his day: the relation of the Christian system of salvation to the Mosaic Law. Paul insists that all saving grace and holiness is a gift of God. Paul, one-time student of Rabbi Gamaliel and ardent Pharisee, uses Hebrew Scripture as a source text and Jewish methods of biblical interpretation to make his case. His style of writing, however, is individual and requires careful attention. In explaining one thing, he touches on another that he will come to later, and then as he elaborates on the new theme he refers to the old matter again in a new perspective. His texts are an interweaving and interlocking of ideas, usually with some new thought added.

Rembrandt's painting of the Apostle Paul (in the Widener Collection, National Gallery of Art, Washington, D.C.) shows Paul at his desk meditating with pen in hand. The colors in the picture are dark brown and red, and the apostle's face glows in the light coming down from above. A sword (artistic symbol for Paul, who was decapitated in Nero's persecution of A.D. 67), leans against the wall.

Introductory Passage

Addressing a Greek-reading audience, Paul writes in the style of ancient Greek letters. He begins by identifying himself and the people to whom he is writing. He adds a profession of his Christian faith, short prayers of thanksgiving and petition and then, in verses 16–17, Paul states his theme.

Romans 1:1–17

1 Paul, a servant of Jesus Christ, called to be an apostle, set apart for the gospel of God ²which he promised beforehand through his prophets in the holy scriptures, ³the gospel concerning his Son, who was descended from David according to the flesh ⁴and designated Son of God in power according to the Spirit of holiness by his resurrection from the dead, Jesus Christ our Lord, ⁵through whom we have received grace and apostleship to bring about the obedience of faith for the sake of his name among all the nations, ⁶including yourselves who are called to belong to Jesus Christ;

7 To all God's beloved in Rome, who are called to be saints:

Grace to you and peace from God our Father and the Lord Jesus Christ.

8 First, I thank my God through Jesus Christ for all of you, because your faith is proclaimed in all the world. ⁹For God is my witness, whom I serve with my spirit in the gospel of his Son, that without ceasing I mention you always in my prayers, ¹⁰asking that somehow by God's will I may now at last succeed in coming to you. ¹¹For I long to see you, that I may impart to you some spiritual gift to strengthen you, ¹²that is, that we may be mutually encouraged by each other's faith, both yours and mine. ¹³I want you to know, brethren, that I have often intended to come to you (but thus far have been prevented), in order that I may reap some harvest among you as well as among the rest of the Gentiles. ¹⁴I am under obligation both to Greeks and to barbarians, both to the wise and to the foolish: ¹⁵so I am eager to preach the gospel to you also who are in Rome.

16 For I am not ashamed of the gospel: it is the power of God for salvation to every one who has faith, to the Jew first and also to the Greek. ¹⁷For in it the righteousness of God is revealed through faith for faith; as it is written, "He who through faith is righteous shall live."

1:1–7 The *Twentieth Century New Testament, a Translation Into Modern English,* first published in 1904, here rearranges and translates: "To all in Rome who are dear to God and have been called to become Christ's People, from Paul, a servant of Jesus Christ. . . ." **1:16** Christians who have maintained missionary enterprises directed toward the conversion of Jews have found in the phrase "To the Jews first" a mandate for their work. Jews hold that Judaism provides them a vital communion with God. Many theologians currently suggest that the proper posture of Jews and Christians toward each other is one of dialogue, conversation. The Second Vatican Council endorsed and promoted dialogue between Christians and Jews in the Declaration on the Relationship of the Church to Non-Christian Religions (Art. 4), just as the Council's Decree on Ecumenism endorsed and promoted dialogue between the separated Christian groups (Art. 9). **1:17** While meditating on this passage in the Black Monastery at Wittenberg, Martin Luther (1483–1546), long troubled at his inability to find peace of conscience through meticulous obedience to the law, suddenly grasped the truth that for him the righteousness of God was not to be understood in terms of God's retributive justice, which rewarded or punished a man on his merits, but rather by the mercy which God extends to the sinner. For by God's standards all men would fall short. Receiving this mercy by faith, the sinner is not only justified in God's sight but is given the power to live by the law. He is enabled to enter into a filial relationship, living the divine life in active obedience to the will of a merciful God.

God Judges All Men

Paul states that Gentiles will be judged by "the law written in their hearts," which many Christians have called the "natural law." Jews, Paul goes on to explain, will be judged by the Law of Moses. This whole section has the form of a dialogue, a philosophical conversation—that is, the sentences are written as responses to questions.

Romans 2:1–29

2 Therefore you have no excuse, O man, whoever you are, when you judge another; for in passing judgment upon him you condemn yourself, because you, the judge are doing the very same things. ²We know that the judgment of God rightly falls upon those who do such things. ³Do you suppose, O man, that when you judge those who do such things and yet do them yourself, you will escape the judgment of God? ⁴Or do you presume upon the riches of his kindness and forbearance and patience? Do you not know that God's kindness is meant to lead you to repentance? ⁵But by your hard and impenitent heart you are storing up wrath for yourself on the day of wrath when God's righteous judgment will be revealed. ⁶For he will render to every man according to his works: ⁷to those who by patience in well-doing seek for glory and honor and immortality, he will give eternal life; ⁸but for those who are factious and do not obey the truth, but obey wickedness, there will be wrath and fury. ⁹There will be tribulation and distress for every human being who does evil, the Jew first and also the Greek, ¹⁰but glory and honor and peace for every one who does good, the Jew first and also the Greek. ¹¹For God shows no partiality.

12 All who have sinned without the law will also perish without the law, and all who have sinned under the law will be judged by the

law. [13] For it is not the hearers of the law who are righteous before God, but the doers of the law who will be justified. [14] When Gentiles who have not the law do by nature what the law requires, they are a law to themselves, even though they do not have the law. [15] They show that what the law requires is written on their hearts, while their conscience also bears witness and their conflicting thoughts accuse or perhaps excuse them [16] on that day when, according to my gospel, God judges the secrets of men by Christ Jesus.

17 But if you call yourself a Jew and rely upon the law and boast of your relation to God [18] and know his will and approve what is excellent, because you are instructed in the law, [19] and if you are sure that you are a guide to the blind, a light to those who are in darkness, [20] a corrector of the foolish, a teacher of children, having in the law the embodiment of knowledge and truth—[21] you then who teach others, will you not teach yourself? While you preach against stealing, do you steal? [22] You who say that one must not commit adultery, do you commit adultery? You who abhor idols, do you rob temples? [23] You who boast in the law, do you dishonor God by breaking the law? [24] For, as it is written, "The name of God is blasphemed among the Gentiles because of you."

25 Circumcision indeed is of value if you obey the law; but if you break the law, your circumcision becomes uncircumcision. [26] So, if a man who is uncircumcised keeps the precepts of the law, will not his uncircumcision be regarded as circumcision? [27] Then those who are physically uncircumcised but keep the law will condemn you who have the written code and circumcision but break the law. [28] For he is not a real Jew who is one outwardly, nor is true circumcision something external and physical. [29] He is a Jew who is one inwardly, and real circumcision is a matter of the heart, spiritual and not literal. His praise is not from men but from God.

2:6 Paul acknowledges here that how a man lives his life and what he does is important to God. But later in the text, 3:21 ff., he will develop the point that all men fall short. They are justified before God by grace, because of the atonement of Jesus and their faith in him as Savior. **2:11** Tyndale: For there is no parcialyte with God. Great Bible: For there is no respect of personnes with God. Geneva Bible: For there is no respect of persons with God. Bishops' Bible and King James Version: For there is no respect of persons with God. Rheims: For there is no acception of persons with God. **2:14** John Calvin (1509–1564) wrote: "Those who rightly judge will always agree that there is an indelible sense of divinity engraven upon men's minds."

Justification Is a Gift of God

Romans 3:9–31

9 What then? Are we Jews any better off? No, not at all; for I have already charged that all men, both Jews and Greeks, are under the power of sin, ¹⁰ as it is written:

"None is righteous, no, not one;
¹¹ no one understands, no one seeks for God.
¹² All have turned aside, together they have gone wrong;
no one does good, not even one."
¹³ "Their throat is an open grave,
they use their tongues to deceive."
"The venom of asps is under their lips."
¹⁴ "Their mouth is full of curses and bitterness."
¹⁵ "Their feet are swift to shed blood,
¹⁶ in their paths are ruin and misery,
¹⁷ and the way of peace they do not know."
¹⁸ "There is no fear of God before their eyes."

19 Now we know that whatever the law says it speaks to those who are under the law, so that every mouth may be stopped, and the whole world may be held accountable to God. ²⁰ For no human being will be justified in his sight by works of the law, since through the law comes knowledge of sin.

21 But now the righteousness of God has been manifested apart from law, although the law and the prophets bear witness to it, ²² the righteousness of God through faith in Jesus Christ for all who believe. For there is no distinction; ²³ since all have sinned and fall short of the glory of God, ²⁴ they are justified by his grace as a gift, through the redemption which is in Christ Jesus, ²⁵ whom God put forward as an expiation by his blood, to be received by faith. This was to show God's righteousness, because in his divine forbearance he had passed over former sins; ²⁶ it was to prove at the present time that he himself is righteous and that he justifies him who has faith in Jesus.

27 Then what becomes of our boasting? It is excluded. On what principle? On the principle of works? No, but on the principle of faith. ²⁸ For we hold that a man is justified by faith apart from works of law. ²⁹ Or is God the God of Jews only? Is he not the God of Gentiles also? Yes, of Gentiles also, ³⁰ since God is one; and he will justify the circumcised on the ground of their faith and the uncircumcised through their faith. ³¹ Do we then overthrow the law by this faith? By no means! On the contrary, we uphold the law.

3:10 Paul made extensive use of Hebrew biblical quotations in his elaboration of Christian views. In his view, Christian teaching was at many points a fulfillment of the promises of Hebrew Scripture. At other points, however, he used Hebrew Bible verses as a foil by which to demonstrate something new or unique in the Christian teaching. Almost always, his quotations are taken from the Septuagint or Greek translation of the Hebrew Bible. They are not always exact renderings of the Hebrew verse. Paul in thus rendering these verses uses them sometimes out of context, or with an emphasis or an interpretation that suits his purpose. **3:10–12** Compare Psalms 14:1–2; 53:1–2. **3:13** Compare Psalms 5:9; 140:3. **3:14** Compare Psalm 10:7. **3:15–17** Compare Isaiah 59:7–8. **3:18** Compare Psalm 36:1. **3:23** Jonathan Edwards (1703–1758), New England preacher, writer and for a short while before his sudden death president of Princeton University, believed this passage gave a true appraisal of human nature and man's need for divine mercy: "Man is wholly under the power of sin and utterly unable, without the interposition of sovereign grace, to do anything that is truly good." **3:25** John Calvin (1509–1564) said: "God, to whom we were hateful through sin, was appeased by the death of his Son, and was made propitious to us." Jews agree that it is doubtful that any man will live his life without sin. On the Day of Atonement Jews confess: ". . . for we are neither so arrogant nor so hardened as to say before thee, O Lord, our God of our fathers, 'We are righteous and have not sinned'; Verily we have sinned." But unlike the Christian, the Jew does not seek atonement for his sins and reconciliation with God through faith in Jesus. Rather, Jews believe that God will accept the Jew's sincere faith in God, his remorse at his shortcomings and his prayerful intention to live by God's law as a sufficient atonement. The Jewish liturgy continues: "Incline our hearts to forsake the path of evil and hasten our salvation. Let the wicked forsake his way and the unrighteous man his thought; let him return unto the Lord, and He will have mercy upon him, for our God is ever ready to pardon." **3:28** Luther added the word "only" to "faith" in his German translation, thus expressing an interpretation of the sentence held by many Protestants. Others, notably Catholic commentators, stress it does not follow from Paul's statement that good works are not necessary for salvation.

Abraham Is a Model for Us
Romans 4:1–8, 13, 16–25

4 When then shall we say about Abraham, our forefather according to the flesh? [2] For if Abraham was justified by works, he has something to boast about, but not before God. [3] For what does the scripture say? "Abraham believed God, and it was reckoned to him as righteousness." [4] Now to one who works, his wages are not reckoned as a gift but as his due. [5] And to one who does not work but trusts him who justifies the ungodly, his faith is reckoned as righteousness. [6] So also David pronounces a blessing upon the man to whom God reckons righteousness apart from works:

[7] "Blessed are those whose iniquities are forgiven, and whose sins are covered;

[8] blessed is the man against whom the Lord will not reckon his sin."

13 The promise to Abraham and his descendants, that they should inherit the world, did not come through the law but through the righteousness of faith.

16 That is why it depends on faith, in order that the promise may rest on grace and be guaranteed to all his descendants—not only to the adherents of the law but also to those who share the faith of Abraham, for he is the father of us all, [17] as it is written, "I have made you the father of many nations"—in the presence of the God in whom he believed, who gives life to the dead and calls into existence the things that do not exist. [18] In hope he believed against hope, that he should become the father of many nations; as he had been told, "So shall your descendants be." [19] He did not weaken in faith when he considered his own body, which was as good as dead because he was about a hundred years old, or when he considered the barrenness of Sarah's womb. [20] No distrust made him waver concerning the promise of God, but he grew strong in his faith as he gave glory to God, [21] fully convinced that God was able to do what he had promised. [22] That is why his faith was "reckoned to him as righteousness." [23] But the words, "it was reckoned to him," were written not for his sake alone, [24] but for ours also. It will be reckoned to us who believe in him that raised from the dead Jesus our Lord, [25] who was put to death for our trespasses and raised for our justification.

We Have Peace with God Through Jesus

Christians who hold the doctrine of original sin regard this as a key passage for understanding it. According to that understanding, "one man's sin" (verse 12) is Adam's sin. Paul contrasts the damage done by Adam's fall with the benefits conferred on mankind by Jesus. For Paul, Jesus is the second Adam bringing the gift of justification. Artists have often alluded to Paul's teaching by depicting a human skull at the foot of Jesus' cross and the blood of the Redeemer falling upon it. The skull signifies Adam and the sin for which Jesus' death makes atonement. Paul insists that whatever man has in the spiritual life he owes to a gift from God.

Romans 5:1–21

5 Therefore, since we are justified by faith, we have peace with God through our Lord Jesus Christ. ²Through him we have obtained access to this grace in which we stand, and we rejoice in our hope of sharing the glory of God. ³More than that, we rejoice in our sufferings, knowing that suffering produces endurance, ⁴and endurance produces character, and character produces hope, ⁵and hope does not disappoint us, because God's love has been poured into our hearts through the Holy Spirit which has been given to us.

6 While we were yet helpless, at the right time Christ died for the ungodly. ⁷Why, one will hardly die for a righteous man—though perhaps for a good man one will dare even to die. ⁸But God shows his love for us in that while we were yet sinners Christ died for us. ⁹Since, therefore, we are now justified by his blood, much more shall we be saved by him from the wrath of God. ¹⁰For if while we were enemies we were reconciled to God by the death of his Son, much more, now that we are reconciled, shall we be saved by his life. ¹¹Not only so, but we also rejoice in God through our Lord Jesus Christ, through whom we have now received our reconciliation.

12 Therefore as sin came into the world through one man and death through sin, and so death spread to all men because all men sinned—¹³sin indeed was in the world before the law was given, but sin is not counted where there is no law. ¹⁴Yet death reigned from Adam to Moses, even over those whose sins were not like the transgression of Adam, who was a type of the one who was to come.

15 But the free gift is not like the trespass. For if many died through one man's trespass, much more have the grace of God and the free gift in the grace of that one man Jesus Christ abounded for many. ¹⁶And the free gift is not like the effect of that one man's sin. For the judgment following one trespass brought condemnation, but the free gift following many trespasses brings justification. ¹⁷If, because of one man's trespass, death reigned through that one man, much more will those who receive the abundance of grace and the free gift of righteousness reign in life through the one man Jesus Christ.

18 Then as one man's trespass led to condemnation for all men, so one man's act of righteousness leads to acquittal and life for all men. ¹⁹For as by one man's disobedience many were made sinners, so by one man's obedience many will be made righteous. ²⁰Law came in, to increase the trespass; but where sin increased, grace abounded all the more, ²¹so that, as sin reigned in death, grace also might reign through righteousness to eternal life through Jesus Christ our Lord.

The Free Gift of God is Eternal Life

Paul explains baptism as a way in which a Christian shares in Jesus'
death and resurrection.

Romans 6:3–6, 12–14, 22–23

3 Do you not know that all of us who have been baptized into
Christ Jesus were baptized into his death? [4] We were buried
therefore with him by baptism into death, so that as Christ was
raised from the dead by the glory of the Father, we too might walk
in newness of life.

5 For if we have been united with him in a death like his, we shall
certainly be united with him in a resurrection like his. [6] We know
that our old self was crucified with him so that the sinful body might
be destroyed, and we might no longer be enslaved to sin.

12 Let not sin therefore reign in your mortal bodies, to make you
obey their passions. [13] Do not yield your members to sin as
instruments of wickedness, but yield yourselves to God as men who
have been brought from death to life, and your members to God as
instruments of righteousness. [14] For sin will have no dominion
over you, since you are not under law but under grace. [22] But now
that you have been set free from sin and have become slaves of God,
the return you get is sanctification and its end, eternal life. [23] For the
wages of sin is death, but the free gift of God is eternal life in Christ
Jesus our Lord.

Two Laws Are at War within Us

As Paul sees it, there is an internal struggle within man, between the
law of God and the law of sin, between the spirit and the flesh.

Romans 7:15–25

15 I do not understand my own actions. For I do not do what I want,
but I do the very thing I hate. [16] Now if I do what I do not want, I
agree that the law is good. [17] So then it is no longer I that do it, but
sin which dwells within me. [18] For I know that nothing good dwells
within me, that is, in my flesh. I can will what is right, but I cannot
do it. [19] For I do not do the good I want, but the evil I do not want is
what I do. [20] Now if I do what I do not want, it is no longer I that do
it, but sin which dwells within me.

21 So I find it to be a law that when I want to do right, evil lies
close at hand. [22] For I delight in the law of God, in my inmost self,
[23] but I see in my members another law at war with the law of my
mind and making me captive to the law of sin which dwells in my
members. [24] Wretched man that I am! Who will deliver me from this
body of death? [25] Thanks be to God through Jesus Christ our Lord!

So then, I of myself serve the law of God with my mind, but with my flesh I serve the law of sin.

The Faithful Are Children and Heirs of God
Romans 8:1–17

8 There is therefore now no condemnation for those who are in Christ Jesus. [2] For the law of the Spirit of life in Christ Jesus has set me free from the law of sin and death. [3] For God has done what the law, weakened by the flesh, could not do: sending his own Son in the likeness of sinful flesh and for sin, he condemned sin in the flesh, [4] in order that the just requirement of the law might be fulfilled in us, who walk not according to the flesh but according to the Spirit. [5] For those who live according to the flesh set their minds on the things of the flesh, but those who live according to the Spirit set their minds on the things of the Spirit. [6] To set the mind on the flesh is death, but to set the mind on the Spirit is life and peace. [7] For the mind that is set on the flesh is hostile to God; it does not submit to God's law, indeed it cannot; [8] and those who are in the flesh cannot please God.

9 But you are not in the flesh, you are in the Spirit, if the Spirit of God really dwells in you. Any one who does not have the Spirit of Christ does not belong to him. [10] But if Christ is in you, although your bodies are dead because of sin, your spirits are alive because of righteousness. [11] If the Spirit of him who raised Jesus from the dead dwells in you, he who raised Christ Jesus from the dead will give life to your mortal bodies also through his Spirit which dwells in you.

12 So then, brethren, we are debtors, not to the flesh, to live according to the flesh—[13] for if you live according to the flesh you will die, but if by the Spirit you put to death the deeds of the body you will live. [14] For all who are led by the Spirit of God are sons of God. [15] For you did not receive the spirit of slavery to fall back into fear, but you have received the spirit of sonship. When we cry, "Abba! Father!" [16] it is the Spirit himself bearing witness with our spirit that we are children of God, [17] and if children, then heirs, heirs of God and fellow heirs with Christ, provided we suffer with him in order that we may also be glorified with him.

Nothing Can Separate Us from the Love of God
Romans 8:28–39

28 We know that in everything God works for good with those who love him, who are called according to his purpose. [29] For those whom he foreknew he also predestined to be conformed to the image of his Son, in order that he might be the first-born among many

brethren. [30] And those whom he predestined he also called; and those whom he called he also justified; and those whom he justified he also glorified.

31 What then shall we say to this? If God is for us, who is against us? [32] He who did not spare his own Son but gave him up for us all, will he not also give us all things with him? [33] Who shall bring any charge against God's elect? It is God who justifies; [34] who is to condemn? Is it Christ Jesus, who died, yes, who was raised from the dead, who is at the right hand of God, who indeed intercedes for us? [35] Who shall separate us from the love of Christ? Shall tribulation, or distress, or persecution, or famine, or nakedness, or peril, or sword? [36] As it is written,

"For thy sake we are being killed all the day long;
we are regarded as sheep to be slaughtered."

[37] No, in all these things we are more than conquerors through him who loved us. [38] For I am sure that neither death, nor life, nor angels, nor principalities, nor things present, nor things to come, nor powers, [39] nor height, nor depth, nor anything else in all creation, will be able to separate us from the love of God in Christ Jesus our Lord.

8:36 Compare Psalm 22:42.

Israel Has Stumbled over a Stone

Why, after a quarter of a century, had the great majority of the Jews not accepted Jesus' claims? Here is Paul's answer.

Romans 9:30–33; 10:1–4

30 What shall we say, then? That Gentiles who did not pursue righteousness have attained it, that is, righteousness through faith; [31] but that Israel who pursued the righteousness which is based on law did not succeed in fulfilling that law. [32] Why? Because they did not pursue it through faith, but as if it were based on works. They have stumbled over the stumbling stone, [33] as it is written,

"Behold, I am laying in Zion a stone that will make men stumble,
a rock that will make them fall;
and he who believes in him will not be put to shame."

10 Brethren, my heart's desire and prayer to God for them is that they may be saved. [2] I bear them witness that they have a zeal for God, but it is not enlightened. [3] For, being ignorant of the righteousness that comes from God, and seeking to establish their own, they did not submit to God's righteousness. [4] For Christ is the end of the law, that every one who has faith may be justified.

Peter Stresses the Role of the Preacher
Romans 10:10–17

10 For man believes with his heart and so is justified, and he confesses with his lips and so is saved. ¹¹ The scripture says, "No one who believes in him will be put to shame." ¹² For there is no distinction between Jew and Greek; the same Lord is Lord of all and bestows his riches upon all who call upon him. ¹³ For, "every one who calls upon the name of the Lord will be saved."

14 But how are men to call upon him in whom they have not believed? And how are they to believe in him of whom they have never heard? And how are they to hear without a preacher? ¹⁵ And how can men preach unless they are sent? As it is written, "How beautiful are the feet of those who preach good news!" ¹⁶ But they have not all heeded the gospel; for Isaiah says, "Lord, who has believed what he has heard from us?" ¹⁷ So faith comes from what is heard, and what is heard comes by the preaching of Christ.

10:11 Compare Isaiah 28:16. **10:12** Jewish scholars point out that in abandoning a distinction between Jew and Greek, circumcised and uncircumcised, Paul expounded a concept that inevitably caused a breach between the Hebrews and the Hebrew-Christian sect. The Jews also look forward to that day when all men will accept the God of Abraham as Lord; but they conceive of the Hebrew nation as "a priest people" for the nations of the world. The universalism of Paul makes no such distinction according to national lines. He provided a concept that enabled Christianity to separate itself from the Hebrew national group and go its own way. Later in history Jewish scholars acknowledged that Christianity had indeed spread a knowledge of God to the far corners of the earth. **10:13** See Joel 2:32. **10:15** See Isaiah 52:7. **10:16** See Isaiah 53:1.

God Still Loves the Jews
Romans 11:1–6, 11–29

11 I ask, then, has God rejected his people? By no means! I myself am an Israelite, a descendant of Abraham, a member of the tribe of Benjamin. ² God has not rejected his people whom he foreknew. Do you not know what the scripture says of Eli′jah, how he pleads with God against Israel? ³ "Lord, they have killed thy prophets, they have demolished thy altars, and I alone am left, and they seek my life." ⁴ But what is God's reply to him? "I have kept for myself seven thousand men who have not bowed the knee to Ba′al." ⁵ So too at the present time there is a remnant, chosen by grace. ⁶ But if it is by grace, it is no longer on the basis of works; otherwise grace would no longer be grace.

11 So I ask, have they stumbled so as to fall? By no means! But through their trespass salvation has come to the Gentiles, so as to make Israel jealous. ¹²Now if their trespass means riches for the world, and if their failure means riches for the Gentiles, how much more will their full inclusion mean!

13 Now I am speaking to you Gentiles. Inasmuch then as I am an apostle to the Gentiles, I magnify my ministry ¹⁴in order to make my fellow Jews jealous, and thus save some of them. ¹⁵For if their rejection means the reconciliation of the world, what will their acceptance mean but life from the dead? ¹⁶If the dough offered as first fruits is holy, so is the whole lump; and if the root is holy, so are the branches.

17 But if some of the branches were broken off, and you, a wild olive shoot, were grafted in their place to share the richness of the olive tree, ¹⁸do not boast over the branches. If you do boast, remember it is not you that support the root, but the root that supports you. ¹⁹You will say, "Branches were broken off so that I might be grafted in." ²⁰That is true. They were broken off because of their unbelief, but you stand fast only through faith. So do not become proud, but stand in awe. ²¹For if God did not spare the natural branches, neither will he spare you. ²²Note then the kindness and the severity of God: severity toward those who have fallen, but God's kindness to you, provided you continue in his kindness; otherwise you too will be cut off. ²³And even the others, if they do not persist in their unbelief, will be grafted in, for God has the power to graft them in again. ²⁴For if you have been cut from what is by nature a wild olive tree, and grafted, contrary to nature, into a cultivated olive tree, how much more will these natural branches be grafted back into their own olive tree.

25 Lest you be wise in your own conceits, I want you to understand this mystery, brethren: a hardening has come upon part of Israel, until the full number of the Gentiles come in, ²⁶and so all Israel will be saved; as it is written,

"The Deliverer will come from Zion,
    he will banish ungodliness from Jacob";
²⁷"and this will be my covenant with them
    when I take away their sins."
²⁸As regards the gospel they are enemies of God, for your sake; but as regards election they are beloved for the sake of their forefathers. ²⁹For the gifts and the call of God are irrevocable.

11:3 Compare 1 Kings 19:14–18. **11:17** Some interpret Paul's metaphor of the olive tree (17–24) as follows: the tree is Israel, the people of God, the branches broken off are Jews who did not accept

Jesus as Christ; branches grafted in are Gentiles who do believe in Jesus. Paul argues that the failure of Jews to believe in Jesus provides the Church the occasion to convert the Gentile world. Despite Jewish enmity to the Gospel, Jews remain dear to God and are favored with His gifts and a calling to His service (11:28–29). Recent Church declarations in an effort to overcome anti-Semitism have pointed to this verse as indication that God has not rejected the Jewish people; they still have a special place in His salvation plan for history.

Overcome Evil with God
Romans 12:1–21

12 I appeal to you therefore, brethren, by the mercies of God, to present your bodies as a living sacrifice, holy and acceptable to God, which is your spiritual worship. [2] Do not be conformed to this world but be transformed by the renewal of your mind, that you may prove what is the will of God, what is good and acceptable and perfect.

3 For by the grace given to me I bid every one among you not to think of himself more highly than he ought to think, but to think with sober judgment, each according to the measure of faith which God has assigned him. [4] For as in one body we have many members, and all the members do not have the same function, [5] so we, though many, are one body in Christ, and individually members one of another. [6] Having gifts that differ according to the grace given to us, let us use them: if prophecy, in proportion to our faith; [7] if service, in our serving; he who teaches, in his teaching; [8] he who exhorts, in his exhortation; he who contributes, in liberality; he who gives aid, with zeal; he who does acts of mercy, with cheerfulness.

9 Let love be genuine; hate what is evil, hold fast to what is good; [10] love one another with brotherly affection; outdo one another in showing honor. [11] Never flag in zeal, be aglow with the Spirit, serve the Lord. [12] Rejoice in your hope, be patient in tribulation, be constant in prayer. [13] Contribute to the needs of the saints, practice hospitality.

14 Bless those who persecute you; bless and do not curse them. [15] Rejoice with those who rejoice, weep with those who weep. [16] Live in harmony with one another; do not be haughty, but associate with the lowly; never be conceited. [17] Repay no one evil for evil, but take thought for what is noble in the sight of all. [18] If possible, so far as it depends upon you, live peaceably with all. [19] Beloved, never avenge yourselves, but leave it to the wrath of God; for it is written, "Vengeance is mine, I will repay, says the Lord." [20] No, "if your enemy is hungry, feed him; if he is thirsty, give him drink; for by so doing you will heap burning coals upon his head." [21] Do not be overcome by evil, but overcome evil with good.

12:1 Richard Francis Weymouth published in England, in 1902, *The New Testament in Modern Speech*, in which he set out to show "how we can with some degree of probability suppose that the inspired writer himself would have expressed his thoughts, had he been writing in our age and country." His version here reads: "I plead with you therefore, brethren, by all the compassions of God, to present all your faculties to Him as a living and holy sacrifice acceptable to Him." **12:16** Compare Proverbs 3:7 and 26:12. **12:17** This passage raises the question of the purpose and function of punishment: does it serve as a vehicle of vengeance, discourage repetition by the offender, rehabilitate the offender, deter others? Compare Proverbs 20:22. **12:9** Compare Leviticus 19:18. **12:20** Compare Proverbs 25:21–22.

We Owe Obedience to Civil Authority
Romans 13:1–7

13 Let every person be subject to the governing authorities. For there is no authority except from God, and those that exist have been instituted by God. ² Therefore he who resists the authorities resists what God has appointed, and those who resist will incur judgment. ³ For rulers are not a terror to good conduct, but to bad. Would you have no fear of him who is in authority? Then do what is good, and you will receive his approval, ⁴ for he is God's servant for your good. But if you do wrong, be afraid, for he does not bear the sword in vain; he is the servant of God to execute his wrath on the wrongdoer. ⁵ Therefore one must be subject, not only to avoid God's wrath but also for the sake of conscience. ⁶ For the same reason you also pay taxes, for the authorities are ministers of God, attending to this very thing. ⁷ Pay all of them their dues, taxes to whom taxes are due, revenue to whom revenue is due, respect to whom respect is due, honor to whom honor is due.

13:1 ff. On this and similar passages (Matthew 22:21; 1 Peter 2:13 f.; Titus 3:1), Luther based his doctrine of the two realms, the Kingdom of Christ and the Kingdom of the World, Church and State. The latter exists prior to, and independently of, the former. Luther did not regard marriage as a sacrament because it is a civil institution; it exists even where the Church has not come. So there are magistrates whose function it is to rule the civil order and whose decrees all citizens presumably should obey. Because the whole of society does not willingly submit to God's rule, it must be kept in order by the civil rulers. Insofar as they administer justice, the latter are agents of the divine purpose. They must therefore accept and exercise their responsibility without pride or self-glorification. "The godly judge," said Luther, "is distressed by the condemnation of the guilty and is truly sorry for the death which justice brings upon them." Luther did not intend, however, that in matters of conscience the Church should be subservient to the State. He believed that civil disobedience was in order when decrees of magistrates violated the Ten Commandments. In this he followed the example, as well as the teaching, of the apostles. Paul here enjoins subjection to the established authority, but when Paul was forbidden by the magistrates in Philippi to preach, he defied them (Acts 16:19–37). When the authorities sought to suppress their witness in Jerusalem, "Peter and the apostles answered, 'We must obey God rather than men'" (Acts 5:29). **13:1–10** Compare Matthew 22:21 and Acts 5:29.

Love Fulfills the Law
Romans 13:8–14

8 Owe no one anything, except to love one another; for he who loves his neighbor has fulfilled the law. ⁹ The commandments, "You shall not commit adultery, You shall not kill, You shall not steal, You shall not covet," and any other commandment, are summed up in this sentence, "You shall love your neighbor as yourself." ¹⁰ Love does no wrong to a neighbor; therefore love is the fulfilling of the law.

11 Besides this you know what hour it is, how it is full time now for you to wake from sleep. For salvation is nearer to us now than when we first believed; ¹² the night is far gone, the day is at hand. Let us then cast off the works of darkness and put on the armor of light; ¹³ let us conduct ourselves becomingly as in the day, not in reveling and drunkenness, not in debauchery and licentiousness, not in quarreling and jealousy. ¹⁴ But put on the Lord Jesus Christ, and make no provision for the flesh, to gratify its desires.

13:13–14 St. Augustine, in his *Confessions* (book 8, chapter 12), describes how he heard the voice of a child from a nearby house repeating over and over in a kind of singsong: "Take up and read." He took up a Bible and read these verses. The experience gave him confidence to turn from a life of dissipation.

Put No Hindrance in the Way of a Brother

There were tensions and antagonisms among the Jewish and Gentile followers of Christ over the Mosaic laws on diet and Sabbath; Paul preaches forbearance, harmony and cooperation.

Romans 14:1–21

14 As for the man who is weak in faith, welcome him, but not for disputes over opinions. ² One believes he may eat anything, while the weak man eats only vegetables. ³ Let not him who eats despise him

who abstains, and let not him who abstains pass judgment on him who eats; for God has welcomed him. ⁴ Who are you to pass judgment on the servant of another? It is before his own master that he stands or falls. And he will be upheld, for the Master is able to make him stand.

5 One man esteems one day as better than another, while another man esteems all days alike. Let every one be fully convinced in his own mind. ⁶ He who observes the day, observes it in honor of the Lord. He also who eats, eats in honor of the Lord, since he gives thanks to God; while he who abstains, abstains in honor of the Lord and gives thanks to God. ⁷ None of us lives to himself, and none of us dies to himself. ⁸ If we live, we live to the Lord, and if we die, we die to the Lord; so then, whether we live or whether we die, we are the Lord's. ⁹ For to this end Christ died and lived again, that he might be Lord both of the dead and of the living.

10 Why do you pass judgment on your brother? Or you, why do you despise your brother? For we shall all stand before the judgment seat of God; ¹¹ for it is written,

"As I live, says the Lord, every knee shall bow to me,
    and every tongue shall give praise to God."

¹² So each of us shall give account of himself to God.

13 Then let us no more pass judgment on one another, but rather decide never to put a stumbling block or hindrance in the way of a brother. ¹⁴ I know and am persuaded in the Lord Jesus that nothing is unclean in itself; but it is unclean for any one who thinks it unclean. ¹⁵ If your brother is being injured by what you eat, you are no longer walking in love. Do not let what you eat cause the ruin of one for whom Christ died. ¹⁶ So do not let what is good to you be spoken of as evil. ¹⁷ For the kingdom of God does not mean food and drink but righteousness and peace and joy in the Holy Spirit; ¹⁸ he who thus serves Christ is acceptable to God and approved by men. ¹⁹ Let us then pursue what makes for peace and for mutual up-building. ²⁰ Do not, for the sake of food, destroy the work of God. Everything is indeed clean, but it is wrong for any one to make others fall by what he eats; ²¹ it is right not to eat meat or drink wine or do anything that makes your brother stumble.

Paul Concludes His Letter

Paul had been collecting money for the needy converts in Jerusalem, and he was ready to bring it to them. He concludes his letter with news, personal notes, greetings for friends and converts (a long list of names—the oldest and most reliable evidence we have about the early Christian community at Rome). He adds: "Greet one another with a holy kiss"—a symbol of brotherly love which became a part of

the liturgical rites in church. This kiss is still used at Solemn Mass.
In the Catholic Church it is called the "Pax," or Kiss of Peace.

Romans 15:24–27

24 I hope to see you in passing as I go to Spain, and to be sped on
my journey there by you, once I have enjoyed your company for a
little. [25] At present, however, I am going to Jerusalem with aid for
the saints. [26] For Macedo'nia and Acha'ia have been pleased to
make some contribution for the poor among the saints at Jerusalem;
[27] they were pleased to do it, and indeed they are in debt to them, for
if the Gentiles have come to share in their spiritual blessings, they
ought also to be of service to them in material blessings.

The First Letter of Paul to the Corinthians

From Ephesus, on the coast of Asia Minor, Paul writes to the Christians in the important city of Corinth, Greece. He had earlier brought the Christian message to that city in one of his missionary journeys (Acts 18:1-11). Now he has heard that there are divisions among the Christian people; they have many questions and problems. In handling all their questions and problems, Paul provides a view of life in an early Christian community, composes a hymn on Christian love (chapter 13), and provides teaching on the resurrection of the body from death (chapter 15). There was evidently a lively correspondence between Paul and the Corinthians. The reference in 1 Corinthians 5:9 to an earlier letter is one of several evidences that three or four letters, written at different times, were combined in an early collection.

Paul Preaches Christ Crucified

1 Corinthians 1:10–31; 2:1–5

10 I appeal to you, brethren, by the name of our Lord Jesus Christ, that all of you agree and that there be no dissensions among you, but that you be united in the same mind and the same judgment. [11] For it has been reported to me by Chlo'e's people that there is quarreling among you, my brethren. [12] What I mean is that each one of you says, "I belong to Paul," or "I belong to Apol'los," or "I belong to Cephas," or "I belong to Christ." [13] Is Christ divided? Was Paul crucified for you? Or were you baptized in the name of Paul? [14] I am thankful that I baptized none of you except Crispus and Ga'ius; [15] lest any one should say that you were baptized in my name. [16] (I did baptize also the household of Steph'anas. Beyond that, I do not know whether I baptized any one else.) [17] For Christ did not send me to baptize but to preach the gospel, and not with eloquent wisdom, lest the cross of Christ be emptied of its power.

18 For the word of the cross is folly to those who are perishing, but to us who are being saved it is the power of God. [19] For it is written,

"I will destroy the wisdom of the wise,
and the cleverness of the clever I will thwart."

[20] Where is the wise man? Where is the scribe? Where is the debater of this age? Has not God made foolish the wisdom of the world?

²¹ For since, in the wisdom of God, the world did not know God through wisdom, it pleased God through the folly of what we preach to save those who believe. ²² For Jews demand signs and Greeks seek wisdom, ²³ but we preach Christ crucified, a stumbling block to Jews and folly to Gentiles, ²⁴ but to those who are called, both Jews and Greeks, Christ the power of God and the wisdom of God. ²⁵ For the foolishness of God is wiser than men, and the weakness of God is stronger than men.

26 For consider your call, brethren; not many of you were wise according to worldly standards, not many were powerful, not many were of noble birth; ²⁷ but God chose what is foolish in the world to shame the wise, God chose what is weak in the world to shame the strong, ²⁸ God chose what is low and despised in the world, even things that are not, to bring to nothing things that are, ²⁹ so that no human being might boast in the presence of God. ³⁰ He is the source of your life in Christ Jesus, whom God made our wisdom, our righteousness and sanctification and redemption; ³¹ therefore, as it is written, "Let him who boasts, boast of the Lord."

2 When I came to you, brethren, I did not come proclaiming to you the testimony of God in lofty words or wisdom. ² For I decided to know nothing among you except Jesus Christ and him crucified. ³ And I was with you in weakness and in much fear and trembling; ⁴ and my speech and my message were not in plausible words of wisdom, but in demonstration of the Spirit and power, ⁵ that your faith might not rest in the wisdom of men but in the power of God.

1:10 Rheims has *schisms*, King James Version has *divisions* for *dissensions*.

"You Are God's Temple"

In his interlocking style, Paul returns to the problem of divisions within the Church. Then with metaphors (field, building, temple) he explains that, because God's spirit dwells in the Christian, providing a special quality, dissensions are unseemly.

1 Corinthians 3:1–9, 16–17

3 But I, brethren, could not address you as spiritual men, but as men of the flesh, as babes in Christ. ² I fed you with milk, not solid food; for you were not ready for it; and even yet you are not ready, ³ for you are still of the flesh. For while there is jealousy and strife among you, are you not of the flesh, and behaving like ordinary men? ⁴ For when one says, "I belong to Paul," and another, "I belong to Apol′los," are you not merely men?

5 What then is Apol′los? What is Paul? Servants through whom you believed, as the Lord assigned to each. ⁶ I planted, Apol′los

watered, but God gave the growth. [7] So neither he who plants nor he who waters is anything, but only God who gives the growth. [8] He who plants and he who waters are equal, and each shall receive his wages according to his labor. [9] For we are fellow workers for God; you are God's field, God's building.

16 Do you not know that you are God's temple and that God's Spirit dwells in you? [17] If any one destroys God's temple, God will destroy him. For God's temple is holy, and that temple you are.

3:16 Here is religious motivation for care of the body, hygienic practices, physical education. Compare 1 Corinthians 6:19–20. It is on the basis of such appreciation for the body that some Christian groups oppose drinking of alcoholic beverages and smoking as a defilement of the body.

What Is to Be Done with a Wicked Brother?

A Christian had married his stepmother. Paul regards the deed as so seriously scandalous (setting such a bad example) that he orders the Christian leaders to dismiss the offender from the community. The process is what came to be known as excommunication (cutting a person off from participation in church privileges). Paul had written an earlier letter (5:9) which had been misinterpreted. He now clarifies his views.

1 Corinthians 5:1–13

5 It is actually reported that there is immorality among you, and of a kind that is not found even among pagans; for a man is living with his father's wife. [2] And you are arrogant! Ought you not rather to mourn? Let him who has done this be removed from among you.

3 For though absent in body I am present in spirit, and as if present, I have already pronounced judgment [4] in the name of the Lord Jesus on the man who has done such a thing. When you are assembled, and my spirit is present, with the power of our Lord Jesus, [5] you are to deliver this man to Satan for the destruction of the flesh, that his spirit may be saved in the day of the Lord Jesus.

6 Your boasting is not good. Do you not know that a little leaven leavens the whole lump? [7] Cleanse out the old leaven that you may be a new lump, as you really are unleavened. For Christ, our paschal lamb, has been sacrificed. [8] Let us, therefore, celebrate the festival, not with the old leaven, the leaven of malice and evil, but with the unleavened bread of sincerity and truth.

9 I wrote to you in my letter not to associate with immoral men; [10] not at all meaning the immoral of this world, or the greedy and robbers, or idolaters, since then you would need to go out of the world. [11] But rather I wrote to you not to associate with any one who

bears the name of brother if he is guilty of immorality or greed, or is an idolater, reviler, drunkard, or robber—not even to eat with such a one. [12] For what have I to do with judging outsiders? Is it not those inside the church whom you are to judge? [13] God judges those outside. "Drive out the wicked person from among you."

5:6–8 Paul interprets the removal of leaven from Jewish homes just before the Passover (cf. Exodus 12:19; 13:17; Deuteronomy 16:3) as a symbol of removing sin (the fermentation process regarded as a kind of corruption, and sin as the corruption of the soul). He calls upon Christians, when worshiping Christ, to cleanse themselves first from sin. **5:7** Some scholars believe this text suggests that some Christians, especially those of Asia Minor, observed Easter coincidentally with the Jewish Passover, which fell invariably on the fourteenth day of the lunar month Nisan. The rest of the Christian world insisted that Easter should always fall on the Sunday after Passover. The First Ecumenical Council, held at Nicaea in A.D. 325, resolved this conflict by making the regulation that Easter should be observed throughout the church on the Sunday following the full moon after the vernal equinox. The observance of Easter was thus separated from the Jewish Passover. The calculation of the date of Easter by reference to lunar cycles, however, meant that it would not be a fixed festival, but would shift constantly within the period March 22–April 25. In both the Protestant and Catholic world debate is still taking place on whether Easter should fall on a fixed date such as Sunday, April 8, or whether the present procedure should be continued. The Second Vatican Council declared in 1963 that the Catholic Church had no objections to a fixed date and revision of the calendar, if the seven-day week is preserved. Jews accept calendar reform only if the seventh day be preserved as the Sabbath.

The Body Is Sacred

The first sentence here is a proverbial way of expressing the idea that the Christians regarded themselves as freed from the rites of the Mosaic Law. Apparently some argued that satisfying sexual desire was like taking food to satisfy one's hunger. Paul rejects that idea. He holds that union with God makes the body holy, keeping man from immoral action.

1 Corinthians 6:12–20

12 "All things are lawful for me," but not all things are helpful. "All things are lawful for me," but I will not be enslaved by anything. [13] "Food is meant for the stomach and the stomach for food"—and God will destroy both one and the other. The body is not meant for immorality, but for the Lord, and the Lord for the body. [14] And God raised the Lord and will also raise us up by his

power. [15]Do you not know that your bodies are members of Christ?
Shall I therefore take the members of Christ and make them
members of a prostitute? Never! [16]Do you not know that he who
joins himself to a prostitute becomes one body with her? For, as it is
written, "The two shall become one." [17]But he who is united to the
Lord becomes one spirit with him. [18]Shun immorality. Every other
sin which a man commits is outside the body; but the immoral man
sins against his own body. [19]Do you not know that your body is a
temple of the Holy Spirit within you, which you have from God?
You are not your own; [20]you were bought with a price. So glorify
God in your body.

Advice for the Married
1 Corinthians 7:1–16

7 Now concerning the matters about which you wrote. It is well for a
man not to touch a woman. [2]But because of the temptation to
immorality, each man should have his own wife and each woman her
own husband. [3]The husband should give to his wife her conjugal
rights, and likewise the wife to her husband. [4]For the wife does not
rule over her own body, but the husband does; likewise the husband
does not rule over his own body, but the wife does. [5]Do not refuse
one another except perhaps by agreement for a season, that you may
devote yourselves to prayer; but then come together again, lest Satan
tempt you through lack of self-control. [6]I say this by way of
concession, not of command. [7]I wish that all were as I myself am.
But each has his own special gift from God, one of one kind and one
of another.

8 To the unmarried and the widows I say that it is well for them
to remain single as I do. [9]But if they cannot exercise self-control,
they should marry. For it is better to marry than to be aflame with
passion.

10 To the married I give charge, not I but the Lord, that the wife
should not separate from her husband [11](but if she does, let her
remain single or else be reconciled to her husband)—and that the
husband should not divorce his wife.

12 To the rest I say, not the Lord, that if any brother has a wife
who is an unbeliever, and she consents to live with him, he should
not divorce her. [13]If any woman has a husband who is an unbeliever,
and he consents to live with her, she should not divorce him. [14]For
the unbelieving husband is consecrated through his wife, and the
unbelieving wife is consecrated through her husband. Otherwise,
your children would be unclean, but as it is they are holy. [15]But if
the unbelieving partner desires to separate, let it be so; in such a case

the brother or sister is not bound. For God has called us to peace. ¹⁶Wife, how do you know whether you will save your husband? Husband, how do you know whether you will save your wife?

7:9 Older translations: "it is better to marry than to burn." **7:15** What is described here has come to be known in Roman Catholic Church law as the "Pauline privilege."

Lead the Life Assigned by God
1 Corinthians 7:17–24

17 Only, let every one lead the life which the Lord has assigned to him, and in which God has called him. This is my rule in all the churches. ¹⁸Was any one at the time of his call already circumcised? Let him not seek to remove the marks of circumcision. Was any one at the time of his call uncircumcised? Let him not seek circumcision. ¹⁹For neither circumcision counts for anything nor uncircumcision, but keeping the commandments of God. ²⁰Every one should remain in the state in which he was called. ²¹Were you a slave when called? Never mind. But if you can gain your freedom, avail yourself of the opportunity. ²²For he who was called in the Lord as a slave is a freed-man of the Lord. Likewise he who was free when called is a slave of Christ. ²³You were bought with a price; do not become slaves of men. ²⁴So, brethren, in whatever state each was called, there let him remain with God.

7:23 Arguments over slavery have made use of this passage. Compare Philemon 1:16 ff.

Advice for the Unmarried
1 Corinthians 7:25–35, 39–40

25 Now concerning the unmarried, I have no command of the Lord, but I give my opinion as one who by the Lord's mercy is trustworthy. ²⁶I think that in view of the impending distress it is well for a person to remain as he is. ²⁷Are you bound to a wife? Do not seek to be free. Are you free from a wife? Do not seek marriage. ²⁸But if you marry, you do not sin, and if a girl marries she does not sin. Yet those who marry will have worldly troubles, and I would spare you that. ²⁹I mean, brethren, the appointed time has grown very short; from now on, let those who have wives live as though they had none, ³⁰and those who mourn as though they were not mourning, and those who rejoice as though they were not rejoicing, and those who buy as though they had no goods, ³¹and those who deal with the world as though they had no dealings with it. For the form of this world is passing away.

32 I want you to be free from anxieties. The unmarried man is

anxious about the affairs of the Lord, how to please the Lord; [33] but the married man is anxious about worldly affairs, how to please his wife, [34] and his interests are divided. And the unmarried woman or girl is anxious about the affairs of the Lord, how to be holy in body and spirit; but the married woman is anxious about worldly affairs, how to please her husband. [35] I say this for your own benefit, not to lay any restraint upon you, but to promote good order and to secure your undivided devotion to the Lord.

39 A wife is bound to her husband as long as he lives. If the husband dies, she is free to be married to whom she wishes, only in the Lord. [40] But in my judgment she is happier if she remains as she is. And I think that I have the Spirit of God.

"For the Sake of the Gospel"
1 Corinthians 9:19–27

19 For though I am free from all men, I have made myself a slave to all, that I might win the more. [20] To the Jews I became as a Jew, in order to win Jews; to those under the law I became as one under the law—though not being myself under the law—that I might win those under the law. [21] To those outside the law I became as one outside the law—not being without law toward God but under the law of Christ—that I might win those outside the law. [22] To the weak I became weak, that I might win the weak. I have become all things to all men, that I might by all means save some. [23] I do it all for the sake of the gospel, that I may share in its blessings.

24 Do you not know that in a race all the runners compete, but only one receives the prize? So run that you may obtain it. [25] Every athlete exercises self-control in all things. They do it to receive a perishable wreath, but we an imperishable. [26] Well, I do not run aimlessly, I do not box as one beating the air; [27] but I pommel my body and subdue it, lest after preaching to others I myself should be disqualified.

9:23 Rheims: that I may be made partaker thereof. King James Version: that I might be partaker thereof with you.

God Will Help When Man Is Tempted
1 Corinthians 10:12–13

12 Therefore let any one who thinks that he stands take heed lest he fall. [13] No temptation has overtaken you that is not common to man. God is faithful, and he will not let you be tempted beyond your strength, but with the temptation will also provide the way of escape, that you may be able to endure it.

Do All to the Glory of God
1 Corinthians 10:31–33

31 So, whether you eat or drink, or whatever you do, do all to the glory of God. ³²Give no offense to Jews or to Greeks or to the church of God, ³³just as I try to please all men in everything I do, not seeking my own advantage, but that of many, that they may be saved.

Women Are to Pray with Covered Head

Paul answers questions about regulations for liturgical assemblies. He bases his answers on what he understands to be the nature of things (as he sees it angels, too, are interested in the order of things). He backs this up with an appeal to the custom in the Christian community. On the basis of this passage it is required in some churches and customary in others that women wear head coverings at worship.

1 Corinthians 11:3–16

3 But I want you to understand that the head of every man is Christ, the head of a woman is her husband, and the head of Christ is God. ⁴Any man who prays or prophesies with his head covered dishonors his head, ⁵but any woman who prays or prophesies with her head unveiled dishonors her head—it is the same as if her head were shaven. ⁶For if a woman will not veil herself, then she should cut off her hair; but if it is disgraceful for a woman to be shorn or shaven, let her wear a veil. ⁷For a man ought not to cover his head, since he is the image and glory of God; but woman is the glory of man. ⁸(For man was not made from woman, but woman from man. ⁹Neither was man created for woman, but woman for man.) ¹⁰That is why a woman ought to have a veil on her head, because of the angels. ¹¹(Nevertheless, in the Lord woman is not independent of man nor man of woman; ¹²for as woman was made from man, so man is now born of woman. And all things are from God.) ¹³Judge for yourselves; is it proper for a woman to pray to God with her head uncovered? ¹⁴Does not nature itself teach you that for a man to wear long hair is degrading to him, ¹⁵but if a woman has long hair, it is her pride? For her hair is given to her for a covering. ¹⁶If any one is disposed to be contentious, we recognize no other practice, nor do the churches of God.

11:4 ff. Among the early Christians, women wore veils at prayer and the men prayed bareheaded. It was probably in part to distinguish themselves from the Christian fashion in prayer that the rabbis in the Talmudic period initiated prayer with head covered. The practice may be due also to the customs of dress derived from the

Babylonian period (A.D. 200–400). In recent years Reform Jews have abandoned the practice and conduct their services bareheaded.

11:11–12 This is paralleled by a Midrashic statement: "Neither man without woman, nor woman without man, and neither of them without the divine spirit" (*Genesis Rabbah* 8:9).

How Should the Eucharist Be Celebrated?
1 Corinthians 11:23–29

23 For I received from the Lord what I also delivered to you, that the Lord Jesus on the night when he was betrayed took bread, ²⁴ and when he had given thanks, he broke it, and said, "This is my body which is for you. Do this in remembrance of me." ²⁵ In the same way also the cup, after supper, saying, "This cup is the new covenant in my blood. Do this, as often as you drink it, in remembrance of me." ²⁶ For as often as you eat this bread and drink the cup, you proclaim the Lord's death until he comes.

27 Whoever, therefore, eats the bread or drinks the cup of the Lord in an unworthy manner will be guilty of profaning the body and blood of the Lord. ²⁸ Let a man examine himself, and so eat of the bread and drink of the cup. ²⁹ For any one who eats and drinks without discerning the body eats and drinks judgment upon himself.

11:23 The Roman Catholic and Orthodox Catholic Churches use this passage in teaching that the Eucharist is really the body and blood of Jesus; that what Jesus is reported doing with the bread and cup is what the Church represents in the Mass each day; that the Mass is a sacrifice, one with the sacrifice of the cross; that in the words "Do this in remembrance of me" Jesus ordained the apostles priests to perpetuate the sacrifice (and so ordination to the priesthood always takes place during a Mass). Protestant views differ on all these points. **11:25** Christ's death on the cross as a sacrificial victim by whose blood the New Covenant is established parallels the account of the covenant sacrifice made by Moses in Exodus 24:8. In the letter to the Hebrews, the death of Christ is set forth as the ultimate sacrifice which surpasses and supplants all the sacrifices of the Old Testament. Although some Orthodox Jews hope that the sacrificial system in a temple in Jerusalem will someday be re-established, most Jews today reject the view that a blood sacrifice is necessary to make atonement with God. "A broken heart and a contrite spirit" are acceptable sacrifices to God.

Christians Are the Body of Christ
1 Corinthians 12:12–31

12 For just as the body is one and has many members, and all the members of the body, though many, are one body, so it is with Christ. ¹³ For by one Spirit we were all baptized into one

body—Jews or Greeks, slaves or free—and all were made to drink of one Spirit.

14 For the body does not consist of one member but of many. [15] If the foot should say, "Because I am not a hand, I do not belong to the body," that would not make it any less a part of the body. [16] And if the ear should say, "Because I am not an eye, I do not belong to the body," that would not make it any less a part of the body. [17] If the whole body were an eye, where would be the hearing? If the whole body were an ear, where would be the sense of smell? [18] But as it is, God arranged the organs in the body, each one of them, as he chose. [19] If all were a single organ, where would the body be? [20] As it is, there are many parts, yet one body. [21] The eye cannot say to the hand, "I have no need of you," nor again the head to the feet, "I have no need of you." [22] On the contrary, the parts of the body which seem to be weaker are indispensable, [23] and those parts of the body which we think less honorable we invest with the greater honor, and our unpresentable parts are treated with greater modesty, [24] which our more presentable parts do not require. But God has so adjusted the body, giving the greater honor to the inferior part, [25] that there may be no discord in the body, but that the members may have the same care for one another. [26] If one member suffers, all suffer together; if one member is honored, all rejoice together.

27 Now you are the body of Christ and individually members of it. [28] And God has appointed in the church first apostles, second prophets, third teachers, then workers of miracles, then healers, helpers, administrators, speakers in various kinds of tongues. [29] Are all apostles? Are all prophets? Are all teachers? Do all work miracles? [30] Do all possess gifts of healing? Do all speak with tongues? Do all interpret? [31] But earnestly desire the higher gifts.

And I will show you a still more excellent way.

The Greatest of Gifts Is Love
1 Corinthians 13:1–13

13 If I speak in the tongues of men and of angels, but have not love, I am a noisy gong or a clanging cymbal. [2] And if I have prophetic powers, and understand all mysteries and all knowledge, and if I have all faith, so as to remove mountains, but have not love, I am nothing. [3] If I give away all I have, and if I deliver my body to be burned, but have not love, I gain nothing.

4 Love is patient and kind; love is not jealous or boastful; [5] it is not arrogant or rude. Love does not insist on its own way; it is not irritable or resentful; [6] it does not rejoice at wrong, but rejoices in the

right. [7] Love bears all things, believes all things, hopes all things, endures all things.

8 Love never ends; as for prophecies, they will pass away; as for tongues, they will cease; as for knowledge, it will pass away. [9] For our knowledge is imperfect and our prophecy is imperfect; [10] but when the perfect comes, the imperfect will pass away. [11] When I was a child, I spoke like a child, I thought like a child, I reasoned like a child; when I became a man, I gave up childish ways. [12] For now we see in a mirror dimly, but then face to face. Now I know in part; then I shall understand fully, even as I have been fully understood. [13] So faith, hope, love abide, these three; but the greatest of these is love.

13:1 Bishops' Bible, Rheims and King James Version have "charity" throughout for "love."

Speak to Instruct
1 Corinthians 14:1–4, 13–19, 26–33

14 Make love your aim, and earnestly desire the spiritual gifts, especially that you may prophesy. [2] For one who speaks in a tongue speaks not to men but to God; for no one understands him, but he utters mysteries in the Spirit. [3] On the other hand, he who prophesies speaks to men for their up-building and encouragement and consolation. [4] He who speaks in a tongue edifies himself, but he who prophesies edifies the church.

13 Therefore, he who speaks in a tongue should pray for the power to interpret. [14] For if I pray in a tongue, my spirit prays but my mind is unfruitful. [15] What am I to do? I will pray with the spirit and I will pray with the mind also; I will sing with the spirit and I will sing with the mind also. [16] Otherwise, if you bless with the spirit, how can any one in the position of an outsider say the "Amen" to your thanksgiving when he does not know what you are saying? [17] For you may give thanks well enough, but the other man is not edified. [18] I thank God that I speak in tongues more than you all; [19] nevertheless, in church I would rather speak five words with my mind, in order to instruct others, than ten thousand words in a tongue.

26 What then, brethren? When you come together, each one has a hymn, a lesson, a revelation, a tongue, or an interpretation. Let all things be done for edification. [27] If any speak in a tongue, let there be only two or at most three, and each in turn; and let one interpret. [28] But if there is no one to interpret, let each of them keep silence in church and speak to himself and to God. [29] Let two or three prophets speak, and let the others weigh what is said. [30] If a revelation is made to another sitting by, let the first be silent. [31] For you can all

prophesy one by one, so that all may learn and all be encouraged; [32] and the spirits of prophets are subject to prophets. [33] For God is not a God of confusion but of peace.

Paul holds that "speaking in tongues" or the "gift of tongues," utterances in languages unintelligible to the community, should be considered subordinate to prophecy (teaching or exhorting under special inspiration of God). What Paul says about women keeping quiet in church is one reason why some Christian churches do not have ordained women clergy.

Paul Summarizes His Message
1 Corinthians 15 : 1–11

15 Now I would remind you, brethren, in what terms I preached to you the gospel, which you received, in which you stand, [2] by which you are saved, if you hold it fast—unless you believed in vain.

3 For I delivered to you as of first importance what I also received, that Christ died for our sins in accordance with the scriptures, [4] that he was buried, that he was raised on the third day in accordance with the scriptures, [5] and that he appeared to Cephas, then to the twelve. [6] Then he appeared to more than five hundred brethren at one time, most of whom are still alive, though some have fallen asleep. [7] Then he appeared to James, then to all the apostles. [8] Last of all, as to one untimely born, he appeared also to me. [9] For I am the least of the apostles, unfit to be called an apostle, because I persecuted the church of God. [10] But by the grace of God I am what I am, and his grace toward me was not in vain. On the contrary, I worked harder than any of them, though it was not I, but the grace of God which is with me. [11] Whether then it was I or they, so we preach and so you believed.

15 : 3 Paul here gives what has been called his kerygma, the kernel of the message that he proclaimed as a herald (*kerygma* from *keryx*, Greek word for herald, refers to the thing spoken by the herald). By Scriptures Paul means that portion of the Bible Christians today call the Old Testament. He holds that Christ fulfilled Old Testament promises. Compare Isaiah 53 : 5– 12. **15 : 4** Compare Psalm 16 : 8– 10.

The Dead Shall Rise
1 Corinthians 15 : 12– 24, 35– 38, 51– 55

12 Now if Christ is preached as raised from the dead, how can some of you say that there is no resurrection of the dead? [13] But if there is no resurrection of the dead, then Christ has not been raised; [14] if Christ has not been raised, then our preaching is in vain and your faith is in vain. [15] We are even found to be misrepresenting God,

because we testified of God that he raised Christ, whom he did not raise if it is true that the dead are not raised. ¹⁶ For if the dead are not raised, then Christ has not been raised. ¹⁷ If Christ has not been raised, your faith is futile and you are still in your sins. ¹⁸ Then those also who have fallen asleep in Christ have perished. ¹⁹ If for this life only we have hoped in Christ, we are of all men most to be pitied.

20 But in fact Christ has been raised from the dead, the first fruits of those who have fallen asleep. ²¹ For as by a man came death, by a man has come also the resurrection of the dead. ²² For as in Adam all die, so also in Christ shall all be made alive. ²³ But each in his own order: Christ the first fruits, then at his coming those who belong to Christ. ²⁴ Then comes the end, when he delivers the kingdom to God the Father after destroying every rule and every authority and power.

35 But some one will ask, "How are the dead raised? With what kind of body do they come?" ³⁶ You foolish man! What you sow does not come to life unless it dies. ³⁷ And what you sow is not the body which is to be, but a bare kernel, perhaps of wheat or of some other grain. ³⁸ But God gives it a body as he has chosen, and to each kind of seed its own body.

51 Lo! I tell you a mystery. We shall not all sleep, but we shall all be changed, ⁵² in a moment, in the twinkling of an eye, at the last trumpet. For the trumpet will sound, and the dead will be raised imperishable, and we shall be changed. ⁵³ For this perishable nature must put on the imperishable, and this mortal nature must put on immortality. ⁵⁴ When the perishable puts on the imperishable, and the mortal puts on immortality, then shall come to pass the saying that is written:

"Death is swallowed up in victory."
⁵⁵ "O death, where is thy victory?
    O death, where is thy sting?"

15:14 This passage (14–55) is often read at funerals. **15:22** It is also a traditional Jewish doctrine that there will be a resurrection of the dead at the end-time when the Messiah will appear. Reform Jews, however, have abandoned this idea and hold instead to a conception of the immortality of the soul. **15:23** ff. At the conclusion of the Passover ceremony, contemporary Jews sing an ancient folksong, "One Only Kid." This song contains a narrative symbolic of man's earthly plight, and concludes with an expression of God's victory, at end-time, over the forces of man and nature—the last enemy to be destroyed will be death. **15:35–38** Paul's conception that in the resurrection men will be given bodily form and will be clothed is similar to the view held by the Pharisees. The Talmud records this description by Rabbi Meir: "If a grain of wheat which is buried naked sprouted forth in many robes, how much more so the righteous who are buried in their raiment" (*Sanhedrin* 90b). Therefore, Orthodox Jews oppose autopsy after death, which mutilates the body, and cremation. It is customary, too, for Orthodox Jews to bedeck their deceased in special shrouds at burial. **15:54–55** Compare Isaiah 25:8; Hosea 13:14.

The Second Letter of Paul to the Corinthians

Paul had many troubles with Corinthians. Some charged that he was not an authentic apostle because he had not seen Jesus in the flesh. From Macedonia he wrote this letter, a vigorous defense of his work and his beliefs. It is the most intensely personal letter in our collection of Paul's writings; in it he reveals his mystical experiences.

Christians Long for Life Eternal

2 Corinthians 4:5–5:5

5 For what we preach is not ourselves, but Jesus Christ as Lord, with ourselves as your servants for Jesus' sake. [6] For it is the God who said, "Let light shine out of darkness," who has shone in our hearts to give the light of the knowledge of the glory of God in the face of Christ.

7 But we have this treasure in earthen vessels, to show that the transcendent power belongs to God and not to us. [8] We are afflicted in every way, but not crushed; perplexed, but not driven to despair; [9] persecuted, but not forsaken; struck down, but not destroyed; [10] always carrying in the body the death of Jesus, so that the life of Jesus may also be manifested in our bodies. [11] For while we live we are always being given up to death for Jesus' sake, so that the life of Jesus may be manifested in our mortal flesh. [12] So death is at work in us, but life in you.

13 Since we have the same spirit of faith as he had who wrote, "I believed, and so I spoke," we too believe, and so we speak, [14] knowing that he who raised the Lord Jesus will raise us also with Jesus and bring us with you into his presence. [15] For it is all for your sake, so that as grace extends to more and more people it may increase thanksgiving, to the glory of God.

16 So we do not lose heart. Though our outer nature is wasting away, our inner nature is being renewed every day. [17] For this slight momentary affliction is preparing for us an eternal weight of glory beyond all comparison, [18] because we look not to the things that are seen but to the things that are unseen; for the things that are seen are transient, but the things that are unseen are eternal.

5 For we know that if the earthly tent we live in is destroyed, we have a building from God, a house not made with hands, eternal in the heavens. [2] Here indeed we groan, and long to put on our heavenly dwelling, [3] so that by putting it on we may not be found

naked. [4] For while we are still in this tent, we sigh with anxiety; not that we would be unclothed, but that we would be further clothed, so that what is mortal may be swallowed up by life. [5] He who has prepared us for this very thing is God, who has given us the Spirit as a guarantee.

5:3 Paul hopes that he will be given his new body before he has to put off his present one. He hopes that he may become immortal without dying first.

Paul Is an Ambassador of Christ

Paul has just asked the Corinthians to contribute to the collection for poor Christians in Jerusalem. The "saints" in verse 12 are the Christians; Paul regards them as sanctified on account of the gifts they have received from God.

2 Corinthians 9:6–15

6 The point is this: he who sows sparingly will also reap sparingly, and he who sows bountifully will also reap bountifully. [7] Each one must do as he has made up his mind, not reluctantly or under compulsion, for God loves a cheerful giver. [8] And God is able to provide you with every blessing in abundance, so that you may always have enough of everything and may provide in abundance for every good work. [9] As it is written,

"He scatters abroad, he gives to the poor;
his righteousness endures for ever."

[10] He who supplies seed to the sower and bread for food will supply and multiply your resources and increase the harvest of your righteousness. [11] You will be enriched in every way for great generosity, which through us will produce thanksgiving to God; [12] for the rendering of this service not only supplies the wants of the saints but also overflows in many thanksgivings to God. [13] Under the test of this service, you will glorify God by your obedience in acknowledging the gospel of Christ, and by the generosity of your contribution for them and for all others; [14] while they long for you and pray for you, because of the surpassing grace of God in you. [15] Thanks be to God for his inexpressible gift!

9:9 Compare Psalm 112:9.

God's Power Is Made Perfect in Weakness

Apparently some were comparing Paul unfavorably with other preachers they had heard. Paul defends himself by "boasting" of his sufferings. When he describes his visions and revelations (12:2–4), Paul speaks of himself in the third person. By the "third heaven" he means the highest bliss.

2 Corinthians 11:1–6, 16–33; 12:1–10

11 I wish you would bear with me in a little foolishness. Do bear with me! ²I feel a divine jealousy for you, for I betrothed you to Christ to present you as a pure bride to her one husband. ³But I am afraid that as the serpent deceived Eve by his cunning, your thoughts will be led astray from a sincere and pure devotion to Christ. ⁴For if some one comes and preaches another Jesus than the one we preached, or if you receive a different spirit from the one you received, or if you accept a different gospel from the one you accepted, you submit to it readily enough. ⁵I think that I am not in the least inferior to these superlative apostles. ⁶Even if I am unskilled in speaking, I am not in knowledge; in every way we have made this plain to you in all things.

16 I repeat, let no one think me foolish; but even if you do, accept me as a fool, so that I too may boast a little. ¹⁷(What I am saying I say not with the Lord's authority but as a fool, in this boastful confidence; ¹⁸since many boast of worldly things, I too will boast.) ¹⁹For you gladly bear with fools, being wise yourselves! ²⁰For you bear it if a man makes slaves of you, or preys upon you, or takes advantage of you, or puts on airs, or strikes you in the face. ²¹To my shame, I must say, we were too weak for that!

But whatever any one dares to boast of—I am speaking as a fool—I also dare to boast of that. ²²Are they Hebrews? So am I. Are they Israelites? So am I. Are they descendants of Abraham? So am I. ²³Are they servants of Christ? I am a better one—I am talking like a madman—with far greater labors, far more imprisonments, with countless beatings, and often near death. ²⁴Five times I have received at the hands of the Jews the forty lashes less one. ²⁵Three times I have been beaten with rods; once I was stoned. Three times I have been shipwrecked; a night and a day I have been adrift at sea; ²⁶on frequent journeys, in danger from rivers, danger from robbers, danger from my own people, danger from Gentiles, danger in the city, danger in the wilderness, danger at sea, danger from false brethren; ²⁷in toil and hardship, through many a sleepless night, in hunger and thirst, often without food, in cold and exposure. ²⁸And, apart from other things, there is the daily pressure upon me of my anxiety for all the churches. ²⁹Who is weak, and I am not weak? Who is made to fall, and I am not indignant?

30 If I must boast, I will boast of the things that show my weakness. ³¹The God and Father of the Lord Jesus, he who is blessed for ever, knows that I do not lie. ³²At Damascus, the governor under King Ar′etas guarded the city of Damascus in order

to seize me, ³³ but I was let down in a basket through a window in the wall, and escaped his hands.

12 I must boast; there is nothing to be gained by it, but I will go on to visions and revelations of the Lord. ²I know a man in Christ who fourteen years ago was caught up to the third heaven—whether in the body or out of the body I do not know, God knows. ³And I know that this man was caught up into Paradise—whether in the body or out of the body I do not know, God knows—⁴and he heard things that cannot be told, which man may not utter. ⁵On behalf of this man I will boast, but on my own behalf I will not boast, except of my weaknesses. ⁶Though if I wish to boast, I shall not be a fool, for I shall be speaking the truth. But I refrain from it, so that no one may think more of me than he sees in me or hears from me. ⁷And to keep me from being too elated by the abundance of revelations, a thorn was given me in the flesh, a messenger of Satan, to harass me, to keep me from being too elated. ⁸Three times I besought the Lord about this, that it should leave me; ⁹but he said to me, "My grace is sufficient for you, for my power is made perfect in weakness." I will all the more gladly boast of my weaknesses, that the power of Christ may rest upon me. ¹⁰For the sake of Christ, then, I am content with weaknesses, insults, hardships, persecutions, and calamities; for when I am weak, then I am strong.

11:2 *Bride of Christ:* We find here invoked the Hebrew image of a marital relationship between Israel and God (cf. Hosea 2:19). Paul replaces this with a conception of the Church betrothed to Christ.

He Gives a Warning and a Blessing

Paul makes it clear that he wants the Christians to correct themselves. The "holy kiss" he refers to is the liturgical embrace we have already read about at the end of the letter to the Romans. The final verse here is the fullest of the blessings that Paul gives at the end of his letters. It has often been observed that the order in this formula is significant: the grace of Jesus leads a person toward the love of God, and the love of God communicated by the Spirit produces fellowship.

2 Corinthians 13:10–14

10 I write this while I am away from you, in order that when I come I may not have to be severe in my use of the authority which the Lord has given me for building up and not for tearing down.

11 Finally, brethren, farewell. Mend your ways, heed my appeal, agree with one another, live in peace, and the God of love and peace will be with you. ¹²Greet one another with a holy kiss. ¹³All the saints greet you.

14 The grace of the Lord Jesus Christ and the love of God and the fellowship of the Holy Spirit be with you all.

The Letter of Paul to the Galatians

In this letter Paul deals with a crisis that had arisen among the churches in Galatia, in central Asia Minor. Some teachers were telling the Galatians that for salvation it was necessary to be circumcised and to observe the prescriptions of the Mosaic Law. In other words, they held that Gentiles had to become both Jews and Christians. This teaching distressed Paul; his letter in answer to it is emotional and sentences are sometimes not completed. The letter has been called the Magna Charta of Christian liberty and the declaration of Christian independence. Some scholars think the letter was written before the Council of Jerusalem took place in A.D. 49 (cf. Acts 15) and that it is therefore the first of Paul's letters. More scholars hold, however, that Paul brought the message of Jesus to Galatia about A.D. 52 and wrote this letter about three years later. He may have written from Ephesus or Antioch.

Justification Is by Faith in Jesus

After insisting upon his apostolic authority and reviewing his credentials, Paul comes to this interesting episode. The sharpness of the division among the early Christians over the observance of the Mosaic Law is here graphically illustrated. Church historians recall this passage when describing differences of opinion among later church authorities.

Galatians 2:1–2, 7–16, 20–21

2 Then after fourteen years I went up again to Jerusalem with Barnabas, taking Titus along with me. [2] I went up by revelation; and I laid before them (but privately before those who were of repute) the gospel which I preach among the Gentiles, lest somehow I should be running or had run in vain.

7 But on the contrary, when they saw that I had been entrusted with the gospel to the uncircumcised, just as Peter had been entrusted with the gospel to the circumcised [8] (for he who worked through Peter for the mission to the circumcised worked through me also for the Gentiles), [9] and when they perceived the grace that was given to me, James and Cephas and John, who were reputed to be pillars, gave to me and Barnabas the right hand of fellowship, that we should go to the Gentiles and they to the circumcised; [10] only they would have us remember the poor, which very thing I was eager to do.

11 But when Cephas came to Antioch I opposed him to his face,

because he stood condemned. [12] For before certain men came from James, he ate with the Gentiles; but when they came he drew back and separated himself, fearing the circumcision party. [13] And with him the rest of the Jews acted insincerely, so that even Barnabas was carried away by their insincerity. [14] But when I saw that they were not straightforward about the truth of the gospel, I said to Cephas before them all, "If you, though a Jew, live like a Gentile and not like a Jew, how can you compel the Gentiles to live like Jews?" [15] We ourselves, who are Jews by birth and not Gentile sinners, [16] yet who know that a man is not justified by works of the law but through faith in Jesus Christ, even we have believed in Christ Jesus, in order to be justified by faith in Christ, and not by works of the law, because by works of the law shall no one be justified.

20 I have been crucified with Christ; it is no longer I who live, but Christ who lives in me; and the life I now live in the flesh I live by faith in the Son of God, who loved me and gave himself for me. [21] I do not nullify the grace of God; for if justification were through the law, then Christ died to no purpose.

> **2:11** Tyndale: for he was worthy to be blamed. Rheims: because he was reprehensible. King James Version: because he was *to be* blamed. **2:16** This theme is repeated in Ephesians 2:8. On June 11, 1738, John Wesley (1703–1791) the founder of Methodism preached from this text before the University of Oxford; from that day on, it was the keynote of his ministry. See also note on Romans 3:21 ff.

There Is Neither Jew Nor Greek

Paul explains his understanding of the relation between the Law of Moses and the Law of Christ: the Law was intended to lead to Jesus. Those who proclaim a faith in Jesus enter the covenant of Abraham.

Galatians 3:16–29

16 Now the promises were made to Abraham and to his offspring. It does not say, "And to offsprings," referring to many; but, referring to one, "And to your offspring," which is Christ. [17] This is what I mean: the law, which came four hundred and thirty years afterward, does not annul a covenant previously ratified by God, so as to make the promise void. [18] For if the inheritance is by the law, it is no longer by promise; but God gave it to Abraham by a promise.

19 Why then the law? It was added because of transgressions, till the offspring should come to whom the promise had been made; and it was ordained by angels through an intermediary. [20] Now an intermediary implies more than one; but God is one.

21 Is the law then against the promises of God? Certainly not; for if a law had been given which could make alive, then righteousness

would indeed be by the law. ²² But the scripture consigned all things to sin, that what was promised to faith in Jesus Christ might be given to those who believe.

23 Now before faith came, we were confined under the law, kept under restraint until faith should be revealed. ²⁴ So that the law was our custodian until Christ came, that we might be justified by faith. ²⁵ But now that faith has come, we are no longer under a custodian; ²⁶ for in Christ Jesus you are all sons of God, through faith. ²⁷ For as many of you as were baptized into Christ have put on Christ. ²⁸ There is neither Jew nor Greek, there is neither slave nor free, there is neither male nor female; for you are all one in Christ Jesus. ²⁹ And if you are Christ's, then you are Abraham's offspring, heirs according to promise.

3:17 Older translations have "promise" for "covenant." **3:25** Tyndale to King James Version: schoolmaster. Rheims: paedagogue ASV: tutor. **3:28** This passage is cited by Christians who claim that the Church must make no distinction between persons on the basis of race, class and sex; and that the Church must accept in its fellowship Christians of every race.

Christians Should Live by the Spirit
Galatians 5:13–26

13 For you were called to freedom, brethren; only do not use your freedom as an opportunity for the flesh, but through love be servants of one another. ¹⁴ For the whole law is fulfilled in one word, "You shall love your neighbor as yourself." ¹⁵ But if you bite and devour one another take heed that you are not consumed by one another.

16 But I say, walk by the Spirit, and do not gratify the desires of the flesh. ¹⁷ For the desires of the flesh are against the Spirit, and the desires of the Spirit are against the flesh; for these are opposed to each other, to prevent you from doing what you would. ¹⁸ But if you are led by the Spirit you are not under the law. ¹⁹ Now the works of the flesh are plain: immorality, impurity, licentiousness, ²⁰ idolatry, sorcery, enmity, strife, jealousy, anger, selfishness, dissension, party spirit, ²¹ envy, drunkenness, carousing, and the like. I warn you, as I warned you before, that those who do such things shall not inherit the kingdom of God. ²² But the fruit of the Spirit is love, joy, peace, patience, kindness, goodness, faithfulness, ²³ gentleness, self-control; against such there is no law. ²⁴ And those who belong to Christ Jesus have crucified the flesh with its passions and desires.

25 If we live by the Spirit, let us also walk by the Spirit. ²⁶ Let us have no self-conceit, no provoking of one another, no envy of one another.

5:13 King James Version: For, brethren, ye have been called unto liberty; only *use* not liberty for an occasion to the flesh, but by love serve one another. By preaching freedom from the Torah and the ceremonial laws Paul created a breach between Judaism and Christianity and set in motion the procedures by which the Hebrew—Christian sect organized itself into a separate religion. In the Jewish view it was held "thou findest no free man except one who occupies himself in the study of the Law" (*Aboth* 6:2). Jews still believe that "obedience to the Law is the most perfect freedom." Although Paul proclaimed the Christian's freedom from the Mosaic Law, it is clear that he gave to licentiousness no license; compare 5:16–24.

Whatever a Man Sows, That He Will Also Reap
Galatians 6:1–18

6 Brethren, if a man is overtaken in any trespass, you who are spiritual should restore him in a spirit of gentleness. Look to yourself, lest you too be tempted. ²Bear one another's burdens, and so fulfil the law of Christ. ³For if any one thinks he is something, when he is nothing, he deceives himself. ⁴But let each one test his own work, and then his reason to boast will be in himself alone and not in his neighbor. ⁵For each man will have to bear his own load.

6 Let him who is taught the word share all good things with him who teaches.

7 Do not be deceived; God is not mocked, for whatever a man sows, that he will also reap. ⁸For he who sows to his own flesh will from the flesh reap corruption; but he who sows to the Spirit will from the Spirit reap eternal life. ⁹And let us not grow weary in well-doing, for in due season we shall reap, if we do not lose heart. ¹⁰So then, as we have opportunity, let us do good to all men, and especially to those who are of the household of faith.

11 See with what large letters I am writing to you with my own hand. ¹²It is those who want to make a good showing in the flesh that would compel you to be circumcised, and only in order that they may not be persecuted for the cross of Christ. ¹³For even those who receive circumcision do not themselves keep the law, but they desire to have you circumcised that they may glory in your flesh. ¹⁴But far be it from me to glory except in the cross of our Lord Jesus Christ, by which the world has been crucified to me, and I to the world. ¹⁵For neither circumcision counts for anything, nor uncircumcision, but a new creation. ¹⁶Peace and mercy be upon all who walk by this rule, upon the Israel of God.

17 Henceforth let no man trouble me; for I bear on my body the marks of Jesus.

18 The grace of our Lord Jesus Christ be with your spirit, brethren. Amen.

6:1 Older translations have "fault" for "trespass."

The Letter of Paul to the Ephesians

There is a tradition that Paul wrote this letter while he was in prison, possibly toward the end of his imprisonment in Rome, in A.D. 63. Some scholars believe that this book was written by a disciple of Paul as a covering letter for the first collection of Paul's letters ever made, and this may explain the lack of the usual personal references customarily found in Paul's writings. Some manuscripts read in the first line of the letter: to the saints "who are at Ephesus," but the earliest manuscripts do not contain this phrase. Its style is impersonal and formal. Many scholars therefore regard this letter as an encyclical ("circular" or circulating letter), a letter distributed to a number of Christian communities. A common theory is that when Paul's letters were gathered for publication, a copy of this letter was obtained from Ephesus, capital of the Roman province of Asia, where mention of Ephesus had been inserted. In this letter, the Church is described as the (mystical) body of Christ, the temple of God and the bride of Christ.

The Father Has a Plan for Us
Ephesians 1:1–10

1 Paul, an apostle of Christ Jesus by the will of God,
To the saints who are also faithful in Christ Jesus:
2 Grace to you and peace from God our Father and the Lord Jesus Christ.

3 Blessed be the God and Father of our Lord Jesus Christ, who has blessed us in Christ with every spiritual blessing in the heavenly places, ⁴even as he chose us in him before the foundation of the world, that we should be holy and blameless before him. ⁵He destined us in love to be his sons through Jesus Christ, according to the purpose of his will, ⁶to the praise of his glorious grace which he freely bestowed on us in the Beloved. ⁷In him we have redemption through his blood, the forgiveness of our trespasses, according to the riches of his grace ⁸which he lavished upon us. ⁹For he has made known to us in all wisdom and insight the mystery of his will, according to his purpose which he set forth in Christ ¹⁰as a plan for the fulness of time, to unite all things in him, things in heaven and things on earth.

1:5 The rendering of the Revised Standard Version here bears on the doctrine of predestination, often thought of as a principal tenet of Calvinism. Primarily a statement about the sovereignty of God, the doctrine was interpreted by the Westminster Assembly in 1643 to mean that "God from all eternity did by the most wise and holy counsel of his own will freely and unchangeably ordain whatsoever comes to pass." Corollaries of this are that "some men and angels are predestinated unto everlasting life, and others foreordained to everlasting death"; and that "Elect infants, dying in infancy, are regenerated and saved by Christ through the Spirit, who, when, and where, and how he pleaseth." In 1906 the General Assembly of what is now the United Presbyterian Church, U.S.A., made a clarifying statement: "The doctrine of God's eternal decree is held in harmony with the doctrine of His love to all mankind, His gift of His Son to be the propitiation for the sins of the whole world, and His readiness to bestow His saving grace on all who seek it." **1:10** Great Bible: set up all things perfectly by Christ. Bishops' Bible: gather together in one all things in Christ. Rheims: to perfit all things in Christ. RV, ASV: to sum up all things in Christ. Confraternity: "to re-establish all things in Christ."

Jesus Reconciled Us to God

Ephesians 2:11–22

11 Therefore remember that at one time you Gentiles in the flesh, called the uncircumcision by what is called the circumcision, which is made in the flesh by hands—[12] remember that you were at that time separated from Christ, alienated from the commonwealth of Israel, and strangers to the covenants of promise, having no hope and without God in the world. [13] But now in Christ Jesus you who once were far off have been brought near in the blood of Christ. [14] For he is our peace, who has made us both one, and has broken down the dividing wall of hostility, [15] by abolishing in his flesh the law of commandments and ordinances, that he might create in himself one new man in place of the two, so making peace, [16] and might reconcile us both to God in one body through the cross, thereby bringing the hostility to an end. [17] And he came and preached peace to you who were far off and peace to those who were near; [18] for through him we both have access in one Spirit to the Father. [19] So then you are no longer strangers and sojourners, but you are fellow citizens with the saints and members of the household of God, [20] built upon the foundation of the apostles and prophets, Christ Jesus himself being the cornerstone, [21] in whom the whole structure is joined together and grows into a holy temple in the Lord; [22] in whom you also are built into it for a dwelling place of God in the Spirit.

2:14–16 This passage is cited by those who believe that it is only through a common faith in Jesus that the whole known world will attain peace. This passage is also cited by those who believe that in Jesus Jews and Christians are united in a special way. Other Christians, recognizing what appears to be an inevitable growth in religious pluralism, have called upon the Church to support human instrumentalities for peace-making such as the United Nations—even though they fall short of the Christian ideal. **2:17** Compare Isaiah 57:19.

Paul Prays for Unity
Ephesians 4:1–7, 11–16

4 I therefore, a prisoner for the Lord, beg you to lead a life worthy of the calling to which you have been called, ² with all lowliness and meekness, with patience, forbearing one another in love, ³ eager to maintain the unity of the Spirit in the bond of peace. ⁴ There is one body and one spirit, just as you were called to the one hope that belongs to your call, ⁵ one Lord, one faith, one baptism, ⁶ one God and Father of us all, who is above all and through all and in all. ⁷ But grace was given to each of us according to the measure of Christ's gift.

11 And his gifts were that some should be apostles, some prophets, some evangelists, some pastors and teachers, ¹² for the equipment of the saints, for the work of ministry, for building up the body of Christ, ¹³ until we all attain to the unity of the faith and of the knowledge of the Son of God, to mature manhood, to the measure of the stature of the fulness of Christ; ¹⁴ so that we may no longer be children, tossed to and fro and carried about with every wind of doctrine, by the cunning of men, by their craftiness in deceitful wiles. ¹⁵ Rather, speaking the truth in love, we are to grow up in every way into him who is the head, into Christ, ¹⁶ from whom the whole body, joined and knit together by every joint with which it is supplied, when each part is working properly, makes bodily growth and upbuilds itself in love.

4:11 While the New Testament assumes that all believers are "a chosen race, a royal priesthood, a holy nation" (1 Peter 2:9), it also assumes within the community a division of labor and a variety of vocations. The "apostles" in the early Church were those who, through association with Jesus, were regarded as founding fathers. The prophets appear to have been preachers to whom "the word of the Lord came," enabling them to set the ancient texts in new light. The evangelists were missionaries to their generation. By contrast with these three offices, each of which required itineration, the "pastors and teachers" carried on a settled ministry. Whatever one's

assignment, it is important to remember that it is God's gift. **4:12**
Tyndale: that the saynctes might have all things necessary to work
and minister with all, to the edifying of the body of Christ. Geneva
Bible: For the gathering together of the Saints for the work of the
ministerie, (and) for the edification of the body of Christ. Rheims: to
the consummation of the saints, unto the work of the ministerie, unto
the edifying of the body of Christ. King James Version: for the
perfecting of the saints for the work of the ministry, for the edifying
of the body of Christ.

Be Imitators of God
Ephesians 4:18–5:2

18 They are darkened in their understanding, alienated from the life
of God because of the ignorance that is in them, due to their
hardness of heart; 19 they have become callous and have given
themselves up to licentiousness, greedy to practice every kind of
uncleanness. 20 You did not so learn Christ!—21 assuming that you
have heard about him and were taught in him, as the truth is in
Jesus. 22 Put off your old nature which belongs to your former
manner of life and is corrupt through deceitful lusts, 23 and be
renewed in the spirit of your minds, 24 and put on the new nature,
created after the likeness of God in true righteousness and holiness.

25 Therefore, putting away falsehood, let every one speak the
truth with his neighbor, for we are members one of another. 26 Be
angry but do not sin; do not let the sun go down on your anger,
27 and give no opportunity to the devil. 28 Let the thief no longer
steal, but rather let him labor, doing honest work with his hands, so
that he may be able to give to those in need. 29 Let no evil talk come
out of your mouths, but only such as is good for edifying, as fits the
occasion, that it may impart grace to those who hear. 30 And do not
grieve the Holy Spirit of God, in whom you were sealed for the day
of redemption. 31 Let all bitterness and wrath and anger and clamor
and slander be put away from you, with all malice, 32 and be kind to
one another, tenderhearted, forgiving one another, as God in Christ
forgave you.
5 Therefore be imitators of God, as beloved children. 2 And walk in
love, as Christ loved us and gave himself up for us, a fragrant
offering and sacrifice to God.

5:1 A similar sentiment that man, in his ethical life, should try to
imitate the ways of God as revealed in Scripture is also to be found in
Judaism. The sainted Rabbi Nahum of Tzernosil said: "Every man
should imitate God of whom it is said: He doeth good to the wicked
as well as to the good."

Put on the New Nature

Ephesians 4:22–27, 31–32; 5:1–2, 5–17

22 Put off your old nature which belongs to your former manner of life and is corrupt through deceitful lusts, [23] and be renewed in the spirit of your minds, [24] and put on the new nature, created after the likeness of God in true righteousness and holiness.

25 Therefore, putting away falsehood, let every one speak the truth with his neighbor, for we are members one of another. [26] Be angry but do not sin; do not let the sun go down on your anger, [27] and give no opportunity to the devil.

31 Let all bitterness and wrath and anger and clamor and slander be put away from you, with all malice, [32] and be kind to one another, tenderhearted, forgiving one another, as God in Christ forgave you.

5 Therefore be imitators of God, as beloved children. [2] And walk in love, as Christ loved us and gave himself up for us, a fragrant offering and sacrifice to God.

5 Be sure of this, that no immoral or impure man, or one who is covetous (that is, an idolater), has any inheritance in the kingdom of Christ and of God. [6] Let no one deceive you with empty words, for it is because of these things that the wrath of God comes upon the sons of disobedience. [7] Therefore do not associate with them, [8] for once you were darkness, but now you are light in the Lord; walk as children of light [9] (for the fruit of light is found in all that is good and right and true), [10] and try to learn what is pleasing to the Lord. [11] Take no part in the unfruitful works of darkness, but instead expose them. [12] For it is a shame even to speak of the things that they do in secret; [13] but when anything is exposed by the light it becomes visible, for anything that becomes visible is light. [14] Therefore it is said,

"Awake, O sleeper, and arise from the dead,
and Christ shall give you light."

15 Look carefully then how you walk, not as unwise men but as wise, [16] making the most of the time, because the days are evil. [17] Therefore do not be foolish, but understand what the will of the Lord is.

5:16 The Greek word, here translated "time," refers not to the succession of moments ticked off by a clock, but rather it signifies the right opportunity, the propitious moment, the right time. Karl Barth (1886–1968) emphasized that each of us lives in a day of opportunity, of crisis, and of judgment.

Paul Describes the Christian Household

Ephesians 5:21–33; 6:1–4

21 Be subject to one another out of reverence for Christ. [22] Wives, be subject to your husbands, as to the Lord. [23] For the husband is the head of the wife as Christ is the head of the church, his body, and is himself its Savior. [24] As the church is subject to Christ, so let wives also be subject in everything to their husbands. [25] Husbands, love your wives, as Christ loved the church and gave himself up for her, [26] that he might sanctify her, having cleansed her by the washing of water with the word, [27] that he might present the church to himself in splendor, without spot or wrinkle or any such thing, that she might be holy and without blemish. [28] Even so husbands should love their wives as their own bodies. He who loves his wife loves himself. [29] For no man ever hates his own flesh, but nourishes and cherishes it, as Christ does the church, [30] because we are members of his body. [31] "For this reason a man shall leave his father and mother and be joined to his wife, and the two shall become one." [32] This is a great mystery, and I take it to mean Christ and the church; [33] however, let each one of you love his wife as himself, and let the wife see that she respects her husband.

6 Children, obey your parents in the Lord, for this is right. [2] "Honor your father and mother" (this is the first commandment with a promise), [3] "that it may be well with you and that you may live long on the earth." [4] Fathers, do not provoke your children to anger, but bring them up in the discipline and instruction of the Lord.

5:22 Verses 22–33 are read in the Wedding Mass (also called the Nuptial Mass). **5:25–29** Husbands should love their wives: The Talmud puts this thought in the following words: "Of a man who loved his wife more than himself, Scripture (Job 5:24) says: 'And thou shalt know that thy tent is in peace'" (*Yebamath* 62b). Rabbi Helbo said: "Be careful about the honor of your wife, for blessing enters the house because of her" (*Babba Metziah* 59a). **6:1** ff. Rabbinic writings similarly abound with words of advice to parents and children. The Rabbis say: "Three combine in the making of man: God, father and mother. If men honor their father and mother, God says, 'I reckon it to them as if I dwelt among them and they honored me'" (*Kiddushin* 30b). Rabbi Zĕ'era said: One must not promise to give something to a child and not give it to him, because he is thereby taught to lie (*Sukkoth* 46b). Ras Huna would eat no breakfast until he had taken a boy to school (*Kiddushin* 30a). Jerusalem was destroyed only because the children did not attend school and loitered in the streets (*Sabbath* 119b).

Put on the Whole Armor of God

Ephesians 6:10–17

10 Finally, be strong in the Lord and in the strength of his might. ¹¹ Put on the whole armor of God, that you may be able to stand against the wiles of the devil. ¹² For we are not contending against flesh and blood, but against the principalities, against the powers, against the world rulers of this present darkness, against the spiritual hosts of wickedness in the heavenly places. ¹³ Therefore take the whole armor of God, that you may be able to withstand in the evil day, and having done all, to stand. ¹⁴ Stand therefore, having girded your loins with truth, and having put on the breastplate of righteousness, ¹⁵ and having shod your feet with the equipment of the gospel of peace; ¹⁶ above all taking the shield of faith, with which you can quench all the flaming darts of the evil one. ¹⁷ And take the helmet of salvation, and the sword of the Spirit, which is the word of God.

6:12 Condemned by the established order, Martin Luther said: "In this solitude there are a thousand battles with Satan. It is much easier to fight against the incarnate Devil—that is, against men—than against wickedness in the heavenly places." **6:13** The imagery of the armor was no doubt suggested to Paul by the accoutrement of the Roman soldiers guarding him. Martin Luther King, Jr. (1929–1968) wrote a "Letter from Birmingham City Jail," in which he said: "I too am compelled to carry the gospel of freedom beyond my particular home town." He said to his followers: "Some of you have knives, and I ask you to put them up. Some of you have arms, and I ask you to put them up. Get the weapon of non-violence, the breastplate of righteousness, the armor of truth and just keep marching." **6:14** Compare Isaiah 11:5, 59:17. **6:15** Compare Isaiah 52:7.

The Letter of Paul to the Philippians

The church at Philippi was the first Christian community Paul had established on European soil. The Philippians had sent a man to be Paul's companion and servant, and they had given him money to take to Paul. Paul writes from prison, where he was awaiting trial, to thank them. It is not clear which one of his imprisonments this one was. References to the praetorian guard and Caesar's household suggest it was the imprisonment in Rome, A.D. 61–63, but it could be an earlier imprisonment at Caesarea or at Ephesus.

Strive for the Faith of the Gospel
Philippians 1 : 12–14, 21–30

12 I want you to know, brethren, that what has happened to me has really served to advance the gospel, [13] so that it has become known throughout the whole praetorian guard and to all the rest that my imprisonment is for Christ; [14] and most of the brethren have been made confident in the Lord because of my imprisonment, and are much more bold to speak the word of God without fear.

21 For to me to live is Christ, and to die is gain. [22] If it is to be life in the flesh, that means fruitful labor for me. Yet which I shall choose I cannot tell. [23] I am hard pressed between the two. My desire is to depart and be with Christ, for that is far better. [24] But to remain in the flesh is more necessary on your account. [25] Convinced of this, I know that I shall remain and continue with you all, for your progress and joy in the faith, [26] so that in me you may have ample cause to glory in Christ Jesus, because of my coming to you again.

27 Only let your manner of life be worthy of the gospel of Christ, so that whether I come and see you or am absent, I may hear of you that you stand firm in one spirit, with one mind striving side by side for the faith of the gospel, [28] and not frightened in anything by your opponents. This is a clear omen to them of their destruction, but of your salvation, and that from God. [29] For it has been granted to you that for the sake of Christ you should not only believe in him but also suffer for his sake, [30] engaged in the same conflict which you saw and now hear to be mine.

1:21 Martin Luther (1483–1546) said: "True faith is that assured trust and firm assent of heart by which Christ is laid hold of, so that Christ is the object of faith. Yet he is not merely the object of faith; but in the very faith, so to speak, Christ is present."

Jesus Is a Model for Us
Philippians 2:5–13

5 Have this mind among yourselves, which you have in Christ Jesus, [6] who, though he was in the form of God, did not count equality with God a thing to be grasped, [7] but emptied himself, taking the form of a servant, being born in the likeness of men. [8] And being found in human form he humbled himself and became obedient unto death, even death on a cross. [9] Therefore God has highly exalted him and bestowed on him the name which is above every name, [10] that at the name of Jesus every knee should bow, in heaven and on earth and under the earth, [11] and every tongue confess that Jesus Christ is Lord, to the glory of God the Father.

12 Therefore, my beloved, as you have always obeyed, so now, not only as in my presence but much more in my absence, work out your own salvation with fear and trembling; [13] for God is at work in you, both to will and to work for his good pleasure.

2:5–8 Martin Luther (1483–1546) was much impressed with the doctrine of the Incarnation: "that the ineffable Majesty should stoop to take upon himself our flesh, subject to hunger and cold, death and desperation. We see him lying in the feeding-box of a donkey, laboring in a carpenter's shop, dying a derelict under the sins of the world. The gospel is not so much a miracle as a marvel, and every line is suffused with wonder." **2:9–11** Luther said: "Now Christ reigns, not in visible, public manner, but through the word, just as we see the sun through a cloud. We see the light, but not the sun itself. But then the clouds are gone, then we see at the same time both light and sun." *At the name of Jesus:* this hope expressed by Paul is paralleled in the Jewish prayer book. In the climactic prayer known as the Adoration, the Jews say three times daily: "Let all the inhabitants of the world perceive and know that unto Thee every knee must bend, every tongue must swear. Before thee O Lord our God let them bow and fall and unto thy glorious Name let them give honor. Let them all accept the yoke of thy kingdom and do thou reign over them speedily and for ever and ever." Substituting the name of Jesus for the name of God, thus violating the Jewish tradition that the Messiah was human and to be distinguished from God, Paul furthered the breach between the Hebrew-Christians and the Jews.

Our Citizenship Is in Heaven
Philippians 3:1–21

3 Finally, my brethren, rejoice in the Lord. To write the same things to you is not irksome to me, and is safe for you.

2 Look out for the dogs, look out for the evil-workers, look out for

those who mutilate the flesh. [3] For we are the true circumcision, who worship God in spirit, and glory in Christ Jesus, and put no confidence in the flesh. [4] Though I myself have reason for confidence in the flesh also. If any other man thinks he has reason for confidence in the flesh, I have more: [5] circumcised on the eighth day, of the people of Israel, of the tribe of Benjamin, a Hebrew born of Hebrews; as to the law a Pharisee, [6] as to zeal a persecutor of the church, as to righteousness under the law blameless. [7] But whatever gain I had, I counted as loss for the sake of Christ. [8] Indeed I count everything as loss because of the surpassing worth of knowing Christ Jesus my Lord. For his sake I have suffered the loss of all things, and count them as refuse, in order that I may gain Christ [9] and be found in him, not having a righteousness of my own, based on law, but that which is through faith in Christ, the righteousness from God that depends on faith; [10] that I may know him and the power of his resurrection, and may share his sufferings, becoming like him in his death, [11] that if possible I may attain the resurrection from the dead.

12 Not that I have already obtained this or am already perfect; but I press on to make it my own, because Christ Jesus has made me his own. [13] Brethren, I do not consider that I have made it my own; but one thing I do, forgetting what lies behind and straining forward to what lies ahead, [14] I press on toward the goal for the prize of the upward call of God in Christ Jesus. [15] Let those of us who are mature be thus minded; and if in anything you are otherwise minded, God will reveal that also to you. [16] Only let us hold true to what we have attained.

17 Brethren, join in imitating me, and mark those who so live as you have an example in us. [18] For many, of whom I have often told you and now tell you even with tears, live as enemies of the cross of Christ. [19] Their end is destruction, their god is the belly, and they glory in their shame, with minds set on earthly things. [20] But our commonwealth is in heaven, and from it we await a Savior, the Lord Jesus Christ, [21] who will change our lowly body to be like his glorious body, by the power which enables him even to subject all things to himself.

3:2 The word "dogs" in verse 2 is a bitter reference to preachers who had appeared claiming that circumcision was necessary for salvation. Paul's reaction is scathing because he felt they were trying to undo his preaching. Such passages provided inspiration for the allegorical figures of church and synagogue seen in many old European cathedrals. F. R. Webber writes: "High up on the south transept of Rheims, next to one of the great rose windows, was a splendid figure of the Church, shown as a fair woman, crowned, holding a chalice in her right hand and a tall, slender staff in her left, the staff terminating in a cross. On the opposite side of the rose window was the figure of the Synagogue, shown as a swaying female figure, blindfolded, with her crown slipping from her head. This idea is quite common in medieval art. In our own day, and in a land where every man enjoys religious freedom, such polemical representations have ceased to be used as much as in olden days, for it is difficult to win friends to a cause by using a club" (*Church Symbolism*). Respect for the dignity of others is, in our day, a more adequate reason for rejecting derogatory representation. **3:8** Older translations have "dung" for "refuse." **3:12** Perhaps because of such vigorous language as he uses in Galatians 1:6–9 where he opposed a situation which, in his judgment, imperiled the very essence of the gospel, Paul has often been thought of as boastful, self-righteous and dogmatic. This passage reveals another side of him. Three other Pauline passages, progressively denigrating the author, form an interesting study in the kind of personal humility which may mark a man who is boldly self-confident about the trust others have reposed in him: "I am the least of the apostles" (1 Corinthians 15:9); "I am the very least of all the apostles" (Ephesians 3:8); "I am the foremost of sinners" (1 Timothy 1:15). **3:20** Older translations have "conversation" for "commonwealth." (RV) RSV: "commonwealth." Paul, eager always to employ the language of his readers, here uses a figure of speech which would be understood by the Philippians. The word translated "commonwealth" (RSV) or "conversation" (KJV) is, in Greek, "citizenship." Philippi was one of the communities in other lands upon whose inhabitants Rome had conferred the privileges of citizenship. The Philippians, therefore, were residents of one place, citizens of another. Similarly, Paul suggests, the members of the believing community are residents of one place, but their final allegiance is elsewhere. As the Philippians were an outpost of Rome, so the Christians were a colony of heaven, bound to order the local situation according to the larger pattern.

Rejoice in the Lord Always
Philippians 4:4–8, 13

4 Rejoice in the Lord always; again I will say, Rejoice. ⁵Let all men know your forbearance. The Lord is at hand. ⁶Have no anxiety about anything, but in everything by prayer and supplication with thanksgiving let your requests be made known to God. ⁷And the peace of God, which passes all understanding, will keep your hearts and your minds in Christ Jesus.

8 Finally, brethren, whatever is true, whatever is honorable, whatever is just, whatever is pure, whatever is lovely, whatever is gracious, if there is any excellence, if there is anything worthy of praise, think about these things.

13 I can do all things in him who strengthens me.

The Letter of Paul to the Colossians

Paul had sent some of his converts to Colossae, a town about a hundred miles from Ephesus. A few years later he heard that other teachers were telling the Colossians about "elements of the world" which had to be worshipped because they were the cause of creation and exercised powers over men. Against all this Paul asserts the unique position of Jesus. The letter is very much like the letter to the Ephesians, but shorter.

All Things Were Created Through Jesus and for Him
Colossians 1:1–29

1 Paul, an apostle of Christ Jesus by the will of God, and Timothy our brother,

2 To the saints and faithful brethren in Christ at Colos'sae: Grace to you and peace from God our Father.

3 We always thank God, the Father of our Lord Jesus Christ, when we pray for you, ⁴because we have heard of your faith in Christ Jesus and of the love which you have for all the saints, ⁵because of the hope laid up for you in heaven. Of this you have heard before in the word of the truth, the gospel ⁶which has come to you, as indeed in the whole world it is bearing fruit and growing—so among yourselves, from the day you heard and understood the grace of God in truth, ⁷as you learned it from Ep'aphras our beloved fellow servant. He is a faithful minister of Christ on our behalf ⁸and has made known to us your love in the Spirit.

9 And so, from the day we heard of it, we have not ceased to pray for you, asking that you may be filled with the knowledge of his will in all spiritual wisdom and understanding, ¹⁰to lead a life worthy of the Lord, fully pleasing to him, bearing fruit in every good work and increasing in the knowledge of God. ¹¹May you be strengthened with all power, according to his glorious might, for all endurance and patience with joy, ¹²giving thanks to the Father, who has qualified us to share in the inheritance of the saints in light. ¹³He has delivered us from the dominion of darkness and transferred us to the kingdom of his beloved Son, ¹⁴in whom we have redemption, the forgiveness of sins.

15 He is the image of the invisible God, the first-born of all creation; ¹⁶for in him all things were created, in heaven and on earth, visible and invisible, whether thrones or dominions or

principalities or authorities—all things were created through him and for him. [17] He is before all things, and in him all things hold together. [18] He is the head of the body, the church; he is the beginning, the first-born from the dead, that in everything he might be pre-eminent. [19] For in him all the fulness of God was pleased to dwell, [20] and through him to reconcile to himself all things, whether on earth or in heaven, making peace by the blood of his cross.

21 And you, who once were estranged and hostile in mind, doing evil deeds, [22] he has now reconciled in his body of flesh by his death, in order to present you holy and blameless and irreproachable before him, [23] provided that you continue in the faith, stable and steadfast, not shifting from the hope of the gospel which you heard, which has been preached to every creature under heaven, and of which I, Paul, became a minister.

24 Now I rejoice in my sufferings for your sake, and in my flesh I complete what is lacking in Christ's afflictions for the sake of his body, that is, the church, [25] of which I became a minister according to the divine office which was given to me for you, to make the word of God fully known, [26] the mystery hidden for ages and generations but now made manifest to his saints. [27] To them God chose to make known how great among the Gentiles are the riches of the glory of this mystery, which is Christ in you, the hope of glory. [28] Him we proclaim, warning every man and teaching every man in all wisdom, that we may present every man mature in Christ. [29] For this I toil, striving with all the energy which he mightily inspires within me.

1:17 Compare Proverbs 8:22–31. Jesus is here given the status and position assigned in Hebrew Scripture to the Torah. **1:18** John Calvin (1509–1564) said: "I attribute the highest importance to the connection between the head and the members; to the inhabitation of Christ in our hearts; in a word, to the mystical union by which we enjoy him, so that, being made ours, he makes us partakers of the blessings with which he is furnished."

Do Everything in the Name of the Lord Jesus

In this passage Paul describes the qualities of one who would call himself a Christian.

Colossians 3:1–17

3 If then you have been raised with Christ, seek the things that are above, where Christ is, seated at the right hand of God. [2] Set your minds on things that are above, not on things that are on earth. [3] For you have died, and your life is hid with Christ in God. [4] When Christ who is our life appears, then you also will appear with him in glory.

5 Put to death therefore what is earthly in you: immorality,

impurity, passion, evil desire, and covetousness, which is idolatry.
[6] On account of these the wrath of God is coming. [7] In these you once
walked, when you lived in them. [8] But now put them all away: anger,
wrath, malice, slander, and foul talk from your mouth. [9] Do not lie
to one another, seeing that you have put off the old nature with its
practices [10] and have put on the new nature, which is being renewed
in knowledge after the image of its creator. [11] Here there cannot be
Greek and Jew, circumcised and uncircumcised, barbarian,
Scyth'ian, slave, free man, but Christ is all, and in all.

12 Put on then, as God's chosen ones, holy and beloved, compassion, kindness, lowliness, meekness, and patience, [13] forbearing one
another and, if one has a complaint against another, forgiving each
other; as the Lord has forgiven you, so you also must forgive. [14] And
above all these put on love, which binds everything together in
perfect harmony. [15] And let the peace of Christ rule in your hearts, to
which indeed you were called in the one body. And be thankful.
[16] Let the word of Christ dwell in you richly, as you teach and
admonish one another in all wisdom, and as you sing psalms and
hymns and spiritual songs with thankfulness in your hearts to God.
[17] And whatever you do, in word or deed, do everything in the name
of the Lord Jesus, giving thanks to God the Father through him.

3:9–10 Other translations have "old man" and "new man" for
"old nature" and "new nature." 3:16 This passage led P. T. Forsyth
(18?), an English Protestant clergyman, to assert that there was only
one sacrament, "the sacrament of the Word," which can be conveyed
in a variety of ways: through preaching, Bible reading, baptism, the
Lord's Supper, etc.

The First Letter of Paul to the Thessalonians

Paul had brought the Christian message to Thessalonica (present-day Salonika), capital of Macedonia, during his second missionary journey (Acts 17:1–9). Paul sent Timothy back to find out how things were going and to strengthen the Christian community. Timothy came to Paul in Corinth with the good news that the Christians were still faithful. Paul wrote this letter to express his joy and gratitude and to answer some questions the Thessalonians had asked him. The letter is generally regarded as the earliest of all Paul's letters. If Mark's Gospel was written in the middle or late fifties, the earliest date for it assigned by scholars, then Paul's two letters to the Thessalonians would be the earliest written witness to the Christian faith of all the books in the New Testament. It is generally agreed that the letters were written in the early fifties, and the first one probably in A.D. 50–51.

Will Those Who Die before the Second Coming Meet the Lord?
1 Thessalonians 4:13–18

13 But we would not have you ignorant, brethren, concerning those who are asleep, that you may not grieve as others do who have no hope. ¹⁴ For since we believe that Jesus died and rose again, even so, through Jesus, God will bring with him those who have fallen asleep. ¹⁵ For this we declare to you by the word of the Lord, that we who are alive, who are left until the coming of the Lord, shall not precede those who have fallen asleep. ¹⁶ For the Lord himself will descend from heaven with a cry of command, with the archangel's call, and with the sound of the trumpet of God. And the dead in Christ will rise first; ¹⁷ then we who are alive, who are left, shall be caught up together with them in the clouds to meet the Lord in the air; and so we shall always be with the Lord. ¹⁸ Therefore comfort one another with these words.

4:13 The Catholic Church uses this section as the Epistle (first lesson) in the funeral Mass and thus keeps before the people this earliest written Christian statement on eschatology ("study of the last things"), especially the Second Coming of Jesus (called the *Parousia* in New Testament times).

When Will Jesus Come in Glory?
1 Thessalonians 5:1–22

5 But as to the times and the season, brethren, you have no need to have anything written to you. ²For you yourselves know well that

the day of the Lord will come like a thief in the night. [3] When people say, "There is peace and security," then sudden destruction will come upon them as travail comes upon a woman with child, and there will be no escape. [4] But you are not in darkness, brethren, for that day to surprise you like a thief. [5] For you are all sons of light and sons of the day; we are not of the night or of darkness. [6] So then let us not sleep, as others do, but let us keep awake and be sober. [7] For those who sleep sleep at night, and those who get drunk are drunk at night. [8] But, since we belong to the day, let us be sober, and put on the breastplate of faith and love, and for a helmet the hope of salvation. [9] For God has not destined us for wrath, but to obtain salvation through our Lord Jesus Christ, [10] who died for us so that whether we wake or sleep we might live with him. [11] Therefore encourage one another and build one another up, just as you are doing.

12 But we beseech you, brethren, to respect those who labor among you and are over you in the Lord and admonish you, [13] and to esteem them very highly in love because of their work. Be at peace among yourselves. [14] And we exhort you, brethren, admonish the idle, encourage the fainthearted, help the weak, be patient with them all. [15] See that none of you repays evil for evil, but always seek to do good to one another and to all. [16] Rejoice always, [17] pray constantly, [18] give thanks in all circumstances; for this is the will of God in Christ Jesus for you. [19] Do not quench the Spirit, [20] do not despise prophesying, [21] but test everything; hold fast what is good, [22] abstain from every form of evil.

5:16–18 When the New Jersey Quaker, John Woolman (1720–1772), lay dying of smallpox in the English city of York, friends asked what they could do. He replied: "Rejoice evermore, and in everything give thanks," then added, "This is sometimes hard to come at." **5:18** Martin Luther (1483–1546) said: "All morality is gratitude. It is the irrepressible expression of thankfulness for food and raiment, for earth and sky, and for the inestimable gift of redemption." Dietrich Bonhoeffer (1906–1945) wrote from Hitler's prison: "I am sure of God's hand and guidance. . . . I am thankful to go the way which I am being led. My past life is full of God's mercy, and above all sin stands the forgiving love of the Crucified."

The Second Letter of Paul to the Thessalonians

Paul's second letter came soon after the first. Some thought the Parousia, or Day of the Lord's Second Coming, had already arrived or was imminent. As a result, some had quit their jobs. Paul replies that the Parousia is not at hand and will not come until after a great apostasy (*departing, falling away, rebellion*) and the coming of a mysterious person ("that sinful man" or "the man of sin" in older translations). Apparently Paul's readers understood what he meant by the "man of sin" (or "man of lawlessness"). "Antichrist" is a term that has traditionally been used in describing this mysterious person, but Paul did not use the term. Many conflicting ideas have been expressed about the identity of Antichrist in books and articles throughout the centuries (even more so in connection with the mention of Antichrist in the Apocalypse or Book of Revelation).

The Man of Lawlessness Will come

2 Thessalonians 2 : 1–17

2 Now concerning the coming of our Lord Jesus Christ and our assembling to meet him, we beg you, brethren, [2] not to be quickly shaken in mind or excited, either by spirit or by word, or by letter purporting to be from us, to the effect that the day of the Lord has come. [3] Let no one deceive you in any way; for that day will not come, unless the rebellion comes first, and the man of lawlessness is revealed, the son of perdition, [4] who opposes and exalts himself against every so-called god or object of worship, so that he takes his seat in the temple of God, proclaiming himself to be God. [5] Do you not remember that when I was still with you I told you this? [6] And you know what is restraining him now so that he may be revealed in his time. [7] For the mystery of lawlessness is already at work; only he who now restrains it will do so until he is out of the way. [8] And then the lawless one will be revealed, and the Lord Jesus will slay him with the breath of his mouth and destroy him by his appearing and his coming. [9] The coming of the lawless one by the activity of Satan will be with all power and with pretended signs and wonders, [10] and with all wicked deception for those who are to perish, because they refused to love the truth and so be saved. [11] Therefore God sends upon them a strong delusion, to make them believe what is false, [12] so that all may be condemned who did not believe the truth but had pleasure in unrighteousness.

13 But we are bound to give thanks to God always for you, brethren beloved by the Lord, because God chose you from the beginning to be saved, through sanctification by the Spirit and belief in the truth. [14] To this he called you through our gospel, so that you may obtain the glory of our Lord Jesus Christ. [15] So then, brethren, stand firm and hold to the traditions which you were taught by us, either by word of mouth or by letter.

16 Now may our Lord Jesus Christ himself, and God our Father, who loved us and gave us eternal comfort and good hope through grace, [17] comfort your hearts and establish them in every good work and word.

Work for Your Bread
2 Thessalonians 3:6–13

6 Now we command you, brethren, in the name of our Lord Jesus Christ, that you keep away from any brother who is living in idleness and not in accord with the tradition that you receive from us. [7] For you yourselves know how you ought to imitate us; we were not idle when we were with you, [8] we did not eat any one's bread without paying, but with toil and labor we worked night and day, that we might not burden any of you. [9] It was not because we have not that right, but to give you in our conduct an example to imitate. [10] For even when we were with you, we gave you this command: If any one will not work, let him not eat. [11] For we hear that some of you are living in idleness, mere busybodies, not doing any work. [12] Now such persons we command and exhort in the Lord Jesus Christ to do their work in quietness and to earn their own living. [13] Brethren, do not be weary in well-doing.

3:10 Some Christians long opposed governmental efforts to provide relief, unemployment insurance and social security on the grounds that those who did not work were merely being lazy. The depression of 1929 showed many people that the intricacies of the economy or other causes beyond a person's control may be responsible for unemployment. Society assumes the burden, therefore, of making sure that even those who do not work will not starve.

The First Letter of Paul to Timothy

The two letters to Timothy and the letter to Titus are called the Pastoral Epistles because they are more formal or official in character and treat the work of a pastor dealing with his people. Timothy was the son of a Greek father and a Jewish mother. His mother and grandmother had become Christians, and he was already a member of the church when Paul came to Timothy's home town of Lystra. Paul took him on his missionary voyages, and Timothy took care of some difficult and confidential missions. Eventually, Paul left him in charge of the church at Ephesus. The language and style of the Pastorals are so different from Paul's other letters that some scholars think they were written by someone else—a disciple of Paul putting unpublished letters together some time after Paul's letter, or one of Paul's secretaries putting Paul's ideas in slightly different style and vocabulary.

Hold Faith and a Good Conscience

1 Timothy 1:12–20

12 I thank him who has given me strength for this, Christ Jesus our Lord, because he judged me faithful by appointing me to his service, [13] though I formerly blasphemed and persecuted and insulted him; but I received mercy because I had acted ignorantly in unbelief, [14] and the grace of our Lord overflowed for me with the faith and love that are in Christ Jesus. [15] The saying is sure and worthy of full acceptance, that Christ Jesus came into the world to save sinners. And I am the foremost of sinners; [16] but I received mercy for this reason, that in me, as the foremost, Jesus Christ might display his perfect patience for an example to those who were to believe in him for eternal life. [17] To the King of ages, immortal, invisible, the only God, be honor and glory for ever and ever. Amen.

18 This charge I commit to you, Timothy, my son, in accordance with the prophetic utterances which pointed to you, that inspired by them you may wage the good warfare, [19] holding faith and a good conscience. By rejecting conscience, certain persons have made shipwreck of their faith, [20] among them Hymenae'us and Alexander, whom I have delivered to Satan that they may learn not to blaspheme.

1:20 The apostles had great—but not inexhaustible—patience for those whom they were privileged to confront with the gospel. Paul addresses the Galatians (4:19) as "my little children, with whom I am again in travail until Christ be formed in you," and reminds the Thessalonians (1 Thessalonians 2:7) that his relationship to them was comparable to that of "a nurse taking care of her children." Jesus had taught, however, that not everyone would respond to the gospel: there are some upon whose hearts the Word falls as seed upon rocky ground (Matthew 13:5, 20, 21). The passage to which this note is appended seems to reflect the author's conviction that there is a point beyond which one cannot go in seeking to win the unyielding. Even so, however, the hope is that this deliverance to the powers of evil will not be final but that those thus condemned may be led to repent and so "learn not to blaspheme" (cf. 1 Corinthians 5:5).

Pray for All Men
1 Timothy 2:1–15

2 First of all, then, I urge that supplications, prayers, intercessions, and thanksgivings be made for all men, [2] for kings and all who are in high positions, that we may lead a quiet and peaceable life, godly and respectful in every way. [3] This is good, and it is acceptable in the sight of God our Savior, [4] who desires all men to be saved and to come to the knowledge of the truth. [5] For there is one God, and there is one mediator between God and men, the man Christ Jesus, [6] who gave himself as a ransom for all, the testimony to which was borne at the proper time. [7] For this I was appointed a preacher and apostle (I am telling the truth, I am not lying), a teacher of the Gentiles in faith and truth.

[8] I desire then that in every place the men should pray, lifting holy hands without anger or quarreling; [9] also that women should adorn themselves modestly and sensibly in seemly apparel, not with braided hair or gold or pearls or costly attire [10] but by good deeds, as befits women who profess religion. [11] Let a woman learn in silence with all submissiveness. [12] I permit no woman to teach or to have authority over men; she is to keep silent. [13] For Adam was formed first, then Eve; [14] and Adam was not deceived, but the woman was deceived and became a transgressor. [15] Yet woman will be saved through bearing children, if she continues in faith and love and holiness, with modesty.

2:1 The first two verses here describe what early Christians called a "litany" (a form of prayer in which clergy and congregation take part alternately). The practice and the name continue in many churches. Usually there are invocations of God and Christ, with the response: "Have mercy on us"; then invocations of the saints, with the response "Pray for us"; then prayers for protection from evils, with the response: "Pray for us"; then prayers for protection from evils, with the response: "Deliver us, O Lord"; finally, prayers for favors, for various classes of people (including rulers), with the response: "We beseech Thee, hear us." The Greek, Russian and other Eastern Catholic churches have a number of litanies in the liturgy, as the early Christians did. In the Mass of the Roman Catholic Church only *Kyrie Eleison* and *Christe Eleison* (*Lord have mercy* and *Christ have mercy*) remain of these recitations and responses, except on Holy Saturday when a full litany is recited as part of the Easter vigil; the Litany of the Saints is recited daily by many Catholic orders and congregations. Since litanies were used during processions, the word litanies came to be used for processions (from the sixth century on), which explains the terms Major Litanies and Minor Litanies in the calendar of the Catholic Church.

Paul Describes a Good Minister of Christ
1 Timothy 3:1–15; 4:1–5, 11–16; 5:17–25

3 The saying is sure: If any one aspires to the office of bishop, he desires a noble task. ²Now a bishop must be above reproach, the husband of one wife, temperate, sensible, dignified, hospitable, an apt teacher, ³no drunkard, not violent but gentle, not quarrelsome, and no lover of money. ⁴He must manage his own household well, keeping his children submissive and respectful in every way; ⁵for if a man does not know how to manage his own household, how can he care for God's church? ⁶He must not be a recent convert, or he may be puffed up with conceit and fall into the condemnation of the devil; ⁷moreover he must be well thought of by outsiders, or he may fall into reproach and the snare of the devil.

8 Deacons likewise must be serious, not double-tongued, not addicted to much wine, not greedy for gain; ⁹they must hold the mystery of the faith with a clear conscience. ¹⁰And let them also be tested first; then if they prove themselves blameless let them serve as deacons. ¹¹The women likewise must be serious, no slanderers, but temperate, faithful in all things. ¹²Let deacons be the husband of one wife, and let them manage their children and their households well; ¹³for those who serve well as deacons gain a good standing for themselves and also great confidence in the faith which is in Christ Jesus.

14 I hope to come to you soon, but I am writing these instructions to you so that, ¹⁵if I am delayed, you may know how one ought to behave in the household of God, which is the church of the living God, the pillar and bulwark of the truth.

4 Now the Spirit expressly says that in later times some will depart from the faith by giving heed to deceitful spirits and doctrines of demons, [2] through the pretensions of liars whose consciences are seared, [3] who forbid marriage and enjoin abstinence from foods which God created to be received with thanksgiving by those who believe and know the truth. [4] For everything created by God is good, and nothing is to be rejected if it is received with thanksgiving; [5] for then it is consecrated by the word of God and prayer.

[11] Command and teach these things. [12] Let no one despise your youth, but set the believers an example in speech and conduct, in love, in faith, in purity. [13] Till I come, attend to the public reading of scripture, to preaching, to teaching. [14] Do not neglect the gift you have, which was given you by prophetic utterance when the elders laid their hands upon you. [15] Practice these duties, devote yourself to them, so that all may see your progress. [16] Take heed to yourself and to your teaching; hold to that, for by so doing you will save both yourself and your hearers.

5 [17] Let the elders who rule well be considered worthy of double honor, especially those who labor in preaching and teaching; [18] for the scripture says, "You shall not muzzle an ox when it is treading out the grain," and, "The laborer deserves his wages." [19] Never admit any charge against an elder except on the evidence of two or three witnesses. [20] As for those who persist in sin, rebuke them in the presence of all, so that the rest may stand in fear. [21] In the presence of God and of Christ Jesus and of the elect angels I charge you to keep these rules without favor, doing nothing from partiality. [22] Do not be hasty in the laying on of hands, nor participate in another man's sins; keep yourself pure.

[23] No longer drink only water, but use a little wine for the sake of your stomach and your frequent ailments.

[24] The sins of some men are conspicuous, pointing to judgment, but the sins of others appear later. [25] So also good deeds are conspicuous; and even when they are not, they cannot remain hidden.

3:1–2 *Episkopos* (literally, "overseer"), Paul's word for what we call a bishop today, is the source of the English words "episcopal," "episcopate," etc. **3:8** Older translations have "honest," "grave," "chaste," for "serious." **4:3** Gnostics taught that marriage should be forbidden. They also prohibited certain foods (as did the Jews). Paul asserts the goodness of God's creation. **4:13** The public reading of Scripture, preaching and teaching were elements in the liturgical practices of synagogues; the early Christians took these elements over into their own liturgy. **4:14** Laying on of hands on a candidate's head was a traditional Jewish rite of ordination called *Semicha*—a leaning on. By this rite, full rabbinic authority was conferred. It was believed that the Master thereby transmitted a wisdom and a power ultimately descended from Moses (see Numbers 27:18, 23 and Deuteronomy 34:9). Although this ceremony was abandoned in the Jewish community after the fourth century, it has been reinstated today and is used at the ordination ceremonies of modern rabbis. **5:17** *Elders* (*presbuteroi*, literally "older ones") are generally identified with the *episkopoi* (overseers, bishops), but the Rheims translation has here: "The priests that rule well ..." and the Confraternity translation uses the word "presbyters." **5:18** Compare Deuteronomy 25:4. **5:19** Compare Deuteronomy 19:15.

Advice to the Wealthy and Conclusion
1 Timothy 6:17–21

17 As for the rich in this world, charge them not to be haughty, nor to set their hopes on uncertain riches but on God who richly furnishes us with everything to enjoy. ¹⁸ They are to do good, to be rich in good deeds, liberal and generous, ¹⁹ thus laying up for themselves a good foundation for the future, so that they may take hold of the life which is life indeed.

20 O Timothy, guard what has been entrusted to you. Avoid the godless chatter and contradictions of what is falsely called knowledge, ²¹ for by professing it some have missed the mark as regards the faith.

Grace be with you.

6:20 The Rheims translation has: O Timothee, keepe the *depositum*. The Latin word *depositum* has become a technical term (deposit of faith) in the Catholic Church for the teaching of the apostles to be transmitted to future generations. The expressions "what is falsely called knowledge" refers to the Gnostic teachings which Paul feels contradict Christian teaching.

The Second Letter of Paul to Timothy

Guard the Truth Entrusted to You
2 Timothy 1:1–14

1 Paul, an apostle of Christ Jesus by the will of God according to the promise of the life which is in Christ Jesus,

2 To Timothy, my beloved child:

Grace, mercy, and peace from God the Father and Christ Jesus our Lord.

3 I thank God whom I serve with a clear conscience, as did my fathers, when I remember you constantly in my prayers. ⁴As I remember your tears, I long night and day to see you, that I may be filled with joy. ⁵I am reminded of your sincere faith, a faith that dwelt first in your grandmother Lo'is and your mother Eunice and now, I am sure, dwells in you. ⁶Hence I remind you to rekindle the gift of God that is within you through the laying on of my hands; ⁷for God did not give us a spirit of timidity but a spirit of power and love and self-control.

8 Do not be ashamed then of testifying to our Lord, nor of me his prisoner, but take your share of suffering for the gospel in the power of God, ⁹who saved us and called us with a holy calling, not in virtue of our works but in virtue of his own purpose and the grace which he gave us in Christ Jesus ages ago, ¹⁰and now has manifested through the appearing of our Savior Christ Jesus, who abolished death and brought life and immortality to light through the gospel. ¹¹For this gospel I was appointed a preacher and apostle and teacher, ¹²and therefore I suffer as I do. But I am not ashamed, for I know whom I have believed, and I am sure that he is able to guard until that Day what has been entrusted to me. ¹³Follow the pattern of the sound words which you have heard from me, in the faith and love which are in Christ Jesus; ¹⁴guard the truth that has been entrusted to you by the Holy Spirit who dwells within us.

Take Your Share of Suffering
2 Timothy 2:1–13

2 You then, my son, be strong in the grace that is in Christ Jesus, ²and what you have heard from me before many witnesses entrust to faithful men who will be able to teach others also. ³Take your share of suffering as a good soldier of Christ Jesus. ⁴No soldier on service gets entangled in civilian pursuits, since his aim is to satisfy the one who enlisted him. ⁵An athlete is not crowned unless he competes according to the rules. ⁶It is the hard-working farmer who ought to have the first share of the crops. ⁷Think over what I say, for the Lord will grant you understanding in everything.

8 Remember Jesus Christ, risen from the dead, descended from David, as preached in my gospel, ⁹the gospel for which I am suffering and wearing fetters like a criminal. But the word of God is not fettered. ¹⁰Therefore I endure everything for the sake of the elect, that they also may obtain the salvation which in Christ Jesus goes with eternal glory. ¹¹The saying is sure:

If we have died with him, we shall also live with him;
¹²if we endure, we shall also reign with him;
if we deny him, he also will deny us;
¹³if we are faithless, he remains faithful—
for he cannot deny himself.

2:9 Older translations have "bound" or "tied" for "fettered."

All Scripture Is Inspired
2 Timothy 3:1, 12–17

3 But understand this, that in the last days there will come times of stress.

12 Indeed all who desire to live a godly life in Christ Jesus will be persecuted, ¹³while evil men and impostors will go on from bad to worse, deceivers and deceived. ¹⁴But as for you, continue in what you have learned and have firmly believed, knowing from whom you learned it ¹⁵and how from childhood you have been acquainted with the sacred writings which are able to instruct you for salvation through faith in Christ Jesus. ¹⁶All scripture is inspired by God and profitable for teaching, for reproof, for correction, and for training in righteousness, ¹⁷that the man of God may be complete, equipped for every good work.

3:1 Older translations have "perilous times" for "times of stress." **3:15–17** Heinrich Bullinger (1504–1575), pupil and friend of Zwingli, played an important part in drawing up the first Helvetic Confession (1536) and the second Helvetic Confession (1566), one of the most widely accepted creeds of the Reformed churches. The latter says: "from these Scriptures are to be taken true wisdom and godliness, the reformation and government of churches; as also instruction in all duties of piety; and to be short, the confirmation of doctrines, and the computation of all errors." **3:16** From the time of Ben Sira, the Hebrews had cherished those "books of our fathers" which, having commended themselves by their own self-authenticating wisdom and power, had stood the test of time. The early Christians, assuming the same attitude toward the Old Testament scriptures which they made their own, were now witnessing the creation of other books deemed worthy to stand alongside the Law, the Prophets, and the Writings. 2 Peter 3:16 reveals that letters of Paul deserve the same consideration accorded "the other scriptures." 2 Timothy 3:16 suggests that the test of canonicity is a book's effectiveness in correcting false doctrine, training people to be well-rounded in their righteousness, and equipping them "for every good work." The opening words of this passage are, in Greek, susceptible of another meaning; the American Standard Version rendered it, "Every scripture inspired by God is also profitable for teaching," etc. *The New English Bible* has it, "Every inspired scripture has its use. . . ." Perhaps the most adequate summary of the Christian doctrine of inspiration, one that applies to both Testaments and makes possible the uniting of both Hebrew and Christian thought, is found in 2 Peter 1:21: "men moved by the Holy Spirit spoke from God."

Convince, Rebuke, and Exhort

2 Timothy 4:1–8

4 I charge you in the presence of God and of Christ Jesus who is to judge the living and the dead, and by his appearing and his kingdom: ² preach the word, be urgent in season and out of season, convince, rebuke, and exhort, be unfailing in patience and in teaching. ³ For the time is coming when people will not endure sound teaching, but having itching ears they will accumulate for themselves teachers to suit their own likings, ⁴ and will turn away from listening to the truth and wander into myths. ⁵ As for you, always be steady, endure suffering, do the work of an evangelist, fulfil your ministry.

6 For I am already on the point of being sacrificed; the time of my departure has come. ⁷ I have fought the good fight, I have finished the race, I have kept the faith. ⁸ Henceforth there is laid up for me the crown of righteousness, which the Lord, the righteous judge, will award to me on that Day, and not only to me but also to all who have loved his appearing.

The Letter of Paul to Titus

Titus accompanied Paul and Barnabas to the meeting of the apostles in Jerusalem (Acts 12:5), and later Paul entrusted him with the organization of the church on the island of Crete. This letter (written probably soon after the first letter to Timothy) begins with an outline of the duties of elders or bishops and continues with advice about dealings with other members of the flock.

Give Good Example for the Sake of the Gospel
Titus 2:1–15, 3:1–7

2 But as for you, teach what befits sound doctrine. ²Bid the older men be temperate, serious, sensible, sound in faith, in love, and in steadfastness. ³Bid the older women likewise to be reverent in behavior, not to be slanderers or slaves to drink; they are to teach what is good, ⁴and so train the young women to love their husbands and children, ⁵to be sensible, chaste, domestic, kind, and submissive to their husbands, that the word of God may not be discredited. ⁶Likewise urge the younger men to control themselves. ⁷Show yourself in all respects a model of good deeds, and in your teaching show integrity, gravity, ⁸and sound speech that cannot be censured, so that an opponent may be put to shame, having nothing evil to say of us. ⁹Bid slaves to be submissive to their masters and to give satisfaction in every respect; they are not to be refractory, ¹⁰nor to pilfer, but to show entire and true fidelity, so that in everything they may adorn the doctrine of God our Savior.

11 For the grace of God has appeared for the salvation of all men, ¹²training us to renounce irreligion and worldly passions, and to live sober, upright, and godly lives in this world, ¹³awaiting our blessed hope, the appearing of the glory of our great God and Savior Jesus Christ, ¹⁴who gave himself for us to redeem us from all iniquity and to purify for himself a people of his own who are zealous for good deeds.

15 Declare these things; exhort and reprove with all authority. Let no one disregard you.

3 Remind them to be submissive to rulers and authorities, to be obedient, to be ready for any honest work, ²to speak evil of no one, to avoid quarreling, to be gentle, and to show perfect courtesy toward all men. ³For we ourselves were once foolish, disobedient, led astray, slaves to various passions and pleasures, passing our days in malice and envy, hated by men and hating one another; ⁴but when

the goodness and loving kindness of God our Savior appeared, [5] he
saved us, not because of deeds done by us in righteousness, but in
virtue of his own mercy, by the washing of regeneration and renewal
in the Holy Spirit, [6] which he poured out upon us richly through
Jesus Christ our Savior, [7] so that we might be justified by his grace
and becomes heirs in hope of eternal life.

2:9 f. On the basis of this and such other passages as Ephesians
6:5–9 and 1 Peter 2:18–21, it has sometimes been charged that
Christianity was reactionary in its attitude toward the social evil of
slavery. Masters in the Christian community were commanded to
recognize themselves as servants of One who exhibits no partiality
(Ephesians 6:9). Paul bids Philemon treat Onesimus "no longer as a
slave but more than a slave as a beloved brother" (Philemon verse
16). Could the early Christians, a small minority not identified with
the power structure, have done anything more radical to end slavery
than insist that slaves be treated as brothers?

The Letter of Paul to Philemon

From prison (in Rome, before A.D. 63) Paul writes to the master of a slave who had robbed his master and run away. The slave had been converted to Christianity by Paul (see verse 10). Now Paul writes to the slave's master, Philemon, a resident of Colossae, in Phrygia, who had earlier become a Christian as a result of Paul's preaching. The entire letter is in these twenty-five verses.

Philemon 1–25

1 Paul, a prisoner for Christ Jesus, and Timothy our brother.

To Phile'mon our beloved fellow worker ²and Ap'phia our sister and Archip'pus our fellow soldier, and the church in your house:

3 Grace to you and peace from God our Father and the Lord Jesus Christ.

4 I thank my God always when I remember you in my prayers, ⁵because I hear of your love and of the faith which you have toward the Lord Jesus and all the saints, ⁶and I pray that the sharing of your faith may promote the knowledge of all the good that is ours in Christ. ⁷For I have derived much joy and comfort from your love, my brother, because the hearts of the saints have been refreshed through you.

8 Accordingly, though I am bold enough in Christ to command you to do what is required, ⁹yet for love's sake I prefer to appeal to you—I, Paul, an ambassador and now a prisoner also for Christ Jesus—¹⁰I appeal to you for my child, Ones'imus, whose father I have become in my imprisonment. ¹¹(Formerly he was useless to you, but now he is indeed useful to you and to me.) ¹²I am sending him back to you, sending my very heart. ¹³I would have been glad to keep him with me, in order that he might serve me on your behalf during my imprisonment for the gospel; ¹⁴but I preferred to do nothing without your consent in order that your goodness might not be by compulsion but of your own free will.

15 Perhaps this is why he was parted from you for a while, that you might have him back for ever, ¹⁶no longer as a slave but more than a slave, as a beloved brother, especially to me but how much more to you, both in the flesh and in the Lord. ¹⁷So if you consider me your partner, receive him as you would receive me. ¹⁸If he has wronged you at all, or owes you anything, charge that to my account. ¹⁹I, Paul, write this with my own hand, I will repay it—to

say nothing of your owing me even your own self. [20] Yes, brother, I want some benefit from you in the Lord. Refresh my heart in Christ.

21 Confident of your obedience, I write to you, knowing that you will do even more than I say. [22] At the same time, prepare a guest room for me, for I am hoping through your prayers to be granted to you.

23 Ep'aphras, my fellow prisoner in Christ Jesus, sends greetings to you, [24] and so do Mark, Aristar'chus, Demas, and Luke, my fellow workers.

25 The grace of the Lord Jesus Christ be with your spirit.

1:16 ff. Compare 1 Corinthians 7:23.

The Letter to the Hebrews

This anonymous letter contains the longest sustained argument of
any book in the Bible. Without address or greeting it goes directly
into the argument that Jesus was superior to prophets, angels and
Moses. Apparently some discouraged converts to Christianity were
about to return to their earlier beliefs and practices. Details in the
letter suggest it was written before the fall of Jerusalem and the
destruction of the temple (A.D. 70). The early church did not believe
Paul wrote this letter, and present-day students see its argument and
style as so different from Paul's that authorship by him is unthinkable. After his name became attached to it, some argued that he had
a different secretary to write it; or had someone else (Apollos?
Barnabas?) familiar with Paul's thinking composed this letter? All
these matters—author, date, recipients—are disputed, and some
argue that this is a sermon rather than a letter.

Jesus Is Superior to the Angels

Hebrews 1:1–9

1 In many and various ways God spoke of old to our fathers by
the prophets; ²but in these last days he has spoken to us by a
Son, whom he appointed the heir of all things, through whom
also he created the world. ³He reflects the glory of God and bears
the very stamp of his nature, upholding the universe by his word
of power. When he had made purification for sins, he sat down at
the right hand of the Majesty on high, ⁴having become as much
superior to angels as the name he has obtained is more excellent than
theirs.

5 For to what angel did God ever say,
"Thou art my Son,
today I have begotten thee"?
Or again,
"I will be to him a father,
and he shall be to me a son"?
⁶ And again, when he brings the first-born into the world, he says,
"Let all God's angels worship him."
⁷ Of the angels he says,
"Who makes his angels winds,
and his servants flames of fire."
⁸ But of the Son he says,

"Thy throne, O God, is for ever and ever,
the righteous scepter is the scepter of thy kingdom.
⁹ Thou hast loved righteousness and hated lawlessness;
therefore God, thy God, has anointed thee
with the oil of gladness beyond thy comrades."

Jesus Is Superior to Moses

Hebrews 3:1–6

3 Therefore, holy brethren, who share in a heavenly call, consider Jesus, the apostle and high priest of our confession. ² He was faithful to him who appointed him, just as Moses also was faithful in God's house. ³ Yet Jesus has been counted worthy of as much more glory than Moses as the builder of a house has more honor than the house. ⁴ (For every house is built by some one, but the builder of all things is God.) ⁵ Now Moses was faithful in all God's house as a servant, to testify to the things that were to be spoken later, ⁶ but Christ was faithful over God's house as a son. And we are his house if we hold fast our confidence and pride in our hope.

Jesus Is Superior to the High Priests

Hebrews 4:14–16; 5:1–7; 7:26–27

14 Since then we have a great high priest who has passed through the heavens, Jesus, the Son of God, let us hold fast our confession. ¹⁵ For we have not a high priest who is unable to sympathize with our weaknesses, but one who in every respect has been tempted as we are, yet without sinning. ¹⁶ Let us then with confidence draw near to the throne of grace, that we may receive mercy and find grace to help in time of need.

5 For every high priest chosen from among men is appointed to act on behalf of men in relation to God, to offer gifts and sacrifices for sins. ² He can deal gently with the ignorant and wayward, since he himself is beset with weakness. ³ Because of this he is bound to offer sacrifice for his own sins as well as for those of the people. ⁴ And one does not take the honor upon himself, but he is called by God, just as Aaron was.

5 So also Christ did not exalt himself to be made a high priest, but was appointed by him who said to him,

"Thou art my Son,
today I have begotten thee";
⁶ as he says also in another place,
"Thou art a priest for ever,
after the order of Melchiz'edek."

7 In the days of his flesh, Jesus offered up prayers and supplications, with loud cries and tears, to him who was able to save him from death, and he was heard for his godly fear.

26 For it was fitting that we should have such a high priest, holy, blameless, unstained, separated from sinners, exalted above the heavens. ²⁷ He has no need, like those high priests, to offer sacrifices daily, first for his own sins and then for those of the people; he did this once for all when he offered up himself.

5:6 Compare Psalm 110:4 and Genesis 14:18.

The New Covenant Is Superior to the Old
Hebrews 8:6–13; 9:11–15, 24–28

6 But as it is, Christ has obtained a ministry which is as much more excellent than the old as the covenant he mediates is better, since it is enacted on better promises. ⁷ For if that first covenant had been faultless, there would have been no occasion for a second.

8 For he finds fault with them when he says:
"The days will come, say the Lord,
　when I will establish a new covenant with the house of Israel
　and with the house of Judah:
⁹ not like the covenant that I made with their fathers
　on the day when I took them by the hand
　to lead them out of the land of Egypt;
　for they did not continue in my covenant,
　and so I paid no heed to them, says the Lord.
¹⁰ This is the covenant that I will make with the house of Israel
　after those days, says the Lord:
　I will put my laws into their minds,
　and write them on their hearts,
　and I will be their God,
　and they shall be my people.
¹¹ And they shall not teach every one his fellow
　or every one his brother, saying, 'Know the Lord,'
　for all shall know me,
　from the least of them to the greatest.
¹² For I will be merciful toward their iniquities,
　and I will remember their sins no more."
¹³ In speaking of a new covenant he treats the first as obsolete. And what is becoming obsolete and growing old is ready to vanish away.

9 ¹¹ But when Christ appeared as a high priest of the good things that have come, then through the greater and more perfect tent (not made with hands, that is, not of this creation) ¹² he entered once for

all into the Holy Place, taking not the blood of goats and calves but his own blood, thus securing an eternal redemption. [13] For if the sprinkling of defiled persons with the blood of goats and bulls and with the ashes of a heifer sanctifies for the purification of the flesh, [14] how much more shall the blood of Christ, who through the eternal Spirit offered himself without blemish to God, purify your conscience from dead works to serve the living God.

15 Therefore he is the mediator of a new covenant, so that those who are called may receive the promised eternal inheritance, since a death has occurred which redeems them from the transgressions under the first covenant.

24 For Christ has entered, not into a sanctuary made with hands, a copy of the true one, but into heaven itself, now to appear in the presence of God on our behalf. [25] Nor was it to offer himself repeatedly, as the high priest enters the Holy Place yearly with blood not his own; [26] for then he would have had to suffer repeatedly since the foundation of the world. But as it is, he has appeared once for all at the end of the age to put away sin by the sacrifice of himself. [27] And just as it is appointed for men to die once, and after that comes judgment, [28] so Christ, having been offered once to bear the sins of many, will appear a second time, not to deal with sin but to save those who are eagerly waiting for him.

8:8–12 Jeremiah 31:31–34. **8:13** Some Christian theologians have believed that once the Jews had prepared the way for Jesus, the Jewish religion became obsolete. The renaissance of Jewish life and the vitality of the Jewish religion to this day have occasioned questions regarding the nature of God's covenant with the Jews and the enduring significance of the Mosaic Law, at least until the second coming of Jesus. **9:13** Compare Leviticus 16:6, 16; Numbers 19:1, 17–18.

Confidence Has a Great Reward

Hebrews 10:19–39

19 Therefore, brethren, since we have confidence to enter the sanctuary by the blood of Jesus, [20] by the new and living way which he opened for us through the curtain, that is, through his flesh, [21] and since we have a great priest over the house of God, [22] let us draw near with a true heart in full assurance of faith, with our hearts sprinkled clean from an evil conscience and our bodies washed with pure water. [23] Let us hold fast the confession of our hope without wavering, for he who promised is faithful; [24] and let us consider how to stir up one another to love and good works, [25] not

neglecting to meet together, as is the habit of some, but encouraging one another, and all the more as you see the Day drawing near.

26 For if we sin deliberately after receiving the knowledge of the truth, there no longer remains a sacrifice for sins, [27] but a fearful prospect of judgment, and a fury of fire which will consume the adversaries. [28] A man who has violated the law of Moses dies without mercy at the testimony of two or three witnesses. [29] How much worse punishment do you think will be deserved by the man who has spurned the Son of God, and profaned the blood of the covenant by which he was sanctified, and outraged the Spirit of grace? [30] For we know him who said, "Vengeance is mine, I will repay." And again, "The Lord will judge his people." [31] It is a fearful thing to fall into the hands of the living God.

32 But recall the former days when, after you were enlightened, you endured a hard struggle with sufferings, [33] sometimes being publicly exposed to abuse and affliction, and sometimes being partners with those so treated. [34] For you had compassion on the prisoners, and you joyfully accepted the plundering of your property, since you knew that you yourselves had a better possession and an abiding one. [35] Therefore do not throw away your confidence, which has a great reward. [36] For you have need of endurance, so that you may do the will of God and receive what is promised.

[37] "For yet a little while,
　　and the coming one shall come and shall not tarry;
　[38] but my righteous one shall live by faith,
　　and if he shrinks back,
　　my soul has no pleasure in him."
[39] But we are not of those who shrink back and are destroyed, but of those who have faith and keep their souls.

10:30 Compare Deuteronomy 32:35–36. **10:37** Compare Habakkuk 2:3–4.

Old Testament Witnesses to Faith

This chapter cites heroes and heroines of the Old Testament who were distinguished for their faith. Verse 16 suggests that their desire was for a heavenly city, which is now promised to the followers of Christ. Jewish scholars hold that in that biblical period the desire of the Old Testament heroes was for establishment of God's kingdom on earth.

Hebrews 11:1–4, 8–10, 13–16, 32–40, 12:1–2

11 Now faith is the assurance of things hoped for, the conviction of things not seen. [2] For by it the men of old received divine approval. [3] By faith we understand that the world was created by the word of

God, so that what is seen was made out of things which do not appear.

4 By faith Abel offered to God a more acceptable sacrifice than Cain, through which he received approval as righteous, God bearing witness by accepting his gifts; he died, but through his faith he is still speaking.

8 By faith Abraham obeyed when he was called to go out to a place which he was to receive as an inheritance; and he went out, not knowing where he was to go. [9] By faith he sojourned in the land of promise, as in a foreign land, living in tents with Isaac and Jacob, heirs with him of the same promise. [10] For he looked forward to the city which has foundations, whose builder and maker is God.

13 These all died in faith, not having received what was promised, but having seen it and greeted it from afar, and having acknowledged that they were strangers and exiles on the earth. [14] For people who speak thus make it clear that they are seeking a homeland. [15] If they had been thinking of that land from which they had gone out, they would have had opportunity to return. [16] But as it is, they desire a better country, that is, a heavenly one. Therefore God is not ashamed to be called their God, for he has prepared for them a city.

32 And what more shall I say? For time would fail me to tell of Gideon, Barak, Samson, Jephthah, of David and Samuel and the prophets—[33] who through faith conquered kingdoms, enforced justice, received promises, stopped the mouths of lions, [34] quenched raging fire, escaped the edge of the sword, won strength out of weakness, became mighty in war, put foreign armies to flight. [35] Women received their dead by resurrection. Some were tortured, refusing to accept release, that they might rise again to a better life. [36] Others suffered mocking and scourging, and even chains and imprisonment. [37] They were stoned, they were sawn in two, they were killed with the sword; they went about in skins of sheep and goats, destitute, afflicted, ill-treated—[38] of whom the world was not worthy—wandering over deserts and mountains, and in dens and caves of the earth.

39 And all these, though well attested by their faith, did not receive what was promised, [40] since God had foreseen something better for us, that apart from us they should not be made perfect.

12 Therefore, since we are surrounded by so great a cloud of witnesses, let us also lay aside every weight, and sin which clings so closely, and let us run with perseverance the race that is set before us, [2] looking to Jesus the pioneer and perfecter of our faith, who for the joy that was set before him endured the cross, despising the shame, and is seated at the right hand of the throne of God.

11:1 Tyndale: Fayth is a sure confidence of things which are hoped for, and a certayntie of things which are not seen. Geneva Bible: Now faith is the grounde of things, which are hoped for, and the evidence of things which are not seen. Rheims: And faith is, the substance of things to be hoped for, the argument of things not appearing. King James Version: Now faith is the substance of *things* hoped for, the evidence of things not seen. (RV) ASV: Now faith is assurance of *things* hoped for, a conviction of things not seen. **11:8** Persecuted by the established order and forced to flee his home, Luther wrote to Spalatin: "I am girded like Abraham to go I know not where, but sure of this, that God is everywhere."

"The Lord Is My Helper"
Hebrews 13:1–8

13 Let brotherly love continue. ² Do not neglect to show hospitality to strangers, for thereby some have entertained angels unawares. ³ Remember those who are in prison, as though in prison with them; and those who are ill-treated, since you also are in the body. ⁴ Let marriage be held in honor among all, and let the marriage bed be undefiled; for God will judge the immoral and adulterous. ⁵ Keep your life free from love of money, and be content with what you have; for he has said, "I will never fail you nor forsake you." ⁶ Hence we can confidently say,

"The Lord is my helper,
    I will not be afraid;
    what can man do to me?"

7 Remember your leaders, those who spoke to you the word of God; consider the outcome of their life, and imitate their faith. ⁸ Jesus Christ is the same yesterday and today and for ever.

13:6 Compare Psalm 118:6.

The Letter of James

The letters of James, Peter, John and Jude are frequently called the "catholic" epistles because they seem intended for a wide circle of readers. The James to whom this letter is attributed was James the Less, son of Alpheus (or Cleophas), whose mother was a sister or close relative of Mary, Jesus' mother, and for that reason he was called "the brother of the Lord," according to Jewish custom. James the Less is traditionally regarded as the first bishop of Jerusalem. According to early Church historians, James died a martyr in the spring of A.D. 62. The language and style of the Greek in the letter have inclined scholars to suggest dates of composition all the way from A.D. 49 to the end of the first century. The "letter" is by our practice better called an epistle, since it is addressed to churches in general and is formal in style. It reads like a sermon in the style of the Hebrew prophets such as Amos, denouncing individual immorality and pointing to its social consequences. The *twelve tribes* in the opening verse means the Jewish people scattered throughout the world; in this context the terms refers to the Christians (converted from Judaism) living outside Palestine. The letter is notable for the allusions it makes to the Sermon on the Mount.

Be Doers of the Word, Not Hearers Only
James 1 : 1, 12–27

1 James, a servant of God and of the Lord Jesus Christ,
To the twelve tribes in the Dispersion:
Greeting.

12 Blessed is the man who endures trial, for when he has stood the test he will receive the crown of life which God has promised to those who love him. ¹³ Let no one say when he is tempted, "I am tempted by God"; for God cannot be tempted with evil and he himself tempts no one; ¹⁴ but each person is tempted when he is lured and enticed by his own desire. ¹⁵ Then desire when it has conceived gives birth to sin; and sin when it is full-grown brings forth death.

16 Do not be deceived, my beloved brethren. ¹⁷ Every good endowment and every perfect gift is from above, coming down from the Father of lights with whom there is no variation or shadow due to change. ¹⁸ Of his own will he brought us forth by the word of truth that we should be a kind of first fruits of his creatures.

19 Know this, my beloved brethren. Let every man be quick to hear, slow to speak, slow to anger, ²⁰ for the anger of man does not work the righteousness of God. ²¹ Therefore put away all filthiness

and rank growth of wickedness and receive with meekness the implanted word, which is able to save your souls.

22 But be doers of the word, and not hearers only, deceiving yourselves. [23] For if any one is a hearer of the word and not a doer, he is like a man who observes his natural face in a mirror; [24] for he observes himself and goes away and at once forgets what he was like. [25] But he who looks into the perfect law, the law of liberty, and perseveres, being no hearer that forgets but a doer that acts, he shall be blessed in his doing.

26 If any one thinks he is religious, and does not bridle his tongue but deceives his heart, this man's religion is vain. [27] Religion that is pure and undefiled before God and the Father is this: to visit orphans and widows in their affliction, and to keep oneself unstained from the world.

1:25 James uses many different expressions to describe the gospel of good news about Jesus; the word of truth, the implanted word, the perfect law, the law of liberty. **1:12** Older translations have "temptation" for "trial."

Faith without Works is Dead
James 2:1–26

2 My brethren, show no partiality as you hold the faith of our Lord Jesus Christ, the Lord of glory. [2] For if a man with gold rings and in fine clothing comes into your assembly, and a poor man in shabby clothing also comes in, [3] and you pay attention to the one who wears the fine clothing and say, "Have a seat here, please," while you say to the poor man, "Stand there," or, "Sit at my feet," [4] have you not made distinctions among yourselves, and become judges with evil thoughts? [5] Listen, my beloved brethren. Has not God chosen those who are poor in the world to be rich in faith and heirs of the kingdom which he has promised to those who love him? [6] But you have dishonored the poor man. Is it not the rich who oppress you, is it not they who drag you into court? [7] Is it not they who blaspheme that honorable name by which you are called?

8 If you really fulfil the royal law, according to the scripture, "You shall love your neighbor as yourself," you do well. [9] But if you show partiality, you commit sin, and are convicted by the law as transgressors. [10] For whoever keeps the whole law but fails in one point has become guilty of all of it. [11] For he who said, "Do not commit adultery," said also, "Do not kill." If you do not commit adultery but do kill, you have become a transgressor of the law. [12] So speak and so act as those who are to be judged under the law of

liberty. [13] For judgment is without mercy to one who has shown no mercy; yet mercy triumphs over judgment.

14 What does it profit, my brethren, if a man says he has faith but has not works? Can his faith save him? [15] If a brother or sister is ill-clad and in lack of daily food, [16] and one of you says to them, "Go in peace, be warmed and filled," without giving them the things needed for the body, what does it profit? [17] So faith by itself, if it has no works, is dead.

[18] But some one will say, "You have faith and I have works." Show me your faith apart from your works, and I by my works will show you my faith. [19] You believe that God is one; you do well. Even the demons believe—and shudder. [20] Do you want to be shown, you foolish fellow, that faith apart from works is barren? [21] Was not Abraham our father justified by works, when he offered his son Isaac upon the altar? [22] You see that faith was active along with his works, and faith was completed by works, [23] and the scripture was fulfilled which says, "Abraham believed God, and it was reckoned to him as righteousness"; and he was called the friend of God. [24] You see that a man is justified by works and not by faith alone. [25] And in the same way was not also Rahab the harlot justified by works when she received the messengers and sent them out another way? [26] For as the body apart from the spirit is dead, so faith apart from works is dead.

2:1 Although Martin Luther's emphasis on the Pauline doctrine of grace led him to repudiate the Letter of James, he wrote: "Good works do not make a man good, but a good man does good works . . . the justified man is not obliged to live rightly, but he lives rightly; and he needs no law to teach him to do so." 2:25 Compare Joshua 2:1-21.

Tame the Tongue
James 3:1-18

3 Let not many of you become teachers, my brethren, for you know that we who teach shall be judged with greater strictness. [2] For we all make many mistakes, and if any one makes no mistakes in what he says he is a perfect man, able to bridle the whole body also. [3] If we put bits into the mouths of horses that they may obey us, we guide their whole bodies. [4] Look at the ships also; though they are so great and are driven by strong winds, they are guided by a very small rudder wherever the will of the pilot directs. [5] So the tongue is a little member and boasts of great things. How great a forest is set ablaze by a small fire!

6 And the tongue is a fire. The tongue is an unrighteous world

among our members, staining the whole body, setting on fire the cycle of nature, and set on fire by hell. ⁷ For every kind of beast and bird, of reptile and sea creature, can be tamed and has been tamed by humankind, ⁸ but no human being can tame the tongue—a restless evil, full of deadly poison. ⁹ With it we bless the Lord and Father, and with it we curse men, who are made in the likeness of God. ¹⁰ From the same mouth come blessing and cursing. My brethren, this ought not to be so. ¹¹ Does a spring pour forth from the same opening fresh water and brackish? ¹² Can a fig tree, my brethren, yield olives, or a grapevine figs? No more can salt water yield fresh.

13 Who is wise and understanding among you? By his good life let him show his works in the meekness of wisdom. ¹⁴ But if you have bitter jealousy and selfish ambition in your hearts, do not boast and be false to the truth. ¹⁵ This wisdom is not such as comes down from above, but is earthly, unspiritual, devilish. ¹⁶ For where jealousy and selfish ambition exist, there will be disorder and every vile practice. ¹⁷ But the wisdom from above is first pure, then peaceable, gentle, open to reason, full of mercy and good fruits, without uncertainty or insincerity. ¹⁸ And the harvest of righteousness is sown in peace by those who make peace.

What Causes Wars?

James 4:1–8

4 What causes wars, and what causes fightings among you? Is it not your passions that are at war in your members? ² You desire and do not have; so you kill. And you covet and cannot obtain; so you fight and wage war. You do not have, because you do not ask. ³ You ask and do not receive, because you ask wrongly, to spend it on your passions. ⁴ Unfaithful creatures! Do you not know that friendship with the world is enmity with God? Therefore whoever wishes to be a friend of the world makes himself an enemy of God. ⁵ Or do you suppose it is in vain that the scripture says, "He yearns jealously over the spirit which he has made to dwell in us"? ⁶ But he gives more grace; therefore it says, "God opposes the proud, but gives grace to the humble." ⁷ Submit yourselves therefore to God. Resist the devil and he will flee from you. ⁸ Draw near to God and he will draw near to you. Cleanse your hands, you sinners, and purify your hearts, you men of double mind.

4:4 To understand this passage, it is necessary to keep in mind that, in the New Testament, the word "world" is used—as indeed it is among us—in two quite different senses. On the one hand, the world is God's creation and he called it good; it is in the world that his purposes are being worked out; the world is the scene of his mighty acts; the world is the habitation of man made in his image. On the other hand, the "world" represents life organized apart from God, the belief on the part of his creation in its own self-sufficiency. It is obviously in the latter sense that friends of the world are enemies of God. In the former sense, "God so loved the world that he gave his only Son" (John 3:16). The world that God loves must not be despised by man. **4:6** Compare Proverbs 3:34.

James Attacks Economic Evils
James 5:1–12

5 Come now, you rich, weep and howl for the miseries that are coming upon you. ² Your riches have rotted and your garments are moth-eaten. ³ Your gold and silver have rusted, and their rust will be evidence against you and will eat your flesh like fire. You have laid up treasure for the last days. ⁴ Behold, the wages of the laborers who mowed your fields, which you kept back by fraud, cry out; and the cries of the harvesters have reached the ears of the Lord of hosts. ⁵ You have lived on the earth in luxury and in pleasure; you have fattened your hearts in a day of slaughter. ⁶ You have condemned, you have killed the righteous man; he does not resist you.

7 Be patient, therefore, brethren, until the coming of the Lord. Behold, the farmer waits for the precious fruit of the earth, being patient over it until it receives the early and the late rain. ⁸ You also be patient. Establish your hearts, for the coming of the Lord is at hand. ⁹ Do not grumble, brethren, against one another, that you may not be judged; behold, the Judge is standing at the doors. ¹⁰ As an example of suffering and patience, brethren, take the prophets who spoke in the name of the Lord. ¹¹ Behold, we call those happy who were steadfast. You have heard of the steadfastness of Job, and you have seen the purpose of the Lord, how the Lord is compassionate and merciful.

12 But above all, my brethren, do not swear, either by heaven or by earth or with any other oath, but let your yes be yes and your no be no, that you may not fall under condemnation.

The Power of Prayer
James 5:13–20

13 Is any one among you suffering? Let him pray. Is any cheerful? Let him sing praise. ¹⁴ Is any among you sick? Let him call for the elders of the church, and let them pray over him, anointing him with oil in the name of the Lord; ¹⁵ and the prayer of faith will save the sick man, and the Lord will raise him up; and if he has committed

sins, he will be forgiven. [16] Therefore confess your sins to one another, and pray for one another, that you may be healed. The prayer of a righteous man has great power in its effects. [17] Eli'jah was a man of like nature with ourselves and he prayed fervently that it might not rain, and for three years and six months it did not rain on the earth. [18] Then he prayed again and the heaven gave rain, and the earth brought forth its fruit.

19 My brethren, if any one among you wanders from the truth and some one brings him back, [20] let him know that whoever brings back a sinner from the error of his way will save his soul from death and will cover a multitude of sins.

5:14–15 The Catholic Church holds that these verses describe the sacrament of extreme unction (the last anointing), which is administered to the sick who are in danger of dying. The priest dips his thumb in holy oil and anoints eyes, ears, nose, mouth, hands and feet, praying in each case that God will forgive sins committed by these members. Then he reads this passage from the letter of James and prays that the person may return to good health if it be the will of God. Verses 13–16 are also read in the special Mass for the Sick. Protestants also pray with the sick and sometimes anoint them. They hold that the purpose of the ministry here enjoined is not to prepare the sick man for death, but that he may be made well.

The First Letter of Peter

This letter was apparently written to encourage Christians undergoing persecution in northern Asia Minor. Verse 5:12 states that Silvanus (identified by some with Silas, Paul's missionary companion) had some part in writing the letter.

Christians Are Heir to Israel

The first chapter of the letter sets forth the resurrection of Jesus from the dead as the foundation of Christian hope. Then the writer applies a number of Old Testament passages to Jesus and his followers.

1 Peter 2:1–10

2 So put away all malice and all guile and insincerity and envy and all slander. ² Like newborn babes, long for the pure spiritual milk, that by it you may grow up to salvation; ³ for you have tasted the kindness of the Lord.

4 Come to him, to that living stone, rejected by men but in God's sight chosen and precious; ⁵ and like living stones be yourselves built into a spiritual house, to be a holy priesthood, to offer spiritual sacrifices acceptable to God through Jesus Christ. ⁶ For it stands in scripture:

> "Behold, I am laying in Zion a stone, a cornerstone chosen and precious,
>> and he who believes in him will not be put to shame."

⁷ To you therefore who believe, he is precious, but for those who do not believe,

> "The very stone which the builders rejected
>> has become the head of the corner,"

⁸ and

> "A stone that will make men stumble,
>> a rock that will make them fall";

for they stumble because they disobey the word, as they were destined to do.

9 But you are a chosen race, a royal priesthood, a holy nation, God's own people, that you may declare the wonderful deeds of him who called you out of darkness into his marvelous light. ¹⁰ Once you were no people but now you are God's people; once you had not received mercy but now you have received mercy.

2:6 Compare Isaiah 28:16. **2:7** Compare Psalm 118:22. **2:8–9** See note on Ephesians 1:4–5, Isaiah 8:14–15. **2:9–10** This passage strikingly expressed the Christian claim that Christians have become "the chosen people of God." This issue in the relation between Christian and Jew—each claiming to be God's priest people—is one of the problems that theologians will discuss in inter-religious dialogue.

Live as Free Men

Advice for the citizen (respect for civil authority) and for Christian servants, husbands and wives is followed by a statement of Christian charity (phrased in terms of Psalm 34:12–16) and a statement on Christian suffering. The Christian is instructed to give an account of his beliefs when he is asked to do so.

1 Peter 2:13–17; 3:8–17; 4:7–11

13 Be subject for the Lord's sake to every human institution, whether it be to the emperor as supreme, [14] or to governors as sent by him to punish those who do wrong and to praise those who do right. [15] For it is God's will that by doing right you should put to silence the ignorance of foolish men. [16] Live as free men, yet without using your freedom as a pretext for evil; but live as servants of God. [17] Honor all men. Love the brotherhood. Fear God. Honor the emperor.

3 [8] Finally, all of you, have unity of spirit, sympathy, love of the brethren, a tender heart and a humble mind. [9] Do not return evil for evil or reviling for reviling; but on the contrary bless, for to this you have been called, that you may obtain a blessing. [10] For

"He that would love life
and see good days,
let him keep his tongue from evil
and his lips from speaking guile;
[11] let him turn away from evil and do right;
let him seek peace and pursue it.
[12] For the eyes of the Lord are upon the righteous,
and his ears are open to their prayer.
But the face of the Lord is against those that do evil."

13 Now who is there to harm you if you are zealous for what is right? [14] But even if you do suffer for righteousness' sake, you will be blessed. Have no fear of them, nor be troubled, [15] but in your hearts reverence Christ as Lord. Always be prepared to make a defense to any one who calls you to account for the hope that is in you, yet do it with gentleness and reverence; [16] and keep your conscience clear, so that, when you are abused, those who

revile your good behavior in Christ may be put to shame. [17] For it is better to suffer for doing right, if that should be God's will, than for doing wrong.

4 [7] The end of all things is at hand; therefore keep sane and sober for your prayers. [8] Above all hold unfailing your love for one another, since love covers a multitude of sins. [9] Practice hospitality ungrudgingly to one another. [10] As each has received a gift, employ it for one another, as good stewards of God's varied grace: [11] whoever speaks, as one who utters oracles of God; whoever renders service, as one who renders it by the strength which God supplies; in order that in everything God may be glorified through Jesus Christ. To him belong glory and dominion for ever and ever. Amen.

2:13 and 17 English translations for centuries understandably put "king" for "emperor." **2:16** One of Luther's most effective tracts was entitled "The Freedom of the Christian Man." This treatise rests on the twin propositions: "Christian man is the most free lord of all, and subject to none; a Christian man is the most dutiful servant to all, and subject to everyone." By faith man is subservient only to God; but he is also called to be a most concerned and loving neighbor.

God Gives Grace to the Humble
1 Peter 5:1–14

5 So I exhort the elders among you, as a fellow elder and a witness of the sufferings of Christ as well as a partaker in the glory that is to be revealed. [2] Tend the flock of God that is your charge, not by constraint but willingly, not for shameful gain but eagerly, [3] not as domineering over those in your charge but being examples to the flock. [4] And when the chief Shepherd is manifested you will obtain the unfading crown of glory. [5] Likewise you that are younger be subject to the elders. Clothe yourselves, all of you, with humility toward one another, for "God opposes the proud, but gives grace to the humble."

[6] Humble yourselves therefore under the mighty hand of God, that in due time he may exalt you. [7] Cast all your anxieties on him, for he cares about you. [8] Be sober, be watchful. Your adversary the devil prowls around like a roaring lion, seeking some one to devour. [9] Resist him, firm in your faith, knowing that the same experience of suffering is required of your brotherhood throughout the world. [10] And after you have suffered a little while, the God of all grace, who has called you to his eternal glory in Christ, will himself restore, establish, and strengthen you. [11] To him be the dominion for ever and ever. Amen.

12 By Silva'nus, a faithful brother as I regard him, I have written briefly to you, exhorting and declaring that this is the true grace of God; stand fast in it. ¹³ She who is at Babylon, who is likewise chosen, sends you greetings; and so does my son Mark. ¹⁴ Greet one another with the kiss of love.

Peace to all of you that are in Christ.

The Second Letter of Peter

This letter warns its readers against false teachers and explains the delay of the expected second coming of the Lord. Because the author refers to Paul's letters as if they were already a published collection and equal to "the other scriptures"—details that developed after Peter's death—many scholars think that a secretary or disciple of Peter published it under Peter's name, presenting Peter's point of view, according to an accepted literary convention of the times.

The Day of the Lord Will Come

2 Peter 3:8–18

8 But do not ignore this one fact, beloved, that with the Lord one day is as a thousand years, and a thousand years as one day. 9 The Lord is not slow about his promise as some count slowness, but is forbearing toward you, not wishing that any should perish, but that all should reach repentance. 10 But the day of the Lord will come like a thief, and then the heavens will pass away with a loud noise, and the elements will be dissolved with fire, and the earth and the works that are upon it will be burned up.

11 Since all these things are thus to be dissolved, what sort of persons ought you to be in lives of holiness and godliness, 12 waiting for and hastening the coming of the day of God, because of which the heavens will be kindled and dissolved, and the elements will melt with fire! 13 But according to his promise we wait for new heavens and a new earth in which righteousness dwells.

14 Therefore, beloved, since you wait for these, be zealous to be found by him without spot or blemish, and at peace. 15 And count the forbearance of our Lord as salvation. So also our beloved brother Paul wrote to you according to the wisdom given him, 16 speaking of this as he does in all his letters. There are some things in them hard to understand, which the ignorant and unstable twist to their own destruction, as they do the other scriptures. 17 You therefore, beloved, knowing this beforehand, beware lest you be carried away with the error of lawless men and lose your own stability. 18 But grow in the grace and knowledge of our Lord and Savior Jesus Christ. To him be the glory both now and to the day of eternity. Amen.

3:8 Compare Psalm 90:4. **3:10** Compare current suggestions that life on earth may end by nuclear fission; note in verse 13 a reason why this possibility is not feared by persons of this faith.

The Three Letters of John

Vocabulary, style and ideas associate The First Letter of John with the Gospel according to John. It does not have the usual salutation and ending. It is an epistle ("epistle general," as the Geneva Bible and the King James Version call it), or encyclical, a letter for general circulation, as Catholic writers often call it. It was written to set forth basic truths about love and to reject Gnostic teachings. The Second Letter of John briefly repeats the main teaching of the first letter. The Third Letter of John, also very brief, applies the same basic points to a particular case.

He Who Loves His Brother Is in Light
1 John 1:5–2:11, 15–17

5 This is the message we have heard from him and proclaim to you, that God is light and in him is no darkness at all. ⁶ If we say we have fellowship with him while we walk in darkness, we lie and do not live according to the truth; ⁷ but if we walk in the light, as he is in the light, we have fellowship with one another, and the blood of Jesus his Son cleanses us from all sin. ⁸ If we say we have no sin, we deceive ourselves, and the truth is not in us. ⁹ If we confess our sins, he is faithful and just, and will forgive our sins and cleanse us from all unrighteousness. ¹⁰ If we say we have not sinned, we make him a liar, and his word is not in us.

2 My little children, I am writing this to you so that you may not sin; but if any one does sin, we have an advocate with the Father, Jesus Christ the righteous; ² and he is the expiation for our sins, and not for ours only but also for the sins of the whole world. ³ And by this we may be sure that we know him, if we keep his commandments. ⁴ He who says "I know him" but disobeys his commandments is a liar, and the truth is not in him; ⁵ but whoever keeps his word, in him truly love for God is perfected. By this we may be sure that we are in him: ⁶ he who says he abides in him ought to walk in the same way in which he walked.

7 Beloved, I am writing you no new commandment, but an old commandment which you had from the beginning; the old commandment is the word which you have heard. ⁸ Yet I am writing you a new commandment, which is true in him and in you, because the darkness is passing away and the true light is already shining. ⁹ He who says he is in the light and hates his brother is in the darkness still. ¹⁰ He who loves his brother abides in the light, and in it there is no cause for stumbling. ¹¹ But he who hates his brother is in the

darkness and walks in the darkness, and does not know where he is going, because the darkness has blinded his eyes.

15 Do not love the world or the things in the world. If any one loves the world, love for the Father is not in him. [16] For all that is in the world, the lust of the flesh and the lust of the eyes and the pride of life, is not of the Father but is of the world. [17] And the world passes away, and the lust of it; but he who does the will of God abides for ever.

1:5 This was a favorite passage of Helen Keller (1880–1968), who triumphed over blindness and deafness not only to speak but also to "read" with her fingertips. She was a friend of American presidents, traveled in many parts of the world, and learned several languages. **2:1** Thomas Arnold (1795–1842), headmaster of Rugby, said to his students: "Always expect to succeed, and never think you have succeeded." **2:17** The second part of this text is inscribed on the tombstone of Dwight L. Moody (1837–1899), at Northfield, Mass. A shoe clerk, Moody determined to see what God could do with one wholly surrendered life. He became the best-known evangelist of his time, conducting campaigns in America and Britain. He founded the Northfield Seminary for girls and the Mt. Hermon School for boys, and for him The Moody Bible Institute in Chicago is named.

He Who Does Not Love Remains in Death
1 John 3:2–24

3 [2] Beloved, we are God's children now; it does not yet appear what we shall be, but we know that when he appears we shall be like him, for we shall see him as he is. [3] And every one who thus hopes in him purifies himself as he is pure.

4 Every one who commits sin is guilty of lawlessness; sin is lawlessness. [5] You know that he appeared to take away sins, and in him there is no sin. [6] No one who abides in him sins; no one who sins has either seen him or known him. [7] Little children, let no one deceive you. He who does right is righteous, as he is righteous. [8] He who commits sin is of the devil; for the devil has sinned from the beginning. The reason the Son of God appeared was to destroy the works of the devil. [9] No one born of God commits sin; for God's nature abides in him, and he cannot sin because he is born of God. [10] By this it may be seen who are the children of God, and who are the children of the devil; whoever does not do right is not of God, nor he who does not love his brother.

11 For this is the message which you have heard from the beginning, that we should love one another, [12] and not be like Cain who was of the evil one and murdered his brother. And why did he murder him? Because his own deeds were evil and his brother's

righteous. ¹³ Do not wonder, brethren, that the world hates you.
¹⁴ We know that we have passed out of death into life, because we
love the brethren. He who does not love remains in death. ¹⁵ Any one
who hates his brother is a murderer, and you know that no murderer
has eternal life abiding in him. ¹⁶ By this we know love, that he laid
down his life for us; and we ought to lay down our lives for the
brethren. ¹⁷ But if any one has the world's goods and sees his brother
in need, yet closes his heart against him, how does God's love abide
in him? ¹⁸ Little children, let us not love in word or speech but in
deed and in truth.

19 By this we shall know that we are of the truth, and reassure
our hearts before him ²⁰ whenever our hearts condemn us; for God is
greater than our hearts, and he knows everything. ²¹ Beloved, if our
hearts do not condemn us, we have confidence before God; ²² and we
receive from him whatever we ask, because we keep his commandments and do what pleases him. ²³ And this is his commandment,
that we should believe in the name of his Son Jesus Christ and love
one another, just as he has commanded us. ²⁴ All who keep his
commandments abide in him, and he in them. And by this we know
that he abides in us, by the Spirit which he has given us.

3:6 The verse has been taken to mean that one who abides in
Jesus will not sin habitually; he will not sin as long as he keeps in
communion with Jesus (remains in the "state of grace"). Those who
choose to sin break that relationship.

Perfect Love Casts Out Fear
1 John 4:7–21

7 Beloved, let us love one another; for love is of God, and he who
loves is born of God and knows God. ⁸ He who does not love does not
know God; for God is love. ⁹ In this the love of God was made
manifest among us, that God sent his only Son into the world, so
that we might live through him. ¹⁰ In this is love, not that we loved
God but that he loved us and sent his Son to be the expiation for our
sins. ¹¹ Beloved, if God so loved us, we also ought to love one
another. ¹² No man has ever seen God; if we love one another, God
abides in us and his love is perfected in us.

13 By this we know that we abide in him and he in us, because he
has given us of his own Spirit. ¹⁴ And we have seen and testify that
the Father has sent his Son as the Savior of the world. ¹⁵ Whoever
confesses that Jesus is the Son of God, God abides in him, and he in
God. ¹⁶ So we know and believe the love God has for us. God is love,
and he who abides in love abides in God, and God abides in him.

¹⁷ In this is love perfected with us, that we may have confidence for the day of judgment, because as he is so are we in this world. ¹⁸ There is no fear in love, but perfect love casts out fear. For fear has to do with punishment, and he who fears is not perfected in love. ¹⁹ We love, because he first loved us. ²⁰ If any one says, "I love God," and hates his brother, he is a liar; for he who does not love his brother whom he has seen, cannot love God whom he has not seen. ²¹ And this commandment we have from him, that he who loves God should love his brother also.

4:18 This verse has been taken to mean that when we love God perfectly our fear of judgment diminishes or disappears. Others explain it to mean that perfect love does away with human, servile fear but does not exclude the wholesome fear of God's judgment, because, as Paul wrote (Phil. 2:12), man must work out his salvation with "fear and trembling."

The Letter of Jude

"Jude, a servant of Jesus Christ and brother to James, to those who are called, beloved in God the Father kept for Jesus Christ." The brief letter contains strong language: admission into the Christian community had been "secretly gained" by "ungodly" persons who "pervert the grace of our God into licentiousness and deny our only Master and Lord, Jesus Christ." This letter was probably written about A.D. 80.

Jude verses 12–13, 20–25

12 These are blemishes on your love feasts, as they boldly carouse together, looking after themselves; waterless clouds, carried along by winds; fruitless trees in late autumn, twice dead, uprooted; 13 wild waves of the sea, casting up the foam of their own shame; wandering stars for whom the nether gloom of darkness has been reserved for ever.

20 But you, beloved, build yourselves up on your most holy faith; pray in the Holy Spirit; 21 keep yourselves in the love of God; wait for the mercy of our Lord Jesus Christ unto eternal life. 22 And convince some, who doubt; 23 save some, by snatching them out of the fire; on some have mercy with fear, hating even the garment spotted by the flesh.

24 Now to him who is able to keep you from falling and to present you without blemish before the presence of his glory with rejoicing, 25 to the only God, our Savior through Jesus Christ our Lord, be glory, majesty, dominion, and authority, before all time and now and for ever. Amen.

Jude 24–25 These verses often form the benediction in Protestant worship.

The Revelation to John

The Book of Revelation is also called the Apocalypse, from the Greek word *apocalupsis* (unfolding, revealing or revelation), which is the first word of the book. There have been many interpretations of this book. Some clues may be found in verses 9–20. All agree the book is a collection of visions, which present ideas about God's justice and mercy in His rule of creation. It appears that one major aim of the book is to assure followers of the Lord that He will come in victory. Symbolic use is made of numbers, strange beasts, stars and lampstands and other items—in much the same style that characterized Ezekiel, Daniel and other apocalyptic writings. The author, John, says that he was on the Island of Patmos "on account of the word of God and the testimony of Jesus," meaning that he was exiled there probably by Emperor Domitian, who reigned from A.D. 81 to 96. This book has inspired poets, hymn writers, folksong writers, artists, preachers and devout people for nearly 1,900 years. For a fine arts presentation of the themes of the Apocalypse there is probably nothing in the world like the collection of seventy fourteenth-century tapestries in the castle of Angers, in western France.

The Lord Is the First and the Last

This preparatory vision took place on "the Lord's day," (in Greek *kyriake*, the term still used in the Greek Church and by the Greek people; compare the Scottish work *kirk*. Sunday, the day of Jesus' resurrection, on which the Christians came together for solemn and joyful worship. The vision John sees here of Jesus Christ exalted in majesty has been depicted in many mosaics in the course of history (including the huge mosaic behind the altar of the National Shrine of the Immaculate Conception in Washington, D.C.).

Revelation 1:9–20

9 I John, your brother, who share with you in Jesus the tribulation and the kingdom and the patient endurance, was on the island called Patmos on account of the word of God and the testimony of Jesus. [10] I was in the Spirit on the Lord's day, and I heard behind me a loud voice like a trumpet [11] saying, "Write what you see in a book and send it to the seven churches, to Ephesus and to Smyrna and to Per'gamum and to Thyati'ra and to Sardis and to Philadelphia and to La-odice'a."

12 Then I turned to see the voice that was speaking to me, and on turning I saw seven golden lampstands, [13] and in the midst of the lampstands one like a son of man, clothed with a long robe and with

a golden girdle round his breast; [14] his head and his hair were white as white wool, white as snow; his eyes were like a flame of fire, [15] his feet were like burnished bronze, refined as in a furnace, and his voice was like the sound of many waters; [16] in his right hand he held seven stars, from his mouth issued a sharp two-edged sword, and his face was like the sun shining in full strength.

17 When I saw him, I fell at his feet as though dead. But he laid his right hand upon me, saying, "Fear not, I am the first and the last, [18] and the living one; I died, and behold I am alive for evermore, and I have the keys of Death and Hades. [19] Now write what you see, what is and what is to take place hereafter. [20] As for the mystery of the seven stars which you saw in my right hand, and the seven golden lampstands, the seven stars are the angels of the seven churches and the seven lampstands are the seven churches."

1:16 The two-edged sword is the word of God (see Hebrews 4:12). **1:17** Compare Isaiah 41:4.

I Stand at the Door and Knock

The majestic Lord of the vision then sends seven letters. There is one for each of seven "angels" of churches, or Christian communities, in western Asia Minor: Ephesus, Smyrna, Pergamum, Thyatira, Sardis, Philadelphia and Laodicea.

Revelation 3:14–22

14 "And to the angel of the church in La-odice'a write: 'The words of the Amen, the faithful and true witness, the beginning of God's creation.

15 " 'I know your works: you are neither cold nor hot. Would that you were cold or hot! [16] So, because you are lukewarm, and neither cold nor hot, I will spew you out of my mouth. [17] For you say, I am rich, I have prospered, and I need nothing; not knowing that you are wretched, pitiable, poor, blind, and naked. [18] Therefore I counsel you to buy from me gold refined by fire, that you may be rich, and white garments to clothe you and to keep the shame of your nakedness from being seen, and salve to anoint your eyes, that you may see. [19] Those whom I love, I reprove and chasten; so be zealous and repent. [20] Behold, I stand at the door and knock; if any one hears my voice and opens the door, I will come in to him and eat with him, and he with me. [21] He who conquers, I will grant him to sit with me on my throne, as I myself conquered and sat down with my Father on his throne. [22] He who has an ear, let him hear what the Spirit says to the churches.' "

3:20–22 A famous painting by Holman Hunt in St. Paul's Cathedral, London, England, shows Christ knocking at a door. Observers have not failed to note that the door has no knob or handle on the outside, suggesting that the artist's point is that the heart must be opened from within. The literal translation of this passage has caused perplexity in those parts of the world where visitors with honorable intentions do not knock but rather call out, as in East Africa where one shouts "Hodi!" In these lands it is only the thief who knocks: if he hears a response, he runs away.

Holy, Holy, Holy Is the Lord God

In this vision the glory of God is first described in terms of precious gems. The twenty-four elders (verse 4) have been interpreted to be the twelve patriarchs of the Old Testament and the twelve apostles of the New Testament, but they may simply be a circle of kings paying homage to God and thus showing that God is far above all kings. The four living creatures (verse 6) may be angelic beings representing man and all beasts; the point would be that God is vastly superior to them and their perfections, in knowledge and strength and all things. The author uses imagery from the prophets Ezekiel (chap. 1) and Isaiah (chap. 6).

Revelation 4:1–11

4 After this I looked, and lo, in heaven an open door! And the first voice, which I had heard speaking to me like a trumpet, said, "Come up hither, and I will show you what must take place after this." ²At once I was in the Spirit, and lo, a throne stood in heaven, with one seated on the throne! ³And he who sat there appeared like jasper and carnelian, and round the throne was a rainbow that looked like an emerald. ⁴Round the throne were twenty-four thrones, and seated on the thrones were twenty-four elders, clad in white garments, with golden crowns upon their heads. ⁵From the throne issue flashes of lightning, and voices and peals of thunder, and before the throne burn seven torches of fire, which are the seven spirits of God; ⁶and before the throne there is as it were a sea of glass, like crystal.

And round the throne, on each side of the throne, are four living creatures, full of eyes in front and behind: ⁷the first living creature like a lion, the second living creature like an ox, the third living creature with the face of a man, and the fourth living creature like a flying eagle. ⁸And the four living creatures, each of them with six wings, are full of eyes all round and within, and day and night they never cease to sing,

"Holy, holy, holy, is the Lord God Almighty,
    who was and is and is to come!"

⁹ And whenever the living creatures give glory and honor and thanks to him who is seated on the throne, who lives for ever and ever, ¹⁰ the twenty-four elders fall down before him who is seated on the throne and worship him who lives for ever and ever; they cast their crowns before the throne, singing,

¹¹ "Worthy art thou, our Lord and God,
    to receive glory and honor and power,
    for thou didst create all things,
    and by thy will they existed and were created."

The Lion and the Lamb

The vision of the Scroll and the Lamb refers, it is generally agreed, to Jesus' sacrificial death by which God's purposes (contained in the scroll) are accomplished. This vision and the passages that follow were the inspiration for El Greco's great painting of the Seven Seals now hanging in the Metropolitan Museum, New York. The number seven is a symbol of fullness and perfection. Seven horns, therefore, would mean fullness of power or strength.

Revelation 5:1–14

5 And I saw in the right hand of him who was seated on the throne a scroll written within and on the back, sealed with seven seals; ² and I saw a strong angel proclaiming with a loud voice, "Who is worthy to open the scroll and break its seals?" ³ And no one in heaven or on earth or under the earth was able to open the scroll or to look into it, ⁴ and I wept much that no one was found worthy to open the scroll or to look into it. ⁵ Then one of the elders said to me, "Weep not; lo, the Lion of the tribe of Judah, the Root of David, has conquered, so that he can open the scroll and its seven seals."

6 And between the throne and the four living creatures and among the elders, I saw a Lamb standing, as though it had been slain, with seven horns and with seven eyes, which are the seven spirits of God sent out into all the earth; ⁷ and he went and took the scroll from the right hand of him who was seated on the throne. ⁸ And when he had taken the scroll, the four living creatures and the twenty-four elders fell down before the Lamb, each holding a harp, and with golden bowls full of incense, which are the prayers of the saints; ⁹ and they sang a new song, saying,

"Worthy art thou to take the scroll and to open its seals,
    for thou wast slain and by thy blood didst ransom men for God
    from every tribe and tongue and people and nation,
¹⁰ and hast made them a kingdom and priests to our God,
    and they shall reign on earth."

¹¹ Then I looked, and I heard around the throne and the living creatures and the elders the voice of many angels, numbering myriads of myriads and thousands of thousands, ¹² saying with a loud voice, "Worthy is the Lamb who was slain, to receive power and wealth and wisdom and might and honor and glory and blessing!" ¹³ And I heard every creature in heaven and on earth and under the earth and in the sea, and all therein, saying, "To him who sits upon the throne and to the Lamb be blessing and honor and glory and might for ever and ever!" ¹⁴ And the four living creatures said, "Amen!" and the elders fell down and worshiped.

5 : 6 In early Christian art, the lamb, often with a cross or a flag (banner of victory) having a cross on it, was an emblem of Christ. Sometimes the lamb was surrounded with a halo or nimbus enclosing a cross.

The Lamb Opens the Seals

Each time the Lamb opens a seal, a horse and rider come forth until there are four. The riders are often called the Four Horsemen of the Apocalypse. Many artists have depicted them in paintings. "The Four Horsemen" is the title of a well known novel and a movie. The term was applied to a Notre Dame football backfield famed for its ability to overrun opponents. The phrase is often used to describe crises in history. The first rider, on a white horse, may represent Jesus but some scholars think he represents war; the red horse and rider symbolize war (or civil war); the black horse and rider represent famine; the pale (or pale green) horse has Death for its rider. All these are judgments on mankind, inevitable consequence of man's sins.

Revelation 6 : 1–8

6 Now I saw when the Lamb opened one of the seven seals, and I heard one of the four living creatures say, as with a voice of thunder, "Come!" ² And I saw, and behold, a white horse, and its rider had a bow; and a crown was given to him, and he went out conquering and to conquer.

3 When he opened the second seal, I heard the second living creature say, "Come!" ⁴ And out came another horse, bright red; its rider was permitted to take peace from the earth, so that men should slay one another; and he was given a great sword.

5 When he opened the third seal, I heard the third living creature say, "Come!" And I saw, and behold, a black horse, and its rider had a balance in his hand; ⁶ and I heard what seemed to be a voice in the midst of the four living creatures saying, "A quart of wheat for a

denarius, and three quarts of barley for a denarius, but do not harm oil and wine!''

7 When he opened the fourth seal, I heard the voice of the fourth living creature say, "Come!'' [8] And I saw, and behold, a pale horse, and its rider's name was Death, and Hades followed him; and they were given power over a fourth of the earth to kill with sword and with famine and with pestilence and by wild beasts of the earth.

Israel and All the Nations before the Throne of God

The fifth seal reveals the martyrs in heaven; the sixth seal reveals punishments of evildoers. Then comes a vision of angels.

Revelation 7:1–4, 8–10, 13–17

7 After this I saw four angels standing at the four corners of the earth, holding back the four winds of the earth, that no wind might blow on earth or sea or against any tree. [2] Then I saw another angel ascend from the rising of the sun, with the seal of the living God, and he called with a loud voice to the four angels who had been given power to harm earth and sea, [3] saying, "Do not harm the earth or the sea or the trees, till we have sealed the servants of our God upon their foreheads.'' [4] And I heard the number of the sealed a hundred and forty-four thousand sealed, out of every tribe of the sons of Israel,

8 twelve thousand of the tribe of Zeb'ulun, twelve thousand of the tribe of Joseph, twelve thousand sealed out of the tribe of Benjamin.

9 After this I looked, and behold, a great multitude which no man could number, from every nation, from all tribes and peoples and tongues, standing before the throne and before the Lamb, clothed in white robes, with palm branches in their hands, [10] and crying out with a loud voice, "Salvation belongs to our God who sits upon the throne, and to the Lamb!''

13 Then one of the elders addressed me, saying, "Who are these, clothed in white robes, and whence have they come?'' [14] I said to him, "Sir, you know.'' And he said to me, "These are they who have come out of the great tribulation; they have washed their robes and made them white in the blood of the Lamb.

[15] Therefore are they before the throne of God,
and serve him day and night within his temple;
and he who sits upon the throne will shelter them with his
presence.
[16] They shall hunger no more, neither thirst any more;
the sun shall not strike them, nor any scorching heat.
[17] For the Lamb in the midst of the throne will be their shepherd,
and he will guide them to springs of living water;
and God will wipe away every tear from their eyes.''

The Lord Shall Reign For Ever and Ever

When the lamb opened the seventh seal, "there was silence in heaven for about half an hour" (one of the more perplexing sentences in the Bible). Then the writer says he saw seven angels with seven trumpets. As the first six blow their trumpets, one after the other, there are various calamities in various parts of the universe.

Revelation 11:15–19

15 Then the seventh angel blew his trumpet, and there were loud voices in heaven, saying, "The kingdom of the world has become the kingdom of our Lord and of his Christ, and he shall reign for ever and ever." ¹⁶ And the twenty-four elders who sit on their thrones before God fell on their faces and worshiped God, ¹⁷ saying,

"We give thanks to thee, Lord God Almighty, who art and who wast,
    that thou hast taken thy great power and begun to reign.
¹⁸ The nations raged, but thy wrath came,
    and the time for the dead to be judged,
for rewarding thy servants, the prophets and saints,
    and those who fear thy name, both small and great,
    and for destroying the destroyers of the earth."

19 Then God's temple in heaven was opened, and the ark of his covenant was seen within his temple; and there were flashes of lightning, loud noises, peals of thunder, an earthquake, and heavy hail.

Satan and His Angels Are Cast Out of Heaven

Next come seven great "signs" ("wonders" is the word in many older translations) or portents, meaning illustrations of truths. The first of them (given here) sets the scene for the rest of the book, which describes in various ways the conflict between Satan and the people of God. The woman, therefore, is counted a symbol of the people of God. She is first Israel, from whom Jesus the Messiah was born (verse 5) and then according to what follows in the book, the Christian Church. The dragon is Satan (verse 9). The 1,260 days (verse 6) would then be a symbol for the period between the ascension of the Messiah into heaven and his return at the Parousia or Last Day (Judgment Day).

Revelation 12:1–17

12 And a great portent appeared in heaven, a woman clothed with the sun, with the moon under her feet, and on her head a crown of twelve stars; ² she was with child and she cried out in her pangs of birth, in anguish for delivery. ³ And another portent appeared in heaven; behold, a great red dragon, with seven heads and ten horns, and seven diadems upon his heads. ⁴ His tail swept down a third of

the stars of heaven, and cast them to the earth. And the dragon stood before the woman who was about to bear a child, that he might devour her child when she brought it forth; ⁵ she brought forth a male child, one who is to rule all the nations with a rod of iron, but her child was caught up to God and to his throne, ⁶ and the woman fled into the wilderness, where she has a place prepared by God, in which to be nourished for one thousand two hundred and sixty days.

7 Now war arose in heaven, Michael and his angels fighting against the dragon; and the dragon and his angels fought, ⁸ but they were defeated and there was no longer any place for them in heaven. ⁹ And the great dragon was thrown down, that ancient serpent, who is called the Devil and Satan, the deceiver of the whole world—he was thrown down to the earth, and his angels were thrown down with him. ¹⁰ And I heard a loud voice in heaven, saying, "Now the salvation and the power and the kingdom of our God and the authority of his Christ have come, for the accuser of our brethren has been thrown down, who accuses them day and night before our God. ¹¹ And they have conquered him by the blood of the Lamb and by the word of their testimony, for they loved not their lives even unto death. ¹² Rejoice then, O heaven and you that dwell therein! But woe to you, O earth and sea, for the devil has come down to you in great wrath, because he knows that his time is short!"

13 And when the dragon saw that he had been thrown down to the earth, he pursued the woman who had borne the male child. ¹⁴ But the woman was given the two wings of the great eagle that she might fly from the serpent into the wilderness, to the place where she is to be nourished for a time, and times, and half a time. ¹⁵ The serpent poured water like a river out of his mouth after the woman, to sweep her away with the flood. ¹⁶ But the earth came to the help of the woman, and the earth opened its mouth and swallowed the river which the dragon had poured from his mouth. ¹⁷ Then the dragon was angry with the woman, and went off to make war on the rest of her offspring, on those who keep the commandments of God and bear testimony to Jesus. And he stood on the sand of the sea.

12:1 This verse has been applied (by accommodation) to Mary, the mother of Jesus, in Catholic liturgy and art (the scene is depicted in many paintings entitled "The Immaculate Conception"). Catholic theologians of the Middle Ages saw represented here also the transfigured mother of Jesus. **12:7** Verses 7–12 are often taken as referring to the struggle between the angels and the fall of Lucifer before the world was made. Some take the whole vision as a symbol of the cosmic struggle between good and evil, but it may express rather the struggle between good and bad angels over the souls of men.

The Infamous Number 666

Two beasts appear in this vision, one from the sea and one from the earth. A code number was given to each. The beast from the sea is generally taken to symbolize the Roman Empire, and the second beast the Emperor Nero. Hebrew (and Greek) letters of the alphabet have numerical equivalents; the number of the beast has been taken to be the sum of the letters in his name. In the case of Nero it would be $50 + 200 + 6 + 50 + 100 + 60 + 200 = 666$. Interpreters in every age have branded their enemies with this infamous number. Pope Leo X, Martin Luther, Napoleon, Hitler, Stalin—each in his time was so stigmatized. In itself, the number 666 could mean for ancient peoples "perfect imperfection," since it three times falls short by one of seven (symbol of perfection).

Revelation 13:1–4, 11–12, 18

13 And I saw a beast rising out of the sea, with ten horns and seven heads, with ten diadems upon its horns and a blasphemous name upon its heads. [2] And the beast that I saw was like a leopard, its feet were like a bear's, and its mouth was like a lion's mouth. And to it the dragon gave his power and his throne and great authority. [3] One of its heads seemed to have a mortal wound, but its mortal wound was healed, and the whole earth followed the beast with wonder. [4] Men worshiped the dragon, for he had given his authority to the beast, and they worshiped the beast, saying, "Who is like the beast, and who can fight against it?"

11 Then I saw another beast which rose out of the earth; it had two horns like a lamb and it spoke like a dragon. [12] It exercises all the authority of the first beast in its presence, and makes the earth and its inhabitants worship the first beast, whose mortal wound was healed.

18 This calls for wisdom: let him who has understanding reckon the number of the beast, for it is a human number, its number is six hundred and sixty-six.

Blessed Are Those Who Have Kept the Faith
Revelation 14:9–13

9 And another angel, a third, followed them, saying with a loud voice, "If any one worships the beast and its image, and receives a mark on his forehead or on his hand, [10] he also shall drink the wine of God's wrath, poured unmixed into the cup of his anger, and he shall be tormented with fire and brimstone in the presence of the holy angels and in the presence of the Lamb. [11] And the smoke of their torment goes up for ever and ever; and they have no rest, day

or night, these worshipers of the beast and its image, and whoever receives the mark of its name."

12 Here is a call for the endurance of the saints, those who keep the commandments of God and the faith of Jesus.

13 And I heard a voice from heaven saying, "Write this: Blessed are the dead who die in the Lord henceforth." "Blessed indeed," says the Spirit, "that they may rest from their labors, for their deeds follow them!"

14:9 Many Christians consider the first part of this vision an indication that those who follow Satan will suffer forever in hell for their sins. **14:12** Older translations have: Here is the patience of the saints; here are they that keep the commandments of God and the faith of Jesus. Chicago Bible: On this fact rests the endurance of God's people, who obey God's commands and cling to their faith in Jesus. **14:13** This verse is used by the Catholic Church in the Mass for the Dead.

A Description of the Last Days

This vision describes the victory of Christ and his heavenly armies over the satanic beast and his forces. The concluding passage (20:11–15) has generally been thought to refer to the final judgment.

Revelation 19:11–16, 19–21; 20:1–3, 7–15

11 Then I saw heaven opened, and behold, a white horse! He who sat upon it is called Faithful and True, and in righteousness he judges and makes war. [12] His eyes are like a flame of fire, and on his head are many diadems; and he has a name inscribed which no one knows but himself. [13] He is clad in a robe dipped in blood, and the name by which he is called is The Word of God. [14] And the armies of heaven, arrayed in fine linen, white and pure, followed him on white horses. [15] From his mouth issues a sharp sword with which to smite the nations, and he will rule them with a rod of iron; he will tread the wine press of the fury of the wrath of God the Almighty. [16] On his robe and on his thigh he has a name inscribed, King of kings and Lord of lords.

19 And I saw the beast and the kings of the earth with their armies gathered to make war against him who sits upon the horse and against his army. [20] And the beast was captured, and with it the false prophet who in its presence had worked the signs by which he deceived those who had received the mark of the beast and those who worshiped its image. These two were thrown alive into the lake of fire that burns with brimstone. [21] And the rest were slain by the

sword of him who sits upon the horse, the sword that issues from his mouth; and all the birds were gorged with their flesh.

20 Then I saw an angel coming down from heaven, holding in his hand the key of the bottomless pit and a great chain. ² And he seized the dragon, that ancient serpent, who is the Devil and Satan, and bound him for a thousand years, ³ and threw him into the pit, and shut it and sealed it over him, that he should deceive the nations no more, till the thousand years were ended. After that he must be loosed for a little while.

7 And when the thousand years are ended, Satan will be loosed from his prison ⁸ and will come out to deceive the nations which are at the four corners of the earth, that is, Gog and Magog, to gather them for battle; their number is like the sand of the sea. ⁹ And they marched up over the broad earth and surrounded the camp of the saints and the beloved city; but fire came down from heaven and consumed them, ¹⁰ and the devil who had deceived them was thrown into the lake of fire and brimstone where the beast and the false prophet were, and they will be tormented day and night for ever and ever.

11 Then I saw a great white throne and him who sat upon it; from his presence earth and sky fled away, and no place was found for them. ¹² And I saw the dead, great and small, standing before the throne, and books were opened. Also another book was opened, which is the book of life. And the dead were judged by what was written in the books, by what they had done. ¹³ And the sea gave up the dead in it, Death and Hades gave up the dead in them, and all were judged by what they had done. ¹⁴ Then Death and Hades were thrown into the lake of fire. This is the second death, the lake of fire; ¹⁵ and if any one's name was not found written in the book of life, he was thrown into the lake of fire.

New Heaven and New Earth

The vision of the new heaven and new earth sums up prophecies in the Old Testament and in St. Paul's letters (Isaiah 65:17; 66:22; Romans 8:19–21). The city of Jerusalem, loved by God as a symbol of His people Israel, now symbolizes the new Israel, the Church, according to the most common Christian interpretation. At the beginning of the Bible there was mention of a tree of life in a garden and a river flowing to water the garden. Here at the end of the Bible there is a river, a tree of life and a city. The account of salvation history has evolved from two people in a garden of paradise and has now come to a heavenly city of many citizens. In the garden there was no sickness, no death, and God provided everything abundantly. Here we are told that it will be in the heaven as it was in the paradise described in Genesis.

Revelation 21:1–14, 22–27; 22:1–2

21 Then I saw a new heaven and a new earth; for the first heaven and the first earth had passed away, and the sea was no more. [2] And I saw the holy city, new Jerusalem, coming down out of heaven from God, prepared as a bride adorned for her husband; [3] and I heard a great voice from the throne saying, "Behold, the dwelling of God is with men. He will dwell with them, and they shall be his people, and God himself will be with them; [4] he will wipe away every tear from their eyes, and death shall be no more, neither shall there be mourning nor crying nor pain any more, for the former things have passed away."

5 And he who sat upon the throne said, "Behold, I make all things new." Also he said, "Write this, for these words are trustworthy and true." [6] And he said to me, "It is done! I am the Alpha and the Omega, the beginning and the end. To the thirsty I will give water without price from the fountain of the water of life. [7] He who conquers shall have this heritage, and I will be his God and he shall be my son. [8] But as for the cowardly, the faithless, the polluted, as for murderers, fornicators, sorcerers, idolaters, and all liars, their lot shall be in the lake that burns with fire and brimstone, which is the second death."

9 Then came one of the seven angels who had the seven bowls full of the seven last plagues, and spoke to me, saying, "Come, I will show you the Bride, the wife of the Lamb." [10] And in the Spirit he carried me away to a great, high mountain, and showed me the holy city Jerusalem coming down out of heaven from God, [11] having the glory of God, its radiance like a most rare jewel, like a jasper, clear as crystal. [12] It had a great, high wall, with twelve gates, and at the gates twelve angels, and on the gates the names of the twelve tribes of the sons of Israel were inscribed; [13] on the east three gates, on the north three gates, on the south three gates, and on the west three gates. [14] And the wall of the city had twelve foundations, and on them the twelve names of the twelve apostles of the Lamb.

22 And I saw no temple in the city, for its temple is the Lord God the Almighty and the Lamb. [23] And the city has no need of sun or moon to shine upon it, for the glory of God is its light, and its lamp is the Lamb. [24] By its light shall the nations walk; and the kings of the earth shall bring their glory into it, [25] and its gates shall never be shut by day—and there shall be no night there; [26] they shall bring into it the glory and the honor of the nations. [27] But nothing unclean shall enter it, nor any one who practices abomination or falsehood, but only those who are written in the Lamb's book of life.

22 Then he showed me the river of the water of life, bright as crystal, flowing from the throne of God and of the Lamb ²through the middle of the street of the city; also, on either side of the river, the tree of life with its twelve kinds of fruit, yielding its fruit each month; and the leaves of the tree were for the healing of the nations.

Epilogue

The author closes his book with statements by Jesus, apparently from another vision of the Lord, to which the Church ("Bride") ardently responds: "Come." There are more warnings and exhortations, and the book ends with a prayer.

Revelation 22:8–21

8 I John am he who heard and saw these things. And when I heard and saw them, I fell down to worship at the feet of the angel who showed them to me; ⁹but he said to me, "You must not do that! I am a fellow servant with you and your brethren the prophets, and with those who keep the words of this book. Worship God."

10 And he said to me, "Do not seal up the words of the prophecy of this book, for the time is near. ¹¹Let the evildoer still do evil, and the filthy still be filthy, and the righteous still do right, and the holy still be holy.

12 "Behold, I am coming soon, bringing my recompense, to repay every one for what he has done. ¹³I am the Alpha and the Omega, the first and the last, the beginning and the end."

14 Blessed are those who wash their robes, that they may have the right to the tree of life and that they may enter the city by the gates. ¹⁵Outside are the dogs and sorcerers and fornicators and murderers and idolaters, and every one who loves and practices falsehood.

16 "I Jesus have sent my angel to you with this testimony for the churches. I am the root and the offspring of David, the bright morning star."

17 The Spirit and the Bride say, "Come." And let him who hears say, "Come." And let him who is thirsty come, let him who desires take the water of life without price.

18 I warn every one who hears the words of the prophecy of this book: if any one adds to them, God will add to him the plagues described in this book, ¹⁹and if any one takes away from the words of the book of this prophecy, God will take away his share in the tree of life and in the holy city, which are described in this book.

20 He who testifies to these things says, "Surely I am coming soon." Amen. Come, Lord Jesus!

21 The grace of the Lord Jesus be with all the saints. Amen.

22:9 Rheims: Adore God (Catholic translators have preferred "adore" as more accurate here than "worship," because, as Catholic theologians have worked it out, adoration is worship paid to God alone. Worship, they contend, is a general word; for example, the Lord Mayor of an English or British city is called the Right Worshipful Lord Mayor. **22:15** In the Bible, dogs often symbolize impure and lascivious people, doers of evil in general (see Philippians 3:2), agents of destruction. An exception is the Book of Tobit. **22:20** Tyndale: be it: I come quickly. Geneva Bible: Surely I come quickly. Rheims: Yea I come quickly. King James Version: Surely I come quickly. **22:21** Some ancient authorities add "Christ" after "Lord Jesus"; some do not have "all"; some omit "the saints." Thus many older translations have: The grace of Our Lord Jesus Christ be with you all. Amen.

Appendix I

The Rabbis and Their Literature

Throughout this *Bible Reader* we have used such terms as "the Rabbis taught" or "in Rabbinical tradition it was held that." Such phrases are a form of literary shorthand. To have named the rabbi who first contributed the thought (if known) or the book in which it first appeared, with dates, would have lengthened an already long book and burdened the student. Instead we provide in this Appendix a brief introduction to the development of Rabbinical literature and Rabbinical Judaism.

For the Jews of biblical times the Bible was more than a book of moral and spiritual inspiration. It also provided the laws by which the Hebrew people and nation governed their political and civil existence. For example, the commandment to observe the Sabbath was the word of God. It was a religious law. At the same time, it had a social and economic significance. Work was prohibited on the Sabbath. The question was asked: What kind of work was prohibited? The Bible mentions only three prohibitions: the kindling of fire (Exodus 16:29), leaving one's home on a journey (Exodus 16:23), and the hewing of wood (Numbers 15:32–36). Obviously, if a spirit of rest was to be achieved within the community other regulations were required.

The priestly leaders of the Hebrew nation did, in fact, preserve such a tradition of legislation which they believed had been part of the Law revealed to Moses at Sinai. Thus the prophet legitimately rebuked the people for carrying burdens on the Sabbath (Jeremiah 17 : 21), and Nehemiah, exercising his civic authority, properly drove away the Gentile traders who came to Jerusalem on the Sabbath (Nehemiah 13:15–23). As conditions changed, however, there were always new questions to put to the Law. For example, if a man were ill, might the doctor apply medicine on the Sabbath? Were the prohibitions of the Sabbath absolute or might they be abrogated under certain conditions?

Consider another example: The Bible enjoins that if a man commits an injury to another he must make recompense, "An eye for an eye, a tooth for a tooth." Today we know that when this law was first revealed it represented an effort by the Hebrews to restrict the vengeance that an injured man might exact. But a question emerged: Were the Hebrews really to apply this law in its literal fashion, or was a financial compensation adequate?

Hebrew Scripture does not explicitly answer such questions. Yet, if one wishes to live by the spirit of God's word, the answer to such questions must be found. From the earliest times, therefore, there developed a body of law attributed to Moses that provided such detailed instructions. Such law, not written down, was known by the Hebrews as the "oral law," distinguishing it thereby from the "written law" to be found in Scripture.

The Bible informs us that, at least from the time of Ezra in the fifth century B.C., there was a group of scholars known as scribes (in Hebrew, *sopherim*) who were "skilled in the law of Moses" (Ezra 7 : 6, 10–11). These scribes applied themselves to the study and teaching of the oral law. In most cases an effort was made to find some source or text in the Bible to justify the oral law. The result of such an effort "to inquire" or "investigate" Scripture in order to extract its full implication and meaning was known as *Midrash* (derived from the Hebrew word *darash*—to investigate).

The first *midrashim* (Hebrew plural for midrash) were generally of a legal nature (in Hebrew known as *halacha*, referring to the way in which the Hebrew people were "to go"). There soon appeared legal commentaries that expanded the law to be found in the Book of Exodus (*Mekilta*), Leviticus (*Sifra*) and the Books of Numbers and Deuteronomy (*Sifre*).

At the same time there also developed a form of midrash that was expository, homiletic and moralistic in nature. Known as *Midrash Aggada* (from the Hebrew word meaning "to tell"), these lessons were a commentary on the nonlegal portions of Scripture. Through legend, folktale and homily, the Rabbis told their moral lessons. They provided interpretations on the meaning of Scripture and exhorted the Hebrew people to virtue. Frequently these were the record of sermons delivered on Sabbath afternoons when people would gather to hear an exposition of Scripture. The earliest of such aggadic midrashim were the collections of the wise sayings of the most important Rabbis (*Pirkey Avot*) and the sermons they delivered on the Book of Genesis.

Some Jews objected to what they thought were the far-fetched interpretations of Scriptures to be found in such midrashic material, just as in the United States not all citizens agree with the manner in which the Supreme Court interprets the meaning of the Constitution. In response, the Rabbis insisted that the authority was given them in Scripture itself to make such interpretations. The passage in Psalm 62 : 11, "Once God has spoken; twice I have heard this," provided a source text for the Rabbis justifying their conviction that it was proper "to hear" in a biblical text several interpretations (*Mekilta* 3a, 6a). So the Rabbis expanded the meaning of Scripture and avoided the delimiting consequence of a literal understanding of the word. They also allowed for differences of interpretation when such differences were sincerely held in conscience as the word of God.

In order to avoid complete anarchy in understanding the Bible, however, the Rabbis rigorously distinguished between the *peshat*, a simple in-context appreciation of what the Bible said, and *midrash*, the

interpretations or exegesis of Scripture that were read into the text.
The Rabbis ruled, "Nothing can override the plain meaning of the
text" (*Shabbat* 63a). Care was taken, too, to recall which rabbi
composed each midrash, although there are many where the author's
name has been lost and forgotten. Furthermore, a distinction
between the halachik midrash and the midrash aggada was
emphasized. Law had to be accepted by a majority of the rabbis in
order to have standing, whereas the imagination was given free reign
in holding to nonlegal midrashic interpretations. Finally, there was
an agreed set of rules—known as hermeneutics—by which Scripture
could be expounded to provide new law or homiletic teaching.

What made Jesus appear to be such a threat to the organized
Jewish community was the fact that he taught the law on his own
authority, frequently without revealing his hermeneutical principles
or without consultation with other Rabbinic authorities. To survive,
a society cannot permit individuals to take the law into their own
hands. The Rabbis did not concede that Jesus proclaimed the law as
the Messiah-Redeemer. As this *Bible Reader* reveals, the ethical
teachings proclaimed by Jesus were not in themselves radically
different from those available in Rabbinic Judaism. Many rabbis
could support the ethical teachings of Jesus. It was his individual
manner of declaring the law, on his own authority, that was
provocative.

The era of the *sopherim* covers at least two centuries after Ezra.
The *sopherim* are known to have developed the regulations that
established the basic pattern of Jewish prayer; they instituted the
feasts of Hanukkah and Purim, they established the order and
essential form of Hebrew Scripture. Futhermore, it is recorded that
they made eighteen changes in the actual Hebrew wording of the
Bible in order to avoid any possible denigrating references to God in
human terms, such as anthropomorphisms. (Example, Genesis
18 : 22: "But *Abraham* still stood before the Lord," where the
original had read, "But the *Lord* still stood before Abraham.") They
also modified several offensive and blasphemous terms. (Example,
Job 2 : 9: Job is urged by his wife to "*Curse* God and die"; the
sopherim changed the Hebrew to read, "*Bless* God and die.")

This era came to an end with the high priesthood of Simeon
Ha-Tzadik (Simon the Just) who died in 180 B.C. Simeon Ha-
Tzadik had achieved a nationwide acceptance of the oral law as the
authoritative legislation by which the Jews would govern their
society.

For several generations after Simeon a succession of rabbis serving
in pairs (*Zugot*), as officers of the Jewish religious and civil legislative
body, the Sanhedrin, organized, systemized and expanded the legal
traditions communicated by the scribes. This effort was climaxed in
the teachings of Hillel and Shammai in the first century B.C. Hillel
(whose grandson Gamaliel was a teacher of the apostle Paul, Acts

22 : 3) taught: "Do not unto others that which you would not have them do unto you" (*Shabbat* 31a).

The rabbis who followed Hillel and Shammai are called *Tannaim* (teachers). They generally favored the more liberal interpretations of law proclaimed in the name of Hillel rather than the conservative interpretations proclaimed by Shammai. Finally, through the efforts of a spiritual giant, Rabbi Judah Ha-Nasi (Judah the Prince) the law was codified and written down under the title *Mishnah* (teaching) about A.D. 220.

The Mishnah was divided into six tractates or orders dealing with every phase of law: (1) *Zeraim,* dealing with agriculture; (2) *Moed,* referring to the observance of holy days including the Sabbath; (3) *Nashim,* family law; (4) *Nezikim,* civil and criminal law and the regulation of courts; (5) *Kadoshim,* laws referring to matters of "holiness," that is, Temple ritual and dietary laws; (6) *Taharot,* laws referring to cultic purity and impurity. The Mishnah was not just a dry law code. Interspersed throughout were aggadic or homiletic sayings which explicated the spiritual ideals that inspired the Law. Included in the Mishnah, for example, was the important treatise of moral conduct, *Pirkey Avot,* the "Sayings of the Fathers."

The rabbis who followed Judah Ha-Nasi are called *Amoraim* ("discoursers" or "expounders"). By way of question and answers, they continued to analyze the law in the Mishnah and to apply it to new situations. Their discussions are called *Gemara* ("completion" of the teaching). In A.D. 550 the Babylonian rabbis, Rav Ashi and Ravina, set down in writing the record of discourses that had heretofore, through the centuries, been communicated orally by memory. Their gigantic work, known as the (Babylonian) *Talmud,* includes both the Mishnah and Gemara. A similar process had taken place in Palestine, resulting in a Palestinian or Jerusalem Talmud.

The Babylonian Talmud is the larger and more distinguished of the two works. Written in Aramaic it is divided into thirty-six tractates or books containing two million five hundred thousand words. Many rabbis spend a lifetime in reading and studying it. For the Talmud contains not only discourse on legal matters, but it records as well the sermons, folk-stories, wise sayings of rabbis; i.e., it has both halachik and aggadic materials. The Rabbis believe that the Talmud supplements and fulfills the legislation and ethical teachings to be found in Scripture. It is *the* textbook of Judaism. Thus, one can find in the Talmud the answers to the legal questions posed at the beginning of this essay: one may violate the Sabbath prohibitions in order to save a life; money is adequate compensation for injury.

Until the seventh century some rabbis made further minor additions to the Talmud. They were called *Saboraim* ("reasoners"). Until the twelfth century, however, the Rabbis continued to write comment-aries on the Bible which were published in book form as works of Midrash. Thus the process of interpreting Scripture in order to apply it to life conditions and to extract from it relevant inspirational messages was an on-going one; it extended for a period ranging from fifth century B.C. to twelfth century A.D. This is known as the Talmudic or Rabbinic Period, and the essence of the teachings contained in Midrash and Talmud is known as Rabbinic Judaism. That process of exegesis continues even to this day.

The Talmud held sway over the Jewish community until the development of Reform Judaism in the eighteenth and nineteenth centuries. In fact, Orthodox Judaism to this very day maintains its orthodoxy by fashioning its beliefs and practices according to Rabbinic Judaism. Reform Jews, however, have abandoned the ceremonial and ritual laws of the Halachah, although they still maintain a deep affection for the spiritual and moral insights of the Aggadah and Midrash. According to Reform Jews the legal restrictions and prohibitions of the Talmud had become enormous and onerous over the centuries. When the Jews were emancipated from the ghetto they required a new approach to religion. Reform Judaism stressed the need for a sustained commitment to the spirit of the law rather than the obligation to maintain the letter of the law. They held the ethical teachings of the prophets to be more binding upon them than the patterns of diet, dress and worship that had accumulated over the centuries of Rabbinic Judaism. Reform Jews were also influenced by scientific knowledge. They abandoned religious concepts that violated their credulity, such as the resurrection of a dead body. They were influenced by scholarly research in archaeology and Bible criticism, and they accepted the view that the Bible revealed God's word as understood by men over a period of centuries. Freed from the obligation, therefore, to accept Rabbinic law as final, fixed and binding, Reform Jews made significant changes in Jewish worship and theology.

The student of this *Bible Reader* will find references to practices maintained by Orthodox, traditional or "observing" Jews. Where such adjectives are used, the practices are probably of ancient derivation, and have their source in rabbinic literature. Where we have attributed concepts to Reform or "contemporary" Jews, we mean that these are more modern innovations or ideas that are not universally accepted by all Jews and particularly by Orthodox Jews.

Between the twelfth and sixteenth centuries the Talmud was attacked by Christian authorities throughout Europe as a heretical book. It was alleged to contain blasphemous utterances against Jesus. In actuality the Talmud contains very little reference to Jesus, Christians or Christianity. The first major assault on the Talmud occurred in 1220 when a Jewish apostate, Nicholas Donin, brought before church authorities malicious charges against the Talmud. Jewish scholars were called to the court of King Louis IX of France, and after three days of coerced "disputation" the Talmud was found guilty. Twenty-four carloads of Talmudic texts were put to the fire.

The event is commemorated in a prayer recited in synagogues on the ninth day of Av, a memorial fast day recalling the destruction of the Second Temple.

In 1554 a papal bull, prohibiting Jews from possessing blasphemous books, led to the widespread censorship of Jewish prayer books and the Talmud. Although these charges against the Talmud were ultimately disproved, when Christian scholars mastered enough Hebrew and Aramaic to study the cited passages in their context, the memory of the Talmud as a book hostile to Christianity lingers among anti-Semitic organizations. In some quarters one still hears denigrating references to the Talmud or its alleged contents.

The student of this *Bible Reader* can see for himself, from the many Rabbinic selections from Midrash and Talmud contained herein, that the Talmud is—as Jews believe it to be—a repository of profound spiritual understanding.

There is, however, a more cogent reason for including selected comments from the Rabbis in this *Bible Reader*. Illustrations of Jewish thought could have been taken from medieval biblical commentary, Hasidic lore or contemporary Jewish religious thought, but they were not. The great period of Rabbinic Judaism was roughly contemporaneous with the writing of the New Testament. Our intention, therefore, was to let it be seen: (1) how Jews in the early Christian period understood their own Hebrew Scripture; and (2) how remarkably the New Testament (outside of its central claim about Jesus) parallels in many of its ethical and spiritual teachings the best of the Judaism of its own day.

Thus while the Jews in the synagogue and the Hebrew and Gentile Christians in the Church quarreled vigorously—and we still disagree—over the significance of Jesus' ministry as the Son of God, the Christ, the perfect embodiment of the hopes of ideals of Israel, it is clear, nevertheless, that Jews and Christians shared together—and still do—a Scripture, a means of interpreting Scripture, a pattern of prayer and worship, an ethical approach to man's relation toward his neighbor, a love of God and a hope for man's future blessedness.

Appendix 2

The Documentary Theory and the Hebrew Bible

The Hebrew Bible, usually called by Christians the Old Testament, is the work of many authors in many generations extending from 1200 to 100 B.C.

The Rabbis in the Talmudic period offer the following classic summary of accepted opinion regarding the authorship of the books of the Hebrew Bible: "Moses wrote his own book, the Torah, and the section concerning Balaam (Numbers 22:2; 25:9), and Job. Joshua wrote his own book and eight verses of the Torah (Deuteronomy 34:5–12). Samuel wrote his own book and Judges and Ruth. David together with ten elders wrote the Book of Psalms. Jeremiah wrote his own book and the Book of Kings and Lamentations. Hezekiah and a group of scholars commissioned by him put into writing Isaiah, Proverbs, The Song of Songs and Ecclesiastes. The Men of the Great Synagogue wrote Ezekiel, the Twelve Minor Prophets, Daniel and Esther. Ezra wrote his own book and the genealogies of the Book of Chronicles as far as himself" (*Babba Bathra* 14b–15a).

The Rabbis believed that prophecy ended with Haggai, Zechariah and Malachi, and that no books of the Hebrew Bible were, therefore, written after Ezra. This account of biblical authorship was maintained for many centuries, both by Jews and Christians. Serious students of the Bible, however, soon began to raise critical questions. The Spanish Jewish scholar Abraham Ibn Ezra in 1152 noted twelve passages in Pentateuch that raised doubts for him regarding historic chronology in Scripture, and this led him to question whether Moses had actually written all of the Torah. A Protestant scholar Isaac de la Peyure in 1655 suggested that the pen of several authors appeared evident in the Pentateuch. Other Christian Bible scholars demonstrated that the book of Daniel and some Psalms were composed in the Maccabean period, much later that the accepted tradition would allow. A major contribution was then made in 1678 by the Dutch Jewish philosopher Benedict Spinoza. He contended that the books from Genesis to Second Kings were once a single work compiled by Ezra from documents of differing dates, some of them with contrasting or conflicting accounts. He dated the Book of Chronicles in the Maccabean period and many of the Psalms in the postexilic.

The next comprehensive presentation of the documentary theory and the one most widely publicized, was that of the French Catholic scholar Jean Astruc (1684–1766), physician to Louis XIV of France. He noted that in the Book of Genesis the names for God, "Yahweh" and "Elohim" were not used interchangeably. This led him to the conviction that they represented two strands of biblical writing that, at some later date, had been put together in one book. Altogether, he suggested, there were eleven literary strands reflected in the Five Books of Moses. Astruc's thesis stimulated a wide-ranging effort by Bible scholars, chiefly in England and Germany, to unravel these various strands in the Bible and particularly in the Pentateuch. In 1806 the scholar DeWette observed special literary qualities in the Book of Deuteronomy. He suggested that Deuteronomy could not have been written by the same authors who composed the other books of the Pentateuch. It must have had its own independent author. In 1822 the scholar Friedrich Bleek disclosed evidence suggesting that the book of Joshua had once been part of the Five Books of Moses. Instead of a Pentateuch therefore, there had originally been a Hexateuch. By 1850 the earlier classic idea that Moses himself wrote most of the Pentateuch had been rejected by large numbers of Bible scholars, although many were ready to acknowledge that each strand included a heritage of laws, traditions, ethical teachings and theological formulations that were the contribution of Moses to the shaping of Judaism.

Needless to say, such views came as a shock to many Bible scholars. Those who held to the traditional view of the authorship of the entire Pentateuch by Moses made their effective replies. The distinguished Jewish Bible scholar Dr. Benno Jacob of Gottingen, Germany, in a criticism of the documentary theory in an article in the Jewish Encyclopedia, insisted that the use of Yahweh or Elohim did not indicate "a difference in authorship" but was due "to the different meanings of the two names, the choice of which is considered carefully in each case." Furthermore, Dr. Jacob argued, "the differences of style and treatment did not reflect different authors but are called forth by different subjects. Obviously a description of the Tabernacle will differ in style from a description recounting Israel's experiences at Sinai. The variations in literary method reflect skilled writing, not two authors."

Such objections, however, did not dissuade the proponents of "higher biblical criticism" from continuing their research. In 1865–1866 the Alsatian biblicist Graf, in a climactic summary of the research, maintained that there were at least four major historical narrations that were combined to make up the Pentateuch and the historic books of Joshua, Samuel and Kings. These include what has now become known as the "J", "E", "D" and "P" documents.

Following Graf there appeared a giant work by a Protestant Bible scholar, Julius Wellhausen. He tried to demonstrate according to the documentary theory how Jewish religious ideals and institutions must have evolved. One of his insights, for example, dealt with the emergence of one central sanctuary and the priesthood as recorded in biblical literature. He tried to prove that it was possible to date the biblical books on the basis of this historical fact. The earliest biblical authors, J and E writing between 950–750 B.C., make no restrictions as to where altars may be erected (cf. Exodus 20:24). The priesthood is not restricted to the tribe of the descendants of Aaron. Gideon, Manoah, Saul, Samuel, Elijah all perform acceptable offerings before God. With the reformation of Josiah, in 621 B.C., however, and the creation of a new D history, it becomes clear that the priests are to be exclusively of the Levitical clan and Jerusalem is to be the favored sanctuary (cf. Deuteronomy 18:6–7 and II Kings 23:8–9). Finally, the P authors a century later and the postexilic prophets—Haggai, Zechariah, Malachi—assume without question that there is now but one central sanctuary in Jerusalem and a priesthood that is limited exclusively to Aaron and his descendants, one family of the tribe of Levi.

Unfortunately, Wellhausen's work was too mechanical in its suggestion that religious institutions developed in a consistent linear fashion. He left little room for spontaneity—even for God's revelation—in his deterministic patterns. Furthermore, he maintained very subjective prejudices of his own regarding religion. Frequently he made judgments concerning the Jewish faith that were offensive to Jews and to many Catholic and Protestant Bible scholars as well.

Stimulated by the Graf-Wellhausen thesis, other less restrained and disciplined scholars dismissed as legend and myth whole sections of Scripture. E. Stucken, about 1900, argued that the patriarchal tales were no more than the remnants of Assyrian lunar myths. Others suggested that they were Canaanite gods whom the Hebrews incorporated into their Scripture. One scholar even denied that there was a sojourn in Egypt.

Such extreme forms of "higher criticism" produced a counter reaction that soon received authoritative support from archaeologists who had begun to uncover more and more records from ancient cultures. These records verified the authenticity of many of the biblical accounts and demonstrated beyond doubt the spiritual genius of the Hebrew authors in eradicating from their religion the offensive practices and ideals of pagan idolatry. Soon traditional scholars were able to point out that the oldest patriarchal accounts in Genesis ring true. They were old. They reflect accurately the given era of history in which they were placed. While Moses may not have written all or most of the Torah, he had certainly inspired enthusiasm for maintaining the memory of the traditions of the Hebrew Fathers. Thus when these traditions were later written down, the early stories were well preserved. Ancient practices were described for which the later Hebrew authors had no explanation; in some cases the practices offended their own moral sense, such as Jacob's marriage to two sisters. Yet these ancient narratives were preserved.

All scholars have agreed that the Hebrews did not write their history merely to record events. They brought a point of view to their writing. They saw in the events of Hebrew history a revelation of

God; they were instructed by these events with a new awareness of His will. Serious Bible critics, therefore, more recently have devoted themselves to an elaboration of the points of view reflected in each of the strands that they feel make up the Pentateuch.

The J Document

According to the documentary theory the J document is distinguished by the fact that is uses the word YHWH as the name of God. Some scholars suggest that this strand was written between 950–850 B.C. by historians who lived in the South among the tribes of Judah. Their narrative describes the fulfillment of God's plan in history, particularly His promise to Noah that the Hebrew nation will rule over Canaan (Genesis 9:25–27), and to Abraham that they will be a great nation (Genesis 12:1–3). Written after the defeat of the Philistines by King David, this history of the Hebrew people is a paean of praise to the God of the Hebrews. Its purpose is to further a sense of loyalty on the part of the Hebrew people towards their God and their monarch.

The E Document

The authors of the E document use the word Elohim for the name of God. Scholars suggest that this strand was written between 850–750 B.C. by historians who resided in the Israelite part of the nation. The authors of the E document begin their story with Abraham. Allegedly they reflect more advanced ethical views than the authors of the J version and they provide religious motivations for what might appear to be unseemly behavior on the part of the founders of the Hebrew people. Contrast, for example, J's account of Sarah in Pharaoh's harem in Genesis 12:10–20 with the account given by E of Sarah in the court of Abimelech in Genesis 20:1–18. E tells the story in such a way that we may be certain that Abraham did not tell a whole lie. His motives were good, and Sarah was not violated. E reflects a bias in favor of the Northern tribes as against the Southern tribes. Thus in E's account of the Joseph story it was Reuben, patriarch of the Northern tribes, who tried to save Joseph (Genesis 37:22; 42:37); whereas in the J account it was Judah, after whom the Southern tribes were named (Genesis 37:26; 43:3; 44:16).

Some scholars hold that the E document was written during the reign of King Jeroboam II (787–747 B.C.). At that time the Israelites lived in great prosperity, and there was a widespread introduction of Canaanite practices. By describing God's progressive historic revelations to the Hebrew people the E historians may have hoped to inspire the Hebrew people to remain true to their ancient faith and to repudiate the idolatrous ways of their neighbors. After the fall of the Northern Kingdom to the Assyrians the J and the E documents were joined together by an editor about 650 B.C.

The D Document

The Book of Deuteronomy, by one account, was written not long before its discovery in the Temple in 621 B.C. In a series of didactic sermons it places back into the Mosaic period religious reforms that the prophets wished to achieve at that moment in history. Deuteronomy contains a vigorous attack on the high places that had been permitted in the early days of the monarchy. Such high places were now to be replaced by one central place of worship purified of any vestiges of idolatry (Deuteronomy 12:2–7). Deuteronomy makes it clear that the Lord prefers righteousness and obedience to His law, over offerings of sacrifice (Deuteronomy 10:12–21). Such emphases are reactions to the situation confronting the Hebrews at that time, when in order to maintain themselves following the earlier defeat of the Northern tribes, the people of Judah made a treaty with Assyria, and Assyrian idols, superstitions and cultural practices inevitably infiltrate the land. In addition to the stirring attack on idolatry and the call to loyalty to YHWH, the authors of the D code rewrite some of the earlier Mosaic laws, providing them with ethical motivations. Thus they attempt to show that the Mosaic covenant was relevant to their day (Deuteronomy 5:3).

Many scholars suggest that the D history may have been written specifically during the reign of King Hezekiah (715–687 B.C.), found in 621, and then re-edited and given final form after Judah's exile in 587 B.C. (note allusions to exile in Deuteronomy 4:25–31 and 28:47–57). Other scholars contend that the material in Deuteronomy seems to take the form of public declarations, possibly made at Covenant renewal ceremonies, such as those that had been celebrated in earlier history in the Northern Kingdom (cf. Joshua 24; I Samuel 1–2; I Kings 12:20; Amos 7:13). These inspiring calls to faith were at a later date utilized and adapted by the Southern authors to their own purpose. Whatever their opinion concerning the exact date for the writing of the D account, most·scholars now agree that Moses could not have recited all that the Book of Deuteronomy puts into his speeches. They see in Deuteronomy the use of a popular literary form or device, also to be found in the writings of Greek and Roman historians. Through a series of speeches or addresses alleged to have been delivered by the national hero, the inspired sages of a later era provide sanction for their own reforms and clothe their new insights with authority.

The P Document

When at last the Hebrews were to return from their first exile in 539 B.C., priestly editors decided to recast once again the historic account of their people and to offer a history that would prepare them·for their new situation. Writing between the sixth and fifth centuries B.C. these priest editors hoped to inspire their faithful by the vision of the promise at Sinai: "If you will obey My voice and keep My covenant, you shall be My own possession among all peoples; for the earth is Mine and you shall be to Me a kingdom of priests and a holy nation" (Exodus 19:5–6).

The P authors provide a new sacred history of the religious institutions of the Hebrew faith. They codify the priestly laws. They reveal a concern for details and genealogies, and according to many Bible critics the P authors are responsible for such accounts in Genesis as chapters 5, 10, 25–31, 46 and Exodus 35–40. The cultistic emphasis on the P code in contrast to the ethical concerns of Deuteronomy may be seen by contrasting Leviticus 25 with Deuteronomy 15. Much of the material in the Book of Leviticus is a reflection of their influence.

The Making of the Canon

These various strands—J, E, D and P—are thought to have been joined together finally about 400 B.C. by Ezra or a school of scribes established in his name. At that time the Pentateuch was separated from and elevated above the historical books of Joshua, Judges, Samuel and Kings. These latter books remained important to the Jewish people but were not yet canonized, i.e., decreed as Holy Scripture. This occurred probably in the period, 250–200 B.C., when the "Former Prophets" (Joshua, Judges, Samuel and Kings) and the "Latter Prophets" (Isaiah, Jeremiah, Ezekiel and the Twelve) were also organized as groups edited and recognized as Holy Scripture.

In those days men did not have the same regard as we do today for maintaining the integrity of a man's written word. Authors or committees of historians in one generation felt free to include—without identification or credit—what they wished of an earlier work in their own new writings or even to make changes or add material to the earlier works. So the Hebrew Scripture grew, evolved and changed, ultimately to become the literary heritage of an entire people rather than independent works of a collection of authors. As the law of Moses it revealed God's word for Israel and through Israel to all mankind.

Ben Sira, writing about 180 B.C., knew of the Law (Torah) and the Prophets but he did not consider this category of sacred writing yet closed; he asserted that his own book was prophetically inspired (Ecclesiasticus 24:33). This and other evidence leads biblical scholars to the conclusion that a miscellany of books then circulating were only later collected together in the category known as Writings. These include poetic books such as Psalms, Proverbs and Job; five short literary works: the Song of Songs, Ruth, Lamentations, Ecclesiastes and Esther—these are called in Hebrew the Five Scrolls; a book of prophecy, Daniel; and the books of history: Ezra, Nehemiah and Chronicles.

By virtue of the earlier canonization of the Pentateuch, it had become accepted principle in Jewish law that no book would be considered Holy Writ were it known definitely to have been written after Ezra, for it was thought that after Ezra prophecy disappeared. A book was considered "holy" only if it were prophetic, i.e., inspired by God. Although, according to historic and literary evidence, such books as Daniel, Psalms, Proverbs, Song of Songs and Ecclesiastes may have been written or included material composed much after Ezra, they were accepted into the canon, since they were attributed to authors who lived before prophecy ended. Books such as I Maccabees or Ecclesiasticus, definitely attributed to authors who lived after Ezra, were excluded from Hebrew Scripture even though they had achieved a wide readership among the Hebrew audience and were highly regarded.

The Hebrews were stimulated to fix their canon because of controversy with the early Hebrew Christians as to which books were holy. As indicated, there were many holy writings then in circulation. Some, written in Greek, were included in the Greek translation of the Bible known as the Septuagint. The unsettling conditions of exile and the dispersion of the population required an authoritative listing of writings accepted by the synagogue as the Word of God and worthy of public reading. So the final structuring of the Hebrew Scripture took place at a council at Jamnia, about 90 A.D. under the leadership of Rabbi Johanan Ben Zakkai.

In the final canonization, the Hebrew Bible was limited to twenty-four books. The Five Books of the Law (counting as one book); the eight books of the Prophets (counting the Book of the Twelve as one); eleven books in Writings (counting Ezra and Nehemiah as one and Chronicles I and II as another). All of these had originally been written in Hebrew. None of the books composed in Greek were included; but they remained part of the Septuagint and were thus preserved for Christian and Jewish study.

The Hebrew Bible is known in Hebrew as TaNaK, the name deriving from the first letter of the three Hebrew titles for each section: Torah (Pentateuch), Neviim (Prophets), Ketuvim (Writings).

The Hebrew canonical sequence of books is:

Torah: Genesis, Exodus, Leviticus, Numbers, Deuteronomy.

Prophets: Joshua, Judges, Samuel, Kings—arranged in a chronological sequence. Isaiah, Jeremiah, Ezekiel—arranged not in chronological sequence, but rather by the size of the book, from larger to smaller.

The Twelve: Hosea, Joel, Amos, Obadiah, Jonah, Micah, Nahum, Habakkuk, Zephaniah, Haggai, Zechariah, Malachi.

Writing: Psalms, Proverbs, Job—arranged by the size of the book from larger to smaller.

The Five Scrolls: Song of Songs, Ruth, Lamentations, Ecclesiastes, Esther.

The Historical Writings: Daniel, Ezra (includes Nehemiah), Chronicles.

Appendix 3

The Stories in Genesis and Near Eastern Myths

The stories recorded in Genesis 1–11 provide answers that the Hebrew people offered to account for the creation of the universe and the existence of man: How did man come into being? How account for evil in the world? Why do men speak different languages? What is man's purpose in this world?

In the Jewish religion, these stories in Genesis 1–11 are related directly to the accounts of the patriarchs found in chapters 12–50. The purpose intended by God in the act of creation, Genesis says, will be fulfilled, ultimately, by Abraham and his descendants.

By the creation, God intended man to rule His universe and to establish within it a kingdom of righteousness. Toward that end He provided man with freedom of will and intelligence. But man, by his sinfulness and arrogance, violated God's trust. In punishment, God visited the earth with a flood and dispersed the nations.

Thousands of ancient clay tablets have been uncovered by archeologists in the Mesopotamian area, the birthplace of Abraham and the early Hebrews. Among these tablets are some containing stories of a creation, reminiscences of a "Garden of the Gods" and an account of a flood, all of which have many parallels with the biblical stories of creation, Eden and Noah. Most biblical scholars have decided therefore, that the biblical stories were not intended to be scientific accounts of creation, but rather are part of the literary heritage of the people who lived in the region bounded by the Tigris and Euphrates rivers. Such scholars nevertheless see the spiritual genius of the Hebrews revealed in the way the Hebrews edited, revised and transformed the legends to express moral and spiritual convictions concerning God and His purpose for man.

The Adventure of Archeology

Archeology is the science by which scholars uncover treasures hidden beneath the earth and recount therefrom the story of mankind in the far distant past. The treasures may include bits of pottery, foundation stones of ancient cities, legal, commercial and literary documents carved into clay tablets or stone prisms, fossils, and the like.

Between 1849–1854 British archeologists working in Nineveh uncovered 25,000 tablets decorated with scribbles that we now recognize to be cuneiform writing. George Smith, an employee of the British Museum, deciphered the writings on these tablets, and in December 1872 he excited the world by translating an Assyrian account of a flood story. Several years later Smith also uncovered tablets that contain an Assyrian account of creation. Later other archeologists working in six other cities in the fertile area bordered by the Tigris and Euphrates rivers, uncovered more tablets—some even older—that contained variant readings of the same stories. Since the evidence from the Bible itself indicates that the early Hebrews were among the Semitic nomads who traveled through the Mesopotamian area, it seemed clear to these scholars that the stories in Genesis 1–11 have origins in the folklore and mythology of that particular culture.

Significant foundations of facts underlie these legends, however. For example, the Mesopotamian area is vulnerable to inundation from rains and the flooding of the Tigris and Euphrates rivers. Archeologists have uncovered many cities in that region, revealing deposits of clay silt indicating that they were inundated by flood waters. Similarly Babylonian documents record that great kings built huge towers like the Tower of Babel. They were considered to be the Temple ladders by which their gods could ascend and descend, and so maintain communication with and protect their servant-human followers.

The Creation Account

The Babylonian account of creation is contained in a long poem. It begins with the existence of two gods: Apsu, god of the Fresh Water and Tiamat, goddess of the Salt Water. Intermingling, these gods give birth to several generations of gods who war among themselves until Ea, Earth and Water god, organizes the young gods into a revolt against Apsu and they murder him. The principal god of Babylonia, Marduk, then allies himself with these younger gods and kills the goddess Tiamat, who had sought to revenge the death of her mate. Marduk carves Tiamat's body in two. From one half he fashions the sky and from the other the earth. He establishes the constellations in their courses. Then by bringing together the bone and blood of another murdered god he creates "savage men" whose function is to serve the needs of the gods. Whereupon the gods treat themselves to a divine banquet.

Like elements are to be found in the biblical creation story: the primeval existence of water, the fashioning of earth and sky, the setting of the constellations in their courses, the creation of man. But, how different is the biblical version!

The Bible rejects the conception of multiple gods. Creation is the willful act of a loving God, not the end process of violence and murder. "In the beginning, God . . ." The unity of God dramatized the order and harmony of nature. No magical rites, no sexual cults, no violent ceremonies were required by the Hebrew religion to appease the unruly, cantankerous gods of the Babylonian experience. Man himself is given control over the forces of nature. Regarded by a righteous God with dignity, man is given freedom and purpose. The end act of creation is not the brawling, drunken banquet; it is the Sabbath, a time of spiritual consecration and holiness.

The Epic of Gilgamesh

Tablet 11 of the Assyrian documents deciphered by George Smith contains 200 lines devoted to an account of a flood, the Epic of Gilgamesh. The story recounts the remorse felt by Gilgamesh, king of the city of Uruk (Erech of Genesis 10:10), when his good friend Enkidu dies. Gilgamesh recalls that his ancestor Utanapishtim, alone of men, had attained immortal life. Gilgamesh seeks the secret from his relative. After much cajoling, Utanapishtim relates the story of the great flood: The gods arbitrarily decide to destroy man. In dissent, the god Ea secretly warns Utanapishtim, a resident of Shuruppak, to build a gigantic ark. When the people will inquire of Utanapishtim why he is building such a vessel, he is instructed to answer that the gods are angry with him and he must flee for his life. He builds an ark with six decks. He loads the boat with all manner of possessions, cattle and grain. For six days and nights it rains. The deluge was so fearful, in fact, that even the gods "cowered like dogs" and some regretted their decision. Piloted by a skilled navigator, the. ark at last lands on Mt. Nisir. Utanapishtim releases a dove, then a swallow, and at last a raven which does not return. Thereupon he leaves the ark and offers a sacrifice. The Gods savoring the sweet odor "gather like flies above the sacrifice." When the chief god, Enlil, sees that a human being has been spared, he is fearfully angry. Ea pleads mercy for this human. Enlil relents; he blesses Utanapishtim and his wife with immortal life.

Again, as in the creation story, the similarities between the Epic of Gilgamesh and the story of Noah are numerous. But how different is the Bible version!

In the Bible, it is not by arbitrary decision that God decides to bring a flood, nor is the choice of Noah capricious. Noah's merit is that he is a righteous man. His building of the Ark is meant to be a warning; God would prefer that men repent of their evil ways than that they die. Noah has no pilot to steer his ship; he is dependent entirely upon God's graciousness. God does not grant Noah immortal life; instead, He establishes a covenant through Noah with all of mankind. According to rabbinic tradition the story instructs us: in order to sustain life on earth, man must not murder or steal, he must establish courts of law, he must maintain standards of family devotion and purity, he may not blaspheme God nor orship idols.

Biblical Genealogy

The sons of Noah, according to Genesis 9:18–19, were Shem, Ham, and Japheth; from these "the whole earth was peopled." Archaeological evidence verifies the historicity of the names and peoples referred to in the genealogies that follow in chapters 10 and 11.

The genealogy does not speak of mankind in terms of "Aryan," "Semitic," or "Negroid" races. It knows nothing of the Far East or sub-Sahara Africa. But it is a generally accurate account of the peoples between 2000–1500 B.C. who populated the ancient Near East, extending from the Aegean peninsula in the West to Iran in the East; from the Black Sea in the North to Ethiopia in the Southwest, and Arabia in the Southeast. Pervading this genealogy is the conviction that all families of nations exist under one God, who guides their destinies for His own special purpose; the descendants of Abraham, however are chosen from among all peoples to be God's priest nation. They are to serve as God's witnesses and as custodians of His Law.

According to the account in Genesis 10:10–11, Nimrod's kingdom consisted of Mesopotamia. In the third millennium B.C., the people in control of the area in lower Mesopotamia, around the juncture of the Tigris and Euphrates rivers and the head of the Persian Gulf, called their god "Sumer" (the biblical "Shinar"). They were *Sumerians.* After Sumerian rule declined, a Semitic dynasty was founded by Sargon of Akkad (a city not yet identified). They were called *Akkadians.* The Sumerian and Semitic (Akkadian) peoples produced one creative civilization blending elements of both cultures. They were distinguished by their skill in mathematics and architecture. They leave us a rich heritage of mythology, social legislation, and a storehouse of documents in cuneiform writing.

Related to these people in south Mesopotamia were the *Babylonians* whose city, Babylon, became the capital of a great kingdom, reaching its peak of glory in the eighteenth or seventeenth centuries B.C., under Hammurabi.

To the west were located the *Amorites.*

To the north on the Tigris River were the *Assyrians,* whose capital city of Ashur was named after their chief god.

The Semitic tribes associated with Abraham, according to the biblical record, had their roots in the Mesopotamian region.

The Patriarchs and Their Background

The Bible traces the patriarchs from Ur of Chaldees in South Mesopotamia, near the junction of the Tigris and the Euphrates rivers, to Haran in north Mesopotamia, and from there to Canaan, into Egypt, and then back into Canaan. Abraham calls himself a "Hebrew" (Genesis 14:13), i.e., one who crosses over from place to place, a nomad. And Deuteronomy 26:5 identifies the patriarchs as "nomadic Arameans." In genealogical tables preserved in Scripture (Genesis 11:10–26) Abraham's antecedents reach back: to Shem—son of Noah and father of the Semitic peoples; to Eber—some scholars believe this to be a reference to the "Habiru" people; to Nahor, and then to Terah who fathers three sons, Abram (later Abraham), Nahor, and Haran. All these personal names are also the names of places.

Archaeology verifies the existence of seminomadic tribes within that area. It records also much migratory effort among them shortly after the nineteenth century B.C. due to severe disturbances in the Near East. The area was in upheaval because of invasions by various ethnic groups such as:

Amorites—Semitic tribes who may have included some Arameans; they entered Mesopotamia from the west and populated northern Canaan.

Hurrians—the biblical Horites who may have come from inner Asia through the northern Caucasian and Armenian mountains. The discovery of thousands of clay tablets in 1925 in the Hurrian city of Nuzi throws light on some of the social customs of the Patriarchs as described in Scripture.

Hittites—a people from Asia Minor speaking an Indo-European dialect whose influence extended physically to Hebron in Canaan. Ezekiel 16:3 describes Jerusalem: "Thy father is an Amorite and thy mother a Hittite," leading some scholars to believe that the Jebusites who occupied Jerusalem until it was captured by King David may be related to these Hittites. Abraham purchased a burial place for his wife from a Hittite (Genesis 23:11–16).

Habiru—described as a "troublesome people" in the writings of Egyptians, Babylonians, and Hittites. A seminomadic people, they included many Semitic tribes; they are recorded as being soldiers for pay, hired laborers, craftsmen, smiths, and musicians, who earned their keep wherever they could. They are a people without a land; since in those days each city, each land, had its own god, they are the only people in all the written records that have been uncovered without a god.

Hyksos—a group that included Semitic, Hurrian, Hittite, and Indo-European warriors. The Semitic name Jacob is included among Hyksos rulers around 1600 B.C. They introduced the horse-drawn war chariot into the Near East. At first invincible, they entered and conquered Egypt about 1700 B.C., and they established their capital at Tanis in the Delta of North Egypt. They were finally driven out by the Pharaohs of the eighteenth dynasty about 1570 B.C. Archaeological evidence suggests that these Hyksos and their Egyptian pursuers at that time destroyed many of the cities of Canaan.

Who were the Hebrews? Scholars are not certain. They may have been the Habiru—a people without land or god; they may have been among the Hyksos; they may have been among the Amorites; in fact they may have been among or included in their ranks all of these peoples. From the biblical account it is clear that Abraham mingled easily with all of them. The exact origin of the Hebrews, therefore, from the biblical point of view is not very important. What is significant is that they became, by God's choice, a priestly people. They recognized Abraham, the first to acknowledge God as as their father. They became a people; they were emancipated from slavery, given a Law; and they acquired a land when they entered into a covenant with God. It is at this point that Hebrew history really begins. It is God's history with the Hebrews.

When did the patriarchs live? Estimates of dates for Abraham's migrations range from 1900 to 1550 B.C. Many scholars place Abraham about 1700 B.C.

Some scholars suggest that the stories of Abraham, Isaac, and Jacob are stories of founders of separate Semitic tribes, later welded into one people by King David under service to the Mosaic God YHWH. It is at that time that the Hebrews wrote down their history, the biblical narrative, and identified themselves as the progeny of one family, related to Abraham.

Some scholars point out, also, that the word *El* for "God" goes back to that Canaanite period. There is evidence of an *El* religion among the Canaanites. Exodus 6:3 reports that Moses was first among the patriarchs to recognize YHWH as God. Under the leadership of Moses, Joshua and David, and under the discipline of the prophets, these Semitic tribes cleansed their worship of its idolatrous manifestations; they accepted YHWH as the Lord and made a covenant with Him. They identified their God of old, *El*, with YHWH in a purified monotheistic religion.

Appendix 4

The Bible in English Translation

I

The Bible is sometimes used in English literature courses, but the Bible is not an English book at all. Except for a few portions in Aramaic, the Old Testament is a Hebrew book, the New Testament a Greek book. To these sources translators must continually return; these are our unfailing link with the first great creative era of the Hebrew-Christian tradition. As language changes, ever-new translations are needed to keep us in touch with origins. Old versions of the Bible are sometimes loved as old linen is loved, or old china. Special poetic quality is thought to inhere in them, but this can be illusion. On this subject, Thomas Hardy made a significant entry in his journal in 1918. Makers of English Bibles, he said, "translated into the language of their age; then the years began to corrupt that language as spoken and to add gray lichen to the translation; until the moderns who use the corrupted tongue marvel at the poetry of the old words. When new they were not half so poetical."

Acknowledging that the Hebrew and Greek originals are alone "authentical," one Reformation Confession states that since these languages are not in common use, the Scriptures "are to be translated into the vulgar language of every nation." An earlier Jewish tradition similarly records that it is permitted to write the biblical books in any language (*Megillah* 1:8; *Sotah* 33a); but when some Greek translations appeared in the second century, the rabbis were so dissatisfied that they compared the day of translation to the day when the Israelites danced around the Golden Calf (*Soferim* 1:8–9).

The makers of the King James Version in their preface include theirs among "translations into the vulgar," and are at pains to point out that this "is not a quaint conceit lately taken up." This use of *vulgar* is a good illustration of how language changes. By it the men of the seventeenth century did not mean the language of the gutter, but rather the language in common use. One of the earliest and most influential of all Bible translations takes its name from the realization that it is only in this way that God's Word can be really effective. The Council of Trent declared the Latin Bible of Jerome to be the authoritative Scripture. This translation, made in the latter part of the fourth century, is called the Vulgate, from the Latin word for "crowd."

The first considerable body of literature ever taken out of one language and translated into another involved the Old Testament. From 500 B.C. through the Babylonian exile Aramaic had gradually replaced Hebrew as the spoken language of the residents of Palestine.

Nehemiah 8:8 makes reference to the fact that the biblical word was read and then interpreted into a language that the people would understand, i.e., Aramaic. The first translation of the Bible into Aramaic is called a "Targum," i.e., a running translation offering the intent of the word rather than its literal rendering. Since such a translation carries the danger that the text may be distorted, the rabbis warned: "He who renders a verse as it reads with strict literalness lies, but he who makes additions is a blasphemer." There were many Aramaic Targums available. Eventually the Babylonian Targum ascribed to a scholar named Onkelos achieved dominance as the most authoritative. In the Targum by Onkelos, despite the warning against "additions," one finds changes in the rendering of the Hebrew text that suggest a reinterpretation and a new understanding given to the Scripture message. For example, human traits ascribed to the deity are toned down. God does not "pass over" the Israelites, He "spares" them. Instead of God's "hearing" or "seeing," it was heard or revealed beforehand. Divine appellations may not be used of humans. For example, Moses is to be to Aaron a "master," not a "God." "Who is like unto Thee among the Gods" (Exodus 15:11), has been changed in the Aramaic: "There is no one besides Thee, for thou art God, O Lord." Personification of inanimate objects is disallowed. Ezekiel does not "eat the Torah scroll," he "listens attentively to its contents." Where the Hebrew text reads, "the Fathers have eaten sour grapes and the children's teeth are set on edge," the Aramaic paraphrases: "the Fathers have sinned but the children are punished." An effort is made to protect the honor of the Hebrews: Leah's eyes were "pretty" not "weak."

With the conquest of Palestine by the Greeks and the existence of a large number of Greek-speaking Jews in Egypt, it was inevitable that there be a request for a Greek translation of the Bible. "Without the Greek translation," asserts the Jewish scholar Morgolis, "the Christian conversion of Europe would have been well nigh impossible." There is evidence that most of the Bible was already available in Greek translation before the Christian era, the most important Greek translation of the Bible being that of the Seventy Elders known as the Septuagint. The New Testament writers regularly quote the Septuagint. That is why prophetic quotations appearing in the Gospels and Epistles are seldom identical with what we find in the English Old Testaments translated directly from the Hebrew.

The Septuagint contained some books not finally included in the Hebrew Bible. Called the Apocrypha by some, these books are considered as sacred by those who regard the Septuagint as authoritative. Luther placed them between the Testaments with the indication that, while "not held equal to the sacred Scriptures," they "nevertheless are useful and good to read." The Anglican Church assigns to them a similar significance. Because the writings included in this Septuagint were cited by Hebrew Christians in their disputations with Jews and because of the Septuagint's inclusion of the Apocryphal books, it was banned in A.D. 130 for use in the synagogue. The discouraged rabbis explained: "The Torah cannot be translated exactly as it ought to be." Nevertheless some rabbis were willing still to give it another try. They ordered a new Greek translation by the scholar Aquila. This translation, used by the Greek-speaking Jews far into the Middle Ages, is a literal, word by word rendering of the Hebrew intending to preserve the Hebrew Bible in its authoritative and canonized form. It served as a Hebrew-Greek lexicon. To offset the literalism of Aquila's translation, a Hebrew Christian by the name of Symmachus wrote a commentary in the Greek, paraphrasing the Hebrew text. Finally a direct translation based upon the "commentary" of Symmachus and the "dictionary" of Aquila was written by Theodotion, a convert to Judaism.

The Church Father, Origen (A.D. 185–254), who had studied Hebrew with Rabbi Hillel, published a Hexapla, a book of six columns drawing upon five Greek translations, including these three by Aquila, Symmachus and Theodotion, and the Hebrew. Origen's Hexapla has thus been of inestimable value to Bible scholars as they have tried to determine the exact meaning of the biblical words.

When we think of how the Bible has come down to us in English, a line of James Russell Lowell takes on new meaning:
 "Slowly the Bible of the race is writ."

Attempts to put the Bible into our language are as old as our literature. Caedmon, the earliest English poet known by name, was famed for his paraphrases of Bible stories. In the eighth century, too, the Psalms were translated into Anglo-Saxon. The Venerable Bede, whose history is still a primary source for knowledge of ancient English, died while dictating to his scribe a translation of John's Gospel. "I don't want my boys to read a lie," he said. In the ninth century, King Alfred prefixed to his own laws a translation of the Ten Commandments, and expressed the wish that all the freeborn youth of his kingdom should employ themselves on nothing till they read the Scripture. In the tenth century, the gospels were translated, apparently for public use, and Archbishop Aelfric had interlinear translations prepared for his clergy.

The first complete English Bible (about 1382) was translated by John Wyclif, the morning star of the Reformation, and friends. Wyclif knew only the Latin Bible, and so his version was a translation of a translation. Yet, with spelling modernized, some of his phrases are still ours: "the depe things of God"; "strait is the gate and narewe is the waye"; "the cup of blessing which we blessen." He gave us, too, the phrase *truly, truly* which in recent English Bibles appears where *verily, verily* once stood. Wyclif provided a key phrase in Lincoln's Gettysburg address; he stated in his preface that he had undertaken the arduous labor of translation because the Bible is "for the government of the people, by the people, and for the people."

The first English New Testament made from the original Greek (1525) was the work of William Tyndale. The publication, a few years before, of Erasmus' Greek Testament made translation imperative, but the church authorities did not wish the people to have the Bible in English, and Tyndale was forbidden to proceed. When he went ahead anyway, the bishops referred to his work as a "heretical and damnable book." Because he had been forbidden to do the work in England, Tyndale went to the Continent where Martin Luther's earlier translation had won hospitality for such a pioneering venture. Tyndale's acquaintance with Luther's brilliant German translation of the Bible is not without significance. For Luther's was the first Western European Bible based, not on the official Latin Vulgate, but on the original Greek and Hebrew. Tyndale recognized in Luther's work an inspiration for his own. Luther's Bible drew upon interpretations of the noted scholar Nicolas De Lyra (died 1340) who was himself indebted to the insights of the historic and renowned Jewish Bible commentator, Solomon, son of Isaac, known as Rashi (died 1105). Luther described the importance of Hebrew and Greek scholarship for Bible translation: "They are the sheaf in which the sword of the spirit is encased. They are the box in which this jewel is carried . . . when we, I say, by our neglect let these tongues go, we shall . . . lose the gospel . . ."

Tyndale's English translation, when completed, was still unwelcome in a more restrictive England. It had to be smuggled into the country and Tyndale paid with his life for his devotion to the Bible. For no other crime than having given his people the New Testament in the language they could understand, he was strangled and his body burned. We who can now buy Bibles so cheaply are sometimes unaware of the price that has been paid in human martyrdom and suffering that we should be enabled to read God's book in the English language.

Tyndale did more than any other individual to formulate our English religious vocabulary, and it is a safe guess that he wrote three quarters of our latest English Bible. His translation of Matthew 1 : 23 reads:

>Beholde a mayde shall be with chylde,
>and shall brynge forthe a sonne,
>and they shall call his name Emmanuel,
>which is by interpretation, God with us.

Tyndale's dying words were: "O Lord, open the King of England's eyes." God did indeed open the eyes of Henry VIII. In 1535 there appeared a translation bearing the name of Miles Coverdale. Coverdale was Tyndale's friend and colleague, and the translation bearing his name was largely Tyndale's. In 1537 the second edition of

Coverdale, the first English Bible printed in England, appeared with these words on the title page: "Set forth with the Kynges most gracious license." Some of Coverdale's renderings are memorable: "Is there no treacle in Gilead?" (Jeremiah 8:22); "broke his brainpanne" (Judges 9:53); "Their windows were not looked upon in the daylie handreaching" (Acts 6:1).

Great Bible (so-called from its size) was the name given to the Tyndale-Coverdale rendering when it was permanently embodied in 1539 in what has come to be known as the first authorized version. A royal decree required that a copy be "set up in a convenient place" in every church in the kingdom. This Bible is still much used. The Prayer Book of the Anglican Church took its Psalter and its Lord's Prayer from this version. Anyone who uses the "trespasses" version of the Lord's Prayer is quoting the Great Bible.

Though never authorized, the next English Bible was one of the most important. In the Roman Catholic rule of Queen Mary, English exiles in Switzerland made a translation to which was given the name *Geneva Bible*. The first English version to have verse divisions, this became the Bible of Cromwell's army and the Scottish Covenanters, of John Bunyan and John Knox. It is the Bible of the Puritans, and the Bible which the Pilgrims brought to the bleak New England shore.

By 1568 ecclesiastical opposition to vernacular Bibles had pretty well subsided, and the church authorities issued their own translation, the second authorized version, the Bishops' Bible. This was the official Bible of the Shakespearean era. Its most lasting influence was an unhappy one. In thirty-two instances which Tyndale correctly rendered by *love,* it used *charity.* The third authorized version was the King James of 1611.

Moving on to 1856, the motion was made in the Convocation of Canterbury that work be started on a new translation of the Bible. The discovery of old manuscripts made this imperative; the English Revision, begun in 1870, was published in 1881–1885. Of this, the American Standard (1901) was a variant. The fifth authorized English Bible is the Revised Standard Version, 1946 (New Testament), 1952 (Old and New Testaments), and 1957 (Apocrypha).

The New English Bible New Testament appeared in 1961.

Because of the beauty of its language, the King James Version of the Bible remained for centuries the chief English text from which English translations of the Bible by Jewish scholars were modeled. In America in 1814 in Philadelphia, Isaac Leeser completed the first version of Scriptures in English to be written by a Jewish scholar. It was based on the King James Version with significant changes reflecting the influence of Leeser's knowledge of Hebrew and the scientific work of the German-Jewish school of biblical criticism. In 1916 Abraham Harkavy changed obsolete words and updated the spelling. But more provocatively he paraphrased certain passages in order to achieve greater explicitness (e.g., in Jeremiah 31:20 for "I remember him," Harkavy added, "I remember him *for good*." In Zechariah 3:8 for "My servant the branch," Harkavy added, "My servant the Sprout *of David*").

In 1917 the Jewish Publication Society issued an authoritative Jewish translation of the Hebrew Bible in English. It drew upon the English in the King James Version as well as the later British and American Revised Versions, but with significant changes reflecting the scholarship of the authors, a most learned group of Jewish teachers who were engaged some 17 years in that work of translation. It was the first English translation under Jewish auspices achieved through a cooperative effort of scholarship. Heretofore the translations had been the products of individual creativity. In explaining the reason for their work, the authors wrote: "Apart from the thought that the Christological interpretations in non-Jewish translations are out of place in a Jewish Bible . . . the Jew cannot afford to have his Bible translation prepared for him by others. He cannot have it as a gift, even as he cannot borrow a soul from others."

In 1962 the Jewish Publication Society again issued a new English translation, *Torah* (Pentateuch); and work is proceeding on other books of the TaNaK. An effort has been made through the use of bold type printed across the page to make the reading easier. Language has been simplified. For example, in former translations the text read: ". . . all that were numbered of the camp of Judah being a hundred thousand and four score thousand and six thousand and four hundred." The new JPS *Torah* writes: "The total enrolled in the divisions of Judah were 186,400." Important Hebrew words like YHWH, the name of the Lord, are preserved in the original Hebrew and no effort is made to translate words that are genuinely obscure. Archaeological evidence dictated calling "the Red Sea," "the Reed Sea" and Joseph's "coat of many colors," is now properly translated "an ornamented tunic." Notes are added to help clarify the text. When Genesis 5:29 suggests that "Noah will provide us with relief from our work . . . out of the very soil which the Lord placed under a curse," the notes refer the reader to Genesis 9:20 where it is recorded that Noah was the first to plant a vineyard. Jewish understandings of Scripture are boldly and for the first time written into the translation. See particularly Genesis 1:2 where for the verse describing the Spirit of God hovering over the face of the waters (often understood in Christian scholarship to be a manifestation of the third person of the Trinity) the new JPS translation reads: "And a wind from God sweeping over the water." (The Hebrew word *ruach* can be translated both "spirit" and "wind"; the use of "wind" places the creation story within the context of the earliest stories of creation found among all peoples of the Near East.) The third Commandment is translated so that it forbids, not cursing, but perjury: "He shall not swear falsely by the name of the Lord, your God." Abandoning finally the English model of the King James Version, the authors point out that "[KJV] rendered the Hebrew to a considerable extent word for word rather than idiomatically, a procedure which nearly always results in quaintness or awkardness and not infrequently in obscurity. A translation which is stilted where the original is perfectly intelligible is the very opposite of faithful." The authors of the new JPS have also rejected, at some points, the chapter structure placed on the Hebrew Bible by Christian medieval translations. Instead they draw from the translation of the Hebrew text into Arabic by the noted Jewish sage Gaon Saadye (892–942).

Selections from Leeser, Harkavy, the JPS Holy Scriptures of 1917 and Torah of 1962 are to be found in this *Bible Reader*.

Bible translations, needless to say, are most frequently not the work of one individual or of one church. When the English Revision was undertaken, the project, initiated by the established church, was set up so as "to invite the cooperation of any eminent for scholarship, to whatever nation or religious body they may belong." The committee included Baptist, Congregationalist, Methodist, Presbyterian, and Unitarian, as well as Anglican, members. On the American side, the committee included members of nine denominations. Work on the Revised Standard Version was initiated by the National Council of Churches, and the Denver Assembly referred to the finished product as "a major contribution of this Council to prophetic religion." The New English Bible was "Planned and Directed by Representatives of the Baptist Union of Great Britain and Ireland, the Church of England, the Church of Scotland, the Congregational Union of England and Wales, the Council of Churches for Wales, the London Yearly Meeting of the Society of Friends, the Methodist Church of Great Britain, the Presbyterian Church of England, the United Council of Christian Churches and Religious Communions in Ireland."

This represents a new stage in the sponsorship of Bible translations. As applied to Scripture, the term "authorized" is sometimes used. What does it mean and who does the authorizing? An authorized Bible is one sanctioned by the highest ecclesiastical authority. In the Anglican Church, the highest authority is nominally the reigning monarch, whose right to authorize Bibles resides solely in his ecclesiastical position. Thus it came about that the first authorized English Bible was sanctioned by the notorious Henry VIII, and the version of 1611 by "God's silly vassal," James VI of Scotland, James I of England. In these days when religion is being increasingly disestablished, the denominational assembly or the council of churches is recognized as the appropriate agency for authorizing Bibles.

II

Any individual qualified by linguistic skills to understand the biblical languages and able to express himself effectively in his own mother tongue is free to make his own translation. Because such a version is the work of one person, it is spoken of as a private or individual translation.

In the eighteenth century among those who made contributions to the English Bible are William Mace, who in 1729 published an English translation in the language of his day in parallel columns with a corrected Greek text; Willam Whiston, translator of Josephus, whose "The Primitive New Testament" appeared in 1745; Gilbert Wakefield, who, in 1751, introduced modern paragraphing and relegated verse numbers to the margin; Dr. E. Harwood whose "Liberal Translation" (1768) was "an attempt to translate the Scriptures with the same freedom and elegance lately applied to the Greek classics."

The most important of private translations of the eighteenth century was one intended "for plain unlettered men." The Holy Club at Oxford began when John and Charles Wesley engaged in study of the Greek Testament. This led Wesley to dissatisfaction with the King James Version. "I do not say," he cautiously wrote, "it is incapable of being brought in several places nearer the original. Neither will I affirm that the Greek copies from which this translation was made are always the most correct." The Greek Testament which he knew enabled him—as at Matthew 5:22; 6:4, 6, 18—to introduce textual improvements which anticipate twentieth century versions. Later, in 1755, he published his "New Testament with Explanatory Notes," the preface of which states: "I have never knowingly so much as in one place altered it for altering's sake but there, and there only, where, first, the sense was made better, stronger, clearer, or more consistent with the context; secondly, where, the sense being equally good, the phrase was better or nearer the original."

Some nineteenth century translators were: Charles Thomson, secretary of the Continental Congress, whose 1808 rendering of the Septuagint was the first English version made in the New World; Granville Penn, grandson and biographer of William Penn, whose "The Book of the New Covenant" appeared in 1836; Jonathan Morgan, a lawyer of Portland, Maine, whose translation made use of phonetic spelling; Joseph Bryant Rotherham whose "New Testament Newly Translated and Critically Emphasized" was dated 1872; Farrar Fenton, an industrialist who, fearing Christianity would perish because the King James Version was obsolete, published in 1895 a New Testament which he claimed was the first ever made by a translator who had no historical or theological theories to support; Robert Young, famed for his concordance, published in 1852 a

"Literal Translation of the Holy Bible" which, in revised edition, was issued again in 1953.

An occasional private translation has been associated with denominational movements or designed to bolster a sectarian position. During the eighteenth century Thomas and Alexander Campbell (1788–1866), father and son, came from Ireland to America. Originally Presbyterians, they were disturbed by sectarian strife among Christians, and initiated in Western Pennsylvania "The Christian Association of Washington," adopting as a slogan "where the Scriptures speak, we speak; where the Scriptures are silent, we are silent." Under the title of "Reformers" or "Disciples," the movement grew, and in 1826 Alexander Campbell published a translation of the New Testament which was held to be necessary because of the changes which had taken place in the English language since the reign of James I, and because better Greek texts were available. This new version rested largely upon the work of three British divines: George Campbell (the Gospels), James Macknight (the Epistles), and Philip Doddridge (Acts and Revelation). Campbell wrote an introduction to each book of the New Testament and added notes of his own. Although he introduced the word "immerse" instead of "baptize," he denied any sectarian concern: "I would not give one turn to the meaning of an adverb, preposition, or interjection, to aid any sectarian cause in the world."

In 1850 the American Bible Union was organized for the purpose of issuing an "immersionist" version of the Scripture for the use of those denominations for whom this mode of baptism was a distinctive rite. The New Testament, which appeared in three successive volumes (1862, 1863 and 1864), was united into a single book in 1865. Undertaking to translate the Old Testament, the group published Genesis in 1868, but lack of funds delayed the completion of the project to 1912, at which time there appeared "The Holy Bible—An Improved Edition." This included a revised New Testament reflecting a somewhat less enthusiastic commitment to the original purpose. Whereas the 1865 edition had "immerse" in each reference to baptism, the 1912 edition carried in each case the double rendering: "baptize (immerse)."

For the use of Jehovah's Witnesses there appeared in 1950 the "New World Translation of the Christian Greek Scriptures," by translators who remain anonymous. This was followed in 1953 by the "New World Translation of the Hebrew Scriptures." Published and circulated by the Watch Tower Bible and Tract Society, this version reflects the distinctive doctrines of the sponsoring sect. Clinging to the hybrid (and now generally abandoned) term, "Jehovah," this translation makes Moses say at Exodus 4:10: "Excuse me, Jehovah." At John 1:1 the rendering is "the Word was a god." Convinced that this earth is to be transformed into a paradise for the faithful, this version moves a comma in Luke 23:43 to support this belief: "Truly I tell you today, you will be with me in paradise." The words "torture stake" and "impale" replace "cross" and "crucify." A useful feature of this translation is a simple printer's device by which you (plural) is distinguished from you (singular). In the Greek different forms occur where one form serves in English. Where "you" is singular, this version prints it in ordinary type; where it is plural, in capital letters.

III

Turning to private translations of ecumenical interest, it can be confidently asserted that no age has been so rich in this activity as our own. Translators have experimented with every conceivable device to put the Word of life into the lives of men and women, boys and girls.

The Twentieth Century New Testament, issued in three parts between 1898 and 1901, abandoned the traditional order of the books in favor of an order more nearly chronological; it has an outline of each book, with numerous subdivisions. In 1961, fifty years after publication, the volume was issued in paperback by the Moody Press. The anonymous translators, describing their translation as "a labour of love," commended it "to the goodwill of all English-speaking people."

In 1902 Richard Francis Weymouth, Fellow of University College, London, published "The New Testament in Modern Speech." In 1932 this work was revised by Professor J. A. Robertson, of Aberdeen, who provided maps and additional notes. Editor of *The Resultant Greek Testament*, Weymouth explained that the purpose of his contemporary version was to consider "how we can with some approach to probability suppose that the inspired writer himself would have expressed his thoughts, had he been writing in our age and country." For the non-expert, Weymouth's version is notable for the way in which it takes the reader into the translator's workshop, so he can see what the translator is doing. A typical note explains the "anxiously asked" of Matthew 2:4: "the tense (imperfect) implies that he asked repeatedly, pressed the inquiry."

One of the most effective and influential of private translations is that of James Moffatt, whose New Testament appeared in 1913, whole Bible in 1926. Moffatt was a kind of universal genius who, besides being expert in both Testaments could write authoritatively on English literature, edited the Handbook to the Hymnary of the Scottish Church, and died as professor emeritus of church history. When a religious journal invited ministers to list the ten books that had influenced them most, a Hollywood pastor headed his list with Moffatt's translation of the New Testament which, he said, "colloquially brings home the availability of the energy God poured through Jesus." A Methodist missionary, imprisoned for 14 months in Communist China, recommended Moffatt's translation as the best book to take with one into solitary confinement. "A turn of phrase," he said, "a directness and forcefulness of diction could give new meaning to a whole paragraph and set my mind and heart aglow with new meaning and emotion."

Dr. Moffatt's Scottish origin comes out in his reference in Exodus 2:3 to "a creel made of papyrus reeds." Any play on words is all but impossible to convey in translation. Here Moffatt has succeeded perhaps better than anyone else. A glance at other versions will suggest how much more effective he is in "he looked . . . for right—and lo shrieks from the wronged" (Isaiah 5:7); "if your faith does not hold out, you will never hold out" (Isaiah 7:9); "not one of them perished—only the son of perdition" (John 17:12). Moffatt's translation has been issued in a variety of editions; a concordance to it has been published, with over 60,000 entries, and on it a whole series of commentaries has been based.

In 1923 Edgar J. Goodspeed, of the University of Chicago, published "The New Testament: An American Translation," in which he sought to express biblical ideas in terms commonly understood in the United States. The man of property in Matthew 25:15 entrusted money to his slaves: "He gave one five thousand dollars, and another two thousand, and another one thousand." The word traditionally rendered "Sirs" in Acts 16:30 became "Gentlemen." On the day of the crucifixion, "from noon there was darkness over the whole country until three o' clock" (Matthew 27:45). Goodspeed's intention was also a format that would give the appearance of a book to be "continuously and understandingly read." In 1931 Goodspeed's New Testament was bound up with "The Old Testament translated by a group of scholars under the editorship of J. M. Powis Smith" to form *The Bible: An American Translation,* often called the Chicago Bible from its place of origin.

Stained glass windows in the First Baptist Church, Washington, D.C., exhibit Baptists who have been distinctive for their exemplification of the faith: William Carey, Adoniram Judson, Walter Rauschenbusch. A panel devoted to Bible translators shows not only Edgar J. Goodspeed but also Helen Barrett Montgomery, perhaps the only woman ever to make a published translation of the entire New Testament. Mrs. Montgomery's "Centenary Translation of the New Testament," a two-volume work issued in 1924, celebrated the centennial of the American Baptist Publication Society. In this version, the chapters are subdivided into paragraphs, each carrying a title in dark-faced type. Some of these titles are : "A 'Closeup' of Sin," "Paul's Swan Song," and "Orchestrate your Virtues."

During World War II, a London rector whose church was destroyed in the blitz spent many of the blackout hours translating for his youth group the New Testament epistles. These were published in 1947 as *Letters to Young Churches,* a volume of which C. S. Lewis said: "It would have saved me a great deal of labor if this book had come into my hands when I first seriously began to try to discover what Christianity was." Encouraged by this reception of his work, J. B. Phillips went on to translate *The Gospels, The Young Church in Action,* and *The Book of Revelation.* The four volumes are now bound together as *The New Testament in Modern English.*

Phillips explained that, since the New Testament was originally in colloquial Greek, it must be put into colloquial English. He freely admits, however, that he has often engaged in paraphrase rather than in translation—thus leaving the English reader unsure of precisely what the original said. An American woman who underwent a cancer operation in Durban, South Africa, said that the translation of J. B. Phillips had sustained her in her loneliness and fear: "We believe now that we had this experience of coming to the end of our tether that we might learn to trust, not ourselves, but in God who can raise the dead" (2 Corinthians 1:9). John 1:1 reads, in Phillips, "In the beginning God expressed himself." At Luke 12:19 the rich farmer says to himself: "Soul, relax."

In 1945 Gerrit Verkuyl, a Presbyterian minister born in Holland and whose career was in the United States, published *The Berkeley* Version of the New Testament, named presumably for the translator's home town in California. Under the editorship of Dr. Verkuyl, a group of scholars issued, in 1959, both Testaments under the title, *The Berkeley Version in Modern English,* "and with numerous helpful non-doctrinal notes to aid the understanding of the reader." Although a score of men contributed to the volume, each was responsible for his own work and there was never any mutual criticism or over-all editing. A conservative reviewer said: "Moralistic conclusions, quotations from modern poets and philosophers, parallels in modern history and suggestions about memorization could well be left for the Sunday-school quarterlies." An example of the kind of note deplored by the reviewer is at Exodus 8:28: "As the world tells the Christian, 'Don't move too far away from us; don't differ too much from us!' It could not satisfy Moses." To Exodus 18:23 are appended the words: "Such counselors as Jethro are sorely needed in most churches and all Christian workers may well make these suggestions part of their program."

In 1963 William F. Beck, who had been a guest lecturer at Concordia Seminary, published *The New Testament in the Language of Today,* the result of many years of personal study devoted to ancient biblical manuscripts and papyrus finds. He sees God's guiding hand in the fact that the church did not seek to preserve its Scriptures "by keeping one original copy . . . which men could destroy but by sending out thousands of manuscripts all over the earth." The papyri he compares to "a tape recording of what people said offguard." He believes the world now needs "a spiritual missile," that is, "the sword of the Word in its unveiled power." A feature of his work is the headings he affixes to the sections into which he breaks the New Testament material. The Sermon on the Mount contains 19 sections, with such titles as "Don't Lust," "Don't Swear," "Don't Blow Your Horn," "Don't Worry." Other headings are "If You're Married to an Unchristian" (1 Corinthians 7:12–16), "Follow your Teachers" (Hebrews 13:7–19), "The Devil's Last Battle" (Revelation 20:1–10).

The Anchor Bible, appearing in 38 volumes, is a series of original translations, with introduction and commentary, by different scholars drawn from Protestant, Jewish and Catholic backgrounds. The translators, however, did not work as a committee and each individual is responsible for his own rendering and annotations. Among the twenty-six individual contributors to the multi-volume project are seven Roman Catholics, four Jewish and fifteen Protestant scholars drawn from Israel, Italy, Denmark, and Sweden as well as the United States.

IV

Private translators have sometimes been primarily concerned with the language of their own culture. Noah Webster (1758–1843) was an American lexicographer who did not wish to be remembered either by his dictionary or his blue-backed speller but rather by his *Holy Bible with Amendments* (1833). Webster considered that the King James Version was sometimes immodest, and contained errors in grammar and geography, and he believed that English versions made in America should conform to American idiom. "Whenever words are understood in a sense different from that which they had when the translation was made, they present a wrong signification of false ideas."

Two men named Charles Williams have made translations of the New Testament. In 1937 Charles B. Williams published *The New Testament: A Translation in the Language of the People*. Explaining what he is about, Williams says he has "tried to use the words and phrases that are understandable by the farmer and the fisherman, by the carpenter and the cowboy, by the cobbler and the cab-driver, by the merchant and the miner, by the milkmaid and the house-mistress, by the woodcutter and the trucker. If these can understand it, it is certain that the scholar, the teacher, the minister, the lawyer, the doctor, and all others can." The tense structure of Greek verbs is different from that in English, and a feature of this work is the effort to bring out the full significance of the Greek verb form. Thus 1 John 3:8 f. brings out the progressive action implied in the present tense: "Whoever practices sin belongs to the devil . . . No one born of God makes a practice of sinning." The aorist verb form at John 7:44 is rendered: "No one ventured to lay a hand on him."

Fifteen years later, in 1952, Charles Kingsley Williams, who had taught in both India and what is now Ghana, published *The New Testament: A New Translation in Plain English*. Except for a supplementary list of terms such as Areopagus, Epicurean, parchment, synagogue, traitor, the words are all taken from the British "Interim Report on Vocabulary Selection." Paul's complex sentences have been broken into shorter ones, and connective words have been adjusted to contemporary practice. The whole is designed so that "learners of English may imitate it without fear of being oldfashioned." 1 Corinthians 11 : 1 in this version reads: "Copy me, as I copy Christ."

Originators of Basic English contend that any idea which can be expressed in English can be expressed in the 850 carefully chosen words (including only 18 verbs) of that scientifically structured vocabulary, intended to facilitate world-wide communication in English. S. H. Hooke and his colleagues of the Orthological Institute issued *The New Testament in Basic English*. In 1950 appeared *The Basic Bible, containing the Old and New Testaments in Basic English*. It was found necessary to supplement the 850-word vocabulary with about 150 additional terms, including terms out of the natural world (leopard, thistle, amethyst) and terms out of the Hebrew tradition (rabbi, manna, phylactery). Because of the arbitrarily limited vocabulary circumlocutions often have to be used. "Soldiers" are "fighting men"; "parable" is "teaching in the form of a story"; "beg" is "make requests of money from people in the street."

This can sometimes be effective. Lacking a word for "deceive," James 1:22 becomes "blinding yourselves with false ideas." "Wilderness" is "waste land," and Golgotha "Dead Mans's Head." "Repent" is "have a change of heart." On the other hand, the limits can be hampering. During World War II the effort was made·to put some of Winston Churchill's speeches into Basic English. The best that could be done with "blood, sweat and tears" was "blood, body water, and eyewash."

The American Bible Society published in 1966 *Today's English Version of the New Testament*. Stating that the volume is designed for people who speak English as their "own mother tongue or as an acquired language," the preface explains that "the work does not compare to traditional vocabulary or style" and has avoided, "as much as possible, words and forms of English not in current use." Matthew's genealogy of Jesus is described as "the birth record." Matthew 1:17 refers to "fourteen sets of fathers and sons." Matthew 1:25 affirms of Joseph and Mary: "he had no sexual relations with her before she gave birth to her son." Ephesians 6 : 1 said: "Children, it is your Christian duty to obey your parents, for this is the rightful thing to do."

Clarence L. Jordan, of Koinonia Farm, Americus, Georgia, has published the *Cotton Patch Version* of the new Testament. The letter to the Hebrews in this translation has the sub-title, "A First-Century Manual for Church Renewal." Hebrews 11:1 is rendered: "Now faith is the turning of dreams into deeds; it is betting your life on the unseen realities. It was for such faith that men of old were martyred." The Sermon on the Mount and the Letter of James are published together under the title, "Practical Religion." Matthew 5:13 is rendered: "You all are the earth's salt. But now if you just sit there and don't salt, how will the world ever get salted?" James 1:26 reads, "If a fellow thinks he has religion, but can't keep from running off at the mouth, and if he has a dishonest heart, that man's religion is as dead as a doornail."

V

While the situation in the Roman Catholic Church has been up to the present somewhat different from that followed by Protestant and Jewish translators, there is a notable convergence of interests and procedures, particularly in the recent years.

Mention has been made of Jerome's fourth century translation, the Vulgate. The church of the middle ages continued to use this translation long after Latin had ceased to be the common language. This was the first considerable book published in movable type in the Western world. A United States postage stamp in 1952 carried the picture of a 15th century printing press at Mainz, with the inscription "500th Anniversary of the printing of the first book, the Holy Bible, from moveable type, by Johann Gutenberg." Of more than forty copies of the Gutenberg Bible that have survived into the 20th century, a baker's dozen are in the United States, and the one in the Library of Congress is said to be the most sought-after exhibit there.

In 1546 the Council of Trent made the Vulgate the official version of the Catholic Church. A principal reason for the swift spread of the Reformation was the vernacular Bibles which appeared in many countries. The common people could not understand the Vulgate, and many of the priests had only a rote knowledge of it. This was at first of no concern to the established order. The important thing about the Mass was the renewal of Christ's sacrifice, and if the congregation did not understand the words that were said, spoken, or sung, that was of no consequence.

In Henry's VIII's domain, English Bibles were proving so popular an instrument of reform that the authorities of the Catholic Church reluctantly decided to make a translation of its own. Cardinal Allen, in initiating it, wrote: "Perhaps it would have been more desirable that the Scriptures had never been translated into barbarous tongues; nevertheless at the present day, when either from heresy or other causes, the curiosity of men, even of those who are not bad, is so great, and there is often such need of reading the Scriptures in order to confute our opponents, it is better that there should be a faithful and catholic translation than that men should use a corrupt version to their peril or destruction."

In 1568, the year of the Anglican Bishops' Bible, Catholic refugees from Britain established a college at Douai, in Flanders, and here the project was undertaken of translating the Vulgate into English. In 1578 political events necessitated the removal of the college to the French city of Rheims; in 1593 the institution, compelled to leave Rheims, re-established itself in Douai. Meanwhile, the work of translation had been proceeding, the result being the Rheims-Douai version. The Rheims New Testament was published in 1582, the Douai Old Testament in 1609–1610.

Noting that the translation is "from the authentical Latin," the preface explains that "the Romanist party found it expedient to translate the Bible into the vernacular for the most speedy abolishing . . . of false and impious translations put forth by sundry sects." Because of the veneration paid to the Vulgate, the Rheims-Douai scholars translated it as slightly as possible—that is to say, they simply tried to Anglicize the Latin. The reference in Philippians 3:10 to sharing Christ's sufferings here becomes "the society of his passions." Philippians 2:7 says that Christ "exinanited himself." 1 Corinthians 5:7 is rendered: "Purge the old leaven that you may be a new paste, as you are enzymes."

Old Testament passages are perhaps even more obscure. Isaiah 13:22 has it: "The Syrach owls shall answer, and mermaids in the temple of pleasure." Psalm 57:10 reads: "Before your thorns did understand the old briar: as living so in wrath he swalloweth them." Psalm 23 contains the following: "Thou hast fatted my head with oyle: and my chalice inebriating how goodlie it is! . . . And that I may dwell in the house of our Lord, in longitude of days."

In the 18th century the Rheims-Douai was subjected to extensive revision by Bishop Challoner of London and Archbishop Troy of Dublin. The primacy given to the Vulgate rested on the theory that, although it was itself a translation, it was more ancient than any of the Hebrew and Greek manuscripts used by Protestant scholars. This claim is vitiated by the fact that the text of the Vulgate itself is in a state of confusion, due to copyists' errors, and a papal commission is seeking to arrive at an official text of the Vulgate. Further, twentieth-century scholars have at their disposal textual evidence older than the Vulgate. In view of these two facts, the interpretation has been given that "the Council of Trent, in declaring the Vulgate to be authentic, did not prefer it to the original texts. . . . The Church . . . guarantees its reliable argumentative force in matters pertaining to faith and morals. In other matters the Vulgate possesses no other authority than that of a good old translation." In 1943 Pope Pius XII decreed that Catholic scholars should work directly from the Hebrew and Greek in making new translations.

Roman Catholic scholars of the twentieth century therefore work, as do their Jewish and Protestant counterparts, with the original languages of Scripture. In 1948 there appeared *The Westminster*

Version of the Sacred Scriptures, a Roman Catholic translation made from the original Greek; this was the culmination of a project begun in 1913. In 1941 there was published in Paterson, N.J., *The New Testament of Our Lord and Saviour Jesus Christ Translated from the Latin Vulgate;* "a Revision of the Challoner-Rheims Version Edited by Catholic Scholars Under the Patronage of the Episcopal Committee of the Confraternity of Christian Doctrine." Although the Vulgate is basic to this version, the work is done with reference to the Greek. The Confraternity Old Testament has just (1968) been completed and the New Testament has been replaced by a translation made directly from the Greek.

In 1954 Fathers Kleist and Lilly published *The New Testament Rendered from the Original Greek,* "with explanatory notes" designed "to render the Greek into such modern English as . . . would approve itself to American Catholics." Meanwhile in Britain, Monsignor Ronald Knox published his translation of the New Testament in 1944 and the whole Bible in 1956. The title page of this work indicated the way in which the Roman Church now re-evaluating its traditional version: *The Holy Bible, A Translation from the Latin Vulgate in the Light of the Hebrew and Greek Originals.*

In his "Trials of a Translator" Monsignor Knox explains why he felt the Vulgate basic to his enterprise: "Latin is so imbedded in our liturgy and in all our ecclesiastical language that a serious departure from it causes infinite confusion." With reference to the Englishing of Bibles, Knox contends that the King James Version "is good English only because English writers, for centuries, have treated it as the standard of good English. In itself, it is no better English than the Douay . . . Only the Douay was written in the language of exiles, which became, with time, an exiled language."

The whole situation with respect to English versions in the Roman Church has been changed by the Second Vatican Council. Whereas Monsignor Knox felt that translators had to work from the Vulgate because that was the language of liturgy, the liturgy has now been restored to the vernacular, so that the whole of Christendom is now engaged in a search for timely words in which to express the eternal Word.

In 1966 there appeared the first complete English translation of the Bible made under Roman Catholic auspices without primary reference to the Vulgate. This version, however, suffers from the fact that it, too, is to a large degree a translation of a translation. In 1961 Dominican scholars associated with L'École Biblique in the Holy Land published *La Bible de Jérusalem,* a translation into French made from the Hebrew and Greek originals, with reference to the Dead Sea Scrolls, Ugaritic religion, and other evidence newly brought to light by archaeology. In England, Alexander Jones, assisted by members of the Theological Studies Group of the

Newman Association, working with *La Bible de Jérusalem* and the Hebrew and Greek originals, published *The Jerusalem Bible*. "The introduction and notes are a direct translation from the French," and the whole "preserves the text established and (for the most part) the interpretation adopted by French scholars." With respect to the English dress in which this work now appears, Father Jones explains that "the first duty of a translator is to try to convey as clearly as he can what the original author wrote . . . there is no longer an accepted 'poetic language' which can be used to give artificial dignity to plain statements."

Although translators no longer work from the Vulgate, it is safe to say that the influence of Jerome's Bible will be felt in English versions for a long time to come. The King James Version, like the Rheims-Douai, at many points simply Anglicizes his Latin: "by him all things consist" (Colossians 1:17); "our conversation is in heaven" (Philippians 3:20); "in my Father's house are many mansions" (John 14:2); "in all things ye are too superstitious" (Acts 17:22); "those things which are not convenient" (Romans 1:28). At all these points the true sense of these Latinisms is missed by moderns, and twentieth-century versions replace them with Anglo-Saxon terms. Other terms derived from the Latin Bible will probably not soon disappear: Calvary, publican, Comforter, propitiation.

For four hundred years, from the time of the Protestant Reformers up to nearly the middle of the twentieth century, the divided groups of Christians were suspicious of each others' Bible translations. Through the decades of the twentieth century, however, biblical scholarship, both Catholic and Protestant, became so objective that scholars realized they could generally agree what Hebrew and Greek manuscripts were the best use as a basis of translation, and they began to think it would be possible to agree on a common translation in modern languages.

The possibility of a common Bible text and common Bible translation gradually engaged the attention of Church leaders. In 1964, at a meeting of Protestant Churches and Bible Societies held at Driebergen in Holland, the delegates from countries around the globe voted approval of the movement for a common Bible. The following year Pope Paul VI and the bishops of the Roman Catholic Church assembled in the Second Vatican Council also endorsed the idea of a common Bible: "If, given the opportunity and the approval of Church authority, translations are produced in cooperation with the separated brethren as well, all Christians will be able to use them" (Constitution on Divine Revelation, Art. 22, Nov. 18, 1965). In 1966, Pope Paul entrusted to Augustin Cardinal Bea and the Secretariat he heads the task of studying how cooperation in Bible translation and distribution could be worked out. One of the editors of this book, Father Walter M. Abbott, S.J., was appointed the Cardinal's assistant for direction of the study.

Recognition of objective scholarship and the desire for a common Bible have already produced significant developments: In twenty languages in various parts of the world Catholics are using, with permission of their bishops, translations produced by traditionally Protestant Bible Societies. There are more than one hundred other projects of the Bible Societies in which Catholics are at work with Protestants in translating books of the Bible or in revising existing translations: French, Arabic, Swahili, etc. The quest for a common Bible in English has resulted in a Catholic edition of the Revised Standard Version. British Catholic scholars went over the American Protestant work that had been finished a decade earlier. They made some minor changes in the New Testament translation—mostly changing "brothers" (of Jesus) to "brethren"—which most Catholic reviewers regarded as unnecessary. A year later, in 1965, the Catholic edition of the RSV Old Testament appeared, with no changes in the translation. Several pages of notes added to each testament and the including of the deuterocanonical books fulfilled requirements of Catholic law for Bible publication.

Strictly speaking, a common Bible in any language is the result of scholars of various faiths working together, reaching agreement, and having their work approved by the Churches. The Anchor Bible project, involving Catholic, Protestant, Jewish and other scholars, in this sense is not a "common" Bible, since each volume is the work of an individual who is solely responsible for the translation. A new edition of the Jerusalem Bible in French has introductory essays by Catholic, Protestant, Orthodox, and Jewish scholars, but the translation itself is the work of Catholics. The Catholic edition of the RSV is an interim kind of common Bible, since Catholics went over the original Protestant work and reached virtually complete agreement. The trend toward the RSV was strengthened by Cardinal Cushing's approval of the Oxford Annotated Bible, with a dozen changes in the annotations but no changes at all in the RSV translation of the Old and New Testaments and the appended Apocrypha.

Some of the scholars who worked on the revision of the Confraternity of Christian Doctrine version have asked that their translations be considered as a candidate for the various uses of a common Bible in English. There are others who hope that the New English Bible (Oxford and Cambridge University presses) will be the common Bible when the Old Testament is added to the already published New Testament. The Catholic directors of the Confraternity project announced that the final work was done in consultation with Protestant scholars, and the Protestant directors of the New English Bible have made a similar announcement about the remainder of their project. Since the Revised Standard Version is complete and over the past ten years has been endorsed by many Churches, and since it has the imprimatur of several Roman Catholic bishops (the Archbishop of Edinburgh, Scotland, and the Bishop of St. Cloud, Minn., U.S.A., for the Catholic edition of the RSV: the Archbishop of Boston, Mass., for the edition known as the Oxford Annotated Bible), many consider the RSV as the leading candidate for the title of common Bible.

There are many advantages in having a common translation. It can provide a common witness, a common source of reference, common spellings of names, the same numberings of Commandments and Psalms. If it becomes the basis for atlases and concordances, these books will be much easier for all to use. Since it is the agreed text of the ancient writings that constitutes *the* common Bible—the text that is the basis of all translations—Jewish scholars have the assurance that all must return first to the Hebrew Scriptures. Finally, the international impact of a common English translation, difficult though it may be to achieve, has such attractive advantages that a committee of Roman Catholic bishops from ten countries has been established to find or promote a common liturgy for the English-speaking world. Since much of the liturgy is based on Scripture, both Old and New Testaments, the quest for a common Bible has been given added impetus.

The desire for a common Bible, with all its advantages, especially if it is adopted for liturgical use by all the Churches, does not mean that other new translations would not be needed or wanted. New translations can give insights and nuances that had not been discovered before—a valuable service for the People of God. Besides, modern language is always changing, archaeologists find new evidence, scientists improve skills for dating manuscripts, students of the ancient languages constantly increase their knowledge of the Bible's original texts. The common Bible translation of one generation will have to be revised or done anew by another generation.

Appendix 5

A Summary of History from the Maccabees to the Days of Pontius Pilate

From Zerubbabel to Jonathan Maccabee, 537 to 161 B.C., the Jewish state was reduced to a small district surrounding Jerusalem. Philistia, the coast towns to the west, Trans-Jordania to the east, and Samaria to the north, all once part of the Jewish state were now all independent and dominated by non-Jews. In fact, the Jewish inhabitants of the region of Galilee were so few that Judah Maccabee was able to transfer all of them to Jerusalem at one time to protect them from their enemies (cf. 1 Macc. 5:23).

Following the death of Judah Maccabee, however, the Hasmonean dynasty began to expand the narrow limits of the Jewish state through treaty and military conquest. The most extensive military victories were won by John Hyrcanus, who conquered Samaria, Edom, part of Moab, and lower Galilee, forcibly converting the defeated nations. This policy was particularly repugnant to the Pharisees, who criticized him violently. At a later date the Pharisees were to interpret.the rise of the tyrannous Edomite house of Herod as punishment for this denial of religious freedom.

Judas Aristobulus, son of Hyrcanus, reigned only one year, during which time he conquered upper Galilee. Then Alexander Jannaeus, another son of Hyrcanus, conquered all of Philistia and the fortified cities across the Jordan. The boundaries of the empire were now identical with those in the reigns of King David and King Solomon.

With Judea at its very height, civil war broke out among the sons of Jannaeus. The blood-letting that resulted from the battles between Hyrcanus II and Aristobulus II (65–37 B.C.) weakened and finally destroyed the Jewish empire.

The Roman commander Pompey, allied with Hyrcanus II, seized Jerusalem in the winter of 63 B.C. Whereupon he tore Judea (Roman name for ancient Judah) from the rest of Palestine, removed the title of "king" from Hyrcanus, and permitted him authority only as a High Priest. But the fratricide continued; thousands of Jews slaughtered each other. Control of the government eventually fell into the hands of the Edomite family of Antipater, father of Herod. The rule of Antipater was tyrannous. Three times the Jews appealed to Rome to replace this despotic ruler; but the triumvir Mark Antony, heavily bribed by Herod, put to death the delegation of Hebrews. With the aid of Parthian rebels against Rome, a desperate effort under the leadership of Antigonus II, second son of Aristobulus II, succeeded. Momentarily victorious, Antigonus II established the Maccabean house once again for a period of three years, 40–37 B.C.

Supported mightily by Rome, Herod renewed an attack on the Maccabean house and Judea was plundered by both the Parthians and the successful Romans. The most vigorous fighting during this period took place in Galilee, where Jewish Zealots engaged in bloody guerrilla warfare.

In an effort to cloak himself with the mantle of respectability, Herod married Mariamne, daughter of the union of the daughter of Hyrcanus II and the son of Aristobulus II. When Herod came to the throne in 37 B.C. Jerusalem and all its surrounding area was almost literally a wilderness. It is estimated that 110,000 men were slaughtered in the preceding thirty years. Josephus notes: "Owing to perpetual wars the Jews were no longer capable of revolting against anybody." In such a dispirited atmosphere the messianic hopes of the prophets of old found fertile soil. An independent Jewish state was not to exist again until the recent establishment of the State of Israel.

Herod, viewed as a successful king by his Roman overlords, was a hated ruler. Upon coming to power, he murdered the remnants of the royal family and sought to destroy all memory of the Maccabean house. Herod persuaded Rome to behead the former king Antigonus II, a humiliation never before imposed by the Romans on their vanquished. Even the enormous temple Herod built and furnished in Jerusalem, for which he was famous in the Gentile world, was desecrated by a Golden Eagle, standard of the Roman empire and a source of scandal to the Jews. The faithful in Jerusalem were also outraged by the athletic games, theater and amphitheater—all dedicated to Roman gods—which Herod sponsored. Thus there were numerous plots on his life. In return Herod imposed on Judea a rule of terror, spies, and denial of civil liberties. He appointed and removed high priests at will.

War erupted again when Herod died; and again Roman troops entered the land to put down Jewish rebellion. Again they sacked Jerusalem. Rome established Archelaus, son of Herod, as "ethnarch," leader of the people, over an area half the size of his father's kingdom. For ten years, 4 B.C. to 6 A.D., Archelaus misruled the Jews, until at last, responding to the people's protest, Emperor Augustus exiled him to Gaul and confiscated his property. Judea, Samaria, and Idumea were then attached to Syria and put under the protection of a procurator. Although the high priests maintained a certain degree of authority over religious matters, Judea was ruled by a permanent army stationed in Jerusalem and the prefect in Caesarea. The prefect also had the power to appoint and depose the high priests.

Jewish religious literature at this period now speaks clearly of a Kingdom of Heaven and a Kingdom of Edom (Rome) in conflict with each other. Jews imagined their sufferings to be "the pangs of the Messiah," that were to be experienced prior to the final redemption. There was also sharp antagonism between the Pharisees, the popular religious leaders of the people, and the Sadducees, the conservative followers of the corrupt priests; and between those who counseled pacifism and repentance, the Essenes, and those who wished to force the coming of God's Kingdom through taking up arms against Rome, the Zealots.

In 6 B.C. a new Roman procurator in Syria instituted a census for the sake of fixing taxation. (Some scholars place this census in A.D. 6.) The Jews viewed a census as contrary to the will of God (cf. 2 Samuel 24), and saw it as a symbol of their complete subjugation. They protested vigorously without success. Zealots sprang up, first in Galilee and then elsewhere, to wage violent guerrilla warfare against Rome.

Scholarly judgment on Pontius Pilate (A.D. 26–36) in whose prefecture Jesus was crucified, is mixed. There are too few hard facts about him. He was another of the Roman governors who violated Jewish religious law and sensibilities by allowing the Roman troops to carry their hated insignia into the Roman fortress in Jerusalem, the Antonia, overlooking the Temple.

Herod Antipas was named tetrarch in Galilee and Trans-Jordania (4 B.C.–A.D. 39). Jesus referred to him as "that fox" (Luke 13:32). It was he who beheaded John the Baptist. Pilate turned Jesus over to him for questioning (Luke 23:7).

Jewish Religious Parties in Judea

During the Maccabean era, 175–125 B.C., two significant political groups are mentioned among the Jews: the *Hasidim* (pious observers of the Mosaic Law) and the *Hellenists* (those who adopted Greek culture and accommodated themselves to its idolatrous requirements). The Hasidim in another generation were to provide followers for groups known as the *Essenes* and the *Pharisees*, even as the Hellenists in large numbers were included among the *Sadducees*.

Jewish history for a century prior to the birth of Jesus recounts a sorrowful record of wars, foreign and civil, oppression at the hands of Rome, economic instability and moral retrogression.

It is no wonder, therefore, that at least one party of Jews, the Essenes, abandoned the political world as the center of concern and agitation. They nurtured, instead, a hope for a messianic Redeemer who would establish a kingdom of a spiritual order. Biblical scholars believe that the Essenes have much in common with the Qumran community of the Dead Sea scrolls, and that their views paralleled many of the beliefs held by John the Baptist and Jesus. By the time of Josephus, Essenes numbered about 4,000. They shared a common fund, table and board. The majority worked in agriculture and lived modest lives in the villages. They cherished no possessions of gold or silver; they owned no slaves. They took no oaths. Many did not marry. Before their ritual meals they engaged in a form of baptism; they bathed, totally immersing themselves. They preserved a secret literature of devotions which allegedly provided the faithful a view of the *Shekinah* (Divine Presence) and inspired apocalyptic visions.

The Pharisees, according to some scholars, may be traced back to the pre-Maccabean period. They were the popular religious leaders of the Hebrew people who sought to achieve a more democratic and just society through knowledge of, dedication to, and implementation of the Mosaic Law.

The Pharisees held, with the Essenes, that a divine Providence governed all things; but unlike the Essenes, they stressed man's freedom of will and denied predestination. They maintained high ethical standards in their lives and held themselves aloof from revelry and foolishness. Devoted to the Law as the way to achieve God's kingdom, they developed procedures by which the Law could be interpreted and applied to changing conditions of life. Thus they helped to hold the splintered Jewish community together through an allegiance to a living Law. At the same time they defended the people against the perversion of the Law by some priests and landowners; they protested the tyrannies imposed by foreign rulers. Among the Pharisees were to be found both militant campaigners against Rome as well as pacifists who believed that Jewish survival depended not on might but only on devotion to God's Law. Ultimately, when Jerusalem was destroyed in A.D. 70 and Jewish resistance finally broken in A.D. 135, the Talmudic academies established by pacifist Pharisees enabled Judaism to survive.

The Pharisees believed in the immortality of the soul, the resurrection of the righteous, and destructive hell-fire for the wicked. Jesus found a source for some of his ethical teachings in the Pharisaic heritage. By no means were all Pharisees hostile to him. Some arranged dinner parties for him, and he was often in their homes (Luke 7:36; 11:37; 14:1). Other Pharisees sought to protect Jesus from the wrath of Herod (Luke 13:31). Jesus was invited into the synagogue to teach. Among the Pharisees were some who defended him within the Sanhedrin. One provided him a tomb (Luke 23:50 f.). Another advised caution in dealing with the followers of Jesus (Acts 5:34–39). The apostle Paul continued to identify himself proudly as "a Pharisee" (Philippians 3:5).

Jesus aroused the anger of the Pharisees generally when he proclaimed and changed the Law on his own authority and rejected the legal methods that had been devised for expanding the Law. Christians, who regard Jesus as the promised Messiah, hold that he was only exercising the legitimate power of his office. But to the Pharisees, concerned with the ever-present problem in Palestine of holding a social order together in this world, the course resulting from such a subjective treatment of the Law could lead only to anarchy. Nor did they recognize Jesus as the Messiah.

Believing in the imminent coming of the Kingdom of God, Jesus could not be patient with what must have seemed to him to be an excessive legalism and contentiousness on the part of some of these religious elders. Ultimately, the Christian Church taught that man was redeemed through Jesus' sacrifice. Jews, unable to accept that claim, remain convinced that man fulfills his responsibility to God by fidelity to the Holy Law. In His own time God will send a Redeemer who will cleanse men's hearts of iniquity and establish a kingdom of righteousness and peace.

Not only did Jesus share many of the values of the Pharisees but, as Jewish scholars point out, his attack on hypocrisy and legalism was itself in the spirit of Pharisaism at its best. Undoubtedly, there were hypocrites among the Pharisees, just as in every generation there are those who tend to make of religious faith merely a series of legalistic prescriptions and ceremonies. All human institutions are touched by the distortions that result from man's finitude and his proclivity to routinization and conformity. No harsher judgment on such an externalization of faith could have been made than that which the Rabbis themselves, heirs to the Pharisees, wrote in the Talmud: "A stupid Hasid, and a cunning knave, a female devotee and the *plagues of the Pharisees* are they who destroy the world" (*Mishna Sota* 83:4). The Talmud enumerates seven types of Pharisees: the *Shikhmi* (hunchback); the *Quizzai* (bookkeeping); the *Kiqpi* (knocker); the *M'dokhya* (pestlelike); the Pharisee who insists, "What is my obligation and I will do it"; the Pharisee who is one from fear; and the Pharisee who is one from love (*Sota* 22b). It is not clear today what the first four types describe; the exact meaning of the words has been lost to us. It has been suggested, however, that these Pharisees were so extremist that they distorted truth. The Pharisee who wants to know his obligations so that he may do them at once is not unlike the reward-seeking young man described in Matthew 9:20. Only the man who serves God out of love is approved.

The *Zealots* shared the Messianic hope of the Pharisees that the nation would be restored to glory in a time to come. Being zealous, they took up arms to emancipate their nation and to achieve their purpose. Depending on one's perspective, they were either noble patriots or fanatical revolutionaries. They were always hopelessly outnumbered, and they suffered severe losses. Their violence was often directed against a seemingly recalcitrant Jewish community. Ultimately, therefore, the Talmudic writers described them as "licentious ones," "outlaws," and "assassins." Among the disciples of Jesus was "Simon who was called the Zealot" (Luke 6:15).

A fourth group to hold power in the Jewish community was the *Sadducees*. The leaders were priests from the family of the sons of Zadok. Their ranks were swelled by the Hellenists of the Maccabean period. But they were not at first in favor with the Hasmonean dynasty, whose leaders had themselves usurped the office of the High Priesthood. When the Pharisee party protested the growing tendency of the later Maccabean rulers toward ostentation and tyranny, the Sadducees emerged as the predominant political power. During the reign of Herod, the priests and landowners associated with the house of Boethus were also identified with the Sadducean group. And in traditional Jewish accounts, that group is believed to have apprehended Jesus and persecuted his disciples.

The Sadducees rejected the oral law, which the Pharisees had developed. They believed that the soul dies with the body, and they discounted any concept of life after death. They were more severe than the Pharisees in meting out punishment. They turned aside the Pharisaic effort to have the whole nation share a corporate responsibility for financing the Temple worship; the Sadducees had a vested interest in maintaining the support of the cult within their own ranks. They controlled the sale of sacrifices and the changing of money. Keeping to the letter of the Mosaic Law, the Sadducees permitted themselves iniquities not specifically prohibited by the Law, whereas the Pharisees concerned with the spirit of the Law sought to extend it and to bring a discipline of holiness into all of Jewish life. Many of the Rabbinic Talmudic sayings that the reader will find throughout this text reflect the depth of religious conviction of the Pharisees.

It is clear that Jesus and his followers, loyal Jews all of them, were not particularly identified with any one of these religious parties in Judea and Galilee. The New Testament recounts how Jesus' ministry clashed at some point or another with each group. Nevertheless, the ultimate opposition to Jesus' ministry, according to Jewish scholars, was not to come from the Jewish parties. Rather, it came from a Roman governor and his Jewish priestly vassals who feared that he might be "the king of the Jews" who would lead the Jews in a new rebellion. For the Jewish messianic dream included a hope for the restoration of Jewish political independence as well as a longing for the renewal of religious faith. And—for different reasons—neither Rome nor the Sanhedrin wanted an upset of the status quo.

If the claims of redemption made in the name of the crucified savior did not satisfy the expectations of synagogue leaders, the reader today, of whatever persuasion, may acknowledge that their reluctance to believe in Jesus was based on a legitimate understanding of the biblical faith. On the other hand, those Jews who adored Jesus were also able to make a claim, from the same biblical texts, that Jesus did in his ministry fulfill the promises of the prophets.

Thus it came to pass in the first century A.D. that a new schism erupted in the Jewish community. Jewish-Christians were split off from the synagogue and a tragic pattern in the history of Jews and Christians was set in motion.

Appendix 6

Hammurabi Code and Mosaic Law

During the period covered by Genesis, Canaan was under the influence of Babylonian culture. Biblical law reflects this influence.

There are in fact twenty-four instances of law contained in the Mosaic code that correspond with Hammurabi's code written four hundred years earlier. The most famous of these is the *lex talionis*, "an eye for an eye," and also laws about kidnapping, burglary, assault and others.

It is in the difference between these codes, however, that one discovers ethical insights distinctive of Mosaic law. For example, in Babylonian law the king, priests, aristocrats, commoners and slaves were all treated differently before the law. In biblical law all men were judged by the same law. In Israel the death penalty for crimes involving property was abolished. The slave was considered a human being. A Hebrew slave is punished for his failure to accept freedom rather than as a consequence of his desire of it. A runaway slave may not be returned. In Jewish tradition there is no record of the application of "an eye for an eye;" monetary equivalent for damage was imposed instead.

A most distinctive difference in Mosaic law is its underlying principle that man is holy by virtue of his creation, and that God demands of all men, therefore, that they deal with each other justly and compassionately.

Index to Introductions, Essays and Notes